ASHE Reader Series

THEORETICAL PERSPECTIVES ON COLLEGE STUDENTS

Edited by

Frances K. Stage, New York University

Deborah Faye Carter, Indiana University

Don Hossler, Indiana University

Edward P. St. John, Indiana University

Series Editor

Lenoar Foster, San Diego State University

PEARSON

Custom Publishing

Cover Art: *Two Pebbles* by Christopher B. Stage.

Printed in the United States of America

10 9 8 7 6 5 4 3 2 1

ISBN 0-536-72960-3

BA 997059

LF/NN

Please visit our web site at *www.pearsoncustom.com*

PEARSON CUSTOM PUBLISHING
75 Arlington Street, Suite 300, Boston, MA 02116
A Pearson Education Company

CONTENTS

ACKNOWLEDGMENTS

We would like to thank Hasani C. Carter, doctoral student at New York University for helpful suggestions and aid in gathering materials for this volume. James L. Ratcliff, Performance Associates Postsecondary Consulting, Pueblo West, CO, editor of the reader series and Lori Bittker Acquisitions Editor, Pearson Custom Publishing guided us into and through the commitment to and undertaking of this project. The advice and recommendations of: Anna Ortiz, California State University- Long Beach; Greg Blimling, Appalachian State University; Katie Branch, University of Rhode Island; Flo Hamrick, Iowa State University; Adriana Kezar, University of Maryland, Jeffrey Milem, University of Maryland; Robert Teranishi, New York University; Patrick Terenzini, Pennsylvania State University; and Lemuel Watson, Clemson University shaped the organization and contents. Finally, in addition to our advisory board, we acknowledge countless colleagues who, as users of two earlier versions of this reader, offered commentary and suggestions that actively shaped the current volume. Representatives of the following presses shared copyrighted materials granting us reprint permission: Agathon Press, American College Personnel Association Media, AMS Press, Greenwood Press, Jossey-Bass Higher and Adult Education Series, Lawrence Earlbaum Associates, State University of New York Press, Vanderbilt University Press. Thank you, all.

INTRODUCTION

FRANCES K. STAGE

This is now the third edition of the ASHE Reader on College Students entitled *Theoretical Perspectives on College Students*. This reader is the result of an evolution across two previous editions and stands as more encompassing and complete than the former. According to our readers, the first included classic works in the study of college students, but lacked more current and diverse works that had begun to appear in the literature. Likewise, some readers were disappointed with the second edition that sacrificed classic pieces in favor of newer and more diverse pieces of research. Additionally, each edition had gaps relative to the extensive work on student identity, development, and learning. In this edition, we worked to address these issues.

Purpose

In this volume we hope to highlight the latest in college student research in an effort to inspire both future researchers and future administrators. For the researchers, we hope these exemplars will generate new questions and suggest new ways to address old questions including through relationships with those who work closely with college students. For administrators, we hope to inspire new ways of conceptualizing solutions to campus problems and to empower them to engage in research themselves in addition to working with the research community to address difficult questions. To this end we have included scholarship from several genres including work: 1) that might be characterized as summarizations of traditional college student research; 2) that is transformational, including work that focuses on new populations or that uses new ways of answering old problems; and 3) work that challenges old models and conventional ways of thinking (Stage & Anaya, 1996).

Overview of the Reader

For our purposes in this volume, we divided the extensive literature on college students into five parts. Each section begins with one or two pieces that might be considered classic followed by more recent contributions to the literature. Below is a very brief overview of these sections. More detailed introductions are offered at the start of each section.

Part 1: Getting to College

An important aspect of studying college students that can be overlooked is the process that brings students to college. With the growing interest in student college choice, we include several selections on this important topic. Because this is a relatively new area of study in higher education, there are still some student populations about whom we know little concerning this process. From a public policy perspective, universal access to and participation in postsecondary education have become indicators of social equality. Thus, policy makers have become more interested in the factors that

---

Stage, F.K. & Anaya, G. 1996. A transformational view of college student research. In F. Stage, G. Anaya, J. Bean, D. Hossler & G. Kuh (Eds.) *College Students: The Evolving Nature of Research*.

influence the decisions to attend two or four-year colleges.

Part 2: The College Environment

The role of the college environment in student life and success has been extensively studied and is increasingly generating usable research. In the 1950s and 1960s, researchers began to examine the fit between college environments and student personalities, frequently using a psychological framework. More recent scholarship addresses the different ways individuals perceive their environment and the ways research on student perceptions can inform practice.

Part 3: Student Development and Identity

The section on Student Development and Identity focuses on internal and external influences on individual student growth. The first selection is an overview of key cognitive, psychosocial, and typology theories as they relate to the longitudinal changes of college students. Other selections within the section scholars shift in balance between focus on psychological and sociological influences. The balance between identity, development, and sociological setting create unique experiences for each college student.

Part 4: The Learning Experience

Probably no area of research on college students is growing as fast as that which focuses on college student learning. The Learning Experience focuses on both classroom and academic learning as well as more general learning that is a part of the college student experience as well as the intersection of the two. The first section focuses on primarily on academic learning particularly related to classrooms. The next section contains articles connected with students' cognitive development and the section ends with more general discussions of student learning in the campus context and reviews of recent research on learning.

Part 5: Summary and Considerations for Future Research

Given the wealth and volume of research on college students, we are fortunate to have many who are willing to step back, take a deep breath, and tell us what it all means. The section begins classic pieces, snapshots from a specific period of time, designed to shape the ways we think about and gather information about students. The next set of readings provides recommendations for ways to make our research better informed and more relevant. The section closes with very specific advice regarding methodological approaches for research and assessment.

Bibliography for Further Reading

Finally, we have included a listing of readings relevant to each of the five sections of the book. This can form a beginning source for topics that are of particular interest to the reader. Some of them were included in earlier editions of this reader, others were suggested by the review board but were not included in the final list. Still others were on the original list of readings for this edition, but the press in question charged an amount for the copyright permission that exceeded the project's budget. In those cases, we contacted the authors and replaced the readings with similar articles with less prohibitive costs. At any rate, we hope the bibliography is useful to you.

In constructing this edition, we could easily have included twice as many high quality readings as appear here. We struggled to balance reasonable length and cost to the reader with comprehensiveness. The good news is that the literature on college students is rich, diverse, and expansive. We hope that this volume inspires you to seek the myriad other articles that inform this rich field and to contribute in meaningful ways to our growing knowledge of college students.

A NOTE TO THE READER

The composition of this reader, *Theoretical Perspectives on College Students,* was directly influenced by the instructors and students who used the first two editions. Within four to five years, it is likely that a new reader will be compiled. We continue to encourage all readers to provide commentary on the present work so that we continue to improve future editions.

Please send recommendations, comments, and suggestions for the next edition of the reader to editor:

Frances Stage
Director, Higher Education Program
Dept. of Administration, Leadership & Technology
Suite 300, 239 Greene St.
New York University
NY, NY 10003

To learn more about the ASHE Reader Series or to provide comments or suggestions for additional topics contact series editor:

Lenora Foster
San Diego State University
College of Education
Educational Leadership Department
5500 Campanile Drive
San Diego, CA 92182-1190

PART I

THE PATH TO COLLEGE

PART 1: THE PATH TO COLLEGE

Scholars and policy makers have long been interested in topic of college attendance. Until the last twenty years, however, most of this research was limited to demographic profiles of students participating in higher education, economic research focusing on cost-benefit analyses of the enrollment decision or the relationships between college enrollment and the labor market, and sociological analyses rooted in the status attainment literature. Beginning in the 1980s there was a dramatic increase in research on what has become known as *student college choice.*

Increased interest in student college choice has been the result of several factors. Between 1959 and 1999, the percentage of students going on to some form of higher education rose from 46% to 63% (*Postsecondary Education OPPORTUNITY*, May, 2001). From a public policy perspective, universal access to and participation in postsecondary education have become indicators of social equality. Thus, policy makers have become more interested in the factors that influence the decisions to attend two or four-year colleges.

In addition to public policy makers, institutional policy makers also have a vested interest in student college choice. Competition for students among both private and public colleges and universities has intensified. Higher education systems throughout the world have been moving toward market models to explain the competitive relationships among institutions. In a market model, enrolled students can be a source of tuition revenue, increased state appropriations, prestige, and other important assets that are coveted by faculty and administrators.

With the growing interest in student college choice, in this section, we include selections on this topic. One caveat should be noted, all of this research focuses upon recent high school graduates. There is far less research on the decision making process of returning adult students who tend be commuters who attend local two- and four-year institutions.

The first piece, "Understanding Student College Choice" by Don Hossler, John Braxton, and Georgia Coopersmith (1989), provides a broad overview of factors that influence student college choice and the timing of their decisions. As research on this topic expanded, scholars have become increasingly interested in populations of recent high school graduates who are less likely to continue their formal education and in more targeted populations of college going students. Kassie Freeman and Gail Thomas (2002), in their article, "Black Colleges and College Choice: Characteristics of Students who choose HBCUs", examine the characteristics of African American students who enroll in Historically Black Colleges. In doing so they illuminate college choice decisions for an important part of the college going population.

Alberto Cabrera and Steven La Nasa (2001) in their article "On the Path to College: Three Critical Tasks Facing America's Disadvantaged" provide a more focused look at low income students and the factors that influence their college choice decisions. Similarly, Chapter Six of Patricia McDonough's book, "Choosing Colleges: How Social Class and Schools Structure Opportunities" (1997), summarizes how different the college decision-making process can be for students attending affluent, middle class, and low income high schools.

This section closes with a policy analysis of the significant policy issues connected with student college choice, "Academic Access and Equal Opportunity: Rethinking the Foundations for Policy on Diversity" (2002) by Ed St. John and Glenda Musoba. The authors consider the changing landscape

Mortensen, Tom. (2001, May). *Postsecondary Education OPPORTUNITY*, No. 107. Oskaloosa, IA.

of affirmative action in admissions, shifts away from federal grants to loans, the role of admissions testing in access to higher education, and other policy developments that are exerting an influence upon the college enrollment decisions of students.

CHAPTER 1

UNDERSTANDING STUDENT COLLEGE CHOICE

DON HOSSLER, JOHN BRAXTON AND GEORGIA COOPERSMITH

Increased Interest in Student College Choice

During the past three decades, a diverse set of demographic and public policy issues have fueled increased interest in student college choice. These issues include the emergence of the federal government as a significant source of student financial aid, the declining pool of high school graduates, and past declines in the postsecondary participation rates of black high school students. As a result of these trends, federal, state, and institutional policy-makers, as well as social science researchers, have become interested in understanding the factors that shape the decision to attend a postsecondary educational institution (PEI).

Public policy-makers at the state and federal level have a vested interest in understanding the factors that influence aggregate student enrollments. Both federal and state policy-makers use postsecondary participation rates as indices of economic competitiveness as well as overall quality of life. Although the relationship between education and economic competitiveness and quality of life is mulitivariate, the commonly held belief is that increased levels of education at the state level improve the quality of life for citizens and attract more business and industry.

As the result of increased state and federal investments in student financial aid, state and federal policy-makers can use research on student college choice to more effectively target financial aid dollars. In some states, policy-makers are also committed to maintaining vitality in both the public and private sectors of postsecondary education. A better understanding of student college choice can provide appropriate incentives to help achieve this goal.

Institutional policy-makers have sought to understand the phenomenon of student college choice in order to develop marketing strategies designed to attract the desired number of students. Selective institutions have used student college choice research to help them attract students with desirable academic and nonacademic characteristics.

Among researchers, interest in student college choice has its roots in econometric studies of student demand for higher education and the status attainment literature. More recently, investigators have attempted to answer more applied questions, such as: (1) What are the effects of financial aid upon access to postsecondary education? And (2) what factors determine the selection of one PEI over another?

Student college choice, however, should be of interest to both policy-makers and researchers for reasons that go beyond its relationship to aggregate postsecondary enrollments or the effects of attending college upon status attainment. Students' decisions to continue their formal education beyond high school, as well as where they attend, have important outcomes for society as well as the individual.

"Understanding Student College Choice." Reprinted from *Higher Education: Handbook of Theory and Research* 5, (1989), by permission of Kluwer Academic Publishers.

A wide range of benefits accrue to society as the result of a well-educated populace. The benefits include increased productivity (Denison, 1971; Schultz, 1961), lower welfare and crime rates (Erlich, 1975; Garfinkel and Haveman, 1977; Spiegleman, 1968), a higher rate of technological development, and greater participation in civic and community affairs (Bowen, 1977). Although scholars and policy-makers may differ on the amount of the costs which our society should bear to provide postsecondary education for its people, few would argue that society does not derive both economic and noneconomic benefits from a well-educated citizenry.

From the perspective of the individual, student college choice also has identifiable outcomes. Individuals incur costs and benefits not only by deciding to pursue a postsecondary education, but also by deciding what type of postsecondary educational institution they will attend. Jencks et al. (1972) found that college-educated males have a significant advantage over males with a high school education, even when ability and family background are controlled. Leslie and Brinkman (1986) compared the lifetime income of high school and college graduates and concluded that the individual rate of return for earning a bachelor's degree is 11.8% (p. 214). In addition, college-educated individuals have better employment fringe benefits and lower rates of health problems, and report being more satisfied with their lifestyle (Bowen, 1977). There are also individual outcomes related to the type of postsecondary education a student completes. Leslie and Brinkman (1986) concluded that graduates of four-year institutions received more financial benefits than those who attended two-year institutions, and students who attended more prestigious institutions appear to accrue more benefits than students attending less prestigious four-year PEIs (although this appears to be the result of a greater likelihood to attain more total years of postsecondary education).

Furthermore, student college choice may be linked with student attrition. The attrition literature suggests that there are linkages between the concept of student-institution fit and student persistence (Williams, 1984). Although the relationship between a student's understanding of postsecondary educational options and the student's subsequent persistence has not been empirically examined, logic would suggest that students who employ a more thorough college

selection process are more likely to attend a PEI that matches their needs and interests. In a recent paper on student persistence, Attanasi (1986) concluded that "getting ready" behaviors that high school students engage in prior to postsecondary matriculation are related to student persistence (pp. 14–25). "Getting ready" behaviors include developing a college-going frame of mind and anticipating what college will be like. These "getting ready" behaviors may be similar to the final phase of college choice, where students weigh various postsecondary educational alternatives and choose one PEI on the basis of a cost-benefit analysis or perhaps an intuitive sense of "fit." Although the relationship between persistence and student college choice goes beyond the scope of this chapter, the linkages may be an area worthy of future research.

The literature on student college choice covers a wide range of topics that employ a diverse set of methodological approaches. Studies range from single institutional studies that investigate the information sources that potential postsecondary students find most useful in selecting a specific postsecondary educational institution to attend to causal models which examine the effects of student characteristics upon postsecondary educational attainment. In an attempt to bring order to the literature on student college choice, this chapter has been organized into the following three sections: The first section reviews the conceptual approaches that have been used to frame investigations of student college choice. This section will focus on econometric studies, status attainment research, and models of student college choice. The second section uses a three-stage model of student college choice to integrate the diverse research on factors that influence the decision to attend a postsecondary educational institution and the subsequent decision as to which postsecondary educational institution to attend. The last section presents a summary of empirical studies of student college choice and discusses future research questions and related methodological issues regarding student college choice.

For many students participation in higher education includes some form of advanced vocational training. Therefore, the terms *postsecondary education* and *postsecondary educational institutions*, rather than *college* or *university*, will be used in this chapter. These terms are intended to encompass certificate programs as well as two-

and four-year degree programs housed in colleges, vocational institutions, and universities.

Defining Student College Choice

Although *student college choice* is the term frequently used to describe the process that results in students' decisions to continue their formal education at a PEI (D. Chapman, 1981; R. Chapman, 1979; Hossler and Gallagher, 1987; Jackson, 1982; Litten, 1982; Tierney, 1980a), the term has not been formally defined in the literature. In addition to *student college choice*, terms such as *college plans* (Baird, 1973), *educational goals* (Tillery and Kildegaard, 1973), and *the demand for higher education* (Campbell and Siegel, 1967) have also been used as descriptors by researchers who have investigated correlates of the decision to attend a PEI. Although the correlates of student college choice are easily identified, the choice process it is more difficult to study because student college choice is a longitudinal and cumulative process that begins at an early age and culminates in the decision to attend a PEI (Corrazini et al., 1972). In this chapter, the term *student college choice* will be used to describe the process that results in (1) making a decision to continue formal schooling after high school and (2) deciding which PEI to attend. We define student college choice as:

> a complex, multistage process during which an individual develops aspirations to continue formal education beyond high school, followed later by a decision to attend a specific college, university or institution of advanced vocational training.

Perspectives on Student College Choice

Conceptual approaches to describing the college choice process are found in three categories of models which specify factors leading to college choice as well as the relationship among the factors: econometric, sociological, and combined (Jackson, 1982). Within each of these three categories, various conceptual approaches or models have also been developed and will be reviewed.

Econometric Models

Two strands of econometric models of college choice are present in the literature. One strand seeks to predict enrollments with institutions, states, and the nation as the units of analysis, while the other strand focuses on the individual student as a unit of analysis (Fuller, Manski, and Wise, 1982). To be conceptually consistent with the definition of student college choice used in this chapter, only those econometric models which seek to estimate the choice process of the individual student will receive attention. Within the strand of econometric literature, which focuses on the choices of individual students, two types of choices are modeled. One type of choice is between enrollment in a PEI or the pursuit of a noncollege alternative such as the military or a job (Kohn, Manski, and Mundel, 1976; Bishop, 1977; Fuller, Manski, and Wise, 1982; Manski and Wise, 1983; Nolfi, 1978), while the choice of a particular PEI from a set of PEIs is the second type of choice process (Radner and Miller, 1970; Kohn et al., 1976; R. Chapman, 1979).

Regardless of the type of choice addressed by the various models, all the models reviewed postulate a weighing of various factors to make a choice. To elaborate, an individual student will select a particular PEI if the perceived benefits of attendance outweigh the perceived benefits of attendance at other PEIs or a noncollege alternative. In other words, the individual student strives to maximize the expected utility of the choice to be made. This formulation specifies the relationships among the factors in each of the models presented. Although the type of choice and the specific factors posited to be influential may differ across the various econometric models, underlying formulations concerning the relationships among factors are the same.

College or Noncollege Choice

Five models have been advanced to describe factors posited to be influential in the process of choice between college attendance or a noncollege alternative (Kohn et al., 1976; Bishop, 1977; Nolfi, 1978; Fuller et al., 1982; Manski and Wise, 1983). Such models have also been termed *college-going models* (Kohn et al., 1976).

Expected costs are factors common to all of the college-going models. Expected costs include tuition, net tuition (tuition minus financial aid), room and board, and various living expenses. Earnings forgone due to college attendance are additional expected costs included in models advanced by Bishop (1977) and Fuller et al., (1982).

Future earnings expected either from college attendance (Bishop, 1977; Fuller et al., 1982) or from a noncollege alternative (Bishop, 1977; Nolfi, 1978) are additional economic factors. According to Fuller et al., (1982), expected or future earnings from college attendance are estimated by students through the value expected to accrue from receipt of a college degree. Various student background characteristics are factors also predicted to influence college-going behavior (Kohn et al., 1976; Bishop, 1977; Nolfi, 1978). Such family background characteristics as parental educational level (Kohn et al., 1976; Bishop, 1977), parental level of income (Kohn et al., 1976; Bishop, 1977; Nolfi, 1978), number of siblings, and parental occupation (Bishop, 1977) are among the student background characteristics included in some of these econometric models (Kohn et al., 1976; Bishop, 1977; Nolfi, 1978).

High school characteristics such as the proportion of graduates going to college or some other PEI (Nolfi et al., 1978) and high school quality (Bishop, 1977) are also factors predicted to affect college-going behavior. Aspirations of neighborhood peers are an additional factor identified (Bishop, 1977).

College characteristics are also assumed to affect college-going choice. The underlying assumption behind the inclusion of college characteristics in this type of college choice model is that individual students will make a choice between attending a PEI or a non-PEI based on the maximum utility or benefit received from the "most attractive" college available to the individual student (Kohn et al., 1976). Both Bishop (1977) and Kohn et al., (1976) include college characteristics in their models of college-going behavior.

Among the college characteristics adduced as influential in determining the maximum utility of the "most attractive" college available to the student are admissions standards (Bishop, 1977), the average ability of students attending the college, educational expenditures, breadth of institutional offerings, and the quality of campus life (Kohn et al., 1976).

Choice Among Colleges

The term *choice among colleges* refers to the selection of a particular college from a set of alternative colleges from which an individual student has received offerings of admission. Kohn et al., (1976)

refer to this process as "college choice." Three econometric models of college choice will be discussed in this chapter subsection (Radner and Miller, 1970; Kohn et al., 1976; R. Chapman, 1979).

Like the models of college-going behavior, each of the three models of college choice also identifies costs as factors which influence the choice of one PEI over a set of alternative PEIs. Costs are influential in that students compare PEIs in their set of choices on the basis of their costs and perceived benefits (Kohn et al., 1976). Out-of-pocket expenses to attend different PEIs are one cost factor (Radner and Miller, 1970; R. Chapman, 1979), while tuition costs and net tuition for all possible PEIs are another factor considered to influence the selection process (Kohn et al., 1976). A ratio of college costs to parental income is an additional factor identified (Radner and Miller, 1970). This ratio suggests that if costs for attendance exceed parental discretionary income for a given PEI, then the probability of selecting that particular PEI decreases.

Such student background characteristics as parental income and student academic ability are also posited as factors in the college choice process (Radner and Miller, 1970; Kohn et al., 1976). Presumably such factors enter into the weighting process for alternative PEIs.

College characteristics are understandably included as factors effecting the choice of a PEI. The admission selectivity of a given PEI is identified by Radner and Miller (1970) and by Kohn et al., (1976) as an indicator of college quality, while academic reputation has been suggested by R. Chapman (1979). Quality dimensions are posited as significant, as students would prefer to attend a higher quality college (Kohn et al., 1976). However, at the same time, students would also prefer not to attend a PEI where average student ability is considerably higher than their own. Thus, this factor is accounted for by two of the econometric models of college choice (R. Chapman, 1979; Kohn, Manski, and Mundel, 1976).

In addition to admissions selectivity, the same array of college characteristics identified as important in the college-going model advanced by Kohn et al., (1976) is also postulated to be influential in their econometric model of college choice. Moreover, a range of college attributes such as the size/graduate orientation, masculinity/technical orientation, ruralness, fine arts orientation, and liberalness are also suggested as factors of importance in the college choice process by R. Chapman (1979).

Consumer Model of Choice

A more general model of college choice is offered by Young and Reyes (1987). They identify costs and risks as the principal factors. Moreover, this model is applicable to various stages of the college choice process. In this econometric model, costs are the use of personal resources to earn a degree. Both monetary efforts and non-monetary effort are forms of personal resources or costs. Financial aid is classified as a type of monetary effort. Risks are also monetary and nonmonetary. A monetary risk revolves around the perceived value or benefit of receiving a college degree in relationship to its costs, whereas nonmonetary risks may be social or psychological. Failure to earn a degree is an example of a nonmonetary risk.

Although not directly stated by Young and Reyes, the choice of a PEI rather than a noncollege alternative requires that an individual student estimate a minimal degree of costs and risks associated with college enrollment. However, Young and Reyes do posit that if risks are perceived to be great, then the influence of cost is reduced.

Costs and risks are also related to stages of the college choice process derived from Kotler and Fox (1985). These stages are (1) need arousal, or when an initial interest in college is developed; (2) information gathering; (3) decision evaluation, or the narrowing down of choices to a particular set of choices; and (4) decision execution, or the choice of one PEI over another. Young and Reyes (1987) suggest that such nonmonetary costs and risks as parental and peer expectations are more influential in the need-arousal and information-gathering stages than are monetary costs. However, monetary costs become more influential in the decision to enroll in one PEI over another. At this stage, financial aid is predicted to play a significant role.

Sociological Models

Sociological models of college choice have focused on the identification and interrelationship of factors which influence aspirations for college attendance. Aspirations for college are of interest to sociologists, as aspirations are an integral element in the status attainment process. The status attainment process is concerned with the role played by various factors in the allocation of individual positions or occupations of varying degrees of prestige or status (Sewell and Shah, 1978). Within this allocative process, the role of education is of central importance.

The derivative model of status attainment was developed by Blau and Duncan (1967). In this model, family socioeconomic background and student academic ability are predicted to have a joint positive effect on aspirations for college. Parental encouragement (Sewell and Shah, 1978) and the influence of significant others and high school academic performance (Sewell, Haller, and Portes, 1969; Sewell and Hauser, 1975) were factors subsequently added as refinements to the basic model. Significant others are the students' parents, teachers, and peers.

The influence of significant others and academic performance represent a linkage of social-psychological mechanisms with status attainment (Sewell et al., 1969). To elaborate, mental ability is assumed to affect academic performance in high school. High school performance and family socioeconomic status exert positive influences on the perceptions of significant others concerning the focal student. Aspirations for college are, in turn, affected by the influence of significant others. Significant others such as parents, teachers and friends influence student aspirations either as models or through the behavioral expectations they communicate.

Two additional perspectives on the shaping of aspirations for college are provided by Boyle (1966) and by Alwin and Otto (1977). Although both Boyle and Alwin and Otto focus on the role of high school context, the formulations of these two models are distinctly different and merit closer examination.

Boyle's model is complex and is best described by beginning with those factors predicted to have a direct influence on the shaping of aspirations for college. Two psychological factors—academic ability and motivation—are posited to directly affect college aspirations. Academic ability is largely determined by high school academic standards, which are, in turn, affected by the structural characteristics of the school and by the preparation and motivation of students. More specifically, the centralization or decentralization of autonomy of local school districts in the development of academic standards (standardized examinations) affects standards at the level of the individual high school. Put differently, variability in high school standards is a function of the extent to which autonomy is extended to the individual high school. The high school student body composition also influences the standards and practices of a high school. High schools vary in composition of their student bodies in terms of the preparation and motivations of students. Well-prepared and highly motivated students are more willing to expend effort in their course assignments and are more amenable to instruction. Student body composition also indirectly affects student motivations for college aspirations. The composition of a student body determines the peer group subcultures of a high school, which, in turn, influence the motivation of students to develop plans for attendance. Thus, Boyle's model addresses the influence of both between- and within-school factors on college aspirations.

The model advanced by Alwin and Otto (1977) also accounts for the effects of between- and within-school variables on the formulation of plans for postsecondary education. This model is comprised of two stages. In the first stage, three background characteristics and school context variables are predicted to indirectly affect college aspirations. Gender, socioeconomic level, and academic ability are the student characteristics, while average student socioeconomic background, average student ability, and the proportion of enrollment which is male are the contextual or between-school variables. These variables are exogenous, or not influenced by any other variables within the model, and are predicted to directly affect academic certification and social influences. These, in turn, directly influence aspirations for college. Grades and placement in a college preparatory curriculum are dimensions of academic certification.

In the second stage of this model, the effects of academic certification and social influences on college aspirations are outlined. While academic certification plays a direct role in shaping institutions, this variable also develops the expectations of significant others for the development of postsecondary educational plans. More specifically, such significant others as peers, teachers, and parents use students' high school performance as a basis for the formulation of expectations. Such significant others also take into account the socioeconomic background and aca-demic ability of the student in the development of such expectations.

Moreover, it is also posited that students take into account their academic ability, previous academic achievements, and the expectations of significant others in the development of postsecondary educational plans. This model is depicted in Figure 1-1. Thus, Alwin and Otto (1977) like Sewell, Haller and Portes (1969) also point to the importance of significant others in influencing aspirations for college. However, the formulations regarding the influence of significant others are different.

Combined Models

Although both status-attainment and econometric models have focused on student decision-making in regard to college selection, neither of these conceptual approaches has provided satisfactory explanations of the *process* of college choice. Renewed interest in the subject has caused scholars to look again at both areas from an applied-research tradition in order to better understand consumer decision-making and recruitment efforts (Hanson and Litten, 1982). The new models, by extricating and combining the most powerful indicators in the decision-making process from previous models, provide a conceptual framework that hopes to predict the effects of policy-making interventions. These combined models, as befitting the longitudinal nature of the college choice process, are presented as sequential and as stages in the decision-making process. Institutional and market research have also made their contribution to the combined models by identifying the difference between student *perceptions* of institutional characteristics and objective institutional indicators and by showing the impact of institutional actions on college choice (i.e., recruitment, financial aid, and admissions activities).

Market research has studied the relationship between the type of student and the category of institution to which he or she applied (Zemsky and Oedel, 1983). Demographics, geographic origins, socioeconomic backgrounds, aptitude, and student interests have been analyzed in order to build a profile of the characteristics of students entering individual institutions. Looking for patterns, market research has found a homogeneity that seemingly cuts across all other

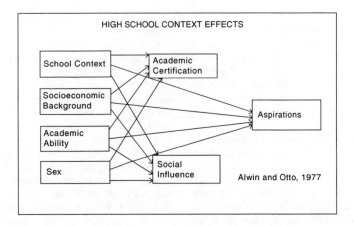

Figure 1-1 Causal diagram for school process model

variables; that is, the personal characteristics of the student—religious and political preferences, levels of sophistication and readiness for college—relate significantly to the existing student body of the college in which she or he enrolls (Clark et al., 1972; Zemsky and Oedel, 1983). From an institutional perspective, the choice process can be likened to a funnel, with a broad pool of prospective students at the top and a narrow pool of students who choose to enroll at the bottom (Litten, 1982).

As in the college-going models advanced by Kohn et al., (1976), Radner and Miller (1970), and R. Chapman (1979), market research indicates that students seek their set of colleges based on their perception of the college community; that is, they seek a college that most closely fits their social preference. These perspectives may be unrealistic. According to R. Chapman (1979), college-bound high school seniors, regardless of the institution they expect to attend, share a highly stereotyped, idealized image of college life, an image that may not be representative of any actual institution. Market research has identified the duality of a college market and the relationship between the structure of student choice and the structure of institutional comparisons—the forces shaping college-bound students' decisions and the institutional consequences of those decisions (Zemsky and Oedel, 1983, p. 25). As market research has shown, the importance of

institutional identity in the college choice process, and these intervening variables, along with those from the status attainment and econometric models, has been incorporated in the combined models now examined.

The major distinction between the combined models and those of status attainment and econometric conceptualizations is that the combined models attempt to identify those factors affecting the decision-making process from a policy analysis perspective; that is, the models attempt to describe the various economic and social forces that affect decision making in order to find opportunities for intervention in the student college choice process. These forces include (1) constraints upon the decision that the researcher and policy-maker should be made aware of and (2) institutional activities that can be undertaken to achieve desired results (beneficial interventions). Because combined models approach the conceptual framework of college choice as applied research and therefore offer opportunities for intervention, they can be more useful to public and institutional policy analysts than could the earlier status-attainment and econometric models.

Two general categories of combined models have been proposed: a three-stage model (Hossler and Gallagher, 1987; Jackson, 1982; Hanson and Litten, 1982) and a multistage model that generally comprises between five and seven stages (Litten, 1982; Kotler, 1976; R. Chapman, 1984)[1] A careful study of both categories reveals much overlap and general consensus (Figure 1-2). In fact, the three-stage model can be viewed as a simplified, "collapsed" version of the other. Differences between the models lie in the description of the intervening variables and in how they define constraining and institution activity.

The elements of a causal model will be used to provide the framework for a comparative discussion of the combined models of college choice. Intervening variables are those between the independent and dependent variable arranged in stages (or in the terminology of behavioral science, they are the intermediant variables of a cause-and-effect sequence). The two types of variables alluded to are (1) constant variables, which include influential factors effecting the process over which the student has no control, and (2) adjunct variables, which consist of auxiliary action taken by the institution that can beneficially affect the outcome of the decision-making process. These combined models are in agreement in regard to the descriptors that make up the independent variables of the model, although a variety of terms are used to describe the characteristics that cause an individual to consider postsecondary education as a viable alternative following graduation from high school. These include "college aspirations" (Hanson and Litten, 1981; Jackson, 1982; Litten,

1982), which is the referent used to describe the desire to attend. The terminology's source comes out of the literature on status attainment and includes factors such as socioeconomic status, aptitude, high school performance, gender, and family background. *Predisposition* (Hossler and Gallagher, 1987) and *general expectations* (D. Chapman, 1981) are also terms that have been used to describe the same set of individual factors.

Kotler (1976) proposed seven stages of the college choice process in his market research theory: (1) decision to attend, (2) information seeking and receiving, (3) specific college inquiries, (4) applications, (5) admission, (6) college choice, and (7) registration. These stages have been retained in subsequent combined models, although most often several of these individual actions have been incorporated into broader categorical stages. Kotler's model correctly identifies many activities of the college selection process. It also reflects his market research orientation. For instance, by separating "information seeking" from "specific college inquiries," Kotler offers institutions an additional opportunity for interaction. In a later publication, Kotler and Fox (1985) propose that in the information seeking stage, people often form images of schools based on inaccurate or limited information. The image formed affects the student's choice of colleges to which he or she will make specific inquiries. Thus, the image of the college,

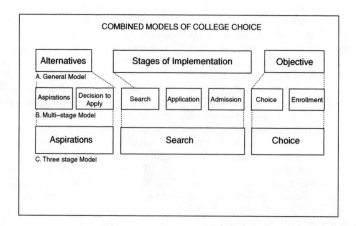

Figure 1-2

realistic or not, has a strong influence on the later stages of selection.

D. Chapman (1981) proposed a model of college choice that attempts to identify important variables and influences affecting student college choice. Unlike the other combined models, Chapman's model does not comprise a series of behavioral stages. Rather, it shows the interrelationship of student characteristics with external forces that result in individual expectations of college life. As such, it may not be as useful for devising intervention strategies, but its clear description of influential factors helps to identify important variables.

The model includes SES, aptitude, level of educational aspiration, and high school performance under the general category of student characteristics. D. Chapman states that students not only enter PEIs at different rates due to their socioeconomic status, they also distribute themselves differently across various types of PEIs. Because many PEIs publish test scores and class rank of their entering class, students self-select colleges prior to application based upon their own assessment of aptitude, as indicated by high school performance (Chapman, 1981, p. 483). Student aspirations include both an estimate of their "prospects" and an expression of their hopes and desires for the future. Under the general heading of external influence, Chapman has included as subcategories significant persons, fixed college characteristics, and college communication efforts.

Research has shown that parents exert the most influence on college choice and that other significant influences can include counselors, peers, teachers, and college admissions officers. Fixed college characteristics are those that help to define the institution such as costs, campus environment, location, and program offerings. Together, these create the institutional image. Even though these characteristics are open to change, the image may remain fixed with students and counselors for a long period of time (ibid, p. 476). The market approach to college admissions believes that institutions can promote an image through their recruitment materials and thereby exert desirable influence on a targeted student population. College communication efforts are described as written publications and recruitment materials. The broad categories of student characteristics and external influences shape the individual's expectations of college life, which in turn influence that student's choice of colleges.

The variables that make up the student characteristics (SES, aptitude, level of aspiration, high school performance) have been described in full in the discussion of status attainment and need not be gone into again.

If the purpose of Chapman's model is to identify the variables important to college choice, Jackson's model (1982) is intended to test the strength of the relationships between variables in order to identify the most effective areas of intervention. Jackson proposes a three-phase model of college choice and describes these phases as (1) preference, (2) exclusion, and (3) evaluation. From the status attainment models, Jackson draws individual characteristics that result in educational and occupational aspirations which result in student preferences for postsecondary education. According to Jackson, the strongest correlate of student aspiration is high school achievement, which is affected by other variables. Next in strength is context, which includes peers, neighborhood, and school. The third correlate of student aspiration is family background. High school aspiration reflects not only a preference for certain options but also the perception of access and availability of certain options.

Jackson's analysis of econometric models suggests that alternatives (PEIs) are initially excluded because of geographic, economic, and academic considerations that act as constraints when they interact with student characteristics. Whereas most PEIs are appropriate for most students, it is the consideration of basic cost, programs and requirements, and location that creates a real difference. Location can add to basic expense when the costs of travel, residence, and out-of-state tuition are considered. Secondly, students don't have access to complete information on all possible college options, and they proceed in the choice process with only partial information. Students also come with their own exclusion criteria that are based on their expectations of financial resources and future economic performance. These conscientiously act as constraints on college choice, causing students to limit their range of options. Thus Jackson describes the processes of phase 2 as the exclusion phase.

The final phase includes the student's evaluation of options, the translation of his or her preferences into a rating scheme, the selection of a choice set, and ultimately, the decision to enroll in a particular college. Although the rating scheme by which students evaluate their choices is not well understood, Jackson contends that family background, academic experience, location, and college costs are most important to this model of student choice. Recruitment information, college characteristics, and job benefits are ranked as having moderate effects college choice. In this model, social context can claim only a weak effect.

In summary, Jackson ranks the effects of different variables found in the general three-stage model of student college choice in order to inform the design of enrollment strategies. This model is presented as a means for evaluating enrollment tactics.

Both Chapman and Jackson present a generalized model of the influence of college choice and their relationship to the outcomes of institutional policy-making in general terms. Litten (1982), Hanson and Litten (1982), R. Chapman (1984) and Hossler and Gallagher (1987), on the other hand, have attempted to create models that show how the *process* of college choice is undertaken and how it is different for different people. The most effective marketing strategies address the needs of different target populations in specific ways, and therefore a model of college choice that takes into account how the college selection process is different for various groups

provides important information for enrollment strategists (Litten, 1982). These multistep, combined models take into account the personal and family background and characteristics that have been borrowed from the status attainment models. Hanson and Litten's (1981) model was used to distinguish how the college selection process is different for men and for women. It also distinguishes between the parallel activities related to the application for college admission and application for financial aid (p. 74). In this model, the six steps of the admission process—(1) desire to attend, (2) decision to attend, (3) investigation of institutions, (4) application for admission, (5) admission, and (6) enrollment—have been organized as three stages (see Figure 1-3). Stage 1 incorporates the desire and decision to attend. The fact of gender is included as one of the predictors of college aspirations in the sociological models and is emphasized as a controlling variable in the Hanson and Litten model. Variables of self-esteem and self-assessment are seen as differing for men and women, thereby affecting educational aspirations (men have tended to be more self-confident). Stage 2 is described as the investigation stage, and parental influence, geographical location, financial considerations, and college environment have been shown to affect women more than men. Women have been more likely to apply for early decision and to apply earlier in general than men, a difference found later in Stage 3.

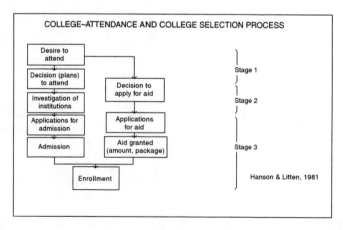

Figure 1-3

Litten later expands this model, drawing upon Chapman's broader, structural model. The "Expanded Model of the College Selection Process" (Litten, 1982, p. 388) draws upon variables from the status-attainment and econometric conceptual approaches. The social attributes of the high school, student performance as indicated by class rank, and high school curriculum are shown to affect student aspirations to attend or not to attend. Likewise, SES and personal attributes— such as academic ability, self-image, and the nature of the economic, political, and cultural environment—are all shown to affect the student's predisposition to attend. At the information-gathering stage, the influence of significant others (parents, peers, close friends) is influential. From market theory, variables of college action (recruitment, policies, publications, media) are demonstrated to have an effect on application. Finally, the college's action to grant or not to grant admission also influences the decision to enroll. Research applied to this model indicated that the timing of steps in the selection process is closely tied in to parental education, especially as it relates to how information on colleges is obtained. By drawing a line around the entire decision-making process, Litten's model illustrates that the control variables have a probable point of principle impact but that they continue to exert influence throughout the process. By developing an awareness of the individual differences in timing, policy-makers may be able to approach targeted groups with information appropriate to their different timetables (Litten, 1982).

R. Chapman (1984) proposes a five-stage theory of how students select a college and adds to the literature by further clarifying the basic terminology used to describe the various behavioral stages. In Chapman's model, the first stage is identified as "Presearch" behavior and is described as that period of time when a student first recognized "the possible need and desirability of a college education." This terminology is close enough to the "college aspirations" or "predisposition stage" of other models to be used interchangeably. By Chapman's definition, the second stage, "Search," is characterized by the active acquisition of alternative variables that characterize colleges, such as cost, quality of life, and academic programs. The search phase concludes when the student decides upon a set of colleges. The set is comprised of the colleges to which applications will be submitted and reveals

a process of self-selection. Research has shown that students apply to those colleges they are likely to be admitted to; likewise, we must assume that the colleges in this set are at least minimally acceptable to them (R. Chapman, 1984). At the application decision, however (stage three), the possibility of financial aid is still an unknown but will effect the next stage, the choice decision. Choice is the decision to select one of several colleges to which the student has been admitted. It is at this point that actual, rather than perceived, college characteristics become of primary importance, along with the factors of financial aid. As with all other models, Chapman's model of the college choice process ends with matriculation, the actual action of enrolling in a college.

The conceptual models of college choice identify significant variables and show the sequence of the decision-making process. Of special interest to researchers and policy-makers are the control variables consisting of constraints (environmental factors or characteristics of the population) and adjuncts (auxiliary actions taken by policy-makers to enhance the process, such as pricing, programming, and recruitment materials). The concept of constraints comes from the economic models, which indicated that students first exclude and then evaluate alternatives. Econometric theory has also been used to predict the impact of change in public policy toward financial aid. Research on the relationship of financial aid and college choice has demonstrated that aid has a significant impact on college attendance and choice of college (R. Chapman, 1979; Fields and LeMay, 1973; Litten, 1986). Likewise, the perception of the out-of-pocket cost of attending a particular institution affects the selection decision (Kohn et al., 1976; Bishop, 1977; Nolfi, 1978; Fuller et al., 1982; Manski and Wise, 1983; Litten, 1986). The importance of identifying constraints, therefore, is that they are variables over which public and institutional policy-makers can exert some control. The combined models of college choice provide useful information for the development of enrollment tactics. By describing the relative strength of different variables, the models also provide the means whereby strategies can be evaluated for projected efficiency and effectiveness.

These three conceptual approaches can also be compared on the range of variables included and on their explanatory power. The combined models are the most inclusive of the three approaches, as a wide range of variables is predicted to influence the college choice process. Moreover, the combined models incorporate more than a single stage of the choice process. The econometric models also include a number of variables of presumed influence and focus on one of two stages in the choice process: college-going and choice behavior. The sociological models, however, include a limited number of variables and focus on only the aspiration stage of the choice process.

When the approaches are compared on their explanatory power, the combined models appear to be limited. Although the models of this category posit relationships between various variables, few assumptions and concepts which seek to explicate the linkages between influential variables are advanced, and those that are have not been investigated. While the econometric models offer the notion of maximum utility of the perceived benefits of one choice alternative over another, assumptions and linking concepts among variables are also lacking. The sociological models not only provide several alternative perspectives on the mechanisms for the development of aspirations of college choice but also move beyond statements of relationships to the advancement of assumptions and concepts which seek to explain these relationships. Thus, the sociological models appear to have the most explanatory power of the three conceptual approaches to the study of college choice.

Given these assessments, we suggest a need for further development of the econometric and the combined models of the college choice process. Such development should focus on enhancing the explanatory power of these conceptual approaches. However, as the combined models appear to be the most inclusive in terms of the stages and factors included, this category of approaches is perhaps the best candidate for further theoretical development. Specific suggestions for such theoretical development are subsequently discussed in this chapter.

A Review of Research on Student College Choice

In addition to the theoretical work that provides a conceptual framework for this chapter, there are numerous studies that have examined various aspects of student college choice. The foci of these studies include the postsecondary aspirations of high school graduating classes, the relationship between high school guidance counseling and postsecondary plans, the impact of financial aid on postsecondary attendance rates, and institutional studies that attempt to determine which factors affect the decision to attend a specific PEI.

For this review, the three-stage model of student college choice proposed by Hossler and Gallagher (1987) will be used as the conceptual framework for organizing empirical investigations of college choice. Although, this model does not capture the complexities of the choice process that are present, for instance, in the model of Kotler (1985), it includes the major stages of the choice process. In addition, this model combines most of the variables found in both econometric and sociological models of student college choice. The model also suggests that institutional variables have an impact on student college choice. By employing a three-stage model, it is possible to bring some order to a diverse, and sometimes chaotic, set of empirical investigations. By employing a theoretical model to organize and review existing research on student college choice, it is possible to conduct a systematic analysis of methodological questions and theory development in the next section of this chapter. The model of Hossler and Gallagher (1987) is based on the work of R. Chapman (1984), Jackson (1982), and Litten (1982). This model of student college choice includes the following stages:

1. Predisposition—The "developmental phase in which students determine whether or not they would like to continue their formal education beyond high school."

2. Search—Searching for the attributes and values which characterize postsecondary educational alternatives as well as learning about and identifying the right attributes to consider.

3. Choice—Formulating a choice (or application set) and deciding which institution to attend. (Hossler and Gallagher, 1987, p. 211)

In this chapter, each stage is examined separately and related research is reviewed. Although this approach integrates and extends our knowledge of student college choice, such an endeavor is not without conceptual and methodological problems.

A review of the research on student college choice quickly reveals that it has not been based upon a common set of theoretical assumptions. Most of the existing research has not been conceptualized in such a way that these studies can easily be categorized into the three-stage model that has been outlined. Many of the investigations, while grounded in concrete practical problems, lack any guiding theoretical constructs. As a result, many studies are based upon a unique set of assumptions. There is great variance in the survey instruments or interview protocols and the results of these college choice studies.

To clarify relationships among variables, available evidence has been carefully reviewed. In addition, causal ordering has been reported whenever such findings were available. Out of necessity, the format of the examination of each stage of student college choice is different. Because there are so many investigations which have examined the correlates of postsecondary enrollment and the demand for higher education, much is known about the factors that influence the predisposition stage of student college choice. The *correlates* of predisposition, as well as some of the *process characteristics* (timing, variability among different students, etc.) of predisposition can be discussed in detail.

Conversely, the search stage has received little attention. Little is known about how students go about collecting and evaluating information about PEIs before they select the institutions to which to apply. Therefore, the discussion of search in this chapter is limited to an examination of the process characteristics (timing and information sources).

The third stage, choice, has received considerable attention from individual institutions. These institutions have studied the correlates of choice in order to understand why students select one PEI over another. It is more difficult to arrive at generalizations similar to those arrived at when examining predisposition. Nevertheless, more is known about the choice stage than is known about the search stage.

Predisposition

During the predisposition phase of student college choice, students arrive at a tentative con-

clusion to continue, or not continue, their formal education after high school graduation. Since few studies of student college choice have been conducted using a college choice model, the predisposition section of this chapter draws primarily upon research that has examined correlates of postsecondary participation. From the perspective of a college choice model, studies that examine such variables as the relationship between SES, or levels of parental encouragement, and postsecondary enrollment provide insights into the factors that influence whether or not a student will attend a PEI. The array of variables that have been found to be correlated with a predisposition toward postsecondary attendance include:

1. Family socioeconomic status is positively associated with postsecondary participation (Corrazini et al., 1972; Ekstrom, 1985; Elsworth et al., 1982; Gilmour et al., 1978; Hause, 1969; Jackson, 1978; Manski and Wise, 1983; Perlman, 1973; Sewell et al., 1972; Sewell and Hauser, 1975; Tuttle, 1981; Yang, 1981).

2. Student academic ability and achievement are positively associated with postsecondary participation (Bishop, 1977; Carpenter and Fleishman, 1987; Hause, 1969; Jackson, 1986; Manski and Wise, 1983; Sewell and Hauser, 1975; Tillery, 1973; Tuttle, 1981; Yang, 1981).

3. Race and ethnicity are associated with postsecondary participation. Caucasians and Asians are more likely to participate, black and Hispanic students are less likely to participate (Hossler, 1984; Litten, 1982; Manski and Wise, 1983; Tuttle, 1981).

4. Gender has little impact on postsecondary participation (Carpenter and Fleishman, 1987; Elsworth, 1982; Hossler and Stage, 1987; Marini and Greenberger, 1978; Stage and Hossler, 1988).

5. Parental levels of education are positively associated with postsecondary participation (Carpenter and Fleishman, 1987; Gilmour et al., 1978; Hossler and Stage, 1988; Jackson, 1986; Solmon and Taubman, 1973; Trent and Medsker, 1967; Tuttle, 1981; Yang, 1981).

6. Family residence—urban or rural location—has differential effects on postsecondary participation (Anderson et al., 1972; Dahl, 1982; Lam and Hoffman, 1979).

7. Parental encouragement and support for postsecondary education are positively associated with postsecondary participation (Carpenter and Fleishman, 1987; Conklin and Dailey, 1981; Ekstrom, 1985; Gilmour et al., 1978; Hossler and Stage, 1988; *Parents, Programs and Pennsylvania Student Plans*, 1984; Russell, 1980).

8. Peer encouragement and support are positively associated with postsecondary participation (Carpenter and Fleishman, 1987; Coleman, 1966; Falsey and Heyns, 1984; Jackson, 1986; Russell, 1980; Tillery, 1973).

9. Encouragement from high school counselors and teachers are positively associated with postsecondary participation (Ekstrom, 1985; Falsey and Heyns, 1984; Tillery, 1973; *Parents, Programs and Pennsylvania Student Plans*, 1984).

10. Student educational aspirations and career plans are positively associated with postsecondary participation (Carpenter and Fleishman, 1987; Dahl, 1982; Gilmour et al., 1978; Hilton, 1982; Jackson, 1978; *Parents, Programs and Pennsylvania Student Plans*, 1984; Peters, 1977; Trent and Medsker, 1968).

11. The quality of the high school and the academic track the student is enrolled during high school are positively associated with postsecondary participation (Alexander et al., 1978; Elsworth, 1982; Harnqvist, 1978; Falsey and Heyns, 1984; Kolstad, 1979; *Parents, Programs and Pennsylvania Student Plans*, 1984; Peters, 1977).

12. The labor market and increased rates of return[2] are positively associated with postsecondary participation (Adkins, 1975; Bishop, 1977; Campbell and Siegel, 1967; Chressanthis, 1986; Corrazini et al., 1972; Dresch and Waldenberg, 1978; Jackson, 1978; Mattila, 1982).

Although each of these variables has been correlated with a predisposition toward enrollment in a PEI, the strength of the association between these variables and predisposition is not consistent across all studies.

Socioeconomic Status

SES is positively associated with a predisposition to attend a PEI. A consistently positive relationship has been found between SES and postsecondary participation rates (Alexander et al., 1978; Corrazini et al., 1972; Ekstrom, 1985; Elsworth et al., 1982; Gilmour et al., 1978; Hause, 1969; Jackson, 1978; Perlman, 1973; Sewell et al., 1972; Tuttle, 1981; Yang, 1981). Elsworth et al. (1982) found that SES explained 9.3% of the variance in postsecondary participation rates among youth in Australia (p. 71). Tuttle (1981) reported that SES accounted for 6.8% of the explained variance in his study of students from the 1980 High School and Beyond study (HSB). The nature of the relationship between SES and predisposition, however, is not specified in all of these studies. In addition, there is some evidence that the impact of SES on predisposition may be different for men and women (Marini and Greenberger, 1978; Stage and Hossler, 1988). In a multivariate analysis of the correlates of postsecondary participation in Australia, Ekstrom (1985) concluded that SES (along with sex, age, and home location) explained most of the variance in participation rates. Gilmour et al. (1978), in a qualitative study of the postsecondary plans of high school seniors in Pennsylvania, reported that as the family income and educational level of parents increased, students started to think about their postsecondary plans earlier.

Not all studies, however, have found SES to play an important role in explaining postsecondary participation rates. Jackson (1986) conducted a comparison of the postsecondary participation rates from the National Longitudinal Study of 1972 (NLS) and the 1980 HSB. Using multiple-regression techniques, he found that SES, while significant, explained only 3.0% of the variance in postsecondary participation rates in the NLS sample and 4.4% of the variance in the HSB sample (Jackson 1986, p. 18). Yang (1981), in a longitudinal study of 1,714 high school seniors that employed multiple-regression techniques, found that SES did not add to the amount of explained variance when parental educational background and parental encouragement were also considered. Similarly, Leslie et al. (1977), in a study of 1,000 high school seniors in Pennsylvania that employed qualitative interview techniques and multiple-regression analysis, found that SES did not have a major impact on student plans to attend a PEI.

Despite the findings of Jackson (1986), Yang (1981), and Leslie et al. (1977), when causal modeling techniques are utilized SES does have a significant, although indirect effect on postsecondary participation. Manski and Wise (1983) used conditional logit analysis to examine the college choice decisions of 23,000 high school students who participated in the National Longitudinal Study of 1972. Their results indicated that SES was associated with the likelihood of postsecondary enrollment (or predisposition), but the effect was not strong. In a pathanalytic study, Tuttle (1981), using HSB data, found that SES had an indirect effect through student ability/achievement on the predisposition stage. Tuttle's results suggest that although SES may not directly influence predisposition, SES does directly influence student achievement in high school, which in turn does exert a positive influence upon the predisposition stage. Similarly, Carpenter and Fleishman (1987) employed path analysis to study student college choice in Australia and reported that the effect of SES was indirect. The effects of SES on the predisposition of these students were mediated through parental encouragement and explained 15% of the variance in parental encouragement for college attendance (p. 94). In support of an indirect effect of SES on predisposition in a LISREL path-analytic study of the postsecondary aspirations of 2,495 high school juniors in Pennsylvania, Marini and Greenberger (1978) found that SES explained 8.9% more of the variance in ambition for boys. Conversely, SES explained 12.2% more of the variance in academic achievement for girls (p. 73).

A review of the findings suggests that SES does have an impact on predisposition; however, the impact may not be direct. Rather, SES has a positive effect upon the academic success of students, their educational aspirations, and the educational expectations they perceive that others have for them.

Student Ability

Trent and Medsker (1967) stated that "There is some question as to whether socioeconomic status or ability has the greater influence on the decision to attend college" (p. 3). Like SES, the empirical evidence supports the assertion that student ability is positively correlated with a predisposition toward postsecondary education (Bishop, 1977; Carpenter and Fleishman, 1987;

Hause, 1969; Jackson, 1978, 1986; Manski and Wise, 1983; Mare, 1980; Peters, 1977; Rumberger, 1982; Tillery, 1973; Tuttle, 1981; Yang, 1981). While Elsworth (1982) did not find that ability added to the amount of variance explained by his path model, this is the only study reviewed that included a measure of ability or achievement and did not find a significant relationship between ability/achievement and a predisposition toward postsecondary education. Manski and Wise (1983) found that high school GPA and SAT scores were the best predictors of who applied to college. In another analysis of NLS data, Peters (1977) concluded that high-ability high school students are eight times more likely to go to college than low-ability students (p. 9). Tillery (1973) reported similar findings. Jackson (1978) analyzed data from the National Longitudinal Study of 1972. He investigated the impact of financial aid on college choice using discriminant analysis. He found that academic standing improved his ability to predict college enrollment by 12% (p. 568). In a later comparative analysis of NLS and HSB data, Jackson (1986) reported that academic test scores explained 6.4% of the variance in postsecondary participation rates for the NLS sample and 8.1% of the variance for the HSB sample. Grades explained 4.2% of the variance in postsecondary participation rates for the NLS sample and 7.9% of the variance for the HSB sample (p. 18). Yang (1981), using multiple regression, also found that high school grades explained 15% of the variance in postsecondary aspirations and 12% of the variance in the actual attendance rates of high school students (p. 13).

Further support for the contribution of ability/academic achievement comes from Carpenter and Fleishman (1987) in their path-analytic study of Australian high school students. They found that academic achievement and ability had a direct effect on postsecondary participation. In addition they noted that achievement interacts with students' self-assessments of their postsecondary potential. They did not find a one-to-one correspondence between ability/achievement and postsecondary participation, however, because some students do not assess themselves realistically. In another path analysis that used HSB data, Tuttle (1981) found that grades explained 6.3% of the variance in the predisposition toward postsecondary education (p. 12). In a LISREL path-analytic study, Hossler and Stage

(1988) also found that student ability was a good predictor of postsecondary aspirations.

The cumulative weight of the findings in these studies reviewed indicates that student ability and student achievement have a significant and direct impact upon the predisposition of high school students toward a postsecondary education. As ability and academic achievement rise, students are more likely to aspire to attend a PEI and they are more likely to follow through on their plans.

Ethnicity

Historically, black students and other minorities were less likely to attend a PEI (Hossler, 1984). Enrollment trends among minority students rose sharply, however, during the 1970s. Between 1966 and 1977 the numbers of black students enrolled in postsecondary education tripled (*Chronicle of Higher Education*, 1978). Through 1986, participation rates slowly declined; however, in 1986 the black student enrollments started to increase (Evangelauf, 1988, p. A33). Such trends make it difficult to anticipate the impact of race on the predisposition phase of college choice. The inclusion of studies that were conducted when the postsecondary participation rates of minority students was higher, or lower, would be misleading since the factors that influenced the participation rates of minority students have changed. In an attempt to try to capture the current impact of race on predisposition, this review has been limited to a sample of recent investigations.

Ekstrom (1985), in an analysis of HSB data, reported that the impact of race upon postsecondary participation rates disappeared when SES was controlled. Tuttle (1981) found similar results; he found that when SES was controlled, minority students of average ability had a 6% higher probability of attendance (p. 13). Manski and Wise (1983), using NLS data, found similar patterns among black students, as did Jackson (1986), who used both NLS and HSB data sets. Hossler and Stage (1987), in a descriptive study of the postsecondary plans of Indiana ninth-grade students, found that ninth-grade minority students reported thinking more about postsecondary education than white students; however, white students were 4% more likely to indicate that they planned to attend a PEI (p. 10).

Similarly, Brown (1982), who compared NLS and HSB data, arrived at some disturbing findings. He found that the numbers of black students aspiring to attend two- and four-year PEIs had increased between the 1972 NLS study and the 1980 HSB study. From an equity perspective, this suggests that although more black students are aspiring to attend PEIs, fewer are actually attending. Attempts to determine the impact of race on predisposition are like tracking a moving target. At the moment, current evidence suggests that any correlation between race and predisposition is the result of other background variables, such as SES, which may be associated with race. Nevertheless, the declining rates of postsecondary participation of black students, when viewed with the knowledge that black students may have higher aspiration rates, give reason to be concerned about access and choice for black students.

Gender

College enrollment patterns for women, like those for minority students, have been in a period of transition. While women have historically been underrepresented in PEIs, there are now more women than men enrolled (*Update*, 1986). The findings from recent studies on the role of gender in aspirations for postsecondary participation are contradictory. Two studies (Hossler and Stage, 1987; Stage and Hossler, 1988) used correlational statistics and LISREL path-analytic techniques to examine the postsecondary aspirations of ninth-grade students in Indiana. They found that women thought more about going to a PEI but received less family support. Carpenter and Fleishman (1987) and Elsworth (1982), who conducted their studies in Australia, found that gender had no impact on postsecondary aspirations and participation. In fact, Tuttle (1981) deleted gender from his path model because it was not significant in the correlation matrix. Based upon these findings the role of gender on predisposition is uncertain. While some evidence suggests that women may receive less encouragement to attend a PEI, the large increase in enrollment rates among women would suggest that gender no longer plays a major role in the predisposition stage of student college choice.

Parental Educational Levels

Several studies have found a relationship between the level of parental education and predisposition (Carpenter and Fleishman, 1987; Gilmour et al., 1978; Hossler and Stage, 1987, 1988; Jackson, 1986; Manski and Wise, 1983; Solmon and Taubman, 1973; Trent and Medsker, 1967; Stage and Hossler, 1988; Tuttle, 1981; Yang, 1981). Carpenter and Fleishman (1987) found a strong relationship between the father's education and postsecondary enrollment. In his study of NLS and HSB participants, Jackson (1986) concluded that each year of parental education increased the likelihood of the student attending a PEI by 6% (p. 13).

Yang (1981) followed 1,714 rural high school seniors during their senior year in high school and their first year in college. Using qualitative data and multivariate analysis, his results revealed that the father's education exerted a stronger influence than the mother's upon the aspiration levels of the students, but the mother's education exerted more influence on actual attendance rates. Gilmour et al. (1978) reported that students with parents who had a college education started thinking earlier about continuing their education after high school. Tuttle (1981), however, using path analysis to study HSB data, found that parental education was not significant in the correlation matrix and therefore deleted it from his path model.

In two separate analyses of a sample of Indiana high school students, employing LISREL, Hossler and Stage (1988) and Stage and Hossler (1988) looked at the effects of parental education upon the postsecondary plans of Indiana ninthgraders. The first study (Hossler and Stage, 1988) found that the combined level of parents' education had a positive indirect and direct effect upon students' educational plans. Parents' education explained 43.5% of the variance in the amount of parental encouragement that parents gave students to attend a PEI (an indirect effect), and in addition, parental education directly explained 9.5% of the variance in students' educational aspirations (p. 7). The second study (Stage and Hossler, 1988) indicated that the mother's level of education had a positive indirect effect upon the educational plans of both male and female students (mediated through parental encouragement), while the father's level of education had both a positive direct and indirect effect upon the postsecondary educational plans of male and female students (total effect was 7.0% for females and 7.6% for males (pp. 20, 21)). In addition, Hossler and Stage (1988) found that the level of parental education was the best predictor of the parents' educational expectations for their children as well as the best predictor of the students' GPAs (explained 34.7% of the variance, p. 7). These findings are similar to those of Manski and Wise (1983), who compared the application probabilities of students whose parents had less than a high school education with those of students whose parents had a college degree or more. Across income levels ranging from $6,000 to $18,000, they found that in most income brackets, students who had parents with a college education more than doubled the probability that they would apply for college (p. 88).

Overall, the evidence suggests that the level of parental education exerts a strong influence upon predisposition toward postsecondary education, more than either SES or student ability.

Family Residence Characteristics

There is some empirical evidence to support the assertion that the location of family residence affects postsecondary participation rates (Anderson et al., 1972; Astin and others, 1980; Dahl, 1982; Lam and Hoffman, 1979; Willingham, 1970). These studies of family residence typically focus upon the impact of living in an urban or rural location, and whether nearness to a PEI influences postsecondary participation rates. Anderson et al. (1972) used multipleregression techniques to analyze SCOPE data (which included postsecondary participation rates from four states). They found that the relationship between distance and college attendance was complex and varied in different states and for students of different ability levels. Generally, students who lived within twenty miles of a PEI were more likely to enroll. The variance in the effects of PEI distance from home ranged from a low of no effect on high-ability men from Illinois to an increase in college-going rates of 22% for low-ability men in Illinois (p. 249). The amount of variance explained by nearness to a PEI was small. Astin and others (1980) and Willingham (1970) reported similar findings.

Anderson et al. (1972) also found that students who lived in urban areas were more likely to attend a PEI. More recently, Dahl (1982), employing discriminant analysis in a longitudinal study of Kentucky high school seniors noted that students who resided in urban areas were more likely to enroll in a PEI. Another study employing discriminant analysis (Lam and Hoffman, 1979), conducted at a single Canadian university, reported that students who lived in rural areas were less likely to enroll in a PEI.

Although the effects of residence characteristics were significant in each of these studies, they did not have a strong or even moderate effect upon a predisposition toward postsecondary education. When ability and SES were controlled, the effects of residence characteristics diminished.

Parental Encouragement

Investigations of student college choice have consistently found that the amount of parental encouragement and support for postsecondary education is related to the likelihood of attendance (Carpenter and Fleishman, 1987; Conklin and Dailey, 1981; Ekstrom, 1985; Gilmour et al., 1978; Hossler and Stage, 1988; Murphy, 1981; *Parents, Programs and Pennsylvania Student Plans*, 1984; Russell, 1980; Stage and Hossler, 1988; Soper, 1971; Tillery, 1973). Several descriptive studies have reported a significant positive relationship between parental expectations and the educational aspirations of high school students (Ekstrom, 1985; *Parents, Programs and Pennsylvania Student Plans*, 1984; Russell, 1980; Soper, 1971; Tillery, 1973). Murphy (1981), in a descriptive study of high school seniors and parents, noted that 42.6% of all students and 50% of all parents said that the idea of attending a PEI was first initiated by parents (p. 143). Hossler and Stage (1988), in their LISREL path model, found that parental encouragement for their students explained 18.2% of the variance in the postsecondary plans of Indiana ninth-graders and exerted the largest direct effect on students' plans.

Carpenter and Fleishman (1987) found that parental expectations did not directly influence the postsecondary enrollment decision. Parental expectations, however, did influence student's perceptions of subjective norms (perceptions of what students believed others thought they should do), which in turn were strongly related to postsecondary enrollment. Furthermore these authors' results demonstrated that as the level of

parental encouragement increases, student achievement also increases. Conklin and Dailey (1981) used multiple-regression techniques to analyze data gathered from a longitudinal study of high school students from their sophomore to senior year. The sample included 2,700 students in southern New York State. They also found that as the level of parental encouragement increased, students were more likely to attend four-year PEIs and More selective PEIs. Sewell and Shah (1978) made an even stronger case for the importance of parental encouragement. Using data from NLS, they found that the amount of parental encouragement explained 37% of the variance in postsecondary aspirations (p. 12). Parental encouragement explained more of the variance than any other variable, including SES and student ability.

When these findings are considered in total, parental encouragement appears to play an important role in the predisposition phase. Parental level of education, combined with parental educational aspirations for their children, may be the best predictors of student postsecondary plans. Carpenter and Fleishman's (1987) finding—that as parental encouragement rises, so does student achievement—also raised possibilities of a reciprocal relationship between parental encouragement, achievement, and predisposition. That is, as students perform better in school, parents provide more encouragement, which in turn provides further motivation for students to further improve their performance.

Peer Support and Encouragement

In addition to parental encouragement, researchers have found a relationship between predisposition toward postsecondary education and the level of support and encouragement of peers (Carpenter and Fleishman, 1987; Coleman, 1966; Falsey and Heyns, 1984; Jackson, 1986; Russell, 1980; Tillery, 1973). Falsey and Heyns (1984) asserted that one of the outcomes of attending private schools is that students establish friendship patterns that result in more contact with students planning to attend PEIs. For students attending private schools, these patterns increase the likelihood that they will attend college. In a study of 13,000 high school students in Manitoba that did not use inferential statistics, Russell (1980) reported that the postsecondary aspirations of friends were cited as one of the most influential factors in determining students' postsecondary plans. Coleman (1966) and Tillery (1973) described similar findings. In his comparison of the NLS and HSB samples, Jackson (1986) found that the presence of college-going peers produced one of the strongest correlations when he attempted to isolate the most important determinants of postsecondary enrollment. Hossler and Stage (1987), however, employed correlational statistics to examine the relationship among postsecondary plans of Indiana ninth-graders and their peers. They found that those students who were not planning to attend a PEI more frequently consulted their peers. This may suggest that students who are not planning to attend college may be more likely to be influenced by their peers than those students who are planning to go to college. The results from these studies suggest that peers also influence the predisposition phase of student college choice. In total, however, the evidence indicates that peer support and encouragement are not strongly associated with predisposition.

Encouragement from High School Counselors and Teachers

Boyer's recent book, *College: The Undergraduate Experience* (1986), asserted that high school counselors and teachers need to work more with high school students so that the student college choice process will be more informed. Some empirical investigations have examined the influence of encouragement from high school counselors and teachers on predisposition (Ekstrom, 1985; Falsey and Heyns, 1984; Lewis and Morrison, 1975; Tillery, 1973; *Parents, Programs and Pennsylvania Student Plans*, 1984). These investigations indicate that counselors and teachers have little impact on the postsecondary aspirations of students (Lewis and Morrison, 1975; Tillery, 1973; *Parents, Programs and Pennsylvania Student Plans*, 1984). Ekstrom (1985), Hossler and Stage (1987), and Lewis and Morrison (1975) did find that low-income and minority students were more likely to consult with counselors. Even among minority students, however, the actual percentage of students that relied on counselors was far below 50% (Hossler and Stage, 1987; Lewis and Morrison, 1975). These findings suggest that counselors and teachers have very little influence upon the predisposition stage of most high school students.

Student Career Plans and Aspirations

Research on the predisposition stage of student college choice indicates that the educational goals and career aspirations of high school students are positively related to enrollment in a PEI (Carpenter and Fleishman, 1987; Dahl, 1982; Gilmour et al., 1978; Hilton, 1982; Jackson, 1978; *Parents, Programs and Pennsylvania Student Plans*, 1984; Peters, 1977; Trent and Medsker, 1968). Several studies reported that over 80% of all high school students who indicate that they plan to enroll in a PEI follow through on their plans (Dahl, 1982; Hilton, 1982; Peters, 1977; Trent and Medsker, 1967). However, when causal models are developed, it appears that student aspirations are influenced by SES, student ability/achievement, and parental expectations (Carpenter and Fleishman 1987; Corazzini et al., 1972; Hossler and Stage, 1988). Thus, while student aspirations may be a good predictor of student outcomes, aspirations may simply reflect the effects of other variables.

School Quality and Academic Track

In addition to all of the variables examined thus far, some investigators have also concluded that the quality of the high school and placement in an academic track influence predisposition (Alexander, 1978; Elsworth, 1982; Falsey and Heyns, 1984; Kolstad, 1979; *Parents, Programs and Pennsylvania Student Plans*, 1984; Peters, 1977). The effects of school quality, however, are contradictory. Alexander (1978), Elsworth (1982) and Falsey and Heyns (1984) reported evidence suggesting that high school quality does effect predisposition. Elsworth's study (1982), however, was conducted in Australia and may not be generalizable to the United States. Falsey and Heyns's (1984) study focused upon the student outcomes of attending private high schools. Their findings may not be generalizable to all types of high schools. Alexander's (1978) study found that the social status of the high school was correlated with attendance at a PEI. Kolstad (1979), however, used multiple-regression analysis with a sample drawn from NLS and concluded that when SES and other background characteristics are held constant, high school quality is only weakly correlated with enrollment in PEIs.

With respect to the high school curriculum, research suggests that being in an academic track has an impact on the predisposition phase (Jackson, 1986; Kolstad, 1979; *Parents, Programs and Pennsylvania Student Plans*, 1984; Peters, 1977). The Pennsylvania study, in fact, found that high school track was a better predictor of attendance in a PEI than grades. Similarly, Jackson (1986) found strong zero-order correlations between academic track and postsecondary enrollment. Kolstad (1979), however, reported that academic track did not exert much influence on postsecondary participation when background characteristics were controlled. Unfortunately, there were no path analytic models to indicate whether other variables have causal links with academic track. It appears that a student's academic track is correlated with the predisposition phase of student college choice, but the precise nature of the relationship between academic track and the decision to attend a PEI cannot be specified. Causal models, however, might be expected to show that SES, ability, and parental encouragement exert a strong influence upon the academic track that students are enrolled in during high school.

Effects of the Rate of Return and Labor Market

Economists as well as education researchers have also investigated the relationship between (1) the labor market, (2) the rate of return, and (3) postsecondary enrollments (Adkins, 1975; Bishop, 1977; Campbell and Siegel, 1967; Chressanthis, 1986; Corazzini et al., 1972; Dresch and Waldenberg, 1978; Jackson, 1978; Mattila, 1982). The questions driving these investigations are:

1. Do the employment opportunities for graduates of PEIs have any impact on decisions to go to a PEI? When the number of jobs for graduates of PEIs decline do postsecondary enrollments decline? When the number of jobs increases, do postsecondary enrollments increase?

2. Are students' decisions to continue their education beyond high school influenced by their perceptions of the rate of return?

In the aggregate, the answer is that the predisposition phase of college choice is not greatly influenced by either labor market activities or the rate of return. Adkins (1975), after comparing postsecondary enrollment trends since the Great Depression to trends in the labor market, stated that the postsecondary enrollments have increased steadily despite shifting trends in the labor market. Corazzini et al. (1972) concluded that during periods of high unemployment students are more likely to attend a PEI rather than be unemployed. Chressanthis (1986) and Hossler (1984) observed the same trend during the recession of the late 1970s.

Changes in the rate of return also have little effect on the predisposition phase of college choice. Despite the well-documented decline in the rate of return during the 1970s (Bird, 1975; Dresch and Waldenberg, 1978; Freeman, 1976), aggregate postsecondary enrollments continued to increase. Mattila (1982) found that enrollment rates among men during the 1970s declined, and he attributed this to changes in draft laws and the declining rate of return. However, Bishop (1977) and Campbell and Siegel (1967) attempted to measure the effects of rate of return on the demand for higher education. Both studies concluded that high school students were either unaware of shifts in the rate of return or discounted future rates of return at such high levels that it had no effect on their postsecondary educational plans. The results of these econometric studies indicate that although some subpopulations of high school students (e.g., males) may be more responsive to economic inducements, in the aggregate, these inducements have little or no impact on the predisposition phase of most high school students.

This review of the correlates of the predisposition indicates that a number of factors influence the predisposition stage of student college choice. Table 1-1 summarizes the strength of the association between these factors and a positive predisposition toward postsecondary education.

Process Characteristics of Predisposition

In addition to the correlates of the predisposition stage, several process characteristics are also involved in the development of a predisposition toward postsecondary education. Gilmour et al. (1978) concluded that the decision to attend a PEI is closely intertwined with the career-decision-making process. The two processes take place simultaneously. A predisposition toward postsecondary education is an evolving process that proceeds at differential rates for different students. Gilmour et al. (1978) noted that the sharpness, or certainty, of students' postsecondary

TABLE 1-1
The Correlates of Predisposition

Variable	Strength of association
Ability/achievement	Strong
Academic track	Strong
Parental levels of education	Strong
Parental encouragement	Strong
Student aspirations	Strong
Peer encouragement	Moderate
Ethnicity	Weak
Family residence	Weak
Gender	Weak
High school counselors and teachers	Weak
Labor market and rate of return	Weak
SES	Weak
School quality	Weak

plans varied greatly among students at the same grade level. For example, when studying two students at the same grade level, one student reported that she wanted to be a premed student at Duke or Stanford, the other student planned to go to a college to be "something better."

These distinctions in the certainty of students' plans are further demonstrated in Ekstrom's (1985) results. Among the students in the HSB study, 41% reported that they decided to attend a PEI by the sixth grade, 53% had decided by the eighth grade, and 61% had decided by the ninth grade (p. 15). Stewart et al. (1987), in a retrospective study conducted at Michigan State University, found that 80% of the students had made the decision to attend a PEI by the end of their junior year in high school (p. 13). Parrish (1979) investigated the postsecondary plans of high school juniors in one high school and reported that 59.8% of the students planned to attend a postsecondary institution and that 22.3% were undecided (p. 3).

Hossler and Stage (1987) found that although nearly 72% of the Indiana ninth-graders in their sample planned to attend a college of vocational institution (p. 8), few ninth-graders had thought beyond the predisposition phase. The ninth-grade questionnaire included a set of questions that asked them to indicate how far they wanted to travel to go to college, the size of the institution they wanted to attend, and whether they wanted to commute or live in campus housing. Most of the respondents were undecided. Students with parents who had more education or who were from high-SES families were more likely to have made some decision about these campus attributes, but over 50% of these students were also undecided (p. 18).

Jackson (1982) observed that the decision to consider attending a PEI was not final. He found that some students who initially planned to attend a PEI eventually decided not to continue their education after high school. The findings from this research review indicate that parents and peers provide information and counseling for students and help shape the predisposition stage. By the end of the junior year in high school, if not sooner, most students have formed their predisposition toward postsecondary education. During the predisposition stage, however, most students think of attending a PEI in global terms and lack specificity in their plans. Table 1-2 outlines the key process characteristics of the predisposition stage.

TABLE 1-2
The Process Characteristics of Predisposition

Duration	Early childhood to the 9th–10th grades
Related factors	Closely related to development of career plans
Specificity of plans	Vague, only certain they want to attend a PEI
Important influences	Parents

Search

Because so little attention has been given to the search stage of student college choice, the format of this section differs from that of the predisposition stage.

Rather than a detailed review of the correlates of the search stage, this section concentrates on a discussion of the process characteristics of this stage.

Timing

The junior year of high school is an eventful year for students in the college choice process. Most students have reached closure on the predisposition stage during the junior year and enter the search stage. Gilmour et al. (1978), in their study of high school students in six Pittsburgh high schools, found that 72% of the students in their sample developed a list of PEIs during their junior year (p. 15). Stewart et al. (1987) also found that 80% of the students who attended Michigan State University started investigating their postsecondary options during their junior year (p. 14).

Gilmour et al. (1978) also discovered that taking the PSAT often precipitated the development of a list of potential PEIs. During the early phase of the search process the list of PEIs included 3–6 institutions (p. 15). Gilmour et al.'s findings suggest that the search process nears completion by the summer of the junior year. They reported that during that summer, most students narrowed their list to 2–4 PEIs (p. 17). However, data collected by Lewis and Morrison (1975), in a series of interviews with high school seniors throughout their senior year in high school, indicated that for many students the search stage continued into the senior year. By October of their senior year, students reported that only 50% of all of the PEIs that they ultimately considered had been added to their list

of potential schools. By the end of January, students had dropped 50% of the PEIs to which they were considering sending applications. The average number of schools considered by students before they began to eliminate institutions was 9.3; as students continued to evaluate institutions, 5.7 was the average number of schools dropped from consideration (p. 17).

Approximately 90% of all PEIs that were considered had been added by February (p. 12). In total, it appears that the junior year and the first months of the senior year in high school are the time frame during which most students move from the search stage to the choice stage of student college choice.

Information Sources

As the search stage started, Gilmour et al. reported that most students had only a casual awareness of PEIs. Some of the first sources they consulted were college guidebooks such as *Peterson's Guide*. Cibik (1982), in a study of high school seniors at a single high school, found that most students first learned of PEIs from friends (50.6%), a personal campus visit (12.7%), or campus publications (11.7%) (p. 101). Tierney (1980b) reported that low-SES students have fewer information sources than high-SES students. This seems to be indirectly supported by Ekstrom (1985), who noted differences in whom students consult when selecting a curriculum in high school. She found that students in general and vocational tracks are more likely only to talk to friends when selecting courses. Students in the college preparatory curriculum consult more sources such as parents, counselors, and friends. Litten (1982) has suggested that low-SES students are less likely to have college-educated parents as well as fewer contacts with well-educated role models. As a result these students are more likely to have access to less information about postsecondary education.

Cibik (1982, p. 100) also asked the high school students in her sample to identify their informational needs. Their information needs were:

Academic quality, 67.6%
Cost, 63.2%
Career availability, 55.4%
Qualification criteria for aid, 55.4%
Helpfulness and instructors, 50.2%

Lewis and Morrison (1975) found that the most frequently used sources of information were (in rank order) catalogs, campus visits, guidance counselors, students already enrolled in college, and admissions officers.

Although many observers have suggested that students are not well informed at any point of the college choice process (Jackson, 1982; Lewis and Morrison, 1975; Litten, 1982), the search stage can be characterized as an active, rather than passive, process. Lewis and Morrison (1975) reported that the search activities most frequently engaged in by high school seniors included (1) writing away for a catalog, (2) campus visits and interviews, (3) talking to guidance counselors, (4) using catalogs available in high schools, and (5) talking to students already in college. The two most frequent activities required students to initiate activities as opposed to using sources of convenience or passively waiting for information to come to them. Caution must be exercised in interpreting these results, however, because this study was conducted before the widespread use of mail marketing techniques (which are possible through the sales of prospective students' names by The College Board, American College Testing, and other organizations). The use of mail marketing techniques may have made the search process more passive.

Limits on Search

During the search stage students establish limits on the process. Gilmour et al. (1978) observed that most of the students in their sample first established geographical and cost limits; then

they determined which institutions offered programs of interest to them. Tierney (1980a) and Astin and others (1980), using larger data sets, also found that geography and cost are important considerations during the search stage.

Table 1-3 presents the key characteristics of the search stage of student college choice.

In total, little information is available about the search stage, and a number of questions remain. Other than the PSAT, are there other key events that influence the search stage? For students who are planning to enter a vocational institution or a two-year college, and who are less likely to take the PSAT, are there any key external events that affect the search stage? Little is known about how students discover the range of PEIs. How do students learn the names of institutions in order to decide which ones to consider? Do PEIs play any role in the search stage? Could they play any role in the search stage? Could state and federal agencies intervene by disseminating more information about financial aid or postsecondary educational opportunities? Although Gilmour et al. (1978), Lewis and Morrison (1975), and Cibik (1982) have suggested that college guides and institutional information are used during the search stage, caution should be exercised in interpreting these findings. Johnson and D. Chapman (1979) reported that many of the written materials PEIs use are above the reading level of most high school students. In addition, D. Chapman (1981) noted that students use most written material from PEIs to confirm decisions they have already made. If this is the case, how do students go about evaluating a range of PEIs?

Questions of equity and access are also important questions during the search stage. Ekstrom (1985), Gilmour et al. (1978) and Tierney (1980b) indicated that low-SES students, as well as students enrolled in vocational and general tracks, have fewer sources of information about PEIs. Miller (1983), in an examination of how PEIs use college SEARCH mailings,[3] reported

TABLE 1-3
The Process Characteristics of Search

Duration	9th–10th grades to fall of senior year
Nature of search behavior	Active, student-initiated
Information sources	Friends, campus visits, campus publications
Most important concerns	Institutional quality, degrees lead to careers, faculty

that many colleges exclude students who reside in low-income zip code areas. This may further exacerbate the lack of information available to low-income students. Although researchers can speculate about the relationships between student characteristics and the search stage, investigations of the search stage are few. Multivariate studies of the search stage could greatly enhance our understanding of this important stage of student college choice.

Choice

Although the search stage of student college choice has not received a great deal of attention, the choice stage has attracted considerable attention. This stage includes (1) the selection of an application set of institutions, that is, the identification of the PEIs students actually apply to, as well as (2) the final matriculation decision. The research literature on the choice stage is dominated by single-institution studies, conducted either at individual high schools or individual PEIs. These studies typically examine the factors that influenced a student's decision to enroll in a specific PEI. There are some well-crafted studies that use larger samples to examine the selection of a PEI. However, they examine aggregate choice decisions such as the selection of a private PEI over a public PEI or the selection of a high-status PEI over a lower status PEI. Research on the choice stage employs a variety of univariate and multivariate statistical designs, as well as qualitative techniques. Missing, however, are studies that employ experimental designs that permit the utilization of causal modeling techniques.

This section on the choice stage will first examine the student correlates of choice. Some of the same variables, such as socioeconomic status or ability, will be used to organize the discussion of student correlates; however, there is little information available about the impact of variables such as gender, peer encouragement, high school quality, or labor market considerations on the choice stage. In this discussion of the choice stage, the institutional correlates of choice (of the institutional characteristics that are associated with selecting one type of public institution over another or in the decision to attend a specific PEI) will be discussed. These institutional characteristics include nonfinancial attributes (e.g., perceived quality and location)

and financial attributes (e.g., tuition costs and financial aid). Finally, some of the process characteristics of the choice stage will be described.

Socioeconomic Status

Although different studies have reported conflicting results as they have attempted to determine the impact of SES on the choice stage, the weight of the evidence suggests that SES is related to both the cost and the quality of PEIs which students apply to and attend. Leslie et al. (1977) did not find a strong correlation between SES and the cost of the institution that students attended. Tierney (1980a, b) used multiple-regression analysis to analyze NLS data and a sample of high school seniors in Pennsylvania. In both studies he found that SES did not affect the cost of the institutions that students applied to, but it was related to institutional status. Lower SES students were less likely to apply to high-status institutions. Maguire and Lay (1981) used discriminant analysis to study the choice stage of applicants to Boston College; they found that low-SES students were just as likely to attend private institutions as high-SES students. Interestingly, Dahl's (1982) analysis of the choice stage for Kentucky high school seniors showed that low-income students were even more likely to choose private PEIs.

Hearn (1984), however, used multivariate techniques to analyze the college choice preferences in a longitudinal sample of students and reported that low-SES students were less likely to apply to high-status PEIs. Spies (1978) used multiple regression to analyze data from a sample of high-ability students. He discovered that middle- and low-income students were less likely to apply to high-status institutions. Maguire and Lay (1981) also found similar results. R. Chapman (1979) concluded that high-SES students are more interested in quality than the cost of attendance. Zemsky and Oedel (1983), in a study sponsored by The College Board, examined the PEI application patterns of students in the New England states. They found that high-income students were more likely to apply to PEIs that were out-of-state with more selective admissions standards. The cumulative evidence suggests that student SES does affect the choice stage of student college choice. High-SES students are more likely to apply to and attend selective PEIs. Surprisingly, however, SES does not seem to be associated with the cost of the PEIs students select.

Ability

Existing research on student ability suggests that if affects the choice stage of student college choice. Dahl (1982) found that high school graduates with the strongest academic credentials were the most likely to select an out-of-state PEI. They were also more likely to attend more selective PEIs. Hearn (1984) also reported that high-ability students were more likely to enroll in more selective institutions. The NLS data analyzed by Jackson (1978) revealed similar student choice patterns. Zemsky and Oedel (1983) found that student ability was directly related to the selectivity of the PEI students applied to as well as where the institutions were located. As student ability rose, the likelihood that students would apply to more selective, out-of-state PEIs also increased. In a single institution study, Maguire and Lay (1981) found that students with higher GPAs were more likely to apply to more selective institutions. Further, their results demonstrated that the preferences of students with high GPAs were more stable; these students were less likely to change their minds. In total, these studies indicate that student ability is positively associated with institutional selectivity. As student ability rises, the selectivity of the PEIs in a student's choice set also increases.

Ethnicity

Fewer studies have been conducted on the impact of ethnicity on the choice stage. In Hearn's (1984) study of this stage, which used longitudinal data from PSAT files, SAT/ACT files, and CIRP data, he found that black students were less likely to apply to more selective institutions. Stewart et al. (1987), in a descriptive study of freshmen at Michigan State University, reported that black students were more concerned about financial aid. He did not control, however, for student SES or ability. Based on these limited findings, we conclude that black students may be less inclined to apply to or enroll in selective PEIs and that they may be more concerned about financial aid and the cost

of attendance. Although research has examined the choice stage for black students, little is known about this stage for other minority groups. This is an area that merits future study.

Parental Levels of Education

The research on this factor is limited. Litten et al. (1983) conducted an investigation into the postsecondary plans of high-ability students in six market regions (Baltimore/Washington, DC, Chicago, Dallas/Ft. Worth, Denver/Boulder, Minneapolis/St. Paul, and San Francisco/Oakland) from which Carleton College attracted students. Using multidimensional scaling they analyzed the characteristics of different market segments in each market region. They found that levels of parental education were positively associated with a preference for private colleges. Gilmour et al. (1978) and Lewis and Morrison (1975), both of whom utilized interview techniques, found that students with college-educated parents applied earlier and to more PEIs. Gilmour et al. (1978) noted that they also made their decision to attend a specific institution earlier. Hearn (1984) concluded that parental education had a positive impact on attending more selective institutions. In total, these studies suggest that as levels of parental education increase, students enter and complete the choice stage earlier and are more likely to choose and attend selective institutions.

Family Residence Characteristics

Where students live may exert a small influence on the choice stage of student college choice. The most thorough discussion of the role of residence is found in Anderson et al.'s (1972) analysis of student enrollment patterns in separate data sets. Anderson and his colleagues analyzed the postsecondary participation patterns of Wisconsin students between 1957 and 1964; and they also examined SCOPE data (from the states of California, Illinois, Massachusetts, and North Carolina) which contained information about the enrollment patterns of twelfth-graders in 1966. The authors employed multiple-regression techniques to analyze the data. They found a weak association between the presence of a local college option and college attendance. However, SES, parental level of education, student ability, and historical college enrollment patterns in various communities and regions had a larger effect upon enrollment rates than the presence of a nearby two- or four-year institution. Litten et al. (1983) and Lewis and Morrison (1975), as well as two single institution studies (Lay and Maguire, 1980; Muffo, 1987), reported that distance from home was negatively related to the likelihood of student application or enrollment. R. Chapman (1979) concluded that for students applying to Carnegie-Mellon University, distance was irrelevant. Maguire and Lay (1981) used multivariate techniques in their study of the application pool at Boston College and found that students who planned to attend a PEI near their homes were more likely to implement their plans. It appears that residence characteristics have a limited effect on choice. While multi-institution studies suggest that residence characteristics have a small impact, single-institution studies suggest that distance has a stronger effect. Factors such as institutional prestige, selectivity, and drawing power may explain the differences across institutions.

Parental Encouragement

The level of parental encouragement for students appears to be correlated with attendance at more selective institutions. Conklin and Dailey (1981) provide the most persuasive evidence of the importance of parental encouragement. Their findings showed that as the level of parental encouragement increased, the likelihood increased that students would (1) attend a PEI, (2) attend a four year PEI, and (3) attend a selective PEI. Keller and McKewon (1984), in a descriptive study of Maryland National Merit finalists, found that students who planned to enroll in private institutions reported more parental support for their educational plans. Welki and Novratil (1987), in a single-institution study that employed conditional logit analysis, also found that parental preference played an important role in the decision to attend the institution. Litten et al. (1983), in his six-market study of the Carleton College applicant pool, noted similarities between the postsecondary preferences of parents and students. The results, however, concluded that parents did not have an effect upon the final matriculation decision. This does not rule out the possibility that parents

influenced students' decisions to consider attending selective institutions such as Carleton.

These studies suggest that parental encouragement plays a role in the choice stage; however, it would appear to be a subtle one which is not currently fully understood. Perhaps the most important parental role comes during the predisposition stage, when parental attitudes greatly influence student aspirations, and during the search stage, when parents may set some of the parameters on net cost and distance from home. During the actual choice stage, parents may not play a central role.

Peer Encouragement and Support

By the time students reach the choice stage, peers do not appear to have an impact. Jackson (1978), in his analysis of NLS data, did not find any relationship between peers and the actual matriculation decision. Gilmour et al. (1978), in his longitudinal study of high school seniors, also reported that peers did not play a role in the decision to attend a specific PEI.

High School Quality

Only one of the studies reviewed examined the relationship between school quality and the choice stage. Falsey and Heyns (1984) concluded that students enrolled in private schools are more likely to enroll in high-status PEIs. They did not control for background characteristics, however, and their findings may be the result of a higher proportion of high-ability and high-SES students attending private schools.

Institutional Attributes

Up to this point in this chapter, the unit of analysis has been the student. Student variables related to predisposition, search, and choice have been examined. This would suggest that PEIs have no impact on the student college choice process. In fact, PEIs have little impact on the predisposition phase. During the predisposition phase students have not sufficiently formulated their postsecondary plans, so that factors such as net cost, size of institution, distance from home, or reputation are not relevant factors. PEIs may, however, have an impact on the search stage; since this stage has not been studied, the effect of institutions on search is unknown. It is likely that students do begin to establish parameters for cost, distance from home, institutional size, specialized programs, and institutional selectivity during the search stage. These probably become important attributes during the search stage, but more research is needed to verify this. Nevertheless, by the time students reach the choice stage, it is clear that their plans are more fully developed and that institutional attributes are important determinants of where students enroll. There is sufficient research on the choice stage to examine some of these institutional attributes.

D. Chapman (1981) described factors such as two- and four-year institutions, academic reputation, size, public or private, and location as "fixed institutional characteristics." Since factors such as public and private, selectivity, and two- and four-year institutions are highly correlated with tuition levels, a discussion of cost is also included. This discussion of cost will focus both on the "list cost" (tuition and fees before financial aid had been awarded) and "net cost" (the cost of attending after financial aid has been awarded). In addition, there are what Hossler (1984) has described as "fluid institutional characteristics," which refer to marketing strategies, offering off-campus programs, and academic program changes designed to attract students. Many studies assert the efficacy of such strategies to attract more applicants and matriculants. For the purposes of this chapter, however, these studies have not been included. Most of these studies rely on anecdotal evidence or lack control groups that permit researchers to assess the effectiveness of such activities. In addition, the literature on this topic would move into a discussion of marketing which is beyond the scope of this chapter. This section will focus on two types of institutional attributes: nonfinancial attributes and financial attributes. Nonfinancial attributes include factors such as academic reputation and social life. Financial attributes include discussions of list and net cost.

Nonfinancial Attributes. A number of studies have been conducted that investigate the characteristics that students rate as most important when they decide to apply to or attend a PEI. Although the precise order of these characteristics varies from study to study, the most frequently mentioned characteristics are listed below in rank order:

1. Special academic programs (major area of study)
2. Tuition costs
3. Financial aid availability
4. General academic reputation/general quality
5. Location (distance from home)
6. Size
7. Social atmosphere

(Sources: Douglas et al., 1983; Bowers and Pugh, 1973; Dahl, 1982; Keller and McKewon, 1984; Konnert and Giese, 1987; Lay and Maguire, 1981; Litten, 1979; Litten et al., 1983; Stewart et al., 1987; R. Chapman and Jackson, 1987).

There are variations in the weighting of these factors by different student populations and for different PEIs. R. Chapman and Jackson (1987) investigated the choice stage of 2,000 academically talented students. Using conditional logit analysis to analyze the data, they concluded that institutional quality was the single most important determinant of the choice stage. Furthermore, they concluded that for high-ability students distance was irrelevant. In their six-market study of academically talented students, Litten et al. (1983) concluded that academic quality had the largest impact on the choice stage. They found, however, that nearness to home, lower costs, and smaller size were also preferred by students in the sample. Keller and McKewon's study of Maryland National Merit Finalists (1984) showed that students planning to attend out-of-state PEIs rated quality as the most important factor in selecting an institution. For students planning to attend an in-state PEI, costs were the most important factor. Leslie et al. (1977) studied the choice stage of 1,000 Pennsylvania high school seniors. They concluded that cost was the most important reason for selecting a PEI among low-income students.

In a study of the applicant pool at Boston College, Lay and Maguire (1980), using factor analysis, determined that the most important factors in deciding who came to Boston College were financial aid (negative), parental preferences, specific academic programs, size, location, and athletic and social activities. In a factor-analytic study of 231 athletes, Mathes and Gurney (1985) found that scholarship athletes placed more emphasis on the academic programs of the institution, while athletes in non-revenue-producing sports placed more emphasis on the coaching staff. In a study of athletes enrolled at colleges in a small college conference that did not award athletic scholarships, Konnert and Giese (1987) indicated that the opportunity to play intercollegiate sports was an important college selection factor for student athletes. Institutional quality and some measure of costs consistently appeared as the two most important reasons that students attend a specific PEI. However, these studies also reveal that there is great variation among students and types of institutions.

Moving beyond the effects of individual institutional attributes, Astin and others (1980) and Zemsky and Oedel (1983) revealed that state policies and the aggregate characteristics of PEIs in a region can influence the choice stage. In states with more generous state scholarship programs, Astin and others (1980) found high school students were more likely to enroll in private PEIs. In addition, students who resided in states with larger private PEI sectors were proportionately more likely enroll in private PEIs. Zemsky and Oedel (1983) also found that in states with a large and diverse range of PEIs, such as Massachusetts, high school students were less likely to attend an out-of-state PEI. It appears that the perceived availability of aid and presence of specific types of PEIs may raise the awareness levels of high school students about postsecondary educational options. Increased awareness may lead to higher attendance rates at all types of PEIs.

Financial Attributes. As already noted in the section on non-financial attributes, students do consider costs when selecting a college in which to enroll. In this section the effects that costs have upon the attendance patterns of different types of students and institutions will be examined. Student self-reports suggest that cost and financial aid are important considerations when applying to a PEI, or when selecting a PEI in which to enroll. Fenske et al. (1979) reviewed several previous studies they had conducted on recipients of Illinois State Scholarships. In 1976–1977, 40% of all of the respondents indicated that they would not have been able to attend the PEI they selected without a state scholarship. An additional 59% indicated that they would not have been able to attend at all without their state aid (pp. 149–151). Fenske et al. estimated that between 15% and 25% would have

attended a public instead of a private PEI if they had not had state scholarships (p. 153). Leslie et al. (1977) indicated that only 25% of their sample of Pennsylvania seniors would not have attended any institution without aid. However, 43.5% of those who indicated that they were only able to enroll in a PEI because of aid were low-income students (p. 280). Lam and Hoffman (1979), in a single-institution study, found that students who did not enroll were more likely to report financial reasons as the cause for their nonattendance.

Although student self-reports suggest that financial aid influences the choice stage of student college choice, multivariate studies demonstrate that the relationship between cost and the choice stage is more complex. Dahl (1982) used discriminant analysis to examine the college enrollment patterns of high school graduates in Kentucky. He reported that those seniors who had planned to enroll but did not were more likely to indicate that low cost and financial aid were important factors in their decisions not to enroll. Hearn (1984), in his longitudinal study of high school students, found that the amount of variance in a student's choice of a PEI that was explained by institutional costs was not very high. Jackson (1978) analyzed NLS data using multiple regression and reported that the amount of aid only increased the likelihood of attending a specific institution by 8.5% (p. 566). Using High School and Beyond data in 1986, Jackson again reported similar results. R. Chapman and Jackson (1987) used conditional logit analysis to study the role of financial aid in the choice stage of academically talented students. They concluded that perceived quality has a greater impact on the choice stage than does the net cost. Their findings showed that on the average, the PEIs that students entered were more expensive than the institutions they did not attend. Furthermore, they found that it would have taken $4,000 in financial aid to move a second-choice institution to be the student's first choice, and $6,000 in financial aid to move a third-choice institution to first choice (p. 38). Freeman (1984), using a sample of students from private colleges in the Great Lakes region who had been awarded no-need merit-based aid, reported similar results.[4] Tierney (1980a) used multiple regression to examine the college choice patterns of 6,444 high school students included in the NLS data set. He found that as private institutions offered more aid, the likelihood of students' enrolling in a private PEI increased. Furthermore, he noted that as the tuition gap between public and private PEIs increased, students were more likely to enroll in a public institution.

An analysis of the impact of cost from the perspective of individual institutions, however, presents a somewhat different set of results. Supporting the findings already cited, R. Chapman (1979), who studied the applicant pool at Carnegie Mellon University, reported that cost had no effect on matriculation patterns. Lay and Maguire (1981), as well as Maguire and Lay (1981), in two investigations of the applicant pool at Boston College, found that the amount of aid did influence the matriculation decision of students. They found that better aid offers from competitor institutions resulted in 32 % of their applicants' attending those institutions, even though they had rated Boston College as their first choice (p. 83). In a study of the applicant pool at Virginia Technical University, Muffo (1987) used multivariate techniques and concluded that high-ability nonmatriculants were more likely to report better financial aid offers from other institutions. This was especially true of high-ability black students. Litten et al. (1983) and Kehoe (1981) also found that students who (1) initially expressed interest in attending out-of-state PEIs and/or private PEIs, but who (2) also stated concerns about the cost of attendance, were more likely to decide to attend a less expensive private or in-state PEI. R. Chapman and Jackson (1987) indicated that when a high-ability student is undecided among two institutions, $1,000 in aid can shift a student's decision in favor of the awarding institution (p. 38).

By this point it should be evident that the relationship between cost and the choice stage is complex. In the aggregate, it appears that aid is not as important as student perceptions of quality. In fact, in the aggregate, net cost exerts only a modest influence on the choice stage. However, individual institutions do not function in the aggregate, and it appears that aid can make a difference to students who are undecided about two or more PEIs. The challenge for most PEIs is that they lack sufficient information about students to know in advance what the effect of financial aid will be. With the rising use of merit aid (Hossler, 1984), it appears that many institutions have decided to make Type I errors, erring on the side of awarding financial aid in order to attract students even though the additional funds may either not be needed or not be sufficient to move the institution to a first-choice institution. In addition, most of the evidence on the impact of financial aid at the institutional level focuses on high-ability students; little is known about the impact of financial aid upon less talented students.

In total, the choice stage of student college choice is a complex phenomenon which exhibits variation for among students and institutions. Table 1-4 summarizes the correlates of the choice stage.

Process Characteristics of the Choice Stage

Although the correlates of the choice stage provide insights into this stage, the correlates do not adequately describe how students enter and complete it. The choice stage has two phases. In the first phase students identify their application set of PEIs. In the second phase students select a PEI to attend. Two qualitative studies of high school seniors provide the most detailed information about this stage (Gilmour et al., 1978; Lewis and Morrison, 1975). The search stage of student college choice ends sometime between the end of the junior year in high school and January of the senior year for most high school students (Lewis and Morrison, 1975).

Stewart et al. (1987), in a retrospective study of freshmen attending Michigan State University, reported that 10% of the students made the decision regarding where they would enroll in their junior year, 70% made the decision sometime during their senior year, and 20% made the decision after their senior year (p. 14). The choice stage begins with a list of the PEIs student's are considering. Students consult a variety of sources while they are evaluating institutions to which to apply. At this point the role of parents and peers diminishes (Gilmour et al., 1978). Cibik (1982), in a descriptive study of high school seniors, found that students were more than twice as likely to report that they alone had the greatest impact on the choice stage (self, 59%; relatives, 21%) (p. 101). Ebberly (1987), however, in a retrospective investigation of freshmen attending Michigan State University, indicated that students used the following sources of information in evaluating their application set: other college students (77%), friends (72%), high school counselors

TABLE 1-4
The Correlates of Choice

Student variables	Strength of association
Ability	Strong; high ability is associated with attending more selective PEIs
Parental encouragement	Strong; positively associated with attending more selective and 4-year PEIs
SES	Strong; positively associated with selectivity
Ethnicity	Moderate; blacks less likely to attend
Parental education	Moderate; students with college educated parents more likely to prefer private PEIs and high-status PEIs
Family residence	Uncertain
High school quality	Weak

Nonfinancial institutional variables	
Academic quality	Strong
Location	Moderate/strong
Financial aid availability	Moderate
Scope of postsecondary system in region	Moderate
Size	Weak
Social atmosphere	Weak

Financial institutional variables	
Net cost	Strong
Receipt of aid	Weak/moderate; depends on student preferences

(70%), and family (61%) (p. 7). Lewis and Morrison (1975) reported that students use global constructs such as size and general quality, as well as specific criteria, such as the quality of the chemistry program, in evaluating PEIs. The reasons for some of the discrepancies reported among other indices are difficult to determine. Sample size and sample representativeness, as well as the types of questions asked, may account for the differences. More systematic research is needed in order to understand how students form and evaluate their application set.

Dahl's (1982) longitudinal study of Kentucky high school seniors, as well as Litten et al.'s (1983) six-market study, shed light on shifts in institutional preferences that take place during this evaluation process. Dahl's (1982) data enabled him to compare stated student preferences with where they actually enrolled. He observed that 75% of all students were involved in a shift among various sectors of postsecondary education (public, private, two-year, and four-

year PEIs) in Kentucky (p. 15). Most changers stayed within their stated preference of two- or four-year institutions; however, they shifted either from public to private, from private to public, or from out-of-state to in-state PEIs. Approximately 66% of all changers shifted from the private sector to the public sector (p. 19). Thirty-three percent of the students who planned to enroll in a PEI out-of-state ended up enrolling in-state (p. 21). Only 13% of those students who planned to enroll in two-year PEIs shifted to another sector (p. 21). The public sector had the best holding power: 88.8% of all students who indicated that they planned to enroll in a public four-year institution followed through on those plans (p. 20). Litten et al. (1983) also found change in students' stated plans and actual enrollment patterns. They found that almost 50% of all students who had indicated a preference for private PEIs in February of their senior year expressed a preference for public PEIs by the summer (p. 102). They also reported an even larger group of changers who had shifted from a preference for highly selective institutions to less selective institutions. Although the time frames on the evaluation process are different as a result of the variance in when these data were gathered, Lewis and Morrison (1975) concluded that evaluation was continuous from early October to early April. After April the application set is established for most students.

The application period varies widely for students. Half of all students apply over a seven-week period, one-fourth of all students send in all of their applications at the same time, and 10% take 21 weeks to send in their applications (p. 22). Black students apply to more PEIs, are accepted by more PEIs, and are rejected by more PEIs. Women start the application process and end the process earlier than men. Jackson (1986) reports that over 90% of all college applicants are accepted by their top-choice institution; 97% are accepted to one of their top three choices (p. 7). By the end of May, most students have received their acceptance notifications and know where they are going to enroll (Lewis and Morrison, 1975).

As Table 1-5 demonstrates, the process characteristics of the choice stage appear to be the most logical and straightforward of the three stages. This may indeed be the case, or this may be because more attention has been paid to the process characteristics of this phase. Further

research on the process characteristics of this stage, as well as the other two stages, is needed.

Student college choice is a complex phenomenon that has not yet been sufficiently researched using theoretical models and a systematic set of questions. There are a number of questions still to be examined regarding the process characteristics of choice. In addition, the role of financial aid and other institutional characteristics in student college choice is poorly understood. At the end of this chapter these questions will be examined. In the context of the research already reviewed, the next section of this chapter will examine methodological issues and questions of theory development.

Suggested Further Directions

This chapter suggests (1) that a three-stage model of student college choice can be a useful conceptual approach for understanding the college choice process and (2) that it illuminates policy options at the federal, state, and institutional level. Although considerable research and numerous models pertaining to the college choice process are in the literature, much work remains to be done. Promising further directions fall into two categories: theory development and suggested further directions for research on the stages of predisposition, search, and choice. The

TABLE 1-5
The Process Characteristics of Choice

Duration	Fall of senior year to spring of senior year
Key influences	Students perceive choice as their own decision, and also recognize importance of parents and peers
Stability of choice	Moderate to high, though some shifting takes place
Application period	50% send in all applications in a 7-week period; there is great variability for the remaining 50%

TABLE 1-6
Important Correlates of Student College Choice

Variable	Predisposition	Search	Choice
Ability	Strong	Strong	Strong
Parental education	Strong	Moderate/strong	Moderate
Parental encouragement	Strong	Strong	Strong
SES	Weak	Moderate	Strong
Institutional characteristics	Weak/none	Weak/moderate	Moderate/strong

suggested directions for each of these categories are presented in the following subsections.

Theory Development

As evidenced by the econometric, sociological, and combined models of college choice reviewed, considerable attention has been devoted to the identification of factors which may influence the choice process, as well as to the interrelationships among these factors. While these models serve to identify salient factors and their interrelationships, most of these models do not specify how each variable interacts within the model. Few of the combined models have undergone attempts to empirically validate them. The work of Boyle (1966) and Alwin and Otto (1977) is an exception. Both studies attempted to explain how family background characteristics interact with high school and community characteristics, as well as student grades and academic track, to influence the college aspirations of students. Needed are a set of concepts which would seek to explain the interrelationships among the various important factors in the college choice process. The extant models and empirical research reviewed might serve as a foundation for the assessment of concepts or theoretical frameworks obtained from various academic disciplines. Alternately, a grounded theory approach could be used to develop such a framework (Glaser and Strauss, 1967). Using naturalistic data-gathering methods, researchers could build a college choice model based upon observations of high school students.

Theory development might also follow the course of the construction of "middle-range" theories, rather than a general theory of college choice (Merton, 1957). To be specific, middle-range theories could be developed for each stage of the choice process. Some of the combined models examined in this chapter represent initial attempts at this. Middle-range theories for each stage are suggested, as the construction of a parsimonious general theory of college choice capable of empirical validation may be too *difficult*, if not an impossible task. For example, while parents may play an important role during the predisposition stage, they appear to be less important during the choice stage. In addition, institutional marketing activities have little effect on the predisposition stage, but their importance grows during the search and choice stages.

A "middle-range theory" for each stage of the college choice process should seek to identify the salient factors associated with the outcomes of each stage. At each stage, theory development should focus on policy implications. For instance, it may be that parental encouragement may still explain a large part of the variance at each stage of the process. If stage-based theories, however, only focus on parental encouragement at each stage this fails to identify other potential areas of intervention. If, however, theories and empirical validations of those theories attempt to hold parental encouragement and other background characteristics constant, then the influence of high school activities and curriculum and institutional marketing activities may be more readily observable.

Further Research Directions

Although much research has focused on identifying factors which influence aspirations or a predisposition toward college attendance, further research on this stage of the choice process is needed. Ethnicity has been found to exert a weak influence on predisposition, especially when SES is controlled. The structure of the development of predispositions toward college attendance, however, may be different for minority and majority students. If parents and teachers are less influential for minority and majority students, are there other peers or role models who can serve as effective substitutes for these students? Thus, future research might focus on the development of separate causal models for each ethnic or minority group of interest. Such research would be of assistance in the development of public policy designed to increase the rate of postsecondary attendance of minority students.

As previously indicated, little is known about the correlates of the search stage of the college choice process. Research on this stage should focus on the role of parental education, SES, and student ability in the identification of attributes and valued characteristics which differentiate college alternatives. Moreover, the influence of the characteristics of PEIs in close proximity to the student's residence might also be considered in additional research on the search stage. A related question might also be to examine how ideal images or preferences for college characteristics develop during the search stage. Kotler and Fox (1985) provide a conceptual lead to the process of image formation. They suggest that during the search stage students form images of PEIs which are often based on incomplete information, yet these images influence both the search and choice stages.

Research on the processes involved in the search stage is also recommended. A variety of questions might guide such research. Additional research might seek to identify critical incidents other than taking the PSAT. Such research would build on the work of Lewis and Morrison (1975) and that of Gilmour et al. (1978), which revealed that taking the PSAT or application deadlines were critical incidents which influenced the college choice process. Academic track choices, which take place in the eighth or ninth grade for most high school students, are one possible critical incident. How do parents, counselors, etc., communicate their educational expectations to students? Other questions include: How do students find out about PEIs? How do they go about collecting information about them? How do they discover the relevant attributes to consider when evaluating PEIs?

Although considerable research has addressed factors which are influential in the choice stage of the college choice process, some additional topics of inquiry on this stage are suggested. The influence of institutional characteristics during the choice stage is a question that merits further examination. Of particular importance is the role of institutional image. The importance of the role of image has been identified by Silber et al. (1961) and by Clark et al. (1972) in the choice process. To date, however, image studies have been done at single institutions. As a result we are unable to determine how students both assess image and then weight these assessments to chose a specific PEI. To rigorously test the effect of image on the choice stage, a multiple-institution study including various types of PEIs with diverse images would need to be conducted.

One approach to assessing the influence of institutional image is suggested by the work of Kuntz (1987). In his research, Kuntz applied Coombs's (1964) "ideal point preference model" to the college choice stage. This application involved the comparison of images of PEIs held by students with their vision of an ideal college, the premise being that college preference is a function of the congruence between the ideal college and students' perceptions of a given set of PEI alternatives. The ideal point preference model could be used in assessing the role of institutional image not only in the development of a choice set of institutions, but also in the actual selection of a particular PEI.

Further research on the processes of the choice stage is also suggested. During the choice stage, how do students evaluate their application set? R. Chapman and Jackson (1987) reported that initial quality rankings at the start of the choice stage are the most important factor for high-ability students. Are these findings generalizable to all students? How much variance in the choice stage is explained by institutional marketing and financial aid practices?

In addition to these suggested research directions for the stages of the choice process, some more general topics of inquiry are in need of exploration. Research on the choice process has focused primarily on traditional-age students. Research on college choice for adult students is scarce and descriptive in nature. Given the increasing proportion of adult students enrolled in PEIs, there is clearly a need for more research on this topic. Similarly, little attention has been paid to the college choice process for community college students. Since adult students and students attending community colleges are more likely to be geographically bound, their choice stage may look very different. This population also merits study.

The full range of topics for further research outlined above can be addressed by the emergence of a systematic research line on student college choice. Longitudinal designs using a variety of institutional types should be the cornerstone for such research. Where quantitative approaches are appropriate for addressing this topic, simultaneous control of relevant factors (e.g., parental education, parental encouragement, student grades) should be used. Qualitative methodology may be particularly well suited for research on the process characteristics of each stage of college choice.

Conclusions

Student college choice is a complex phenomenon. It is not a single event, but the result of a process that begins at an early age for most students with a predisposition toward postsecondary education and ends in the selection of a PEI. For public policy-makers and institutional policy-makers questions of access, equity, and institutional vitality make student college choice a topic worthy of investigation. At each stage of the college choice process, a better understanding of college choice can facilitate more effective policy decisions. At the predisposition stage, the importance of parental encouragement indicates that any efforts to improve postsecondary participation rates should be targeted at parents as well as students. Furthermore, process research on predisposition reveals that most students have made their postsecondary plans by the end of the ninth or tenth grade. Thus, intervention programs need to begin early.

Research on the search stage indicates that developmental events such as taking the PSAT or academic tracking decisions influence the search stage. If public policy-makers wish to intervene during the search stage, the role of these events must be examined. More importantly, the dearth of research on the search stage makes it more difficult for policy-makers to develop intervention strategies. For instance, since little is known about how students identify potential PEIs and evaluate them, the effects of the marketing activities of individual PEIs are uncertain.

During the choice stage, institutional policy-makers can use an enhanced understanding of college choice to improve both marketing activities and student-institution fit. Research on the choice stage provides institutional policy-makers with a reverse lens that enables institutions to see themselves as students see them. This ability to see oneself through students' eyes could be used to recruit prospective students who are more likely to find that the institution meets their expectations.

With respect to marketing, institutional policy-makers can exert some influence by emphasizing quality and cost. Research on the process characteristics of the choice stage also reveals when students begin to apply to and evaluate PEIs. This can be useful information for institutional policy-makers. Nevertheless, many questions regarding the impact of institutional marketing efforts and financial-aid-awarding practices need further examination.

In addition to these applied questions a number of questions remain for the research community to address. This chapter points out the need for "middle-range" theories (Merton, 1957) that can be used to develop theoretical models for each stage of student college choice

as well as models for different ethnic and other minority groups. In the search and choice stages, future studies should include large student sample sizes that examine the search and choice stages for multiple PEIs. Longitudinal studies which follow high school students from their early years in high school to their first year after high school would also be beneficial. Given the importance of parental encouragement, such studies should include the parents of the students. At the search and choice stages, causal modeling techniques should be employed that will enable researchers to untangle the interrelationships among a diverse set of variables.

Systematic, theory-driven research on college choice can enhance the accumulated knowledge on student college choice. It can lead to more effective policy decisions at the federal, state, and institutional levels. Students may also benefit from an improved understanding of college choice, which can lead to aid policies, high school guidance activities, and marketing activities that make college more accessible to students and that increase the likelihood of student fit. This would benefit the research community and policy-makers and extend our understanding of postsecondary institutions and students.

Notes

1. As many as thirteen separate activities were identified by Lewis and Morrison (1975).
2. The income differential between high school graduates, usually computed over a lifetime. For example, an estimated rate of return of 10% indicates that when background characteristics are controlled, the typical college graduate earns 10% more over a lifetime when compared to the typical high school graduate.
3. SEARCH is a service marketed by The College Board in which the names and addresses of potential students are sold to PEIs. PEIs then send these students unsolicited information about themselves. Although ACT and other educational marketing firms also sell prospective student names, the term *search* has become synonymous with this approach to marketing.
4. R. G. Chapman and Jackson (1987) and Freeman (1984) used student samples that were academically talented. There are no high-quality studies using students of average or below-average ability. As a result, the effects of no-need aid on less talented students are unknown.

References

Adkins, D. L. (1975). *The Great American Degree Machine*. New York: McGraw-Hill.

Alexander, K., et al. (1978). *Status Composition and Educational Goals: An Attempt at Clarification*. Washington, DC: National Institute of Education. (ED 160 537)

Alwin, D. F., and Otto, L. B. (1977). Higher school context effects on aspirations. *Sociology of Education* 50: 259–273.

Anderson, C., Bowman, M. J., and Tinto, V. (1972). *Where Colleges Are and Who Attends*. New York: McGraw-Hill.

Astin, A., and others. (1980). *The Impact of Student Financial Aid Programs on Student College Choice*. Washington, DC: Office of Planning. (ED 187 368)

Attanasi, L. (1986). Getting in: Mexican-American student's perceptions of their college-going behavior with implications for their freshman year persistence in the university. Paper presented at Annual Meeting of the Association for the Study of Higher Education, San Antonio, March.

Baird, L. L. (1973). *The Graduates: A Report on the Characteristics and Plans of College Seniors*. Princeton, NJ: Educational Testing Service.

Bird, C. (1975). *The Case Against College*. New York: David McKay.

Bishop, J. (1977). The effect of public policies on the demand for higher education. *Journal of Human Resources* 5(4): 285–307.

Blau, P. M. and Duncan, O. D. (1967). *The American Occupational Structure*. New York: Wiley.

Bowen, H. R. (1977). *Investment in Learning: Individual and Social Value of American Education*. San Francisco: Jossey-Bass.

Bowers, T. and Pugh, R. (1973). Factors underlying college choice by students and parents. *Journal of College Student Personnel* 220–224.

Boyer, E. L. (1987). *College: The Undergraduate Experience in America*. New York: Harper & Row.

Boyle, R. P. (1966). The effect of the high school on student aspirations, *American Journal of Sociology* 71:628–39.

Brown, K. G. (1982). Postsecondary plans of high-school seniors in 1972 and 1980: Implications for student quality. Presented at the AIR Forum, Denver, May. (ED 220 060)

Campbell, R., and Siegel, B. N. (1967). The demand for higher education in the United States, 1919–1964. *American Economic Review* 57: 453–499.

Carpenter, P. G., and Fleishman, J. A. (1987). Linking intentions and behavior: Australian students college plans and college attendance. *American Educational Research Journal: 24(1)*: 79–105.

Chapman, D. W. (1981). A model of student college. *Journal of Higher Education* 52(5): 490–505.

Chapman, R. C. (1979). Pricing policy and the college choice process. *Research in Higher Education* 10: 37–57.

Chapman, R. C. (1984). Toward a theory of college selection: a model of college search and choice behavior. Unpublished manuscript, Alberta, Canada: University of Alberta.

Chapman, R. C., and Jackson, R. (1987). *College Choices of Academically Able Students: The Influence of No-Need Financial Aid and Other Factors*, Research Monograph No. 10. New York: The College Board.

Chressanthis, G. A. (1986). The impacts of tuition rate changes on college graduate head counts and credit hours over time and a case study. *Economics of Education* 5(2): 205–217.

Chronicle of Higher Education (1978). 16(5, November 13): 8.

Cibik, M. A. (1982). College information needs. *College and University* 57: 97–102.

Clark, B. R., Heist, P., McConnell, T. R., Trow, M. A., and Yonge, C. (1972). *Students and Colleges: Interaction and Change*. Berkeley, CA: Center for Research and Development in Higher Education.

Coelho, G. V., Hamburg, D. A., and Murphey, E. B. (1963). Coping strategies in a new learning environment: A study of the American college freshman. *Archives of General Psychiatry* 9: 433–443.

Coleman, J. S. (1966). Peer culture and education in modern society. In T. M. Newcomb and E. K. Wilson, (eds.), *College peer groups: Problems and Prospects for Research*. Chicago: Aldine.

Conklin, M. E., and Dailey, A. R. (1981). Does consistency of parental encouragement matter for secondary students? *Sociology of Education* 54: 254–262.

Coombs, C. H. (1982). *A Theory of Data*. New York: Wiley.

Corazzini, A. J., et al. (1972). Determinants and Distributional aspects of enrollment in U.S. higher education. *Journal of Human Resources* 7: 26–38.

Dahl, R. W. (1982). College attendance and institutional choice. Results from the Kentucky longitudinal study. Paper presented at the Annual Forum of the Association of Institutional Research, Denver, June. (ED 220 227).

Denison, E. F. (1971). In R. W. Wykstra, (ed.) *Human Capital Formation and Manpower Development* New York: Free Press.

Douglas, P., et al. (1983). Factor in the choice of higher educational institutions by academically gifted seniors. *Journal of College Student Personnel* 24: 540–545.

Dresch, S. P., and Waldenberg, A. L. (1978). *Labor Market Incentives, Intellectual Competence, and College Attendance*. New Haven, CT: Institute for Demographic and Economic Studies.

Ebberly, C. G. (1987). Information sources used by high school seniors. Paper presented at the Annual Meeting of the American Association of Counseling and Development, New Orleans, March.

Ekstrom, R. B. (1985). *A Descriptive Study of Public High School Guidance: Report to the Commission for the Study of Precollegiate Guidance and Counseling*. Princeton, NJ: Educational Testing Service.

Elsworth, G., et al. (1982). *From High School to Tertiary Study: Transition to College and University in Victoria*. Hawthorn, Victoria: Australian Council on Education.

Erlich, I. (1975). On the relation between education and crime. In F. J. Juster (ed.), *Education, Income and Human Behavior*. New York, McGraw-Hill.

Falsey, B., and Heyns, B. (1984). The college channel: Private and public schools reconsidered. *Sociology of Education* 57: 111–122.

Fenske, R. H., Boyd, J., and Maxey, E. J. (1979). State financial aid to students: a trend analysis of access and choice of public or private college. *College and University* 54: 139–155.

Fields, C., and LeMay, M. (1973). Student financial aid: Effects on educational decisions and academic achievement. *Journal of College Student Personnel* 14: 425–429.

Freeman, R. (1976). *The Over-educated American*. New York: Academic Press.

Freeman, H. B. (1984). Impact of no-need scholarships on the matriculating decision of academically talented students. Paper presented at the Annual Meeting of the American Association of Higher Education, Chicago, March.

Fuller, W., Manski, C., and Wise, D. (1982). New evidence on the economic determinants of postsecondary schooling choices. *Journal of Human Resources* 17(4): 472–498.

Garfinkel, I., and Haveman, R. (1977). *Earnings Capacity, Poverty and Inequality*. Institute for Research on Poverty Monograph. New York: Basic Books.

Gilmour, J., et al. (1978). *How High School Students Select a College*. Pennsylvania State University. (ED 208 705)

Glaser, B. G., and Strauss, A. L. (1967). *The Discovery of Grounded Theory*. Chicago: Aldine.

Hanson, K. H., and Litten, L. H. (1982). Mapping the road to academia: A review of research on women, men, and the college-selection process. In P. Perun (ed.), *The Undergraduate Woman: Issues in Education*. Lexington, MA: Lexington Books.

Harnqvist, K. (1978). *Individual Demand for Education*. Analytical report. Paris, France: OECD. (ED 159 119)

Hause, J. C. (1969). Ability and schooling as determinants of lifetime earnings, or if you're so smart, why aren't you rich. *American Economic Review* 59: 289–298.

Hearn, J. (1984). The relative roles of academic ascribed and socioeconomic characteristics in college destinations. *Sociology of Education* 57: 22–30.

Hilton, T. L. (1982). *Persistence in Higher Education*. New York: The College Board.

Hossler, D. (1984). *Enrollment Management: An Integrated Approach*. New York: The College Board.

Hossler, D., and Gallagher, K. S. (1987). Studying student college choice: A three-phase model and the implications for policy-makers. *College and University* 2(3): 207–221.

Hossler, D., and Stage, F. (1987). *An Analysis of Student and Parent Data from the Pilot Year of the Indiana College Placement and Assessment Center*. Bloomington: Indiana College Placement and Assessment Center.

Hossler, D., and Stage, F. (1988). Family and high school experience factors' influence on the postsecondary plans of ninth grade students. Paper presented at the Annual Meeting of American Education Research Association, New Orleans, April.

Jackson, G. A. (1978). Financial aid and student enrollment. *Journal of Higher Education* 49: 548–574.

Jackson, G. A. (1982). Public efficiency and private choice in higher education. *Educational Evaluation and Policy Analysis* 4(2): 237–247.

Jackson, G. A. (1986). MISSA, the fall of Saigon, and college choice, 1972 to 1980. Paper presented at the Annual Meeting of the Association for the Study of Higher Education, San Diego, February.

Jencks, C., et al. (1972). *Inequality: A Reassessment of the Effects of Family and Schooling in America*. New York: Basic Books.

Johnson, R. H., and Chapman, D. W. (1979). An assessment of college recruitment literature: Does the high school senior understand it? Presented at Annual Forum of the Association of Institutional Research, San Diego, June. (ED 174 079)

Kehoe, J. J. (1981). Migrational choice patterns in financial aid policy making. *Research in Higher Education* 14(1): 57–69.

Keller, M. J., and McKewon, M. P. (1984). Factors contributing to postsecondary enrollments decisions of Maryland National Merit Scholarship Semifinalists. Paper presented at Annual Meeting of the Association for the Study of Higher Education, Chicago.

Kohn, M. G., Manski, C. F., and Mundel, D. (1976). An empirical investigation of factors influencing college going behaviors. *Annuals of Economic and Social Measurement* 5(4, Fall): 391–419.

Kolstad, A. J. (1979). The influence of high school type and curriculum on enrollment in higher education and postsecondary training. Paper presented at the Annual Meeting of the American Educational Research Association, San Francisco, April. (ED 173 627)

Konnert, W. and Giese, R. (1987). College choice factors of male athletes at private NCAA Division III institutions. *College and University* 63(1): 23–48.

Kotler, P. (1976). Applying marketing theory to college admissions. In *A Role for Marketing in College Admissions*. New York: The College Entrance Examination Board.

Kotler, P. and Fox, K. (1985). *Strategic Marketing for Educational Institutions*. Englewood Cliffs, NJ: Prentice-Hall.

Kuntz, S. S. (1987). A study of student's cognitive structure for colleges. Paper at the Annual Meeting of the American Educational Research Association, Washington, DC, April.

Lam, J., and Hoffman, D. (1979). The study of sequential student participation in University in a changing environment. Manitoba, Canada: Brandon University. (ED 198 785)

Lay, R., and MaGuire, J. (1980). Identifying the competition in higher education. *College and University* 56(1): 53–65.

Lay, R. and Maguire, J. (1981). Coordinating market and evaluation research on the admissions rating process. *Research in Higher Education* 14(1): 71–85.

Leslie, L. L., et al. (1977). The impact of need-based student aid upon the college attendance decision. *Journal of Education Finance* 2: 269–286.

Leslie, L. L., and Brinkman, P. T. (1986). Rates of return to higher education: An intensive examination. In J. Smart (ed.) *Higher Education: Handbook of Theory and Research* Vol. III. New York: Agathon Press.

Lewis, G. H., and Morrison, J. (1975). *A Longitudinal Study of College Selection* Tech. Report No. 2. Pittsburgh: School of Urban Public Affairs, Carnegie-Mellon University.

Litten, L. H. (1982). Different strokes in the applicant pool: some refinements in a model of student college choice. *Journal of Higher Education* 53(4): 383–402.

Litten, L. H. (1986). Perspectives on pricing. In D. Hossler (ed.), *Managing College Enrollments*, New Directions of Higher Education, No. 53. San Francisco: Jossey-Bass.

Litten, L. H., et al. (1983). *Applying Market Research in College Admissions*. New York: The College Board.

Maguire, J., and Lay, R. (1981). Modeling the college choice process. *College and University* 56(2): 123–139.

Manski, C. F., and Wise, D. A. (1983). *College Choice in America*. Cambridge, MA: Harvard University Press.

Mare, R. D. (1980). Social background composition and educational growth. *Demography* 16: 55–71.

Marini, M. M., and Greenberger, E. (1978). Sex differences in educational aspirations and expectations. *American Education Research Journal* 15(1): 67–79.

Mathes, S., and Gurney, G. (1985). Factors in student athletes' choices of colleges. *Journal of College Student Personnel* 26: 327–333.

Mattila, J. P. (1982). Determinants of male school enrollments: A time series analysis. *Review of Economics and Statistics* 64: 242–251.

Mayer, R. R., and Greenwood, E. (1980). *The Design of Social Policy Research* Englewood Cliffs, NJ: Prentice-Hall.

Merton, R. K. (1957). Priorities in scientific discovery. *American Sociological Review* 2: 635–659.

Miller, I. (1983). Higher education: The demography of opportunity. *Journal of College Admissions* 101: 10–13.

Miller, P. W., and Volker, P. A. (1985). On the determination of occupational attainment and mobility. *The Journal of Human Resources* 20(2): 197–213.

Muffo, J. A. (1987). Market segmentation in higher education: A case study. *Journal of Student Financial Aid* 17(3): 31–40.

Murphy, P. E. (1981). Consumer buying roles in college choice. *College and University* 57: 141–150.

Nolfi, G. J. (1978). *Experiences of Recent High School Graduates*. Lexington, MA: Lexington Books.

Parents, Programs and Pennsylvania Student Plans (1984). Harrisburg: Pennsylvania Association of Colleges and Universities.

Parrish, R. E. (1979). *Survey of Educational Goals: Ocean County High School Juniors and Seniors, Spring 1979*, Report 78-79-05. Toms River, NJ: Ocean County College. (ED 179–255)

Perlman, R. (1973). *The Economics of Education: Conceptual Problems and Policy Issues*. New York: McGraw-Hill.

Peters, W. B. (1977). *Fulfillment of Short-Term Educational Plans and Continuance in Education*. Washington, DC: National Center of Educational Statistics.

Powers, S., and Douglas, P. (1985). Gender differences in selecting of an institution of higher education: a discriminant analysis. *Psychological Reports* 56: 295–278.

Radner, R., and Miller, L. S. (1970). Demand and supply in U.S. higher education: a progress report. *American Economic Review* 30: 327–334.

Rumberger, R. W. (1982). Recent high school and college experiences of youth: Variations by sex, race and social class. *Youth and Society* 13: 449–470.

Russell, C. N. (1980). *Survey of Grade 12 Students' Postsecondary Plans and Aspirations.* Manitoba, Canada: Department of Education, September. (ED 201 225)

Schultz, T. W. (1961). Educational and economic growth. In N. B. Henry (ed.), *Social Forces Influencing American Education.* Chicago: National Society for the Study of Education.

Sewell, W. H., Haller, A. O., and Ohlendorf, G. (1971). The educational and early occupational status attainment process: replication and revision. *American Sociological Review* 35: 1014–1027.

Sewell, W. H., Haller, A. O., and Portes, A. (1969). The educational and early occupational attainment process. *American Sociological Review* 34: 82–92.

Sewell, W. H., and Hauser, R. M. (1975). *Education, Occupation and Earnings: Achievement in Early Career.* New York: Academic Press.

Sewell, W. H., and Shah, V. P. (1978). Social class, parental encouragement, and educational aspirations. *American Journal of Sociology* 3: 559–572.

Sewell, W. H., et al. (1972). The educational and early occupational status attainment process: replication and revision. *American Sociological Review* 40(1): 1014–1027.

Silber, E., et al. (1961). Competent adolescents coping with college decisions. *Archives of General Psychiatry* 5: 517–527.

Solmon, L. C., and Taubman, P. J. (1973). *Does College Matter?* New York: Academic Press.

Soper, E. L. (1971). *A Study of Factors Influencing the Postsecondary Educational Plans of Utah High School Students.* Washington, DC: National Center for Educational Statistics.

Spaeth, J. L. (1967). Occupational prestige expectations among male college graduates. *American Journal of Sociology* 73(5): 548–558.

Spiegleman, R. G. (1968). A benefit/cost model to evaluate educational programs. *Socio-economic Planning Sciences* 1: 443–460.

Spies, R. (1978). *The Effects of Rising Costs on College Choice. A Study of the Application Decision of High Ability Students.* New York: The College Board.

Stage, F., and Hossler, D. Differences in family influences on college attendance plans for male and female ninth graders. *Research in Higher Education* 30:3.

Stewart, N. R., et al. (1987). Counselor impact on college choice. Paper presented at the Annual Meeting of the American Educational Research Association, Washington, DC.

Tierney, M. (1980a). Student college choice sets: Toward an empirical characterization. Paper presented at the Annual Meeting of the Association for the Study of Higher Education, Washington, DC, March.

Tierney, M. (1980b). The impact of financial aid on student demand for public/private higher education. *Journal of Higher Education* 51: 527–545.

Tillery, D. (1973). *Distribution and Differentiation of Youth: A Study of Transition from School to College.* Cambridge, MA: Ballinger.

Tillery, D., and Kildegaard, T. (1973). *Educational Goals, Attitudes and Behaviors: A Comparative Study of High School Seniors.* Cambridge, MA: Ballinger.

Trent, J., and Medsker, L. (1967). *Beyond High School: A Psychological Study of 10,000 High School Graduates.* San Francisco: Jossey-Bass.

Tuttle, R. (1981). *A Path Analytical Model of the College Going Decision.* Boone, NC: Appalachian State University. (ED 224 434)

Update. (1986, January). A report from the Washington Office of the College Board. Washington, DC: The College Board.

Welki, A. M., and Novratil, F. J. (1987). The role of applicant's perceptions in the choice of college. *College and University* 62(2): 147–160.

Williams, T. W. (1984). Recruiting graduates: Understanding student institutional fit. In D. Hossler (ed.), *Enrollment Management: An Integrated Approach.* New York: The College Board.

Willingham, W. W. (1970). *Free Access to Higher Education.* New York: The College Board.

Yang, S. W. (1981). Rural youth's decisions to attend college: aspirations and realizations. Paper presented at the Annual Meeting of the Rural Sociological Association, Guelph, Ontario, July. (ED 207 765)

Young, M. E., and Reyes, P. (1987). Conceptualizing enrollment behavior. *Journal of Student Financial Aid* 17(3): 41–49.

Zemsky, R., and Oedel, P. (1983). *The Structure of College Choice.* New York: The College Board.

CHAPTER 2

BLACK COLLEGES AND COLLEGE CHOICE:
CHARACTERISTICS OF STUDENTS
WHO CHOOSE HBCUS

KASSIE FREEMAN AND GAIL E. THOMAS

While researchers know a great deal about the experiences of African Americans in different types of higher education institutions (e.g, Allen, 1992; Epps, 1972; Fleming, 1984; Nettles, 1988; Wilson, 1994), curiously less is known about the characteristics of African American students who choose to attend HBCUs. Our intent in this research is to increase researchers' and educators' understanding of African American high school students who choose to attend HBCUs. We examine the characteristics of students who chose to attend HBCUs in the past and compare them with students who are currently choosing to attend HBCUs.

To deepen our understanding of these students, this study examines three questions: (a) How are African American high school students who currently choose HBCUs different from those who have historically attended HBCUs? (b) Who and/or what influences their consideration of HBCUs? (c) What challenges will HBCUs face in continuing to attract a broad range of African American students? We compare some research in Thomas's (1981) early edited volume, which was a forerunner in studies of African Americans' participation in education, with Freeman's (1997, 1999) more recent research, which has focused on African Americans' college choices.

This comparison is significant in three ways. First, Thomas's edited volume reviewed quantitative data and Freeman focused on qualitative data. It is therefore noteworthy and more thorough to construct the similarities and differences in outcomes by examining the findings from different methods and from a historical perspective. Second, as William Trent indicated in his presentation at the American Educational Research Association (AERA) annual meeting in 2000, we need both methods (quantitative and qualitative) to fully comprehend the picture and story of African American students. Finally, this comparison is important because it helps to develop a composite of the data and challenges facing HBCUs in recruiting African American students.

Because African American students today have more choices in the institutions they can attend, it is important to better understand the characteristics of those choosing to attend HBCUs. There is a general perception that African Americans who choose to attend HBCUs are less well prepared academically and therefore have fewer options. This research explores this assumption.

Knowing more about the characteristics of African Americans who choose to attend HBCUs is also useful to admissions officers at HBCUs. Some HBCUs have a goal of increasing their enrollments

(Benavides, 1996), and HBCUs are seeking ways to attract top African American high school graduates to their institutions. Furthermore, to better understand the retention at various higher education institutions, it is helpful to understand how students made their selections in the first place. Academic and social integration is more easily achieved if students are committed to the higher education institution they selected to attend.

HBCU Matriculation: A Historical Overview

According to Davis (1998), it is very important to understand the historical context of HBCUs because "the present situation of these schools and their students cannot be understood and appreciated without some knowledge of historical events that influenced the development and current state of these institutions" (p. 144). When the first Black colleges were founded over 150 years ago, they filled an important gap in the educational terrain of Black America (Willie & Edmonds, 1978). As early as 1837, these institutions exhibited a remarkable capacity for survival, serving as a cultural and intellectual enclave for America's Black populace (Murty & Roebuck, 1993).

During the decade following the Emancipation Proclamation (1863), it became evident that a system of formal education must be established to meet the relevant needs and conditions of the newly freed Black citizens (Bullock, 1967). "Education, then, according to the more liberal and dominant segments of missionary philanthropists, was intended to prepare a college-bred Black leadership to uplift the Black masses from the legacy of slavery and the restraints of the postbellum caste system" (Anderson, 1988, pp. 240–241; capitalization standardized). Although, according to Anderson, there may have been differences of opinion about the type of education Blacks should receive at HBCUs, there was little doubt that HBCUs should serve the central role of uplifting Black people. Despite "different educational ideologies and reform movements," the "central goal" of Black education was "preparing Black leaders or 'social guides,' as they were sometimes called, for participation in the political economy of the New South" (p. 239).

As recently as two decades ago, the majority of African Americans in college were attending HBCUs (Wilson, 1994). African Americans were limited in their access to types of higher education institutions, partly because most African Americans of college age resided in the South where segregation barriers made it impossible to select PWIs and partly because admissions barriers at northern PWIs also limited the access of African Americans (Gurin & Epps, 1975).

Two events "dramatically changed" both the number of African American participants and their geographic distribution throughout American higher education institutions (Wilson, 1994, p. 198). The first was the G.I. Bill, which increased by the thousands the number of African American veterans able to attend college. The second was the Civil Rights Act (1964), which increased the opportunities of African Americans to select PWIs. However, it was not until the 1970s that more African Americans began to select PWIs. By 1980, only 20% of African American students in higher education were attending HBCUs (Wilson, 1994, p. 198). In spite of these decreased numbers, HBCUs still continue to play a unique role in American higher education. These institutions have been extraordinary in their achievement of producing an overwhelming percentage of African American leaders "in the face of considerable obstacles, such as discriminatory public funding, hostility of the White power structure, low church support, [and] minimal response from the White philanthropic community and foundations" (Wilson, 1994, p. 198).

Although in the 1980s more African Americans were electing to attend PWIs, in the 1990s, many African American students were reconsidering HBCUs because of their interest in embracing history and tradition (Benavides, 1996). Additionally, studies of African American students experiences suggest that many have negative experiences at PWIs and that they suffer lower achievement and higher attrition than White students (Allen, 1992; Nettles, 1988). In contrast, African American students at HBCUs experience higher intellectual gains and have more favorable psychosocial adjustment, more positive self-images, stronger racial pride, and higher aspirations (Fleming, 1984; Gurin & Epps, 1975).

African Americans Choosing HBCU in 1970s

In the 1970s, according to Gurin and Epps (1975), approximately 60% of African Americans at Black colleges and approximately 45% of African Americans at PWIs had fathers who had not graduated from high school. Since, according to Gurin and Epps, many African Americans' occupations have been in semiskilled or unskilled jobs, a significant difference between African Americans who selected HBCUs and PWIs was their financial support. That is, according to Gurin and Epps, "Only one-third of Black students in Black colleges but one-half of those in White colleges held scholarships or grants that covered most of their college expenses" (p. 29). Therefore, the availability of financial aid has likely influenced African American students' selection of higher education institutions. Financial considerations also tend to encourage matriculation at colleges close to home. Gurin and Epps (1975) estimated that 90% of students attending HBCUs in the South were southerners (p. 29).

In Thomas's edited volume, Astin and Cross (1981) reported on the characteristics of Blacks choosing to attend HBCUs. In contrast to the findings of Gurin and Epps (1975), Astin and Cross found that these students "tended to have somewhat better educated fathers" *and* better educated mothers than those of Black students attending PWIs (p. 36). Although Astin and Cross found that Blacks attending White insti-

tutions "tended to have made better grades in high school and to have applied to and been accepted by more postsecondary institutions" than Blacks at HBCUs, they also found that this second group aspired more often to the Ph.D. or Ed.D. than their counterparts at White institutions (p. 43). Another noteworthy characteristic is that Black students in Black institutions "were more concerned about the political structure and community action, whereas those attending White institutions gave higher priority to financial and status goal" (Astin & Cross, 1981, p. 43).

African Americans who attend HBCUs are generally thought to have lower high school GPAs and lower standardized test scores, and to live nearby (Allen, 1992). However, Allen (1992) and Davis (1998) warn that the selectivity of the colleges and the socioeconomic status of students attending private and public HBCUs mean that caution should be used in generalizing about the background characteristics of all students attending HBCUs.

Current African American Students at HBCUs

Despite the varied profile of students who currently choose to attend HBCUs, they show some common characteristics with students who chose HBCUs in the 1970s. In a recently completed qualitative, longitudinal study that Freeman (1999) conducted on 21 high-achieving African

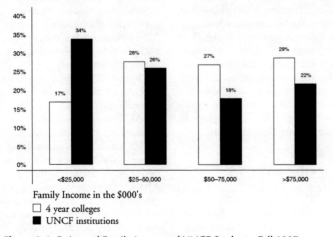

Family Income in the $000's
☐ 4 year colleges
■ UNCF institutions

Figure 2-1 Estimated Family Income of UNCF Students, Fall 1997

American students, she found that background characteristics of students choosing HBCUs was not distinguishable from those choosing PWIs. For example, the academic achievements of these high-achievers were similar, all grew up in predominantly Black environments, and all attended predominantly Black high schools. Only five of the 21 students had parents who were college graduates. Of those five, two chose to attend HBCUs. Obviously they did not choose HBCUs because they were limited in their choices by academic abilities nor socioeconomic background.

Regardless of the type of institution they selected, all 21 students indicated that financial aid was one of their biggest considerations in college choice. The often-constricted financial resources of HBCUs could limit their ability to attract a broader range of students. For example, as Figure 2-1 indicates, the largest percentage of students attending United Negro College Fund (UNCF) schools come from families that earn less than $25,000. This is understandable because the highest percentage of African Americans in this country are concentrated in the lowest salaries. However, at the high end, families with incomes greater than $75,000 show that the gap narrows between UNCF school participants and students attending other types of higher education institutions. In short, "College Fund institutions serve students from various socioeconomic backgrounds" (Freeman, Perna, & King, 1998, p. 17).

In summary, the characteristics of African Americans choosing to attend HBCUs have been somewhat consistent over time; however, recent qualitative findings (Freeman, 1999) show that HBCUs are currently attracting more academically capable students. Still, it is necessary to desegregate the data by type, just as with any other type of higher education institutions. The most consistent finding about African American students across higher education type continues to be the importance of financial aid because of so many African American families still cannot afford to finance higher education for their children.

Influences on Students Choosing HBCUs

Hossler and Gallagher (1987) describe the search phase as a courtship between the preferences of the applicant and the attributes of the college or university. Astin and Cross (1981) found that Black students' attending Black colleges in the 1970s were strongly influenced by relatives, teachers, or another personal acquaintance who had attended HBCUs, although they were also influenced by academic reputation. (See Table 2-1) Black students selected predominantly White institutions (PWIs) for financial assistance and HBCUs for low tuition. Therefore, financial considerations have and continue to be an important considerations for Blacks in choosing a higher education institution. Hossler and Gallagher's (1987) findings support the importance of financial aid, particularly for African Americans, but found that White students required a large increase in financial aid to move them from their first choice to their second. The socioeconomic composition of the school also influenced students. According to Hanson and Litten (1989), students from a high school with higher SES tended to attend a more selective college or university.

Freeman (1999), McDonough, Antonio, and Trent (1995) and Hearn, Griswold, Marine, and McFarland (1995) have conducted the most recent studies on African Americans' choices about higher education institutions. Hearn et al. found that SES and African Americans' background, academic ability, high-school track, tenth-grade expectations, and having siblings in college positively influenced 12-grade expectations about college matriculation. A finding they reported with a recommendation for further study showed that the percentage of White students, the percentage of disadvantaged, the student/teacher ratio, and the student/counselor ratio had negative effects on high African American expectations about college matriculation: "The more a school is populated by those from backgrounds socioeconomically disadvantaged in one respect or another, the more likely aspiring lower-SES students are to receive [the] support and encouragement they need to fulfill their dreams" (pp. 15–16).

McDonough, Antonio, and Trent (1995), in a quantitative study on African Americans' choice of HBCUs, found that students' religion (being Baptist), the school's reputation, and relatives' desire were the top influences. Influences for African Americans choosing PWIs were being "recruited by an athletic department," wanting to "live near home," and valuing "the college's academic reputation" (p. 27). They also found that most students applied to three or fewer col-

TABLE 2-1
Reasons for Black Students' Choice of HCBU or PWI

	Blacks in Black Institutions		Blacks in White Institutions	
	Men	Women	Men	Women
My relatives wanted me to come here.	15.8[a]	13.6	9.3	8.6
My teacher advised me.	10.9	4.3	5.0	8.4
This college has a very good academic reputation.	51.9	56.4	48.3	59.1
I was offered financial assistance.	28.0	24.5	32.1	34.1
I was not accepted anywhere else.	5.3	3.3	2.9	2.4
Someone who had been here before advised me to go.	20.7	18.5	12.8	10.1
This college offers special educational programs.	35.0	30.1	25.6	33.7
This college has low tuition.	18.2	12.6	10.8	16.2
My guidance counselor advised me.	11.7	8.8	9.8	12.1
I wanted to live at home.	11.5	11.8	7.3	4.0
A friend suggested attending.	12.6	10.5	7.7	4.2
A college representative recruited me.	10.0	7.1	15.1	9.2

[a] Percentages represent the proportion of students who checked the response category "very important."
Source: Astin & Cross, 1981, pp. 11–17.

leges and that about three-quarters were accepted at their first choice. However, African American students are accepted at their first choice less frequently (55%) than the national average (70%). This finding seems reasonable, given that African Americans attending inner-city schools are less likely than their counterparts at private high schools to be admitted to PWIs. The percentage of acceptance for African American students whose first choice is an HBCU is slightly higher (59%).

Freeman's (1999) qualitative study found three major influences on selecting an HBCU: (a) knowing someone who attends an HBCU (cultural affinity), (b) seeking roots, and (c) lack of cultural awareness. African American students, regardless of high school types, were more likely to consider HBCUs if they had a family member, a teacher/counselor, or a friend who was connected with an HBCU. This influence has remained consistent since the 1970s (Astin & Cross, 1981). (See Table 2-1.)

However, probing deeper into African American students' motivations for considering HBCUs, Freeman (1999) found that the more African American students were isolated from their cultural heritage, the more they longed for a deeper understanding of it and the more motivated they were to attend an HBCU. Even students who attended predominantly White private high schools and who considered prestigious PWIs also considered HBCUs and most often reported, as their motivation, a desire to search for their roots in or find a connection to the African American community.

In contrast, students attending predominantly Black high schools strongly favored considering PWIs (Freeman, 1999). These students reported a need to share their culture with other groups and wanted a PWI because "the real world is not Black."

HBCUs Recruitment Challenges

Our study indicates that the profile of students choosing to attend HBCUs has been somewhat consistent over time. That is, it is difficult to predict by education and SES of parents alone the college choice pattern of African American high school students. Other influential factors are the type of high school attended and the degree to which the students perceive themselves as missing cultural connections. This latter finding was particularly true of students in predominantly White high schools, expressed as a desire to "lift up the race" and a frustration that their curriculum to that point had not met their need for greater cultural identification. Reinforcing this pattern is the parallel finding that students attending predominantly Black high schools indicated a need to be in a mixed environment.

As in the 1970s and 1980s, financial aid is still a major influence on the type of higher education institution (HBCU or PWI) African American students choose to attend. Therefore, contrary to popular belief, high-achieving students will choose to attend HBCUs that can offer comparable financial aid.

For HBCUs to remain competitive in recruiting students, this research suggests a more strategic use of HBCU connections, more focus on a range of high school types (including private high schools), and proactive involvement of the leadership in the admissions process. These findings suggest that HBCU admissions officers could make better use of their alumni, teachers, and counselors at all high school types, while more extensive recruitment at private schools and predominantly White high schools might provide a good long-term return on their investment. Over time, establishing a relationship at these schools, especially with counselors and teachers, would provide access to at least some high-achieving students. An important recruiting strategy to use at these schools is responding to the desire of African American students to become more connected to their culture (Freeman, 1999).

These findings suggest that HBCUs are positioned to African American students from a wide range of high school types, academic abilities, and socioeconomic backgrounds and that this pattern has been consistent over time.

References

Allen, W. (1992). The color of success: African American college student outcomes at predominantly White and historically Black colleges. *Harvard Educational Review, 62,* 26–44.

Anderson, J. (1988). *The Education of Blacks in the South, 1860–1935.* Chapel Hill: University of North Carolina Press.

Astin, H. S., & Cross, P. H. (1981). Black students in Black and White institutions. In G. E. Thomas (Ed.), *Black students in higher education: Conditions and experiences in the 1970s* (pp. 11–17). Westport, CT: Greenwood Press.

Benavides, I. (1996, February 19). Historically Black colleges buying muscle to up enrollment. *Tennessecan, 1A.*

Bullock, H. (1967). *A history of Negro education in the South.* Cambridge, MA: Harvard University Press.

Davis, J. E. (1998). Cultural capital and the role of historically Black colleges and universities in educational reproduction. In K. Freeman (Ed.), *African American Culture and Heritage in Higher Education Research and Practice* (pp. 143–154). Westport, CT: Praeger.

Epps, E. G. (1972). Higher education and Black Americans: Implications for the future. In E. G. Epps (Ed.), *Black students in White schools* (pp. 102–111). Worthington, OH:Charles A. Jones Publishing.

Fleming, J. (1984). *Blacks in college.* San Francisco: Jossey-Bass.

Freeman, K. (1997). Increasing African Americans' participation in higher education: African American students' perspective. *Journal of Higher Education, 68*(5), 523–550.

Freeman, K. (1999). HBCUs or PWIs? African American high school students' consideration of higher education institution types. *Review of Higher Education, 23*(1), 91–106.

Freeman, K. E., Perna, L. W., & King, N. J. (1998). *The United Negro College Fund statistical report 1998.* Fairfax, VA: United Negro College Fund, Frederick D. Patterson Research Institute.

Gurin, P., & Epps, E. G. (1975). *Black consciousness, identity, and achievement: A study of students in historically Black colleges.* New York: John Wiley & Sons.

Hanson, K. H., & Litten, L. H. (1989). Mapping the road to academe: A review of research on women, men, and the college-selection process. In P. J. Perun (Ed.), *The undergraduate woman: Issues in educational equity* (pp. 73–98). Lexington, MA: Lexington Books.

Hearn, J. C., Griswold, C. P., Marine, G. M., & Mcfarland, M. L. (1995). *Dreams realized and dreams deferred: A causal analysis of six years of educational expectations and attainment.* Paper presented at the 1995 meeting of the American Educational Research Association, New York.

Hossler, D., & Gallagher, K. (1987). Student College Choice: A three-phase model and the implications for policymakers. *College & University, 62*(3), 207–221.

McDonough, P., Antonio, A., & Trent, J. (1995). *Black students, Black colleges: An African American college choice model*. Paper presented at the meeting of the American Educational Research Association, San Francisco.

Murty, K. S., & Roebuck, J. B. (1993). *Historically Black colleges and universities: Their place in American higher education*. Westport, CT: Praeger.

Nettles, M. (Ed.). (1988) *Toward Black undergraduate student equity in American higher education*. Westport, CT: Greenwood Press.

Thomas, G. E. (Ed.). *Black students in higher education: Conditions and experiences in the 1970s*. Westport, CT: Greenwood Press.

Willie, C., & Edmonds, R. (1978). *Black colleges in America: Challenges, development and survival*. New York: Teachers College Press.

Wilson, R. (1994). The participation of African Americans in American higher education. In M. J. Justiz, R. Wilson, & L. G. Bjork (Eds.), *Minorities in higher education* (pp. 195–211). Phoenix, AZ: Oryx Press.

CHAPTER 3

ON THE PATH TO COLLEGE: THREE CRITICAL TASKS FACING AMERICA'S DISADVANTAGED

ALBERTO F. CABRERA AND STEVEN M. LA NASA

A middle high school student's likelihood of continuing on to college or university rests on the completion of at least three critical tasks: (a) acquiring at least minimal college qualification, (b) actually graduating from high school, and (c) applying to a 4-year college or university. Eighty-one percent of those 1988 eighth graders who completed these three tasks enrolled in college by 1994. The path to college among socioeconomically disadvantaged middle high school students can best be characterized as hazardous. By 1994, just 1 out of 10 of the original class of 1988 poor eighth graders was attending a 4-year institution. Comparative analyses of lowest and highest SES students reveal substantial differences between these two groups, favoring upper-SES individuals at each of the three tasks on the path to college. These substantial SES-gaps are reduced, if not eliminated, once a number of influential school-based and family background variables are taken into account.

On his path to immortality, Hercules faced 12 tasks of increasing difficulty. Each task demanded different skills, strengths, and endurance. He managed to overcome each task not only because of his physical and intellectual prowess, but also thanks to the assistance of divine and human intervention at key points. Similar to Hercules' odyssey, college enrollment requires the successful completion of critical tasks as described in recent literature (Adelman, 1999b; Berkner and Chavez, 1997; Horn and Nuñez, 2000). Each task is completed not only through the merits of the student, but when he or she receives critical support and assistance.

Literature suggests that acquisition of college qualifications, graduation from high school, and applying to college is embedded into what is known as the college-choice process (Hossler, Braxton, and Coopersmith, 1989). In undergoing each phase of the college-choice process, the high school student develops *predispositions* to attend college, *searches* for general information about college, and makes college attendance *choices*. As a precondition for the final stage, choice, the student must first meet two tasks: securing college qualifications and graduating from high school. Acquisition of college qualifications, in turn, is a byproduct of a student's ability and early development of educational plans to attend college, as well as parental encouragement and involvement.

Our examination of the college-choice process experienced by a nationally representative sample of 1988 eighth graders confirms that college enrollment is, indeed, a byproduct of these three tasks (see Figure 3-1). When one examines a student's progression through these three critical checkpoints,

"On the Path to College: Three Critical Tasks Facing America's Disadvantaged." Reprinted from *Research in Higher Education* 42, no. 2 (2001), by permission of Human Sciences Press, Inc.

we find the defining characteristic of the college enrollee is the acquisition of college qualifications[1] that begins as early as the eighth grade (see Figure 3-1).[2] Students who secure college qualifications while in high school have a higher chance of enrolling in college than those who do not. Sixty-nine percent of college-qualified high school graduates enrolled in a four-year institution[3] immediately following high school completion, while only 9.9% of those who did not secure college qualifications enrolled. Even obtaining only a minimum level of college qualifications increased a student's likelihood of enrolling in a 4-year institution. Thirty percent of those eighth graders who secured only minimum college qualifications during high school enrolled in a 4-year institution after graduation.

Figure 1 also shows the importance of securing college qualifications as an important precondition of high school graduation. Nearly all students securing minimal qualifications and above completed high school, whereas only 77% of those students not meeting college qualifications secured a high school diploma.

As important as it is to become college qualified and obtain a high school diploma to enroll in a 4-year institution, college attendance can only be triggered when the student actually submits college applications. The application process in itself presents numerous hurdles. Those hurdles include concerns over college costs, uncertainties in the selection of major, completion of college application forms, and filling out extremely complex financial aid forms. Even for the most college-qualified students, the application process may present intimidating challenges. Eighteen percent of those most qualified students did not apply to a 4-year institution. Regardless of qualifications, if students opt not to apply, they are not eligible to enroll.

Substantial differences in the patterns of college choice emerge when one takes into account a student's socioeconomic status (SES). Seventy-one percent of the lowest-SES students do not obtain the academic qualifications necessary to support college enrollment (see Figure 3-2). Lowest-SES students are 24.2% less likely to be qualified than the national average; fully 71% of lowest-SES students fail to gain the requisite qualifications. In contrast, only 30.3% of the highest-SES students do not obtain the requisite college qualifications (see Figure 3-3). Interestingly, the graduation rates among the lowest-SES students at least minimally qualified are indistinguishable from the corresponding graduation rates for the highest-SES students (see Figure 3-2 and 3-3). Apparently, once students overcome the college qualification hurdle, the chances for lowest-SES students to obtain a high school diploma even out.

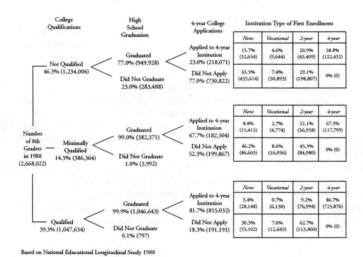

Based on National Educational Longitudinal Study 1988

Figure 3-1 College choice process for 1988 eighth grade students

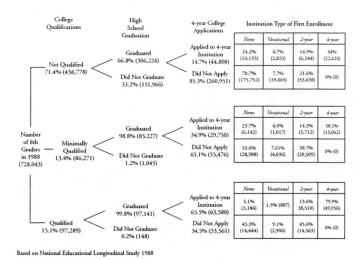

Based on National Educational Longitudinal Study 1988

Figure 3-2 College choice process for lowest SES students

Completing the third task, actually applying to a 4-year institution, appears to be particularly challenging for the lowest-SES students. Only 65.5% of the college-qualified, high school graduates from lowest-SES backgrounds actually apply to a 4-year institution. This rate is 16% and 22% below the national rate of similarly qualified eighth graders and the rate for students from high-SES background, respectively (see Figure 3-1 and 3-3).

Once lowest-SES students complete the third task and submit an application, their chances of enrolling in a 4-year institution improve dramatically to the point of closely resembling the national average and the rate for the highest-SES students (see Figure 3-2 and 3-3). Among qualified, lowest-SES, high school graduates, 80% enroll in a 4-year institution. College attendance rates for the high-SES and average eighth graders were 88.8% and 87%, respectively

Purpose

This study sought to gain a better understanding of how economically and sociologically underprivileged Americans ready themselves for college. In so doing, it highlights those factors that affect the chances for lowest-SES students to secure college qualifications, graduate from high school, and apply to a 4-year institution. This study builds upon the extant literature through analysis of the National Education Longitudinal Study of 1988 (NELS:88). The NELS data follows a representative sample of students from the eighth grade until after high school graduation.

Theoretical Background

This study rests on a framework that views a student's college choice as a complex and interwoven by-product of numerous family- and school-based factors that enable a student to go to college (Cabrera and La Nasa, 2000). Such an approach is consistent with the extant literature showing that collegiate experiences and outcomes are intrinsically and unavoidably linked with the decisions, plans, and actions students and their families undertook at the secondary level (e.g., Hossler, Schmit, and Vesper, 1999; St. John, Paulsen, and Starkey, 1996).

In this framework, parental encouragement and involvement, a pivotal force in the emergence of occupational and educational aspirations, is conditioned by the ability and high school preparation of the child, parental and sibling educational attainment, and access to information about college and costs (Berkner and Chavez, 1997; Flint, 1993, 1997; Horn, 1997; Hossler and Vesper, 1993; Hossler, Schmit, and Vesper, 1999; Perna, 2000; Sewell and Hauser, 1975; Stage and Hossler, 1989; St. John, 1990;

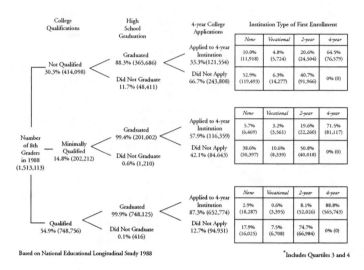

Based on National Educational Longitudinal Study 1988

*Includes Quartiles 3 and 4

Figure 3-3 College choice process for high* SES students

Terenzini, Cabrera, and Bernal, in press). Parental encouragement, the availability of information about college and perceived cost/benefit analysis of attending college also shape the institution set the student and family will seriously consider (e.g., McDonough, 1997; Hossler, Braxton, and Coopersmith, 1989). In turn, the final decision depends on the saliency of institutions, parental encouragement, financial considerations, the student's high school academic resources, the student's educational and occupational aspirations, and, of course, the student's academic abilities.

Planning for college begins as early as the eighth grade, and by the ninth grade most students have already developed occupational and educational aspirations[4] (Eckstrom, 1985; Stage and Hossler, 1989). During this period, the junior high school student comes to value a particular occupation and begins to see attending college as crucial in securing his or her occupational goals. Early college plans seems to play the role of a trigger mechanism in securing critical cultural capital. It enables eighth graders and their parents to plan for college-track curriculum and extracurricular activities, maintaining good academic performance, and securing information about ways to finance college (e.g., Hossler, Schmit, and Vesper, 1999; McDonough, 1997).

Planning for college is affected by many factors that interact in a complex manner (Alexander and Eckland, 1975). Higher socioeconomic

status parents are more likely to talk to their children about college (Stage and Hossler, 1989). They are also more predisposed to make financial plans to pay for college (Flint, 1992) and are more knowledgeable of financial aid programs (Olson and Rosenfeld, 1984; Tierney, 1980). Among the factors predicting students' early educational plans, parental encouragement is the strongest (Conklin and Dailey, 1981; Hossler, Schmit, and Vesper, 1999; Stage and Hossler, 1989).

Research suggests parental encouragement has two dimensions. The first is motivational: Parents maintain high educational expectations for their children. The second is proactive: Parents become involved in school matters, discuss college plans with their children, and save for college (Flint, 1992, 1993; Henderson and Berla, 1994; Hossler and Vesper, 1993; Miller, 1997; Perna, 2000; Stage and Hossler, 1989).

Development and maintenance of postsecondary education aspirations among high school students is proportionally related to the frequency and consistency with which parents provide encouragement (Flint, 1992). Conklin and Daily (1981), for instance, found that high school graduates entering a 4-year college were more likely to report consistent parental encouragement from 9th grade through the 12th grade. In contrast, students entering 2-year institutions were more prone to report mixed parental support across the high school years.

Applying to college and actually enrolling has been scrutinized under two lenses, one is economic in nature, the other is sociological (St. John, Paulsen, and Starkey, 1996). The economic perspective regards enrollment as the result of a rational process in which an individual estimates the economic and social benefits of attending college, comparing them to those of competing alternatives (Manski and Wise, 1983). The sociological approach examines the extent to which high school graduates' socioeconomic characteristics and academic preparation predispose them to enroll at a particular type of college and to aspire to a particular level of postsecondary educational attainment. As noted by St. John, Paulsen, and Starkey both approaches converge in portraying low-income students as sensitive to financial considerations and academic preparation for college. Our analysis incorporates elements and prior research from both perspectives.

For three decades, socioeconomic factors also have mediated student access to information about college. Using data from the National Longitudinal Study of the High School Class of 1972 (NLS:72), Tierney (1980) reported lowest-SES students had fewer information sources than upper-level SES students. Leslie, Johnson, and Carlson (1977) report similar findings. These researchers found lowest-SES students relied on high school counselors as the single most likely source of information about college. In contrast, upper-income students report a variety of sources including parents, students, catalogs, college representatives, and private guidance counselors. While low-income students may be limited in their access to a variety of sources of information, availability of high school-based academic information resources seems to level the playing field (King, 1996).

Parental education also conditions the extent to which parents are knowledgeable about college-qualification criteria and with financial strategies to pay for college. Olson and Rosenfeld (1984), based on the Parent Survey from the High School and Beyond Study, found that net of a parents' gender and college expectations for the child, having college education and children in college exerted the strongest effects on parental knowledge of financial aid programs. Strategies followed in securing information also affect the amount of knowledge the parents have regarding avenues to finance their children's college education. Olson and Rosenfeld reported that parents' knowledge of financial aid increased the most when they employed a variety of information-seeking strategies, including consulting with high school guidance counselors and bank loan officers, as well as by reading a variety of college financing pamphlets and books. Ikenberry and Hartle (1998) found that the amount and quality of information on college financing varies proportionally with socioeconomic status. Overall, upper-income families were more knowledgeable.

SES as an Indicator of Wealth

Research on college choice has approached "wealth" in several ways (see Appendix). Family income is the prevailing measure of wealth. Fourteen out of the 24 seminal college-choice studies we examined relied on family income as a wealth measure. Unfortunately, most income-based studies relied on students' self-reported information (8 out of 14). The literature also shows a growing number of recent studies employing SES as a proxy of wealth. Thirty-three percent of the college-choice studies we examined relied on SES (see Appendix).

This study relies on SES as an indicator of wealth. Several considerations guided this selection. Income, after all, reflects the availability of resources at a given point of time, masking all resources parents may have to provide for educational opportunities to their children (Oliver and Shapiro, 1995). Socioeconomic status indexes[5] also capture critical dimensions of social and cultural capital (such as parental education), which helps to explain social and occupational attainment (Bourdieu, 1977; Coleman, 1988). In addition to its comprehensive nature as a measure of wealth, SES indexes have been found to be more valid and reliable than income measures, especially when the data are self reported (Adelman, 1998). Fetters, Stowe, and Owins (1984), for instance, found low levels of agreement between students' and parents' reports of family income and parental occupation. Fetters and his colleagues, however, reported high validity coefficients when income, parental education, and parental occupation were combined into a single indicator, such as socioeconomic status.

Methodology

This section describes the database, weights employed, and variables used in the analysis. Descriptive statistics for all relevant variables are presented in Table 3-1.

Database

The National Education Longitudinal Study of 1988 database (NELS: 88 NCES; CD#: NCES 96–130) tracks nearly 15,000 1988 eighth graders, with follow up surveys in 1990 (10th grade), 1992 (12th grade), and 1994 (2 years out of high school).

Of the several national databases available to researchers, this database is best suited to examine the three tasks critical to college choice because it tracks students from the eighth grade until after high school graduation. At present, the vast explanatory potential of the NELS database has not been fully used to explain how low-income students make college attendance decisions.

Weights Employed

Analysis relied on the 1988 Panel weight (F3PNLWT) in order to adjust the NELS:88 data to reflect the number of eighth graders in the

TABLE 3-1
Descriptive Statistics for the Variables Employed in the Logistic Regression Models

Variable	N	% Cell	Mean	S.D.
SES				
Lowest	3,658	24.5		
Middle Lowest	3,653	24.5		
Middle Upper	3,682	24.7		
Upper	3,921	26.3		
Gender				
Male	7,473	50.1		
Female	7,441	49.9		
Ethnicity				
Hispanic	1,542	10.5		
African American	1,987	13.5		
Asian American	525	3.6		
White	10,642	72.4		
Planned for college at eighth grade				
Yes	11,620	78.9		
No	3,117	21.1		
Parental involvement	12,750	—	2.05	.45
Test score at eighth grade (math and writing)	14,364	—	50.59	10.04
At-risk factors	11,188	—	1.04	1.08
At least minimally college qualified				
Yes	6,200	53.9		
No	7,205	46.2		
Four-year college qualified	13406	—	2.31	1.46
Not qualified	6200	46.3		
Minimally qualified	1941	14.5		
Somewhat qualified	1771	13.2		
Very qualified	1940	14.5		
Highly qualified	1554	11.6		

TABLE 3-1 (*continued*)
Descriptive Statistics for the Variables Employed in the Logistic Regression Models

Variable	N	% Cell	Mean	S.D.
High school graduate				
Yes	13,128	88.0		
No	1,783	12.0		
Information Sources on Financial Aid	11,842	—	2.23	1.68
Applied to a 4-year institution				
Yes	9,585	64.3	—	—
No	5,320	35.7		
Highest parental expectations				
No PSE or unsure	1,421	11.8		
Some college	1,868	15.5		
Bachelor's	4,609	38.4		
Advanced degree (MS/PHD/Prof)	4,114	34.2		
Educational expectations in 1992				
No PSE expectations	2,190	15.3		
Some College	3,789	26.4		
Bachelor's	4,377	30.5		
Advanced degree (MS/PhD/Prof)	3,992	27.8		
Planned ever to attend PSE				
No PSE	503	4.1		
2-yr, or trade school	4,583	37.3		
4-yr college	7,210	58.6		
High School-based support				
College application	5,495	46.8		
Application essay assistance	4,483	38.0		
Financial aid application	3,572	30.6		

population in 1988 (*N* = 2,968,427). Following recommendations by Perna (2000), the panel weight F3PNLWT was divided by the average weight in the sample (average weight = 199.02) resulting in DWEIGHT. This adjusted weight minimizes the effect of large sample size on standard errors brought about by stratified weights. The weighted sample using F3PNLWT produces 2,968,427 cases, whereas DWEIGHT yielded 14,915. All logistic regression results are based on DWEIGHT.

Variables

Background Variables

Gender (F3SEX) coded as 0 (Male) and 1 (Female) and ethnicity (F3RACE). Ethnic cate-gories included Hispanic (1), African American (2), Asian American (3), and White (4). Native Americans, due to their small number, were excluded from the logistic regression analyses.

Socioeconomic Status

Quartile coding of base year SES (BYSESQ) was used in this study. This variable was built upon respondent's socioeconomic status at the time he or she was an eighth grader in 1988. Socioeconomic status, as defined by variables within NCES datasets, includes the following measures: parental education, parental occupation, items in the home (i.e., dishwasher, books, etc.), and family income. This variable ranged from 1 (Lowest-SES) to 4 (Upper-SES).

Ability at Eighth Grade

Composite standardized score (BY2XCOMP) of the NELS reading and mathematic tests administered to all subjects in 1988 captures student ability. The test score ranges from 30.93 to 75.81.

College Qualification Index

Developed by Berkner and Chavez (1997), the college-qualification index (CQCOMV2) attempts to approximate college admissions criteria. Thus, the index is based on cumulative academic course GPA, senior class rank, the 1992 NELS aptitude test scores, and the SAT and ACTS scores. Moreover, Berkner and Chavez adjusted this index to account for having taken rigorous high school academic work. The college qualification index ranges from 1 (not qualified) to 5 (very highly qualified). We found the college-qualification index to correlate significantly with the HIGHMATH, a scale developed after Adelman's HSB/So HIGHMATH variable (1999). The correlation between CQCOMV2 and HIGHMATH was .723. Berkner and Chavez reported that meeting minimal college qualifications significantly predicts college enrollment. To maintain

consistency with Berkner and Chavez's approach, we dichotomized the college-qualification index to reflect the absence (0) or presence of being at least minimally college qualified. We used this dichotomized variable as both dependent and predictor in logistic regression models depicted in Tables 3-2 and 3-3. CQCOMV2, in its original metric, was used in the regression model displayed in Table 3-4.

At-Risk Factors

Composite of five dichotomous NELS:88 variables indicating whether the eighth grader came from a single-parent family (BYFCOMP), had siblings who dropped out of high school (asked in the 10th grade [F1S94]), changed school two or more times from first to eighth grade (BY40), had average grades of C or lower from sixth to eighth grade (BYGRD68), and repeated an earlier grade from first to eighth grade (BYS74). The scale ranges from 0 to 5.

Parental Involvement in Students' Education

Composite of six items reflecting the extent to which subjects agree having discussed with par-

TABLE 3-2

Change in the Probability of Securing at Least Minimal College Qualifications by 12th Grade Due to Background, Planning for College at Eighth Grade, Parental Involvement, Ability, and At-Risk Factors

Factor	All	Socioeconomic Status			
		Lowest	Middle Lowest	Middle Upper	Upper
Second Lowest-SES	−0.015	—	—	—	—
Upper Middle-SES	0.058**	—	—	—	—
Upper-SES	0.146***	—	—	—	—
Female	0.026	0.021	0.049	0.032	−0.002
Hispanic	0.014	0.029	0.067	0.018	−0.080
African American	0.014	0.077	0.046	0.043	−0.163***
Asian American	0.132***	0.147	0.125	0.209***	0.030
Planned for college at eighth grade	0.168***	0.121***	0.191***	0.184***	0.102***
Parental involvement	0.181***	0.150***	0.157***	0.134***	0.146***
Ability at eighth grade	0.029***	0.025***	0.031***	0.030***	0.018***
At-risk factors at eighth grade	−0.110***	−0.084***	−0.116***	−0.125***	−0.054***
Number of cases	8,808	1,896	2,130	2,298	2,484
Baseline-p	0.537	0.286	0.454	0.589	0.796
Model χ^2, df	4,078,11***	526,44,8***	879,87,8***	881,89,8***	653,93,8***
PCP	78.9%	75.6%	75.3%	77.7%	85.6%

TABLE 3-3
Change in the Probability of Securing a High School Diploma Due to Background,
Planning for College at Eighth Grade, Parental Involvement, Ability,
At-Risk Factors and Securing Minimal College Qualifications

Factor	All	Socioeconomic Status			
		Lowest	Middle Lowest	Middle Upper	Upper
Second Lowest-SES	.009	—	—	—	—
Upper Middle-SES	.055***	—	—	—	—
Upper-SES	.076***	—	—	—	—
Female	−.033**	−0.040	−0.017	−0.075**	−0.001
Hispanic	.019	0.130***	0.006	−0.151***	0.006
African American	−.002	0.091*	−0.084*	−0.015	0.017
Asian American	.035	0.073	0.028	0.019	0.011
Planned for college at eighth grade	.024*	0.003	0.067***	−0.011	−0.001
Parental involvement	.053***	0.092**	0.006	0.051***	0.014
Ability at eighth grade	.007***	0.011***	0.008***	0.006***	0.001
At-risk factors	−.046***	−.053***	−0.085***	−0.021*	−0.005
College qualified	0.114***	.256***	0.131***	0.056***	0.019***
Number of cases	8,807	1,896	2,130	2,298	2,483
Baseline-p	0.881	0.733	0.863	0.939	0.980
Model X^2, df	1459,45,12***	327,08,9***	448,34,9***	256,13,9***	80,45,9***
PCP	93.9%	85.4%	92.2%	96.9%	99.1%

ents: (a) school courses (F1S105A), (b) school activities (F1S105B), (c) thing studied in class (F1S105C), (d) school grades (F1S105D), (e) how to prepare for the ACT/SAT test (F1S105F), and (f) going to college (F1S105G). Each item was assessed in a Likert scale ranging from 1 (never) to 3 (often). Perna (2000) found these six items factoring into a single highly reliable ($r = .83$) and predictive scale of college enrollment for the 1992 high school class.

Highest Parental Expectations

Derived from the highest expectations respondents' felt either their mother (F2S42B) or father (F2S42A) had for them in their education, this variable is made of the following categories: (1) parents had no postsecondary expectations or the respondent was unsure what their expectations were, (2) parents expected the respondent to attend either a 2-year academic or technical college, a trade school, or some college, (3) parents expected the respondent to complete a bachelor's degree, and (4) parents expected the respondent to secure advanced degrees (MS/PhD/Professional).

Information Sources on Financial Aid

A factorially derived scale made up of five NELS:88 items indicated whether the 12th grader read information on aid from the U.S. Department of Education (F2S58D) or colleges/universities (F2S58E), or talked to high school counselors (F2S58A), college representatives (F2S58B), loan officers (F2S58C) or adults (F2S58G) about financial aid. The factor solution accounted for 48.4% of the correlation matrix. The corresponding scale has an alpha reliability of 0.73. Factor loadings are reported below.

Information Sources on Financial Aid	Loadings
Teachers/counselors (F2S58A)	0.704
College representative (F2S58B)	0.706
Read DOE information about financial aid (F2S58D)	0.599
Read information on aid from colleges/universities (F2S58E)	0.761
Other adults (F2S58G)	0.700

TABLE 3-4

Changes in the Probability of Applying to College Among 12th Graders Due to Background, At-Risk Factors, Parental Involvement, Parental Educational Expectations, College Qualifications, Information and Resources, and Degree Aspirations

Factor	All	Socioeconomic Status			
		Lowest	Middle Lowest	Middle Upper	Upper
Second Lowest-SES	.020	—	—	—	—
Upper Middle-SES	.145***	—	—	—	—
Upper-SES	.264***	—	—	—	—
Female	−.009	−.025	.038	.019	−.053
Hispanic	−.000	.009*	−.110	−.077	.009
African American	.125***	.108*	.129*	.225***	.005
Asian American	.125***	.171	.198	.109	.026
Risk factors	−.065***	−.052***	−.073***	−.029	−.065***
Parental involvement	.072***	−.030	.143***	.052	.059
Parent expected some college	−.002	.009	−.037	−.064	.106
Parent expected bachelor's	.255***	.235***	.285***	.219***	.166***
Parent expected advanced degree	.219***	.171**	.212***	.184***	.166***
College-qualifications	.140***	.122***	.137***	.127***	.091***
Information on financial aid	.050***	.053***	.064***	.050***	.016
Help in college application	.113***	.067	.091*	.164***	.050
Help in financial aid procedures	.029	.022	.028	.018	.021
Help in college essays	.081***	.060	.070	.047	.071**
Aspired for some college	−.014	.008	.011	−.054	−.042
Aspired for a bachelor's	.276***	.306***	.300***	.246***	.137***
Aspired for advanced degree	.336***	.388***	.333***	.288***	.186***
Number of cases	7,417	1,393	1,732	2,022	2,270
Baseline-p	.467	.213	.342	.537	.755
Model χ^2, df	44422.51,20***	666,15,17***	1,031,06,17***	1,014,28,17***	791,78,17***
PCP	82.8	82.8	81.0	80.4	87.0

High School-Based Support

Three variables were identified signifying as to whether the student received help from his or her high school with college (F2S57A) and financial aid (F2S57C) application procedures, and assistance in writing college application essays (F2S57B).

Planned for College at Eighth Grade

Relied upon by Berkner and Chavez (1997), BYS45 identifies the highest degree planned to obtain by the eighth grader. We created a dichotomous variable signifying whether the eighth grader planned to obtain at least a 4-year degree (1) or not (0).

Planned Ever to Attend PSE

Developed by Berkner and Chavez (1997), PLANS92 captures 12th-grader plans to continue their formal education at some point after high school completion. Berkner and Chavez coded plans in terms of type of institution planned to attend. The categories are : (1) no postsecondary institution, (2) student planned to attend either a 2-year academic or technical college, or a trade school, and (3) respondent planned to attend a 4-year college.

Educational Expectations in 1992

Developed by Bekner and Chavez (1997), F2ASPIRE92 captures 12th graders' highest educational expectations after high school completion. The categories are: (1) no postsecondary education, (2) respondent expected to complete trade or vocational school or some college, (3) respondent expected to complete a bachelor's degree, and (4) respondent expected to complete an advanced degree (MS/PhD/Professional).

Applied to a 4-Year Institution

Developed by Berkner and Chavez (1997), EVR4YRA signifies whether or not the 12th grader applied to a 4-year institution. Although based on self-reported data, Berkner and Chavez corrected missing cases as having applied if subjects enrolled at a 4-year institution.

First Type of Institution Attended as of 1994

Developed by Berkner and Chavez (1997), F3SEC2A1 tracks type of institution attended as of 1994. The categories they developed include: (1) no postsecondary enrollment as of 1994, (2) private, not for profit less-than-year, (3) public less-than-2-year, (4) public 2-year, (5) private, not-for-profit 4-year, and (5) public 4-year. For the purpose of this study categories 2–3 were collapsed into a single category termed: Vocational. Based on the information provided in Berkner and Chavez, institution types 2 and 3 did not appear to offer a degree at the associate level. Moreover, several of the analyses they conducted made a clear distinction between category types 2 and 3 and 2-year and 4-year institutional types. Categories 5–6 were collapsed to form the category 4-year.

Data Analysis

Due to the dichotomous nature of the dependent variables, logistic regression was used to assess the effect of school-based and family-based variables on the probability of becoming college qualified, graduating from high school, and applying

to college (see Tables 3-2, 2-3, and 3-4). Several measures of fit were used when judging the significance of each logistic regression model. These include: the χ^2 of the model, Delta-ps, and PCPs. A significant χ^2 indicates that the independent variables as a group correlate with the dependent variable. The Delta-p represents the change in the probability in the dependent variable due to a unit change in the factor variable under consideration. PCP represents the percent of cases correctly predicted by the model. PCPs higher than 55% signify a good fit for the model. Referred as Baseline-p, Tables 3-2, 3-3, and 3-4 also report observed probabilities of becoming college qualified, graduating from high school, and applying to college. For instance, the observed probability that lowest-SES eighth graders would meet minimal college qualifications by 12th grade is .286, or 28.6 of them got qualified (see Table 3-4). Baseline-p, also referred to as unadjusted probability, serves as a benchmark to assist in assessing how much each independent variable contributes to the probability of the dependent variable (see Cabrera, 1994).

Results

Distinguishing Characteristics: Parental Education and At-Risk Factors

To become college qualified and graduate from high school, the role of parental education plays a pivotal role (Perna, 2000; McDonough, 1997). Research also shows that familiarity with college helps parents in their efforts to assist their children prepare for college. Using a sample of low-income high school students who took the SAT in 1995, King (1996) noted that low-income high school seniors reporting *planning* to attend college at higher rates than expected had parents familiar with higher education. When considering those parents with at least some exposure to the requirements of college and the college-choice process, our results indicate that, at most, 23% of lowest-SES parents can provide their children with any guidance based on first-hand collegiate experiences. In contrast, nearly all of highest-SES students (99.3%) grew up in families knowledgeable of postsecondary education.

Parental education is not, however, the only differential factor that is affecting lowest-SES students on the path to college. Lowest-SES students also tend to be differentially at risk. Chen and Kauffman (1997) found that the likelihood of dropping out of high school was in direct proportion to the extent the student has: (a) a record of poor academic performance during junior high school, (b) a history of high school dropouts in the family, (c) been held back a grade, (d) been raised by a single parent, and (e) changed schools more than twice. These five risk factors tend to be associated with lowest-SES students more so than students from other SES groups. The degree of association for three of Chen and Kauffman's risk factors and SES is fairly high and warrants attention. Lowest-SES students are 35% more likely to receive lower grades during the sixth through eighth grades than are their high-SES counterparts. This period may be critically important, as this is the point where powerful predispositions toward college attendance are formed. Furthermore, this is the time when students lay the academic foundation upon which other subject matter is built during high school. Failure to achieve adequate academic preparations, even at this early stage, may inhibit a student's future prospects. Additionally, lowest-SES students are almost 23% more likely to have older siblings that have opted to not complete high school. This characteristic may be extremely damaging to a student's prospects because firsthand knowledge of dropping out may increase acceptance of this path as a viable alternative. Finally, lowest-SES students tend to be held back one grade more often that their higher socioeconomic peers. Only 9% of high-SES students are held back a grade, whereas 30% of lowest-SES students are held back at least once during their academic career. Not only do each of these five risk factors tend to affect lowest-SES students more when the factors are considered individually, but when examining the risk factors as a group, they are more prevalent among the lowest-SES students.

The frequency with which eighth graders experience at-risk factors correlates negatively with their socioeconomic status ($r = -.294$). The higher a student's socioeconomic status the less likely the student is to be influenced adversely by the presence of risk factors. On average, lowest-SES students tend to have at least one risk factor influencing their high school performance, whereas the upper middle and highest-SES students have less than one factor exerting an influence on their chance of success. This difference, though small, is withstanding. Chen and Kauff-

man (1997) showed that an increase in just one more at-risk factor could quadruple the likelihood of dropping out from high school.

Thus far, the present study highlights the vast discrepancies between the back-grounds and experiences of the lowest-SES and highest-SES students on the path to college. Particular attention has been directed at the roles played by obtaining college qualifications, graduating from high school, and applying to a 4-year institution. Our findings and the supporting college choice literature suggest that these three tasks are critical to college enrollment. Evidence shows a clear disparity between the lowest- and highest-SES students with respect to the successful completion of these tasks. Therefore, the following sections examine the extent to which risk factors, along with other factors important to the college-choice process, affect the acquisition of college qualifications, graduation from high school, and application to a 4-year institution. We first examine college qualifications and graduation from high school.

Acquisition of College Qualifications and Graduation from High School

In following the 1988 eighth graders from lowest-SES backgrounds on the path to college, less than one third secured some degree of college qualifications by the end of their senior year (see Baseline-*ps* in Table 3-2). Of them, 15% were college qualified. Thirteen percent obtained minimal college qualifications. By 1992, 73% of the original class of 1988 lowest-SES eighth graders graduated from high school (see Baseline-*ps* in Table 3-3). In contrast, 80%, or four fifths, of a similar group of upper-SES students secured some degree of college qualifications by their senior year (see Baseline-*ps* in Table 3-2). The majority, 55%, was qualified to begin collegiate work. By 1992, 98% of upper-SES seniors graduated from high school (see Baseline-*p* in Table 3-3).

The literature shows that parental encouragement matters for lowest-SES students' postsecondary plans. King (1996) noted that parental encouragement was a decisive factor in formulating postsecondary plans among a sample of 1995 low-income high school students. Low-income seniors, unsure whether their fathers were pleased with their postsecondary plans, were less likely than their better-off peers within their cohort to aspire to attend a public 4-year college or university. King also concluded that income has a pervasive effect on postsecondary plans.

Our results regarding the connection between SES and early postsecondary plans are consistent with King's findings. Lowest-SES eighth graders were 34.5%, 25.7%, and 13.6% less likely to develop postsecondary plans than are their upper, middle-upper, and middle-lowest SES counterparts.

Perna (2000) has shown that parental involvement in school activities, as early as junior high, predicts whether or not the student would enroll in a 4-year college or university after high school graduation. Our examination of NELS:88 indicates that parental involvement in eighth graders' school activities varies in direct relation with SES ($r = .252$). On average, upper-SES students reported higher levels of parental involvement than their lower SES counterparts.

Research on occupational attainment also indicates that parents provide the most encouragement to the child with the highest academic ability (Hossler, Braxton, and Coopersmith, 1989). Ability does correlate with socioeconomic status among eighth graders ($r = .442$) Our results also show that lowest-SES eighth graders displayed lower standardized scores in math and reading. And, consistently with the extant literature, we find a significant relationship between parental involvement and a student's ability. However, this correlation is weak ($r = .169$).

Adelman (1999) and Berkner and Chavez (1997) have shown that securing college qualifications is a pivotal force in a student's decision to enroll in college. In the aggregate, discrepancies in college-preparation rates between socioeconomically advantaged and disadvantaged students are vast. Lowest-SES students are 51%, 30%, and 18% less likely to secure minimal college qualifications than their upper, middle-upper, and middle-lowest counterparts (see Baseline-p in Table 3-2). The degree of association between meeting minimal college qualifications and SES was moderately high ($r = .377$).

Factors Influencing Acquisition of College Qualifications

A series of logistic regressions were run to control for the effects of background, ability, parental encouragement, and at-risk factors on the probability of securing at least minimal college qualifications by the end of 12th grade. Before

controlling for these important college-choice factors, the difference between SES groups is substantial. The lowest-SES students are 51% less likely than highest-SES students to secure college qualifications (see Baseline-p in Table 3-2). The large SES-difference narrows dramatically when controlling for college plans in the eighth grade, ability in the eighth grade, steady parental involvement, and at-risk factors. After taking these college-choice factors into account, the net difference between lowest-SES and highest-SES students falls to only 15% (see Table 3-2).

Regardless of SES and ability, planning for college as early as the eighth grade and having parents involved in one's education are key factors that increase the likelihood of securing minimal college qualifications by the end of the senior year. Parental involvement increases the likelihood of meeting minimal college qualifications by 18%, whereas early planning for college increases this likelihood by 17% (see Table 3-2). Being at risk has a consistent negative effect on the likelihood of securing minimum college qualifications, regardless of the eighth grader's socioeconomic status. Across all students, being at risk decreases the chances of becoming minimally qualified for college by the senior year by 11% (see Table 3-2).

Table 3-2 also shows the resulting effects of background, encouragement, ability, and at-risk factors on the probability of securing minimal qualifications within each SES quartile. The most remarkable finding is the fact that ability in the eighth grade, consistent parental involvement, postsecondary planning in the eighth grade, and at-risk factors play an important and consistent role within each of the SES categories. Our findings lead us to conclude that these influences are universal.

Factors Influencing High School Graduation

The rate at which 1988 eighth graders graduated from high school correlates with their socioeconomic status ($r = .291$). Overall, lowest-SES students are 25%, 21%, and 13% less likely to graduate than their upper, middle-upper, and middle-lowest SES counterparts (see Baseline-p in Table 3). Once college-choice factors are taken into account, the differences in high school graduation rates between upper-SES and lowest-SES students are reduced from 25% to 8% (see Table 3).

Securing college qualifications also increases the likelihood of graduating from high school by 11% (see Table 3-3). Moreover, securing college qualifications along with parental involvement, ability in the eighth grade, and at-risk factors increases the likelihood of graduating from high school across each of the four SES categories. Among the poorest students, securing a minimum level of college qualifications increases the chance of graduating from high school by over 26%.

Applying to College

The third task on the path to college is overcoming the multiple hurdles embedded in the college application process. As is the case with securing college qualifications and completing high school, we find that the lowest-SES students are less likely to complete this task. Twenty-one percent of the lowest-SES eighth graders applied to a 4-year institution by the time they were seniors in high school (see Baseline-ps in Table 3-4). In contrast, 76% of the high-SES eighth graders applied to a 4-year institution (see Baseline-ps in Table 3-4). In other words, high-SES students were 55% more likely to apply than their lowest-SES counterparts.

In planning for college, 1992 high school seniors relied on a wide variety of sources of information, a pattern closely resembling the one documented by King (1996). Sources included: talking to high school teachers and counselors, speaking to college representatives, speaking to other adults, and reading information on federal and institutional programs. Financial aid concerns dominate lowest-SES students' information collection activities. Lowest-SES seniors were 5% and 4% more likely to discuss financial aid with high school staff and college representatives, respectively. Also noteworthy is the fact that a substantially large proportion of the highest-SES seniors also report consulting with high school and college personnel concerning financing college.

Research shows that applying to college is in part the result of accumulation and assimilation of information necessary to develop the student's short list of institutions to which the 12th grader will apply. Securing college-related information is heavily influenced by parental encouragement (Conklin and Dailiey, 1981; Flint, 1992; Litten, 1982). When focusing only on sources of information about financial aid, we find a weak cor-

relation between parental encouragement and expectations for postsecondary education and sources of information. These correlations are .182 (involving highest parental expectations) and .157 (parental involvement in student's education).

Also noteworthy is the fact that lowest-SES students, in relation to high-SES students, are less likely to receive high levels of parental encouragement. In other words, the population most in need is the least likely to receive this form of cultural capital. While 92% of upper-SES 12th graders have parents expecting them to secure at least a bachelor's degree, only 54% of the lowest-SES students report having parents holding such expectations. The correlation between parental expectations and socioeconomic status is .320.

Factors that Influence Applying to College

Our review of the literature identified a substantial gap regarding the factors that compel students to apply for college admission. With few notable exceptions (e.g., Berkner and Chavez, 1997; Jackson, 1978; St. John and Noell, 1989), the literature concentrates on enrollment. In so doing, a key linkage has been overlooked: College attendance can only take place *if, and only if,* a student submits college applications. Moreover, applying to college triggers access to more information about the institutions themselves and available academic and financial aid assistance that otherwise would not be accessible to the students and their families. This information, along with financial aid offers, can be enough to motivate actual enrollment. Jackson (1978), for instance, found that receiving offers of financial aid on the part of the institutions increased the likelihood of college enrollment by 15% among lowest-SES 1972 high school graduates.

It stands to reason from a policy perspective that intervention strategies will be more successful if they seek to influence those factors that predispose students to actually apply to college. Our findings emphasize that when lowest-SES seniors apply to a 4-year institution, they do enroll at rates almost identical to other SES groups (see Figure 3-2 and 3-3). Applying to college is strongly associated with a student's SES ($r = .414$). Lowest-SES seniors are 55% less likely to apply to a 4-year institution than are their high-SES counterparts (see Baseline-p in Table 3-4). These proportions fail to consider the powerful effects of those factors most likely affecting application to college; namely parental involvement, securing the necessary college qualifications, aspirations, school-based assistance, and background factors. Once we control for these college-choice factors, the 55% gap separating the lowest- from the highest-SES students narrows to 26.4%. In fact, there is no significant difference in the likelihood of applying to college for those students in the bottom half of the SES distribution (see Table 3-4). However, in relation to middle-upper SES students, the lowest-SES students are still 15% less likely to apply.

High school seniors' postsecondary education expectations are a powerful predictor of eventual application to a 4-year institution. Those aspiring for at least a bachelor's degree are 28% more likely to apply than those with no post-secondary education aspirations. Those aspiring for an advanced degree are even more likely to submit a college application (34%). Having parents with high educational expectations matters. Those 12th graders whose parents expected them to earn at least a bachelor's degree were 26% more likely to apply to a 4-year institution. Parental expectations beyond the bachelor's degree improves 12th graders' likelihood of applying by 22%.

The extant literature shows that quality and intensity of the high school curriculum, along with meeting other qualification factors, most affects the likelihood of college attendance and success (Adelman, 1999b; Berkner and Chavez, 1997). Those findings also apply when considering application to a 4-year college or university. For every 1-unit increase in a student's college qualification score, the likelihood of submitting college applications rises by 14% (see Table 3-4).

Accumulating information on financial aid and receiving school-based assistance with the college application process also makes a difference. For every 1-unit increase in the amount of financial aid information, a high school student improves his or her likelihood of applying by 5%. Receiving help with application materials and college essays at school enhances the chances of applying by 11% and 8%, respectively.

Earlier, we reported that being at risk of dropping out from high school significantly decreased an eighth grader's chances of becoming college-qualified and graduating from high school. Similarly, we find that being at risk

decreases the likelihood of applying to college by the 12th grade. Every at-risk factor, possessed as early as the eighth grade, decreases the likelihood of applying to college by the 12th grade by 7%.

African Americans and Asian Americans are 13% more likely to apply to college than their White counterparts. Female 12th graders do not differ in the likelihood to apply. These results confirm Perna's (2000) recent findings regarding the probability of enrolling in a 4-year institution among 1992 high school graduates.

Factors affecting all 12th graders' chances of applying to college are remarkably similar to those affecting the most disadvantaged high school students (Column 2 compared to Column 3 in Table 3-4). Notable differences include the lack of affect that parental involvement and high school-based resources play in a lowest-SES student's chance of applying to college (see Table 3-4). The reasons for these results are apparent; on average lowest-SES students simply do not receive adequate parental involvement and their parents tend to hold low educational expectations. Additionally, a lowest-SES 12th grader has, on average, 33.4% less information than his or her middle-upper SES counterpart.

The significance of this finding is in the fact that the most disadvantaged students are not substantially different than students from higher-SES groups when it comes to the factors that encourage application to 4-year institutions. We conclude that the factors promoting college attendance are universal. It is important to note that even after controlling for relevant college-choice factors, there still is a 26.4% gap in the college application rate between lowest-SES students and highest-SES students. Reasons for this gap may include substantial differences in ability to pay for college, the quality of information, and aspects of cultural capital beyond the scope of this study.

Discussion and Conclusion

Enrolling in a 4-year institution rests on the completion of at least three critical tasks: (a) meeting minimal college qualifications, (b) graduating from high school, and (c) applying to a 4-year college or university. Eighty-one percent of those 1988 eighth graders who completed these three tasks enrolled in college by 1994 (see Figure 3-1). The path to college among socioeconomically disadvantaged middle high school students can best be characterized as Darwinian in nature. Of the original class of 728,043 eighth graders who began their path to college in 1988, less than one third of them had secured minimal college qualifications by the end of their senior year (see Figure 3-2). Seventy-three percent of them graduated from high school by 1992. By their senior year, one fifth of them applied to a 4-year institution. By 1994, just 1 out of 10 of the original class of 1988 poor eighth graders was attending a 4-year institution. Comparative analysis of lowest- and highest-SES patterns associated with the completion of these three tasks reveals substantial differences between the two groups.

In order to explain the factors that encourage students to complete each task, we examined the role played by a student's academic ability, the amount and quality of parental encouragement and involvement received, his or her early educational and occupational aspirations, the amount information available about college, and his or her acquisition of college qualifications. Because many of the college-choice variables examined are intertwined, we used logistic regression to single out the net effects of individual variables at each step on the path to college. The steps examined by our analysis were: (a) acquisition of college qualifications, (b) graduation from high school, and (c) applying to a 4-year college or university. In testing the effects of these college-choice variables, we were limited by the availability of indicators in the NELS:88 file. Nevertheless, the richness of this data enabled our analysis to test most of the propositions embedded into our college-choice model. SES-gaps are reduced, if not eliminated, once a number of influential school-based and family-originated factors are taken into account. In other words, family-based, school-based, and individual-based practices are as important if not more than is family's SES in becoming college qualified, graduating from high school, and applying to a 4-year institution.

Our results clearly show that intervention strategies seeking to increase college participation rates among socioeconomically disadvantaged high school students need to be holistic. Given the high degree of interdependence between family- and school-based resources, it is unrealistic to assume that one "single shot" policy by itself would facilitate their success on the path to college.

Targeting the acquisition of college qualifications seems to be a most fruitful area for policy intervention. Its importance reverberates in two out of the three tasks examined by this study. The critical importance of being college qualified extends well beyond the application process. As masterfully shown by Adelman (1999b), the academic resources secured at the elementary and secondary education levels make completion of a college degree a certainty. Programs must ensure that sixth, seventh, and eighth graders—and especially their parents—are aware of curriculum needed to succeed in college.

Becoming college qualified, in turn, presupposes high parental involvement in school activities as well as early planning for college (Henderson and Berla, 1994). And, as our literature review shows, parental involvement is directly related to the amount of information parents themselves have regarding college. Firsthand exposure to postsecondary education greatly facilitates access to this information. College educated parents are more likely to see the long-term benefits associated with a college degree and to communicate this information to their children (Coleman, 1988). They are also more knowledgeable of the curricular requirements and mechanisms to finance college education (Flint, 1992, 1993; McDonough, 1997). In this respect, lowest-SES students are most disadvantaged. Whereas 99.3% of upper-SES parents have some formal college education, barely 23% of lowest-SES parents have been exposed to higher education. It stands to reason that information efforts targeting lowest-SES parents would yield the highest pay-off.

Parental involvement in children's school activities, as well as parental educational expectations are likely to be enhanced if lowest-SES parents see a connection between a college degree and economic and social benefits. Equally important is parental knowledge of curricular strategies and financial planning needed to meet the goal of securing a college education. Information on financial planning need not be detailed; providing parents with general, concise, and clear data on college costs and financial aid may suffice to motivate them to start saving for their children's postsecondary education and to learn about different financial aid packages (Hossler, Schmit, and Vesper, 1999; Olivas, 1985). A plausible source of this information is the postsecondary institution itself (Adelman, 1999a).

Colleges and universities are in the unique position of explaining to parents the importance of curriculum planning as early as in the eighth grade. They are well aware of the specific academic skills and knowledge needed to undertake different academic majors. Moreover, colleges' and universities' expertise with financial aid application procedures uniquely qualify them to assist lowest-SES parents to overcome their fears of qualifying for need-based financial aid (Olivas, 1985).

School partnerships, as early as the elementary level, constitute another promising domain in which parental involvement can be fostered the most. A lowest-SES student's acquisition of study habits, literacy skills, and commitment to life-long learning seems to be fostered the most when involvement comes from both parents and schools (Clark, 1983). Partnerships have an extra advantage: They provide information and skills lowest-SES parents themselves may need to become involved in decisions pertaining to curricular planning and school activities for their own children (Henderson and Berla, 1994).

Being aware of the curriculum and other college-related requirements one needs to meet may not suffice when the elementary and secondary institutions do not provide what Adelman (1999a) dubs an "opportunity-to-learn." As noted by McDonough (1997), differences in college attendance rates among varied SES groups can be explained in part by the quality of the high school they attended. Little change would take place if the nation's lowest-SES students attend schools lacking labs, engaging and adequate curriculum, innovative instructional techniques, qualified teachers, appropriate computer equipment, books, and academic and career advising to make this "opportunity-to-learn" a vibrant reality.

Based on the findings of our analysis, it stands to reason that programs focusing their attention on those factors enabling students to successfully complete the three critical tasks on their path to college will most benefit lowest-SES students. The Talent Search and the GEAR UP initiatives are illustrative of such comprehensive approach.

Acknowledgments. Support for this study was provided by two grants from the Association for Institutional Research (Contract Numbers: 99-114-0 and 00-107). The College Board provided additional funding (Contract No. 412-13 CB Low Income Students, 24450). The opinions expressed here do not necessarily reflect the opinions or policies of either funding organization, and no official endorsement should be inferred. The authors are indebted to two anonymous reviewers and the editor for the invaluable suggestions. Special thanks go to Clifford Adelman, Aurora D'Amico, Cynthia L. Barton, Lutz Berkner, Dennis Carrol, Susan Choy, Vicky Dingler and Anne-Marie Nuñez who constantly came to our rescue while navigating the unfamiliar NELS:88 waters. We are also grateful to Larry E. Gladieux and W. Scott Swail for their encouragement and very useful insights throughout the whole project.

Appendix: Definitions of Wealth

An extensive review of the literature on college choice was conducted in search of seminal papers examining the role of wealth related indicators (e.g., income, parental education, socioeconomic status). Twenty-four seminal studies were identified through ERIC database searches and solicitations of the expertise of 24 top scholars researching issues of access and persistence in higher education. The studies used a variety of methodologies and data sets to assess the impact of wealth measures on a range of higher education issues. Each study was analyzed to ascertain collegiate outcome(s) addressed, data source, and definition of wealth. Wealth measures varied widely across the studies being family income the most commonly used (58%). Thirty-three percent of the college-choice studies relied on SES.

Notes

1. Developed by Berkner and Chavez (1997), the college-qualification index approximates college admissions criteria by collapsing cumulative academic course GPA, senior class rank, aptitude test scores, and the SAT and ACTS scores (see Methodology section).
2. Figures 3-1 – 3-3 are based on panel weight (F3PNLWT), which estimated the population of eighth graders to be 2,968,427 in 1988 (see Methodology section). Of them, only 89.1% (2,668,022) had valid information in the college-qualification index. Subjects with missing values for high school completion and four-year applications have also been excluded from analysis.

Researchers	Outcome(s)	BPS: 89–90	NPSAS	HSB:So	HSB:Sr	NLS-72	NELS: 88	Inst.	Multi-Inst	Definitions of Wealth
Adelman (1998, 1999b)	Choice & Persistence to graduation	X				X				2 Lowest-SES and SESINC composite quintiles
Berkner and Chavez (1997)	Enrollment						X			Low income (<$25,000), middle-income ($25,000–$74,999) and high-income ($75,000 or more). Income reported by parents in 1988.
Choy (2000)	Financing College						X			Income below 125% of the federally established poverty threshold given family size
Choy and Ottinger (1998)	College choice		X							Low income (<$30,000, middle income ($30,000–$69,999) and high income ($70,000) or more. Dependent students.
Choy and Premo, MPR (1996)	Financing College	X	X							Income below 125% of the federally established poverty threshold given family size
Cuccaro-Alamin and Choy (1998)	Financing College	X	X							Lowest-SES quartile (middle 2 combined)
Flint (1992)	College Choice								X	Self-reported family income by $10,000's (compared to Census %). no breakdown analysis for low income students
Flint (1997)	College Choice		X							Self-reported family income by $10,000's (compared to Census %). no breakdown analysis for low income students
Hearn (1992)	College Choice				X					SES scores
Horn and Chen, MPR (1998)	College Choice & Persistence						X			Lowest-SES quartile and 5 at-risk factors
Horn and Nuñez (2000)	Enrollment								X	1991 Parents' reported income Low (<$25,000): middle ($25,000–$74,999) and high ($75,000 or higher)

Researchers	Outcome(s)	BPS: 89–90	NPSAS	HSB:So	HSB:Sr	NLS-72	NELS: 88	Inst.	Multi-Inst	Definitions of Wealth
Jackson (1978)	College Choice-Application Stage					X				Lowest-SES third
King (1996)	College Choice: Planning to attend								X	Self-reported <$20,000 (lowest quartile nationally)
Leslie, Johnson and Carlson (1977)	College Choice: Planning to attend							X		Self-reported Low ($7,500); middle ($7,500–$15,000); and high (>$15,000)
Leslie and Brinkman (1998)	College Choice								X	Summary of 25 different institutional research studies
Manski and Wise (1983)	College Choice & Persistence					X				Self-reported family income Lower (<$16,900); Middle ($16,900–$21,700) & Upper (>$21,700)
McPherson and Schapiro (1998)	College Choice								X	1980 <$10,000; $10,000–$15,000; $15,000–$30,000; $30,000–$50,000; $50,000–$100,000; and >$100,000 1994 <$20,000; $20,000–$30,000; $30,000–$60,000; $60,000–$100,000; $100,000–$200,000; and >$200,000
Nuñez and Cuccaro-Alamin, MPR (1998)	First Generation College Students	X								Lowest-SES quartile (middle 2 combined)
Perna (2000)	Enrollment						X			Parents' education from (1) less than high school to (5) advanced degree

Researchers	Outcome(s)	BPS: 89–90	NPSAS	HSB:So	HSB:Sr	NLS-72	NELS: 88	Inst.	Multi-Inst	Definitions of Wealth
St. John and Noell (1989)	College Choice: Applying & Enrolling				X	X				Self-reported family income, no breakdown analysis for low income students
St. John (1990)	College Choice: Enrollment			X						Self-reported family income: <$15,000, $15,000–24,999, $25,000–39,999, and >$40,000
St. John (1994)	Pricing			X						SES quartiles and 3 Need simulations (1-mostly Pell grants, 2-eligibility for other need-based aid, 3-not considered eligible for need-based aid).
St. John et al. (1996)	Choice & Persistence			X						<$11,000; $11,000–29,999; $30,000–$59,999, and >$60,000, no breakdown analysis for low-income students

3. College enrollment was ascertained using F3SEC2A1, an index developed by Berkner and Chavez tracking first type of institution attended as of 1994 (see Methodology section).
4. Eckstrom, (1985) found that 61% of those high school graduates who enrolled in college had made the decision to go to college by ninth grade.
5. Although Duncan (1961) developed the widely used socioeconomic index (SEI) to predict occupational prestige, socioeconomic status (SES) has become the preferred yardstick to reflect potential for social and economic mobility bestowed by one's family background.

References

Adelman, C. (1998). Academic resources: Developing an alternative index of individual student capital. Paper presented at the meeting of the Association for Institutional Research, Minneapolis, MN.

Adelman, C. (1999a). The rest of the river. *University Business,* 43–48.

Adelman, C. (1999b). *Answers in the tool box: Academic intensity, attendance patterns, and bachelor's degree attainment.* Document #PLLI 1999-8021. Washington, DC: U.S. Department of Education, Office of Educational Research and Improvement.

Alexander, K. L., and Eckland, B. K. (1975). Basic attainment processes: a replication and extension. *Sociology of Education* 48: 457–495.

Berkner, L. K., and Chavez, L. (1997, October). *Access to postsecondary education for the 1992 high school graduates.* Statistical Analysis Report, NCES 98-105. Washington, DC: U.S. Department of Education, Office of Educational Research and Improvement, National Center for Education Statistics.

Bourdieu, P. (1977). Cultural reproduction and social reproduction. In J. Karabel and A. Halsey (eds.), *Power and Ideology in Education.* New York: Oxford University Press.

Cabrera, A. F. (1994). Logistic regression analysis in higher education: an applied perspective. In John C. Smart (ed.), *Higher Education: Handbook for the Study of Higher Education* Vol. 10, pp. 225–256. New York: Agathon Press.

Cabrera, A. F., and La Nasa, S. M. (2000). *On the path to college: three critical tasks on facing America's disadvantaged.* Report to the Association for Institutional Research. University Park: Center for the Study of Higher Education, The Pennsylvania State University.

Chen, X., and Kauffman, P. (1997). Risk and resilience: The effects of dropping out of school, Paper presented before the annual meeting of the American Association of Education Research. Chicago, Illinois.

Choy, S. P. (2000, April). *Low-income students: who they are and how they pay for their education.* Postsecondary Education Descriptive Analysis Reports, NCES 2000-169. Washington, DC: U.S. Department of Education, Office of Educational Research and Improvement, National Center for Education Statistics.

Choy, S. P., and Ottinger, C. (1998, November). *Choosing a postsecondary institution.* Statistical Analysis Report, NCES 98-080. Washington, DC: U.S. Department of Education, Office of Educational Research and Improvement, National Center for Education Statistics.

Choy, S. P., and Premo, M. D. (1996). *How low-income undergraduates financed postsecondary education: 1992–93.* Statistical Analysis Report #NCES 96-161. Washington, DC: U.S. Department of Education, National Center for Education Statistics.

Clark, R. M. (1983). *Family Life and School Achievement.* Chicago: University of Chicago Press.

Coleman, J. S. (1988). Social capital in the creation of human capital. *American Journal of Sociology* 94: 95–120.

Conklin, M. E., and Dailey, A. R. (1981). Does consistency of parental educational encouragement matter for secondary students? *Sociology of Education* 54(4): 254–262.

Cuccaro-Alamin, S., and Choy, S. P. (1998). *Postsecondary financing strategies: how undergraduates combine work, borrowing, and attendance.* Statistical Analysis Report, No. NCES 98-088. Washington, DC: U.S. Department of Education, National Center for Education Statistics.

Duncan, O. (1961). A socioeconomic index for all occupations. In A. J. Reiss (ed.), *Occupations and Social Status,* pp. 109–138. New York: Free Press.

Eckstrom, R. B. (1985). *A Descriptive Study of the Public High School Guidance: A Report to the Commission for the Study of Precollegiate Guidance and Counseling.* Princeton, NJ: Education Testing Service.

Fetters, W. B., Stowe, P. S., and Owins, J. A. (1984). *Quality of Responses of High School Students to Questionnaire Items.* Washington, DC: U.S. Department of Education, National Center for Educational Statistics.

Flint, T. A. (1992). Parental and planning influences on the formation of student college choice sets. *Research in Higher Education* 33(6): 689–708.

Flint, T. A. (1993). Early awareness of college financial aid: does it expand choice? *Review of Higher Education* 16(3): 309–327.

Flint, T. A. (1997). Intergenerational effects of paying for college. *Research in Higher Education* 38(3): 313–344.

Hearn, J. C. (1992). Emerging variations in postsecondary attendance patterns: an investigation of part-time, delayed, and nondegree enrollment. *Research in Higher Education* 33(6): 657–687.

Henderson, A. T., and Berla, N. (1994). A New Generation of Evidence: The Family is Critical on Student Achievement. Washington, DC: National Committee for Citizens in Education.

Horn, L. (1997). *Confronting the odds: Students at risk and the pipeline to higher education,* Statistical Analysis Report No. NCES 98-084. Washington, DC: U.S. Department of Education, Office of Educational Research and Improvement, National Center for Education Statistics.

Horn, L., and Nuñez, A. M. (2000). *Mapping the road to college: first generation students' math track, planning strategies, and context of support.* Statistical Analysis Report No. NCES 2000-154. Washington, DC.: US Department of Education, National Center for Education.

Horn, L. J., and Chen, X. (1998). *Toward resiliency: At-risk students who make it to college* Report No. PLLI 98-8056. Washington, DC: U.S. Department of Education, Office of Educational Research and Improvement.

Hossler, D., Braxton, J., and Coopersmith, G. (1989). Understanding student college choice. In J. Smart (ed.), *Higher Education: Handbook of Theory and Research,* Vol. 5. New York: Agathon.

Hossler, D., Schmit, J., and Vesper, N. (1999). *Going to College: How Social, Economic, and Educational Factors Influence the Decisions Students Make.* Baltimore: Johns Hopkins University Press.

Hossler, D., and Vesper, N. (1993). An exploratory study of the factors associated with parental saving for postsecondary education. *Journal of Higher Education* 64(2): 140–165.

Ikenberry, S. O., and Hartle, T. W. (1998). *Too Little Knowledge is a Dangerous Thing: What the Public Thinks and Knows About Paying for College.* Washington, DC: American Council on Education.

Jackson, G. (1978). Financial aid and student enrollment. *Journal of Higher Education* 49(6): 548–574.

King, J. E. (1996). *The Decision to Go to College: Attitudes and Experiences Associated with College Attendance Among Low-Income Students.* Washington, DC: The College Board.

Leslie, L. L., and Brinkman, P. T. (1988). *The Economic Value of Higher Education.* New York: Collier Macmillan.

Leslie, L. L., Johnson, G. P., and Carlson, J. (1977). The impact of need-based student aid upon the college attendance decision. *Journal of Education Finance* 2: 269–285.

Litten, L. H. (1982). Different strokes in the applicant pool: some refinements in a model of student college choice. *Journal of Higher Education* 53(4): 383–401.

Manski, C. F., and Wise, D. A. (1983). *College Choice in America.* Cambridge, MA: Harvard University Press.

McDonough, P. (1997). *Choosing Colleges: How Social Class and Schools Structure Opportunity.* Albany: State University of New York Press.

McPherson, M. S., and Schapiro, M. O. (1998). *The Student Aid Game: Meeting Need and Rewarding Talent in American Higher Education.* Princeton, NJ: Princeton University Press.

Miller, E. I. (1997). Parents' views on the value of a college education and how they will pay for it. *Journal of Student Financial Aid* 27(1): 20.

Nuñez, A., and Cuccaro-Alamin, S. (1998). *First-generation students: undergraduates whose parents never enrolled in postsecondary education.* Statistical Analysis Reports #NCES 98-082. Washington, DC: U.S. Department of Education, National Center for Education Statistics.

Olivas, M. A. (1985). Financial aid packaging policies: Access and ideology. *Journal of Higher Education* 56: 462–475.

Oliver, M. L., and Shapiro, T. M. (1995). *Black Wealth/white Wealth: A New Perspective on Racial Inequality.* New York: Routledge.

Olson, L., and Rosenfeld, R. A. (1984). Parents and the process of gaining access to student financial aid. *Journal of Higher Education* 55(4): 455–480.

Perna, L. W. (2000). Differences in the decision to attend college among African Americans, Hispanics, and Whites. *Journal of Higher Education* 71(2): 117–141.

Sewell, W. H., and Hauser, R. M. (1975). *Education, Occupation, and Earnings: Achievement in the Early Career.* New York: Academic Press.

St. John, E. P. (1990). Price response in enrollment decisions: an analysis of the high school and beyond sophomore cohort. *Research in Higher Education* 31(2): 161–176.

St. John, E. P. (1994). Assessing tuition and student aid strategies: using price-response measures to simulate pricing alternatives. *Research in Higher Education* 35(3): 301–335.

St. John, E. P., and Noell, J. (1989). The effects of student financial aid on access to higher education: An analysis of progress with special consideration of minority enrollment. *Research in Higher Education* 30(6): 563–581.

St. John, E. P., Paulsen, M. B., and Starkey, J. B. (1996). The nexus between college choice and persistence. *Research in Higher Education* 37(2): 175–220.

Stage, F. K., and Hossler, D. (1989). Differences in family influences on college attendance plans for male and female ninth graders. *Research in Higher Education* 30(3): 301–315.

Terenzini, P. T., Cabrera, A. F., and Bernal, E. M. (in press). *Swimming Against the Tide: The Poor in American Higher Education*. The College Board.

Tierney, M. S. (1980). The impact of financial aid on student demand for public/private higher education. *Journal of Higher Education* 51(5): 527–545.

CHAPTER 4

COLLEGE CHOICE IN A CULTURAL CONTEXT

P. M. McDONOUGH

Findings

This book has shown the myriad ways in which students navigate through the process of choosing a college: from considering a range of appropriate colleges to gathering information on those schools under consideration to making a decision. Students make college choices in the context of implicit and explicit messages from their social and organizational networks. Sometimes the cultural context of the students' communities, schools, and families are in agreement, and sometimes they are not.

To use the image of a mobile, the students in this study differ in how they weigh different factors in the college choice process; thus, the mobile shifts and hangs in many different ways. For some students in this study, the family, in effect, was silent. Carol Lincoln's parents provide one example of this. They felt they did not know much about college and had little of value to contribute to their daughter's decision. In the framework of this book, they lacked the cultural capital relevant to college choice.

From Carol's point of view, not only was her parents' participation limited, but she felt equally let down by her school. Her poor course counseling in junior high school left her without needed high school science courses and consequently left her having to enroll in remedial classes in her freshman year of college. Her college counselor offered little help in her decision making, other than telling her that the two schools she was interested in were "pretty" campuses near the beach.

Carol's friends were the factors in her mobile that carried the most weight. Carol serendipitously decided to apply to a California State University because some of her high school friends were applying. Both Carol and her friends chose a less well-known route to college, something other than her high school's well-worn path to the local community colleges. As Carol articulated it, she decided on this choice after she watched her friends apply; she herself applied "just for the heck of it."

This college choice process is not the economist's rational choice model of a world with perfect information, nor is it a policy maker's model of informed consumer choice accounting for cost and comfort considerations. It is a teenager left to her own devices in making what she called a "spur of the moment" decision. This spontaneous action was similar to many of Carol's college preparatory actions: studying for the SATs consisted of buying a book two days before the exam and practicing "a little."

Some might ask, "What's wrong with this approach? Carol is attending a decent college." Evidence suggests that where one attends college affects one's chances of getting the bachelor's degree, as well as other educational and occupational attainment evidence also suggests that controlling for students' input characteristics at four-year colleges showed little differences in outcomes. However, many of the high SES parents in this study believe and act on cultural capital and habitus—that certain colleges are "helpful to you in the future" and provide "ins" in one's later professional world. Moreover, there are differences among specific institutions, even if there are no differences in types of institutions. At Carol's college, only 30 percent of entering freshmen graduate.

Not all college-bound students face equal choices if they start out with different family and school resources that enable or constrain their educational and occupational mobility possibilities. These differential resources contribute to the persistence and reproduction of a social-class-based stratified system of postsecondary opportunity that thwarts meritocratic ideals.

The students from Paloma and Gate of Heaven had counselors who were able to offer more resources and time than counselors at the other two high schools. Moreover, Paloma students' parents had first-hand college information that they brought to bear on their daughters' choice processes, and they have other relevant cultural capital. For example, Mr. Ornstein knew his daughter's SAT scores (which were comparable to Carol's) could be improved through formal coaching, and he hired a private counselor to help identify schools at which those SAT scores would not be an admissions hindrance.

In other students' college choice decision making processes, parents, regardless of whether they possessed the relevant cultural capital, were relatively passive because of their competing time demands. Susan Harriman's parents, although involved somewhat, left much of the college choice decision making process up to their daughter, which made Susan, her friends, and Paloma School more influential pieces of her college choice mobile. Mrs. Harriman bought private school resources and attention and counted on Susan's home, school, and friendship circles to be mutually reinforcing regarding college aspirations. Nonetheless, Susan felt relatively misunderstood and unsupported by her parents throughout her college choice process.

Lareau (1989) notes that cultural capital, effectively used, provides needed advantages to individuals in their interactions with social institutions. This study documents that cultural capital also confers needed advantages in making the transitions between social institutions by further advantaging those students who have and use family, financial, and network capital to supplement their organizational habitus in trying to maximize their educational choices and eventual returns on investment.

Families and schools are in a mutually influencing process that affects individual student outcomes. Some families have consciously chosen to enhance their daughters' educations by placing them in private high schools or hiring tutors or private counselors. Other parents move to certain neighborhoods to place their children in better school districts. Still other families do not have conscious, educational game plans, and instead react to their children's opportunities based on what school personnel say is possible given their children's demonstrated achievement.

Students' values also enter into the picture. Every student filters her college options through the lenses of her academic achievement, her economic circumstances, her field of vision, and her values. Given these ability, economic, and value constraints, a student eventually narrows down the 3,600 colleges and universities to a piece of the opportunity structure that she believes is within her grasp. This personal schema, including known options and preferences, is the synthesis of what Bourdieu (1977b) calls the objective probabilities and subjective assessments of an individual's chances for mobility.

Although an individual develops her own personally synthesized aspirations, college-bound students of relatively the same academic achievement and similar social class backgrounds make remarkably similar college choices. And those choices are qualitatively different from the choices made by relatively equal-ability students from different social class backgrounds. It is not a coincidence that individuals from the same social class come to relatively similar aspirational schemata. The patterns of students' aspirations in this study were shaped by the class context of the communities, families, and schools in which these students lived their daily lives. These class-based patterns stand in stark contrast to traditional aspiration or expectation research that assumes an individual-level analysis.

The world of choosing a college is much more complex and different than either functionalist or policy maker frameworks suggest. Functionalist educational attainment theory posits that abilities and achievements determine aspirations and subsequent attainment. In this view, college-bound individuals locate their place in the academic hierarchy by matching their prior achievements with appropriate openings. Traditional policy making assumes the same structure of opportunity. The California Master Plan for Higher Education specifies different opportunities for different segments of the college-going population:

- the top 12 percent of California's high school graduates are eligible for University of California campuses,
- the California State University is available to the top one-third of California's high school graduates, and
- the community college system is open to all high school graduates.

In elaborating on Bourdieu's work, I have introduced the concept of "entitlement": students believe they are entitled to a particular kind of collegiate education based on their family's and/or high school's habitus. Class socialization precedes and significantly shapes the formation of aspirations—students develop college plans based on their families' and communities' values and assessments of appropriate goals.

Paloma students felt entitled to the best education they could secure: private when available, or the best public education as a backup. University High School students were, for the most part, from the same geographic and social class communities as Paloma students and felt entitled to at least the best public education and certainly the best private education they could afford. Gate of Heaven students felt entitled to a generic notion of college and whatever was available locally, while Mission Cerrito students felt entitled to the local community colleges.

Class-based patterns of aspirations are a joint product of family and school influences. When families who can afford it choose to send their daughters to private schools like Paloma, they are buying college preparatory services, as well as peace of mind from the perceived problems at public high schools. Other families, like some at University High School, make the most of the college guidance capacity of their daughters' public school environment. Most high SES families in this study knew better than their low SES counterparts how, when, and why they should interact with the school about their

daughters' college choice processes. The high SES families had the cultural capital to be aware of nonschool-based admissions management services (McDonough 1994) such as SAT tutoring and private counselors and had the financial resources to then make it possible to purchase those services to supplement their existing family and school resources.

Paloma's college preparatory efforts were comprehensive, proactive, and nurturing. Gate of Heaven's college counseling program also was proactive, providing information and attempting to engage students in exercises designed to stretch their conceptions of appropriate college choices. Gate of Heaven's support for college planning was multi-level and used teachers, students, alumni, computers, and counselors to inform and encourage students.

University High School's counselor conveyed basic and necessary information to large numbers of students about the most popular college choices, but left the college choice decision making process to individual students or their families and could not help students who wanted to consider anomalous choices. Mission Cerrito initiated its college counseling when students were in the final lap of their college choice race—senior year. Students made their choices without much assistance from the school, except for school mailings and bulletins that assumed the best option was community college.

Each of these schools offered different organizational environments for college choice decision making in terms of

1. the actual structure and resources of the school devoted to college preparation—timing, availability, and support for college advising; and
2. the normative structure of the high school
    - an organizational mission which more or less emphasizes college, most explicitly through curricular options;
    - assumptions of students' cultural capital that the official guidance program can and did build upon; and
    - counselor role expectations and enactment that display and reinforce the taken-for-granted nature of a subset of the 3,600 U.S. colleges that counselors have firsthand knowledge of and recommend that students attend.

Each of these organizational environment features presented to the students in those schools a particular organizational habitus, the impact of a cultural group or social class on an individual's behavior through an intermediate organization. These organizational habiti presented different views of the college opportunity structure and thus framed and enabled students' college aspirations. Organizational habitus demonstrates how high schools' organizational cultures are linked to wider socioeconomic status cultures, how social class operates through high schools to shape students' perceptions of appropriate college choices, thereby affecting patterns of educational attainment, and how individuals and schools mutually shape and reshape each other.

Each of the guidance counselors constructed norms for behavior and expectations for students making assessments of the objective probabilities of individual students and each school's average student's chances for college admissions. The counselors offered their assessments to students through handbooks, the array of college representatives they invited to the school, the information packets they kept on hand to pass out to students, and through the collective seminars and individual advisement sessions. The counselors were aware of and some were sensitive to parental demands or expectations for "appropriate" colleges or information. However, the central role of habitus is in defining and limiting what is seen by an actor and how it is interpreted. For Paloma students, cost was not perceived as a big factor, geography was unlimited, and current academic achievement was manipulable. For University High School students, cost was a modest factor, geography was somewhat unlimited, and achievement often was viewed as subject to enhancement much the same as Paloma students viewed it.

For Gate of Heaven students, cost was a substantial factor, achievement was a modest limitation, and geography was cast in narrow and local terms when considering schools twenty-five to fifty miles away, but most often when attending colleges within five to fifteen miles of their homes. For these Catholic school students and their parents, a private high school education was a hedge against "bad" public high schools and minimal protection against drugs and teen pregnancy. However, public colleges were seen as providing a more-than-sufficient and cost-effective education. For Mission Cerrito students, cost, achievement, and geographical distance were substantial factors. Most of these students did not see their high school preparation as adequate and focused their college sights primarily on nearby junior colleges. The local community colleges, which were some of the best in the state, were viewed by these students and their families as a good investment, a way to "try out" college, and to "sharpen their limited academic skills" in a safe, familiar environment. Even though 55 percent of Mission Cerrito college-bound students went on to attend two-year community colleges, there still was a stigma attached to these colleges.

College admissions environments also shaped the organizational structure and culture of high schools as they related to college guidance. Paloma and University High Schools' organizational habiti were influenced by a national, volatile, competitive college admissions environment that was highly stressful and competitive. These students also lived in a community that was focused on prestige. Mission Cerrito and Gate of Heaven's organizational habiti were shaped by a local opportunity structure and limited family financial resources. Consistent with the research literature, the low SES students looked for low-cost colleges and tight vocational linkages in their educational programs.

At all four schools, students looked at colleges with some concept of habitus, although never calling it that. Some students looked for colleges that matched some aspect of their high school habitus, such as the same supportive environment that had nurtured them during high school. Other students looked for a college habitus that contrasted with their high school experience or was consistent with their own personal values or personalities.

Parents also enabled or constrained their daughters' views of the college opportunity structure, with regard to what were feasible costs, how far from home was appropriate, and whether college was something you entered, or left, with clear career expectations. High SES students' worlds had a seamless quality, while deciding on college was characterized by conflict and challenge for low SES students. Low SES students considered cost in identifying a range of affordable institutions, and these students assumed that the burden of paying for college was theirs. The high SES students usually deferred to their parents on the issue of defining a financially acceptable range of college choices and assumed that the major burden of paying for college lay with their parents.

Enrollment and competition dynamics in the college admissions environment played an enormous role in the process of choosing a college for many of the high SES students in this study. This current method of applying to college is full of uncertainty and heightened anxiety. Many high SES, college-bound students engage in a highly rationalized, managed application process, often employing professional assistance. I described a whole range of new, nonschool-based admissions support services, especially the use of private counselors and characterized students' use of these support services as admissions management behaviors that respond to the heightened admissions competition resulting from colleges implementing marketing and enrollment management practices. Students' admissions management behaviors are individual, class, and organizational responses to a changed, uncertain environment.

Implications

Of what concern is and what conclusions can be drawn from a California study regarding wider populations of college-bound individuals? First, California enrolls 14 percent of all U.S. postsecondary students (Snyder and Hoffman 1995), so in and of itself it is worth understanding how, within a single sizable component of the higher-education opportunity structure, individuals perceive and act on their options. Most states, and certainly the U.S. system in the aggregate, do not have such a highly stratified structure for higher education as does California. However, this book's insights into the college choice processes of its students and their families are instructive to future parents, policy makers, high school counselors, and college admissions officers in and out of California. What is most important is that this study has used naturalistic inquiry to understand how individuals make sense of and move through their social and organizational worlds. Both the findings reported here, and qualitative methods in general, have much to add to understanding and conceptualizing college choice and therefore to understanding the dynamics of college access today.

Through this research, I found that individuals' cultural capital is evident in a sense of "entitlement": students believe they are entitled to a particular kind of collegiate education based on their family's habitus or class status and organize their college searches around a range of acceptable institutions. Paloma students only perceived college opportunities within "the same ten schools, with the Ivy's and all that." University High School students' felt entitled to UC campuses, with elite private colleges as "reaches" and CSU campuses as "safeties." Gate of Heaven girls often found it hard, in an implicit cost-benefit analysis, to justify CSU over community colleges. Finally, Mission Cerrito students most often went to community colleges and those who felt entitled to more, most often went to local CSU campuses and the local private university.

Moreover, high school context plays a significant role in shaping student tastes for particular types of postsecondary institutions. This study demonstrated how high schools' organizational arrangements and processes and the linkages between high schools and colleges help define and mediate individuals' achievements and aspirations.

This study also showed that the cognitive constraints on decision making that bound students' rationality are coupled with individual and organizational cultural and affective premises and satisficing behaviors. Students college choice alternatives often were influenced by their geographical location, social network, and high school stimuli, as well as by their anticipated college goals and consequences. Moreover, within single high schools, the organizational evoking mechanism—the college guidance operation—had a differential impact on students from different class backgrounds. Individual student behavior in each of these high schools was influenced by the flow and content of college information and the school's explicit expectations that highlighted or downplayed specific options. Assumptions about how familiar students were with basic college information, curriculum prerequisites, and specialized college choice vocabularies had different impacts on students' who did not met or who exceeded those expected levels of knowledge.

Habitus exists not only in families and communities but also in *organizational contexts*.

Organizational habitus is a way to understand schools' roles in reproducing social inequalities. Organizational habitus refers to the impact of a social class culture on individual behavior through an intermediate organization, in this case, the high school. These high schools were nested in social class communities that powerfully shaped the specific, current patterns of college choice options highlighted and downplayed by each school, which was reinforced or challenged by the habitus of family and friends. Organizational habitus made possible individual decisions by bounding the search parameters: different schools offered different views of the college opportunity structure.

Organizational habitus is distinct from organizational culture, climate, context, and structure and brings social class back into organizational analyses by showing

- how organizational habitus similarities exist across the upper-middle class communities of Paloma and University High School, and the working-class communities of Mission Cerrito and Gate of Heaven;

- how differences exist between upper-middle class and working-class high schools' organizational habitis; and

- how high schools' internal organizational cultures and habiti are shaped by their larger socioeconomic environment.

Current organizational culture research does not capture the social class complexities of organizational contexts and does not clarify why particular types of high schools produce regular patterns of college outcomes. This study demonstrates the need to reassess equity in college choice and reorient policies to increase students' cultural capital and to reexamine school contexts for equity.

There are implications for policy, practice, research, and theory in these findings. A major implication of this study is the need to redefine equal opportunity in a way that accounts for the cultural dimension of individual opportunity. Clearly, individual students in this study did not always have equal opportunities in fact.

Policy: Cultural and Organizational Equality of Opportunity

In some cases, the schools provided different and unequal resources that enabled different outcomes. In other cases, the parents of these students gave their daughters' financial or cognitive resources to make their college choices. In still other cases, when the school or the family had reached its limits in assisting the college-bound daughter, the family paid for the services of a private counselor.

Scholars and policy makers need to continue to address issues of ability and finances in access to college. However, this study points to both the sociocultural and organizational barriers to the ideal of a truly meritocratic, higher-education opportunity structure. It also highlights the need to discover strategies for expanding cultural and organizational equality of educational opportunities for U.S. high school students. One way to do that would be to increase support for college guidance in public high schools. But, in California and in the rest of the United States, the fiscal outlook for education is likely to remain bleak. What can be done to eliminate or lessen the impact of these organizational and cultural barriers to full equal educational opportunity?

From the perspective of organizational opportunity, better counselor-to-student ratios could offer modest help to college-bound students who lack the family resources to find the "right" college opportunities. For those students whose parents have attended college, more attention to their organizational and counseling needs could be helpful in dealing with the stresses and pressures in much the way that Mrs. Ball does at Paloma. Public high schools could review their college counseling programs to analyze the habitus they are fostering and to make any changes they deem necessary. Public high schools in California need to clearly address their lack of college advising services and to see how they might restructure their current operations, or supplement those operations with new services.

There also is a role for colleges and universities. Admissions offices not only need to rethink their outreach to low SES students, but need to rethink how they might de-escalate the uncertainty and competition for many high SES students. Teacher-educator programs at colleges and universities could also evaluate programs and make future educators aware of the issues presented here and offer suggestions about how they can help future students see the entire college opportunity structure.

Given that the major restructuring of public education necessary for equal opportunity at the organizational level is unlikely any time soon, what else can be done? The corporate sector could be enlisted to help schools provide better college guidance services. Besides corporate grants to improve services, corporate professional staff could work with schools to help students discover a wider range of colleges; students could be matched with mentors who could tell them about a full range of college opportunities.

Colleges and universities could launch a major media campaign targeted to inform not only students but also their parents about the whole range of colleges across the country. The campaign should be aimed to reach junior high and early high school students so they can enroll in the appropriate classes and begin the long process of becoming emotionally adjusted to either going away to college or going to a college "where people are different." This type of media campaign would work best if good consumer information like graduation rates (or transfer rates for community colleges) were part of the message. However, this idea is likely to be met with serious resistance on the part of colleges with low graduation or transfer rates.

Theory and Scholarship

At the level of theory and scholarship, there are implications for scholars conducting status attainment and school climate research, as well as organizational theory and interpretative social science. Scholars concerned with equity in college access should consider how to best study how and why students make decisions about which colleges to attend. I have proposed the extension of Bourdieu's concept of habitus to the organization. Organizational habitus is the impact of a cultural group or social class on an individual's behavior through an intermediate organization and family habitus that is reasonable or rational behavior in context. This study

has attempted to show how organizational habitus makes individual decisions possible by bounding the search parameters. Depending on the family resources of the individual student, this organizational habitus reinforces or challenges the habitus of family and friends.

Class-based patterns of organizational habitus cut across individual schools, albeit with slight variations. Future research with a larger sample of schools might specify the general dimensions of school organizational habitus that vary by social class and aim to measure their effects, independent of family variables. Future ethnographic research might explore, in more depth or across more contexts, the social class norms that produce similar organizational context effects and how that influences outcomes and reproduces social inequalities (Anyon 1980).

Future quantitative research should more thoroughly investigate organizational contexts. With specification and operationalization of the indicators of organizational habitus, future researchers might employ multi-level modeling techniques such as Hierarchical Linear Modeling (HLM) to address the equity implications of different types of organizational habiti.

Research about organizational habitus can extend one's understanding of the impact of high school counselors on college-bound students, especially in the case of first-generation college-bound students. Counselors can have an impact on students either through the one-on-one advising situation or, more likely, in the organizational conditions they create for college counseling and planning. For example, Constance Evans who attended University High School and was from a low SES family, found the counselor, the school's "Four-Year Plan," and her peers' assistance invaluable. Her school and friends filled in the gaps resulting from her family's lack of college resources by informing her about PSATs, insisting that she visit campuses before choosing a final destination, and advising and supporting her through the resources of her school's career center.

The data in this study identify the social class and organizational context patterns of a small sample of young women's college application processes. These patterns should be tested with different research populations: males, other racial and ethnic categories, and the highest-and lowest-ability students. One study already has used a quantitative analysis to demonstrate a habitus for African American college-bound students, in deciding between historically black and predominantly white colleges (McDonough, Antonio, and Trent 1997). Extending the research base and assumedly the understanding of organizational or cultural habitus would help policy makers, scholars, and administrators address issues of equality of access in general, as well as increase the flow of low income students and students of color into the academic pipeline.

This study contributes to an emerging sociological tradition of integrating studies of status groups and organizations. Karabel (1984) conducted a historical study of three elite universities and their admissions processes as a case of organizational self-interest. David Karen (1990) examined the organizational context of selective university admissions processes and demonstrated the ways in which meritocratic and class-based factors influence admissions. This project extends that work by demonstrating the dialectical mating of family and school resources in status and educational attainment.

The construct of organizational habitus developed in this study might be extended to research in other organizational contexts. However, this construct may be relevant only to organizations that are in the business of status transmission or educational certification. Future research could test the generalizability of organizational habitus. For example, it could be included and tested in Useem and Karabel's (1986) model of corporate mobility. Such research might discover the diverse habiti of distinctive subpopulations of classes and organizations. The research would have to address questions of specificity: In what kinds of organizations and where or when in all organizations is habitus evident?

Although I offer conclusions and suggestions here about the college choice decision-making process, the framework of cultural capital and habitus also can be applied to studies about how individuals choose either proprietary schools or enter the workforce. Work regarding internal labor markets (ILMs) has shown that occupational information, opportunities, and mobility are structured by different occupations, industries, and organizational arrangements (Doeringer and Piore 1971). This line of research also has shown that there are many job ladders and that individuals progress up the ladder on which they begin. I have shown similar differential structuring of information, opportunity, and mobility in the educational organizations I studied. Future research could extend this line of inquiry to examine other high schools and analyze, in general, if high schools provide entry points on particular educational opportunity ladders in the same way ILMs set a person on a particular corporate track.

This book could have implications for the conceptualization and conduct of status attainment research. A useful refinement of status attainment models could include indicators of organizational habitus and high school-college linkages. Furthermore, given this study's findings regarding bounded rationality, more attention to the role of perceptions is called for and future status attainment models might be expanded to include students' perceived options, independent of aspirations. The status attainment model's focus on individual-level effects has obscured the organizational level effects that channel individual action. Future research needs to make visible schools' roles in channelling and shaping certain repertoires of college choice behaviors.

There also are implications for qualitative research. Qualitative and quantitative researchers need to work together more closely and learn from each others' research. More ethnographic, small-scale studies are needed about school contexts to understand the formation, maintenance, and effects of school and college habiti.

What also needs to be better understood is inter-institutional linkages, such as the one between high schools and colleges. Scholars need to direct their attention to the implications of public high schools' virtual divestment of college guidance. Moreover, they need to study the inter-institutional linkages between families and schools (Anyon 1980; Lareau 1989).

I have examined the process individuals go through in choosing a college. Also identified were the patterns of social class influences on the resources individuals have at their disposal to make these college choices. Clearly, this study is limited because it is a small sample of California students from four high schools, students who made their choices constrained by a highly stratified, public postsecondary educational system. However, the decision-making process and its influences are important across other contexts. The California public education system may present particular patterns of variation in aspirational schemata, but further research will show that the choice process is, in essence, similar in other states. This is a likely result of the strong social class effects shown here that are present even in states where the system of public higher education is not so stratified.

This research has demonstrated that the specific choice of any single individual, illuminating or noteworthy though it may be, is not the only important part of this story. The choice process students go through and the set of outcomes students, their peers, families, and schools define as acceptable also are a main point. The social class and financial abilities of each of these students affected the resources they had at their disposal to make choices about where to go to college, as it does for every student facing these and other kinds of social mobility decisions.

The schools, peers, families, and communities all influenced these college-bound seniors by shaping their range of aspirations, the ways in which they made their final choices, and what they defined as the college education they were entitled to have. It is this influence and shaping of students' aspirations in the context of a class-based sense of entitlement that makes college choice an important issue of educational equity.

This reconceptualization of college admissions problems and prospects reframes issues of educational equity to emphasize the inter-institutional linkages between the secondary and postsecondary educational systems. In conclusion, until the issues of cultural and organizational barriers to equal educational opportunity are addressed, students will perceive many unequal opportunity structures, rather than one to which all will have equal access.

CHAPTER 5

ACADEMIC ACCESS AND EQUAL OPPORTUNITY: RETHINKING THE FOUNDATIONS FOR POLICY ON DIVERSITY

EDWARD P. ST. JOHN & GLENDA D. MUSOBA

For a very brief period in the 1970s, public policy was aligned with the goal of overcoming the vestiges of segregation in American higher education. After centuries of legal segregation, the federal courts began to promote desegregation of public colleges after the *Adams* decision in 1977 (Williams, 1988). This reform effort built on a strong foundation provided by the Great Society education reforms of President Johnson. Federal student aid programs were organized around the principle of promoting equal opportunity and were adequately funded (Gladieux & Wolanin, 1976), and school reform focused on improving opportunity for historically disadvantaged students (Wong, in press). In the late 1970s, traditional college-age African Americans participated in higher education at essentially the same rate as Whites (U.S. Department of Education, 1998). Unfortunately, soon after the 1980 election of Ronald Reagan the federal government essentially dismantled the entire structure of federal policies that promoted equal opportunity and diversity in higher education.

At the start of the twenty-first century, a new set of public policies no longer overtly supports improvements in diversity. During the middle 1990s, federal policy on higher education desegregation shifted from promoting desegregation of predominantly White colleges to promoting the desegregation of historically Black colleges (St. John & Hossler, 1998; Williams, 1997), before all of the *Adams* states had their initial plans approved by the federal government (Brown & Hendrickson, 1997; Williams, 1997). School reform shifted to a focus on outcomes—and to an overt emphasis on standardized tests—replacing the former emphasis on ensuring equal opportunity and equal resources (Finn, 1990). Federal student grants declined during the last two decades of the century, increasing the net costs for low-income students beyond the point of affordability (Advisory Committee on Student Financial Assistance, 2001; St. John, 1994). More recently, the federal courts have begun to reconsider the legality of Affirmative Action in college admission (e.g., *Hopwood v. State of Texas*) and other courts are following the precedence (e.g., *Gratz and Hamacher v. Bollinger, et al.*). College participation rates for traditional college-age African Americans have lagged behind Whites by about ten percentage points for more than a decade (U.S. Department of Education, 1998).

Unfortunately, it is unlikely that the strategies used to advocate for equal opportunity during the last half of the twentieth century will be persuasive in the new century. Instead, a new policy context requires a fundamental rethinking of both research questions and advocacy strategies. This

"Academic Access and Equal Opportunity: Rethinking the Foundations for Policy on Diversity." Reprinted from *Equity and Access in Higher Education: Changing the Definition of Educational Opportunity—Readings on Equal Education* 18, (2002), by permission of AMS Press.

chapter takes a step toward such a rethinking process. First, the changing policy context is examined, with an explicit focus on the role of federal and state policy in promoting equal educational opportunity and encouraging diversity. Then, we suggest a new set of foundations for guiding practical strategies for equalizing opportunity and promoting academic access for diverse groups in American society. Finally, we conclude by suggesting an agenda that can inform policymakers who are concerned about improving equity in educational opportunity.

A Changing Policy Context

During the last two decades of the twentieth century, the foundations for educational policy in the United States were systematically restructured, shifting the focus from promoting equal opportunity to promoting excellence at a lower taxpayer cost. The courts have also shifted their focus away from racial preference in college admissions and from system-wide access to a remedy for college segregation at historically Black colleges and universities (HBCUs). Given judicial trends, it is probably not reasonable to expect the courts to reverse their new positions by suddenly accepting rationales they have previously rejected. It is also unlikely that voters will elect a new Congress and President that will substantially expand resources for equalizing educational opportunity. Rather, it is crucial for advocates of diversity in higher education to build an understanding of the new policy context before rethinking their research and advocacy strategies.

Desegregation at a Crossroads

Efforts to understand the new policy context appropriately start with a reexamination of policy on desegregation in education. The position of the courts on desegregation in both K-12 education and higher education changed during the 1990s, creating a new climate, disappointing those who expected judicial activism to remedy the vestiges of segregation.

The failure of federal efforts to desegregate urban schools creates a perplexing context for efforts to promote access in higher education. The federal courts have essentially declared victory by ending forced desegregation in many cities (Fossey, 1998; Orfield & Eaton, 1996). However,

this is a hollow victory at best, given that America's schools were more segregated in the late 1990s than they were before the Supreme Court's 1954 decision in *Brown v. Board of Education* (Fossey, 1998; Fossey, in press). Both urban communities and urban schools are now predominantly minority. Further, since most African Americans attend urban K-12 schools, efforts to promote diversity through college admissions must contend with the fact that many African American, as well as White, students will have attended segregated schools prior to attending college.

Higher education desegregation decisions have recently focused on desegregation of public HBCUs (St. John, 1998; Williams, 1997), a development that could erode one of the traditional educational pathways for African American students. Research on HBCUs indicates that they provide a supportive environment for African American students (Allen, Epps, & Haniff, 1991; Fleming, 1984; McDonough, Antonio, & Trent, 1997). However, the courts are now focused on providing opportunities for White students to attend HBCUs rather than for minority students to attend predominantly White institutions (Conrad, Brier, & Braxton, 1997). This could diminish some of the advantages associated with the supportive environment a predominantly Black college provides African American students. African Americans who attended segregated K-12 schools may need the opportunity to attend HBCUs for both academic and social support. Recent court decisions could shift attention away from maintaining a culture that supports African American student development (Hossler, 1997).

Thus, not only are K-12 schools more segregated, but there is the potential for a breakdown of one of the proven educational pathways for students from racially isolated K-12 schools to attend predominantly Black colleges that provide a supportive culture. This context complicates college admissions and other efforts to equalize opportunity. If segregated schools contribute to inequities in educational opportunity, then we need to ask whether there has been sufficient improvement in schools to overcome these inequities. If desegregation did not solve the problems of racial isolation and unequal opportunity in K-12 schools, then we need to ask whether the educational improvements implemented as a result of the desegregation plans and other reforms improved schools for those who suffered the most from racial isolation. Evidence from research on urban school reform suggests that reform has failed urban schools (Miron & St. John, in press), which means that the deficiencies in educational opportunity have not been resolved.

A better understanding of high school contexts is needed in college admissions, if not in efforts to support academic achievement of diverse students in colleges and universities. If HBCUs are under mandates to desegregate in order to receive funding, therefore potentially disrupting their supportive communities, and if the total opportunity to attend other four-year colleges is limited, then it is possible that children who attended racially isolated or academically inadequate urban schools will be at a competitive disadvantage for admission and success in four-year colleges.

The Decline of Affirmative Action

If it were still acceptable to use racial preferences in college admissions, then it would be easier to equalize opportunity to attend college for under-represented groups (i.e., Hispanics and African Americans). Advocates of Affirmative Action argue that the use of racial preferences can overcome some of the historic disadvantages associated with racial isolation and underfunding of urban schools. There is also some evidence to support this proposition (Bowen & Bok, 1998; Gurin, 1999). However, both the courts and the majority of voters in several states have taken an opposing position to this traditional position on Affirmative Action.

Public colleges and universities are losing the freedom to consider race explicitly in their admissions processes. In California and Washington, voters have required colleges and universities to abandon Affirmative Action. In the Texas *Hopwood* decision, the federal court ruled that the University of Texas could not give preferential treatment to African Americans and Hispanics in college admissions. Recently, the federal court also ruled that the University of Michigan's former admissions process had illegally used racial preferences (*Gratz and Hamacher v. Bollinger, et al.*). The rationale for the explicit use of racial preferences has fallen out of favor.

The origins of racial preferences in college admissions were situated in efforts to rectify injustices of segregated and inequitable educational systems. However, the rationale for ending racial preferences is rooted in the U.S. Constitution, which requires people to be treated in fair and equal ways regardless of their race or gender (Schmidt, 1998). In one sense, the position one takes on the issue of racial preferences depends on the definition of fairness one holds. As Rawls' theory of justice (1971) argues, there is a need to balance arguments about fairness for all with special consideration of those with disadvantages. Given the great disparity in K-12 schools and the consequences of racial isolation of urban schools, it is important to recognize that the vestiges of unequal education have not been removed. Fairness in admissions must be consonant with fairness of opportunities for educational preparation prior to admissions. This means that we need to find new ways to balance both types of justice considerations in this new legal context.

One possible path involves evolving new rationales for racial preference. A number of noted scholars have taken this path, including Derek Bok and Howard Bowen (1998). There is a new wave of research that indicates that integrated education and especially enrollment in courses that consider issues related to multicultural education actually contribute to intellectual development in college for all students, including majority students (Hurtado, 1999, in press). However, while this research is compelling, there is reason to question whether it will provide a sufficient rationale for continuing to use racial preferences in admissions. The argument is currently going through the federal courts in the University of Michigan undergraduate admissions case (*Gratz and Hamacher v. Bollinger, et al.*). Lower court rulings held that the University's current admissions practice was legal but its former practice (1995–1998) was illegal. The rulings are under appeal with the U.S. Sixth Circuit Court at the time of this writing.

An alternative for advocates of social justice is to consider new legal ways of constructing admissions decisions. Since the court decisions on Affirmative Action have focused explicitly on the legality of assigning points to students from underrepresented racial-ethnic groups, it should be possible to construct alternative admission criteria that ensure diversity without explicitly considering race-ethnicity as an admission criterion (Goggin, 1999). Recent simulations illustrating this can be a workable approach (see St. John, Simmons, & Musoba, 2002).

However, regardless of the path chosen, there is a need to think through the strategies for achieving diversity in college admissions in the post-Affirmative Action period. Since there are substantial inequities in educational opportunities for school children, it is possible that explicit recognition of deficiencies in the prior schools the students attended can overcome some of the vestiges of inequity in college admissions. However, admission is only part of the new problem with racial inequality.

The Decline of Federal Need-Based Grants

Federal need-based grant aid has declined substantially since 1980 (College Board, 2000; St. John, 1994;). While federal loans have expanded, the total student aid available to low-income students is inadequate (Advisory Committee on Student Financial Assistance, 2001). In 1992-93, the average college freshman from a low-income family (i.e., families earning less than $25,000) paid $4,922 in four-year public colleges after grants, loans, and other aid (Berkner & Chavez, 1997). College costs have risen faster than federal student aid since that time (College Board, 2000), so these problems have worsened. Further, low-income students borrow substantially more than middle- and high-income students. These conditions have serious consequences for both the opportunities to attend four-year colleges and to persist to degree completion. Since more than half of the African American freshmen who attended college in 1992–93 were from families earning less than $25,000 (Berkner & Chavez, 1997), the inadequacy of federal aid contributed to the opportunity gap.

The decline in federal need-based grants has contributed directly to the widening of the opportunity gap since 1980. Using a standard of academic qualification comparable to admittance to a four-year college, an NCES report on access found that in 1994, 22.3% of college-qualified, low-income students in the freshman age group had not attended college two years after high school (Berkner & Chavez, 1997). Further, barely over half (52.5%) of the low-income high school graduates were academically qualified, indicating that many had inadequate opportunities in their K-12 education. Thus, there are both financial and academic aspects of the access problem.

The financial aspect of the access problem is not only evident in the lower college participation rate by low-income students, but also in persistence. Recent analyses of national databases indicate that low-income students are not only more likely to choose college because of low tuition and high aid than for degree or educational opportunities, but that grant aid is inadequate to promote continuous enrollment (Paulsen & St. John, 2002). Further, persistence studies using national databases not only show that low-income students are less likely to persist than middle-income students, controlling for achievement, but that debt is negatively associated with persistence (Cofer & Somers, 2000). Since low-income students usually accumulate more debt, dropping out because of inadequate finances is especially problematic. Thus, even if they can afford college enrollment initially, low-income students have substantially less financial capacity to afford continuous enrollment.

The cuts in federal grants were fueled by a new conservative ideology that maintained colleges were wasteful and that student aid was ineffectual (Bennett, 1987; Carnes, 1987; Finn, 1988; Hansen, 1983). This rationale persuaded Congress to reduce funding for federal grant programs (Cook, 1998; Parsons, 1997). However, the new policy of reducing grants and expanding loans was a primary cause of the opportunity gap. The Advisory Committee on Student Financial Assistance (2001) has recently released a report, titled *Access Denied*, that called attention to this issue, arguing that the decline in student grants has contributed to the opportunity gap.

The Apparent Failure of K-12 School Reform

Conservative criticism of the Advisory Committee's *Access Denied* (2001) report has argued that improvement in K-12 schools is needed to expand access, and if there was sufficient improvement in schools, then fewer people would need college (Finn, 2001). In the 1980s, the Reagan administration shifted the focus on federal school reform from equalizing opportunity (i.e., providing supplemental educational resources to the children most at risk) to focusing on test scores and curriculum alignment for all schools (Finn, 1990). Given that these reforms have had a nearly 20-year trial, it seems reasonable to ask whether they have contributed to an expansion in opportunity. If they have not, then such reforms are not the answer to reducing the opportunity gap.

One indicator of the efficacy of school reforms is whether they have improved the percentage of students who graduate from high school. Since the mid 1970s, high school graduation rates have actually declined slightly (U.S. Department of Education, 2001), indicating that educational opportunity has not increased as a result of these reforms. One recent study examined the impact of implementing a high stakes graduation test in Indiana (Manset & Washburn, in press), finding that special education students and urban schools were negatively impacted by the new tests because fewer of these students graduated. This study illustrates an underlying problem with test-driven reform ideology. By introducing more tests into the system and forcing an alignment of curriculum with tests, educational systems can force students out who need special assistance and force more students into special education.

The latest wave of federal education reform has emphasized using "research based" methods. Both the *Reading Excellence Act* and the *Comprehensive School Reform Demonstration Act* provide funding for schools to adopt reforms that have a proven research base. Initial studies on these reforms indicate that some reform models actually do reduce special education referral and grade retention in elementary schools (St. John, Manset, Chung, Musoba, et al., in press; St. John, Manset, Chung, Simmons, in press). Thus, there is an obvious need for more research on the effects of these reforms. It is also apparent that providing schools the opportunity to adopt reform models that have a research base could be a viable approach for keeping more children in the educational system and for increasing the percentage of students who are prepared for college.

Clearly, K-12 school reform must be part of the solution to the access problem through enhancing academic preparation. However, it is crucial to recognize that past reforms have contributed to the problem. While the newest wave of research-based reforms provides reasonable hope, substantial gains must be made just to regain the equity level that has been lost.

Breakdown in Education Policy

The current education policy context has many impediments to equal opportunity in both K-12 education and higher education. While the test-driven reforms overtly promote opportunity for all, they speed the decline in equity. The cuts in federal student grants may be the primary cause of the new inequality in opportunity, but failed efforts at K-12 reform have also contributed to the problem.

In this context, the shifting focus of higher education desegregation to desegregating HBCUs from desegregating Predominately White Institutions (PWIs) and the decline in Affirmative Action limit the mechanisms that can be used to remedy the problem. Historically colleges used racial preferences to ensure diversity in college admissions, but their ability to follow this path has been curtailed, if not extinguished. Unfortunately, the notion that equal educational opportunity should be an outcome of college desegregation is no longer the focus of federal desegregation litigation in the post-*Fordice* environment (St. John, 1998; Williams, 1988). We clearly need to take a fresh look at the challenge of promoting equal opportunity.

Rethinking Advocacy

Current conditions surrounding academic access and opportunity necessitate a rethinking of policy strategies by those who are committed to promoting equal educational opportunity. Before considering alternative strategies, however, we should revisit the theory of social justice, as a foundation for rethinking policy strategies.

Refocusing on Social Justice

Rawls (1971) identified two principles of justice. The first, "each person is to have an equal right to the most extensive total system of equal basic liberties compatible with a similar system of liberty for all" (p. 302), and the second, "social and economic inequalities are to be arranged so that they are both: (a) to the greatest benefit to the least advantaged, consistent with the just savings principle, and (b) attached to offices and positions of fair equality of opportunity" (p. 302). The first principle clearly argued for equal treatment, a rationale related to arguments for eliminating racial preferences in admissions. However, before we leap to the conclusion that it should be applied to the current access problem, we need to consider Rawls's first priority rule for applying the principles:

> The principles of justice are ranked in lexical order and therefore liberty can be restricted only for the sake of liberty. There are two cases: (a) a less extensive liberty must strengthen the total system of liberty shared by all; (b) a less than equal liberty must be acceptable to those with lesser liberty. (p. 302)

Whether individuals argue for affirmative methods of intervention depends on the way they view the evidence relative to "fair and equal opportunity." In higher education there was fair and equal opportunity in the late 1970s (1976–78), at least as measured by the near equal participation rates. As the previous review indicates, policies have shifted in ways during the intervening twenty years that have increased inequities. We think it is too early to eliminate the emphasis on racial preference and equal opportunity (e.g., St. John & Hossler, 1998; St. John, Simmons, & Musoba, 2002). However, we also recognize it may no longer be possible to rest policy arguments on this principle alone.

The new legal environment clearly argues that Rawls's first principle rather than the second should be applied in college admissions. Federal desegregation strategies now promote desegregation of historically Black colleges more ardently than they promote desegregation of predominantly White colleges. The decline of Affirmative Action further illustrates there has been a shift in emphasis and logic used to litigate and orchestrate. The new challenge for advocates of social justice in educational policy is to promote access in ways that are compatible with the equal treatment principle, especially with respect to the elimination of racial preference, yet help remedy the inequality in economic opportunity that has emerged.

Financial Access

Since financial access has surfaced as a problem in higher education, it is important to start with a workable definition of financial access. We have defined financial access as: "the ability to afford continuous enrollment in the lowest cost two-year and four-year program available to appli-

cants, given their ability and prior performance" (St. John, Musoba, & Simmons, 2001, p. 2). This definition of financial access is consistent with the first principle of justice, with respect to racial preference, but also provides a basis for constructing and assessing policy aimed at promoting equal opportunity across racial and economic groups. The erosion of federal student aid programs has limited the ability of states to ensure financial access for their citizens. The unmet need for the average low-income student in public college with average costs is currently too high to maintain continuous enrollment unless there is supplemental grant support from states and/or institutions.

A recent analysis of the 21st Century Scholars Program in Indiana illustrates that the financial access problem can be resolved by states, but it takes a substantial financial commitment to need-based student grants (St. John, Musoba, & Simmons, 2001). This program asked low-income eighth graders (i.e., those eligible for free or reduced lunch) to make commitments to prepare for college academically and to remain alcohol and drug-free. In 1997–98 the average freshman in the program received a state grant of over three thousand dollars, an amount nearly equal to the average unmet need after Pell grants, the largest federal need-based grant. Our analyses of within-year persistence by freshmen revealed that recipients of 21st Century grants were more likely to persist than were unaided students and that low-income students had the same probability of persisting as other students (St. John, Musoba, & Simmons, 2001). Further, a series of studies of within-year persistence by college students in Indiana in the 1990s, a period when federal grants declined and Indiana grants climbed, indicated financial aid remained adequate to equalize the opportunity to persist (Hu & St. John, 2001; St. John, Hu, & Weber, 2000, 2001). Thus, the 21st Century Scholars Program in Indiana was an integral part of a state finance strategy that has ensured financial access.

The solution to the financial access problem relates directly to the adequacy of state student financial aid, given the inadequacy of federal student aid and the ongoing conservative call to reduce federal taxes. Thus, advocates of equal educational opportunity must promote adequate funding of need-based state grant programs. Promoting greater cooperation between states and the federal government on a second-tier grant strategy might also be a viable approach. However, it is unlikely that the federal government will reinvest in federal grants at a level approximating the investment made in the 1970s.

Academic Access

Our definition of financial access leaves colleges and universities in control of academic access, whether students are qualified for initial and continued enrollment. The admitting institution retains responsibility for determining academic access while the K-12 education system and the student are responsible for adequate academic preparation. This definition of academic access is not only consistent with the notions of academic qualification used by the National Center for Education Statistics (e.g., Berkner & Chavez, 1997), but also provides a basis for rethinking strategies that promote financial access. We explicitly consider admissions policy, postsecondary encouragement, and school reform.

Admissions Policy. While states may set general policies for admission standards and admission practices, the process of admitting and educating students remains an institutional responsibility. In reaction to the post Affirmative Action litigation, some states have emphasized high school grade point averages instead of test scores as part of the criteria used in admissions. This approach implicitly adjusts for inequities in high schools, consistent with the assumption that students should not be penalized for attending low-quality high schools. This assumption is compatible with the second principle of justice, but does not use racial-ethnic preferences as a basis for promoting equity. If we hold to this assumption, then there are at least four possible approaches to promoting equal opportunity in academic admission processes in public universities:

- Using grade point averages, an approach recommended by Olivas (1997, 1999) and used in Texas, Florida, and California, states that have adjusted to the post-Affirmative Action environment.

- Adjusting test scores using a merit index constructed from the high school average, an approach proposed by Goggin (1999) and empirically tested by St. John, Simmons, & Musoba (2002).

- Creating an empirical index for high school quality in a state, based on high school achievement test scores and other indicators, an approach that is conceptually consistent with Goggin's merit aware approach and potentially more equitable than adjusting test scores.

- Adjusting applications for SES indicators, a class based affirmative action advocated by Kahlenberg (1996), and tested with mixed results (Bernal, Cabrera, & Terenzini, 2000).

Of the possible approaches, we think the methods that index for academic inequities among high schools (i.e., SAT or high school achievement tests) hold the greatest potential because they hold children harmless for high school effects without inducing grade inflation. Using GPA as a primary criterion for admissions can encourage grade inflation in high schools. However, adjusting standardized tests avoids this problem, while encouraging equity in admissions decisions and encouraging more students to take admissions tests. However, there is a need for more research on all possible methods, as a means of testing how well they work in practice. Recently we collaborated on a study that estimated effects of the SAT and the merit index on persistence (St. John, Hu, Simmons, & Musoba, 2001). We found that the merit index, an adjustment of the SAT for the high school average, predicted persistence as well as the SAT. We think that further experimentation and testing of different approaches to adapting admission standards is appropriate and needed.

The challenge of providing fair and just admissions practices will likely become more acute in the future given the relative erosion of opportunity for African Americans and Hispanics to attend public four-year colleges. Between 1990 and 1996 the number of full time equivalent (FTE) students enrolled in public four-year colleges actually declined while the number in public two-year colleges and private four-year colleges increased (U.S. Department of Education, 1998). This erosion in opportunity was attributable to a new set of financial circumstances, including rising tuition and reduced grant aid. States have reduced spending on public four-year colleges, which has influenced tuition to rise. Higher costs of attending and lower student aid have contributed to the financial access problem (Advisory Committee on Student Financial Aid, 2001).

Further, given the need to expand access in the next few decades, it is possible that states will expand two-year systems rather than four-year systems (Council for Aid to Education, 1997; National Center for Public Policy and Higher Education, 2000). If this happens, then there will be more competition for limited opportunity to attend four-year colleges. Thus, it is crucial to evolve fair and just approaches to admissions that maintain academic access for diverse groups.

Academic Support. Once students are admitted, a tacit contract is formed between a college and a student. Essentially the student is agreeing to work at a level sufficient to maintain enrollment while colleges are agreeing that the student has the capability to maintain enrollment, provided the institution offers sufficient academic opportunity and support. We think that when colleges admit students who are at risk of failure without providing adequate support opportunities, they are contributing to a "revolving door" (Cope & Hannah, 1975), rather than fulfilling the commitment they make at admission, even open admission. This standard is infrequently discussed in academic meetings, but should be a central concern for both admissions officers and academic administrators, as well as for the assessment of academic programs.

The persistence studies of college students enrolled in public higher education in Indiana reveal that achieving below C grades is a major predictor of dropout (St. John, Hu, & Weber, 2000, in press), especially for minority students (Hu & St. John, 2001) and freshmen (St. John, Musoba, & Simmons, 2001). These studies reveal that even when financial access is guaranteed by states, that academic access, especially the ability to remain academically qualified for continuous enrollment, remains a challenge for public colleges and universities, at least in Indiana.

Postsecondary Encouragement: A new federal program—Gaining Early Awareness and Readiness for Undergraduate Programs (GEAR UP)—funds organizations that provide encouragement to students to attend college. The theory behind this approach to promoting access is that students will be more likely to prepare for college if they are aware of the opportunities available and of financial resources available to them. There is substantial evidence that postsecondary encouragement can improve college participation rates if there is adequate student aid (Hossler & Schmit, 1995).

However, as long as substantial numbers of academically qualified and highly motivated students do not attend college, a situation that obviously exists at the present time (Berkner & Chavez, 1997), there is little reason to assume expanding encouragement will make a difference for students from low-income families. In spite of this limitation, there is reason to expect that providing early encouragement to students in middle school and high school can promote better preparation (Hossler, Schmit, & Vesper, 1998), if the schools have adequate course offerings.

School Reform: School reform potentially provides the fourth component of a coherent strategy aimed at expanding academic access and equalizing the opportunity to attend college. However, it is crucial that K-12 education shift away from tightening tests and curriculum in ways that force more children out of the mainstream. The alternative is to engage schools in reform processes that enable more children to maintain academic progress at a sufficient level to stay in the educational mainstream. Toward this end, we think that researchers need to assess whether reforms actually reduce failure (i.e., retention and special education referral) and improve the percentage of children who complete high school and who are prepared for college.

An Agenda: Research Informing Policy

We can now propose an agenda for researchers and reformers who are concerned about improving equity in educational attainment. A central feature of this strategy involves treating opportunity-related outcomes as goals of education, goals that merit attention along with more frequently measured achievement related outcomes. We think that opportunity and achievement should be put back into balance in education policy. Specifically, we recommend that:

- K-12 school reform should be evaluated based on whether it improves the percentage of children achieving on or above grade level (i.e., reducing dropout, grade retention, and referral to special education) and high school graduation rates, along with achievement test scores and pass rates.

- Financial access should be evaluated based on whether economically diverse students who are academically qualified have equal opportunity to enroll, as well as by whether low-income and minority students have equal probabilities of persisting, controlling for academic achievement.

- Academic preparation should be evaluated based on how well high schools prepared students for college, as measured by percentages of students, by income level, completing a college preparatory curriculum and standardized-test scores and pass rates.

- Academic access should be evaluated by percentage of academically prepared students, by income group, who attend college. This is a minimum standard. Ideally students with college preparatory coursework would go to four-year colleges.

In addition, equal opportunity can be given more explicit consideration if researchers and policymakers consider how these outcomes vary for economically and ethnically diverse groups in state educational systems. This research-based approach provides a workable alternative to the current direction of education policy, which does not give adequate consideration to equity issues.

It is crucial that we reconsider measures of equal opportunity along with the traditional measures of educational achievement that are now used to evaluate education policy in the U.S. Educational policy is overly focused on the academic outcomes without adequately considering opportunity-related outcomes. Thus, a more balanced approach is needed in education policy in states and at the federal level.

Notes

1. This approach is potentially more equitable because states have relatively complete information on high schools and only a limited percentage of students from high schools actually take the SAT test.

References

Advisory Committee on Student Financial Assistance. (2001). *Access denied.* Washington, DC: Authors.

Allen, W. A., Epps, E. G., & Haniff, N. Z. (Eds.) (1991). *College in Black and White: African American students in predominantly White and in historically Black public universities.* Albany, NY: State University of New York Press.

Bennett, W. J. (1987). Our greedy colleges. *New York Times,* 18 February, I 31.

Berkner, L., & Chavez, L. (1997). *Access to postsecondary education for the 1992 high school graduates.* Washington, DC: U.S. Dept. of Education, Office of Educational Research and Improvement.

Bernal, E. M., Cabrera, A. F., & Terenzini, P. T. (2000). The relationship between race and socioeconomic status (SES): Implications for institutional research and admissions policies. *Removing Vestiges,* (1), 6–13.

Bowen, W. G., & Bok, D. (1998). *The shape of the river: Long-term consequences of considering race in college and university admissions.* Princeton, NJ: Princeton University Press.

Brown, M. C., & Hendrickson, R. M. (1997). Public historically Black colleges at the crossroads: *United States v. Fordice* and higher education desegregation. *Journal for a Just and Caring Education, 3* (1), 95–113.

Carnes, B. M. (1987). The campus cost explosion: College tuitions are unnecessarily high. *Policy Review, 40,* 68–71.

Cofer, J., & Somers, P. (2000). A comparison of the influence of debtload on the persistence of students at public and private colleges. *Journal of Student Financial Aid 30* (2), 39–58.

College Board. (2000). *Trends in student aid.* Washington, D.C.: College Board.

Conrad, C. F., Brier, E. M., & Braxton, J. M. (1997). Factors contributing to the matriculation of White students in public HBCUs. *Journal for a Just and Caring Education, 3* (1), 37–62.

Cook, C. (1998). *Lobbying for higher education: How colleges and universities influence federal policy.* Nashville, TN: Vanderbilt University Press.

Cope, R., & Hannah, W. (1975). *Revolving college doors: The causes and consequences of dropping out, stopping out, and transferring.* New York: Wiley.

Council for Aid to Education. (1997). *Breaking the social contract: The fiscal crisis in higher education.* Santa Monica, CA: RAND.

Finn, C. E., Jr. (1988, July/August). Judgment time for higher education: In the court of public opinion. *Change*, 35–38.

Finn, C. E., Jr. (1990). The biggest reform of all. *Phi-Delta-Kappan, 71* (8), 584–92.

Finn, C. E., Jr. (2001, February 21). College isn't for everyone. *USA Today*, p. 14A.

Fleming, J. (1984). *Blacks in college*. San Francisco: Jossey-Bass Publishers.

Fossey, R. E. (1998). Desegregation is not enough: Facing the truth about urban schools. In R. E. Fossey (ed.), *Readings on equal education, Vol. 15, Race, the courts, and equal education: The limits of the law*. New York: AMS Press.

Fossey, R. E. (in press). Desegregation is over in the inner cities: What do we do now? In L. Miron & E. P. St. John (eds.), *Reinterpreting urban school reform*. Albany, NY: State University of New York Press.

Gladieux, L. E., & Wolanin, T. (1976). *Congress and the colleges: The national politics of higher education*. Lexington, MA: Lexington Books.

Goggin, W. J. (1999, May). A "merit-aware" model for college admissions and affirmative action. *Postsecondary Education Opportunity Newsletter*, (Published by Tom Mortenson), 6–12.

Gurin, P. (1999). Expert report of Patricia Gurin. In *The compelling need for diversity in higher education* [On line.] Available at http://www.umich.edu/;slurel/admissions/legal/expert/gurintoc.html.

Hansen, W. L. (1983). The impact of student financial aid on access. In J. Froomkin (ed.), *The crisis in higher education*. New York: Academy of Political Science.

Hossler, D. (1997). Scholarly research and personal reflections. *Just and Caring Education, 3* (1), 114–126.

Hossler, D. & Schmit, J. (1995). Postsecondary encouragement programs: The Indiana experiment. In E. P. St. John (ed.), *Rethinking tuition and student aid strategies*. New Directions in Higher Education, No. 89, 27–40. San Francisco: Jossey-Bass.

Hossler, D., Schmit, J., & Vesper, N. (1998). *Going to college: How social, economic, and educational factors influence the decisions students make*. Baltimore: Johns Hopkins University Press.

Hu, S., & St. John, E. P. (2001). Student persistence in a public higher education system: Understanding racial/ethnic differences. *Journal of Higher Education, 72* (3), 265–286.

Hurtado, S. (1999). Reaffirming educators' judgment: Educational value of diversity, *Journal of Liberal Education*, Spring, 24–31. Washington, DC: American Association of Colleges and Universities.

Hurtado, S. (in press). Linking diversity with educational purpose: College outcomes associated with diversity in the faculty and student body. In G. Orfield and C. Edley (eds.), Harvard Civil Rights Project.

Kahlenberg, R. D. (1996). *The remedy: Class, race and affirmative action*. New York: Basic Books.

Manset, G. & Washburn, S. (in press) Inclusive education in high stakes, high poverty environments: The case of students with learning disabilities in Indiana's urban schools and the Graduation Qualifying Exam. In L. F. Miron & E. P. St. John (eds.), *Reinterpreting urban school reforms: A critical-empirical review*. NY: SUNY Press.

McDonough, P. M., Antonio, A. L., & Trent, J. W. (1997). Black students, Black colleges: An African American college choice model. *Journal for a Just and Caring Education 3* (1), 9–36.

Miron, L. F. & St. John, E. P., (eds.) (in press) *Reinterpreting urban school reform: A critical-empirical review*. Albany, NY: SUNY Press.

National Center for Public Policy and Higher Education. (2000). *Measuring up 2000*. Washington, DC: Authors.

Olivas, M. A. (1997). Constitutional criteria: The social science and common law of admissions decisions in higher education. *University of Colorado Law Review, 68* (4), 1065–1121.

Olivas, M. A. (1999). Higher education admissions and the search for one important thing. *University of Arkansas at Little Rock Law Review, 21*, 993–1024.

Orfield, G., & Eaton, S. E. (1996). *Dismantling desegregation: The quiet reversal of Brown v. Board of Education*. New York: Free Press.

Parsons, M. D. (1997). *Power and politics: Federal higher education policymaking in the 1990s*. Albany, NY: State University of New York Press.

Paulsen, M. B., & St. John, E. P. (2002). Social class and college costs: Examining the financial nexus between college choice and persistence. *Journal of Higher Education, 73*, 189–236.

Rawls, J. (1971). *A theory of justice*. Cambridge, MA: Belknap Press of Harvard University Press.

St. John, E. P. (1994). *Prices, productivity and investment: Assessing financial strategies in higher education*. ASHE/ERIC Higher Education Report, No. 3. Washington, D.C.: George Washington University.

St. John, E. P. (1998). Higher education desegregation in the post-Fordice legal environment: An historical perspective. In R. E. Fossey (ed.), *Readings on equal education, Vol. 15, Race, the courts, and equal education: The limits of the law* (pp. 101–122). New York: AMS Press.

St. John, E. P., & Hossler, D. (1998). Higher education desegregation in the post-*Fordice* legal environment: A critical-empirical perspective. In R. E. Fossey, (ed.), *Readings on equal education, Vol. 15, Race, the courts, and equal education: The limits of the law* (pp. 123–156). New York: AMS Press.

St. John, E. P., Hu, S., Simmons, A., & Musoba, G. D. (2001). Aptitude versus merit: What matters in persistence. *Review of Higher Education, 24,* 131–152.

St. John, E. P., Hu, S., & Weber, J. (2000). Keeping public colleges affordable: A study of persistence in Indiana's public colleges and universities. *Journal of Student Financial Aid, 29* (2), 21–32.

St. John, E. P., Hu, S., & Weber, J. (2001). State policy and the affordability of public higher education: The influence of state grants on persistence in Indiana. *Research in Higher Education, 42,* 401–428.

St. John, E. P., Manset, G., Chung, C. G., Musoba, G. D., Loescher, S., Simmons, A. B., Gordon, D., & Hossler, C. A. (in press). Comprehensive school reform: An exploratory study. In L. F. Miron & E. P. St. John (eds.), *Reinterpreting urban school reform: A critical-empirical review.* Albany, NY: State University of New York Press.

St. John, E. P., Manset, G., Chung, C. G., Simmons, A. B., Musoba, G. D., Manoil, K., & Worthington, K. (in press). Research-based reading reform: The impact of state-funded interventions on educational outcomes in urban schools. In L. F. Miron & E. P. St. John (eds.), *Reinterpreting urban school reform: A critical-empirical review.* Albany, NY: State University of New York Press.

St. John, E. P., Musoba, G. D., & Simmons, A. B. (2001). *Keeping the promise: The impact of Indiana's 21st century scholars program.* Paper presented at the 18th Annual Student Financial Aid Research Network Conference: A Joint NASSGAP/NCHELP Project.

St. John, E. P., Simmons, A., & Musoba, G. D. (2001). Merit-aware admissions in public universities: Increasing diversity. *Thought and Action, 27* (2), 35–46.

Schmidt, P. (1998, October 30). U. of Michigan prepares to defend admissions policy in court. *Chronicle of Higher Education,* p. A32.

U.S. Department of Education, National Center for Education Statistics. (1998). *The condition of education 1998.* Washington, D.C.: U.S. Government Printing Office.

U.S. Department of Education, National Center for Education Statistics. (2001). *Digest of Education Statistics, 2000.* NCES 2001–034. By Thomas D. Snyder. Project Dir., Charlene M. Hoffman. Prod. Mgr. Washington, DC: NCES. [On-line] Available at: http://nces.ed.gov; shpubs2001/digest/

U.S. Department of Education (1997). Comprehensive School Reform Act. Public Law 105–78. Appropriations Act. Conference Report: House Report No. 105–309. [On-line] Available at: http://www.ed.gov/offices/OESE/compreform.

U.S. Department of Education (1999). Title VIII—Reading Excellence Act. An amendment to the Elementary and Secondary Education Act. [On-line] Available at: http://www.ed.gov/offices/OESE/REA/

Williams, J. B. (1988). Title VI regulation of higher education. In J. B. Williams (ed.), *Desegregating America's colleges and universities: Title VI regulation of higher education* (pp. 33–53). New York: Teachers College Press.

Williams, J. B. (1997). *Race discrimination in higher education.* New York: Praeger.

Wong, K. K. (in press). Federal Title I as a reform strategy in urban schools. In L. F. Miron & E. P. St. John (eds.), *Reinterpreting urban school reform: A critical-empirical review.* Albany, NY: SUNY Press.

Table of Legal Cases

Regents of Univ. of California. v. Bakke, 438 U.S. 265, 287, 98 S. Ct. 2733, 2746, 57 L. Ed. 2d 750 (1978)

Brown v. The Board of Education of Topeka, Kansas, 349 U.S. 294 (1955).

Gratz and Hamacher v. Bollinger, et al., No. 97–75231.

Hopwood v. State of Texas, 78 F.3d 932 (5th Cir. 1996) cert. Denied, 116 S. Ct. 2581 (1996).

United States v. Fordice, 505 U.S. 717 (1992).

PART II

THE COLLEGE ENVIRONMENT

PART 2: THE COLLEGE ENVIRONMENT

The role of the college environment in student life and success has been extensively studied and is increasingly generating usable research. In the 1950s and 1960s, researchers began to examine the fit between college environments and student personalities, frequently using a psychological framework. Leonard Baird's (1988) "The college environment revision: A review of research and theory" provides a comprehensive review of the development of college environment surveys. While many of the early survey instruments used a psychological theory of individual fit with their colleges as organizations, the basic premises of this line of inquiry evolved and changed because the initial premises were not always supported by research evidence. More recent scholarship addresses the different ways individuals perceive their environment and the ways research on student perceptions can inform practice.

Social theory on college students' integration into their colleges as learning environments became a widely studied topic in the 1970s. Vincent Tinto's (1986) "Theories of student departure revisited" not only elaborates on his well referenced social theory of student integration, but also reviews other theories of student departure providing an overview of other lines of inquiry about persistence. In addition to emphasizing the central importance of student social and academic integration in this restatement, Tinto acknowledged that low-income students may face financial barriers to persistence and that integration theories do not explicitly focus on mechanisms for encouraging student integration.

By the 1990s theoretical conceptions about educational environments began to focus more explicitly on issues germane to individual experience. Sylvia Hurtado, Jeffrey Milem, Alma Clayton-Pedersen, and Walter Allen's (1998) "Enhancing campus climates for racial/ethnic diversity: Education policy and practice" reviews the research on diversity in higher education with a focus on interventions that facilitate diversity. More recently theorists and researchers have begun to explicitly focus on issues related to facilitating diversity in education learning environments.

Glen Godwin and William Markham (1996), in "First encounters of the bureaucratic kind: Early freshman experiences with a campus bureaucracy" uncover some of the ways that the procedures can be adapted to make college learning environments more supportive of new students. Louis Attinasi's (1989) "Getting in: Mexican American's perceptions of university attendance and the implications for freshman year persistence," one of the first qualitative studies of the early college experiences, challenges readers to rethink strategies to encourage and support enrollment by diverse students. Anna Ortiz and Iris Heavy Runner's (2003) "Student access, retention and success: Models for inclusion and support" examines research on Native American students in higher education, identifying strategies that can be used to encourage and facilitate attainment. Finally, Kevin Dougherty (1992), in "Community college and baccalaureate attainment," provides a thoughtful review of research on transfer between two-year and four-year colleges and strategies institutions can use to support attainment by students who start out in community colleges.

99

CHAPTER 6

THE COLLEGE ENVIRONMENT REVISITED: A REVIEW OF RESEARCH AND THEORY

LEONARD L. BAIRD

Researchers' interest in the important, but extremely complex and slippery topic of the college environment has waxed and waned over the last 30 years. Beginning with Pace and Stern's (1958) development of the College Characteristics Index to measure perceptions of environmental press, a great variety of approaches and instruments were developed to assess the psychological climates of colleges (Baird and Hartnett, 1980). The availability of these instruments, joined with an increased interest in college student development, led to a great deal of research on the perceptions of the environment by different groups and the effects of different environments in the 1960s and early 1970s (Feldman and Newcomb, 1969; Pascarella, 1985). From the mid-1970s to recent years, the focus seems to have turned to relatively specific aspects of the environment or of subgroups, perhaps because these aspects are more subject to intervention and manipulation, and because they may impinge more directly on students' lives than the global environment (Baird and Hartnett, 1980; Moos, 1979). Although the listings in *Higher Education Abstracts* suggest that researchers' interest in the college environment has remained at about the same level in recent years, it has not regained its popularity of the 1960s.

However, several recent developments have renewed interest in the college environment. First is the call for increased quality in the undergraduate *experience* (e.g., Boyer, 1986), which entails the environment. For example, the recommendations of several national reports recommend changes in the *process* of education as the pathway to excellence (e.g., Study Group on the Conditions of Excellence in American Higher Education, 1984). Second is the interest of researchers in finding better theoretical concepts to explain the ways in which the colleges affect students, as reflected in the development of models of student-environment interaction to account for student attrition (e.g., Pascarella and Terenzini, 1983; Tinto, 1987). These models use concepts which refer, at least partly, to the faculty and peer environments of colleges. A third is the "ecological" approach to guidance and counseling that has emerged in the last few years, which attempts to analyze information about students and their environments and to identify matches and mismatches for the purposes of intervention (e.g., Huebner, 1980).

The purpose of this chapter is to examine the various conceptions of the college environment and to suggest appropriate assessment strategies. In so doing, I will discuss the history of problems in conceptualizing and assessing the environment, evidence from studies of college impact on students, criteria for theories, the issues of the level of analysis, and the validity of different kinds of

"The College Environment Revisited: A Review of Research and Theory." Reprinted from *Higher Education: Handbook of Theory and Research* 4, (1988), by permission of Kluwer Academic Publishers.

measures. Finally, potentially useful conceptions from research into organizational behavior will be discussed.

A History of Approaches to the College Environment

Approaches to studying the college environment can be categorized as demographic, perceptual, behavioral, and multimethod approaches (Menne, 1967; Feldman, 1972; Huebner, 1980). Demographic methods are primarily descriptive and are based on data of record such as enrollment, distribution of majors, and library books per student. The perceptual approach relies on students', faculty's, and administrators' responses to items and scales designed to assess their perceptions of their institutions. The behavioral approach attempts to assess the environment by measuring detailed observable behavioral regularities of students, faculty, and staff. The multimethod approach combines the other three into a single assessment. Probably the best way to understand these approaches is to examine them in their context in the history of research on college students and their institutions. In general, this history seems to have followed two main streams: one stream focused on understanding and assessing the environment per se, or environmental description, and a second stream assessed the environment as a part of research that focused on other concerns, such as the development of talent, the course of vocational choices, or attrition. Eventually these streams merged.

The First Stream: Environmental Description

The approaches that developed in this stream are mainly organized around specific instruments which are the operational definitions of various approaches to the environment. For this reason, this section of the chapter will describe these measures in some detail. Although there were many implicit theoretical approaches to the college environment, with attendant assessment procedures, reviewed by Barton (1960), the first formal proposal for measuring the college environment lies in the work of Pace and Stern (1958). During the 1950s at Syracuse University, Pace and Stern began to work with the idea that a student's behavior depends not only on personal-ity but also on the demands of the college and the interaction between the student's personality and the college. For example, a rigid student may do well in a formal, structured college but poorly in an informal, unstructured one. Specifically, Pace and Stern attempted to implement the ideas of Harvard psychologist Henry Murray about the personality "needs" of an individual and the "presses" of the environment that influence the individual's behavior. *Needs* are manifested by a tendency to perform actions of a certain kind; for example, a "need for achievement" might be manifested by working hard for grades. A *press* is a property or attribute of an environment which encourages or discourages the individual to behave in particular ways (Stern, 1970).

Presses are of two types, first as they exist in reality or an objective inquiry discloses them to be (alpha press), and second as they are perceived or interpreted by the individual (beta press). The beta press is further composed of a *private press* based on the unique and personal view each person holds about his or her experience and a *consensual press*, which is the common or mutual interpretation of experiences shared by people participating in events. For example, a course in calculus could be judged as relatively difficult or easy by an external expert in mathematics who also had some information about the prior mathematics training and performance of the students. This would be the alpha press. An individual student could feel that the work was easy or difficult (private beta press) but could sense the class's collective view of its difficulty (consensual or aggregated beta press). Thus, an individual's perception of the environment is based partly on his or her own interpretation of experience and partly on the interpretations of important reference groups.

It is this perceived environment that Pace and Stern attempted to assess with the College Characteristics Index (CCI), designed to parallel the measure of needs tapped in the Activities Index (AI). Although Murray's theories did not require that needs and presses be conceived of as parallel, for the purpose of exploring the potential value of the CCI Pace and Stern included scales to parallel those of the AI. The scales were derived from Murray's list of "needs" (1938) and included such variables as affiliation, autonomy, order, and understanding. In other words, the 30 scales of the CCI were part of a strategy to find environmental presses that bore directly on the satisfaction or frustration of a psychological need. In some cases, this strategy had face validity; for example, the AI need-for-change scale was paralleled by the CCI change-press scale, which included items on whether course and procedures were frequently revised and whether the student body was diverse in background, opinions, and behavior. Other scales seemed to be stretching to find environmental parallels of needs. For example, "harm avoidance" included items on fire drills, health campaigns, housing requirements, and the absence of such "rough" activities as intramural sports. The parallelism, not intended by Murray in any case, seems strained and even misleading as a guide to the environment. In any case, the approach seemed to focus on the individual's perceptions of the environment. Stern (1970) subsequently argued that these individual perceptions of the environment from the CCI could be aggregated and averaged to yield a portrait of the collective environment.

Empirical studies showed that the CCI did indeed differentiate among colleges; for example, the profiles for Bennington and Syracuse differed. However, the original hope that the parallelism would reveal a person-environment "fit" which would affect academic performance and student satisfaction was not realized. Although one would expect, for example, students with needs for affiliation to get better grades and to be more satisfied in colleges with high average scores on the CCI affiliation scale, most studies showed no effect of congruence on satisfaction or achievement and have shown negative effects as often as positive effects (see Walsh, 1973, and Huebner, 1980, for summaries of evidence). Further, little has been written to show how the CCI could be used to improve the student-college fit, even if it were shown to make a difference, and less has been written on how CCI results could be specifically used to improve "congruence" on campuses.

These negative results are partly due to the multiple scales on the CCI (i.e., there are 30 possible "fit" scores), and to the fact that the psychometric strategy used to develop the CCI was to examine the variance between individuals, rather than the differences among colleges. That is, differences in CCI scores were based on differences in how different students saw colleges, some portion of which were due to their per-

sonalities, attitudes, and so on, and on another indeterminant portion which was due to differences among the colleges they were attending. This was because Stern used the student as the unit of analysis rather than the college. These limitations led Pace (1969), who had moved to UCLA at this time, to use a different strategy. Pace abandoned the press-need parallelism, used the average scores of colleges as the unit of analysis, and selected items that seemed directly relevant to the college experience. Pace used the statistical techniques of cluster analysis and factor analysis and used the college as the unit of analysis to reduce the number of scales to reflect only the major ways *colleges* differed from one another. Finally, for the final selection of items, Pace used a scoring system that was designed to reflect "consensus." An item is counted toward a score in a scale only if two thirds of the respondents agree (or disagree) in the scored direction. For example, if 69% agreed that "students are encouraged to take an active part in social reforms or political programs," it would count for one point for a college on the awareness scale; if only 62 % agreed, it would not count.

The outcome of Pace's analyses was the College and University Environment Scales (CUES). CUES originally consisted of 150 items drawn from the CCI and provided 30-item scales on five dimensions: pragmatism, reflecting the college's emphasis on practicality, status, and college fun; community, reflecting the friendliness and warmth of the campus; awareness, reflecting an active cultural and intellectual life; propriety, reflecting properness and conventionality; and scholarship, reflecting the academic rigor of the college. Eventually, CUES also included a 22-item scale of campus morale, and an 11-item scale of quality of teaching (faculty-student relationships). Pace (1969) related these scales to a variety of other information about colleges to establish their validity. For example, among colleges with high scholarship scores, a greater proportion of the faculty held doctorates. Small colleges were more likely than large colleges to have high community scores.

In a subsequent study with CUES, Pace (1974) compared the activities of upperclassmen and alumni of 100 institutions. Pace found that these eight types of institutions, selected to reflect the diversity of American higher education, had quite different patterns of CUES scores. For example, selective universities, engineering schools, and selective liberal arts colleges had similar high scores on the scholarship dimension, but engineering schools had very low awareness scores, while the other two had very high scores; less selective liberal arts colleges had community scores as high as selective liberal arts colleges but had lower scholarship and awareness scores. The other types of colleges—general comprehensive universities, strongly denominational colleges, and teacher's colleges—also showed distinctive patterns on CUES.

However, the most important results of Pace's study for questions of validity were the correlations between CUES scores and the activities and attitudes of students and alumni. For example, the art-activity scale measured whether students and alumni read about art, talk about it, went to galleries and museums to see it, bought it, and expressed themselves through it. The art-activity scale correlated .67 among upperclassmen and .62 among alumni with their college's score on the CUES awareness scale. A college scoring high on this scale would have "an environment that encourages concern about social and political problems, individuality and expressiveness through the arts, and tolerance of criticism" (Pace, 1974). Although one would expect people who experience an environment that encourages expressiveness through the arts to be active in art, colleges that score high on the CUES awareness scale are seldom art schools; usually they are private liberal arts colleges, many of which do not consider themselves to place an extraordinary emphasis on art education. And they are not necessarily highly selective, so the high scores on art activity received by these schools' upperclassmen and alumni cannot be explained simply by the caliber of students that the college attracts. Thus, the art activity of these students and alumni may be a result of the lively intellectual atmospheres of their colleges.

This study also found many other relationships between CUES scores and student and alumni sense of educational progress on a variety of areas, such as writing, understanding science, and critical thinking. In general, students or alumni reported stronger evaluations of their progress in colleges with high CUES scores in areas related to the area of progress. Although not nearly as strong as evidence from studies of student change, these self-reports of amount of progress suggest that the aspects of the envi-

ronment measured by CUES may be related to the impact of colleges; at least, they are related to satisfaction.

CUES has also been used to compare the perceptions of different campus subgroups, with results indicating that most groups perceive the overall environment in approximately the same way (e.g., Berdie, 1967), although administrators often have a much more positive view of their colleges than do students (Pascarella, 1974). Pace (1972) also showed that the CUES scores of 80 protestant colleges were related to the strength of their legal ties to their denominations: "The more firmly and zealously a college is related to a church the more clearly it emerges as a distinctive college environment. And this distinctiveness is defined by uniformly high scores on the characteristics labeled community, propriety, and practicality" (p. 37).

CUES was also used in a great many studies that compared the scores of incoming freshmen with those of upperclassmen (Feldman and Newcomb, 1969, reviewed many of these studies). In general, incoming freshmen seemed to share a general idealized image of college as friendly, stimulating, and vigorous, regardless of the description provided by students who had actually experienced the environment. Stern (1970) called this the "freshman myth." Some studies suggested that students quickly formed a less idealistic view of their college, sometimes within a few weeks. However, there is little evidence that this "disillusion" has any long-lasting effects.

CUES has also been used by other researchers to examine other topics. For example, Chickering, McDowell, and Campagna (1969) studied institutional differences and student development. Although, like other researchers, they found little relationship between environmental scores and changes in personality, measured in this study by the Omnibus Personality Inventory, they did find relationships with college "orientations." Specifically, students in colleges with high practicality scores tended to shift out of the "nonconformist" orientation, and students in colleges with high community or scholarship scales tended to shift away from the vocational orientation, intellectual students moved into academic orientations, and practical students shifted into vocational and collegiate orientations. All of this suggests some interactions between student characteristics and college environments. Unfortunately, there are very few other studies examining the influence of the variables measured by CUES and change in students. Thus, the main evidence for the influence of the environment as measured by CUES is correlational.

The development of CUES suggests several issues that apply to all measures of the environment and that will be considered again in the concluding section of the chapter. These problems include finding an appropriate theoretical scheme to conceptualize the environment, generalizing from *individual* perceptions or characteristics to a group or total environment, finding conceptually and statistically sound units of analysis and methods of scoring, and establishing the validity of the environmental measure.

Stern (1970) attempted to deal with one of the limitations of the CCI approach: its large number of *a priori* variables and scales. Stern factor-analyzed the CCI, using individual students' responses as the unit of analysis. Technically, this meant he had analyzed the variance between students' perceptions of colleges in general, rather than the variance between colleges per se. The dimensions identified are therefore the dimensions of how different students view their colleges, as well as the dimensions of how colleges differ from one another as reflected in the perceptions of their students. Stern has reported second-order factor analyses of the CCI and has developed versions for use in high schools, evening colleges, and organizations. Stern has also attempted to describe the "culture" of colleges by factor-analyzing the Activities Index and the CCI together, and then describing colleges in joint terms of the characteristics of their students and the students' perceptions of the environment. This procedure seems to finesse another question about the college environment: Is it due more to the characteristics of the people in the college, or is it due more to the characteristics of the institution independent of its students?

Although Stern (1970) does not provide a satisfactory definition of college "culture" or give a convincing rationale for his analyses, the idea of simultaneously analyzing average individual characteristics and aggregate perceptions of the environment appears to have merit. Stern used institutions as the unit of analysis, and he used average scores on the AI need factors and CCI press factors as variables. The second-order factor analysis recorded five "culture" factors:

the expressive, a non-work-oriented, nonconforming climate peopled by students with nonapplied interests, who do not value orderliness; the intellectual, characterized by intellectually demanding courses and faculty, opportunities for expressiveness, little bureaucratic control, peopled by students with high levels of interest in academic achievement and ideas; the protective, characterized by a highly organized, supportive environment and a relatively dependent, submissive student body; the vocational, characterized by heavily applied programs, conventionality, and authoritarianism, with students who tend to be selfish and manipulative; and the collegiate, characterized by extensive facilities for student recreation and amusement, ambiguous standards of achievement, and uncertain administrative practices, with friendly and assertive students.

Stern also proposed three additional indexes: dispersion, deviancy, and dissonance. The dispersion index is the average variation around the college or group mean. For example, a college with a small dispersion index score would presumably have a high degree of consensus on desirable behavior and characteristics; a college with a large dispersion index would have little such consensus. The deviancy index is simply the *individual's* distance from the college mean. The dissonance index is the discrepancy between the need component and the press component of each culture score. This index can be calculated for individuals for assessing intraindividual dissonance or for groups, to assess what Stern calls "cultural dissonance." As intriguing as these indexes are, they, like the "culture" idea, have not been used systematically in subsequent work.

Other Environmental Measures

The interest in the environment *per se* and student characteristics in the mid-1960s led to a variety of additional measures, most of which were developed at the Educational Testing Service. The first of these was the College Student Questionnaire (CSQ; Peterson, 1968), a lengthy survey which was designed to do two things: first, to assess student characteristics that presumably will affect their adjustment to college or could be affected by their college experiences, and second, to assess aspects of the environment that could influence that adjustment or development. Obviously, the questionnaire mixes student and institutional characteristics. However, one of its chief values has been its utility in studying *changes* in groups on variables that one would hope would be affected by college study. It consists of two parts.

Part I, covering students' backgrounds, attitudes, and plans, was designed to be used with entering students; Part II, which obtains information about students' educational and vocational plans, college activities, and attitudes toward their college, is designed to be used with students who have had one or more years of college. Each questionnaire consists of 200 multiple-choice questions, some of which are fairly complex. Part I can be scored for 7 scales: Family Independence, Peer Independence, Liberalism, Social Conscience, Cultural Sophistication, Motivation for Grades, and Family Social Status. Part II can be scored for 11 scales: the first five described for Part I plus Satisfaction with Faculty, Satisfaction with Administration, Satisfaction with Major, Satisfaction with Students, Study Habits, and Extracurricular Involvement. Although the CSQ was developed atheoretically, there is an *implicit* theory of college impact in these scales; that is, one would hope that as students move through college, they would become independent of their families and independent of peer pressures, would develop greater social consciousness, would become more culturally sophisticated, and, depending on one's political views, would become more liberal in their attitudes. One might also hope that students would be satisfied with their professors, their majors, their peers, and the administrative policies and procedures, which, together, would reflect satisfaction with the environment. That is, again implicitly, the CSQ assumes that the most salient feature of the environment is whether students feel satisfied that it is meeting their educational needs.

Because its format is designed to study change, the CSQ has been used in a wide variety of studies of student groups, particularly residence groups such as those in fraternities and sororities and residence halls (Longino and Kart, 1974). Wilder et al. (1986), for example, studied three cohorts of students at Bucknell, with data gathered when they were freshmen and upperclassmen in the 1960s, the 1970s, and the 1980s. In each time period, "Greek" students tended to score lower than independent or former Greek students on the scales assessing family and peer independence, cultural sophistication, social

conscience, and liberalism. The Greeks also gained less on these scales during college. However, the most intriguing finding was that the students of the 1980s *also* scored lower on these measures and gained less. This result belies the belief that today's students start college at a higher level of maturity than students in the past.

The CSQ was also used in a great many studies of the "subcultures" in the Clark and Trow (1966) typology, consisting of the academic, nonconformist, collegiate, and vocational subcultures. Although the CSQ actually measures the "orientation" that a student prefers among those described in four paragraphs, it has, nevertheless, been the operational definition used in studies which find a number of differences among the four groups of students (e.g., Terenzini and Pascarella, 1977; Doucet, 1977).

The next environmental approach measure, the Institutional Functioning Inventory (IFI), was developed in the "environmental description" tradition with a project to assess "institutional vitality," that is, to identify the characteristics of colleges that seemed to have strong, individual atmospheres. This effort changed to one of identifying the major dimensions of how colleges *function* (Peterson et al., 1970). In addition, the authors realized that, in order to understand how colleges function, they would need to assess the perceptions of faculty and administrators, as well as students. The 11 scales in the IFI thus represent the aspects that the authors considered the most important for institutional functioning: Intellectual-Aesthetic Curriculum; Freedom; Human Diversity; Concern for the Improvement of Society; Concern for Undergraduate Learning; Democratic Governance; Meeting Local Needs; Self-Study and Planning; Concern for Advancing Knowledge; Concern for Innovation; and Intellectual Esprit. Although a factor analysis of average faculty scores on these scales suggested that they could be more parsimoniously described by only four factors (liberal atmosphere, sense of community, intellectual climate, and ivory tower outlook), the authors contend that the conceptual distinctions among the scales warrant their retention.

The "validity" of the scales was suggested by correlating them with data of record, CUES scores, and a study of student protest (Sasajima, Davis, and Peterson, 1968). The correlations seemed plausible; for example, library size and research funds were correlated with the

Advancement of Knowledge Scale (.77 and .72, respectively), the Concern for the Improvement of Society Scale correlated with the CUES awareness scale (.68), and the Concern for Undergraduate Learning Scale was negatively correlated with the incidence of student complaints and demonstrations about the quality of teaching. In addition, a multigroup-multiscale analysis showed that faculty, administrators, and students generally described their campuses the same way, with the interesting exception of the Democratic Governance Scale. On this scale, students often perceived much less democracy than did their professors and administrators.

The IFI seems to be sensitive to the actual differences among colleges. For example, although there is a positive correlation between the Institutional Esprit and Democratic Governance scores across all colleges, the profile of one of the armed service academies shows a very high score on Institutional Esprit and a very low score on Democratic Governance; in contrast, a selective liberal arts college renowned for its flexibility had a very high score on Democratic Governance and a very low score on Institutional Esprit.

One of the most extensive studies using the IFI was conducted by Anderson (1983), who compared the "functioning" of a number of colleges, defined by scores on the IFI obtained between 1968 and 1972 and scores obtained between 1979 and 1981, and related these scores to the financial conditions of the colleges. Overall, colleges' scores on the IFI suggested greater human diversity and less democratic governance in the later period. However, state-supported institutions reported gains on all 11 scales, while community colleges declined on 4 scales. Most important, Anderson found little relationship between changes in finances and changes in the IFI. For example, faculty morale was less affected by salaries and institutional finances than by participation in governance. As this study illustrates, the IFI assesses perceptions of components of the environment that are important to faculty, as well as components that are important to students. In that sense, it involves an implicit recognition that there are multiple environments that are based on the experiences of the respondents. For example, faculty would generally have little knowledge of student social life or groups, and students would have little knowledge of the institution's policies on publication and tenure, although these are extremely important to the

groups that can report on them. However, it is unlikely that most people who are knowledgeable about college affairs would agree that the IFI adequately describes how colleges actually work, or how their daily activities are carried out.

Another approach to the environment was taken from the literature on organizational theory and behavior. One consistent theme in that literature is that it is critical to understand the *goals* of an organization in order to understand how it functions (e.g., Georgion, 1973). This idea has been applied to universities by sociologists Gross and Grambsch (1968, 1974), who studied the goals of 68 Ph.D.-granting universities as seen by faculty and administrators in two different time periods. The results were basically that the universities in both periods were heavily committed to research and scholarly pursuits, with much less attention given to students and their needs. Peterson and Uhl (1977) adapted the Gross and Grambsch strategy by designing an Institutional Goal Inventory (IGI) so that respondents can rate each of 90 statements of goals both according to how those goals are currently emphasized at the college and according to how they believe the goals should be emphasized. The differences between these "is" and "should be" ratings show how closely present campus goals match the goals that people prefer, and they identify areas where changes may be needed. Furthermore, differences among groups of respondents on their preferred goals show how much agreement exists about institutional purposes and objectives.

The IGI consists of 20 scales. Most of the goal statements form scales that comprise 13 *outcomes*, or substantive objectives, that a college may seek to achieve: Academic Development, Intellectual Orientation, Individual Personal Development, Humanism/Altruism, Cultural/Esthetic Awareness, Traditional Religiousness, Vocational Preparation, Advanced Training, Research, Meeting Local Needs, Public Service, Social Egalitarianism, and Social Criticism/Activism. The remaining statements form 7 scales relating to educational or institutional *process* goals: Freedom, Democratic Governance, Community, Intellectual/Esthetic Environment, Innovation, Off-Campus Learning, and Accountability/Efficiency.

These scales are based on the perceptions of respondents in response to items concerning their institution's goals. For example, in the Academic

Development Scale, respondents report their perceptions of the importance their institution currently gives to such goals as "to help students acquire depth of knowledge in at least one academic discipline" and "to hold students throughout the institution to high standards of intellectual performance."

Although IGI scores correlated with such published institutional data as proportion of faculty with doctorates and sectarian control, the most interesting study was an analysis of the views of faculty, students, administrators, and other members of the institution's community, such as residents and legislators, which showed that different types of institutions differed dramatically on the IGI, reflecting their sharply different missions. In a study of 105 California colleges, Peterson and Uhl (1977) reported that differences were especially large on the scales of Research, (universities high, community colleges low), Vocational Preparation and Social Egalitarianism (community colleges high, private institutions low).

It is striking that for all institutions combined, the "should be" scores were higher than the "is" scores on every scale, suggesting that few institutions are currently meeting their goals, according to their constituencies. The discrepancy was particularly large for the scales of Community, Intellectual Orientation, Individual Personal Development, and Vocational Preparation. In addition, a study comparing the IGI scores of the students, faculty, administrators, chancellors, regents, and residents of local communities of the University of California revealed some large differences *within* the institutions.

As with the IFI, factor analysis revealed a much simpler structure:

> In summary, five factors were identified in the analyses of present importance ratings: (1) humanistic development, which emphasized the personal and ethical development of the student; (2) a liberal, flexible environment characterized by freedom in many activities; (3) service to society; (4) research and graduate training; and (5) academic and intellectual development of students and the associated academic and intellectual climate. With only two minor exceptions, these factors were consistent for each participating group.
>
> The results of the analyses of preferred importance ratings are very similar to the analyses of present importance ratings with two exceptions: (1) the academic and intellectual development factor was not isolated as a separate factor; and (2) for the faculty and administrator groups only, an ivory-tower factor was identified, which included Factor 3 (service to society) at one pole and Factor 4 (research and graduate training) at the other pole. (Peterson and Uhl, 1977, p. 55)

Although an analysis of institutional goals is commonly considered critical in order to understand a college's policies and procedures, most goals are specifically tied to the history, the clientele, and the particular programs of the colleges. Therefore, it may not appear to be especially fruitful to many observers to examine *general* goals as the approach of the IGI does (Lunneborg, 1978). A better strategy would be a consideration of *detailed* goals. However, for research purposes, this general approach may allow for comparisons among institutions that would not be possible in the clutter of particular institutions' goals.

Despite its "goal" rationale, it should be obvious that the IGI, at least in the "is" section, is basically a perceptual measure, and thus, it is not surprising that the factors found in the factor analysis are fairly similar to those found in analyses of other perceptual measures. And these factors tend to reflect the general ways in which perceptions of colleges differ from one another, which do not necessarily correspond to other information about colleges or the people in them.

A Shift in Environmental Assessment Research

The possible limitations of the perceptual approach led to two strategies: the first was to use multiple sources of information about colleges, and the second was to make environmental assessments more specific and practical. The first strategy was used by Centra (1970, 1973) in the development of the Questionnaire on Student and College Characteristics (QSCC) to describe the college environment accurately by including information on students' perceptions of their institutions, their behavior during college, and their personal backgrounds and characteristics. After an initial tryout in 8 colleges, Centra (1970) obtained data from a sample of students in 214 colleges, which were subjected to a variety of factor analyses. First, the 77 items that asked for students' perceptions were analyzed separately. (These items asked students either to indicate whether statements were true or false or to rate their agreement with statements on a 4-point scale.) A typical item was "Faculty members tend to be aloof and somewhat formal with students." The factors obtained were termed Restrictiveness, Faculty-Student Interaction, Activism, Nonacademic Emphasis, Curriculum Flexibility, Challenge (academic), Laboratory Facilities, and Cultural Facilities. From these analyses, factor scores based on two to nine items per factor were computed. The median coefficient alpha reliabilities of the scales were .86, and six of the eight scales had reliabilities of .84 or higher.

In a second analysis, the eight factor scores just described were included with 34 student self-report items about their behavior in college (for example, the extent of their involvement in intramural athletics or dramatic productions), plus objective information about the colleges (such as the percentage of students in residence halls, the number of books in the library per student, and student SAT scores). A factor analysis yielded six factors: athletic emphasis versus cultural activities, size and cliquishness, academic elitism, activism and flexibility, students' satisfaction with their college, and social life. A second, multimethod factor analysis yielded 10 factors. The first 4 were similar to those obtained in the standard factor analysis, supporting the meaning and stability of those factors. The remaining 6 factors were regulation, fraternity and sorority emphasis, emphasis on science, and three other factors with unclear meanings. The variety of these factor solutions suggests the dependence of the description of the environment on the methods used in analysis.

In an interesting precursor to the student consumerism movement, the colleges that had participated in the administration of the QSCC had been encouraged to use the results in their self-descriptions for the "College Life" section of the College Board's *College Handbook*. Interestingly, 53% did not use the results at all, 9% used them for only one to three sentences, 13% used them for as much as a short paragraph, and only 25% used them extensively.

However, the key finding, again, is that the dimensions of the environment that are found are considerably dependent on the methods used

to assess them. The point was also made by Chickering (1972), who found that "Colleges which are bedfellows on CUES, where students give their general impressions, may not even be roommates on an instrument like the ECQ [Experience of College Questionnaire], where they report their daily experiences and behaviors, although they may remain in the same dormitory. Conversely, strangers on one instrument may find themselves friends or acquaintances on another" (p. 141). This point will be discussed in greater detail later in the chapter.

The second strategy for increasing the value of environmental measures was to make them more specific and practical. As Baird (1974) pointed out, most measures were so "global as to be unrelated to concepts suggesting practical actions" (p. 307). This is partly due to the fact that most have been perceptual measures, relying on generalizations, and that they were designed to reflect interinstitutional variance, or how colleges as units vary from one another. This means that local or specifically important concerns may not be reflected in the measures in any useful detail. For this reason, some researchers attempted to develop more detailed measures or techniques.

For example, Warren and Roelfs (1972) developed the Student Reactions to College questionnaire for colleges to use in identifying students' views of institutional strengths and weaknesses. To maximize the instrument's usefulness to staff members and its relevance to students, Warren and Roelfs did not simply develop their own questions; instead, they interviewed students, faculty members, and administrators about what they thought was important to know about their colleges. And on a pretest version of the form, students were asked to write in issues of importance to them that were not covered in the questionnaire. Its first 150 items cover such areas as instruction, grading, faculty and staff contact with students, registration and class scheduling, student activities, financial problems, housing, food services, and transportation. In addition, the questionnaire includes 9 background questions about the student and space for 20 questions that the college can develop itself. The items ask students if they feel their needs are being met.

Betz, Klingensmith, and Menne (1970) reviewed industrial research on job satisfaction for its insights into students' satisfaction with their colleges, and after a variety of analyses, they developed the College Student Satisfaction Questionnaire, which assesses satisfaction with fairly specific areas: (1) Policies and Procedures (for example, choice of classes); (2) Working Conditions (for example, comfort of residence); (3) Compensation (for example, amount of study required to attain good grades); (4) Quality of Education (for example, making friends); and (6) Recognition (for example, faculty acceptance of the student as worthwhile).

An even more specific technique, the Environmental Referent, has been developed by Huebner and Corrazini (1978), which asks respondents to provide written descriptions of the factors that caused them to experience a particular situation as stressful and incongruent or enhancing and congruent. When common themes appear, the concrete situation is analyzed so that corrective actions can be taken.

In general, then, in recent years, the "environmental description" stream of research has seemed to focus more on relatively specific aspects of the environment that are related to student satisfaction. What began with the rather abstract theoretical concept of need-press congruence, across colleges, has come to emphasize the concrete practical details of specific local conditions.

The Second Stream: Approaches to the College Environment Developed as Part of Other Research Questions

A variety of approaches to the college environment are the result of research projects which attempted to understand an issue in higher education where the environment was of secondary importance. For example, one of the major concerns of research in the late 1950s and the 1960s was the development of "talent," which usually meant some form of academic achievement. Knapp and Goodrich (1952) and Knapp and Greenbaum (1953) conducted some of the earliest of these studies that touched on the college environment. Knapp and Goodrich calculated the *rate* at which colleges' baccalaureates were later listed in *American Men of Science*, and Knapp and Greenbaum examined the rate at which they later won graduate fellowships or earned doctorate degrees. Knapp and Goodrich correlated various factual characteristics of the colleges with the rate of "success" and found that the

most productive institutions had moderate rather than high costs, were often small liberal arts colleges, and drew many students from semirural areas. For example, the 10 most productive institutions in this study were, in descending order, Reed, Cal Tech, Kalamazoo, Earlham, Oberlin, University of Massachusetts, Hope, DePauw, Nebraska Wesleyan, and Iowa Wesleyan. Intrigued that these colleges outperformed such institutions as Harvard, Yale, Princeton, Berkeley, Michigan, and Columbia, none of which were in the top 50 in the production of scientists, Knapp and Goodrich did case studies of the institutions to attempt to understand why some colleges were so unexpectedly productive. They examined their histories, finances, students, faculty, and curricula. Although each institution was unique, in general, they were characterized by "a student body in which the scholar is the hero rather than the athlete or socialite" (p. 94). They also did a study of ratings of faculty and found that "productive" colleges had faculty characterized as "masterful," as exemplified by rigorous standards of grading and a high level of energy; as "warm," as illustrated by the use of humor and concern for students; and as having "intellectual distinction," as manifested in intellectual mastery of the field and scholarly production.

As the Cold War progressed in the 1950s, the concern about America's "talent resources" increased greatly (e.g., Wolfle, 1954). One of the consequences was the founding of the National Merit Scholarship Corporation (NMSC) in 1955. The Merit Corporation was founded with the purpose of identifying the nation's most talented high school students and providing financial assistance for their college education. Supported by funds from the Ford Foundation and the National Science Foundation, the NMSC tested several million high school students each year. After a number of studies of the predictors of the academic accomplishment of the very bright students who received scholarships, the NMSC research staff began to explore the conditions in colleges that were associated with the educational attainments of the Merit Scholars, particularly plans to attend graduate or professional school, and to obtain the Ph.D.

One group of these studies stemmed directly from the work of Knapp and his associates. Thistlethwaite (1960, 1963) and Thistlethwaite and Wheeler (1966) conducted a series of analyses using samples of current students, all of whom had taken the NMSC examination in high school. The criteria in the last of these studies were degree aspirations and plans for entry into graduate school of the students as seniors. Statistical controls for initial aspirations, sex, test scores, social class, finances, and initial major were used. Thistlethwaite developed a perceptual measure designed to assess the environmental factors that might influence educational aspirations. There were 14 lower division scales (9 for faculty press and 5 for student press) and 20 upper division scales (12 for faculty press and 8 for student press). Factor analysis of the press scales suggested six factors: excellence of faculty in major field, lower division humanistic and intellectual press, upper division student intellectualism, lower division faculty supportiveness and enthusiasm (all these factors were positively related to plans and aspirations for advanced study), student camaraderie and playfulness, and faculty press for vocationalism and compliance (both negatively related to plans and aspirations). However, it should be noted that none of these variables was as strongly related to plans after the controls were applied as were undergraduate grade-point average and the proportion of the students' friends who were entering graduate school immediately after college. In any case, Thistlethwaite's measures were another perceptually based attempt to analyze the subtleties of the environment, which resulted in dimensions that were quite similar to those found by Pace and other researchers, although the research question was quite different.

The next development at the National Merit Scholarship Corporation was a fairly direct extension of John Holland's (1962, 1966) theory of vocational choice. Holland theorizes that there are six types of vocational choices corresponding to six personality groupings (the Realistic, Scientific, Artistic, Social, Conventional, and Enterprising), and that there are six corresponding types of environments. The environments are consistent with the interests, needs, habits, and interpersonal styles of the personalities. When personality and environment type match, this congruence leads to satisfaction and reinforcement of the individual's characteristics. When they are incongruent, the result is dissatisfaction and dissonance. (A formal statement of the theory will be discussed later in the chapter.) Therefore, in order to study this theory of voca-

tional choice among college students, Astin and Holland (1961) developed the Environmental Assessment Technique (EAT), which is based on the assumption that

> the college environment depends on the personal characteristics of the students, faculty, administration and staff of the institution. Since the undergraduate's personal contacts are chiefly with fellow students, it is further assumed that the major portion of the student's environment is determined by the characteristics of his fellow students. Accordingly the environment was defined in terms of eight characteristics of the student body; average intelligence, size, and six personal orientations based on the proportions of the students in six broad areas of study. (p. 308)

The "orientations" were based on Holland's theory of vocational choice and were estimated by the percentage of students majoring in realistic (or technical) fields, scientific fields, social fields, conventional (or clerical) fields, enterprising (or business and sales) fields, and artistic fields. How did this relatively simple system work? Astin and Holland first found that the EAT variables correlated with the perceptual CCI scores. For example, the average intelligence of students was strongly related to the CCI Understanding Scale, and the Realistic Scale had a highly negative relation with the CCI Humanism Scale.

Astin (1963b) later showed that the EAT correlated with seniors' ratings of their colleges at 82 colleges. For example, he reported that size correlated .57 with the percentage of students reporting that "many of the social groups on campus have a definite snob appeal." Intelligence level correlated .63 with the percentage reporting that "The typical student spends a lot of time in the library"; the realistic orientation correlated .57 with students' reports that their attitudes toward fraternities and sororities had become more positive; intellectual (or scientific) orientation was correlated—.58 with the percentage who agreed that "Many of the students are interested primarily in getting married and raising families"; the social orientation was correlated .41 with the percentage who agreed that "A student who is not very skilled in etiquette or social graces would probably feel out of place on the campus"; the conventional orientation was correlated .56 with the percentage who agreed that "Faculty members usually don't like the student to question their judgment or point of view"; the enterprising orientation correlated .42 with the percentage who agreed that "Students are always ready to argue or debate almost any issue"; and the artistic orientation correlated—.47 with the percentage who felt that their interest in sports had increased during college. Most of the relations were both sizable and plausible. Altogether, Astin and Holland martialed substantial evidence that the characteristics of the student body have a considerable influence on the total environment.

Richards, Seligman, and Jones (1970) provided evidence that the characteristics of the faculty and the curriculum, as well as the students, have an influence on the environment. These researchers modified the EAT strategy to derive measurements of school environments by counting the number of courses, the numbers of degrees, and the number of faculty members rather than using the proportions of students in the six types of fields derived from Holland's theory.

These three measures correlated with each other, but at a lower level than one might expect, so that scores based on one data source would provide a different "environment" score than scores based on another. For example, faculty and student scores correlated .53 for enterprising and—.18 for conventional. Perhaps more important, the faculty scores correlated only moderately with CUES scores; the highest correlation was—.43 between faculty intellectual (scientific) scores and CUES practicality scores. Correlations between faculty scores and CUES scores that one would predict to be higher often were not. For example, faculty social scores correlated .12 with CUES community scores, faculty artistic scores correlated .19 with CUES awareness scores, and faculty realistic scores correlated .04 with CUES practicality scores. Perhaps a perceptual measure for faculty, like the IFI, would correlate more highly. However, it is plausible to think that if one were studying faculty, these faculty measures might be of value, and if one were studying curriculum, the curricular measures could be used.

Astin (1962) was subsequently motivated by a researcher's desire to provide other researchers "with a more limited set of empirical dimensions which account for the major variations among institutions" for use as independent variables in their studies. Astin's strategy was to factor-analyze the factual information that can be

obtained from college directories and fact books such as tuition and number of books in the library. Astin did this for 33 variables concerning four-year colleges and obtained six dimensions that accounted for many of the differences on these variables between colleges (80% of the variance). He called the six dimensions affluence or wealth, size, private versus public control, proportion of males in the student body, technical emphasis, and homogeneity of curriculum and EAT scores. Astin (1963a) then used these measures to show that very bright students were less likely to aspire to the Ph.D. degree in large colleges, predominantly male colleges, and colleges emphasizing clerical curricula. Astin (1965) showed that these scores correlated with student characteristics (e.g., degree aspirations and high school accomplishments) and differed by college types (e.g., technological institutions and liberal arts colleges). He also reported scores for most individual four-year colleges for the purpose of guiding students in their choice of college.

Astin's strategy was subsequently used with junior colleges by Richards, Rand, and Rand (1966), who found six factors: cultural affluence, technological specialization, size, age, transfer emphasis, and business orientation. Richards and Braskamp (1969) showed that these factors were related to a wide variety of average student characteristics. The junior college factors had a few similarities with the four-year college factors. Subsequently, Richards, Rand, and Rand (1968) used the same strategy with medical schools and found four factors: affluence, Canadian versus United States admissions practice, size, and hospital training emphasis. The limitations of these various factual approaches will be discussed later in the chapter.

After moving to the American Council on Education, Astin (1968, 1972) decided that the perceptual approach was too ambiguous, and that what he called the "student characteristics" approach provided too little information about the educational process to be adequate for assessing the college environment. He proposed another approach to the environment, which he called a "stimulus" approach. His idea was that the actual behavior of students and faculty and specific features of the college represent stimuli that have an impact on each student's perceptions of the college as well as on his or her own behavior. An environmental stimulus is "any behavior, event, or other observable characteristic of the institution capable of changing the student's sensory input, the existence of which can be confirmed by independent observation" (p. 5). Astin asked students to respond to 275 relatively specific items concerning their own behaviors and the characteristics of their peers, classrooms, college rules, and so on. In addition, students responded to 75 items that were similar to CUES items to analyze their "image" of their college. Astin separately analyzed the items referring to the "peer," "classroom," "administrative" and "physical" environments and found 27 dimensions on which colleges differed from one another. Analysis of the "image" items produced eight additional factors, resulting in 35 dimensions to describe the college environment.

The content of the factors was clearly dependent on the particular items Astin had used. For example, the "peer environment" factors ranged from the general factor "competitiveness versus cooperativeness" to "regularity of sleeping habits." All of the "administrative" environment scales consisted of factors whose names began with "severity of administrative policy against . . ." since all the original items referred to rules. Although some students may be strongly affected by rules and their enforcement, most students are affected in more areas of their behavior by such administrative decisions as tuition, registration, and degree requirements. And, of course, students are also influenced, albeit indirectly, by administrative policies that are usually beyond their knowledge, such as requirements for hiring and promotion of faculty and the allocation of the budget. Thus, Astin's description, in spite of its 35 dimensions, seems quite limited in some areas, even if we accept Astin's "stimulus" idea. There are other aspects of the college that serve as unperceived or indirect "stimuli."

In addition, although the interpretations of original factors are based on all the loadings in a factor analysis, the actual "scales" used in the Inventory of College Activities are amazingly short. Of the 25 "stimulus" scales, 12 are three items long, six are two items long, and seven consist of one item. Sometimes the content is peculiar, as often happens in studies based on the factor analysis of a hodge-podge of variables. For example, the percentages of students who said that in the past year they had gambled with cards or dice, had *not* participated in an informal group sing, and had *not* voted in a student election are weighted and summed to measure "competitiveness versus cooperativeness," "Informal dating" was measured solely by the percentage of students who said they had fallen in love in the past year.

Furthermore, many of the items seemed problematical; some seemed as "perceptual" as other instruments, for example, the three items that composed the "Extraversion of the Instructor" scale; "The instructor was enthusiastic," "The instructor had a good sense of humor," and (scored negatively), "The instructor was often dull and uninteresting." More generally, it is hard to see how many of the items which refer to private behavior that is usually unobservable by other people could be "stimuli" for other students in the aggregate, for example, "I had a blind date," "I took weight-reducing or dietary formula," and "I overslept and missed a class or appointment." In sum, although the general *idea* of examining the physical, social, intellectual, and organizational stimuli that impinge upon students for keys to the environment seems to have considerable potential, this particular attempt does not seem to fulfill that potential. An approach that is based more on theoretically, or even intuitively, based ideas and less on a shotgun approach would be much better. I shall return to this point later in the chapter.

Creager and Astin (1968) factor-analyzed ICA scores from the research just described as well as variables from earlier factual analyses: the colleges' affluence, size, and so on, and such "commonsense" variables as type of control and region of the country. Most of the resulting dimensions placed great weight on the commonsense and factual data. This suggests the possibility that we may be able to infer a good deal about a college from a few basic facts without a much more extensive investigation. For example, the first factor, Drinking versus Religiousness, has high negative loadings on selectivity, status, and private nonsectarian control as well as high positive loadings on severity of the policies against drinking, sex, and aggression. Thus, if we knew that a college was private, nonsectarian, highly selective, and prestigious, we could make a pretty good guess that it would be a free and open campus with regard to drinking, sex, and so on. The greatest weight on the second factor was given to the proportion of males at the school, the third factor to the size of the student body, the fourth to the presence of

Roman Catholic colleges in the sample, and the fifth to technical institutes. The rest of the weights on these factors were consistent with general expectations about such institutions and consisted of the "stimulus" and "image" factors as well as other commonsense variables. In general, many of the differences between colleges were associated with commonsense distinctions, suggesting that some typology of institutions could be developed that would provide us with a great deal of information about colleges. For example, we know a lot about a college just by knowing that it is a selective engineering college in the Northeast or an unselective womens' Catholic college in the Midwest.

In contrast, when Astin and Panos (1969) studied the influence of college environments on the vocational and educational plans and achievements of college students, the stimulus and image measures had a considerable influence, independent of and sometimes larger than the commonsense or factual variables. In predicting 28 criteria after controlling for input, commonsense and factual environmental variables appeared in the equations 88 times, while "stimulus" and "image" factors appeared 68 times. Although the stimulus and image factors seemed to have more powerful influences on educational aspirations and plans than upon career choices, which were influenced by the composition of the student body, they seemed to be getting at something unique in college environments that influence students' development. Thus, while we may know a good deal just by knowing the facts about a college, we still need to know more to really understand its environment.

Recent Research on the College Environment

Interest in the topic of the general college environment seemed to subside in the 1970s. Instead, researchers began to focus on subenvironments and more specific aspects of the college experience, which more directly impinge upon the behavior of students. The two major research efforts in these areas were conducted by Moos, who concentrated on subenvironments, and Pace, who concentrated on student experiences.

Moos (1979), who began his career studying therapeutic milieus, turned his attention to res-

idence units in colleges. The eventual product of his research was the University Residential Environment Scales (URES). Partly from his psychiatric background, Moos proposed that environments can be seen as having three domains of social climate and their related dimensions: *relationship* dimensions, which assess the extent to which people are involved in the setting, the extent to which they support and help one another, and the extent to which they express themselves freely and openly; *personal growth* or goal orientation dimensions, which measure the basic goals of the setting, that is, the areas in which personal developmental self-enchancement tends to occur; and *system maintenance and change* dimensions, which measure the extent to which the environment is orderly and clear in its expectations, maintains control, and responds to change.

The URES designed to measure these constructs consist of 9–10 items each and measure 10 dimensions, which are grouped into "domains." These 10 scales, with typical items, are as follows:

Relationship Domain

1. Involvement ("There is a feeling of unity and cohesion here").
2. Emotional Support ("People here are concerned with helping and supporting one another").

Personal Growth Domain

3. Independence ("People here pretty much act and think freely without too much regard for social opinion").
4. Traditional Social Orientation ("Dating is a recurring topic of conversation around here").
5. Competition ("Around here, discussions frequently turn into verbal duels").
6. Academic Achievement ("People here work hard to get top grades").
7. Intellectuality ("People around here talk a lot about political and social issues").

System Maintenance and Change Domain

8. Order and Organization ("House activities are pretty carefully planned here").

9. Student Influence ("The students formulate almost all the rules here").

10. Innovation ("New approaches to things are often tried here").

The validity of the URES approach was suggested by a series of studies. Some correlated URES data about dormitories with other information about dormitories (Gerst and Sweetwood, 1973); others used the URES to construct a typology of student living groups (Moos et al., 1975); some related URES scores to the influence of living groups on students' vocational choices (Hearn and Moos, 1976); and still others studied the effects of "megadorms" (Wilcox and Holahan, 1976).

Moos (1979) also developed a College Experiences Questionnaire, which was designed to assess the consequences of college attendance in four general areas: styles of coping with college life; personal interests and values; self-concept, mood, and health-related behaviors; and aspiration and achievement levels. Moos and his associates administered this instrument to students in 52 living groups on two campuses at the beginning and at the end of their freshman year. Moos also administered the URES. Moos first identified clusters of living groups based on the similarity of their URES profiles. These clusters include relationship-oriented groups, traditionally socially oriented groups, supportive achievement-oriented groups, competitive groups, independence-oriented groups, and intellectually oriented groups. When Moos compared the changes in group scores using a comparison of residuals (actual versus predicted scores), there were distinctive impacts of each grouping, with the interesting exception that competitive groups had no significant effects on any outcome. Residence groups had no influence on any of the measures of self-concept and mood, or on the coping style of "hostile interaction", but had a considerable effect on "student body involvement" (such as attending a school political rally and voting in a student election); academic orientation (participating in a science contest or being a member of a scholastic honor society);

and achievement level (grade-point average). Other research examined the influence of the groups on students' health. Moos and Van Dort (1977), for example, found that groups with low social and emotional support and high competition had higher than average reports of stress and physical complaints.

Additional evidence about the idea of the importance of the environment of living groups comes from a variety of studies. For example, Winston, Hutson, and McCaffry (1980) found that while the fraternities with the highest grades on one campus had no higher average SAT scores than the fraternities with the lowest grades, their URES scores showed that the high-achieving fraternities scored significantly higher on the Academic Achievement and Intellectuality scales and lower on the Independence scale. However, occasional negative results, at least those using Moos's approach, cast doubt upon the idea that the residence group environment influences grades. For example, Ballou (1985) found numerous differences among types of residence halls on the URES, but the type of residence was unrelated to grades, student participation in campus activities, and health habits. These inconsistent or complex, even muddled, results are much like those in a good deal of the research on residential units.

However, Moos's strategy can be seen as a fairly direct continuation of Astin and Panos's (1969) comment on their extensive analyses of the influences on the vocational and educational development of a large sample of students and institutions:

> Since most of the environmental effects of our 246 institutions appeared to be mediated through the peer environment rather than the classroom, administrative, or physical environments, further study of the nature and influence of undergraduate peer groups is clearly indicated. At the same time, a greater effort should be devoted to the identification of other effective environmental variables which are more directly manipulatable and not so highly dependent on the characteristics of the entering students. (p. 158)

Residence groups are clearly a major force in the peer environment, and one that can often be manipulated to have rather different characteristics. More generally, Moos's strategy represents a move away from interest in the global or distal environment and toward a concern with the local or proximal environment and the use of important subgroups rather than the institution as a whole as the unit of analysis, which may be a more fruitful research approach.

Pace's attempt to assess students' quality of effort, while not designed to provide a measure of the environment, does, in fact, demonstrate large differences among types of colleges not only in the average "level of effort," but in the specific incidence of particular experiences of students, some of which must be due as much to the type of college they attend as to their own effort.

The instrument Pace developed to assess these ideas was the College Student Experiences questionnaire (CSEQ), a standardized self-report survey of how students spend their time and the nature and quality of their activities (Pace, 1987). Students respond by checking "never," "occasionally," "often," or "very often" for activities in 14 clusters of mostly 10 items: Library Experiences; Course Learning; Art, Music, and Theater; Science Lab Activities; Student Union; Athletic and Recreation Facilities; Dormitory or Fraternity/Sorority; Experiences with Faculty; Clubs and Organizations; Experiences in Writing; Personal Experiences; Student Acquaintances; Topics of Conversation; and Information in Conversation. The items are arranged in a hierarchy so that participation in a high-level activity is qualitatively different from participation in a lower level activity.

Although not designed to measure environments, the norm group information by type of college suggests major differences in the experiences of students among types of institutions which, if the "aggregate behavior" approach is used, would play a larger role than the characteristics of the students in defining the character of the environment. Baird (1987) compared CSEQ scores of doctoral universities, comprehensive colleges, and universities, selective liberal arts colleges, general liberal arts colleges, and community colleges and found fairly sizable differences. Although the community college students understandably reported a lower rate of activity and involvement in many out-of-classroom areas, especially in athletics and recreation, clubs and organizations, art, music and theatre, and student acquaintances, they reported an activity rate equal to other types of

colleges in the areas of library usage, writing, and interactions with faculty. Thus, the *academic* side of the college experience was strong in community colleges, but the nonacademic side was not, probably due to the high rate of commuting. In contrast, doctoral universities were below average in library usage, writing, and interactions with faculty. Comprehensive colleges and universities were below average in athletics and recreation, clubs and organizations, and student acquaintances. General liberal arts colleges' students reported a high rate of activity in interactions with faculty, use of the student union, athletics and reaction, and clubs and organizations. Selective liberal arts college students reported the highest levels of activity of all groups in the areas of use of the library; interaction with faculty; art, music, and theater; student union; athletics and recreation; clubs and organizations; and student acquaintances.

More specifically, students at doctoral universities reported the lowest frequency of any type of college of "working on a paper or project where you had to integrate ideas from various sources," "talked with a professor," "asked your instructor for information related to a course you were taking (grades, make-up work, assignments, etc.)," "visited informally and briefly with an instructor after class," and "made friends with students whose age was very different from yours."

The comparison of doctoral universities, which were only average in most areas, and which were below average in several, with selective liberal arts colleges, which were superior to other colleges in a variety of areas, suggests several points. First, these differences held, although these two types of colleges are fairly comparable in quality of facilities and faculty. Thus, it is not so much the *presence* of facilities, funding, and staff, but the uses to which they are put that determines their educational impact. The second point is the importance of the emphasis that different types of colleges place on undergraduate education in the quality of the experience for students. Both of these points illustrate how different environments can influence behavior.

An interesting demonstration of the interaction of environment and "effort" is shown in some results provided by Pace (1984) in which the the predictors of student satisfaction and students' sense of gain in five areas were studied. The independent variables were the "quality of effort" scales, student background characteristics, a brief student assessment of the college environment (nine items for nine characteristics), and college status. The brief environment scores were the best predictors of the criterion of satisfaction in every type of college. Turning to sense of gain, college status variables (class, major, degree plans, grades, residence, and hours employed) accounted for the largest amount of variance (increases in R^2 ranged from .19 to .33), but the environment items made the next largest contribution to prediction in three of five areas (ranging from .11 to .14). Quality-of-effort scales were next in these three areas and were next to background in the other two areas.

In sum, current work in college environments seems to be concentrating on subenvironments or is concerned with more specific aspects of the environment that can be used for particular research projects. Examples of the latter include types of student-faculty interaction (Pascarella and Terenzini, 1978, 1980); academic alienation and political climate (Long, 1976, 1977); student perceptions of cheating and attitude toward cheating of other students (Haines et al., 1986); minority students' feelings about the level of discrimination and the quality of peer relations (Nettles, Thoeny, and Gosman, 1986); and compatibility of the work environment among graduate faculty (Baird, 1986). Additional measures of environment have been developed in secondary analyses of existing data sets. For example, Pascarella (1984) reanalyzed data from a longitudinal sample of college students and developed three very brief scales of "academic or intellectual competition," "impersonalism and inaccessible faculty," and "conventional or conformist press." These variables had modest effects on students' aspirations. Although these variables are much more appropriate to the research problems involved in the studies than global measures of the environments, they do not in themselves further our understanding of how the overall college operates and how it influences students and faculty.

Criticisms of Currently Available Approaches to the Environment

Although there is a long research history devoted to the college environment, there are many problems in the area. These can be divided into the technical-logical and the theoretical. Many of the approaches to the college environment are based on an assessment of the perceptions of students, faculty, administrators, and sometimes others. Measures of student and faculty perceptions of the environment have several difficulties. The first is the ambiguity of what an aggregate perception of an environment means. A person's perceptions of a social situation depend on many things, as Feldman (1972) and Chickering (1972) have pointed out. Students' interests and characteristics help determine the colleges they choose to attend. Students' characteristics then form part of the total environment. For example, the presence of many bright, intellectual students may lead an individual student to perceive the whole college as intellectual. In addition, students select subgroups, major fields, courses, and activities consistent with their interests and characteristics. Professors and administrators likewise have different patterns of experiences. These experiences compose their sampling of the total physical and interpersonal environment and thus the way in which they perceive the environment. And even these perceptions are influenced by their personal characteristics and social position. For example, students who think of their college may think first of their classes, a president may have uppermost in his or her thoughts the budget, a professor his or her research, and a dean his or her work with curriculum reform.

This problem may be particularly difficult when there are distinct subenvironments in the campus, since the scoring of most instruments sums across the subenvironments. For example, at a highly politicized college, the disparate perceptions of a leftist subgroup and a conservative subgroup may cancel each other out, and the college would appear to be nonpolitical on the environmental measure. Having said this, we should note that the evidence about the influence of personal characteristics on perceptions of the college environment is limited. For example, Pace (1966), Hartnett and Centra (1974), and Moos and Bromet (1978) have provided evidence that personal characteristics have little influence on environmental perceptions, and that environmental scores for subgroups are seldom different from the scores of the majority. Although subgroups may have different college experiences, they seem to describe the total environment in much the same way (e.g., Berdie, 1967).

It is also clear that the accuracy of perceptions depends on the knowledge of the respondent, a factor which varies from person to person and from area to area. For example, most students know very little about some aspects of faculty life, and commuting students have little to say about life in the dormitories. Furthermore, some respondents may report stereotypes or rumors, particularly when an item refers to activities that are not publicly visible, for example, when a student believes that other students do not study very much, just because he or she cannot see them study.

A major limitation of the perceptual approach is that a person can describe only those aspects of the college covered by the items in the instrument and only in the particular way the items allow. This difficulty is increased since the items in environmental instruments, of necessity, tend to be general and without precise referents. The items must refer to things that are common to all or most colleges and then must be phrased in such a way that they can be answered by people from any subgroup of the college.

Since many of the important aspects of the atmosphere of a college tend to be elusive and can be captured only by items that ask for the respondent's overall impressions, even the most skillfully prepared items will appear vague or ambiguous. This ambiguity can lead to descriptions of environments that may bear little relationship to the realities of campus life. For example, Chickering (1972) found extremely large differences among four colleges in their students' reports of the percentage of their classroom time they spent in different behaviors (e.g., listening and taking notes primarily to remember, thinking about the ideas presented); studying outside of class (memorizing, synthesizing ideas); or using information (applying concepts or principles to new problems, interpreting). The colleges also differed greatly in descriptions of specific instructor behaviors, students' reasons for studying, feelings about courses, and patterns of academic work (pace and promptness). However, on the CUES Quality of Teaching and Faculty Student Relationship scale, the colleges were very similar. In contrast, at the two colleges with the highest CUES scholarship scores, students spent the least time thinking about ideas in class and spent the least amount of studying time synthesizing, applying, and interpreting their assignments. In short, this study raises the pos-

sibility that general impressions may not correspond to specific behaviors.

Of course, there are the ambiguities that arise when the responses of individuals to each item are combined with those of the other respondents. These combined responses thus reflect the degree of consensus among the reporters as well as the intensity of the environment. For example, when half the students only moderately agree that "the college encourages individual freedom," it is quite different from when half strongly agree and half strongly disagree with the item. The items are also typically summed on a scale, the meaning of which has been decided by the authors of the instrument. In many cases, the items have been selected for strictly statistical reasons and may have slight coherent meaning. For example, the Inventory of College Activities "Cohesiveness" scale consists of the items "I discussed how to make money with other students" and "Freshmen have to take orders from upperclassmen for a period of time."

Because of the generality and ambiguity of perceptual measures, they are not very useful to people who want to evaluate or change their colleges. For example, what can an administrator do with the finding that his or her college scored at the 50th percentile on a scale of "friendliness"? The administrator finds nothing in the score to serve as a guide to action; doesn't know if the 50th percentile is good or bad; and is not sure what the "friendliness" scale really measures. However, an unexpectedly high or low score can be a "red flag" that can identify potential problem areas that can be the subject of more pointed, detailed investigation. A student choosing a college may find perceptual scores more useful.

Perhaps the most fundamental problem with the perceptual approach is its assumption that reports of individual perceptions in fact represent some kind of agreed-upon reality. That is, how can we logically move from the level of an individual's view of an institution to the level of a characteristic of the entire institution for everyone? As Feldman and Newcomb (1969) pointed out:

> To know whether the "is" of the environment represents pressures on students, one needs to know such things as the degree to which there is shared awareness about the desirability of certain attitudes and behaviors, the

structural arrangements and systems of rewards and punishments that implement and ensure conformity to norms, and the degree to which individuals accept these norms. (p. 72)

A central problem for the perceptual approach, then, is to find procedures to determine "shared awareness," and to determine how "shared awareness" and individual perceptions interact to form an environment. Even more important is what the "environment" really represents, and whether and how it influences behavior.

Factual Approaches

Demographic, financial, and other "objective" information about institutions can tell us a good deal about institutions and can also be quite misleading. For example, one might make many assumptions about the character of small Roman Catholic liberal arts colleges for women that are located in large cities. However, this category includes Alverno College in Milwaukee, Mundelein College in Chicago, and Mount Vernon College in the District of Columbia, which are very different institutions. Size, a variable found in many studies, and used as evidence of "validity" in others, has rather problematical significance. For example, Ohio State, with the largest enrollment in the United States on one campus, actually spends a larger *proportion* of its budget on instruction than many smaller institutions. Michigan State, another extremely large campus, has made great efforts to create separate"subcolleges" within the university.

More generally, the problem with size, as with "objective" measures, is that it is, in reality, no more objective than any other piece of information. That is, to be objectively valid, a piece of information must lead to accurate and meaningful interpretations of current phenomena and have logical and empirical connections to, or predictions of, other phenomena (Cronbach, 1969). What does an enrollment of a certain size mean? What are its psychological and sociological implications? Do the students at a college with an enrollment of 1,000 feel they are in an institution that is twice as "large" as one with an enrollment of 500? What about an enrollment of 40,000 compared to one of 20,000? The point is, without theories and evidence about the measuring of such factual variables, such as

Barker's behavior-setting theory (1968), we are using them based only on vague intuitions. In addition, "objective" data can vary to a much greater extent than is sometimes assumed. For example, there are many ways to calculate enrollment, based on varying definitions of students—full-time equivalents, etc.—and these can be calculated in different ways. For example, an institution may report one figure on enrollment to the legislature if an enrollment-driven budget system is used but may use quite another figure when it is calculating its average student-faculty ratio for reporting in recruiting literature.

Another example of the problematical meaning of factual measures is "affluence" or the wealth of the institution per student. Although one might assume that larger endowments and operating budgets would make life more pleasant for students, the monies may be spent in very different ways. In some calculations prepared by Charles Elton (1987) comparing the budgets of institutions with the highest rated graduate programs, the dollar amounts and the percentages of the budget spent on instruction, research, and service varied dramatically, even though all the institutions were relatively wealthy. Detailed analyses of the budgets of these institutions may reveal even greater differences in how funds are actually spent, which may indicate that interpretations of the categories based on their face value are based on erroneous assumptions. For example. much of the money spent on instruction may actually go to support some "stars" on the faculty, who may see very few students, or the funds spent for minority student affairs may chiefly go to administrators and their staffs, not to students. To illustrate the point another way, no one would confuse New York University and Dartmouth. However, the values of their endowments are very similar. In short, to properly use "factual" information to understand institutions, we need to examine it in considerable detail just to see if the data represent what we think they do. However, the most fundamental problem with "factual" information is that it is, in itself, *not* the environment. Factors such as size or affluence create the conditions for the environment but should be kept distinctly separate in our thinking about the environment. They are probably best considered contextual variables.

Theoretical Criticisms of Current Approaches to the College Environment

There are many approaches to the college environment, but few of them provide comprehensive accounts of how colleges and universities operate and influence students. To some extent this is understandable, since colleges and universities are very complex social institutions. Although the research efforts just reviewed are based on various notions of what is important to attend to in the college environment (e.g., needs and press, "fit," institutional "functioning," goals, the characteristics of people in the institution), they have, in fact, very few theoretical propositions that can be tested unambiguously—and fewer conceptions of *mechanisms* to explain how colleges operate and affect the people in them.

For example, the needs-press approach has essentially one proposition: that when students' personal characteristics "fit" or are "congruent" with the environment, the students are more satisfied, perform at a higher level, and have greater commitment to the institution. Why and how these consequences follow is not really explained; that is, there is no mechanism to explain the operations and effects of "congruence" except for a vague idea of needs being "met." Further, one might argue with the basic concept, based on the ideas of Feldman and Newcomb (1969), Chickering (1969), and such theorists as Loevinger (Wethersby, 1981) and Perry (1981), who emphasize the critical role of challenge in promoting change and growth in college students. That is, it is not *congruency* that is conducive to growth, achievement, and, eventually, satisfaction, but *incongruity*, that is, a challenging, if supportive, environment.

The approach used by Astin and Holland in the EAT, quoted earlier, and by Richards in subsequent work (Richards et al., 1970) is that characteristics of individuals compose the environment operationally (the basic assumption of the EAT is that "students make the college," according to Richards et al.). The sheer number of people in a given category of occupational or major choice therefore defines the environment. Holland's (1985) explanation is that, since people in a given vocational or major

group tend to have similar personalities, they will respond to many situations and problems in similar ways and will therefore create characteristic interpersonal environments. Again, it is unclear why this is supposed to be the case; that is, there is no mechanism other than an equally general idea of "reinforcement" to explain the contention. In other words, *how* do people with similar personalities create environments? Do they agree on goals? Do they create contingencies or rewards and punishments that promote certain behaviors and attitudes just by being together? How does reinforcement work?

Beyond the contention that the personal characteristics of the members define the environment, the remaining proposition of Holland's theory is, in structure, the same as in need-press theory: congruence. Holland (1985) does expand upon the concepts:

> People find environments reinforcing and satisfying when environmental patterns resemble their personality patterns. This situation makes for stability of behavior because persons receive a good deal of selective reinforcement of their behavior. The greater the discrepancy between people's personality patterns and environmental patterns, the more dissatisfying, uncomfortable, and destructive these interactions become. . . .

Incongruent interactions stimulate change in human behavior; conversely, congruent interactions encourage stability of behavior. Persons tend to change or become like the dominant persons in the environment. This tendency is greater, the greater the degree of congruence is between person and environment. Those persons who are most incongruent will be changed least. Or, the closer a person is to the core of an environment, the greater the influence of the environment.

A person resolves incongruence by seeking a new and congruent environment, by remaking the present environment, or by changing personal behavior and perceptions.

A. Differentiation and consistency of personality pattern as well as identity usually make for a change of environment in the face of an incongruent environment.

B. Persons with differentiated and consistent personality patterns and clear identity are more apt to remake the environment itself, if they cannot leave it, to achieve greater congruence. For example, people usually hire people whom they like or see as congenial.

C. Persons with undifferentiated and inconsistent personality patterns and diffuse identity tend to adapt to incongruence by changing their own behavior and personality pattern to achieve greater congruence with their environment.

D. A person's tendency to leave an environment increases as the incongruity of the interaction increases. (pp. 53–54)

Although there are some inconsistent propositions in this statement, the key *mechanism* lies in the phrase "reinforcing and satisfying" and "selective reinforcement," and in the idea that people who are sure of themselves will change their environments, while people who are unsure of themselves will be changed by their environments, although there is little explication of how this works.

The remainder of the approaches to the environment are chiefly atheoretical, although they sometimes have implicit theories, as have been noted when these approaches were described. Perhaps this atheoretical quality is due to the difficulty in conceptualizing something as complex as colleges' environments, as suggested in the following section.

The Road Ahead: Needed Theoretical and Empirical Work

The review of the majority of the work in analyzing and understanding the college environment covered a great deal of research activity through the 1960s that continued into the early 1970s. This work raised many fundamental issues, suggested in the description of the research, which seemed to have resulted in some very difficult questions, such as the following:

1. Is there such a phenomenon as a "college environment" that somehow includes and also exists beyond the perceptions and characteristics of the individuals in it?

2. How, specifically, can we logically and empirically deduce the characteristics of a group or an overall environment from the perceptions and characteristics of its members?

3. How, specifically, can we relate financial and organizational conditions to the characteristics of the overall environment?

4. What are the most salient and potent aspects of the environment? For which criteria?

5. How can we best conceive of these aspects and their interaction?

6. How, specifically, do environments influence the individuals in them?

7. What are the "subenvironments" on campuses (which may not correspond to traditional groupings at all)?

8. How do "subenvironments" interact with the overall environment?

9. How do we deal, conceptually and technically, with the multiple overlap among subenvironments? For example, a student may be a sophomore, an English major, a member of a fraternity, enrolled in ROTC, a member of an intramural team, and work part time in the book store. How can we assess the influence of these different possible subenvironments, let alone others which may escape our categorizations, as, for example, students who are fervent fans of a particular rock group?

It is easy to recognize the difficulty, perhaps even the intractability, of these questions about the overall environment, but we should note that many of them apply equally well to assessments of parts or details of colleges that are only apparently more easily conceptualized and assessed. However that may be, the key tasks seem to be to develop better theories of college environments and to deal with the problems of interrelating individual perceptions or characteristics to those of the global environment.

Organizational Research Contributions to Understanding and Assessing the Environment

Contributions of Organizational Research to Considerations of the Level of Analysis

One of the recurring problems in research on the college environment is the level of analysis. That is, how do we relate the levels of the individual, the subgroup, and the overall environment? Researchers in organizational behavior, particularly organizational climate, have attempted to deal with this issue in considerable detail. Rousseau (1985) described some of the complexities and distinctions. The object of the research (individual, subgroup, or total institution) is the *focal unit*. Research on the focal unit involves two kinds of levels: *level of measurement*, which refers to the unit to which data are directly attached (for example, self-reports of personal behaviors are usually at the individual level, the number of people is measured at the group level, the and degree of bureaucracy at the organizational level). The *level of analysis* is the unit to which data are assigned for hypothesis testing and statistical analysis.

However, Rousseau points out that, in practice, the level of measurment and the level of analysis may not correspond, and that neither may be the level to which generalizations are made. This leads to the error of misspecification which "occurs when we attribute an observed relationship other than the actual behavioral or responsive unit." For example, if faculty's scores on the IFI Democratic Governance Scale at a particular college were correlated with the number of articles they published, it would be a mistake to conclude that democratic governance leads to research productivity; that is, we risk misspecification. Another common error lies in the aggregation of data based on homogeneous groups which, when correlated, yield higher results than when individual data are used, or are actually artifacts due to other factors. For example, the correlation between college mean SAT scores and the percentage of seniors planning to go to graduate school is higher than the correlation between SAT scores and graduate school plans based on individuals. A related error is the cross-level fallacy, which exists when the same construct is used inappropriately to characterize phenomena at different levels. For example, *colleges* don't behave; *individuals* behave.

The contribution made by organizational researchers is to compose models and logical rules that provide for careful reasoning about evidence of the influence of one level on another. For example, the overall college culture may create group norms that influence individual behavior. The task for researchers is to assess each of these kinds of variables, (i.e., culture, group norms, and individual behaviors) and to analyze how they influence each other. As Burstein (1980) has pointed out, different variables may enter a model at different levels and may mean different things at different levels. For example, in the international mathematics study, the perceptions of the teachers' friendliness may mean something quite different when the individual student, the classroom, the school, the school system, or the country is the unit of analysis. Burstein (1980) and others have developed statistical procedures for giving the proper weight to these different levels in the prediction of achievement; that is, they have partitioned the variance.

Some of the models that organizational researchers have developed to deal with multiple levels include composition models, which relate nondependent variables across levels; cross-level models, which relate independent and dependent variables at different levels; and multilevel models, which relate independent and dependent variables generalizing across two or more levels (see Rousseau, 1985, for an explication of these models). An example of a composition model is provided by James (1982), who argues that when the definitions of organizational "climate," are the same at the individual and the unit levels, then psychological and organizational climate represent the same construct. For example, when professors' academic rigor means the same thing at the level of the individual student and at the level of the classroom as a whole, then it is the same construct. The criterion for equivalent definitions is perceptual agreement, according to James. When unit members perceive the unit in the same way, they share psychological meaning, perceptual agreement exists, and therefore, psychological and organizational climate represent the same construct. However, it is important to keep the levels distinct and carefully in mind when we study a particular criterion.

For example, Hulin and Rousseau (1980) report a series of studies that demonstrate these differences. Studying a phenomenon that is comparable to attrition among college students, employee turnover, they found that while economic factors explain 70% of the variance in unit-level turnover rates, individual attitudes and behavioral intentions explain 70% of the variance in *individual* turnover rates.

Cross-level models would include studies of such phenomena as the influence of college environmental characteristics, such as CUES community scores, on individual behavior, such as the individual's satisfaction with the social life of the college, and would use contextual moderators, such as a college's location or private-public status, that affect these relationships.

The third type of model, the multilevel model, examines phenomena and their consequences at individual, group, and organizational levels. For example, Staw, Sandelands, and Dutton (1981) examined the parallel processes by which individuals, groups, and organizations cope with adversity. The general process that was common across levels was that threat produced rigidity, a process that the behavior and the decisions at each level reinforced and solidified.

There are many other examples of these models in organizational research, but the lesson for researchers in higher education is that fellow researchers have wrestled with the same issues and types of constructs that concern researchers studying the college environment. Organizational researchers provide guidelines and techniques for careful reasoning about relating data, variables, and constructs from one level to another (see Roberts and Burstein, 1980, for discussions of statistical methods). One possible application would be to study in a single model the individual, peer-group, and college influences on students' aspirations toward graduate school.

Insights and Possibilities from Organizational Theory

In organizational research, there are many potential contributions of theory to the understanding and assessment of college environments. First is the variety of theories that have been considered (Benson, 1983; Hauser, 1980; Lawler, Nadler, and Cammann, 1980). Some of the more recent of these theorists include, at one extreme, the demythologizers, who argue that the idea that organizations are rationally articulated structures organized to meet specific goals is a myth, especially as it applies to educational institutions (e.g., Meyer and Rowan, 1978; Weick, 1976). What is important, according to this view, is to keep a particular coalition in power. Rituals and symbolism are used to convince others of the legitimacy and rationality of the organization. For example, a university has a variety of rituals

to assume legitimacy among other people, including hiring a ritually approved staff, offering a conventional curriculum, granting credentials, and satisfying accrediting agencies and professional associations. However, the university goes to great lengths to be sure that the core of the teaching and learning process is not evaluated by external groups. Given that the goal is simply the perpetuation of the organization, not the rational meeting of goals, the organization can allow opposing interests to exist and can use multiple nonaccountable administrative structures. However, this very nonrational structure allows the organization to be quite adaptable to changing conditions. The demythologizers would have us look less at organizational structures in colleges and more at rituals, symbols, and their functions, and at how colleges construct our views of reality.

Another class of recent theorists are termed the "politicizers" by Benson (1983), because they argue that power considerations, particularly the control of resources, are the key to organizations. For example, organizational decisions may be made as much to maintain or enhance the control of a power coalition as to enhance efficiency and effectiveness. Even technical decisions may be largely based on political considerations (Pfeffer, 1981). This group of theorists would argue that in order to understand why environments have the characteristics they do, we need to examine the underlying power coalitions in colleges at universities and how their relations affect decisions, rather than the colleges' purported educational goals.

Another group, the "ecologizers" (Aldrich, 1979; Hanf and Scharpf, 1978), go beyond the single organization to focus on interorganizational power-dependence relations. These theorists would have us concentrate on the relations between colleges, state legislatures, major economic groups, and professional agencies and examine how those relations influence the environment. For example, part of the growing environmental press for "vocationalism" on many campuses may stem from the demands of professional organizations and state or federal agencies.

Another group of innovative theorists are the "totalizers," who examine how organizations are entangled in the economic and political structure of the total society, as well as their role in the reproduction or maintenance of that structure.

The totalizers concentrate on the place of organizations, networks of organizations, and populations of organizations in the total social structure. Thus, they would have us examine how colleges and universities have been and are linked to technological and economic developments. They would then have us examine how these developments influence the internal structure of colleges, following a Weberian analysis (McNeil, 1978) or how they are part of a capitalistic domination, following a Marxian analysis (Clegg and Dunkerley, 1980). The view of colleges and universities in Collins's *The Credential Society* (1979) and the views of the true purpose of liberal education by Rossides (1984) can be considered in this category.

Other theorists have studied a variety of additional concepts, including that of organizational evolution (Tushman and Romanelli, 1985), focusing on considerations of forces for stability and forces for fundamental change, and identifying the reasons for periods of relative calm or convergence and periods of reorientation or divergence. These are associated with internal requirements for coordinated action and external demands or challenges for the organization. This research has led some even to propose institutional "life cycles," although this concept is controversial (Cameron and Whetten, 1983). In any case, this approach suggests determining where an organization is in its evolution in order to understand its priorities, structure, and functioning, Kimberly (1980) provides an example of this kind of analysis in a study of an innovative medical school.

Another approach, developed by Albert and Whetten (1985), is that of "extended metaphor analysis" in which the organization being analyzed is compared to a set of alternative organizations. Albert and Whetten developed this method when they attempted to define organizational identity, that is, how an organization answers the questions "Who are we?" and "What do we want to be?" They proposed that organizational identity is composed of a claimed central character, claimed distinctiveness from other organizations, and claimed continuity and consistency over time. However, these authors found that institutions can often have dual, even multiple, identities, illustrating this idea with the modern research university. To explicate the dual identity of the university, these authors used the metaphors of the church and the business organ-

ization. They compared these organizations in terms of their ideological claims, their socialization procedures, their organizational pattern, and, most important, their normative versus utilitarian functions. These have implications for decisions during times of retrenchment, attitudes toward leadership, and attitudes toward marketing the organization. The method of extended metaphor analysis, then, also suggests different ways of viewing the college environment.

Another potentially useful approach is the study of organizational demography (Pfeffer, 1983). Particularly appropriate for the faculty environment, this approach examines the demographic characteristics of the staff, such as age, sex, ethnicity, SES, and especially length of service. These characteristics influence such variables as acceptance of innovation and adaptability, the form of control employed and the size of the administrative staff, cohort identity, and mobility aspirations. The effects of organizational demography in colleges can be seen in such areas as the "graying of the professoriate" and the increasing numbers of "new students" and "returning students." Although these factors have been discussed on a national level, the effects of the demographics of the student body, the professors, and the administrators on individual college environments have not been explored systematically. However, it seems very plausible that the environments of colleges with a high proportion of returning or older students would be different from colleges with low proportions. These possibilities are worth exploring.

One significant contribution of organizational behavior research is the explication of the idea of *fit*. As described by Nadler and Tushman (1980), there are at least six definitions of *fit*, as shown in Table 6-1.

The drawback of this delineation of the varieties of fit, or congruence, is that it does not show how to deal with multiple fits. For example, a student may fit quite well in a residence group which has an antiacademic, social orientation, which does not fit with the college's academic orientation. When the residence group is involved in a "task" that has an academic purpose, there may be a further lack of fit. Situations like this may explain why studies of congruence have obtained such disappointing results. That is, a student can be congruent with some aspects of a college and incongruent with others. It may be the total *level* of congruency, or his or her

TABLE 6-1
Definitions of Fits

Fit	The issues
Individual-organization	To what extent individual needs are met by the organizational arrangements, to what extent individuals hold clear or distorted perceptions of organizational structures, and the convergence of individual and organizational goals
Individual-task	To what extent the needs of individuals are met by the tasks, to what extent individuals have skills and abilities to meet task demands
Individual-informal organization	To what extent individual needs are met by the informal organization, to what extent the informal organization makes use of individual resources, consistent with informal goals
Task-organization	Whether the organizational arrangements are adequate to meet the demands of the task, whether organizational arrangements tend to motivate behavior consistent with task demands
Task-informal organization	Whether the informal organization structure facilitates task performance, whether it hinders or promotes meeting the demands of the task
Organization-informal organization	Whether the goals, rewards, and structures of the informal organization are consistent with those of the formal organization

Source: Nadler and Tushman (1980).

degree of congruency with the elements of the environment, that is most *important* to him or her, or congruence with the areas that are most *salient* to a particular criterion that will play the largest role. Although it is extremely difficult to distinguish among these multiple interactions in our research, it is important to attempt to assess their influence.

In sum, organizational behavior research includes many concepts that can be applied to several of the problems in the study of the college environment that were identified in the review of research. These include clarification of the meaning of perceptions, clarity concerning the level of analysis, and recognition of the multiple meanings of *fit*. In addition, organizational theory provides many useful perspectives on the college environment, suggesting reconceptualizations of their structure and functioning.

Conclusion

This review of research on the college environment has discussed a wide variety of concepts and assessment techniques. This variety might be expected. The "environment" can be an elusive concept, since it includes such components as campus mores and traditions; standards of achievement; political atmosphere; physical facilities and architecture; values and priorities; organizational structure; and long-standing issues and controversies (Dressell, 1976). In addition, each of these components affects members of the environment through other people, so that the characteristics of the individual members of the environment help determine its overiding features. For example, a college could have stringent academic standards, but the environment for learning would be very different if these standards were upheld by friendly, supportive faculty or by martinets. Although it is important to analyze the separate components and to distinguish between general characteristics and individual behaviors, it is an even more important and difficult task to analyze the ways in which they interact to form an overall "evironment" (Glick, 1985). A related conceptual problem is whether it is the local or "proximal" environment or subenvironment or the total or "distal" environment or "climate" that is most important (Pace and Baird, 1966; Moran and Volkwein, 1987).

Another issue with far-reaching consequences is whether we conceive of the environment as an individual psychological variable or a group of organizational variables. In addition to the problems in analysis and statistics that this issue creates, it leads to very different consequences for our research methods. If we consider the environment a psychological issue, we might attempt to examine each individual's ideas about the environment by assessing the person's "construct space," akin to semantic space. We would be less concerned with the "objectivity" of the descriptions of the environment than with the consequences for the individual's behavior. We would examine the individual's coping mechanisms and other psychological reactions to the environment. (Moos, 1979, has proposed something along this line.) We would also turn to environmental psychology for insights and methods (e.g., Holahan, 1986). If we consider the environment as a sociological or social psychological issue, we would concentrate on identifying norms, sanctions, controls for deviancy, patterns of affiliation, power relations, and so on, using the group or the organization as the unit of analysis.

Since the interaction of the individual with his or her environments involves many complexities and subtleties, consideration should be given to qualitative research methods (Jacob, 1987). These methods include cognitive anthropology, symbolic interaction, and ethnography. Ethnography seems particularly appropriate to the analysis of the environment. Originally developed in anthropology, ethnography is today an "extended family" of techniques, but its key focus is on analyzing the cultural patterns of a defined group and on describing the culture as it is seen by participants in the culture (Hammersley and Atkinson, 1983). Therefore, it involves participation, observation, interviewing, and documentation of behaviors and attitudes (Clammer, 1984). Although it has rarely been applied to higher education, ethnography has been profitably used to study medical education (Atkinson, 1981) and such educational units as high schools (e.g., Peshkin, 1978).

The problem is, of course, that the "environment" is where the individual mind, the social group, and the organizational structure meet and interact. And these interactions create many conceptual and statistical difficulties. However, it seems that, in order to understand how colleges educate and influence their students, we will have to deal with these difficulties. The recent research in organizational

behavior offers some very helpful insights and techniques. However, the greatest need is for comprehensive theories that will allow us to deal with the complexities of the person-environment interaction in all its richness.

More specifically, my opinion is that future research will be more fruitful if it moves in certain directions. The first is to continue the trend of movement away from analyses of specific measures and toward the identification of the psychological and social *processes* that create the environment. That is, it would be profitable to concentrate on understanding how students are attracted to one another, how informal groups form, how cohesiveness operates, how peers influence one another, how norms are formed and enforced, how people become identified with their group and college, how social judgments are formed, and how the social roles on campuses conflict with or reinforce each other. It would also be very useful to have better ways of identifying the real subgroups on campuses. That is, almost all research involving college subgroups uses nominal groups, such as the residence group, the major field, and student organizations, which may not have any true social interaction and cohesiveness. Research projects that could identify the real norm and peer groups of students would be very valuable. A related advance in research methodology would be technique for assessing students' degree of *involvement* in different groups and methods of assessing their *saliency* in different areas. For example, a student might base his or her ideas of the right number of hours to study on interactions with the members of an informal study group in a math class but might base his or her drinking behavior upon a group of friends in his or her residence hall. Different groups are salient for different behaviors.

A more general issue is that of the general level of involvement in campus life. Many students today experience little of the college. Nationally, 42% of students are enrolled part time. Of freshmen, 40% do not live on campus, and this percentage increases as students progress toward their degrees. As commuting and working students, they come to college only to attend classes or to do required assignments. What is the "environment" for these students? Clearly, our usual conceptions of the environment, which are based on the fully involved student, are inadequate for understanding how the college affects such students.

Whatever the topic pursued, researchers should keep the distinctions between *levels* of measurement in mind and should develop measures that are appropriate for the individual psychological environment, the group social-psychological environment, and the global or college culture environment. Likewise, researchers should use statistical methods that properly link data at different levels.

Finally, progress can be made if we recognize that a good deal of research bears on the analysis of the college environment, even if it is concerned with another topic. For example, a recent study of the characteristics of productive research departments included a variety of measure of the environments of graduate programs (Baird, 1986). These kinds of research should be brought into our thinking about the environment. Likewise, I hope this review will encourage researchers working on a variety of topics in higher education to include assessments of environments in their designs.

In summary, this review of the extensive history of research efforts to understand and assess the college environment indicates that the general concept is alive and well and is living in the minds of more than a few researchers.

References

Albert, S., and Whetten, D. A. (1985). Organizational identity. In Cummings and Staw, *Research in Organizational Behavior*, Vol. 7.

Aldrich, H. E. (1979). *Organizations and Environments*. Englewood Cliffs, NJ: Prentice-Hall.

Anderson, R. E. (1983). *Finance and Effectiveness: A Study of College Environments*. Princeton, NJ: Educational Testing Service.

Ashforth, B. E. (1985). Climate formation: issues and extensions. *Academy of Management Review* 10: 837–847.

Astin, A. W. (1962). An empirical characterization of higher educational institutions. *Journal of Educational Psychology* 53: 224–229.

Astin, A. W. (1963a). Differential effects on the motivation of talented students to pursue the Ph.D. degree. *Journal of Educational Psychology* 54: 63–71.

Astin, A. W. (1963b). Further validation of the environmental assessment technique. *Journal of Educational Psychology* 54: 217–226.

Astin, A. W. (1965). *Who Goes Where to College?* Chicago: Science Research Associates.

Astin, A. W. (1968). *The College Environment*. Washington, DC: American Council on Education.

Astin, A. W. (1972). *Manual for the Inventory of College Activities*. Minneapolis: National Computer Systems.

Astin, A. W., and Holland, J. (1961). The environmental assessment technique: a way to measure college environments. *Journal of Educational Psychology* 52: 308–316.

Astin, A. W., and Panos, R. J. (1969). *The Educational and Vocational Development of College Students*. Washington, DC: American Council on Education.

Atkinson, P. (1981). *The Clinical Experience*. Farnsborough, U.K.: Gower.

Baird, L. L. (1974). The practical utility of measures of college environments. *Review of Educational Research* 44(3): 307–329.

Baird, L. L. (1986). What characterizes a productive research department? *Research in Higher Education* 25(3): 211–225.

Baird, L. L. (1987). The undergraduate experience: commonalities and differences among colleges. Paper presented at 1987 Meetings of the Association for the Study of Higher Education, February, San Diego.

Baird, L. L., and Hartnett, R. T. (1980). *Understanding Student and Faculty Life*. San Francisco: Jossey-Bass.

Ballou, R. A. (1985). An analysis of freshman students perceptions of the living environment, behavior, and academic achievement in the residence hall systems of twelve colleges and universities. Paper read at National Association of Student Personnel Administrators Meetings.

Barker, R. G. (1968). *Ecological Psychology: Concepts and Methods for Studying the Environment of Human Behavior*. Stanford, CA: Stanford University Press.

Barton, A. H. (1960). Organizational measurement and its bearing on the study of college environments. *Research Monograph No. 2*. New York: College Entrance Examination Board.

Benson, J. K. (1983). Paradigm and praxis in organizational analysis. In Cummings and Staw, *Research in Organizational Behavior*, Vol. 5.

Berdie, R. F. (1967). A university is a many-faceted thing. *Personnel and Guidance Journal* 45: 269–277.

Betz, E. L., Klingensmith, J. E., and Menne, J. W. (1970). The measurement and analysis of college student satisfaction. *Measurement and Evaluation in Guidance* 3: 110–118.

Boyer, E. L. (1987). *College: The Undergraduate Experience in America*. New York: Harper & Row.

Burstein, L. (1980). The analysis of multilevel data in educational research and evaluation. In D. E. Berliner (ed.), *Review of Research in Education*, Vol. 8. Washington, DC: American Educational Research Association.

Cameron, K. S., and Whetten, D. A. (1983). Models of the organizational life cycle: applications to higher education. *Review of Higher Education* 6: 269–299.

Centra, J. A. (1970). The college environment revisited: current descriptions and a comparison of three methods of assessment. *Research Bulletin 70–44*. Princeton, NJ: Educational Testing Service.

Centra, J. A. (1973). Comparison of three methods of assessing college environments. *Journal of Educational Psychology* 63: 56–62.

Chickering, A. W. (1969). *Education and Identity*. San Francisco: Jossey-Bass.

Chickering, A. W. (1972). Undergraduate academic experience. *Journal of Educational Psychology* 63(2): 134–143.

Chickering, A. W., McDowell, J., and Campagna, D. (1969). Institutional differences and student development. *Journal of Educational Psychology* 60: 315–326.

Clammer, J. (1984). Approaches to ethnographic research. In R. F. Ellen (ed.), *Ethnographic Research: A Guide to General Conduct*. London: Academic Press.

Clark, B. R., and Trow, M. (1966). The organizational context. In T. M. Newcomb and E. K. Wilson (eds.), *College Peer Groups: Problems and Prospects for Research*. Chicago: Aldine.

Clegg, S., and Dunkerley, D., eds. (1980). *Organization, Class and Control*. Boston: Routledge & Kegan Paul.

Collins, R. (1979). *The Credential Society*. New York: Academic Press.

Creager, J. A., and Astin, A. W. (1968). Alternative methods of describing characteristics of colleges and universities. *Educational and Psychological Measurement* 28: 719–734.

Cronbach, L. J. (1969). *Essentials of Psychological Testing*. New York: Harper & Row.

Cummings, L. L., and Staw, B. M., eds. (annual, 1978–). *Research in Organizational Behavior*. Greenwich, CT: JAI Press.

Deutch, M., and Krauss, R. M. (1965). *Theories in Social Psychology*. New York: Basic Books.

Doucet, J. A. (1977). The implications of rank-ordering on the Clark-Trow typology. *Journal of College Student Personnel* 18(1): 25–31.

Dressell, P. L. (1976). *Handbook of Academic Evaluation*. San Francisco: Jossey-Bass.

Elton, C. F. (1987). Unpublished analyses, University of Kentucky.

Feldman, K. A. (1972). Measuring college environments: some uses of path analysis. *American Educational Research Journal* 8: 51–70.

Feldman, K. A., and Newcomb, T. M. (1969). *The Impact of College on Students*. San Francisco: Jossey-Bass.

Georgion, P. (1973). The goal paradigm and notes toward a counter paradigm. *Administrative Science Quarterly* 18: 291–310.

Gerst, M. S., and Sweetwood, H. (1973). Correlates of dormitory social climate. *Environment and Behavior* 5: 440–464.

Glick, W. H. (1985). Conceptualizing and measuring organizational and psychological climate: pitfalls in multilevel research. *Academy of Management Review* 10: 601–616.

Gross, E., and Grambsch, P. V. (1968). *University Goals and Academic Power*. Washington, DC: American Council on Education.

Gross, E., and Grambsch, P. V. (1974). *Changes in University Organization, 1964–1971*. New York: McGraw-Hill.

Guion, R. M. (1973). A note on organizational climate. *Organizational Behavior and Human Performance* 9: 120–125.

Haines, V. J., Deifhoff, G. M., LaBeff, E. G., and Clark, R. E. (1986). College cheating: immaturity, lack of commitment and the neutralizing attitudes. *Research in Higher Education* 25(4): 342–354.

Hammersley, M., and Atkinson, P. (1983). *Ethnography: Principles in Practice*. New York: Tavistock.

Hanf, K., and Scharpf, F., eds. (1978). *Interorganizational Policy Making, Limits to Coordination and Central Control*. Beverly Hills: Sage.

Hartnett, R. T., and Centra, J. A. (1974). Faculty views of the academic environment: Situational vs. institutional perspectives. *Sociology of Education* 47: 159–169.

Hauser, D. L. (1980). Comparison of different models for organizational analysis. In Lawler et al., *Organizational Assessment*.

Hearn, J. C., and Moos, R. H. (1976). Social climate and major choice: A test of Holland's theory in university student living groups. *Journal of Vocational Behavior* 8: 293–305.

Holahan, C. J. (1986). Environmental psychology. *Annual Review of Psychology, 1986* 37: 381–407.

Holland, J. L. (1962). Some explorations of a theory of vocational choice: one-and two year longitudinal studies. *Psychological Monographs* 76(26): entire issue.

Holland, J. L. (1966). *The Psychology of Vocational Choice: A Theory of Personality Types and Model Environments.* Waltham, MA: Blaisdell.

Holland, J. L. (1973). *Making Vocational Choices: A Theory of Careers.* Englewood Cliffs, NJ: Prentice-Hall.

Holland, J. L. (1985). *Making Vocational Choices* (2nd ed.). Englewood Cliffs, NJ: Prentice-Hall.

Huebner, L. A. (1980). Interaction of student and campus. In U. Delworth and G. R. Hanson (eds.), *Student Services: A Handbook for the Profession.* San Francisco: Jossey-Bass.

Huebner, L. A., and Corrazini, J. G. (1978). Ecomapping: a dynamic model for intentional campus design. *Journal Supplement Abstract Service.* Am. Psychol. Assn.

Hulin, C. L., and Rousseau, D. M. (1980). Analyzing infrequent events: once you find them your troubles begin. In R. H. Roberts and L. Burstein (eds.), *Issues in Aggregation: New Directions for Methodology of Social and Behavioral Science,* Vol. 6. San Francisco: Jossey-Bass.

Jacob, E. (1987). Qualitative research traditions: a review. *Review of Educational Research* 57(1): 1–50.

James, L. R. (1982). Aggregation bias in estimates of perceptual agreement. *Journal of Applied Psychology* 67: 219–229.

James, L. R., and Jones, A. P. (1974). Organizational climate: a review of theory and research. *Psychological Bulletin* 81: 1096–1112.

Johannesson, R. E. (1973). Some problems in the measurement of organizational climate. *Organizational Behavior and Human Performance* 10: 118–144.

Kimberly, J. R. (1980). Initiation, innovation, and institutionalization in the creation process. In J. R. Kimberly and R. H. Miles (eds.), *The Organizational Life Cycle.* San Francisco: Jossey-Bass.

Knapp, R. H., and Goodrich, H. B. (1952). *Origins of American Scientists.* Chicago: University of Chicago Press.

Knapp, R. H., and Greenbaum, J. J. (1953). *The Younger American Scholar.* Chicago: University of Chicago Press.

Lawler, E. E., Nadler, D. A., and Cammann, C., eds. (1980). *Organizational Assessment.* New York: Wiley.

Long, S. (1976). Sociopolitical ideology as a determinant of students' perceptions of the university. *Higher Education* 5: 423–435.

Long, S. (1977). Dimensions of student academic alienation. *Educational Administration Quarterly* 13: 16–20.

Longino, C. F., and Kart, C. S. (1974). The college fraternity: an assessment of theory and research. *Journal of College Student Personnel* 14: 118–125.

Lord, R. G. (1985). An information processing approach to social perceptions, leadership, and behavioral measurement in organizations. In Cummings and Staw, *Research in Organizational Behavior,* Vol. 7.

Lunneborg, C. E. (1978). Review of the institutional goals inventory. In O. K. Buros (ed.), *The Eighth Mental Measurements Yearbook.* Highland Park, NJ: Gryphon Press.

McNeil, K. (1978). Understanding organizational power: building on the Weberian legacy. *Administrative Science Quarterly* 23: 65–90.

Menne, J. W. (1967). Techniques for evaluating the college environment. *Journal of Educational Measurement* 4: 219–225.

Meyer, J. W., and Rowan, B. (1978). The structure of educational organizations. In W. Meyer and Associates (eds.), *Environments and Organizations.* San Francisco: Jossey-Bass.

Moos, R. H. (1979). *Evaluating Educational Environments.* San Francisco: Jossey-Bass.

Moos, R. H., et al. (1975). A typology of university student living groups. *Journal of Educational Psychology* 67: 359–367.

Moos, R. H., and Bromet, E. (1978). Relation of patient attributes to perceptions of the treatment environment. *Journal of Consulting and Clinical Psychology* 46: 350–351.

Moos, R. H., and Van Dort, B. (1977). Physical and emotional symptoms and campus health center utilization. *Social Psychiatry* 12: 107–115.

Moran, E. T., and Volkwein, I. (1987). Organizational climate of institutions of higher education: construct determination and relationship to organizational effectiveness criteria. Paper presented at Association for the Study of Higher Education meetings, San Diego.

Murray, H. A. (1938). *Explorations in Personality.* New York: Oxford University Press.

Nadler, D. A. (1980). Role of models in organizational assessment. In Lawler et al., *Organizational Assessment.*

Nadler, D. A., and Tushman, M. L. (1980). A congruence model for organizational assessment. In Lawler et al., *Organizational Assessment.*

Naylor, J. P., Pritchard, R. D., and Ilgen, D. R. (1980). *A Theory of Behavior in Organizations.* New York: Academic Press.

Nettles, M. T., Thoeny, A. R., and Gosman, E. F. (1986). Comparative and predictive analyses of black and white students' college achievement and experiences. *Journal of Higher Education* 57: 289–318.

Pace, C. R. (1966). *Comparisons of CUES Results from Different Groups of Reporters*. (College Entrance Examination Board Report No. 1.) Los Angeles: University of California.

Pace, C. R. (1969). *College and University Environment Scales: Technical Manual* (2nd ed.). Princeton, NJ: Educational Testing Service.

Pace, C. R. (1972). *Education and Evangelism: A Profile of Protestant Colleges*. New York: McGraw-Hill.

Pace, C. R. (1974). *The Demise of Diversity? A Comparative Profile of Eight Types of Institutions*. New York: McGraw-Hill.

Pace, C. R. (1984). *Measuring the Quality of College Student Experiences*. Los Angeles: UCLA-Higher Education Research Institute.

Pace, C. R. (1987). *CSEQ: Test Manual and Norms: College Student Experiences Questionnaire*. Los Angeles: The Center for the Study of Evaluation, Graduate School of Education, University of California, Los Angeles.

Pace, C. R., and Baird, L. L. (1966). Attainment patterns in the environmental press of college subcultures. In T. M. Newcomb and E. K. Wilson (eds.), *College Peer Groups*. Chicago: Aldine.

Pace, C. R., and Stern, G. G. (1958). An approach to the measurement of psychological characteristics of college environments. *Journal of Educational Psychology* 49: 269–277.

Pascarella, E. T. (1974). Students' perceptions of the college environment: how well are they understood by administrators? *Journal of College Student Personnel* 15: 370–375.

Pascarella, E. T. (1984). College environmental influences on students' educational aspirations. *Journal of Higher Education* 55: 751–771.

Pascarella, E. T. (1985). College influences on learning and cognitive development. In J. Smart (ed.), *Higher Education: Handbook of Theory and Research*, Vol. 1. New York: Agathon Press.

Pascarella, E., and Terenzini, P. (1978). Student-faculty informal relationships and freshman-year educational outcomes. *Journal of Educational Research* 71: 183–189.

Pascarella, E., and Terenzini, P. (1980). Student-faculty and student-peer relationships as mediators of the structural effects of undergraduate residence arrangement. *Journal of Educational Research* 73: 344–353.

Pascarella, E., and Terenzini, P. (1983). Predicting voluntary freshmen-year persistence/ withdrawal behavior in a residential university: a path analytic validation of Tinto's model. *Journal of Educational Psychology* 75: 215–226.

Perry, W. G. (1981). Cognitive and ethical growth: the making of meaning. In A. W. Chickering and Associates (eds.), *The Modern American College*. San Francisco: Jossey-Bass.

Peshkin, A. (1978). *Growing Up American: Schooling and the Survival of Community*. Chicago: University of Chicago Press.

Peterson, M. W., Cameron, K. S., Mets, L. A., Jones, P., and Ettington, D. (1986). *The Organizational Context for Teaching and Learning: A Review of the Research Literature*. Ann Arbor, MI: National Center for Research to Improve Postsecondary Teaching and Learning.

Peterson, R. E. (1968). *College Student Questionnaire: Technical Manual*. Princeton: Educational Testing Service.

Peterson, R. E., et al. (1970). *Institutional Functioning Inventory: Preliminary Technical Manual*. Princeton: Educational Testing Service.

Peterson, R. E., and Uhl, N. P. (1977). *Formulating College and University Goals: A Guide for Using the IGI*. Princeton: Educational Testing Service.

Pfeffer, J. (1981). *Power in Organizations*. Marshfield, MA: Pittman.

Pfeffer, J. (1982). *Organizations and Organization Theory*. Boston: Pittman.

Pfeffer, J. (1983). Organizational demography. In Cummings and Staw, *Research in Organizational Behavior*, Vol. 5.

Richards, J. M., Jr., and Braskamp, L. A. (1969). Who goes where to junior college. In L. A. Munday (ed.), *The Two-Year College and Its Students: An Empirical Report*. Iowa City: American College Testing Program.

Richards, J. M., Jr., Rand, L. M., and Rand, L. P. (1966). Description of junior colleges. *Journal of Educational Psychology* 57: 207–214.

Richards, J. M., Jr., Rand, L. M., and Rand, L. P. (1968). A description of medical college environments. *American Educational Research Journal* 5: 647–658.

Richards, J. M., Jr., Seligman, R., and Jones, P. K. (1970). Faculty and curriculum as measures of college environment. *Journal of Educational Psychology* 61: 324–332.

Roberts, K. H., and Burstein, K., eds. (1980). *Issues in Aggregation: New Directions for Methodology of Social and Behavioral Science*, Vol. 6. San Francisco: Jossey-Bass.

Rossides, D. W. (1984). What is the purpose of education: the worthless debate continues. *Change* 16(3): 14–46.

Rousseau, D. M. (1985). Issues of level in organizational research: multi-level and cross-level perspectives. In Cummings and Staw, *Research in Organizational Behavior*, Vol. 7.

Sasajima, M., Davis, J. A., and Peterson, R. E. (1968). Organized student protest and institutional climate. *American Educational Research Journal* 5: 291–304.

Schneider, B. (1975). Organizational climates: an essay. *Personnel Psychology* 28: 447–479.

Schneider, B. (1983). Work climates: an interactionist perspective. In N. W. Feimer and E. S. Geller (eds.), *Environmental Psychology: Directions and Perspectives*. New York: Praeger.

Staw, B., Sandelands, L. E., and Dutton, J. E. (1981). Threat-rigidity effects in organizational behavior: a multi-level analysis. *Administrative Science Quarterly* 26: 501–524.

Stern, G. G. (1970). *People in Context*. New York: Wiley.

Study Group on the Conditions of Excellence in American Higher Education. (1984). *Involvement in Learning*. Washington, DC: U.S. Department of Education.

Terenzini, P. T., and Pascarella, E. T. (1977). An assessment of the construct validity of the Clark-Trow typology of college student subcultures. *American Educational Research Journal* 14: 225–248.

Thistlethwaite, D. T. (1960). College press and changes in study plans of talented students. *Journal of Educational Psychology* 51: 222–234.

Thistlethwaite, D. T. (1963). Rival hypotheses for explaining the effects of different learning environments. *Journal of Educational Psychology* 53: 310–315.

Thistlethwaite, D. T., and Wheeler, N. (1966). Effects of teaching and peer subcultures upon student aspirations. *Journal of Educational Psychology* 57: 35–47.

Tinto, V. (1987). *Leaving College*. Chicago: University of Chicago Press.

Tushman, M. L., and Romanelli, E. (1985). Organizational evolution: a metamorphosis model of convergence and reorientation. In Cummings and Staw, *Research in Organizational Behavior*, Vol. 7.

Van deVen, A. H., and Drayin, R. (1985). The concept of fit in contingency theory. In Cummings and Staw, *Research in Organizational Behavior*, Vol. 7.

Walsh, W. B. (1973). *Theories of Person-Environment Interaction: Implications for the College Student*. Iowa City: American College Testing Program.

Warren, J. R., and Roelfs, P. J. (1972). Student reactions to college: the development of a questionnaire through which junior college students describe their college experiences. *Research Project Report 72–23*. Princeton: Educational Testing Service.

Weick, K. (1976). Educational organizations as loosely coupled systems. *Administrative Science Quarterly* 21: 1–19.

Weick, K. (1977). Repunctuating the problem. In P. S. Goodman and J. M. Pennings (eds.), *New Perspectives on Organizational Effectiveness*. San Francisco: Jossey-Bass.

Wethersby, R. P. (1981). Ego development. In A. W. Chickering and Associates (eds.), *The Modern American College*. San Francisco: Jossey-Bass.

Wilcox, B., and Holahan, C. J. (1976). Social ecology of the megadorm in university student housing. *Journal of Educational Psychology* 68: 453–458.

Wilder, D. H., Hoyt, A. K., Surbeck, B. S., Wilder, J. C., and Carney, P. I. (1986). Greek affiliation and attitude change in college students. *Journal of College Student Personnel* 27(6): 510–518.

Williams, T. E. (1986). Optimizing student-institution fit: an interactionist perspective. *College and University* 61: 141–152.

Winston, R. B., Jr., Hutson, G. S., and McCaffry, S. S. (1980). Environmental influences on fraternity academic achievement. *Journal of College Student Personnel* 21: 449–455.

Wolfle, D. (1954). *America's Resources of Specialized Talent*. New York: Harper Bros.

CHAPTER 7

Theories of Student Departure Revisited

Vincent Tinto

The past decade has witnessed a marked increase in studies of student retention in higher education. Fueled in large measure by the onset of declining numbers of college entrants, there has been renewed interest in the study of the forces that shape student departure from institutions of higher education. Understandably, there has also been increased interest in the construction of models, and sometimes theories, of student departure to explain both the patterning and the longitudinal occurrence of student departure from varying institutions of higher education.[1]

With this explosion in attention has come some confusion. While we have learned much about the character of student departure, the construction of different theories has led to some disagreement, if not confusion, about the appropriate explanation of student departure in higher education. That this should be the case is understandable, indeed desirable. The advance of our understanding of social phenomena is always the result of our first opening up new ways of thinking about explaining the phenomena we observe. The inevitable conflict that arises between different views is a necessary part of the process through which new insights into social phenomena are gained. New questions are almost always the sources of new answers. But at some point in our debate, we must stand back to reassess where we have been and where we seek to go in the future. At some stage of our work, we need to develop a more synthetic view of departure that integrates the diverse findings of the past and points our way to new questions for future inquiry.

It is to that long-term goal, that of eventually producing a more synthetic theory of student departure, that this chapter is directed. Specifically, it is concerned with the first step in the process of synthesis, namely, the critical assessment.[2] In the pages that follow, we first direct our attention to a critical review of the existing models that have been espoused as providing an explanation for the process of student departure from higher education. That review is followed by an extended discussion of some of the changes that would have to be included in a new theoretical synthesis of student departure. To that end, the outline of a possible synthetic model of student departure is proposed, one that highlights the interactive, longitudinal character of student experience in institutions of higher education. The chapter concludes with an agenda for future research that identifies the critical questions that need be resolved if we are to make further advances in our understanding of the process of student departure from higher education.

The State of Current Theory on Student Departure

One way of distinguishing theories of student departure from one another is by the emphasis they give to different individual and environmental forces in the shaping of student behavior. Roughly

"Theories of Student Departure Revisited." Reprinted from *Higher Education: Handbook of Theory and Research*, (1986), by permission of Kluwer Academic Publishers.

speaking, it is possible to categorize past theories as falling into one of five types of theory, each with its own particular focus and level of analysis. These can be described by the terms *psychological, societal, economic, organizational,* and *interactional.*[3]

The first, psychological, is the category of theory that, as the name implies, emphasizes the role of individual psychological attributes in the departure process. The second, third, and fourth are theories that emphasize in different ways the impact of environmental forces on student behavior. Organizational theories stress the influence of immediate organizational characteristics on student behavior, whereas societal and economic theories look toward broader social and economic attributes and the impact that external social and economic forces have on the process of student departure. The last category, interactional, is the form of theory that sees student behavior as being influenced both by individual attributes and by environmental forces, especially those within the immediate setting of the institution in which students find themselves.

Psychological Theories of Student Departure

Psychological models of student departure, those that dominated our thinking about retention in the decades immediately following World War II, argue that student behavior is primarily the reflection of student attributes, specifically those that describe the individual's psychological characteristics. Models such as those by Summerskill (1962) and Marks (1967) point to the importance of intellectual attributes as shaping the individual's ability to meet the academic challenges of college life, while those by Heilbrun (1965), Rose and Elton (1966), Hanson and Taylor (1970), Rossmann and Kirk (1970), Hannah (1971), and Waterman and Waterman (1972) stress the role that personality, motivational, and dispositional characteristics play in influencing the student's ability and/or willingness to meet those challenges.

Typically, research of the psychological type has sought to distinguish stayers and leavers in terms of attributes of personality that help account for their differing response to supposedly similar educational circumstances. Heilbrun (1965), for example, in comparing stayers and leavers, argued that dropouts were likely to be less mature, more likely to rebel against authority, and more likely to be less serious in their endeavors and less dependable than persisters. More to the point, Rose and Elton (1966) argued that student leaving is an immediate reflection of maladjustment and directed hostility. Students with high hostility who are unable to adjust to the college tend to direct their hostility for their problems toward the institution and either leave higher education altogether or transfer to another institution.

However framed, all these views of departure share a common theme, namely, that retention and departure are primarily the reflection of individual actions and therefore are largely due to the ability or willingness of the individual to complete successfully the tasks associated with college attendance. More important, such models invariably see student departure as reflecting some shortcoming and/or weakness in the individual. Leaving is, in this view, assumed to be reflective of a personal failure of the individual to measure up to the demands of college life. Though external forces may matter, the individual alone bears the primary responsibility for persistence.

There is, of course, some merit to this view of student departure. There can be little doubt that individual actions matter and that differences in intellectual and personality attributes influence student persistence. But at the same time, there is no substantial body of evidence to suggest, as do these theories, that leavers are consistently different in personality from stayers or that such a thing as a "dropout" personality exists. Rather, one is led to the conclusion that observed differences in personality attributes of stayers and leavers are situationally determined.

The work of Sharp and Chason (1978) is, in this respect, most revealing. Though their first study of departure showed differences between stayers and leavers in personality scores on the Minnesota Multiphasic Personality Inventory, their attempt to replicate the results on a subsequent sample of students in the same institution proved negative. As a result, they and others (e.g., Cope and Hannah; 1975) concluded that the significant relationships shown in prior research between broad personality traits and persistence were situational and sample-specific.

The difficulty, then, with the psychological view of student leaving is that it is not truly explanatory. Because it has largely ignored the impact situations may have on student behaviors, the psychological perspective does not provide a suitable model of departure for either institutional research or institutional policy. Though it does point up the necessary role of personality in individual responses to educational situations, this perspective has not yet been able to tell us why it is that some personality attributes appear to describe differences among stayers and leavers in some situations but not in others. As a result, it does not yet provide a suitable guide either for researchers who seek to better explain the departure of different types of students from different types of institutional settings or for institutional officials who seek to enhance student retention by altering institutional actions.

Societal Theories of Student Departure

At the other end of the spectrum from psychological theories are environmental theories of student departure which emphasize the impact of wider social and economic forces on the behavior of students in institutions of higher education. One variant of the environmental perspective, societal theories of student departure, sees educational attainment as only one part of the broader process of social attainment and the success or failure of students in higher education as being molded by the same forces that shape social success generally. Rather than focusing on individual dispositions, societal theories have concerned themselves with those attributes of individuals, institutions, and society, such as social status, race, institutional prestige, and opportunity structures, that describe the person's and the institution's place in the broader social hierarchy of society.

But the manner in which they have done so has varied considerably. Societal theories of departure, like the social theories from which they derive, have differed because their view of the underlying causes of social success has also differed. Take, for example, the work of Karabel (1972) and Pincus (1980). Like most conflict theorists, these authors have argued that social institutions generally and higher education in particular are structured to serve the interests of the prevailing social and educational elites. In their view, student departure must be understood not as an isolated individual event but as part of a larger process of social stratification, which operates to preserve existing patterns of educational and social inequality. Student departure must be seen in light of how its patterned occurrence among different persons and institutions serves to reinforce social inequality generally. Thus, it is argued that individual social status, race, and sex are particularly important predictors of student success and that high rates of departure in two-year colleges reflect the intentional desire of educational organizations to restrict educational and social opportunity to particular groups in society (Clark, 1960; Pincus, 1980).

Other theorists, who share in the structural-functional view of society, see the outcome of schooling as reflecting the largely meritocratic contest among individuals for social attainment (Duncan et al., 1972; Sewell and Hauser, 1973; Featherman and Hauser, 1978). In their view, differences in educational attainment—and therefore, patterns of student departure—tend to mirror differences in individual skills and abilities rather than social status *per se*. Though social origins as defined by social status and race matter, they tend to be less important than those attributes of individuals and organizations that impact directly on their ability to compete in the academic marketplace.

Whether a derivative of conflict theory or structural-functional theory, societal theories of departure stress the role of external forces in the process of student persistence, often at the expense of institutional forces. Consequently, such theories are frequently insensitive to the institution-specific character of student retention and to important variations in staying and leaving. Though useful in the aggregate, that is in describing broad trends in retention in society generally, these theories are much less useful in explaining the institution-specific forces that shape varying forms of student institutional departure.

Economic Theories of Student Departure

This is not as true for those environmental theories of schooling which stress the importance of economic forces in student decisions to stay or leave. Derived from economic theories of educational attainment, the work of researchers such as Manski and Wise (1984), Iwai and Churchill (1982), Jensen (1981), and Voorhees

(1984) share the view that individual decisions about persistence are not different in substance from any other economic decision that weighs the costs and benefits of alternative ways of investing one's scarce economic resources. Thus, retention and departure mirror economic forces, especially those that influence both the economic benefits accruing to a college education and the financial resources that individuals can bring to bear on their investment in continued college attendance.

Understandably, all such theories emphasize the importance of individual finances and financial aid in student retention (e.g., Iwai and Churchill, 1982). More importantly, economic theories, unlike societal theories generally, take account of institution-specific forces by arguing that individual weighing of costs and benefits necessarily reflects individual experiences within a given institutional setting. Nevertheless, economic theories do so only as measured by economic factors. They are generally insensitive to the social or nonpecuniary forces inside and outside institutions that color individual decisions regarding persistence. Though such theories are useful for the study of certain problems, for instance the analysis of the effect of financial aid and tuition upon retention, their ability to explain departure in its various forms has thus far been quite limited.

In any case, there is little evidence to support the contention that financial forces are paramount to individual retention decisions. Though there is little doubt that financial considerations are important to the continued persistence of some students, most notably those from working-class and disadvantaged backgrounds, they tend to be of secondary importance to the decisions of most students. The reasons are twofold: First, the effect of finances upon persistence is most often taken up in decisions regarding college entry, that is, whether to attend and where to attend (Manski and Wise, 1984). Second, though students frequently cite finances as reasons for withdrawing, those reasons normally reflect other forces unassociated with finances, such as dissatisfaction with the institution. When students are satisfied with their institutional experience, they frequently accept a great economic burden in order to continue.[4]

This is not to say, however, that short-term fluctuations in financial resources do not lead to departure among some students, especially those from disadvantaged backgrounds. But such events are most often short-term in character and cannot explain the continuing long-term patterns of student departure that we observe in higher education. A general theory of student departure, if it is to be fully explanatory, must be able to account for the latter as well as the former mode of student departure.

Organizational Theories of Student Departure

Organizational theories of student departure, like environmental theories generally, are also concerned with the impact of environmental forces on student behavior. But rather than focus on broad social or economic forces, they center on the effect of the organization of higher educational institutions. Like studies of role socialization and worker productivity and turnover, from which they are derived, organizational theories of departure, such as those of Kamens (1971) and Bean (1983), see the occurrence of student departure as reflecting the impact that the organization has on the socialization and satisfaction of students. Their central tenet has been that departure is as much, if not more, a reflection of institutional behavior as it is of the individuals within it.

Typically, researchers have looked at the effect of organizational dimensions such as bureaucratic structure, size, faculty-student ratios, and institutional resources and goals on the aggregate rates of student institutional departure. Though individual attributes are sometimes included, they are not of primary theoretical interest. Kamens's multi-institutional study (1971), for instance, focused on the impact of organizational size and complexity on student role socialization and retention. He argued that larger institutions with distinct college "charters" would have lower rates of attrition because of their superior capacity to allocate students to the more prestigious positions in society. Such "charters" are a reflection not only of institutional resources but also of the links that larger institutions maintain with different occupational and economic groups (Kamens, 1971, pp. 271–272). Bean's study (1983) takes a somewhat different view of departure. An offshoot of an industrial model of work turnover (Price, 1977; Price and Mueller, 1981), this study looked at the impact of organizational attributes (e.g., routinization, participation, and communication) and rewards (e.g., grades, practical value, and development) on retention through their impact on student satisfaction. As in work organizations, it is argued that institutional rates of retention—that is, student turnover—would be heightened by institutional policies that increase students' participation and enhance the rewards they obtain for their "work" in the institution.

The strength of the organizational view of student departure lies in its reminding us that the organization of educational institutions—their formal structures, resources, and patterns of association—do impact on student retention. As in formal organizations generally, organizational decisions within higher education necessarily impact on the satisfaction of all members within the organization, students as well as faculty and staff. In this respect, organizational models are especially appealing to institutional planners concerned with the restructuring of organizations to achieve greater institutional effectiveness, for they focus on organizational attributes that are directly alterable by administrative action. These models should also be appealing to researchers interested in the comparative analysis of institutional retention.

As a theory of student departure, however, organizational theories such as Bean's (1983) and to a lesser extent Kamens's (1971) lack in explanatory power in that they do not enable us to understand how organizational attributes eventually impact on student decisions to stay or leave. That is the case, in part, because these theories normally do not point out the intervening factors, such as student subcultures and patterns of student-faculty interaction, that serve to transmit the effect of the organization to student behaviors.[5] Nor do they enable us to understand why it is that different types of students may take on different types of leaving behaviors within the institution. In this regard, these theories implicitly assume that all leavings arise from the same sources—an assumption we know not to be correct.

Though organizational models may be especially suited to comparative studies of rates of retention in different types of higher education organizational settings—for which they have unfortunately been rarely used—they are much less useful in the study of intraorganizational variations in student behaviors. They are not well suited to the task of explaining the patterns of student departure that arise among different types of students within the institution. For this purpose, one has to look elsewhere, specifically to interactional theories of student departure.

Interactional Theories of Student Departure

Interactional theories of student departure, those that have now come to dominate current views of student leaving, take student behavior as reflecting both individual and organizational attributes. But rather than being a simple compilation of psychological and organizational theories, they represent a dynamic, interactive view of student experience, one that has its origins in social anthropological and ethnomethodological studies of human behavior. From the former, interactional theories of student departure have taken the view that student leaving reflects individuals' experience in the total culture of the institution as manifested in both the formal and the informal organization of the institution. Rather than focusing on formal organization alone, they stress the role of informal social organizations (e.g., student peer groups) and subcultures in student departure. From the latter, they have come to argue that student departure necessarily reflects the interpretation and meaning that individuals attach to their experiences within the institution. Though individual attributes matter, their impact cannot be understood without reference to how they relate to the understandings that different students have of events within the institution.

In this fashion, interactional theories see student leaving as reflecting the dynamic reciprocal interaction between environments and individuals. The two cannot be separated and are intimately intertwined in the manner in which each comes to shape the interpretations that differing individuals give to their experiences. In the final analysis, what matters is the individual's understanding of the situation—an interpretation of events that is necessarily a dynamic outcome of how the individual interacts with other persons and with the broader setting of which he or she is a part.

There are several variants of the interactional view of student departure. The least complex are those that use the notion of role socialization and "person-role fit" to describe student departure (Pervin and Rubin, 1967; Rootman, 1972). For them, socialization into the student role is central to the retention process. As a consequence, the more closely aligned the individual sees himself or herself as being with that role, the more likely is he or she is to stay rather than to leave. Conversely, the greater the perceived discrepancy between the individual's perception of the self and the student role, the greater the likelihood of departure.

Though evidence seems to bear out this view, it does so only for some types of leaving, primarily from relatively homogeneous institutional settings where the notion of *student role* may be more clearly articulated and representative of the wider college culture. In heterogeneous settings or in those with no dominant student subculture (e.g., non-residential colleges), the same notion may provide a less suitable account of student departure. In any event, like other views of departure, the "person-role fit" model tends to assume that all leavings are the same in character and in source—an assumption that we know to be incorrect. Only some forms of leaving appear to fall within the notion of *person-role fit*. Many others appear to arise from different sources.[6]

A more complex form of the interactional view of departure, and perhaps the most widely cited, is that of Tinto (1975). A derivative of Spady's earlier work (1970), it draws its theoretical origins from the work of the French sociologist Emile Durkheim, in particular his study of social communities and individual suicide. As applied to the question of student leaving, Tinto's model argues that colleges are very much like other human communities, and that the process of persistence—and by extension, that of departure—is very much like those processes within communities that influence the establishing of community membership. In the multifaceted world of the college, student decisions to leave are seen as directly and indirectly influenced by the individual's social (personal) and intellectual (normative) experiences in the various communities that make up the world of the college. Specifically, they reflect the impact that those experiences have on individual goals and commitments both to the goal of degree completion and to the institution. Thus, decisions to leave reflect the individual's interpretation of those experiences and therefore those personal attributes that are associated with how individuals interact with and come to attach meaning to the world around them.

Though quite complex, interactional models provide a more inclusive view of the departure process, one that integrates both the organizational and the psychological view of departure, while enabling researchers to sort out the various forms of leaving that are typically subsumed under the label *dropout* (Tinto, 1982, 1985b). More importantly, they also highlight the various mechanisms through which organization and personality impact upon departure (Pascarella and Terenzini, 1979). By so doing, they move from a largely descriptive view of departure to an explanatory theory that is amenable to the development of testable hypotheses. That is, they go beyond the description of differences between stayers and leavers to an explanation of how those differences arise within the context of a specific institution.

The interactional model is, as Peterson (1985, p. 8) noted, the only theory of student departure to have generated a systematic testing of its ability to explain student departure from institutions of higher education (e.g., Pascarella and Terenzini, 1979; Munro, 1981; Pascarella and Chapman, 1983; Pascarella and Terenzini, 1983; Donovan, 1984; Pascarella and Wolfle, 1985; Pascarella et al., 1985; Fox, 1985; Hall et al., 1985; Cash and Bissell, 1985; Weidman, 1985). For that reason, interactional theories of departure, particularly Tinto's, appear to offer the firmest and most complete foundation on which future developments in theories of student departure can occur.

Nevertheless, the interactional theory of departure is also subject to some important limitations (Tinto, 1982). Not the least of these pertain to its failure to take explicit account of either the formal organizational or external forces (e.g., external communities) which impact upon student participation in college.[7] For that reason, current forms of interactional theory are neither particularly well suited to the study of non-residential institutions and/or of departure among commuting students, nor easily adapted to the practical needs of administrative planners. Tinto's (1975) theory of departure, for instance, is more clearly a social science theory of departure than an administrative one designed for the formulation of policy. More importantly, as is true for virtually all models of student departure, the interactional view of student leaving is not truly longitudinal. Though it is longitudinal in nature, it does not provide substantive details of the manner in which the departure process may vary over time. It assumes, in effect, that the process of leaving is largely uniform over time.

If we wish to produce a truly synthetic theory of departure, we must extend current theory to meet these needs. Specifically we need to address three major areas of concern, namely the need for a more complete longitudinal model of departure over time, for a model which takes account of the effect of external forces upon departure, and for one which allows us to map out the impact of the formal organization of the institution upon student departure.

Directions for Future Theory on Student Departure

The Longitudinal Nature of Student Withdrawal: The Stages of Institutional Departure

To address the issue of the longitudinal nature of student departure, we turn to the field of social anthropology and studies of the temporal process of establishing membership in traditional societies. Specifically, we can turn to the work of the Dutch anthropologist Arnold Van Gennep and his study of the rites of membership in tribal societies.[8] Of his numerous concerns, the one most directly related to the process of student departure is his focus on the movement of individuals from membership in one group to membership in another, especially as it occurs in the ascendancy of individuals from youth to adult status in society. In his classic study entitled *The Rites of Passage*, Van Gennep (1960) argued that the process of the transmission of relationships between succeeding groups is marked by three distinct phases or stages, each with its own specialized ceremonies and rituals: separation, transition, and incorporation. Each serves to move individuals from youthful participation to full membership in adult society. They provide, through the use of ceremony and ritual, for the orderly transmission of the beliefs and norms of the society to the next generation of adults and/or new members. In that fashion, such rites serve to ensure the stability of society over time, while also enabling younger generations to assume responsibility from older ones.

According to Van Gennep, each stage in the rites of passage to adulthood consists of a change in patterns of interaction between the individual and other members of society. The first, separation, is characterized by a marked decline in interactions with members of the group from which the person has come. Frequently involving ceremonies whose purpose it is to mark as outmoded the views and norms that characterize that group, separation requires the individual to remove herself or himself, in both physical and normative terms, from past forms of association and patterns of behavior.

The second stage, transition, is a period during which the person begins to interact in new ways with members of the new group in which membership is sought. Isolation, training, and sometimes ordeals are employed as mechanisms to ensure the separation of the individual from past associations and the adoption of behaviors and norms appropriate to membership in the new group. It is during this transitional stage that individuals acquire the knowledge and skills required for the performance of their specific role in the new group. Having given up past forms of association, individuals now prepare themselves for full membership in the new communities of the future.

The third and last phase, incorporation, involves taking on new patterns of interaction with members of the new group and establishing competent membership in that group as a participant. Full membership in or incorporation into the new group is marked by special ceremonies that announce and certify not only the rewards of membership but also the responsibilities associated with it. Though the person may begin to interact once again with past associations, he or she now does so as a member of the new group. He or she has completed the movement from the past and is now fully integrated into the culture of the new group.

Van Gennep believed that the notions of rites of passage could be applied to a variety of situations, especially those involving the movement of a person or group from one place to another.[9] In that movement, the individual or group leaves an old territory or community (separation); in some fashion crosses a border, whether it be physical or ceremonial, to a new setting (transition); and takes up residence in the new location or community (incorporation). For the individual, such movements necessarily entail moving from a position as a known member in one group to that of a stranger in the new setting. The result is often feelings of weakness and isolation not very different from those Durkheim described as being "anomic." Having given up the norms and beliefs of past associations and not yet having adopted those appropriate to membership in a new community, the individual is left in a state of at least temporary normlessness. A consequence of normlessness—that is, of the absence of guiding norms and beliefs—is the likelihood of departure from the community before incorporation.

The work of Van Gennep provides us with a way of thinking about the longitudinal process of student persistence in college and, by extension, about the time-dependent process of student departure.[10] College students are, after all, moving from one community or set of communities to another. Like other persons in the wider society, they too must separate themselves, to some degree, from past associations in order to make the transition to eventual incorporation into the life of the college. In attempting to make such transitions, they too are likely to encounter difficulties that are as much a reflection of the problems inherent in shifts of community membership as they are either of the personality of individuals or of the institution in which membership is sought.

The longitudinal process of institutional persistence can therefore be envisioned as consisting of three major stages or passages through which students must typically pass in order to complete their degree programs. These are, as in the work of Van Gennep, the stages of separation, transition and incorporation. By extension, the process of institutional departure can be seen as being differentially shaped by the difficulties that students encounter in attempting to navigate successfully those stages and to become incorporated into the life of the college.

Separation from the Past. The first stage of the college career, separation, requires students to disassociate themselves, in varying degrees, from membership in past communities, most typically those associated with the local high school and place of residence. Depending in part on the character of those communities, especially their views regarding the worth of college attendance, separation may be quite difficult or merely an accepted part of the process of movement that most persons are expected to make in the course of their lives. Nevertheless, all separations, however small, entail some form of parting from past habits and patterns of affiliation. The adoption of the behaviors and norms appropriate to the college almost always requires some degree of transformation and perhaps rejection of those of the past communities. However close, the life of families and high schools and the demands that they impose on their members are qualitatively different from those that characterize most colleges.

For virtually all students, the process of separation from the past is at least somewhat stressful. For some, it may be so severe as to constrain persistence in college. This may be especially true for individuals who, for the first time, move away from their local high-school communities and families to live away at a distant college, and/or whose colleges are markedly different in social and intellectual orientation from that of the family and the local community. In order to become fully integrated into the communities of the college, these individuals have to disassociate physically as well as socially from the communities of the past. In a very real sense, their persistence depends on their ability to depart from the norms of their former communities.

This may not apply to persons who stay at home while attending college. They need not disassociate themselves from local communities in order to establish membership in the new communities of the college. By the same token, they may be unable to take full advantage of those communities for integration into the social and intellectual life of the college. Though such persons may find movement into the world of the college less stressful, they may also find it less rewarding. They may not be able to reap the full social and intellectual rewards that social membership in college communities brings. Thus, the irony is that though they may find the task of persistence initially easier, it may be measurably more difficult over the long run."

Transition to College. The second stage of the college career, transition, is a period of passage between the old and the new, between the associations of the past and the hoped-for associations with communities of the present. Having begun the process of separating themselves from the past, new students have yet to acquire the norms and patterns of behavior appropriate to integration into the new communities of the college. They have not yet established the personal bonds that underlie community membership. As a result, they are neither bound as strongly to the past, nor firmly tied to the future.

The stress and sense of loss and bewilderment, if not desolation, that sometimes accompany the transition to college can pose serious problems for the individual attempting to persist in college. Though most students are able to cope with the problems of adjusting to the social and intellectual life of the college, many find it measurably more difficult. As a result, many withdraw from college very early in the academic year. They do less from an inability to become integrated into the social and academic communities of the college than from an inability to withstand and cope with the stresses that such transitions commonly induce.

Besides the obvious role of personality, differences in individual coping skills and in educational goals and commitments have much to do with individual responses to the stresses of separation and transition. Quite simply, some students are unable to cope with such situations. They have not learned how to direct their energies to solving the problems they face. Without institutional assistance, they often flounder and withdraw without having made a serious attempt to adjust to the life of the college. But some students stick it out even under the most severe conditions, while others withdraw even under minimal stress. The unavoidable fact is that some students are unwilling to put up with the stresses of transition because they are not sufficiently committed either to the goals of education and/or to the institution into which entry is first made. Others, however, are so committed to those goals that they will do virtually anything to persist.

The point here is simply that the problems associated with both separation and transition are problems that, though stressful, need not in themselves lead to departure. It is the individual's responses to these problems that finally determine staying or leaving. By extension, institutions can do much to assist new students in dealing with conditions that are inherent in the first two stages of the college career.

It should be noted that the scope of the transition stage—that is, the degree of change that it entails—depends on a number of factors, not the least of which is the degree of difference between the norms and patterns of behavior of the past and those required for integration into the life of the college. For example, persons from families, communities, and/or schools that are very different in behavior and norms from those of the college are faced with especially difficult problems in seeking to achieve membership in the communities of the college. Their past experiences are unlikely to have prepared them for the new life of the college in the same way as have the experiences of those persons who come from families that are themselves college-educated. In the "typical" institution, one would therefore expect persons from minority backgrounds and/or from very poor families, older adults, and persons from very small rural communities to be more likely to experience such problems than would other students.

The same may also apply to persons who reside at home during college. In seeking to avoid the pains of separation, they may fail to perceive the need to adjust to the new demands of the college and to become involved in its ongoing intellectual and social life. As a consequence, they may limit the amount of the time they spend on campus. The resulting restriction on their interaction with other members of the college communities may severely constrain the learning of the norms and patterns of behavior required for full incorporation into the life of the college. In the particular case of nonresidential two-year colleges, such transitions are rarely required. Nor is full integration into the life of the institution. Again, what one gains in the way of easier persistence early in the college career, one may pay for in difficulty in persistence later on.

Incorporation into College. After passing through the stages of separation and transition, the individual is faced with the task of becoming integrated, or to use Van Gennep's term, *incorporated* into the community of the college. Having moved away from the norms and behavioral patterns of past associations, the person now faces the problem of finding and adopting norms appropriate to the new college setting and of establishing competent membership in the social and intellectual communities of college life. As social interactions are the primary vehicle through which such integrative associations arise, individuals have to establish contact with other members of the institution, student and faculty alike. Failure to do so may lead to the absence of integration and to its associated sense of isolation. These, in turn, may lead to departure from the institution.

But unlike incorporation into traditional societies, individuals in college are not always provided with formal rituals and ceremonies whereby such contacts are ensured. Nor are they always clearly informed either of the character of the local communities or of the behaviors and norms appropriate to membership in them. Of course, most institutions, especially residential ones, do provide a variety of formal and informal mechanisms for that purpose. Fraternities, sororities, student dormitory associations, student unions, frequent faculty and visiting-scholar series, extracurricular programs, and intramural athletics, for example, may all serve to provide individuals with opportunities to establish repetitive contact with other members of the institution in circumstances that lead to the possibility of integration.

Not all individuals, especially those recently removed from the long-known confines of the family and local high-school communities, are able to make such contacts on their own. As a result, they do not all come to be incorporated into the life of the college and do not establish competent membership in its intellectual and social communities. Many eventually leave because of the ensuing isolation that they experience.

But some students may leave because they choose not to become incorporated into the communities of the college. Having established contact with other members of the institution, some new students may find that the social and intellectual communities of the college are not to their liking. Rather than adopting values and behavioral styles that they see as discordant with their own, they may decide to voluntarily withdraw in order to seek membership in other settings. Their leaving is more a reflection of a perceived lack of fit between themselves and the life of the college than it is of personal isolation. Though isolation may occur, it is the result of their prior decision not to become integrated.

Reflections on the Stages of Institutional Departure and Current Theories of Student Departure. Several observations should be made before we proceed to other areas of theory. The first concerns the relationship between this view of institutional departure and the interactional theories of departure, in particular that of the author. The view described here can be seen as complementary to that theory. Rather than offering a conflicting view of departure, it adds a time dimension to the theory by describing the longitudinal stages of the process of integration, in par-

ticular the early phases of separation and transition that precede incorporation into the life of the college. This view is, in effect, a description of the longitudinal character of the student career as it proceeds toward incorporation into the communities of the college, that is, persistence.

The inclusion of the notion of stages or passages also highlights the sorts of difficulties that students typically face in each of those stages. It argues that all students, regardless of personality and prior experience, will encounter difficulties, in some form, that are characteristic of the college career. Consequently, it also argues that institutions must carefully frame and time their actions on behalf of student retention to meet the changing needs of students as they arise at different points during the college career.

It should also be observed that college communities are both academic and social. Persistence in college may arise in either the academic or the social system of the institution and may reflect both the personal and the intellectual integration or incorporation of the individual into the communities of the college. By extension, the longitudinal process of student institutional departure can be seen as being marked by the difficulties that individuals experience in making the social and/or the intellectual adjustment to the formal and informal academic and social life of the new communities of the college. The general notion of stages of passage may be seen, therefore, as applying to the separate passages that new students must make to become incorporated into both the social and the intellectual life of the college.[12]

Finally, it must be recognized that the stages of passage that we have described are abstractions that necessarily simplify, for purposes of analysis, the more complex phenomena that we understand as student departure. In using the stages of separation, transition, and incorporation in our analysis of student departure, we do not mean to oversimplify what is a very complex and quite fluid situation. Though these stages may apply to the process of departure in an abstract form, they need not apply without modification to each and every case. Some students may hardly be aware of the transition required in becoming integrated into the life of the college. Others may not experience the separate stages at the same time or in the same way. For still other students, any or all of the stages may significantly overlap and may occur simultaneously.

Even so, the tasks and problems associated with each stage must be encountered and overcome for all students to become fully incorporated—that is, integrated—into the life of the communities of the college. Most students are eventually faced with very much the same sorts of problems and experience similar types of difficulties in attempting to establish competent membership within the communities of the college that they enter. These are as much a reflection of the process of persistence in college as they are of either the attributes of the persons experiencing them or the institution in which they occur. By extension, the longitudinal process of departure from institutions of higher education is similarly marked in time by difficulties associated with the individual's inability to attend to the problems that arise in those stages. Though the process of departure necessarily reflects the absence of integration into the life of the college, it may arise at differing points of time from different problems. In short, lack of integration, which has been posited elsewhere as a primary cause of student departure, is not necessarily a reflection of an absence of incorporation alone. It may also result from the inability of students to separate themselves from past associations and/or to make the transition to new ones.

External Forces and the Concept of Competing Communities

All this is not to say, however, that individual decisions regarding staying in college are unaffected by events external to college. We know this not to be the case. Though interactional and organizational models of student departure emphasize the role of intrainstitutional experiences, they do not exclude the possibility that external forces may also sway individual decisions regarding departure.

One can think of the problem of external forces in terms of internal and external communities. External communities (e.g., families, neighborhoods, peer groups, and work settings), like those internal to the college, have their own social and normative structure and patterns of interaction, leading to community membership. For any individual, participation in external communities may serve to counter, rather than to support, participation in college communities. This is so not only because the demands of the

former may take away time from participation in the latter but also because the requirements of membership in one may work counter to those of membership in the other.

The normative requirements of membership in one's local peer group external to the college, for instance, may be such as to downplay the appropriateness of membership in the intellectual communities of the college. Membership in the latter may be seen as being a deviant form of activity within the former. Individuals in such situations may be forced to choose between membership in possibly long-standing external communities and membership in the relatively new, still tenuous communities of the college. When these latter communities are either weak—as they may be in nonresidential, commuting institutions—or when one's experiences in them are unsatisfactory, the effect of external communities on decisions to persist may be quite substantial. The direction of their impact may spell the difference between staying and leaving. For persons who are only weakly affiliated with any college community and/or whose local community may be marginal to the life of the institution, the effect of such external forces may be sufficiently great to alter their goals and commitments so as to induce them to leave the college for other pursuits.

External events may also influence departure by altering the mix of competing opportunities for the investment of individual resources. As pointed out by economic models of departure, individual judgments about continued participation in college may be viewed as a weighing of the costs and benefits of college persistence relative to alternative investments of one's time, energies, and scarce resources. Significant alteration in the external mix of opportunities and/or in their relative benefits may change decisions in favor of noncollege activities. Increases in the demand for non-college-graduates or heightened unemployment among college graduates may, for instance, induce some persons to leave college for potentially greener pastures. Similarly, the removal of restrictions that limit the range of external options, such as occurred with the cessation of the draft and the opening up of white colleges to black students, may lead others to do the same.

In this regard, the research of Chacon et al. (1982) on dropouts among Latina women in colleges in the Southwest reminds us of the way in which excessive external demands—in this case, of one's local and extended family—can effectively prevent persistence within college. The demands of the former are so great as to prevent the transition to the world of the college. Though contact within the college may help, for some it may be insufficient to counter the deeply rooted demands of families and family roles on students' time and energies.

This last notion, that of roles, suggests, perhaps, another fruitful area of exploration: role theory and role conflict. Though it is not our intent here to develop this possibility, it should be pointed out that one can envision the conflict between external and internal forces as being comparable to the conflict between competing roles. Persistence requires the individual to successfully play the role of student, whereas family life requires the person to play different roles. When the two are in conflict, that is, when each requires of the person different forms of behavior and allocation of time and energies, the person is placed in a potentially quite stressful situation. Unless individuals are able to cope with that stress, departure from college (or from the family) may be the only viable way of resolving a potentially damaging situation.

Having made this point, we must also observe that student departure most frequently arises because of a change in the person's evaluation of the relative benefits of college activities. This may result not only from a change in the external benefits accruing to college graduates but also from an alteration in the intrinsic rewards arising from college attendance. As argued in Tinto's model of departure, these intrinsic rewards are largely the consequence of one's social and intellectual integration into the communities of the college. The absence of such integration may alter the person's judgment of the relative costs and benefits of continued persistence, regardless of changes in the world external to the college.

The point here is quite simple. Though external events may be important for some students, especially those from less affluent backgrounds, for most students they are of secondary importance relative to experience within the college. While external forces may influence decisions to go to college and may greatly constrain the choice of which college to attend, their impact on departure following entry is generally quite minor.[13] Recent research on retention in a two-year commuting college tends to support this view (Neumann, 1985). Even in that setting, where on-campus contact with faculty is so limited, social and intellectual contact with persons within the institution matters. Students who might not otherwise be expected to finish their degree program apparently do so because of the relationships they establish with other persons on campus.

Bringing in the Organization: The Mediating Effect of Social and Intellectual Communities

To the same degree that organizational theories of student departure have largely ignored the subtle effects of the informal world of the college, so, too, have interactional models of departure tended to overlook the effect of the formal organization of the institution on student behavior. This need not be the case. As noted earlier, the latter models can very easily be modified to include the effect of organizational attributes on student behavior.

A number of different perspectives on organizations can serve this purpose. In addition to the model of worker turnover used by Bean (1983), one can make reference to Hirschman's analysis (1970) of the effect of participation on worker loyalty, Barker and Gump's study (1964) of the effect of school size on student participation and satisfaction, or Stroup's extended essay (1966) on bureaucracy in higher education. Any of these models of organizations can provide us with a framework for understanding the many ways in which organizational attributes eventually reach down and impact on the lives of students.

But here an important caveat is called for. The application of theories of work organizations, for instance, to the study of student departure must be carried out with care. The primary difficulty with such applications is that they make the implicit assumption that higher education organizations are essentially the same as those in the world of work and, therefore, that one can think of students in those organizations as one would of workers in factories or offices. While the analogy may be stretched to fit faculty and staff, it is doubtful that students would see themselves in the same light as would workers generally. Though the analogy of worker productivity to that of student performance is especially appealing, as it can provide us with a way of addressing both the issue of retention and the issue of student learning, we must be careful not to push such analogies too far. Perhaps we should consider looking to other models of organizations, such as those of the professional or socializing type, as possible guides to our study of the effect of organizations on student departure.

Whatever our referent, it is important that the adoption of organizational models enable us to trace more accurately the direct and indirect effects of organizations on student behavior. Available evidence leads us to believe, for instance, that one of the primary effects of the organization on student departure is indirect, through its influence on the character of the social and intellectual communities within the college. For example, formal academic policies, such as requiring faculty to take attendance, may alter not only the nature of classroom interactions but also the character of the academic communities of the college. By so doing, such policies may have wider, though often unintended, impacts on student retention that extend beyond initial policy goals. In this example, they may undermine rather than aid student learning by affecting how students and faculty view their mutual responsibility in the learning process.

By allowing us to map out the multiple effects of the organization on students, the inclusion of organizational variables in current interactional theories of departures can also lead to a more complete guide for administrative policy formation. They may do so by pointing out the various and often unintended ways in which formal administrative actions impact directly and indirectly on student departure. Currently, interactional theories of departure are, in this regard, particularly weak.

Combined interaction and organizational theories may also serve as an effective tool for the comparative study of student departure in different institutional settings. They may enable us, for instance, to analyze more carefully the ways in which different organizational structures impact upon institutional rates of student departure. Though some very informative attempts have been made to use existing interactional models for this purpose (e.g., Pascarella and Chapman, 1983; Pascarella and Wolfle, 1985), we have only begun to scratch the surface of the multi-layered effects of different institutional settings on student departure.

Concluding Comments: Commonalities In the Development of a General Theory of Student Departure

The above discussion leads us finally to consider some of the major elements of a general theory of student departure and some of the research we would have to pursue to develop that theory. Here it would seem to be the case that recent research provides a reasonable guide to what we can expect in the future, namely, that a general theory of student departure will result from an extension and elaboration of the interactional view of departure. That view, especially as elaborated by Tinto (1975), Pascarella and Terenzini (1979), Pascarella et al. (1983), and Tinto (in press), seems to provide the most inclusive theoretical base on which future developments in a theory of student departure can be built. This is the case because it already contains many of the elements that are essential to a general theory of student departure.

First, this view enables researchers to sort out the various forms of leaving that are typically subsumed under the label *dropout*. For instance, it allows one to distinguish voluntary withdrawal from forced dismissal and, within the former, to separate the various roots of voluntary withdrawal. Here, current research is still lacking. Though we have distinguished between forced and voluntary leaving, we have not yet adequately isolated the events that lead persons to leave because of lack of fit from those that give rise to leaving because of social and/or intellectual isolation. Until we do so, it should not be surprising that our models of departure will continue to explain relatively small percentages of variance in leaving behaviors.

Second, this view offers an inclusive model of departure that integrates, in a dynamic and interactive fashion, the full range of environmental and individual influences that impinge on the withdrawal process. It includes both social and academic forces and the formal and informal impact of both personal and intellectual experiences on individual decisions to stay in college. Furthermore, it can, with some of the revisions suggested above, also capture the various direct and indirect effects of the formal organization of the institution on student behavior. In this fashion, it provides us with a way of tracing out the direct and indirect effects that formal organizational structures have on student retention and of isolating how informal structures (e.g., peer subcultures) serve to mediate and sometimes to alter the intended impact of formal administrative decisions.

The mapping out of those effects requires, however, that we carry out many more multi-institutional comparative studies of student departure. Only through carefully drawn comparisons between institutions or settings of different organizational attributes can we come to understand the multidimensional impacts that settings have on student retention. For example, we need to look not only at the experiences of similar types of students in different institutional settings but also at the differences in the experiences of different types of students (e.g., black and white, male and female) in those varying settings. Though the recent work of Pascarella and Wolfle (1985) is a move in the right direction, it is only a first step. Rather than relying on large databases drawn from many institutions—in the case of Pascarella and Wolfle's study, 10,326 students attending 487 colleges and universities—we need to carefully select a few institutions from which we sample a much larger number of students. Only in that way can we expect to tease out the complex patterns of interactions that are likely to describe the experiences of different students in different institutional settings.

Third, this view is a longitudinal explanatory model of retention that can be extended to provide explanatory detail of the time-variable dimension of the process of student departure.[14] A relatively simple extension of the model to include the concept of passages is, as described above, only one possible way to achieve that end. Here is where the need for additional research is clearest. We need to carry out research that explores the character of departure at differing points in the student career. For instance, we must look at departure during the first several months of college separately from departure that occurs at the end of the first year, and we must study departure that arises early in the student career separately from departure in the last years of college. And we must do so for different types of students as they enter and progress through varying types of institutions.

However constructed, future theory must also lead to or be derived from the perceptions that the actors themselves have of the situation. It must be based on the meanings that students place on their experiences. In other words, future theory must be grounded in the everyday reality of the lives of students and must make sense of their experiences in the various realms of college life. Future theory must, in this sense, be understandable to the actors themselves. It must distinguish situations of personal failure from those that represent successful individual adaptation to changing educational circumstances. For the most part, our current theories of departure, with several notable exceptions, continue to treat all leaving as dropout and therefore as reflective of some form of personal failure.

It is for this reason that an agenda for future research must also include more careful qualitative studies of student departure. Though there is much merit in present efforts to provide quantitative tests of existing theory, we should not overlook the important contributions that grounded qualitative research can make to the development of theory. Regrettably, serious qualitative studies of student departure, such as that by Neumann (1985), are infrequent and far between. The development of complete, grounded theory of student departure requires that we carry out similar qualitative studies that explore the experiences of different students (e.g., adult, minority, and part-time) in varying institutional settings (e.g., two-year and nonresidential). We must more frequently combine the strengths of comparative longitudinal studies of departure with those of detailed qualitative studies of the character of those departures.

Finally, in looking at the experiences of students, future theory must be able to make sense of research that indicates the importance of "quality of student effort" and student "involvement in learning" to both retention and the quality of student learning (e.g., Pace, 1984). In pursuing their educational mission, institutions of higher education must act to enhance the quality of student effort and to involve students in the learning enterprise in ways that lead not only to retention but to further education (see Endo and Harpel, 1982). To that end, our theories of student retention and departure must also be theories of student involvement and learning—theories that point up how institutional experiences serve to heighten or hinder student involvement and to enhance or reduce the quality of effort that they are willing to expend on behalf of their own education. In the final analysis, our theories of student departure must also be translatable into theories of student education. Otherwise, they will always be only marginally relevant to the important needs of both students and institutions of higher education.

Notes

1. The distinction between models and theories is not a trivial one. Not all so-called theories of student departure are theories in the social science sense of the word. Only infrequently have we had theories of student departure that provide for a systematic set of relationships or underlying principles which could be said to explain the observed phenomena of student leaving and that lead to the specification of hypotheses which could be tested and verified by research. Most so-called theories are, in fact, models of departure which focus on some, but by no means all, of the factors and relationships that would account for students' leaving. Though they may be inspired by a theory of behavior, they are more limited in scope than the theories from which they derive. Nevertheless, in the discussion that follows, we will refer to current models of departure as if they were theories of student departure. We will do so because it is our intent to highlight not only the theoretical orientations from which they derive, but also the essential differences in theoretical assumptions that describe their varying approaches to the question of explanation.

2. In many respects, the current discussion parallels that by the author over ten years ago (Tinto, 1975). As in that article, the current chapter reflects an attempt to provide a theoretical assessment of our current state of knowledge about the process of student departure. But now we have the benefit of the considerable body of research and theory development that has taken place over the past decade. Though there are still major gaps in our knowledge of student departure, we are much better informed today of the roots of leaving than we were a decade ago.

3. There are a number of other ways of categorizing theory. We could also distinguish theories by the theoretical orientations from which they spring (e.g., conflict versus structural) or by the levels of analyses they use to study departure (e.g., individual, group, or societal). In this case, the distinction between psychological, societal, economic, organizational, and interactional serves to highlight the essential differences between theories in the assumptions they make about the primary causes of student attrition. Of equal importance, this distinction enables us to consider ways in which these disparate perspectives may someday be fused by highlighting the different levels of analysis (individual, organizational, and societal) that can be applied to the study of student leaving.

4. A study by Collins, Turner and Maguire (1979) at Boston College is one of a number of institutional studies which reinforce this contention, namely that student response to economic hardships is dependent upon their level of satisfaction with their educational experience.

5. Bean and Kuh (1984) has recently modified his original model to include both the attributes of and individual forms of participation in the social and intellectual communities of the institution. In this sense, then, his more recent work appears to be an attempt to integrate his organizational model with the interactional models of retention which now have such wide currency.

6. Studies which have supported the notion of student-role fit have been of relatively small and/or quite homogenous institutions such as military academies (Rootman, 1972) and church-related colleges (Cash, 1985). In much larger, heterogeneous institutions, even potentially deviant students sometimes manage to find a niche and stay until degree completion (Simpson, Baker and Mellinger, 1980).

7. It should be noted that most current interactional theories of student departure assume a largely functionalist view of behavior. In arguing that integration is central to persistence, they have made the implicit assumption that retention is functional for both the individual and the institution. But that assumption is not the only one which can be used to frame a theory of student retention. The conflict tradition, already noted, makes the assumption that social structure will reflect the interests of the prevailing social elites. As a result, it is possible that retention may sometimes further the interests of the institution at the expense of the individual. The phenomenological tradition, however, would argue that theorists should suspend judgment until they made reference to the understanding various actors have of retention. Rather than invest in research which seeks to validate preexisting theories, phenomenologists would have theory evolve from the grounded discovery of the meaning different individuals give to student leaving.

8. A year after having completed the first draft of this paper, the author learned of the work of John Gardiner of the University of South Carolina on the same theme. Having worked independent of one another, we had arrived at the same point, namely the application of the notion of Rites of Passage to the study of student persistence. For that reason the reader is urged to look at Gardiner and Jewler (1985) as an example of another application of the same concept to the problems of educational continuance.

9. Solon Kimball, in his introduction to the English translation of Van Gennep's classic *Rites of Passage*, argues that Van Gennep's "scheme du les rites de passage" might be more appropriately translated as "dynamics of the rites of transition", with the term dynamics implying both a sense of process and structure (Van Gennep, 1960, pp. v–xxii). In his view Van Gennep was as much concerned with the process of transitions as with the structure of the ceremonies which marked those transitions.

10. For a more complete discussion of the application of Van Gennep's work to the study of student departure the reader is urged to see Tinto (1985a).

11. It should also be pointed out that by staying at home, students expose themselves to a number of potential risks, not the least of which is the exposure to external forces which pull the person away from incorporation into the communities of the college. If the orientation of the family or local peer group does not support, indeed opposes, participation in higher education, early separation and transition may be measurably more difficult. It may require the person to reject the values of the family or the local peers in order to adopt those appropriate to the college.

12. These varying passages and the differing forms of adjustment that they entail are inextricably linked. In the interactive life of colleges, experiences in adjusting in one domain of the college necessarily impacts on those in other domains of the college. Difficulties that new students encounter in adjusting to the social life of the college, for instance, may affect their ability to adapt to the academic demands of the college. Similarly, problems that new students experience in adjusting to the informal intellectual style of academic life may impact on their ability to make the transition to the formal demands of academic life.

13. Not all institutions would agree with this view. For those institutions, such as the urban two-year colleges, that serve large proportions of part-time and/or less well-to-do students the importance of external events cannot be underestimated. In a similar fashion, technical-vocational institutions that provide direct access to work opportunities are more likely to feel the effects of alterations in job markets than are other institutions.

14. Of course the same can be said of other models of departure. The organizational model, for instance, can also be extended for this purpose. Here, the notion of worker-role socialization may be useful in helping researchers to think about the longitudinal process by which new workers come to adopt behaviors appropriate to their new setting.

References

Barker, R. G., and Gump, P. V., (1964). *Big school, small school.* Stanford, CA: Stanford University Press.

Bean, J. P. (1983). The application of a model of turnover in work organizations to the student attrition process. *The Review of Higher Education* 6: 129–148.

Bean, J. P., and Kuh, G. (1984) The reciprocity between student-faculty informal contact and academic performance of university undergraduate students. *Research in Higher Education* 21: 461–477.

Cash, R. W., and Bissell, H. (1985). Testing Tinto's model of attrition on the church-related campus. A paper presented at the annual meeting of the Association for Institutional Research, Portland, OR.

Chacon, M., Cohen, E. G., Camarena, M., Gonzalez, J., and Stover, S. (1982). *Chicanas in postsecondary education.* Stanford, CA: Center for Research on Women, Stanford University.

Clark, B. (1960). The "cooling-out" function in higher education. *American Journal of Sociology* 64: 569–576.

Collins, J. S., Turner, R. M., and Maguire, J. G. (1979). Unmet Need: How the gap is filled. *Journal of Student Financial Aid* 9: 4–15.

Cope, R., and Hannah, W. (1975). *Revolving college doors: the causes and consequences of dropping out, stopping out, and transferring.* New York: Wiley.

Donovan, R. (1984). Path analysis of a theoretical model of persistence in higher education among low-income black youth. *Research in Higher Education* 21: 243–259.

Duncan, O. D., Featherman, D. L., and Duncan, B. (1972). *Socioeconomic background and achievement.* New York: Seminar Press.

Endo, J., and Harpel, R. L. (1982). The effect of student-faculty interaction on students' educational outcomes. *Research in Higher Education* 16: 115–135.

Featherman, R. L., and Hauser, R. M. (1978). *Opportunity and change*. New York: Academic Press.

Fox, R. N. (1985). Application of a conceptual model of college withdrawal to disadvantaged students. A paper presented to the annual meeting of the American Educational Research Association, Chicago.

Gardner, J. N., and Jewler, A. J. (1985). *College is only the beginning*. Belmont, CA: Wadsworth.

Hall, E. R., Mickelson, D., and Pollard, D. (1985). Academic and social integration and student persistence at a commuter university. A paper presented at the annual meeting of the American Education Research Association, Chicago.

Hannah, W. (1971). Personality differentials between lower division dropouts and stay-ins. *Journal of College Student Personnel* 12: 16–19.

Hanson, G. R., and Taylor, R. G. (1970). Interaction of ability and personality: another look at the dropout problem in an Institute of Technology. *Journal of Counseling Psychology* 17: 540–545.

Heilbrun, A. B. (1965). Personality factors in college dropouts. *Journal of Applied Psychology* 49: 1–7.

Hirschman, A. (1970). *Exit, voice and loyalty*. Cambridge: Harvard University Press.

Iwai, S. I., and Churchill, W. D. (1982). College attrition and the financial support systems of students. *Research in Higher Education* 17: 105–113.

Jensen, E. L. (1981). Student financial aid and persistence in college. *Journal of Higher Education* 52: 280–294.

Kamens, D. (1971). The college "charter" and college size: effects on occupational choice and college attrition. *Sociology of Education* 44: 270–296.

Karabel, J. (1972). Community colleges and social stratification. *Harvard Educational Review* 42: 521–562.

Manski, C. F., and Wise, D. A. (1983). *College choice in America*. Cambridge: Harvard University Press.

Marks, E. (1967). Student perceptions of college persistence and their intellective, personality and performance correlates. *Journal of Educational Psychology* 58: 210–211.

Munro, B. (1981). Dropouts from higher education: path analysis of a national sample. *American Education Research Journal* 18: 133–141.

Neumann, W. (1985). Persistence in the community college: the student perspective. An unpublished Ph.D. dissertation, Syracuse University.

Pace, R. (1984). *Measuring the quality of college student experiences*. Los Angeles: Higher Education Research Institute, University of California, Los Angeles.

Pascarella, E., and Chapman, D. (1983). A multi-institutional, path analytic validation of Tinto's model of college withdrawal. *American Educational Research Journal* 20: 87–102.

Pascarella, E., Smart, J., and Ethington, C. (1985). Tracing the long-term persistence/withdrawal behavior of two-year college students: test of a causal model. A paper presented to the annual meeting of the American Educational Research Association, Chicago.

Pascarella, E., and Terenzini, P. (1979). Interaction effects in Spady's and Tinto's conceptual models of college dropout. *Sociology of Education* 52: 197–210.

Pascarella, E., and Terenzini, P. (1983). Predicting voluntary freshman year persistence/withdrawal behavior in a residential university: a path analytic validation of Tinto's model. *Journal of Educational Psychology* 75: 215–226.

Pascarella, E., and Wolfle, L. (1985). Persistence in higher education: a nine-year test of a theoretical model. A paper presented to the annual meeting of the American Educational Research Association, Chicago.

Pervin, L., and Rubin, D. (1967). Student dissatisfaction with college and the college dropout: a transactional approach. *The Journal of Social Psychology* 72: 285–295.

Peterson, M. W. (1985). Emerging developments in postsecondary organization theory and research: fragmentation or integration. *Educational Researcher* 14: 5–12.

Pincus, F. (1980). The false promise of community colleges: Class conflict and vocational education. *Harvard Educational Review* 50: 332–361.

Price, J. L. (1977). *The study of turnover*. Ames: Iowa State University Press.

Price, J. L., and Mueller, C. W. (1981). A causal model of turnover for nurses. *Academy of Management Journal* 24: 543–565.

Rootman, I. (1972). Voluntary withdrawal from a total adult socialization organization: a model. *Sociology of Education* 45: 258–270.

Rose, R. A., and Elton, C. F. (1966). Another look at the college dropout. *Journal of Counseling Psychology* 13: 242–245.

Rossmann, J. E., and Kirk, B. A. (1970). Factors related to persistence and withdrawal among university students. *Journal of Counseling Psychology* 17:56–62.

Sewell, W., and Hauser, R. (1975). *Education, occupation and earnings*. New York: Academic Press.

Sharp, L. F., and Chason, L. R. (1974). Use of moderator variables in predicting college student attrition. *Journal of College Student Personnel* 19: 388–393.

Spady, W. (1970). Dropouts from higher education: an interdisciplinary review and synthesis. *Interchange* 1: 64–85.

Stroup, H. (1966). *Bureaucracy in higher education.* New York: Free Press.

Summerskill, J. (1962). Dropouts from college. In N. Sanford (ed.), *The American college.* New York: Wiley.

Tinto, V. (1975). Dropout from higher education: a theoretical synthesis of recent *research. Review of Educational Research* 45: 89–125.

Tinto, V. (1982). Limits of theory and practice in student attrition. *Journal of Higher Education* 53: 687–700.

Tinto, V. (1985a). Rites of passage and the stages of institutional departure. A paper presented at the annual meeting of the American Educational Research Association, Chicago.

Tinto, V. (1985b). Dropping out and other forms of withdrawal from college. In L. Noel (ed.) *Improving student retention.* San Francisco: Jossey-Bass.

Tinto, V. (in press). *Leaving college: Rethinking the causes and cures of student attrition.* Chicago: University of Chicago Press.

Van Gennep, A. (1960). *The rites of passage,* trans. by M. Viedon and G. Caffee. Chicago: University of Chicago Press.

Voorhees, R. A. (1984). Financial aid and new freshman persistence: an exploratory model. A paper presented at the annual meeting of the Association for Institutional Research, Fort Worth.

Waterman, A. S., and Waterman, C. K. (1972). Relationship between freshman ego identity status and subsequent academic behavior: a test of the predictive validity of Marcia's categorization system for identity status. *Developmental Psychology* 6: 179.

Weidman, J. (1985). Retention of non-traditional students in postsecondary education. A paper presented at the annual meeting of the American Educational Research Association, Chicago.

CHAPTER 8

ENHANCING CAMPUS CLIMATES FOR RACIAL/ETHNIC DIVERSITY: EDUCATIONAL POLICY AND PRACTICE

SYLVIA HURTADO, JEFFREY F. MILEM,
ALMA R. CLAYTON-PEDERSEN, AND WALTER R. ALLEN

Probably few policy areas of higher education have received more recent attention than the issue of race on campus. Evidence appears in policies and programs related to college admissions, financial aid, affirmative action, discrimination and harassment, and desegregation. Yet, at the same time, probably no area of campus life has been so devoid of policy initiatives as the racial climate at individual institutions. Until recently, there has been no common framework for understanding the campus racial climate in a way that helps develop policies and practices that can be used to enhance the campus climate.

We pose four possible explanations for this phenomenon. First, higher education leaders and higher education institutions have taken the *laissez-faire* approach that people will (should) work things out interactively and that it is wrong to intervene too closely in student interactions (Horowitz, 1987). The second explanation involves ambiguity in the role that colleges and universities perform as agents of socialization. Administrators and faculty recognize that students bring with them to college a sense of identity and purpose shaped by their parents, their communities, their religions, etc., and that these influences are critically important to students' growth and development. The quandary lies in just how much of a resocializing agent higher education institutions wish to be. Higher education has not decided whether it should merely reflect our society or whether it should try to consciously shape the society. Third, while research findings document the important role that faculty serve as the "designated socializing agents" in higher education (Feldman & Newcomb, 1969, p. 227), policy initiatives that address faculty attitudes and behaviors have been implemented only with great hesitation and caution. Until now, it seems that only the most problematic discriminatory behaviors of faculty have been addressed. Finally, the situation has been exacerbated by neglect. A rich history of research on issues that affect the campus racial climate has existed for some time. However, this research has not always been valued by the higher education community. A study analyzing the major paradigms used in manuscripts published in "major" higher education journals found that fewer than 2% used paradigms that addressed issues of race from a critical perspective with the goal of producing meaningful change (Milam, 1989).

Attorneys, policy-makers, and institutional leaders across the country are searching for research evidence that demonstrates the benefits of diversity and documents persistent discrimination and inequality in higher education. Perhaps at no other time in our history have higher education scholars had the opportunity to provide evidence of the educational outcomes of diversity in a way that puts the benefits of diversity at the center of the educational enterprise. The purpose of this paper is to illustrate how research on issues related to campus racial climate can be used to enhance educational policy and practice. Both classic and contemporary research can inform national policy and debates surrounding affirmative action and other policies to create diverse learning environments (Hurtado, Milem, Clayton-Pedersen, & Allen, in press). What is needed are vehicles that translate higher education research into thoughtful policies incorporating the goal of educating diverse students. While such vehicles, or "translation documents," can be written in any number of higher education policy arenas, this paper focuses on the critical need for sustaining progress in educating diverse students.

We conducted an extensive multidisciplinary analysis of the research literature on the sources and outcomes of campus racial climate and developed a framework for understanding and describing the campus climate. It is our hope that policy-makers, institutional leaders, and scholars of higher education will find this framework useful as they seek to create comfortable, diverse environments for learning and socializing that facilitate the intellectual and social development of all students.

A Framework for Understanding Campus Climate

Considerable research on various racial/ethnic students in higher education addresses an array of cognitive and affective outcomes and group differences in educational attainments (Durán, 1983; Pascarella & Terenzini, 1991; Sedlacek, 1987). While these earlier research syntheses represent scholarly work on the achievement of various racial/ethnic groups, they contain almost no specific references to the institutional climate's potential influence on diversity. Some literature refers to the climate as important but "intangible." Recently, both qualitative and quantitative researchers have provided greater definition for this "intangible" quality by examining how students, faculty, and administrators perceive the institutional climate for racial/ethnic diversity, their experiences with campus diversity, and their own attitudes and interactions with different racial/ethnic groups. Multi-institutional studies have also shown, using a variety of measures, that the climate for diversity varies substantially from one institutional context to another (El-Khawas, 1989; Gilliard, 1996; Hurtado, 1992; Peterson, Blackburn, Gamson, Arce, Davenport, & Mingle, 1978).

This chapter provides a framework for understanding four dimensions of the campus climate and a conceptual handle for understanding elements of the environment that were once thought too complex to comprehend. This framework was first introduced in a study of the climate for Latino students (Hurtado, 1994) and further developed in a synthesis of research done for practitioners (Hurtado, Milem, Clayton-Pedersen, & Alien, in press). It makes concrete observations of institutions and individuals. It also defines areas where research has been conducted and, more importantly, where practical or programmatic solutions can be targeted.

Most institutions, when considering diversity on campus, tend to focus on increasing the numbers of racial/ethnic students. While this area of institutional effort is important, the four-part framework underscores other elements that require also attention, defining key areas upon which to focus diversity efforts. The studies we reviewed contain specific references to these various dimensions of the climate, describe the climate's impact on students from different racial/ethnic groups, and capture the experiences or unique perspectives of racial/ethnic groups that have historically been underrepresented in higher education.

Central to the conceptualization of a campus climate for diversity is the concept that students are educated in distinct racial contexts. These contexts in higher education are shaped by external and internal (institutional) forces. We represent the external components of climate as two domains: (a) the impact of governmental policy, programs, and initiatives and (b) the impact of sociohistorical forces on campus racial climate. Examples of the first include financial aid policies and programs, state and federal policy on affirmative action, court decisions on the desegregation of higher education, and the manner in which states provide for institutional differentiation within their state system of higher education. Sociohistoric forces influencing the climate for diversity on campus are events or issues in the larger society, nearly always originating outside the campus, that influence how people view racial diversity in society. They stimulate discussion or other activity within the campus. Obviously, these two domains influence each other. Tierney (1997) points out, "No policy can be isolated from the social arena in which it is enacted" (p. 177). While research literature documents the effect of governmental policy, programs, and initiatives (particularly in financial aid), there are fewer studies of the influence of sociohistorical forces on the campus racial climate.

The institutional context contains four dimensions resulting from educational programs and practices. They include an institution's historical legacy of inclusion or exclusion of various racial/ethnic groups, its structural diversity in terms of numerical representation of various racial/ethnic groups, the psychological climate of perceptions and attitudes between and among groups, and the behavioral climate dimension, characterized by intergroup relations on campus. We conceive the institutional climate as a product of these various elements.

It is important to note that these dimensions are connected, not discrete. For example, the historical vestiges of segregation have an impact on an institution's ability to improve its racial/ethnic student enrollments, and the underrepresentation of specific groups contributes to stereotypical attitudes among individuals within the learning and work environment that affect the psychological and behavioral climate. In short, while some institutions are now trying to take a "multi-layered" approach toward assessing diversity on their campuses and are developing programs to address the climate on campus, very few recognize the importance of the dynamics of these interrelated elements of the climate.

The Institutional Context
Historical Legacy of Inclusion or Exclusion

In many ways, the historical vestiges of segregated schools and colleges continue to affect the climate for racial/ethnic diversity on college campuses. The best example is resistance to desegregation in communities and specific campus settings, the maintenance of old campus policies at predominantly White institutions that best serve a homogeneous population, and attitudes and behaviors that prevent interaction across race and ethnicity. Because they are embedded in the culture of a historically segregated environment, many campuses sustain long-standing, often unrecognized, benefits for particular student groups (Duster, 1993).

Desegregation policies in schools and colleges were designed to alter their racial/ethnic composition, improve educational opportunity, and ultimately, change the environments of our educational institutions. Research on the outcomes of desegregation suggests that individuals who attend desegregated schools and colleges accept desegregation as adults in other educational settings, occupations, and social situations. Moreover, White adults who attended desegregated schools have fewer racial stereotypes and less fear of hostile reactions in interracial settings (Braddock, 1980, 1985; Braddock, Crain, & McPartland, 1984; Braddock & Dawkins, 1981; Braddock & McPartland, 1982, 1989; Green, 1982; Scott & McPartland, 1982).

While some campuses have a history of admitting and graduating students of color since their founding days, most predominantly White institutions (PWIs) have a history of limited access and exclusion (Thelin, 1985). A college's historical legacy of exclusion can determine the prevailing climate and influence current practices (Hurtado, 1992). Various institutional case studies document the impact of the historical context on the climate for diversity and on attempts to create a supportive climate for students of color (Peterson et al., 1978; Richardson & Skinner, 1991). Researchers found that success in creating supportive campus environments often depends on an institution's initial response to the entrance of students of color. Among important factors were the institutional philosophy of education for students of color, commitment to affirmative action, institutional intent for minority-specific programs, and attention to the psychological climate and intergroup relations on campus (Peterson et al., 1978). Higher education has had a long history of resistance to desegregation. The need for legal pressures and extended litigation to require institutions to accept their obligation to serve equitably a more diverse group of students has conveyed not only the message of institutional resistance but, in some cases, outright hostility toward people of diverse backgrounds.

Historically Black colleges and universities (HBCUs) and American Indian colleges (AICs) have historic commitments to serve populations previously excluded from higher education. These students continue to face seemingly intractable problems at PWIs. In recent years, due to dramatic changes in Latino enrollment, Hispanic-serving institutions (HSIs) have also begun to emphasize their commitment to educating Latino students. Today, as before, HBCUs, AICs, and HSIs not only represent alternative choices for students but also include attention to the cultural and academic development of these students and their communities as part of their mission.

Research that has examined differences in outcomes for African American students who have attended HBCUs as compared to students who have attended PWIs suggest that HBCUs provide more social and psychological support, higher levels of satisfaction and sense of community, and a greater likelihood that students will persist and complete their degrees (Allen, 1992; Allen, Epps, & Haniff, 1991; R. Davis, 1991; Jackson & Swan, 1991; Pascarella, Smart, Ethington, & Nettles, 1987). Recent findings from the National Study of Student Learning indicate that HBCUs also provide educational environments that support their students' intellectual development (Pascarella, Whitt, Nora, Edison, Hagedorn, Terenzini, 1996).

However, most racially and ethnically diverse students are educated in predominantly White environments (Carter & Wilson, 1993); therefore, PWIs's responses to desegregation are key in defining the campus racial climate. A positive response requires a clear definition of desegregation and strategic planning by the institution (Stewart, 1991). Further, the goals of desegregation plans must be precisely articulated with the objective of increasing overall representation of the historically excluded group.

Implications for Policy and Practice

Colleges and universities cannot change their past histories of exclusion nor should they deny that they exist. However, they can take steps to insure that diversity becomes a central value of their educational enterprise. Campus leaders should not assume that members of their community (particularly incoming students) know these histories, nor should they assume that teaching about these histories will lead to dissatisfaction. By being clear about an institution's past history of exclusion and the detrimental impact that this history has had on the campus, colleges and universities may garner broader support for their efforts to become more diverse through affirmative action programs and other programs and services designed to improve the climate for diversity. Moreover, acknowledging a past history of exclusion implies an institutional willingness to actively shed its exclusionary past. Such efforts may be even more effective if they are coupled with a clearly articulated vision for a more inclusive future.

In assessing the influence of the campus's history, leaders must consider whether "embedded benefits" may still exist on their campus. Institutions with a history of exclusion are likely to have evolved in ways that disproportionately benefit some group. For example, at many PWIs, fraternities and sororities have been a part of campus life much longer than people of color. Predominantly White fraternities and sororities frequently have houses that provide members with a place to meet or to live that are centrally located on campus or directly adjacent to the campus while the Greek system is deeply involved in daily campus activities, politics, socials, etc. In contrast, African American fraternities and sororities at these institutions seldom have been able to accumulate similar benefits for their members. The likelihood of finding the same quality of houses in equally convenient locations is quite low. In fact, students in these organizations may struggle to find places that they can meet on or near some campuses. Research shows that these organizations are critically important to the students who join them, but African American fraternities and sororities frequently seem less central than their White counterparts in daily campus activities, politics, and socials. As campus leaders thoughtfully consider their histories of exclusion, they are likely to find many more examples.

The success of legislation and litigation regarding desegregation in higher education has been mixed at best (Williams, 1988). In the prevailing climate, the federal government is taking a somewhat passive role and deferring to states.

Even where the willingness to pursue desegregation exists, the capacity for most states to regulate their colleges and universities (particularly their flagship institutions) has been limited (Williams, 1988). Hence, efforts to maintain a commitment to desegregation and equality of opportunity in higher education are most likely to succeed at the campus level with provisions for support at the state level. Desegregating predominantly White institutions is particularly important in states and communities where high-school segregation has continued; as a result, college may be the first chance for many students to encounter and interact with someone of different race or ethnicity.

According to the Southern Education Foundation (1995), HBCUs and PWIs are the result of "purposeful, state-imposed segregation," hence "no set of institutions has any more right than another to survive. The burden of desegregation should not fall exclusively or disproportionately on HBCUs" (p. xix). To require this effort would be unfair and unwise. E. B. Davis (1993) explains: "Institutions that retain a specifically black identity will not easily be able to reach the level of integration which reflects the population. They are being challenged to change their very character, while historically White schools are being asked only to broaden access" (p. 523). HBCUs serve an essential role in the higher education system by providing educational environments that facilitate positive social, psychological, and intellectual outcomes for students who attend them. Hence, they must be maintained. Moreover, PWIs can learn much from HBCUs, AICs, and HSIs about enhancing their environments to insure the success of students of color on campus.

Structural Diversity and Its Impact on Students

Given recent assaults on affirmative action in states like California and judicial rulings like that in *Hopwood*, it is critically important to understand how changes in the enrollment of racial/ethnic students (or the lack thereof) transform into educational benefits for students. Research supports the concept that increasing the structural diversity of an institution is an important initial step toward improving the climate. First, environments with highly skewed distributions of students shape the dynamics of social interaction (Kanter, 1977). Campuses with high proportions of White students provide limited opportunities for interaction across race/ethnicity barriers and limit student learning experiences with socially and culturally diverse groups (Hurtado, Dey, & Treviño, 1994). Second, in environments that lack diverse populations, underrepresented groups are viewed as tokens. Tokenism contributes to the heightened visibility of the underrepresented group, exaggeration of group differences, and the distortion of images to fit existing stereotypes (Kanter, 1977). The sheer fact that racial and ethnic students remain minorities in majority White environments contributes to their social stigma (Steele, 1992) and can produce minority status stress (Prillerman, Myers, & Smedley, 1989; Smedley, Myers, & Harrell, 1993). Third, an institution's stance on increasing the representation of diverse racial/ethnic groups communicates whether maintaining a multicultural environment is a high institutional priority. For example, African American, Chicano, and White students tended to report that commitment to diversity was a high institutional priority on campuses with relatively high percentages of African American and Latino students (Hurtado, 1990).

Loo and Rolison (1986) conclude that sufficient racial/ethnic enrollments can give potential recruits the impression that the campus is hospitable: "No matter how outstanding the academic institution, ethnic minority students can feel alienated if their ethnic representation on campus is small" (p. 72). However, increasing the numbers of students of color on campus is not free from problems. The racial/ethnic restructuring of student enrollments can trigger conflict and resistance among groups. It can also create a need for institutional changes more substantial than first envisioned. Resulting changes affect both the academic and social life of the institution, resulting in, for example, the development of ethnic studies programs, diverse student organizations, specific academic support programs, and multicultural programming (Muñoz, 1989; Peterson et al., 1978; Treviño, 1992).

Increases in diverse student enrollment, however, have also become problematic for the White majority and racial/ethnic minority groups. Race relations theorists hypothesize that the larger the relative size of the minority group, the more likely it is that there will be minority/majority conflict over limited resources (Blalock, 1967). On campuses where Asian American enrollments have increased substantially, Asian American students have reported more personal experiences of discrimination than any other group (Asian Pacific, 1990). White students tend to perceive racial tension on predominantly White campuses with relatively high African American enrollments (Hurtado, 1992). However, results from this study also show that, when students feel that they are valued and that faculty and administrators are devoted to their development, they are less likely to report racial/ethnic tension on campus. This finding suggests that campuses can minimize racial tension and competition among groups by creating more "student-centered" environments.

Chang (1996) found that maximizing cross-racial interaction and encouraging ongoing discussions about race are educational practices that benefit all students. However, when minority enrollments increased without implementing these activities, students of color reported less overall satisfaction with their college experience (Chang, 1996). Thus, increasing only the structural diversity of an institution without considering the influence of each of the other dimensions of the campus racial climate is likely to produce problems for students at these institutions.

Implications for Policy and Practice

Clearly, one important step toward improving the campus climate for diversity is to increase the representation of people of color on campus. Hence, institutional and government policy must insure that access to college is available to all members of our society. Admissions practices and financial aid policies are two areas in which changes can be made that will have prompt, positive effects.

Some critics have suggested that college and graduate/professional admissions policies and practices place too much emphasis on standardized test scores and not enough on evidence of previous achievement such as high school or college grade point averages and a student's drive to achieve (Frierson, 1991; Guanier, 1997). Guanier (1997) has suggested that college and graduate/professional school admission committees decide on a minimum acceptable score, then hold a lottery to draw the entering class from the pool of candidates meeting that criterion. Students who offer qualities considered valuable to the institution would have their names entered more than once to increase the likelihood that they would be selected. "These could be students who have overcome adversity, who have particular skills and credentials, who have outstanding academic records, or who have special and worthy career aspirations" (Guanier, 1997, p. 60).

Another approach to college admissions can be found in a proposal offered in response to the *Bakke* decision (Astin, 1985; Astin, Fuller, & Green, 1978). The authors reported that standardized tests presented a significant obstacle for students from historically disadvantaged backgrounds and that the negative impact of these tests increases dramatically as the selection ratio (number of applicants compared to the number of students admitted) increases at institutions. They suggested the use of a "disadvantagement index" derived from parental income, father's educational level, and mother's educational level. This index assumes that affluent parents are more likely to provide their children with greater access to educational opportunities and are more likely to live in communities where local schools are better funded and have more educational resources.

Neither proposal is likely to provide a single best answer about reforming the college admissions process to insure that diverse people are appropriately represented. Indeed, in the case of the disadvantagement index, critics might argue that class is an insufficient proxy for race (Tierney, 1997). However, in discussing the relative merits of such approaches, a discussion might begin on how college admissions policies and programs can be reformed to insure appropriate levels of structural diversity.

Without a doubt, state and federal financial aid policies have increased the diversity of college enrollments. Researchers of student financial aid have found that financial aid generally does what it was designed to do: It increases access to higher education by increasing the probability that students will attend college (St. John 1991a; Stampen & Fenske, 1988). While all forms of aid are positively associated with the decision to attend college when *all* students are considered, not all forms of aid are equally effective for students from historically disadvantaged backgrounds. Aid packages with loans are less consistently significant in facilitating access for minority applicants than for White applicants (St. John, 1991a), and Black, Latino, and American Indian students borrow considerably less than White or Asian students (Stampen, 1985).

Maintaining appropriate forms of financial aid at the state, federal, and institutional levels is critical in increasing the diversity of student enrollments. However, federal funding has not kept pace with increases in tuition in recent years (Orfield, 1992). Recent federal policies related to financial aid still disadvantage poor families from various racial/ethnic groups, thus reducing equity and college access for them (Olivas, 1986; Orfield, 1992). The expanded availability of and extended eligibility for loan dollars (and the decreased availability of grant and work study funds) has increased access for students from middle-income families while restricting access for students from low-income backgrounds. A key component of any longterm *and* short-term response to these trends should involve substantial increases in federal student grant funding, rather than an increased emphasis on loans (Astin, 1982; St. John, 1991b). Moreover, additional investment in financial aid programs makes good fiscal sense. Funding federal financial aid programs provides a substantial return on investment of public funds (St. John & Masten, 1990).

Recent research on the impact of financial aid provides an example of how external factors (governmental policy, programs, and initiatives) influence the campus climate for diversity. Campuses must find ways to counteract the negative consequences of changes in financial aid programs for students from historically disadvantaged backgrounds. If schools are sincere in their effort to attract more diverse students, they should change institutional aid policies so that they offer as much aid as possible in grants. Moreover, institutional leaders should work with state and federal policy-makers for appropriate levels of funding for financial aid and put this money into the aid programs that are most helpful to students from historically disadvantaged backgrounds—i.e., grants and work study programs.

Campus leaders and policy-makers should not expect to substantively improve the campus racial climate by increasing only the structural diversity of institutions. In fact, problems are likely to arise without improvements in other aspects of campus climate. Increased structural diversity will likely fail in achieving its goals unless accompanied by efforts to make institu-

tions more "student-centered" in approaches to teaching and learning (Hurtado, 1992) and by regular and on-going opportunities for students to communicate and interact cross-racially (Chang, 1996).

The Psychological Dimension of Climate and Its Impact on Students

The psychological dimension of the campus racial climate involves individuals' views of group relations, institutional responses to diversity, perceptions of discrimination or racial conflict, and attitudes toward those from other racial/ethnic backgrounds than one's own. It is important to note that more recent studies show that racially and ethnically diverse administrators, students, and faculty tend to view the campus climate differently. Thus, an individual's position and power within the organization and his or her status as "insider" or "outsider" strongly influence attitudes (Collins, 1986). In other words, who you are and where you are positioned in an institution will affect how you experience and view the institution. For example, Loo and Rolison (1986) found that 68 percent of White students thought their university was generally supportive of minority students; only 28 percent of the African American and Chicano students expressed the same opinion. Cabrera and Nora (1994) found that students of color were more sensitive to different forms of prejudice and discrimination; White students were less likely to perceive nuances. Variations within ethnic groups also occur, depending on the student's background and sense of ethnic identity. For example, one study found that American Indian students who closely held to American Indian values were likely to report more negative racial encounters in college than other students (Huffman, 1991). These perceptual differences of the college experience are significant, for perception is both a product of the environment and potential determinant of future interactions and outcomes (Astin, 1968; Tierney, 1987). As past and contemporary research reveals, these differing perceptions and experiences have real consequences for individuals.

General student perceptions of discrimination have a significant and negative effect on African American students' grades (Nettles,

1988; Prillerman et al., 1989; Smedley et al., 1993). First-year students who felt that they were singled out or treated differently in the classroom reported a higher sense of alienation at the end of their freshman year (Cabrera & Nora, 1994). While significant for all racial/ethnic groups, this form of discrimination was particularly detrimental to African Americans. A longitudinal study of highly talented Latino students found that perceptions of racial tension between groups on campus in the first year had a consistently negative effect on academic and psychological adjustment in subsequent college years (Hurtado, Carter, & Spuler, 1996). The study also found that while reports of overt instances of personal harassment/discrimination did not significantly affect academic and personal-emotional adjustment, they diminished Latino students' feelings of attachment to the institution. Another study of freshman minority students found that perceptions of discrimination affected their academic and social experiences but not their persistence in college (Nora & Cabrera, 1996). It may be that, although academically confident students of color continue to feel marginalized, they learn how to deal with discrimination (Tracey & Sedlacek, 1985).

However, even students of color who persist through graduation may feel high levels of alienation: one study found less satisfaction and more social alienation among African American and Asian American students who stayed at the institution as compared to those who left the university, presumably for better environments (Bennett & Okinaka, 1990). Introducing ways for students to report and seek redress for negative experiences is important, but campuses must also be aware that many psychological aspects of the college climate go unreported. A study of California State institutions revealed that Asian Pacific Americans often do not use formal grievance procedures when they experience discrimination or harassment (Asian Pacific, 1994). Native American students confirmed that perceptions of racial hostility were strongly associated with feelings of isolation, but the effect on their attitudes toward college or grade point average was not decisively significant (Lin, LaCounte, & Eder, 1988).

In a multi-campus study, Gilliard (1996) found that the most significant climate measure for Black students was their perceptions of racial discrimination by college administrators. She

also found that White students' sense of belonging was negatively affected by a poor racial climate but was positively tied to having non-White friends and to perceptions that the campus accepted and respected African American students. Similarly, Nora and Cabrera (1996) found that White students' persistence in college was both directly and indirectly affected by perceptions of discrimination. These studies show that White students are also affected by the climate for racial/ethnic diversity.

Research on the impact of peer groups and other reference groups is helpful in understanding another important aspect of the psychological dimension of climate on campus. Peer groups influence students' attitudes and behavior through the norms that they communicate to their members. While faculty play an important role in the educational development of students, most researchers believe that student peer groups are principally responsible for socialization (Chickering, 1969; Feldman & Newcomb, 1969). This finding does not minimize the role of faculty; rather, it suggests that their normative influence will be amplified or attenuated by the interactions students have with their peers. While peer groups clearly have the greatest impact in the undergraduate socialization process, recent research on the impact of college on students' racial attitudes, cultural awareness/acceptance, and social/political attitudes suggests that faculty may have a larger, more important role than traditionally believed (Hurtado, 1990, 1992; Milem, 1992, 1994, 1998).

Implications for Policy and Practice

Institutional leaders can significantly strengthen the psychological climate on their campuses by purposefully becoming deliberate agents of socialization. They can begin by designing and implementing systematic and comprehensive educational programs to help all members of the campus community to identify and confront the stereotypes and myths that people have about those who are different from them. While much of what is known about the development and reduction of prejudice and bias comes from the research of college and university faculty, many businesses and organizations in the private sector have shown a greater willingness to apply these findings in the hope of strengthening their organizational effectiveness. If these activities provide opportunities for cross-racial interaction, the magnitude of difference in perceptions of the racial climate between White students and students of color on campus is likely to be dramatically reduced (Pascarella et al., 1996).

Because perceptions of discrimination have consequences for all students, institutions should do all that they can to insure that students perceive the institutional climate as fair and just. Hence, institutions must have clearly stated policies and procedures to help the campus community confront and resolve incidents of harassment and discrimination. These policies and procedures should include formal processes for resolving conflicts or disputes that involve representatives from all members of the campus community (students, faculty, staff).

As we discussed earlier, there will almost certainly be significant differences in perceptions of the climate based on the experience and position of the person being asked. Campus leaders should insure that the perspectives of all members of the campus community be considered in decision-making processes. Hence, institutions must implement regular and on-going assessments of the campus climate for diversity.

Research findings clearly document the important role of ethnic student organizations and other student support services for students of color on predominantly White campuses. Hence, campuses must insure that these services and organizations have enough staff, funding, and resources to serve students successfully.

An emerging body of research on mentoring suggests that academe poorly socializes graduate students of color into the culture of academic departments. Students of color who pursue research on issues relevant to their cultural/ethnic background frequently report difficulty in finding faculty who encourage and support their work. This faculty indifference probably influences negatively student perceptions of the climate of the institution and may have a detrimental effect on their graduate student experience (Nealy, 1996; Turner & Thompson, 1993; Willie, Grady, & Hope, 1991). Institutional leaders can address these concerns by providing formal mentoring programs where students are matched with faculty who will support them and their work as emerging scholars.

The research in social psychology and higher education has suggested for some time that peer groups are critical in students' educa-

tional experience. However, institutions of higher education have not done all that they can to incorporate these groups into the formal educational process. Rather than leaving cross-racial interactions among students to chance, educators should make peer groups a deliberate and positive part of the educational process in colleges and universities.

Recent research also suggests that faculty serve a more important role in influencing students' attitudes and values than had been previously thought. It is time to shift the debate from whether faculty can (or should) be "objective" to how to give faculty support and guidance in becoming aware of their biases and the effect of these biases on their students.

The Behavioral Dimension of Climate and Its Impact on Students

The behavioral dimension of the institutional climate consists of (a) actual reports of general social interaction, (b) interaction between and among individuals from different racial/ethnic backgrounds, and (c) the nature of intergroup relations on campus. Student involvement plays a central role in undergraduates' successful educational experience; it enhances cognitive and affective student outcomes (Astin 1988, 1991, 1993; Kuh, Schuh, Whitt, Andreas, Lyons, Strange, Krehbiel, & MacKay, 1991; Pascarella & Terenzini, 1991) and retention (Tinto 1987, 1993). "Involving colleges" foster high expectations for student performance, minimize status distinctions, and have an unwavering commitment to multiculturalism (Kuh et al., 1991).

The prevailing contemporary view is that campus race relations are poor, social interaction is low, and students from different racial/ethnic groups are segregating themselves from other groups (Altbach & Lomotey, 1991; Bunzel, 1992). To be sure, incidents of overt racism and harassment occurred with greater frequency at the end of the 1980s and received much press coverage (Farrell & Jones, 1988). However, several research studies based on students' interactions and relations on campus paint a different picture. White students interpreted ethnic group clustering as racial segregation, while minority students viewed this behavior as cultural support within a larger unsupportive environment (Loo & Rolison, 1986). Chicano, Asian American, and African American students reported widespread and frequent interaction across race/ethnicity in various informal situations (i.e., dining, roommates, dating, socializing), but White students were least likely to report any of these activities as interracial (Hurtado, Dey, & Treviño, 1994). Although African Americans and Asian Americans reported more frequent racial/ethnic harassment (32% and 30% respectively), such experiences did not significantly diminish interaction across race/ethnicity for these groups.

The absence of interracial contact clearly influences students' views toward others, support for campus initiatives, and educational outcomes. White students who had the least social interaction with someone of a different background were less likely to hold positive attitudes toward multiculturalism on campus (Globetti, Globetti, Brown, & Smith, 1993). Conversely, White students who had socialized with someone of another race, had discussed racial/ethnic issues with other students, or had attended racial/cultural awareness workshops were more likely to value the goal of promoting racial understanding (Milem, 1992, 1994, 1998). Another study revealed that socializing across race and discussing racial/ethnic issues have a positive effect on students' retention, overall satisfaction with college, intellectual self-concept, and social self-concept (Chang, 1996). After studying the complex dynamics of interaction on the U.C. Berkeley campus, where dramatic changes in racial/ethnic enrollments have occurred, Duster (1993) suggested continued support for strong ethnic identities and affiliations as well as institutional encouragement for multiracial contacts.

Although some suggest that racial/ethnic student organizations and minority programs contribute to campus segregation, a series of studies refutes this perspective. These studies have empirically demonstrated that students join racial/student organizations because they are identity enhancing and that such increased identity comfort may lead to a greater interest in both cultural and cross-cultural activities (Treviño, 1992; Mitchell & Dell, 1992). Treviño (1992) found that members of racial/ethnic student organizations were more likely to participate in racial/cultural awareness workshops. Students in such organizations also report more frequent

informal interactions across race/ethnicity (Hurtado, Dey, & Treviño, 1994). In addition, Gilliard (1996) found that participation in racially focused cultural activities and support programs (e.g., Black Student Union, minority peer support services) was correlated with African Americans' higher social involvement, informal social interactions with faculty, and higher use of general support services.

Implications for Policy and Practice

Research on the behavioral dimension of racial climate suggests a wide range of beneficial practices for students. While institutions cannot change their pasts, they can clearly articulate to all members of the community the expectation that interracial dialogue and interaction are highly valued on campus. They should try to provide students with opportunities for cross-racial interaction whenever possible—both in and out of the classroom. This interaction should be structured so that it will be positive for participants. The contact should be regular, on-going, and viewed as equal in status by all participants. Finally, the contact should occur in an environment characterized by cooperation and not competition (Allport, 1954).

Faculty can facilitate positive interaction in the classroom by insuring that racial/ethnic diversity is part of the course content. Moreover, faculty can promote interaction across racial/ethnic groups and student achievement. Cooperative learning activities, inside and outside of the classroom, increase interaction across race/ethnicity and lead to intergroup friendships (Slavin, 1985). When students work cooperatively on course content, they learn more about one another as well as about the specific content areas. Faculty members should also consider how to modify their classroom practices to reduce competition in the classroom. Finally, given the important role of faculty contact (in and out of the classroom), institutions should provide abundant opportunities for all faculty-student contact in and out of the classroom. Given the academic reward structure at many institutions, institutional leaders may need to provide incentives to encourage faculty to engage students in this way.

Cross-race interactions can be also enhanced by the programs and activities of multicultural centers. These centers frequently house the ethnic student organizations that are critical to the educational success of the students they represent. Given the importance of these organizations in affirming a sense of identity for students and in their role of encouraging students to become involved in other aspects of campus life, campus leaders should vigorously support these organizations for all students, communicating their importance as essential educational resources. Such an approach should help overcome the problem that, while multicultural centers are frequently the center of activity and support for students of color, White students are less likely to be involved in these centers' programs and activities.

Finally, research in race relations indicates that increased structural diversity is usually accompanied by increased levels of conflict. However, conflict should not be viewed as a destabilizing force in higher education institutions. Parker Palmer (1987) suggests that conflict is an essential component of meaningful communities, which he defines "as a capacity for relatedness within individuals—relatedness not only to people but to events in history, to nature, to world of ideas, and yes, to things of the spirit" (p. 24). In communities that are not perceived as supportive, conflict is likely viewed as a threat to be avoided. Hence, it is essential that institutions provide ways for members of the campus community to successfully understand and resolve conflict. Then conflict can become a stimulus for creativity and community-building. Dialogue groups can provide both a structure and process for addressing the intergroup dynamics of multiculturalism within the learning environment. Activities for the learning process include the opportunity to break down barriers, challenge the ignorance inside and outside oneself, create new insights, forge new connections and identities, and finally, build coalitions to work toward a common goal (Zúñiga & Nagda, 1992). The issue of group conflict and social attitudes surrounding communities of difference addressed in dialogue groups are "not easily resolvable as long as the lack of adequate structures and processes for intergroup interactions in the college community maintains the invisible, but psychologically real walls that separate different groups" (Zúñiga and Nagda, 1992, p. 251).

From Research to Policy and Practice: Strategies for Improving Campus Diversity

Recent research on the campus climate for diversity has enabled campuses to better understand institutions and their impact on students, student responses to climate issues, and relationships that develop among diverse students and faculty. While many institutions are still contending with issues of diversifying their campus enrollments, more campuses need information to help them address the psychological and behavioral dimensions of the climate. At national higher education conferences, more individuals are talking about improving the climate and are sharing practices that work. The empirical evidence and policy recommendations provided here will help institutional administrators and program planners use a wealth of research, about both specific institutions and national samples of students and institutions. In addition, many institutions are undertaking assessments of their climate for diversity to understand better their own institutional contexts. While a wealth of knowledge is now available and institutions are better informed as they begin self-examinations, designing an action plan that will significantly improve the quality of experiences for undergraduates is perhaps the next important challenge in the process.

Campuses are complex social systems defined by the relationships between the people, bureaucratic procedures, structural arrangements, institutional goals and values, traditions, and larger socio-historical environments. Therefore, any effort to redesign campuses with the goal of improving the climate for racial and cultural diversity must be comprehensive and long term. Institutions change slowly. It is the nature of a stable system of higher education. Therefore, the success of efforts to achieve institutional change will rely on leadership, firm commitment, adequate resources, collaboration, monitoring, and long-range planning.

Institutional change can be implemented at several levels. Most important is the structural level. An institution should increase at all levels the number of previously excluded and underrepresented racial/ethnic minorities (i.e., students, faculty, staff, administrators). Ideally minorities should be represented on the campus in proportionate numbers. While efforts to increase the representation of minorities on campus and to remove barriers to their participation are crucial, these steps alone are not sufficient to achieve the goal of improving the climate for diversity.

Beyond the observable make-up of the students and faculty are the attitudinal and behavioral characteristics of how particular groups of individuals "feel" about and relate to one another. How does the campus "feel" to minority individuals (e.g., Do they feel welcome? Do they sense hostility? Do they feel valued?). How does the campus respond to racially and culturally different groups (e.g., Does the campus strive to change to incorporate these students or does the campus communicate that adaptation is the job of only the minority students? Does the campus genuinely value diversity?).

In short, two sets of issues are important when considering the success of efforts to improve the campus racial climate: (a) How diverse does the campus look in its representation of different cultural groups? and (b) To what extent do campus operations demonstrate that racial and ethnic diversity is an essential value?

References

Allen, W. R. (1992). The color of success: African-American college student outcomes at predominantly white and historically black public colleges and universities. *Harvard Educational Review, 62*(1), 26–44.

Allen, W. R., Epps, E. G., & Haniff, N. Z. (Eds). (1991). *College in Black and White: African American students in predominantly White and in historically Black public universities.* Albany: State University of New York Press.

Allport, G. W. (1954). *The nature of prejudice.* Reading, MA: Addison-Wesley.

Altbach, P. G., & Lomotey, K. (Eds.). (1991). *The racial crisis in American higher education.* Albany: State University of New York Press.

Asian Pacific American Education Advisory Committee. (1990). *Enriching California's future: Asian Pacific Americans in the CSU.* Long Beach, CA: Office of the Chancellor, The California State University.

Asian Pacific American Education Advisory Committee. (1994). *Asian Pacific Americans in the California State University: A follow-up report.* Long Beach, CA: Office of the Chancellor, The California State University.

Astin, A. W. (1968). *The college environment.* Washington, DC: American Council on Education.

Astin, A. W. (1982). *Minorities in American higher education.* San Francisco: Jossey-Bass.

Astin, A. W. (1985). *Achieving educational excellence.* San Francisco: Jossey-Bass.

Astin, A. W. (1988). Student involvement: A developmental theory for higher education. *Journal of College Student Personnel, 25*(4), 297–308.

Astin, A. W. (1991). *Assessment for excellence: The philosophy and practice of assessment and evaluation in higher education.* New York: Macmillan.

Astin, A. W. (1993). *What matters in college: Four critical years revisited.* San Francisco: Jossey-Bass.

Astin, A. W., Fuller, B., & Green, K. C. (1978). *Admitting and assisting students after Bakke.* New Directions for Higher Education, No. 23. San Francisco: Jossey-Bass.

Bennett, C., & Okinaka, A. M. (1990, March). Factors related to persistence among Asian, Black, Hispanic, and White undergraduates at a predominantly White university: Comparison between first and fourth year cohorts. *Urban Review, 22*(1), 33–60.

Blalock, J. M. (1967). *Toward a theory of minority-group relations.* New York: Wiley.

Braddock, J. H. (1980). The perpetuation of segregation across levels of education: A behavioral assessment of the contact hypothesis. *Sociology of Education, 53,* 178–186.

Braddock, J. H. (1985). School desegregation and Black assimilation. *Journal of Social Issues, 41*(3), 9–22.

Braddock, J. H., Crain, R. L., & McPartland, J. M. (1984, December). A long-term view of school desegregation: Some recent studies of graduates as adults. *Phi Delta Kappan,* 259–264.

Braddock, J. H., & Dawkins, M. (1981). Predicting achievement in higher education. *Journal of Negro Education, 50,* 319–327.

Braddock, J. H., & McPartland, J. M. (1982). Assessing school desegregation effects: New directions in research. In A. C. Kerckhoff (Ed.) & R. C. Corwin (Guest Ed.), *Research in Sociology of Education and Socialization, Vol. 3* (pp. 259–292). Greenwich, CT: JAI.

Braddock, J. H., & McPartland, J. M. (1989). Social-psychological processes that perpetuate racial segregation: The relationship between school and employment desegregation. *Journal of Black Studies, 19*(3), 267–289.

Bunzel, J. H. (1992). *Race Relations on Campus: Stanford Students Speak.* Stanford, CA: Stanford Alumni Association.

Cabrera, A. F., & Nora, A. (1994). College student perceptions of prejudice and discrimination and their feelings of alienation: A construct validation approach. *Review of Education/Pedagogy/Cultural Studies, 16*(3–4), 387–409.

Carter, D. J., & Wilson, R. (1993). *Minorities in higher education: Eleventh annual status report.* Washington DC: American Council on Education.

Chang, M. J. (1996). *Racial diversity in higher education: Does a racially mixed student population affect educational outcomes?* Unpublished doctoral dissertation, University of California, Los Angeles.

Chickering, A. W. (1969). *Education and identity.* San Francisco: Jossey-Bass.

Collins, P. H. (1986). Learning from the outsider within: The sociological significance of Black feminist thought. *Social Problems, 33*(6), 514–532.

Davis, E. B. (1993). Desegregation in higher education: Twenty-five years of controversy from Geier to Ayers. *Journal of Law and Education, 22*(4), 519–524.

Davis, R. (1991). Social support networks and undergraduate student academic-success-related outcomes: A comparison of Black students on Black and White campuses. In W. R. Allen, E. G. Epps, & N. Z. Haniff (Eds.), *College in Black and White: African n American students in predominantly White and in historically Black public universities* (pp. 143–57). Albany: SUNY Press.

Durán, R. P. (1983). *Hispanics' education and background: Predictors of college achievement.* New York: College Board Publications.

Duster, T. (1993). The diversity of California at Berkeley: An emerging reformulation of "competence" in an increasingly multicultural world. In B. W. Thompson and Sangeeta Tyagi (Eds.), *Beyond a dream deferred: Multicultural education and the politics of excellence* (pp. 231–255). Minneapolis, MN: University of Minnesota Press.

El-Khawas, E. (1989). *Campus Trends, 1989.* Higher Education Panel Reports, No. 78. Washington, DC: American Council on Education.

Farrell, W. C., Jr., & Jones, C. K. (1988). Recent racial incidents in higher education: A preliminary perspective. *Urban Review, 20*(3), 211–233.

Feldman, K. A., & Newcomb, T. M. (1969). *The impact of college on students, Vol. 1.* San Francisco: Jossey-Bass.

Frierson, H. T. (1991). Intervention can make a difference: The impact on standardized tests and classroom performance. In W. R. Allen, E. G. Epps, & N. Z. Haniff (Eds.), *College in Black and White: African American Students in predominantly White and in historically Black public universities* (pp. 225–238). Albany: SUNY Press.

Gilliard, M. D. (1996). *Racial climate and institutional support factors affecting success in predominantly White Institutions: An examination of African Amer-*

ican and White student experiences. Unpublished doctoral dissertation, University of Michigan.

Globetti, E. C., Globetti, G., Brown, C. L., & Smith, R. E. (1993). Social interaction and multiculturalism. *NASPA Journal, 30*(3), 209–218.

Green, K. C. (1982). *The impact of neighborhood and secondary school integration on educational achievement and occupational attainment of college-bound Blacks.* Unpublished doctoral dissertation, University of California, Los Angeles.

Guanier, L. (1997, August 7). The real bias in higher education. *Black Issues in Higher Education,* p. 60.

Horowitz, H. L. (1987). *Campus life: Undergraduate cultures from the end of the eighteenth century to the present.* Chicago: University of Chicago.

Huffman, T. E. (1991). The experiences, perceptions, and consequences of campus racism among Northern Plains Indians. *Journal of American Indian Education, 30*(2), 25–34.

Hurtado, S. (1990). *Campus racial climates and educational outcomes.* Unpublished doctoral dissertation, University of California, Los Angeles. Ann Arbor: University Microfilms International, No. 9111328.

Hurtado, S. (1992). The campus racial climate: Contexts for conflict. *The Journal of Higher Education, 63*(5), 539–569.

Hurtado, S. (1994). The institutional climate for talented Latino students. *Research in Higher Education, 35*(1), 21–41.

Hurtado, S., Dey, E., & Treviño, J. (1994). *Exclusion or self-segregation? Interaction across racial/ethnic groups on college campuses.* Paper presented at the American Educational Research Association conference, New Orleans.

Hurtado, S., Carter, D. F., & Spuler, A. (1996). Latino student transition to college. *Research in Higher Education, 37*(2), 135–157.

Hurtado, S., Milem, J. F., Clayton-Pedersen, A. R., & Allen, W. R. (in press). *Enacting diverse learning environments: Improving the campus climate for racial/ethnic diversity.* ASHE/ERIC Higher Education Report Series.

Jackson, K. W. & Swan, L. A. (1991). Institutional and individual factors affecting Black undergraduate student performance: Campus race and student gender. In W. R. Allen, E. G. Epps, & N. Z. Haniff (Eds.), *College in Black and White: African American students in predominantly White and in historically Black public universities* (pp. 127–141). Albany: SUNY Press.

Kanter, R. M. (1977). Some effects of proportions on group life: Skewed sex ratios and responses to token women. *American Journal of Sociology, 82,* 965–989.

Kuh, G., Schuh, J. S., Whitt, E. J., Andreas, R. E., Lyons, J. W., Strange, C. C., Krehbiel, L. E., & MacKay, K. A. (1991). *Involving colleges: Successful approaches to fostering student learning and personal development outside the classroom.* San Francisco: Jossey-Bass.

Lin, R., LaCounte, D., and Eder, J. (1988). A study of Native American students in a predominantly White college. *Journal of American Indian Education, 27*(3), 8–15.

Loo, C. M., & Rolison, G. (1986). Alienation of ethnic minority students at a predominately White university. *Journal of Higher Education, 57*, 58–77.

Milam, J. H. (1989). The presence of paradigms in the core higher education journal literature. *Research in Higher Education, 32*(6), 651–668.

Milem, J. F. (1992). *The impact of college on students' racial attitudes and levels of racial awareness.* Unpublished doctoral dissertation, UCLA. Ann Arbor: University Microforms International (UMI), No. 9301968.

Milem, J. F. (1994). College, students, and racial understanding. *Thought and Action, 9*(2), 51–92.

Milem, J. F. (1998). Attitude change in college students: Examining the effect of college peer groups and faculty normative groups. *Journal of Higher Education, 69*(2), 117–140.

Mitchell, S. L., & Dell, D. M. (1992). The relationship between Black students' racial identity attitude and participation in campus organizations. *Journal of College Student Development, 33*, 39–43.

Muñoz, C. (1989). *Youth, identity, and power in the Chicano movement.* New York: Verso.

Nealy, C. (1996). *The musing of an at-risk student.* Paper presented at the annual meeting of the American Educational Research Association, New York.

Nettles, M. (Ed.). (1988). *Toward Black undergraduate student equality in American higher education.* Westport, CT: Greenwood Press.

Nora, A., & Cabrera, A. F. (1996). The role of perceptions of prejudice and discrimination on the adjustment of minority students to college. *Journal of Higher Education, 67*(2), 119–148.

Olivas, M. A. (1986). The retreat from access. *Academe, 72*(6), 16–18.

Orfield, G. (1992). Money, equity, and college access. *Harvard Educational Review, 62*(3), 337–372.

Palmer, P. J. (1987). Community, conflict, and ways of knowing. *Change, 19*(5), 20–25.

Pascarella, E. T., & Terenzini, P. T. (1991). *How college affects students: Findings and insights from twenty years of research.* San Francisco: Jossey-Bass.

Pascarella, E. T., Smart, J. C., Ethington, C., & Nettles, M. (1987). The influence of college on self-concept: A consideration of race and gender differences. *American Educational Research Journal, 24*, 49–77.

Pascarella, E. T., Whitt, E. J., Nora, A., Edison, M., Hagedorn, L. S., & Terenzini, P. T. (1996). What have we learned from the first year of the national study of student learning? *Journal of College Student Development, 37*(2), 182–192.

Peterson, M. W., Blackburn, R. T., Gamson, Z. F., Arce, C. H., Davenport, R. W., & Mingle, J. R. (1978). *Black students on White campuses: The impacts of increased Blacks enrollments.* Ann Arbor: Institute for Social Research, University of Michigan.

Prillerman, S. L., Myers, H. F., & Smedley, B. D. (1989). Stress, well-being, and academic achievement in college. In G. L. Berry and J. K. Asamen (Eds.) *Black students: Psychosocial issues and academic achievement* (pp. 198–217). Newbury Park, CA: Sage.

Richardson, R., & Skinner, E. (1991). *Achieving diversity.* Washington, DC: ACE/Macmillan.

Scott, R. R., & McPartland, J. M. (1982). Desegregation as national policy: Correlates of racial attitudes. *American Educational Research Journal, 19*(3), 397–414.

Sedlacek, W. (1987). Black students on White campuses: 20 years of research. *Journal of College Student Personnel, 28*(6) 484–95.

Slavin, R. E. (1985). Cooperative learning: Applying contact theory in desegregated schools. *Journal of Social Issues, 41*(1), 45–62.

Smedley, B. D., Myers, H. F., & Harrell, S. P. (1993). Minority-status stresses and the college adjustment of ethnic minority freshmen. *Journal of Higher Education, 64*(4), 434–452.

Southern Education Foundation. (1995). *Redeeming the American promise: Report of the panel on educational opportunity and postsecondary desegregation.* Atlanta: Southern Education Foundation.

St. John, E. P. (1991a). The impact of student financial aid: A review of recent research. *Journal of Student Financial Aid, 21*(1), 18–32.

St. John, E. P. (1991b). What really influences minority attendance? Sequential analyses of the high school and beyond sophomore cohort. *Research in Higher Education, 32*(2), 141–158.

St. John, E. P., & Masten, C. L. (1990). Return on investment in student financial aid: An assessment for the high school class of 1972. *Journal of Student Financial Aid, 20*(3), 4–23.

Stampen, J. O. (1985). *Student aid and public higher education: Recent changes.* Washington, DC: American Association of State Colleges and Universities.

Stampen, J. O., & Fenske, R. H. (1988). The impact of financial aid on ethnic minorities. *Review of Higher Education, 11*(4), 337–353.

Steele, C. M. (1992, April). Race and the schooling of Black Americans. *Atlantic Monthly,* 68–78.

Stewart, J. B. (1991). Planning for cultural diversity: A case study. In H. E. Cheatham (Ed.), *Cultural Pluralism on Campus* (pp. 161–191). N.p.: American College Personnel Association.

Thelin, J. (1985). Beyond the background music: Historical research on admissions and access in higher education. In John C. Smart (Ed.), *Higher Education Handbook of Theory and Research, Vol. 1.* (pp. 349–380). New York: Agathon.

Tierney, W. G. (1997). The parameters of affirmative action: Equity and excellence in the academy. *Review of Educational Research, 67*(2), 165–196.

Tinto, V. (1987). *Leaving college: Rethinking the causes and cures of student attrition* (1st ed.) Chicago: University of Chicago Press.

Tinto, V. (1993). *Leaving college: Rethinking the causes and cures of student attrition* (2nd ed.). Chicago: University of Chicago Press.

Turner, C., & Thompson, J. (1993). Socializing women doctoral students: Minority and majority experiences. *The Review of Higher Education, 16*, 355–370.

Tracey, T. J., & Sedlacek, W. E. (1985). The relationship of noncognitive variables to academic success: A longitudinal comparison by race. *Journal of College Student Personnel, 26*, 405–410.

Treviño, J. G. (1992). *Participating in ethnic/racial student organizations.* Unpublished doctoral dissertation, University of California, Los Angeles.

Williams, John B., III. (1988). Title VI regulation of higher education. In J. B. Williams (Ed.), *Desegregating America's Colleges and Universities* (pp. 3–53). New York: Teachers College Press.

Willie, C., Grady, M., & Hope, R. (1991). *African-Americans and the doctoral experience: Implications for policy.* New York: Teachers College.

Zúñiga, X., & Nagda, B. A. (1992). Dialogue groups: An innovative approach to multicultural learning. In David Schoem (Ed.), *Multicultural teaching at the university* (pp. 233–248). New York: Praeger.

CHAPTER 9

FIRST ENCOUNTERS OF THE BUREAUCRATIC KIND:
EARLY FRESHMAN EXPERIENCES
WITH A CAMPUS BUREAUCRACY

GLEN J. GODWIN AND WILLIAM T. MARKHAM

As the dominant organizational form in our society [17], bureaucracy provides the framework within which much everyday activity takes place [38], shaping and constraining the behavior of most everyone [10, 25]. Learning to operate in a bureaucracy is therefore a crucial aspect of socialization [45, 25]. Yet adapting to bureaucratic roles is not always easy, especially for "lower participants" [11] in organizations, such as clients and ordinary employees [2, 25]. Lower participants may find themselves alienated [25], disempowered [8, 37], and confused or frustrated by bureaucratic dysfunctions [27]—ranging from red tape and rigidity [29] to communications breakdowns[9]. It is therefore not surprising that overt protests by lower participants stemming partly from dissatisfaction with bureaucratic requirements appear episodically, as in the case of the student revolts of the 1960s and 70s.

Nevertheless, despite occasional protests, the organizational landscape is clearly characterized more frequently by stability and acquiescence to bureaucracy than by sharp dissent. Several explanations for the widespread acceptance of bureaucracy despite its problems have been proposed. Bureaucracy may be less aggravating than sometimes claimed [36], or coercion and managerial chicanery may overcome resistance [10]. Mechanisms for compromising the interests of leaders and lower-participants may defuse conflict [7], or clients and employees may accept bureaucracy's disadvantages in return for a steady flow of benefits [18].

But despite its importance, the question of how and why lower participants come to give assent to bureaucratic requirements remains surprisingly neglected in research [25, 42], especially research in higher education. This study broadens our knowledge in this area through an in-depth study of an especially interesting set of lower participants—traditional-age college freshmen at a large state university. Its purpose is to determine how these students' interpretations of and adaptations to the campus bureaucracy allow the bureaucracy to remain stable and continue to function with few challenges and relatively little overt conflict—despite all the problems that bureaucracy is alleged to raise for clients. Answering this question requires an examination of the properties of bureaucracy and the problems it may present for students. It requires as well in-depth investigation of how students as bureaucratic clients develop understandings of the bureaucratic milieu, how they define their situations and options, how they negotiate patterns of interaction with their peers and superordinates, and how they cope with stresses that their experience with and adaptations to the bureaucracy engender.

"First Encounters of the Bureaucratic Kind: Early Freshman Experiences with a Campus Bureaucracy." Reprinted from *Journal of Higher Education* 67, no. 6 (1996), Ohio State University Press.

Although newcomers to the university have been neglected in past studies of bureaucracy, this population is theoretically and practically strategic. Traditional-age freshmen are newcomers to a large and complex campus bureaucracy. Examining their emerging views of the bureaucracy and the patterns of action they develop to cope with it provides an especially clear view of the stresses built into bureaucratic roles—stresses to which more seasoned participants in the campus bureaucracy might already have become inured. By investigating the socializing experiences of newcomers, we gain insight into how patterns of acquiescence and coping become established—as well as how the pressures of bureaucracy occasionally lead to active resistance or exit from the university.

Furthermore, for many traditional-age freshmen, encounters with the campus bureaucracy are among their first *adult* experiences with bureaucracy, and for those without work experience in large organizations these encounters can be their very first. Learning to fit into a bureaucratic society is, of course, one part of the "hidden curriculum" of elementary and secondary schools [15, 19], but freshmen encounter bureaucracy in a new way—as adults. They must now transact business with strangers who provide minimal help and emotional support. They must assume more personal responsibility, and they receive fewer allowances for immaturity and inexperience. Consequently, young adults' early encounters with bureaucracy can be difficult learning experiences, and their early interpretations of and adaptations to bureaucracy can set the pattern for later ones.

Our investigation has three parts. First, we reviewed existing literature about the problems that clients—especially newcomers—face adapting to bureaucracy. Past work on organizational socialization [45] and student life [33] is almost completely silent on this topic, but other bodies of work provide useful leads. We reviewed studies of dysfunctions of bureaucracy that confuse and frustrate clients, studies of client powerlessness and its effects, literature about how organizational actors go about defining their situations and the implications of their definitions, and studies of how clients negotiate their roles and adapt to bureaucracy.

Second, we conducted preliminary field observation of students as they encountered the campus bureaucracy in various university offices.

These observations helped us to see how well issues and patterns described in the general literature about clients in bureaucracy applied to students on campus and identify unique issues that this particular bureaucracy poses for students. The observations also provided hints about how students define their experiences with the campus bureaucracy and direct information about their coping behaviors. We used this information in combination with ideas from the literature review to construct questions for subsequent interviews with Freshmen students and staff and as a validity check on students' reports about their dealings with the bureaucracy.

Finally, we conducted semistructured interviews with samples of traditional-age freshmen and staff in the offices that deal with them. The interviews with freshmen provide extensive information about their interpretations of the campus bureaucracy, the problems it posed for them, and their adaptations to it. The staff interviews provide the staff's insights about student behavior, and they also tell us how staff members' own views and behavior affect their interaction with students.

Bureaucratic Dysfunctions and Powerlessness as Problems for Clients in a Bureaucracy

Bureaucracies combine rules, specialization, hierarchy, impersonality, and records to create an orderly, efficient structure that processes work quickly [16, 35, 47]. Yet despite its vaunted efficiency, existing literature suggests that bureaucracy can also develop irritating and frustrating dysfunctions [9, 27]. Bureaucratic rules can become too numerous, rigid, conflicting, and confusing [9, 25, 27, 32]. Officials may develop "bureaucratic personalities," placing more emphasis on rules than on client needs [29]. Clients may have to revisit offices repeatedly, endure long waits, and follow complex procedures. Proliferation of specialized departments can lead to poor coordination [23, 27], duplication of requests for information [25], to situations in which no one seems to have the authority or information to act effectively, and a tendency for departments to put their own priorities ahead of client needs [9, 27]. Powerful officials can impose onerous requirements that clients lack the power to contest [8]. Managers—who often lack substantive expertise but want to display their initiative nonetheless—may implement procedures that impede client service [9, 44, 49]. Bureaucratic impersonality can make clients feel poorly served or denigrated because their unique needs go unacknowledged [24], alienating them from officials and exacerbating tensions [25]. Impersonality also encourages officials to distance themselves emotionally from clients and rigidly follow procedures to avoid criticism [25, 29]. Finally, "red tape" can become oppressive, with endless forms to complete [1, 22, 25], errors in records can deprive clients of benefits, and staff may use paperwork requirements to control or punish clients [25, 42].

Bureaucracy can also subordinate individual independence to bureaucratic imperatives [2, 6, 7]. As lower participants, clients typically occupy roles with few resources for gaining power. Authority is delegated to staff [44, 47], who have authority over clients. Clients are often predisposed by past socialization to follow bureaucratic requirements, and they may be awed by officials' titles, presumed expertise, or symbols of authority [3, 44]. They also depend on staff for help in negotiating the system and reaching their goals [3, 25, 42], and bureaucratic procedures and appeals processes frequently make challenging the system difficult [25]. Clients thus often must forego their own preferences to conform to staff demands [8, 47]. Because managers, staff, and clients frequently have different goals, this power imbalance is problematic for clients [25]. Lack of power therefore has considerable potential to produce anxiety and frustration for clients.

Clients' Definitions of the Bureaucratic Situation

Bureaucratic dysfunctions and disempowerment thus pose a set of potential problems for bureaucratic clients, especially newcomers, to solve [46]. Newcomers must make sense of a new situation, decide what possibilities it offers, and negotiate their own roles and solutions to its challenges. We could locate no studies of how this process occurs among college students, but symbolic interaction theory [41, 46] and scattered studies of clients in other bureaucracies provide some points of departure.

Symbolic interaction theory suggests that, in their initial encounters with bureaucracy, clients base their definitions of their situation on past experience and their own interpretation of their current experiences [5, 43]. They might also actively seek information about how to adapt to the system and reach their ends [25, 31]. The physical setting of offices, waiting areas, ropes, counters, and lines, might provide additional cues [5, 26, 30]. Clients cannot define situations capriciously, because the bureaucracies are highly structured and desired outcomes are more likely to accrue to those who fit into existing forms [46]. Nevertheless, bureaucracy never fully determines behavior, and clients' actions depend to a significant extent on their own definitions.

Defining situations and negotiating a solution to the problems that bureaucracy poses for them is often difficult for clients because their definitions of the situation do not agree with the world view of bureaucratic officials [24]. A client's emergency may be an official's routine problem, and paperwork and procedures that appear clear to bureaucrats may mystify clients [42]. Clients usually prefer personalized attention, but staff may be rewarded for adhering to procedure and fast processing of cases, not for providing personal attention [4, 29]. Understanding both clients' and officials' definitions is thus crucial for explaining how clients cope with bureaucracy.

Clients, Staff, and Negotiated Order

Symbolic interaction theory suggests that, based on their definitions of situation, clients and staff attempt to choose actions that let them interact successfully, reach their goals, play their roles as they understand them, maintain consistent and favorable self-images, and adapt to the situation [5, 21]. Research in other settings suggests that accomplishing this can pose a number of dilemmas for bureaucratic clients, who must decide how much inconvenience they will tolerate and how much autonomy they are willing to sacrifice to obtain services [39]. To the extent that bureaucracy causes them problems, clients must choose among strategies such as resisting bureaucratic controls, complaining about bureaucratic dysfunctions, questioning authority, learning about and embracing the requirements, or superficially acquiescing and "working the system" to reach their goals. Alternatively, they may choose to exit physically [25] or psychologically [2]. Staff also face choices. They may pursue their goals by instructing clients about rules and requirements and finding ways to control them [25]. They may make genuine efforts to meet individual needs, or—pressured by understaffing, quantitative performance measures, or sanctions for breaking rules—they may become unresponsive, orient themselves toward quotas or minutiae, or withdraw psychologically [4, 25, 29]. How they resolve these dilemmas affects clients' situation.

Because clients are usually at a power disadvantage, the heavier burden of adjustment generally falls on them. They usually face strong pressure to acquaint themselves with bureaucratic procedures and follow them, even when doing so is unpleasant [18, 48]. Nevertheless, past research shows that clients are not without resources for balancing power informally [25, 28, 37]. They can cause inconvenience by filing appeals or grievances (which must be taken seriously in rule-bound environments) or disrupt operations by making a scene [25]. They also can become "prison lawyers," acquiring enough knowledge of the rules to argue their cases effectively. They can cultivate personal relationships with bureaucrats, enlist the support of powerful outsiders [25, 42], or cultivate styles of self-presentations that make them more persuasive [13, 14].

Despite the obstacles created by differing definitions of the situation or goals, existing research suggests that clients and staff often do develop understandings and strategies that let them adapt and accomplish many of their goals [4, 25, 48]. Although clients are at a power disadvantage, the patterns of interaction that emerge are generally negotiated, not imposed unilaterally by staff [14]. For bureaucracy to operate, the two groups need not have identical definitions of situation and goals, but they must develop a working consensus to follow patterns of behavior that lets interaction proceed [48]. For example, clients can appear to acquiesce, "playing along" with irritating requirements and hiding their frustration [14]. The organization can then continue to function despite underlying disagreements [48].

The Research Setting

Our case study of newcomers' adaptations to bureaucracy focuses on traditional-age freshmen at a state university with well over ten thousand students. We examine how these newcomers—

some with little previous adult experience with bureaucracy—cope with a highly bureaucratized setting, which potentially presents freshmen with many of the problems described above. Our inquiry focuses on freshmen's experiences with four offices that most encounter almost immediately on arrival.

The *Registrar's Office* registers students for classes at a central site in the Student Center. It handles preregistration, regular registration, and schedule adjustments. To register, a student must present a schedule card, signed by his or her faculty advisor. Registration is by appointment, so students usually wait less than 30 minutes, but waits can be much longer, especially during the "add/drop" period. Freshmen register last, so they are more likely to encounter closed classes, which become even more common during "add/drops." If a class is closed, students may change sections on their own, but a new signature is required to change courses.

The *Academic Advising Office*, located in the administration building, helps with problems faculty advisors cannot resolve, places students on probation or suspension, processes petitions for exceptions to requirements and requests to declare or change majors, provides general academic counseling, and attempts to schedule "progress-assessment" appointments with first semester freshmen. Advisors ordinarily see students by appointment or on a walk-in basis. However, at the beginning of the semester, when Academic Advising is busiest, all students are seen only on a walk-in basis. They must sign in, indicate their business, and wait to be called. Students are ordinarily called in the order they have signed in, but those with simple needs are sometimes seen first.

The *Financial Aid Office*, located in a third building, administers student aid and handles work-study assignments. About half of students receive financial aid. Students who apply for federal aid must submit an elaborate Financial Aid Form to an office in another state, which determines their eligibility—sometimes only after requests for supplemental information. The Financial Aid Office then makes aid awards. Ordinarily, notices of awards are issued before a semester begins. However, delays do occur, and students may not receive the notices until after arrival on campus. Students must file a new application for each year, providing evidence of adequate academic progress. During most of the semester, Financial Aid staff see students, either by appointment or on a walk-in basis, during specified "counseling hours." But at the beginning of the fall semester, counselors are available for extended hours to see students on a walk-in basis only. Students must sign in and indicate the reason for their visit. Waits can be up to three hours because problems are being resolved and work study assignments made.

The Office of Residence Life handles room assignments and administration of meal plans for students who live on campus. It also handles requests for repairs or alterations to rooms. Students who wish to live in residence halls complete an application before arriving on campus or during the preceding semester and are assigned rooms in order of application. Residence Life conducts business at two offices, both in the same dormitory. Waits are usually short.

Other Offices. Students pick up financial aid checks and pay bills at the Cashier's Office in the Administration Building. They must present a validated ID and proceed to color-coded stations to pick up aid checks, sign checks, pay tuition and fees, and receive receipts. Long lines form at the beginning of the semester. The ID Center is located in an upstairs office in the Student Center. Existing ID's can be validated and ID's issued to new students only with proof of registration. Students with campus jobs must also present a social security card and other identification and have their completion of a federal I-9 form witnessed at the ID Center. Lines can be very long, but processing usually goes quickly and waits do not usually exceed 30 minutes.

The complex campus bureaucracy presents many potential problems for students. Some afflict bureaucratic clients generally, while others are specific to this particular setting. There are waiting lines, multiple forms to complete, impersonal processing, complicated rules. As clients, students are relatively powerless. Because offices are highly specialized, staff members may not know the details of procedures and requirements in other offices, and no one has overall responsibility for a given student's affairs. When things go wrong, it is the student who must try to coordinate the efforts of the offices and persuade staff to act. Moreover, offices that perform related functions are geographically dispersed, so staff in different offices cannot easily meet to resolve issues. Students with problems that involve several offices must go from office to office and try to communicate the results of discussions in one office to staff in another. This arrangement is conducive to communications problems that require multiple trips to different offices to resolve. Finally, many of the campus bureaucracy's procedures are long-linked technologies, so breakdowns at one step can produce a domino effect of problems later. For example, if Financial Aid sends confirmation of students' aid awards to the Cashier late, students may subsequently find their registrations canceled by the Registrar, their room contracts revoked by Housing, and their meal plans canceled by the Dining Service.

Existing theory and research suggested that traditional-age freshmen would encounter at least some problems with the campus bureaucracy and that how they defined their situation and the problems it presented would be key to understanding how they coped. However, it leaves many questions unanswered. What specific aspects of the campus bureaucracy are most and least troubling to freshmen? How do they define their experiences? What coping mechanisms do they use to deal with any frustrations caused by bureaucratic dysfunctions and their relative powerlessness? What strategies do they develop to gather information and gain their objectives? How do they relate to the staff, who may have different perceptions, needs, and goals than students? When does a working consensus that lets interaction proceed develop, and under what conditions do relations between freshmen and staff become conflictual or break down?

Data Collection and Analysis

We tailored our approach to data collection and analysis to the level of development of past literature and our research goals. Many past studies suggest that bureaucracy frequently poses problems for clients, whom it usually places at a considerable power disadvantage. The literature also identifies specific problems clients have commonly encountered in specific settings, though it gives little attention to college students as clients. Symbolic interaction theory emphasizes the importance of actors' definitions of a situation and suggested general processes by which clients develop such definitions of and strategies for coping with new or problematic settings, but it gives relatively little attention to clients in a bureaucracy. Scattered studies suggest mechanisms that clients sometimes use to manage their relationships with bureaucracies, but none look at college students as clients.

Our research strategy used a combination of nonparticipant observation and semistructured interviews to both ascertain the extent to which patterns found in previous studies recur among college freshmen and to allow the discovery of new concepts and patterns to build a grounded theory [12]. We attempted to determine whether insights from past formal theory—such as Merton's work on the dysfunctions of bureaucratic rules—and existing substantive theories about the dynamics of bureaucracy in particular settings—such as Susser's [42] insight that excessive paperwork requirements are often used to punish recalcitrant welfare clients—appeared in this setting by mapping our observational and interview data into these categories. However, we were careful to avoid forcing our data into these categories so that new categories and relationships could emerge from the data [12]. This approach, a modification of the constant comparative method [12] allowed us to discover, for example, that many freshmen did not feel especially burdened by what we might have coded as rigid rules because the rules were so institutionalized as to blend into the background of "just how it is," but that, in this setting, a pattern of events freshmen referred to as "the runaround" was a special burden.

Ten days of intensive nonparticipant observation was conducted in the offices described above and in related campus settings in the fall semester, from the beginning of freshman orientation through the end of the "add/drop" period. Observation was most intensive during the first few days, when most students on campus were freshmen. The first author, then a graduate student, attended freshman orientation sessions and circulated among the offices described above, where he waited in line and sat in waiting areas. He attempted to visit offices at peak times but limited his stay in any area to 30 minutes—less if there was little activity. He also ate in the dining hall and spent time in the student center. To avoid influencing events, he minimized interaction with other students, speaking only if addressed. He recorded observations as they were made. (Writing in a notebook is not unusual on campus.) He encountered no evidence of suspicion from students, who usually leave a site immediately after completing their

business. On three occasions, he showed a letter explaining the project to staff who questioned his presence.

Field notes were typed daily, and both researchers reviewed them. We noted (a) observations relevant to topics of theoretical importance identified by the literature review and (b) observations that were part of other unanticipated but recurrent patterns of interest (such as students' tendency to try to understand a situation by watching what went on rather than by asking questions). We discussed these unanticipated patterns as they appeared and began to seek further examples of them to understand their place in the larger picture.

The bulk of our data came from semistructured interviews conducted early in the spring semester with a systematic sample of freshmen drawn from the student directory. The directory, which lists all students enrolled after fall registration, was ideal for our purposes because freshmen who were still enrolled at the time of our interviews had just completed their second registration cycle but still had relatively little experience on campus. After eliminating students who had dropped out of school, were older than 20, or had been on campus more than two semesters, 33 eligible subjects remained. We obtained interviews with 20, 19 of whom lived on campus. Sixty-five percent were female, about the same as among all traditional-age freshmen. The semistructured interview schedule contained questions derived from the literature review and our observations. To avoid forcing data into preexisting categories, we included questions that asked about students' early and most memorable experiences in the four offices without specific guidance about what they should cover. Follow-up questions focused on more specific topics that the literature review and observational analysis suggested might be important. These included rules, paperwork, waiting, relations with staff, "runarounds," complaining, and coping strategies—and experience in other organizations. Interviews averaged 30 to 45 minutes in length.

Interviews were tape-recorded, and transcripts were typed using Ethnograph, a qualitative data analysis program that allows attaching one or more codes to relevant passages in the interview transcripts. With this program, all segments of the notes linked to any code or combination of codes can be recalled and displayed for use in data analysis. We derived the initial codes we used from the literature review and field observations. However, a careful review of pretest and early interview transcripts by both investigators led to some modifications of the original coding scheme to reflect emergent categories and relationships in the data.

Staff interviewees were chosen from individuals who had worked in the four offices for over a year and whom the directors described as having frequent, direct student contact. In one office, the director selected 5 employees for interviews. The other three directors provided us with lists totaling 21 staff members; we selected 5 at random from each office. All staff members selected agreed to participate. The interviews, which averaged about an hour in length, were also based on a semistructured interview schedule. They focused on relationships with students and colleagues, causes of students' problems, students' adaptation to the bureaucracy, and staff perceptions of their offices' effectiveness and problems. To encourage frankness, we did not tape-record the interviews. Transcripts were compiled from detailed notes and coded and analyzed as described above.

Several drafts of each segment of our analysis were written by the first author and reviewed by the second—who also read a sample of interview transcripts—for clarity, mutual exclusiveness of categories, and fit between the raw data and the categories and relationships suggested. Issues raised by this procedure were resolved by an iterative process in which our discussions of drafts were followed by further review of the raw data and revised drafts of the manuscript. In later drafts we paid special attention to how the categories and relationships we found constituted an overall pattern that could help to answer our original research question.

Points of Friction in the Campus Bureaucracy

Students did sometimes experience their encounters with the campus bureaucracy as annoying, frustrating, and confusing. However, their reactions were mediated by both their relative powerlessness and their interpretations of their experiences and options. Their comments about their problems with the bureaucracy centered around five major themes, lines and waiting, impersonality, rules, "the runaround," and paperwork.

Lines and Waiting

When we asked freshmen open-ended questions about what they remembered about the campus offices, lines and waiting were the most frequently mentioned source of frustration. Freshmen reported waits from 5 minutes to 3 hours. The longest occurred in offices where appointments were not accepted and individualized processing, such as making financial aid awards rather than mass production, was required [50].

Even though freshmen often complained about lines and waiting, not all interpreted waiting the same way. For example, a wait of 30 minutes was defined as "just horrible" by one student, but as "no big deal" by another. Three factors helped to predict how negatively freshmen's viewed waiting. When processing was *visible*, as at registration, students could usually see that the staff was moving as fast as possible, making the students more tolerant. Where processing occurred in private offices, as in Financial Aid, the process was opaque, arousing more frustration and anxiety. As one interviewee said, "It may have been that there was someone in every single office and four people in front of me, but that still doesn't account for an hour and a half." The *predictability* of waits was also salient. Lines where people moved at a relatively steady pace allowed students to estimate how long they would have to wait. Two freshmen even reported counting the number of people in front of them. Sign up sheets produced more frustration because position in the queue was hard to determine in a crowded waiting room. Students could try to estimate their wait by checking the sign-up sheet, but they were sometimes misled, because the order in which students were seen depended partly on the nature of their business. Nor was asking staff about probable waiting times effective. Several staff members reported that they lacked the information to answer such questions. Unpredictability led students to become irritated with situations that they saw as chaotic. Less often, *favorable treatment* affected how students defined waits. For example, one freshman enrolled at the last minute because her program was canceled at another college. Although her application was filed late, Financial Aid agreed to process it. She described a 30-minute wait to register as "horrible" but a similar wait in Financial Aid as "kind of annoying" but understandable because of the office's workload.

But despite the inconvenience, our observations showed that students invariably at least outwardly accepted the lines—even when the waits were long. The interview data provided considerable insight into how and why this happened. First, many students saw lines as normal. As one put it, "I just did it and followed the rest of the sheep." Indeed, the observational data showed that students entering a setting often actually looked for lines and sometimes asked others where the line formed. Freshmen also explained that they saw lines as a legitimate, fair way to order an otherwise ambiguous situation. Observation showed that lines were governed by informal equity norms. Students could leave the line briefly to visit the restroom or recover a forgotten item and reclaim their places. On the other hand, they sometimes complained when staff brought someone to the front of the line, violating the equity the line created. But so long as the norms were followed, lines were usually accepted even when they proved frustrating. In one instructive instance, an interviewee cut a class to get to the add/drop period early to avoid being closed out of a class. When the person in line just ahead of her took the last vacancy, she, even though frustrated, did not complain, because she believed the queue was fair.

Some freshmen said that they didn't mind waiting much; however, for others, overt acceptance of long lines masked stronger feelings. One said simply, "I hated it; I just hated it." Lines could also exacerbate anxiety created by uncertainty about other problems in the bureaucracy: "[I would sit there], hoping that [my problem with the office] would eventually work out and never knowing when it would work out." Nevertheless, only three students, two of whom were already frustrated by lost paperwork, reported becoming really angry about waiting. Only two students expressed anger overtly to staff, and they too accepted the wait in the end. Eight of 20 staff interviewees said that students never complain about lines, and 3 reported minimal complaining. Given the large number of students, this also suggests that complaints are infrequent. In short, freshmen accepted waiting, even when they found it frustrating. As one said, "Waiting is just something you have to go through."

Staff Impersonality

Campus offices pursue efficiency and fairness by basing decisions on regulations, not personal considerations. When asked about their own approach to students, 14 of the 20 staff interviewees said that they tried to remain detached, though 6 added that this did not mean callous indifference. Staff explained their impersonal approach by noting that there are too many students to allow staff to cater to individual needs, that students need to learn to deal with bureaucracy on their own, not be babied by staff, and that for staff to become personally involved would undermine their effectiveness.

Some freshmen praised staff members who went out of their way to help by telling them where to go for assistance, helping them choose courses or majors, and providing personal attention. Nevertheless, the majority perceived staff's approach as impersonal. One freshman said, "They just did what they had to do and didn't have . . . too much contact with students." Others said that students were treated simply as cases to be processed. One remarked, "I felt like I was being herded, actually . . . like one of the masses, a number maybe." Another viewed this impersonality as a striking contrast to earlier experiences: "When you go through life, you're a person. People care about you. Then [when] you go to college, it's like a totally new world." Two students interpreted impersonal treatment as indicating that the staff member was having a bad day, and a few complained that staff were rude. Still others felt that staff didn't care about them: "They just want to get you in there and get you out so they can go on to the next person, and they could care less about what you have to get done." Interestingly, students had fewer such complaints about student assistants. They felt that shared experiences linked them to student staff, who understood their problems.

Yet despite these negative feelings, freshmen once again defined an irritating situation as "just the way it is," often ruefully repeating some of the staff's own rationales for impersonal treatment. One said, "I guess in situations like that they can't treat everyone personally. . . . It's got to be 'get it done' or the line will back up a lot longer." Freshmen's desire to complete their own tasks expeditiously inclined them to accept the impersonal treatment, which they saw as necessary to reach their goals. One freshmen explained that he accepted impersonal treatment in the Academic Advising office because, "If they did sit down with everyone, . . . you would be there probably three [or] four hours waiting." Ironically, their acceptance of bureaucratic impersonality meant that freshmen rarely asked for help, making it impossible for staff to work personally with those who needed special assistance.

Rules

The literature suggests that excessive, rigid, and contradictory rules are among the most frustrating aspects of bureaucracy, and the campus bureaucracy manifests an extensive, complicated set of rules. Some staff interviewees claimed that the rules were flexible and that they sometimes made exceptions. Staff did sometimes make exceptions, but the observational data also revealed many instances of strict application of rules. For example, although staff sometimes suggested alternative signers to students having trouble obtaining required signatures on their advising cards, they invariably insisted on an authorized signature, even when the change was minor. In interviews, some staff members explained that they purposefully granted exceptions sparingly, made students work to get exceptions, and warned students that further exceptions would not be given because they did not want students to think the rules were unimportant. Making too many exceptions might cause problems later if word spread and other students expected the same treatment. Several staff members also argued that the students who had the most trouble with the rules were typically too egocentric to understand that the rules were intended to be fair to everyone. Staff believed that the rules were generally fair and efficient, and they tried to communicate the importance they placed on following rules to students.

Despite the prevalence of formalized procedures, when we asked freshmen about rules, we found that they were of two minds. On the one hand, there was considerable equanimity toward rules. This evidently occurred in part because rules were so much a part of the bureaucratic landscape that many students gave them little thought. Indeed, when asked how they felt about rules and procedures, some interviewees needed examples to clarify the question. One explained, "When I went in, I really wasn't con-

scious of the rules and procedures. . . . I really didn't think about there being rules and procedures. I just went in." Another carried this theme to the extreme, reporting, "There weren't any rules." Indeed, some students used the word "rule" *only* to refer to regulations that caused them trouble.

When asked directly about rules, most freshmen said that they saw them as necessary to keep things organized. One student whose classes were canceled because of the strict application of a rule about payment due dates nevertheless concluded, "[Without the rules], everything would have gotten all screwed up worse." Several also noted that rules helped them to make sense of a new and unfamiliar environment. As one pointed out, "I didn't have a problem with the [existence of] rules because I didn't know what was to be expected." Most also believed that the rules worked to help them reach their goals. One reasoned, I think [the rules], were necessary . . . because [the university is] offering me the chance to earn money to get an education . . . [therefore] I think its necessary that I take care of everything.

On the other hand, some freshmen, usually those who had been inconvenienced, did have complaints about rules. The requirement that faculty advisors sign registration schedules often proved especially irritating. Advisors could be hard to find, occasionally signed cards without really providing any help—sometimes without even looking at them—and had to be sought out anew for each schedule change. The rule that assigned the lowest registration priority to freshmen was another source of frustration, because it meant that freshmen encountered many closed courses. "They say you're supposed to graduate in four years, and you can't because you want to take a class that's filled up, but then you can't take that class, so you have to keep going back to different classes." There were also complaints about ambiguous or conflicting rules. As one freshman said, "No one seems to have the same story about what to do about anything." Another characterized rules as intimidating. For a brand new person, the [rules and procedures] are not very straightforward. . . . I felt that it was very confusing, and that just scares you even more. . . . It was very nerve-racking." Finally, there were complaints about inflexible rules and bureaucratic personalities. One freshman criticized a clerk who told her that office procedures meant that a check sent in by the student's mother could not be matched to her paperwork. Cancellation of her registration would probably result. She said that the staff member declined to take an interest in the problem, claiming that nothing could be done.

But in even these instances, our interviewees grudgingly followed the rules, and no one asked for an exception. In part this was because freshmen were not aware of the existence of exceptions or of procedures for obtaining one; in part it was because freshmen tended to perceive rules as immutable and to define their own difficulties as idiosyncratic or as minor hassles. Finally, even freshmen with major problems usually concluded that obeying rules was the best way to reach their goals.

"The Runaround"

Specialized offices scattered across various buildings caused problems for students, who frequently had to visit several offices, often in a specific sequence, to complete their business. Worse still, it was not always clear which office handled a problem. For example, several students were surprised that an office named Academic Advising could not sign class registration cards. As a result, some students found themselves rushing from office to office, sometimes revisiting the same office several times, to solve a problem. Office specialization also contributed to chain reaction foul-ups. For example, two students found that when their financial aid applications failed to go through on time, registrations and meal plans were canceled. Similarly, paperwork lost by one office could not be forwarded to others, resulting in problems down the line.

Five of 20 freshmen reported serious problems with such "runarounds," and 10 others mentioned minor difficulties. Several complained that they had to make repeated visits to faculty advisors for minor schedule changes. Another complained bitterly about problems finding information about what courses could be substituted for a particular requirement. I've gone there . . . for something, and they've chased me all around the world. . . . They sent me everywhere except where I was supposed to be." One victim of a chain reaction foul-up commented, "I was kind of starting to get angry that people were sending me all over campus to figure out

something that they had originally screwed up." Others simply found trying to make all the required stops confusing and frustrating: "I've got to get here. I've go to get there. Your mind's one step ahead of your body."

Other students had trouble understanding that secretaries or receptionists did not have the skill or authority to help with many of their problems. After a receptionist asked one student we observed if she could help, but then took his name and told him to have a seat, he commented to another student, "Isn't it stupid how she asks if she can help you and then tells you to sit down? She'll do it every time. Watch."

Staff members said that they tried to avoid giving students the runaround, but some acknowledged that office specialization and the limited authority of individual officials could produce problems anyway. Two even noted that it is easy for the staff to forget that students have difficulty understanding how the bureaucracy is set up. On the other hand, some staff responses contained hints of victim-blaming [40]. Staff were more likely to blame freshmen's problems on failure to read the rules and acquaint themselves with the system and overreliance on help from parents and friends than on the system itself.

Although victims of major "runarounds" sometimes complained bitterly, most freshmen viewed their experiences as—at worst—mildly annoying. Many resolved their problems fairly quickly. But even those who were seriously inconvenienced rarely directed their complaints to staff. Instead, they chose to accede to the bureaucracy, albeit sometimes reluctantly. They saw the problems with the system as, "just the way it is."

Paperwork

Excessive, redundant paperwork is legendary in bureaucracy; however, the majority of our interviewees found paperwork to be—at most—somewhat annoying. One said, "[The paperwork] was a little tiresome, but I thought it was necessary. . . . It made sense." In fact, students often received more help with paperwork than with other aspects of the campus bureaucracy. Parents usually filled out the most complicated and problematic form, the Financial Aid Form, and staff were available to help with other paperwork. In addition, freshmen generally defined paperwork as a means to their goals: registration and financial aid. One freshman's reaction to the required I-9 (citizenship verification) form was typical. "It didn't bother me. It's required; if I didn't fill it out, I didn't get my paycheck. And if I didn't get my paycheck, I wouldn't be here."

Nevertheless, paperwork did cause problems for some. Lost paperwork and inaccurate records, in particular, caused consternation. One freshman reported recurrent difficulty with her scholarship check.

> They send me a card in the mail saying . . . your scholarship check has come in and you need to come in and sign your check on this day between these times, and I'll go. And your name is supposed to be on a little colored card. My name—never fails—is never on a card. And yet they send me this thing that says . . . come get your check. So I have to get out my ID, and they have to fill out a card for me. So I stand around and wait for that. Then I'll go up and they can't find my file. They don't understand what kind of scholarship I got.

Others complained about redundant requests for information.

> There's way too much repetition of information. They send you nine to ten forms to fill out the very same information. It's like they lost it the first eight times. I'll be happy to tell you anything you want to know, but don't ask for the same information again and again and again. It gets old.

Another occasional complaint was that required paperwork was not clear or that staff were poorly informed and unwilling to help.

> I ask them the question, and they said to me, "Well if you'd read the form, you'd find your answer in the form." And I said, "Well I read the form. . . ." And they read it and said, "Oh." And it wasn't in the form.

Freshmen were especially likely to become angry when they defined paperwork as pointless. One became frustrated when told that, although it would probably not be possible for him to change roommates, he should complete the forms requesting the change anyway. He complained, "It just seemed like a lot of red tape crap that you had to just do for no apparent reason." Another, recalling problems with complex financial aid requirements, complained bitterly, "It must have been 20 pages of paperwork for $100

[more financial aid]." Yet even students who found paperwork frustrating or pointless almost always yielded to the requirements without overt complaint.

Staff members displayed ambivalence about paperwork. Most acknowledged that paperwork, especially the dreaded Financial Aid Form, was a problem for some students, and some agreed that forms could be redundant, lack complete instructions, or implicitly assume too much knowledge. A few complained that paperwork requirements interfered with meeting students' needs. Nevertheless, many staff also insisted that most problems arose because students did not read the instructions, did not ask for assistance, and relied too heavily on parents.

Student Acquiescence to the Campus Bureaucracy

The literature suggested that freshmen might have trouble adapting to the campus bureaucracy, and our interviews showed that many found the bureaucracy annoying at times, while a few experienced considerable frustration. Nevertheless, both the interviews and observational data showed that students rarely displayed *overt* anger about lines, closed courses, paperwork, and runarounds, suggesting that most elected to deal with the campus bureaucracy without verbal complaint, confrontation, or formal appeals. Staff members also reported relatively little complaining and arguing, especially from freshmen, explaining that new students were timid, uncertain, and afraid; however, several noted that freshmen's body language could betray suppressed frustration and anger. Students generally expressed anger overtly only in extreme cases. For example, one victim of an extended runaround later experienced further consternation when he wanted to give a financial aid check directly to a receptionist. She insisted that he give her a personal check instead, as the financial aid award was not yet in the computer system. Although he became angry with her and argued vociferously, he too ultimately gave in and followed the required procedure.

Freshmen's explanations of how they viewed the bureaucratic requirements and their own situation provide considerable insight into their acquiescence. They identified five interrelated reasons for accepting the campus bureaucracy.

One major reason for the lack of overt complaining and confrontation was that freshmen almost always interpreted the campus bureaucracy as the natural order of things. The bureaucracy was so well institutionalized that most had difficulty imagining options—even when an outsider might conclude that alternatives, such as adding more staff to speed up processing, were available. Thus, one student explained, "I just didn't know how they could do anything better than they were"; another commented, "I was upset that it happened, but there was nothing that any of them could really do." Long lines, frustrating rules and the like were seen as beyond anyone's control, and the few freshmen who suggested improvements often qualified their ideas by saying that they really didn't know whether they would work better. Even those who experienced serious problems sometimes emphasized bureaucracy's strong points, viewing their difficulties as isolated and defining the bureaucracy as generally effective. A few also blamed themselves for their problems, acknowledging that they had not read or followed the procedures.

This definition of the situation led students to accept the bureaucracy—at least grudgingly. As one put it, "That's the way it's supposed to be; that's the way it's going to be." Another said, "That's just part of the rules and regulations. Got to do it; can't cry about it." Consequently, even when bureaucratic requirements and procedures caused them annoyance and frustration, freshmen usually acceded to them. One victim of an extended wait explained his feelings this way, "At that point, I had to stand in line. . . . I didn't really have a choice. I mean, I was hungry. I wanted to go to lunch, but I didn't have a choice, so I just stood there."

Second, freshmen reported that past experiences, such as waiting in a doctor's office, paid jobs, and working in high-school student government, helped them to understand and adjust to the campus bureaucracy. Most also mentioned high school itself as preparation, including— somewhat surprisingly—two who believed that high school had been even more bureaucratic than the university. More typical were those who said that high-school bureaucracy was similar, but on a smaller scale. "[High school] was a taste, so when I came here, it really wasn't anything different. . . . I wasn't really as surprised as I think I would have been if I hadn't had some pre-

vious experience." However, some had little experience at all with bureaucracy. Four students, all of whom found adapting to the university bureaucracy difficult, indicated that high school had been much less bureaucratic, offering attentive, supportive assistance.

Third, freshmen interviewees said that they lacked information needed to challenge the system. Knowledge is an important basis for power in organizations [37], and freshmen, as newcomers, had not had enough experience in the campus bureaucracy to understand it very well. As one explained, "I was a freshman; I didn't realize what the hell I was supposed to be doing." Sometimes, ironically, there was even too much information, that is, too much new information to comprehend at once. As one freshman noted, "I didn't know what to expect, so I didn't know how to take it all in." Lacking a clear picture of how things worked, freshmen found it difficult to question the established order, and the limited information they had predisposed them to do things the organization way. For example, lack of knowledge of the existence of exceptions or, even more often, procedures for obtaining one predisposed freshmen simply to accept the general procedures established for everyone.

Fourth, interviewees' accepted the campus bureaucracy because they believed they had little power. Some believed that it was inappropriate for newcomers at the bottom of the hierarchy to challenge the system. One said simply, "I just don't feel like it's my place [to argue]." They allowed their behavior to be guided by staff, even when they disagreed or did not understand, because they respected authority and expected staff to be in charge. One freshman explained, "[When a receptionist] tells you to sit down, that's what you do." In addition, most freshmen concluded that they were potentially at the mercy of campus bureaucrats. With their superior knowledge of the rules and their ability to enforce them rigorously if they chose, staff could make students' lives more difficult or help them to reach their goals. Thus, 13 of 20 staff interviewees said that they sometimes overlooked minor rule violations—a practice that gave them considerable leverage. Students concluded that it was safer to accept instructions from staff than to risk offending them by complaining. Two freshmen reported that they even "made up" majors on the spot to satisfy a staff member's insistent demand that they list one. Another said that if she complained, "maybe they wouldn't help me as much as they would if I were calm." A few also said they feared that failure to comply might earn them the label of troublemakers, a supposition that also received some support from staff interviews.

This is not to say that the exercise of staff power involved much overt conflict. Staff usually exercised power politely and prudently, and their superior knowledge made it easy for them to persuade students to do things the organization way—in the process socializing them into the bureaucracy [25, 34]. They simply offered polite advice about what students needed to do, presenting their suggestions as in students' best interest. The widespread reliance on lines, rules, and procedures also reduced the need for staff to issue direct orders, and they rarely gave them. Like rules, staff power blended into the background, and even staff themselves seemed almost unconscious of it.

When students violated their expectations, staff often found indirect ways to get them to conform. The observational data showed that students who forged to the front of a line saying that they had only a quick question were simply ignored. It was also obvious that staff members used informal but fairly rigid "scripts" to structure interaction, especially when many students had to be processed quickly. If a student rambled on or took too much time, staff members displayed enough impatience to bring him or her back into line.

As a result, although freshmen sometimes resented being at the bottom of the totem pole, they usually did not feel that they were being ordered around. Students generally complied with staff requests and suggestions, allowing staff to control their behavior almost without fully realizing it. One freshman explained her compliance with a staff member's request for an appointment this way:

> The lady called me and made an appointment with me, which I think is a bit more pressing than my making an appointment with her . . . [so] it's important for me to get my tail over there and do stuff. I mean . . . she's calling me and doing [things for me].

The final and most immediate reason for freshmen's compliance was that they almost invariably concluded that cooperating with the

bureaucracy was the best approach to reaching goals that were important to them. As one freshman explained, "I basically realized that there was no choice. If I wanted to take classes this semester, . . . I had to do what it takes, so I did." For most students, cooperating with the bureaucracy and accepting what they defined as just minor annoyances without complaint led simply and directly to meeting their objectives. So it is not surprising that they elected to cooperate. But even freshmen who had experienced serious problems were apt to adopt this outlook. For them, the bureaucracy "worked" only in the limited sense that, after considerable frustration, they finally did achieve their goals. Nevertheless, the circumstances that persuaded other students that working with the system was the best course also elicited compliance from them, albeit with a more negative view of the bureaucracy and occasional overt protest. As one said, "I don't see another . . . way to solve the problem, so I guess I'll have to deal with it [their way]."

Coping with Campus Bureaucracy

Freshmen usually accepted the campus bureaucracy as "just the way things are," elected to cooperate with it, and rarely challenged it overtly. Yet their compliance was often somewhat grudging, and at times they were irritated and frustrated by their powerlessness and the campus bureaucracy's requirements and dysfunctions. Hence, they had to develop strategies for coping with the problems the bureaucracy caused them. By ameliorating the problems the students face, these coping strategies help the bureaucracy to maintain itself and function despite its drawbacks.

Finding Out How the Bureaucracy Works

As newcomers, freshmen need information about which offices to consult for various services, what materials or information to bring, and the order in which events must occur. Several staff people noted that freshmen are bombarded with so much confusing information that they have trouble determining what is important or understanding any of what they have been told. Students also often cited lack of good information as a key reason for many of their problems with the campus bureaucracy. They mentioned confusing instruction sheets, inadequate orientation sessions, and staff who assumed that freshmen understood everything in advance. As one said, "They acted like I was supposed to know all this stuff, and I don't know where the hell I was supposed to find out about it."

Our interviewees adopted various strategies to sort things out and decide what they should do. Some adopted a "watch and learn" strategy. From what they saw, they inferred how they should interact with staff, what paperwork was needed, and what procedures were in use. For example, students were observed leaving the ID Center after they saw that others had brought receipts from the Cashier's Office, commenting that they were going to get their receipts. In some offices, ropes that guided lines and signs on the walls also provided information. Several freshmen said that they purposefully observed what occurred in the campus offices to gain information, but for many "watch and learn" was not a systematically planned strategy. Instead, their need for information made them ready to note and absorb whatever data crossed their paths. Several staff members and students pointed out that students preferred to learn by watching rather than by asking questions because they did not know what to ask and wanted to avoid appearing naive or bothering staff.

Freshmen sometimes did ask directly for information or advice from staff as well as from friends or parents, who sometimes accompanied them. Students accompanied by friends and parents were a common sight during our observations, but most freshmen reported that they did not rely heavily on them for advice. Most of the freshmen's friends were also freshmen, and interviewees told us that neither they nor parents had much useful information. Staff tended to emphasize the help students received from friends or parents more than the freshmen, usually citing instances of bad advice.

Strategies for Getting What You Want

The campus bureaucracy and students' relative powerlessness could make reaching their objectives frustrating. It was therefore to their advantage to find ways to "get around" the bureaucracy to get what they wanted more directly than they could by going thorough official channels. If successful, use of unsanctioned or unofficial methods to reach their goals has the potential to defuse tensions that might otherwise build up in interacting with the campus bureaucracy.

One obvious strategy for achieving one's ends is to violate the rules, but most freshmen interviewees said they never did so. The requirement that the faculty advisor sign the registration card is a good example. The requirement could be aggravating, and the opportunity for rule violation was obvious. Many freshmen said they knew that others had forged a signature, and the chance of being caught was low. Yet only four students said that they had considered forgery, and only two had done so. Staff also noted that a few students failed to follow the requirement to inform Financial Aid when they dropped below a full course load, but they said this violation was rare, and none of our interviewees mentioned it.

Freshmen gave several reasons for hewing to the rules. A few said that they were afraid of being caught. Others believed that following rules was fairly easy, so breaking them was not worth it. Some said that they did not yet know the system well enough to guess what they could get by with but might break more rules later. Many seemed to take rules so much for granted that breaking them was almost unthinkable. Thus one labeled the advisor's signature rule as "written in stone."

Fibbing is another potentially effective way to shortcut the bureaucratic process and reach one's goals. Staff interviewees reported occasional instances of students who lied about what other staff members had told them. Some of these "lies" may actually have been the result of student misunderstandings of what other staff had told them, and none of our student interviewees reported lying.

Another possible strategy is to enlist the help of parents. Both observational data and freshmen interviews indicated that parents accompanied students fairly often, especially to Financial Aid, where they could provide needed information. Nevertheless, only two instances of parents intervening directly were noted in the observations, and only the two student interviewees who experienced the worst problems said they had asked their parents to help. Nevertheless, the mere presence of parents may have helped to ensure more responsive treatment. One freshman explained,

"I think the way they treated me was different when my mom was there and when my mom wasn't there. It's like, 'Well, here's your daughter; we're going to treat her good; everything is going to be fine.' Then whoa! Mom's gone, and it's like, 'Now we're going to treat you like we really want to treat you.'"

Usually however, the bureaucracy worked well enough that students preferred to handle things themselves. And indeed, some parents insisted that they do so.

Staff members had a different view of parental intervention; 19 of 20 reported that students sometimes brought parents along, and 17 said that parents were very active in assisting students, helping them with paperwork, interceding when dorm repairs were not completed promptly or when mistakes in processing paperwork occurred, and even helping students to select courses. Several commented about parents who insisted on doing all the talking, often to the student's embarrassment. But staff also reported instances in which students asked parents to accompany them because they believed this would help to get what they wanted. Freshmen may have underreported parents' assistance because it threatened their self-esteem, and staff's strong negative reaction to parents' involvement may have led them selectively to remember times when parents intervened. Staff have good reason to dislike parental intervention. Dealing with parents takes time, creates conflict between trying to satisfy the parent and avoiding unfair exceptions, and may affect job performance ratings or job security. Perhaps partly for these reasons, most staff believe that students should handle their own affairs.

Filing complaints and appeals is another strategy for getting one's way in bureaucracy [25]. The campus bureaucracy offers several ways for students to appeal decisions, through the offices themselves, to faculty committees, or through the administration. Although our interviewees did not know the details of these procedures, most were aware that complaints were an option. Some had actively considered mounting a formal complaint, but no one had actually done so, and staff reported that formal complaints were rare. When we asked students who had encountered problems why they did not complain, some said that they had just never been pushed far enough. Others claimed that

complaining was not in their nature: "I guess I'm not that kind of person, to really go and complain about things." Others were afraid that appeals would succeed only in offending powerful staff members.

Despite the irritation and frustration—and occasional genuine anger—that dealing with the bureaucracy could engender, both the observational and interview data indicate that students generally chose to be nonconfrontational. This could require using "fronts" [13] to conceal true feelings. Through speech, gestures, and manner, they presented a calm, rational outward demeanor, even when inwardly angry. They often tried to appear "mature" and cooperative and conform to the norms of the bureaucracy. Our freshmen interviewees believed that such fronts were the best way to maintain superficially pleasant relations with staff, make a favorable impression, and reach their goals. By acting this way, students contributed to the development of a "working consensus" [13], supporting staff's view that the bureaucracy worked relatively smoothly.

Most direct encounters with staff did not last long, so it was not too hard for students to maintain their "performances." Nevertheless, some did lapse, at least momentarily. For example, one student was observed to become overtly hostile when a staff member asked her if her papers had been checked. Rather than respond to the anger, the staff member ignored it, and the student soon resumed her calm "performance." Staff members believed that it was important to maintain calm outward appearances and to avoid dealing with obviously angry students, therefore they usually did not react to such lapses or to student body language that signaled frustration or anger.

Dealing with Frustration

Whatever their strategies, students did not always get what they wanted immediately and they sometimes had to put up with considerable inconvenience before they reached their objectives. Hence, they needed to find ways to deal with the resulting frustration. By reducing or managing frustration, these safety valve strategies made it easier for students to maintain smooth relations with the campus bureaucracy.

A few freshmen tried to reduce their frustration with the campus bureaucracy by simple avoidance. One explained, "I haven't dropped or added a class just because I didn't want to have to go through the crap. It just seemed like too much of an ordeal." For most, however, avoidance was not feasible. They had to find other ways to reduce or manage frustration.

One approach was to create psychological distance. Students sometimes responded to staff impersonality by viewing staff just as impersonally as the staff viewed them. If staff members were affectively distant, our interviewees would transform them into just another part of the bureaucratic apparatus, expressing only partly concealed resentment by referring to them as "Miss Whatever" or "the poor little lady." Or as another put it, "A receptionist is a receptionist is a receptionist." By creating interpersonal distance, students could avoid damage to their self-esteem by deciding that staff opinions of them did not matter and justify expressing resentment toward staff.

Another set of strategies for reducing frustration centered around waiting in line. Both observation and interview data indicate that students in lines spent much time talking to one another, allowing them to build social networks and pass the time. Indeed, 5 of our 20 interviewees actually recruited friends to go with them to a campus office. As one said, "It would have been a lot worse if I hadn't had someone to wait with me." Others were accompanied by parents for the same reason. Some freshmen reported using waiting time to conduct "symbolic rehearsals" [41] of upcoming interaction with staff. Others passed the time and reduced their anxiety by tracking their progress: "I just watched the line in front of me and noticed how much time each person was taking and tried to evaluate how much longer until I would be seen."

Because freshmen were unwilling to vent their frustration to staff, they turned elsewhere to express their feelings. The ends of lines, for example, provided "back regions" where students could "come out of character" [13] and voice their complaints to other students. When staff members were near, these complaints were suppressed or muted in the interest of avoiding friction with staff. Friends, roommates, and parents could also provide a sympathetic ear for students needing to blow off steam.

Staff Coping Behaviors

Staff members too experienced difficulties trying to make the system work and managing their sometimes conflictual relationships with students. Staff dealt with conflict primarily by attempting to maintain a businesslike attitude when dealing with students. By emphasizing following the rules, making clear that they expected to be treated respectfully, and maintaining emotional distance between themselves and students, staff could insulate themselves from the emotional demands of their work while reassuring themselves that they were providing fast, equitable service [25, 30]. All staff members said that they tried to avoid conducting business with visibly angry or agitated students. They tried to calm them, encouraged them to leave the office, and referred the most problematic cases to supervisors. Similarly, decisions about student petitions were made in private. Students were informed by mail, protecting staff from the immediate anger of students whose petitions were denied. Strategies like these reduced the emotional strain on staff, helping to stabilize the system.

Staff also developed shared interpretations of why students had difficulties—some of them self-serving ones that protected their self-images and commitment to the system. Although some did concede that runarounds and confusing jargon caused some problems for students, staff attributed most problems to students who looked for short cuts, put things off, accepted poor advice from parents and friends, and—most of all—failed to read and follow rules. Staff reported that students who were too dependent on parents, those from small towns, and freshmen had the most difficulty. They characterized freshmen as lost, "green," and too accustomed to having their parents take care of things.

Staff also sometimes engaged in "victim-blaming" [25, 40]. For example, we heard uncooperative students described as having "attitude problems," parents characterized as "domineering," and students who advised others as merely "thinking that they know what's going on." Although probably true in some instances, staff's ready reliance on such characterizations reassures them that the system is sound and that most problems come from uncooperative individuals.

Like students who were irritated by the bureaucracy, staff who were frustrated by aggressive students or difficult decisions turned to peers for counsel and support. Backstage conversations allowed them to vent frustrations, make light of student peccadillos, reassure one another of the soundness of the procedures, and obtain advice about how to handle problematic cases. Several noted that conversations with colleagues let them "talk out" their frustration with students who had angered them rather than directing the anger back toward students.

Implications

Bureaucracy is the dominant organizational form in our society, and learning to adapt to it is an important aspect of socialization. College freshmen's first experiences with bureaucracy are theoretically and practically strategic because, as putative adults, freshmen must learn to deal with bureaucracy and its problems without the protection and support of parents and sympathetic teachers. They must define a new situation, adapt to bureaucratic constraints, and learn to operate successfully in a bureaucratic context. Because their encounters are early ones, freshmen's experiences reveal the dynamics of adapting to bureaucracy especially well. They may also set the pattern for later encounters, helping us to understand how bureaucracy perpetuates itself despite built-in strains.

Bureaucracy uses specialization, rules, hierarchical authority, records, and impersonal decision making to achieve efficiency, accuracy, and speed by tightly structuring behavior, minimizing wasted effort, and encouraging rationality [47]. Yet bureaucracy carries a price, especially for lower participants. Bureaucratic dysfunctions, such as runarounds, waiting in line, and communication breakdowns, are not just obstacles to efficiency. They are also sources of irritation and frustration for clients. Moreover, because bureaucracy works by tightly controlling behavior, lower participants sometimes find working within its confines annoying and unpleasant [2, 46].

Bureaucracy thus presents a paradox for clients seeking services. Like most social structures [7, 8], bureaucracies have a positive side, meeting needs in an orderly way, and a conflictual side, controlling client behavior in ways that impose costs. As newcomers to bureaucracy,

freshmen confront this paradox immediately. The bureaucracy often operates predictably, equitably, and relatively efficiently to meet their needs [20]. When it does, it elicits trust and compliance [3]. But to get bureaucracy to meet their needs, students must pay a price, subordinating personal preferences to the bureaucracy's demands, standing in lines, accepting impersonal treatment, filling out required paperwork, following rules, and accepting staff guidance. Control does not come merely from having to take orders [8], but also from a complex apparatus of rules, physical barriers, records, indirect cues about proper behavior, and rewards for conformity and punishments for deviance [10, 25]. Adapting to these constraints can be unpleasant, so motivating clients to conform can be problematic [24].

Yet freshmen do in fact usually conform, even when inconvenienced or frustrated. The forces that produce their compliance form a complex, interactive system, which is especially persuasive for newcomers. Socialization teaches them to define bureaucracy as the normal and best way to accomplish complex tasks. For many, successful encounters with bureaucracy reinforce this view [20]. Freshmen often lack the previous experience or knowledge needed to visualize arrangements that might work better, and they do not see challenging the system as appropriate behavior for neophytes in a subordinate role. They see staff members as having authority, and they fear that challenging the system might cause staff to retaliate by withholding the information or help they need [3]. Although they may acknowledge minor flaws in the bureaucracy, staff are generally committed to the system that employs them and puts them in control of interaction. They communicate this commitment and their expectations to students, and they withhold cooperation from those who do not conform.

Faced with these conditions, it is very likely that most clients, especially organizational newcomers like college freshmen, will define bureaucracy as part of the natural order of things and as relatively efficient, viewing any problems they encounter as minor irritants or isolated incidents. The minority who encounter more serious difficulties often have more reservations and complaints about the bureaucracy, providing greater potential for conflict [24]. But these clients interpret and act on their experiences within the context of a larger group who define the bureaucracy as normal and efficient. Almost all respond by concluding that it is to their advantage to conform overtly to bureaucracy's demands, maintaining a compliant, cooperative front in their brief interactions with staff. They see conformity as a more promising path to their goals than protest. Staff members encourage and reward this behavior, and staff's willingness to make exceptions and overlook minor rule violations helps to defuse some of the most serious conflicts. Freshmen who experience problems reduce their own anxiety and frustration by gathering information about how the bureaucracy works, by developing strategies to manipulate the system to get what they want, by blowing off steam in backstage settings, by seeking emotional support from family and friends, and by developing strategies for reducing frustration.

The result is a bureaucratic system that continues to elicit acceptance and cooperation from lower participants whom it sometimes does not serve well. Complaints are repressed or expressed only in muted terms. Freshmen fit their actions to bureaucratic constraints, and behavior flows through well-worn bureaucratic channels, even when they and staff define things differently [48]. So long as both groups follow bureaucratic procedures, the organization can continue to function.

As today's freshmen evolve into tomorrow's seniors, they often become more accustomed to the system, more adept at working within in, and a bit more willing to bend rules or complain. Nevertheless the definitions of situation and patterns of behavior laid down early persist at the university and are probably carried to new organizations—just as experiences from high school and early job experiences help to shape the definitions and behavior of freshmen.

The reactions of students who differ in age, gender, class, or regional background might depart in detail from our findings, but the pattern of conformity and acceptance reported here is apparent on many other campuses, as well as in other client-serving bureaucracies [25], and it outlived the student revolts of the 1960s and 1970s. Fxamination of its roots helps us to understand how bureaucracy endures despite tensions inherent in it, both on the university campus and beyond.

References

1. Argyris, C. "Selections from the Impact of Budgets on People." In *Organizations: Structure and Behavior*, edited by J. A. Litterer, pp. 251–263. New York: Wiley, 1952.
2. Argyris, C. *Personality and Organization*. New York: Harper, 1957.
3. Bidwell, C. E. "Students and Schools: Some Observations on Client Trust in Client-Serving Organizations." In *Organizations and Clients: Essays in the Sociology of Service*, edited by W. R. Rosengren and M. Lefton, pp. 37–69. Columbus, OH: Bobbs-Merrill, 1970.
4. Blau, P. M. *The Dynamics of Bureaucracy*. Chicago: University of Chicago, 1955.
5. Blumer, H. "Society as Symbolic Interaction." In *Symbolic Interaction: A Reader in Social Psychology*, edited by J. Manis and B. Meltzer, pp. 145–153. Boston: Allyn and Bacon, 1972.
6. Braverman, H. *Labor and Monopoly Capital: The Degradation of Work in the Twentieth Century*. New York: Monthly Review Press, 1975.
7. Dahrendorf, R. "Out of Utopia: Toward a Reorientation of Sociological Analysis." *American Journal of Sociology*, 64 (September 1958), 115–127.
8. Dahrendorf, R. *Class and Class Conflict in Industrial Society*. Stanford, CA: Stanford University Press, 1959.
9. Downs, A. *Inside Bureaucracy*. Boston: Little, Brown, 1966.
10. Edwards, R. *Contested Terrain*. New York: Basic Books, 1979.
11. Etzioni, A. *A Comparative Analysis of Complex Organizations*. New York: Free Press, 1975.
12. Glaser, B. G., and A. L. Strauss. *The Discovery of Grounded Theory*. Chicago: Aldine, 1967.
13. Goffman, E. *The Presentation of Self in Everyday Life*. Garden City, NY: Anchor Books, 1959.
14. Goffman, E. "The Interaction Order." *American Sociological Review*, 48 (February 1983), 1–17.
15. Gracey, H. "Learning the Student Role: Kindergarten as Academic Boot Camp." In *Readings in Introductory Sociology*, edited by D. Wrong and H. Gracey, pp. 347–361. New York: Macmillan, 1972.
16. Gulick, L. H. "Notes on the Theory of Organization." In *Classics of Public Administration*, edited by J. Shafritz and A. Hyde, pp. 80–89. Pacific Grove, CA: Brooks/Cole, 1992.
17. Hall, R. H. *Organizations: Structures, Processes, and Outcomes*. Englewood Cliffs, NJ: Prentice-Hall, 1991.

18. Homans, G. C. *Social Behavior: Its Elementary Forms*. New York: Harcourt Brace Jovanovich, 1974.

19. Jackson, P. W. *Life in Classrooms*. New York: Holt, Rinehart, and Winston, 1968.

20. Katz, D., B. A. Gutek, R. L. Kahn, and E. Barton. *Bureaucratic Encounters: A Pilot Study in the Evaluation of Government Services*. Ann Arbor, MI: Survey Research Center, Institute for Social Research, 1975.

21. Lauer, R. H. *Social Psychology*. Boston: Houghton Miflin, 1977.

22. Lawler, E. E. III, and J. G. Rhodes. *Information and Control in Organizations*. Santa Monica, CA: Goodyear, 1976.

23. Lawrence, P. R., and J. W. Lorsch. *Organization and Environment*. Cambridge, MA: Harvard University Press, 1967

24. Lefton, M. "Client Characteristics and Structural Outcomes: Toward Specification of Linkages." In *Organizations and Clients: Essays in the Sociology of Service*, edited by W. R. Rosengren and M. Lefton, pp. 17–36. Columbus, OH: Bobbs-Merrill, 1970.

25. Lipsky, M. *Street-level Bureaucracy: Dilemmas of the Individual in Public Services*. New York: Russell Sage Foundation, 1980.

26. Mann, L. "Queue Culture: The Waiting Line as a Social System." *American Journal of Sociology*, 75 (November 1969), 340–354.

27. March, J. G., and H. A. Simon. *Organizations*. New York: John Wiley, 1958.

28. Mechanic, D. "Sources of Power of Lower Participants in Complex Organizations." *Administrative Science Quarterly*, 7 (December 1962), 349–364

29. Merton, R. K. "Bureaucratic Structure and Personality." In *Social Theory and Social Structure*, by R. K. Merton, pp. 249–261. New York: Free Press, 1968.

30. Milgram, S., H. J. Liberty, R. Toledo, and J. Wackenhut. "Response to Intrusion into Waiting Lines." *Journal of Personality and Social Psychology*, 51 (1986), 683–689.

31. Miller, D. C., and W. H. Form. *Industrial Sociology: Work in Organizational Life*. New York: Harper and Row, 1980.

32. Mintzberg, H. *The Structuring of Organizations: A Synthesis of the Research*. Englewood Cliffs, NJ: Prentice-Hall, 1979.

33. Pascarella, E. T., and P. T. Terenzini. *How College Affects Students: Insights from Twenty Years of Research*. San Francisco: Jossey-Bass, 1992.

34. Parelius, R. J., and A. P. Parelius. *The Sociology of Education*. Englewood Cliffs, NJ: Prentice-Hall, 1987.

35. Perrow, C. *Complex Organizations: A Critical Essay*. Glenview, IL: Scott Foresman, 1986.

36. Perrow, C. "A Framework for the Analysis of Organizations." *American Sociological Review*, 32 (April, 1967), 194–208.

37. Pfeffer, J. *Power in Organizations*. London: Pitman Publishing, 1981.

38. Presthus, R. *The Organizational Society*. New York: St. Martin's, 1978.

39. Rosengren, W. R. "The Social Economics of Membership." In *Organizations and Clients: Essays in the Sociology of Service*, edited by W. R. Rosengren and M. Lefton, pp. 205–222. Columbus, OH: Bobbs-Merrill, 1970.

40. Ryan, W. *Blaming the Victim*. New York: Vintage Books, 1976.

41. Stryker, S. *Symbolic Interactionism*. Menlo Park, CA: Benjamin/Cummings, 1980.

42. Susser, I. *Norman Street*. New York: Oxford University Press, 1982.

43. Thomas, W. I. "The Definition of the Situation," In *Symbolic Interaction: A Reader in Social Psychology*, edited by J. Manis and B. Meltzer, pp. 331–336. Boston: Allyn and Bacon, 1972.

44. Thompson, V. A. *Modern Organizations*. New York: Alfred A. Knopf, 1961.

45. Van Maanen J. "Organizational Socialization." In *Handbook of Work Organization and Society*, edited by R. Dubin, pp. 67–130. Chicago: Rand McNally, 1976.

46. Vaughan, T. R., and G. Sjoberg. "The Individual and the Bureaucracy: An Alternative Median Interpretation." *Journal of Applied Behavioral Science*, 20 (January 1984) 57–69.

47. Weber, M. 1946. *From Max Weber: Essays in Sociology*. New York: Oxford University Press, 1946.

48. Weik, K. *The Social Psychology of Organizing*. Reading, MA: Addison-Wesley, 1979.

49. Wilensky, H. *Organizational Intelligence*. New York: Basic Books, 1967.

50. Woodward, J. *Industrial Organization: Theory and Practice*. New York: Oxford University Press, 1985.

CHAPTER 10

GETTING IN: MEXICAN AMERICANS' PERCEPTIONS OF UNIVERSITY ATTENDANCE AND THE IMPLICATIONS FOR FRESHMAN YEAR PERSISTENCE

LOUIS C. ATTINASI, JR.

In view of its importance for social advancement [11] and its contribution to the improvement of personal well-being [2, 51], it is not surprising that higher education in the United States has become a cynosure for efforts to improve the condition of economically and socially disadvantaged subpopulations. Ironically, the present condition of these subpopulations exists because, in the past, higher education's service as an instrument for social mobility was seldom indiscriminate. America's racial and ethnic minorities have been and continue to be "grossly underrepresented in higher education and in almost all occupational fields that require a college education" [2], and do not, as a consequence, enjoy equitable participation in the larger society's social, economic, and political life.

One racial minority that has been particularly underserved by American higher education, in general, and by the four-year institution, in particular, is the Mexican American. In 1979, according to an estimate by the Bureau of the Census [47], the rate of baccalaureate degree attainment in the general population was more than four times the rate in the Mexican American subpopulation alone. Data presented by Brown [10] tend to confirm the link between social and economic advancement and college graduation. Relative to the total population, Mexican Americans are overrepresented in lower-level, poorer-paying positions, such as those occupied by service workers, artisans, operatives, farm and nonfarm laborers; they are underrepresented in more prestigious, better-paying positions, including those held by professional and technical workers, managers and administrators, and farmers and farm managers.

The low percentage of the Mexican American subpopulation graduating from college is attributable, in part, to high attrition rates at the elementary and secondary school levels, which effectively decrease the number of individuals eligible for college attendance, and to the failure of a substantial number of high school graduates from the subpopulation to enroll in college. Data based on the Bureau of the Census' Current Population Surveys from 1974 through 1978 [2] indicate nationwide a rate of high school completion for Mexican Americans of 51 percent and a rate of college entry of 23 percent. The corresponding rates for whites are 83 percent and 38 percent, respectively.

"Getting In: Mexican Americans' Perceptions of University Attendance and the Implications for Freshman Year Persistence." Reprinted from *Journal of Higher Education* 60, (1989), Ohio State University Press.

The Persistence of Mexican Americans in College

The low percentage of college graduates among Mexican Americans is also due to the failure of many Chicanos, once enrolled in an institution of higher education, to persist to degree completion. Numerous studies involving national [4], regional [11], state [13], and institutional [23, 36, 37] data have shown that Mexican American students graduate from college within a normal time frame—four to five years—at a rate that is from one and a half to two times smaller than the rate for Anglo students. Even if a longer time frame—nine or ten years—is considered, the discrepancy persists. Tracking students who entered college in 1971 until 1980, Astin [2] found that 55 percent of the Anglos but only 40 percent of the Mexican Americans in his national sample had achieved baccalaureate degrees during the nine-year period.

It is clear that addressing the low percentage of college graduates in the Chicano subpopulation necessitates examinations of Mexican American school-going behavior before, at the point of, and after college entry. The study of Chicano persistence in the elementary and secondary schools [28] has a history of several decades, beginning, most notably, with the U.S. Commission on Civil Rights' Mexican American Education Study in 1971 [48]. Similarly, there has been extensive investigation of the issue of Mexican American access to college [28, 38]. Much less attention, however, has been focused on the persistence of Chicanos at the baccalaureate level.

Of the few attempts to date to isolate factors that influence the persistence of Mexican Americans in college, the most significant is a study by Astin and Burciaga [3] for the Commission on Minorities in Higher Education. Astin and Burciaga analyzed data based on two different longitudinal samples—one covering the first two years of undergraduate work (1975 freshmen followed up in 1977) and the other a nine-year span covering undergraduate and graduate work (1971 freshmen followed up in 1980). For the first sample, persistence was examined as continuous enrollment over the first two years of college; for the second, as attainment of the baccalaureate degree by the ninth year following matriculation. In each case, analysis was by means of a two-stage stepwise linear multi-

ple regression "so that the students' entering characteristics were first controlled before any attempt was made to assess the influence of environmental characteristics" [2, p. 90].

Astin and Burciaga [3] found that the persistence of Chicanos is related statistically to a number of factors including performance and preparation in high school, the education and occupational status of parents, various expectations about the college experience, the nature of financial support, and the institution of initial matriculation. As their analysis was not theory-driven, however, Astin and Burciaga could provide no overarching conceptualization to tie these statistical associations together. Establishing the associations did not lead to a coherent explanation of Chicano persistence in college.

Methods of Studying Persistence in College

Astin and Burciaga's study is not atypical of research on the persistence/attrition of college students. Studies of this subject have either lacked the guidance of a conceptual framework or have uncritically accepted frameworks developed for other sociopsychological phenomena. Investigators not using conceptual frameworks have been content with establishing the correlates of persistence, rather than understanding the phenomenon as a dynamic process.

Since 1967 a number of "models" of persistence/attrition behavior have been developed and tested. These models have been based on selective findings of the correlational research, together with certain sociological and/or psychological constructs adapted from theoretical frameworks for explaining other social phenomena. For example, both Spady [41] and Tinto [45, 46] have proposed conceptualizations of attrition behavior heavily influenced by Durkheim's [15] sociological explanation of suicide. Other prominent models [7, 42] derive their basic theoretical orientations from one or another of the recent conceptualizations of disengagement from work (for example, Price's [34] model of work turnover or Dawis, Lofquist, and Weiss' [12] theory of work adjustment).

Undoubtedly, with the emergence of these conceptual models, the study of student persistence in college has moved in a potentially more fruitful direction. As the preoccupation with the identification of correlates has been replaced by an interest in explaining the processes that lead to persistence and withdrawal behaviors, the models have held out the possibility of reaching an understanding of the underlying dynamics of persistence/attrition phenomena. Still, none of the available models has proved more than very modestly successful in explicating those dynamics [31]. This is the result, in my judgment, of certain conceptual and methodological shortcomings shared by the existing models.

First, as mentioned above, each of the present persistence/attrition theorists has chosen to ground his model in a framework used to explain some other social or sociopsychological phenomenon. But an assumption *at the outset* that dropping out of college is like committing suicide or leaving a job has turned out to be too severe a constraint upon the conceptualizing process [31]. In addition, the models have been developed on the basis of, and tested with, data collected from institutional records and/or by means of fixed-choice questionnaires. These are methods of data collection that effectively strip away the context surrounding the student's decision to persist or not to persist in college and exclude from consideration the student's own perceptions of the process.

Yet, given the present level of our understanding of that decision, it is precisely those characteristics—the context of the decision and the student's perspective on the context—that investigations of student persistence in college must include. What are needed then are naturalistic, descriptive studies guided by research perspectives that emphasize the insider's point of view [46].[1]

An Exploratory Study

In this chapter, I report an exploratory study undertaken to collect and analyze qualitative data describing, from the Mexican American student's point of view, the context surrounding his or her decision to persist or not to persist in the university and, on the basis of that description, to develop concepts of the university-going process. The concepts so developed were used to propose hypotheses about the context within which Mexican American students make decisions to persist or not to persist in the university.

In lieu of one of the existing conceptual frameworks of persistence/attrition, the study was guided only by a broad research perspective—the sociology of everyday life [14]. The latter is actually a collection of research perspectives in sociology, all of which focus on everyday social interaction in natural situations and have as their starting points (1) the experience and observation of people interacting in concrete, face-to-face situations, and (2) an analysis of the actors' meanings.

In particular, two of the sociologies of everyday life—symbolic interactionism and ethnomethodology—were used in conducting the inquiry. Symbolic interactionism emphasizes social interaction as a process that forms human conduct: It is from the interaction of the individual with others that the meanings of things arise, and it is on the basis of their meaning that the individual acts toward things. The concern of symbolic interactionists then is shared emergent meanings. Ethnomethodology seeks to understand how actors go about the task of seeing, describing, and explaining the world in which they live, that is, the process of creating shared emergent meanings and using them to account for things in one's everyday world. Two assumptions, following from the research perspective, underlay the study: (1) Persistence behavior is the consequence of a process in which the student is an active participant: He or she takes account of various things in his or her everyday world and acts on the basis of how he or she interprets them. (2) Persistence behavior is related to the manner in which the university becomes and remains, through everyday social interaction, a reality for the student.

Data Collection and Analysis

The conceptualization of Chicano university-going reported here is based on Mexican American university students' perceptions of their own and others' college-going experiences and attitudes, as reported to the author in open-ended interviews. Eighteen students and former students from a single entering class of a large, public southwestern university were interviewed by the author eight to eleven months following the end of their freshman year to obtain their perceptions of their college-going behavior during, and prior to, their freshman year.

Informants for the study were selected from a list provided to the author by the Office of Academic Computing Services at the study university. The list contained the names, addresses, and telephone numbers of individuals who: (1) were new freshmen at the university in the fall of 1981, (2) were registered as full-time students (more than eleven credit hours) for that semester, (3) at the time of admission reported their ethnicity to be Hispanic,[2] and (4) at the time of admission were citizens or permanent residents. The list also indicated whether or not and, if so, when each student had withdrawn from the university prior to the twenty-first day of the fall semester of 1982.

The selection of informants from the sampling frame was guided by a single consideration: the sample had to include both persisting and nonpersisting students. In all other respects, the selection process was arbitrary, producing, in essence, a sample of convenience. Individuals who agreed to be interviewed and did, in fact, participate in interviews constituted the sample. Representativeness was not an important consideration in the selection process because the purpose of the study was to discover, rather than to validate, the patterns in a process as it naturally occurs and is understood.

Thirteen of the informants were persisters, that is, they exhibited continuous enrollment through the beginning of their sophomore year; the other five were nonpersisters, having withdrawn at some point between the beginning of the freshman year and the beginning of the sophomore year. A demographic and academic profile of the informants is provided in table 10-1, together with comparable profiles of all new full-time Hispanic freshmen and of all new full-time freshmen matriculating at the study university in fall 1981. Table 10-2 identifies (pseudonymously) the eighteen informants and provides additional background information on them.

Open-ended interviewing, that is, interviewing without an interview schedule, was used in the study so that the author would be free to pursue any area of inquiry suggested by an informant's responses, and the informant would be free to draw upon his or her own experience, rather than prestated alternatives, in responding to the author's questions. The interviews were in-depth modified "life history" interviews; the informants were encouraged to think back over their lives and recount experiences related to their own and others' college-going behavior. For each experience, informants were asked to describe the ways in which other persons were involved in the experience and to recall their own perceptions of it. The interviews were conducted in person at sites of the informants' choosing.

Analysis of the data was accomplished by qualitative induction [17]. That is, concepts and hypotheses emerged from an examination of concrete data collected in the field. The induction process was constrained only by the research perspective: any concept or hypothesis that emerged would, perforce, be consistent with the assumptions of the sociology of everyday life.

To initiate the analysis, the interviews were open-coded, that is, the contents were coded in as many different ways as possible [9]. A total of one hundred nineteen codes were used in this study. These related to context and setting, informants' definitions of situations, informants' ways of thinking about people and objects, process, activities, events, strategies, and relationships. Some coding categories—those most related to the study's research perspective—were more likely to be used than others. Examples of the former are everyday social interaction and perceptions of the university. Often the coding categories were labeled with the very words (for example, "getting in" and "preparing") used by the informants themselves.

Coding was followed by a data reduction step in which the number of coding categories was reduced and the analysis became more conceptually oriented. Decisions about the retention, merging, and discarding of codes initially were made on the basis of the saliency of the categories, that is, the number of cases they contained and the extent of their relationships to other categories. Further data reduction was accomplished by "clustering" [44] the remaining coding categories. Connections or linkages between categories were established by identifying higher-order categories under which a number of coding categories fit. Conceptually, the coding categories became subcategories or properties of the higher-order category. For example, the categories "scaling down" and "getting to know" were seen to be linked, because they were both processes that helped students negotiate, or penetrate, the campus geographies. Thus, it was possible to "reduce" these two categories to form the broader category "getting in." "Scaling

TABLE 10-1
Demographic and Academic Profiles of Various Groups of Fall 1981
Matriculants at the Study University

	All Full-Time, First-Time Freshmen	All Full-Time, First-Time Hispanic Freshmen	The Informants
Number:	3126	147	18
Gender:			
% Male	48.9	50.3	44.4
% Female	51.1	49.7	55.6
Residency status:			
% Resident of state	77.2	81.0	88.9
% Non-resident of state	22.8	19.0	11.1
Average age:	18.4	18.5	18.6
Average rank in high-school graduating class (% from the top):	N/A	24.3	23.1
Average ACT composite score:	N/A	18.5	18.7
Area of major:			
% Agriculture	0.6	0.7	
% Business Administration	23.2	24.5	27.9
% Communication	6.1	2.1	
% Computer Science	6.0	6.8	5.6
% Education	3.3	6.9	
% Engineering	15.2	15.0	16.7
% English	0.5	0.7	
% Fine Arts	5.0	5.5	
% Home Economics	0.7	1.4	11.1
% Mathematics & Natural Science	2.8	2.1	
% Medical Technology	0.6		
% Pre-Professional	13.2	14.4	22.4
% Pre-Architectural	5.2	4.8	5.6
% Pre-Criminal Justice	0.5	0.7	5.6
% Pre-Law	2.5	2.7	5.6
% Pre-Medicine	2.8	3.4	5.6
% Pre-Nursing	1.8	1.4	
% Pre-Social Work	0.4	1.4	
% Psychology	2.0		
% Social Science	2.2	1.4	5.6
% Spanish	0.1	0.7	
% Other foreign language	0.3		
% No Major	18.1	18.4	11.1
Freshman-Year Persistence Status:			
% Persisting	83.5	68.7	72.2
% Not Persisting	16.5	31.3	27.8

TABLE 10-2
Comparative Background Data for Informants

Name	Sex	Age*	Marital Status	Location Of High School(s) Attended	Location of Residence While Attending University	Academic Major*	Persistence Status
Anita[†]	F	18	Single	In-state	On-campus	Bus./Pre-Law	Persister
Barbara	F	18	Single	In-state	Off-campus	Undecided	Persister
Carlos	M	18	Single	In-state	Off-campus	Computer Sci.	Persister
David	M	18	Single	Out-of-state/ In-state	Pre-Medicine Off-campus		Persister
Emmanuel	M	18	Single	In-state	On-campus	Electr. Eng.	Persister
Frances	F	18	Single	In-state	On-campus	Electr. Eng.	Persister
Gregory	M	18	Single	In-state	Off-campus	Bus. Adm.	Persister
Helen	F	17	Single	In-state	Off-campus	Home Ec.	Non-Persister
Isabelle	F	19	Single	In-state	Off-campus	Pre-Architect.	Persister
Jose	M	19	Single	Out-of-state/ In-state	Off-campus	Management	Persister
Karen	F	18	Single	In-state	On-campus	Crim. Justice	Persister
Linda	F	17	Single	In-state	On-campus	Sociology	Persister
Michael	M	17	Single	In-state	Off-campus	Aerospace Eng.	Non-Persister
Natalie	F	19	Single	Out-of-state	Off-campus/ On-campus	Marketing	Persister
Thomas	M	19	Single	Out-of-state	On-campus	Pre-Law	Persister
Peter	M	23	Married	In-state	Off-campus	Gen. Construction	Non-Persister
Theresa	F	18	Single	In-state	Off-campus	Home Ec.	Non-Persister
Rose	F	18	Single	In-state	Off-campus	Bus. Adm.	Non-Persister

* At time of matriculation
† All names are fictitious.

down" and "getting to know" then became sub-categories of "getting in."

This process of "moving out of the data" was facilitated by the writing of research memos [16]. Research memos were notes of varying length that the author wrote to himself in order to capture, on the spot, insights into the data and its analysis. As the analysis proceeded, there was increasing interplay between data reduction and memo writing. Progress in reducing the data and generating conceptual categories expanded the contents of memos and suggested connections between the ideas in separate memos. The latter resulted in "rememoing," that is, writing memos based on other memos. At the same time, memoing and rememoing facilitated data reduc-tion by suggesting how categories might be collapsed into other categories, and, thus, categories of a higher conceptual level generated.

Getting Ready

Two conceptual schemes for interpreting the college-going behavior of Chicano university students emerged from the study. One of these schemes has reference to behaviors and attitudes of these students prior to college matriculation, the other to behaviors and attitudes after matriculation. Each scheme centers around a major organizing concept. For prematriculation experiences, the concept is "getting ready"; for post-matriculation experiences, it is "getting in."

TABLE 10-3
Dimensions of the "Getting Ready" Categories

Category	Type of Activity	Other Participants	Message Conveyed	Outcome
Initial expectation engendering	Oral communication	Parents Friends Classmates	*You* are a *future* college-goer.	Expectation of being a college student.
Fraternal modeling	Observation Oral communication (a description)	Siblings Other relatives	*You* are a *future* college-goer. This is what college is like for me, your brother.	Expectation of being a college student. Expectation of what being a college student is like.
Mentor modeling	Oral communication (a description)	High-school teachers (especially mentors)	This is what college *was* like for me, your teacher.	Expectation of what being a college student is like.
Indirect simulation	Oral communication (a prescription or prediction)	High-School teachers (especially mentors)	This is what you *should do* in college. This is what college *will be* like for you.	Expectation of what being a college student is like.
Direct simulation	Participant observation	Campus people	Oh, so this is what college will be like for me, the informant.	Expectation/ experience of what being a college student is like.

Among experiences before college attendance reported by the informants were activities that variously engendered a college-going frame of mind; modeled college-going behavior; or simulated, in some way, the experience of going to college. These experiences were seen to constitute five categories, or patterns, of getting-ready behavior: (1) Initial expectation engendering, (2) Fraternal modeling, (3) Mentor modeling, (4) Indirect simulation, and (5) Direct simulation (table 10-3).

"Initial expectation engendering" refers to experiences very early in the life of an informant that led to a belief or perception, held long before actual college attendance, that the informant would be going to college. Although such an expectation could be encouraged by elementary school teachers and classmates, it was most frequently perceived to be the result of parental exhortation. For example, Julius (all names are pseudonyms) recalled: "That's all [my father]

ever preached—college." Rose, after quoting her father's advice: " 'Go to college. Go to college,' " added, "You know, going to college and getting an education was just everything to my father."

Despite the obvious importance of parents and others in engendering this early college-going expectation, the informants often described the expectation as though it were a conclusion they had reached independently. Some recalled coming to think about college as part of a natural progression. In the words of Anita: "So I thought: 'After high school comes college, after college comes work'." Other informants linked college-going to future benefits. For example, David recalled this sentiment: "I knew I wanted to go to college anyway because I wanted to be better off." Frances specifically connected the self-realization aspect with the influence-of-others aspect of initial expectation engendering: "Deep down [my sister] doesn't really want to go to school but it's been expected and she knows if she wants to make anything of herself and if she really wants to do something she's going to have to go."

Whatever the particular characteristics of the initial expectation engendering process, the outcome was always perceived to be an expectation that the informant would be a college-goer. Experiences belonging to the remaining categories of getting ready provided substance, in the form of descriptions, prescriptions, and predictions *about* college-going, for the generalized expectation *of* college-going that resulted from initial expectation engendering.

"Fraternal modeling" refers to the informant's having observed, and/or having received information about, the college-going behavior of a relative, usually a sibling. There appear to have been at least two aspects, or features, of this category of getting ready. First, the informant's knowing *that* his or her relative had gone to college often led to a kind of "turn-taking" mind set. Linda provides a description of this feature: "When my brother first went to college, . . . I just assumed at that point, that when I was that age, I would go to college."

The second aspect of fraternal modeling involved the informant's coming to know something *about* the college-going behavior of the relative. Cues given by the relative provided the informant with information about how one went about being a college student, about negotiating the college campus. Oral cues were forthcoming during face-to-face interactions when the relative returned home from college, or, occasionally, over the telephone. Barbara recounted what she learned from her sister: "Well, my sister was in engineering. And she was one of the few girls, which made things worse. She talked about some of her classes and stuff which I knew from then I didn't want to get into anything that I was going to have to be that involved and that so precise and everything." A few informants actually observed, if only in limited contexts, the college-going behavior of a sibling during visits to the campus. Anita reported: "I came and visited my sister a couple of times and . . . I remember going through all the hassles of getting her registered and everything and it was just like uh, it was a big hassle."

Knowing something about the experiences and/or attitudes of the modeler sometimes led to early apprehension about college-going. As a result of experiences like the one described above

and of her sister's expressed anxieties, Anita recalled being "scared" about the idea of going to college. This kind of knowledge also resulted in "negative exampling," that is, the modeler's behavior causing the informant to decide to approach college-going differently than the modeler. Barbara's remarks about how her sister's experiences with the engineering major influenced her own choice of major are quoted above. Barbara also made this observation:"I saw the mistake my sister made of thinking she was going to get A's and then she didn't and so I taught myself to be the opposite way around, to know that I wasn't going to."

Modeling behavior which provided the informants with knowledge about college-going behaviors and attitudes also was exhibited by particular high-school instructors. Because the informants reported close relationships with these instructors, they are referred to here as mentors. Invariably, "mentoring modeling" took the form of the mentor relating his or her own experiences in, and attitudes about, college. Anita recalled a high school physics teacher who talked a lot about the subject: "He went [to college] all over but [mentions a university by name] was mostly what he talked about. . . . He is really intelligent and anything he said, we knew it was true." Barbara provided a very specific example of her mentor's influence on her attitude development toward college-going: "One of my high school teachers, probably the best teacher I ever had, flunked out of college two times. He didn't tell his parents when he flunked out. . . . He was real good because all my life everybody's always expecting me to get A's. . . . So that was the first time I really had a different perspective."

In the case of fraternal or mentor modeling, informants came to have knowledge about college-going as the result of interactions that produced *descriptions* of college-going behaviors and attitudes. Such knowledge could also be the consequence of interactions that led to *prescriptive* or *predictive* statements about college-going. Experiences of the latter kind are examples of "indirect simulation."

Two subcategories of indirect simulation can be differentiated on the basis of the formality of the simulative experience. First, there were the formal, well-planned simulative experiences. These included preparation for college classes. David provided this description of a "college class" that he had taken in high school: "They told us about ACT's and college. It was mainly . . . to prepare us. . . . That's the only class where they really pushed us to go [to college]." Career-day seminars were also simulative experiences of this kind.

Although planned simulations seem to be common to all informants, simulations that were less formal and more spontaneous apparently made a stronger impression. Anita recalled vividly a prediction her high-school chemistry teacher had made about what college-going was going to be like for her and her classmates: "He would expect everybody to go to college, right? And he'd say, 'You think I'm easy now but wait until you get to the university. Those profs are just going to eat you alive if you're like this in class.' He goes, 'I'm very easy compared to some of those profs that you're going to meet'."

While indirect simulations, like modeling experiences, involved the informants in the vicarious acquisition of knowledge about college-going behavior and attitudes, the final category of getting ready—"direct simulation"—includes a whole range of what might be called "quasi-college-going" experiences involving the informants' actual participation. Sorting of these experiences into subcategories of direct simula-

tion (table 10-4) was accomplished by evaluating them in the light of six criteria: (1) the intention of the informant, that is, whether his or her purpose was essentially or incidentally related to college-going; (2) the nature of the informant's activity, particularly the kinds of interactions he or she had with campus people; (3) the extent of such interactions; (4) the nature and extent of the informant's use of campus resources; (5) the duration of the experience; and (6) the role the informant occupied during the experience.

"Incidental visiting" refers to experiences that were essentially unrelated to college-going activity, that were typically short in duration and not recurrent, and that involved limited interaction with campus people and limited use of resources. An example is Peter's infrequent visits to the campus to use the gym. Experiences that belong to the subcategory called "related visiting" were related to college-going but indirectly, that is, to the college-going of a person other than the informant, or prospectively, that is, to the anticipated college-going of the informant. Like incidental visiting, related visiting tended to be characterized by limited interaction with campus people, limited use of campus resources, and a time frame that was short. Informants who participated in visiting experiences often reported

TABLE 10-4
Subcategories of "Direct Simulation" and their Dimensions

Subcategory	Intention	Example(s) of Activities	Amount of Interaction	Duration	Use of Resources	Role of Informant
Incidental visiting	Not related to college-going	Taking test Going to gym	None or limited	Short limited	Very limited	User
Related visiting (I)	Related to college-going (prospectively)	Touring campus	Limited	Short	Very limited	Tourist
Related visiting (II)	Related to college-going (indirectly)	Accompanying sibling	Variable but usually limited	Variable but generally short	Limited	Visitor
Attending (I)	Variable	Participating in summer workshop	Extensive	Relatively long	Relatively extensive	Pseudo-student
Attending (II)	Related to college-going (directly)	Going to college class	Extensive	Long	Extensive	Quasi-student

that they came away feeling that they had "just barely walked on campus" (Isabel) and had not been "exposed to the real aspect of the university being a university" (Linda).

Experiences that involved extensive use of campus resources, extensive interaction with campus people, and extended or repeated presence on the college campus belong to a subcategory of direct simulation called "attending." One kind of attending (Attending I) refers to activities that extensively imitated college-going behavior. Such activities may or may not have been related to college-going per se. Nevertheless, each experience of this type involved the informant in considerable interaction with campus people, extensive usage of campus resources, and a relatively lengthy or recurrent campus stay. Emmanuel recounted his participation in a summer institute sponsored by the study university: "In the summer of my junior year, between my junior and my senior year, the university, the engineering department, sent me to a summer institute, a seminar for a week. And they try to familiarize you with the campus."

A second level of attending (Attending II) included experiences that, to some degree, constituted college-going, for example, attending college classes as an official enrollee or as the companion of an official enrollee. As an example of the latter, Natalie reported: "My mother was also going to college while I was in high school. So I used to go to classes with her. Sometimes I would just accompany her . . . or if she said that she had a interesting class, I'd listen to it. . . . [I'd go] to classes and the cafeteria." Participation in Attending II experiences blurred the boundary between simulation and the true experience, and it is difficult, on the basis of the available data, to estimate the extent to which such experiences only simulated postmatriculation college-going experiences vis-à-vis actually embodying them. Still, the findings to be presented in the next section indicate that having had Attending II experiences did not exempt informants, after official matriculation at the university, from obstacles to their effective negotiation of the university campus.

It should be clear to the reader that each getting-ready experience resulted in either (1) an expectation that the informant would eventually go to college, or (2) an expectation of what it would be like to be college-going. Expectations resulting from experiences belonging to all categories, save direct simulation, were externally prompted, that is, the impetus for the expectation was something said or done by an individual other than the informant. Expectations from direct simulation experiences tended to derive from self-reflexive activity and, hence, were internally prompted.

Each expectation may be understood to be the outcome of an evaluative experience. That is, associated with the prompting of the expectation was a valuation—either positive or negative—of college-going. All of the experiences identified as instances of initial expectation engendering involved only positive valuations. It is hypothesized that experiences of this kind involving negative evaluations do occur, probably to individuals who decide not to attend college. Experiences assigned to the other four categories involved both positive and negative valuations. An interesting case of the latter (an example is described above) is the high-school teacher's use of future college-going as a disciplinary mechanism. However, most experiences in these categories reported by the informants resulted in positive valuations of college-going.

Although experiences belonging to any single category of getting ready were not temporally discrete from those belonging to all others, there was an overall chronological pattern to the occurrence of the experiences relative to their categorical assignments. For example, initial expectation engendering, as is implied by its name, generally took place very early in an informant's life. Fraternal modeling, mentor modeling, and indirect simulation were experienced, more or less simultaneously, some variable length of time after initial expectation engendering. Direct simulation was characteristic of late precollegiate life.

One consequence of this patterning was that experiences belonging to later occurring categories tended to build upon those belonging to earlier ones. As noted above, experiences of the fraternal modeling, mentor modeling, and indirect simulation types provided substance, in the form of descriptions, prescriptions, and predictions about college-going, for the kind of generalized expectation of college-going that resulted from initial expectation engendering. The self-expectation that characterized experiences in the direct simulation category was the result of a valuation of college-going that took into account not only the immediate events but also valuations and expectations resulting from (earlier) experiences belonging to the other categories.

Getting In

Postmatriculation behaviors and attitudes can be understood in terms of a second organizing concept—"getting in." In describing their early impressions of the university, the informants were virtually unanimous in emphasizing a perception of "bigness." The descriptor "big" turned out to be a gloss for articulating the perceived dimensions; namely, mass, distance, and complexity, of three campus geographies: (1) the physical geography, (2) the social geography, and (3) the academic/cognitive geography (table 10-5).

For example, mass, distance, and complexity of the physical geography referred to the fact that for some informants the campus was larger in size than their entire hometowns (mass), that from one end of the campus to the other was much longer than the single block their high schools occupied (distance), and that it was not easy to resolve the physical campus into what would be for the informants logical and easily recognizable spaces (complexity). As an aspect of the social geography, mass was often described in terms of the literally hundreds of students with whom the informants attended class, distance as the gap between student and instructor that prevented a close working relationship, and complexity as the total ignorance of one another's lives exhibited by members (including the informants) of the campus population. Mass as an aspect of the academic/

cognitive geography exhibited itself in what was perceived to be a seemingly unlimited number of potential fields of study, distance as the giant cognitive step the informants had to make in moving from "easy" high-school curricula to "hard" university ones, and complexity as the perceived obtuseness of professor talk. The inability to deal with these dimensions led to feelings of "being lost" in one or more of the geographies.[3]

Many of the postmatriculation behaviors reported by the informants may be understood as strategies to fix themselves in the physical, social, and/or academic/cognitive geographies. The behaviors employed in this way, which constitute the categories of getting in, took account, quite naturally, of the perceived dimensions of the geographies. Each represents a potential component of the process by which the informant initiated his or her negotiation of the geographies. Two categories of getting in emerged from an analysis of the data: (1) "getting to know" and (2) "scaling down."

A seemingly obvious way for an individual to deal with a milieu that overwhelmed him or her with its size, placed him or her at a distance from important people and things, and posed complexity was to increase his or her familiarity with that milieu. The informants reported two different sets of behaviors that led to increased knowledge of the campus geographies. The first set, called "mentoring," involved interactive experiences with students, already at the university for some time when the informant matriculated, who functioned as guides or interpreters

TABLE 10-5
The Perceived Geographies and Their Features

Feature	Geography		
	Physical	Social	Academic/Cognitive
Mass	"Is this place large!"	"So many people!"	"So many fields, so many classes one could take."
Distance	"You can't see from one side of the campus to the other."	"I was like in an audience and he had a microphone."	"High school to college is a bigger step."
Complexity	"There were all these little signs telling you to go over here, go over there. I got lost."	"You're constantly running into people you don't know."	"They made instruction more complicated than it had to be."

of the geographies. Frances reported such a person, who had had a profound influence on her early behavior at the university: "She influenced my decision to stay here [in the dorm]. . . . She told me basically what goes on around here and how to get along around here. . . . Some of the things she said, you know, about the Engineering College and about how band was. I wanted to be in a good band so. And engineering—she told me a lot of things that go on in engineering. She told me what classes to take my first semester because [from] the trouble she had . . . she knew, you know, what you should do first. . . . She just kind of paved the way and guided me through making decisions, you know, as to where to go."

The second set of getting-to-know experiences—"peer knowledge sharing"—includes experiences with fellow newcomers in which there was a kind of cooperative exploring of the geographies. Barbara provides a good description of such activity: "It kind of helps if you have somebody to relate to and somebody who's having the same problem. And they find out something you're suppose to do that you didn't know about. So just kind of giving information back and forth." In Barbara's case, it was with high-school friends, co-matriculants at the university, that she engaged in peer knowledge sharing. In other cases, peer knowledge sharing occurred with individuals who were not known to the informants prior to their arrival on campus. Anita reported her strategy of sitting by someone in each class and introducing herself to that person: "That way it makes the class a lot easier. . . . Because, you know, they learn it different, they can explain it in their terms and you can catch on easily and that way you're not so insecure when you go in [-to class]."

Scaling down refers to behaviors and attitudes which resulted in the informant's perception of a more narrowly defined geography, effectively reducing the amount of the geography with which the informant had to be familiar in order to locate himself or herself. In effect, the mass, distance, and complexity dimensions of the geographies were "scaled down." Barbara, for example, explained how she had learned to avoid the "biggest places" on campus. Rather, she ran her "own little circle": "It's not like I'm at [the university]. It's kind of like I'm here in this part of it."

One focus of both the getting-to-know and the scaling-down kinds of experiences was the process of "majoring in." In addition to its manifest function—initiating a focused study of that area of the curriculum that is most closely related to one's life and career goals, selecting an academic major had another, more latent function: it provided a vehicle for locating oneself in the physical, social, and academic geographies; it provided a way of getting in. For the informants, the assumption of an academic major meant that the physical environment was circumscribed, the curriculum was bracketed, an important element of one's self-identity vis-à-vis the campus community was created, and a cynosure for social activities was realized. Hence, the expression, "I am majoring in _____" [a particular academic major is named] or, more simply, "I am in _____" [a particular academic major is named], was not merely an idiom but an oral affirmation of the locating function of the academic major. With respect to the role of the major in negotiating the social geography, it is interesting to note that the campus organization most frequently mentioned by the informants—an organization for Hispanic business students—had as its *raison d'être* the sharing of an academic major (figure 10-1).

Theoretical Interpretations and Hypotheses

Following Stern [44], who argues that the process of concept development in qualitative research is facilitated by selective sampling of the literature for concepts that can be compared as data, the author looked for available social and/or sociopsychological constructs that could be used to draw out the theoretical significance of the getting ready and getting in concepts.

The construct "significant other," particularly as worked out by Haller and Woelfel [18], is useful for considering the significance of getting ready. In their study of the occupational and educational goals of high-school students, Haller and Woelfel [18, pp. 594–95] came to define a "significant other" as:

> A person, known to the focal individual, who either through direct interaction (a definer) or by example (a model) provides information which influences the focal individual's conception of himself in relation to educational or occupational roles or influences his conception of such roles (a conception of an object).

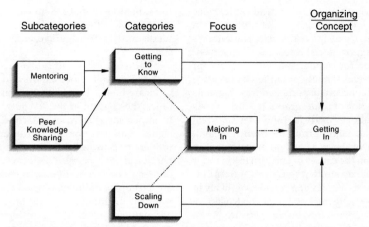

Figure 10.1 The Categories and Subcategories of "Getting In" and their Relationship to "Majoring In."

In the present study, parents, high-school teachers and, less frequently, siblings were definers with respect to college-going: These individuals communicated to the informant the fact that he or she belonged to the category of future college-goers and defined for him or her what it meant to be a college-goer. In addition, high-school teachers and siblings created expectations with respect to college-going by modeling college-going behavior. The mere departure of an older sibling for college might have signalled to the informant his or her membership in the category of (future) college-goers. Subsequently, the informant's observations of college-going behavior by siblings and teachers provided insight into the nature of the college-going role.

A second construct that was useful for drawing out the theoretical significance of getting ready was anticipatory socialization.[4] Anticipatory socialization refers to a premature taking on or identification with the behavior and attitudes of an *aspired to* group which "may serve the twin functions of aiding [an individual's] rise into [the aspired to] group and of easing his adjustment after he has become part of it" [24, p. 87]. The concept has been primarily worked out in relation to occupational preparation [33] and the formation of political views [39], but there has been some consideration of it with respect to the role of college student.

Parsons [30], for example, has argued that because, as early as elementary school, high achievers are culled from their classmates so they can be directed toward a college preparatory curriculum, the decision of a high achiever to attend college may be the result of a long period of anticipatory socialization. Silber and his colleagues [40] have reported that some high-school students prepare themselves for college by rehearsing forms of behavior they associate with college students. This role rehearsing may include taking special courses that are viewed as trial college experiences and carrying out assignments the teacher identifies as what one does in college.

Role-rehearsing was clearly an element of the getting ready experiences recorded here. It may have been very indirect as, for example, the simulation of certain aspects of college-going in college preparatory classes. A more direct kind of rehearsing occurred when the individual participated in on-campus activities: living in dormitories, going to parties, attending classroom lectures. Another component of anticipatory socialization, the forecasting of future situations, was a feature of getting ready; as, for example, when the informant, upon observing an older sibling depart for college, predicted his or her own matriculation, or when a high-school teacher predicted that college professors would treat the informant and his or her co-students much differently than he or she (the high-school teacher) did.

In drawing out the theoretical significance of the concept "getting in," the author again referred to two existing constructs. The author's consideration of "social integration" as a theoretical datum for comparison with the concept of getting in was initially prompted by his reading of other conceptually oriented investigations of the behavior of undergraduate students. As mentioned above, Spady [41] and later Tinto [45] borrowed the concept from the French sociologist Emile Durkheim as he had elaborated it in his treatise on the causes of suicide [15], in order to conceptualize student withdrawal from college. Durkheim argued that suicide was likely in populations where rates of interaction (collective affiliation) were too low, because this leads to a lack of common sentiments and values (moral consensus) and the precedence of individual interests over social ones. As the individual increasingly frees himself or herself from the social control of the group, he or she removes himself or herself from its prophylactic influence and finds little meaning in life, which comes to appear as an intolerable burden.

Spady (and Tinto after him), in adapting these concepts to an explanation of student withdrawal from college, specified a lack of collective affiliation (friendship) and a lack of moral consensus (cognitive congruence) as having separate effects on dropping out behavior, that is, independently influencing the level of one's social integration. Neither Durkheim nor Spady provides a clear definition of the construct "social integration."

The results of the study reported here suggest that moral consensus is neither the (principal) outcome of collective affiliation (as postulated by Durkheim) nor an independent cause of one's persisting in life or college (as indicated by Spady and Tinto). A student's interaction with others is important for his or her persistence in college not simply or primarily because it leads to the sharing of general values and orientations, but because it assists the student in developing specific strategies for negotiating the physical, social, and cognitive/academic geographies. The getting-to-know category of getting in defines "collective affiliations" with specific individuals—mentors and peers—that "integrate" the student into the physical and academic/cognitive geographies as well as the social geography by providing him or her with knowledge of these geographies and

the skills to negotiate them. According to this interpretation, then, students become integrated for distinctly more cognitive, and less moral, reasons.

In theorizing about how exactly students, with the assistance of mentors and peers, come to locate themselves in the perceived geographies, the concept of the "cognitive map" may be important. It is hypothesized [43] that when significant environments (for example, a large university campus) are too large to be apprehended at once, people will form "conceptions" of them. These conceptions, or cognitive maps, are a complex of things learned about the environment, including expectations, stereotypes, and value judgments. In developing cognitive maps of large and complex spaces, individuals make certain simplifications and adjustments in accordance with their own needs and experience. This means, of course, that cognitive maps and mapmaking exhibit considerable interpersonal variation.

The basis of cognitive map formation is the identification of significant objects in the environment, the establishment of the connectedness of the objects to one another and to the observer, and the assignment of meaning, whether emotional or practical, to the objects and their relationships. As the word "map" implies, the origin and major implication of the cognitive map lie in the spatial domain. But people are thought to organize other phenomena, for example, social interrelations, affective bonds, and temporal relationships, in the same way [22]. Cognitive mapping is similar to the "sense-making activity" of organizational members as described by Weick [49, pp. 148–49]:

> People in organizations try to sort . . . chaos [which is flowing and equivocal] into items, events, and parts which are then connected, threaded into sequences, serially ordered, and related. . . . [Because it is] the individual [who] breaks up chaos so that other forms of order can be created, . . . it stands to reason that what is eventually available for inspection is something very much of the individual's own making.

The student's initial perceptions of the campus geographies may be understood to reflect the absence of cognitive maps. Thus the geographies were perceived to be large-scale environments (mass) in which objects stood separated from one another (distance) and seemed incapable of being resolved into meaningful components (complexity). The student's strategies for getting in are conceptualized to be mechanisms for facilitating the acquisition of these maps. For example, getting-to-know behaviors—knowledge sharing with other neophytes and mentoring relationships with veteran students—are shortcuts to acquiring representations of specific objects within the various geographies and the associations between these representations. Scaling-down behaviors result in more detailed maps of smaller portions of the geographies—areas of particular concern to the individual.[5,6]

On the basis of the findings and theoretical interpretations of the research reported here, the following hypotheses regarding the context of the Mexican American's decision to persist in the university are proposed.

(1) For Mexican American freshmen, the effects of so called "background" variables (for example, high school curriculum, parents' education, parents' occupations) on persistence in college are mediated by significant-other influences. Most of the existing models of college student persistence/withdrawal posit, and are successfully used to test for, the influence of prematriculation factors on persistence. The findings of the present study suggest that where these factors influence the persistence of Mexican Americans in the university it is because they increase these students' exposure to modeling and defining experiences relative to college-going.

(2) For Mexican American freshmen, the extent and nature of anticipatory socialization for college-going has an influence not only on the decision to go to college but, once there, on the decision to stay. Haller and Woelfel [18] have shown that the level of anticipatory socialization for college, in the form of defining and modeling experiences, has a positive impact on an individual's educational goals, that is, the decision to go to college. The results of the present study suggest that these experiences also have an impact on the decision to remain in college. That is, a student's willingness to "stick it out" may reflect early and thorough socializing by family, teachers, and friends for college-going.

(3) For Mexican American freshmen, the extent to which social integration influences persistence is not the extent to which it promotes the individual's moral conformity to the institution but rather the extent to which it endows the indi-

vidual with the capacity to cognitively manage the university environment, that is, helps him or her to perceive the physical, social, and academic/cognitive geographies as negotiable.

(4) For Mexican American freshmen, persisting at the university is positively related to the development and use of cognitive maps of the physical, social, and academic/cognitive geographies. The persister is more likely to employ strategies (the result of other cognitive maps?) that facilitate the development of such maps.

Implications for Practice

The results of the research reported here suggest a number of strategies that the university might adopt to improve the college-going experience of Mexican Americans and promote their persistence during the freshman year. Consider, for example, early anticipatory socialization for college-going. Parents, teachers, and siblings are generally the key agents for such socialization, and it is not easy to conceive of how the university community could have much direct impact upon it. There are ways, however. An example is an experimental program currently underway at the study university in which members of the staff of the Student Affairs Office are bringing Chicano junior high-school girls and their mothers to the campus in order to introduce them, gradually, to the university and to the college-going process. Each of the girls in the project was selected from a family without any previous college experience. By including mothers, the project directors have acknowledged the important role of parents in socialization for college attendance.

The opportunities for constructive intervention by the university in later anticipatory socialization are many and varied. Indeed, most institutions, including the study university, already play a role in this kind of socialization. For example, universities regularly provide tours of their campuses for high-school students and conduct college day programs. But it is common for host institutions to look upon such events as nothing more than marketing strategies. This is unfortunate, because the results of the present study suggest their potential for significant socialization to college-going; they represent opportunities for orienting the prematriculant to the university experience.

For example, the traditional campus tour might be conducted in such a way that it assists the student to begin to develop a cognitive map of the physical geography. This would involve, for example, the tour director highlighting the importance of places (not just their histories) and indicating their connections with one another. Visual aids might include, in addition to commercial products, sketch maps of the university drawn by veteran students.

Of course, in those situations where the high-school student is on the university campus for an extended period of time, the opportunity for influencing his or her socialization to college-going is maximal. Each case of an extended stay mentioned by the informants in the present study (for example, a yearbook editors' conference and a statewide summer enrichment program) was the result of an effort underwritten by the high school. The university itself should sponsor extended stays, so that students (particularly those being little socialized to college-going at home) can "practice" going to the university.

Still another way for the university to influence later anticipatory socialization would be involvement in the design of curricula for college preparatory classes (for example, writing for college) which are offered by many high schools. Again, the object would be to assist the prematriculant to initiate the processes of developing cognitive maps of the campus geographies.

With respect to getting-in phenomena, the results of the present study have several implications for university intervention to positively influence the process of college-going after matriculation. For example, most institutions, including the study university, introduce new freshmen to their campus by conducting a special program, traditionally called "freshman orientation."[7] The duration of the program varies from institution to institution, being as short as a day and as long a several weeks. Its purpose is to "orient" individuals to a new environment.

The present study should prove useful to the university student affairs office in the conduct of the freshman orientation for Chicano freshmen inasmuch as it provides a conceptualization of how these students "orient" themselves. They build up internal mental representations, or cognitive maps, of the physical, social and academic/cognitive geographies; these maps are mechanisms for finding one's way in a large-scale environment. The map-making process is gradual and apparently exhibits interpersonal variation. For example, students who persist through their freshman year may form maps more quickly than those who do not. This, in turn, may be related to the possession by the persisters of still other cognitive maps—cognitive maps that are, essentially, instructions on how to negotiate new environments. It would behoove university personnel designing orientation sessions to understand the components (for example, knowledge-sharing and mentoring strategies) of such "how to" cognitive maps so that such information can be passed on early to new students. The results of this study also argue for an orientation that continues through the freshman year rather than being limited to one or two weeks at the beginning of the fall semester. This would reflect the gradualness of the process of building cognitive maps and, hence, the importance of monitoring it on a continuous basis.

Future Research

In-depth, nonscheduled interviews of Mexican American university students and former university students conducted from the perspective of the sociology of everyday life proved useful for generating concepts of Chicano university-going. But these concepts need to be refined and verified in subsequent research. This can be accomplished, in the first place, by expanding the qualitative data base on Mexican American university-going initiated by the present study. Although further in-depth interviewing of university sophomores and nonpersisting members of their freshman classes would be useful, interviews of individuals at other points in the life cycle should be conducted as well. The research reported here suggests that the nature of college-going in the freshman year is influenced profoundly by experiences that occur much earlier in life.

Undoubtedly, it would be illuminating to interview individuals on a continuous basis from, say, the time they entered first grade in order to ascertain their immediate perceptions of people and events ultimately influencing their college-going and persistence at the university. To do so would be logistically and financially impractical. More feasible is a research design in which informants are interviewed periodically from the time they enter high school until the time they complete, or fail to complete, their freshman year of college. At minimum, the research design of the present study should be extended so that individuals are interviewed *while* they are in their freshman year.

The findings of the present study suggest specific areas of inquiry for future interviewing. Thus, questioning ought to be focused, for example, on experiences in which college-going is modeled or defined for future college-goers, or on social interactions that contribute to the development and use of cognitive maps of the university. Information on these topics would be collected by means of an interviewing technique that was more structured than that used here so that data obtained from different individuals would be more comparable. In addition to the question-and-answer format, other procedures for eliciting information would be employed. For example, the notion that there is variation among students in the acquisition and use of cognitive maps might be "tested" by having individuals draw maps of the campus geographies or list categories of objects to be found within them [20].

Qualitative data collection by methods other than interviewing also should be considered in future research. Two of these methods would seem to be particularly useful. Because experiences related to college-going and persistence at the university are extensive in time and occur ubiquitously, the possibility of a researcher's observing and recording even a fraction of these experiences is nil. This problem cannot be circumvented, but comparable kinds of data can be collected by having informants be the observers and recorders of their own experiences. Cooperative and articulate individuals would be trained to record in diaries or logs their experiences and their immediate reactions to their experiences. Periodically, these individuals would be debriefed by the researcher.

The extensiveness of the temporal and spatial contexts of behavior related to college-going and persistence does not mean that direct observation of such behavior is lost to the researcher as a strategy for data collection. The results of the present study (and presumably of interviews in follow-up studies) suggest (or will suggest) places where and times when observation of behavior related to college-going can be conducted most propitiously. For example, on the basis of the present investigation, a researcher

wishing to observe various getting-ready experiences might focus on the college preparatory class, the university tour, and/or the high-school career day. Foci for observation of getting-in experiences would include freshman-level classes of varying sizes and extracurricular organizations (such as the Hispanic Business Students' Association) that form around the academic major.

In addition to initiating a qualitative database on Mexican American college-going, the present study has hypothesized factors that influence the persistence of Chicanos at the university during the freshman year. Future research should seek to test the relationships specified in these hypotheses. Most likely, this would involve the design of a survey instrument and its administration to a large, random sample of Chicano students stratified on the basis of whether or not they persisted into the sophomore year. Alternatively, first-time university freshmen could be surveyed and their persistence status subsequently ascertained.

Still another way in which the research described here might be followed up would involve examining, with comparable research methods, the college-going and persistence of students from other ethnic backgrounds, of other academic levels, and in other kinds of institutions. One wonders, for example, to what extent the patterns of college-going and persistence described in this study are tied to unique aspects of Mexican American culture. Ramírez and Castañeda [35] have identified four major value clusters within the Mexican American value system, including identification with family, community and ethnic group; personalization of interpersonal relationships; status and role definition in family and community; and Mexican Catholic ideology. Given the centrality of the family to the total socialization of the Chicano child, the importance of parents, siblings, and other relatives for getting-ready behavior is not surprising. Should we expect that for Anglos significant others for socialization to college-going might be drawn more heavily from among elementary and secondary school teachers and counselors? Similarly, in what ways do cultural differences between minority and Anglo students affect how and how effectively cognitive maps of the university environment are "drawn" and utilized?

The present dearth of meaningful studies of Hispanic college students[8] parallels the primitive state of research on Latino education in general

[27]. The investigation reported here was undertaken in the spirit of Olivas' [27] call for improvement in both the quality of Hispanic data and theoretical constructs for explaining them. The author hopes it will encourage others to begin to fill the "fertile void in the literature of Hispanic students" [27, p. 136].

Notes

1. This approach was adopted by Neumann [25] in a study of the persistence of community college students.
2. Virtually all of the Hispanics who attend the university are Mexican American. For purposes of university reporting, ethnic/racial background is based on the student's response to an item on the university's admission form. Because an unknown number of Hispanics either (along with Anglos) selects the alternative "Other" or declines to respond at all to this item, it is unlikely that the list included *all* new full-time Hispanic freshmen entering in fall 1981. For the purpose of the research reported here, it was not necessary that it do so (see below).
3. Mass, distance and complexity all seem to be related to the sociopsychological concept of alienation, which has been defined as [19, p. 9]: "Different kinds of dissociation, break or rupture between human beings and their objects, whether the latter be other persons or the natural world, or their own creations in art, science and society; and subjectively, the corresponding states of disequilibrium, disturbance, strangeness and anxiety."
4. Other researchers [8, 21, 31] have noted the potential usefulness of this concept for understanding persistence in college.
5. Scaling down behavior may be an example of what Weick [50] calls the "small win" strategy. According to Weick [50, p. 44]: "People with limited rationality have sufficient variety to visualize, manage, and monitor the smaller amount of variety present in scaled-down problem environments. When people initiate small-scale projects there is less play between cause and effect; local regularities can be created, observed, and trusted; and feedback is immediate and can be used to revise theories. Events cohere and can be observed in their entirety when their scale is reduced."
6. The nature of scaling down attitudes and behavior presumably would be of interest to campus ecologists [5] who wish to understand how specific groups and even individual students visualize and use the campus, in order to design environments that better meet these students' needs [6].
7. Pascarella and his colleagues [31] have found participation in freshman orientation to have a significant indirect effect (through social integration) upon the persistence of college students.
8. The recently published *Latino College Students* [28], an edited volume of research studies, is an attempt to address this omission.

References

1. Anderson, K. L. "Student Retention Focused Dialogue: Opening Presentation." Paper presented at the annual meeting of the Association for the Study of Higher Education, Chicago, 1985.
2. Astin, A. W. *Minorities in Higher Education: Recent Trends, Current Prospects, and Recommendations.* San Francisco: Jossey-Bass, 1982.
3. Astin, H. S., and C. P. Burciaga. *Chicanos in Higher Education: Progress and Attainment.* ERIC 226–690. Los Angeles: Higher Education Research Institute, 1981.
4. Astin, H. S., and P. H. Cross. *Student Financial Aid and Persistence in College.* ERIC 221–078. Los Angeles: Higher Education Research Institute, 1979.
5. Banning, J. H. "The Campus Ecology Manager Role." In *Student Services: A Handbook for the Profession*, edited by U. Delworth, G. R. Hanson and Associates, pp. 209–27. San Francisco: Jossey-Bass, 1980.
6. Banning, J. H., and L. Kaiser. "An Ecological Perspective and Model for Campus Design." *Pesonnel and Guidance Journal*, 52 (February 1974), 370–75.
7. Bean, J. P. "The Application of a Model of Turnover in Work Organizations to the Student Attrition Process." *Review of Higher Education*, 6 (Winter 1983), 129–48.
8. ———. "Interaction Effects Based on Class Level in an Explanatory Model of College Student Dropout Syndrome." *American Educational Research Journal*, 22 (Spring 1985), 35–64.
9. Bogdan, R. C., and S. K. Biklen. *Qualitative Research for Education: An Introduction to Theory and Methods.* Boston: Allyn & Bacon, 1982.
10. Brown, G. H. "The Outcomes of Education." In *The Condition of Education for Hispanic Americans*, edited by G. H. Brown et al., pp. 117–215. Washington, D.C.: U.S. Government Printing Office, 1980.
11. Carter, T. P., and R. D. Segura. *Mexican Americans in School: A Decade of Change.* New York: College Entrance Examination Board, 1979.

12. Dawis, R. V., L. H. Lofquist, and D. J. Weiss. *A Theory of Work Adjustment. A Revision*. Minnesota Studies in Vocational Rehabilitation, No. 23. Minneapolis: Center for Industrial Relations, University of Minnesota, 1968.

13. De Los Santos, A. G., Jr., J. Montemayor, and E. Solis. *Chicano Students in Institutions of Higher Education: Access, Attrition, and Achievement*. Research Report Series, Vol. 1, No. 1. ERIC 205–360. Austin: Office for Advanced Research in Hispanic Education, College of Education, University of Texas at Austin, 1980.

14. Douglas, J. D. "Introduction to the Sociologies of Everyday Life." In *Introduction to the Sociologies of Everyday Life*, edited by J. D. Douglas, pp. 1–19. Boston: Allyn & Bacon, 1980.

15. Durkheim, E. *Suicide: A Study in Sociology*. Edited by G. Simpson. Translated by J. A. Spaulding and G. Simpson. Glencoe, Ill.: Free Press, 1951. (Originally published 1897.)

16. Glaser, B. G., and A. L. Strauss. *The Discovery of Grounded Theory: Strategies for Qualitative Research*. New York: Aldine, 1967.

17. Goetz, J. P., and M. D. LeCompte. *Ethnography and Qualitative Design in Educational Research*. Orlando, Fla.: Academic Press, 1984.

18. Haller, A. D., and J. Woelfel. "Significant Others and Their Expectations: Concepts and Instruments to Measure Interpersonal Influence on Status Aspirations." *Rural Sociology*, 37 (December 1972), 591–622.

19. Heinemann, F. H. *Existentialism and the Modern Predicament*. New York: Harper Torchbooks, 1958.

20. Herman, J. F., R. V. Kail, and A. W. Siegel. "Cognitive Maps of a College Campus: A New Look at Freshman Orientation." *Bulletin of the Psychonomic Society*, 13 (March 1979), 183–86.

21. Iverson, B. K., E. T. Pascarella, and P. T. Terenzini. "Informal Faculty-Student Contact and Commuter College Freshmen." *Research in Higher Education*, 21 (1984), 123–36.

22. Kaplan, S., and R. Kaplan. "Introduction to Chapter 3." In *Humanscape: Environments for People*, edited by S. Kaplan and R. Kaplan, pp. 42–43. North Scituate, Mass.: Duxbury Press, 1978.

23. Kissler, G. R. *Retention and Transfer: University of California Undergraduate Enrollment Study*. ERIC 215–597. Berkeley: Calif.: Office of the Academic Vice President, University of California, 1980.

24. Merton, R. K., and A. S. Kitt. "Contributions to the Theory of Reference Group Behavior." In *Continuities in Social Research: Studies in the Scope and Method of 'The American Soldier'*, edited by R. K. Merton and P. F. Lazarsfeld, pp. 40–105. Glencoe, Ill.: Free Press, 1950.

25. Neumann, W. F. "Persistence in the Community College: The Student Perspective." Ph.D. Dissertation, Syracuse University, 1985.

26. Olivas, M. A. *The Dilemma of Access: Minorities in Two-year Colleges*. Washington, D.C.: Howard University Press, 1979.

27. ———. "Research and Theory on Hispanic Education: Students, Finance, and Governance." *Aztlan*, 14 (Spring 1983), 111–46.

28. ———(ed.). *Latino College Students*. New York: Teachers College Press, 1986.

29. Ortiz, V. "Generational Status, Family Background, and Educational Attainment Among Hispanic Youth and Non-Hispanic White Youth." In *Latino College Students*, edited by M. A. Olivas, pp. 29–46. New York: Teachers College Press, 1986.

30. Parsons, T. "The School Class as a Social System: Some of Its Functions in American Society." *Harvard Educational Review*, 29 (Fall 1959), 297–318.

31. Pascarella, E. T., and D. W. Chapman. "A Multi-institutional, Path Analytic Validation of Tinto's Model of College Withdrawal." *American Educational Research Journal*, 20 (Spring 1983), 87–102.

32. Pascarella, E. T., P. T. Terenzini, and L. M. Wolfle. "Orientation to College and Freshman Year Persistence/Withdrawal Decisions." *Journal of Higher Education*, 57 (March/April 1986), 155–75.

33. Pavalko, R. M. *Sociology of Occupations and Professions*. Itasca, Ill.: Peacock, 1971.

34. Price, J. L. *The Study of Turnover*. Ames, Iowa: Iowa State University Press, 1977.

35. Ramírez, M., III, and A. Castañeda. *Cultural Democracy, Bicognitive Development, and Education*. New York: Academic Press, 1974.

36. Richardson, R. C., Jr., and L. C. Attinasi, Jr. *Persistence of Undergraduate Students at Arizona State University: A Research Report on the Class Entering in Fall, 1976*. ERIC 223–138. Tempe, Ariz.: College of Education, Arizona State University, 1982.

37. Rosenthal, W. *Summer 1980 Report of Persistence-Attrition of Members of Ethnic Groups*. ERIC 191–412. East Lansing, Mich.: Office of Institutional Research, Michigan State University, 1980.

38. Santos, R. "Hispanic High School Graduates: Making Choices." In *Latino College Students*, edited by M. A. Olivas, pp. 104–27. New York: Teachers College Press, 1986.

39. Sheinkopf, K. G. "Family Communication Patterns and Anticipatory Socialization." *Journalism Quarterly*, 50 (Spring 1973), 24–30, 133.

40. Silber, E., et al. "Adaptive Behavior in Competent Adolescents: Coping with the Anticipation of College." *Archives of General Psychiatry*, 5 (October 1961), 354–65.

41. Spady, W. G. "Dropouts from Higher Education: An Interdisciplinary Review and Synthesis." *Interchange*, 1 (April 1970), 109–21.

42. Starr, A., E. L. Betz, and J. Menne. "Differences in College Student Satisfaction: Academic Dropouts, Nonacademic Dropouts, and Nondropouts." *Journal of Counseling Psychology*, 19 (July 1972), 318–22.

43. Stea, D. "The Measurement of Mental Maps: An Experimental Model for Studying Conceptual Spaces." In *Behavioral Problems in Geography: A Symposium* (Northwestern University Studies in Geography, No. 17), edited by K. R. Cox and R. G. Golledge, pp. 228–53. Evanston, Ill.: Department of Geography, Northwestern University, 1969.

44. Stern, P. N. "Grounded Theory Methodology: Its Uses and Processes." *Image*, 12 (February 1980), 20–23.

45. Tinto, V. "Dropout From Higher Education: A Theoretical Synthesis of Recent Research." *Review of Educational Research*, 45 (Winter 1975), 89–125.

46. ———. *Student Leaving: Rethinking the Causes and Cures of Student Attrition*. Chicago: University of Chicago Press, 1987.

47. U.S. Bureau of the Census. *Persons of Spanish Origin in the United States: March 1979*. Current Population Reports, Series P-20, No. 354. Washington, D.C.: U.S. Government Printing Office, 1980.

48. U.S. Commission on Civil Rights. *The Unfinished Education: Outcomes for Minorities in the Five Southwestern States*. Mexican American Educational Series, Report 2. Washington, D.C.: U.S. Government Printing Office, 1971.

49. Weick, K. E. *The Social Psychology of Organizing*. 2nd ed. Reading, Mass.: Addison-Wesley, 1979.

50. ———. "Small Wins: Redefining the Scale of Social Problems." *American Psychologist*, 39 (January 1984), 40–49.

51. Withey, S. B. "Summary and Conclusions." In *A Degree and What Else: Correlates and Consequences of a College Education*, edited by S. B. Withey, pp. 127–32. New York: McGraw-Hill, 1971.

CHAPTER 11

STUDENT ACCESS, RETENTION, AND SUCCESS: MODELS OF INCLUSION AND SUPPORT

ANNA M. ORTIZ AND IRIS HEAVY RUNNER

Introduction

Betty began attending classes after she was divorced. She lived about 30 miles from the college campus. Betty excelled and made the honor roll every semester she attended. During the fall semester, her car broke down and she could not afford to fix it. She also became ill and missed two weeks of class. Her ex-husband refused to give her any financial support, and she was nearly evicted from her home because she had no money to pay the rent. Betty came to the counselor and said she intended to withdraw from college. The counselor suggested that she not withdraw until the counselor had spoken to the instructors. Later, Betty came to the counselor to report that the instructors had gone to their church congregations and asked for donations to help her buy a car. They were able to raise enough money so Betty could buy a used car. As she told her story to the counselor, Betty was so overcome by their concern that she couldn't stop crying. Thanks to two caring instructors, Betty continued to do well in her classes and graduated in 2001.

(Personal communication, April 20, 2000)

Tribal colleges and universities (TCUs) have helped students like Betty overcome personal and family problems while attending those institutions. Many tribal college students begin classes with good intentions and high expectations. Unfortunately, for more than half who enroll, these expectations of completing college and finding a better life are not realized. Students bring with them the baggage of many years of failure—failed marriages and relationships, periods of unemployment and welfare dependency, and, for some, histories of drug and alcohol addiction (Bowker, 1992; Ewen, 1997; O'Brien, 1992). Enrolling in college represents a new beginning, but to succeed, the students need to learn strategies to overcome the failures of the past.

The story of Native Americans in higher education is filled with successes and challenges. As with other ethnic minority groups, Native Americans' participation in higher education is a complex picture. Although the proportion who participate in higher education is slightly higher than their representation in the nation's population, thus indicating parity[1] (1% versus .09%, respectively), their numbers remain small. Of the more than 14.2 million students in our nation's colleges and universities, only 145,300 are American Indian (all statistics in this section are drawn from the *Chronicle of Higher Education*, 2001). African American and Hispanic students participate below parity, but far

"Student Access, Retention and Success: Models of Inclusion and Support." Reprinted from *The Renaissance of Native American Higher Education: Capturing the Dream*, (2003), Lawrence Erlbaum Associates, Inc.

greater numbers of these students attend college than do Native Americans (see Table 11-1). Because the presence of a significant number of coethnics on campus leads to greater individual success in terms of retention and satisfaction with college, the fine distinctions between parity and achievement of critical mass are important (Tinto, 1997).

A close look at patterns of participation of Native American students reveals areas of additional concern as well as evidence of success. For instance, in academic year 1997–1998, Native Americans received only .6% of the bachelor's degrees .5% of the master's degrees, and .4% of the doctoral degrees awarded in the United States (see Table 11-2). A study of the educational progression of freshmen admitted in 1989–1990 indicates that only 15.8% of Native American students who began their college careers received their bachelor's degree by 1994 and only 11.9% received their associate's degree (*Chronicle of Higher Education*, 2001). These numbers are lower than those cited by Brandt (1992) who found a dropout rate of 50.9% among Navajo students. However, there are strong signs of improvement. For instance, the number of Native Americans enrolling in higher education has been rising each year since 1976. In fact, current rates of participation are twice as high in 1976. In addition, in the past several years, Native Americans' patterns of attendance in sectors of higher education have shifted from majority enrollment in

2-year colleges to majority enrollment in 4-year colleges and universities (50.4%). This shift is significant because there is ample evidence that attaining a bachelor's degree confers fringe benefits that exceed those gained by earning an associate's degree (Astin, 1985). This shift may also signify tribal colleges' success in having student transfer to 4-year higher education institutions.

Part of the enrollment picture includes the vast number of Native American students who choose to begin their college careers at a local TCU. This choice is appropriate for students who wish to or need to remain close to home, who value culturally relevant higher education, and who find the low cost of TCUs attractive (Wright, 1989). Enrollment patterns in the 33 tribal colleges that have been established over the past three decades have also evidenced shift and growth. In 1982, 2,100 American Indians were enrolled in tribal colleges. By 1991, tribal colleges were serving almost *seven times* that many students, with an enrollment of 13,800 full- and part-time students, representing 14% of the American Indians enrolled in higher education [American Indian Higher Education Consortium (AIHEC), 1999]. By 1995–1996, enrollment over the 12-month academic period reached 24,363 undergraduates and 260 graduate students (AIHEC, 1999). Enrollment continues to climb rapidly, and many TCUs are struggling to keep up with the growing demand (Boyer, 1997a).

TABLE 11-1
Participation in Two- and Four-Year Institutions by Ethnic Group

Ethnic Group	Two-Year Institution	Four-Year Institution	Total Population	Total Student Population
Native American	72,100 (49.6)	73,400 (50.4)	(0.9)	145,300 (1.0)
Asian American	355,800 (39)	553,900 (61)	(3.6)	909,700 (6.0)
African American	687,700 (41)	962,000 (59	(12.3)	1,640,700 (11.5)
Hispanic	735,100 (55.8)	581,400 (44.2)	(12.5)	1,316,600 (9.2)
White	3,670,400 (35.8)	6,592,200 (64.2)	(75.1)	10,262,500 (71.9)
Total	5,512,100 (38.6) (38.7)	8,762,700 (61.4)		14,274,800

Note. Foreign students were not included in the analysis. Percentage of ethnic group distribution in percentages.

Another piece of the picture includes the participation of women and older students in higher education, which has changed quite dramatically over the past 20 years, and this pattern is also evident in TCUs. For instance, in fall 1996, 56% of the undergraduates at all public institutions were women, as compared to 64% at tribal colleges (U.S. Department of Education, 1990–1997).[2] In fact, from the beginning of the tribal college movement in 1968, most tribal college students have been older and most have been women. The typical tribal college student is often described as a single mother in her early 30s [American Indian College Fund (AICF), 2000]. Tribal college officials explain that this population is the least served by higher education, yet it is the most eager to receive a degree. American Indian women with children, especially, are often determined to get off welfare and provide for their families, but they are unable or unwilling to leave home and attend schools in distant cities. For them, tribal colleges are the only option (Boyer, 1989). The fact is that, even with the recent surge of interest in persistence, we still know relatively little about the specific attributes of attrition among older women. Yet, common experience tells us that the experience of older students and of females differs, at least in part, from that of younger male college students (Tinto, 1997).

With near exponential growth over the past 20 years, TCUs serve over a third of all native students in 2-year colleges. As is illustrated elsewhere in this book and in this chapter, this growth has occurred in environments with sig-nificant challenges. Whereas the institutions confront problems with financing, governance, and tribal relations, the Native American student faces problems of equal complexity. Experiences in college often include difficulties of how to juggle academic, family, and community responsibilities as well as academic challenges that their precollege experiences have not prepared them for. These challenges, in addition to issues about cultural continuity, are explored in this chapter. The chapter concludes with examples of model programs that have been developed to specifically address the concerns of the Native American student.

Half the Battle: Getting to College

Tribal communities, in which most of the tribal colleges are located, face staggering unemployment rates, ranging from 45% to 90% (AIHEC, 1999; Boyer, 1997b; Karger & Stoesz, 1998; Stein, 1992). In addition to economic hurdles, tribal college students and their families face many social obstacles. For example, the suicide rate for American Indians is more than twice that of other racial/ethnic minority groups, the death rate from alcohol-related causes is very high, and the already large number of single-parent households continues to increase (O'Brien, 1992). Students' K-12 experiences often reflect the effects of poverty and family difficulties. As with other patterns of educational achievement, success in college reflects students' high school experiences and socialization in the home community.

TABLE 11-2
Degrees Conferred in 1997–1998 by Ethnic Group

Ethnic Group	Associate Degree	Bachelor's Degree	Master's Degree	Doctorate Degree	Professional Degree
American Indian	6,200 (1.0)	7,894 (0.6)	2,049 (0.5)	187 (0.4)	561 (0.7)
Asian American	25,047 (4.4)	71,592 (6.0)	21,088 (4.9)	2,334 (5.0)	7,712 (9.8)
African American	55,008 (9.8)	98,132 (8.2)	30,097 (7.0)	2,066 (4.4)	5,483 (6.9)
Hispanic	45,627 (8.2)	65,937 (5.6)	16,215 (3.8)	1,270 (2.7)	3,547 (4.5)
White	411,336 (73.6)	900,317 (76.0)	307,587 (71.5)	28,747 (62.5)	59,273 (75.4)

Note. Percentages of total degree category in parentheses.

Students often find the cultural disconnect between school and community to be an obstacle to their academic success. Reyhner, Lee, and Gabbard (1993) found that it was not environmental or cognitive deficits that caused poor performance in high school, but rather cultural discontinuity between home and school. They found that high schools did little to make the curriculum or teaching styles culturally relevant to students. However, Ambler (1998) questioned the soundness of cultural infusion at the expense of basic education stating, "In their attempt to emphasize culture, programs may not devote enough attention to science, resulting in students who are ghettoized and competent to enter only their local tribal employment market" (p. 8). Instead, she advocated the creation of curricula that reflect the experiences of Native American students, where they can see themselves in literature read in English courses and where native interpretations help students learn science.

Disagreements about the curriculum and its effects are compounded by the treatment Native Americans often receive from their nonnative teachers. In addition to a feeling that such teachers may not care about or understand native students (Shields, 1999), they often have lower expectations for these students, which tends to reinforce belief in a cultural deficit model. Teachers often make judgments about students' home, family, and resources that affect how they work with these students. Shields found this pattern in her study of native high school students and their teachers. Teachers believed that students generally came from one-parent families, had few modern conveniences in the home, had families that were unsupportive of educational goals, and came from communities that did not nurture Navajo culture.

However, Shields (1999) did not characterize their homes in this way. More than half of the students reported that their homes had electricity and running water, and two thirds lived in two-parent homes. More than 80% said that their primary identification was Navajo, and nearly as many reported that they could speak Navajo fluently. Further, the students' home environment seemed to promote education. The average number of books in the home was 50, and reading materials were purchased on a regular basis.[3] Nearly all students said that their parents would not let them quit school. Students in Shields' study also reported that they were involved in

their high school through both academics and extracurricular activities. Other studies have confirmed these findings. Brandt (1992) found that Navajo families did encourage and support education and were regularly involved in school activities. Ewen's (1997) study supported the above-mentioned findings. Students in that study also primarily identified themselves with their Indian nation and did not experience a negative impact on their education from living on a reservation.

It is important to remember that the kinds of family systems native youth experience in their communities do vary. Although the evidence cited earlier demonstrates that students often persist and achieve in concert with their native identity and despite negative images or stereotypes that educators may hold, there are also times when family systems and cycles of poverty do interfere with students' educational pursuits. At times, family responsibilities disrupt school attendance, primarily because the student's earnings are needed to sustain the family (Dehyle, 1992).

Bowker (1992) found that some students attributed their lack of success in high school to the traditional orientation of their families. They thought they were not encouraged to succeed in school due to expectations that they assume traditional roles in the family and community. Ewen's (1997) study confirmed these findings as students reported that they dropped out primarily due to problems at home or a lack of encouragement from their families to excel. However, Bowker also noted that just as many students from traditional backgrounds did succeed. There is evidence that students' families, whether traditional or nontraditional, are critical to their academic success in college (Lin, 1990; Wenzlaff & Biewer, 1996).

Critics also have cited the communities that many Native American high school students live in as being related to academic underachievement. However, researchers have found that the problem is more complex than socioeconomic factors and also includes the lack of the presence of mentors and models who let students know that education is a valued path to success that can be achieved while still maintaining and nurturing one's native identity. When students see educated community members employed in low-paying jobs in the community, they are less likely to see the value of educational success (Dehyle, 1992; Reyhner et al., 1993). Shields'

(1999) findings were related, but notably different. In her study, students could not explain how educational attainment related to success in life, but they believed that they could achieve their goals through education.

Researchers have also speculated that students often view academic success in a negative way, as leading to a future identity as part of the dominant culture in contrast to their Indian identity. This kind of resistance to the dominant culture plays an important, and complex role in how Native American youth interpret their academic experience and commitment to success. The students in Dehyle's (1992) study said they rejected the path to college because they saw that choice as "non-Indian." Students who did achieve felt separated from their Indian peers. A student who was in college-prep mathematics said, "I was the only Indian! So I moved back to basic math. I knew it all 'cause I had it before, but it was all Indian and I felt better. I was the top in that class" (p. 37). Other students like that one commonly report that they are bored in remedial courses. Boredom in class and a dislike of school are often precursors to a host of behavioral difficulties. Indeed, behavioral difficulties stemming from an active dislike of the school experience were the cause of attrition for one third of the students in Dehyle's study.

In the literature on precollege experiences of native youth, there is ample evidence of success despite difficulty. Although Dehyle (1992) found that students might drop out due to attitudes toward school, she did not find evidence of attrition due to academic problems, marriage, or pregnancy. Similarly, Bowker (1992) found that despite living in poverty, prevalence of teen pregnancy, various kinds of abuse, and alcoholism, more than half the women in his study "survived the environment, graduate from high school (and often college), and became very productive citizens within their tribal group, and for some, leaders in their tribes and in their states and nation" (p. 14). Certainly, these are the stories of success that also characterize native experience in higher education.

College Experiences

Experiences of Native American students in college vary by the type of institution they attend and by their family circumstances. Many of the same factors that contribute to success in high school also contribute to success in college. Likewise, barriers that make achieving an education difficult in high school have similar effects in college. And in college, as in high school, native students achieve great success even in the face of seemingly insurmountable odds. However, the fact remains that Native American students have the lowest educational attainment of all ethnic/racial groups and that their participation in higher education is skewed toward 2-year colleges (*Chronicle of Higher Education*, 2001). Of course, the prevalence of Native American students in 2-year institutions is explained by their participation in TCUs, which are predominantly 2-year colleges. Many of the differences in native students' college experiences are associated with whether they attend TCUs or predominantly white universities. Whereas many native students experience a highly supportive environment (the tribal college), others encounter one that is often hostile to their presence (the predominantly white institution).

Factors Affecting Success in College

The connection between family members' experience and history in higher education cannot be overstated. Because Native American students often remain with their families or live in close proximity to them, family members continue to play an important role in students' academic progress. The phenomenon of the first-generation college student is often used as an explanation for the poor performance of native students in higher education (Boyer, 1997a).

Conversely, when students have close relatives and role models who have had successful experiences in college, they are more likely to be successful themselves (Wenzlaff & Biewer, 1996). Support from same-gender family members has been found to play a critical role in academic success. In Bowker's (1992) study of successful college graduates, he found that:

> one factor which seemed to stand out above all others in the lives of girls who succeeded . . . was the support of their families and particularly that of their mothers and grandmothers. In the case of those who graduated from college, there was often tremendous family support which extended beyond the immediate family. (p. 16)

Furthermore, the nature of the family, for example whether it is modern or traditional, has an influence on the student attending college. Students from modern families (delineated by the mother's education level), were more likely to get support and encouragement in college and felt less of a disconnect between home and college (Lin, 1990). However, students from traditional families were more likely to exhibit behaviors that led to success in college, such as being task and achievement oriented, earning higher grade point averages, and spending more time doing homework (Lin, 1990). These findings are good example of the complex interactions between family and education for native students. Other researchers (Falk & Aitken, 1984; Pavel & Padilla, 1993) confirmed the link between retention and academic success and family support and educational attainment. In fact, college retention was facilitated by family support (Falk & Aitken, 1984).

Although family support is important, family obligations often make it difficult for native students to succeed in college. Tate and Schwartz (1993) discovered that two thirds of the students they studied had family obligations that were serious enough to interfere with school. These problems centered on being nontraditional students with child care, transportation, alcoholism, drug abuse, domestic violence, and employment concerns (Boyer, 1997b). When native students attend predominantly white universities, these family concerns are often dramatically different from those of their white peers (Taylor, 2001). For instance, in Wenzlaff and Biewer's (1996) study, one woman said, "If anything happened to a family member, I would leave in a second to be at home with them" (p. 41). This student thought her white peers would react differently in such a situation.

Academic preparation also plays a significant role in the college success of native students. Although Falk and Aitken (1984) reported that family support was most important in retention, they noted that academic preparation, in the form of study skills, mathematics skills, and career information, reached a close second. Poor academic preparation often offsets Scholastic Aptitude Test (SAT) scores for Native American students, who score higher on this standard test than do African Americans and Latino/as (Reddy, 1993). Remediation becomes a significant barrier for students because they need to spend time and tuition dollars on remedial courses before they can advance to do college

level work (Boyer, 1997a). However, students' educational aspirations can counteract the effects of poor academic preparation and might be considered an element of academic preparation. In fact, researchers have found that having high educational aspirations is an important ingredient for success (Brown & Robinson-Kurpius, 1997; Pavel & Padilla, 1993).

Tribal College Experiences

TCUs offer opportunities for Native American students to participate in higher education in ways that support their identity as native people. TCUs recognize the unique challenges in attending college given complex factors such as economics and family dynamics, hence these institutions offer culturally relevant learning that serves to promote the individual and the group. Students at tribal colleges experience a better "institutional fit" that often compensates for the usual 2-year college effects that inhibit transfer and student development (Machamer, 1998). This fit is achieved through integration of Indian thought into the entire curriculum, thus making subjects more accessible and relevant to students (Boyer, 1989). Many TCUs also offer cultural sensitivity training for non-Indian service providers. For students who have spent little time away from the family or the reservation, these measures help to make college less of a disorienting experience.

Students report high satisfaction with tribal colleges even though these institutions are more poorly resourced than traditional 2- and 4-year colleges. Many tribal colleges have student service programs that offer native students additional support that they might not experience in a predominantly white institution. Tutors and academic support and assistance programs offered at tribal colleges give students individual attention, taking into account varied levels of college preparation and the time constraints students may have from fulfilling multiple life roles (e.g., parent and student; Machamer, 1998). Because poor academic preparation is a key factor in attrition once students transfer to 4-year institutions (Falk & Aitken, 1984), these support programs are critical in helping native students meet their higher education goals. Tribal colleges also give students an opportunity to take remedial courses in a supportive environment that is less expensive than a 4-year institution.

Courses in basic writing and mathematics skills, and Native American studies are highly valued by students (Wright, 1989).

Faculty members at tribal colleges play key roles in students' success (see Tippeconnic & McKinney, chap. 12). Students at these colleges experience high levels of support from faculty, which helps prevent academic isolation and, ultimately, enhances retention (Buckley, 1997). Boyer (1997b) reported that students often awarded "heroic" status to their professors, whom they perceived as being completely dedicated to their success. When students transferred to predominantly white 4-year institutions, their expectations of faculty were elevated due to the close relationships they thought they had with their tribal college faculty. However, students also felt that tribal college faculty should have higher academic expectations of students (Boyer, 1997b). Support needed to be balanced with appropriate challenges so that students could succeed in a predominantly white environment.

Although tribal colleges provide culturally relevant curricula and supportive institutional climates for Native American students, they experience many of the same afflictions that affect these students' success in higher education. Students face difficulties with poverty, financing higher education, alcohol and drug abuse, language differences, and family dysfunction (Dodd, Garcia, Meccage, & Nelson, 1995). Similarly, the institutions suffer from insufficient academic and financial resources (see also Stein, Shanley, & Sanchez, chap. 4). Students may find that the tribal college in their community has limited offerings of majors and programs, and therefore they leave the institution (Boyer, 1997a; Wright, 1989).

The tribal communities and governance structures that create and support TCUs may, at times, interfere with the institutions' ability to function smoothly. Political conflicts and resource-distribution disagreements within the tribal community often affect the leaders of the tribal college (see Stein chap. 2; Shanley chap. 3; Stein, Shanley, & Sanchez chap. 4, this volume). The tribal council may serve as the college's board of trustees, thus exerting influence on the academic program and personnel decisions that influence the education students receive. Students commonly know of these conflicts and experience their effects. Machamer (1998) found that conflicts between staff, admin-istrators, faculty, and boards of trustees also took their toll on students' satisfaction with their college. Because resources in tribal communities can be scarce, many tribal colleges also have poorly maintained facilities and lack of space to conduct college business (Boyer, 1997a).

Experiences at Predominantly White Institutions

Ideally, tribal colleges help students develop the self-esteem and academic skills they need to succeed at predominantly white institutions when they transfer to earn a baccalaureate degree. Native Americans must go to these campuses fully prepared because they face considerable obstacles in predominantly white institutions. No longer are student services all located in one office; rather, they are dispersed throughout the campus. Wenzlaff and Biewer (1996) recommend that students connect early with people who can help them negotiate the larger, more complex environment. Students in Taylor's (2001) study spoke of at least one person at the university who encouraged them and motivated them to succeed. They acknowledged that a connection with more than one person is also important as students need to develop strong bonds with native peers and faculty. This is critical when students leave home and the tribal community to attend college. Data indicate that native students are incredibly resilient. Lin, LaCounte, and Eder (1988) found that, although Native American students achieved lower grade point averages and felt more hostility and isolation than their white peers, they were more positive about their college experience and had educational aspirations similar to those of their white peers.

At predominantly white colleges, academic and social integration are strong predictors of retention and degree completion (Tinto, 1997). The same was confirmed for native students in a study by Pavel and Padilla (1993), who found that academic integration and students' intentions to complete their degrees were among the most important variables that directly and indirectly affect postsecondary outcomes. Academic integration is important because precollege academic factors such as high school rank, SAT scores, and grade point averages do not predict college success for native students. High-achieving students were found to be just as likely to have difficulty as their less prepared native peers (Benjamin, Chambers, & Rieterman, 1993). Academic integration is a function not only of success in courses, but also of relationships with faculty and staff. Students reported that having professors who were caring and willing to find answers helped them succeed in college (Dodd et al., 1995). Staff and/or faculty at TCUs provide native students who are the first in their families to attend college with academic advice and guidance that others may receive from family members who have college experience (Taylor, 2001).

Social integration also plays a significant role in the success of native students. Friendships in general (Dodd et al., 1995) and those formed through student organizations and activities enhance student retention (Wenzlaff & Biewer, 1996). Students in Taylor's (2001) study speculated that having native cultural centers on campus, places that symbolize the center of the community, would promote student retention. Cultural centers are key because it is important for students to feel that they are a part of the institutional culture and experiences. Institutional and student culture and values need to be congruent for social integration to be successful. Tinto (1997) posited that when students are in close alignment with the culture of the institution, their social integration is more complete. When students' values differ significantly form those of the mainstream institution, the incongruence can lead to a sense of isolation and early attrition. Taylor (2001) found that native students believed that their values were incongruent with those of the mainstream institution. They felt the university had capitalist values, was Christian in nature, had a competitive ethos, was materialistic, and had a Western orientation. They also thought the university had limited definitions of family and family obligations, making it difficult for native students to manage their family obligations and succeed academically.

Tinto (1997) also argued that if there is a critical mass of students at the institution, students can form strong subcultures that, although marginal, play important roles in social integration and retention. Native students find their subculture through staff and support services directed at the native student community and through native student organizations on campus. The notion of critical mass is important because there must be enough native students at a particular campus to form a supportive group.

Native students also experience discrimination, racism, and other "microagressions" that alienate them from the college environment. Despite some evidence that there are no differences in retention rates for students, who experience discrimination (Brown & Robinson-Kurpius, 1997), the problem is persistent enough for students to feel isolated on campus without the presence of a native student community on campus.

Predominantly white institutions do offer support services that benefit many native students. Larger institutions may have offices specifically designated for native student support services and cultural programs, but this model is rare in typical 4-year institutions. Most often, support programs for all "minority" students are streamlined in a common office, with cultural-program implementation being delegated to the native student organization on campus. Efforts made by administrators of predominantly white institutions often are not highly valued by Native American students. In Taylor's (2001) interview study of native students at a mainstream institution, students neglected to mention many institutional initiatives (special support services, native student organizations, summer programs, and Native American studies programs) designed to support native and other minority students as sources of support for retention. Neither did they mention that the institution had given the native student organization $70,000 to fund their annual pow wow. Students explained that one of the reasons support programs and administrators were seen as unsupportive was that staff members from those offices seldom came to events and had little contact with native students. When administrators learned of this dissatisfaction, they became frustrated because they believed the funding itself was sufficient to meet student needs.

Faculty in predominantly white institutions also pose challenges to Native American students. Because academic integration is important for student success in higher education, faculty play a crucial role in the lives of native students (Bowker, 1992; Dehyle, 1992; Tate & Schwartz, 1993). Faculty determine the pedagogy that will be used in the classroom. Some evidence has indicated that native and white students learn differently. Wilson (1997) found that native students tended to prefer an active-experimentation orientation to learning, in which they learn by engaging in projects and small-group discussions. This contradicts the preferred style of white students (abstract conceptualization) and the dominant form of teaching in the university—lecturing. Nearly half of the nation's faculty reported that they used extensive lecturing in their courses (Sax, Astin, Arredondo, & Korn, 1996). In contrast, only a third of the faculty used cooperative learning methods and only 20% used experiential learning (Sax et al., 1996). The content of courses is also important. Faculty play an instrumental role in making sure that Native Americans are depicted in the material used in class. They have the ability to provide some of the assets of the tribal college experience through integrating tribal culture and values into the course (Boyer, 1997a; Taylor, 2001).

Faculty who are accessible, approachable, and available motivate students to succeed (Wilson, 1997). In Boyer's (1997b) study, many students expected their professors at 4-year institutions to be similar to the faculty at their tribal college, where students perceived faculty as being more than dedicated to students. Conversely, Tate and Schwartz (1993) found that poor faculty contact was a barrier to retention. Further, students thought that faculty at mainstream institutions did not understand their educational needs or family responsibilities.

Effective Models and Programs

The Native American Higher Education Initiative (NAHEI) programs and models demonstrate exceptional examples of increasing native students' access to and retention in higher education. Collaborations between TCUs and mainstream institutions of higher education (IHEs) include programs in which resources are shared, course content and scheduling are realigned to fit articulation agreements, and student support services are connected and streamlined. These initiatives have been developed over the course of 5 or more years, bolstered with funding from the W. K. Kellogg Foundation in 1996. One of the key objectives of the NAHEI project was to develop and enhance student support programs, in addition to several other objectives focusing on the institutions and their associated communities. In this section, several of these projects are highlighted as examples of programs that have been successful in attracting students to higher education and retaining them

once they are enrolled. These initiatives answer the call in the literature presented earlier in this chapter. They show that education that is connected to culture, services that are responsive to diverse family and community relationships, and programs designed to build the efficacy of native communities can be instrumental in enhancing student progress and success.

A Focus on Students and Their Families: Family Education Model

The Family Education Model (FEM) is an integrated system designed to improve retention rates among students at TCUs. The FEM, based on principles of education and social work, was developed and implemented at four tribal colleges in Montana (Blackfeet Community College, Salish/Kootenai College, Stone Child College, and Fort Peck Community College). The model shifts the paradigm from a focus on drop-outs to a family-centered approach, building on student and family strengths. "The strengths based perspective is an approach honoring the innate wisdom of the human spirit, the inherent capacity for transformation of even the most humbled and abused" (Saleeby, 1996, p. 3). In the FEM, the focus is on seeing students not at-risk, but at-promise. From their inception, tribal colleges have been at the forefront of providing student support services that view students in the context of their extended kinship structures and traditional cultural values.

The FEM offers strategies to help tribal college students develop a sense of connection with the college. Students' families are involved in cultural activities such as social dancing, feasting, storytelling, traditional dressmaking, gardening, and cooking. In this way, the entire family feels a part of the college experience, instead of resenting the time the student spends on his or her studies. These activities continue throughout the student's involvement in the college (e.g., orientation, registration, midterm, and graduation). Establishing and maintaining a sense of "family" both at home and at college is a critical factor in the retention of American Indian students (Dodd et al., 1995; Mainor, 2001; Rousey & Longie, 2001; Shanley, 1999; Wenzlaff & Biewer, 1996).

As another strategy, faculty initiate the Search and Rescue Team, a form of intrusive monitoring, when students appear to be at-risk for leaving college. For example, the team receives a referral from faculty and sends a post-card asking the student to contact student support services. When one student, Sara (not her real name), received such a postcard and contacted the counselor, she said she was ready to withdraw. The counselor asked her to explain why she felt she could not continue in college. Sara said she had a 6-month-old baby with a cold and the day-care center would not take her. Because Sara had no one who could care for her baby, she stayed home with her. Sara also told the counselor that she had been walking from her apartment to the day-care center downtown and then walking more than a mile to the classroom building. As the weather turned colder, she did not like taking the baby out.

After team members were told about Sara's situation, they went to work. The assigned team member contacted Sara's instructors, who provided her home-study assignments so that she could make up the work she had missed. The financial-aid officer helped Sara obtain a $300 supplemental grant so she could purchase a used car. Sara's name did not appear on the referral list thereafter, and she completed the semester with a 2.3 grade point average. The frequency and perceived worth of interaction with faculty, staff, and other students, is one of the strongest predictors not only of student persistence, but also of student development (Tinto, 1997).

A third strategy of the model, family life skills, covers such topics as resource management, decision-making skills, communication skills, conflict resolution, parenting skills, anger management, star quilt making, traditional food preparation, and the study of native plants. Students are encouraged to attend the seminars with their spouses and children. Gilda Ferguson, director of Family Focus in Chicago's North Lawndale neighborhood, believes that if parents are nurtured, they in turn can nurture their children (Schorr, 1997). Likewise, if the families of tribal college students are nurtured, they in turn will nurture these students.

Linkages Between TCUs and IHEs: Leech Lake Tribal College and Bemidji State University

Leech Lake Tribal College (LLTC) and Bemidji State University (BSU) developed strategies to help LLTC students transfer to BSU. Specifically,

having a NAHEI-funded native mediator/counselor resulted in a 50% decrease in early withdrawals, a 38% increase in LLTC student transfers, a 200% increase in enrollment of LLTC students at BSU, and a 300% increase in the number of Indian students earning 4-year degrees in the 1998–1999 academic year.

Focus on Student Affairs Professionals: The National Institute for Native Leadership in Higher Education (NINLHE)

The National Institute for Native Leadership in Higher Education (NINLHE), founded in 1993, is a national nonprofit organization affiliated with the University of New Mexico. Members of the strategic alliance include 125 educational professionals from more than 95 public and private universities, TCUs, and national education organizations across the United States and Canada. Through the Training Fellowship Program, those responsible for designing and implementing effective retention programs share their expertise with others who will then attempt to replicate this success in their own institutions and organizations. In their evaluations, participants consistently give the training fellowship program top marks, not only for skills training and networking, but also for personal empowerment and spiritual renewal. The annual meeting brings together native students from mainstream post-secondary institutions throughout the country for an intensive leadership development program. Participants are asked to approach the gathering as they would a ceremony—in a good way, with minds and bodies unclouded by alcohol or other drugs and with hearts and spirits open to giving, receiving, and sharing.

As native people, we know that humor is often the best medicine, so each Institute starts with icebreaker games, and the first evening is devoted to playing NINLHE's own game show, Indians in Jeopardy. Each day begins with prayer and reflection by elders-in-residence who also lead activities such as sweat lodge ceremonies, talking circles, and a sunrise ceremony. Participants take time each day for personal reflection and physical exercise by making use of the walking trails and sports facilities at the meeting site. In all these ways, the training is designed to help participants make connections to each other and reclaim a balance among the physical, intellectual, emotional, and spiritual aspects of themselves.

Rather than work directly with students, as several other organizations already do, NINLHE works to bolster the skills and staying power of those professionals responsible for improving Native American recruitment, retention, and graduation rates. By strengthening these key individuals, NINLHE can, by extension, improve the educational experience of thousands of native college students. At the institutional level, NINLHE works to improve retention rates among native students and student affairs professionals by changing higher education institutions into more supportive learning and working environments for Native Americans.

A Culturally Relevant Academic Programs: Crownpoint Institute of Technology (CIT)

The literature has indicated that learning is enhanced when students can connect content and theory to real life experiences. The Crownpoint Institute of Technology's (CIT) Alternative Livestock and Veterinary Science Program is an example of this theory-to-practice relationship. The program, which involves raising elk and llamas, provides genetic-research opportunities in embryo transfer, artificial insemination, and other reproductive technologies. The project has pursued a small business and entrepreneurship program marketing elk velvet antler products as health supplements rather than raising the elk for the marketing of meat products. As a means of increasing student retention, the project offers cultural-awareness activities for students. These activities include workshops and presentations by Diné elders, who use tribal history and language to teach about traditional medicines and animal health practices.

Providing Access Through Distance Education: Salish Kootenai College (SKC)

As a leading institution in distance education, Salish Kootenai College (SKC) developed the Expanded Access to Guided Learning Environments (Eagle) Project in which two upper division baccalaureate degree programs were developed, one in environmental science and the other in tribal human services. By fall 2000, SKC faculty had designed 22 of 52 upper level courses

required for the new baccalaureate degree programs. The degrees are offered to 27 TCUs offering only associate of arts degrees. In anticipation of receiving approval from its accrediting body to offer degrees through online education, SKC tested and implemented a system for online student admissions and registration. In November, 2000, SKC hosted the first International Indigenous Peoples Distance Education Conference. The objectives of the conference were to embrace learning from ancient wisdom, share experiences, understand how education in cyberspace can preserve tribal culture, and develop a networking forum with indigenous professionals from around the globe.

Partnerships to Build a Virtual University: The North Dakota Intertribal College Partnership

The North Dakota Intertribal College Partnership is a consortium of six tribal colleges serving American Indian students and communities in North and South Dakota. The purpose of this statewide collaboration is to develop a virtual college (i.e., a way to serve students in several colleges by sharing courses using distance education technology) to increase access for native students to higher education. By August, 2000, 11 interactive video network (IVN) courses had been provided to 233 students; these courses generated 23 hours of credit. Twenty-six Internet courses were being offered on the North Dakota Association of Tribal Colleges (NDATC) Website. The courses range from the arts and sciences, to macro and microeconomics, to speech classes. Some courses provide unique viewpoints that are rarely available in mainstream institutions of higher education (e.g., Holocaust From a Native American Perspective).

A Native-based Teacher Education Program: OKSALE

The lack of Native American teachers in native communities is a significant issue in the academic progress of students in K—12 systems. Native American teachers' ability to connect with the experiences of native children and to teach in a way that honors native culture and language is key to academic success. In an effort to "grow our own," Northwest Indian College (NWIC) and Washington State University (WSU), through an NAHEI-funded partnership, implemented the baccalaureate-level OKSALE Native Teacher Education Program, which reaches out to native K—12 students in native communities and tribes within the entire state. The partnership secured a $10 million 5-year grant from the U.S. Department of Education, which provides subcontracts to its partner TCU and public and tribal schools in the state that serve native students. Through teacher training as well as technical training and assistance, the subcontracts focus on improving the ways in which the educational needs of native students are met. Enhancing this NAHEI-initiated partnership is the inclusion of tribal governments in the form of a tribal advisory board to WSU, comprising of tribal chairpersons from participating tribal governments.

Developing K-12 Educational Leaders: The Oyate Consortium

Professional development of teachers is also enhanced by opportunities to participate in graduate education. When graduate education is provided within the framework of native education, teachers can be trained to be more effective with native youth. The Oyate Consortium (Oglala Lakota College, Si Tanka College, Sitting Bull College, Sinte Gleska University, and Sisseton Wahpeton Community College) in collaboration with the University of South Dakota established the *Akicita Oyuha Waste* (warriors making things work well) master's degree program with an emphasis on educational administration for K-12 school principals. Program personnel have worked with the University of South Dakota to gain state board of education approval for the degree. Forty graduate students are enrolled in the master's degree program. In the year 2000, the first student graduated with a master's of arts degree. Currently, graduate courses are being offered at Oglala Lakota College, Si Tanka College, and Sitting Bull College. This is the only tribal college graduate program nationwide that leads to state certification as a principal.

Recommendations

The story of Native Americans' success in TCUs and in higher education in general has diffi-

culties, but, in general, improvement has been consistent and meaningful in recent years. TCUs have been particularly adept at providing education that meets the needs of students who are seeking vocational training, high school equivalency, academic preparation for higher education, and transfer to four-year institutions. They have done all this with limited resources, little supportive centralization, and largely without state or federal support. Several recommendations are made here in the hope of strengthening the educational experiences of students at TCUs.

Recommendation #1: That a Student Database System be Designed That is Both Evaluative and Educational in Nature

TCUs would benefit from a consistent, high-quality, and collaborative system of tracking students' aspirations and progress. Having a national database for all 33 TCUs would help to reflect more accurately the impact of these institutions on student success and on the tribal communities in which they reside. At a minimum, the database could house enrollment statistics, academic outcomes such as grade point average, program-completion information, credit-taking patterns, and transfer rates. A more sophisticated database could also record student characteristics that have been shown to affect retention, participation in support programs designed to enhance persistence, and program completion. If collected annually, information on these variables can be linked to show what experiences and characteristics contribute to departure, as well as where students are interfacing with the institution in meaningful ways. The student database system can assist TCUs and mainstream IHEs track and report progress in student retention in terms of recruitment, placement, advising, financial aid, and tutoring. In addition to providing important feedback to the institution about the progress of its students and the effectiveness of its programs, a collective database for the TCU sector of higher education can also help in securing philanthropic and government funds for additional programs and resources.

Recommendation #2: Institutional Staff (i.e., Retention Officer, Student Support Services, Counselor, Financial Aid Officer, Faculty, Distance Education Coordinator) Should Design Systems-Oriented Interventions to Reduce the Number of Withdrawals

Systems-oriented interventions focus on the reciprocal interactions between college and family and assist individual students see how they contribute to their own persistence. Tribal college staff with this orientation draw heavily on cultural/interaction theory, assisting students learn to express their needs and feelings in non-threatening ways and to listen attentively; such staff model for students effective problem-solving skills (Hepworth, Rooney, & Larsen, 1997). Systems-oriented student support services acknowledge that students must be successful in several areas of life in order to effectively navigate and succeed in higher education. The examples cited in this chapter characterize a systems approach to student support. The programs attend to the learner's academic needs, to the learner's responsibilities (such as families), to the learner's culture, and to the learner's tribal community. When these systems are synchronous, the learner stands a better opportunity for success. As a part of such systems, retention efforts that are grounded in the concepts of cultural resilience (e.g., feasts, humor, elders, spirituality), family kinship, and community can help students achieve their educational goals.

Recommendation #3: Native Students Should be Helped to Negotiate the Policy Maze of Higher Education

First-generation college students often rely on high school and college administrators and advisors to help them understand the myriad policies that govern participation in higher education. Tribal college student service staff can help students understand financial aid policies and how their attendance patterns may affect their eligibility for aid. For instance, students who simply leave college, rather than officially withdrawing, risk severe consequences in terms of financial aid if they decide to return to college in the future. This point is critical because more than 90% of TCU students receive financial aid.

Attendance and course-taking patterns also impact other policies. Unexpected absences due to family emergencies or planned absences due to tribal ceremonies may negatively affect student's grades. Students should be encouraged to work closely with professors so that they will not be penalized for these absences. Advisors can also help students to understand how the grade point average can affect financial aid eligibility and the ability to continue at a particular institution. The importance of making good academic progress needs to be stressed. Advisors and faculty at TCUs should be informed in articulation or transfer agreements with 4-year institutions. In this way, they can guide students in selecting courses that will meet their overall degree requirements. Finally, advisors should consistently help students to understand time to degree policies. Whereas undergraduate students are seldom affected by these policies, they are strictly enforced for graduate students. Advisors and faculty working with undergraduate students planning to attend graduate school should make sure that these policies are understood.

Recommendation #4: Native Youth Should be Encouraged to Attend TCUs as a Way to Prepare for Transferring to Mainstream Institutions of Higher Education

Not all students who attend TCUs aspire to attain a baccalaureate degree. Those who do are increasingly able to complete the degree at a TCU or through distance-education partnerships with mainstream institutions of higher education. However, many students who aspire to attain a baccalaureate intend to do so at a predominantly white 4-year institution. Students who are underprepared academically for study at these institutions should be encouraged to attend tribal colleges to prepare for transfer. Tribal colleges are better designed to provide a supportive environment for remedial education. Students can take remedial courses at a lower cost than at a 4-year institution, often without the stigma associated with taking these courses at a mainstream institution. Students can also take advantage of the support services and culturally relevant course content and pedagogy characteristic of tribal college educational experiences.

Recommendation #5: Native Students Should be Helped to Choose an Appropriate College

Many tribal college students find that their educational and career aspirations can be met at the tribal college, but others might want to pursue undergraduate or graduate education at a predominantly white institution. K-12 school and college advisers, and community leaders can help native students choose the institutions that have the greatest potential to help them meet their goals. Ample research has demonstrated the importance of a critical mass of native students in enhancing retention. Native students should be encouraged to attend institutions where there are significant numbers of native students in attendance. Students should ask about the vitality of native student organizations and their activities. Campuses with solid support programs designed specifically for native students should especially be encouraged. Because many "satellites" of support have been found to be important for retention, students should consider campuses where there are visible and involved native faculty and staff, and where there are evident linkages to nearby native communities.

Recommendation #6: TCUs Should Continue to Establish and Enhance High-Quality Student Support Services

Much of the research on student satisfaction has indicated that tribal college students are most influenced by faculty and staff. Excellent and caring staff leading effective advising and support programs make a significant difference at institutions that are poor in terms of physical and financial resources, yet rich in human resources. The rescue teams at Fort Peck are an ideal example of how staff and faculty can network to create a safety net for students. These networks can be expanded through the use of peer mentor programs and regular visits from students who have "made it," either in their chosen occupations, tribal leadership, or mainstream institutions of higher education. An extensive team of support individuals can help students overcome the challenges they face as they attempt to fulfill their educational goals while managing childrearing and care issues, transportation difficulties, and the residuals of substance abuse.

Final Reflections

Great strides have been made in tribal college education and in the persistence of native students in higher education. TCU and mainstream student affairs professionals can continue to work to decrease the occurrence of student attrition in higher education by creating supportive learning environments in which native students can attain their educational goals, thereby improving their own lives and those of their families. These efforts require the collaboration that has been shown in AIHEC, NAHEI, and the numerous partnerships among native communities, tribal colleges, and mainstream institutions of higher education. Just as collaboration among these sectors and organizations of higher education is necessary, we must also be mindful that students have their own networks of collaborations, which include family responsibilities, financial commitments, and personal goals. Helping students meet all of these challenges while staying focused on their prize is the noble goal we hope to fulfill.

Notes

1. When participation in an educational institution matches the proportion of that ethnic or racial group in the population, that group is judged to have reached parity in terms of participation.
2. These figures vary by institution; 76% of the students at Sisseton Wahpeton Community College were women as compared to 46% at Haskell Indian Nations University (U.S. Department of Education, 1990–1997).
3. The number of books in the house and regular purchase of reading materials are common variables in studies of the effect of the home environment on educational persistence and literacy.

References

Ambler, M. (1998, Fall). Land-based colleges offer science students a sense of place. *Tribal College Journal of American Indian Higher Education, 10*(1), 6–8.

American Indian College Fund. (2000). *Annual report*. Denver, CO: Mansfield, Brewer & Cadue.

American Indian Higher Education Consortium and the Institute for Higher Education Policy. (1999). *Tribal colleges: An introduction*. Washington DC: Author.

Astin, A. W. (1985). *Achieving educational excellence*. San Francisco: Jossey-Bass.

Benjamin, D., Chambers, S., & Rieterman, G. (1993). A focus on American Indian college persistence. *Journal of American Indian Education, 29*(3), 25–40.

Bowker, A. (1992, May). The American Indian female dropout. *Journal of American Indian Education, 31*(3), 3–20.

Boyer, P. (1989, Summer). Higher education and Native American society. *Tribal College of American Indian Higher Education, 1*(1), 10–18.

Boyer, P. (1997a). *Native American colleges: Progress and prospects*. Princeton, NJ: Jossey-Bass.

Boyer, P. (1997b). First survey of tribal college students reveals attitudes. *Tribal College Journal of American Indian Higher Education, 11*(2), 36–41.

Brandt, E. A. (1992). The Navajo area student dropout study: Findings and implications. *Journal of American Indian Education, 31*(2), 48–63.

Brown, L. L., & Robinson-Kurpius, S. E. (1997). Psychosocial factors influencing academic persistence of American Indian college students. *Journal of College Student Development, 38*(1), 3–12.

Buckley, A. (1997). *Threads of nations: American Indian graduate and professional students*. (ERIC Document Reproduction Services No. ED 444771).

Chronicle of Higher Education. (2001). http://chronicle.com.free/almanac/2001/index.htm

Dehyle, D. (1992, January). Constructing failure and maintaining cultural identity: Navajo and Ute school leavers. *Journal of American Indian Education, 31*(2), 24–47.

Dodd, J. M., Garcia, F., Meccage, C., & Nelson, J. R. (1995). American Indian retention. *NASPA Journal, 33*(1), 72–78.

Ewen, A. (1997, Winter). Generation X in Indian country. *Native American, 14*(4), 24–29.

Falk, D. R., & Aitken, L. P. (1984). Promoting retention among American Indian college students. *Journal of American Indian Education, 23*(2), 24–31.

Hepworth, D. H., Rooney, R. H., & Larsen, J. (1997). *Direct social work practice: Theory and skills* (5th ed.). Pacific Grove, CA: Brooks/Cole Publishing Company.

Karger, H., & Stoesz, D. (1998). *American social welfare policy: A pluralist approach* (2nd ed.). New York: Longman.

Lin, R. (1990, May). Perception of family background and personal characteristics among Indian college students. *Journal of American Indian Education, 29*(3), 19–28.

Lin, R., LaCounte, D., & Eder, J. (1988, May). A study of Native American students in a predominantly White college. *Journal of American Indian Education, 27*(3), 8–15.

Machamer, A. M. (1998). Survey reflects student development at D-Q University. *Tribal College Journal of American Indian Higher Education, 10*(2), 38–43.

Mainor, P. (2001). Family matters: Fort Peck Community College tests holistic approach to student success. *Tribal College Journal of American Indian Higher Education, 12*(4), 10–13.

O'Brien, E. M. (1992). American Indians in higher education. *Research Briefs, 3*(3). Washington, DC: American Council on Education.

Pavel, D. M., & Padilla, R. V. (1993). American Indian and Alaska native postsecondary departure: An example of assessing a mainstream model using national longitudinal data. *Journal of American Indian Education, 32*(12), 1–23

Reddy, M. A. (Ed.). (1993). *Statistical record of native North Americans*. Washington, DC: Gale Research.

Reyhner, J., Lee, H., & Gabbard, D. (1993, Spring). A specialized knowledge base for teaching American Indian and Alaska Native students. *Tribal College Journal of American Indian Higher Education, 4*(4), 26–32.

Rousey, A. & Longie, E. (2001). The tribal college as family support system. *American Behavioral Scientist, 44*(9), 1492–1504.

Saleeby, D. (Ed.). (1996). *The strengths perspective on social work practice*. New York: MacMillan.

Sax, L. J., Astin, A. W., Arredondo, M., & Korn, W. S. (1996). *The American college teacher: National norms for the 1995–96 HERI faculty survey*. Los Angeles: University of California, Los Angeles, Higher Education Research Institute.

Schorr, E. (1997). *Common purpose: Strengthening families and neighborhoods to rebuild America*. New York: Anchor Books.

Shanley, J. (1999). Traditional Assiniboine family values: Let us bring back something beautiful. *Tribal College Journal of American Indian Higher Education, 11*(1), 12–17.

Shields, C. M. (1999). Learning from students about representation, identity, and community. *Educational Administration Quarterly, 35*(1), 106–129.

Stein, W. (1992). *Tribally controlled colleges: Making good medicine*. New York: Peter Lang.

Tate, D. S., & Schwartz, C. L. (1993, Fall). Increasing the retention of American Indian students in professional programs in higher education. *Journal of American Indian Education, 33*(1), 21–31.

Taylor, J. S. (2001, April). *Through a critical lens: Native American alienation from higher education*. Paper presented at the Annual Meeting of the American Educational Research Association, Seattle, WA.

Tinto, V. (1997). *Leaving college: Rethinking the causes and cures of student attrition* (2nd ed.). Chicago: University of Chicago Press

U.S. Department of Education, National Center for Educational Statistics. (1990–1997).

Wenzlaff, T. L. & Biewer, A. (1996). Native American students define factors for success. *Tribal College Journal, 12*(4), 40–44.

Wilson, P. (1997). Key factors in the performance and achievement of minority students at the University of Alaska, Fairbanks. *American Indian Quarterly, 21*(3), 535–544.

Wright, B. (1989). Tribally controlled community colleges: An assessment of student satisfaction. *Community/Junior College Quarterly, 13*, 119–128.

CHAPTER 12

COMMUNITY COLLEGES AND
BACCALAUREATE ATTAINMENT

KEVIN J. DOUGHERTY

In recent years, several critics of the community college have raised the cry that baccalaureate aspirants are much less likely to receive a bachelor's degree if they enter a community college rather than a four-year college [11; 14, p. 209; 15, p. 226; 27; and 55, pp. 13–15]. For example, Steven Brint and Jerome Karabel [15, p. 227] recently declared: "The very fact of attending a two-year rather than a four-year institution lowers the likelihood that a student will obtain a bachelor's degree."

This claim has not gone unchallenged. Defenders of the community college have argued that the critics are comparing apples and oranges. Students who enter the community college, they note, are much less likely than four-year college entrants to want a baccalaureate degree. Moreover, even if they have such a desire, they are hampered by weaker academic skills, less certain plans, and shakier confidence than four-year college entrants. Hence, any simple comparison of baccalaureate-attainment rates is highly deceptive [24, p. 44; 72, pp. 11–12].

This debate is important. Despite the community college's strong commitment to occupational, remedial, and community and adult education, it still enrolls many students who aspire to a baccalaureate degree. They still make up 30 to 40 percent of all community college entrants [24, pp. 49–52; 27, p. 87; and 55, pp. 10–11].[1] Moreover, the community college's role in baccalaureate preparation has been under great scrutiny in recent years [23; 55; 58].

The importance of the debate over the community college's impact on its baccalaureate aspirants and the heat it has generated demands a careful investigation of the best available evidence on this question. Too often, the debaters have replied to each other with data of poor quality: anecdotes and surveys drawn from a small and unrepresentative sample of colleges. In this article I propose to examine the results of the best available national longitudinal surveys of student educational attainment. These surveys include all the variables that need to be controlled in order to allow a valid comparison of the effects of community colleges and four-year colleges apart from the influence of student backgrounds, aptitudes, and aspirations. That is, these surveys allow us to establish the *institutional* effect of the community college, controlling for the fact that its students tend to differ in many regards from those entering four-year colleges.

Is There Really a Baccalaureate Gap?

Social surveys routinely find a large gap between community college entrants and four-year college entrants in rates of attaining a bachelor's degree. Three different national surveys found that, on

"Community Colleges and Baccalaureate Attainment." Reprinted from *Journal of Higher Education* 63, no. 2 (1992), Ohio State University Press.

the average, 70 percent of four-year college entrants received a baccalaureate degree when followed up four to fourteen years later, whereas only 26 percent of public two-year college entrants reached the same destination [7, 10, 73]. One of these surveys also indicated that four-year college entrants on the average secure one-half more year of education than two-year entrants [2].

However, as defenders of the community college have pointed out, the existence of a baccalaureate gap should not be surprising, given that community college students differ greatly from four-year college entrants in ways that affect how well they will do educationally. On the average, community college students are poorer, more often nonwhite, less academically apt, less ambitious, and less likely to attend full-time than are four-year college students [24, pp. 30–51], and it is well known that all these student characteristics are associated with lower rates of baccalaureate attainment [4, 5, 65].

Nonetheless, defenders of the community college must face the fact that these differences

in student characteristics do not entirely explain away the baccalaureate gap. Even when comparing students of equivalent background, ability, high-school record, and aspirations, several different studies have found that students entering the community college receive 11 to 19 percent fewer bachelor's degrees and average one-eighth to one-fourth a year less of higher education than similar students entering four-year colleges. In short, the lower baccalaureate attainment of community-college entrants is not attributable only to their traits; it is also due to the nature of the institution they are entering.

This is a difficult conclusion to accept, so let us carefully examine the studies from which it emerges. The findings and key characteristics of these studies are summarized in table 12-1.

Using the National Longitudinal Survey of the High-School Class of 1972 (NLS-72), Charlene Nunley and David Breneman [49] examined the educational records of *baccalaureate aspirants* who entered college in October 1972 and were followed up in October 1979. They found that those entering community colleges received 11.5

TABLE 12-1
Difference between Four-Year and Two-year College Students in Baccalaureate Attainment and Years of Education

	Nunley, Breneman (1988)	Velez (1985)	Anderson (1984)	Astin et al. (1982)
Study Characteristics				
Data set used	NLS-72	NLS-72	NLS-72	ACE[a]
Population covered	all US	all US	all US	all US
Year students began college	1972	1972	1972	1971
Year students followed up	1979	1979	1979	1980
Aspirations of respondents	B.A. + above	Acad. prog.	Acad. prog.	B.A. + above
Findings				
Difference in Percent Attaining B.A.				
no controls	NA	48.0%	23.9%	44.0%[a]
with controls	11.5%[b]	18.7%*	14.0%*	NA[c]*
Difference in Average Years of Education Attained				
no controls	NA		0.46	
with controls	0.16[b]		0.25*	

Note: Appendix Table A1 reports the data in full and lists the control variables.
[a] Figures are for Whites only. Study does not report figures for all races together.
[b] Presents significance level only for comparison with those not in college.
[c] Reports *partial correlations* between college type and attainment of a baccalaureate for five racial or ethnic groups. The partial correlations for public two-year college entrants range from –0.20 to 0.01 (with four of five correlations significant at *p* less than 0.05), whereas the correlations for public four-year nonuniversity college entrants range from –0.08 to 0.08 (with only one being significant). See discussion in text.
*Significant at the 0.05 level.

percent fewer bachelor's degrees and averaged 0.16 fewer years of education than those entering four-year colleges, even after controlling for differences between the two sets of students in family background, high-school record, and educational aspirations (pp. 80–81). (The variables controlled are indicated in table A1 in the Appendix.) These findings were replicated in two other studies using the NLS-72 1979 followup but focusing instead on students who entered the *academic* programs of community colleges and four-year colleges in the fall of 1972. William Velez [73] found that, even after controlling for various pre- and postmatriculation differences, community-college entrants still received 18.7 percent fewer baccalaureate degrees than comparable four-year college entrants [73, p. 199]. Kristine Anderson [2], meanwhile, found that students who entered community colleges secured 14 percent fewer bachelor's degrees and 0.25 fewer years of education than comparable students who entered state four-year colleges [2, pp. 33–34].

It could be argued that these findings are peculiar to the NLS-72. But an analysis of an entirely separate national survey discovered the same pattern. Alexander Astin and colleagues [7] in 1980 followed up freshmen surveyed in 1971 as part of the American Council on Education's yearly national survey of full-time freshmen. Concentrating on those aspiring to at least a bachelor's degree, they found that nine years later the two-year-college entrants had less often attained a baccalaureate degree than had four-year-college entrants, even after controlling for their differing personal characteristics. For example, for Whites, the partial *correlation* between community-college entrance and attaining a bachelor's degree was –0.14, whereas the partial correlation between entrance to one of four types of four-year college and attaining a bachelor's degree ranged between –0.04 and 0.15. (This pattern held as well for Blacks, Chicanos, and American Indians, although not for Puerto Ricans.)

In sum, the poorer outcomes encountered by baccalaureate aspirants entering community colleges rather than four-year colleges cannot be attributed only to the fact that the former entrants are generally of more modest backgrounds, abilities, and aspirations. Even when we compare students with similar traits, we find that baccalaureate aspirants entering the community college are still significantly less likely to

realize their hopes. This is an *institutional* effect that cannot be explained by differences in student characteristics.

Explaining the Baccalaureate Gap

But if the critics have been correct that there is an institutional impact, they have been less clear on what precise features of the community college account for it. Synthesizing a broad array of research on the community college and on colleges more generally, I have found that baccalaureate aspirants in the community college encounter institutional obstacles at three stages: surviving in the community college, transferring to a four-year college, and persisting in the four-year college. (For reasons of space, the following discussion is quite condensed. An extended treatment can be found in Dougherty [29].)

Attrition in the Community College

The first challenge community college entrants face is to survive the first difficult years of college when dropout is at its highest. Community college entrants drop out considerably more frequently than four-year college students. Personal characteristics play a role in this. Dropout rates are highest for students who are nonwhite, low in social class, or of modest academic aptitude, and the community college has more of these students than do four-year colleges [4; 50, p. 44; 69, pp. 22, 135–36, 150; 70, pp. 19–28]. However, even when we control for these differences, we find that community college students still drop out more frequently. As table 12-2 shows, community college entrants are 10–18 percent more likely to drop out in those first two years than are four-year college entrants of similar background, ability, and aspirations. (See Appendix table A2 for the control variables.)

The key institutional factor here is the community college's weaker ability to integrate its students into the academic and social life of the institution.[2] In his theory of the process of college withdrawal, Vincent Tinto [64, 65] has powerfully illuminated the nature of academic and social integration. He holds that dropout arises from a poor fit between an institution and its students and powerfully synthesizes and extends previous theory and research. He argues that dropout decisions are most immediately the product of a breakdown

TABLE 12-2
Attrition from Higher Education

	National Center Ed. Stats. (1990a)	Pascarella, Astin (1975)	Chapman (1983)[a]	Anderson (1981)[b]	Anderson (1984)[b]
Study Characteristics					
Dates set used	HS&B	ACE	own	NLS-72	NLS-72
Year students began college	1982	1968	1978	1972	1972
Year students followed up	1986	1972	1979	1973,1974	1973
Aspirations of students	any post second'y	B.A.+ above	any post second'y	academic program	academic program
Findings on Percentage Dropping Out					
Difference in Percent at the End of One Year					
no controls			NA	NA	10.6%
with controls[c]			10.0%*	5.0%**	3.9%[d]
Difference in Percent at the End of Two Years					
no controls			NA		
with controls[c]			14.0%**		
Difference in Percent at the End of Four Years					
no controls	12.0%	18.4% (male)[d]			
		27.3% (female)[d]			
with controls[c]		10.0% (male)[d]			
		18.0% (female)[d]			

[a]Pascarella and Chapman's attrition figures are for withdrawal from the institution rather than from higher education as a whole.
[b]Anderson counts as withdrawal not only dropping out of higher education but also moving out of the academic program into the vocational program. The figure in the table under her 1984 study is the difference between the dropout rates at community colleges and state four-year colleges (excluding universities).
[c]See Appendix table A2 for control variables.
[d]No significance level reported.
*Significant at the 0.05 level.   **Significant at the 0.01 level.

in commitment to staying at a given college (in the case of withdrawal from an institution) or in commitment to securing a college degree (in the case of dropout from the higher education system as a whole). This breakdown in turn is precipitated by inadequate *academic integration* (marked by poor college grades, low attendance, weak academic contact with teachers and students, and lack of a sense that one is developing intellectually) and poor *social integration* (evidenced by low participation in extracurricular activities, little extra-academic contact with faculty, and few friends on campus). The central features of Tinto's model have been repeatedly validated by a host of studies [2, 3, 47, 53, 63].

Various studies indicate that community colleges do not integrate their students socially and

academically as strongly as do four-year colleges. Socially, community college students are much less involved in extracurricular activities and extra-academic contact with faculty and peers [19, p. 316]. Although this in good part reflects the attitudes and interests of community college students themselves, it also reflects the nature of the institutions. The most important institutional feature is that community colleges very rarely afford their students the opportunity to live on campus, whereas the majority of four-year colleges do. Using the NLS-72, Anderson [2, p. 14] found that only 8.9 percent of entrants to academic programs in public two-year colleges lived on campus, where-as for four-year colleges the percentage ranged from 38.8 percent at public universities to 58 percent at private universities. Living on campus has been found to have a significant positive effect on students' persistence into the sophomore year, even with controls for students' back-ground, aspirations, and high-school achievement, and various characteristics of the college [1, p. 12; 2, pp. 15–18; 3, p. 173; 4, pp. 91–92, 165–68; 5, p. 109, 217; 73, pp. 196–97]. On-campus residence powerfully contributes to student social integration into collegiate life if only by reducing the costs in time, money, and safety of participation in campus life. This greater participation takes the form of wider contact with faculty and other students, greater involvement in extracurricular activities, and deeper satisfaction with campus life. This greater social integration in turn promotes greater commitment to staying at the institution for the full course and securing a degree. Campus residence fosters this effect in good part by weakening home and neighborhood obligations and allegiances, which often divert time and energy from school work. More positively, campus residence exposes students more to fellow students and college faculty and thus enhances involvement in college activities [5; 53; 54; 64, pp. 107, 109–10; and 73, pp. 198–99].[3]

Finally, community colleges are less able to integrate their students academically. Their lower academic selectivity tends to create diminished expectations among faculty, and these diminished expectations interact with considerable ambivalence among working class and minority students toward the value and possibility of attaining a baccalaureate [7, pp. 101–02; 45, chaps. 2–5; 76, pp. 84–93, 134–37, 153–54]. Community colleges are less selective academically due to their open-door admissions policy. This goal is admirable, but it has an unanticipated consequence: it hinders students' academic integration and thus causes lower persistence. Several studies have pointed to the positive impact of college selectivity on persistence even when controlling for student traits and other college characteristics [2, pp. 15–17, 33, 36; 7, pp. 101–02; 22, pp. 55–56; and 64, pp. 114–15]. The community college's low academic selectivity impinges on its students' academic integration, and thus on dropout rates, in three ways. Less selective institutions provide a smaller payoff to their students, thus providing less incentive to finish college [37]. In addition, because community colleges are less selective, community college entrants more often find themselves surrounded by peers who are

not interested in or good at academic work and discourage those who are. This anti-academic student culture is partly rooted in the ambivalence of many working-class and minority students toward education. Most of these students want to do well, but they are also afraid of failing. Furthermore, they view academic success as requiring them to take on the culture of an alien group and to repudiate (and be repudiated by) their family and peers. Hence, working-class and minority students often develop powerful norms against taking academic work seriously [15, p. 180; 45, chaps. 3–4; 48, p. 58; and 76, pp. 102, 122, 134–37, 153–54]. This negative attitude is then amplified in that community college teachers provide less academic encouragement to their students than do four-year college teachers. Noting the unselective character of their institutions, community college teachers tend to have low expectations of their students, perceiving them as largely lacking academic ability and motivation [15, p. 179; 24, pp. 65, 82–84, 242; 45, chaps. 2, 5; 48, p. 61; 58, p. 36; 61; and 76, pp. 84, 89–90, 93]. For example, a survey of community college humanities instructors in 1975 found that only 12 percent rated their students' enthusiasm for learning as excellent and 39 percent put it as fair or poor [21, pp. 139, 148]. And another nationwide survey of community college science instructors found that—when asked "what would it take to make yours a better course?"—over half of them responded: "Students better prepared to handle course requirements" [13, p. 32]. To blunt the sharp edge of their disappointment, many community college teachers concentrate on reaching a few students and largely give up on the rest [45, chaps. 2, 5; and 76, pp. 84–93].

While we have moved down to psychological causes of the greater attrition among community college students, we have to remain firmly aware that they are anchored in institutional factors: particularly, lack of dormitories and consequently weak social integration of students; and unselective admissions and consequently weak academic integration. This attention to the effects of an unselective admissions policy does not mean that community colleges should abandon their open-door policy. Far from it: it is one of the glories of the community college. But we do need to find ways to neutralize its harmful side effects.

Difficulty Transferring to Four-Year Colleges

If baccalaureate aspirants survive the first one or two years of community college, they face a second obstacle: transferring to a four-year college in order to continue to pursue their degree. Regrettably, community college entrants continue onto the upper division of four-year colleges at a lower rate than comparable four-year college entrants.[4] It has been estimated that only about 15 percent of community college entrants eventually transfer to a four-year college [15, p. 129; 24, p. 53; and 55, pp. 11–13]. Again, this reflects in part the greater proportion of community college students of modest background, ability, and ambition. But even when we control for this difference, we find that community college entrants are at a disadvantage relative to similar four-year entrants. An analysis of the National Longitudinal Survey of the High-School Class of 1972 found that among baccalaureate aspirants who survived the first two years of college, only 49.3 percent of the community college entrants, but 96.2 percent of the four-year college entrants, reached the junior year at a four-year college [68].

This transfer gap arises in part because community college entrants less often try to move on to the upper division than do four-year entrants. Community college entrants have to move to a new school, perhaps in a different community, where they might stay only two or three years [79, p. 240n]. Four-year college entrants find no such chasm lying between their sophomore and junior years. Moving from the lower to the upper division is simply a matter of registering for next semester's classes at what now is a familiar institution. Hence, four-year college natives need very little encouragement from their college teachers and counselors to continue into the junior year.

Clearly, the hesitation of community college students needs to be overcome by strong encouragement on the part of the institution. However, several studies have found that far too many community colleges provide at best cursory and haphazard encouragement and advice for their transfer aspirants [11, p. 37; 23, pp. 180–81; 57, pp. 317–21; 58, p. 152]. For example, a recent nationwide survey of community college faculty found that only a small number had frequent meetings with students to discuss transfer and

only one-third had information on their students' transfer intentions [25, p. 90]. Meanwhile, a survey of community college students who had transferred to nine urban universities found that the majority did so without benefit of advice from community college faculty or advisors [58, p. 152]. The dearth of activity and information in favor of transfer education reflects the weak commitment to the transfer program of too many community colleges today. A national survey of faculty teaching *college transfer courses* at twenty-four community colleges nationwide found that only 19 percent believed that "the primary function of the community college should be to prepare students for transfer to four-year colleges or universities" and only 34 percent agreed with the statement that "first time freshmen in community colleges should be encouraged to earn, at the very least, the baccalaureate degree" [25, pp. 81–82].

In addition to providing inadequate transfer advice, community colleges often inadvertently dampen student interest in transfer by drawing them into their occupational programs. These programs are much more attractively packaged and vigorously publicized than transfer programs 58, p. 41]. Though occupational education is no longer an absolute barrier to transfer, it still poses an obstacle. At the individual level, Crook and Lavin [26] found that community college students who enrolled in the vocational curriculum received 13 percent fewer baccalaureate degrees than those who enrolled in the liberal arts, even when they controlled for the students' background, aspirations, and abilities at college entrance, their college freshman grades, the number of remedial courses they took in college, and whether they worked in college. At the institutional level, it has been found that the more vocational a community college is the lower its transfer rate. The California state community college board found that vocationally oriented community colleges have significantly lower transfer rates to the University of California than do transfer-oriented community colleges, even controlling for differences in student-body composition (race and grades) and proximity to the university [16, pp. 17–19]. Finally, at the systemic level, Grubb [32] found that the more vocational a state's community college system was (as measured by the vocational proportion of its associate degree output in 1970–71) the lower the proportion of its high-school graduates receiving baccalaureate degrees ten years later, even with controls for differences between states in their social characteristics and labor market conditions. (This negative association was statistically significant in the case of women but not of men.)

Even if they do attempt to transfer, community college entrants still encounter institutional obstacles. Many four-year colleges still are reluctant to take transfers, accepting them only if they cannot fill their classes with freshmen [58, p. 81; 77, pp. 5–6, 25–26; 79, pp. 246–49]. And even institutions that are committed to accepting transfers, such as the California state universities, turn them away because of insufficient room [17, pp. 7–8]. In addition, would-be transfers secure less financial aid than do four-year college natives. According to the NLS-72, students who transferred from two-year colleges received fewer scholarships and other grants than students who initially entered four-year colleges (19.3 percent versus 38.9 percent), although they received as many loans (22.1 percent versus 23.8 percent) [69, p. 34]. The financial aid gap is probably smaller today, yet there is still no federal program specifically for transfer students, and

many states have taken little initiative in this area. This shortfall in financial aid clearly undermines transfer. A study of transfer applicants to the University of California who were accepted but did not matriculate (19 percent of those accepted) found that a major reason was finances [9, p. 6]. Meanwhile, a survey of minority transfers with high GPAs found that one-third could not have transferred if they had not received a scholarship [55, p. 34].

Attrition in the Four-Year College

Even after transferring to four-year colleges, community college entrants are still at greater risk of failing to secure a baccalaureate. Several studies have found that, three to five years after transferring, about a third of all transfers have dropped out. And after a few more years, even more are felled. By comparison, four-year college natives entering the junior year have a considerably lower dropout rate. This process can be seen in the figures reported in table 12-3 below.

A good part of this difference in dropout rate is no doubt due to the lower ability and weaker

TABLE 12-3
Educational Outcomes for Two-Year Transfers and Four-Year Natives

Study Characteristics	Calif. Community Colleges (1984)[a]	Fla. State Ed. Dept. (1983)[b]	Holmstrom and Bisconti (1974)	Trent and Medsker (1968)	Folger et al. (1970)	Knoell and Medsker (1965)
Coverage	Calif.	Fla.	U.S.	U.S.	U.S.	U.S.
Year began college	NA	NA	1968	1959	1960	1958
Year transferred	1975	1976	NA[b]	NA[b]	NA[b]	1960
Year followed up	1980	1978	1972	1963	1965	1963
Findings on Percent Dropping Out						
Two years after transfer						
two-year transfers		32.0%	14.3%	21.0%		
four-year natives		19.8%				
Three years after transfer						
two-year transfers					32.0%	29.0%
Five years after transfer						
two-year transfers	35.6%					
four-year natives	23.9%					

[a] The California data compare fall 1975 transfers to the California State University system (CSU) who came in as juniors and CSU natives who became juniors the same year. The Florida data are for fall 1976 transfers to three state universities who came in as juniors and university natives who became juniors at the same time.
[b] Holmstrom and Bisconti [34], Trent and Medsker [66], and Folger et al. [31] did not report the time elapsed between the year transfer students entered four-year colleges and the year they were followed up. But because the majority of students transfer between sophomore and junior year, the followup probably came after two years at the four-year college in Holmstrom and Bisconti's and Trent and Medsker's studies and after three years in the Folger et al. study.

motivation of two-year college transfers [68, pp. 32, 75]. But these student-centered factors are unlikely to explain the entirety of this difference. Other evidence indicates that several features of the U.S. higher education system contribute to the higher mortality of community college transfers. These students less often receive financial aid. Their lower-division credits are less often recognized by senior colleges. They are not as well integrated socially into four-year colleges. And they are prepared less well by their community colleges for the kind of work they will have to do at four-year colleges. Let us review each of these factors in turn.

As stated in the section on transfer difficulties, transfer students less often receive financial aid than native four-year college students [69, 34]. One of the reasons is that many community college students have largely exhausted their eligibility by the time they transfer, having enrolled in the community college for three or more years. In addition, transfer students transferring between the fall and spring semesters often find that, even when they do receive financial aid, this aid is not increased to reflect the sharp increase in tuition and living expenses accompanying the move to a four-year college [58, pp. 56–57, 112]. This gap in financial aid increases the probability that transfer students will have to withdraw for lack of money. This is the main reason given by transfer students who withdraw of their own volition [41, p. 71]. In addition, as we will see below, lack of financial aid also hinders transfer students' academic and social integration into four-year colleges.

A sizable number of transfer students lose credits in transit to four-year colleges, thus slowing their educational progress and endangering their ability to finance their college career [24, p. 54; 56; 58, p. 80].[5] A recent study of community college transfers at nine urban universities across the country found that 58 percent reported losing credits in transferring, with 29 percent losing ten or more credits. In addition, 25 percent reported that even when the university gave them credit for certain courses, those credits were not counted against their majors. For 11 percent, this loss of major credit involved ten or more credits [58, p. 148]. Similarly, a recent study of transfers from Maryland community colleges found that 6 percent lost thirteen or more credit hours (that is, at least one semester) [46, p. 12].

Credit loss stems from several sources. Com-

munity colleges have been criticized for often making little effort to ensure that their transfer courses indeed parallel university courses in credit hours, course sequencing, and prerequisites. Moreover, community college transfer students interviewed at nine urban universities often complained that their community college counselors frequently did not know which courses were transferrable, with the result that they had to retake courses [58, pp. 40, 159–60, 164]. At the same time, four-year colleges deserve a share of the blame. They routinely refuse credit for community college courses that have no counterpart in their curriculum, such as many vocational education courses.[6] Moreover, four-year colleges often deny credit to courses that they consider as belonging in the upper division. This has been a major problem in the area of business education. The American Association of Collegiate Schools of Business discourages university students from enrolling in business courses until their junior year, when they have gotten their general education requirements out of the way. As a result, university business schools rarely give credit for community college business courses, because they are considered as having been taken out of proper sequence [12, 60]. In addition, four-year colleges often give no credit or only partial credit for community college courses for which a student received a D, although four-year college natives are not so penalized. A random survey of 541 four-year institutions in 1982 found that 64 percent refused even to give credit toward the general residence requirement (quite apart from credit toward the major) for transfer courses carrying a D [75, p. 222]. Finally, many four-year colleges refuse to give credit for more than two years of courses [39, chap. 2; 41, p. 61; 46, p. 12; 58, p. 193; and 78, pp. 189–90]. Of 541 four-year colleges surveyed in 1982, 22 percent limited to two years' worth the number of courses students could transfer for credit [75, pp. 224–25].

Transfer students also encounter obstacles to educational success in the form of various hindrances to social integration in four-year colleges [4, p. 154, 168; and 41, p. 68].[7] Because of lack of financial aid, transfer students more often have to work to support themselves and thus have less time for mixing with their peers on campus. Orientation programs directed specifically to transfer students are rare, and clubs and other extracurricular activities at four-year colleges usually focus their recruitment efforts on freshmen. In addition, transfer students often fail to get campus housing because many four-year colleges give first priority to freshmen. Furthermore, students transferring from community colleges with large minority populations may find it hard to adjust to four-year colleges if they have small minority populations or are suffering from the spasms of racial tension that have shaken such well-known institutions as the University of Massachusetts and the University of Michigan. As a consequence of these various impediments, transfer students often complain that they find it difficult to join student activities and take part in the general social life of the college [58, pp. 82–83, 161; 59, pp. 7–9].

Poorer social integration leads in turn to greater likelihood of academic failure. Pincus and DeCamp [56] found, in a study of high-achieving minority students who transferred to four-year colleges in the early 1970s and were followed up in 1986, that those who failed to graduate were less often members of student clubs or organizations at the four-year college and were less likely to report that their classmates encouraged them to graduate. Similarly, a study of Los Angeles community college transfers to UCLA found that those who dropped out were significantly less likely to have most of their friends within UCLA than those who remained [40, pp. 9–10].

Finally, transfer students run afoul of obstacles to integrating themselves academically into four-year colleges. Studies repeatedly find that they tend to suffer a sharp drop in grades in the first year after transfer [23, pp. 101–02; 24, p. 53;33;39; and 41, pp. 27–28]. For example, the median GPA of fall 1982 community college transfers to the University of California and California State University systems dropped by one-half point at UC and one-third point at CSU from their community college medians [16, pp. 26, 30, F-2]. Similarly, in the fall of 1979 Illinois community college transfers to Illinois public and private universities suffered an average drop of about one-third grade point between their community college GPAs and their first-year university GPAs [35, p. 11].

It is often claimed that transfers' upper-division grades soon recover from "transfer shock." However, this claim is misleading. It is based on comparing the grades of students two or three years past transfer to those of students the first year of transfer. Even when the same cohort is involved, no correction is made for the fact that the older students no longer include the many students who did badly after transfer and dropped out. A study of Illinois transfers found that, whereas those who eventually graduated with a baccalaureate largely did rally from their transfer shock, those who dropped out never did fully recover [36, pp. 12–15].

Not surprisingly, transfer shock in the form of bad grades is significantly associated with greater attrition, whether through academic dismissal or voluntary withdrawal. Two studies document this connection. Kissler, et al. [40, pp. 9–10] found that Los Angeles community college transfers to UCLA who dropped out had significantly lower grades at UCLA than those who continued. Similarly, Johnson [38, pp. 324–25] found that community college students transferring to a large urban commuter university in the Southwest in the fall of 1984 were significantly less likely to return for the spring semester if they had lower grades, even if one controlled for educational aspirations, academic self-concept, perception of practical value of education, rating of academic difficulties, academic satisfaction, and degree of academic integration.

Clearly, a good part of the grade shock encountered by transfer students stems from a collision between their abilities and the tougher standards of the four-year colleges. But it also stems from institutional factors: particularly, less access to financial aid and poorer academic preparation in the community college.

As noted above, transfer students receive less financial aid than four-year college natives. And this exclusion significantly depresses their upper-division grades and persistence rates. A study of fall 1977 transfers from Los Angeles community colleges to UCLA found that the students' grades at UCLA were negatively and significantly associated with their amount of unmet financial need, even when their community college GPAs and community college preparation were controlled [40, pp. 6–8].

Community college transfers also get poorer upper-division grades than four-year college natives because their lower-division preparation is, on average, inferior [8, pp. 116–18; 11, pp. 36–38; 40, pp. 12–13; 41, pp. 60, 98; and 58, pp. 27–28, 34–36, 46–48]. Evidence of this is Crook and Lavin's [26] finding that, for 1970–72 entrants to the City University of New York, freshman grades are significantly less predictive of B.A. attainment by 1984 among community college entrants than four-year college entrants. In separate regressions, an increase of one point in first-year GPA increased the probability of getting a baccaluareate degree by 20 percent among four-year entrants but only 11 percent among community college entrants, even when their differences in background, aspirations, high-school record, and college experiences were controlled.

Programs ostensibly designed to prepare students for eventual transfer to four-year colleges have become essentially open door programs with virtually no entry or exit requirements. Many transfer courses do not have prerequisites, with the result that students do not have to progress in their learning and can avoid difficult courses. As a result, transfer courses are often not up to university standards of instruction [11, p. 38; 23, p. 100; 51, pp. 210, 213, 226–28]. Moreover, community college instructors often do not communicate and enforce high academic expectations for their students. They more often grade relative to the class norm (rather than an abstract standard) than do university instructors. They cover less material in class. And they less often assign difficult reading and essay examinations [11, pp. 36–37; 58, pp. 27–28, 34–36, 46–48]. In a survey of 1977 community college transfers to UCLA, only one-third reported that in the community college they frequently had to write papers integrating ideas from various parts of a course; yet two-thirds stated that at UCLA they had to do this frequently [42, pp. 2, 8–9]. A similar pattern of neglect of higher order cognitive skills appears in national data. A national survey of community college instructors found that only 27 percent allocated more than a quarter of the final course grade to essay examinations [25, p. 90]. Moreover, community college students were required to write papers in only one-fourth of their humanities courses and one-tenth of their science courses [22, p. 156]. Though only part of their academic malpreparation, community college students' lack of writing experience nonetheless has a seriously deleterious effect. Among the UCLA transfers described above, lack of writing experience in the community college had a significant impact on upper-divison grades and persistence rates, even after controlling for students' social background, community college grades, and course-taking and study habits in the community college [42, pp. 2, 8–9].

Conclusions

We must take seriously, then, the claim that baccalaureate aspirants are less likely to receive this degree if they enter a community college rather than a four-year college. There really is a baccalaureate gap, and it is only partially explained by the different characteristics of the two student bodies. Even when these differences are controlled, students entering community college with the hope of receiving a bachelor's degree are 11 to 19 percent less likely to do so than *comparable* students entering four-year colleges. This gap effect is attributable to various *institutional* characteristics of the community college and of the higher educational system generally that produce lower rates of persistence, transfer to the upper division, and persistence in the upper-division than is the case for four-year colleges. This finding is made all the more distressing by the fact that the community college has become the main point of entry into higher education for working class and minority students. Consequently, it plays no small role in the ongoing decline over the last fifteen years in the number of Blacks receiving baccalaureate degrees [52, p. 62]. As a result, we must begin to look beyond remedying the deficiencies of community college students to reforming the institution itself in fundamental ways.

A wide variety of proposals have been made to address the obstacles that baccalaureate aspirants face upon entering the community college. Some, that might be termed operational reforms, call for improving transfer education, without fundamentally changing the community college. Others, which might go by the name of structural reforms, have called for a radical alteration in the community college's very structure.[8]

Operational reformers have offered a host of ideas for improving institutional performance in the areas of persistence in the community colleges, transfer to four-year colleges, and persistence in the four-year colleges. To reduce attrition in the community college, operational reformers have proposed strengthening students' academic and social integration into college life through such means as providing more jobs on campus, holding more campus events, and encouraging greater interaction between faculty and students through formal conferences in the office and informal contact outside [6, pp. 132–33; 18, pp. 100–102; 23, p. 182; and 55, p. 4].

Transfer rates would be increased by better transfer advising, familiarizing would-be transfer students with four-year colleges through campus visits, and more financial aid tailored to transfer students' special needs. Transfer advising in particular would be improved by clearly labeling transfer courses, establishing centers at community colleges to centralize and disseminate transfer information, and creating computerized systems to track student progress and indicate how well they are meeting transfer requirements [6, pp. 132–33; 11, p. 37; 18, pp. 99–102; 23, pp. 180–81; 51, pp. 332–34; 55, pp. 3, 7; 58, pp. 38–39, 108–9, 173–74, 206–13, 219; and 79, pp. 240–46].

Finally, post-transfer retention would be promoted through more and better packaged financial aid, greater social integration of transfer students, more rigorous pretransfer academic preparation, and greater acceptance of credits. Pretransfer academic preparation would be improved by familiarizing community college teachers with the universities' academic expectations for students and by more rigorously testing students when they enter the community college and not allowing them to enter transfer courses until they are functioning at a collegiate level of preparation. Credit transfer would be eased by better exchange of information between community colleges and four-year colleges about transferability, creating common course numbers across two- and four-year colleges, having state governments require public four-year colleges to give full credit to general education courses taken in the community college, and reducing the obstacles to transfer of vocational credits by establishing more "capstone" or "inverted major" programs in which students get their technical training at the community college and their general education at the senior college [18, pp. 99–101; 23, pp. 19, 160–61, 179–81; 51, p. 333; 55, pp. 3–5, 7, 40–41, 44; 57, pp. 323–24; 58, pp. 56–57, 82–83, 112, 147, 169–70, 184–85, 207–18].

These operational reforms would be highly beneficial and should be vigorously pursued. However, they also have their limits. The operational reformers have been criticized by structural reformers for focusing exclusively on revamping how the community college operates while largely ignoring the need to change its very structure and position within the higher education system. These critics argue that as long as the community college remains a two-year, commuter institution that is structurally separate from the four-year colleges that baccalaureate aspirants must eventually enter, its baccalaureate aspirants will encounter major obstacles to their success. The structural reformers therefore have called for fundamentally reshaping the community college and its relationship with the rest of higher education. These fundamental reforms have evident problems, but they also deserve careful consideration by scholars and policymakers.

Some structural reformers have argued that we should consider turning the community colleges into four-year colleges [79, pp. 251–52]. The hope is that these new community colleges could dramatically reduce their rates of attrition by no longer requiring students to transfer in order to pursue their upper-division education and by more effectively integrating their students academically and socially. This proposal has been criticized, however, on the grounds that it would be utterly impracticable politically; it would be horrendously expensive and inefficient; it would fuel educational inflation and overeducation by producing too many bachelor's degree holders; it would fail to meet the needs of the 60 to 70 percent of community college entrants who are not baccalaureate aspirants; it would still leave the community college low in the higher education prestige hierarchy; or alternatively, it would embolden the community college to push for graduate programs [20].

These objections to transforming community colleges into four-year colleges may not be as convincing as the critics believe. Nonetheless, they suggest the need to examine other routes to restructuring the community college and its position within higher education. One idea that has gone unmentioned in current debates over the future of the community college but bears careful consideration is that of converting community colleges into branches of the state universities. Such systems of two-year university branches exist today in Alaska, Connecticut, Hawaii, Kentucky, Louisiana, New Mexico, Ohio, Pennsylvania, and South Carolina. This policy might garner most of the benefits and avoid most of the problems of transforming community colleges into four-year colleges. Because of their strong connections to the universities, university two-year branches apparently make it much easier for students to transfer than do community colleges. But unlike transforming community colleges into four-year colleges, converting community colleges into university branches would be less expensive and much less likely to catalyze the opposition of the state universities [28].

But even as we focus on reforming the community college operationally and structurally in order to remove the institutional obstacles it places in the way of its baccalaureate aspirants, we must keep in mind that it should not be saddled with this task alone. Four-year colleges must also confront the ways in which they obstruct the path of community college transfers. Moreover, elementary and secondary schools must address their contribution to the academic and motivational deficiencies of the students they send on to community colleges. The fact that many of them are lower class or nonwhite cannot be allowed to be an excuse for poor precollegiate preparation. Elementary and secondary schools must do a better job of preparing all their students, whatever their backgrounds.

APPENDIX

TABLE A1
Educational Attainment of Entrants to Two-Year Colleges and Four-Year Colleges

	Nunley, Breneman (1988)	Lavin, Crook (1990)	Nunley, Breneman (1988)	Velez (1985)	Anderson (1984)	Astin et al. (1982)
Study Characteristics						
Data set used	NLS-72	CUNY	NLS-72	NLS-72	NLS-72	ACE
Population covered	all US	N.Y City	all US	all US	all US	all US
Year students began college	1972	1970–72	1972	1972	1972	1971
Year students followed up	1979	1984	1979	1979	1979	1980
Aspirations of respondents	any post second'y	any post second'y	B.A. + above	Acad. prog.	Acad. prog.	B.A. + above
Findings						
Percent Attaining B.A.						
Four-year colleges						
public and private	NA		NA	79.0%		73.0%[a]
public only		74%				
state college only					NA	
Two-year colleges						
public and private				31.0%		29.0%[a]
any public	NA		NA		NA	
community colleges		31%				
Difference in Percentage						
no controls	NA	43.0%	NA	48.0%	23.9%	44.0%[a]
with controls	11.4%*	17.0*	11.5%[b]	18.7%*	14.0%*	NA[c]
Years of Education Attained						
Four-year colleges						
public and private	NA		NA			
state college only					14.49	
Two-year colleges						
any public	NA		NA		14.03	
Difference in Years						
no controls	NA		NA		0.46	
with controls	0.12*		0.16[b]		0.25*	

TABLE A1 (*continued*)
Educational Attainment of Entrants to Two-Year Colleges and Four-Year Colleges

	Nunley, Breneman (1988)	Lavin, Crook (1990)	Nunley, Breneman (1988)	Velez (1985)	Anderson (1984)	Astin et al. (1982)
Control Variables						
Social background						
Sex	X	X	X	X	X	X
Race	X	X	X	X	X	X
SES	X	X	X	X	X	X
Age		X	X			X
Language spoken at home	X		X			
Religion				X	X	
Marital status	X		X			
Location of home	X		X			
Aspirations						
Student's educ. asps.	X	X	X[d]	X	X	X[d]
Student's occ. asps.					X	X
Parents' educ. asps.	X		X	X	X	
Peers' post-HS plans	X		X			
College decision date	X		X			
Student's perception of college ability	X	X	X		X	
Importance of gen. ed.		X				
High School Experiences						
Test scores				X	X	X
Grades or class rank	X	X	X	X	X	X
Curriculum or track	X	X	X	X	X	X
Hours spent on homework	X		X			
Hours spent at job	X		X			
Location of high school	X		X			
Racial composition of high school						X
College Experiences						
FT or PT enrollment	X					
Living arrangements	X		X	X		
Hours spent at job	X	X	X			
Work on campus				X		
College program	X	X	X	X[c]	X[c]	
Number of remedial courses taken		X				
College grades	X		X	X		
Children while in college	X		X			
Married in college	X		X			

[a] Figures are for Whites only. Does not report figures for all races together.
[b] Presents significance level only for comparison with those not in college.
[c] *Partial correlations* between college type and attainment of B.A. for five racial/ethnic groups. The partial correlations for public two-year college entrants range from –0.20 to 0.01 (with four of five correlations significant at *p* less than 0.05), whereas the correlations for public four-year nonuniversity college entrants range from –0.08 to 0.08 (with one significant).
[d] The sample included only those aspiring to a baccalaureate degree.
[e] The sample included only those students in the academic program.
*Significant at the 0.05 level.

TABLE A2
Attrition from Higher Education

	National Center Ed. Stats. (1990a)	Astin (1975)	Pascarella, Chapman (1983a)[a]	Anderson (1981)[b]	Anderson (1984)[b]
Study Characteristics					
Data set used	HS&B	ACE	own	NLS-72	NLS-72
Year students began college	1982	1968	1978	1972	1972
Year students followed up	1986	1972	1979	1973,1974	1973
Aspirations of students	any post second'y	B.A. + above	any post second'y	academic program	academic program
Findings on Percentage Dropping Out					
Percent at the End of One Year					
Public two-year colleges			NA	30.9	
Community Colleges			NA		
All four-year colleges			NA	NA	
State four-year colleges				20.3	
Difference					
no controls (gross)			NA	NA	10.6
with controls (net)			10.0*	5.0**	3.9[c]
Percent at the End of Two Years					
Public two-year colleges				NA	
Community colleges					
All four-year colleges				NA	
State four-year colleges					
Difference					
no controls (gross)				NA	
with controls (net)				14.0**	
Percent at the End of Four Years					
All two-year colleges	42.6%				
Public two-year colleges		56.0 (male) 59.0 (female)			
Community colleges					
All four-year colleges	30.6%				
All colleges		37.6 (male) 31.7 (female)			
Difference in Percentage					
no controls (gross)	12.0	18.4 (male)[c] 27.3 (female)[c]			
with controls (net)		10.0 (male)[c] 18.0 (female)[c]			
Control Variables					
Social background					
Sex		X	X	X	X
Race		X		X	X
Age			X		
SES		X	X	X	X
Religion		X		X	X

TABLE A2 (*continued*
Attrition from Higher Education

	National Center Ed. Stats. (1990a)	Astin (1975)	Pascarella, Chapman (1983a)[a]	Anderson (1981)[b]	Anderson (1984)[b]
Aspirations and Other					
Student educ. asps.	X			X	X
Student's occ. asps.				X	X
Parents' educ. asps.				X	X
Peers' post-HS plans				X	
College entrance date					X
Student's perception of college ability				X	X
Affiliation needs			X		
Achievement needs			X		
High-School Experiences					
Test scores				X	X
Grades or class rank	X		X	X	X
Curriculum or track				X	X
College Experiences					
Living arrangements				X	
Work on campus			X	X	
Academic major			X		
Size of institution			X		
% of undergraduates living on campus			X		
Academic integration			X		
Social integration			X		

[a] Pascarella and Chapman's attrition figures are for withdrawal from the institution rather than from higher education as a whole.
[b] Anderson counts as withdrawal not only dropping out of higher education but also moving out of the academic program into the vocational program.
[c] Level of significance not reported
*Significant at 0.05 level
**Significant at 0.01 level

Notes

1. A frequently stated misestimate of the number of baccalaureate aspirants is that they run as high as two-thirds to three-quarters of all community college students. The mistake often derives from basing the estimate on figures in the annual freshman survey of the American Council on Education. This survey questions only full-time students who make up only 58 percent of community college entrants but tend to have higher aspirations than part-time students [27, p. 87; 62; and 67, p. 53]. The vagueness and volatility of many students' ambitions makes it very difficult to determine exactly rates of baccalaureate aspiration. A question one has to confront is whether one should take what students say as the only valid indication, even if those statements are not reflected in baccalaureate-oriented behavior, or whether one should only class as baccalaureate aspirants those who take concrete steps in this direction? Arthur Cohen and Florence Brawer and their associates at the Center for the Study of Community Colleges [25] and Stephen Sheldon [62] and his associates in the California community colleges have taken important steps toward developing a sophisticated method for measuring baccalaureate aspirations.

2. In addition, it has been claimed that community college students drop out more often because they are given less financial aid than students at public four-year colleges, despite the fact that they are considerably less well off [51]. In fact, the 1987 National Postsecondary Student Aid Study found that only 28.5 percent of public two-year college students received student aid of any kind in 1986, whereas the comparable percentage for those at public universities was 46.8 percent [71, p. 286]. However, it is not clear that community college students have to bear a larger *net* cost of education than do four-year college entrants. Although they get less financial aid, they also have considerably smaller tuitions. On the other hand, community college students are poorer, so that even if their net cost is smaller, it might represent a larger proportion of their income. Clearly this question deserves more research.

3. The finding that differences in social integration lead to differences in persistence between community colleges and four-year colleges does not contradict the repeated finding that social integration is of little importance in explaining differences in persistence *among* community college entrants alone [53, pp. 98–99; 54, pp. 37, 43–44; 69, pp. 178, 184]. Social integration cannot have much impact on differences in persistence among community college students alone because there is little variation among community colleges in social integration and its causes, such as campus residence. Because the independent variable varies little, it is by definition unable to explain differences in the dependent variable. However, social integration can be significantly associated with differences in persistence between community college and four-year college entrants because it varies greatly between the two types of institutions.

4. Moreover, these transfer problems are greater for students who are female, non-white, and low in socioeconomic status than for students with the obverse characteristics [44; 68, pp. 8, 11, 13, 28, 32, 70, 73; 74].

5. Indirect evidence of the impact of credit loss is that Illinois community college students transferring to four-year colleges with 60 or more credits are considerably more likely to receive a baccalaureate degree eventually than those transferring 14 credit hours or less: 65 percent versus 41 percent [36, p. 75].

6. This problem has eased in recent years as many four-year colleges have established "capstone" programs in technical fields. Under these programs, four-year colleges give credit for community-college vocational courses and require students to cap them with liberal arts courses. However, the complaint has been made that such programs rarely operate effectively after a few years. Once established, their faculty give admissions preference to native freshmen rather than community college transfers [58].

7. See the section on lower-division persistence for a discussion of the general research literature on the importance of social and academic integration for remaining in college.

8. These proposals are only covered very briefly below. Their content and relative costs and benefits are evaluated at length in Dougherty [28; 29].

References

1. Anderson, K. "Post-High School Experiences and College Attrition." *Sociology of Education*, 54 (January 1981), 1–15.

2. ———. "Institutional Differences in College Effects." ERIC 256–204. Boca Raton, FL: Florida Atlantic University, 1984.

3. ———. "The Impact of Colleges and the Involvement of Male and Female Students." *Sociology of Education*, 61 (July 1988), 160–78.

4. Astin, A. *Preventing Students from Dropping Out*. San Francisco: Jossey-Bass, 1975.

5. *Four Critical Years*. San Francisco: Jossey-Bass, 1977.

6. ———. "Strengthening Transfer Education." In *Issues for Community College Leaders in a New Era*, edited by G. Vaughan, pp. 122–138. San Francisco: Jossey-Bass, 1983.

7. Astin, A., et al. *Minorities in Higher Education*. San Francisco: Jossey-Bass, 1982.

8. Aulston, M. D. "Black Transfer Students in White Colleges." *NASPA Journal*, 12 (1974), 116–23.

9. Baratta, F., and E. Apodaca. "A Profile of California Community College Transfer Students at the University of California." ERIC 260–754. Berkeley, Calif.: University of California, 1984.

10. Bayer, A. E., J. T. Royer, and R. M. Webb. *Four Years after College Entry*. American Council on Education Research Reports 8(1). ERIC 077–329. Washington, D.C.: Government Printing Office, 1973.

11. Bernstein, A. "The Devaluation of Transfer." In *The Community College and Its Critics*, edited by L. Steven Zwerling, pp. 31–40. New Directions for Community Colleges No. 54. ERIC 271–169. San Francisco: Jossey-Bass, 1986.

12. Blood, M. "Transferring Credit from Four-Year Colleges: Business School Official Replies." *Chronicle of Higher Education*, 33 (April 8, 1987), 45.

13. Brawer, F., and J. Friedlander. "Science and Social Science in the Two-Year College." Topical Paper No. 69. ERIC 172–854. Los Angeles: ERIC Clearinghouse for Junior Colleges, 1979.

14. Breneman, D. W., and S. C. Nelson. *Financing Community Colleges*. Washington, D.C.: Brookings Institution, 1981.

15. Brint, S., and J. Karabel. *The Diverted Dream*. New York: Oxford University Press, 1989.

16. California Community Colleges. *Transfer Education*. ERIC 250–025. Sacramento: Office of the Chancellor, 1984.

17. California Postsecondary Education Commission. *Update of Community College Transfer Statistics, 1988–89*. ERIC 313–073. Sacramento: California Postsecondary Education Commission, 1989.

18. Center for the Study of Community Colleges. *An Assessment of Urban Community College Transfer Opportunity Program*. ERIC 293–573. Los Angeles: University of California at Los Angeles, 1988.

19. Chapman, D. W., and E. T. Pascarella. "Predictors of Academic and Social Integration of College Students." *Research in Higher Education*, 19 (1983), 295–322.

20. Clark, B. R. "The 'Cooling Out' Function Revisited." In *Questioning the Community College Role*, edited by George Vaughan, pp. 15–31. New Directions for Community Colleges No. 32. San Francisco: Jossey-Bass, 1980.

21. Cohen, A. M., and F. B. Brawer. *The Two- Year College Instructor Today*. New York: Praeger, 1977.

22. ———. *The American Community College*. 1st ed. San Francisco: Jossey-Bass, 1982.

23. ———. *The Collegiate Function of the Community College*. San Francisco: Jossey-Bass, 1987.

24. ———. *The American Community College*. 2nd ed. San Francisco: Jossey-Bass, 1989.

25. Cohen A. M., F. B. Brawer, and E. Bensimon. *Transfer Education in American Community Colleges*. ERIC 255–250. Los Angeles: UCLA Center for the Study of Community Colleges, 1985.

26. Crook, D. B., and D. E. Lavin. "The Community College Effect Revisited: The Long Term Impact of Community College Entry on Baccalaureate Attainment." Paper presented to the American Educational Research Association, San Francisco, 1989.

27. Dougherty, K. J. "The Effects of Community Colleges: Aid or Hindrance to Socioeconomic Attainment?" *Sociology of Education*, 60 (April 1987), 86–103.

28. ———. "The Community College at the Crossroads: The Need for Structural Reforms." *Harvard Educational Review*, 61 (August 1991), 311–36.

29. ———. *The Contradictory College: The Political Origins, Current Impact, and Likely Future of the Community College*. Unpublished book manuscript, Department of Sociology, Manhattan College, 1991.

30. Florida State Education Department. *A Longitudinal Study Comparing University Native and Community College Transfer Students in the State University System of Florida*. ERIC 156–849. Tallahassee: Florida State Education Department, 1983.

31. Folger, J., H. Astin, and A. E. Bayer. *Human Resources and Higher Education*. New York: Russell Sage, 1970.

32. Grubb, W. N. "Vocationalizing Higher Education: The Causes of Enrollment and Completion in Public Two-Year Colleges, 1970–1980." *Economics of Education Review*, 7, (1989), 301–19.

33. Hills, J. R. "Transfer Shock: The Academic Performance of the Junior College Transfer." *Journal of Experimental Education*, 33 (1965), 201–15.

34. Holmstrom, E., and A. Bisconti. *Transfers from Junior to Senior Colleges*. Washington, D.C.: American Council on Education, 1974.

35. Illinois Community College Board. *Fall 1979 Transfer Study, Report 4: Third and Fourth Year Persistence and Achievement*. ERIC 254–275. Springfield: Illinois Community College Board, 1984.

36. ———. *Illinois Community College Board Transfer Study: A Five Year Study of Students Transferring from Illinois Two Year Colleges to Illinois Senior Colleges in the Fall of 1979*. ERIC 270–148. Springfield: Illinois Community College Board, 1986.

37. Jencks, C. S., et al. *Who Gets Ahead?*. New York: Basic Books, 1979.

38. Johnson, N. "Academic Factors that Affect Transfer Student Persistence." *Journal of College Student Personnel*, 28 (July 1987), 323–29.

39. Kintzer, F. and J. L. Wattenbarger. *The Articulation/Transfer Phenomenon*. ERIC 257–539. Washington, D.C.: American Association of Community and Junior Colleges, 1985.

40. Kissler, G., J. Lara, and J. Cardinal. "Factors Contributing to the Academic Difficulties Encountered by Students Who Transfer from Community Colleges to Four-Year Institutions." ERIC 203–920. Unpublished paper, University of California at Los Angeles, 1981.

41. Knoell, D. M., and L. L. Medsker. *From Junior College to Senior College*. Washington, D.C.: American Council on Education, 1965.

42. Lara, J. "Differences in Quality of Academic Effort between Successful and Unsuccessful Community College Transfer Students." ERIC 201–359. Unpublished paper, University of California, Los Angeles, 1981.

43. Lavin, D. E., and D. B. Crook. "Open Admissions and Its Outcomes: Ethnic Differences in Long-Term Educational Attainment." *American Journal of Education*, 98 (August 1990), 389–425.

44. Lee, V., and K. Frank. "Student Characteristics that Facilitate the Transfer from Two-Year to Four-Year Colleges." *Sociology of Education*, 63 (July 1990), 178–93.

45. London, H. *The Culture of a Community College.* New York: Praeger, 1990.

46. Maryland State Board for Community Colleges. *The Role of Community Colleges in Preparing Students for Transfer to Four-Year Colleges and Universities*. ERIC 230–255. Annapolis: Maryland State Board for Community Colleges, 1983.

47. Munro, B. "Dropouts from Higher Education." *American Educational Research Journal*, 18 (1980), 133–41.

48. Neumann, W., and D. Riesman. "The Community College Elite." In *Questioning the Community College Role*, edited by George Vaughan, pp. 53–71. New Directions in Community Colleges, No. 32. San Francisco: Jossey-Bass, 1980.

49. Nunley, C. R., and D. W. Breneman. "Defining and Measuring Quality in Community College Education." In *Colleges of Choice*, edited by Judith Eaton, pp. 62–92. New York: Macmillan, 1988.

50. Olivas, M. *The Dilemma of Access: Minorities in Two-Year Colleges*. Washington, D.C.: Howard University Press, 1979.

51. Orfield, G., et al. *The Chicago Study of Access and Choice in Higher Education*. ERIC 249–929. Chicago: University of Chicago, Committee on Public Policy, 1984.

52. Orfield, G., and F. Paul. "Declines in Minority Access: A Tale of Five Cities." *Educational Record*, 68–69 (Fall-Winter 1987–1988), 57–62.

53. Pascarella, E. T., and D. W. Chapman. "A Multi-Institutional, Path Analytic Validation of Tinto's Model of College Withdrawal." *American Educational Research Journal*, 20 (1983a), 87–102.

54. ———. "Validation of a Theoretical Model of College Withdrawal." *Research in Higher Education*, 19 (1983b), 25–48.

55. Pincus, F. L., and E. Archer. *Bridges to Opportunity? Are Community Colleges Meeting the Transfer Needs of Minority Students?* New York: College Board, 1989.

56. Pincus, F. L., and S. DeCamp. "Minority College Students who Transfer to Four-Year Colleges: A Study of a Matched Sample of B.A. Recipients and Non-Recipients." *Community and Junior College Quarterly of Research and Practice*, 13 (1990), 191–219.

57. Rendon, L., and T. Matthews. "Success of Community College Students." *Education and Urban Society*, 21 (May 1989), 312–27.

58. Richardson, R., and L. Bender. *Fostering Minority Access and Achievement in Higher Education*. San Francisco: Jossey-Bass, 1987.

59. Sandeen, A., and T. Goodale. *The Transfer Student*. ERIC 154–750. Gainesville, Fla.: University of Florida, 1976.

60. Savage, D. "It's Time to Stop Thwarting Students Who Try to Transfer Business Credits to Four-Year Colleges." *Chronicle of Higher Education*, 33 (April 18, 1987), 56–57.

61. Seidman, E. *In the Words of the Faculty*. San Francisco: Jossey-Bass, 1985.

62. Sheldon, S. *Statewide Longitudinal Study. Report on Academic Years, 1978–1981. Part 5: Final Report*. ERIC 217–917. Sacramento: California Community Colleges, 1982.

63. Terenzini, P., and E. T. Pascarella. "Toward the Validation of Tinto's Model of College Student Attrition: A Review of Recent Studies." *Research in Higher Education*, 12 (1980), 271–82.

64. Tinto, V. "Dropout from Higher Education: A Theoretical Synthesis of Recent Research." *Review of Educational Research*, 45 (1975), 89–125.

65. ———. *Leaving College*. Chicago: University of Chicago Press, 1987.

66. Trent, J., and L. L. Medsker. *Beyond High School*. San Francisco: Jossey-Bass, 1968.

67. U.S. Bureau of the Census. *School Enrollment—Social and Economic Characteristics of Students: October 1986*. Current Population Reports, Series P-20, No. 429. Washington, D.C.: Government Printing Office, 1989.

68. U.S. National Center for Education Statistics. *Transfer Students in Institutions of Higher Education*. American Statistical Index 1977 4586–1.19. Washington, D.C.: Government Printing Office, 1977a.

69. ———. *Withdrawal from Institutions of Higher Education*. American Statistical Index 1978 4586–1.26. Washington, D.C.: Government Printing Office, 1977b.

70. ———. *Patterns and Trends of Stopping Out from Postsecondary Education: 1972, 1980, 1982 High School Graduates*. American Statistical Index 1990 4842–41. Washington, D.C.: Government Printing Office, 1990a.

71. ———. *Digest of Education Statistics, 1990*. Washington, D.C.: Government Printing Office, 1990.

72. Vaughan, G. "Introduction." In *Questioning the Community College Role*, edited by George Vaughan, pp. 3–14. New Directions for Community Colleges, No. 32. San Francisco: Jossey-Bass, 1980.

73. Velez, W. "Finishing College: The Effects of College Type." *Sociology of Education*, 58 (1985), 191–200.

74. Velez, W., and R. G. Javalgi. "Two-Year College to Four-Year College: The Likelihood of Transfer." *American Journal of Education*, 96 (November 1987), 81–94.

75. Walton, K. "Transfer of Undergraduate Credit." *College and University*, 58 (1984), 217–28.

76. Weis, L. *Between Two Worlds: Black Students in an Urban Community College*. Boston: Routledge and Kegan Paul, 1985.

77. Willingham, W., and N. Findikyan. *Patterns of Admission for Transfer Students*. New York: College Entrance Examination Board, 1969.

78. Winandy, D., and R. McGrath. "A Study of Admissions Policies and Practices for Transfer Students in Illinois." *College and University*, 45 (1970), 186–92.

79. Zwerling, L. S. *Second Best: The Crisis of the Junior College*. New York: McGraw-Hill, 1976.

PART III

STUDENT DEVELOPMENT AND IDENTITY

PART 3: STUDENT DEVELOPMENT AND IDENTITY

The section on Student Development and Identity focuses on internal and external influences on individual student growth. Bob Rodgers's (1990). "Recent Theories and Research Underlying Student Development" describes theoretical contexts for understanding college student development. This chapter is an appropriate beginning to this section because it gives an overview of key cognitive, psychosocial, and typology theories as they relate to the longitudinal changes of college students.

Deborah Faye Carter's (2002) article, "College Students' Degree Aspirations: A Theoretical Model and Literature Review With a Focus on African American and Latino Students," focuses on the sociological and structural processes related to college students' degree aspirations. Carter's article is a slight departure from the other articles and chapters featured in this section in that the article focuses sociological and structural processes while the focus of most of the other articles in this section relate psychological processes to student development. The article highlights the individual factors in connection with the college environmental processes as they affect student degree aspirations.

The next three articles in this section focus on racial identity development and the identity development of gay, lesbian, and bisexual students. Janet Helms (1990), in "Toward a model of White racial identity development," describes the previous research and theoretical development pertaining to White racial identity. Helms is noted for the model of White racial identity development and describes each stage in this article. Helms specifically details how each stage of the model features its own set of attitudes, behaviors, and emotions, and that attitudes are hypothesized to change more quickly than behaviors.

In "Cross's Nigrescence Model: From Theory to Scale to Theory," Beverly Vandiver, Peony Fhagen-Smith, Kevin Cokley, William Cross, and Frank Worrell (2001) illustrate the ways in which Cross' 1971 Nigrescence Identity Model has evolved in the thirty years since its original publication. The authors describe how they modified the theory based on additional theoretical and empirical investigation. This expanded nigrescence model was developed as a result of comprehensive research studies, and the authors conclude that relying only on empirical research or only on theoretical considerations may present an incomplete picture of a specific phenomenon. Their approach uncovered layers and complexities in people's identity development that were only discovered through the use of theory and empirical research.

The article by Heidi Levine and Nancy Evans (1991), "The Development of Gay, Lesbian, Bisexual Identities," covers the development of gay, lesbian, and bisexual identities, and the authors review theoretical models that examine psychological influences and social processes on GLB identity development. Levine and Evans make the important point that lesbian and bisexual identity development has not been studied to the extent that gay male identity development has been.

The concluding piece in the section focuses on a validation of Holland's theory and how the theory can be incorporated into existing theories of college student development. John Smart, Kenneth Feldman, and Corinna Ethington (2000), "Educational and Organizational Implications of Holland's Theory in Higher Education Settings," completed a comprehensive study validating Holland's theory, and the chapter of their book included in this section examines the research and policy implications of the findings of their study. The authors make a powerful argument – that previous research has been lacking in terms of properly taking into account academic disciplines and how these environments affect student-learning outcomes. Further, they assert that the framework of Holland's theory may influence the development of different programmatic practices and organizational changes in academic programs.

CHAPTER 13

RECENT THEORIES AND RESEARCH UNDERLYING STUDENT DEVELOPMENT

ROBERT F. [BOB] RODGERS

Treated simplistically, the concept of "student development" entails characterizing a *student* and characterizing *development* and then applying the concept of development to a student. Student development comprises, in this context, the ways that a student grows, progresses, or increases his or her developmental capacities as a result of enrollment in an institution of higher education. The concept of student development has come to represent more, however, than this descriptive meaning suggests. The concept is used, for example, to represent the body of research and theories on late-adolescent and life-span adult development. In particular, works in the families of theory termed *person-environment interaction, psychosocial, cognitive-developmental*, and *typological* are called the theories of student development (Knefelkamp, Widick, & Parker, 1978; Rodgers, 1980).

The concept of student development can also be used as a philosophy. Student development can be considered as the ideological basis for actions or the rationale for programs. In the *Student Personnel Point of View* (American Council on Education, 1937, 1949) and the reports of the Council of Student Personnel Associations (Cooper, 1971, 1972), for example, this ideological use is plainly stated and openly advocated. The philosophical usage is prescriptive. It takes a value stand on the purpose of higher education and on the question of what higher education ought to seek as an outcome. In this usage, student development is synonymous with student affairs' central, historical educational value, *concern for the development of the whole student*.

A third usage of the concept of student development is programmatic. Student development is what student affairs staff and faculty members do to facilitate learning and development. It consists of the environments (i.e., services, workshops, classes, programs, policies) provided. This programmatic usage may or may not use the theories and research on student and adult development as the bases for programmatic efforts. In this chapter, however, it will be assumed that programmatic efforts are based on these theories and research about them, and the chapter will concentrate on an update of the families of theory and research that can be used to plan those programmatic efforts. Because the major reviews of these theories and research occurred in the late 1970s (Drum, 1980; Knefelkamp et al., 1978; Rodgers, 1980), this update will emphasize theories and research published since 1980 and thus will supplement those major reviews.

"Recent Theories and Research Underlying Student Development." Reprinted from *Journal of College Student Development*, (1990), American College Personnel Associates.

Person-Environment Interaction Theories

In the 1980s, it became clear that in using developmental theories without the person-environment interaction perspective, student development efforts tacitly focused mostly on the person (*P*) and often neglected the environment (*E*) and the interaction (×). Similarly, in using the person-environment perspective without using developmental theories, campus ecology projects did not assess, redesign, or evaluate for development per se. The two approaches are compatible and integratable, that is, student development can be *integrated into* the person-environment way of thinking, with both approaches profiting as a result. Campus ecology [$B = f(P \times E)$], therefore, has become the most basic way of thinking about the work of student affairs, and theories of adult development give the ecology model developmental substance. The following will elaborate on these points using recent research and evaluation studies.

Campus Ecology Without Student Development

William Perry (1970) opened his book *Forms of Intellectual and Ethical Development in the College Years* by describing and analyzing three students' reactions to a classroom lecture. Building upon Perry's hypothetical scene, let's imagine these three students are once again headed for class. Each student is thinking about an announced history lecture on the causes of the Civil War while walking toward the lecture hall. Student A is thinking, "Well, the professor is going to tell us why we had the Civil War. As he lectures, I'll write down the answers in my notes. Later I'll memorize my notes, and then on the test I'll prove to the professor that I've learned why we had the Civil War."

Student B thinks, "Well, I want to know why we had the Civil War so I can make a good grade in this class. I hope the professor gives us the answers. If he does, I'll take good notes and then give the answers back to the professor on the test. Professors, however, sometimes want you to learn to think critically rather than just learn the facts. So, instead of giving you the answers, which they could do, they give you a set of questions and criteria, lecture on various views of

what happened, and then expect you to work out the correct answer. That is all right as long as the material is not too vague. I wonder what our professor is going to do today?"

Student C assumes, "I'm going to class to learn about the various points of view on the question of why we had the Civil War, the evidence that supports the various theories, and their limitations. After the lecture, I'll read the important sources and then I'll try to work out a synthesis of why I think we had the Civil War."

The professor has to lecture from some point of view. Let us assume he covers four theories on the causes of the Civil War, does a devastating critique of each one, and then says, "Class dismissed!" Let us assume all three of our students have the same academic advisor. After class, student A rushes to see the advisor. "I want out of my history class," he says. "I don't understand anything the professor is saying. You cannot learn anything in the class. I have no idea why we had the Civil War after listening to the professor's lectures. I know I can't pass a test in this class. Why did the university hire him anyway? He doesn't know very much about history. I am so confused. I want to drop this class."

The next day Student B arrives at the advisor's office. "I need to talk," he says, "I don't know about history. I think I understand the questions about the cause of the Civil War, but I'm really confused about which theory is correct. The professor is so difficult to understand. I don't know if I can handle this class or not!"

A week later Student C visits the advisor. "I can't tell you how much I'm enjoying history," Student C says. "The professor is so stimulating. You should have heard his wonderful lectures on the Civil War."

At this point the academic advisor is scratching his or her head and thinking, "Could this have been the same professor on the same day in the same set of lectures with the students reacting so differently?" Evaluation using the Perry scheme, of course, makes this range of reactions possible. Students A, B, and C are making meaning of their experience in the same history class in different ways; they are at different positions of intellectual development. Nevertheless, the advisor who is not familiar with Perry's work but is familiar with the ecosystems model of examining person and environment interaction, decides to visit the history professor, and they discuss Students A, B, and C, the class, and the possibility of studying the situation. The professor agrees to join the advisor in studying the environment of the history class using an ecosystems methodology. A working group of students, the professor, and the advisor design a tailor-made instrument to assess the syllabus, reading list, each major assignment, the tests, the professor's lectures, and the recitation discussion groups. Students are asked to evaluate their degree of satisfaction with each of these elements in the class environment. For items with a high degree of dissatisfaction, students are asked through an Environmental Referent (ER) form for suggestions to correct the situation. Data are collected and analyzed, with the following results:

1. On the ER, a majority of the 150 students in the class report that the professor's lectures are confusing. They have difficulty understanding him and judging which point of view is the right one. They recommend simpler lectures. "Tell us clearly," says one student, "which theory is the right view on the topic." "Be more straight forward," says another.

2. A majority of the students also say that the discussions in the recitation section are a waste of time. "We don't learn anything in these so-called discussions," say a representative student. "It would be better, especially for passing tests, if the teaching assistant lectured and made sure we've learned the material for the tests."

3. The students report having difficulty with the professor's tests. Each test is half essay and half objective questions. The students do not like the essays and recommend that they be dropped and the entire test be clear-cut and objective.

Should the class be redesigned based on these recommendations? Should the professor simplify his lectures and present a single point of view clearly and carefully? Should he switch to objective tests and make the recitation sessions into lectures to prepare students for the tests? Upon *what grounds* should the planning group or the professor make decisions? Would the recommended changes be appropriate for the development of the students? For satisfaction with the class? For better grades.

This illustration is typical of most ecosystems studies that were completed and published in the 1970s and 1980s. These person-environment interaction studies were mostly atheoretical studies of students' perceived dissatisfactions with a given environment. They assumed that reducing the perceived dissatisfactions would result in improved satisfaction, performance, and development. These assumptions may or may not be valid. In terms of development, for example, reducing perceived dissatisfactions would facilitate development if the recommendations were congruent with the environmental conditions that seem to facilitate development. In the illustration, the recommendations are largely incongruent with the kind of classroom environment that seems to facilitate intellectual development for students making meaning in dualistic or relativistic ways, but may be congruent with improved satisfaction for dualists and perhaps improved performance in terms of making higher grades. Hence, if the recommendations for the history class were implemented, satisfaction might improve for many but not all students in the class. Performance in the class might improve provided the goals of the course were compatible with the changes, or the professor amended the goals to be compatible with the changes. It is doubtful, however, that the ability to think in more complex ways (i.e., intellectual development) would be enhanced.

Assessment of Ecosystems Studies

Although the intent of campus ecology studies has been to assess and then, if needed, redesign campus environments for increased satisfaction, better performance, and personal, intellectual, and social development (Banning & Kaiser, 1974; Blocker, 1974; Fawcett, Huebner, & Banning, 1978; Huebner, 1979; Huebner & Corazzini, 1978; Kaiser, 1978; Morrill, Hurst, & Oetting, 1980), most of the published works and dissertations on campus ecology have not mirrored these intents. In residence halls, for example, Schuh's (1979), Livingston's (1980), Fries's (1983), and Reynolds's (1984) studies are atheoretical assessments of students' perceived satisfaction with the environment, not studies of development or performance per se. Schroeder's (1976, 1980a, 1980b, 1981; Schroeder & Belmonte, 1979) works with residence halls are theoretically based. He used theories of territoriality, person-environment interaction, and Jungian personality type in his assessments and environmental redesigns. His pre- and posttest measures of the impact of redesigned environments, however, focus on perceived satisfaction, behaviors on administrative indices such as renewal and damage rates, or Moos's (1979) perceived social climate. None of these measures are developmental per se.

Dietrich's (1972) ecosystem study of campus ministries, Sabock's (1980) ecosystem assessment of intercollegiate athletic academic support services, Treadway (1979) report on a campuswide assessment and redesign project, and Mintz's (1970) assessment of a national Greek pledge educational system similarly are atheoretical assessments of perceived environments without using any criteria derived from developmental theory. With the exception of Treadway's study, these studies also have not reported on satisfaction, group performance, or developmental outcomes that may have resulted from redesigned environments. Treadway reported on follow-up atheoretical campuswide assessment after redesign. The redesigns did not use criteria derived from developmental perspectives, and the evaluation did not examine developmental changes that may have occurred.

Huebner, Royer, Moore, Cordes, and Paul (1979) and Hurst and Ragle (1979) advocated the use of developmental perspectives in assessments and evaluations of outcomes; however, the projects they described failed to implement these recommendations. Huebner's work on stress and medical school environments and Hurst and Ragle's brief descriptions of ombudsman and minority student assessments all used tailor-made local instruments, interviews, or institutional atheoretical data bases for assessments. No studies of redesigned environments were reported.

Hence, most campus ecology studies seem to have used tailor-made, local atheoretical environmental assessments or, when theories have been used, they have not been developmental theories. Reports on evaluations of environmental redesigns are less numerous but also have not included developmental variables. At best therefore, published studies have assumed that redesigned environments based upon recommendations from students' atheoretical perception of the environment would result in development. The studies have not dealt with the issue of development directly, and the assumption that development occurs may or may not be the case. Hence, in the 1980s the question became, *How might student development principle be integrated directly into campus ecology methodologies* (Rodgers, 1984a)?

Integrating Student Development and Campus Ecology Principles

The integration of student development and campus ecology theories and methodologies initially requires an analysis of the basic constructs of both. Campus ecology examines the interaction of students and their campus environments of subenvironments. Given the same environment, some students may succeed (Student C in the history class), whereas others may fail (Students A and B). Some may be satisfied (Student C), and others (Students A and B) may not be. Some may develop (Student C); others (Students A and B) may not.

The *student*, the *environment*, and their *interaction* are involved in these differential outcomes, not just the student or the environment. Students have different genetic heritages and histories of development. These students can experience the same environment differently. Similarly, when the environment is altered, development, performance, and satisfaction also may be altered for different students differentially. In short, the essence of the ecological perspective is a belief that human behavior results from the *interaction* of the *individual* and the *campus environment*.

In one of its three usages, student development is a name given to deliberate attempts to help students learn and develop by designing campus environments using adult developmental theories. The *deliberate* and *theory-in-practice* nature of these efforts often are put into operation through the use of process models (Rodgers, 1980). *Process models* are conceptualizations of the steps that help practitioners use theory in practice. They are not developmental theories per se. They cannot tell deans or counselors anything about the nature of development, how development is facilitated, or how it is measured. The theories themselves inform the practitioner of the types of development possible for college students, the criteria for deliberately designing environments that facilitate development, and the instruments or other means for measuring development. The means of measurement link the theories to developmental assessments of persons and evaluations of redesigns. The criteria for designing facilitative environments link theories to environmental assessments and redesign efforts. Process models tell the practitioner *when* and *how* to use the theories, their criteria for designing facilitative environments, and the means of measurement.

Campus ecology studies often have used ecosystems (Aulepp & Delworth, 1978) or related process models (Fawcett et al., 1978; Huebner & Corazzini, 1978) to implement their projects. Similar to all other process models, ecosystems models cannot define student development, specify criteria for facilitating developmental change, or specify means for measuring student development. Ecosystems models specify the nature and order the steps needed to assess an environment, redesign the environment, and evaluate the results of redesign. As indicated, when theories have been used in campus ecology, these theories have been person-environment interaction theories such as those of Moos (1979), Stern (1970), or Pervin (1967, 1968). These theories are not developmental per se (Rodgers, 1980). Hence, the campus ecology studies completed and published so far have not focused on student development per se and have not used developmental theories as criteria for designing facilitative environments or as means of measurement in the steps of their process models.

To correct the situation, Lewin's (1936) famous equation

$$B = f(P \times E) \qquad (1)$$

can be restated in a more complex form as follows:

$$B_p = f(P_d \times E_s) \qquad (2)$$

where, B_p is the probability of facilitating growth in a specific kind of development [e.g., intellectual development as defined by the Perry (1970) scheme] or two or more kinds of development [e.g., development on the Perry scheme and psychosocial development as defined by Chickering's (1969) vectors]; f represents the phrase "is a function of"; P_d is the developmental level of a person in a given developmental area(s) such as the Perry scheme or Chickering's vectors; E_s is the external stimuli of the environment as described by criteria for facilitating development derived from the developmental area(s) under consideration (e.g., the Perry scheme or Chickering's vectors); and $\times$ is the interaction defined by the degree of compatibility between a person and the environment as evaluated by the criteria for facilitating development derived from the theories under consideration. It is important to note that *both* the person and the environment

are assessed, not just one or the other, and *both* are evaluated in terms of *interaction* as defined by the *same developmental theories*.

When student development and campus ecology are combined, both P_d and E_s can be defined by various kinds of developmental theories. For example,

$$P_d = f(P_{cd}, P_{ps}, P_{pei}, P_t, \text{and/or } P_s) \qquad (3)$$

where P_{cd} represents cognitive developmental theories of human development such as those of Perry (1970), Kohlberg (1984), and Kegan (1982); P_{ps} represents psychosocial theories of development such as those of Erikson (1968), Chickering (1969), Levinson (1978), Josselson (1987); P_{pei} represents person-environment interaction theories and models such as those of Moos (1979), Pervin (1967), Barker (1968), and Stern (1970); P_t represents typological models and theories of personality type such as those of Jung (1971), Kolb (1976), Keirsey and Bates (1978), and Heath (1964); and P_s represents academic and life coping skills and attitudes such as assertiveness, problem-solving, interpersonal care-giving, and reading or note-taking skills.

Similarly, for E_s

$$E_s = f(E_{cd}, E_{ps}, E_{pei}, E_t, \text{and/or } E_s) \qquad (4)$$

where the subscripts represent the same families of theory as P_d.

Figure 13-1 summarizes this integration of student development theories into the person-environment interaction perspective. The person, the environment, and their interaction can be conceptualized and assessed from behavioral, psychosocial, cognitive-structural, humanistic-existential, person-environment, or typological points of view. The *same theoretical perspective(s) need to be used for all three assessments (P, E, and X)* and not one or the other. Mutual assumptions, constructs, and research bases allow for consistent interpretation of assessments, goal setting, environmental design criteria, and evaluation of outcomes.

If campus ecology is to focus on development in environmental redesign, then at least *one developmental theory* must be used in assessing the persons and the environment, in analyzing their interaction, in making decisions about redesigning the environment, and in evaluating the outcomes of the redesigned environment. It is important to note, however, that the use of *several*

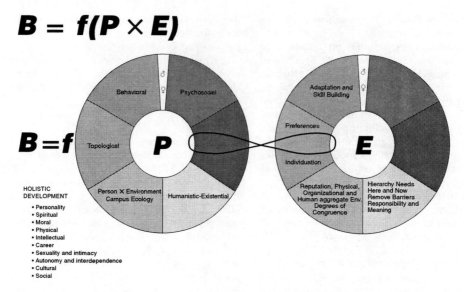

Integrating Student Development With Person-Environment Interaction

Figure 13-1 Integrating Student Development With Person-Environment Interaction

theoretical perspectives permits more sophisticated person-and-environment assessment and environmental design than the use of a single theory or no theory at all (Rodgers, 1983).

To sum up, in order to integrate student development within campus ecology and to focus on student development as an outcome, the following recommendations and observations are offered:

1. Use the person-environment interaction as the basic general paradigm for your work and then integrate developmental and other relevant theories into it;

2. Person-environment interaction models serve as reminders to assess three things, not just one or two of the following: (a) the *students*, (b) their *environment*, and (c) the degree of congruence or incongruence in their *interaction*;

3. Use theory, including at least one developmental theory, in making campus developmental and other theoretical ecological assessments; do not limit assessments to common-sense and atheoretical variables;

4. If *multiple types* of developmental and other theoretical frameworks are used, the

degree of individuation in environmental designs can be increased;

5. To determine whether or not environmental redesign is needed, use criteria derived from theories and your educational values to analyze and make judgments on the interaction data;

6. If redesign is needed, the nature of the redesign also derives from the assessment data as evaluated by theoretical criteria; and finally,

7. Evaluate outcomes of redesigned environments using measures of the developmental and other theories and atheoretical variables selected for a given project.

Cognitive-Developmental Theories

Cognitive-developmental theories attempt to describe the increasing degrees of complexity with which individuals make meaning of their experience with moral questions (Kohlberg, 1984), questions of knowing and valuing (Kitchener & King, 1981; Perry, 1970), questions of faith (Fowler, 1981), and questions of what is self and object (Kegan, 1982; Loevinger, 1976).

During the 1980s, with the exception of the theories of Carol Gilligan (1982, 1986a, 1986b) and Robert Kegan (1982), major new cognitive-developmental theories were not introduced as they were in the 1960s and especially in the 1970s. The past 10 years have been more of a period of testing the validity of these theories. More specifically, during the last 10 years some researchers have been examining questions of possible gender and cultural-ethnic differences in cognitive structural development. Other researchers have been conducting longitudinal studies in order to validate theoretical constructs or propositions.

Gender-Related Research

If you were planning a career development workshop, if you were counseling a married couple, if you were teaching a history course, if you were contemplating a set of policies and processes for student retention, or if you were mediating a residence hall roommate conflict, and if you were trying to use your students' cognitive-developmental levels as a guide to doing your work, would your work inherently be biased against women? Because many cognitive-developmental theories were developed using male subjects, the question has been raised whether cognitive-structural theories are gender-biased in favor of men. In other words, if you use cognitive-structural theories to plan your practice, are you inherently helping the development of men more than the development of women?

This issue of whether men and women make meaning in similar or different cognitive-structural ways has been the focus of research and speculation throughout the 1980s. The most famous theory in this regard is Gilligan's (1982) two voices of development, and the best known debate or discussion involves Kohlberg (1984) and Gilligan (1986a, 1986b). Kegan's (1982) theory and the Perry scheme (1970), however, also have been foci for research on gender issues.

Gilligan's Theory and the Kohlberg-Gilligan Debate/Discussion

While Gilligan was studying the relationships between moral reasoning and moral behavior using as subjects women who were considering whether or not to have abortions, she discovered a form of moral reasoning that she believed to be different from the reasoning described by Kohlberg (Gilligan, 1982). She called this different way of reasoning the *care and responsibility voice*, and, following Kohlberg's use of language, she called his descriptions of reasoning *the justice voice*.

The *care voice* may be characterized (Gilligan, 1982; Lyons, 1983) as emphasizing relationships between persons and seeing self and others as embedded in their specific situations. Within these situations care seeks to understand what the other needs and then to respond to these needs as defined by the other and not by the self. Moral dilemmas, therefore, are seen in terms of relationships, collaboration, maintaining and restoring relationships, and preventing psychological or physical harm, and are resolved through actions of support, healing, and care. On the night before he died, for example, Jesus of Nazareth is reported to have ministered to his disciples. He washed their feet, expressed love and care for them just as they were to love and serve others, and tried to prepare them to maintain their relationships with each other and with him through a new ritual of bread and wine. At the same time he claimed that one disciple would deny and another betray their relationship.

The *justice voice*, in contrast, is characterized as emphasizing the effects of moral choice on the self or on the other as the self would see it from the other's shoes. These effects are evaluated through rules and principles of fairness and relationships of reciprocity. Moral dilemmas are analyzed in terms of issues and conflicting claims among competing individuals or options. Duty and obligation are the result of impartial analysis using rules and principles of justice. For example, on the night before his death, in contrast to Jesus, Socrates and his friends engaged in a dispassionate analysis of the competing options open to him to escape or to stay in prison and face death. Using starting principles and logical analysis, Socrates concluded that he should not escape but stay in prison and die. His duty was clear.

Although the care voice was discovered using a female sample, Gilligan was careful to point out that subsequent research indicated that all men and women use both voices, but everyone prefers one voice over the other. The preferred voice is used most often and is probably better developed; the other voice is used sometimes even though it is not preferred. In the research reported by Gilligan and her colleagues (Gilligan, 1982, 1986a, 1986b; Lyons, 1983) most (about 80%) but not all women preferred the care voice, and most (about 70%) but not all men preferred the justice voice. Some women (about 20%) preferred the justice voice and some men (about 30%) preferred the care voice.

These associations of voice with majority and minority gender groups were not overridden even when care-voiced persons of both sexes were presented with a hypothetical dilemma that was formulated in terms of conflicting rights, and justice-voiced persons of both sexes were presented with a dilemma of conflicting responsibilities and relationships (Gilligan, 1986a; Johnston, 1985; Langdale, 1983). Both kinds of reasoning were used by both voices in response to both dilemmas. The care-voiced persons' use of justice reasoning increased on the justice dilemma and the justice-voiced persons' use of care reasoning increased on the relationships dilemma. Nevertheless, individuals' preferences were not overridden by the nature of the dilemma. Both groups still preferred and used most often the preferred voice. Hence, the situation (the nature of the dilemma) does affect reasoning, but does not seem to cancel voice preferences.

Kohlberg's scoring system uses justice-oriented dilemmas as the stimuli to which subjects respond, and his scoring manual is based on justice criteria for assigning stages to protocols. If such stimuli bring forth more justice responses, even from care-voiced persons, and if such rating criteria bring forth scores representing a care person as lower in developmental level than comparable justice persons, then there may be a systematic bias against the care voice in Kohlberg's theory and measure. Gilligan (1982, 1986a) believed that these biases do exist, and that care-voiced persons are handicapped within Kohlberg's theory and measurement system.

Kohlberg rejected Gilligan's proposition that his theory is biased and not universally applicable both to women and men. He argued (Kohlberg, 1984) that there is one justice structure of moral reasoning with two *styles* of expressing it. Gilligan's care voice is not a separate cognitive structure but a style that is similar to his substage A. Similarly, Gilligan's justice voice is his substage B, a second style for the *same* stage structures. Furthermore, if age, occupation,

and educational level are held constant, then Kohlberg maintained that the research (Denny, 1988; Gibbs, Arnold, & Burkhart, 1984; Walker, 1984) does not support the conclusion that men score higher than women using his or Gibbs's (Gibbs & Widaman, 1982) scoring systems.

Countering, Gilligan (1986a, 1986b) claimed that in two recent studies (Baumrind, 1986; Haan, 1985) where educational levels were controlled, women scored lower than men. In addition, Langdale (1983) performed a third study controlled for age, occupational level, and educational level; she found that persons with care orientations (86% women, 14% men) had significantly lower Kohlberg stage scores than did individuals with predominantly justice orientations (69% men, 31% women). This suggests ". . . that gender differences reported in Kohlberg's measure derive not from the fact of gender per se but rather from the greater tendency of females (and some males) to frame and resolve moral problems in the care orientation. . . . This finding in turn reflects the fact that Kohlberg conceived moral judgment within the single perspective of the justice orientation" (Gilligan, 1986a, p. 45).

So, the debate continues. The issues are not yet resolved. Is there one structure with two styles, or are there two structures? Is Kohlberg's measurement biased against the care orientation? Or, as he claims, do substages A and B correct for this criticism?

The debate is important because the differences in the two voices have practical implications for student affairs. Is it possible that *most* college teaching, student affairs programs, and even educational policies help one voice (justice) to be a detriment to the other (care)? For example, if classroom or workshop procedures focus only on the adequacy of a student's justice reasoning and perhaps use a debate as a forum for learning and as a stimulus for cognitive development, then that classroom or workshop is based on the assumption that care-voiced students learn best in the same environment as justice-voiced students. The development of care students has been equated with their ability to accept the questions, definitions, and teaching methods of the justice voice. Such processes may not be optimal for facilitating development of a care-oriented student.

Care-voiced persons seem to prefer *dialogue discussions*, where students rely on each other and their teacher or facilitator for understanding, comfort, and support (Gilligan, 1986a, p. 50). They prefer collaborative, supportive discussions instead of competitive debates. They prefer an interdependent atmosphere that empowers them to build and evolve relationships with each other and staff members and then to learn from one another by listening to each other. They do not prefer hierarchical classrooms or organizations that are structured around dominance and subordination or autonomous competition.

Gilligan (1986a; Lyons, 1983) also believed that the two voices have consequences beyond cognitive-structural development per se. There also may be two kinds of *identity formation*, two different processes for *resolving psychosocial issues* such as vocational choice, and two different ways of *constructing problems, making decisions*, and *resolving conflict*. Identity formation for a care-voiced person, for example, may best be facilitated within a framework of relationships and dialogue. Such a dialogue process places emphasis ". . . on speaking and listening, on being heard and making oneself understood, ties self-definition to an active engagement with others and turns attention to the process of communication" (Gilligan, 1986a, p. 51). In short, counseling rather than objective critical self-analysis would be a more appropriate paradigm for facilitating identity formation for care-voiced persons.

Gilligan argued that the two voices cannot be integrated into a single, unified entity. They are always in tension with each other. They are complementary processes for development, ways to construct problems and find solutions, and forms of identity. Sometimes justice might benefit from the *inclusiveness* of care; sometimes care might benefit from the *rational analysis* of justice. Nevertheless, to educate both voices requires student affairs to use processes applicable to both orientations and to give up what Perry (1970) might call the dualist's single right road to development.

Finally, if many women and some men prefer the care voice, what can said about the origins of the voices? Gilligan (1986b) described the type of activities that might lead women behaviorally to a care perspective, where Rodgers (1988) conceptualized the problem in terms of Jung/Myers personality types. Rodgers hypothesized that the underlying distinction between the two voices may be the Thinking (T) and Feeling (F) judgment preference as defined by Jung

(1971) and Myers (1980). He studied the voice orientations of equal numbers of dominant male and female Fs and dominant male and female Ts. Without exceptions, so far, he has found all of the Fs (both male and female) to be care-voiced and all of the Ts (both male and female) to be justice-voiced using Lyons's (1983) interview to measure voice. It is important to note that the T and F scales are the only dimension of the Myers-Briggs Type Indicator that also has revealed a gender difference in the population. Similar to Gilligan's findings, about 75% of the women have F preferences and 25% have T preferences, and about 75% of the men have T preferences and 25% have F preferences. These preliminary findings lend some support to an interpretation that the two voices originate in personality type at birth rather than in social conditioning. Cultural expectations for the sexes may bring experiences that reinforce personality type preference voices (e.g., female Fs and male Ts) or make some voices/types "swim upstream" (e.g., female Ts and male Fs). The voices of college students, therefore, may be exemplifications both of personality type preferences and social conditioning.

Robert Kegan's Theory

Robert Kegan's (1979, 1980a, 1980b, 1982) theory of ego development attempts to describe how we make meaning of *what is self* and *what is other*. That is, his theory describes the processes of differentiating *self* from *other* and then integrating *self* with *other* as the ego evolves throughout the life course. In addition, his work also helps clarify some of the issues that divide Gilligan and Kohlberg.

Kegan posited six cognitive structural stages similar to but broader than Kohlberg's stages. Kegan called his stages *temporary truces*—an equilibrium people establish for a time that provides the boundary between self/subject and other/object. Stages, therefore, are the ways a person settles the issue of what is *me* and what is *other*. It is the *psycho-logic* of individuals' meaning making. It is their *truth*. It defines *who they are*.

Thus, for example, at the stage of interpersonalism (Stage 3, the stage of many college students), people *are* their relationships. They are, in Kegan's terms, embedded in mutuality with their primary peer group. They cannot *be* without being in relationship. Hence, for many college students, nothing is as influential as the peer group, for "who they are" is defined by their relationships in these groups. Therefore, in a property damage situation in a residence hall, the self would rather help pay the damages than risk disapproval of the group by reporting the person actually responsible.

When the Stage 3 self evolves or develops, people differentiate the self as interpersonalism and make the psycho-logic of interpersonalism into an object. As individuals move to Stage 4 (institutionalism), they *have* relationships with peer groups as opposed to *being* those relationships. However, at Stage 4, the self is embedded in ideology, autonomy, and competence. People are now autonomous, ideological selves and self-consistency with their ideology is more important than relationships. Hence, they may act in opposition to peer norms and report the person responsible for damages. However, the institutional way of defining the self cannot be differ-

entiated; this self cannot yet examine itself as an object.

The stages of the evolving self are summarized in Table 1, which begins on page 000. The underlying tension in the evolution of the self outlined in Table 13-1 is the yearning toward *inclusion* and *connectedness* (Gilligan's care voice) and the yearning toward *autonomy* and *independence* (the justice voice). The nature of the self's boundaries emphasizes one and then the other yearning as individuals progress through life. Stages 1, 3, and 5 emphasize inclusion and connectedness. Stages 0, 2, and 4 emphasize separateness and autonomy.

Kegan argued that this alternating emphasis has significant implications for relationships, working with groups, and counseling. As indicated, at the interpersonal stage, college students are embedded in mutuality, in their relationships. They cannot separate who they are from their relationships. If their relationships with lovers

TABLE 13-1
The Evolving Self

Stage	What is Self? Subject? "I am this way of making meaning."	Become Object	What is Other? Object? "I relate to these old selves as object."
0: Incorporate Self	I am my reflexes such as moving, sensing. ↓ *new self*	↘	None.
1: Impulsive Self	I am my impulses and perceptions. ↓ *new self*	↘	I can relate to and consciously manipulate my reflexes, moving, sensing. ↓
2: Imperial Self	I am my needs, interests, and wishes. ↓ *new self*	↘	I now have and can consciously control my impulses and perceptions. ↓
3: Interpersonal Self	I am my interpersonal relationships, mutuality. ↓ *new self*	↘	I now have needs, interests, and I can control them. ↓
4: Institutional Self	I am my autonomy, my ideology, my identity. ↓ *new self*	↘	I now have interpersonal relationships but they don't define me. ↓
5: Interindividual Self	I am the interpenetrability of self systems. ↓ *new self*	↘	I now have self-definition ability, an ideology, identity, but I control them; they don't define me. ↓
6: ??	??		??

*Adapted from Kegan (1982). Adapted with permission of the publisher. From *The Evolving Self: Problem and Process in Human Development* by Robert Kegan, Cambridge, MA: Harvard University Press. Copyright © 1982 by the President and Fellows of Harvard College.

or fraternal groups come to an end, they may have strong feelings of dependency and loss of self. They may leave school rather than face peers without their lover or without being pledged to the right fraternal group.

Students at Stage 3 cannot settle or resolve conflicts between different but important interpersonal relationships. For example, the peer group and parents may have different norms on the issue of drinking alcoholic beverages before being of legal age. The student may behave one way with peers and another way at home. In each case, the student behaves according to the norms of the group, even though they are inconsistent. If these two worlds come together, however, such students often report feeling sad, wounded, or incomplete, but not angry at their friends or parents. They may become *depressed* and express their depression as feeling lonely, deserted, betrayed, and strained. The tension behind the depression results from being both vulnerable to what peers and family think of them and yet feeling selfish and uncaring if they begin to put themselves and a new set of values first.

Similarly to this analysis of Stage 3 and parallel with transitions between different stages of ego development, Kegan postulated three kinds of depression, each corresponding to the failure or inadequacy of a previous stage of ego development (see Table 13-2).

Sensitive staff and counselors can use both the stages and forms of depression in understanding and intervening with college students. The stages help them understand how students may be defining "self" and "other" as they attempt to resolve psychosocial developmental tasks. Emotional autonomy, for example, may require a student to move from seeing self as his or her relationships (Stage 3) to *having* relationships and *being* his or her autonomous ideology (Stage 4). Hence resolving the emotional autonomy aspect of Chickering's "developing autonomy may require a Stage 3 to Stage 4 cognitive-structural transition as a necessary but not sufficient condition for psychosocial developmental change.

The three forms of depressions may help student affairs professionals understand the pain often associated with cognitive-structural change. Students resist growth—because what must be given up is who they are, their being, their truth. Transition from one stage to another is a slow, painful, and sometimes *depressing* process. Kegan's theory (1982) helps student affairs professionals understand the differential kinds of depression students often experience and how to support them differentially through their process of change.

Gender Research on Intellectual or Epistemological Development

Just as Gilligan explored possible gender differences in moral development, similar gender-based questions have been explored for the Perry scheme and to some degree for Kitchener and King's (1981, 1985a, 1985b; King, 1982; King, Kitchener, Davison, Parker, & Wood, 1983; Kitchener, 1986) Reflective Judgment model. Do college women systematically score lower than

TABLE 13-2
Types of Depression

Type of Depression	Transition	Characteristics
Type A	Concerns transition from Stage 2 to 3	Concern over loss of needs; unhappiness at cost of meeting needs; feels constrained, controlled, yet feels compromised.
Type B	Concerns transition from Stage 3 to 4	Concern with loss and damage to interpersonal relationships; feels lonely, deserted, betrayed, abandoned; feels tension between being vulnerable to fusion with others and feeling selfish, heartless, and cold if puts self first. "If I lose my relationships, I will cease to be."
Type C	Concerns transition from Stage 4 to 5	Concern with failure to meet own standards, to control oneself or perform as one should or is expected to perform. Feels humiliated, out of control; life is unfair and meaningless. Feels tension between self-criticism and isolation and feeling out of control, ineffective, and evil.

*Adapted from Kegan (1982). Adapted with permission of the publisher. From *The Evolving Self: Problem and Process in Human Development* by Robert Kegan. Cambridge, MA: Harvard University Press. Copyright © 1982 by the President and Fellows of Harvard College.

college men on intellectual or epistemological development? If you use Perry's or Kitchener and King's theories to plan your practice, are you inherently helping men more than women? Do women reason with different epistemological structures than men? Or, if they do not use different structures, are there different styles of making meaning within the same structures? If there are different structures or styles, what difference does it make for professional practice?

Upon entry to college, generally women have scored slightly higher than men on intellectual development in several studies at various institutions (Heidke, 1982; Omahan, 1982; Rodgers, 1974–1988), or no differences have been found between the genders (Baxter Magolda, 1987, 1988a, 1988b, 1989; Brabeck, 1984; Kitchener & King, 1985a; Kitchener & King, 1985b; Moore, 1982). First-year students have scored predominantly at Position 2, between 2 and 3, or at Position 3, using both theories.

Seniors, on the other hand, generally have scored between Positions 3 and 4 or at Position 4, also on both theories, with men usually scoring slightly higher than women (Heidke, 1982; Kitchener & King, 1985a, 1985b; Omahan, 1982; Welfe & Davison, 1986). Hence, it seems that women start college slightly ahead of or equal to men; however, they finish college slightly behind. Institutions of higher education, therefore, seem to have more effect on the intellectual or epistemological development of men than the development of women. Why is that? What in the environment of the college experience might account for this difference? Are there two structures or styles of epistemological development, and is the college experience biased toward one more than the other? Belenky, Clinchy, Goldberger, and Tarule (1986) and Baxter Magolda (1987, 1988a, 1988b, 1989) explored these issues, and their works deserve careful consideration and analysis.

In *Women's Ways of Knowing*, Belenky et al. (1986) described five ways of knowing derived from their study of women. Their five positions seem to share epistemological structures with Perry's scheme; however, there are significant differences in how Perry's men and Belenky's women come to change their ways of knowing and how the positions are expressed once known. Table 13-3 summarizes *both* schemes and contrasts their similarities and differences.

An analysis of this table indicates that the differences in men and women occur in the categories of View of Self and View of Authority. They do not occur in the View of Knowledge. The structural category is View of Knowledge, whereas View of Self and View of Authority are behavioral correlates with the structures. Hence, the differences found by Belenky et al. (1986) seem to be *stylistic* rather than *structural*. Baxter Magolda (1987, 1988a, 1988b, 1989) independently reached similar conclusions.

Baxter Magolda (1988a, 1988b) is studying possible gender differences longitudinally with a male and female sample using her measure of the Perry scheme, the Measure of Epistemological Reflection (MER), and a semi-structured interview. The MER (Baxter Magolda & Porterfield, 1985) was developed and normed using both men and women; therefore it should be sensitive to stylistic differences between the sexes. The interviews were designed to examine possible structural differences. After 2 years in college, her sample has revealed stylistic but not structural differences during both years. Specifically, Position 2 women wanted authorities to provide them with answers while they listened, wanted a relaxed and nonconfrontive atmosphere, wanted others to ask the questions, and advocated studying together in groups. They saw areas of uncertainty as places where authorities had different opinions about the facts. Men, on the other hand, felt authorities expected them to look up answers and not just listen, expected learning to be interesting, and saw evaluation as a time to be corrected. Uncertainty was seen as caused by different degrees of detail among authorities.

At Position 3, women gained a new perspective through discussions, sought the support of teachers, preferred experiential learning and organized classes, and believed they would find answers to uncertainties sometime in the future or by adding up positive factors associated with options. Men emphasized being forced to think, identified with their teachers, sought fairness in evaluation, and evaluated using logic. Hence, Baxter Magolda's findings are similar to the results of Belenky et al. and Gilligan.

To sum up, Belenky et al. and Perry seem to describe two different styles of knowing within one epistemological structure. Baxter Magolda's MER seems to be sensitive to both styles, and she

TABLE 13-3
Perry Scheme Compared to *Women's Ways of Knowing*

Position	*Perry* Name	*Belenky et al.* Name	Similarities	Differences
1	Basic Quality	Silence	*View of Knowledge* • Single absolute right and wrong answers. Cannot perceive authority as making errors • Knowing is observing, hearing without evaluation, and then obeying *View of Authority* • Tell you what to do, not why *View of Self as Learner* • Concrete and not conceptual • Silent, passive, obedient • Dependent on authorities and obey blindly • Authorities are right and overpowering	
2	Multiplicity Prelegitimate	Received Knowledge	*View of Knowledge* • What is known is true, absolutely • Good authorities have truth; bad ones do not • Learners receive truth from authorities • Questions are right or wrong, true or false • You collect right answers; you do not construct them • Facts are true; opinion does not count • Diversity is due to poor authorities who are wrong; therefore, diversity is an illusion *View of Authority* • Have right answers and give them to you • Bad authorities are mistaken or wrong *View of Self as Learner* • Listening is the way to learn • Receive knowledge, not source of it • Intolerant of ambiguity; literalist in interpretation	*View of Authority* • (W) are awed by authorities; do not identify with authorities; authorities are they, not we • (M) do identify with authorities; authorities are we *View of Self as Learner* • (W) not confident of ability to contribute • (M) speak up to let authorities know that they've learned

continued

TABLE 13-3 (*continued*)
Perry Scheme Compared to *Women's Ways of Knowing*

Position	*Perry Name*	*Belenky et al. Name*	*Similarities*	*Differences*
2 (continued)			*View of Self as Learner* • Prefer clarity, predictability, structure, precise and detailed expectations • Perceive diversity of opinion exists	*View of Self as Learner* • (W) listen to authorities or to discussions of peers who know; listen actively; dislike debate • (M) listen and argue or debate; discussion is waste of time because only authorities have truth; peers do not
3 Perry only	Multiplicity Subordinate	Comparable position not described	None because no equivalent described	*Male View of Knowledge* • Some knowledge is known absolutely; all is knowable in principle • We may not know yet; someday we will • When we know, it must be right. If we don't know yet, then how do we search? Absolutize the method of search • Diversity of opinion is legitimate in areas where don't know yet *View of Authority* • Authorities tell us what is right when we know, and teach us how to search when we don't know *View of Self as Learner* • Receive by listening, observing when we know; helping search when we don't know • Learn methods of searching and use them because they are the right processes
3 Belenky et al.		No such position		
4 Perry	Multiplicity	Subjective knowledge	*View of Knowledge* • No longer absolute right or wrong • Is subjective, right only for me and nobody else • All opinions are of equal value because there are no absolute criteria for deciding • Each person has own truth	

TABLE 13-3 (*continued*)
Perry Scheme Compared to *Women's Ways of Knowing*

Position	Perry Name	Belenky et al. Name	Similarities	Differences
4 Perry (*continued*)			*View of Authority* • Not absolute authorities • Redefine authority as just another outside opinion no better than mine • Do not have to accept what they say • Their opinions can be bad for you *View of Self as Learner* • Active explorer for own opinions and beliefs • Liberated from tyranny of absoluteness • New sense of autonomy and self-directedness • Can hold contradictory beliefs	*View of Self as Learner* • (W) Self's truth is personally intuited and perhaps uncommunicable • (M) Self is defender of everyone's *right* to have own opinion; resist authorities who pretend to to have answers; publicly give their opinion • (W) Style is less public; opinion held inside and often not expressed; fear open expression of opinions and desires • (W) Less confident about their opinions and beliefs and want others to affirm their views • (W) Subjective truth is felt and is not thought about logically; tolerate differences rather than being an advocate for rights. Advocation can lead to unpleasant conflicts • (W) Distrust logic and analysis • (M) Opinions tend to be expressed and thought out logically
4 Belenky et al. 5 Perry	Relativism	Procedural knowledge	*View of Knowledge* • Results from use of nonabsolute criteria such as reasoned reflection • Subjective truth can be wrong or hurtful • Move from subjective to rational criteria for making judgments on what is known	

continued

TABLE 13-3 (*continued*)
Perry Scheme Compared to *Women's Ways of Knowing*

Position	Perry Name	Belenky et al. Name	Similarities	Differences
5 Perry (*continued*)			*View of Self as Learner* • Try new way of thinking that authority recommends	*View of Self as Learner* • (W) *Procedural preoccupation* with obtaining and passing on knowledge; especially prefer a sensitive counselor/teacher • (M) New way to think is a logical argument to meet standards of an impersonal authority in the field; need to master a field objectively • (W) New way is an inner need to understand and to have a personal connection with knowledge, to develop a commitment to it • (M) *Separate* knowing style *Be doubting*: doubt and apply logical criticism, especially to ideas based on feelings *Use reason*: learn to analyze and evaluate arguments. Use critical discourse with others, whether know them or not *Debate*: paradigm of desired adversarial process of learning and growth is a debate *Be adversarial and competitive*: learning procedures are adversarial, but with fair rules. Competitive comparisons are emphasized *Public*: public presentation of views for criticisms by others is emphasized *Separate self from ideas (objective)*: impersonal analysis is valued; must learn to divorce self from your ideas; personal beliefs or commitments are excluded and not trusted

TABLE 13-3 (*continued*)
Perry Scheme Compared to *Women's Ways of Knowing*

Position	Perry Name	Belenky et al. Name	Similarities	Differences
5 Perry (*continued*)				• (W) *Connected* learning style *Experiential base*: The most trusted knowledge comes from personal experience. How does one gain access to the experiential and personal bases of others' views of a theory? *Empathetic*: Empathetic listening, drawing out, and clarifying are preferred means of knowing and developing. Establish connected knowing groups before sharing and learning together *Conversation, not debate*: Clinical-like interview is paradigm of the valueed procedure. Tell one's story without interruption, then clarify. Question only when relationship is established and listening and clarification has occurred *Clarify, don't judge*: Listen, draw out, understand but don't judge others' views. Must build trust to have a relationship. Must have relationship to get at understanding. Judgment destroys trust. That is, judgment is a threat to connectedness *Collaborative and personal*: Bring tentative ideas to a connected group and collaboratively work on them. Nurture ideas given and help clarify them. Person and ideas stay connected in a personal journey for knowledge

continued

TABLE 13-3 (*continued*)
Perry Scheme Compared to *Women's Ways of Knowing*

Position	*Perry* *Name*	*Belenky et al.* *Name*	*Similarities*	*Differences*

5
Both
Belenky
et al. &
Perry
	Relativity	Constructed
		knowledge
			View of Knowledge
			• Constructed: Knowledge
			  is constructed and knower
			  is part of known
			• Contextual: Knowledge is
			  contextual and answers of
			  better or worse vary due to
			  context in which question
			  is asked and personality and
			  experience of person asking
			• Never-ending: Search for
			  truth is a never-ending
			  construction	

			View of Self as Learner and
			View of Authority
			• Self and authorities are on a
			  joint journey to construct
			  truth
			• Competence, not role,
			  defines authority
				View of Self as Learner
				• (W) *Passion and*
				  commitment: Passionate
				  pursuit and commitment of
				  self to understand and
				  connect with others'
				  constructions. Attend to
				  others, feel related to them,
				  and seek to understand
				  their assumptions and
				  experience. Encounter them
				  only after hearing their story
				  and clarifying it.
				• (W) Self is related to what
				  it is trying to understand
				  and know
				• (W) *Connected learning*
				  style
				• (M) *Separate knowing style*

also finds similar stylistic differences between her male and female students, but not structural differences. Stylistic differences are important because of their implications for differential ways of teaching and offering student affairs programs. Given that men seem to enter college behind or equal to women in intellectual development and leave college ahead, there is some support to conclude that the environments of colleges cater more to the male, Separate, or T style than to the female, Connected, or F style. As Gilligan emphasized, if one voice, style, or type goes untutored due to biased learning environments, then everything we do in student affairs and college teaching may need to be systematically redesigned to accommodate two voices, styles, or types.

Recently Astin (1987) and Palmer (1987) seemed to agree. They characterized the environment of higher education as competitive rather than collaborative, individualistic rather than communal, objective rather than related, and exclusive rather than inclusive. They called for radical reform, not just of structures but also of higher education's inherent *ways* of *knowing*. If the way of knowing stays in the *separate* style, they believed reform efforts would fail. Reform efforts should, from their viewpoint, accommodate the care voice, the connected and communal way of knowing, and the F form of judgment. Furthermore, the reform efforts must manifest themselves in the reward structures, desired outcomes, how programs are taught and what programs and services are offered, and who is hired as faculty and staff.

Psychosocial Theories

Psychosocial development refers to the issues, tasks, and events that occur throughout the life span, and to a given person's pattern of resolution of the issues and tasks, and adaptation to the events (Rodgers, 1984b). Some of the issues, tasks, and events are *age-graded*, that is, their timing, duration, and nature are similar for many individuals of the same chronological age. For example, most 18- to 23-years-olds in our culture struggle to determine who they are (identity), who they will love (sexuality and intimacy), and what they will believe (values and lifestyle). Some of the issues, tasks, and events are *history-graded*, that is, they are normative for a given age group due to the group's unique historical experience. The civil rights era or Great Depression, for example, are unique historical events that have influenced the development of a given cohort of college students but not others. Finally, some are *unanticipated life events*. For example, an unexpected illness or death of a parent can influence the development of a college student in negative ways.

College environments (e.g., programs, relationships, policies) appropriately challenge and facilitate the resolution of tasks and adaptations to events or get in the way and hinder development. The *content* of the tasks and events, the *skills* needed to cope with them, and the dynamics or *processes* involved in resolution and adaptation all provide the criteria for evaluating or designing college environments. A review follows of selective research on psychosocial age-graded tasks of college students in terms of content, skills, and processes.

Similar to the cognitive developmental family of theory, research on psychosocial development during the 1980s concentrated more on testing and validating theories than on introducing new theories. Gender, socioeconomic, and cultural-ethnic differences once again were the foci of research. Studies examined the degree to which the psychosocial development of men and women, Blacks and Whites, rural and urban populations, or individuals in various socioeconomic classes is the same or different. Each of these issues is important and will be viewed selectively.

Gender Research

In research on women, Baruch, Barnett, and Rivers (1983) studied the sources of feelings of mastery and pleasure in women's lives, Straub and Rodgers (1986) and Straub (1987) the development of autonomy, and Josselson (1987) the development of identity. In research on men, Farrell and Rosenberg (1981) studied development in the 20s and 40s age ranges for various socioeconomic classes in both urban and rural environments. Finally, for both sexes, Branch-Simpson (1984) studied the developmental tasks of traditionally aged Black college students and compared the results with Chickering's vectors.

Baruch and Barnett (1980) and Baruch et al. (1983) studied how the number and types of roles in a woman's life may act as moderating variables in how women adapt to life events and resolve adult developmental tasks. The patterns of life roles under study were: (a) never married, (b) married with children, (c) married without children, and (d) divorced with children. The sample was randomly selected from a single town in Massachusetts. All the never-married and divorced women in the sample were employed, as were half of the married women selected. Random selection led to approximately equal numbers of high-, medium-, and low-prestige jobs.

Generally, Baruch and Barnett sought to describe the sources of pleasure and mastery in the lives of women in the different role patterns. They found that 88% of all these women had a strong sense of pleasure and mastery. The main source of mastery was competent skill in a job that had high prestige. The main sources of pleasure were relationships with spouse, children, family of origin, friends, or work colleagues. Many women in all of the life patterns reported satisfying lives; however, the right combination of roles seemed to be the key to well-being.

Divorce as a life event forced the divorced women in this study to grow. It forced them to provide both materially and psychologically for themselves. These women became more instrumentally and emotionally self-sufficient rather than dependent.

Marriage and children generally were sources of pleasure; however, if a woman overidentified with her spouse or her children, she was vulnerable. The loss of spouse or children would leave such a woman without an identity because she defined the self almost exclusively in terms of others. Married women at home with children were satisfied but also felt that current society viewed their traditional combination of roles negatively.

Never-married women scored lower than married women; however, single women with high-prestige jobs scored high enough to have very satisfying lives. The problem for single women, therefore, was not being single per se but the combination of being single combined with a low-prestige job. This combination of roles yielded the lowest sense of pleasure and mastery.

The best combination of roles was wife, mother, and high-prestige job holder. These women reported the highest levels of pleasure and mastery, and they did not report the high levels of stress predicted for this combination of roles.

It seems, therefore, that counselors and student affairs staff should note that both single women with careers and women with husbands, children, and jobs can have satisfying lives. There was not a single psychosocial pattern of well-being for women in this study. In addition, the work implies that the development of instrumental and emotional autonomy (Chickering, 1969) during the college years may be especially important for the well-being of women in later adulthood.

Straub and Rodgers (1986) and Straub (1987) studied the achievement of autonomy in women, and their work can help illuminate the types of experiences that have helped women internalize the capacity for instrumental and emotional self-sufficiency. Using the Bem Sex Role Inventory, Straub and Rodgers (1986) found that college women with androgynous and masculine orientations tended to resolve the tasks of instrumental and emotional autonomy during college. Feminine and Undifferentiated women, on the other hand, not only did not become autonomous individuals during college, but they tended to remain dependent well into their late 30s. Is it the case that Feminine and Undifferentiated college women become the mothers Baruch and Barnett (1980) described who overidentify with their spouses and children and are dependently vulnerable at mid-life? Additional research is needed to answer questions such as this.

Straub (1987) followed up with the women who scored high in autonomy. She conducted critical incident interviews with these women to discover the types of events that contributed to their development of autonomy and the aspects of those events that were significant or meaningful. Briefly, the categories of events associated with achieving autonomy included: (a) significant relationships with men or parents (38.5%), (b) educational experiences (37%) both in the classroom (15.5%) and student affairs areas such as residence halls or student organizations (21%), (c) work experiences (4%), (d) uprooting family experiences (10%), and (e) personal experiences with counseling or personal growth workshops (8%). The significant aspects of these experiences were: (a) having to be "on their own" in a residence hall and then in an apartment (33%), (b) "taking risks" that lead to insights about oneself and about sources of personal stress (24%), (c) "overcoming obstacles" in academic or job achievement (7%), and (d) learning that dependence on men or parents results in enormous personal losses in areas such as career, educational pursuits, and personal identity (17%). Seventy three percent of the events related directly to instrumental or emotional autonomy as conceptualized by Chickering (1969), and 27% related to developing autonomy through freeing interpersonal relationships with significant others or parents.

In terms of the college environment, 22% of the experiences related to classroom or academic obstacles and 29% related to experiences with student affairs programs and services outside the classroom. Combining classroom and student affairs experiences, 51% of the events occurred in the college environment and 49% occurred in other environments.

Finally, Josselson's (1987) longitudinal study of identity development in women from their first year in college through age 34 seems especially significant. Josselson's research is based on Marcia's (1966, 1976, 1980; Marcia & Friedman, 1970) model and research on identity statuses. Guided by Erikson, Marcia described two dimensions in identity formation: (a) conscious experience of an identity crisis to be resolved and (b) commitment to a sense of self or identity after deliberate exploration of options. The combination of the two dimensions yields four paths as summarized in Table 13-4.

Each of these paths has important characteristics and dynamics that student affairs professionals could profit from knowing.

TABLE 13-4
Marcia's Identity Model

		Conscious of an identity crisis and its issues	
		NO	YES
Commitment to identity after exploring options	NO	Diffuse	Moratorium
	YES	Foreclosed	Achieved

Notes.
Foreclosed: Women who have never felt an identity crisis or explored options but who are rigidly committed to a childhood vision of their identity.
Diffuse: Women who never experienced an identity crisis in college, never explored options, and have not committed to an identity at the end of college.
Moratorium: Women who felt an identity crisis during college, explored identity issues, but left college still exploring and unresolved.
Achieved: Women who felt an identity crisis during college, explored options, achieved an individualized sense of self, and have committed to an identity.

Foreclosed

At the end of college, 24% of Josselson's women were "foreclosed." (The percentages are based upon 34 of the original 60 subjects in the study.) They had made commitments to an identity without experiencing a crisis or deliberately exploring options. These women needed *to feel loved and cared for.* They saw only one course for their lives—getting married, having children, and having close family relationships. Security and harmony were prominent needs. A close-knit family, turned in on itself, was their source of security. Childhood identifications with family of origin seemed to be the source of their foreclosed identity. They held their goals rigidly and without doubt. These women were going to continue the beliefs, sex-role orientations, and values on sexual behavior of their parents without rethinking or testing them in any way. They resisted the influences of the classroom, extracurricular college experiences, and peer influences during college. They did not change.

These foreclosed women had histories of difficult peer relationships and never identified with a primary peer group during college. They had possessive and fearful mothers and warm fathers. They passed through college remaining close to their mothers, did not experiment, and graduated seeing things as their mothers did. They were judgmental rather than empathic, and their judgments were absolutely right or wrong.

At age 34 these foreclosed women had high self-esteem and low anxiety. They seemed to be functioning well and still held rigidly to their college views of an ideal life. They had not changed at all. They had resisted today's pluralistic culture just as they had resisted college's potential influences for change. Many had fulltime jobs but cared only about their private family lives. Career success was not a goal in their lives. They had a strong sense of duty to family and conservative moral values. Their identities continued to be assigned from the outside and held rigidly. They had not resolved issues of autonomy or interdependence. The only hint of Baruch and Barnett's vulnerability for overidentified women was found in those who experienced divorce. Divorce precipitated an identity crisis on foreclosed women, forcing them to change to deal with issues of self-sufficiency.

Hence, from the freshman year in college until age 34, foreclosed women apparently derive both a sense of mastery and pleasure from relationships in their families. They make meaning in Perry's dualism during college and adulthood. They are not autonomous or interdependent. They identify totally with their families and rigidly hold conservative values. Most were functioning well and satisfied with their lives at age 34, but the clouds of mid-life were on the horizon.

Diffuse

At the end of college, 23% of Josselson's women were identity diffuse. They had not experienced a crisis, explored options, nor committed to an

TABLE 13-5
Four Patterns of Diffusion

Subgroup name	(Percentage)		Percentage
Severe psychopathology	(Not reported)		
Many unresolved previous developmental tasks	(Not reported)	[Combined]	50%
Moratorium diffuse	(19%)		
Foreclosure diffuse	(31%)	[Combined]	50%

identity. Josselson differentiated this group into four (4) subgroups (see Table 13-5).

The subgroup labeled *severe psychopathology* and *previously unresolved tasks* had histories of traumatic abuse or neglect by unhealthy parents. By their freshman year, nothing was working in their lives. They had undifferentiated sex-role orientations. They were impulsive (similar to Kegan's Stage 2 of ego development), tried to avoid feeling guilty, and were unstable and unreliable. They failed to develop the inner capacities for intimacy, autonomy, or interdependence. The self fluctuated widely and there was no inner sense of self. They were at the mercy of today's experiences and impulses without the capacity to learn from their experiences.

The *moratorium diffuse* subgroup (19%), in contrast, had experienced an identity crisis; however, their crises were deeper than those of most of the other women in the study. They struggled with deep philosophical questions about the meaning of life and explored radical options involving drugs, sex, and religious sects. Their college years were characterized by movements in and out of moratorium and diffusion.

The *foreclosed diffuse* subgroup (31%) were characterized as acting on the demands of their immediate situation without a consistent sense of direction. This group's parents were also diffuse and left all decision making in the hands of their daughters. The parents could offer neither guidance nor role models. The women seemed to cling to what little security their families could provide and then waited to see what fate would bring. They adopted, in turn, whatever came. They graduated with nowhere to go and had no idea how to proceed with their lives.

By age 34, the moratorium and foreclosure subgroups had been in and out of counseling on several occasions. Their solution to the identity issue was to not solve it. They moved in and out

of jobs and accepted whatever the environment seemed to be saying that they should be. Various authority figures organized a temporary self for them. From the four combined subgroups, 33% briefly tried to create identities and then fell back into diffusion; 33% established some kind of identity through the help of authorities who structured their lives; 22% died in their 20s, and 11% were still trying to establish identity.

Moratorium

At the end of college, 29% of the longitudinal sample were classified as being in *moratorium*. As college students, these women were aware that they had to make choices to define themselves but they were not yet able to do so. They seemed to be paralyzed in their crisis and awareness.

These women were concerned about social problems, had a capacity for empathy, and were concerned about philosophical questions. They had dreams of careers in helping others and solving social problems but did not know how to make their idealistic dreams become reality. They tested and searched. They had lower self-esteem and greater levels of anxiety than achieved or foreclosed women. By age 34, three had achieved identity, one was still struggling in moratorium, and six had retreated into more-or-less foreclosed identities similar to those of their childhood families.

The dynamics of the college years for moratorium women are especially important for student affairs professionals because they may provide cues for developmental interventions. Women classified in moratorium did loosen family ties, unlike foreclosed and diffuse women. They tended to find boyfriends who were different from their families. The boyfriends they chose, however, often became substitute parents. That is, the women remained dependent or even more dependent on their controlling boyfriends than they had been on their parents.

Like the foreclosed women, the moratorium women had overprotective mothers who indulged them, and they felt guilty over betraying the norms of their mothers, especially in sexual behavior. Those who were able to tolerate their guilt went on to achieve identity; those who could not, retreated toward foreclosure.

These women would daydream rather than really exploring careers. They needed relationships to bolster their self-esteem and to show them how to be different or uniquely themselves. They needed healthy models, but more often chose and obeyed controlling boyfriends with different sexual values. They were not yet autonomous or interdependent at graduation and usually chose the wrong resources to help them achieve these inner capacities. They needed supportive rather than controlling relationships during college.

Achieved

Twenty four percent of Josselson's longitudinal sample were identity achieved. These women had felt an identity crisis, separated from their families, explored options, and chosen their own identities and life-styles. Although the content of their identities differed, they used a common process.

All of the achieved women were able to separate themselves from needing parental or peer group sanctions. They became individualized persons, capable of inner self-reliance. This internal liberation involved several common ingredients: These women did not retreat from rejections, even though they were painful; they developed an internalized sense of competence in and out of the classroom; and they had the capacity to tolerate their sense of guilt as they explored options.

The common process also involved a common pattern; that is, all of these women defined the self as a *self in relationships*. They emphasized interdependence rather than autonomy. Their identity was a related identity, usually with a boyfriend with whom they had a mutually supportive, interdependent relationship. Their boyfriends were not controlling but supportive.

As adults, the achieved women had consciously examined and reworked their identities by age 34. They had the highest self-esteem and low levels of anxiety. They were flexible, open to new experiences, self-confident, and not dependent on external sources for meaning. Work was a source of mastery and pleasure but was not the key ingredient in their identity as it was for men of this age (Levinson, 1978; Vaillant, 1977). The adult self was a *balance* of work, relationships, and other interests, with *relationships* being the key ingredient in the balance.

Summary and Comparison

Each of Baruch and Barnett's role combinations (married with no children, married with children but no job, married with children and job, single) are found in each of the four different identity statuses of Josselson's women. One could infer from Josselson's data that the pattern of roles may not be as important in the well-being of women as the identity status of the individual. For example, a woman in her mid-30s could be married with children and be foreclosed, diffuse, achieved, or in moratorium. Only foreclosed and achieved women seemed to have a sense of well-being, and a high-status job did not seem to be a central issue for either.

Of Kegan's two basic issues in life, *separateness* and *togetherness*, togetherness, or connectedness, was central to the identity development of most of Josselson's women. Those who achieved identity opted to stay attached as they became self-confident, assertive, and masters of their own lives. Their problem was how to separate, how to be different, and yet how to stay connected as they went through this process.

The process and nature of identity formation for Josselson's women were different, therefore, from those of men. Whereas men often separate from their families as they form and live their identities, these women tended to stay connected. The issues that concern men and women as they separate also tended to differ. Whereas Josselson reported that men focus on politics, religion, and careers in separating themselves from their families, her women were concerned with religious traditions, whom to choose as friends, sexual behavior, and whom and when to marry. Most of Josselson's women used relationships with men, staff, or friends to help them separate from their mothers' priorities.

Work was important but secondary in the lives of Josselson's women, and even avocational interests could be more important than careers in defining the self. When career was the most important thing in a woman's life, the woman had a mentor with whom she had a supportive, facilitative relationship. The absence of a mentor had significant consequences for using career as an anchor for identity. In order to be an anchor for identity, ". . . work has to matter to someone who matters to her" (Josselson, 1987, p. 177).

Many identity achieved women became disillusioned with work. Most of these women's career goals included "helping others," and this goal often was not a top priority of the bureaucracies and businesses in which they worked. As a consequence, for these women, avocations rather than their jobs often became the outlet for this goal.

Finally, friendships were the anchor relationships for identity achieved women only if other relationships were tried and rejected. Friends came to play some of the same roles as husbands and mentors, that is, they were people with whom the women could discuss a problem, find support, and obtain logistical help.

Farrell and Rosenberg's (1981) study of men offers the closest comparative study to Josselson's women. Farrell and Rosenberg studied 500 men, 200 between 25 and 30 years old and 300 between 38 and 48. They identified urban, suburban, and rural districts in the northeast zone of the United States, and then classified each area by socioeconomic class (SEC). Districts, neighborhoods, blocks, and houses were then selected randomly by SEC, and the authors studied the men who lived in the houses selected. The resulting sample was statistically representative of the general population of men in this country.

Generally, regardless of SEC or rural-urban background, Farrell and Rosenberg found that a common set of issues tended to confront each of their subjects at mid-life. Some of these issues seemed to be biologically determined, but the majority seemed to be derived from psychological or societal motivations.

Mid-life was a time of fundamental reassessment but not necessarily a crisis for the men in this study. They reexamined their careers, their marital relationships, and relationships with their children, parents, and friends. Approximately 33% of the sample confronted and resolved these issues. Most (approximately 67%) denied or avoided the issues. The common set of issues and differential outcomes are especially instructive.

In their 20s, regardless of SEC or urban or rural background, the men in this study were absorbed in their world of work. Whether their careers were foreclosed, unstable and drifting, purposefully in exploration, or mature commitments, identity and relationships were *organized around work*. For many men, however, work was a source of defeat rather than success. Socioeconomic class and past developmental history correlated with differential career outcomes.

At mid-life, most of these men felt committed *both* to work and family relationships; however, internal self-experience became more focused on the family for the first time. That is, many of these men began to view wife, children, and material characteristics of the home as expressions of and support for the self, a self often frustrated at work. At mid-life, however, children were beginning their separation or individuation from the family, and spouses often were becoming more autonomous and achievement-oriented. Many wives in this study wanted to move away from being expressions of and support for their husbands, just as the husbands wanted "nothing to change." Thus, for many men in this study, the development of family members disrupted their use of family to make up for career frustrations. They were being asked to facilitate and support the others rather than use the others as their refuge. They, in effect, were being asked to switch to a more connected identity from a separate identity, to support more rather than be supported. The problem was to establish intimate, care-oriented relationships with spouse, children, and parents; for these men, this was a more complex and difficult task than their career problems. Work, however, also was a mid-life issue.

Career possibilities were shrinking at mid-life for these men. There were fewer illusions about advancement, fewer openings, and stiffer competition. Dreams were measured against realities, whether the men were foreclosed, searching, diffuse, or achieved. The expansive future of youth gave way to particular options in the present, or lack thereof.

At mid-life, biological or physical body decline was clearly present. This decline also affected these men's images of themselves and how they related to the world.

Finally, just as men were expected to be at their height of social and family responsibility and to be pillars of emotional strength for others, they needed a moratorium in order to explore the changes that were going on within themselves. They needed to negotiate a new or revised identity.

A factor analysis of data received from these men yielded four styles of coping with the demands of mid-life and four outcomes. The two dimensions that define the four styles are as follows: (a) alienation—integration, and (b) denial—openness. The four developmental pathways are summarized in Table 13-6.

Generative

Professional, middle-class men who lived in urban areas had the best internal and external resources to resolve the issues of mid-life, and this group made up most but not all of the 33% who successfully negotiated mid-life. Careers and autonomy became less important for these men, whereas intimacy and interdependence with spouse, children, and parents became more important. They reformed their identities, adjusted their life structures (Levinson, 1978), became or stayed open to feelings and new experiences, and facilitated the individuation of their young adult children. They paralleled Josselson's identity achieved group, although the nature of their issues differed.

Punitive-Disenchanted

Unskilled laborers in rural and urban locations had the least internal and external resources to deal with mid-life. These men had the same personal disorientations and psychopathology as Josselson's diffuse women. They began the college years developmentally behind and they never recovered. In their 20s these men were alienated, unstable, and prejudiced. By mid-life they denied that they had faults and projected the negative happenings in their lives onto minority groups and their own children. They were authoritarian, reported high degrees of anxiety and depression, and had many physical illnesses. They roamed from job to job and did not have stable relationships. They were in serious physical and mental decline.

Pseudodeveloped

The majority of the sample were lower- and middle-class skilled workers, clerical personnel, and owners of small businesses. These men divided into two groups, one called "pseudo-developed" and the other "crisis type." The "pseudo-developed" group resembled Josselson's foreclosed group in their psychological makeup. They *denied* that they were experiencing the stress and issues of mid-life and *tried to avoid* dealing with them. They claimed to be satisfied with their lives, yet their attitudes were rigid and prejudiced. They denied feelings. They exhibited a great deal of authoritarianism and covert depression and anxiety. They avoided new situations, people, or ideas, and rigidly tried to hang onto their highly structured and self-centered lives.

TABLE 13-6
Four Developmental Pathways for Men

	Denial	Openness
	Punitive-Disenchanted	**Crisis Type**
	Deny issues and stresses	Openly confront stress and issues
Alienation	Alienated	
	Unstable and bigoted history of unresolved issues	Alienated, with a developmental
	Pseudodeveloped	**Generative**
	Deny issues and stresses	Openly confront stress and issues
Integration	Satisfied and trying to prevent changes	Have a positive developmental history
		Have resolved issues and integrated a revised identity

*Adapted from Farrell & Rosenberg (1981). Used with permission. From *Men at Midlife* (pp. 32, 75) by Michael P. Farrell and Stanley Rosenberg, Dover, MA: Auburn House, an imprint of Greenwood Publishing Group Inc. Copyright © 1980 by Auburn House Publishing Company

Crisis Type

The crisis type resembled Josselson's moratorium group. These men were very well aware that they were in a total identity crisis, but their poor developmental histories left them highly handicapped. They cast themselves as anti-heroes trying to find a sense of wholeness and ability to cope, but they were failing. Being highly dependent but self-aware, they lamented their lack of ability to deal with the growing demands of their wives, children, and parents. They had, in essence, given up on themselves. They had a vivid sense of futility and were in depressive decline.

Summary and Implications

As with Josselson's women, the casualty rate for men at mid-life is high. Only one fourth to one third of the group remain developmentally healthy at mid-life. The distinguishing variables seem to be societal expectations, internal psychological resources, and life circumstances.

Our society's norms for men seem to be externally and materially defined. Most young men strive for identity through external achievement in school, work, athletics, and marriage. These norms may neglect or even punish a care orientation and the inner capacity for intimacy. At mid-life, however, the capacity for care and intimacy must be developed if the issues are to be resolved.

Past developmental history also seems to affect mid-life outcomes. Previous developmental success affects men's openness to the experiences, stresses, and needed psychological capacities of mid-life. If the tasks of previous stages have been more rather than less resolved, then men have a better chance of resolving the issues of mid-life.

Socioeconomic class and educational level, in turn, also seem to affect the experiences that influence resolution of tasks. Urban, educated, middle- and upper-class men have better chances of dealing with adult developmental tasks than rural, less educated, and lower socioeconomic class men.

In higher education, it may be important to reflect on these findings. For example, it may be important to support alternatives to the dominant social expectations for men and women during adulthood. Identity through autonomous achievement may leave care, support, and intimacy retarded in adolescence. The college years are critical for developing capacities for free and intimate interpersonal relationships as well as autonomy (Chickering, 1969). For men, freeing interpersonal relationships is swimming upstream to dominant societal norms, and apparently many men leave college without resolving these issues. Nevertheless, for men at mid-life, a capacity for care and intimacy is critically important. Must many men wait until mid-life to develop these capacities? Could more men develop them during the college years as many women apparently do?

Research With Black Students

Branch-Simpson (1984) studied the degree to which Black students' psychosocial developmental tasks were similar to those reported by Chickering (1969) as well as other theories based on White subjects. Instead of using Chickering's vectors as a basis for studying Black students, the author conducted psychosocial biographical interviews with Black male and female college students and used content analysis to identify developmental tasks descriptive of their experience. She found many areas of overlap with Chickering's vectors; however, there were some differences, which are highlighted in Table 13-7.

Although Branch-Simpson's (1984) work is very preliminary, it is interesting to speculate on the implications of this work for student affairs. For example, the religious and spiritual dimension was prominent in the developmental processes these Black students described. Spiritual or faith development has not been a major focus of Euro-American psychology or student affairs programs. Amendments may be needed. Also, Branch-Simpson found the theme of interpersonal relationships in several psychosocial domains and in ways of knowing. Although there were differences between the Black men and women in the degree of this emphasis, clearly this theme was more pervasive than it is in descriptions of the development of White men, if not White women. Or, considering the pervasive influence of the family and extended family on Black students, student development educators may need to study the family's influence and family development much more seriously if they are going to use theory to design programs and services for Black students.

TABLE 13-7
Black Student Development Compared to Chickering's Vectors and Ways of Knowing

Issue	Chickering	Branch-Simpson
Competence	Sense of competence is resolved during first 2 years if student stays in college.	Sense of competence is an issue throughout undergraduate years. Continued stress and hard work.
Autonomy	Separation from family is part of process of developing emotional and instrumental autonomy. Women develop these capacities well ahead of men. Women stay related to parents as they separate.	Both sexes tend to stay connected to family and supports development of autonomy, women more so than men. Women develop these capacities well ahead of men.
Intimacy	Women develop these capacities well ahead of men.	Women develop these capacities well ahead of men. Many men graduate without developing these capacities.
Values	Religion is seldom mentioned in humanizing or personalizing issues.	Religion or spiritual dimension is part of both sexes' lives and is used to resolve values questions.
Identity formation	Separate and achievement-oriented for men; relationship-oriented in a balanced pattern of relationships for women.	Identity is achieved in relationships with extended family, including deity, for both sexes. Men more instrumental and career achievement oriented than women. Role models are Black humanitarian figures or family members.
Ways of knowing	Separate knowing for most men and connected knowing for most women.	Connected learning for men and women. Knowing must be personal. Students want relationships with their teachers, men less so than women, however.
Weltanschauung* (Worldview)	Value acquisition of objects. Knowing is cognitive. Justice logic dominates. Trust in technology and science.	Value interpersonal relationships. Knowing is symbolic imagery. Logic is a union of opposites. Trust networks of human and spiritual interrelationships.

*Worldview is not a part of Chickering's theory (see Nichols, 1988).

Typological Theories

Typological theories describe permanent or semipermanent stylistic, temperament, or personality type preferences. There is not a single unifying theoretical perspective for these theories, and, with the exception of the theories of Jung (1971) and Myers (1980), they are not developmental per se. They relate to college student development, however, because psychosocial and cognitive-structural development takes place within a type or style, and type or style affects preferred ways of learning, being motivated, relating with others, and being satisfied. If student development programs are to be appropriately challenging and supportive, then how students learn, are motivated, relate with others, and are satisfied should be taken into account.

Because Claxton and Murrell (1987) published a recent major review of typological theories and because one of the typological models is used more than the others in student affairs, this section will focus on recent theoretical debates related to the most used and general of the typological instruments, the Myers-Briggs Type Indicator (MBTI) (Myers & McCaulley, 1985). The debate centers on whether theories of *type* or theories of *temperament* are more valid for interpreting and predicting behavior. For example, MBTI preferences can be interpreted in terms of Jung/Myers (Jung, 1971; Myers, 1980) personality *types* or Keirsey (Keirsey & Bates, 1978; Keirsey, 1988) or other (Osmond, Siegler, & Smoke, 1983) personality *temperaments*. Type and temperament not only offer differing interpretations of MBTI preferences, but also sometimes offer different prescriptions for practitioners. Hence, the assumptions and major propositions of each need to be examined.

Keirsey's Temperaments

Temperament theory (Keirsey, 1988; Keirsey & Bates, 1978; Keirsey & Brownsword, 1983) asserts that persons are *systemic, self-regulating wholes*. Personality has an inborn pattern of or propensity toward certain behavior, and it is the total pattern that is called *temperament*. The focus is on the governing whole, not the parts.

These patterns are socially imprinted or conditioned, however (Keirsey & Brownsword, 1983). That is, the patterns emerge, survive, and flourish if the social environment facilitates their emergence and growth. If not, various pathologies emerge (Keirsey, 1988). The environment does not create the patterns, however. "The pattern is there from the start" (Keirsey & Brownsword, p. 6). Temperament, therefore, is an inborn propensity for constancy of behavior.

Keirsey (1988) divided temperaments into MBTI Sensors (concrete and component perceivers) or Intuitives (abstract and wholistic perceivers) and subdivided these two subgroups each. The letters in the Keirsey Temperaments' box correspond to Jungian/Myers names for mental functions and attitudes to be covered later in this chapter; however, Keirsey believes that persons functions as patterned wholes and he does not accept the concepts of mental functions and attitudes per se. Nevertheless, the letters in the box are used symbolically as follows: S stands for Sensors, N for Intuitives, E for Extroverts, I for Introverts, T for Thinkers, F for Feelers, P for Perceptive type, and J for Judgment type.

Keirsey Temperaments			
	SJ	Epimethian or Guardian Temperament	
S		ISTJ	ISFJ
		ESTJ	ESFJ
	SP	Dionysian or Artisan Temperament	
		ISTP	ISFP
		ESTP	ESFP
	NT	Promethian or Rational Temperament	
N		INTJ	INTP
		ENTJ	ENTP
	NF	Apollonian or Idealistic Temperament	
		INFP	ENFP
		INFJ	ENFJ

The four Jungian types listed under each temperament subgroup are believed to share common behavior patterns, and the common pattern guides behavior more than do differences among patterns. The SJ temperament, for example, has a strong sense of duty. SJ type individuals establish and maintain social institutions such as family, church, or corporations. Belonging to such organizations must be earned. Structure, order, and planning are valued and reflected in their behavior. These individuals relate to others in terms of their status and roles in structured hierarchies. They are not risk takers; they are conservers. They desire stability and predictability. They are stable, responsible, dependable, and practical in their behavior. Hence, they learn and develop best in environments that are preplanned, concrete, experiential, routine, sequential, structured, and inductive— that is, proceeding from a particular instance to the generalization.

The SP temperament, on the other hand, wants to be free and spontaneous. SP type individuals do not want to be preplanned, restricted, or obligated. They are action-oriented. Spontaneous action based on here-and-now impulses is characteristic of their behavior. Hence, they enjoy life and its sensual pleasures. They are fun-loving, exciting, generous, and congenial. They are competitive and take risks. If they have goals and plans, these would be highly pragmatic, formulated at the last moment, and changeable. They learn best, therefore, through sensual involvement with spontaneous action in competitive contexts that also provide enjoyment, some risk taking, and excitement.

Among the two Intuitive temperaments, NT type individuals are centered on competence. They search for intellectual understanding, explanation, prediction, and control. They enjoy abstract reasoning and intellectual achievement. They read and build abstract theories or systems, and are interested in the principles that underlie their theories and not the facts or specifics of particular instances. Generally, they are competent with language and complex problem solving. Hence, they learn and develop best in environments that involve impersonal analysis, exploration of ideas, critique, debate, classification, and exploration of the possibilities of underlying principles.

Finally, NF temperaments characterize people in the process of becoming. Their goals are self-development and self-actualization. They are emotive, sensitive, and skilled in interpersonal relationships. They search for meaning in their experiences and value authenticity rather than role behavior or facades. They are abstract reasoners and have a personal flair for influencing others with their speech or writing. They learn and develop best in environments that involve the exploration of possibilities with people, understanding of self and others, empathic discussions, development of personal relationships, creativity and imagination, and personalization of knowledge.

Given these four basic patterns of behavior, Keirsey (Keirsey & Brownsword, 1983) believed that the parts of the whole that Jung called mental *functions* and *attitudes* have meaning mostly in relationship to the total pattern, not by themselves. In other words, temperament precedes type. A particular function in one temperament may mean a different behavior in another temperament. For example, Jung/Myers described ISTPs and INTPs as similar "introverted thinking" types. They share the same dominant function, T, and it is expressed in an introverted manner for both types. Hence, both share a propensity, according to Jung/Myers, for introverted logical analysis (one of concepts and the other of sensual facts). Keirsey (Keirsey & Bates, 1978) claimed that "even a cursory observation of a few clearcut ISTPs will show how striking the contrast, and how trivial the resemblance" (p. 203). ISTPs are interested in doing, not thinking, in spontaneous real-world action, and do not reflect even on their sensations. The primary differences between ISTPs and INTPs are their symbolic-abstract *intuition* and real-concrete *sensations*, not the sharing of the Jungian dominant function of Thinking and attitude of Introversion. Temperament precedes type.

Jung/Myers Types

In contrast to Keirsey's *holistic* emphasis on static patterns of behavior, Jung/Myers (Jung, 1971; Myers, 1980; Myers & McCaulley, 1985) emphasized a *dynamic parts* theory whose constructs *develop* over the life span. Their theory, therefore, is a dynamic model of ego development involving four functions (Sensing, Intuition, Thinking, Feeling), two attitudes (Extroversion and Introversion), and two lifestyles (Judgment and Perception).

The four functions attempt to describe the functioning and development of the ego. Sensing (S) and Intuition (N) are polar processes for taking in information, for perceiving. Everyone has both processes within themselves but everyone prefers to use one more often than the other. Sensing is the taking in and coordinating of concrete, here-and-now experiences through the five external senses and through the internal body senses. Sense perceiving is believed to be spontaneous, concrete, linear, accurate, and concerned with components of the whole. In contrast, Intuition (N) is the spontaneous perception of the significance of experience, that is, the insights generated by experience. It is the perception of symbols, images, ideas, and abstractions rather than the concrete components of experience. Intuition is an ideational process concerned with abstract, symbolic, nonpractical, holistic comprehension. That is, it allows individuals to grasp the symbolic and abstract whole, and it probably exceeds their capacity to express it with language (Newman, 1986).

Thinking (T) and Feeling (F) are polar rational processes of judgments that everyone is capable of using. One process is preferred, however, and it is used most often and is better differentiated than the nonpreferred alternative. Thinking is judgment based on an objective, impersonal, and logical sorting and analysis. Thinking relates perceptions to existing knowledge and allows them to be expressed in a logical manner. Behaviorally, thinkers are critical and believe personal considerations should be left out of decisions. Feeling, on the other hand, is an experiential process of judgment based on a complex coordination of a variety of emotional reactions to perception and value-oriented criteria. It is sensitive to and coordinates the feelings of self and others and regulates individuals' emotional life. It is associated with cognitive capacities to image and visualize, control body states, and think with metaphors (Newman, 1987). Behaviorally, Fs use personal consideration in making decisions, and are good at projecting the impact of decisions on people.

The two attitudes, Extroversion and Introversion, are basic and fundamentally different ways of relating the self to the world. One is preferred and more differentiated, although everyone experiences both. Extroversion focuses on the external world of people, places, and things, whereas Introversion relates to the internal world of thought, awareness, and reflection. Behaviorally, Extroverts need more outside involvements, seek affirmation and confirmation of themselves from others, are comparatively good at meeting people and at interpersonal interaction, speak often at meetings, and in fact speak in order to sort out judgments. Introverts need more time alone, seek inner understanding, and must internally sort and analyze before they speak. They often have better writing than verbal skills, and are more difficult to get to know than Extroverts.

Finally the two life-styles are polar opposite preferences for Judgment (T or F) or Perception (S or N) in individuals' extroverted environment. Judgment (J) prefers an organized, planned life-style. Js like to get things settled, dislike interruptions or changes in the schedule, and get things done on time. Perceivers (P) prefer flexibility and therefore adapt better to changing circumstances. Ps are open to new perceptions, make decisions more slowly, start more often than finish, and are often late in finishing if they finish at all.

Unlike Keirsey in the use of Sensing and Intuition, Jung first divided types on Extroversion and Introversion, and then added the functions, and Myers added the life-styles. In addition, Jung believed that one of the four functions is the *dominant* function in ego development and expression. This is the most important function in personality and its development. The *auxiliary* function also is preferred but is not dominant. Rather than being in opposition to the dominant function, however, Jung believed the auxiliary serves the dominant function but is less differentiated.

Jung's constructs yield 16 personality types. They represent 16 different tracks of development toward wholeness or individuation. During the first half of life (until age 40), development ought to focus on the dominant function and a fairly well-differentiated auxiliary. In the college years, the opposite of the auxiliary (called the third function) can become the object of development, while the inferior function, the opposite of the dominant, is more consciously felt and is differentiated only after mid-life. Hence, for Jung/Myers, an ISTP type has T as a dominant function and S as the auxiliary. For good type development, Thinking is expressed introvertedly, whereas Sensing is

expressed extrovertedly. During college, therefore, development would be facilitated by a major calling for introverted, logical reflection on concrete external data from Sensing. The third function is Intuition, the opposite of Sensing, and some experiences differentiating this function also would be prescribed. Feeling processes probably should be minimized during college for this type.

Summary and Comparison of Temperament and Type

To sum up, Keirsey would interpret MBTI preferences in terms of four temperaments, SJ, SP, NF, and NT. These, he believes, are systemic, holistic patterns of behavior, not particular mental functions. The patterns of behavior are static and not developmental per se. The patterns are more important and override the influence of any particular mental function, if such exists. Temperament precedes and overrides type.

In contrast, Jung/Myers would interpret MBTI preferences in terms of particular psychological cognitive processes or functions, attitudes, and life-style patterns. The 16 types have different dynamic paths for development. Type development includes having a clearly preferred and differentiated perceiving and judging function, attitudes, and life-style. The dominant function operates mainly in the preferred attitude, whereas the auxiliary provides attitude and functional balance and operates mainly in the non-preferred attitude. Early in life, development should concentrate on the dominant function, along with the supporting auxiliary. Later the third and inferior functions should receive attention. Behavior is influenced by all four preferences, not just the pairs Keirsey highlighted. Keirsey's temperaments in fact are only four of several preference combinations that could be used to describe patterns of behavior. Osmond et al. (1983), Arthur (1985), and Brownsword (1988), for example, described the behavior of functional pairs (NT, NF, ST, SF), whereas Brownsword (1988) also described the behavior of attitude pairs (EJ, EP, IJ, and IP) and extroverted pairs (SP, NP, TJ, and FJ). All combinations of preferences could be considered as temperaments; they do not precede or override type, however. They simply highlight selected behavioral aspects of type.

What seems to be needed in order to clarify some of the differences between Keirsey and Jung/Myers is research on the actual behavioral characteristics of types and temperaments. Berens (1985) cautioned that valid interpretation of such research on Ss, Ns, Ts, Fs, Es, Is, Ps, Js, or any combination of letters cannot be made unless samples include balanced representation from all of the other preferences. The study of the behavior of SPs for example must include balanced representation of ESFPs, ISFPs, ISTPs, and ESTPs, and not be biased by the absence or over-representation of any one of the SP types. Given the above, McCarley and Carskadon (1986) and Ruhl and Rodgers (in press) asked college students of all 16 types to rate the accuracy of each individual element in Keirsey and Bates's (1978) and Myers's (1980) type descriptions. Both studies found the ratings of Myers's and Keirsey's descriptions virtually identical in accuracy; hence, on the preliminary data available, neither theory seems to be more accurate than the other in describing behavior. Both interpretations of MBTI preferences, therefore, seem to be acceptable as a basis for planning student affairs programs.

Keirsey and Brownsword (1983) agreed that both are useful and that a practitioner's choice is not "either-or" but "both." This can be illustrated by analyzing the behavior of an ESTJ and ESFJ student leader. These two leaders would have similar SJ temperaments, but would be very different functional types.

The ESTJ leader has a "no-nonsense, impersonal, sometimes hot tempered style" (Keirsey & Brownsword, 1983, p. 8). This leader is socially active but also decisive, dependable, and demanding. She believes she is right on most issues and she does not easily compromise her rightness for harmony among members of her group. She gives orders, makes assignments, and gets things done.

On the other hand, the ESFJ leader could take over a student government that is full of conflict and within a few weeks everyone would be working harmoniously together (Keirsey & Brownsword, 1983). Before meetings, this leader spends much time figuring out how to minimize conflict and maximize harmony and commitment. The ESFJ leader rarely gives orders, rarely speaks in a commanding way, and is likely to ask for information when the intent is to ask the other to do something. Type, therefore, would predict these T versus F differences in leadership emphasis and style. Temperament would not. Both of these leaders, however, also share the SJ traditionalist or guardian temperament. Both respect the university governance system and keep their organizations within policy guidelines. They follow rules, get things done on time, and accomplish the details of organizational life. Temperament works, also.

Using MBTI, Type, and Temperament

To use the MBTI, type theory, and temperament theory, practitioners must know the theories and instrument well and use them (Rodgers, 1983). Self-analysis is a good way to start. Look at your own behavior through the perspectives of type and temperament. Similarly, look at the behavior of the students with whom you work. This usually leads to greater understanding of self and other, acceptance of what cannot be changed, and awareness of what can be changed. It also can lead to designing programs that facilitate psychosocial and cognitive-structural development through the use of type characteristics. This student development use of type has been aptly demonstrated in teaching (Golay, 1982; Lawrence, 1982), counseling (Provost, 1984), retention (Kalsbeek, 1987), residential programs (Schroeder & Jackson, 1987), student activities (Provost & Anchors, 1987), academic advising (Anchors, 1987), career development (Golden & Provost, 1987; Myers & McCaulley, 1985), and student development as defined by Chickering's vectors (Lynch, 1987).

Use and Abuse of Theory

As this review of recent theory and research underlying student development concludes, a few remarks about the abuse of theory may be in order. Brownsword (1987) provided a brief synopsis of this important topic. He reminded student affairs professionals that thorough knowledge of theory is both professionally powerful and subject to abuse. If professionals use knowledge to stereotype or limit themselves or others, then they are abusing their knowledge of theory.

"Oh, he's only a Kohlberg Stage 3, we can't pick him."

"She's an ISTJ, she'd never make a career in student affairs."

Similarly, when a professional uses knowledge of theory as an excuse for behavior, he or she is abusing theory.

Other: "You missed our appointment again."

Self: "What can you expect, I'm a P!"

"He's a Kegan 3 and that's why he let his friends into the back gate of the concert. What else can you expect?"

Awareness, understanding, appreciation, and facilitation of the growth of developmental and typological differences are not the same as excuses, stereotypes, and preemptive limitations. Seek the former; avoid the latter.

References

American Council on Education. (1937). *The student personnel point of view*. American Council on Education Studies, Series 1. Washington, DC: Author.

American Council on Education. (1949). *The student personnel point of view* (rev. ed.). American Council on Education Studies, Series 6. Washington, DC: Author.

Anchors, S. (1987). Academic advising. In J. Provost & S. Anchors (Eds.), *Applications of the Myers-Briggs Type Indicator in higher education* (pp. 109–123). Palo Alto, CA: Consulting Psychologists Press.

Arthur, S. (1985). The most closely related types. *Bulletin of Psychological Type, 8*(1), 24–25.

Astin, A. W. (1987, Sept./Oct.). Competition or cooperation. *Change, 19*(2), 12–19.

Aulepp, L., & Delworth, U. (1978). A team approach to environmental assessment. In J. H. Banning (Ed.), *Campus ecology: A perspective for student affairs* (pp. 51–71). Washington, DC: National Association of Student Personnel Administrators.

Banning, J., & Kaiser, L. (1974). An ecological perspective and model for campus design. *Personnel and Guidance Journal, 52*, 370–375.

Barker, R. G. (1968). *Ecological psychology: Concepts and methods for studying the environment of human behavior*. Stanford, CA: Stanford University.

Baruch, G., & Barnett, R. (1980, December 7). A new start for women at midlife. *New York Times Magazine*, pp. 196–201.

Baruch, G., Barnett, R., & Rivers, C. (1983). *Lifeprints*. New York: Signet.

Baumrind, D. (1986). Sex differences in moral reasoning: Response to Walker's (1984) conclusion that there are none. *Child Development, 5*(2), 511–521.

Baxter Magolda, M. B. (1987). A comparison of open-ended interview and standardized instrument measures of intellectual development on the Perry scheme. *Journal of College Student Personnel, 28*, 443–448.

Baxter Magolda, M. B. (1988a). Measuring gender differences in intellectual development: A comparison of assessment methods. *Journal of College Student Development, 29*, 528–537.

Baxter Magolda, M. B. (1988b, March). *Validity of the measure of epistemological reflection for assessing gender differences*. A paper presented at the annual conference, American College Personnel Association, Miami, FL.

Baxter Magolda, M. B. (1989). Gender differences in cognitive development: An analysis of cognitive complexity and learning styles. *Journal of College Student Development, 30*, 213–220.

Baxter Magolda, M. B., & Porterfield, W. D. (1985). A new approach to assess intellectual development on the Perry scheme. *Journal of College Student Personnel, 26*, 343–351.

Belenky, M. F., Clinchy, B. M., Goldberger, N. R., & Tarule, J. M. (1986). *Women's ways of knowing: The development of self, voice and mind*. New York: Basic Books.

Berens, L. (1985). Differences that make a difference: Theory and research. *MBTI News, 7*, 8–10.

Blocker, D. H. (1974). Toward an ecology of student development. *Personnel and Guidance Journal, 52*(6), 360–365.

Brabeck, M. (1984). Longitudinal studies of intellectual development during adulthood: Theoretical and research models. *Journal of Research and Development in Education, 17*, 12–27.

Branch-Simpson, G. (1984). *A study of the patterns in the development of black students at The Ohio State University*. Unpublished doctoral dissertation, The Ohio State University, Columbus.

Brownsword, A. W. (1987). *It takes all types!* Washington, DC: Baytree.

Brownsword, A. W. (1988). *Psychological type: An introduction*. Washington, DC: Baytree.

Chickering, A. W. (1969). *Education and identity*. San Francisco: Jossey-Bass.

Claxton, C. S., & Murrell, P. H. (1987). *Learning styles: Implications for improving educational practices*, Report 4, ASHE-ERIC Higher Education Reports. Washington, DC: ERIC Clearinghouse on Higher Education.

Cooper, A. C. (1971). *A proposal for professional preparation of the college student development educators*. Report from Commission on Professional Development. Council of Student Personnel Associations. Washington, DC: Council of Student Personnel Associations.

Cooper, A. C. (1972). *Student development services in higher education.* Report from Commission on Professional Development, Council of Student Personnel Associations. Washington, DC: Council of Student Personnel Associations.

Denny, N. (1988). *Socio-moral development variability: Comparisons of Kohlberg's moral reasoning stages for Jung's Thinking-Feeling student process, educational level, and gender.* Unpublished doctoral dissertation, The Ohio State University, Columbus.

Dietrich, M. K. (1972). *Goal setting for The Ohio State University Campus Ministry Association using The Delphi Technique as a data-based intervention strategy.* Unpublished master's thesis, The Ohio State University, Columbus.

Drum, D. (1980). Understanding student development. In W. H. Morrill, J. C. Hurst, & E. R. Oetting (Eds.), *Dimensions of intervention for student development* (pp. 14–38). New York: Wiley.

Erikson, E. H. (1968). *Identity, youth, and crisis.* New York: Norton.

Farrell, M. P., & Rosenberg, S. D. (1981). *Men at midlife.* Dover, MA: Auburn House.

Fawcett, G., Huebner, L. A., & Banning, J. H. (1978). Campus ecology: Implementing the design process. In J. H. Banning, (Ed.), *Campus ecology: A perspective for student affairs* (pp. 32–50). Washington, DC: National Association of Student Personnel Administrators.

Fowler, J. (1981). *Stages of faith.* New York: Harper & Row.

Fries, S. (1983). *Black and white students' perceptions of the Olentangy Residence Halls: An ecosystems approach.* Unpublished master's thesis, The Ohio State University, Columbus.

Gibbs, J. C., Arnold, K. D., & Burkhart, J. E. (1984). Sex differences in the expression of moral judgment. *Child Development, 55,* 1040–1043.

Gibbs, J. C., & Widaman, K. F., with A. Colby. (1982). *Social intelligence: Measuring the development of sociomoral reflection.* Englewood Cliffs, NJ: Prentice-Hall.

Gilligan, C. (1982). *In a different voice: Psychological theory and women's development.* Cambridge, MA: Harvard University Press.

Gilligan, C. (1986a). Remapping development: The power of divergent data. In L. Cirillo & S. Wapner (Eds.), *Value presuppositions in theories of human development* (pp. 37–61). Hillsdale, NJ: Lawrence Erlbaum Associates.

Gilligan, C. (1986b). Reply by Carol Gilligan. *Signs: Journal of Women in Culture and Society, II,* 304–333.

Golay, K. (1982). *Learning patterns and temperament styles.* Fullerton, CA: Manis Systems.

Golden, V. & Provost, J. (1987). The MBTI and career development. In J. Provost & S. Anchors, (Eds.), *Applications of the Myers-Briggs Type Indicator in higher education* (pp. 151–179). Palo Alto, CA: Consulting Psychologists Press.

Haan, N. (1985). With regard to Walker (1984) on sex "differences" in moral reasoning. Mimeographed paper. Berkeley, CA: University of California, Berkeley, Institute of Human Development.

Heath, R. (1964). *The reasonable adventurer.* Pittsburgh, PA: University of Pittsburgh Press.

Heidke, J. (1982). *A study of cognitive-intellectual and psychosocial development of women at Kenyon College and The Ohio State University.* Unpublished doctoral dissertation, The Ohio State University, Columbus.

Huebner, L. A. (1979). Emergent issues of theory and practice. In L. A. Huebner (Ed.), *Redesigning campus environments* (pp. 1–21). New Directions for Student Services Series, No. 8. San Francisco: Jossey-Bass.

Huebner, L. A., & Corazzini, J. G. (1978). Ecomapping: A dynamic model for intentional campus design. *Journal Supplement Abstract Service, Catalogue of Selected Documents on Psychology, 8(9),* 9.

Huebner, L. A., Royer, J. A., Moore, J., Cordes, D. L., & Paul, S. C. (1979). Stress management through an ecosystem model in a school of medicine. In L. A. Huebner (Ed.), *Redesigning campus environments* (pp. 51–67). New Directions for Student Services Series, No. 8. San Francisco: Jossey-Bass.

Hurst, J. C., & Ragle, J. D. (1979). Application of the ecosystem perspective to a Dean of Students office. In L. A. Huebner (Ed.), *Redesigning campus environments* (pp. 69–84). New Directions for Student Services Series, No. 8. San Francisco: Jossey-Bass.

Johnston, D. K. (1985). *Two moral orientations—two problem-solving strategies: Adolescents' solutions to dilemmas in fables.* Unpublished doctoral dissertation, Harvard University, School of Education, Cambridge, MA.

Josselson, R. (1987). *Finding herself: Pathways to identity development in women.* San Francisco: Jossey-Bass.

Jung, C. G. (1971). *Psychological types.* In H. Read, M. Fordham, G. Adler, & W. McGuire (Eds.), R. F. C. Hull (Trans.), *Vol. 6 of Collected works.* Bollingen Series, XX. Princeton, NJ: Princeton University Press.

Kaiser, L. (1978). Campus ecology and campus design. In J. H. Banning (Ed.), *Campus ecology: A perspective for student affairs* (pp. 24–31). Washington, DC: National Association of Student Personnel Administrators.

Kalsbeek, D. (1987). Campus retention: The MBTI and institutional self-studies. In J. Provost & S. Anchors, (Eds.), *Applications of the Myers-Briggs Type Indicator in higher education* (pp. 31–63). Palo Alto, CA: Consulting Psychologists Press.

Kegan, R. (1979). The evolving self: A process conception for ego psychology. *The Counseling Psychologist, 8,* 5–34.

Kegan, R. (1980a). Making meaning: The constructive-developmental approach to persons and practice. *The Personnel and Guidance Journal, 58,* 373–380.

Kegan, R. (1980b). *There the dance is: Religious dimensions of a developmental framework. Toward moral and religious maturity.* Morristown, NJ: Silver-Burdett.

Kegan, R. (1982). *The evolving self: Problems and process in human development.* Cambridge, MA: Harvard University Press.

Keirsey, D. (1988). *Portraits of temperaments.* Del Mar, CA: Prometheus Nemesis.

Keirsey, D., & Bates, M. (1978). *Please understand me: Character and temperament types* (3rd ed.). Del Mar, CA: Prometheus Nemesis.

Keirsey, D., & Brownsword, A. (1983). Temperament theory and the theory of functions. *MBTI News, 6*(1), 5–10.

King, P. M. (1982, November). *Perry's Scheme and the Reflective Judgment model: First cousins once removed.* Paper presented at the Annual Conference of the Association for Moral Education, Minneapolis, MN.

King, P. M., Kitchener, K. S., Davison, M. L., Parker, C. A., & Wood, P. L. (1983). The justification of beliefs in young adults: A longitudinal study. *Human Development, 26,* 106–116.

Kitchener, K. S. (1986). The reflective judgment model: Characteristics, evidence, and measurement. In R. A. Mines & K. S. Kitchener (Eds.), *Adult cognitive development: Methods and models* (pp. 76–91). New York: Praeger.

Kitchener, K. S., & King, P. M. (1981). Reflective judgment: Concepts of justification and their relationship to age and education. *Journal of Applied Developmental Psychology, 2,* 89–116.

Kitchener, K. S., & King, P. M. (1985a). *Reflective judgment theory and research: Insights into the process of knowing in adulthood.* (ERIC Document Reproduction Service No. ED 263 821.) Denver: University of Denver.

Kitchener, K. S., & King, P. M. (1985b, June). *The reflective judgement model: Ten years of research.* Paper presented at the Beyond Formal Operations Symposium, Boston, MA.

Knefelkamp, L., Widick, C., & Parker, C. A. (1978). *Applying new developmental findings.* San Francisco: Jossey-Bass.

Kohlberg, L. (1984). *Essays on moral development: Volume II—The psychology of moral development: The nature and validity of moral stages.* San Francisco: Harper & Row.

Kolb, D. A. (1976). *Learning Style Inventory technical manual.* Boston: McBer.

Langdale, S. (1983). *Moral orientations and moral development: The analysis of care and justice reasoning across different dilemmas in females and males from childhood to adulthood.* Unpublished doctoral dissertation, Harvard University, School of Education, Cambridge, MA.

Lawrence, G. (1982). *People types and tiger stripes* (2nd ed.). Gainesville, FL: Center for Applications of Psychological Type.

Levinson, D. J. (1978). *The seasons of a man's life.* New York: Knopf.

Lewin, K. (1936). *Principles of topological psychology.* New York: McGraw-Hill.

Livingston, M. D. (1980). *An ecological assessment of the residence halls' environment at the University of Iowa.* Unpublished doctoral dissertation, Michigan State University, East Lansing.

Loevinger, J. (1976). *Ego development: Conceptions and theories.* San Francisco: Jossey-Bass.

Lynch, A. (1987). Type development and student development. In J. Provost & S. Anchors (Eds.), *Applications of the Myers-Briggs Type Indicator in higher education* (pp. 5–29). Palo Alto, CA: Consulting Psychologists Press.

Lyons, N. P. (1983). Two perspectives: On self, relationships, and morality. *Harvard Educational Review, 53,* 125–145.

Marcia, J. E. (1966). Development and validation of ego identity status. *Journal of Personality and Social Psychology, 3,* 551–558.

Marcia, J. E. (1976). Identity six years after: A follow-up study. *Journal of Youth and Adolescence, 5,* 145–160.

Marcia, J. E. (1980). Identity in adolescence. In J. Adelson (Ed.), *Handbook of adolescent psychology* (pp. 159–187). New York: Wiley.

Marcia, J. E., & Friedman, M. (1970). Ego identity status in college women. *Journal of Personality, 38,* 249–263.

McCarley, N., & Carskadon, T. G. (1986). The perceived accuracy of elements of the 16 type descriptions of Myers and Keirsey among men and women: Which elements are most accurate, should the type descriptions be different for men and women, and do the type descriptions stereotype sensing types: *Journal of Psychological Type, 11*, 2–29.

Mintz, R. B. (1976). *Goal setting for the future: An application of context evaluation to fraternity life*. Unpublished master's thesis, The Ohio State University, Columbus.

Moore, W. (1982). *The measure of intellectual development: A brief review*. Baltimore, MD: University of Maryland, Center for Application of Developmental Instruction.

Moos, R. H. (1979). *Evaluating educational environments*. San Francisco: Jossey-Bass.

Morrill, W. H., Hurst, J. C., & Oetting, E. R. (1980). *Dimensions of intervention for student development*. New York: Wiley.

Myers, I. B. (1980). *Gifts differing*. Palo Alto, CA: Consulting Psychologists Press.

Myers, I. B., & McCaulley, M. H. (1985). *Manual: A guide to the development and use of the Myers-Briggs Type Indicator*. Palo Alto, CA: Consulting Psychologists Press.

Newman, J. (1986). Intuition as a cognitive process. *Bulletin of Psychological Type, 9*(1), 4–6.

Newman, J. (1987). Thinking as a cognitive process. *Bulletin of Psychological Type, 10*(2), 13, 25–27.

Nichols, E. J. (1988, July). *Managing in a multicultural community*. Paper presented at the 14th annual Richard F. Stevens NASPA/ACE Institute on Leadership and Administration of Student Affairs in Higher Education, Annapolis, MD.

Omahan, D. (1982). *Cognitive-intellectual and psychosocial development of male students at a small private college and a large public university*. Unpublished doctoral dissertation, The Ohio State University, Columbus.

Osmond, H., Siegler, M., & Smoke, R. (1983). Typology revisited: A new perspective. *MBTI News, 5*(2), 1, 10–13.

Palmer, P. J. (1987, September/October). Community, conflict, and ways of knowing. *Change, 19*(2), 20–25.

Perry, W., Jr. (1970). *Forms of intellectual and ethical development in the college years: A scheme*. New York: Holt, Rinehart & Winston.

Pervin, L. A. (1967). A twenty-college study of student x college interaction using TAPE: Rationale, reliability, and validity. *Journal of Educational Psychology, 58*, 290–302.

Pervin, L. A. (1968). Performance and satisfaction as a function of individual-environment fit. *Psychological Bulletin, 69*, 56–68.

Provost, J. (1984). *A case book: Applications of the Myers-Briggs Type Indicator in counseling*. Gainesville, FL: Center for Applications of Psychological Type.

Provost, J., & Anchors, S. (1987). *Applications of the Myers-Briggs Type Indicator in higher education*. Palo Alto, CA: Consulting Psychologists Press.

Reynolds, A. (1984). *A graduate housing ecosystem: An international-North American student comparison*. Unpublished master's thesis, The Ohio State University, Columbus.

Rodgers, R. (1974–1988). *Perry level of entering freshmen*. Unpublished research studies. Columbus, OH: The Ohio State University.

Rodgers, R. (1988, September). *Origins of the care voice: Gender or type?* Paper presented at Association for Psychological Type Great Lakes Regional Conference, Indianapolis, IN.

Rodgers, R. F. (1980). Theories underlying student development. In D. G. Creamer (Ed.), *Student development in higher education: Theories, practices, & future directions* (pp. 10–95). Alexandria, VA: American College Personnel Association.

Rodgers, R. F. (1983). Using theory in practice. In T. K. Miller, R. B. Winston, & W. R. Mendenhall (Eds.), *Administration and leadership in student affairs* (pp. 111–144). Muncie, IN: Accelerated Development.

Rodgers, R. F. (1984a, June). *Student development through campus ecology*. Paper presented at Annual Conference on Campus Ecology, Pingree Park, CO.

Rodgers, R. F. (1984b). Theories of adult development: Research status and counseling implications. In S. Brown & R. Lent (Eds.), *Handbook of counseling psychology* (pp. 479–519). New York: Wiley.

Ruhl, D., & Rodgers, R. (in press). The perceived accuracy of the 16 type descriptions of Jung/Myers and Keirsey: A replication of McCarley and Carskadon's (1986) study. *Journal of Psychological Type*.

Sabock, A. F. (1980). *A context evaluation of female athletes' perceptions of study tables, tutoring, academic advising and scheduling, counseling, and social life at The Ohio State University*. Unpublished master's thesis, The Ohio State University, Columbus.

Schroeder, C. (1976). New strategies for structuring residential environments. *Journal of College Student Personnel, 17*, 386–391.

Schroeder, C. (1980a). Designing college environments for students. In F. B. Newton & K. L. Ender (Eds.), *Student development practices* (pp. 52–79). Springfield, IL: Charles C Thomas.

Schroeder, C. (1980b). Territoriality: An imperative for personal development and residence education. In D. DeCoster & P. Mable (Eds.), *Personal education and community development in college residence halls* (pp. 114–132). Alexandria, VA: American College Personnel Association.

Schroeder, C. (1981). Student development through environmental management. In G. Blimling & J. Schuh (Eds.), *Increasing the educational role of residence halls* (pp. 35–49). San Francisco: Jossey-Bass.

Schroeder, C., & Belmonte, A. (1979). The influence of residence environment on pre-pharmacy student achievement and satisfaction. *American Journal of Pharmaceutical Education, 43,* 16–19.

Schroeder, C., & Jackson, S. (1987). Designing residential environments. In J. Provost & S. Anchors (Eds.), *Applications of the Myers-Briggs Type Indicator in higher education* (pp. 65–88). Palo Alto, CA: Consulting Psychologists Press.

Schuh, J. H. (1979). Assessment and redesign in residence halls. In L. A. Huebner (Ed.), *Redesigning campus environments* (pp. 23–36). New Directions for Student Services Series, No. 8. San Francisco: Jossey-Bass.

Stern, G. G. (1970). *People in context*. New York: Wiley.

Straub, C. (1987). Women's development of autonomy and Chickering's theory. *Journal of College Student Personnel, 28,* 198–205.

Straub, C., & Rodgers, R. F. (1986). An exploration of Chickering's theory and women's development. *Journal of College Student Personnel, 27,* 216–224.

Treadway, D. M. (1979). Use of campus-wide ecosystem surveys to monitor a changing institution. In L. A. Huebner (Ed.), *Redesigning campus environments* (pp. 37–49). New Directions for Student Services Series, No. 8. San Francisco: Jossey-Bass.

Vaillant, G. E. (1977). *Adaptation to life*. Boston: Little, Brown.

Walker, L. (1984). Sex differences in the development of moral reasoning: A critical review. *Child Development, 55,* 667–691.

Welfel, E. R., & Davison, M. L. (1986). The development of reflective judgment in the college years: A four year longitudinal study. *Journal of College Student Personnel, 27,* 209–216.

CHAPTER 14

COLLEGE STUDENTS' DEGREE ASPIRATIONS:
A THEORETICAL MODEL AND LITERATURE REVIEW
WITH A FOCUS ON AFRICAN AMERICAN
AND LATINO STUDENTS

DEBORAH FAYE CARTER

Quite a few comprehensive studies on undergraduate experiences and general models of degree attainment and attrition have highlighted the importance of measuring educational aspirations. Many researchers theorize that student educational aspirations have strong effects on (or strong relationships with) a variety of outcomes, particularly college choice, student retention, and graduate school enrollment (Astin, 1977; Tinto, 1993).

However, educational aspirations are less often studied as *outcomes*. A few higher education researchers have studied the factors that influence educational aspirations (e.g. Astin, 1977, 1993; Hearn, 1987, 1991; Pascarella, 1984), but scholars and researchers still have cursory knowledge about why the aspirations of racial/ethnic minority students and White students differ significantly.

The purpose of this chapter is to review and synthesize the literature related to educational aspirations. This review attempts to summarize what is known about aspirations in general and the aspirations of African American and Latinos specifically. I also posit a research and conceptual model, based on empirical research and existing theory, for understanding what affects educational aspirations.

Much of the literature described in this chapter has its foundations in sociology. Students' educational goals are the function of several elements, including internal psychological processes, social interactions, and structural processes; in this chapter I will focus on the formation and change of aspirations as a result of social interactions and structural processes. The main reason for this emphasis is that the concepts presented can contribute to theoretical advances in the study of educational aspirations and have practical implications for campus programming and institutional policies.

In a review of aspirations studies of the 1960s and 1970s, Pascarella (1984) stated that researchers tend to use methods relying on empirical examinations of aspirations as opposed to theoretical examinations of aspirations. Pascarella developed a model of affective outcomes that posits that individual characteristics and secondary school achievement will have stronger effects on later educational aspirations than institutional environment variables. Pascarella's model has proven useful in understanding the process by which students' aspirations change over time, but there is still a need for

"College Students' Degree Aspirations: A Theoretical Model and Literature Review With a Focus on African American and Latino Students." Reprinted from *Higher Education: A Handbook of Theory and Research* 17, (2002), by permission of Kluwer Academic Publishers.

understanding the unique processes by which the aspirations of students of color change over time.

The study of aspirations in general can be characterized as lacking in clarity. One key area that researchers have noted as needing greater understanding and theoretical specificity is the formation and maintenance of educational aspirations—particularly in populations who continue to be underrepresented in higher education institutions (Kao & Tienda, 1998).

The aspirations of students of color often do not fall into easily predictable patterns. In several studies, African American students tend to have higher than expected aspirations (Astin, 1990; Hanson, 1994), which some researchers have called "unrealistic," while other researchers have found that high aspirations for African Americans are the mediating factor in whether they attend college (St. John. 1991).

As early as the 1960s, research comparing the college going behaviors and attainments of African American and White youth discovered significant differences in the aspirations and aspirations change process between the two racial groups. In some studies, the researchers found that African American youth had lower aspirations than White youth while in others, the aspirations of African American youth were higher than or similar to those of White youth (Portes & Wilson, 1976; St. John, 1991). Regardless of the direction (or lack) of difference in aspirations levels, it has been clear that the variables affecting aspirations can differ in magnitude and direction between the racial groups.

There has been much less research on the aspirations of Latino high school and college students. The educational attainment rates of Latinos are at crisis levels; Latinos (particularly Mexican Americans) have much lower high school completion rates and college going rates than White students, and tend to be concentrated in two year institutions.

Researchers have suggested that "increasing minority participation in graduate programs is an important national goal to be realized. . . . It is for the collective benefit of society that the representation of minority group persons among those earning advanced degrees he increased" (National Board on Graduate Education cited in Deskins, Jr., 1994, p. 144). Indeed, a recent study found that the racial representation of physicians affects available health care in poor and minority communities (Komaromy, Grumbach, Drake, Vranizan, Lurie, Keane. & Bindman, 1996). Therefore, the aspirations and subsequent graduate degree attainments of minority students not only have an impact on individual factors such as income, but also can have an impact on the welfare of entire communities.

This chapter is organized in two parts: the first addresses theoretical foundations relating to the study of aspirations, and the second describes a model of educational aspirations and highlights the empirical studies that relate to aspects of the model.

Theoretical Foundations for Aspirations Studies

Status Attainment

Status attainment literature in the field of sociology provides the main foundation for the study of the educational aspirations of high school and college students. Blau and Duncan (1967) developed the first status attainment model, which focused on the occupational attainments of males from White and African American populations. Blau and Duncan's model assumes that ascriptive characteristics (father's education and income) determine the male's occupational attainment. The model is quite parsimonious and is composed of the five following variables: father's educational attainment and father's occupational status, and the respondent's educational attainment and first-job status. The first two are predictors of the latter two, and all four variables are predictors of the respondents' eventual occupational attainment. Educational aspirations were not included in Blau and Duncan's original model, but subsequent status attainment research has developed the model to take aspirations into account.

Many researchers have noted one main weakness in Blau and Duncan's model: the relationships between the variables could not be sufficiently explained (Kerckhoff, 1984; Sewell, Haller, & Ohlendorf, 1970; Sewell, Haller, & Portes, 1969). The model has been criticized because there seems to be little theoretical support for the concept that fathers' education determines sons' occupational attainments besides a strict notion of social reproduction (that is, people's socioeconomic status is determined by the status of their parents and there is little mobility between generations). In attempting to further enhance Blau and Duncan's model by explaining the processes by which a parent's socioeconomic status can affect the status of the adult child, Sewell, et al. (1969) and others expanded the model to include social psychological variables. In developing this expanded model, called the social psychological model of status attainment, the "Wisconsin model", or a socialization model, it was the position of the researchers that social psychological variables, previously shown to be important to educational attainment, were valuable to examine as intervening variables with respect to educational and occupational attainment. Such variables as significant others, reference groups, self-concept, aspirations, and experience of school success are all constructs whose effects on attainments had been proven in research completed in the late 1950s and early 1960s (Sewell, et al., 1969). Measures of ability were particularly highlighted as important for researchers to take into account because mental ability (as measured by IQ and other standardized tests) was assumed to affect the student's "academic performance and the influence significant others have on him [or her]" (Sewell, et al., 1970, p. 1015).

The social psychological model of status attainment assumes that the socioeconomic status and ability of the student affect the encouragement and support the student receives from significant others, which in turn, affect the student's goals and aspirations (Kerckhoff, 1976). The Wisconsin model posits causal arguments "linking social origins and ability with educational and early occupational status attainments by means of intervening behavioral mechanisms" (Sewell, et al., 1970, p. 1015). In developing this theory, Sewell, et al. (1969) applied the work of previous psychological researchers who, as early as 1935, concluded that individuals obtain their "social behavior tendencies largely through the influence of others" (p. 85) and that "one's conception of the educational behavior others think appropriate to him [or her] is highly correlated with [the] level of educational aspiration" (p. 85).

Sewell, et al.'s (1969) model presents four sets of causal relationships in a 1957 study of a homogenous sample (all White, farm youth) of Wisconsin high school male seniors: 1) social structural (socioeconomic status, or SES) and psychological factors (mental ability) affect sig-

nificant others' influences; 2) significant others' influences affect educational and occupational aspirations; 3) aspirations affect attainment; and 4) educational attainment affects occupational attainment. Significant others (in this study) refers to parents, peers, and instructors.

Sewell, Haller, and Ohlendorf (1970) describe the patterns of effects in greater detail. Generally, social structural and psychological factors affect young men's academic performance and the influences that significant others have on them. The influences of significant others and the students' academic ability affect their levels of educational and occupational aspiration. The levels of aspiration affect educational and occupational status attainment.

The social psychological (or socialization) model of status attainment views aspirations as a central element in the status attainment process and states that aspirations "are formed in social interaction" (Knotterus, 1987, p. 116). Knotterus (1987), in an examination of status attainment researchers' view of society, states that in the social psychological model of status attainment, "aspirations develop in response to the evaluations one receives from significant others and the self-assessment of one's potential based upon academic performance" (p. 116). The social psychological model assumes that social interaction is structured by socioeconomic status groups. The implication being that "significant others—for example, teachers and peers—tend to be drawn from socioeconomic positions somewhat similar to those of the youth's parents and provide encouragement from a similar value orientation" (Otto & Haller, 1979 cited in Knotterus, p. 116). This perspective seems to assume relative homogeneity in the socioeconomic statuses of the population of any given high school.

Status attainment research primarily has been conducted on high school student populations and shows that through interactions with parents, teachers, peers, and other "significant others," students are socialized as to the value of achievement and appropriate educational goals. In this way, the status attainment perspective views society as "a mass of social actors, motivated by universalistic values and functioning in an open structure, are free to pursue their goals" (Knotterus, 1987, pp. 116-7).

Therefore, in the late 1960s, two theories of the process of status attainment (and by implication the development of educational aspirations and degree plans) emerged: one perspective is that educational aspirations and attainment are the direct result of socioeconomic/ascriptive factors (the Blau & Duncan model). The modification of Blau & Duncan's model is the socialization model, which holds that a student's socioeconomic status affects the way he or she interacts with others (and in turn how others interact with the student), which affect aspirations and ultimately attainment (Sewell, et al., 1969). Both theories of the status attainment process were supported by the research completed through the early 1970s, but the social psychological models explain more of the variance in attainments than the ascriptive, Blau and Duncan model (Sewell, et al., 1970).

Another perspective on status attainment was developed in response to what some researchers felt were the theoretical shortcomings of the social psychological model. This perspective, first advanced by Kerckhoff (1976), is called social allocation. Kerckhoff's view is that the process of status attainment is not so much a process of socialization than it is a process of social allocation. Kerckhoff's criticism of the Wisconsin model is that the model views an individual as relatively free to move through society; attainment is determined by what the individual chooses to do and how well the individual does it. The social allocation perspective views the individual as constrained by social structure—an individual's attainments are determined by what he or she is allowed to do. Researchers have found strong associations between "ambition" and attainment; therefore, the socialization model assumes that a student's goals direct and motivate the student's efforts which lead to attainment (Kerckhoff, 1976). On the other hand, the measures of ambition used in the past research do not measure motivation as much as they measure "knowledge of 'the real world'" (Kerckhoff, p. 370). Most questions measuring motivation and ambition ask for students' plans or expectations, not their wishes or aspirations (Kerckhoff, 1976). Kerckhoff feels that the difference between *wishes* and *plans* are the most important distinctions between the socialization and social allocation perspectives. The social allocation perspective purports that:

> Expectations are strongly associated with attainments because [students] become suf-

ficiently knowledgeable to be able to estimate the probabilities of various outcomes. . . . People's observations of the attainments of others like themselves undoubtedly do have a feedback effect on their expectations, [Kerckhoff, 1976, p. 371].

It is assumed that individuals may *want* the same outcomes, but that they may expect different outcomes based on their assessments of their life chances. Therefore, while the social psychological model of status attainment views the individual as unconstrained by society and success as determined by the individual's abilities, the social allocation model views the individual as constrained by society. The social psychological model views aspirations as resulting from an individual's social interactions and abilities. An assumption of the model is that a reason certain students are not upwardly mobile is because they are of low ability and/or that they do not have the goals and motivation to succeed. The social allocation interpretation views individuals as constrained by their life circumstances. Individuals only have degree expectations that they think they can achieve given the system constraints in which they live. Kerckhoff (1976, 1984) admitted that it may be difficult to empirically distinguish between the socialization and the social allocation interpretations of the status attainment model. However, Kerckhoff considers the social allocation perspective a different explanation for the same phenomenon.

One problem with Kerckhoff's perspective is that few researchers have demonstrated clear empirical differences between what students' want to happen versus what they expect to happen. In addition, there has not been uniform measurement of aspirations—some measure aspirations as likes or wants (Agnew & Jones, 1988), expectations (Weiler, 1993), and plans (Pascarella, 1984).

A second problem with Kerchkoff's perspective is the role that the concept of "opportunity" plays in the national culture of the people in the United States. "From the earliest days of the Republic, Americans have possessed an abiding faith that theirs is a land of opportunity" (Brint & Karabel, 1989, p. 3). The United States, unlike European societies, was founded on the belief that people have limitless opportunities and can succeed through hard work and ability (a notion that is referred to as "contest mobility" and will be described in greater detail in the next section of this chapter). The uniqueness of U.S. society bears out in modern times: when the U.S. is compared with other industrial nations, no other country sends as many individuals to postsecondary educational institutions as the United States (Brint & Karabel, 1989).

The issue is that millions more individuals in this country aspire to high levels of education and prestigious occupations than the educational and occupational systems can support. "For example, over half of high school seniors [in the early 1980s] 'planned' careers in professional/technical jobs . . . but in that same year, only 13 percent of the labor force was employed in such jobs" (Brint & Karabel, p. 8). Thus, drawing a distinction between what a student wants and expects may be a particularly difficult and unique problem, especially for a population of students who have already reached postsecondary education and are faced with a changing job market.

Contest versus Sponsored Mobility

Tuner (1960) proposed a framework for understanding the differences in the educational systems of the United States and England. Turner's view is that the U.S. educational system resembles a "contest" system of mobility where access to elite status is an open contest. An established elite does not have control over the final outcome of who may attain upward mobility and therefore education is a field in which open competition is the means by which people can improve their statuses. On the other hand, sponsored mobility is a system in which the elite controls the process. "Elite status is *given* on the basis of some criterion of supposed merit and cannot be *taken* by any amount of effort or strategy" (emphasis in original, Turner, 1960, p. 856). Turner compares upward mobility in a sponsored system to gaining entrance into a private club:

> Each candidate must be 'sponsored' by one or more of the members. . . . The governing objective of contest mobility is to give elite status to those who earn it, while the goal of sponsored mobility is to make the best use of the talents in society by sorting persons into their proper niches [Turner, 1960, pp. 856–857].

Turner also discusses how the societies ensure and maintain loyalty to the social system. In a contest mobility system, individuals think of themselves as competing for positions in the elite. When individuals think of themselves as future members of the elite, they begin to identify with the members of the upper classes, view high status society members as "ordinary" people, and begin to form the conviction that they may become members of the elite in the future. A contest mobility system influences the internalization of high achievement values in most members of society—especially those in the lower socioeconomic strata. Those members of society who are unambitious are "individual deviants" and not a threat to the cohesiveness of society. In a contest mobility system, education is considered an "opportunity" whereby an individual who has strong initiative and drive may make the best use of it. Turner describes the fact that researchers found the "general level of occupational aspiration reported by high school students is quite unrealistic in relation to the actual distribution of job opportunities" (p. 858) as proof that the United States educational system is primarily a contest mobility system. Lower SES students' aspirations are not lowered (or kept low) early in the educational process, as would be predicted in a sponsored mobility system.

In a sponsored mobility system, social control is maintained by guiding the members of the lower socioeconomic classes to feel inferior to the elite. The future members of the elite are selected very early in their schooling so that the others can be "taught to accept their inferiority and to make 'realistic' rather than [f]antasy plans" (p. 859). Early selection of future members of the elite prevents the "masses" from raising their hopes and thereby becoming powerful members of a discontented force.

The assumptions of contest mobility systems are similar to the assumptions of a meritocracy and of the social psychological models of status attainment: individuals' achievement affect their educational aspirations, expectations, and attainments. Sponsored mobility, and the social allocation perspective of mobility, view the individual as constrained by what the members of the elite will allow the individual to do: individuals' achievement is largely dependent upon their statuses at birth.

Critiques of States Attainment & Contest/Sponsored Mobility

The status attainment model is the primary way in which aspirations have been studied over the past thirty years. This section discusses critiques of status attainment research (and therefore much of the research on aspirations that use the status attainment model). Status attainment research—Blau and Duncan's model and social-ization models—have been found to work well for samples of White males. When the models have been tested on White females and students of color of both genders, the models explain lit-tle of the variance. This section posits some rea-sons for lack of success of the status attainment research in explaining the outcomes of minor-ity students and White females.

One of the main criticisms of the status attainment model is that it offers little to explain gender and ethnic differences, and probably that is a reason why the social psychological status attainment model has been cited sporadically in research articles in the last ten years. The socialization model explained very little of the variance in aspirations and attainment for women of all ethnicities and minority men (Berman & Haug, 1979), and often the pattern of relationships between the White samples and the minority samples were completely different (Portes & Wilson, 1976). Campbell (1983) com-pleted a critique of the status attainment models and concluded that an important and necessary direction for status attainment research is in the area of "minority group differences in achieve-ment processes . . . [and] it will be possible to determine if there might be a 'minority group status attainment process' which applies to racial minorities . . ." (p. 59). In addition to the criticism that the model has limited application to minor-ity populations and women, there are several other critiques of the model and studies of aspi-rations in general (Kerchoff, 1984).

A second criticism of status attainment research, which may be related to the model's limited explanatory power for White female stu-dents and minority students, is that one of the core assumptions of the status attainment model is that the United States society functions as a meritocracy. In other words, the researchers who study students using the attainment model view educational systems as functioning mostly on merit—the students who are the most able will have the highest aspirations and attain the high-est degrees. Eckland (1964) responded to previ-ous researchers who stated that SES affects who attends college but has little relationship to who graduates from college:

> . . . Social class differences will increasingly determine who graduates among the college entrants of the [future]. . . . To the extent that higher education develops the same mass conditions as our system of secondary edu-cation in which dropout has been so closely associated with social status, a similar pro-cess will occur in our colleges [p. 50].

Other researchers emphasize that the unequal opportunities for lower SES students are encour-aged by an educational system that purports to reward students based solely on merit. Educa-tional institutions transmit inequality by legiti-mating ascriptive statuses through academic achievement (Morrow & Torres, 1995). Therefore, a student's life chances can be determined by the student's circumstances at birth. This is counter to the assumptions of a meritocracy.

Contest mobility may describe the educa-tional opportunities of certain members of the United States population, but at the time Turner published his article, the *Brown v. Board of Edu-cation* decision concerning the unequal and biased nature of African American elementary education was barely six years old. "The Amer-ican system of stratification and mobility has caused Black mobility to approximate Turner's sponsored mobility" (Porter, 1974, p. 313). African Americans had and continue to have legal battles to gain entrance to the educational institutions where the "meritocratic contests" were supposedly taking place. All members of United States society could not participate in an "equal contest" for upward mobility, and status attainment models assume that the United States is an open opportunity structure (Wilson Sadberry, Winfield, & Royster, 1991). This assumption seems to be incorrect, especially when one considers occupational outcomes. Women earn lower salaries than men and the situation is particularly startling for African Americans and Latinos: in 1980, Black women and Black men tended to earn salaries that were, respectively, 46% and 68% of those earned by White men (Grubb & Wilson, 1989). It seems that the system of mobility in the United States can-not be broadly categorized as a "contest" for all groups, but the patterns of mobility may vary greatly by ethnicity, SES, and gender. Therefore, it is reasonable to say that the assumption of meritocracy may be one problem with the applicability of the status attainment model to different populations.

A third criticism of status attainment literature is the dated nature of the research. Much of the status attainment research was completed in the 1960s and 1970s and may not take into account the increasing diversity on college campuses. The effects of affirmative action programs and financial and programs on increasing access (in the 1970s) and limiting access (in the 1980s to present) are not examined. There are policy and structural issues that have long term impacts on college student outcomes that are not addressed in status attainment models.

A fourth criticism of the early status attainment literature (although this is less true of recent educational aspirations studies by higher education researchers) is the focus on individual characteristics and lack of or limited use of institutional variables. Researchers have suggested that status attainment studies should take into account the characteristics and effects of the educational institution in addition to individual characteristics (Kerckhoff, 1976). Educational institutions are not equal in terms of resources and they affect the outcomes of students differently. Studies need to take this into account as well as individual differences between students (Pascarella, 1984).

A final criticism of the status attainment literature is more pertinent for the social allocation analysis than for the socialization perspective. Social allocation tends to view the process of status attainment and aspirations development as deterministic. Structural constraints in society limit the aspirations and attainments of individuals such that those whose parents are from the lower socioeconomic statuses will, more likely than not, remain at the same status through adulthood. However, there are individuals in society who resist the mechanisms of reproduction and succeed. Resistance theory posits that individuals in the lower socioeconomic classes of society resist the upper classes' control of resources through subtle or direct means (Giroux, 1983). Resistance has taken the form of direct confrontation in student protests and in more subtle means by way of students' rejection of messages from others that claim they

cannot succeed (Feagin, Vera, & Imani, 1996; Hurtado, 1990).

A key element of resistance theory is the transformation of institutional structures. High aspirations may help increased mumbers of African Americans and Latinos to achieve high levels of educational attainment. Perhaps maintaining high aspirations is one way minority students refuse to internalize "do not succeed" messages. Indeed, in spite of economic inequality, African Americans have historically maintained high hopes of becoming upwardly mobile through the education process (Knight & Wing, 1995).

Cultural and Social Capital

Status attainment and contest and sponsored mobility are well-established theoretical frameworks within which to study educational aspirations. Another theoretical framework that is gaining more prominence in recent higher education literature is based on Bourdieu's work on cultural capital and on the concept of social capital.

The terms "social capital" and "cultural capital" have their origins in Marxist analyses of class conflict and in Bourdieu's publications about French society. Both are terms used in many sociological theories of reproduction, which assume that society reproduces status (particularly class) differences within particular institutions.

Social capital can be defined as the relationships and institutions that shape a social group's (or society's) interactions. Researchers have linked the status attainment research to the concept of social capital in that "children's achievement is facilitated by . . . social capital involving parent-child interactions in learning activities" (Hao & Bonstead-Bruns, 1998, p. 177). Therefore, the quality of the interactions between parents and children affect the children's achievement.

Cultural capital is knowledge transmitted from upper- and middle-class families to their children. This knowledge adds to the economic capital that is already transmitted in the families. Cultural and social capital perspectives have been applied to higher education relatively recently. Researchers have used Bourdieu's framework as a way of explaining why class is so significant in affecting student outcomes and discussing the application of cultural capital to various outcomes including retention and college choice (Berger, 2000; McDonough, 1997).

Cultural capital may explain why lower SES students have lower aspirations. More-educated parents may socialize their children early to prepare their children for professional careers. Middle- and upper-class students may have more information about their post-secondary options and therefore would be more likely not only to attend college, but to attend higher status institutions that may afford them greater benefits later.

A significant limitation of many reproduction theories (including the discussions of social and cultural capital) is that the notions of agency and resistance are not examined thoroughly. In addition, many of systems of oppression in U.S. society are gender- and race/ethnicity-based in addition to being class-based. Since most reproduction theories focus on class differences, there is a gap in the literature regarding theories that can account for complex relationships between gender, race, and class. Some researchers have begun to fill that gap, noting the specific interactions of gender and race in how groups relate to each other (Luttrell, 1989; Morrow & Torres, 1995).

Explanations for the Low Aspirations of Minority Youth

The previous sections described the three main theoretical explanations for aspirations: status attainment, contest and sponsored mobility, and social/cultural capital. This section of the chapter discusses theories explaining why African American and Latino students have lower aspirations (and lower attainments) than White students.

African Americans

In the United States, African Americans have low educational and occupational attainments in comparison to White individuals. One explanation is the cultural deficit perspective. This perspective assumes that "Black cultural values, as transmitted through the family and specifically the parents, are dysfunctional, and therefore the reason for Blacks' low educational . . . attainment" (Solorzano, 1992, p. 30). The cultural deficit perspective also assumes that some African Americans do not place as high a value on education as do White individuals. Although

Black parents tend to communicate to their children the need to work hard, Black children do not put a lot of effort into their schooling for three reasons:

> (a) perseverance at academic tasks has not developed as a part of their cultural tradition; (b) the actual texture of their parents' lives of unemployment, underemployment, and discrimination convey a powerful message that counteracts parental verbal encouragement; and (c) children learn from observing older members of their community that school success does not necessarily lead to jobs and other necessary and important things in adult life [Ogbu, 1983, p. 181].

Ogbu argues that because of the history of poor education of African American youth in this country, Black parents and children have a deep distrust for schooling. This distrust prevents Black children from internalizing the "values of the schools, accept[ing] school criteria for success, or follow[ing] school rules of behavior for achievement" (p. 181). Thus, because Black children do not internalize the values of schools, they tend to do much more poorly than White students.

Ogbu's research on the educational experiences of African American students has led to the development of the caste theory explanation of school failure. This theory asserts the following: (1) there is a caste system in the United States based primarily on race/ethnicity; (2) there is a typology of experiences of minority group members whereby "involuntary" minorities and "voluntary" minorities have historical differences with respect to their relationships with the country and the negative historical experiences that "involuntary" minority group members endured continue in the present; (3) in response to oppression and limited opportunities, "involuntary" minority group members develop various adaptive or survival strategies that are quite often negative adaptations (Foley, 1991; Ogbu, 1983).

Ogbu identifies Mexican Americans, Native Americans (American Indians), and African Americans as the primary involuntary minority groups in the United States. Ogbu feels that involuntary and voluntary minority group members "perceive their historical deprivation" quite differently (Foley, p. 65). Ogbu's thesis is that recent immigrant groups ("voluntary" minority group members) "do not perceive the racial barriers and the lack of opportunity in . . . American society" and therefore they view the United States as a "land of opportunity" in comparison to their country of origin. Because of this, voluntary minority group members have a sense of optimism about their future and do better in schools (Foley, p. 65). On the other hand, involuntary minority group members have negative views of society and of their chances to succeed in society. Ogbu's primary emphasis is on the negative adaptive strategies of involuntary minority group members:

> [Involuntary minority group members] are overwhelmed by the 'community forces' of a job ceiling and racial oppression, and by a variety of 'school forces.' Their typical psychological and cultural adaptation is self-defeating in several ways. They succumb to the dominant societies' myths about them as inferior. They are unable to create a folk theory of schooling that is optimistic about their future. They develop a dysfunctional oppositional culture that leads them to believe that they cannot be both academically successful and ethnically different . . . Caste theory makes a powerful case that involuntary minorities are not likely to succeed in school or in life [Foley, 1991, p. 67].

In addition, Fordham and Ogbu (1986) postulate that Black students, who are capable of doing well in school, do not do well because they do not want to be accused of "acting White." Certain behaviors are conceptualized by Black students as inappropriate because those behaviors are characteristic of White students.

Although there have been several critiques of Ogbu's research, one critique is the most salient for this chapter: Ogbu's emphasis on the negative adaptive patterns of involuntary minority group members (Foley, 1991). Ogbu theorizes that oppressed minority group members develop oppositional cultures, and these oppositional cultures come "trapped in a counterproductive pattern of reacting to racial stereotypes and myths" (Foley, p. 76). In this way, Ogbu's conception of African American school behavior resembles the oft maligned "culture of poverty" concept. However, in the "culture of poverty" perspective of African Americans in inner cities, African Americans are psychologically damaged: they have low self-esteem, pessimism, and a sense of fatalism. Ogbu's view of African Americans is not so much that the group is psychologically dam-

aged, but that African Americans are "discouraged and trapped in the racist myths of the dominant society. They are unable to see that they can be both successful and Black" (Foley, p. 77). Caste theory does tend to ignore the ways in which oppressed groups engage in "positive" resistance. Thus, caste theorists tend to "underestimate the capacity of ethnic resistance movements to empower individuals" (Foley, p. 78).

Ogbu's research has parallels to the social allocation model of status attainment: members of involuntary minority group members see their opportunities as constrained by society, and that affects their behavior in schools. Ogbu's research in the United States has primarily focused on the school *failure* of African American children. Given that postsecondary education attendees are already successful by many standards. Ogbu's caste theory may have limited applicability to college students.

Latinos

The discussion of Ogbu's work has parallels for Latino students, who (particularly Mexican Americans) are considered involuntary minorities. As such, they are similar to African Americans in status and in educational attainment patterns. Therefore, Mexican American students may tend to feel negatively toward society and have a distrust of schooling. In addition to Ogbu's work, the work of Barrera is particularly applicable in explaining racial inequality.

Barrera (1997) describes three major deficiency theories of racial inequality: biological, cultural, and social structural. Biological theories assert that there are essential differences between members of racial groups that explain the respective gaps in levels of educational achievement, attainment, and socioeconomic success. Social structural theories argue that historical and social structure factors in the U.S. society have produced weak family structures for some racial/ethnic minority group members (e.g. African American, Latinos, American Indians) and have led to emotional problems and low educational attainment. Cultural deficiency theories argue that it is the culture of minority groups that contribute to their lower attainment rates and lower SES. These theorists have characterized African Americans and Latinos as having a "culture of poverty" where they have a "present orientation rather than [a] future orientation, a lack of work discipline, and so on" (Barrera, p. 5). "Individuals who share this 'culture' do poorly in school, and their educational attainment creates conditions of poverty and powerlessness, which interact with each other and create a vicious circle to perpetuate educational inequalities" (p. 5). In particular, theorists argue that Latinos suffer from a "language handicap" and lack of a success orientation, and because of their relatively lower SES, they suffer from a "cultural disadvantage." Chicano culture is often portrayed as "highly traditional and nonadapted to the requirements of upward mobility in an industrial society" (p. 6).

Barrera concludes that "as an approach to explaining racial inequality, then, deficiency models based on social structure are inelegant methodologically—different deficiencies have to be found for each racial group" (p. 7). While negative traits of the cultures of racial/ethnic minority groups are accentuated in such theories, the theories often do not examine accompanying positive traits (see Foley's critique of Ogbu in the previous section). Furthermore, thorough examinations of the positive and negative traits of the dominant cultural group are often not taken into account.

Ethnic Differences in Aspirations Studies

Latinos

Few studies have been done comparing the aspirations of Latino populations to other groups. However, two studies do provide some understanding of the issues that are particular to Latinos' aspirations. In a comparison of the aspirations of African American, Latino, Asian American, and White students using the National Educational Longitudinal Study (NELS) dataset, Latino youth had the lowest aspirations of the four groups (Kao & Tienda, 1998). Kao and Tienda supplemented their quantitative analyses with focus group interviews with African American and Latino youth. Based on their analyses, they conclude that Latino youth had optimistic educational aspirations—taking into account the lower socioeconomic status of their parents. Despite their relatively high aspirations, Latino youth in general did not have adequate information about college options and financial aid packages: "some students believed that their parents' financial status makes college

an impossible dream, while others believe they can obtain a full scholarship simply because they are [Latino] or athletes" (p. 379).

Kao and Tienda also assert (as do other scholars who study the effects of aspirations on attainments—see St. John, 1991) that "educational aspirations mediate the influence of family backgrounds and significant others on ultimate educational attainments" (p. 380). What remains a question after years of research in this area is: if the deficit theories are accurate and there are negative pressures in the schools and cultures of African Americans and Latinos that limit attainments, why don't these pressures similarly constrain aspirations?

One answer to this question is the role that Latino parents play in the aspirations of their children. So (1987) found that Latino parents "have high aspirations for their children and want their children . . . to go to college as much as White parents want their children to do so" (pp. 49–50). So further found that Latino parents "started forming aspirations for college attainment when their children were still in elementary school" (p.52).

African Americans

Researchers typically cannot pinpoint why the patterns of relationships between variables in models explaining African Americans' aspirations differ so greatly from the relationships in White student samples. When African Americans students have high aspirations, they have been referred to as "unrealistic," and when lower income students and/or African Americans inflate their educational expectations it has been labeled an adaptation to deprivation (Agnew & Jones, 1988). Students categorized as having "unrealistic expectations" do achieve their dreams (attend college, or complete a college degree, for instance), though perhaps in smaller numbers than their higher income, higher scoring peers (Agnew & Jones, 1988). Referring to African Americans specifically as having "unrealistic" aspirations seems especially unnecessary given the high aspirations of the people of the U.S. and that researchers have noted that low SES/White students have had higher than "realistic" aspirations for several decades (Brint & Karabel, 1989). In fact, research indicates that high aspirations may at least partially mitigate the negative effects of low SES on college attendance (St. John, 1991). Therefore, high aspirations have assisted African American students in achieving their goals.

In the 1960s, African Americans were thought to have lower levels of aspirations than White students, but in studies where socioeconomic class is controlled, African Americans were found to have as high or higher aspirations within socioeconomic stratification groups (Portes & Wilson, 1976). These findings have led researchers to conclude that White students' higher attainments is due to their advantages in background variables and characteristics (Portes & Wilson, 1976). In fact, while minority students have "the aspirations, the ability, and the qualifications to go to a four-year college, they do not attend the college of their choice to the degree that Whites do." (Labovitz, 1975, p. 248).

In addition, the cultural deficit view of attainment "has become the social scientific norm even though little empirical evidence exists to support many of its claims" (Solorzano, 1992, p. 31). As has been discussed, African American students tend to have as high or higher aspirations than White students—especially when SES characteristics are controlled (St. John, 1991). Thus, the cultural deficit model seems to have little foundation in empirical research. The assumptions of the cultural deficit model may hold true for some selected groups of African Americans (Ogbu, 1983), but has yet to be demonstrated to be a universal norm, especially through national databases (Solorzano, 1992).

What is especially lacking in discussions of the educational aspirations of African American, Latino, and White students is the role that educational institutions play in the development and maintenance of aspirations. Focusing on the ways in which institutions contribute to the development of aspirations moves the discussion away from cultural and individual characteristics and toward the types of educational environments that are most conducive for student achievement. In this way, the literature on college impact and on the experiences of college students informs status attainment research.

College Students' Degree Aspirations and College Impact

The literature on college students' degree aspirations, that is, the literature on college students' plans to attend graduate school, is more sparse than the high-school-to-college literature. Pascarella (1984) both applauds and criticizes previous studies of college students' aspirations. On the one hand, Pascarella contends that the research of Astin (1977) and his colleagues make some contributions to an understanding of the institutional characteristics that influence students' aspirations. On the other hand, these research publications "have a number of methodological problems . . . the most important of these . . . is the orientation toward an empirical rather than theoretical framework for the data analyses" (Pascarella, 1984, p. 753). Few researchers have theorized why and how the characteristics of an institution impact an individual student's degree plans.

The social psychological status attainment model is the foundation of college student aspirations studies. College students are considered individual actors who have access to several parts of the campus and interact with the individuals they choose. Many researchers do recognize the ways in which institutional structures can constrain the behavior of individuals (Astin, 1993), but why is it that some institutions have higher proportions of student degree completion than others? Particular institutional characteristics and students' college experiences work to produce positive student educational outcomes. For example, African American students who attend historically Black colleges and universities (HBCUs) tend to go to graduate school in greater numbers than African Americans who attend predominantly White institutions (PWIs). Women who attend women's colleges attend graduate school in greater numbers and have more positive affective development than women attending co-educational institutions (Smith, 1990).

College choice literature also centers on the discussion of aspirations. The literature has evolved over the years into the formulation of a three stage model: predisposition, search, and choice (Hossler & Gallagher, 1987). The predisposition stage has particular parallels to the study of aspirations. Predisposition is described as "a developmental phase in which students determine whether or not they would like to continue their education beyond high school" (Hossler & Gallagher, 1987, p. 209). The theoretical underpinnings for the predisposition stage is grounded in the status attainment literature (Hossler, Braxton, & Coopersmith, 1989). Much of the research on the predisposition stage finds significant relationships between level of aspirations and ethnicity, size of family, parents' education attainments, parents' income, student academic ability and achievement, and peer and teacher influences (Paulsen, 1990).

Person environment fit—the degree to which an individual belongs in (is congruent with) an environment—has been a popular explanation for why some students seem to succeed and some fail in a given institution (Feldman & Newcomb, 1969).

> Students from lower status backgrounds differ from those of higher status backgrounds in ways that presumably produce greater incongruence between the lower status group and the demands and opportunities of the college environment. Thus entering students of lower socioeconomic status, in comparison to their higher status counterparts, (1) are less culturally sophisticated . . . : (2) have had a more restricted range of experiences . . . : and (3) are more likely to be oriented to college in terms of vocational or professional training and less likely to be oriented in terms of intellectual growth [Feldman & Newcomb, p. 277].

One problem with the traditional person-environment fit perspective is that the burden of congruence is placed on the student. Little responsibility is placed on the members of the campus community who have constructed and maintained the campus environment. The person-environment fit explanation of college impact—especially as it relates to SES—corresponds best with the contest view of social mobility (as described in previous sections). Those persons who are most like the environment they enter will be the most successful—although, since lower SES students tend to be less successful, perhaps a form of sponsored mobility is at work.

African Americans in Higher Education

Although there are few articles that specifically test models of degree aspirations on African American college students, the author of this *chapter* has been able to locate very few published studies that test models of degree aspirations on Latino college students. The following section describes previous empirical research on African American college students' aspirations.

The models that have been tested on Black students are substantially different from models tested on White students. Therefore, it is important to understand the processes by which students develop and maintain educational aspirations and expectations, if only to understand the educational experiences of African American students. In a study of High School and Beyond (HSB) participants who graduated from college. Weiler (1993) found that roughly the same percentage of minority and White students who enrolled in graduate school initially did not expect to attend. However, there were large differences between the numbers of minority and White students who had expected to attend graduate school and then did not. Weiler concluded that "the key reason for lower post-baccalaureate attendance of minorities is the fact that a relatively large fraction of them who planned to continue their education beyond the baccalaureate at the time they entered college changed their minds" (p. 446). It is important to study the individual and institutional attributes of the process by which some college students are "cooled out" from graduate study. The process of cooling out is one in which the "socializing agents" in colleges—faculty and peers, the curriculum, and administrative procedures—all influence the lowering of educational plans (Clark, 1960; Pascarella & Terenzini, 1991).

Feagin, et al. (1996) detail some of the negative experiences African Americans have in PWIs. A central theme in the study is that of Black invisibility. Much like the main character of Ralph Ellison's book, African American students in Feagin, et al.'s study are not seen by "White professors, students, staff members and administrators . . . as full human beings with distinctive talents, virtues, interests and problems" (p. 14). Black students at PWIs often feel anxiety and fear at being the only one or one of a few African Americans in a particular environment. This anxiety can mean that African Americans look for the increased company of other African Americans for their support. Feagin, et al. also report that "a recent survey of Black students at mostly White universities found they were so concerned about intellectual survival that they were unable to devote as much attention to their personal, social, and cultural development as they should" (p. 75).

As with high school studies, researchers studying college students have implied that African Americans have unrealistic educational aspirations. Astin (1990) stated that Black students' aspirations are inconsistent with their career choices given the fact that 15.7%, 14.3%, and 37.7% of African Americans planned to earn doctoral, advanced professional (MD, JD), or, Master's degrees respectively, while only 11%, 10.1%, and 36.9% of White students planned to earn such degrees. In addition, African Americans planned to be businesspersons or computer programmers 4%–6% more than White students. Doctorates are not necessarily required for such professions as businesspersons and computer programmers, and thus Astin feels Black students have unrealistic educational aspirations.

In a study using prestige scores for occupations (instead of discrete categories). White students tended to have nearly the same short range occupational expectations as Black students at HBCUs and PWIs, and the long-range occupational expectations of White students tended to be slightly higher or about the same as the expectations of Black students (Dawkins, 1982). So, perhaps the career expectations of African American college students are not found to be so inconsistent when different measures and statistical controls are employed.

The degree to which college students' aspirations for graduate education are "unrealistic" is perhaps difficult to determine, particularly since students who attend postsecondary institutions have already demonstrated success. They completed secondary education and have the personal goals, initiative, and achievement necessary to apply to college and be admitted. College students are successful, talented, and capable—even likely—to earn graduate degrees. However, as research reviewed in this section demonstrates, there are significant patterns of stratification within higher education: African American students disproportionately attend less "prestigious" institutions, drop out of post secondary institutions and tend not to go on to earn graduate degrees in similar numbers as White students (Carter & Wilson, 1996).

Description of a Theoretical Model

The competing assumptions of educational mobility focus on conceptions of individual students' aspirations and attainment as being functions of social constraints (social allocation or sponsored mobility theoretical perspectives) or as being free of social constraints and subject to individual agency (status attainment or contest mobility theoretical perspectives). Empirical evidence supports both assumptions, but in addition, it seems evident that the processes of aspirations development are different for African American, Latino, and White students. Although it may be possible to develop a theoretical model of aspirations development that encompasses the experiences of African American, Latino, and White students, the model should be tested *separately* for each group because African American, Latino, and White students begin college with different backgrounds, attend different types of institutions, and have different experiences in college (Carter, 1999b; Kao & Tienda, 1998).

In addition, the theoretical conceptualizations of the role of institutions in the development of students' aspirations are lacking. Pascarella (1984) critiqued educational aspirations research as being atheoretical, and found few direct effects of institutional measures on students' degree aspirations. A few studies show that the structural characteristics of institutions do have direct effects on students' aspirations and that the role of institutional characteristics in the development of students' degree goals needs to be linked with the theoretical perspectives of status attainment (Carter, 2001).

Therefore, students' degree goals are a function of their own individual backgrounds and circumstances, their institutional choices (such as they are), and the socializing influences of institutions. Theories of students' degree aspirations and achievement that encapsulate the multi-faceted nature of student decision-making as well as the ways in which institutional environments affect students' decisions can better conceptualize the processes by which students make decisions about their futures.

Figure 14-1 shows a theoretical model based on the findings of previous studies and theoretical foundations previously discussed. This section of the chapter will focus on previous empirical research; the theoretical frameworks discussed in the first half of the chapter are the lenses through which these relationships in the model can be interpreted.

The research and conceptual model posed is perhaps most appropriate for quantitative research where the specific effects of variables

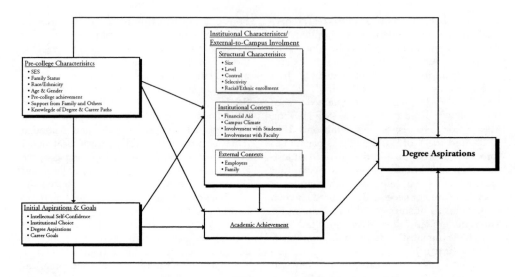

Figure 14-1 Theoretical and Conceptual Model of Factors Influencing College Students' Degree Aspirations.

can be tested on an outcome. However, there is a need for extensive qualitative work on students' degree aspirations (Kao & Tienda, 1998) and the model presented may assist qualitative researchers in studying about how students' aspirations are shaped.

The model represents race/ethnicity as an exogenous variable in the model, but we may need to consider it specifically since the aspirations of racial/ethnic groups differ to such a degree. Generally, the ways in which students' degree aspirations are influenced can be described in four stages:

1. *Pre-college characteristics* (e.g. socioeconomic status, age, gender, family status, pre-college achievement, support from family and peers, knowledge of degree and career path) affect *students' initial aspirations and goals* (e.g. self-confidence, college choice behavior, initial degree aspirations, career goals).

2. *Pre-college characteristics* and *initial aspirations and goals* affect *institutional experiences and involvement.*

3. All three groups of variables in turn affect *academic achievement.*

4. Finally, *pre-college characteristics, initial aspirations, institutional experiences, and academic achievement* all affect later *degree aspirations.*

First, pre-college characteristics in the form of SES, age, family status, and pre-college achievement affect initial aspirations, students' career and life goals, levels of intellectual self-confidence, and college choices. There is significant evidence that socioeconomic status affects students' degree goals. Since many researchers argue that both contest and sponsored mobility processes affect the ways in which students develop their aspirations, pre-college achievement is an important measure to incorporate. Age and family status are variables that specifically distinguish between traditional and nontraditional students in higher education. Close to 50% of the higher education population are more than 24 years old, and older students tend to be married and/or have children (Choy & Premo, 1995). Since such a significant population of our higher education institutions is so different from traditional 18-year-old students who have been the focus of higher education research, considerations that uniquely affect the aspirations of nontraditional students needs to be taken into account as well. In addition, the support individuals receive from family and peers regarding their academic and career goals and the knowledge students have about career and degree paths all need to be considered as affecting students' initial aspirations and goals upon college entry.

Initial orientations, goals, aspirations, and institutional choice measures are important to incorporate into a model of degree aspirations because they can show the students' levels of intellectual and academic self-confidence, their initial degree and career goals, and the reasons they chose the institution they are attending (e.g. students' choice of institution was constrained by financial or social circumstances).

Second, pre-college characteristics and initial aspirations/goals affect institutional experiences and involvement. Students are not randomly assigned to higher education institutions. Pre-college characteristics and initial aspirations and goals affect the kinds of institutions students attend. The results of previous studies show that students interact in particular institutional contexts that influence their aspirations (Allen, 1992). For instance, the type of institution students attend (four year or two year, high cost vs. low cost, high percentage of minority enrollment, faculty-student ratio) affects the kind of financial assistance they can receive, their perceptions of campus climate, and their involvement with students and faculty. The financial aid students receive (especially students with work study awards, working on- or off-campus) affect the students' involvement with faculty, staff, and students on campus and their involvement with individuals external to the campus community. Student perceptions of the campus climate and the structural characteristics of the campus jointly can influence students' interactions with individuals off campus—particularly if the students are nontraditional students or have interests that are not well-represented on-campus. Perceptions of campus climate may have indirect effects on aspirations by affecting the level of involvement students have with other students, faculty, and staff. In addition, students' involvement in communities that are external to the campus community also may be important factors affecting students' aspirations. In predominantly White institutions. African American and Latino students may have frequent interactions with their families, friends and others that may counteract the negative experiences.

Third, all three groups of variables in turn affect academic achievement. Students' experiences in institutional and external-to-the-institution contexts may affect their levels of college achievement. *Finally, all of the preceding variables affect later aspirations.* The following section details the empirical findings for each section of the model.

Pre College Characteristics

Higher education research suggests several background characteristics affect student aspirations. African American students have been found to have aspirations as high as, or higher than, those of White students over several years of studies (Allen, 1991; Astin, 1977, 1993). However, the aspirations models tend not to work as well for African American populations (Blau & Duncan, 1967; Epps & Jackson, 1985; Portes & Wilson, 1976). Portes and Wilson (1976) found that African Americans out perform White students (i.e. Black students receive higher grades and have higher aspirations, when SES is controlled) at each stage of the attainment process. Given this finding, they suggest that White students' advantage in attainment "depends directly on their initial advantages in the input variables" (p. 423).

As mentioned earlier, Latino students tend to have lower aspirations than White or African American students, and statistical models tend to predict their aspirations well (Carter, 1999b; Kao & Tienda, 1998). Labovitz (1975) studied the effect of ethnicity, SES and fulfillment of college aspirations. Labovitz's model included measures of IQ, SES, college plans, GPA, school SES, and neighborhood SES as predictors of college attendance for 1966 San Diego high school seniors. Minority students were found to "have the aspirations, the ability, and the qualifications to go to a four-year college, [but] they do not attend the colleges of their choice to the degree that White [students] do" (p. 248). Again, the notion of contest mobility with respect to minority students is questioned. In Labovitz's study, attendance at a four-year college is not simply the result of an even "contest" based on ability and goals. There are other factors—unexamined in the study—that seem to disadvantage minority students in the college attendance process. This is particularly true when you consider that the students in Labovitz's study graduated from high school thirty years ago.

Women have lower aspirations than men, on average (McClelland, 1990), tend to be more adversely affected by delays in entry to higher education (Kempner & Kinnick, 1990), have more unexplained variance in aspirations models than men (Hearn, 1987), and tend to be less likely to pursue a post-baccalaureate degree immediately after college graduation (Isaac, Malaney, & Karras, 1992). Astin (1977) found that over a four-year period, almost uniformly women had lowered aspirations. However, women who attend women's colleges significantly raise their degree aspirations over a four-year period (Smith, 1990).

Socioeconomic status is the variable most often studied in status attainment models. Sewell and Shah (1967) completed a study to determine which affects college-going and completion more: ability or socio-economic status. They found that SES and intelligence have positive relationships to college attendance for both males and females. Further, for men, the effect of SES decreases over time, and SES has comparably lower effects on college outcomes than intelligence does. However, the same is not true for females. SES has a much greater effect on the outcome measures than intelligence (measured by scores on the Henmon-Nelson Test of Mental Maturity). The main point of their study is "that along with intelligence, socioeconomic status continues to influence college graduation even after socioeconomic selection has taken place in the process of determining who will attend college" (p. 20). Therefore, socioeconomic status plays a part in determining who can participate in the contest for upward mobility. It is known from the literature that lower income students, and students whose parents achieved lower levels of education, tend to have lower aspirations and expectations than higher SES students. SES seems to affect the aspirations and achievement of women and minority students more than it affects the aspirations and achievement of White male students (Burke & Hoelter, 1988). Other researchers have concluded that the educational attainment of the same-sex parent is what most affects the educational behaviors of the student (Isaac, Malaney, & Karras, 1992).

The research on ability reveals complicated effects on aspirations. Ancis and Sedlacek (1997) state that "SAT scores tend to under-predict women's grades" and the use of other variables "provides for a more accurate and complete understanding of women's educational development" (p. 6). When colleges and universities rely on SAT scores to make academic decisions (financial aid based on "merit," and admissions decisions) they may be limiting the extent to which talented women students can obtain financial aid or participate in certain programs, and may restrict the admission of women students to certain institutions (Ancis & Sedlacek, 1997). In addition, academic advisors may have lower expectations of women students' achievement if they judge ability only by SAT scores. This has direct implications to the socialization view of social mobility: Significant others influence the goals of students. If the basis by which significant others' expectations of what women students are able to do is not a "true" measure of their ability (e.g. the SAT score), this could unnecessarily constrict students' future goals. When ability is measured by aptitude tests and grade point average, ability seems to have mostly indirect effects on educational aspirations. Perhaps this is because aptitude has been found to be strongly related to socioeconomic status (Thomas, Alexander, & Eckland, 1979). However, another study found that ability (as measured by IQ and GPA) has clear direct effects on the aspirations of White students, but no direct effects on the aspirations of African American students (Burke & Hoelter, 1988). Several researchers have found significant relationships between high college GPAs and high aspirations (Astin, 1977; Hearn, 1987; Pascarella, 1985), though in other studies, grade point average had no significant relationship to aspirations (Burke & Hoelter, 1988). These conflicting results suggest that tests of direct effects taking into account other background characteristics are important in determining the relationship of ability measures to aspirations.

Age and family status have not often been considered in models of degree aspirations. Two studies found that age is a significant predictor of White students' degree aspirations but not a significant predictor of African American and Latino students' aspirations. Younger White students tended to have higher aspirations after two and four years of college than older White students. Therefore, nontraditional students seem to have their aspirations constrained over time (Carter, 1999a; 1999b).

Knowledge of career and degree paths is an important element to consider in aspirations models. If students are not knowledgeable about the paths to graduate degrees and/or the necessary educational requirements for certain professions, their aspirations may change considerably over time. There is some evidence that African American students spend a shorter time preparing for college than White students. In a study conducted by the American College Testing (ACT) organization—the organization that administers one of the two most-used standardized tests for college admission—African American students attending their first-choice college tended to have lower ACT scores than those attending second- or third- or other-choice colleges. Explanations offered for this finding are that "students receiving higher scores on the ACT lift their aspirations, are recruited by other colleges, or find that financial aid opportunities have increased for them" (Maxey, Lee, & McClure, 1995, p. 101). This is not surprising, given that 81% of African American students were in twelfth grade when they took the ACT, as opposed to less than 70% of White students. African Americans may need more support than White students in developing post-secondary education plans (Maxey, et al., 1995).

Initial Aspirations and Goals

Burke and Hoelter (1988) use identity theory to conceptualize their approach to status attainment. They assert that people choose behaviors that correspond to their self-concept or identities. Thus, they assume that people who have strong, positive academic self-concepts should have higher educational aspirations and goals. Burke and Hoelter also take the same approach to studying aspirations as the Wisconsin (or social psychological) model, in that social psychological variables (e.g. academic identity/self-concept) mediate the effects of SES on educational intentions (Sewell, et al., 1969). They found that academic identity (as defined by students' evaluation of work independent of grades, perceived academic ability, and perceived ability to achieve high grades) mediates the effects of the main predictor variables—IQ and grade point average, for instance—on the educational plans of three of their sub-groups. Academic identity impacted the educational plans of White males and females, and African American females, but not of African American males.

The researchers offer very little explanation for the different findings for African American males, noting only that the meaning of educa-

tional expectations may differ for this particular group, and that the source of academic identity differs for the groups. Teacher influence has effects for the three groups, but not for Black males, and family background impacts White students' academic identity but not the identity of Black students. Burke and Hoelter suggest that "many of the variables of the traditional Wisconsin model are thus not relevant for [African Americans], even though, for [African American] females, academic identity is" (p. 41).

Burke and Hoelter believe that their study provided support for the notion that different models may be needed for separate ethnic and gender populations and showed support for their assumption that identity theory can be used successfully to broaden the Wisconsin model. Given that the researchers could not explain why the African American male students did not fit their identity theory assumptions, the usefulness of self-concept measures with respect to predicting aspirations may be limited. Burke and Hoelter's recommendation that self-concept variables should be incorporated into the Wisconsin status attainment model—without verifying the utility of the construct for African American males—remains an insupportable conclusion of their research.

The explanatory power of the social psychological model (the Wisconsin model) for the African American young men in the sample is much lower than for the young White men (Portes & Wilson, 1976). The correlations between self-esteem (measured in part by the Rosenberg Self-Esteem scale) with educational aspirations is .24 for White students, in contrast to the .13 value for African American students. The model explains 35% of the variance in educational aspirations for White students as opposed to 13% of the variance for African Americans. Portes and Wilson believe that African Americans are able to move through the educational and occupational systems due to self-reliance and ambition, while White students also use these attributes as well as benefiting from a social structural system that can "carry them along to higher levels of attainment" (p. 430). Portes and Wilson's findings seem to support a notion that aspirations are a function of individual attributes (contest mobility) as well as structural limitations (sponsored mobility).

There is some evidence in aspirations studies that the longer a student holds an aspiration, the more likely he or she will meet that goal. Alexander and Cook (1979) found that students who, before the 10th grade, planned to go to college were about 47% more likely to attend college as students who decided in the 12th grade to go to college. Therefore, early and sustained aspirations are important in the future attainments of students.

Astin (1977) incorporated analyses of students' degree aspirations in his study of the four-year effects of college. Astin found that "the student's degree aspirations at the time of college entrance are the most potent predictors of enrollment in graduate or professional schools" (p. 112). In terms of change in students' aspirations, several of Astin's findings (1977) are particularly interesting: Astin found that students' degree aspirations increase after college entrance—at the time of the study, 51% of first year students planned to achieve a post-graduate degree and four years later, this percentage increases to 65% of the students. What is also important about the findings of Astin's study is that students' changes in degree plans increase gradually over the four years. About 4% of students increase their aspirations each year of the study.

Astin updated his 1977 study in 1993 and found that 63 percent of students entering college in 1985 planned to earn a post baccalaureate degree. By the fourth year of college, the number of students with postgraduate degree aspirations were 68 percent. In addition, there is only a .35 correlation between 1985 and 1989 aspirations, which suggests that most of the students change their aspirations over time, or that changes in aspirations are due primarily to college experiences. There continues to be a positive correlation between those who have high 1985 aspirations and graduate school attendance. The positive predictors of high aspirations are intellectual self-esteem, and "[indicating] 'to prepare for graduate or professional school' as an important reason for attending college" (p. 265). Astin's findings seem to support the previous findings that academic identity is related to educational aspirations (Burke & Hoelter, 1988).

The college choice literature acknowledges the effects of individual attributes and structural limitations. As was explained earlier, college choice literature intersects with aspirations literature in many ways, and there are direct implications of college choice on college student

outcomes. The type of institution a student attends has significant implications for the student's future degree attainment and future occupational earnings. The process by which students choose institutions is an important element of understanding the process of educational aspirations development. A significantly lower proportion of African American students compared with White students attend their first choice institution (Hurtado, Inkelas, Briggs, & Rhee, 1997; (Maxey, et al., 1995).

Institutional Characteristics

Institutional characteristics and experiences can mediate or counteract background characteristics (Alwin, 1974), and can independently affect several educational outcomes including academic achievement and aspirations. This is especially true for African American students:

> The educational goals and activities of Black students are acted out in specific social environments that influence not only their ambitions, but also the possibility that they will realize their goals. Actors or agents in a particular setting—indeed, the setting itself—can either facilitate or frustrate the academic achievement of Black students. [Allen, 1992, p. 40]

Researchers have tried to broaden the status attainment models by introducing measures of students' experiences in educational institutions. Otto (1976) sought to expand Blau and Duncan's model by investigating the extent to which social integration (as defined by participation in school activities) affects educational attainment. According to Otto, past research on high school effects on educational attainment have found that within-school effects are far more important than between school effects. Since Spady (1970) hypothesized that membership in extracurricular activities can provide opportunities for students to acquire, develop and rehearse attitudes and skills, Otto decided to study whether extracurricular involvement impacts educational attainment.

Studying a sample of 1957 Michigan high school graduates who participated in a follow-up study in 1972, Otto (1976) hypothesized that prior social integration (participation in extra-curricular activities) facilitates the "acquisition, development, and rehearsal of achievement-related attitudes" (p. 1379) and that the benefits of social integration should apply to outcomes other than educational attainment. Otto's hypothesis is partially supported by the research. Social integration is the only variable in the model that has a significant total effect on the three main outcomes: educational attainment, income, and occupational attainment. However, most of the effect of social integration on occupational attainment and income is mediated by educational attainment. The explanation for the mixed results is that social integration may be a proxy for aspirations and that a study of the effect of social integration needs to be completed while aspirations are controlled. This suggests that aspirations studies should take into account college experiences where students benefit from peer socialization.

In addition to college experiences, particular aspects of environments seem to affect student outcomes. Tuition cost is an institutional characteristic that affects attainment. Pascarella, Smart, and Smylie (1992) found that the cost of an institution had an independent effect on occupational attainment. Students who attended high cost institutions tended to have higher occupational attainments than students who attended lower cost institutions. High tuition has also been shown to influence persistence (educational attainment) negatively. The higher the tuition, the less likely students will persist (St. John, Oescher, & Andrieu, 1992).

Astin, Tsui, and Avalos (1996) found that private universities (as compared to religious colleges, private colleges, and public colleges and universities) have the highest nine-year degree attainment rates for every racial/ethnic group (72% overall). Catholic institutions have the second highest attainment rates at 54.9%. Therefore, attendance at a private university more than attendance at other institutional types can insure that a student earns a Bachelor's degree. Since the link between attendance at a private university and degree achievement is so strong, perhaps institutional type has an impact on the development of degree aspirations.

Attending a large college (in terms of size of student body) tends to lower educational aspirations of African American men in predominantly White institutions (PWIs) and historically Black colleges and universities (HBCUs) (Smith, 1988). Highly selective institutions tend to have a positive effect on aspirations for White students and Latinos (Carter, 1999b; Pascarella, 1985). In a national study of undergraduates, Astin (1977) found that students attending more highly selective institutions tend to increase their aspirations over time, while students attending selective, public institutions and large institutions tend to lower their aspirations. In a follow-up study in 1993, Astin also found that the percentage of women in the student body was a positive predictor of increased aspirations among students. In contrast, a study of the effects of institutional type on educational aspirations found that many of the institutional effects on aspirations were modest, leading to assertions that institutional environments have primarily indirect effects on aspirations, being mediated by variables like achievement (Pascarella, 1984).

There are clearly conflicting conceptions of the ways in which institutional differences affect individual students' aspirations. The effect of community colleges on the aspirations and attainments of students has been a point of controversy for several decades. Clark (1960) discussed the role of the community college in the educational and occupational attainment of students. Clark believed that lower SES students were directed to two-year colleges and were thus "cooled out" (lowered their aspirations) as a result of their experiences in the institutions. As stated before, the process of cooling out is one in which the "socializing agents" in the two-year college—faculty and peers, the curriculum, and administrative procedures—all influence the lowering of educational plans (Pascarella & Terenzini, 1991). There is considerable evidence that the mere fact that a student attends a two-year college as opposed to a four-year college lowers that student's chances of attaining a Bachelor's degree by 19% (Brint & Karabel, 1989; Vélez, 1985).

> Community colleges are significantly less able than four-year colleges to facilitate the educational and economic attainment of the approximately 30 to 40 percent of community college entrants seeking bachelor's degrees . . . [G]enerally baccalaureate aspirants entering community colleges secure significantly fewer bachelor's degrees, fewer years of education, less prestigious jobs and in the long run, poorer paying jobs than comparable students entering four-year colleges . . . [Dougherty, 1987, pp. 99–100]

In this way, community colleges function as a form of "tracking" in higher education, such that the more able, higher SES students go directly to four-year colleges and institutions while the lower SES, less able students attain two-year degrees. The function of community colleges in terms of lowering attainment (and presumably aspirations) has been described by some researchers as part of society's role in "managing ambition": the United States society generates more ambition than the opportunity structure can support; therefore, the attendance of lower SES students at community colleges is one structural way of depressing high ambitions (Brint & Karabel, 1989).

The institutional effects of HBCUs and PWIs on African American student achievement has been the focus of several studies over the past two decades. Given the fact that HBCUs comprise 9% of the nation's baccalaureate-granting institutions, but "account for more than 30 percent of the all Bachelor's degrees awarded" (Trent, 1991, p. 56) to African Americans, it seems that there is something unique about the way HBCUs facilitate aspirations and attainment. Many of the studies find that African American students tend to experience social isolation and suffer identity problems in PWIs that may interfere with academic achievement (Jackson & Swan, 1991). On the other hand, HBCUs have been described as providing a "very mediocre educational experience," given their comparative lack of resources (Jackson & Swan, 1991, p. 127). However, some researchers suggest that despite HBCUs' relative disadvantages with respect to resources, the colleges have "been able to create a social psychological campus climate that not only fosters students' satisfaction, sense of community, and adjustment to college, but also increases the likelihood of persistence and degree completion" (Bohr, Pascarella, Nora, & Terenzini, 1995, p. 82).

Research showing the positive effects of HBCUs on students' achievement has been contrasted with the research on African American students' educational experiences in PWIs.

> Black students on White campuses, compared with their counterparts who graduate from [HBCUs], generally have lower grade point averages, lower persistence rates, lower academic achievement levels, higher attrition rates, less likelihood of enrolling in advanced degree programs, poorer overall psychological adjustment, and lower post graduate attainments and earnings. [Darden, Bagaka's, & Kamel, 1996, p. 56]

According to Fleming (1984), HBCUs facilitate students' academic development in three ways: friendship among peers, faculty, and staff: participation in the life of the campus; and feelings of academic success. HBCUs encourage African American students to interact with peers, faculty and staff to a greater degree than PWIs; African American students hold more positions of leadership in HBCUs than in White colleges; finally, the academic successes of African American students are more encouraged (and perhaps *noticed*) by faculty in HBCUs than in PWIs (Fleming, 1984).

In addition, attendance at HBCUs has been shown to enhance the life circumstances of students. African American students who attend HBCUs tend to have higher incomes twenty years later than students who attended other kinds of postsecondary institutions (Constantine, 1995). As far as educational aspirations, one study found that African American students attending HBCUs tend to aspire to doctoral degrees in greater numbers than African American students at PWIs—although the students at PWIs tend to aspire to more "prestigious" professional degrees (e.g. law and medical degrees) than the students at HBCUs (Allen & Haniff, 1991).

Besides research on the comparative experiences of African American students at PWIs and HBCUs, there is very little knowledge on the degree to which the percentage enrollments of racial/ethnic minority students affect their educational outcomes. The structural diversity of an institution (the numerical representation of various racial/ethnic groups) is an important characteristic of colleges and universities. College environments with very high percentages of White students (in comparison to students of color) tend to provide few cross-race interactions for White students, tend to treat students from minority groups as symbols rather than as individuals, and tend to convey the message that maintaining a campus multicultural environment is a low institutional priority (Loo & Rolison, 1986; Hurtado, Milem, Clayton-Pederson, & Allen, 1999). In addition, minority students have experienced significant levels of alienation and harassment based on their ethnic group membership (Loo & Rolison, 1986). Minority students have been described as highly "visible" on campus and "often viewed as outsiders and isolated from the mainstream" (Nagasawa & Wong, 1999, p. 81). Students of color at PWIs can experience minority status stress and alienation from the campus community (Loo & Rolison, 1986; Smedley, Myers, & Harrell, 1993). Thus, the racial composition of the students in a postsecondary educational institution can affect students' outcomes independent of other characteristics.

There are competing views as to whether large numbers of racial/ethnic minority group members will positively or negative affect student outcomes. On the one hand, in environments that have lower numbers of certain groups, underrepresented minority group members may be viewed as "tokens"—symbols rather than as individuals—which can heighten the visibility of the group members and exaggerate differences between groups (Hurtado, et al., 1999). On the other hand, large numbers of minority group members "can hinder their absorption into the campus culture" (Nagasawa & Wong, 1999, p. 87). What seems clear is that a critical mass of underrepresented minority group members is necessary for students to form supportive peer groups and feel comfortable on college campuses (Smedley, et al., 1993; Nagasawa & Wong, 1999). Having a larger number of racial/ethnic minority students on a college campus may communicate the message that the campus is committed to the success of minority students (Hurtado, 1990; Loo & Rolison, 1986). This may be true, since one study found that African American, Latino, and White students attending campuses with higher minority enrollments—taking into account the selectivity of the institutions—tended to have higher aspirations after four years (Carter, 1999b).

In addition, it is important to consider how the students at particular institutions differ. Students are not randomly distributed throughout the different college levels and types; different colleges attract different types of students (Feldman & Newcomb, 1969). A student's socioeconomic status is significantly related to the type of college he or she attends. Karabel and Astin (1975) studied the effect of SES, academic ability and college selectivity and found that a "student's social origin is significantly related to the status of the college he [sic] attends" (p. 394). The lower the SES, the more likely a student will go to a less-expensive, public, and less-selective institution (Karabel & Astin, 1975; Pascarella, Smart, & Smylie, 1992). Hearn (1991) studied the types of colleges 1980 high school graduates attended and concluded that "the most stubborn barriers to meritocracy seem to be those that are directly and indirectly based in SES, rather than those that are based in race, ethnicity, or gender" (p. 168). In other words, although more students are attending postsecondary institutions, lower SES students attend less selective institutions more often than higher SES students. African Americans may have had comparable access to educational institutions in Hearn's study, but their educational and occupational outcomes are far lower than White students.

The college choice theoretical perspective coupled with the above research showing the relationship between SES and type of college a student attends may indicate that income plays an indirect role in the development of degree aspirations and that institutional characteristics play a direct role in developing or constraining students' aspirations. However, after finding few significant effects of institutional type on degree aspirations. Pascarella (1984) suggests that institutional characteristics play an indirect role in affecting students' aspirations. Whether the effect of institutional type is direct or indirect, these findings of studies on the effect of institutional characteristics on student outcomes highlight the importance of controlling for background characteristics in order to assess the true effect of institutional characteristics.

The Effect of Financial Aid Variables

There is very little research on the effect of financial aid on educational aspirations. Financial aid can be seen as representative of both institutional financial support and of individual financial need. Traditionally, broad financial aid support for students to attend college was intended to lessen any financial difficulties students may have in paying tuition. The Higher Education Act of 1965 is the first example of broad federal support for attendance at postsecondary institutions. This act featured grants and low interest government insured loans (Rippa, 1997). Therefore, financial aid awards to lower SES students should mediate the financial limitations of their backgrounds and increase the probability they will attend four year institutions and desire to continue on to post baccalaureate education.

The type of aid students receive, and the degree to which their financial need is met, may impact their degree expectations. Institutional type and individual characteristics should both influence financial aid measures.

Very few studies incorporate financial aid variables into their models of educational outcomes. Unfortunately, quite a few of the financial aid studies are a decade or more old, which means that we will not know the effect of recent federal policies limiting financial aid for several years. The United States government policies from the 1960s and 1970s, geared toward increasing access to higher education by offering aid to financially needy students, were significantly weakened in the 1980s (Baker & Vélez, 1996). The result of the weakening in financial support to low income postsecondary students is that fewer funds for grants and more aid in the form of loans were made available to students. This study does examine the effect of financial aid on the degree aspirations of college students in the late 1980s and early 1990s.

St. John and Noell (1989) found that all types of financial aid packages had positive impacts on student enrollment decisions, particularly minority student enrollment. However, a review of the literature on access to postsecondary education noted that one reason for the decline of African American college attendees in the 1980s is that "African Americans are less willing to borrow for higher education for purely economic reasons . . . given that African American students are increasingly from low-income families in which a typical $10,000–12,000 debt will often be larger than his or her annual family income" (Baker & Vélez, 1996, p. 88).

What is known about the effect of financial aid (in unspecified forms) is that it facilitates students' peer social interactions (Cabrera, Nora, & Casteñeda, 1992). "Financial aid may provide recipients with enough freedom to engage in social activities . . . [or] remove anxieties, time, and effort associated with securing additional funds to finance their education" (p. 589). Students in work study programs may benefit in particular because they tend to have more frequent contact with faculty, staff and institutional policies (Hossler, 1984). Increased interaction with faculty and staff may increase students' knowledge of degree options and may encourage students to aspire to post-baccalaureate degrees.

Since financial aid has been found to affect access, retention, and degree progress, it is likely that aid will affect students' degree expectations. Perhaps, more importantly, the form of aid (loans vs. grants) may deter students from pursuing (or wanting to pursue) advanced degrees.

Academic Achievement

Several researchers have found significant, positive relationships between college GPAs and aspirations (Astin, 1977; Carter, 2001; Hearn, 1987; Pascarella, 1985). Clearly, the status attainment framework suggests that a student's educational aspiration level is affected by his or her prior academic performance. Thus, it seems that students may adjust their aspiration levels in college based on their college academic performance. Examining the role of academic ability in the development of degree aspirations is particularly important in determining what affects the patterns of mobility for African American, Latino, and White students.

Conclusions

The main theoretical framework described in this chapter can be summarized by discussing three themes presented in this paper: 1) the roles of ascribed status or merit in influencing students' aspirations; 2) the effects of institutional characteristics and experiences, and 3) the unique experiences and characteristics of African American and Latino students in higher education.

The social psychological status attainment model (Sewell, et al., 1969; 1970). Turner's (1960) contest vs. sponsored mobility, and cultural capital are the main lenses through which the roles of ascribed status and merit in affecting students' aspirations are examined. The status attainment model. Turner's theory of the mobility processes, and cultural capital hold significant assumptions about the ways in which students achieve (or acquire) status and how their aspirations are affected over time.

Institutional characteristics and experiences can have as strong an effect on students' aspirations as socioeconomic status or individual achievement. Each institution (or institutional type) has particular social environments that can independently affect academic outcomes. Specifically, certain characteristics of institutions may increase access to students from lower SES backgrounds and may particularly affect the educational goals of African American students.

African American and Latino students are populations of students who tend to come from lower income backgrounds and have lower rates of college enrollment than White students. Furthermore, researchers have not been wholly successful in explaining what affects African American and Latino students' degree aspirations. Future research needs to explain better the reasons why there are racial/ethnic group differences in educational aspirations.

The model posed in this *chapter* advances previous perspectives on college students' degree aspirations by incorporating previous empirical research into the dominant theoretical frameworks used in sociology. The unique experiences of African American and Latino students have not been explained well by existing research. Elements of the proposed model should help researchers explore the racial/ethnic differences between groups and, perhaps, given the proper data, will illuminate appropriate institutional responses to increasing students' degree goals and therefore increasing students' educational attainments. More research is also needed on the role of institutional environments on students' degree aspirations. Aspirations are individually and socially constructed; the pre-college elements of the social and individual construction are well-identified—theoretically, if not empirically. However, the gap remains in explaining how institutions affect students' degree goals and why racial/ethnic groups differ in their degree goals. This chapter and the proposed model take the first step by synthesizing previous research and theoretical perspectives to explain the changes in college students' aspirations over time—with emphasis on institutional environments.

There remain several significant gaps in current research on students' educational aspirations. First, as researchers and practitioners, we need to identify and make clear our assumptions about educational aspirations. For instance, although the lowering of aspirations may not be ideal, it ultimately might be a positive result given a student's circumstance. If a student from a low SES background aspires to be a physician, but achieves "only" a Bachelor's degree, that still is a success for the student. Understanding our assumptions about aspirations may help clarify models and theories that can explain the pro-

cesses by which students' change their educational goals.

A second, related gap in research on students' aspirations is in what affects nontraditional students' aspirations. Nontraditional students are a majority of the individuals attending post-secondary institutions and additional research needs to be done to understand influences on their degree goals. It would be inappropriate to use theoretical models that assume direct high school-to-college mobility for college students who are in their late 20s and above.

Third, the existing theoretical frameworks discussed in this chapter, in conjunction with the empirical research reviewed, need to be supplemented with other theoretical approaches. Other disciplinary approaches (e.g. organizational theory, anthropology, psychology, racial identity theory) may help explain student aspirations in addition to the theoretical approaches from sociology. For example, racial identity theory may account for the negative characteristics related to minority group status but also may account for positive behavior like the effect of role models on student outcomes.

A final gap in the research on students' educational aspirations results from the methodology used in many studies. Much of the research on students' aspirations has been done using quantitative data analyses. The contribution of this body of work as a whole is significant, because researchers have been able to demonstrate the differences that occur between different student groups and have shown various direct and indirect effects on aspirations. However, qualitative research is a necessary new direction for study in this field. The process by which students set educational goals and change them over time is complex. Understanding *why* students change their goals and the many factors that affect their educational goals are important future directions for aspirations research.

References

Agnew, R. & Jones, D.H. (1988). Adapting to deprivation: An examination of inflated educational expectations. *The Sociological Quarterly*, 29(2), 315–337.

Alexander, K.L. & Cook, M.A. (1979). The motivational relevance of educational plans: Questioning the conventional wisdom. *Social Psychology Quarterly*, 42(3), 202–213.

Allen, W.R. (1991). Introduction. In W.R. Allen, E.G. Epps, and N.Z. Haniff (eds.) *College in Black and White: African American students in predominantly White and in historically Black public universities* (pp. 1–14). Albany: State University of New York Press.

Allen, W.R. (1992). The color of success: African-American college student outcomes at predominantly White and historically Black public colleges and universities. *Harvard Educational Review*, 62(1), 26–44.

Allen, W.R. & Haniff, N.Z. (1991). Race, gender, and academic performance in U.S. higher education. In W.R. Allen, E.G. Epps, and N.Z. Haniff (eds.) *College in Black and White: African American students in predominantly White and in historically Black public universities* (pp. 95–109). Albany: State University of New York Press.

Alwin, D.F. (1974). College effects on educational and occupational attainments. *American Sociological Review*, 39(April), 210–223.

Ancis, J.R. & Sedlacek, W.E. (1997). Predicting the academic achievement of female students using the SAT and noncognitive variables. *College and University*, 72(3), 2–8.

Astin, A.W. (1977). *Four critical years*. San Francisco: Jossey-Bass Publishers.

Astin, A.W. (1990). *The Black undergraduate: Current status and trends in the characteristics of freshman*. Los Angeles: Higher Education Research Institute.

Astin, A.W. (1993). *What matters in college?: Four critical years revisited*. San Francisco: Jossey-Bass Publishers.

Astin, A.W., Tsui, L. & Avalos, J. (1996). *Degree attainment rates at American colleges and universities: Effects of race, gender, and institutional type*. Los Angeles: Higher Educational Research Institute, University of California.

Baker, T.I. & Vélez, W. (1996). Access to and opportunity in postsecondary education in the United States: A review. *Sociology of Education*, (Extra Issue), 82–101.

Barrera, M. (1997). A theory of racial inequality. In A. Darder, R.D. Torres, and H. Gutierrez (eds.). *Latinos and Education: A Critical Reader* (pp. 3–44). New York: Routledge.

Berger, J. B. (2000). Optimizing capital, social reproduction, and undergraduate persistence: A sociological perspective. In J. M. Braxton (ed.) *Reworking the Student Departure Puzzle* (pp. 95–124). Nashville, TN: Vanderbilt University Press.

Berman, G.S. & Haug, M.R. (1975). Occupational and educational goals and expectations: The effects of race and sex. *Social Problems*, 23, 166–181.

Blau, P.M. & Duncan, O.D. (1967). *The American occupational structure*. New York: John Wiley & Sons, Inc.

Bohr, L., Pascarella, E.T., Nora, A., & Terenzini, P.T. (1995). Do Black students learn more at historically Black or predominantly White colleges? *Journal of College Student Development*, 36(1), 75–85.

Brint, S. & Karabel, J. (1989). *The diverted dream: Community colleges and the promise of educational opportunity in America, 1900–1985*. New York: Oxford University Press.

Burke, P.J. & Hoelter, J.W. (1988). Identity and sex-race differences in educational and occupational aspirations formation. *Social Science Research*, 17, 29–47.

Cabrera, A.F., Nora, A., and Castañeda, M.B. (1992). The role of finances in the persistence process: A structural model. *Research in Higher Education*, 33(5), 571–593.

Campbell, R.T. (1983). Status attainment research: End of the beginning or beginning of the end? *Sociology of Education*, 56(January), 47–62.

Carter, D.F. (2001). *A Dream Deferred? Examining the Degree Aspirations of African American and White College Students*, New York: Garland.

Carter, D.F. (1999a). The impact of institutional choice and environments on African American and White students degree expectations. *Research in Higher Education*, 40(1), 17–41.

Carter, D.F. (1999b). *Institutional diversity and the degree expectations of college students*. Paper presented at the meeting of the Association for the Study of Higher Education, Miami, FL.

Carter, D.J. & Wilson, R.T. (1996). *Minorities in higher education: 14th annual status report*. Washington, D.C.: American Council on Education.

Choy, S.P. & Premo, M.K. (1995). *Profile of older undergraduates: 1989–90*. National Center for Education Statistics, Statistical Analysis Report 95–167. Washington, D.C.: U.S. Department of Education. Office of Educational Research and Improvement.

Clark, B. (1960). The "cooling out" function in higher education. *American Journal of Sociology*, 65, 569–576.

Constantine, J.M. (1995). The effect of attending historically Black colleges and universities on future wages of Black students. *Industrial and Labor Relations Review*, 48(3), 531–546.

Darden, J.T., Bagaka's, J.G. & Kamel, S.M. (1996). Historically Black institutions and desegregation: The dilemma revisited. *Equity & Excellence in Education*, 29(2), 56–68.

Dawkins, M.P. (1982). Occupational prestige expectations among Black and White college students: A multivariate analysis, *College Student Journal*, 16(3), 233–242.

Deskins, Jr., D.R. (1994). Prospects for minority doctorates in the year 2000. Employment opportunities in a changing American society. In M. Holden, Jr. (ed.) *The challenge to racial stratification: National political science review* (volume 4) (pp. 98–148). News Brunswick: Transaction Publishers.

Dougherty, K. (1987). The effects of community colleges: Aid or hindrance to socioeconomic attainment: *Sociology of Education*, 60(April), 86–103.

Eckland, B.K. (1964). Social class and college graduation: Some misconceptions corrected. *American Journal of Sociology*, 70, 60–72.

Epps, E.G. and Jackson, K.W. (1985). *Educational and occupational aspirations and early attainment of Black males and females*. Atlanta, Georgia: Southern Education Foundation.

Feagin, J.R., Vera H., and Imani, N. (1996). *The agony of education: Black students at White colleges and universities*. New York: Routledge.

Feldman, K. & Newcomb, T. (1969). *The impact of college on students*. San Francisco: Jossey-Bass.

Fleming, J. (1984). *Blacks in college*. San Francisco: Jossey-Bass.

Foley, D.E. (1991). Reconsidering anthropological explanations of ethnic school failure. *Anthropology & Education Quarterly*, 22, 60–86.

Fordham, S. & Ogbu, J. U. (1986). Black students' school success: Coping with the "burden of 'acting White' " *The Urban Review*, 18(3), 176–206.

Giroux, H.A. (1983). Theories of reproduction and resistance in the new sociology of education: A critical analysis. *Harvard Education Review*, 53(3), 257–293.

Grubb, W.N. & Wilson, R.H. (1989). Sources of increasing Inequality in wages and salaries, 1960–80. *Monthly Labor Review*, 112(4), 3–13.

Hanson, S.I. (1994). Lost talent: Unrealized educational aspirations and expectations among E.S. youths, *Sociology of Education*, 67(July), 159–183.

Hao, L. and Bonstead Burns, M. (1998). Parent-child differences in educational expectations and the academic achievement of immigrant and native students. *Sociology of Education*, 71(3), 175–198.

Hearn, J.C. (1987). Impacts of undergraduate experiences on aspirations and plans for graduate and professional education. *Research in Higher Education*, 27(2), 119–141.

Hearn, J.C. (1991). Academic and nonacademic influences on the college destinations of 1980 high school graduates. *Sociology of Education*, 64(July), 158–171.

Hossler, D. (1984). *Enrollment management*. New York: College Entrance Examination Board.

Hossler, D., Braxton, J., & Coopersmith, G. (1989). Understanding student college choice. In Smart, J.C. (Ed.). *Higher Education: Handbook of Theory and Research* (volume 5). New York: Agathon Press.

Hossler, D. & Gallagher, K.S. (1987). Studying student college choice: A three-phase model and the implications for policymakers. *College and University*, 62(3), 207–221.

Hurtado, S. (1990). *Campus racial climates and educational outcomes*. Unpublished doctoral dissertation, University of California, Los Angeles.

Hurtado, S., Inkelas, K.K., Briggs, C., & Rhee, B. (1997): Differences in college access and choice among racial ethnic groups: Identifying continuing barriers. *Research in Higher Education*, 38(1), 43–75.

Hurtado, S., Milem, J.F., Clayton-Pedersen, A.R., & Allen, W.R. (1999). Enacting diverse learning environments. Improving the climate for racial ethnic diversity. *ASHE-ERIC Higher Education Report* Volume 26, No. 8. Washington, D.C.: The George Washington University, Graduate School of Education and Human Development.

Isaac. P.D., Malaney, G.D., & Karras, J.E. (1992). Parental educational level, gender differences, and seniors' aspirations for advanced study. *Research in Higher Education*, 33(5), 595–606.

Jackson, K.W., & Swan, L.A. (1991). Institutional and individual factors affecting Black undergraduate student performance: Campus race and student gender. In W.R. Allen, E.G. Epps, and N.Z. Haniff (eds.) *College in Black and White: African American students in predominantly White and in historically Black public universities* (pp. 127–141). Albany: State University of New York Press.

Kao, G. & Tienda, M. (1998). Educational aspirations of minority youth. *American Journal of Education*, 106(5), 349–384.

Karabel, J. & Astin, A.W. (1975). Social class, academic quality, and college "quality". *Social Forces*, 53(3), 381–398.

Kempner, K. & Kinnick, M. (1990). Catching the window of opportunity: Being on time for higher education. *Journal of Higher Education*, 61(5), 535–547.

Kerckhoff, A.C. (1976). The status attainment process: Socialization or allocation? *Social Forces*, 55(2), 368–381.

Kerckhoff, A.C. (1984). The current state of social mobility research. *The Socialization Quarterly*, 25 (Spring), 139–153.

Knight, W.H. & Wing, A. (1995). Weep not, little ones: An essay to our children about affirmative action. In J.H. Franklin & G. R. McNeil (eds.) African Americans and the living Constitution. Washington: Smithsonian Institution Press.

Knotterus, J.D. (1987). Status attainment research and its image of society. American *Sociological Review*, 52(February): 113–121.

Komaromy, M., Grumbach, K., Drake, M., Vranizan, K., Lurie, N, Keane, D., & Bindman, A.B. (1996, May 16). The role of Black and Hispanic physicians in providing health care for underserved populations. *New England Journal of Medicine*, 334(20), 1305–1310.

Labovitz, E.M. (1975). Race, SES, contexts and fulfillment of college aspirations. *The Sociological Quarterly*, 16, 241–249.

Loo, C.M. & Rolison, G. (1986). Alienation of ethnic minority students at a predominantly White university. *Journal of Higher Education*, 57(1), 58–77.

Luttrell, W. (1989). Working class women's ways of knowing: Effects of gender, race, and class. *Sociology of Education*, 62(1), 33–46.

Maxey, J., Lee, J.S., & McLure, G.T. (1995). Are Black students less likely to enroll at their first-choice college? *Journal of Blacks in Higher Education*, 7, 100–101.

McClelland, K. (1990). Cumulative disadvantage among the highly ambitious. *Sociology of Education*, 63(April), 102–121.

McDonough, P.M. 1997. *Choosing colleges: How social class and schools structure opportunity*. Albany, NY: State University of New York Press.

Morrow, R.A., & Torres, C.A. (1995). *Social theory and education: A critique of theories of social and cultural reproduction*. Albany, NY: State University of New York Press.

Nagasawa, R. & Wong, P. (1999). A theory of minority students' survival in college. *Sociological Inquiry*, 69(1), 76–90.

Ogbu, J.U. (1983). Minority status and schooling in plural societies. *Comparative Education Review*, 27(2), 168–190.

Otto, I.B. (1976). Social integration and the status attainment process. *American Journal of Sociology*, 81(6), 1360–1383.

Pascarella, E.T. (1984). College environmental influences on students' educational aspirations. *Journal of Higher Education*, 55(6), 751–771.

Pascarella, E.T. (1985). Students' affective development within the college environment. *Journal of Higher Education*, 56(6), 640–663.

Pascarella, E.T., Smart, J.C., & Smylie, M.A. (1992). College tuition costs and early career socioeconomic achievement: Do you get what you pay for? *Higher Education*, 24(3), 275–291.

Pascarella, E.T. & Terenzini, P.T. (1991). *How college affects students*. San Francisco: Jossey-Bass.

Paulsen, M.B. (1990). College choice: Understanding student enrollment behavior. *ASHE-ERIC Higher Education Report No. 6*. Washington, D.C.: The George Washington University, School of Education and Human Development.

Porter, J.N. (1974). Race, socialization and mobility in educational and early occupational attainment. *American Sociological Review*, 39(June), 303–16.

Portes, A. & Wilson, K.L. (1976). Black-White differences in educational attainment. *American Sociological Review*, 41(June), 414–431.

Rippa, S.A. (1997). *Education in a free society: An American history*, (8th ed.). New York: Longman.

Sewell, W.H., Haller, A.O. & Ohlendorf, G.W. (1970). The educational and early occupational status attainment process. Replication and revision. *American Sociological Review*, 35, 1014–1027.

Sewell, W.H. Haller, A.O. & Portes, A. (1969). The educational and early occupational attainment process. *American Sociological Review*, 34(February), 82–92.

Sewell, W.H. & Shah, V.P. (1967). Socioeconomic status, intelligence, and the attainment of higher education. *Sociology of Education*, 40(1), 1–23.

Smedley, B.D., Myers, H.F., & Harrell, S.P. (1993). Minority status stresses and the college adjustment of ethnic minority freshmen. *Journal of Higher Education*, 64(4), 434–452.

Smith, A.W. (1988). In double jeopardy: Collegiate academic outcomes of Black females vs. Black males. *National Journal of Sociology*, 2, 3–33.

Smith, D.G. (1990). Women's colleges and coed colleges: Is there a difference for women? *Journal of Higher Education*, 61(2), 181–195.

So, A.Y. (1987). The educational aspirations of Hispanic parents. *Educational Research Quarterly*, 11, 47–53.

Solorzano, D.G. (1992). An exploratory analysis of the effects of race, class, and gender on student and parent mobility aspirations, *Journal of Negro Education*, 61(1), 30–43.

Spady, W.G. (1970). Lament for the letterman: Effects of peer status and extracurricular activities on goals and achievement, *American Journal of Sociology*, 75(January), 680–702.

St. John, E.P. (1991). What really influences minority attendance? Sequential analyses of the High School and Beyond sophomore cohort. *Research in Higher Education*, 32(2), 141–158.

St. John, E.P. & Noell, J. (1989). The effects of student financial aid on access to higher education: An analysis of progress with special consideration of minority enrollment. *Research in Higher Education*, 30(6), 563–581.

St. John, E.P., Oescher, J. & Andrieu, S. (1992). The influence of prices on within year persistence by traditional college age students in four-year colleges. *Journal of Student Financial Aid*, 22(1), 27–38.

Thomas, G.E., Alexander, K.I., & Eckland, B.K. (1979). Access to higher education: The importance of race, sex, social class, and academic credentials. *School Review*, 87(2), 133–156.

Tinto, V. (1993). *Leaving college*. Chicago: University of Chicago Press.

Trent, W.I. (1991). Focus on equity: race and gender differences in degree attainment, 1975–76; 1980–81. In W.R. Allen, E.G. Epps, and N.Z. Haniff (eds.) *College in Black and White: African American students in predominantly White and in historically Black public universities* (pp. 41–59). Albany: State University of New York Press.

Turner, R.H. (1960). Sponsored and contest mobility and the school system. *American Sociological Review*, 25, 855–867.

Vélez, W. (1985). Finishing college: The effects of college type. *Sociology of Education*, 58(July), 191–200.

Weiler, W.C. (1993). Post baccalaureate educational choices of minority students. *The Review of Higher Education*, 16(4), 439–460.

Wilson Sadberry, K.R., Winfield, J.F., & Royster, D.A. (1991). Resilience and persistence of African American males in postsecondary enrollment. *Education and Urban Society*, 24(1), 87–102.

Chapter 15

Toward a Model of
White Racial Identity Development

Janet E. Helms

The development of White identity in the United States is closely intertwined with the development and progress of racism in this country. The greater the extent that racism exists and is denied, the less possible it is to develop a positive White identity. J. M. Jones (1972, 1981) has identified three types of racism: (a) individual, that is, personal attitudes, beliefs, and behaviors designed to convince oneself of the superiority of Whites and the inferiority of non-White racial groups; (b) institutional, meaning social policies, laws, and regulations whose purpose is to maintain the economic and social advantages of Whites over non-Whites; and (c) cultural, that is, societal beliefs and customs that promote the assumption that the products of White culture (e.g., language, traditions, appearance) are superior to those of non-White cultures.

Because each of these three types of racism is so much a part of the cultural milieu, each can become a part of the White person's racial identity or consciousness ipso facto. In order to develop a healthy White identity, defined in part as a nonracist identity, virtually every White person in the United States must overcome one or more of these aspects of racism. Additionally, he or she must accept his or her own Whiteness, the cultural implications of being White, and define a view of Self as a racial being that does not depend on the perceived superiority of one racial group over another.

Thus, the evolution of a positive White racial identity consists of two processes, the abandonment of racism and the development of a non-racist White identity. Because White racism in the United States seems to have developed as a means of justifying the enslavement of Black Americans during the slavery eras of the 1700s and 1800s (cf. Comer, 1980; Cross et al., in press; Giddings, 1984), Blacks and/or Black culture have been the primary "outgroup" or reference group around which White racial identity development issues revolve. Thus, as is the case with Black racial identity, White racial identity contains parallel beliefs and attitudes about Whites as well as Blacks.

For the most part, theories or models of White racial identity development have focused on defining racism. Some of these perspectives are summarized in Table 15-1. As shown in Table 15-1, most of these models are typologies, that is, they assume that racists can be classified according to various categories. Moreover, most of these early perspectives were fueled by the implicit assumption that racism was only damaging to the victims of the resulting oppression but did not consider their effects on the beneficiaries or perpetrators of racism.

Only recently have theorists begun to speculate about the harmful consequences of racism on the perpetuators of racism, which include the absence of a positive White racial identity. In presenting

"Toward a Model of White Racial Identity Development." Reprinted from *Black and White Racial Identity: Theory, Research, and Practice*, (1990), Greenwood Publishing Group, Inc.

TABLE 15-1
Summary of White Racial Identity Models

Author	Model Type	Components Name	Description
Carney & Kahn (1984)	Stage	1. Stage 1	1. Knowledge of ethnically dissimilar people is based on stereotypes.
		2. Stage 2	2. Recognizes own cultural embeddedness, but deals with other groups in detached scholarly manner.
		3. Stage 3	3. Either denies the importance of race or expresses anger toward her/his own cultural group.
		4. Stage 4	4. Begins blending aspects of her/his cultural reference group with those of other groups to form a new self-identity.
		5. Stage 5	5. Attempts to act to promote social equality and cultural pluralism.
Ganter (1977)	Stage	1. Phase 1	1. Protest and denial that Whites are patrons and pawns of racism.
		2. Phase 2	2. Guilt and despair as racism is acknowledged.
		3. Phase 3	3. Integrates awareness of Whites' collective loss of human integrity and attempts to free oneself from racism.
Hardiman (1979)	Stage	1. Acceptance	1. Active or passive acceptance of White superiority.
		2. Resistance	2. Person becomes aware of own racial identity for the first time.
		3. Redefinition	3. Attempts to redefine Whiteness from a non-racist perspective.
		4. Internalization	4. Internalizes non-racist White identity.
Helms (1984)	Stage	1. Contact	1. Obliviousness to own racial identity.
		2. Disintegration	2. First acknowledgment of White identity.
		3. Reintergration	3. Idealizes Whites /denigrates Blacks.
		4. Pseudo-Independence	4. Intellectualized acceptance of own and others' race.
		5. Immersion / Emersion	5. Honest appraisal of racism and significance of Whiteness.
		6. Autonomy	6. Internalizes a multi-cultural identity with non-racist Whiteness as its core.
Kovel (1970) Gaertner (1976) Jones (1972)	Type	1. Dominative racist	1. Openly seeks to keep Black people in inferior positions and will use force to do so.
		2. Aversive Dominative racist	2. Believes in White superiority, but tries to ignore the existence of Black people to avoid intrapsychic conflict.
		3. Aversive Liberal racist	3. Despite aversion to Blacks, uses impersonal social reforms to improve Blacks' conditions.
		4. Ambivalent	4. Expresses exaggeratedly positive or negative responses toward Blacks depending on the consequences to the White person.
		5. Non-racist	5. Does not reveal any racist tendencies.

TABLE 15-1 (*continued*)
Summary of White Racial Identity Models

Author	Model Type	Components Name	Description
Terry (1977)		1. Color blind	1. Attempts to ignore race; feels one can exonerate self from being White by asserting one's humanness; equates acknowledgment of color with racism.
		2. White Blacks	2. Abandons Whiteness in favor of overidentifying with Blacks; denies own Whiteness; tries to gain personal recognition from Blacks for being "almost Black".
		3. New Whites	3. Holds a pluralistic racial view of the world; recognizes that racism is a White problem and attempts to eliminate it.

Note: Gaerther (1976) and J. M. Jones (1972) elaborated the typology originally proposed by Kovel (1970).

the case for the need to help Whites develop a positive White identity, various authors have discussed the defense mechanisms by which Whites pretend that they are not White. For instance, J. Katz and Ivey (1977) noted that when faced with the question of their racial identification, Whites merely deny that they are White. They observed: "Ask a White person what he or she is racially and you may get the answer "Italian," "English," "Catholic," or "Jewish." *White people do not see themselves as White*" (p. 486). Relatedly, Terry (1981) commented, "To be white in America is not to have to think about it. Except for hard-core racial supremacists, the meaning of being White is having the choice of attending to or ignoring one's own Whiteness" (p. 120). If these authors' surmises are accurate, then it appears that most Whites may have no consistent conception of a positive White identity or consciousness. As a consequence, Whites may feel threatened by the actual or presupposed presence of racial consciousness in non-White racial groups.

In exploring the emotional consequences of racism to Whites, Karp (1981) indicated that major concomitants of racism and Whites' distorted views of racial identity are negative feelings such as "self-deception," "self-hate," and "guilt and shame, along with feeling bad about being white (sometimes expressed as a flip side—rigid pride in 'superiority')" (p. 89). She further suggests that these feelings can contribute to distorted behaviors as well as distorted views of the world. Dennis (1981) discussed the many "selves" into which a White person must compartmentalize her or his feelings and

thoughts in order to be accepted by other Whites. In passing, it should be noted that theorists and researchers have viewed similar symptoms (e.g., racial denial, self-hate, feelings of inferiority, etc.) as cause for alarm and serious psychological intervention in Black communities. However, it does not seem that similar enthusiasm has been expended in promoting healthy White racial identity development.

Implicit in much of the contemporary writings on White racial identity development is the awareness that, in spite of the pervasive socialization toward racism, some White people do appear not only to have developed a White consciousness, but one that is not predominated by racial distortions. Some authors have even loosely described an orderly process by which a White person can move from a racist identity to a positive White consciousness. In describing the process by which some Whites have overcome racism, Dennis observed: "one sees them moving from 'knowing' Blacks to knowing Blacks, from deracialization to reracialization, toward a more 'objective' approach to race with a clearer understanding of the role of race and culture in society" (p. 74). Karp (1981) described the process as follows: "Whites [must address] their feelings of oppression [must seek out] accurate information, [must discharge] feelings related to racism, and [consequently change] their attitudes and behaviors" (p. 88). Thus, Dennis essentially proposes a cognitive process of White identity development, whereas Karp emphasizes the interrelatedness of emotions, attitudes, and behaviors.

At least two of the White identity typologists (Pettigrew, 1981; Terry, 1981) have speculated more systematically about the relationship of White racial identity to Whites' psychological health. Applying Jahoda's (1958) trichotomy of "sick," "not healthy," and "well" to describe the psychological consequences to Whites of racism, Pettigrew (1981) concluded that roughly 15 to 75% of Whites were in the categories of sick or not healthy as a consequence of internalizing some form of personal racial bigotry. Terry's (1977) categorical system recognized that there were different ways that one could acknowledge and, consequently, be White (see Table 15.1); just as there were different ways that one could be racist. However, from none of the typological perspectives is it clear how or whether a person can shift from one type of identity or category to another.

Working independently, in separate places and at different times, Hardiman (1979) and Helms (1984b) proposed developmental models of White racial identity development. Both models are similar in that they propose a linear process of attitudinal development in which the White person potentially progresses through a series of stages differing in the extent to which they involve acknowledgment of racism and consciousness of Whiteness. They differ in the particulars of some of the stages, though both agree that the highest stage involves an awareness of personal responsibility for racism, consistent acknowledgment of one's Whiteness, and abandonment of racism in any of its forms as a defining aspect of one's personality. Hardiman's theoretical model is summarized in Table 15.1. However, since Helms's model has been subjected to empirical investigation and (to the author's knowledge) Hardiman's has not, Helms's model is the primary theoretical basis for the subsequent presentation of White racial identity development. Consequently, it will be presented in some detail.

Stages of White Racial Identity Development

One of the concomitants of being a White person in the United States is that one is a member of a numerical majority as well as the socioeconomically and politically dominant group. One result of this racial status is that, as Dennis (1981) points out, even if one has few resources oneself, as long as one has White skin in America, one is entitled to feel superior to Blacks. This sense of entitlement seems to be a basic norm of White society.

Perhaps more importantly, as previously noted, if one is a White person in the United States, it is still possible to exist without ever having to acknowledge that reality. In fact, it is only when Whites come in contact with the idea of Blacks (or other visible racial/ethnic groups) that Whiteness becomes a potential issue. Whether or not this initial contact has any implications for racial identity development depends upon the extent to which it is unavoidable. Thus, if the Black (in this instance) presence "intrudes" into the White person's environment, and the intrusion cannot be ignored or controlled, then the White person is likely to be forced to deal with White racial identity issues somewhat. However, to the extent that such intrusions can be avoided, which may still be the case in much of White America, one can avoid resolving White racial identity issues. That is, one can choose to be oblivious to race and the differential effects of race on how one is perceived and treated by society at large; or one can decide to remain fixated at one of the identity stages to be described subsequently.

There are two primary ways by which one can become aware of the presence of Blacks as an outgroup: vicariously or directly. Vicarious awareness occurs when significant persons in one's life (e.g., media, parents, peers) inform one of the existence of Blacks as well as how one ought to think about them. Dennis (1981) does an excellent job of describing how Whites are socialized directly and indirectly to fear and devalue Blacks. Direct awareness occurs when the White person interacts with Blacks himself or herself. These two means of awareness are not necessarily exclusive, as Dennis points out. Nevertheless, though one's own initial experiences with Blacks may be pleasant and non-individually racist, significant White persons in one's environment may use the socialization pressures available to them to ensure that the White person learns the rules of being a socially accepted White person. A number of autobiographical accounts (e.g., McLaurin, 1987; L. Smith, 1961), usually written from a Southern perspective, describe how Whites are taught to develop individual racism.

Recall that institutional and cultural racism are so much a part of the White (or Black) individual's world that he or she is often blind to their presence. Thus, the White person's developmental tasks with regard to development of a healthy White identity, according to both Hardiman's (1979) and Helms's (1984b) perspectives, require the abandonment of individual racism as well as the recognition of and active opposition to institutional and cultural racism. Concurrently, the person must become aware of her or his Whiteness, learn to accept Whiteness as an important part of herself or himself, and to internalize a realistically positive view of what it means to be White.

Helms (1984) originally proposed that White racial identity development occurred via a five-stage process, each involving attitudes, emotions, and behaviors in which Whites as well as Blacks are referents. More recently, she has included a sixth stage, Immersion/Emersion, to reflect Hardiman's (1979) contention that it is possible for Whites to seek out accurate information about their historical, political, and cultural contributions to the world, and that the process of self-examination within this context is an important component of the process of defining a positive White identity.

Thus, presently, Helms conceptualizes a two-phase process of White identity development. As illustrated in Figure 15.1, Phase 1, the abandonment of racism, begins with the Contact stage and ends with the Reintegration stage. Phase 2, defining a positive White identity, begins with the Pseudo-Independent stage and ends with the Autonomy stage.

Contact

As soon as one encounters the idea or the actuality of Black people, one has entered the Contact stage of identity. Depending somewhat upon one's racial (particularly) familial environment, one will enter Contact with either naive curiosity or timidity and trepidation about Blacks and a superficial and inconsistent awareness of being White. When one is in Contact, if one exhibits individual racism, it is probably exhibited in a weak and unsophisticated form since the person is just beginning to try her or his racial wings. Nevertheless, the person in Contact automatically benefits from institutional and cultural racism without necessarily being aware that he or she is doing so.

Oddly enough, the person in Contact may enjoy being a racist more than persons at the other stages simply because he or she has not had to confront the moral dilemmas resulting from such an identification. The Contact person's White racial identification is equally subtle. Thus, although such a person evaluates Blacks according to White criteria (e.g., White physical appearance, standardized tests, etc.), he or she does so automatically without awareness that other criteria are possible, and that he or she might be as legitimately evaluated according to other racial/cultural groups' criteria.

Behaviors thought to characterize Contact people are limited interracial social or occupational interaction with Blacks, unless the interaction is initiated by Blacks who "seem" White except for skin color or other "Black" physical

Stages and Phases of White Racial Identity Development

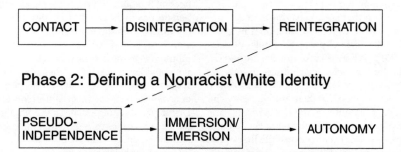

Figure 15-1 States and Phases of White Racial Identity Development

characteristics. In such interactions, the White person uses the Black person to teach him or her about what Black people in general are like and often uses societal stereotypes of Blacks as the standard against which the Black person is evaluated. Comments such as "You don't act like a Black person," or "I don't notice what race a person is," are likely to be made by Contact persons.

Affectively, Contact persons can be expected to have positive self-esteem because they have not yet learned to compartmentalize and differentially value their different selves (cf. Dennis, 1981). They should generally have positive feelings about the "idea" of Blacks and fair treatment of Blacks; though trait anxiety should be low, state anxiety or arousal may be present when actual interactions with Blacks are experienced or anticipated.

One's longevity in the Contact stage depends upon the kinds of experiences one has with Blacks and Whites with respect to racial issues. For instance, as the White person becomes aware of Blacks, if this awareness is based on vicarious information rather than actual experiences, then he or she is likely to remain in the Contact stage, particularly the aspect of the stage associated with fearfulness and caution. This supposition is based on the common observation (e.g., Karp, 1981; Reid, 1979) that the bulk of information available to Whites (and Blacks) about Blacks is negative. In such cases, the person is likely to continue to engage in minimal cross-racial interaction, is unlikely to be forced to rethink her or his racial perspective, is tolerated by her or his racial peers if he or she makes known her or his Contact perspective, and, of course, is warmly accepted if he or she remains silent about it.

On the other hand, if the Contact person continues to interact with Blacks, sooner or later significant others in the person's environment will make it known that such behavior is unacceptable if one wishes to remain a member in good standing of the "White" group (cf. Boyle, 1962; L. Smith, 1961). Where Blacks are concerned, if Whites in the Contact stage continue to interact with them, sooner or later the Contact person will have to acknowledge that there are differences in how Blacks and Whites in the United States are treated regardless of economic status. Sometimes this awareness may occur because the Black person points out the differences; sometimes it occurs because of obvious acts of discrimination (e.g., cab drivers who pass by Blacks regardless of how they are dressed, but stop for their White associates). Moreover, many Blacks will not join the Contact person in pretending that he or she is also Black (see Terry, 1980). When enough of these "socialization" experiences penetrate the White person's identity system, then he or she can enter the Disintegration stage.

Disintegration

Entry into the Disintegration stage implies conscious, though conflicted, acknowledgment of one's Whiteness. Moreover, it triggers the recognition of moral dilemmas associated with being White as described by Dennis (1981). If some of his dilemmas are reworded to refer to Whites regardless of religion or geographic origin, then they can be summarized as follows:

(a) the desire to be a religious or moral person versus the recognition that to be accepted by Whites one must treat Blacks immorally;

"[b] the belief in freedom and democracy versus the belief in racial inequality";

"[c] the desire to show love and compassion versus the desire to keep Blacks in their place at all costs";

(d) the belief in treating others with dignity and respect versus the belief that Blacks are not worthy of dignity or respect;

"[e] the belief that each person should be treated according to his or her individual merits versus the belief that Blacks should be evaluated as a group without regard to individual merits and talents" (p. 78).

Accompanying the conflicted White identification is a questioning of the racial realities the person has been taught to believe. It is probably during this stage, for instance, that the person first comes to realize that in spite of mouthings to the contrary, Blacks and Whites are not considered equals and negative social consequences can besiege the White person who does not respect the inequalities. Moreover, the Disintegration stage may be the time in which the person comes to realize that the social skills and mores he or she has been taught to use in interacting with Blacks rarely work. Thus, the person in Disintegration may not only perceive for the first time that he or she is caught between two racial groups, but may also come to realize that his or her position amongst Whites depends upon his or her ability to successfully "split" her or his personality.

Self-actualization personality theorists such as Rogers (1951) suggest that emotional discomfort, which Rogers calls "incongruence," results when one must markedly alter one's real self in order to be accepted by significant others in one's environment. The feelings of guilt, depression, helplessness, and anxiety described by various authors (e.g., J. Baldwin, 1963; Karp, 1981; J. Katz, 1976) as correlates of Whiteness probably have their origins in the Disintegration stage.

Festinger (1957) theorized that when two or more of a person's cognitions (e.g., beliefs or feelings about oneself) are in conflict, an uncomfortable psychological state that he calls "dissonance" likely results. He suggests that when dissonance is present, a person will not only attempt to reduce it, but will also take steps to avoid situations and information that are likely to increase it. Thus, if one thinks of the uncomfortable feelings resulting from White moral ambivalence as previously described as dissonance, then it seems plausible that the same sorts of strategies used to reduce dissonance in general may also be used to reduce race-related dissonance.

Festinger proposed three ways of reducing dissonance: (a) changing a behavior, (b) changing an environmental belief, and (c) developing new beliefs. Accordingly, the person in the Disintegration stage might reduce discomfort by (a) avoiding further contact with Blacks (changing a behavior), (b) attempting to convince significant others in her or his environment that Blacks are not so inferior (changing an environmental belief), or (c) seeking information from Blacks or Whites to the effect that either racism is not the White person's fault or does not really exist (adding new beliefs). Additionally, as a means of avoiding an increase in dissonance, the person may selectively attend only to information that gives him or her greater confidence in the new beliefs and/or he or she will interact only with those who can be counted on to support the new belief.

Which alternative the White person chooses probably depends on the extent to which her or his cross-racial interactions are voluntary. It seems likely that the person who can remove herself or himself from interracial environments or can remove Blacks from White environments will do so. Given the racial differences in social and economic power, most Whites can choose this option. If they do so, they will receive much support in an exclusively White environment for the development of individual racism as well as the maintenance of cultural and institutional racism.

Attempts to change others' attitudes probably occur initially amongst Whites who were raised and/or socialized in an environment in which White "liberal" attitudes (though not necessarily behaviors) were expressed. However, due to the racial naiveté with which this approach may be undertaken and the person's ambivalent racial identification, this dissonance-reducing strategy is likely to be met with rejection by Whites as well as Blacks.

To the extent that cross-racial interaction is unavoidable, the White person will attempt to develop new beliefs. However, the desire to be accepted by one's own racial group and the prevalence in the White group of the covert and overt belief in White superiority and Black inferiority virtually dictates that the content of the person's belief system will also change in a similar direction. As this reshaping of the person's cognitions or beliefs occurs, he or she enters the Reintegration stage.

Reintegration

In the Reintegration stage, the person consciously acknowledges a White identity. In the absence of contradictory experiences, to be White in America is to believe that one is superior to people of color. Consequently, the Reintegration person accepts the belief in White racial superiority and Black inferiority. He or she comes to believe that institutional and cultural racism are the White person's due because he or she has earned such privileges and preferences. Race-related negative conditions are assumed to result from Black people's inferior social, moral, and intellectual qualities, and thus, it is not unusual to find persons in the Reintegration stage selectively attending to and/or reinterpreting information to conform to societal stereotypes of Black people. Cross-racial similarities are minimized and/or denied.

Any residual feelings of guilt and anxiety are transformed into fear and anger toward Black people. Much of the person's cross-racial behavior is motivated by these feelings. Though the feelings may not be overtly expressed, they lie just below the surface of the person's awareness, and it only takes an event(s) that can be characterized (whether or not it actually is) by the White person as personally threatening for these feelings to be unleashed.

Behaviorally, people in the Reintegration stage may express their beliefs and feelings either passively or actively. Passive expression involves deliberate removal of oneself and/or avoidance of environments in which one might encounter Black people. In this instance, honest discussion of racial matters is most likely to occur among same-race peers who share or are believed to share a similar view of the world. Active expression may include treating Blacks as inferior and involve acts of violence or exclusion designed to protect White privilege.

In this society, it is fairly easy to remain or fixate at the Reintegration stage, particularly if one is relatively passive in one's expression of it. A personally jarring event is probably necessary for the person to begin to abandon this essentially racist identity. Again, the event can be direct or vicarious; it can be caused by painful or insightful encounters with Black or White persons. Changes in the environmental racial climate may also trigger transition from the Reintegration stage, For instance, the Civil Rights Movement of the 1960s and the Vietnam War caused some Whites to question their racial identity, though hopefully the catalyst for such self-examination does not have to be so major. Be that as it may, once the person begins to question her or his previous definition of Whiteness and the justifiability of racism in any of its forms, then he or she has begun the movement into the Pseudo-Independent or Liberal stage.

Pseudo-Independent

Pseudo-Independent is the first stage of redefining a positive White identity. In this stage, the person begins actively to question the proposition that Blacks are innately inferior to Whites. Instead, in this stage, the person begins to acknowledge the responsibility of Whites for racism and to see how he or she wittingly and unwittingly perpetuates racism. Consequently, he or she is no longer comfortable with a racist identity and begins to search for ways to redefine her or his White identity. Usually the redefining process takes the form of intellectual acceptance and curiosity about Blacks.

The Pseudo-Independent stage is primarily a stage of intellectualization in which the person attempts to submerge the tumultuous feelings about Whiteness that were aroused in previous stages. To the extent that feelings concerning racial identity issues are allowed to emerge, they are apt to be feelings of commiseration with Blacks and perhaps disquietude concerning racial issues in White peer groups.

Nevertheless, though the person in the Pseudo-Independent stage is abandoning the belief in White superiority/Black inferiority, he or she may still behave in ways that unwittingly perpetuate this belief system. That is, though the person may seek greater interaction with Blacks, much of this interaction involves helping Blacks to change themselves so that they function more like Whites on White criteria for success and acceptability rather than recognizing that such criteria might be inappropriate and/or too narrowly defined. Furthermore, cultural or racial differences are likely to be interpreted by using White life experiences as the standards. Moreover, the Pseudo-Independent person still looks to Black rather than White people to explain racism and seeks solutions for it in hypothetical Black cultural dysfunctionalities.

Although the person in the Pseudo-Independent stage no longer has a negative White identity or consciousness, neither does he or she have a positive one. The paucity of White models of positive Whiteness means that the person usually has no visible standards against which to compare and/or modify himself or herself. Additionally, such a person is likely to be met with considerable suspicion from other Whites as well as Blacks.

Many Whites will treat the Pseudo-Independent person, who actively expresses this identity, as though he or she has violated White racial norms. Many Black people will be suspicious of the motives of a person who devotes so much attention to helping Blacks rather than changing Whites. Consequently, the Pseudo-Independent person may not feel entirely comfortable with her or his White identity, but overidentification with Blacks is also not likely to be very comfortable. Thus, the person may come to feel rather marginal where race and racial issues are concerned. However, if the personal rewards (e.g.,

Figure 15-2 A Workshop Activity on Self-Assessing White Racial Identity

For each of the subsequent items, use the following scale to indicate the extent to which the item is true of you.

4—Strongly Agree
3—Agree
2—Disagree
1—Strongly Disagree

Write the numbers of your responses on the line next to the item. Add together your responses to the item precededs by the same combination of letters and plot your scores on the graph. Draw a line to connect your C total, R total, D total, P total, E total, and A total. Draw another line to connect the totals preceded by double letters (e.g., CB). This will give you a racial identity profile.

C1   _____   There is no race problem in the United States.

C2.   _____   Racism only exists in the minds of a few Black people.

C3.   _____   I personally do not notice what race a person is.

        _____   C TOTAL

CB1.   _____   I have asked or would ask a Black person to help me understand how I might be prejudiced.

CB2.   _____   I contribute or would contribute money or time to social programs to help Blacks.

CB3.   _____   I participate or would participate in an activity to help Blacks overcome their poor environment.

        _____   CB TOTAL

R1.   _____   I believe that White culture or Western civilization is the most highly developed, sophisticated culture ever to have existed on earth.

R2.   _____   Africans and Blacks are more sexually promiscuous than Europeans and Whites.

R3.   _____   The White race will be polluted by intermarriage with Blacks.

        _____   R TOTAL

RB1.   _____   When a Black male stranger sits or stands next to me in a public place, I move away from him.

RB2.   _____   I live or would live in a segregated (White) neighborhood.

RB3.   _____   The people I do my non-business related socializing with either are Whites or Blacks who "act White."

        _____   RB TOTAL

D1.   _____   American society is sick, evil, and racist.

D2.   _____   There is nothing I can do to prevent racism.

D3.   _____   I avoid thinking about racial issues.

        _____   D TOTAL

P1.   _____   It is White people's responsibility to eliminate racism in the United States.

P2.   _____   Eliminating racism would help Whites feel better about themselves.

P3.   _____   White people should help Black people become equal to Whites.

        _____   P TOTAL

PB1.   _____   I have boycotted a company or its products because of its racist programs.

PB2.   _____   For Martin Luther King's Birthday, I attend or would attend a commemorative event.

PB3.   _____   I have tried to help Whites understand Blacks.

        _____   LB TOTAL

E1.   _____   White culture and society must be restructured to eliminate racism and opposition.

E2.   _____   Whites and White culture are not superior to Blacks and Black culture.

E3.   _____   A multi-cultural society cannot exist unless Whites give up their racism.

        _____   E TOTAL

continued

Figure 15-2 (*continued*)

EB1. _____ I have studied the history of White and Western European people.

EB2. _____ I meet with Whites to discuss our feelings and attitudes about being White and White racism.

EB3. _____ I have conducted activities to help Whites overcome their racism.

_____ EB TOTAL

A1. _____ I accept that being White does not make me superior to any other racial group.

A2. _____ Being a member of a multi-racial environment is a must for me.

A3. _____ My Whiteness is an important part of who I am.

_____ A TOTAL

AB1. _____ I speak up in a White group situation when I feel that a White person is being racist.

AB2. _____ I express my honest opinion when a Black person is present without worrying about whether I appear racist.

AB3. _____ I attempt to explain to White friends and relatives the relationship of racism to other forms of oppression.

_____ AB TOTAL

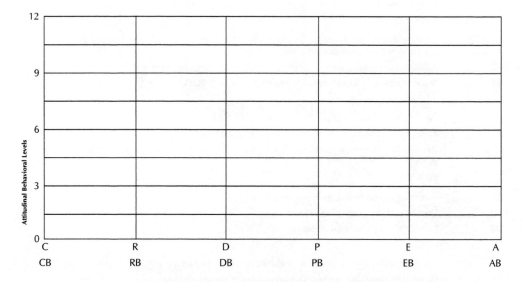

This workshop activity is adapted from Hardiman (1979) and Helms (1984). These items are not from a validated scale and are presented here for the reader's possible self-exploration. Abbreviations are: C = Contact attitudes, CB = Contact behavior, R = Reintegration attitudes, RB = Reintegration behavior, D = Disintegration attitudes, DB = Disintegration behavior, P = Pseudo-Independent attitudes, PB = Pseudo-Independent behavior, E = Emersion attitudes, EB = Emersion behavior, A = Autonomy attitudes, AB = Autonomy behavior. Higher scores indicate higher levels of the attitudes/behaviors.

self-esteem, monetary, etc.) are great enough to encourage continued strengthening of a positive White identity, then the person may begin the quest for those positive aspects of Whiteness that are unrelated to racism. The quest for a better definition of Whiteness signals the person's entry into the Immersion/Emersion stage.

Immersion/Emersion

Redefining a positive White identity requires that the person replace White and Black myths and stereotypes with accurate information about what it means and has meant to be White in the United States as well as in the world in general. The person in this stage is searching for the answers to the questions: "Who am I racially?" and "Who do I want to be?" and "Who are you really?"

Often such a person will immerse herself or himself in biographies and autobiographies of Whites who have made similar identity journeys. He or she may participate in White consciousness-raising groups whose purpose is to help the person discover her or his individual self-interest in abandoning racism and acknowledging a White racial identity. Changing Black people is no longer the focus of her or his activities, but rather the goal of changing White people becomes salient.

Emotional as well as cognitive restructuring can happen during this stage. Successful resolution of this stage apparently requires emotional catharsis in which the person reexperiences previous emotions that were denied or distorted (cf. Lipsky, 1978). Once these negative feelings are expressed, the person may begin to feel a euphoria perhaps akin to a religious rebirth. These positive feelings not only help to buttress the newly developing White identity, but provide the fuel by which the person can truly begin to tackle racism and oppression in its various forms.

Autonomy

Internalizing, nurturing, and applying the new definition of Whiteness evolved in the earlier stages are major goals of the Autonomy stage. In this stage, the person no longer feels a need to oppress, idealize, or denigrate people on the basis of group membership characteristics such as race because race no longer symbolizes threat to him or her. Since he or she no longer reacts out of rigid world views, it is possible for him or her to abandon cultural and institutional racism as well as personal racism. Thus, one finds the Autonomous person actively seeking opportunities to learn from other cultural groups. One also finds him or her actively becoming increasingly aware of how other forms of oppression (e.g., sexism, ageism) are related to racism and acting to eliminate them as well. Terry's (1977) description of the characteristics of the New White (see Table 15.1) seems to describe the Autonomous person.

Although Autonomy represents the highest level of White racial identlity and might be thought of as racial self-actualization or transcendence, perhaps it is best to think of it as an ongoing process. It is a process wherein the person is continually open to new information and new ways of thinking about racial and cultural variables. Nevertheless, reaching the Autonomy stage does not necessarily mean that the person is perfect with respect to all aspects of her or his identity. Chances are if the person had a grouchy personality (i.e., personal identity) before he or she began movement through the racial identity development process, then he or she will still be a grouch once the process is completed. It is just that his or her grouchiness will no longer be governed by cultural or racial determinants. In other words, one might find a variety of personality characteristics and styles among people who have reached the Autonomy stage.

Conclusions

As might be apparent, each of the White racial identity stages is hypothesized to have its own unique effect on attitudes, behaviors, and emotions. Nevertheless, it is probably not the case that each of these develops at the same rate. In fact, studies of symbolic racism (e.g., McConaghy & Hough, 1976) suggest that attitudes (at least racist attitudes as opposed to White identity attitudes) may change faster than behaviors. As an example of how this is possible, the reader might wish to try out the workshop exercise in Figure 15.2. It seems reasonable to speculate that the greatest discomfort occurs for those individuals whose attitudes, emotions, and behaviors are not in harmony.

CHAPTER 16

CROSS'S NIGRESCENCE MODEL:
FROM THEORY TO SCALE TO THEORY

BEVERLY J. VANDIVER, PEONY E. FHAGEN-SMITH, KEVIN O. COKLEY,
WILLIAM E. CROSS, JR., AND FRANK C. WORRELL

This chapter describes the process of developing a new scale to measure the revised nigrescence model (Cross, 1991). First, the identity clusters that characterize the nigrescence theory and that are measured in the Cross Racial Identity Scale (CRIS; Vandiver et al., 2000) are presented by stage. Thus, we first discuss the Pre-Encounter identity clusters, then the Immersion-Emersion identity clusters and third, the Internalization identity clusters. The second section of the chapter chronicles the evolution of four scale-development phases of the CRIS and the subsequent changes to the scale and theory at the end of each phase. For a more detailed summary of nigrescence theory and the changes to it over time, readers are referred to Cross (1971, 1991) and to Cross and Vandiver (2001).

Historical and Theoretical Considerations

Pre-encounter: A Mariska [Matryoshka] Puzzle

Like the multinested Mariska [Matryoshka] dolls, Cross's (1971, 1991) Black racial identity stage of Pre-Encounter (Stage 1) is deceiving. On the surface, Pre-Encounter seems to reflect a unitary construct, composed of two polar aspects of Black identity: pro-White and anti-Black attitudes. In the original nigrescence model (Cross, 1971), Pre-Encounter Blacks were believed to operate from an assimilation-integration paradigm, internalizing a "pro-White" identity that affirms "White-Anglo-Saxon-Protestant" characteristics and negates non-WASP behavior (Cross, 1971, p. 16). Blacks who were viewed as pro-White were believed to be anti-Black and self-hating and to have low self-esteem (poor mental health). However, after an extensive review of the Black identity literature, Cross (1991) concluded that Pre-Encounter was more complex than originally conceived, and Pre-Encounter is now believed to be characterized by at least three identity clusters (Cross & Vandiver, 2001). In addition, psychological functioning or self-esteem is no longer directly linked to racial group preference.

Pre-Encounter and Black self-hatred. The term *Black self-hatred*, which can be defined as a Black person's hatred of the self because of race, has a long history in the discourse on Black identity. As early as the 1930s, scholars believed that Blacks' preference to be White was indicative of self-hatred, and, thus, reflective of an identity problem (see Clark & Clark, 1947; Horowitz, 1939). Kardiner and

"Cross's Nigrescence Model: From Theory to Scale to Theory." Reprinted from *Journal of Multicultural Counseling and Development* 29, no. 3 (2001), American Counseling Association.

Ovesey (1951) noted that *Black self-hatred* (a term traced to their work) could be revealed by indirect and direct evidence. Definitive statements reflecting anti-Black feelings or beliefs (e.g., "I hate being Black" or "I dislike my Black features") were seen as direct evidence of self-hatred. Examples of indirect evidence included Blacks' idealization of White people and White culture (e.g., through assimilationist behavior and attitudes). Both direct and indirect manifestations of Black self-hatred were included in the original description of the Pre-Encounter stage (Cross, 1971) and in other Black identity change theories (e.g., Fanon, 1967; Memmi, 1965; Milliones, 1973; Thomas, 1971).

The Pre-Encounter subscales of both the Black Racial Identity Attitude Scale (RIAS-B; Parham & Helms, 1981) and the Developmental Inventory of Black Consciousness (DIBC, Milliones, 1973; Taylor, Brown, & Denton, 1996) included direct (anti-Black) and indirect (pro-White) self-hatred items. Researchers who used the RIAS-B reported evidence linking the Pre-Encounter identity to poor ego identity development (Looney, 1988), low levels of self-actualization, feelings of inferiority, anxiety, and a lack of self-acceptance (Carter, 1991; Parham & Helms, 1985a, 1985b), as well as low personal autonomy and interpersonal difficulties (Taub & McEwen, 1992). Results from studies using the DIBC linked the Pre-Encounter stage to low self-esteem, depression, low levels of self-actualization, aggressive social attitudes, and a propensity toward asocial behavior, such as committing violent crimes (Taylor, 1986; Taylor et al., 1996). These and other findings (see Carter, 1996; Cross, 1991, for reviews) established that the Pre-Encounter identity reflected a single theme—Black self-hatred.

The link between Black self-hatred and pro-White attitudes began to be questioned in the 1980s. Empirical studies on Blacks across the age span (Cross, 1991; Gordon, 1980; Porter & Washington, 1979; White & Parham, 1990), using other measures of Black identity (e.g., Q-sorts), revealed a weak or near zero correlation between pro-White attitudes and self-esteem. The discrepancy in findings can be explained by the way that the DIBC and the RIAS-B are scored. Although both the DIBC and RIAS-B consist of pro-White and anti-Black items, more anti-Black items are contained in these measures. Summing the ratings of the pro-White and anti-Black items to create a total Pre-Encounter score may result in an artificial link between pro-White attitudes and low self-esteem.

Using separate pro-White and anti-Black subscales, two studies (Cross, Swim, & Fhagen-Smith, 1995; Johnson, 1972) illustrated the possible differential link between self-esteem and pro-White and anti-Black items. Johnson found that, in both high school and college samples, high scores on the anti-Black subscale were positively related to high scores on anomie, intolerance of ambiguity, alienation, stoicism, and rigidity, whereas few of these variables related to pro-Whiteness. More evidence for two Pre-Encounter identities was provided in a study conducted by Cross et al. (1995). The researchers administered a modified version of the RIAS-B (Parham & Helms, 1981), with additional pro-White and anti-Black items, and the Rosenberg Self-Esteem Scale (RSES; Rosenberg, 1965) to 64 African American college students attending a large, predominately White, mid-Atlantic university. The composite Pre-Encounter score, consisting of pro-White and anti-Black items, was significantly and negatively correlated with global self-esteem ($r = -29, p < .01$). However, when the Pre-Encounter composite score was divided into pro-White and anti-Black items, self-esteem was found to be related to the anti-Black score ($r = -.31, p < .007$) but not to the pro-White score ($r = .09, p > .05$). Despite the study's limitations (e.g., small sample size, no validity and reliability information on the modified RIAS-B subscales), these and other findings (e.g., Gordon, 1980; Johnson, 1972) supported Cross's (1991) contention that a pro-White attitude is not related to self-esteem and is not a valid indicator of Black self-hatred. In addition, these findings challenged the characterization of Pre-Encounter as a single identity, suggesting instead that at least two Pre-Encounter dimensions exist.

Two Pre-Encounter identities. In the revised model, Cross (1991) delineated two Pre-Encounter identity clusters: Assimilation and Anti-Black. The Pre-Encounter Assimilation identity describes a cluster of people who show low salience for race but a strong reference group orientation centered on being an American. In contrast, the Anti-Black identity represents the original feature of the 1971 version of Pre-Encounter: Black self-hatred or anti-Blackness. Pre-Encounter Anti-Black depicts a Black person who holds extremely negative views about Black people (high, negative race salience), and these views are internalized as Black self-hatred. Cross (1991) pointed out that it is difficult for any Black person to pass through the formal education system without being exposed to certain historical distortions about Africa and the African American experience. When a Black person begins to believe these distortions, he or she evidences the trait called *miseducation*, a term attributed to Woodson (1933). The internalization of negative stereotypes about Blacks results in individuals questioning their own self-worth as a Black person. Black self-hatred is the result of extreme miseducation.

The Two Sides of Immersion-Emersion

Cross (1991) described the Immersion-Emersion stage as "the most sensational aspect of Black identity development, for it represents the vortex of psychological nigrescence" (Cross, 1991, pp. 201–202). Although Cross (e.g., Cross, 1991, 1995; Cross & Vandiver, 2001) has changed the number of identities in the immersion process, the nature of the Immersion-Emersion experience, as described almost three decades ago, has not changed. Once viewed as a reflection of only one identity, the Immersion phase describes a bifurcation of vision regarding the world and society. These two visions are considered to encompass two separate, but related, Immersion identities: Everything Black or Afrocentric is good (Intense Black Involvement), and everything White or Eurocentric is evil (Anti-White).

Intense Black Involvement. In the original nigrescence model (Cross, 1971; Hall, Freedle, & Cross, 1972) the Immersion-Emersion stage was described as a period when everything important must be relevant to Blackness. Individuals in this stage are described as hungrily consuming "Black literature and [devoting] much contemplation to the forms of being Black" (Hall et al., 1972, p. 6). As Cross, Parham and Helms (1991) pointed out, nigrescence means "to become Black" (p. 320). *Immersion* into Blackness, characterized by the excessive embracing of everything Black, is the first step on the journey toward an "internalized" Black identity.

One of the positive aspects of Intense Black Involvement is the unbridled enthusiasm for information about Africa and African Americans. The Immersion-Emersion process may lead to well-informed individuals who have a sense of their place in the world and of the contributions that they and their ancestors have made over the years. Cross (1991) noted that there is also a tangible benefit to society in general. Immersion activities have resulted "in an explosion of articles, books, newsletters, journals and any number of new organizations" (p. 203). However, there is a price that is paid by the individual and, often, by society as well. Rage, anxiety, and guilt, emotions that are potentially destructive when uncontrolled, fuel these explorations of Blackness.

"How could *they* do this to me?" "How could *they* do this to us?" "How could I have failed to see what society was like before now?" These questions are critical ones for the Immersion-Emersion individual, and they act as the motivators in the quest for nigrescence. The questions represent a wellspring of rage, anxiety, and guilt. Individuals in Immersion feel a profound rage at society—translated as White America—for deceiving them all these years. They are also enraged with themselves for allowing the deception to take place. These individuals also feel a tremendous sense of guilt for betraying Blacks by ignoring or downplaying the impact of race in everyday life, and the immersion into Black activities is a symbolic attempt to baptize themselves into a new way of being.

As has been indicated, the outward behavioral manifestations involve immersion in everything Black. There are two other behavioral manifestations that are emotionally based. One of these is an unforgiving stance toward other African Americans who are perceived to be Pre-Encounter or Multiculturalist. The intense Black-involved individual is not able to distinguish between these two identity frameworks, seeing both as pro-White and, therefore, anti-Black. A second manifestation is a virulent anti-White attitude that can be manifested in social interactions and public behavior.

Anti-White attitudes. Originally, Cross (1978) conceptualized anti-White attitudes as a secondary aspect of a Black person's immersion process. During this process, individuals have "a tendency to denigrate White people and White culture" (p. 17). Anti-White attitudes are an inevitable consequence of immersing oneself in Blackness and becoming fully enamored with Black people, culture, and history. Building on these tenets from his original model, Cross (1991) noted in the revised model that the outward expression of disdain for Whites was less likely to occur in the present-day social milieu than during and immediately after the Civil Rights movement. He suggested that anti-White attitudes held during the immersion period were "worked through as daydreams or fantasies such as the urge to rip off the first White person one passes on a particular day" (Cross, 1991, p. 206). Cross also contended that these fantasies about hurting White people are experienced by Blacks regardless of age, sex, or class background. Furthermore, he suggested that anti-White attitudes can become a permanent part of one's Black racial identity (i.e., an identity based on the hatred and negation of White people). Thus, extreme anti-White attitudes can emerge as a unique Immersion identity, separate from the Intense Black Involvement Immersion identity.

In support of Cross's current view of an Anti-White identity, hooks (1992) also differentiated between anti-Whiteness in response to White oppression and anti-Whiteness on the basis of stereotypes of White people. hooks described anti-White sentiments this way:

> . . . I want to focus on that representation of Whiteness that is not formed in reaction to stereotypes but emerges as a response to the traumatic pain and anguish that remains a consequence of White racist domination, a psychic state that forms and shapes the way Black folks "see" Whiteness. (p. 169)

In hooks's view, then, the anti-White sentiment of Immersion-Emersion is not only understandable, it is rational.

The Internalization Stages

Early nigrescence models (e.g., Cross, 1971; Milliones, 1973; Thomas, 1971) assumed that the final stage of Black racial identity resulted in self-actualization (Cross, 1991). The term *Black self-actualization* was used to infer not only the acceptance of a positive Black identity but also an improvement in psychological functioning or self-concept. In the revised nigrescence model, Cross (1991) underscored the importance of Black acceptance and pride, rather than self-actualization, in the Internalization stage.

The Original Stages of Internalization

Two stages of Internalization, Internalization and Internalization-Commitment, were proposed in the original nigrescence model (Cross, 1971). During Internalization (Stage 4), individuals put aside the anger and guilt of Immersion-Emersion and accept themselves as Blacks without romanticizing Blackness or hating Whiteness. The fifth and final stage of nigrescence (Internalization-Commitment) marked a racial identity that was based on involvement and activism and was evidenced in regular involvement in diverse organizations. Moving into the Internalization stage resulted in "self-healing" (Cross, 1995, p. 96), with feelings of inferiority and insecurity replaced by "Black pride" and "self-love" (Cross, 1991, p. 159). Because few attitudinal differences exist between the psychology of Blacks in the Internalization and Internalization-Commitment stages, these two stages are combined, and, in further discussion, are collectively termed *Internalization*.

Internalization Revised

Cross's (1991) critical review of empirical studies on Black racial identity led to the implementation of two major theoretical changes in the Internalization stage. First, Internalization was no longer synonymous with a universal or humanist view about relationships among diverse cultural groups. Rather, internalized Blacks could differ in their acceptance of members from diverse cultural groups. The second change in the revised Internalization stages was the uncoupling of Black self-acceptance and mental health. Cross (1995) argued that changes from pro-White to pro-Black attitudes might result in changes in a person's worldview, value system, ideology, or reference group orientation, but not in general psychological functioning or personality. In other words, acceptance of Blackness does not guarantee a positive change in a Black person's level of psychological functioning. The acceptance of Blackness does not insulate Blacks from depression, nor does it change fundamental personality characteristics (Cross, 1991, 1995).

Rather, the primary shift for internalized individuals is in reference group orientation. Internalized Blacks slough off the stereotypical and unjustified pro-race and anti-race attitudes once held. Being comfortable with their Blackness frees individuals to concentrate on issues beyond the parameters of a personal sense of Blackness. The diversity of internalized identities is evidenced by Cross's (1991, 1995) delineation of three independent ideologies: Black Nationalism, Biculturalism, and Multiculturalism.

Black Nationalism

Of all of the identities of Cross's (1971, 1991) nigrescence theory, Black Nationalism is perhaps the most complex and controversial and, consequently, the most misunderstood. The challenge of fully understanding Black Nationalism is due, in part, to the negative connotations associated with any type of nationalism, particularly a racial or ethnic form. Media coverage of nationalism often results in sensationalistic portrayals of racial/ethnic tensions and rarely offers insight into the complexity of the psychological processes underlying nationalist expressions. Even Black scholars (e.g., West, 1993) often treat Black Nationalism monolithically, by focusing on its extreme elements rather than acknowledging its multiple expressions.

Black Nationalism is characterized by a focus on Black empowerment, economic independence, and a heightened awareness of Black history and culture. Its goal is to acknowledge and honor the dignity and humanity of Black people (Frederickson, 1995). To understand Cross's (1971, 1991, 1995) theorizing about the psychological role of Black Nationalism, the primary types of Black Nationalism are briefly explicated. Two primary forms of Black Nationalism (separatism and inclusion) exist.

Separatist views. The separatist view of Black Nationalism emerged from the Pan-Africanist ideology advocated by immigrants such as Crummell, Blyden, and Garvey (Frederickson, 1995) in the late nineteenth and early twentieth centuries. The Pan-Africanist ideology called on people of African descent in America (a) to go back to Africa or (b) to establish a separate all-Black nation within the United States. The Nation of Islam, a religious manifestation of Black Nationalism that emerged in the 1950s (Frederickson, 1995), made similar separatist calls, advocating self-sufficiency within the United States. The African cultural nationalism movement, another separatist form of Black Nationalism, surfaced in the 1960s and 1970s. Led by Karenga (1993), African cultural nationalism stressed racial separatism and emphasized the importance of African culture, with proponents wearing African clothes and hairstyles and changing their American names to African ones

(Frederickson, 1995).

Inclusion movements. In contrast, DuBois's view of Black Nationalism emphasized a strong Black consciousness situated within American educational, political, and cultural institutions, with Blacks achieving the same political and civil rights as their White counterparts. A related, but distinct, Black Nationalism ideology of political inclusion—anti-capitalist socialism—surfaced during the Black Power movement in the 1960s and 1970s. Greatly influenced by Marxist thought, anti-capitalist socialism was inclusive of non-Blacks as long as they supported the dismantling of capitalism and White oppression (Frederickson, 1995). Other nationalist movements that stressed Black empowerment, but did not represent separatist or inclusive ideologies (e.g., Afrocentricity; Asante, 1980; Nobles, 1991), emerged during the latter part of the Black Civil Rights movement and became central in the Black identity discourse beginning in the 1980s and continuing to the present.

The original nigrescence model and Black Nationalism. In Cross's (1971) original model, Black Nationalism was not addressed directly. However, some of the beliefs associated with the Intense Black Involvement of the Immersion-Emersion stage (e.g., joining only all-Black organizations, attending pro-Black functions, wearing African clothing, taking African names) were related to Black Nationalist perspectives, such as the Afrocentrist or separatist. However, the pro-Black/nationalist orientation of Immersion-Emersion was also characterized by cognitive inflexibility, as well as "oversimplified" and "racist" beliefs about White people (Cross, 1971, p. 20). Viewed from the perspective of Immersion-Emersion, then, Black Nationalists did not have a "psychologically healthy" Black identity.

Nationalism in the revised nigrescence model. Critics (e.g., Karenga, 1993) argued that Cross's 1971 characterization of Black Nationalism, although implicit, was limited and pejorative and failed to recognize "the role [that] Black Nationalism plays in the lives of many who achieve Internalization" (Cross, 1995, p. 97). Many Black Nationalists hold well-articulated ideologies that are used to achieve Black empowerment and economic equity. For example, Cross's (1991) description of Internalization-Commitment seems to parallel the anti-capitalist, Black Nationalist ideology. In response to these critiques, Cross (1991) explicitly addressed the role of Black Nationalism in the revised nigrescence model. Black Nationalism, regardless of the diverse ideologies, is no longer implicitly situated in the Immersion-Emersion stage. Instead Black Nationalism is now viewed as serving a vital and positive role in the lives of those who reach the Internalization stage. However, Cross (1991) noted that Black Nationalist identities, although internalized, carry with them "possibilities of conflict over how to relate to the other [American] half of their cultural-historical makeup" (p. 213).

Cross (1991) also explicitly addressed Afrocentricity in the Internalization stage. Although a form of Black Nationalism, a variety of definitions of Afrocentricity exist. Cross (1991) defined *Afrocentricity* as a "Black American interpretation of what it means to have an African perspective" (p. 222). In 1971, Cross stated that nigrescence was not enough to liberate the minds of Black scholars from Western thought and contended that exposure to non-Western ideology was a necessity. The inclusion of Afrocentricity as a type of nationalist in the final stage of nigrescence (Cross, 1991) offers one possible non-Western framework that internalized Blacks may rely on to diminish the hegemonic influence of a Eurocentric worldview.

Internalization Beyond Race

The words *bicultural, humanist,* and *cross-cultural* were used to describe individuals in the original Internalization stages (Cross, 1978; Parham, 1989). Blacks who were in the Internalization stages were open to other cultures and worldviews, but they still opposed societal racism and oppression. With acceptance of being Black as their foundation, internalized individuals were united around the perspective of a universalist/humanist. Increased contact with people from diverse cultural backgrounds increased the likelihood that Blacks in the Internalization stages would become culturally adept. However, in addition to negotiating the identities of race and nationality, other cultural aspects of internalized individuals were not addressed. Thus, a bicultural/multicultural perspective undergirded the original Internalization stages, with the primary focus on race. In Cross's (1991) revision of the Internalization stage, he delineated bicultural and multicultural reference group orientations and expanded the focus of these identities beyond only race.

An internalized Bicultural identity. The development of an internalized Bicultural identity describes the acceptance of being both Black and American. The positive aspects of both identities are accepted without romanticizing race, as in the Immersion-Emersion stage, or nationality, as in the Pre-Encounter stage.

An internalized Multicultural identity. As with all internalized identity clusters, Black self-acceptance is at the heart of the Multicultural identity. Being Black is salient, but at least two other identity categories are also given nearly equal status in the dynamics of the person's identity. The acceptance of others from diverse racial backgrounds is also seen as being part of an internalized Multicultural identity. For example, a person may stress being Black, gay, female, and disabled or Black, deeply religious, and male (Cross & Vandiver, 2001) and will be open to working on causes alongside cultural groups other than African Americans.

Method

Four phases of scale development are presented. In Phase 1, the goal was to develop a pool of items that reflected the attitudes of the nigrescence identity clusters. Phases 2 through 4 describe the initial scale development of the CRIS with three independent samples of African American college students and the subsequent impact on the nigrescence model and scale. The goals of Phases 2 through 4 were to establish a stable measure with minimum reliability estimates of .70 for subscale scores and subscale intercorrelations of |.30| and below. An additional goal of Phase 3 was to establish initial construct validity through exploratory factor analysis (EFA).

Phase 1

Content Validity of the CRIS Items

Content validity of the CRIS items was established in two ways. We and the other members of the CRIS research team discussed and wrote items based on the identity cluster constructs described in the revised nigrescence model (Cross, 1991). This process produced 250 items that, after review and further discussion, were reduced to 126. To maximize the content validity of the CRIS items, external judges, who were knowledgeable about the revised nigrescence theory, were identified and asked to evaluate the content of the 126 CRIS items. The judges were advanced graduate students, staff psychologists, and university faculty in multicultural psychology. Twenty of the 45 experts who agreed to participate returned ratings of the CRIS items. Final selection and refinement of items for the first version of the CRIS were based on the judges' ratings and our discussion of the items. The specific criteria used to select items from the judges' ratings are described in detail by Cross and Vandiver (2001).

Nigrescence Identity Cluster Constructs

Six of the seven identity clusters described by Cross (1991) were used for item development: two Pre-Encounter clusters, Assimilation and Anti-Black; two Immersion-Emersion clusters, Intense Black Involvement and Anti-White; and two Internalization clusters, Black Nationalist and Multiculturalist. Stage 2 (Encounter) and the Emersion phase of the Immersion-Emersion stage (Stage 3) were not measured, because neither an encounter nor emersion from the emotional upheaval of immersion is assumed to represent specific identity clusters (Cross, 1991). Rather, the Encounter stage describes unique individualistic racial experiences or events that may precipitate a possible reevaluation of the person's Black identity (Cross, 1991). In addition, the Emersion phase chronicles the transition to the Internalization stage. We decided not to measure the Internalization Biculturalist identity cluster because of its nested relationship with the Internalization Multiculturalist identity cluster. Items designated for the Biculturalist identity are just as likely to be rated similarly by those believed to have a Multiculturalist identity. In addition, the combination of the Internalization stages resulted in the development of Internalization items to capture both the essence of Internalization and the activism component of Internalization-Commitment. For the Black Nationalist, social activism is described in terms of uplifting the Black community, whereas for the Multiculturalist, activism is depicted in terms of creating coalitions among diverse cultural groups.

Pre-Encounter identity clusters. Pre-Encounter is characterized by varying degrees of race salience and is seen as having two identity clus-

ters: Assimilation and Anti-Black. The focus of the Assimilation identity cluster was specifically on a Black person's preference for an American worldview and culture. An example of an Assimilation item was "I prefer to socialize with European Americans." The Anti-Black cluster identity incorporated two themes of rejecting a Black identity: miseducation and self-hatred. Items were written to address both anti-Black themes as representative of one identity cluster. A typical miseducation item was "African Americans do not stress education and training," whereas "I secretly dislike my skin color and physical features" exemplified the self-hatred items.

Immersion-Emersion identity clusters. Intense Black Involvement describes the immersion into Black culture and the romanticizing of everything Black. A typical Intense Black Involvement item reflects an extreme, emotional pro-Black view (e.g., "Sometimes I cannot help myself and I 'go off' on someone who thinks like a typical 'Negro' "). The Anti-White identity cluster describes demonizing White culture and people. Items for the Anti-White identity cluster reflected hatred for all things associated with White people (e.g., "I hate White people").

Internalization identity clusters. The Internalization identity clusters reflect Black self-acceptance. Because the Black Nationalist identity represents a myriad of ideologies, items were initially developed that represented a composite of the more prominent Black Nationalist ideologies (Afrocentrism, separatism, traditional Black Nationalism) existing in the United States (Frederickson, 1995). Key words were used to establish a link among the Black Nationalist items and to delineate the Black Nationalist items from the Intense Black Involvement items. A typical Black Nationalist item was "As a Black Nationalist, I support combating racism through Black solidarity."

Items for the Multiculturalist subscale were written to link Black self-acceptance with connections to or appreciation for individuals from diverse cultural groups. On some Multiculturalist items, references were made to other cultural groups (e.g., Latinos/as, Whites, gays/lesbians) by including a parenthetical statement listing these groups. The parenthetical listing helped to demarcate the Multiculturalist identity cluster from the Pre-Encounter Assimilation identity cluster, which does not emphasize cultural diversity. A typical Multiculturalist item was "Because I feel comfortable with my Black identity, I seek interactions with people who represent other racial and ethnic groups (e.g., Latinos/as, Whites, gays/lesbians)."

Data Collection Summary for Phases 2 Through 4

Participants

Three independent samples of African American college students were the participants for Phases 2 through 4. 16-1 contains a summary of each sample's characteristics. The first two samples were collected from the same mid-Atlantic, predominately White university, with data collection more than 1 year apart. In Phase 4, the sample

came from a predominately White university in New England. The mean age of participants across the three samples was approximately 21 years ($SD = 3.47$), and more women than men participated in each phase. Most participants self-designated as African American or Black, and most were undergraduates. The samples did not differ significantly by sex representation, age, racial self-designation, or academic class standing across phases.

Measures

Participants in each sample received a survey packet that contained the current version of the CRIS and a background information sheet. Participants in Phase 2 also completed the RSES

TABLE 16-1
Description of Samples for Phases 2 Through 4

Demographic	Phase 2	Phase 3	Phase 4
Sample location	Mid-Atlantic	Mid-Atlantic	New England
Sample size	119	142	149
Sex			
Women	78	92	99
Men	31	50	48
Unknown	10	0	2
Age			
Range	17–47	17–40	17–35
M	21.26	20.62	20.46
SD	4.56	3.17	2.69
Unknown	10	3	16
Racial designation			
African American/Black	91	122	109
Other Black	18	20	31
Unknown	10	0	9
Academic class standing			
Freshman/sophomores	50	74	77
Juniors/seniors	58	66	66
Other	0	1	5
Unknown	11	1	1
Incentives	None	Monetary	Monetary
Measures			
CRIS	57 items	76 items	64 items
Background sheet	Yes	Yes	Yes
RSES	Yes	No	No

Note. CRIS = Cross Racial Identity Scale; RSES = Rosenberg Self-Esteem Scale.

(Rosenberg, 1965). Background information collected from each sample included sex, racial designation, and academic class status.

Procedure

In all the phases, we and other members of the research team, using flyers, announcements in the campus newspaper, and individual contact, recruited participants across the campuses to participate in a social attitude survey. In Phases 3 and 4, monetary raffles were used in addition to the other recruitment methods previously described to increase the motivation of students to participate. All measures were randomly ordered in the packets to control for order effects. Typically, participants were able to complete the packet in about 20 minutes.

Phase 2

The first version of the CRIS was composed of 57 items distributed across six subscales: Pre-Encounter Assimilation (9 items), Pre-Encounter Anti-Black (9 items), Immersion-Emersion Intense Black Involvement (11 items), Immersion-Emersion Anti-White (9 items), Internalization Black Nationalist (9 items), and Internalization Multiculturalist (10 items). All CRIS items were rated on a 7-point Likert rating scale, which ranged from 1 *(strongly disagree)* to 7 *(strongly agree)*, and a mean score was derived for each subscale. To measure global self-esteem, the RSES (Rosenberg, 1965) was used. The RSES con-

sists of 10 items and measures global self-esteem on a 4-point rating scale, ranging from 1 *(strongly disagree)* to 4 *(strongly agree)*. Higher scores reflect higher levels of self-esteem. Reliability estimates for the RSES scores have ranged from .70 to .90 (Wylie, 1989).

Phase 2: Results and Discussion

Table 16-2 provides the reliability estimates and intercorrelations for the CRIS subscale scores and the RSES score. Reliability estimates for the CRIS subscale scores ranged from .59 to .83 (*Mdn* = .71). Subscale intercorrelations ranged from −.50 to .64 (*Mdn* = .04), with 7 of the 15 CRIS subscale intercorrelations at or above |.30|. The Multiculturalist subscale was not significantly correlated to any of the other CRIS subscales. The Anti-Black subscale was only correlated with the Assimilation subscale, sharing approximately 22% of the variance. Individuals who rated themselves high on an American worldview (Assimilation) had more anti-Black views. In contrast, the Assimilation subscale was significantly correlated with all CRIS subscales with the exception of the Multiculturalist subscale. The Assimilation subscale had negative relationships with both Immersion-Emersion subscales (Intense Black Involvement and Anti-White) and the Internalization Black Nationalist subscale. Assimilationists were likely to rate themselves lower on pro-Black (Intensive Black Involvement, Black Nationalist) and anti-White (Anti-White) subscales. The two Immersion-Emersion

TABLE 16-2
Phase 2 Subscale Intercorrelations and Reliability Estimates of CRIS and RSES Scores (*N* = 119)

Subscale	RSES (10)[a]	PA (9)	PAB (9)	IEIBI (11)	IEAW (9)	IBN (9)	IMC (10)	α
RSES	—							.83
PA	−.12	—						.68
PAB	−.20*	.47**	—					.73
IEIBI	−.08	−.34**	.14	—				.75
IEAW	−.09	−.31**	.05	.44**	—			.83
IBN	−.03	−.50**	−.05	.63**	.43**	—		.69
IMC	−.09	.11	.04	−.04	−.10	.01	—	.59

Note. See Table 16-1 *Note.* PA = Pre-Encounter Assimilation; PAB = Pre-Encounter Anti-Black; IEIBI = Immersion-Emersion Intense Black Involvement; IEAW = Immersion-Emersion Anti-White; IBN = Internalization Black Nationalist; IMC = Internalization Multiculturalist.

[a]Number in parentheses indicates number of items in each scale or subscale.
*p < .05. **p < .001.

subscales and the Internalization Black Nationalist subscale were positively correlated with each other, sharing approximately 19% to 40% of the variance. Those who reported Black views also had pro-Black and anti-White views. An inverse relationship was only found between self-esteem on the RSES and anti-Black scores on the CRIS at the .05 probability level, accounting for approximately 4% of the variance.

In summary, the goals for Phase 2 were partially supported. Reliability estimates for three subscale scores (Anti-Black, Intense Black Involvement, and Anti-White) were at or above .70. In addition, the Multiculturalist subscale correlated below |.30| with the other CRIS subscales, and the Anti-Black subscale had a significant relationship with one other subscale. Furthermore, as predicted by the nigrescence theory, only the Anti-Black subscale was found to have a relationship with the RSES, albeit with shared variance of less than 10% and not at the established significance level of .001. In conclusion, the Anti-Black subscale's moderate relationship with the Assimilation subscale and the strength of the relationships among four of the CRIS subscales (Assimilation, Intense Black Involvement, Anti-White, & Black Nationalist) indicated too great an overlap in measurement and the need for further delineation of the CRIS constructs.

Item Revisions for Phase 3

On the basis of the Phase 2 findings, items on the CRIS subscales were revised to create a clearer delineation among the subscales. Item correlations across subscales and reliability analyses were used to identify items that made a robust contribution to the designated subscale's variance but that did not correlate above |.30| with items from a different CRIS subscale. In addition, correlations between the Pre-Encounter items and the self-esteem score were examined.

Revisions of the Pre-Encounter Assimilation items resulted in a more obvious shift from a pro-White (European American) preference to an American preference, with the hope of muting the relationship between the Assimilation and Anti-White subscales. Assimilation items and most of the Anti-Black items were not significantly correlated to global self-esteem. However, three Anti-Black self-hatred items had correlations above |.30| with global self-esteem. Revision of the Pre-Encounter Anti-Black subscale involved clarify-

ing the miseducation items and the self-hatred items. The revised miseducation items focused on reference group orientation by referring to negative beliefs about how Blacks functioned generally, whereas self-hatred items focused on the pain individuals felt about being Black, a reflection of their personal identity. Both strands, self-hatred and miseducation, were still believed to represent the overarching construct of anti-Blackness and were included in one subscale.

Intense Black Involvement items were revised to be more extreme, with the use of words such as "absolutely," "totally," and "constantly." In addition, Intense Black Involvement items were written to emphasize the rejection of other Blacks for not having a "pure" Afrocentric or pro-Black perspective. The Anti-White items were streamlined to focus on the hatred of Whites without using the words "European American." To separate anti-White sentiments from the Black Nationalist worldview, Black Nationalist items were revised to emphasize the lack of White hatred while still focusing on Black empowerment.

Two issues emerged regarding the Multiculturalist items. First, although *multiculturalists* were defined as Blacks who connected primarily to other racial minorities, only 2 of the 10 Multiculturalist items referred to Whites. Second, some Black participants who rated themselves high on race-related Multiculturalist items did not endorse the statements that included Whites, lesbians, and gay men. Data collectors reported that some of the study's participants (primarily associated with religious organizations) objected to statements including gay men and lesbians. In essence, the Multiculturalist subscale was not measuring a multiculturalist as articulated by Cross (1991): that is, Blacks who are accepting of their Blackness and willing to create coalitions with people of diverse cultural backgrounds, not only with other racial minorities. To maintain consistency between nigrescence theory and the Multiculturalist subscale, more items included Whites and other broad cultural referents in parenthetical statements (e.g., Whites, lesbians/gays, Native Americans).

Phase 3

In Phase 3, participants completed the second version of the CRIS and a background information sheet. This version of the CRIS, consisting of 76 items, included revised and new items distributed across the same six subscales: Pre-Encounter Assimilation (14 items), Pre-Encounter Anti-Black (18 items, 9 miseducation and 9 self-hatred), Immersion-Emersion Intense Black Involvement (17 items), Immersion-Emersion Anti-White (11 items), Internalization Black Nationalist (12 items), and Internalization Multiculturalist (13 items). The items were rated and scored the same as in Phase 2.

Phase 3: Results and Discussion

Table 16-3 presents the subscale intercorrelations and reliability estimates of the Phase 3 CRIS scores. Reliability estimates ranged from .69 to .87 ($Mdn = .75$), and intercorrelations ranged from −.29 to .55 ($Mdn = .22$), and only five subscale intercorrelations were at or above |.30|. The Assimilation subscale did not correlate above |.30| with any of other CRIS subscales, and the Anti-Black and Multiculturalist subscales each had one correlation at or above |.30|. The most notable subscale intercorrelations were between the Immersion-Emersion subscales and the Black Nationalist subscale. The Intense Black Involvement, Anti-White, and Black Nationalist subscales shared approximately 14% to 30% of their variance. Participants who rated themselves high on Intense Black Involvement also rated themselves high on anti-White sentiment and Black Nationalism.

The substantial increase in correlation between Anti-Black and Intense Black Involvement (from .14 to .33) and the poor performance of the Anti-Black self-hatred items in reliability analyses led to a closer examination of the items on the Anti-Black subscale. Interitem correlations and reliability statistics revealed that the self-hatred and miseducation items were not working well together on that subscale. Subsequent analyses revealed that scores on the self-hatred items resulted in a reliability estimate of .62, whereas the reliability estimate for scores on the miseducation items was .73. Removal of items with low item-total correlations resulted in improved reliability estimates for both sets of scores, to .71 for self-hatred and .76 for miseducation items. To examine if the miseducation and self-hatred items represented unique constructs, separate subscales were created and correlated with the other CRIS subscales. Table 16-4 provides a summary of the correlational pattern among all the CRIS subscales, using three Pre-Encounter subscales (Assimilation, Miseducation, and Self-Hatred). Correlations among the three Pre-Encounter subscales ranged from .07 to .33, and none of the three subscales had correlations at or above |.30| with the other CRIS subscales.

At the end of Phase 3, scale properties were closer to the established goals than at the end of Phase 2 (see Table 16-4). All but one (Assimilation) of the reliability estimates for CRIS subscale scores were above .70. Only four subscale intercorrelations were above |.30|. However, the intercorrelations among Intense Black Involvement, Anti-White, and Black Nationalist subscales continued to be higher than desired.

TABLE 16-3
Phase 3 Reliability Estimates and Subscale Correlations of CRIS Scores
Using One Anti-Black Subscale ($N = 141$)

Subscale	PA (14)[a]	PAB (18)	IEIBI (17)	IEAW (11)	IBN (12)	IMC (13)	α
PA	—						.69
PAB	.29**	—					.75
IEIBI	−.05	.33**	—				.84
IEAW	−.29**	.17	.49**	—			.87
IBN	−.12	−.02	.55**	.37**	—		.75
IMC	.22*	−.14	.10	−.29**	.30**	—	.77

Note. See Tables 16-1 and 16-2 Notes.

[a]Number in parentheses indicates number of items in each subscale.
*$p < .01$. ** $p < .001$.

TABLE 16-4
Phase 3 Reliability Estimates and Subscale Intercorrelates of CRIS Scores
Using Two Anti-Black Subscales (N = 141)

Subscale	PA (14)[a]	PM (7)	PSH (6)	IEIBI (17)	IEAW (11)	IBN (12)	IMC (13)	α
PA	—							.69
PM	.33**	—						.76
PSH	.07	.24*	—					.71
IEIBI	−.05	.22**	.14	—				.84
IEAW	−.29*	.07	.21	.49**	—			.87
IBN	−.12	.01	−.16	.55**	.37**	—		.75
IMC	.22*	−.06	−.26*	.10	−.29**	.30**	—	.77

Note. See Tables 16-1 and 16-2. Notes. PM = Pre-Encounter Miseducation; PSH = Pre-Encounter Self-Hatred.

[a]Number in parentheses indicates number of items in each subscale.
*$p < .01$. **$p < .001$.

Pre-Encounter Revisited

Cross (1991) had theorized that the Pre-Encounter stage was representative of two distinct identity clusters, Assimilation and Anti-Black, with the latter consisting of miseducation and self-hatred. However, the empirical evidence at the end of Phase 3 did not support a unitary anti-Black construct. Miseducation and self-hatred, as measured by the CRIS items, reflected two constructs and necessitated two separate subscales. Consequently, the term *anti-Black* was dropped, and the subscales were designated as Pre-Encounter Miseducation and Pre-Encounter Self-Hatred.

Item Revisions for Phase 4

Revisions of items at this stage focused on refining the measurement of each CRIS subscale by trying to capture the essence of each identity cluster, again using correlational analyses and reliability estimates to identify core items. Assimilation items continued to focus on a preference for mainstream American society, with the goal of diminishing the relationship between the Assimilation and Anti-White items. Miseducation items were narrowed to reflect the more negative views that are commonly attributed to Blacks (e.g., being lazy or criminal). In contrast, the Self-Hatred items focused on the personal dislike of being Black. Because more muted Anti-White items, such as distrust of Whites, had

stronger correlations with other CRIS subscales, all anti-White items were revised to reflect a passionate hatred of Whites.

The Intense Black Involvement items continued to reflect a positive and extremely emotional view of Blackness. In contrast, rational ideology was emphasized in the Black Nationalist items. To minimize the connection between the Black Nationalist and Anti-White items, phrases denouncing anti-White sentiments, which had been anchored to the Black Nationalist ideology, were moderated. A Phase 3 item, which read "I do not hate Whites; I simply love Black people and want to support all of our efforts at building a strong, Afrocentric, and self-sustaining Black community," was revised to read "I support all of our efforts at building a strong, Afrocentric, and self-sustaining Black community in order for us to compete, side by side, with other racial groups."

Substantial revisions were also made to the Multiculturalist items despite the improved reliability of the scores. In Phase 3, some Multiculturalist items seemed too universal, resulting in low item-total score correlations. In addition, participants' responses to Multculturalist items suggested that the items were still bifurcated along cultural inclusion and exclusion. Some students marked through the words, "Whites" and "gays/lesbians," or otherwise edited the items before rating themselves on the statements. Other students wrote comments next to the culturally inclusive items, indicating that they would rate themselves differently on these items if either Whites or gay men and lesbians were not included.

Internalization Revisited

Feedback about the Multiculturalist items from two consecutive data collection periods resulted in a reexamination of the Multiculturalist identity cluster as articulated by Cross (1991). For instance, it is possible to be a multiculturalist and not be accepting of all diverse cultural groups, or are there steps along the path to being accepting of all cultures? Being mistrustful of White society can be rational (hooks, 1992) and does not preclude Black self-acceptance. To examine the existence of a multiculturalist with a minority racial focus, another Internalization identity cluster was proposed, and a new CRIS subscale was created.

The new Internalization identity and subscale were named Internalization Multiculturalist Racial and were characterized by Black self-acceptance and the acceptance of members of racial minority groups. The original Multiculturalist subscale was renamed Internalization Multiculturalist Inclusive and was based on accepting all people, including Whites, gay men, and lesbians. The Multiculturalist Racial and the Multiculturalist Inclusive items were contrasted by the referents placed in parentheses at the end of each sentence. The Multicultualist Inclusive (cultural inclusion) items continued to list Whites, gay men and lesbians, whereas the Multiculturalist Racial (cultural exclusion) items only listed members of racial minority groups.

Phase 4

The third version of the CRIS consisted of 64 items, distributed across eight subscales: Pre-Encounter Assimilation (10 items), Pre-Encounter Miseducation (6 items), Pre-Encounter Self-Hatred (10 items), Immersion-Emersion Intense Black Involvement (9 items), Immersion-Emersion Anti-White (9 items), Internalization Black Nationalist (10 items), Internalization Multiculturalist Inclusive (10 items), and Internalization Multiculturalist Racial (10 items). All items were rated and scored as in the original CRIS.

Phase 4: Results and Discussion— Descriptive Statistics

Subscale intercorrelations and reliability analyses of the CRIS subscale scores are presented in Table 16-5. Reliability estimates of the scores ranged from .63 to .84 (Mdn = .81), and the subscale intercorrelations ranged from −.51 to .80 (Mdn = .06). Seven of the 29 intercorrelations were above |.30|. None of the Pre-Encounter subscales were substantially correlated to the other CRIS subscales. As in Phase 3, the Assimilation and Miseducation subscales were significantly correlated, sharing 23% of the variance, but Self-Hatred was not correlated to the other Pre-Encounter subscales. Moderate correlations

TABLE 16-5
Phase 4 Reliability Estimates and Subscale Intercorrelates of CRIS Scores (N = 149)

Subscale	PA (10)[a]	PM (6)	PSH (10)	IEIBI (9)	IEAW (9)	IBN (10)	IMCI (10)	IMCR (10)	α
PA	—								.81
PM	.48**	—							.80
PSH	.16	.13	—						.84
IEIBI	−.17	−.06	−.05	—					.63
IEAW	−.21**	−.06	.01	.32**	—				.91
IBN	−.20	.02	−.13	.50**	.38**	—			.65
IMCI	.11	.13	−.12	.11	−.51**	.06	—		.83
IMCR	.10	.11	−.15	.14**	−.41**	−.03	.80**	—	.76

Note. See Table 16-1. 16-2. 16-4. *Notes.* IMCI = Internalization Multiculturalist Inclusive; IMCR = Internalization Multiculturalist Racial.

[a]Number in parentheses indicates number of items in each subscale.
*p < .01 ** p < .001.

among the Immersion-Emersion subscales and the Black Nationalist subscale continued to exist, ranging from .32 to .50. The two Multiculturalist subscales shared 64% of their variance, and both had moderate inverse correlations with the Anti-White subscale. Because the two Multiculturalist subscales were strongly correlated ($r = .80$), indicating that substantial revisions would be needed, and Multiculturalist Inclusive was seen as the critical Internalization subscale, the Multiculturalist Racial subscale was omitted from subsequent analyses.

Phase 4: Results and Discussion—EFA

First, EFAs were used to examine the integrity of the individual subscales (see Floyd & Widaman, 1995; Smith & McCarthy, 1995). Using principal axis factor (PAF) extraction, both oblique and orthogonal rotations were run and examined. Several criteria for factor retention and interpretation were used, including parallel analysis, the scree test, a minimum number of four items per factor, structure coefficients above |.40|, and the interpretability of the factors (Thompson & Daniel, 1996). Table 16-6 summarizes the EFA findings for the individual CRIS subscales. Five of the subscales yielded single-factor solutions. However, analysis of the 10 Assimilation items resulted in two factors. The 6 items making up the first factor best represented the theoretical construct of Assimilation and were retained for this subscale. A two-factor solution was also identified for the 10 Black Nationalist items. The emphasis of the 6 items on Factor 1 was the lack

of racial hatred, whereas the 4 Factor 2 items reflected achieving Black empowerment. Factor 2 also had lower correlations with the Anti-White and Intense Black Involvement subscales. Consequently, the 4 items that loaded on Factor 2 were selected to reflect the Black Nationalism construct. After refining each subscale by identifying the best items, 26 items were discarded, and 38 items were retained for further analyses.

These 38 CRIS items were all submitted to an EFA, using a PAF extraction and oblique rotation. The same factor retention and interpretation criteria were used. Despite the approximately 4:1 sample size ($N = 149$) ratio to number variables (38), the stability of the EFA was supported by the level of the communality of the variables (MacCallum, Widaman, Zhang, & Hong, 1999). The values of the CRIS items' communality ranged from .38 to .81 ($Mdn = .62$). MacCallum et al. stated, "When communalities are consistently high (probably all greater than .60) . . . [g]ood recovery of population factors can be achieved with samples that would be traditionally be considered too small for factor analytic studies, even when N is well below 100" (p. 96).

Although a seven-factor solution was proposed based on the number of subscales on the CRIS, a five-factor solution was the most viable, meeting all of the factor-retention criteria. On both the seven-factor and six-factor solutions, only 2 items loaded on Factor 6 with structure coefficients above |.40|. With the five-factor solution, the three Pre-Encounter subscales loaded on separate factors with structure coefficients ranging from |.53| to |.79|: Factor 2, Pre-Encounter

TABLE 16-6
Summary of Exploratory Factor Analysis (EFA) Findings for the Individual Subscales of the CRIS

Subscale	N	Number of Factors Extracted	Number of Items Retained	Range of Structure Coefficients for Retained Items
PA 148	148	2	6 (10)[a]	.52–.73
PM 148	148	1	5 (6)	.57–.83
PSH 147	147	1	7 (10)	.58–.74
IEIBI 144	144	1	5 (9)	.44–.67
IEAW 145	145	1	5 (9)	.75–.85
IBN 144	144	2	4 (10)	.42–.77
IMCI 146	146	1	6 (10)	.54–.71

Note. See Tables 16-1 16-5 and 5 Notes.

[a] Number in parentheses indicates original number of items on subscale.

Self-Hatred; Factor 3, Pre-Encounter Assimilation; Factor 5, Pre-Encounter Miseducation. The Anti-White items loaded negatively on Factor 1, with structure coefficients ranging from −.69 to −.81, and the Multiculturalist Inclusive items loaded positively on the same factor, with structure coefficients from .49 to .63. The Intense Black Involvement and Black Nationalist items loaded on Factor 4, with structure coefficients ranging from .29 to .59.

The Pre-Encounter subscales emerged as independent constructs, but the Immersion-Emersion and Internalization subscales did not. A pro-Black dimension seemed to undergird the Intense Black Involvement and the Black Nationalist subscales, and the inverse relationship of the Anti-White and Multiculturalist Inclusive items seemed to reflect a cultural inclusion/exclusion dimension. Thus, the measurement of the Immersion-Emersion and Internalization identity clusters did not match the theory, which postulated separate constructs.

Because the Black Nationalist construct is a unique Internalization identity, and we believed that the Intense Black Involvement individuals were endorsing Black Nationalist items, a decision was made to examine the factor structure of the CRIS without the Intense Black Involvement items. Again using PAF extractions with oblique rotations, five-factor and six-factor EFAs were run on 33 items, excluding the 5 Intense Black Involvement items. In the five-factor solution, the items for the Pre-Encounter subscales loaded on separate factors: Factor 2, Pre-Encounter Self-Hatred; Factor 3, Pre-Encounter Assimilation; and Factor 5, Pre-Encounter Miseducation. Two Miseducation and 2 Assimilation items cross-loaded at or above |.30| between the respective subscales but did not reach |.40|. However, the first and fourth factors were not as clearly delineated. Four of the 6 Multiculturalist Inclusive and all of the Black Nationalist items loaded exclusively on Factor 4. Two of the Multiculturalist Inclusive items and all the Anti-White items loaded primarily on Factor 1, with the remaining Multiculturalist Inclusive items cross-loading on Factor 1. In addition, the structure coefficients for the Multiculturalist Inclusive and Black Nationalist items were all in the .40 and .50 range, whereas the ranges of scores were higher (between .50 and .70) on the six-factor solution.

On the six-factor solution, the Pre-Encounter subscales loaded on the same factors (2, 3, & 5)

with essentially the same pattern as in the five-factor solution. Black Nationalist items loaded cleanly on Factor 4, and no other items cross-loaded onto that factor. The Anti-White and Multiculturalist Inclusive items loaded on Factors 1 and 6, respectively, with inverse cross-loadings in the .30 to .40 range. In summary, the six-factor solution was cleaner and in keeping with the nigrescence model. Furthermore, the strong inverse relationship between Multiculturalist Inclusive and Anti-White items made theoretical sense. Thus, the decision was made to accept the six-factor solution, presented in Table 16-7. As can be seen in Table 16-7, construct reliabilities of all but one subscale (Black Nationalist) are at or above .80, and only the correlation between the Anti-White and Multiculturalist Inclusive subscales is above .32.

In retrospect, the Intense Black Involvement items seemed to moderate the relationship between Anti-White and Multiculturalist Inclusive items, as well as loading on the same factor with Black Nationalist items. Without the Intense Black Involvement items, the preliminary findings support the Pre-Encounter and Black Nationalist subscales as relatively independent constructs. Separate, but related, Immersion-Emersion Anti-White and Internalization Multiculturalist Inclusive constructs were partially demonstrated. The goals for subsequent scale development of the CRIS are to test the stability of the three Pre-Encounter subscales, to improve the internal consistency of scores on the Black Nationalist subscale, and to delineate more clearly the Anti-White and Multiculturalist Inclusive subscales (Vandiver, Cross, Worrell, & Fhagen-Smith, in press).

General Discussion

The development of the CRIS (Vandiver et al., 2000) was begun in an attempt to measure the revised nigrescence model (Cross, 1991, 1995). The findings from independent samples across three data collection periods resulted in an expanded nigrescence model (Cross & Vandiver, 2001). The tentative conclusion is that there are at least three independent Pre-Encounter identity clusters, with all three operationalized on the CRIS; two Immersion-Emersion identity clusters, with one operationalized on the CRIS; and three Internalization identity clusters, with two measured on the CRIS. Moreover, scores on the six

TABLE 16-7
Structure Coefficients of Principal Axis Analysis With
Oblique Rotation of Phase 4 CRIS Scores[a]

Item	Factor 1 IEAW	Factor 2 PSH	Factor 3 PA	Factor 4 IBN	Factor 5 PM	Factor 6 IMCI
IEAW22	−.84	.07	−.08	−.07	.06	−.43
IEAW31	−.83	−.03	−.11	.13	.06	−.52
IEAW73	−.81	−.05	−.09	−.01	.04	−.49
IEAW15	−.77	.01	−.10	.01	.07	−.36
IEAW61	−.75	−.16	−.19	.11	.19	−.42
PSH5	.02	.76	.16	−.13	−.17	.03
PSH17	−.08	.71	.12	−.09	−.05	.05
PSH39	−.09	.71	.11	−.22	−.05	−.17
PSH74	.03	.70	.17	−.13	−.10	−.12
PSH80	.05	.69	.14	−.11	−.12	−.02
PSH55	.14	.64	.02	−.22	−.10	−.04
PSH27	.08	.57	−.03	−.26	−.07	−.02
PA64	.15	.08	.75	−.13	−.37	.03
PA51	−.03	.14	.69	−.28	−.21	−.08
PA37	.19	−.01	.61	−.04	−.24	.15
PA10	.19	.15	.60	.02	−.32	.09
PA3	−.12	.07	.58	−.23	−.18	−.05
PA25	.07	.19	.53	−.12	−.11	−.08
IBN18	−.09	−.15	−.16	.72	.03	.09
IBN21	−.02	−.23	−.20	.53	.06	.05
IBN6	.14	−.10	.00	.52	−.07	.25
IBN50	−.11	−.10	−.10	.41	−.08	.02
PM47	.02	.12	.28	.10	−.79	.03
PM23	.09	−.01	.15	.04	−.69	.14
PM35	−.07	.14	.38	−.12	−.66	.05
PM43	.10	.23	.18	−.02	−.64	−.01
PM12	.12	−.01	.30	.19	−.59	.18
IMCI36	.35	−.09	.14	.01	−.18	.76
IMCI72	.45	.12	.21	.18	−.24	.65
IMC114	.31	−.01	−.03	.10	−.08	.62
IMCI65	.38	−.04	−.09	.20	−.01	.59
IMCI54	.32	−.02	−.12	.13	−.02	.58
IMCI75	.33	−.08	.01	.20	.08	.56
Eigenvalues	5.60	4.68	3.22	2.34	1.65	1.43
% of Variance	16.96	14.19	9.77	7.09	5.01	4.34
Alpha	.90	.87	.80	.62	.81	.80

Factor Correlation Matrix

Factor 1	—					
Factor 2	.04	—				
Factor 3	.09	.13	—			
Factor 4	−.01	−.21	−.15	—		
Factor 5	−.07	−.12	−.32	−.04	—	
Factor 6	.46	−.05	.03	.17	−.10	—

Note. See Tables 16-1, 16-2, 16-4, 16-5 *Notes.* Boldface indicates highest loadings on each factor.

[a] N = 149.

CRIS subscales are generally reliable. In addition, using PAF analyses, four subscales emerged as separate factors, and two subscales were relatively independent. Despite the lack of full support for the CRIS, these findings are in need of replication and also open the door to a new era in examining the nigrescence model as operationalized on the CRIS.

The Interconnectedness of Theory and Research

The Pre-Encounter Identities

Originally, the Pre-Encounter stage was believed to be a unidimensional representation of Black self-hatred (Cross, 1971, 1978). Reviews of early empirical studies led to a revision of Pre-Encounter, and Cross (1991) argued that the Pre-Encounter stage was composed of pro-American and anti-Black or self-hating identity clusters. Cross also introduced the term *miseducation* to the discussion of Anti-Black identity. The current data suggest that African Americans can have negative stereotypes of Blacks (miseducation) that do not reflect self-hatred. By psychometrically isolating three Pre-Encounter identity clusters, the empirical findings forced a re-examination of the Anti-Black identity and the roles of self-hatred and miseducation in the Pre-Encounter stage. Additional empirical work will determine whether these three Pre-Encounter themes depict unique Black racial identities. Finally, the relationship between global self-esteem and the Self-Hatred subscale still requires further exploration. The preliminary finding does not support the premise of the revised nigrescence theory that self-hatred and low self-esteem are linked.

The Immersion-Emersion Identities

The Immersion-Emersion stage continues to be an area needing examination. The strong pro-Black feelings of this stage are matched, at least in the beginning, with equally potent anti-White feelings. In developing the CRIS, we and other members of the research team attempted to capture Intense Black Involvement and Anti-White sentiment as two related, but separate, constructs. This goal was only partially accomplished. Although the present version of the CRIS contains an Anti-White subscale, which yields reliable scores, the instrument does not have a subscale measuring Intense Black Involvement. In part, this is a theoretical issue. The two Immersion-Emersion identity clusters (Intense Black Involvement and Anti-White) are described as concomitants of the immersion process (Cross, 1991) and may be difficult to measure independently. Work continues on developing an Intense Black Involvement subscale. However, the Anti-White subscale of the CRIS will allow researchers to examine, in part, the Immersion-Emersion stage of Black identity development.

Internalization Identities

Whereas the original nigrescence model (Cross, 1971) described the essence of Internalization, Black self-acceptance, the revised nigrescence model (Cross, 1991) detailed three possible manifestations of Internalization: a pro-Black, non-racist orientation (Black Nationalism), with the focus solely on race; a biculturalist orientation, with Black acceptance and another cultural identity (typically nationality) both salient; and a multiculturalist orientation, with Black self-acceptance intertwined with two or more salient cultural identities. The results of this series of studies contribute to the expanded nigrescence model (Cross & Vandiver, 2001). These results suggest that there are at least two types of multiculturalists (racial and inclusive), a finding that raises questions for Cross's (1991) theory: What is at the heart of internalized identity clusters, and can one reach the Internalization stage and not be accepting of others? The incorporation of an Internalization Black Nationalist identity suggests that Cross has already taken a step toward addressing this issue. Our findings suggest that the Black Nationalist construct is multifaceted, with some strands being more separatist than others. At the end of Phase 4, we decided to use Black empowerment items as the core of the Black Nationalist subscale. However, there are other definitions of nationalism that require further study and that Cross will need to address from a theoretical standpoint. Finally, the results indicate that scores on the Multiculturalist Inclusive subscale are reliable but that more work is needed either to empirically demarcate more clearly the relationship between the Anti-White and Multiculturalist subscales or to reconceptualize the nature of these identities in the nigrescence model.

Conclusion

As detailed in the revised nigrescence model (Cross, 1991), examining Pre-Encounter construct is similar to examining a Russian Mariska [Matryoshka] doll. At first glance, Pre-Encounter seemed to be represented by the Self-Hatred identity, the doll that was clearly visible. However, just as when the top Mariska [Matryoshka] doll is lifted up, another doll appears, so too the peeling away of Self-Hatred led to the discovery of the Assimilation identity, and then to the discovery of the Miseducation identity. This metaphor can also be applied to the other two stages. The inclusive self-acceptance of the original conception of Internalization masked the self-acceptance of the Black Nationalist and Multiculturalist Racial identities. The data also indicate that a way needs to be found to tease apart the Intense Black Involvement identity and the Black Nationalist identity, as well as the relationship between Anti-White and the Multiculturalist Inclusive identities. Just as new identity clusters emerged in the scale-development process, in the same way the Mariska [Matryoshka] doll metaphor symbolizes the relationship between theory and research. Relying too much on theory or research can result in an incomplete picture of a phenomenon if theory and research are not used reciprocally to peel away layers. Advancing the understanding of Black identity development is best served by a healthy interaction between theory and research.

References

Asante, M. K. (1980). *Afrocentricity: The theory of social change*. Buffalo, NY: Amulefi.

Carter, R. T. (1991). Racial identity attitudes and psychological functioning. *Journal of Multicultural Counseling and Development, 19*, 105–114.

Carter, R. T. (1996). Exploring the complexity of racial identity attitude measures. In G. R. Sodowsky & J. Impara (Eds.), *Multicultural assessment in counseling and clinical psychology* (pp. 192–223). Lincoln, NE: Buros Institute of Mental Measurement.

Clark, K. B., & Clark, M. P. (1947). Racial identification and preference in Negro children. In T. M. Newcomb & E. L. Hartley (Eds.), *Readings in social psychology* (pp. 169–178). New York: Holt.

Cross, W. E., Jr. (1971, July). The Negro-to-Black conversion experience. *Black World*, 13–27.

Cross, W. E., Jr. (1978). The Thomas and Cross models of psychological nigrescence: A review. *Journal of Black Psychology, 5*, 13–31.

Cross, W. E., Jr. (1991). *Shades of Black: Diversity in African-American identity*. Philadelphia: Temple University Press.

Cross, W. E., Jr. (1995). The psychology of nigrescence: Revising the Cross model. In J. G. Ponterotto, J. M. Casas, L. A. Suzuki, & C. M. Alexander (Eds.), *Handbook of multicultural counseling* (pp. 93–122). Thousand Oaks, CA: Sage.

Cross, W. E., Jr., Parham, T. A., & Helms, J. E. (1991). The stages of Black identity development: Nigrescence models. In R. L. Jones (Ed.), *Black psychology* (3rd ed., pp. 319–338). Berkeley, CA: Cobb & Henry.

Cross, W. E., Jr., Swim, J., & Fhagen-Smith, P. E. (1995). *Black identity: Nigrescence and the search for the smallest Mariska doll*. Unpublished manuscript, The Pennsylvania State University, University Park.

Cross, W. E., Jr., & Vandiver, B. J. (2001). Nigrescence theory and measurement: Introducing the Cross Racial Identity Scale (CRIS). In J. G. Ponterotto, J. M. Casas, L. M. Suzuki, & C. M. Alexander (Eds.), *Handbook of multicultural counseling* (2nd ed., pp. 371–393). Thousand Oaks, CA: Sage.

Fanon, F. (1967). *Black skins, White masks* (C. L. Markmann, Trans.). New York: Grove Press.

Floyd, F. J., & Widaman, K. F. (1995). Factor analysis in the development and refinement of clinical assessment instruments. *Psychological Assessment, 7*, 286–299.

Frederickson, G. (1995). *Black liberation: A comparative history of Black ideologies in the United States and South Africa*. New York: Oxford Press.

Gordon, V. V. (1980). *The self-concept of Black Americans*. Washington, DC: University Press of America.

Hall, W. S., Freedle, R., & Cross, W. E., Jr. (1972). *Stages in the development of a Black identity*. Iowa City, IA: American College Testing Program.

hooks, b. (1992). Representations of Whiteness. In b. hooks (Ed.), *Black looks: Race and representation* (pp. 165–178). Boston: South End Press.

Horowitz, R. (1939). Racial aspects of self-identification in nursery school children. *Journal of Psychology, 7*, 91–99.

Johnson, L. P. (1972). *The correlates of the Black identity complex*. Unpublished doctoral dissertation, University of Minnesota, Minneapolis.

Kardiner, A., & Ovesey, L. (1951). *The mark of oppression*. New York: Norton.

Karenga, M. (1993). *Introduction to Black studies* (2nd ed.). Los Angeles: University of Sankore Press.

Looney, J. (1988). Ego development and Black identity. *Journal of Black Psychology, 15*, 41–56.

MacCallum, R. C., Widaman, K. F., Zhang, S., & Hong, S. (1999). Sample size in factor analysis. *Psychological Methods, 4*, 84–99.

Memmi, A. (1965). *The colonizer and the colonized* (H. Greenfield, Trans.). Boston: Beacon Press.

Milliones, J. (1973). *Construction of the Developmental Inventory of Black Consciousness.* Unpublished doctoral dissertation, University of Pittsburgh.

Nobles, W. (1991). African philosophy: Foundations for Black psychology. In R. L. Jones (Ed.), *Black psychology* (3rd ed., pp. 47–63). New York: Harper & Row.

Parham, T. A. (1989). Cycles of psychological nigrescence. *The Counseling Psychologist, 17*, 187–226.

Parham, T. A., & Helms, J. E. (1981). The influence of Black students' racial identity attitudes on preference for counselor's race. *Journal of Counseling Psychology, 28*, 250–258.

Parham, T. A., & Helms, J. E. (1985a). Attitudes of racial identity and self-esteem of Black students: An exploratory study. *Journal of College Student Personnel, 26*, 143–147.

Parham, T. A., & Helms, J. E. (1985b). Relation of racial identity attitudes to self-actualization and affective states of Black students. *Journal of Counseling Psychology, 32*, 431–440.

Porter, J. D., & Washington, R. E. (1979). Black identity and self-esteem: A review of studies of Black self-concept, 1968–1978. *Annual Review of Sociology, 5*, 53–74.

Rosenberg, M. (1965). *Society and the adolescent self-image.* Princeton, NJ: Princeton University Press.

Smith, G. T., & McCarthy, D. M. (1995). Methodological considerations in the refinement of clinical assessment instruments. *Psychological Assessment, 7*, 300–308.

Taub, D. J., & McEwen, M. K. (1992). The relationship of racial identity attitudes to autonomy and mature interpersonal relationships in Black and White undergraduate women. *Journal of College Student Development, 33*, 439–446.

Taylor, J. (1998). Cultural conversion experiences: Implications for mental health research and treatment. In R. L. Jones (Ed.), *African American development* (pp. 85–97). Hampton, VA: Cobbs & Henry.

Taylor, J., Brown, A., & Denton, S. (1996). Milliones' Developmental Inventory of Black Consciousness. In R. L. Jones (Ed.), *Handbook of tests and measurements for Black populations* (Vol. 2, pp. 191–206). Hampton, VA: Cobb & Henry.

Thomas, C. (1971). *Boys no more.* Beverly Hills, CA: Glencoe Press.

Thompson, B., & Daniel, L. G. (1996). Factor analytic evidence for the construct validity of scores: A historical overview and some guidelines. *Educational and Psychological Measurement, 56*, 197–208.

Vandiver, B. J., Cross, W. E., Jr., Fhagen-Smith, P. E., Worrell, F. C., Swim, J., & Caldwell, L. (2000). *The Cross Racial Identity Scale.* Unpublished scale.

Vandiver, B. J., Cross, W. E., Jr., Worrell, F. C., & Fhagen-Smith, P. E. (in press). Validating the Cross Racial Identity Scale. *Journal of Counseling Psychology.*

West, C. (1993). *Beyond Eurocentrism and multiculturalism.* Monroe, ME: Common Courage Press.

White, J., & Parham, T. A. (1990). *The psychology of Blacks.* Englewood Cliffs, NJ: Prentice-Hall.

Woodson, C. G. (1933). *The mis-education of the Negro.* Washington, DC: Associated Press.

Wylie, R. C. (1989). *Measures of self-concept* (pp. 25–35). Lincoln, NE: University of Nebraska Press.

CHAPTER 17

THE DEVELOPMENT OF GAY, LESBIAN, AND BISEXUAL IDENTITIES

HEIDI LEVINE AND NANCY J. EVANS

To understand the issues faced by gay, lesbian, and bisexual people on college campuses, we must first examine the life experiences of these individuals. What it means to be gay, lesbian, or bisexual is unique to each person; but some commonalities exist as individuals become aware of their attraction to others of the same sex and integrate these feelings into other aspects of their identity.

The research that considers timing and age factors in the gay and lesbian identity development process suggests that many developmental issues occur during the traditional undergraduate years (Bell, Weinberg, & Hammersmith, 1981; McDonald, 1982). As student development professionals, we know that this is a key time for identity development in general (Chickering, 1969; Erikson, 1968; Moore & Upcraft, 1990). College and university students are faced with many areas in which they need to reconsider their self-perceptions, develop new skills, and master developmental tasks. The possibility or certainty that one is gay, lesbian, or bisexual complicates these developmental challenges and adds an additional set of complicated issues that must be resolved. This chapter examines gay, lesbian, and bisexual identity development as it is experienced in Western society.

Much confusion exists in the literature concerning the terms *homosexual, gay,* and *lesbian* as well as what the concepts of identity and identity development mean. This *chapter* thus begins by clarifying terms used in relation to the development of a gay, lesbian, or bisexual identity. Gay identity development models are then reviewed, with special attention given to the model proposed by Cass (1979). Distinctions are made between social and psychological models, and the advantages of Cass' psychosocial approach are noted.

Most models of development have failed to consider gender differences, and none have taken into account bisexuality. Therefore, unique aspects of lesbian identity development and special concerns of bisexual individuals are next considered to complement discussion of the major models of gay identity development. The chapter ends with a summary and critique of the work done to date related to gay, lesbian, and bisexual identity development.

Definitional Issues

Researchers and theorists have paid little attention to the factors involved in the development of a gay, lesbian, or bisexual identity. Richardson (1981b) suggested that the development of gay, lesbian, and bisexual identities has been neglected for three reasons: (a) the study of homosexuality has focused almost exclusively on determining its causes, (b) homosexuality has been defined in

"The Development of Gay, Lesbian, and Bisexual Identities." Reprinted from *Beyond Tolerance: Gays, Lesbians, and Bisexuals on Campus*, (1991), by permission of American College Personnel Association.

terms of sexual acts, and (c) homosexuality has been viewed as a pathological state.

Until as recently as the 1970s, the focus of all discussions of homosexuality was etiology. Various biological and psychological causes of homosexual behavior were hypothesized, investigated, and hotly debated. The assumption in this debate was that homosexuality is a universal experience and that homosexuals are a specific type of being who exhibit predictable behaviors (Browning, 1984; Plummer, 1981). More recent writers do not assume that an individual is born with a homosexual identity but rather suggest that such an identity is socially constructed and maintained through interaction with others (Richardson, 1981a).

A number of writers have noted that homosexual *identity* must be distinguished from homosexual *acts* because individuals frequency engage in homosexual behavior without identifying themselves as homosexual (Cass, 1983–1984; Marmor, 1980; Nungesser, 1983; Richardson & Hart, 1981; Weinberg, 1978). Often, same-sex sexual activity is a precursor to developing a gay identity (Cass, 1983–1984; Weinberg, 1978).

Few writers have taken the time to define clearly the concept of homosexual or gay identity. Cass (1983–1984) identified a number of conflicting definitions in her review of the literature, including "(1) defining oneself as gay, (2) a sense of self as gay, (3) image of self as homosexual, (4) the way a homosexual person is, and (5) consistent behavior in relation to homosexual-related activity" (p. 108). She pointed out that some of these definitions are interpersonally focused, others are intrapersonal, and occasionally still others are both. The lack of clarity and agreement, as well as the difficulty in operationalizing these potential definitions, is troublesome.

Homosexual identity must be recognized as only one aspect of the person's total identity. Troiden (1984) defined identity as "organized sets of characteristics an individual perceives as definitively representing the self in relation to a social situation" (p. 102). Homosexual identity, then, is "a perception of self as homosexual in relation to a social setting" (p. 103). Minton and McDonald (1984) saw identity as including "the ascribed, achieved, and adopted roles characteristically enacted by the individual" (p. 91); sexual identity is one of these roles. They went on to define homosexual identity formation as "a life-span, developmental process that is part of the general maturational process of achieving a coherent sense of personal identity" (p. 91).

A distinction must be made between the terms *homosexual identity* and *gay identity*. Homosexual identity is a narrower term, referring to sexual behavior only, whereas gay identity suggests the total experience of being gay (Warren, 1974). The use of the term *homosexual identity* is often viewed negatively by the gay and lesbian community because it has been used as a diagnostic label by many clinicians and is often associated with a negative self-image. *Gay identity*, however, has a positive connotation within the gay and lesbian communities and is seen as encompassing emotional, lifestyle, and political aspects of life rather than being exclusively sexual (Beane, 1981).

Jandt and Darsey (1981) noted that all definitions of homosexual or gay identity have in common a shift in perception of self as a member of the majority to self as a member of the minority. Along with this change in perception comes adoption of a new set of values and a redefinition of acceptable behavior. As such, development of a gay, lesbian, or bisexual identity is mainly an internal, psychological process.

As various models of homosexual identity development are examined, the reader needs to note problems related to definition. Some theorists and researchers are careful to define their terms, but others assume the reader will know what they mean. In addition, terms such as *homosexual* or *gay identity* and labels given to various stages of gay or lesbian identity development often have different connotations in various models of development.

Identity Development Models

Models addressing homosexual or gay identity development evolved throughout the 1970s and 1980s. During this period, research started to move from a focus of "becoming homosexual" to one of "developing a homosexual identity." A great deal of overlap is evident in this research, as is some ambivalence about what is being studied.

One issue to be aware of in reviewing these models is that given their focus on gay men's development, they may not accurately reflect the perspectives of lesbian women. Similarly, there is little or no room in these models for the attainment of a healthy bisexual identity. Indeed, an inherent assumption of some is that a "healthy bisexual identity" would be a contradiction in terms! These issues are specifically addressed in later sections of this chapter.

Shively and deCecco's (1977) article on aspects of homosexual identity provided a good example of this early trend. They identified biological sex, gender identity, social sex role, and sexual orientation as the four components of sexual identity. Although the last component (orientation) encompasses physical and affectional preference, no mention is made of the establishment of identity as a gay or lesbian person.

At the same time, others were beginning to look at how a gay or lesbian identity is formed. Models based on developmental perspectives, and outlining a series of stages through which an individual moves in acquiring a homosexual identity, were proposed. These models fit loosely into two categories: those addressing social factors and those focusing on psychological changes. Many, however, encompass both areas. Those models that present specific stages of development (Lee, 1977; Coleman, 1981–1982; Plummer, 1975; Troiden. 1979; Minton & McDonald, 1984; Cass, 1979) are shown in the table.

Social Models

One of the first works to address the concept of gay identity was that of Dank (1971). In his study of men coming out within the gay community, Dank looked at the time lapse and (to a lesser extent) process involved in moving from first awareness of attraction to other men and then to self-labeling as homosexual. He suggested that identity development is based on the meanings that an individual ascribes to homosexuality and made clear that identification as gay and self-acceptance do not necessarily occur at the same time. Although a clear portrait of how movement through these levels occurs is not presented in this paradigm, it gave an early way to look at homosexual identity and its development.

The impact of the gay community and development of a social role have been the focus of several studies. As mentioned before, Warren (1974) was one of the first to make a distinction between homosexual and gay identities. She described gay identity as being based on the degree of affiliation that an individual has with the gay community. Generally this attachment follows engagement in homosexual (sexual) behavior and the development of a homosexual identity. In addition to the impact of the gay community, she described a "conversion effect" involved in the formation of gay identity. Through this process societal stigmas are converted into a positive identity as myths about homosexuality are encountered and challenged.

In a more radical exploration of gay identity, DuBay (1987) suggested that identity development is based on an interaction between social contacts and roles. He challenged the belief that there is an inherent, internal quality about an individual that leads to the development of a specific identity. Rather, he saw *identity* or *role* (terms that he used interchangeably) as being made up of a number of more distinct roles, which for gay and lesbian individuals serve the purpose of dealing with societal homophobia. He suggested that gay identity is made up of the merging of self-concept and sexuality, which becomes the central component in the individual's self-view. DuBay advocated dropping such roles, moving away from the concept of a gay identity, and, instead, looking at sexuality as one part of the person's total identity.

A number of writers who have approached gay identity from the social perspective focus on the coming out process. *Coming out* is an aspect of gay identity development that has been defined in various ways. In the 1960s coming out was seen as a specific occasion—a person's initial acknowledgement of same-sex attraction to another person (Gramick, 1984). Now writers stress the ongoing developmental nature of coming out, beginning when individuals start to question their sexual orientation and continuing through ongoing self-discovery and disclosure to others of their identity (Ponse, 1980; Richardson, 1981b).

Lee (1977) (see table 17-1) described coming out as one facet of a three-stage model of homosexual self-identity. His emphasis was on individuals' movement from privately recognizing themselves as homosexual to publicly sharing this identity. In the first stage, individuals self-label homosexual fantasies or experiences as deviant; then in the second stage, they begin to enter the gay culture, selectively disclose their identity, and become involved in political and

TABLE 17-1
Stage Models of Gay Identity Theory

Stage	Social Models		Psychological Models			Psychosocial Model
	Lee (1977)	Coleman (1981–1982)	Plummer (1975)	Troiden (1979)	Minton and McDonald (1984)	Cass (1979)
I. First Awareness	Signification	Pre Coming Out		Symbiotic		
		Coming Out	Sensitization	Sensitization		Identity Confusion
				Dissociation and Signification	Egocentric	Identity Comparison
II. Self-Labeling						Identity Tolerance
III. Community Involvement and Disclosure	Coming Out	Exploration	Signification			
			Coming Out	Coming Out	Sociocentric	Identity Acceptance
	Going Public	First Relationships				Identity Pride
IV. Identity Integration		Integration	Stabilization	Commitment	Universalistic	Identity Synthesis

social organizations. The third stage clearly builds on stage two, with individuals becoming more public in their activities and willing to be spokespersons.

Another approach that has been taken to coming out is to frame it as a developmental process encompassing both social and psychological factors. Hencken and O'Dowd (1977) suggested that there are three levels to this process: (1) awareness, (2) behavioral acceptance, and (3) public identification. At each level an individual comes out in a key area (e.g., coming out of ignorance and into awareness of feelings in the first stage), building a framework for future growth.

A more fully conceptualized model of the coming out process was offered by Coleman (1981–1982). Coleman presented a five-stage developmental model of coming out (see table), with the establishment of a gay identity centering around interpersonal relationships. As individuals progress through the stages, developmental tasks are confronted, the resolution of which determines whether movement to a new level will occur. Although such social/relational issues as seeking validation through self-disclosure, exploring sexual relationships, and establishing emotional intimacy are primary areas of focus, attention is also paid to more psychological issues. Coleman discussed ways in which these developmental tasks have impact on self-esteem and self-view, and presented stage 5 (Integration) as the point at which individuals develop a sense of both personal and interpersonal wholeness.

Psychological Models

Another perspective for looking at the development of gay identity focuses on the psychological (rather than social) processes involved. One of the first such models to be proposed was that of Plummer (1975) (see table). He identified four stages of identity development, moving from early awareness to the attainment of an integrated and stable identity.

Building on Plummer's work, Troiden (1979) (see table) suggested that there are four stages of gay identity acquisition. As movement through the stages occurs, feelings that the individual experiences shift from being ego-dystonic (dissonant with self-perceptions) to positively integrated and ego-syntonic (consistent with self-perceptions). As is true of several of the models discussed above, Troiden distinguished between homosexual and gay identities, with the latter reflecting involvement in a committed relationship and commitment to this identity. This last point notwithstanding, he also stated that identity is fluid and is never completely acquired in all aspects of an individual's life.

Looking at homosexual identity formation as one aspect of a lifelong developmental process, Minton and McDonald (1984) had as their foundation a nonlinear ego development model (see table). Growth is based on the interaction between the individual and societal values and beliefs. The two primary developmental tasks involved in this process are (1) forming a homosexual self-image, which culminates in attaining a positive gay identity, and (2) identity management, choosing the extent to which this identity will be shared. The goal of this model is to achieve identity synthesis (versus having a fragmented personal identity), which requires integration of all aspects of personal identity.

Cass' Psychosocial Model of Sexual Identity Formation (SIF)

To varying extents, each of the social and psychological models discussed in the preceding sections addresses the variables that have an impact on how gay identity develops. This process is a complex one, with development being affected by such diverse factors as self-image, social support, and even geography. As Troiden (1979) pointed out, gay identity evolves slowly and with some struggle. The presence (or absence) of information, resources, and a supportive community, along with such factors as family attitudes and individual personality, help determine how much struggle any one individual faces in developing an identity as a gay, lesbian, or bisexual person.

Vivienne Cass (1984) has pointed out the need for integration of the social and psychological elements of identity development and for consideration of the changes involved at the cognitive, emotional, and behavioral levels. In her model of Sexual Identity Formation (SIF), Cass (1979) fully described each of the six stages into which she divides the identity development process (see table), specifying the challenges found at each stage. Cass' model provides an exceptionally comprehensive description of gay identity development. Cass has also conducted extensive research on her theory, something which is lacking with several of the other models.

Cass' SIF model is built upon a theoretical base that addresses the interaction between psychological and sociological factors. Progression from one stage to another is motivated by incongruities felt by the individual within what Cass described as the "intrapersonal matrix." The components that make up this matrix are individuals' self-perceptions, perceptions of their behavior, and perceptions of others' response to them. At each stage, some conflict will be experienced either within or between areas of the intrapersonal matrix. This conflict is resolved either through advancement to a new stage or identity foreclosure.

The first stage (Identity Confusion) is ushered in by a growing awareness of thoughts, feelings, or behaviors that may be homosexual in nature. These self-perceptions are incongruent with earlier assumptions of personal heterosexuality and constitute the first developmental conflict of the model. How individuals perceive these characteristics or behaviors will influence the way in which they seek to resolve the incongruence, either through repression (identity foreclosure) or by moving into the second stage.

Identity Comparison (stage 2) allows individuals to begin checking out those qualities first experienced in stage 1. As they begin to gather information and seek out contacts with gay others, there is increasing congruence between self-perceptions and behaviors but increased conflict with others. As this sense of conflict heightens, individuals may move into stage 3, Identity Tolerance. This stage is marked by increased contact with the gay community, leading to feelings of greater empowerment. At this point individuals hold an increasingly strong homosexual self-image but continue to present themselves (outside the community) as heterosexual.

Moving into stage 4, Identity Acceptance, the conflict between the self and nongay others' perceptions is at an intense level. This conflict may be resolved through either passing as "straight," limited contact with heterosexuals, or selectively disclosing to significant (heterosexual) others. Those who find that these strategies effectively manage the conflict may stay at this level comfortably; otherwise the continuing conflict pushes the individual into the fifth stage of Identity Pride. In this stage the conflict is managed through fostering a dichotomized homosexual (valued) and heterosexual (devalued) world view. Stage 5 is marked not only by strong pride in the gay community and identity but also by intense anger directed toward and isolation from the heterosexual society.

How others, particularly those who are not gay, respond to the expression of these feelings influences whether individuals move into the final stage, Identity Synthesis. Movement into the sixth stage is most likely when individuals experience positive reactions from heterosexual others, creating new incongruence in their perceptions. Individuals in stage 6 perceive similarities and dissimilarities with both homosexuals and heterosexuals, and sexuality is seen as one part of their total identity. Although some conflict is always present, it is at the lowest and most manageable point in this stage.

To test her theory, Cass (1984) developed factors that describe elements of each of her six stages of homosexual identity formation. For each factor she identified the underlying cognitive, behavioral, and affective dimensions. These dimensions provided criteria for assigning individuals to one of the six stages of identity development. Cass compared participants' assignment to a specific stage according to these criteria with self-ratings on her Stage Allocation Measure (SAM). She found that individuals both matched the profile for the stage to which they had been assigned and could be placed into that same stage according to the SAM. Cass suggested these findings support the concept that individuals who perceive homosexuality to be relevant to them will have characteristics identified in her model.

Summary of Identity Development Models

The six models presented in table 17-1 approach the question of how individuals develop an identity as a gay or lesbian person from a fairly wide range of perspectives. Of these models, Lee's (1977) presentation of gay self-identification conceptualizes this process with the most narrowly social focus.

Although varying degrees of balance between personal and social factors are found across the theories, there is a general trend toward a more psychological perspective in the later models. Those theories developed earlier present coming out as a culminating event or marker, followed only by a stage of integration or further commitment. In contrast, the models of Coleman (1981–1982), Minton and McDonald (1984), and Cass (1979) place coming out very early in the process, and the latter two do not identify it as a separate stage at all.

These differences notwithstanding, there is a general pattern of developmental levels that emerges across the models. We have identified four levels, which are used as a basis of comparison in table 17-1 (in column 1). Although the models presented do not all fit into this conceptualization at exactly the same points, each passes through and refers to the tasks found in all four levels.

The level of First Awareness is a distinct component of all but one model (Minton & McDonald, 1984). At this first level individuals are becoming conscious of homoerotic feelings and behaviors, generally with no sense of these feelings being "okay." Two models (Coleman, 1981–1982; Minton & McDonald, 1984) explicitly mentioned stages before this first level, and Cass (1984) discussed assumptions about individuals' beliefs prior to entering her first stage.

The second level that we have identified is Self-Labeling. This point centers around individuals beginning to identify themselves as being gay and having early contacts with the gay community. The main distinction between the second level and the third (Community Involvement and Disclosure) is in the growing sense of acceptance of a gay identity and increasing comfort with sharing this aspect of the self with non-gay others. The fourth and final level is Identity Integration, which involves incorporating gay identity into individuals' total sense of self.

Lesbian Identity Development

Differences in Identity Development Between Gay Men and Lesbians

Largely because of differences in the way men and women are socialized in Western society, a number of variations are evident in the patterns of identity development and lifestyles of gay men and lesbians (Cass, 1979).

The timing of events associated with the process of developing a gay or lesbian identity is different for men and women. Lesbians exhibit more variation than gay men in age at which awareness of attraction to individuals of the same sex occurs (Moses & Hawkins, 1986), and evidence suggests that gay men become aware of same-sex attractions, act on those attractions, and self-identify as gay at earlier ages than do lesbians. Men also disclose their homosexual identity earlier than women (DeMonteflores & Schultz, 1978; Sohier, 1985–1986; Troiden, 1988). Henderson (1984) proposed two hypotheses in reference to these timing variations: (1) women's sexual orientation may be more variable than men's and more tied to particular relationships, or (2) women are more likely to be influenced by societal norms that expect everyone to be heterosexual and so adhere longer to heterosexual behavior patterns and a heterosexual identity. Gramick (1984) concurred with the latter point of view.

Lesbians tend to establish ongoing love relationships earlier than gay men (Troiden, 1988) and are more likely to commit to a homosexual identity within the context of an intense emotional relationship, whereas gay men do so within the context of their sexual experiences (Groves & Ventura, 1983; Sohier, 1985–1986; Troiden, 1988). In general, emotional attachment is the most significant aspect of relationship for lesbians, but sexual activity is most important for gay men (DeMonteflores & Schultz, 1978; Gramick, 1984). As a result, lesbians tend to look for and maintain more stable, long-term relationships than do gay men (Gramick, 1984).

Although this pattern may be changing because of concern arising from the spread of AIDS, historically, gay men have been involved with many more one-time-only sexual partners than have lesbians (Kimmel, 1978; Marmor, 1980). This pattern, again, can be related to differences in the manner in which men and women are socialized; men are expected to be interested in sex before love, whereas women look for love before sex (Henderson, 1984; Westfall, 1988). Men are also encouraged to experiment sexually more than women (Coleman, 1981–1982). As one might expect given these socialization patterns, "tricking" (picking up unknown individuals for brief sexual liaisons) has been much more common among gay men than among lesbians who tend to meet others and interact in more intimate, private settings (Cronin, 1974; Gramick, 1984; Nuehring, Fein, & Tyler, 1974).

DeMonteflores and Schultz (1978) suggested that lesbians often use feelings to avoid thinking of themselves as homosexual whereas men use denial of feelings as a way to avoid self-labeling as gay. Women use the rationale that they merely love one particular woman, but men view their homosexual activity as insignificant because they are not emotionally involved with their partners.

Some researchers (Bell & Weinberg, 1978; Sohier, 1985–1986) have suggested that acceptance of homosexuality is easier for women than for men since sexual relationships between women are less stigmatized than those between men (DeMonteflores & Schultz, 1978; Marmor, 1980; Paul, 1984). The women's movement may have assisted lesbians to come out; there has been no comparable movement for men (DeMonteflores & Schultz, 1978). Also, since many lesbians become aware of their identity at later ages, they may have resolved other identity issues and be more adept at handling the coming out process than gay men who generally self-identify during their teens (Paul, 1984).

A number of writers have suggested that lesbians are more likely to view their sexuality as a choice, whereas gay men see it as a discovery (Henderson, 1984; Kimmel, 1978; Westfall, 1988). This distinction is particularly true for feminist lesbians. Feminist lesbians also identify more strongly with the political-philosophical aspects of their lifestyle, whereas gay men are more concerned with the physical-social aspects (Jandt & Darsey, 1981).

With regard to relationship development, lesbians more closely resemble other women than they do gay men (Marmor, 1980). Women, in general, are more concerned with the relational aspects of their attachments to other people and focus on establishing intimate, long-term relationships. Because they fear displeasing others, they may have difficulty breaking norms and acknowledging that they cannot accept the roles family, friends, and society have identified for them. Men, however, are taught to be independent, competitive, and autonomous. These factors appear to play an important role in the differences exhibited between lesbians and gay men.

Relational Versus Political Lesbians

Great variation exists in the way lesbians describe themselves and how they come to identify themselves as lesbian (Miller & Fowlkes, 1980). And as Golden (1987) noted, feelings, behaviors, and self-identification do not always agree nor do they always remain the same over time. Two major philosophical approaches to lesbianism can be identified in the literature, however: a traditional relational viewpoint that focuses on emotional and sexual attraction to other women (Moses, 1978; Ponse, 1980) and a radical feminist perspective that views the lesbian lifestyle as a political statement (Faraday, 1981; Lewis, 1979).

A number of theorists note that a distinction must be made between women who view their lesbianism as beyond their control and those who see it as a choice (Golden, 1987; Richardson, 1981b). Generally, lesbian feminists adhere to the latter viewpoint, but relational lesbians take the former position (Richardson, 1981b; Sophie, 1987).

In a small study of 20 self-identified lesbians, Henderson (1979) distinguished three groups: (1) *ideological lesbians*, women who can be viewed as radical feminists for whom a lesbian lifestyle is politically correct; (2) *personal lesbians*, women concerned with establishing an independent identity who find homosexuality supportive of this goal and who view lesbianism as a choice; and (3) *interpersonal lesbians*, women who find themselves involved with another woman, often to their chagrin, and who experience their involvement as a discovery rather than a choice.

Development of a Lesbian Identity

Although a number of writers believe that sexual activity between women has become more acceptable as a result of the women's movement and the freeing of sexual norms (Blumstein & Schwartz, 1974; Henderson, 1979), the developmental process of identifying oneself as a lesbian is still difficult.

Many lesbians recall being "tomboys" as youngsters: a preference for "masculine" rather than "feminine" activities as a child is often the first indication that they do not fit the heterosexual pattern (Lewis, 1979). This awareness intensifies during puberty when the adolescent finds herself attracted to women rather than men. This discovery can lead to intense feelings of loneliness. Because of the difficulty young lesbians experience in finding a support group of other lesbians or identifying positive role models, this period is particularly difficult in the person's life (Sophie, 1982).

Most lesbians have a history of sexual involvement with men and, contrary to popular belief, become involved with women not because of unsatisfactory relationships with men but rather because they experience greater emotional and sexual satisfaction from women (Groves & Ventura, 1983). Indeed, women frequently identify themselves as bisexual prior to adopting a lesbian identity.

It needs to be noted that most lesbians go through a period during which they reject their identity because they are unable to deal with the stigma associated with the label *lesbian* (Groves & Ventura, 1983). Often they seek security and an escape from their feelings of isolation and anxiety in heterosexual activity or marriage (Lewis, 1979; Sophie, 1982).

Usually involvement in an intense, all-encompassing love relationship with another woman is the decisive factor in embracing a lesbian identity (Groves & Ventura, 1983; Lewis, 1979). Such an involvement often develops slowly, starting out as a friendship.

Sophie (1982) noted that it is difficult for lesbians to feel good about themselves until they reconceptualize the term *lesbian* into positive terms. This process rarely occurs in isolation. Interaction with other lesbians and other sources of information about positive aspects of a lesbian lifestyle are helpful.

Coming out, both to other lesbians and to accepting heterosexuals, is also supportive of establishment of a lesbian identity (Richardson, 1981b; Sophie, 1982). Often the individual decides to come out because it takes too much energy to maintain a heterosexual image. Usually the individual comes out first to close friends who appear trustworthy Lewis, 1979. As the woman becomes involved in the lesbian community, pressure is often applied to come out publicly (Lewis, 1979). Doing so can be viewed as the final step in the solidification of a lesbian identity.

Identity Development Models

A number of theorists have proposed models of identity development specific for lesbians. Ponse (1980) noted three steps in lesbian identity development: becoming aware of feeling different because of sexual-emotional attraction to other women, becoming involved in a lesbian relationship, and seeking out other lesbians. This model differs from many of the gay male models in that a serious relationship is formed *before* the individual becomes involved in the lesbian community.

Gramick (1984) pointed out that in attempting to make meaning of their experiences, many lesbians reinterpret past events, feelings, and behaviors as sexual that were not perceived as such at the time they occurred. She suggested that the process of developing a lesbian identity first involves strong emotional attachment to other women leading to a feeling of "differentness" within the context of the social environment but without a recognition that this difference might be labeled as lesbian. In adolescence, heterosexual socialization patterns strongly influence all young women and often delay development of homosexual identity. Meeting other lesbians and becoming emotionally and sexually involved with another woman are usually key events in confirming and accepting a lesbian identity. In Gramick's model, supportive others, as well as sexual involvements, play a crucial role in identity development.

Lewis (1979) identified five stages in the development of a lesbian identity and focused more on the political aspects of lesbianism. Her stages include (1) experience of discomfort with the heterosexual and patriarchal nature of socialization, (2) labeling self as different from other

women, (3) becoming aware of lesbianism, (4) finding and becoming involved in a lesbian community, and (5) educating self about the lesbian lifestyle.

Also writing from a feminist perspective, Faderman (1984) questioned the appropriateness of Minton and McDonald's (1984) model of identity development for lesbian feminists. She suggested that the developmental progression for these women is roughly the opposite of the model they proposed. The first step for lesbian feminists, according to Faderman, involves rejection of societal norms concerning the role of women and acceptance of a lesbian identity. This step is followed by experiences of prejudice and discrimination resulting in feelings of aloneness outside of the community of radical feminists and, finally, by sexual experiences with other women. Faderman suggested that because lesbian feminists are exposed to and accept the movement's political philosophy prior to their first homosexual experience they may not experience the guilt and shame felt by other lesbians and gay men.

In line with the two philosophical perspectives evident within the lesbian community, Sophie (1982) identified two endpoints for lesbians who have achieved identity synthesis: *integration*, that is, living as an open lesbian in both the lesbian and nonlesbian communities; and *separation*, that is, limiting one's interactions to the lesbian community as much as possible.

Bisexual Identity

The gay rights movement has generally ignored bisexual men and women. Although Kinsey and his colleagues (Kinsey, Pomeroy, & Martin, 1948; Kinsey, Pomeroy, Martin, & Gebhard, 1953) discovered that more individuals are bisexual than strictly homosexual, later researchers and theorists have held to a rigid dichotomization of sexual behavior as either heterosexual or homosexual (Klein, Sepekoff, & Wolf, 1985). Acknowledging and attempting to understand the variation and fluidity of sexual attraction and behavior are important if we are to advance our knowledge of human sexuality and sexual identity development (Paul, 1985).

Bisexuality, particularly among women, seems to have increased in Western society, perhaps as a result of more relaxed sexual norms and the women's movement (MacDonald, 1981). A study based on a questionnaire published in *Forum* magazine found that male bisexuals outnumber female bisexuals, bisexual activity increases over the lifetime, and sexual preference changes over time (Klein, Sepekoff, & Wolf, 1985). The biased sample upon which this study was based (*Forum* readers who responded to a questionnaire) must be kept in mind, however.

Bisexuality comes in many forms. MacDonald (1982) identified four areas of variation: (1) individuals may have a preference for one gender over the other or may have no preference; (2) they may have partners of both sexes either simultaneously or sequentially; (3) they may be monogomous or have several partners; and (4) their bisexuality may be transitory, transitional, a basis for homosexual denial, or an enduring pattern. Zinik (1985) proposed the following criteria for assuming a bisexual identity: (1) being sexually aroused by both males and females, (2) desiring sexual activity with both, and (3) adopting bisexuality as a sexual identity label.

Two contrasting theories have been offered to account for bisexuality (Zinik, 1985): The conflict model suggests that bisexuality is associated with conflict, confusion, ambivalence, and an inability to determine one's sexual preference; the flexibility model hypothesizes that bisexuality is characterized by flexibility, personal growth, and fulfillment. The media tends to adhere to the former view, presenting bisexuality as a confused or conflicted lifestyle, as retarded sexual development, or as a denial of a true heterosexual or homosexual identity (Hansen & Evans, 1985).

Because the stigma attached to bisexuality is greater in many ways than that associated with homosexuality, many people who are bisexual in behavior do not identify themselves as such (Blumstein & Schwartz, 1974; Golden, 1987; Hansen & Evans, 1985; Paul, 1984; Zinik, 1985). Although some individuals are quite open about their identity, others hide it from both the heterosexual and the homosexual communities (Blumstein & Schwartz, 1977a). MacDonald (1981) suggested that bisexuals are less willing to disclose their identity than any other group because they believe that neither gays nor heterosexuals will accept them.

Bisexuals experience the same type of oppression as gay men and lesbians because society tends to group bisexuals with homosexuals. Heterosexuals assume that individuals are trying to excuse their homosexual inclinations by labeling themselves as bisexual (Blumstein & Schwartz, 1977a).

Because they do not conform to heterosexist culture, many bisexuals tend to align themselves with the gay and lesbian communities (Shuster, 1987). However, an individual's self-identification as bisexual is frequently met with skepticism in the homosexual community as well and viewed as an attempt to avoid the stigma of, or commitment to, a gay or lesbian lifestyle (Paul, 1984). The lesbian community, in particular, seems to have difficulty accepting bisexuality (Golden, 1987). Bisexuals are faced with considerable pressure to identify as homosexual and to behave in an exclusively homosexual manner (Blumstein & Schwartz, 1974; Hansen & Evans, 1985; Paul, 1985). Frequently, bisexuals respond to this pressure by pretending to be either exclusively homosexual or heterosexual depending on the social situation (Zinik, 1985).

Results of a study of 156 bisexuals conducted in the early 1970s (Blumstein & Schwartz, 1976, 1977a, 1977b) suggested that no identifiable bisexual life script exists and that identity and partner preferences change over the life course. Sexual experience and identity are not necessarily synonymous. The researchers identified several conditions that they saw as necessary for assumption of a bisexual identity: labeling, conflicting homosexual and heterosexual experiences, and contact with other bisexuals.

Zinik (1985) suggested that bisexual identity development may occur in stages similar to those proposed by Cass (1979) for homosexual identity formation. As with gay men and lesbians, the coming out process is one of both self-acknowledgement and disclosure to others (Shuster, 1987). Wide variation exists, however, in the timing and ordering of sexual experiences leading to a bisexual identification. In addition, because bisexuality lacks societal and scientific affirmation, acceptance of such an identity requires a high tolerance for ambiguity and is even harder than acceptance of a homosexual identity (MacDonald, 1981, Richardson & Hart, 1981). In most cases, bisexuals tend to identify in terms of particular relationships in which they are involved rather than with the abstract label bisexual (Shuster, 1987).

Although gay men and lesbians have formed support groups and political organizations, few such groups of bisexuals exist (Paul, 1985). As

MacDonald (1981) noted, there is no "bisexual liberation movement" (p. 21). As a result, no clear bisexual identity exists, and little scientific research has examined the life experiences of bisexual men and women.

Critique and Summary

Over the past two decades a number of theorists and researchers have addressed the question of how individuals develop identities as gay, lesbian, and bisexual men and women. The shift in focus from "why" or "how" individuals "become homosexual" to understanding the process whereby they develop a gay, lesbian, or bisexual identity speaks to a more positive and healthy perspective on homosexuality. There are, however, a number of areas that need to be addressed.

One area of concern involves the datedness of some of the models discussed in this chapter. The concept of a gay identity first began to be addressed in the early 1970s, the years immediately following the Stonewall riots. The focus on coming out as a discrete step and social statement in models such as those of Dank (1971) and Lee (1977) clearly reflected the mood of the early gay-rights era. Similarly, these models are based on a social culture that has changed significantly, due in large part to the impact of the AIDS crisis, and do not necessarily describe today's realities.

Many of the models of lesbian identity development also were shaped by the political and social forces of the 1970s. The early feminist movement had tremendous influence on many of these models, leading to conceptualizations of identity centered around breaking away from patriarchal and oppressive social norms (Browning, 1984; Faraday, 1981; Lewis, 1979).

The political climate today is much different than that of 15 or even 10 years ago. There is general consensus that a conservative backlash took place during the 1980s, but we have not looked at what impact this change has had on the development and maintenance of a gay or lesbian identity. Although many (or even most) aspects of identity development have probably remained relatively constant, these models need to be reconsidered in light of a new societal context.

A second area needing consideration deals with the problems inherent in working with stage models of development. By nature, these models break the process of development into discrete, stable, and clearly discernible levels. In reality, growth is rarely so clear cut.

McDonald (1982) suggested that linear developmental models do not account or leave room for individual differences and variations in development. He found that there are clearly milestone events in the coming out process for gay men, and that these events occur in a fairly stable pattern. There is sufficient variety in the timing and direction of these events, however, to justify moving away from a linear conceptualization of the process.

Another writer who has questioned the developmental stage concept is Troiden (1984). He suggested that rather than attaining one identity, individuals develop one self-concept (or self-image) and a variety of identities that are used to assist the individual specifically in social situations. Within this framework, homosexual identity presents a way of placing self in a defined social category. The interplay between self-concept and identities shifts over time, as social contexts change, thus creating a fluid sense of identity(ies).

In the only study that has focused on women in the process of developing a lesbian identity, Sophie (1985–1986) found extensive variety in the sequence and timing of significant events. She found that events such as self-definition, contact with other lesbians, and involvement in a significant same-sex relationship occur at different points in the identity development process for different women. She pointed out that looking at this process through a linear lens is difficult and becomes more problematic as the process advances and greater individual differences emerge.

In general, there are a great needs for more research on the identity development process. For example, more research testing the models that have been (and are being) developed is needed. One of the reasons Cass' (1979) model has found wide acceptance is that she has conducted fairly extensive testing of her theory (Cass, 1984). Rather than considering external criteria as a means of validating her model, Cass compared two techniques based on her own theory for estimating level of development. Studies that contrast models or determine and measure underlying factors will add to the creation of a strong research base in this area.

As has been pointed out throughout this chapter, an area that has been severely overlooked has been identity development among lesbian and bisexual persons. Sophie's (1985–1986) study is the only one to date that looked specifically at the development of a lesbian identity, and there are no models that describe the attainment of a bisexual identity. The little research that has been conducted with these two groups clearly shows that the male-oriented models that have been developed do not adequately describe their different experiences. We need to address and fill the gaps in our understanding of these processes.

A similar gap in the research involves identity development among college and university students. Working through questions about the relevance of homosexuality or bisexuality in one's own life while also dealing with the challenges of being a college or university student adds to the magnitude of transition and potential for experiencing periods of crisis. We need to conduct research that helps us to understand the interplay between student development and the acquisition of gay, lesbian, and bisexual identities.

One issue that is of concern in all research with gay, lesbian, and bisexual people is that of obtaining truly random samples. This problem is most apparent with the *Forum* article (Klein, Sepekoff, & Wolf, 1985) mentioned earlier in this chapter. The issue of having a nonrandom sample is inherent, however, in any study that utilizes a group of individuals who self-identify as gay, lesbian, or bisexual.

The models and studies discussed in this chapter give us the foundations for this future work. We know much about college and university students and are learning about what it means to be a gay, lesbian, or bisexual person in our society. The framework is there, and our challenge is to move ahead toward expanding and bringing together these areas of understanding.

References

Beane, J. (1981). "I'd rather be dead than gay": Counseling gay men who are coming out. *Personnel and Guidance Journal, 60,* 222–226.

Bell, A. P., & Weinberg, M. S. (1978). *Homosexualities: A study of diversity among men and women.* New York: Simon and Schuster.

Bell, A. P., Weinberg, M. S., & Hammersmith, S. K. (1981). *Sexual preference: Its development in men and women.* Bloomington: Indiana University.

Blumstein, P. W., & Schwartz, P. (1974). Lesbianism and bisexuality. In E. Goode & R. R. Troiden (Eds.), *Sexual deviance and sexual deviants* (pp. 278–295). New York: Morrow.

Blumstein, P. W., & Schwartz, P. (1976). Bisexuality in women. *Archives of Sexual Behavior, 5,* 171–181.

Blumstein, P. W., & Schwartz, P. (1977a). Bisexuality in men. In C. A. B. Warren (Ed.), *Sexuality: Encounters, identities, and relationships* (pp. 79–98). Beverly Hills, CA: Sage.

Blumstein, P. W., & Schwartz, P. (1977b). Bisexuality: Some social psychological issues. *Journal of Social Issues, 33,* 30–45.

Browning, C. (1984). Changing theories of lesbianism: Challenging the stereotypes. In T. Darty & S. Potter (Eds.), *Women-identified women* (pp. 11–30). Palo Alto, CA: Mayfield.

Cass, V. C. (1979). Homosexual identity formation: A theoretical model. *Journal of Homosexuality, 4,* 219–235.

Cass, V. C. (1983–1984). Homosexual identity: A concept in need of definition. *Journal of Homosexuality, 9*(2/3), 105–126.

Cass, V. C. (1984). Homosexual identity formation: Testing a theoretical model. *Journal of Sex Research, 20,* 143–167.

Chickering, A. W. (1969). *Education and identity.* San Francisco: Jossey-Bass.

Coleman, E. (1981–1982). Developmental stages of the coming out process. *Journal of Homosexuality, 7,* 31–43.

Cronin, D. M. (1974). Coming out among lesbians. In E. Goode & R. R. Troiden (Eds.), *Sexual deviance and sexual deviants* (pp. 268–277). New York: Morrow.

Dank, B. M. (1971). Coming out in the gay world. *Psychiatry, 34*(2), 180–197.

DeMonteflores, C., & Schultz, S. (1978). Coming out: Similarities and differences for lesbians and gay men. *Journal of Social Issues, 34*(3), 59–72.

DuBay, W. H. (1987). *Gay identity: The self under ban.* Jefferson, NC: McFarland.

Erikson, E. H. (1968). *Identity: Youth and crisis.* New York: Norton.

Faderman, L. (1984). The "new gay" lesbians. *Journal of Homosexuality, 10*(3/4), 85–95.

Faraday, A. (1981). Liberating lesbian research. In K. Plummer (Ed.), *The making of the modern homosexual* (pp. 112–129). Totowa, NJ: Barnes & Noble.

Golden, C. (1987). Diversity and variability in women's sexual identities. In Boston Lesbian Psychologies Collective (Eds.), *Lesbian psychologies: Explorations and challenges* (pp. 19–34). Urbana, IL: University of Illinois Press.

Gramick, J. (1984). Developing a lesbian identity. In T. Darty & S. Potter (Eds.), *Women-identified women.* (pp. 31–44). Palo Alto, CA: Mayfield.

Groves, P. A., & Ventura, L. A. (1983). The lesbian coming out process: Therapeutic considerations. *Personnel and Guidance Journal, 62,* 146–149.

Hansen, C. E., & Evans, A. (1985). Bisexuality reconsidered: An idea in pursuit of a definition. In F. Klein & T. J. Wolf (Eds.), *Bisexualities: Theory and research* (pp. 1–6). New York: Haworth.

Hencken, J. D., & O'Dowd, W. T. (1977). Coming out as an aspect of identity formation. *Gai Saber, 1*(1), 18–22.

Henderson, A. F. (1979). College age lesbianism as a developmental phenomenon. *Journal of American College Health, 28*(3), 176–178.

Henderson, A. F. (1984). Homosexuality in the college years: Development differences between men and women. *Journal of American College Health, 32,* 216–219.

Jandt, F. E., & Darsey, J. (1981). Coming out as a communicative process. In J. W. Chesebro (Ed.), *Gayspeak* (pp. 12–27). New York: Pilgrim.

Kimmel, D. C. (1978). Adult development and aging: A gay perspective. *Journal of Social Issues, 34,* 113–130.

Kinsey, A. C., Pomeroy, W. B., & Martin, C. E. (1948). *Sexual behavior in the human male.* Philadelphia: Saunders.

Kinsey, A. C., Pomeroy, W. B., Martin, C. E., & Gebhard, P. H. (1953). *Sexual behavior in the human female.* Philadelphia: Saunders.

Klein, F., Sepekoff, B., & Wolf, T. J. (1985). Sexual orientation: A multivariable dynamic process. In F. Klein & T. J. Wolf (Eds.), *Bisexualities: Theory and research* (pp. 35–49). New York: Haworth.

Lee, J. A. (1977). Going public: A study in the sociology of homosexual liberation. *Journal of Homosexuality, 3*(1), 49–78.

Lewis, S. G. (1979). *Sunday's women: A report on lesbian life today.* Boston: Beacon.

MacDonald, Jr., A. P. (1981). Bisexuality: Some comments on research and theory. *Journal of Homosexuality, 6*(3), 21–35.

MacDonald, Jr., A. P. (1982). Research on sexual orientation: A bridge that touches both shores but doesn't meet in the middle. *Journal of Sex Education and Therapy, 8,* 9–13.

Marmor, J. (1980). Overview: The multiple roots of homosexual behavior. In J. Marmor (Ed.), *Homosexual behavior: A modern reappraisal* (pp. 3–22). New York: Basic Books.

McDonald, G. J. (1982). Individual differences in the coming out process for gay men: Implications for theoretical models. *Journal of Homosexuality, 8*(1), 47–90.

Miller, P. Y., & Fowlkes, M. R. (1980). Social and behavior constructions of female sexuality. *Signs, 5,* 783–800.

Minton, H. L., & McDonald, G. J. (1984). Homosexual identity formation as a developmental process. *Journal of Homosexuality, 9*(2/3), 91–104.

Moore, L. V., & Upcraft, M. L. (1990). Theory in student affairs: Evolving perspectives. In L. V. Moore (Ed.), *Evolving theoretical perspectives on students.* (pp. 3–23). *New Directions for Student Services,* No. 51. San Francisco: Jossey-Bass.

Moses, A. E. (1978). *Identity management in lesbian women.* New York: Praeger.

Moses, A. E., & Hawkins, R. O. (1986). *Counseling lesbian women and gay men: A life issues approach.* Columbus, OH: Merrill.

Nuehring, E., Fein, S. B., & Tyler, M. (1974). The gay college student: Perspectives for mental health professionals. *The Counseling Psychologist, 4,* 64–72.

Nungesser, L. G. (1983). *Homosexual acts, actors, and identities.* New York: Praeger.

Paul, J. P. (1984). The bisexual identity: An idea without social recognition. In J. P. DeCecco & M. G. Shively (Eds.), *Bisexual and homosexual identities: Critical theoretical issues* (pp. 45–63). New York: Haworth.

Paul, J. (1985). Bisexuality: Reassessing our paradigms of sexuality. In F. Klein & T. J. Wolf (Eds.), *Bisexualities: Theory and research* (pp. 21–34). New York: Haworth.

Plummer, K. (1975). *Sexual stigma: An interactionist account.* London: Routledge & Kegan Paul.

Plummer, K. (1981). Going gay: Identities, life cycles, and lifestyles in the male gay world. In J. Hart & D. Richardson (Eds.), *The theory and practice of homosexuality* (pp. 93–110). London: Routledge & Kegan Paul.

Ponse, B. (1980). Lesbians and their worlds. In J. Marmor (Ed.), *Homosexual behavior: A modern reappraisal.* (pp. 157–175). New York: Basic Books.

Richardson, D. (1981a). Theoretical perspectives on homosexuality. In J. Hart & D. Richardson (Eds.), *The theory and practice of homosexuality* (pp. 5–37). London: Routledge & Kegan Paul.

Richardson, D. (1981b). Lesbian identities. In J. Hart & D. Richardson (Eds.), *The theory and practice of homosexuality* (pp. 111–124). London: Routledge & Kegan Paul.

Richardson, D., & Hart, J. (1981). The development and maintenance of a homosexual identity. In J. Hart & D. Richardson (Eds.), *The theory and practice of homosexuality* (pp. 73–92). London: Routledge & Kegan Paul.

Shively, M. G., & deCecco, J. P. (1977). Components of sexual identity. *Journal of Homosexuality, 3,* 41–48.

Shuster, R. (1987). Sexuality as a continuum: The bisexual identity. In Boston Lesbian Psychologies Collective (Eds.), *Lesbian psychologies: Explorations and challenges* (pp. 56–71). Urbana, IL: University of Illinois Press.

Sohier, R. (1985–1986). Homosexual mutuality: Variation on a theme by E. Erikson. *Journal of Homosexuality, 12*(2), 25–38.

Sophie, J. (1982). Counseling lesbians. *Personnel and Guidance Journal, 60*(6), 341–344.

Sophie, J. (1985–1986). A critical examination of stage theories of lesbian identity development. *Journal of Homosexuality, 12*(2), 39–51.

Sophie, J. (1987). Internalized homophobia and lesbian identity. *Journal of Homosexuality, 14*, 53–65.

Troiden, R. R. (1979). Becoming homosexual: A model of gay identity acquisition. *Psychiatry, 42*, 362–373.

Troiden, R. R. (1984). Self, self-concept, identity, and homosexual identity: Constructs in need of definition and differentiation. *Journal of Homosexuality, 10*(3/4), 97–109.

Troiden, R. R. (1988). Homosexual identity development. *Journal of Adolescent Health Care, 9*(2), 105–113.

Warren, C. A. B. (1974). *Identity and community in the gay world.* New York: Wiley.

Weinberg, T. S. (1978). On "doing" and "being" gay: Sexual behavior and homosexual male self-identity. *Journal of Homosexuality, 4*(2), 143–156.

Westfall, S. B. (1988). Gay and lesbian college students: Identity issues and student affairs. *Journal of the Indiana University Student Personnel Association, 1–6.*

Zinik, G. (1985). Identity conflict or adaptive flexibility? Bisexuality reconsidered. In F. Klein & T. J. Wolf (Eds.), *Bisexualities: Theory and research* (pp. 7–19). New York: Haworth.

CHAPTER 18

EDUCATIONAL AND ORGANIZATIONAL IMPLICATIONS OF HOLLAND'S THEORY IN HIGHER EDUCATION SETTINGS

JOHN SMART, KENNETH FLEDMAN, AND CORINNA ETHINGTON

Organizational Diversity in American Higher Education

Finn and Manno (1996), in documenting many of the dramatic changes in American higher education throughout the past five decades, note that "the culture of higher education is expansion oriented" (p. 46). One manifestation of this expansion is the sheer growth in the number of institutions from seventeen hundred before World War II to over thirty-seven hundred today. Numerous scholars contend, however, that the growing number of institutions has not contributed to organizational diversity in American higher education because newer institutions tend to imitate existing institutional forms (Birnbaum, 1983; Fairweather, 1996; Jencks & Riesman, 1968; Newman, 1971; Riesman, 1956).

The orientation of higher education toward expansion has also been manifested within individual colleges and universities in terms of the greater heterogeneity of students enrolled, the proliferation of programs offered, and the services rendered to meet the many distinctive needs of these students (Callan, 1997; Finn & Manno, 1996). As Mitchell (1997) maintains, such dramatic changes "in the kinds of people who attend as students and work as faculty alter the nature of the enterprise in fundamental ways" (p. 268). The trends noted by Finn and Manno seem unlikely to diminish, for the next generation of college students will be "the most diverse in higher education's history" (Callan, 1997, p. 104). These and other developments that have been evolving over the past two decades have led scholars to conclude that organizational diversity in American higher education is more evident within institutions than between them (Carnegie Council, 1980; Stadtman, 1980; Trow, 1988).

Organizational diversity is critical to the long-term vitality of higher education because it affects the system's capacity to respond to pressures of the environment and to maintain its essential character and integrity (Altbach & Berdahl, 1981; Birnbaum, 1983; Bok, 1986; Huisman, 1998; Mitchell, 1997; Pace, 1974; Trow, 1988). The perceptions of scholars about the relative salience of diversity, both within and between educational institutions, also have important research implications for those

"Educational and Organizational Implications of Holland's Theory in Higher Education." Reprinted from *Academic Disciplines: Holland's Theory and the Study of College Students and Faculty*, (2000), by permission of Vanderbilt University Press.

who study the organization and management of colleges as well as for those who study the attitudes and performance of college faculty and students, for these perceptions influence what researchers actually study in their investigations. With respect to college students, for example, those persuaded that diversity *between* institutions is paramount will focus their attention on whether or not different kinds of institutions (e.g., control, selectivity, size) have differential influence on student change and stability during college, whereas those who advocate the growing importance of diversity *within* institutions will focus their attention on determining the relative influence of different collegiate environments or experiences within institutions (e.g., residency patterns, academic majors, student-faculty interactions) on student change and stability. As for research on college faculty, the institutional setting and the academic discipline of faculty are commonly regarded as the two major influences on the norms, values, and activities of the American professoriate (Bowen & Schuster, 1986; Clark, 1987a; Finkelstein, 1984; Light, 1974a; Light, Mardsen, & Corl, 1973; Rothblatt, 1997). Researchers who believe that between-institution diversity is paramount will concentrate on differences in the norms, values, and activities of faculty based on the type of institution with which faculty are affiliated, whereas researchers who advocate the growing importance of within-institution diversity will concentrate on differences in the norms, values, and activities of faculty affiliated with different academic disciplines within their institutional settings.

Although diversity has long been noted as the central distinguishing feature of American higher education and the major determinant of faculty life, little sustained, systematic, theory-based research exists on this phenomenon. True, there have been literally hundreds of what Hobbs and Francis (1973) term "analysis and recommendation" descriptive studies, but there have been relatively few systematic, theory-based inquiries. The potential of Holland's theory to ameliorate this neglect is the central consideration of this chapter. We spell out this potential by providing some examples of how Holland's theory can be used to understand and promote student learning and to enhance the organizational structure and managerial processes of colleges and universities.

Understanding and Promoting Student Learning

We first note that scholars who study college effects on students might associate only cognitive outcomes with college majors and not consider the impact of major fields on the development of students' affective traits. We think this is a mistake given the findings reported by Feldman and Newcomb (1969), as well as our own syntheses in chapters 5, 6, and 7 of the research literature concerning Holland's theory. Furthermore, we wish to emphasize that our findings on the differential patterns of longitudinal change in students' abilities and interests are based on a broad repertoire of cognitive and affective attributes of students. This repertoire includes a broad range of measures of students' self-reported abilities (e.g., academic, artistic, leadership, mathematical, writing), self-concepts (e.g., intellectual and social self-confidence, popularity), and interests (e.g., making a theoretical contribution to science, writing original works, helping to promote racial understanding, being very well off financially). Also included are students' perceptions of their gains over the four-year period across a diverse array of common college outcomes (e.g., problem-solving skills, cultural awareness, tolerance of other people with different beliefs, competitiveness). In sum, it is clear that our findings pertaining to the differential patterns of change in students associated with their major field of study are based on a wide array of both cognitive and affective college outcomes.

We now explore how the use of Holland's theory might contribute to a greater understanding and promotion of student learning in its broader sense. We offer some observations regarding the potential of the theory to advance knowledge of patterns of change and stability in college students, and we then discuss the possible use of the theory in curricular design.

Research on Patterns of Change and Stability in College Students

We began this book by providing a rationale for our belief that knowledge of academic disciplines is a prerequisite to understanding academic lives through a comparison of the general perspective(s) of scholars who study college faculty with the general perspective(s) of those who study college students. In comparing these two streams of research, we noted that those who study the professional lives of faculty have largely assumed and accepted the centrality of academic disciplines in their inquiries, whereas this has not been the case—especially in more recent years—for those who study longitudinal change and stability of college students. We suggested that this difference has both conceptual and methodological implications for the research agendas and research methods evident in the two domains of inquiry.

With particular reference to the differential importance of academic disciplines in the respective literatures on patterns of change and stability in college students' abilities and interests reviewed by Feldman and Newcomb (1969) and Pascarella and Terenzini (1991), we wonder whether the stronger influences of academic disciplines discerned by the former authors may have resulted from their greater reliance on certain earlier analysts who had a more sociologically oriented research paradigm, while the weaker influences of academic disciplines discerned by the latter authors may be a consequence of their relying on a more psychologically oriented research paradigm by some contemporary scholars. In the end, we raised the possibility that what scholars find in their inquiries may be influenced by what they look for and that the weaker influence of academic disciplines on patterns of change and stability in students' abilities and interests may be due to the fact that these considerations of the possible impacts of academic disciplines as well as other group influences in colleges and universities are not as important in the psychological-research paradigm as they are in the sociological-research paradigm.

At any rate, we believe that the evidence we have presented in the intervening chapters—based on our review of the extant research literature and our own empirical findings—clearly supports our fundamental premise that academic disciplines are a highly important source of influence on the academic lives of both college faculty and students. The fundamental differences in the professional norms and values of college faculty in the four distinct academic environments and the different change and stability patterns in the abilities and interests of students in these respective environments were summarized in the previous chapter.

The collective evidence we have presented leads us to reaffirm our initial contention that academic disciplines are an essential component in efforts to understand how students change as a result of their collegiate experiences. We have presented consistent evidence from the extant literature and our own empirical findings that faculty members in different clusters of academic disciplines create distinctly different academic environments as a consequence of their preference for alternative goals for undergraduate education, their emphasis on alternative teaching goals and student competencies in their respective classes, and their reliance on different approaches to classroom instruction and ways of interacting with students inside and outside their classes. We have also presented consistent empirical evidence that these distinctive academic environments created by their respective faculties have a strong socializing influence on change and stability in students' abilities and interests—that is, what students do and do not learn or acquire as a consequence of their collegiate experiences. In general, our findings support the conclusion reached by Pace (1990) that academic disciplines (environments) are a primary influence on "the extent and direction of student progress in college" (p. 76). In essence, students learn what they study, which is to say the distinctive repertoire of professional and personal self-perceptions, competencies, attitudes, interests, and values that their respective academic disciplines/environments distinctly reinforce and reward (in addition to the specific content/factual knowledge associated with the discipline).

Such a conclusion may not appear to be profound on the surface, but we think it has important implications for understanding the apparent conflict in the respective conclusions reached by Feldman and Newcomb (1969) and Pascarella and Terenzini (1991) concerning the relative influence of academic disciplines on change and stability of college students. In addition we feel that this conclusion has implications for future research on this phenomenon. What follows in this section are our observations and concerns about the fundamental nature of contemporary research on how colleges affect change and stability in college students and our suggestions to improve this important line of inquiry through theory-based studies.

Many of the models—that have guided research over the past two decades on how colleges affect students incorporate elements of student-faculty interactions within and outside the classroom, and studies grounded in these models often incorporate some indicator of the students' academic major. Why then are the reviews of the findings of this literature by Feldman and Newcomb (1969) and Pascarella and Terenzini (1991) in such seeming contradiction?

We think the answer is twofold and is a consequence of (1) the manner by which scholars classify academic majors/environments and (2) the nature of the measures used in their studies to explain the relative importance of alternative features in overall collegiate experiences contributing to student growth—or lack thereof. The following is a discussion of how these two possible factors may have contributed to the seeming contradiction in the findings of Feldman and Newcomb (1969) and Pascarella and Terenzini (1991), as well as our suggestions of how reliance on Holland's theory might ameliorate such difficulties in future research on understanding and promoting student learning in colleges and universities.

Theory-based classifications of academic environments. As we previously noted in this chapter scholars who study change and stability of college students have not been as inclined as their peers who study college faculty to assume and accept the centrality of academic disciplines in their studies. One consequence of this neglect is that substantive conceptual and empirical knowledge about the classification of students' academic majors or environments is not as evident in the literature concerning how colleges affect students as in the literature on differences in faculty attitudes and behaviors. For instance, it is much more common to find classifications of students' academic majors based on such idiosyncratic and crude indicators as science versus nonscience and liberal arts versus professional than on systematic classifications based on empirically (Biglan, 1973a, 1973b) or theoretically (Holland, 1966, 1973, 1985, 1997) derived typologies of academic disciplines. The use of such crude and simplistic classification schemas for students' academic majors/environments may well have contributed to weaker findings regarding the impact of those majors on students' patterns of change and stability.

We encourage scholars to classify students' academic majors or environments in ways that have theoretical merit and are empirically defensible in future efforts to discern those environments' potential influences on student learning. Holland's theory appears to be especially useful in this respect given its strong theoretical grounding and the abundant empirical evidence supporting its premises *The College Majors Finder* (Rosen, Holmberg, & Holland, 1989, pp. 4–22) and the *Dictionary of Holland Occupational Codes* (Gottfredson & Holland, 1996a, pp. 675–693) are especially valuable references in that they classify literally hundreds of specific academic majors into the six academic environments. Both references also give three-letter Holland codes for each academic major, thus allowing more fine-grained analyses of differences *within* each of the six academic environments.

We offer this suggestion not to imply that Holland's theory provides the only basis for such classification, but rather to point out that it is a well-established theoretical framework that is germane to such inquiries and one that has been validated in dozens of studies. We believe that reliance on such a theoretically based and empirically defensible classification scheme of academic environments is a more valid way of capturing the inherent diversity of academic disciplines than the more simplistic, unsystematic classifications commonly used; it thus has more potential to contribute to greater understanding of the extent to which academic disciplines influence student learning. In addition, reliance on such a classification scheme would facilitate efforts to synthesize the evolving literature on the extent to which academic disciplines influence student learning, thereby contributing to a more systematic understanding of this important phenomenon than does adherence to idiosyncratic classification schemas prevalent in contemporary research.

Measures incorporated in prevalent college-impact models. Many of the models that have guided much contemporary research on the effects of colleges on students, in fact, include measures of student-faculty interaction inside and outside formal classroom settings—for example, measures of the teaching behaviors students encounter in class settings and the frequency and nature of student-faculty interactions outside formal classes. The inclusion of such measures is consistent with Pascarella and Terenzini's (1991) statement that "one of the most inescapable and unequivocal conclusions we can make is that the impact of college is largely determined by the individual's quality of effort and level of involvement in both academic and nonacademic activities" (p. 610) and their advice to researchers to focus "more on such factors as curricular experiences and course work patterns, the quality of teaching, the frequency and focus of student-faculty nonclassroom interaction, the nature of peer group and extracurricular activities, and the extent to which institutional structures and policies facilitate student academic and social involvement" (p. 596). The difficulty associated with such measures is that they are very global or general in character and lack theoretical grounding; they essentially tap the extent to which students take advantage of people within the general institutional setting and the multitude of services and facilities provided by colleges and universities.

The global character of such measures and the ways they are commonly employed in contemporary research on student learning contribute to three concerns we have that could be ameliorated by reliance on theory-based measures. Our first concern is simply that the commonly used measures lack strong theoretical underpinnings in terms of explaining why students should learn more from their greater frequency of either formal or informal interaction with others (e.g., peers, faculty) or from their greater frequency of use of available services or facilities provided by their institutions. What theoretical premise explains, for example, why students who interact more frequently with other students and faculty and who are more engaged in active learning activities should achieve greater growth in such diverse areas as general education, literature, history, philosophy, arts, writing, synthesizing knowledge, and knowledge of the world in general? The failure to ground inquiries in appropriate theories contributes to an unguided search for the correlates of student learning—correlates that most often lack theoretical origins and acquire legitimacy only by virtue of the fact that others have found these correlates to be important, significant predictors of the specific student outcome being explored.

Although it is true that the current approach has contributed to the accumulation of growing and increasingly consistent evidence showing that some predictors have more influence on student learning than others, such efforts have also contributed to an emerging tendency to search for and endorse uniform "good practices for undergraduate education" (Chickering, Gamson, & Barsi, 1989; Kuh & Vespers, 1997), a tendency that is in direct conflict with the inherent diversity of American higher education noted earlier in this chapter. This leads to our second concern that the relative importance of such measures of "good practice" may differ depending on the specific student competencies (outcomes) that particular academic environments seek to develop in their respective student bodies. Simply put, "good practices" may well vary across different academic environments whose faculties emphasize different teaching and learning goals and use different instructional approaches.

Our portraits of the academic environments created by faculty and our summary of research findings provide a number of examples of how academic environments differ on measures commonly used to understand which particular facets of collegiate experiences are most related to students' patterns of change and stability. To give but a single illustration, faculty in Investigative environments rely predominantly on structured and formal teaching-learning strategies that are decidedly subject-matter centered; they believe that students learn best by meeting specific, clear-cut a priori course requirements; and they place high value on examinations and grades. In comparison, their colleagues in Artistic environments use a blending of both subject-matter and student-centered instructional approaches, place a high value on student freedom and independence in the learning process, prefer a collegial mode of interaction with students, and believe that students do their best work when they are on their own. Thus, although we have shown that both Investigative and Artistic academic environments are comparably successful in promoting their respective patterns of student learning, they do so in different ways.

Why then should one assume or expect that there are generic "good practices" that promote the distinctive patterns of student outcomes that the respective academic environments seek to reward and reinforce in their students? We think it is more plausible to assume that different teaching or instructional approaches are related to different student outcomes. Searching for uniform "good practices for undergraduate education" in the face of this clear diversity of actual practices by faculty in these disparate academic environments has the potential to be misleading and to inject a search for uniformity that runs counter to the inherent diversity of American higher education.

Our third concern is in part related to our second one. The use of global measures—such as measures of frequency of general student-faculty interaction and teaching behaviors students generally encounter—to explain and understand patterns of change and stability in students also runs counter to extant knowledge that it is these very kinds of interaction and behaviors that vary among faculty in the four academic environments. As we have shown, faculty members in Investigative, Artistic, Social, and Enterprising academic environments have decidedly different preferences for how they interact with students, and they use different instructional approaches in their respective classes and interactions with students. The consequence of including global or general measures in studies of student learning leads to our third concern—that much of the potential influence of the particular and specific academic majors/environments (however classified) is lost to these general measures of faculty members' instructional approaches and interactions with students. That is to say, if analysts ignore the manner by which faculty in specific sorts of academic environments teach students in their classrooms and interact with students outside class settings—if analysts, in essence, subsume these specific matters under a more general assessment—then much of the potential influence of the specific academic major/environment on patterns of student change and stability is hidden or masked.

The underlying bases for these three concerns are our convictions (1) that there are theory-based linkages between what students learn and the instructional approaches faculty employ to promote learning and (2) that academic disciplines—which differentially emphasize the relative importance of different student outcomes and which employ alternative instructional approaches to achieve student leaning of these different outcomes—constitute the fundamental element for these theoretical linkages. We encourage scholars to ground their studies of student learning in theoretical frameworks that rec-

ognize the centrality of academic environments and their faculties to student learning. Such theoretical grounding would result in the selection of both dependent and independent variables that have theoretical meaning. That is to say, for example, that future research would benefit from focusing on student outcomes (dependent variables) that are an integral component of an appropriate theory and on explanatory/independent variables that have an assumed theoretical relationship with whatever student outcome is of interest to the particular investigator(s). Holland's theory provides such a framework through a theoretical classification of academic disciplines that incorporates theory-based assumptions of the respective student abilities and interests reinforced and rewarded by the distinctive academic environments. Subsequent research has assisted in understanding how the alternative instructional approaches and distinctive patterns of interaction with students used in each environment contribute to student learning of the distinctive abilities and interests that the faculties of those respective environments reinforce and reward.

Detecting disciplinary effects. Being guided by theory for the appropriate selection of measures, however, is a necessary but not sufficient condition for the detection of disciplinary effects. Even if classifications of disciplines are theoretically sound and the selection of measures to include in studies are theoretically based and specifically related to the discipline classifications and outcomes under study, the use of statistical techniques such as multiple regression or analysis of covariance will continue to preclude the appearance of discipline effects. If the purpose of the research is to understand how disciplines contribute to *change* in students, these approaches do not allow the assessment of actual change a repeated-measures approach is more appropriate to assess magnitude and direction of change. If the purpose is to assess the influence or impact of disciplines on outcomes, the inclusion in the statistical models of both discipline classifications *and* instructional practices and types of faculty-student interactions specific to the disciplines statistically equates the disciplines on characteristics that differentiate between disciplines. Once these characteristics are controlled for and the faculty "equated" across the respective academic environments, the disciplinary effect has been controlled—that is, it has already been accounted for by other measures in the analysis. There may not be a direct impact of discipline if the discipline effect is completely manifested through the instructional practices and types of faculty-student interactions.

An alternative to the approach based on standard regression/analysis of covariance is the use of path-analytic procedures. The utility of path analysis in studying the influence of disciplines on student outcomes is twofold. First, path analysis calls for a strong theory that links student experiences with student outcomes; second, the influence of disciplines on student outcomes that is manifested indirectly through the differing teaching practices and types of interactions can be measured and tested. We believe the adoption of these suggestions is likely to yield a more "true" estimate of the influence of academic environments and that such estimates will affirm the importance of academic environments to what students do and do not learn as a result of their college experiences.

Path-analytic models are already commonly used to examine the effects of colleges on students, but we think such models have been misdirected because they have not been especially well grounded in theory. That is, theory has not guided either the classification of academic departments or the assumed linkages among students' college experiences and the student outcomes under investigation. In essence, we believe that the "cause-effect" premises of most models have little theoretical grounding and that Holland's theory provides a strong theoretical basis for formulating and testing such models since it provides a theoretical basis for both the classification of academic environments and the linkages among the instructional approaches of faculty and longitudinal patterns of student change and stability.

Reliance on a theory such as Holland's would have at least two major benefits. First, variation in patterns of student learning would be theoretically linked to specific academic environments. Take, for example, two studies that seek, respectively, to examine change and stability of students in terms of their critical thinking and interpersonal skills. According to Holland's theory, the first study would assume that development of critical thinking skills would be greater among students majoring in an Investigative academic environment because that environment reinforces and rewards stu-

dents for the display of such attributes as being analytical, critical, independent, and rational; alternatively, the second study would assume that development of interpersonal skills would be greater among students majoring in a Social academic environment because that environment reinforces and rewards students for seeing themselves as liking to help others, understanding others, and being cooperative, empathic, and sociable. Thus, in the first study the author(s) might create a dichotomous measure of academic environments distinguishing between students who had majored in Investigative academic environments versus students who had chosen other academic environments, while in the second study the author(s) might create a dichotomous measure of academic environments distinguishing between students who had majored in Social environments versus students who had majored in other academic environments. The point emphasized here is that there is a direct theoretical link between specific academic environments and specific student outcomes.

Second, there would be a theoretical connection between the specific experiences students encounter in their collegiate careers and the particular outcome under investigation. In terms of the two student outcomes just discussed, Holland's theory, together with the accumulated research evidence on the alternative instructional approaches used by faculty in the respective academic environments, would lead to the selection of different college experiences for inclusion in the model. For example, the study of critical thinking skills might incorporate measures of the extent to which the learning experiences of students were predominantly in structured and formal settings that were subject-matter centered (e.g., lecture-discussion); that placed a strong emphasis on their learning specific, clear-cut a priori requirements; and that placed a high value on examinations and grades since these are reflective of the prevailing instructional approaches used by faculty in Investigative environments. Alternatively, the study of interpersonal skills might incorporate measures of the extent to which the learning experiences of students were predominantly in less structured and more informal settings that were more student-centered (e.g., small-group discussions) and that placed a stronger emphasis on student freedom and independence in the learning process and a more collegial mode of student-faculty interaction, since these are reflective of the prevailing instructional approaches used by faculty in Social environments. The point we wish to emphasize here is that there is a clear theoretical link between students' learning experiences and their learning outcomes.

We believe that the use of path-analytic procedures incorporating these features will yield a better estimate of the influence of academic disciplines on student learning than has resulted from the use of less-theory-based inquiries in recent years. The use of Holland's theory to link alternative student outcomes to theory-based categories of academic environments has the potential to yield more accurate, and we believe stronger, estimates of the *direct effects* of academic disciplines on students' learning because the disciplines would not be "expected" to influence student learning on outcomes that they do not reinforce and reward. The use of Holland's theory to establish specific theory-based links between specific student experiences and specific student learning outcomes also has the potential to yield more accurate, and we believe stronger, estimates of the *indirect effects* of academic disciplines on student learning since the studies would be based on analyzing instructional approaches that are at least theoretically related to the specific student learning outcome(s) being investigated.

Curricular Design: Alternative Schemas

Holland's theory has implications for the design of alternative curricular patterns. These implications, however, vary rather dramatically depending on the intended outcomes to be achieved. We provide two illustrations. The first focuses on efforts to enhance student persistence in the freshman year and thus has a very specific objective and a relatively short-term time frame. The second provides an example of how Holland's theory might be used to promote a more systematic broadening of students' learning experiences and patterns of learning over the duration of the students' undergraduate careers and thus is more general in character with a longer time frame.

Enhancing freshman year persistence. The topic of student attrition is of major importance to both students and their institutions. A college education is a major investment for students and their families, and it has important consequences for students' growth and development as well as students' long-term career and economic success. Student attrition is also a salient issue to institutions, for college tuition is a primary source of their total revenue. Because student attrition is most acute in the freshman year, any effort or intervention that might diminish the likelihood of student attrition would have important positive implications for both students and their institutions.

The typical curricular pattern of most colleges and universities is for freshmen to take a variety of general-education courses in their first (and often second) year of enrollment. One consequence of this pattern is that students are required (or encouraged) to enroll in a wide variety of course work immediately following matriculation, and many of these courses are new and foreign to students' primary interests and abilities. It is quite possible that this requirement could contribute to lower levels of student stability, satisfaction, and success during the critical freshman year given the congruence assumption of Holland's theory, which suggests that college students are most likely to flourish in congruent academic environments or majors because these environments provide opportunities, activities, tasks, and roles that correspond to the competencies, interests, and self-perceptions of students.

An alternative curricular pattern that appears potentially useful for reducing the current level of student attrition (and for promoting satisfaction and success) in the freshman year is to allow students to take a greater proportion of course work in subject-matter areas that are more congruent with their personality types. Holland's theory offers particular promise in this respect because of the associated measures to determine both students' personality types and the relative congruence of alternative academic environments and their respective courses. Students' personality types could be discerned from the use of several well-established and validated instruments, such as the Self-Directed Search, the Vocational Preference Inventory, and the Strong-Campbell Interest Inventory. The relative congruence between students' dominant personality types and the alternative academic environments would be discerned from use of the hexagonal model shown in Figure 18-1. For example, students with a dominant Enterprising personality type would be encouraged as freshmen to take a greater proportion of course work in equivalent (Enterprising) or adjacent (Social, Conventional) academic environments, while those freshmen with a dominant Investigative personality type would be encouraged to take a greater proportion of course work in equivalent (Investigative) or adjacent (Realistic, Artistic) academic environments. Such a charge in curricular patterns in the freshman year would appear to have the potential for promoting student persistence, satisfaction, and success in this critical year of college enrollment (given the congruence assumption of Holland's theory).

Such a change, which would be a dramatic shift from past and current practices, may appear to promote greater narrowness in student learning. This outcome need not necessarily be the case, however, assuming that "disciplines are not inherently narrow," as Rothblatt (1997, p. 249) contends, and that "all, even the most vocational [disciplines], can effectively stretch the mind . . . [since they have] a capacity for breadth, connecting certain forms of knowing and their methods with others, reaching outward into adjacent disciplines and fields of interest, and encouraging exploration by means of connected and systematic systems of evidence gathering and evaluation" (Rothblatt, 1997, p. 249). What might well be necessary, however, would be to assure that freshman courses in the respective academic disciplines/environments do in fact achieve their inherent "capacity for breadth" suggested by Rothblatt.

Promoting systematic growth of multiple competencies. The preceding comments have focused specifically on the freshman year as critical to the issue of student retention and persistence. Thus a relatively short time frame is involved: the suggestions are designed to achieve specific outcomes—persistence, satisfaction, success—in the freshman year. The hexagonal model shown in Figure 18.1 and the logic of its use might also be used over the duration of students' total academic careers to provide a theory-based and systematic curricular design that is intended to broaden students' learning over this longer time interval. The hexagonal model suggests a specific progression for broadening students' abilities and

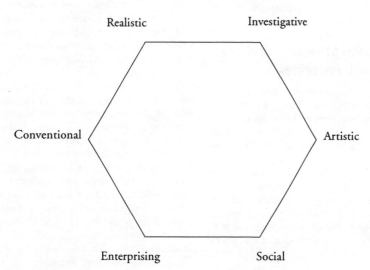

Figure 18-1 Hexagonal Model for Defining Psychological Resemblances among Personality Types and Academic Environments

interests during their college years. For example, and as just discussed, a greater proportion of students' course work in the freshman year would be devoted to subjects in either congruent or adjacent academic environments. In subsequent years, however, students would be required or encouraged to take course work in academic environments that are progressively dissimilar to their dominant personality types, perhaps returning in their final year to capstone or culminating courses in their specific academic majors/environments. For example, entering students with a dominant Social personality type would be encouraged or required to take course work in the analogous (Social) or adjacent (Artistic, Enterprising) academic environments during the freshman year; they would take courses in adjacent (Artistic, Enterprising) or once-removed (Investigative, Conventional) environments during the sophomore year; they would study courses in the once-removed (Investigative, Conventional) and distant (Realistic) environments their junior year; and they would return to capstone and culminating course work in their analogous environment (Social) in their senior year. Our aim here is not to provide a mechanistic format for individualized programs of study based on students' dominant personality type, but rather to illustrate the utility of Holland's theory to promote focused and broadening student learning over both short-term and long-term time frames of students' college careers.

Organizational Structure and Administrative Processes

In this *section* we first provide a series of illustrations depicting the basic utility of Holland's theory to the organization and management of institutions of higher learning and to research on the performance of those institutions. We focus initially on the organizational structure of colleges and universities. This is followed by a discussion of managerial and leadership practices within these institutions. We provide in *each section* a description of the policy or practice implications of Holland's theory as well as research hypotheses that flow from adoption of the inherent assumptions of the theory.

Organizational Structure: Making Sense of Diversity

Structure is obviously a common feature of all organizations, though the particular nature of that structure may vary substantially according to such attributes as the organization's specific goals, strategies, size, core processes, and workforce nature. Structure is a primary way by which complex organizations seek to balance the inherent tension between internal coordination and adaptation to the external environment. Although organizational structure is often conceived of as machinelike and inflexible, there is a growing tendency to design structures that are more flexible and emphasize the participation of organizations' members. For example, Bolman and Deal (1997), in illustrating their fundamental point that "successful organizations employ a variety of methods to coordinate individual and group efforts and to link them with desired goals" (p. 41), juxtapose the tightly controlled and highly centralized structure of McDonald's (where most major decisions are made at the top) with the decidedly more decentralized structure of Harvard University (where most major decisions are made at the lowest possible level in the organization).

Holland's theory has clear implications for the organizational structure of institutions of higher learning. These institutions traditionally are organized on the basis of schools and colleges, with the assumption that there are more common interests within these organizational units than across them. Yet the assignment of specific academic departments to colleges (or schools) historically has been made without the benefit of theory-based understanding of the similarities and differences among diverse academic environments/departments. The consequence is that we have colleges structured along the lines of external accreditation agencies and general professional associations (e.g., colleges of business, education, engineering, etc.), creating collegiate units that often include academic departments whose orientations are markedly dissimilar in terms of the premises of Holland's theory.

The hexagonal model shown in Figure 18.1, in conjunction with the *Dictionary of Holland Occupational Codes* (Gottfredson & Holland,

1996a) and *The College Majors Finder* (Rosen, Holmberg, & Holland, 1989), provides a theoretically based and empirically supported method for the assignment of specific academic departments to broader collegiate units. Table 18.1 provides an illustrative comparison between the traditional assignment of academic departments (columns) characterizing the typical structure of contemporary colleges and universities and the assignment (rows) suggested by the hexagonal model shown in Figure 18.1 and based on the first-letter code of academic disciplines (that is, their primary type).

It is readily apparent from Table 18.1 that each traditional collegiate unit (columns) is composed of multiple types of academic departments based on the classification of specific academic departments to the six academic environments proposed by Holland (based upon classifications using the *Dictionary of Holland Occupational Codes* and *The College Majors Finder*). For example, Colleges of Education often are composed of academic departments or programs that are members of five of Holland's academic environments; the academic departments in Colleges of Arts and Sciences customarily represent at least four of the academic environments; and Colleges of Business typically include academic departments that are members of three environments.

Holland (1997) proposes that organizations with high levels of congruence will be more likely "to interact with mutually satisfying relationships . . . to have members with higher levels of involvement and satisfaction . . . [and] be economically productive" (p. 54). These theory-based premises suggest that the realignment of academic departments into collegiate units consistent with the hexagonal model (reflected in the rows in Table 18.1) would enhance faculty involvement, job satisfaction, and productivity. Thus, Holland's theory provides both (1) a theoretical framework for the organizational structure of academic departments into broader collegiate units and (2) a set of theory-based propositions of the benefits that would be expected to accrue from implementation of this framework.

Similarly, various premises regarding the internal diversity of existing collegiate units are evident from Holland's premise that congruence is positively related to vocational and educational stability, satisfaction, and success. The

TABLE 18-1
Alternative Collegiate Organizational Structures

Traditional Colleges of			
Holland Environments	Education	Business	Arts and Sciences
REALISTIC	Agricultural Educ.	(none)	(none)
	Industrial Arts Educ.	(none)	(none)
INVESTIGATIVE	Science Education	Business Economics	Economics
	Mathematics Educ.	Systems Analysis	Mathematics
	Educational Research	Operations Research	Physics
			Statistics
ARTISTIC	Art Education	(none)	Art History
	Music Education	(none)	Music
	Foreign Lang. Educ.	(none)	French
			Theater/Drama
SOCIAL	Elementary Education	(none)	Philosophy
	Educ. Administration	(none)	Area Studies
	Special Education	(none)	Political Science
	Counselor Education	(none)	History
ENTERPRISING	Business Education	Marketing	Communications
	Higher Ed. Research	Labor Relations	Journalism
		Personnel Mgmt.	
		Advertising	
CONVENTIONAL	(none)	Accounting	(none)

basic expectation is that faculty members in academic departments that are most congruent with the college's norms and values should be more stable, satisfied, and successful than those in departments that are not congruent with the college's norms and values. Let us illustrate this contention by using the description of Colleges of Education in Table 18.1. These colleges are composed predominantly of Social academic departments (e.g., elementary education, educational administration, special education, counselor education), and secondarily of Realistic (agricultural and industrial arts education), Investigative (science and mathematics education, educational research), Artistic (art, music, and foreign language education), and Enterprising (business education, higher education research) departments. Based on the hexagonal model shown in Figure 18.1 and with all other things being equal (e.g., seniority and pay of faculty, size and prestige of department), it would be expected that Education faculty members in Social departments would be the most stable, satisfied, and successful, followed by their colleagues in Artistic and Enterprising departments; those in Investigative and Realistic departments would be the least stable, satisfied, and successful. Obviously these and other premises from Holland's theory regarding the organizational structure of colleges and universities need to be subjected to empirical study before they can be accepted.

Just as Holland's theory provides a basis for the assignment of specific academic disciplines to theory-based collegiate organizational units, so too it provides a basis for understanding similarities and differences *within* these units (i.e., the rows in Table 18.1) Both the *Dictionary of Holland Occupational Codes* and *The College Majors Finder* provide three-letter codes for each academic discipline. The use of the first-letter code to assign specific disciplines to theory-based collegiate units in Table 18.1 is intended to provide an overall organizational structure in which disciplines within the respective collegiate units share more in common with one another than they do with those in other units. Disciplinary differences within these theory-based collegiate units will still exist, however. The use of the second-letter code of disciplines—their secondary type—provides a basis for understanding similarities and differences among disciplines within these

theory-based collegiate units. For example, of the ten Investigative disciplines in Table 18.1 two have an Artistic second-letter code (Business Economics, Economics), one has an Enterprising second-letter code (Systems Analysis), and the remaining seven have a Realistic second-letter code. The premises just discussed concerning faculty stability, satisfaction, and success within the overall collegiate units also would be applicable to understanding diversity within these specific units. For instance faculty in the discipline within the Investigative collegiate unit in Table 18.1 that has an Enterprising second-letter code (Systems Analysis) should be less stable, satisfied, and successful than those that have either a Realistic or Artistic second-letter code because the latter are adjacent to the Investigative type in the hexagonal model shown in Figure 2.1.

The point here is simply that Holland's theory might guide those responsible for restructuring institutions of higher learning by providing a theory-based framework that, if followed, offers the promise of improving the professional stability, satisfaction, and success of faculty within these institutions. At the same time his theory provides a series of theory-based hypotheses for assessing variations in the current levels of stability, satisfaction, and success of colleges and universities as organizational entities in addition to the variability in the stability, satisfaction, and success of their individual members. We predict, for instance, that the extent to which colleges and universities are structured in ways consistent with the premises of Holland's theory will be positively related to their successful performance as measured by the collective levels of their members' stability (e.g., lower turnover), satisfaction (e.g., higher involvement and participation), and success or achievement (e.g., more effective teaching, higher research productivity, and greater service contributions).

Administrative Processes: The Management of Diversity

The diversity that characterizes American higher education imposes a major challenge to those responsible for the administration of these diverse institutions—namely, establishing administrative policies and procedures that are fair and equitable (uniform), on the one hand,

and that reflect the unique (differentiated) norms and values of the diverse academic units that constitute these institutions, on the other hand. To strike a balance between these two seemingly contradictory objectives is made difficult by the conflict and competition for power among individual members and interest groups entrenched by their enduring differences regarding the appropriateness of alternative values, beliefs, information, interests, and perceptions. Although it might be "normal" to conceive of such conflict as abnormal and counterproductive, Bolman and Deal (1997)—and other organizational theorists such as Quinn (1988)—note that "conflict is inevitable" (p. 164) and that "it is naive and romantic to hope that politics can be eliminated in organizations" (pp. 165–166). Hearn and Anderson (1998) have observed, for example, that colleges and universities are certainly not immune from the ubiquity of conflict that characterizes all complex organizations. These analysts have provided an excellent summary of research findings demonstrating conflicts among academic departments in terms of their preferences for alternative governance models, approaches to academic program cuts, peer-review processes for promotion and tenure, research priorities, and roles within the academy (e.g., teacher vs. researcher).

The first step in managing large and complex organizations and in developing strategies and tactics to cope with inevitable conflict is to understand the fundamental diversity of these organizations and the leadership and managerial implications that naturally accrue from this diversity. Here again Holland's theory has much utility. Our review of the research literature on college faculty and our own empirical findings, as presented in chapter 4, show wide differences in the work environments of faculty in academic departments classified according to Holland's academic environments. The collective findings from the extant studies reveal substantial differences in academic departments classified according to Holland's six academic environments in terms of organizational and teaching goals, instructional practices, student competencies emphasized by faculty, the nature of student-faculty interactions within the environments, the duties performed by department heads/chairs and the sources of their overall job satisfaction, and the level of graduate students'

satisfaction with the program. In addition, our own findings reveal broad differences among faculty members in the academic environments as to their preferences for alternative goals for undergraduate education, their comfort with the current level of curricular specialization, and the types of undergraduate courses and students they prefer to teach.

These collective findings, which clearly indicate the broad and theoretically consistent differences among faculty in the six academic environments proposed by Holland, demonstrate the usefulness of Holland's theory in understanding the inherent internal diversity of American colleges and universities and in formulating administrative policies and procedures that are equitable and, at the same time, recognize this internal diversity. This balancing between equitability and diversity is perhaps most evident in the formulation of criteria and performance standards used to evaluate the performance of faculty and academic programs. While institutional officials may use common criteria in these evaluations, the standards of their performance should differ given the unique characteristics of the six clusters of academic departments noted earlier. The lesson to be learned from extant findings is twofold. First, the use of universalistic criteria is questionable given the demonstrated internal diversity of institutions. Second, regardless of the criteria employed, the formulation of performance standards for program and personnel evaluations should recognize differences among diverse academic departments—diversity which is generally both systematic and consistent with the premises of Holland's theory.

Suggestions for Future Research Using Holland's Theory

The collective findings presented in chapters 4 through 8 testify to the potential of Holland's theory to guide systematic research on the differential patterns of longitudinal change in the abilities and interests of college students. We hope that these findings, will stimulate scholars to conduct similar theory-based studies in this important area of inquiry. We offer here some suggestions for those who are interested in grounding their research in the context of Holland's theory. Our intent is not to be exhaustive, but rather to select and present a few suggestions that we consider important. We begin with a consideration of Holland's caveat of "other things being equal." This consideration is followed by a discussion of the need to explore the socialization mechanisms of academic environments in an effort to undersand how these environments contribute to the differential patterns of longitudinal change in students' abilities and interests (such as those presented in preceeding chapters). Finally, we offer some suggestions about how Holland's theory might be used to guide research on student persistence in colleges and universities.

Other Things Being Equal: The Importance of Conditional Effects

Holland (1997), in noting that his theory "cannot be applied successfully without the observation of a few boundary conditions" (p. 13), offers the general caveat that the validity of the basic assumptions of the theory is conditional on the premise of "other things being equal" (p. 13). He refers specifically to the need to consider such factors as the "intelligence, social class, gender, and educational level" (p. 40) of the individuals in research on the validity of the assumptions of the theory, and he notes that "the 'other things being equal' clauses in the theory need more attention" (p. 166).

Our response to this caution was to examine the extent to which our findings were equally true for male and female students and for those with similar ("primary recruits") and dissimilar ("secondary recruits") initial and final choice of academic majors in our sample. Our findings reveal several instances of differences between male and female students and between primary and secondary recruits, though, as we repeatedly noted, these differences were basically in the magnitude of change rather than in the substance of the patterns of change. Nonetheless, we believe that our set of findings affirm the wisdom of Holland's warning that other things may not always be equal; and we suggest that subsequent research on Holland's theory also use research designs that enable scholars to examine possible conditional effects. Given our findings, we specifically encourage those who use Holland's theory to study differential patterns of change and stability in students' abilities and interests to examine the extent to which their findings are applicable for both males and females and for primary and secondary recruits to academic majors. Other attributes of individuals that Holland suggests should be incorporated in research include their age, intelligence, ethnicity, and social class.

Socialization Mechanisms of Academic Environments

While our findings as a whole support the validity of all three basic assumptions in Holland's theory, albeit with varying degrees of strength, we examined the relative merits of the congruence and socialization assumptions referring to the former as the "personality dynamic" in the theory and the latter as the "socialization dynamic." Our findings clearly show the primacy of the socialization dynamic in that the effect of any one of the four academic environments is essentially equivalent irrespective of whether or not the student has the "right personality type" for the environment. We think this is an important finding that has broad implications for subsequent research based on Holland's theory, especially given the paucity of research on environments. We refer specifically to the need to explore more systematically the socialization mechanisms of academic environments that in part produce the differential patterns of longitudinal change in the college students' abilities and interests.

Holland (1997) offers a number of potential explanations for the differential success of environments in reinforcing and rewarding the characteristic patterns of abilities and interests of their associated personality types. In general, he notes that highly differentiated environments and those with strong identity are more successful in reinforcing their preferred pattern of abilities and interests than are those that are undifferentiated and have a diffuse identity. Highly differentiated environments are defined as encouraging a narrow range of behaviors in explicit ways, whereas undifferentiated environments stimulate a broader range of behaviors and offer ambiguous guidance to individuals. Similarly, environments with high identity have a limited set of consistent and explicit goals, whereas those with a diffuse identity are characterized by a large set of conflicting and poorly defined goals. Thus, the constructs of environmental differentiation and identity, essentially define the clarity and focus of academic subenvironments.

It seems reasonable to assume that one possible explanation for the differential success of the four academic environments in our study in promoting student change over the four-year period in a manner consistent with the characteristic pattern of abilities and interests of their associated personality types could be differences in the levels of their environmental differentiation and identity. Are, for example, Investigative, Artistic, and Enterprising academic environments more highly differentiated and do they have higher identity levels than Social environments? Do faculty in Investigative, Artistic and Enterprising environments in fact encourage a more narrow range of behaviors in explicit ways, and are the goals of these faculty members more explicit and consistent than those of their colleagues in Social environments? These are important questions in efforts to develop deeper understanding of the differential success of socialization mechanisms used by academic environments in promoting self-defined goals and objectives for student change.

To date, Holland's theory has been especially helpful in providing theory-based explanations of differential patterns of change and stability in the abilities and interests of students based upon their selection of and involvement in disparate groups of academic majors. Little attention, however, has been given to specific organizational features of academic environments (e.g., their clarity and focus) and to specific socialization mechanisms (e.g., classroom practices, out-of-class faculty-student interactions) employed within such environments that might be related to differential success in promoting their own self-defined goals and objectives for student change. The time has clearly arrived for such in-depth analyses in order to advance our understanding of the differential success of these academic subenvironments in promoting student learning.

We suggest specifically focusing on the collective and individual efforts of faculty members in these disparate academic environments. The collective actions of faculty contribute to the overall clarity and focus (i.e., environmental differentiation and identity) of the respective environments. While it is known that there are statistically significant differences in the educational goals of the different subenvironments

(Smart & McLaughlin, 1974; Smart, 1982), we are not aware of any research that examines the extent to which the alternative academic environments espouse a narrow range of behavior in explicit ways (environmental differentiation) or embrace a limited set of consistent and explicit goals (environmental identity). Similarly, statistically significant differences in classroom learning climates have been found across the disparate environments (Astin, 1965; Hearn & Moos, 1978) as have differences in the extent to which faculty in these environments emphasize the development of alternative competencies in their students (Thompson & Smart, 1998); yet more research is needed like that of Peters (1974), which examines the extent to which individual faculty members in the respective academic environments actually employ different instructional approaches in classroom settings, or vary in terms of the amount and nature of their interactions with students outside of formal class settings. Such research has the potential to advance our understanding of why some academic environments are more successful than others in promoting their own self-defined goals and objectives for student change.

In addition to the suggestions based on Holland's work, we think the conceptual model of undergraduate socialization proposed by Weidman (1989) would be useful in efforts to advance systematic knowledge of the socialization mechanisms of academic environments. His model incorporates situational and individual developmental constraints that limit student choices in academic environments as well as a set of socialization processes that influence the normative contexts and the interpersonal relations among faculty and students in academic environments.

Holland's Theory and Research on College Student Persistence

The vast majority of studies of student persistence are grounded in the premises of Tinto's (1970, 1987, 1993) theory of college student departure or extensions of that theory by Bean (1985) and Cabrera, Nora, and Castanda (1993). While occasionally using other terminology, all of these models or theories are essentially theories of person-environment fit, and seek to assess the extent to which students fit or conform to institutional norms. And yet none of these theories has an operational definition of the extent to which students fit with the norms and expectations of their campus environments. The concept of fit is often described in terms of the degree to which students become integrated into or conform to the academic and social norms of their institutions. It is generally assumed that "more is better"—that is, the higher students' scores on measures of academic and social integration, the more likely the students are to persist. But institutions as well as individuals have different norms and values, and the question of how much academic or social integration reflects what level of fit with any institution is not addressed.

Holland's theory too is a theory of person-environment fit. It differs, however, from the theories just noted by providing specific ways for assessing the degree of fit between students and their institutions. This assessment may be accomplished through use of the Environmental Assessment Technique (EAT) The EAT is predicated on the assumption of Holland and others "that the attributes of people, not the nature of the external environment, or organizational technology, or organizational structure, are the fundamental determinants of organizational behavior" (Schneider, 1987, p. 437). Holland (1997) similarly notes that "many of the psychologically important features of the environment consist of or are transmitted by the people in it" (p. 48).

This logic led to the formulation of the EAT which, when used in colleges and universities, is a straightforward census of the academic majors of college students and/or academic department affiliation of college faculty, since choice of an academic major or department is an expression of one's personality type. The EAT thus yields a profile or distribution for each institution and there is abundant empirical evidence showing that perceptions of the overall environments of colleges and universities, as measured by the College Characteristics Index (Pace, 1969) and the College and University Environment Scales (Pace & Stern, 1958), vary in accordance with the distribution of students and faculty across the six personality types. The EAT is thus a means of measuring institutional environments, and the profile that it yields is a three-level classification of the distribution or proportion of students and/or faculty members on a given campus across the six personality

types. Take, for instance, an institution that has the following distribution of faculty members (and/or students): 25 percent in Realistic departments; 35 percent in Investigative departments; 25 percent in Artistic departments; 10 percent in Social departments; 10 percent in Enterprising departments; and 5 percent in Conventional departments. This campus would have an EAT code of "IRA" since most faculty are in Investigative departments, followed by those in Realistic and Artistic departments, respectively.

The personality types of students can also be measured in a variety of ways with individuals given a three-level code based upon their primary, secondary, and tertiary scores on measures of their resemblance to each of the six personality types. It thus becomes possible to determine the degree of congruence or fit between individual students and their respective campus environments. Given Holland's assumption that educational stability is dependent on the fit between students and their institutions, and given the underlying assumption of person-environment fit of Tinto's (and other related) theory, it is reasonable, for example, to assume that a student with a dominant Artistic personality type would be more likely to persist in an institution that has an "AIS" EAT code than one that has a "CRE" EAT code. The point we wish to make here is simply that Holland's theory provides an operational definition of the degree of person-environment congruence or fit capable of being integrated with the primary constructs in the person-environment fit theories, which themselves have been so instrumental in increasing our understanding of the factors that contribute to students' persistence in or withdrawal from colleges and universities.[2]

A Concluding Comment

No doubt the possibility exists of misusing Holland's theory and the associated findings in ways that would be harmful to faculty and students. This potential for misuse is most evident in the context of "social engineering"—using the theory to assess students' personality types and to require students to enter academic majors that are "right for them." We do not think the theory is designed for that purpose, nor do we think the accumulated research evidence is sufficiently strong to warrant such actions. Our intent throughout this chapter has been to show how Holland's theory might contribute to theory-based research on college students and to greater understanding of the disciplinary work environments of faculty, as well as the educational and organizational implications of the theory in higher education settings. All of these efforts have been to understand the diversity that has historically characterized American higher education for the ultimate purpose of serving individuals better and improving the performances of colleges and universities.

Notes

1. More than a dozen different indices of the degree of congruence or fit between individuals and their environments have been developed and their respective strengths and weaknesses have been reviewed by Assouline and Meir (1987), Brown and Gore (1994), Camp and Chartrand (1992), Holland (1997), and Spokane (1985). Most of these indices provide much more complex and precise measurements of the degree of person-environment fit than used in this example.

PART IV

THE LEARNING EXPERIENCE

PART 4: THE LEARNING EXPERIENCE

Probably no area of research on college students is growing as fast as that which focuses on college student learning. The Learning Experience focuses on both classroom and academic learning as well as more general learning that is a part of the college student experience as well as the intersection of the two. The first section focuses on primarily on academic learning particularly related to classrooms. The next section contains articles connected with students' cognitive development and the section ends with more general discussions of student learning in the campus context and reviews of recent research on learning. We begin with the late Robert Menges' (1988) work, "Research on Teaching and Learning: The Relevant and the Redundant." Menges was one of the first higher education scholars to seriously examine student learning on campus. His classic work reviews scholarship on learning to that point then sets an agenda for future research on learning—an agenda that remains as relevant today as it was over 15 years ago. In a more recent work, "Setting the Context: Psychological Theories of Learning," Frances Stage (1996) provides a review of theories that contribute to an understanding of college student learning. The article concludes with suggestions for the use of those theories in attempts to study or promote learning on college campuses.

Ana Martinez Aleman (1997) in "Understanding and Investigating Female Friendship's Educative Value" provides a unique perspective on academe. Her research suggests ways that women's friendships are the basis for learning and intellectual play and performance. The value and power of these relationships in higher education for pedagogy, research, and practice are discussed. Similarly, Marcia Baxter Magolda (1999) in "The Evolution of Epistemology: Refining Contextual Knowledge at Twentysomething" examines the evolution of complex thinking of students through college and beyond. In her research she identifies themes that have direct relevance for student affairs. Finally,"A Multicultural View Is a More Cognitively Complex View: Cognitive Development and Multicultural Education" by Patricia King and Bettina Shuford (1996) suggests that reasoning skills developed in adulthood are relevant to multicultural education. The authors provide suggestions for promoting intellectual development in that context.

Lemuel Watson and Frances Stage (1999) in "A Framework to Enhance Student Learning," present Watson's (1996) model for considering learning within the context of students lives and the campus context. It can be used by administrators on a campus to promote learning, involvement, and other educational outcomes. In "Student's out-of-class experiences and their influence on learning and cognitive development: A literature review," Patrick Terenzini, Ernest Pascarella, and Gregory Blimling (1996) review research that examines the effects of college students' out-of-class experiences on various academic outcomes. They discuss relevant relationships between student affairs and academic affairs.

This section closes with Patricia Cross' (1999) "What Do We Know about Students' Learning, and How Do We Know It?," provides a review of recent work on college students' cognitive development. For the reader, she distills 30 years of work that focuses on the topic and provides critique for those who will continue to study learning. She enjoins us to seek multiple sources as we seek answers to questions about this important topic.

CHAPTER 19

RESEARCH ON TEACHING AND LEARNING: THE RELEVANT AND THE REDUNDANT

ROBERT J. MENGES

Some years ago, Bernard Berelson and Gary Steiner published an important reference book, *Human Behavior: An Inventory of Scientific Findings* (1964). In some seven hundred pages, they summarized and attempted to integrate more than one thousand verified generalizations which they called social science "findings." The story goes that when Berelson later looked back on this work, reflecting on what was learned from all those studies, he made three succinct points. Today, I suppose we would call them his meta-findings. About these studies of human behavior he said: (1) some do, some don't; (2) the differences aren't very great; and (3) it's more complicated than that.

Critical bibliographers, meta-analysts, and other reviewers of research easily empathize with those sentiments. They also provide a structure for my comments about research on teaching-learning processes in postsecondary education.

Some Things Do Work

First, here is an instance of a relatively clear positive finding. It has long been accepted that an immediate mastery test helps a student retain information. Decades ago in the *Archives of Psychology*, Jones (1923) documented a forgetting curve for lecture material. The average student's recollection of lecture content was initially 62 percent, but it declined to 45 percent after three or four days and to only 24 percent after eight weeks. If students took an immediate examination, however, they retained almost twice as much material after eight weeks, both for "thought questions" and for "fact questions."

Replications and refinements of such studies have substantiated the positive effect of immediate testing or other forms of required review. It is one of the things that work. More studies of it would be redundant.

Even though further studies of this effect are unnecessary, we do need better ways of understanding why teachers fail to apply that well-established principle. Our students' learning would certainly be enhanced if, as a condition for leaving the classroom, they had to demonstrate mastery of the day's instruction. Yet few of us use such tactics in our teaching. Our profession badly needs investigations exploring resistance to implementing established principles of teaching and learning; such a project would be highly relevant.

Some Things Don't Work

On the negative side, some research has *not* fulfilled its early promise. Studies of trait-treatment interactions illustrate one approach to research on teaching and learning that has failed to deliver strong results. For example, consider a large, late 1960s project by Goldberg (1972). He varied instructional method (lecture versus self-study) and student product (quiz versus papers) and, for each of 800 students, derived more than 350 scores on personality tests and other measures. Virtually no significant statistical interactions were found involving these measures and the outcomes of student learning, student satisfaction, and amount of extracurricular reading. The few relationships identified in one class failed to withstand cross-validation in another class.

Other trait-treatment and aptitude-treatment studies have similarly and redundantly found few strong interactions. This situation may change with more sophisticated conceptual analysis or with more adequate design and measurement techniques. Rickards and Slife (1987), for example, recently demonstrated that students' dogmatism (high versus low) interacted with the rhetorical structure of prose passages read to them, affecting their recall of the content of those passages. Identifying classroom implications of such findings, based as they are on laboratory studies of extreme-scoring students, is a daunting challenge. Meanwhile, in most trait-treatment and aptitude-treatment interaction studies, as in studies of many other teaching and learning topics, the differences apparently aren't very great.

Most Things Are More Complicated

These results, need not lead to despair. Indeed, as Berelson noted, things are more complicated. After all, most of these studies represent one research approach, positivism, now badly battered by its critics. The studies come from an earlier time, a time when psychology was appropriating the experimental methods of physical science and when educationists, in turn, were applying psychologists' methods to classroom research. The optimistic expectation was that tightly controlled experiments would yield a body of relevant knowledge about teaching through, as Douglass wrote in 1929, "hundreds

and thousands of tiny but reliable accretions" (p. 273). Studies of this kind were quite common in the early decades of this century. So many had accumulated by 1920, that Klapper, while observing that "the field of college pedagogics is still virgin soil" (1920, 43), could nevertheless fill nearly 600 pages with comments about scholarly publications on that topic. Of course, not everyone agreed about the quality of this work. In 1935, Payne and Spieth synthesized more than 400 sources, attempting to spare teachers the decision of which parts of that literature were valuable and which were not. They and others agreed that much was not, but the flow of research using controlled, experimental methods continued unabated.

Trait-treatment and aptitude-treatment interaction studies came into vogue somewhat later, aided by the power and convenience of computer-assisted data analysis. More sophisticated in both conception and technique, these studies nevertheless perpetuated the positivist's search for universally applicable generalizations by which behavior could be predicted and controlled.

The positivist paradigm is now in disrepute, and there is considerable discussion about what might replace it. For descriptions of alternative paradigms and for illustrative research examples, see the volumes edited by Ashworth, Giorgi, and de Koning (1986); Reason and Rowan (1981); Sarbin (1986); and von Eckartsberg (1986). An especially provocative framework is the "interpretive approach," as described by contributors to the collection, *Interpretive Social Science: A Reader* (Rabinow and Sullivan, 1979). This approach emphasizes multiple meanings rather than fixed findings (particularly seeking meanings for events as held by the persons being studied), searches for understanding and insight rather than for prediction and control, attempts to explicate particular contexts rather than to discover universal generalizations, and attends to the intentional and value-laden aspects of human action and interaction. It is clear that the studies cited earlier did not reflect this framework.

Neugarten characterizes the interpretive approach this way:

> The study of the human world can never be context-free; the observer can never stand outside his subject-matter but must always share the context of cultures, languages and symbols that constitute that world. In this

view the observer stands within the same circles of human meaning as do the objects of his studies, and there is no outside, detached standpoint from which to gather observations. . . . Social scientists are all caught in a hermeneutic circle: Ultimately a good explanation is one that makes sense of the behavior we see, but what makes sense is itself based on the kinds of sense we can make. In different words, there is no "objective" nor absolute verification procedure to fall back on. We can only continue to offer interpretations (1985, 292).

To illustrate how easily we become trapped in our own meanings for events and in our own ways of making sense of the world—thereby failing to gain insight into the meanings held by those we study—I shall refer to research on student evaluations of courses and teachers. Even the name by which these studies have come to be known, "the student ratings literature," complicates and trivializes them through associations with popularity contests or, perhaps more aptly in our television age, with estimates of the percentage of viewers who are tuned in.

Reviews of this research, meticulously documented over the past decade by Feldman (for example 1978) and Marsh (1984), present some clear findings. It is clear from this research that teaching evaluations involve distinguishable dimensions, although there is some dispute about the number of dimensions and the names by which they are properly called. Student ratings are relatively free from bias and sufficiently reliable to differentiate levels of perceived teaching performance and to document changes in teaching performance over time. There is also evidence for the validity of student ratings, although validity estimates vary with the criterion used.

Identifying a validity criterion for student ratings represents one formidable problem. If end-of-course evaluations are to stand as valid, against what independent measure of teaching effectiveness should their validity be determined? Here are some possibilities: other evaluative information from students, such as interviews, essays, or letters; ratings of the same teacher by nonstudents, such as colleagues, administrators, or alumni; or alternative evidence of effective teaching (for example, examination scores and course grades, enrollment of one's students in advanced courses, or faculty excellence in other areas, such as scholarly pub-

lication). Of course, nothing is a perfect proxy for teaching effectiveness, at least not as our rhetoric rather grandly portrays effective teaching.

The most defended validity criterion is student learning, usually measured by examination scores. Student evaluations do correlate positively with that criterion, although the correlation is relatively modest. Yet none of us can feel satisfied that our teaching effectiveness is sufficiently captured by student performance on examinations. We need much more sensitive evidence about the quality of students' experiences with teachers to reach an adequate understanding of the validity of student ratings.

Another way of seeing that things are more complicated in this student ratings research is to critique the language of evaluation forms. As Tom Wilson (1987) points out, the language of items and response categories implies a world where the teacher is active and where students are reactive or passive. It is a world where students are objectified as the recipients of another's action, since, insofar as students do participate, it is the teacher who sets the conditions of their participation. It is a world where knowledge exists outside of the learner—that is, where the teacher organizes knowledge for learners and subsequently verifies how well they have acquired it. The world implied by these evaluation questionnaires rarely takes account of learners as active makers of meaning, of the dialogic relationship of teachers with learners, or of knowledge as the creation of a community.

Research Questions and Methods for an Interpretive Approach

Impersonal and objective language, as used for example in student ratings questionnaires, along with other conventions of the scientific search for universally applicable generalizations, distances researchers from the experiences ostensibly under study. But we do not need distance from these experiences. We need more direct access to them, both during the experience itself and as it is subsequently recollected.

We also need to attend to more than individual experience. Although that level might be considered fundamental, the context in which individual experience occurs is pertinent, even indispensable. For teaching and learning research, context includes the course, the department or school, the institution, and society as a whole.

Research Questions

Using those five levels as a framework, I here present some researchable questions about teaching-learning issues. I believe that these questions lend themselves to an interpretive approach and that their answers will help to improve educational practice and to further research. These questions focus on critical events and situations about which students and teachers can reflect and about which they can communicate using their own structures of meaning rather than only the predetermined categories and language of the investigator.

At the level of experience of the individual student:

- Why do students sometimes choose to learn what is *not* required and perhaps not even rewarded? What consequences does that choice have for learning what *is* required?

- Why do students sometimes show the "desire to appear to know" (Coe, 1929, 7) or, in other words, why do they sometimes show the "appearance of a desire to know"?

The course level is the aggregate of students and the teacher. At that level, critical issues of power and authority deserve investigation:

- Why do students sometimes sabotage their peers' learning, and under what conditions do they support the success of peers?

- Why do teachers sometimes take upon their own shoulders nearly the entire responsibility for their students' learning? (a situation called the Atlas Complex by Finkel and Monk, 1983).

The department and school level is the aggregate of teachers as well as of students and includes issues outside as well as inside the classroom:

- What is most puzzling for teachers about the teaching-learning process, and how are those puzzles confronted or avoided in conversations with other faculty, during office hours with students, and in policy discussions?

- As a result of student evaluations, how do teachers perceive the instructional process differently, behave differently as teachers, and act differently with colleagues?

At the campus level, our view extends across departments and schools:

- What course events, if any, help students to make sense of their experiences in residence halls and playing fields and with friends and family members off campus, and how does that differ from major to major?

- What change goals do faculty set for themselves related to their teaching, what role do students play in the selection and implementation of the goals, and how do the goals differ across academic fields?

The societal level permits exploration of links between campus and situations elsewhere:

- How much similarity is there among students (and what are the key differences among students) in their responses to off-campus work experience?

- Under what conditions do members of the nonacademic community become active users of postsecondary education facilities to further their own learning, and how do they define "learning" for these purposes?

Other questions might bridge two or more levels and thus be of even greater consequence.

Research Methods

Methods appropriate for gathering data to answer questions like these are not the methods typically used by laboratory investigators. Appropriate methods must fit the natural environment of students' classrooms and places of study and must accommodate the respondents' own styles of expression. They must be flexible enough to accommodate frames of reference possibly quite different from those originally held by researchers. Techniques of data collection should be dialogical, since inquiry is itself an interactive teaching-learning encounter. Discussion of results is likely to be more elaborative than reductive, and conclusions are likely to be more suggestive than definitive.

One suitable use of the interpretive approach to capture meanings that people give to events is through analysis of their verbal reports. Verbal reports in the form of conversations and relatively unstructured interviews can retain the spontaneity of improvised communication. Responses to fixed, written questions may also be useful; they can take the form of short essays or be spoken and later transcribed. Once entered for computer analysis, verbal reports may be examined in a variety of ways.

When respondents formulate verbal reports, they are constructing narratives about their experience. It appears that even complex experiences and sequences of experiences can be captured coherently in this way. Bruner, for example, has been studying a topic that is literally as large as life itself by asking people to tell the stories of their lives, constrained by a thirty-minute time limit. His research is actually less about lives as such than about how people view, construe, and even guide their lives. He observes, "I believe that the ways of telling and the ways of conceptualizing that go with them become so habitual that they finally become recipes for structuring experience itself, for laying down roots into memory, for not only guiding the life narrative up to the present but directing it into the future" (1987, p. 31).

A narrative study of classroom experience is likewise less about what actually occurs than about how the actors perceive events and relationships. For example, in one study we asked students to describe classroom incidents they found satisfying and others they found dissatisfying. When these accounts were examined, there seemed to be few differences between the two categories and little similarity within them, until particular features of the course were examined. Then it became clear that satisfying incidents tended to occur in courses where there was consistency in such features as teaching method, class size, and instructional objectives. (A simple example of consistency would be using the lecture method in a large class where the teacher's goal is information transmission.) In classes where unsatisfactory incidents occurred, consistency was less likely (Menges & Kulieke, 1984). A study not incorporating narratives would probably have missed these relationships, since they were not part of the framework from which the study was originally designed.

The interpretive approach can employ a variety of techniques. Students may be asked to construct problems or to solve them (intellectual tasks), or they may be presented with tasks calling for communication or interaction with others (social tasks). The resulting performance records take narrative form: commentaries about events as the events unfold or as stimulated by a recording. Alternatively, the narrative may be in response to structured but ambiguous stimuli such as drawings and photographs used in thematic apperception or Rorschach tests.

At other times, investigators themselves may stimulate events of interest deliberately and openly. For example, it is of interest to know how people go about increasing the quality and quantity of student contributions to class discussions. To study that problem, the researcher would work with other teachers and students who have similar goals. The investigator would document thoughts and behaviors of each of them, including his or her own, note circumstances facilitating or inhibiting change, and ascertain consequences. For these studies, the researcher participates in events that are intended to induce change. Such research is an important counter to approaches where investigators keep their distance, merely documenting the status quo.

When there is reason for researchers to think that verbal reports are less than complete or candid or when they desire more extensive contextual information, they should add data from other sources. Detailed descriptions of behavior and of the context in which behavior occurs are appropriate for this purpose. The family of research methods known as participant observation is consistent with the interpretive approach. Erickson characterizes these methods as most interested in "human meaning in social life and in its elucidation and exposition by the researcher" (1986, 119).

Regardless of labels used, the guiding principle is that method be regarded as the servant of the question being asked. It is no more correct to say that all inquiry is fully served by an interpretive approach than it is to say that all inquiry is fully served by positivist science. Greater tolerance of diversity makes it more likely that a research approach is properly matched with the issue under study.

In conclusion, it remains to be seen how productive these research questions and methods will be in reducing redundancy and increasing relevance. (Of course, that depends in part on the paradigms governing our definitions of "productive.") Put broadly, our task is to shape research so that it is not redundant with the scholarship that has gone before and so that it provides insights relevant to postsecondary education in the years ahead.

References

Ashworth, Peter D., Amedeo Giorgi, and Andre J. J. de Koning, eds. *Qualitative Research in Psychology*. Pittsburgh: Duquesne University Press, 1986.

Berelson, Bernard, and Gary A. Steiner. *Human Behavior: An Inventory of Scientific Findings*. New York: Harcourt, Brace and World, 1964.

Coe, George A. "Byproducts of the College Classroom." In *Am I Getting an Education?* edited by G. A. Coe and Associate, 5–13. Garden City, NY: Doubleday, Doran, 1929.

Douglass, H. R. *Controlled Experimentation in the Study of Methods of College Teaching*. University of Oregon Education Series, 1929, 1, (1929): 265–316.

Erickson, Frederick. "Qualitative Methods in Research on Teaching." In *Handbook of Research on Teaching*, edited by M. C. Wittrock, 119–61. 3rd ed. New York: Macmillan, 1986.

Feldman, Kenneth A. "Course Characteristics and College Students Ratings of their Teachers: What we Know and What we Don't." *Research in Higher Education* 9 (1978): 199–242.

Finkel, Donald L., and Stephen G. Monk. "Teachers and Learning Groups: Dissolution of the Atlas Complex." *New Directions for Teaching and Learning No. 14* (1983): 83–97.

Goldberg, Lewis R. "Student Personality Characteristics and Optimal College Learning Conditions: An Extensive Search for Trait-by-Treatment Interaction Effects."*Instructional Science 1* (1972): 153–210.

Jones, Harold E. "Experimental Studies of College Teaching: The Effect of Examinations on Permanence of Learning." *Archives of Psychology* No. 68, 10 (1923): 5–70.

Klapper, Paul, ed. *College Teaching: Studies in Methods of Teaching in the College*. Yonkers-on-Hudson, NY: World Book Company, 1920.

Marsh, Herbert W. "Students' Evaluations of University Teaching: Dimensionality, Reliability, Validity, Potential Biases, and Utility." *Journal of Educational Psychology 76* (1984): 707–54.

Menges, Robert J., and Marilynn J. Kulieke. "Satisfaction and Dissatisfaction in the College Classroom." *Higher Education* 13 (1984): 255–64.

Neugarten, Bernice L. "Interpretive Social Science and Research on Aging." In *Gender and the Life Course*, edited by S. Rossi, 291–300. Chicago: Aldine, 1985.

Payne, Fernandus, and Evelyn W. Spieth. *An Open Letter to College Teachers*. Bloomington, Ind.: Principia Press, 1935.

Rabinow, Paul, and William M. Sullivan, eds. *Interpretive Social Science: A Reader*. Berkeley: University of California Press, 1979.

Reason, Peter, and John Rowan, eds. *Human Inquiry: A Sourcebook of New Paradigm Research*. New York: Wiley, 1981.

Richards, John P., and Brent D. Slife. "Interaction of Dogmatism and Rhetorical Structure in Text Recall." *American Educational Research Journal* 24 (1987): 635–41.

Sarbin, Theodore R., ed. *Narrative Psychology: The Storied Nature of Human Conduct*. New York: Praeger, 1986.

von Eckartsberg, Rolf. *Life-world Experience: Existential-Phenomenological Research Approaches in Psychology*. Washington, D.C.: University Press of America, 1986.

Wilson, Tom C. *Pedagogical Justice and Student Evaluation of Teaching Forms: A Critical Perspective*. Paper presented at the American Educational Research Association, Washington, D.C., 1987.

CHAPTER 20

SETTING THE CONTEXT:
PSYCHOLOGICAL THEORIES OF LEARNING

FRANCES K. STAGE

> Learning theories can provide guidance to student affairs professionals as they create a context for
> learning for college students on their own campuses.

Recently, the student affairs profession has renewed efforts to demonstrate its many contributions
to undergraduate education. (Chickering & Gamson, 1987; Chickering & Reisser, 1993; Kuh, Schuh,
Whitt, & Associates, 1991; Schroeder, 1993; Schroeder & Mable, 1994). *The Student Learning Imperative (SLI)* (American College Personnel Association [ACPA], 1994) in particular has focused increased
attention on the important role student affairs educators play in enhancing student learning and educational attainment. As student affairs seeks to emphasize its own role in student learning and to
underscore collaboration with other campus units, knowledge of psychological theories of learning
is both necessary and useful.

Although this focus on connections between learning and student affairs is not new (see Banning, 1989; Blimling & Schuh, 1981; Brown, 1968, 1989; DeCoster, 1968; Greenleaf, Forsythe, Godfrey, Hudson, & Thompson, 1967; Schroeder, 1973, 1988; Schroeder & Belmonte, 1979), it is perhaps
more urgent given the current higher education climate. Resources that seemed tight through the
1980s became almost non-existent in the 1990s. Often the burden of cuts to colleges and universities
was shifted from academic units to student affairs and other departments considered supportive
of, but not central to, the academic mission. Additionally, legislators', trustees', parents', and students' demands for accountability put pressure on all aspects of college life. Today, as never before,
student affairs and academic units must demonstrate their necessity and centrality to undergraduate education and their unique contributions to student learning.

As the *SLI* describes the importance of student affairs to the learning process of college students, it makes distinctions between *student learning* and *personal development*. The distinction is an
important one because much of our theory about college students focuses on the latter and not the
former. The *SLI* describes student affairs' relationship to learning in ways that can be enhanced by
knowledge of psychological learning theories as well.

Usefulness of Theory

Parker (1977) discussed the use of theories by professionals and described informal theories as "the
body of common knowledge that allows us to make implicit connections among the events and

---

"Setting the Context: Psychological Theories of Learning." Reprinted from *Journal of College Student Development* 32, no. 2
(1996), by permission of the American College Personnel Association.

persons in our environment and upon which we act in everyday life" (p. 420). Several reasons exist for incorporating formal psychological theory into our work with college students. First, theory provides a framework with which to connect our experiences and observations about college students. In other words, theory can help us "ground" our practice and our decision making. Second, through language, theory allows us to communicate with others and connect our own experiences with others' experiences. Such "linking" enables us to take advantage of the wide-ranging works of other theorists and researchers. For example, by reading articles in the *Journal of College Student Development* (as well as by publishing our own articles in this and other journals) and by attending and facilitating sessions at professional conferences, we can link our limited knowledge and experiences with those of others who share similar goals. Additionally, theory guides our "experiments" (whether based on research or on daily practice) so that we can observe whether our theories work and, if so, how well they work.

Yet another compelling reason exists for incorporating psychological learning theories in our efforts to enhance student learning. We work in an academic milieu where information is currency. Theory provides us with the language and the currency of our colleagues to talk about rationales for approaches taken, decisions made, and programs designed and managed. Using theory to improve our practice enables us to make an intellectual connection that helps others on campus—administrators, academics, and graduate students understand us and the importance of our relationships to student learning.

Using psychological theories should seem familiar to many student affairs professionals. For over 3 decades, interest in theories of college student development has steadily increased (Stage, 1991). Student development theories are most familiar to student affairs professionals. These theories, which largely focus on personal development, enable educators to describe observed differences between students and often can be the basis for creating programs and activities that facilitate development. For the most part, these theories focus on how students reason when faced with decisions. For example, an academic advisor can more readily recognize a dualistic student's desire to be given firm advice and provide the student with a more limited set of choices for an elective, based on the advisor's knowledge of that students' strengths and previous selections (Perry, 1981). A faculty advisor of a judicial board can listen to a student judge's struggles with relativism and then ask the student to consider whose rights are violated when some people are given complete freedom of expression (Kitchener & King, 1990).

Other theorists have focused on tasks faced by college students (Chickering, 1969; Heath, 1968) and on characteristics of learners within their environments (Holland, 1985; Myers, 1980). Student affairs professionals have found these theories useful when working with college students who have communication or lifestyle differences that cause roommate problems. Still other theorists have talked about "Theories of Involvement " and have documented important relationships between involvement and learning (Astin, 1984; Black, 1985; Kuh et al, 1991; Pace, 1979, 1990.)

Although these theories help us understand much about students' behaviors on campus and students' personal development, they do not completely contribute to our understanding of the ways in which students learn. Psychological theories of learning can assist educators as they work within the framework provided by *SLI* to enhance learning on college campuses.

Psychological Theories of Learning

In the first part of this century, psychological theorists took a behavioristic view of humans and their interactions with the world around them. The most well-known of these theorists were J. B. Watson (1924) and B. F. Skinner (1953, 1968). Behaviorists believed the goal of psychology was to predict and control behavior. As a result, learning was often studied within carefully controlled experimental settings, often far removed from the complex realities of actual learning. Behavioristic theorists still influence the ways in which students are taught today.

In recent decades however, psychological theorists have taken a cognitive approach to learning (Ausubel, 1963; Bruner, Goodnow, & Austin, 1956; Neisser, 1967). With these cognitive approaches to understanding learning, researchers have begun to recognize that the learning context is more important than once thought. Often, much of the learning for college students occurs embedded within a classroom setting. Translation of that learning into job related activities and decision making is often challenging (Glover, Ronning, & Bruning, 1990). Psychologists have learned that "knowledge in human memory seems to be 'stored' in contextual fashion" (Glover, Ronning, & Bruning, 1990, p. 23). Because no classroom exercise or set of exercises (as they currently exist) can fully represent the complexity of job situations, other experiences can contribute much to the learning process. For example, leadership opportunities, service learning experiences, judicial activities, and tutoring, rendered within the framework of students affairs, can provide contexts within which students can interpret their classroom learning experiences.

As student affairs professionals, we have the educational role of providing contexts within which student learning takes place. As *context setters*, student affairs professionals, working with faculty, students, and others, can help provide experiences that give structure and meaning to classroom learning for college students.

One theory often used to enhance classroom learning readers is Kolb's (1981) typology of four learning styles. The Kolb types—converger, diverger, assimilator, and accommodator—have been documented among college students as well as faculty (Rothschadl & Russell, 1992; Russell & Rothschadl, 1991). Most faculty tend to be assimilators who tend to teach and require work that favors students who are also assimilators (Stage & Manning, 1992). The theory has been used to encourage faculty to broaden their scope of teaching and to incorporate the strengths of a wider range of students (Rothschadl & Russell, 1992; Russell & Rothschadl, 1991; Stage & Manning, 1992).

In addition to Kolb's 1981 approach, several cognitive psychological theories hold particular relevance for student affairs professionals. Because many theories of learning exist, only a few relevant ones are included in this review. As with student development theories, overlap and similarities exist that should be comforting to us as various scholars attempt to describe the phenomenon of human learning. Those similarities help us see connections between one theory and the next, and highlight the most important aspects of human learning. Similarities enable us to carry our knowledge of theories in general to our practice in particular (Stage, 1991).

For example, a common theme repeated below is the importance of the individual's view of self as learner. After seeing the importance that a variety of scholars attribute to this concept, we can carry this knowledge back to our work with students by striving to create positive learning experiences for all students across the range of abilities on our campuses. Also, we are reminded of the importance cognitive development theorists place on creating challenges that are not overwhelming for students. After discussing these theories, I will summarize the ways that the theories (as well as their overlapping principles) can be useful to readers seeking to implement the *SLI*. Together they enable us to set the context for learning on college campuses.

Motivation Theories

Today, motivational theories are widely recognized as critical in influencing behavior and learning (McKeachie, Pintrich, Lin, Smith, & Sharma, 1990). The *SLI* calls on educators to "create conditions that motivate and inspire students to devote time and energy to educationally-purposeful activities, both in and outside the classroom" (ACPA, 1994, p. 1). Regularly in our lives we hear about motivation of athletic teams for the big game, discuss the seeming lack of motivation of a student of high ability who fails to achieve in classes, and lament our own lack of motivation to get up early and exercise. Despite the pervasive references to the importance of motivation in our lives, one rarely hears a discussion about motivating college students to learn. In fact, many researchers assume that merely by enrolling in college, a student has demonstrated that motivation. From our own work with college students we know differently.

Motivation was first described in 1913 by Thorndike: "Learning . . . is strengthened when it is followed by a satisfying state of affairs—satisfying of course, to the learner" (quoted in Sprinthall, Sprinthall, & Oja, 1993, p. 527). In attempts to describe these influences Maslow (1954) established a hierarchy of needs that motivate humans. According to Maslow's theory, needs at one level must be somewhat satisfied before an individual is motivated to satisfy higher level needs. The first levels, *physiological needs* (food, drink, sex, and shelter) and *safety needs* (security, order, protection, and family stability) are often taken for granted but can sometimes interfere with college students' pursuit of higher level needs. The next two, *love needs* (affection, group affiliation, and personal acceptance) and *esteem needs* (self-respect, prestige, reputation, and social status) are likely to be central to college students' lives. Additionally, according to Maslow, these two types of needs must be somewhat satisfied before an individual begins to focus on *self-actualization needs* (self-fulfillment and achievement of lifetime personal goals).

McKeachie, Pintrich, Lin, Smith, and Sharma (1990), in a review of theories of teaching and learning took an expectation approach to motivation. With this approach they described a complex web of relationships among student goals, perceived value of and student efficacy at learning tasks, test anxiety, and expected outcomes; all are related to student motivation. Chickering and Gamson's (1987) principles for undergraduate education, for example, remind us that "good practice communicates high expectations" (p. 3). Expecting more from all students, regardless of ability level, can provide the motivation for a given student to succeed.

Recently motivational theorists have focused on the role that intrinsic goals play in the learning and development process. College students who develop their own internal goals for learning, aside from any official or familial coercion, are more likely to achieve success, whether inside or outside the classroom. Also, student affairs efforts that focus on learning skills and test anxiety and that seek to help students match their learning experiences with their personal goals are obvious ways that motivation might be positively influenced.

Perceived Self-efficacy

Bandura (1986, 1993, 1994, in press) described the importance of perceived self-efficacy in learning. He defined self-efficacy as individuals' "beliefs about their capabilities to produce designated levels of performance that exercise influence over events that affect their lives" (Bandura, 1994, p. 71). Perceptions of self-efficacy are related to motivation in that they can enhance or decrease motivation. Bandura and his colleagues demonstrated that both the beliefs of students and the collective beliefs of teachers (in their own instructional efficacy) contributed significantly to students' levels of academic achievement in school settings (Bandura, 1993).

For the college student, prior conceptions of ability (often based on experiences in previous educational settings), social comparisons (within classes, living environments, and extracurricular contexts), framing of feedback (achieved progress or shortfalls), and perceived controllability (locus of control) all combine for the development of self-efficacy. Bandura's (1993) work on self-efficacy forms an important basis for consideration of learning on the college campus. The campus community can provide the context within which a student who does not excel in the classroom discovers skills and capacities that are useful and valued in the real life arena. As students' beliefs about themselves become increasingly positive, their motivation to perform and, ultimately, performance are enhanced. With success, beliefs about self-efficacy become even more positive, the student is more motivated, and performance proceeds in a continual reciprocal relationship.

For students, self-efficacy beliefs shape choices of activities and environments, and thereby shape their lives. Choices of educational opportunities, social networks, and careers are influenced by students' perceived self-efficacy. In focusing specifically on the transition from adolescence to adulthood, Bandura (in press) describes the particular importance of structured transitions such as those provided within the context of colleges and universities.

Self-efficacy is linked to other behaviors through motivation, which, in turn, is influenced by expectations regarding outcomes of behavior and the value of those outcomes. Explicit challenging goals enhance and sustain motivation. People set challenging goals for themselves and thereby create a state of disequilibrium, which they then reduce by accomplishing the goals. College students constantly set goals, fail or succeed, readjust the goals, and begin the cycle again in a dynamic and continual process of self regulation, adjustment, and reevaluation. Affective processes form an emotional component of self-efficacy. Students' beliefs in their own capabilities affect the amount of stress and depression they experience in difficult situations, either academic or social. This can be seen, for example, when disturbing thought patterns lead to test anxiety and interfere with a student's ability to perform.

Self-efficacy is highly domain specific (Pressley & McCormick, 1995). For example, a college student might have high self-efficacy with respect to math and science, but low self-efficacy with regard to writing or leadership skills. Beliefs about personal efficacy play a key role in an individual's choice of career and major. They can also be restrictive. For example, a college student might choose a major because it does not have a mathematics requirement. They can likewise be enabling for a student who has positive beliefs about his or her own ability to learn difficult material (Bandura, in press). As students move through college and into adulthood, knowledge of self-efficacy is likely to crystallize. Tasks that are challenging to the learner (and are met successfully) can increase self-efficacy in ways that promote future attempts at challenging tasks. Conversely, tasks that are too challenging can erode an individual's sense of efficacy and thwart ambition.

Beliefs about efficacy are developed through four main sources of influence: mastery experiences, vicarious experiences, social persuasion, and somatic and emotional states (Bandura, 1994). In various campus contexts students can engage successfully in activities to experience mastery, watch others like themselves succeed and thus experience success vicariously, and be persuaded by their peers to participate in challenging activities, thereby developing positive, less stressful reactions to challenges.

The *SLI* encourages us to capitalize on students' beliefs in their self-efficacy by developing learning activities both related to and outside of regular college classroom activities. Part of our role in student affairs is to help students find contexts in which they can develop their self-efficacy by capitalizing on their diverse talents and ways of learning (Chickering & Gamson, 1987).

Attribution Theory

Attributions can be described as the reasons students give for their success (or failure) at various tasks. These attributions might include skill, luck, persistence, bad timing, illness, fatigue, native intelligence, and so on. Weiner (1980) categorized these attributions on dimensions according to *locus* (internal or external), *stability*, and *controllability*. Depending on the combination of attribution categories, future performance may be enhanced or thwarted.

The relationship of attribution to success is neither simple nor linear. For example, students who perform well and believe their performance to be related to skill or intelligence would expect to perform well in the future. On the other hand, students who perform well and believe their good performance to be related to luck and extra effort, might not have such high expectations for future performances (unless the same level of effort is expended, accompanied by the same degree of luck).

Not quite conversely however, students who perform poorly and believe their performance to be related to skill or intelligence would expect to perform poorly in the future. Again, those who perform poorly and believe their performance to be related to bad luck or lack of effort might expect to perform better in the future if they adjust their effort and have better luck. Not surprisingly, these attributions for success or failure affect students' motivation to invest effort in a similar task in the future (Pressley & McCormick, 1995).

Student affairs efforts that promote the importance and development of learning skills can contribute to positive attributions of success and failure. Programs that enable students to develop knowledge of their learning strengths and to improve weaknesses their can aid students in their learning efforts. As student affairs professionals "collaborate with other institutional agents and agencies to promote student learning and personal development" (ACPA, 1994, p. 1), they communicate to other constituents the importance of respecting "diverse talents and ways of learning" (Chickering & Gamson, 1987, p. 3). The value of skills and experiences, particularly those outside the classroom arena, can contribute to students' positive development and learning in the classroom.

Constructivist Theories of Learning

Constructivist theories of learning are most popular in elementary and secondary mathematics and science classrooms. Yet the principles of constructivist learning are logical and easily extend to other contexts. Constructivists emphasize the importance of learning within the context of reality. At the extreme, a constructivist believes that, given sufficient equipment and time, and minimal guidance in a laboratory, a student would discover all he or she needed to know about, for example, biology.

In a modification of constructivist theory, Driver, Asoko, Leach, Moritmer, and Scott (1994) described much learning and particularly mathematics and science as "social constructivism". In conjunction with discovery, the learner is "initiated into scientific ways of knowing" (p. 6). As the young scientist makes 'discoveries' the teacher helps the student place his or her discoveries within the framework of science as described by current scientists. "The objects of science are not the phenomena of nature, but the constructs that are advanced by the scientific community to interpret nature." (p. 5). These constructs (e.g., rates of chemical reactions, atoms, genes and chromosomes) are unlikely to be discovered by individuals through observation. Science educators then help their learners mediate scientific knowledge and make personal sense of the ways in which knowledge claims are generated and validated rather than to organize their own individual sense-makings about the natural world (Driver et al., 1994). Learning and understanding then occur when "individuals engage socially in talk and activity about shared problems or tasks" (p. 7). The teacher serves as mediator and guide.

Many campus learning situations rely on a constructivist approach to learning. As examples, student government and Greek leadership positions, residence hall and educational organizations, and intramural athletic activities often provide "real life" experiences for students, particularly when the activities are supported by an advisor who provides intellectual links between the activities and interpretation in an academic context.

Many campuses have established service-learning programs that embrace many of the tenets of social constructivism. These approaches move beyond traditional internships, volunteerism, and community service efforts. Within these programs guidance and mentoring are provided to help students to make intellectual links with their practical learning. Ideally, such links would be related to the students' academic coursework (Muller & Stage, 1995). This "guided learning" is the hallmark of service learning and does not take for granted that learning occurs merely because a student is engaged in the activity. Rather, service learning provides the context and suggests the links as students work toward incorporation of varied experiences into classroom learning.

For example, on an individual basis, a student leader learning to manage an organization might experiment with ways of working with various student groups. Over the course of several months or a year even a very gifted student leader might not be able to "discover" satisfactory patterns for working with everyone. Using a social constructivist approach, an advisor might guide the student's discoveries by introducing basic readings in management theory and personal communication styles. Alternatively, the student might have already read relevant leadership materials in business and psychology classes, and the discovery process could be facilitated by that knowledge. The advisor might discuss those materials with the student and help analyze their usefulness or relevance. The hallmark of social constructivist learning is a focus on the context or the reality of day to day life, not in place of other types of learning, but in close connection with them.

Using Theory to Set The Context

Heath and McLaughlin (1994) argued that a typically academic focus on knowledge ignores learning that takes place in everyday life. Speaking to precollege educators, they focused on the curricula of youth organizations—Boy Scouts and Girl Scouts, grassroots athletic organizations, and apprenticeship experiences—as they relate to learning. Heath and McLaughlin proposed that such experiences might provide the bases for the "authentic" experiences and evaluations being sought in elementary and secondary education as described by Delandshere and Petrosky (1994).

The arguement is not unfamiliar. Many of us have engaged in campus discussions about the value of learning in the student affairs context, as well as possible links to classroom learning. A few have attempted to assess such learning (Mentkowski & Doherty, 1984). Theories of learning could help us to extend those discussions. And following Heath and McLaughlin's advice, we might make efforts to evaluate such learning experiences as evidence of the "authenticity" of college students' learning.

Consider the following examples. A service learning program that links experience to classroom based theories of learning could be evaluated by comparing the related class outcomes for students who participated in the service activities with the outcomes for students who did not (controlling for incoming abilities). For student leaders, leadership abilities might be evaluated and then compared to their abilities after linking their experiences with theories of group behavior and leadership.

Students who are struggling with grades and are on academic probation might be encouraged to take a lighter course load, take a learning skills development course, and engage in a limited way in activities and experiences congruent with past successes. A former high school swimmer might be given internship credits for managing the swimming team; a business major might be encouraged to work as an intern for 10 hours a week with a city program for start-up businesses; and a natural resource major might work with physical plant operations on campus. These students could gain reinforcement for expansion of their already strong skills, acquire knowledge to develop their self-efficacy, and build motivation to work toward academic goals. In addition, they could be required to work on study skills that might enhance their chances of succeeding.

Theories of learning provide us with cues for linking student affairs to learning both inside and outside the classroom. As advisors, leaders, and guides, we establish contexts within which the learning of the classroom can crystallize. "The process of learning is located at the interface of people's biography and the sociocultural milieu in which they live" (Jarvis, 1992, p. 17). College students have experienced much of their biographies in the classroom. The milieu in which they live is a colorful combination of social, athletic, academic, and artistic events, all of which often provide meaning for their classroom learning.

Other Theories

The theories I have described here are but a sampling of the wealth of psychology based knowledge about learning. Other theories and models could be helpful as well. For example, Gardner and Hatch (1989) provided a description and summary of research and practice based on the theory of multiple intelligences, in which intelligence is seen as moving beyond the limited notion that all intelligence can be described through verbal and mathematical measures. As another relevant example, Friere's (1970, 1985)

conscientization theory, focused on social dimensions of learning. Friere described learning as an active process and describes learning as movement from one level of consciousness to another, ultimately resulting in a deepening awareness of sociocultural reality (Muller & Stage, 1995). Similarly, Gamson's (1994) description of collaborative learning and Smith's (1991) descriptions of learning communities can provide important guidance to those who seek to learn ways of implementing some of the theoretical principles I have discussed here. Finally, Fincher (1994) and Stage and Muller (1995) described several additional theories and research on learning specifically related to the college classroom.

Conclusion

As we take the *SLI* to our own campuses, I suggest that we direct our attention squarely on theories of learning. By focusing on theories related to learning we can more fully describe our own efforts as well as design new efforts that complement and support academic programs on our campuses. More importantly, we can continue to do what we do best—provide contexts that maximize opportunities for student learning.

References

American College Personnel Association (ACPA) (1994). *The student learning imperative: Implications for student affairs*. Washington, DC: Author.

Astin, A. (1984). Student involvement: A developmental theory for higher education. *Journal of College Student Development, 25*, 297–308.

Ausubel, D. P. (1963). *The psychology of meaningful verbal learning*. New York: Grune & Stratton.

Bandura, A. (1986). *Social foundations of thought and action: A social cognitive theory*. Englewood Cliffs, NJ: Prentice-Hall.

Bandura, A. (1993). Perceived self-efficacy in cognitive development and functioning. *Educational Psychologist, 28*, 117–148.

Bandura, A. (1994). Self-efficacy. In V. S. Ramachaudran (Ed.), *Encyclopedia of Human Behavior* (Vol. 4, pp. 71–81). New York: Academic Press.

Bandura, A. (in press). *Self-efficacy: The exercise of control*. New York: Freeman.

Banning, J. H. (1989). Creating a climate for successful student development: The campus ecology model. In U. Delworth, G. Hanson, & Associates (Eds.), *Student services: A handbook for the profession* (2nd ed.) San Francisco: Jossey-Bass.

Blake, J. H. (1985). Approaching minority students as assets. *Academe, 71*(6), 19–21.

Blimling, G. S., & Schuh, J. H. (1981). *Increasing the Educational Role of Residence Halls.* (New Directions for Student Services, No. 13) San Francisco: Jossey-Bass.

Bruner, J. S., Goodnow, J. J., & Austin, G. A. (1956). *A study of thinking.* New York: Wiley.

Brown, R. (1968). Manipulation of the environmental press in a college residence hall. *Personnel and Guidance Journal, 46,* 555–560.

Brown, R. (1989). Fostering intellectual and personal growth: The student development role. In U. Delworth, G. Hanson, & Associates, *Student services: A handbook for the profession,* (2nd ed.) San Francisco: Jossey-Bass.

Chickering, A. W. (1969). *Education and identity.* San Francisco: Jossey-Bass.

Chickering, A. W., & Gamson, Z. F. (1987). Seven good practices in undergraduate education. *AAHE Bulletin, 39*(7), 3–7.

Chickering, A. W., & Reisser, L. (1993). *Education and identity* (2nd Ed.) San Francisco: Jossey-Bass.

DeCoster, D. (1968). Effects of homogeneous housing assignments for high ability students. *Journal of College Student Personnel, 8,* 75–78.

Delandshere, G., & Petrosky, A. R. (1994). Capturing teachers' knowledge: Performance assessment: *Educational Researcher, 23*(5), 11–18.

Driver, R., Asoko, H., Leach, J., Mortimer, E., & Scott, P. (1994). Constructing scientific knowledge in the classroom. *Educational Researcher, 23*(7), 5–12.

Fincher, C. (1994). Learning theory and research. In K. A. Feldman & M. B. Paulsen (Eds.), *Teaching and learning in the college classroom* (ASHE Reader Series, pp. 47–74). Needham Heights, MA: Ginn.

Friere, P. (1970). *Pedagogy of the oppressed.* New York: Herder & Herder.

Friere, P. (1985). *An invitation to conscientization and deschooling: The politics of education.* South Hadley: Bergin & Garvey.

Gamson, Z. F. (1994). Collaborative learning comes of age. *Change, 26,* 44–49.

Gardner, H., & Hatch, T. (1989). Multiple intelligences go to school. *Educational Researcher, 18*(8), 4–9.

Glover, J. A. Ronning, R. A., & Bruning, R. H. (1990). *Cognitive psychology for teachers.* New York: Macmillan Publishing Company.

Greenleaf, E. A., Forsythe, M., Godfrey, H., Hudson, B., & Thompson, F. (1967). *Undergraduate students as members of the residence hall staff.* Bloomington, IN: National Association of Women Deans and Counselors.

Heath, D. H. (1968). *Growing up in college: Liberal education and authority.* San Francisco: Jossey-Bass.

Heath, S. B., & McLaughlin, M. W. (1994). Learning for anything everyday. *Journal of Curriculum Studies, 26,* 471–489.

Holland, J. L. (1985). *Making vocational choices.* Englewood Cliffs, NJ: Prentice-Hall.

Jarvis, P. (1992). *Paradoxes of learning: On becoming an individual in society.* San Francisco: Jossey-Bass.

Kitchener, K., & King, P. (1990). The reflective judgement model: Ten years of research. In M. Commons, C. Armon, L. Kohlberg, R. Richards, T. Grotzer, & J. Sinnott (Eds.), *Adult development: Models and methods in the study of adolescent and adult thought.* New York: Praeger.

Kolb, D. A. (1981). Learning styles and disciplinary differences. In A. W. Chickering & Associates (Eds.). *The modern American college* (pp. 232–255). San Francisco: Jossey-Bass.

Kuh, G., Schuh, J., Whitt, E., & Associates (1991). *Involving Colleges.* San Francisco: Jossey-Bass.

Maslow, A. H. (1954). *Motivation and personality.* New York: Harper & Row.

McKeachie, W. J., Pintrich, P. R., Lin, Y-G., Smith, D. A. F., & Sharma, R. (1990). *Teaching and learning in the college classroom: A review of the research literature* (2nd ed.). Ann Arbor, MI: Regents of the University of Michigan.

Mentkowski, M., & Doherty, A. (1984). Abilities that last a lifetime: Outcomes of the Alverno experience. *American Association for Higher Education Bulletin, 36,* 5–6, 11–14.

Muller, P., & Stage, F. K. (1995). Service-learning: Transforming volunteerism and community service to maximize student learning and personal development. (Chapter under review for American College Personnel Association Media).

Myers, I. (1980). *Gifts differing.* Palo Alto, CA: Consulting Psychologists Press.

Neisser, U. (1967). *Cognitive psychology.* New York: Appleton-Century-Crofts.

Pace, C. R. (1979). *Measuring outcomes of college: Fifty years of findings and recommendations for the future.* San Francisco: Jossey-Bass.

Pace, C. R. (1990). *The undergraduates: A report of their activities and progress in college in the 1980s.* Los Angeles: University of California, Center for the Study of Evaluation.

Parker (1977). On modelling reality. *Journal of College Student Personnel, 18,* 419–425.

Perry, W. (1981). Cognitive and ethical growth: The making of meaning. In A. Chickering & Associates (Eds.), *The modern American college* (pp. 76–116). San Francisco: Jossey-Bass.

Pressley, M., & Mcormick, C. B. (1995). *Advanced educational psychology for educators, researchers, and policymakers.* New York: HarperCollins.

Rothschadl, A. M., & Russell, R. V. (1992). Improving teaching effectiveness: Addressing modes of learning in the college classroom. *Schole: A Journal of Recreation Education and Leisure Studies, 7.*

Russell, R. V., & Rothschadl, A. M. (1991). Learning styles: Another view of the college classroom? *Schole: A Journal of Recreation Education and Leisure Studies, 6.*

Schroeder, C. C. (1973). Sex differences and growth toward self-actualization during the freshman year. *Psychological Reports, 32,* 416–418.

Schroeder, C. C. (1988). "Student affairs—academic affairs: Opportunities for bridging the gap." *ACPA Developments,* Fall.

Schroeder, C. C. (1993). New students—new learning styles. *Change, 25*(4), 21–26.

Schroeder, C. C., & Belmonte, A. (1979). The influence of residential environment on prepharmacy student achievement and satisfaction. *Journal of Pharmaceutical Education, 43,* 16–19.

Schroeder, C. C., & Mable, P. (1994). *Realizing the educational potential of residence halls.* New Directions for Higher and Adult Education. San Francisco: Jossey-Bass.

Skinner, B. F. (1953). *Science and human behavior.* New York: Macmillan.

Skinner, B. F. (1968). *The technology of teaching.* New York: Appleton-Century-Crofts.

Smith, B. L. (1991). Taking structure seriously: The learning community model. *Liberal Education, 77*(2), 42–48.

Sprinthall, N. A., Sprinthall, R. C., & Oja, S. N. (1993). *Educational psychology: A developmental approach* (6th ed.). New York: McGraw-Hill.

Stage, F. K. (1991). Common elements of theory: A framework for college student development. *Journal of College Student Development, 32,* 56–61.

Stage, F. K., & Manning, K. (1992). *Enhancing the multicultural campus environment: A cultural brokering approach* (New Directions for Student Services No. 60) San Francisco: Jossey-Bass.

Stage, F. K., & Muller, P. M. (1995). Theories of learning for college students. (Chapter under review for American College Personnel Association Media).

Watson, J. B. (1924). *Behaviorism.* New York: Norton.

Weiner, B. (1980). *Human Motivation.* New York: Holt, Rinehart, & Winston.

CHAPTER 21

UNDERSTANDING AND INVESTIGATING FEMALE FRIENDSHIP'S EDUCATIVE VALUE

ANA M. MARTÍNEZ ALEMÁN

Introduction: A Heuristic Hunch

In the small midwestern coeducational college where I extol the virtues and value of feminist research and pedagogy, I am struck by how the talk of young women students with each other marks the conversational buzz in the hallways between class sessions. Conversational quizzing and animated exchanges are resonant in these corridors. With full-bodied richness, this female friendship talk carries tales of literary theory, of chemistry labs and global economic predicaments. Fashioned by spirited female voices, mathematical queries move sharply and confidently from doorway to doorway, social movements theorizing is spun with poised intellectual ease. Consciously, I listen and try to gauge the energetic yet relaxed and daring manner with which these young women collegians venture into the realm of scholarly speech and commentary with one another. I marvel at the fact that it is their female voices, and not those of their male collegiate class mates, which configure the discourse seemingly spilled over from the classroom. As I wait for my class to commence structurally disconnected from this instructional thoroughfare, I smile and silently celebrate this feminist educational coup. *These* are Wollstonecraft's professional women! *These* are Woolf's feminine intelligentsia! *These* are Sor Juana's illuminati! Yet, their public articulation of thinking, of knowing, of higher learning, the sound of female voices publicly raising objections, positing alternative hypotheses, and soliciting critique, disturbs me.

What do I make of the nagging suspicion that once these young women enter the college classroom—even my feminist classroom, warm and not "chilly"—their voices will find hiatus in quiet listening and reflection, in conversational reticence and insecurity? Why don't they speak in class as they have spoken to each other, as I have heard them speak in stairwells and study nooks? How does the assertive, suggestive, inquiring, probing, and nurturing female friendship talk of the corridor become the timid, pleasing, and reluctant chat of the classroom? Or does it? Is that talk simply relegated to the corridors, to the walkways, to the dormitories and lunch tables where female friendship is moderated? Why is the talk of college female friends left outside our classroom doors, even outside our feminist classrooms? There's something to this talk, in this talk for women's intellectual development, I tell myself. I have a hunch that these friendships are educationally powerful relationships for undergraduate women.

"Understanding and Investigating Female Friendship's Educative Value." Reprinted from *Journal of Higher Education* 68, no. 2 (1997), Ohio State University Press.

Review of the Literature

Feminist Research

Educators and social science researchers have explored a variety of issues affecting women in American colleges and universities and have argued that in order to effectively educate "the majority," our institutions of higher education must understand "the culture of women" (Shavlik & Touchton, 1992), p. 47). Feminist researchers have reasoned that in order for women students to be taken seriously in our classrooms, we must recognize "the structure of the classroom interaction as a major reason [why] many women find the classroom inhospitable" (Kramarae & Treichler, 1990, p. 42), and that any deviance from the male norms of classroom participation could lead faculty to perceive young women students as uninvested and thus, pedagogically unimportant (Hall, 1985). Perhaps more to the point, researchers have acknowledged that it is higher education's "obligation" to provide women students with "a sense of autonomy and self-worth (Astin & Kent, 1983, p. 309), an obligation, which if met, would certainly resolve many of our chilly classroom difficulties.

Complex, dynamic, and variable, the "culture of women" that Shavlik and Touchton address is, in my mind, not a spontaneous occurrence nor a biologically essential phenomenon. Rather, it is a series of women's integrated patterns of social and intellectual behaviors in a particular educational setting. In the case of college women, this "culture," or perhaps more accurately, "cultures," is often about the patterns of behaviors in which women engage in institutions traditionally hostile to them. Women's presence in higher education, and in particular, their presence alongside men, has been about the development of their cultures in an enterprise specifically designed for men, not one for and about women.

Women's marginalization in the intellectual worlds of certain classes and races of men in the United States has been about their gendered positions within patriarchal systems. As Florence Howe reminds us in her 1978 essay, "Myths of Coeducation," postsecondary coeducation is the "education of women with men;" it is not the education of genderless students. It is, as Howe so astutely notes, about the "maleness of education," about women laying claim to male privilege (p. 208). Because "institutionalized educational settings are a major site where women's subordination is reaffirmed and the ideology of women's social place is reproduced" (Lewis, 1993, p. 146), the "culture of women" in coeducational colleges can thus be viewed as collections of gendered behaviors which play out in an oppositional environment.

In the last twenty years, researchers have investigated the legacy of "maleness" in our postsecondary classrooms in a variety of different ways. According to Williams's (1990) review of the research literature on postsecondary classroom climate for women, "many studies have found that women students do not participate as much as men students in the classroom" and that research has not "investigated what contributes to this lack of participation by females" (p. 40). Hall and Sandler (1983) asserted that the coeducational college classroom climate could discourage women from participating in class discussions and from engaging in traditional classroom argumentation, a phenomenon disturbingly reminiscent of "female inhibition" behavior studies (Megargee, 1969; Cronin, 1980). In these studies of adolescence, researchers describe girls lowering their performance levels in order to avoid defeating males. Other researchers have concluded that many women find classroom conditions detrimental to their participation (Brooks, 1982; Banks, 1988; Lewis, 1993; Guinier, Fine, & Balin, 1994; Fassinger, 1995), underscoring Hall's and Sandler's "chilly climate" appraisal. Though some researchers have argued that college students' assessment of classroom climate varies fundamentally not by sex but by class year (Heller, Puff, & Mills, 1985), the recent work by Kramarae and Treichler (1990), Guinier, Fine, and Balin (1994), and Fassinger (1995) suggests that men and women do differ in their assessment of classroom behavior and conversation and that the conditions under which they feel comfortable talking in class has much to do with the same problematic "chilly" climate conditions suggested by Hall and Sandler (1983). Taunya Lovell Banks's 1988 study of gender bias in the coeducational law school classroom, for example, suggested that women's classroom silence has much to do with their position as "outsiders" in legal education and about their perception that their views carry no weight and their questions lack merit.

This "chilly climate" for women in coeducational college classrooms has led some researchers to examine particular aspects of the structure of college classroom climate and their effects on women's learning. Feminist scholars such as Magda Lewis have considered and examined pedagogy and women's classroom silence. In *Without a Word: Teaching Beyond Women's Silence* (1993), Lewis claims that women's classroom silence has been "framed within an ideology of deficiency" (p. 3) and challenges the idea that it is "an example of women's lack" (p. 41). Instead, writes Lewis, women's classroom silence is a political act, especially when we understand the relationship between public speaking and power: "That language, discourse, speaking, and writing are not neutral but political acts becomes clear when we realize that who "speaks" and by what authority their "speaking" is governed cannot be disassociated from these relations of power that mark the social, political, economic structures within which individuals live their daily lives" (p. 114). Thus, studies whose findings suggest that women are less verbally active than men and readily yield to men's opinions may, in fact, be gender "identifying behaviors" in the classroom spilled over from society (Lockheed & Hall, 1976). These patterns of coeducational behavior appear to begin in early schooling when boys and girls learn what is stereotypically inappropriate for their sex (Stein & Smithells, 1969) and continue into adulthood. Women in law school, for example, understand that "becoming gentlemen," the mark of a skillful legal mind, often requires behavior antithetical to their socialization as females (Guinier, Fine, & Balin, 1994).

Feminist scholars have suggested that "chosen, negotiated, achieved, not simply given" connections between women (Martin, 1988, p. 96) have taken many forms throughout space and time but, more importantly, have served many educative purposes. In nineteenth- and twentieth-century North America, for example, quilting groups, settlement houses, women's clubs, and consciousness raising groups have been places where women gathered in the absence of men in order to make connections with those with whom experiences and meanings were shared. Within these and other networks of female friendships, many of the constraints and obstacles to self-expression, learning, and female relatedness that existed in

women's lives were dissolved. Many women's clubs, unions, and religious and secular organizations sought to provide women the opportunities to form and maintain female friendships where, as in the case of certain white women's groups, a "sense of freedom" prevailed (Rothman, 1978). As an act of resistance, it is a freedom, I suspect, which included, and perhaps centered around, women's intellectual autonomy and liberty. Activist African-American women's groups' designed to undermine racist institutions were sororities in which women's self-definition and self-valuation were affected by a woman-centered ethos (Hill Collins, 1990). Such women tested moral paradigms—abolition, temperance, voting rights, educational opportunity, reproductive freedom—acts that philosopher Marilyn Friedman would consider morally transformative and which facilitated moral autonomy (Friedman, 1993). As Friedman suggests, women learning from women friends, unlike learning from books, is learning that is about talking on one's own terms, in response to one's own inquiries, in a language understood by both, and marked by "an authenticity and spontaneity not available in novels" (p. 201). Friedman is suggesting, I believe, that the friendship of women with each other has an educative character, a character absent in traditional ways of college classroom learning. Much like Belenky's, Clinchy's, Goldberger's, and Tarule's "connected knowers" (1986), meaning, and thus learning, results from engaging in collaborative investigations in which individuals are marked by authenticity and authority.

Woman-woman friendships appear to enable women to reflect critically on their concrete experiences, as we see in the case of feminist Lila Abu-Lughod's account of the sex-segregated world of Bedouin women of the Egyptian Western Desert (Abu-Lughod, 1995). Women's segregation and their interactions with each other, writes Abu-Lughod, are marked by a respect for personal characteristics commonly valued in men. "Energy, industry, enterprise, and emotional and physical toughness" are attributes women value in each other, and most importantly, through storytelling and singing, women demonstrate their "wisdom, intelligence, and verbal skill" to other women (p. 31). These relations appear to enhance self-knowledge, personal development, and autonomy. Their sex-segregated social intimacy brings about opportunities to "indulge in minor defiances of the system and the men in control"; "allows for the development of social responsibility"; gives women the opportunity to be moral "arbiters" and to exchange knowledge critical for the survival of the group (e.g., household management, agrarian practices, health and child-rearing knowledge) (p. 29). As authentic speakers, these women educate each other in a world hostile to their sex and sexuality, in a world in which woman-woman relationships are the sources for personal and intellectual autonomy.

Social Science Research

The psychological, sociological, and anthropological research literature on college women's friendships is scarce in part due to the relative newness of adult friendship research. Despite recognition of its importance by early Greek thinkers such as Aristotle and Plato (Rankin, 1914), research on adult friendship is a rather modern phenomenon. Though research on other relationships, such as parent-child and children's peer relationships, has been ongoing in the United States since the 1920s, much of the research on adult friendship as a primary relationship has emerged only in the past twenty-five years. Treated as attributes of individuals in earlier studies, adult friendship, as Blieszner and Adams (1992) note, has only recently been viewed as a relationship of significance. More recent studies begin to reflect a general interest in gender and sex differences in friendships (Sherrod, 1989; Reisman, 1990; Wright, 1982; and Aukett, Ritchie, & Mill, 1988) but have not had college women's friendships as a central point, let alone consider their cognitive worth. Researchers' attentions usually focus on the structure, processes, and phases of same-sex relationships, often considering an "essential nature" of friendship between women (Becker, 1987), or a "central feature of women's friendships" (Aries & Johnson, 1983), such as their talk and conversations (Caldwell & Peplau, 1982; Davidson & Duberman, 1982). Though some researchers, like Becker (1987), use college women friends to consider relationship aspects deemed necessary for their friendships (aspects such as caring, trust, equality, and respect), one is unlikely to find a study dedicated to the consideration of the cognitive power and learning character of women's friendships, let alone *college* women's friendships. If mention is made of any cognitive or intellectual value of women's friendships, researchers, because their attention is fixed elsewhere, treat such observations as superfluous. For example, Hays (1989) ascertains that a benefit of same-sex friendships is "feeling intellectually stimulated and receiving useful information" (p. 25), yet we find no discussion of the implications of such a finding, nor does educational research appear to spring from such a finding.

Sex-role research that examines same-sex friendship stipulates that female same-sex friendships show greater involvement than male same-sex friendships (Levinger, 1980), greater depth (Altman & Taylor, 1973), and are longer lasting (Caldwell & Peplau, 1982; Wright, 1982). In Barth's and Kinder's (1988) assessment of gender identification and same-sex friendship studies, we are assured that "female same-sex friendships are more involved than those of males" and that women "seek friends to whom they can relate on many levels" (p. 359), thus implying that this multileveled, in-depth relation has possibilities for learning. Together with deep conversational patterns (Aries & Johnson, 1983), woman-woman friendships' multidimensional relatedness suggests that these relationships are epistemic gold mines.

Educational research on chosen peer relationships has followed a similar course. For example, some educational research on friendship has considered these relationships within the context of college students' intellectual development (Perry, 1978; 1981; Clinchy & Zimmerman, 1982), but primarily as it applies to approaches to conceptions of learning and study habits. Often studies of friendships among college students seek to understand social support and emotional needs (Wohlgemuth & Betz, 1991), or examine student friendships as active elements of the "cocurriculum" (Baxter-Magolda, 1992). Research on cooperative learning and small group learning yields little insight into the educational character of college women's friendships specifically, and it is really only in the literature on peer-assisted learning that same-sex friendship emerges as a critical criterion for academic success (Alexander, Gur, Gur, & Patterson, 1974). Analyses of group and peer learning which posit that self-selection of learning partners minimizes dysfunctional conflict in group learning (Latting & Raffoul, 1991) support these claims.

If, as professors and researchers we believe that the purpose of articulating thoughts and raising questions in the public forum of the college classroom is to strengthen and deepen women's intellectual development (Belenky, M. F., Clinchy, N., Goldberger, N., & Tarule, 1986; McKeachie, W. J., 1990), it becomes important to investigate those experiences in which college women are not silent and in which they formulate ideas without the fear of embarrassment or degradation (Crawford, M. & MacLeod, M., 1990; Guinier, 1994). This said, how do I begin to assess the speculation that college women's friendships are indeed learning relationships? How can I begin to explain and understand a women's postsecondary learning relationship in context? How does one investigate a relationship that researchers have not previously characterized as educative and that has been unexplored and uncharted in higher education and gender research? How can this project bring together feminist theory, higher education research, and sociopsychological scholarship on women? This project, then, will seek to understand a particular phenomenon—college women's female friendships—at the intersection of these three research traditions.

Grounded Theory and Research

Grounding the investigation in doctoral work I had previously done on John Dewey's concepts of sociality and the individual (Martínez Alemán, 1992), and in the work of Janice Raymond (1986), and Nel Noddings (1991), I drafted a project to assess my suspicions about college women's female friendships. Theoretically anchoring this investigation was not only good research practice, it also allowed me to maintain a steady and reliable research framework. I make note of this simply because given the nature of this topic—its absence from the literature and the demand that I join and thus relate feminist theory on self and relatedness with psychological, sociological, and educational empirical investigations—my hallway hunch would not have weathered the investigative storm. Too many connections needed to be made. This demanded a solid and trustworthy foundation.

John Dewey's Individual and Sociality

The work of John Dewey is an important theoretical anchor for this study because it is Dewey, in his dismissal of both dualistic thinking and the purported tension between the individual and society and between autonomy and interdependence, who provides a framework for understanding who women are as individuals and as knowers in friendship relationships. Dewey's view of the individual as an integrated, interdependent, and interactive knower allows for the possibility that learning can take place within a relationship characterized by the existence of both a mutuality of interests and autonomous growth.

Dewey's individual is an integrated individuality whose aims are not purely personal, nor purely social. Such an individual, he insisted, is not ready-made. We are capacities for development that is always incomplete and evolving (Dewey, 1930) and absolutely dependent upon others. In this way, Dewey allows for a feminist reconstruction of women as individuals characterized by their gendered (thus social) relationships and their particularity as human beings. Dewey's individual is not an isolated, ego-centered, asocial individual. Rather, she is an individual in relation with the world, a relationality in which communication is critical. For Dewey, communication, intelligence, and interaction are the conditions necessary for the development of individuals and, more specifically, for learning (Dewey, 1916). In Dewey's view, "relationship," or in the pragmatic vernacular, "experience," is a condition necessary for learning.

This mutual dependence between individuals is characterized by a reciprocity of interests and relationality. The individuals in Dewey's social unit share purposes and are mutually sympathetic. The "worth" of relationships can be measured by the degree to which interests are shared, cooperation is enacted, and individuals experience growth. In his assessment of group sociality, Dewey asserted that the degree to which interests are consciously shared by individuals are "numerous and varied" and "full and free" (Dewey, 1916, p. 83) is indicative of the learning potential of relationships. He warns that barriers which prevent the sharing of common interests, "barriers to free intercourse and communication of experience," prevent the development of the individual. Let's remember that for Dewey, the more fruitful the association and intercourse between human beings, the greater their experience, the greater the potential for learning. The greater their experience, the more progressive an individual's growth. And progressive growth, according to Dewey, is the distinguishing trait of intelligence (Dewey, 1916, pp. 81–99).

Dewey's sociality necessarily requires the freedom to be autonomous. It must have those "positive conditions, forming the prevailing state of culture," which release individuals from "oppressions and repressions" (Dewey, 1939, p. 7). In effect, it is a sociality which requires autonomy. In Deweyan sociality, it appears, individuals are free to self-direct, self-govern, or simply put, choose for themselves. It is the freedom of self-determination which must characterize Dewey's "autonomy," not a right to act as one chooses. To have the opportunities for self-determination—to be able to ascertain what I want to do, to articulate these thoughts, and to act upon them—demands an accessible experiential world, which for women in patriarchal systems is often restricted and checked.

Feminist Female Friendship and Interpersonal Reasoning

Janice Raymond writes in *A Passion for Friends: Toward a Philosophy of Female Affection* (1986), that female friendship is the "foundation for and consequence of feminism" (1986, p. 13) and "part of the history of feminist discernment" (p. 20). Inspired and motivated by women's search for meaning, female friendship seems to be a means through which women have attained an understanding of their circumstances, their possibilities, and their intellectual worth. It is a relationship that feminist philosopher María Lugones would characterize as one which is "guided by a concern for the friend in her particularity," and is "significantly constituted by understanding of the other" (Lugones, 1995, p. 142).

It is from a sociocultural constructivist perspective that Janice Raymond develops her thesis on female friendship. In *A Passion for Friends* Raymond states simply that women don't have a "biological edge on the more humane qualities of human existence" (p. 21). For Raymond it is the conditions and realities of women's lives that create the "social trust" called female friendship. The attraction of women for women is for Raymond "neither natural nor ontological" but the manifestation of a desire to recognize relatedness in patriarchal realities. The "heteroreality" of women's lives, contends Raymond, places women in social, political, and economic associations that are "ordained" by men and are only woman-to-man associations (pp. 5–8). Relatedness and freedom to choose relations are missing for women in such a scheme, and thus they experience a need for female friendship. Female friendship, then, emerges from "women's search for meaning" about herself and others like herself (p. 20).

Female friendship's starting point is for Raymond, the "companionship of Self," the experience of knowing oneself as a unique individual. It is a "Self" that Raymond defines as an "authentic" self that women are "recreating"; it is not a self that is "grafted" onto women by patriarchy (Raymond, 1986, p. 4). Given that Raymond believes in a sociocultural construction of woman, we can take her use of the term "Self" not be an essential self but rather an identity that women construct individually and one that is not prescribed by patriarchal forces. For Raymond to say that the female "Self" is "authentic" and constantly being recreated by woman, she infers not that an essential self is present, but that a self constructed by and for woman is possible.

It is the "affinity a woman has with her vital Self" that enables her to care about others like herself (Raymond, 1986, pp. 5–6). This may hint at a kind of self-knowledge and appreciation that is self-serving and individualistic, but I do not think that Raymond is suggesting this at all. On the contrary, the assertion is that through a real knowledge of Self, a meaningful knowledge, one is able to reason and consider the Self in relation to others. The real self, discovered through thinking, is uniquely fundamental and original, yet consonant with others, and not obsessively self-involved (1986, p. 222).

Raymond's view that women's attraction for other women rests on the belief that there is an integration, a healthy dynamic between Self and Others, between female friends. As a "social trust," female friendships involve "reciprocal assurances based on honor, loyalty and affection" (Raymond, 1986, p. 9), a trust I assert, that is extremely rare between women and men, given our well-practiced patriarchal ethos. That female friendships have managed to get beyond sociocultural barriers, or what Raymond calls the "female state of atrocity" (1991, p. 350), is testament to the strength of the human "longing for relatedness" (Noddings, 1984, p. 104) and self-affirmation. Somehow, women have known that, given the realities of patriarchy, the coming together of women in the absence of men allows for the freeing and subsequent affirmation of Self, an act Dewey would name "educative." As "an understanding that is continually renewed [and] revitalized" (Raymond, 1986, p. 9), female friendship demands conditions conducive for individual and shared growth. Raymond puts forth four conditions necessary for feminist female friendship: thoughtfulness, passion, worldliness, and happiness.

It is through thinking that a person can discover her real Self; it is thinking restored of "thoughtfulness," however. Raymond views thinking as theory and thoughtfulness as theory applied, theory practiced. Searching for meaning is thinking; thoughtfulness injects into thinking's rational orientation a consideration and caring for others and respect for their needs. Knowledge without meaning is useless for association. It is simply "know-how" and lacks the thoughtful experience of knowing "why" something or someone is so (Raymond, 1986, p. 218). Echoing Dewey's concern for connection as necessary for meaning and thus intelligence, Raymond's thoughtfulness is "the intentional endeavor to discover specific connections between something we do and the consequences which result" (Dewey, 1916, p. 145).

Because Raymond's female friendship begins with knowing the Self, thinking about oneself must be a fundamental necessity of female friendship, and such is the case. Raymond emphasizes what she calls the "duality of thinking . . . that is, the duality of 'myself with myself' . . . the one who asks and the one who answers" (1986, p. 222). In Raymond's view, such meaningful thinking will enable conversation with Others because in understanding Self we understand our need for association. Each participant in friendship conducts the same personal dialogue, setting up the dialectical movement where being an "original Self" and a friend is simultaneously possible. Thinking individuals, then, maintain their integrity while at the same time attaining group membership through friendship. Intelli-

gent (thoughtful) thinking communicated and shared will undoubtedly lead to intelligent action, a formula that Dewey would find made to order, and one that is clearly educative.

In "Stories in Dialogue: Caring and Interpersonal Reasoning" (Noddings & Witherell, 1991), Nel Noddings considers the development and composition of a relationality that resonates with Raymond's feminist friendship and Dewey's sociality, giving us language to investigate the educative character of female friendships. "Interpersonal reasoning," writes Noddings, "is guided by an attitude that values the relationship of the reasoners over any particular outcome, and it is marked by attachment and connection rather than by separation and abstraction" (p. 158). An inductive reasoning, it is marked by its openness, flexibility, and genuine concern for the relationship. Building each other's self-esteem and confidence is a central component of interpersonal reasoning and is developed through dialogue (pp. 163–164).

A "thinking heart" is the manifestation of another condition, that of passion, for Raymond's female friendship. A "thoughtful passion," according to Raymond, does not place thinking and passion at polar ends. Instead, their integration and connection allow for the positive action that ensures the growth of both the individual and the friendship (Raymond, 1986, pp. 223–225). To influence, to act on, to move and impress, and in turn, to be influenced by, acted upon, moved and impressed by others, is the thoughtful Gyn/affection of female friendships (1986, p. 8). For Raymond, friendship that is distinguished by "thoughtful passions ensures that a friend does not lose her Self in the heightened awareness of and attachment to another" (p. 225).

Friendship provides a location in the public and private worlds of our realities, and this, contends Raymond, is a critical significance for female friendship. Both a personal and political space, "worldliness" seems to be the practiced intelligent, passionate action of female friends. It is both personal and political, and it must be given female friendship's relational thinking. Engaged in association, the Self transcends the alleged boundaries between private and public and acknowledges both direct and indirect consequences of association. In this sense, Raymond's worldliness underscores Dewey's contention that we do not exist as solitary beings whose involvement is inconsequential or unimportant. For women, Raymond's worldliness introduces her Self as female Self to man-made political space, and her subsequent participation thus becomes meaningful. The worldly woman, then, lives with integrity in the world.

But Raymond also adds that it is woman's worldliness which enables her to maintain the feminist vision necessary to change those aspects of the world's realities that are unfriendly to her. This positions the individual, in this case woman, as agent for change, agency that "acts with respect to the other on the basis of shared understanding" (Gould, 1988, p. 75). Such agency allows for the fuller development of the individual.

Research Rationale

Taking Lather's (1991) feminist analysis of educational and human science research to heart, I constructed a study that would reflect women's cognitive styles and learning conditions. Much like Holland's and Eisenhart's (1990) inquiry into the culture of romance among college women, this investigation of college women's friendship sought to understand women's experience in a particular educational context. In the summer of 1993 I sketched out a research plan to assess the cognitive nature, power, and educational value of college women's friendships. I reasoned that I could come to some understanding of how some college women view the educational value of their friendships with each other through the use of qualitative/naturalistic research methods that would yield a "telling" of the friendship relationship. This project, I believed, required research methods that could tap meaning-rich narratives and dialogue that would bring into relief, a relationship of knowledge unexplored. My confidence in the use of dialogue in the form of semi-structured interviews is supported by Grumet's critical assessment of narratives, storytelling, and dialogue as "forms for educational research and criticism" (Noddings & Witherell, 1991, p. 67). I believe that Grumet is correct when she writes, "our stories are the masks through which we can be seen, and with every telling we stop the flood and swirl of thought so someone can get a glimpse of us, and maybe catch us if they can" (p. 69). Thus, in order to "get a glimpse" of female friendship's educative value, methods had to provide the conditions for the "telling" of friendship.

Because it is through listening to their talk that I first observed qualities judged necessary for learning (qualities discussed in Marton, Dall'alba, & Beaty, 1993; Saljo, 1979; Solano, 1986; Blieszner & Adams, 1992), I chose to examine college women's friendship talk as the site for research consideration. "Talk is the substance of women's friendships;" it is the "central feature of women's friendships" (Aries & Johnson, 1983, p. 354). It is in talk, in conversation with women friends, that women's intellectual abilities and potential are respected. According to Aries and Johnson, it is in conversation with each other that women friends "develop a sense of inner security and self-esteem" (p. 355).

To measure the learning character of woman-woman friendships among undergraduates at my small midwestern college, I looked at the work of Marton, Dall'alba, and Beaty (1993), Solano (1986) and other learning researchers. In Marton's, Dall'alba's and Beaty's (1993) updating of Saljo's (1979) phenomenographical study on the conceptualization of learning, university students were interviewed in order to "give more precise characterization of the differing conceptions of learning" and to "identify relationships between the conceptions" (Marton, Dall'alba, & Beaty, 1993, p. 279). Saljo's initial findings had suggested that students recognized learning as academic in nature and that learning was about the increase of knowledge, about memorizing, the acquiring of facts or skills, understanding meaning, and the interpretation of reality (Saljo, 1979). Students interviewed by Marton et al. reiterated Saljo's five categories with one addition: learning as changing as a person. When one finds a new way of seeing phenomena, it means that one sees the world or an aspect of it differently. This new view or "seeing the world differently means that you change as a person" (Marton, Dall'alba, & Beaty, 1993, p. 292).

These six conceptualizations of learning are analogous to Solano's (1986) functions of friendship and Blieszner's and Adams's (1992) descriptions of the cognitive processes resident in adult friendships. Solano submits that friendships function to meet certain needs. Meeting such needs as information provides friends with a feeling of security, while meeting such cognitive needs as conversation, ideas, and experiences provides a way of assessing self. Emotional needs such as acceptance, trust, and love are also met through friendship. Blieszner's and Adams's (1992) survey of the literature on adult friendship reveals that integral to the cognitive processes involved in adult friendships is the requirement of "ongoing growth and change" (p. 62).

What of friendships between women? In her "structural description" of friendships between women, Carol Becker (1987) posits that women's friendships with each other involve a maturing dialogue between autonomous but interdependent agents and are relationships that provide "a context for each woman becoming herself, personally and interpersonally" (p. 65). Here again we find that friendship between women is a site for growth, growth that results from an "evolving dialogue" between interdependent agents. In Johnson's and Aries's (1983) examination of the talk of women friends several themes emerge that reinforce Becker's (1987) and Marton, Dall'alba's, and Beaty's (1993) work. Johnson and Aries found that women friends engage in noncritical listening, describe the relationship as supportive and interdependent; women friends reported that they positively affected each other's self-worth and viewed each other as necessary for self-discovery and growth (pp. 357–358).

What this research on learning, learning relationships, women's and college students' friendships suggested to me was that for college women's friendships to be educative, to be a site for college women's intellectual and academic development, these relationships must provide college women a site for assessing meaning of self and of reality, a site for the experience of different perspectives and viewpoints, and an opportunity for growth through interdependency.

Thus, beginning in the autumn of 1993 and ending in the spring of 1995, I asked 44 undergraduate women to participate in a qualitative study designed to help me understand the educative nature of their friendships with other college women. The qualitative character of this study was drawn from research strategies described in Lincoln and Guba (1985) and Ely, Anzul, Friedman, Garner, and Steinmetz (1991). For example, categorizing techniques, establishing categories, developing themes, and member-checking strategies reflect these researchers' desire to make a "three dimensional whole" of data through which I can understand such relational phenomena as female friendship (Ely, Anzul, Friedman, Garner & Steinmetz, 1991). The use of semistructured interviews was an important element of this feminist research, because it offered me "access to [women's] ideas, thoughts, and memories," a condition critical for feminist research (Reinharz, 1992, p. 19). As Reinharz notes, the use of interviewing in feminist research "is particularly important for the study of women, because in this way learning from women is an antidote to centuries of ignoring women's ideas altogether or having men speak for women" (p. 19). In a study that is about the consideration of an aspect of women's relationships that is customarily ignored, the use of the semistructured interview made feminist methodological sense.

By the autumn of 1994 participants in the study had completed surveys and informal interviews, and by December of that year, 24 of the original cohort participated in an in-depth discussion of the phenomenon. Of these 24 college women, 16—by then all juniors and seniors—had spent additional time with me in a lengthier semistructured research interview, in which they talked about the performative nature of the relationship, its role in their academic successes, and their perceptions of its significance to their cognition. It is important to note here that as these women talked about their friendships and about themselves as students in the classroom, it became clear that who they were as speakers and knowers in the college classroom and who they were as speakers and knowers in female friendship was incompatible. The differences they expressed suggest to me that the coeducational classroom can still be viewed as inhospitable for many women and that a feminist pedagogy that has as its central ethos collaborative or friendship work may be a vehicle for many college women to come to an intellectual and academic voice outside of their female friendships.

Method and Data Sources

A purposeful sample of undergraduate women participants from enrolled students in five undergraduate classes[1] at a small liberal arts college in the rural Midwest of the United States of America was collected. They included 7 seniors, 17 juniors and 20 sophomores. Given the study's focus on established close female friendships, it was decided that no first-year/first-semester women would take part in the analysis. This participant restriction was necessary because first-year/first-semester women are not "information rich cases that manifest the phenomenon of [close female college friendship] intensely" (Patton, 1990, p. 171). For such intensity sampling (Patton, 1990), first-year/first-semester women were clearly ineligible. The women participating were of traditional college age, ranging from 18 years to 23 years, with the vast majority (93%) between the ages of 19 and 21. Much to my disappointment, racial and ethnic distribution within the pool of participants made it impossible to glean any understanding of Latina, Asian, or African American women's friendships, because only one Latina and no Asian American women participated in the study. I had hoped that the participation by four African American women would allow for some discussion on these particular African American college women's friendships, but given the cursory responses by each of the four African American women participants and the limits of a standardized open-ended interview (Patton, 1990, p. 287), I gleaned little insight into the cognitive character of their friendships. Much the same can be said of the distribution of heterosexual, bisexual, and lesbian participants: Two women self-identified as bisexual, 3 women as lesbian, and 38 as heterosexual.

Participants were asked to share their perceptions about their friendships with college women by completing a questionnaire and answering several standardized open-ended questions posed by trained interviewers. Participants were told that the entire exercise would take no more than 50 minutes, a time determined by pretests on participants made ineligible for the study during the preceding summer. No participant expressed the need for extra time nor did anyone suggest that the time allotted was inadequate. All participants were asked to read the introductory page of the questionnaire explaining the purpose of the study, their rights and responsibilities, and confidentiality (Appendix C).

In both the interviews and survey, I asked women to describe the purposes they thought that their conversations with a close female friend served. The initial survey asked the participant women to choose one particular female friend who attended the college and, with her in mind, to complete a questionnaire consisting of five open-ended/multiple response questions designed to solicit from participants the topics of their conversations with their friends and words used to describe intellectual and academic properties of their friendships. Such questions would allow me to explore the participants' views of reality—in this case, female friendship—and develop theories about this phenomenon (Reinharz, 1992). These items were constructed for the purposes of testing their perceptions of these friendships against Raymond's model of female friendship (1986) and as sources of comparison for the standardized open-ended interview. The following open-ended questions were posed:

1. What ten words would you use to describe your relationship?

2. Think of the same close female college friend. What ten words characterize your conversations?

3. What do you and this close friend talk about?

4. What words would you use to characterize the role you each play in the other's intellectual growth?

5. What words would you use to characterize the role you each play in the other's academic performance?

The questions designed to ascertain their perceptions of their conversations' purposes were framed to suggest that "academic" and "intellectual" objectives were our focus, that I was interested in knowing how their talk was "academic"—about matters of school (course content, exams, papers, etc.)—and how they were about "intellectual" matter—ideas, theories, knowing "outside" the realm of undergraduate course work and requirements.

The addition of a 13-item Likert scale served as a final source of comparison for the interview. The items on the scaled response section reflect conceptions of learning as discussed in Marton, Dall'alba and Beaty (1993). The use of these different types of measures (open-ended/multiple response questions, scaled responses, open-ended question interview) was an attempt at triangulation and convergence as discussed in Lincoln and Guba (1985), Ahern and Baker (1990), Patton (1990), and Reinharz (1992). Many of the qualitative research features employed in this study were informed by techniques suggested in Lincoln and Guba (1985) and Bogdan and Biklen (1982).

Each questionnaire was reviewed to make sure that all entries to all questions were legible. Entries for Questions 1 through 5 that could not be recognized were discarded. Each entry for each of the five questions was then recorded and tallied by two 2-person research teams.

Question 1 ("What ten words would you use to describe your relationship?") and Question 2 ("Think of the same close female college friend. What ten words characterize your conversations?") were coded for the conditions of female friendship discussed in Raymond (1986), "thoughtfulness," "passion," "worldliness," and "happiness." In order to "test" for the feminist character of the relationship, two separate research teams coded the responses for: "thoughtfulness," defined by Raymond as the ability to reason with considerateness and caring; "worldliness," a term used to describe a friend's position as "inside outsider" in college culture; and "passion," a term Raymond defines as the thinking heart that "move[s], stir[s], influence[s], and affect[s]" the other woman (Raymond, 1990, pp. 218–229). Responses were coded as "Questionable" by both teams if no agreement could be reached among team members and then between teams. A final list of coded responses was produced by comparing each team's codes, discussing questionable responses and coming to agreement on responses that had been coded differently across teams. Final response distribution can be found in Appendix B.

Responses to Question 3 ("What do you and this close friend talk about?") were coded in the same way as Questions 1 and 2 according to the categories "intellectual," "academic" and "personal lives" (Appendix E). These categories were an attempt to "test" the perception of the alleged tension between what participants perceive as intellectual and what they perceive as academic. These variables, or category sets, were chosen after researchers engaged in a process of data categorizing described in Lincoln and Guba (1985). These three emergent categories correlate with Johnson's and Aries's (1983) findings on the composition of conversations between female friends. Research teams used marginal tabulation categories (Borg & Gall, 1983) to code responses to both Question 4 ("What words would you use to characterize the role you play in each other's intellectual growth?") and Question 5 ("What words would you use to characterize the role you each play in each other's

academic performance?"). The distribution of responses can be found in Appendixes F and G.

Responses to the last component of the questionnaire, the 13-item Likert scale, were tallied within question and across category (Appendix H). In addition, a percentage of "Agree" and "Strongly Agree" responses was calculated for each of the 13 items.

Immediately upon the completion of the questionnaire, participants were asked to read descriptions of two sets of friendships (Appendix C) and to take a few minutes to think about these relationships. Participants were then asked to engage in a semistructured, limited survey interview (Lincoln & Guba, 1985), which was tape recorded. Transcripts of the tapes were compiled and emergent data categories developed. Data categories and their descriptions were given to research assistants who coded interview responses according to the categories.

Emergent Themes

What became apparent after reading the completed surveys is that for these college women, their conversations with their female friend served as (1) a respite from academic stress and anxiety; (2) as validation and support of their thinking and their ideas; (3) as testing sites for ideas; (4) as risk-free testing sites for their ideas; (5) as a source for different and diverse perspectives; and (6) as sources of information and advice. Subtle differences suggest that the "intellectual" purposes of these conversations are more about growth from association, identity development, and non-performative characteristics, while the "academic" purposes appear to be about performance, individual validation, resources acquisition, and hiatus.

Respite from Academic Stress

As a respite from academic stress and anxiety, these conversations do serve different purposes, depending on whether they were identified as "academic" or "intellectual." For example, comments such as: "we keep one another from going too hard," and "it's really a stress reliever," and

> she stops me from being too intense. I have a tendency to be way over intense and so she comes down and makes me stop reading for awhile. And that's probably a healthy thing academically.

indicate that the relationship is a site where academic performance is not demanded nor expected. These conversations seem to be places free of the anxiety and stress-producing performative elements of academics—tests, papers, presentations, class participation. Women often characterized talking with their female friend as

> getting away from your work, getting away from reminders of your work,

and that "getting away" often had to do with respite from the demands of academic performance and being evaluated. As one undergraduate women noted, "I use it to diffuse stress" produced by exams and papers and speaking in class. Somehow these college women's talk is not perceived to be evaluated nor evaluative in this friendship relationship.

When the theme emerges as a response to the intellectual purposes of their talk, the following is the typical response:

> To stimulate me to go out . . . and read a different book or we actually hand the book to the other person; then to question things like the existence of God or something more interesting than just the academic.

It appears that this type of hiatus is not about safe-haven from the academic onslaught but about an opportunity for cognitive growth. Somehow, "thinking" within the intellectual conversation is not about academic performance but about the freedom from judgment.

Risk-Free Test Sites

This same subtlety rang true when participants talked about these conversations as risk-free testing sites for ideas. Often, participants would present their conversations as opportunities to try out ideas related to a class in a "safe" environment, an environment free of criticism and directed argumentation. Note the following participant comments:

> It's nice to have someone that you can talk to about ideas and not worry about being shot down in an academic setting.

> We do create kind of a safe environment for one another.

One gets the impression that female friends create a temporary mock classroom void of the elements they deem inhospitable in the classroom. Women are listened to, and they don't feel attacked:

> I think that I'm a lot less hesitant when I'm with her to say things. It's at an individual level and it's not talking to the whole class and I know that she'll understand and listen to me.

> Comparing them with conversations I have with my male friends, they are challenging; they might challenge my position but at the same time not in a combative way.

> Just talking it out is good for me, in a comfortable environment and to be able to say something in an environment where I know I won't be killed, yelled at or something.

Female friendship provides them with a stage for the rehearsal of their thinking; it is a rehearsal space in which they do not struggle with performance anxiety, the possibility of public humiliation. It is a space in which their gendered identities as women are not poised against the demand for validation. It is as if they knew that in female friendship they will be listened to unconditionally. In female friendship, criticism and the request for help to clarify thinking are components of a congenial learning process and not threats to self-worth:

> She offers critiques but not criticism, direct criticism.

> If I'm not clear on something, I'm using her as a sounding board, to bounce off an idea: "Does this make sense to you?" Or: "This is my idea for a paper. Do you think this will work?"

When asked about the "intellectual" purposes of their conversations, participant comments within this theme were not about performative safety. Instead, their comments suggested that these conversations were sites for intellectual play.

> We're trying ideas on each other just for the sake of ideas. It's not to help academics.

> You can try out new ideas and stuff . . . it would allow me to try out this new theory I learned in class.

> . . . clarifying my ideas on things and . . . I get new ideas from her.

It's just a more comfortable way of express- ing ideas or different thoughts about things, which is a good way of rethinking or restruc- turing different things I've learned.

To view such female friendship talk as a site of intellectual play is to suggest that for these women, friendship learning has an interactive, independent, informal, and unbound quality that sets it apart from learning in their con- ditional, self-supported and sustained class- rooms. Perceived by the participants as personally and academically inconsequential, this learning, this intellectual practice and play, seems to provide a bridge between cognitive self and college.

Source of Information and Advice

Perhaps the most striking difference between the "intellectual" and the "academic" purposes of their conversations resides in the conceptualiza- tion of conversation as a source of information and advice. These conversations seem to serve as both pragmatic academic resources—advice about course requirements and responsibilities— and as a site for identity construction and self- assessment. Note the following sample of the responses to the question regarding "academic" purposes:

We give each other advice about classes or how to deal with the workload, . . . how to go about preparing for class. . . . We usually do a lot of explaining, a lot of clarifying . . . things that have to do with grammar and things of that nature.

I had to make a presentation in an education class and I went over it with her first.

She's taken this class before me and so aca- demically it's very nice to have someone who's taken the class already.

These college women saw their friendships as a relationship from which they could learn to nav- igate college terrain, and from which they could extract the information necessary to improve the chances for academic success. Their female friendships are practical and functional in that they serve as resources for effective skills: antic- ipating what the professor wants, setting work- load priorities, and proofreading.

The responses to the question about "intel- lectual" purposes of their conversations suggest that women's friendships with each other serve to enhance self-knowledge, and often, to under- stand their place in the world as gendered selves:

We do talk about the role of women and the society and where we are [in it].

It's intellectually rewarding that I learn things about myself. I learn, I question things about myself that I might not otherwise do. Like I question why I'm going to college, what I'm doing after college.

It helps me to learn more about myself, learn more about other people when I have con- versations where [there's] a completely dif- ferent perspective.

I think that she causes me to question myself a lot, . . . because she'll ask why I have that view, and it turns out that it's something I've never really asked myself.

I think that intellectually our discussions help me kind of focus a little better or kind of place myself a little better. I kind of fig- ure out a little better who I am in relation to the outer world outside of [the College].

But it is a knowledge about self that is interde- pendent with enhancing self-knowledge for friends. Women talked about the development of knowledge of self in relation to the development of self-knowledge in their friend. This mutual- ity is characteristic of their friendship exchanges:

We'll pick up different things from what's going on . . . and say "look, did you know this?" . . . and whatever's going on—bring it out and check out if it's worth knowing.

I think that we've both gotten a lot out of our relationship—like growing as a person and changing who you are.

I can be telling a story I've told a hundred times before and suddenly it sounds differ- ently. I think about it and she asks the right questions and you get a little more in depth. And it's very good. I learn a lot about myself. I learn a lot about her.

. . . allowed me to become more of a political person. . . . I hadn't formulated my feminist identity yet, so that was something she was in part responsible for—helping me do that. And I think that I helped her do that a little bit too.

It almost seems that when viewed as "intellectual," these conversations are not a reaction to a situation, to an immediate performative reality. Instead, they are about some refinement or development of self-definition for each friend. The "intellectual," here, is about self and *for* self, and for other, while the "academic" appears to be about performing self for someone (a professor) or something (grades). Even when describing how these conversations serve as sites for the validation of ideas, when the ideas are about academics, these conversations serve as sights of risk-free practice. Intellectual validation of ideas, on the other hand, is about "nourishing and replenishing." As in Noddings's "interpersonal reasoning" (1991), friendship talk is the means through which these women reason as contextualized, concrete and interdependent agents.

Consequences

It appears, then, that for female friends in college, conversations with each other serve as vehicles to transgress the limits of dualistic thinking, of dichotomous ideology. I say this because it is in their conversations with each other that college women friends contest the boundaries of the classroom and the hallways, and of the autonomous academic self and interdependent intellectual self. If intellectual work is nonperformative and if academic work is performative, it becomes necessary to find some means of linking what these college women perceive to be separate cognitive spheres. Their conversations prove effective means; their friendship proves an effective site for this process.

Why the need for such a site? Why the need for such a means? The easy answer to these questions is to remember the prevalence of an ideology in higher education that presents the academic as solely an individual enterprise, as individual performance, and as autonomous cognition. If the academic is perceived by college women as being about autonomy and self-directed performance—as the women who participated in this query suggest it is—and they define the intellectual as an interdependency with trusted, supportive, nurturing friend; and they maintain that they are intellectual independents as well—as the women who participated in this query suggest it does—then college women's friendships are sites where learning is an interdependent activity where self is not per-

ceived as lost. There is no "loss of Self" in learning relation; there is a "thoughtful passion [which] ensures that a friend does not lose her Self in the heightened awareness of and attachment to another" or another's ideas or perspectives (Raymond, 1986, p. 225).

What became clear to me from the interviews of these college women is that female friendship, unlike the overwhelming majority of their college classrooms, is a site for the execution of knowledge, for the realization of their thinking. In this relationship, talk is fundamentally about authorship and about academic and intellectual agency. Unlike Judith Butler's performative nature of gender (Butler, 1990), an understanding of gender as actions produced by social practices that regulate what it means to be a woman or a man, female friendship for these college women, is a place where the articulation of their thinking and knowing—their "performance"—does constitute their identity. It appears that in female friendship, a woman's identity is not as "it is purported to be" (Butler, 1990, p. 25) but as that which is developing, becoming more complex and sophisticated. It is an identity in process and not a "given" of gendered education. It is in this friendship talk that these college women spirit not a parody—again to use Butler's notion of gender construction (p. 31)—of academic argumentation, but an active, dynamic exchange characterized by mutuality, suspended judgment, and helpful challenges. It is as if in these friendships women shed their gendered educational conditioning and revealed a self hidden by years of gendered socialization. As Valerie Walkerdine notes in "Femininity as Performance" (1994):

> As girls at school, as women at work, we are used to performing. We are used, too, to dramaturgical metaphors that tell us that life is a performance in which we do nothing but act out a series of roles or indeed that these roles can be peeled away like layers of an onion to reveal a repressed core, a true self, which has been inhibited, clouded by layers of social conditioning which obscure it. Such views form much of the common sense ideas about socialization in relation to education. Girls are conditioned into passivity (p. 57).

In my view, female friendship for the college women in this study is an educational site in which "performance" abandons its gendered passivity.

As suggested by the following comment by a senior woman participant, speaking in class, "performing" in class, is often conditionally inhospitable:

> I guess my idea of thinking in the classroom is that it's not a process that can be done out loud unlike in your friendship; it's a process that has to take place internally and then it's allowed to come out and it's supposed to be polished.

"Thinking out loud" is not a process that is valued in the classroom. Rather, she maintains that thought must be pre-processed, positioned and directed, definitive, and must be "well" articulated. For these college women, speaking in a classroom is fundamentally an act of disconnected, perfunctory "academic" performance and not an act of "connected knowing" (Belenky, et al., 1986); it is *not* an opportunity to develop self, voice, and mind as a totality. This holds especially true when subject areas, disciplines, or professorial style are perceived to be disconnected or distanced from "real" life, as when course content is presented as "abstract" and unrelated to their experiences. For example, a senior mathematics major makes the distinction between friendship talk as life-related and higher mathematics as too "abstract" to be "related" to her life experience. Often, these women speak in class just to fulfill some ill-defined and ambiguous requirement called "class participation," making only "safe" and "polished" comments. Many described this speech as commentary that was not "exploratory," "controversial," or "risky." It seems, then, that classroom performance for these undergraduate women is less about a genuine intellectual exercise and more about safety, or about little possibility of penalty.

The "risks" associated with classroom performance, according to these junior and senior women, are forged by what is perceived to be an equation that results in the judgment of the individual. It appears that for these undergraduates, the lack of intimacy between themselves and their classmates does not allow for the development of trust between individuals, a trust that appears to be critical for these women to engage in the kind of dynamic, relational, and critical thinking they deem necessary for knowing and understanding. Interestingly enough, the professor—the class member institutionally sanctioned to judge and criticize—is a secondary variable in this equation. Women spoke much, much more of their concerns about peer judgment than of professors' evaluations.

> I don't know these people [other students] well and I'm afraid they might criticize me, . . . you don't know what they are going to say. You don't know if they're going to totally criticize you, if they're going to think that you're an idiot.

> I've always wondered why I'm so timid in class, why I don't want to bring issues up. I keep my mouth shut just out of fear that I'll be shot down and because there's a lot of times when there are competitions in our classroom. The competition is there and sometimes I don't think that I would match up because I have a tendency to listen to other people, to hear what they say, to listen to their views. In a classroom [listening] can be perceived as you're weak.

> I'm sitting in classes with twenty other people and I don't know them. I make a comment and it's kind of the only thing they have. I mean., you don't have any relationship with them outside of class. You don't know them as a person, you don't know anything about them; . . . the one component [making a comment in class] becomes all-important. [With a friend such a comment/position taking] is just one component of you that they assimilate in forming the picture they have of you.

Classmates, as "strangers" who only know them by what they say in class, will judge their intelligence based on the one or two comments expressed throughout the semester. Faculty, on the other hand, have more than one or two opportunities (papers, exams, office meetings) to assess their intellectual worth before making judgment.

The fear of being judged, especially being judged as unintelligent, is what many of the women expressed as the reason for perceiving classroom performance as risky and thus why they are unlikely to ask questions, express a minority opinion, play the devil's advocate, or publicly wrestle with ideas.

> [With a friend] you can take risks because you have this trust that your friend doesn't think you're dumb. They value you for other things other than your intelligence.

I think that's [being judged as intelligent] something that's very, very important at [the college]. It's not necessarily academic performance, but some level of intelligence is very important . . . this defines you as a [college] student.

Classmates are often viewed as "strangers" who must be impressed by intelligence performed.

The people in the classroom—the only basis they have for knowing me is the fact that I'm in class with them; . . . it's the only thing they have to base their opinion of me, or whether or not they want to get to know me. I'm sitting back there [in class] going "Okay, are they going to think that if I say this. . . ." How do I think it will make them perceive me? It's ironic because it's such a small school and you would think that they wouldn't be strangers.

Much like verbal messages communicated in high context cultures, who the speaker is important, and even more important is the distinction of stranger versus trusted insider (Hall, 1976).

These college women see the classroom as a place for traditional argumentation, a pedagogy they see as inhospitable. They do not see the win-lose/debate paradigm as intellectually challenging. On the contrary, traditional argumentation is not viewed as a way to challenge thinking; it is perceived as "antagonistic," as "degrading" of individual thinking, and as a static cognitive activity—her thinking remains unchanged, unenhanced, and unexplored. Power relations in the classroom are constructed by these college women as a dynamic, which does not allow for the meaningful challenge of their thinking, thus it does not allow for knowing as an evolutionary and effectual exchange. The classroom, unlike their female friendship, is a site that "cuts off" or stalls the thinking process. These female friends do not seem to "interrupt" each other's thinking. Instead, they are likely to ask probing questions meant to gain understanding rather than the argumentative upper hand. One gets the impression that college women understand their knowing, their intellectual growth, to be about relatedness, exchange, mutuality, and an autonomy that is essentially about interdependence. And it is in describing their female friendship talk that one begins to understand that it is there that these women find a hospitable performative platform.

In my view, it is certain that the crux of this performance is rooted in intimacy and trust. Women often gauged the risk of speaking in class by the degree to which they "knew" the other class members and the degree to which classmates "knew" them. "Knowing" a person, for these undergraduates, means that one can be trusted not to criticize thinking in a way that is degrading, nor to engage in a "competitive" discussion, and to be assured that power in the dialogue will not be framed as dominance and submission—that the objective of the talk is not to have a winner and a loser, and thus have one's thinking dominate or be unequivocally "right."

In female friendship, college women can experience the free-flowing, playful, and risk-free performance that for them constitutes purposeful, practical, and productive learning. The talk of undergraduate female friends is characterized as a performance in which intellectual confidence is restored, in which expressing "minority opinions" is commendatory, and unlike classroom performance, it is one filled with questions and play circumscribed by safety. Women frequently described how in their female friendship, each woman often takes on the devil's advocate position in order to help the other develop her thinking. In female friendship, it seems, performing the less accepted or approved cause is done less for the sake of "pure" argument than for the sake of self-determined knowing. It is also true that these women did not feel that taking a "devil's advocate" position was risky for them. It is as if the friend's self-determination, the friend's journey towards knowing, is given primacy. Being the "devil's advocate" is in female friendship, a performance which benefits both actors: for one, it is about the evolution of knowledge; for the other, it is about the facilitation of knowledge for a trusted other.

Discussion

In January of 1995 I concluded my examination believing that I had posed more questions than I had answered. Though I was confident that I had proven my presuppositions about college women's friendship talk, I was left with a series of pragmatic educational questions: What *are* the implications of the realization of the educative power of female friendships for higher education pedagogies, curricula, and classrooms? What is there to be done with this new insight?

Pedagogies, even feminist pedagogies in higher education, I now believe, will need to reconsider and view in a new light the value of familiarity and interdependency among women students. These relationships appear to be resources for academic success. Can they be identified and put to good use? Can, for example, feminist pedagogies appropriate fundamental characteristics of such female friendships in order to better the learning conditions of *all* students? One suggestion is that college women's friendships can serve as models for educational research on the dynamics of autonomy and interdependence, and consequently, as models for university and college instructors who wish to create the types of feminist classrooms that develop voice, mind, and self.

Female friendships can be models for peer-assisted learning in higher education. As pointed out by Alexander, Gur, Gur, and Patterson (1974), peer-assisted learning is an "often neglected but potent resource inherent in a student population" (p. 175). Their studies reaffirm the suspicion that arbitrary partnerships within pedagogical practices are problematic and that success of these learning partnerships is attributed to friendship (p. 179). The college women I interviewed indicate that arbitrary groupings in courses are problematic but become less so if two conditions are imposed: the size of the group and the length of time that the group is asked to work together are critical for attaining intimacy and trust, for "knowing" the other group members. All of the women spoke about the size of the group in terms of its correlation, whether positively or negatively, to intimacy and, consequently, their ability to voice concerns, ask questions, negotiate demands, and "think out loud." A handful of these women spoke of one particular class in which they were asked to form small groups in which membership was freely chosen. These all-women groups were together for the whole semester, working each week for a required number of hours, and periodically presenting research to the whole class. This type of grouping seemed to contain the important elements of intellectual performance that they described in their female friendships; it allowed the members to get to know each other more thoroughly, thus avoiding the pitfall of being "strangers" engaged

in a mini-classroom. As the semester progressed and students got to know each other better, the women felt that they were far more vocal, that their thinking was challenged, that they were able to ask questions that would generate discussion, and that they were able to test their ideas without fear of humiliation or dismissal. As the intimacy of the group increased, so did the students' participation. Points and opinions were negotiated; thinking evolved over the course of what was described as a "continuous and shared conversation"; decisions/judgments could be suspended. Thus, if one of the more bothersome burrs in the collaborative learning theoretics is the conflict between individualistic tendencies and the requirement for interdependence, it appears that women's friendships' reconciliation of this tension can provide insight into this educational quandary and can provide an effective model for peer-assisted, cooperative learning situations.

It seems, then, that a pedagogy patterned after their female friendship can be a site for intellectual performance. To replicate the conditions of female friendship (risk-free testing sites for ideas, source for different perspectives, validation for thinking) in our university and college classrooms and as sources for information, may not be an easy task but it is, as these undergraduate women made known, nonetheless possible. If Perry's (1978; 1981) conclusions, which suggest that intellectual development among college and university students relies strongly on supportive relationships, and if Astin's (1992) assessment that peer group is the most important influence on academic and cognitive growth in post-secondary students are correct, then it would seem reasonable that we consider ways to implement such pedagogies designed to improve the conditions for our women's intellectual growth and academic success.

Often, the college women I interviewed spoke of the ways in which they "make time" to talk to their female friend, action which is a consequence of the demands of an academically rigorous semester system and the need for study. Time appears to be at a premium for these women, and most women expressed that the stresses of school work and academic schedules did not leave much time for friendship talk. Thus, another consideration for post-secondary institutions concerned with the quality of women's intellectual development is to assess how institutions and institutional policies provide opportunities and space for these conversations.

The reason most cited for interfering with female friendship is, quite plainly, "school." Because of this, these college women either purposely schedule time with their friend, either on or off campus, or hope for the spontaneous opportunities that may or may not arise on this small campus in the dormitories or in off-campus houses. Often, when women feel the pressure of academic work, engaging in friendship talk is deemed reasonable only when an urgency is sensed:

> Sometimes I feel like I only want to talk when I have something important to say,

or when talk can be legitimized as a "study break" or a "stress reliever." Several women remarked that talking over lunch or dinner is good use of time and are hence less likely to feel as if they were taking time away from school work. However, when friends do take time "for themselves," as one senior women describes it:

> You have it in the back of your mind that I should be doing this or that kind of [work].

In many cases, friendship talk appears to be viewed as a dereliction of student duties. It is as if time spent talking with a female friend held no academic value, no educational worth, and were somehow frivolous and irresponsible.

Privacy, private space and residential arrangement also seem to be important for engaging in friendship talk. Many women noted the advantages of living in off-campus houses, a living arrangement that, unlike the dorm, seems more practical and convenient.

> Because I live with my close friend, there's a lot of time when normally I wouldn't be studying. . . . So after dinner, when I'm brushing my teeth and getting ready, putting my books together to go to the library, I'm spending time with [her].

> Being off-campus helps you mentally separate yourself from school work.

The implications for higher education student affairs/cocurricular programs are obvious. Residential systems and student space should be assessed based on the knowledge that for college women time spent with female friends can be educational, can be part of learning in the "cocurriculum" (Baxter-Magolda, 1992). Institutions can consider such issues as the availability of private space for after dinner conversations in the dining halls or in the student pay cafeteria. As a senior woman remarked, when she and her friend do manage to take time after dinner to sit and talk over hot chocolate, they are quickly ushered out by the dining hall staff after the last meal is served. Early closing hours at the college's pay cafeteria presents them with a similar problem.

Publicly validating female friendship's educative potential is, in my opinion, one of the more proactive campaigns to validate women's intellectual development. Understanding that women's friendships and talk are vehicles for learning and cognitive growth, does the institution publicly prize women's academic partnerships, an act implicitly (if not explicitly) validating these ways of knowing and cognition? Does the institution revere academic sorority? Providing evidence that such partnerships are important and educationally useful gives women students a sense that their interdependency with women can be academically profitable. Institutions of higher learning can present through colloquia, symposia, panel presentations, and other public forums, examples of effective collaboration between women friends. In our own classrooms we frequently use texts, essays, and research by female friendship collaborations. Do we make a point of this successful intellectual interdependence thus validating this kind of relationship? In my own class on American feminist educational theory, I can now imagine how our discussion of *The Feminist Classroom* by Frances A. Maher and Mary Kay Thompson Tetreault (1994), or our analysis of the collaboratively authored *Women's Ways of Knowing* (1986) can be framed as thinking, knowing, understanding, and investigating through female friendship. I can bring to my students' attention the fact that Mary Belenky talks about writing *Women's Ways of Knowing* (1986) as "a world of "pajama parties" that gave the women friends the "luxury of sustained conversation" (Ashton-Jones & Thomas, 1990, p. 275), and that this serious and formal collaboration between women friends was about excitement, loving, and hard-nosed assessment and critique (p. 280), Embarrassingly, I now note that in the years in which I have taught this course and on those occasions when

I have discussed these books with students, I have never reinforced the works' most formidable educative characteristic: the friendship among the women.

At the conclusion of this investigation, I remarked to my best female friend that I was cer-

tain that I had continued to raise far more questions than I could, at least for the moment, adequately and confidently address. She reminded me that this heuristic hunch of mine seemed more like a commitment to theorizing that would, in all inevitability, incite further research,

APPENDIX A
Demographic Data

Q1		Q2 Major	
Seniors	7	Anthropology	3
Juniors	17	Anthropology and Environmental Studies	1
Sophomores	20	Biology	4
		Classics	1
Q3 Concentration		English	6
AfroAmerican Studies	1	History	4
English/History	1	Music	1
Environmental Science	1	Philosophy	1
Gender Women Studies	1	Physics/Math	1
Latin American Studies	1	Political Science	3
Not answered	14	Psychology	9
Psychology	1	Religious Studies	1
REES	1	Sociology	5
Social Work	1	Spanish	2
		Theater	1
Q4 Age		Undeclared	4
18	2		
19	15		
20	14		
21	10		
22	1		
23	1		

APPENDIX B
Demographic Data

Q5 Race		Q6 Cultural Identity	
African-American	4	African-American	2
Asian-American	0	American	29
Bi-Racial	2	German	1
Caucasian/White	36	German-African American	1
Latina	1	Greek	1
Q7		Haitian	1
Heterosexual	38	Hungarian	1
Homosexual	3	Irish-German American	2
Bi-Sexual	2	Jewish	3
		Latina-American	1
		Slovak	1

APPENDIX C
The Cognitive Value of College Women's Friendships: A Case Study Research Questionnaire

Today you are being asked to share your perceptions about your friendships with college women. You will be asked to consider the intellectual and cognitive worth of these relationships, as well as their impact on your learning. It is the researchers' contention that your friendships with college women may serve as learning relationships. You will be asked to provide the researchers with descriptions of your friendships with college women as they pertain to your assessment of their cognitive nature, power and value. The researchers hope to consider how institutions of higher learning can encourage and provide undergraduate women the opportunities and environments for such relationships. You may find that this exercise will bring you a greater awareness and appreciation of your friendships with college women.

The completion of the questionnaire and several open-ended questions should take about 50 minutes. Your responses to these questions will be tape recorded and transcribed for use by the researchers only. After this short interview, a researcher will answer any questions you may have about the research and address any of your concerns. You may withdraw your participation from this study at any time without penalty and are encouraged to contact Prof. Martínez Alemán (Steiner 303, X4218, Box C-4) should you have any questions after your participation. A summary and status of the research will be mailed to you early in the Spring semester. The researchers respect your privacy and appreciate your willingness to participate in this project. All responses to questionnaire items and questions are confidential, as is your name and college address. Should reference be made to any of your responses in a manuscript, a pseudonym will be assigned.

Please sign below if you agree to participate in this research. Your signature indicates that you have read the above and understand your rights and responsibilities.

Thank you.

_____ _____ P.O. Box _____

Date   Signature

Please turn to Page 1 of the Questionnaire and begin.
Thank You.

APPENDIX C
Page 1

Please complete the following and be assured that all data will remain confidential.

1. Year in College   _____
2. Academic Major   _____
3. Academic Concentration   _____
4. Age   _____
5. Race   _____
6. Ethnicity/Cultural Identity _____
7. Sexual/Affectional Preference _____

Throughout this research questionnaire, as the basis for your responses, please choose *one* particular close female friend who attends this college and answer the questions as best you can.

1. What ten words would you use to describe your relationship?

1. _____   6. _____
2. _____   7. _____
3. _____   8. _____
4. _____   9. _____
5. _____   10. _____

2. Think of the same close female college friend. What ten words characterize your conversations?

1. _____   6. _____
2. _____   7. _____
3. _____   8. _____
4. _____   9. _____
5. _____   10. _____

Please turn to Page 2 and continue.

APPENDIX C
Page 2

3. What do you and this close friend talk about?

1. _____   6. _____
2. _____   7. _____
3. _____   8. _____
4. _____   9. _____
5. _____   10. _____

4. What words would you use to characterize the role you each play in each other's intellectual growth?

1. _____   6. _____
2. _____   7. _____
3. _____   8. _____
4. _____   9. _____
5. _____   10. _____

5. What words would you use to characterize the role you each play in each other's academic performance?

1. _____   6. _____
2. _____   7. _____
3. _____   8. _____
4. _____   9. _____
5. _____   10. _____

Please turn to Page 3 and continue.

APPENDIX C
Page 3

Keeping in mind the same close female college friend referred to in your responses to the previous items, please circle the one response you feel best reflects your thinking to each statement below: There are five possible responses: Strongly Disagree (SD), Disagree (D), Neutral (N), Agree (A), and Strongly Agree (SA).

1. As I think back over the academic work I've done in college, my relationship with my friend has positively affected my understanding of course material.	SD	D	N	A	SA
2. I feel comfortable when my friend and I discuss important issues.	SD	D	N	A	SA
3. I gain confidence in my intellectual abilities through my relationship with my friend	SD	D	N	A	SA
4. Though we share thoughts and have similar opinions, I feel that my friend and I are intellectually independent individuals.	SD	D	N	A	SA

5. Our friendship provides a location for me to take intellectual risks. I can try out ideas, thoughts, theories and not risk ridicule or condemnation.	SD	D	N	A	SA
6. I feel that my friend respects my intelligence.	SD	D	N	A	SA
7. My friend often encourages me to consider a different angle on a problem or an issue.	SD	D	N	A	SA
8. My friend is a source of valuable information.	SD	D	N	A	SA
9. My friend frequently presents a view different from mine.	SD	D	N	A	SA
10. I feel that my friendship with her has positively affected my test performances and course grades.	SD	D	N	A	SA
11. Through my relationship with my friend, I am able to gain a broader view of things.	SD	D	N	A	SA
12. Because I have gained broader perspectives through my friendship, I feel that I have changed as a person for the better.	SD	D	N	A	SA
13. I feel that my friendship with her facilitates my intellectual growth.	SD	D	N	A	SA

Please turn to Page 4 and continue.

APPENDIX C
Page 4

Please read the following paragraphs. Take some time to think about these relationships. When you are ready, a researcher will ask you a few questions.

Janice and Lauren

Janice and Lauren are junior Biology majors at the College. They have been close friends for over a year, having met as first year students in an introductory literature course. They socialize together often, either alone or with mutual friends. This semester they share one class and meet to study once a week for 2 to 3 hours. When they meet to study, they discuss lab procedures, or review lecture notes, or work through problem sets. Janice and Lauren share information about their papers, tests, lab reports, and other assignments to get advice and encouragement from each other. Both women feel that this aspect of their friendship is very valuable because it increases each woman's confidence in her academic abilities.

Patricia and Sandra

Patricia is a senior Economics major and Sandra a senior Poli Sci major. The two women met as first year students playing on the College's Women's Soccer team. They have many of the same friends, interests and social activities. Each considers the other a very close friend. Patricia and Sandra frequently meet for lunch or coffee. Their conversations are usually peppered with tales of happenings in their classes, news about their mutual friends, and personal plans, but both women feel that the real worth of their talk is when they discuss political issues, current events, and when they "try out" on each other a theory covered in class. Sandra and Patricia view these conversations with each other as intellectually energizing, challenging and risk-free.

Please let the researcher know when you are ready to answer his/her questions.

APPENDIX D

All	Thoughtfulness	Q1 Worldliness	Passion	Questionables	Total
Raw	110	54	196	20	380
%	29	14	52	5	/
Seniors (7) (16)*					
Raw	13	10	30	8	61
%	21	16	49	13	16**
Juniors (16)(38)*					
Raw	37	20	73	12	142
%	26	14	51	8	37**
Sophomores (20)(47)*					
Raw	60	24	93	0	1
%	34	14	52	/	49**

All	Thoughtfulness	Q2 Worldliness	Passion	Questionables	Total
Raw	133	67	170	21	391
%	34	17	43	5	/
Seniors (7)(16)*					
Raw	17	15	30	2	64
%	27	23	47	3	16**
Juniors (16)(38)*					
Raw	49	21	72	6	148
%	33	14	49	4	38**
Sophomores (20)(47)*					
Raw	67	31	68	13	179
%	37	17	38	7	46**

* (# Participants) (% of all participants)
** % of total participant responses

APPENDIX E

"intellectual"			Q3 "academic"			"personal lives"		
73			5			258		
19%			15%			66%		
			Total words = 388					

examples:

issues	(14)	4%	classes	(28)	7%	friends/others	(37)	9%
books	(10)	3%	course work	(11)	3%	family	(28)	7%
sexuality	(7)							college
experiences	(5)		relationships	(24)				
romantic/sexual	6%							
values/beliefs	(5)		professors	(3)		men	(16)	4%
			exams	(2)		sports	(9)	
			stress	(2)		women	(2)	

APPENDIX F

positive	null, equal	Q4 Role in Intellectual Growth negative	?
234	6*	6	4
75%	2%	2%	

Total words = 312

* equal (2)
  mutual
  partners (2)
  symbolic

Most Frequent		"Practical"
challenge(12)	4%	books
encouraging (13)	4%	computers
Informative (14)	4%	*conversation*
helpful (12)	4%	discusssion (2)
stimulate (10)	3%	edifying
supportive (23)	7%	exchanges (4)
		proof-reader (2)
		resource (4)
		sounding-board (6)
		Total = 22 = 7%

APPENDIX G

positive	null, equal*	Q5 Role in Academic Growth negative	questionable
224	21	18	17
81%	8%	7%	

Total Words = 275

		Questionable
* equals		competition (5)
irrelevant		emotional
marginal		friendly (5)
mututal		independent
oblivious		parent
random		purging
reciprocal		time consuming
unimportant		touchy

APPENDIX G (*continued*)

Q5 Role in Academic Growth (continued)

Most Frequent

advice (8)	3%
encouraging (18)	7%
helpful (22)	8%
relaxing (6)	2%
supportive (34)	12%

"Practical"

cheering
comfort
confidante
confidence booster (5)
console
emotional
encouraging (18)
guidance
hopeful
listener
nurturing
reaffirming
reassurance (2)
supportive (34)
sympathetic

Total = 70 = 25%

APPENDIX H

		Scaled Responses					
		SD	D	N	A	SA	A+SA
1	Positive effect on course understanding	1	4	8	22	8	70
2	Safety	0	0	2	7	34	95
3	Confidence in intellectual abilities	0	1	3	13	26	91
4	Intellectual independents	1	0	1	6	35	95
5	Risk free-intellectual safety	0	1	1	15	26	95
6	Friend respects intelligence	0	0	1	11	31	98
7	Encourages perspective	0	2	7	15	19	79
8	Source of information	0	0	4	11	28	91
9	Different view	0	7	7	25	4	67
10	Positive effect on grades, tests	2	7	17	13	4	39
11	Wider perspective	0	0	3	18	22	93
12	Positive change in self	0	0	6	15	22	86
13	Facilitates intellectual growth	0	0	3	18	22	93

generate more concrete and more tangible "discoveries." She's right, of course. My goal here has been to present a possibility, to ascertain the character of the phenomenon, and to suggest considerations. Understanding and investigating female friendship's educative value is territory I encourage us to explore, discuss and deliberate. Whether as practitioners, researchers or theorists, female friendships are relationships in which, I submit, we can come to understanding in greater depth, women's knowing, thinking, and cognition. It is an expedition worth taking.

Notes

1. Students were recruited from classes other than my own.

References

Abu-Lughod, L. (1995). A community of secrets: The separate world of Bedouin women. In M. Friedman, & P. A. Weiss (Eds.), *Feminism and community*. Philadelphia: Temple University Press.

Alexander, L. T., Gur, R., Gur, R., & Patterson, L. (1974). Peer-assisted learning. *Improving Human Performance Quarterly, 3*(4), 175–186.

Altman, I., & Taylor, D. A. (1973). *Social penetration: The development of interpersonal relationships*. New York: Holt, Rinehart & Winston.

Aries, E. J., & Johnson. F. L. (1993). The talk of women friends. *Women's Studies International Forum, 6*(4), 353–361.

Ashton-Jones, E., & Thomas, D. K. (1990). Composition, collaboration, and women's ways of knowing: A conversation with Mary Belenky. *Journal of Advanced Composition, 10*(2), 275–292.

Astin, A. W. (1992). *What matters in college: Four critical years revisited*. San Francisco: Jossey-Bass.

Astin, H. S., & Kent, L. (1983). Gender roles in transition. *Journal of Higher Education, 54*, 309–324.

Aukett, R., Ritchie, J., & Mill, K. (1988). Gender differences in friendship patterns. *Sex Roles, 19*(1–2), 57–65.

Baker, G., & Ahern, T. M. (1990). Triangulation: Strengthening your best guess. *Performance Improvement Quarterly, 3*(3), 27–35.

Banks, T. L. (1988). Gender bias in the classroom. *Journal of Legal Education, 38*(1–2), 137–146

Barth, R. J., & Kinder, B. N. (1988). A theoretical analysis of sex differences in same-sex-friendships. *Sex Roles, 19*(5, 6), 349–363.

Baxter-Magolda, M. B. (1992). *Knowing and reasoning in college: Gender-related patterns in students' intellectual development*. San Francisco: Jossey-Bass.

Becker, C. S. (1987). Friendship between women: A phenomenological study of best friends. *Journal of Phenomenological Psychology, 18*, 59–72.

Belenky, M. F., Clinchy, B. M., Goldberger, N. R., & Tarule, J. M. (1986). *Women's ways of knowing: The development of self, voice and mind*. New York: Basic Books.

Blieszner, C., & Adams, R. G. (1992). *Adult friendship*. Newbury Park, CA: Sage.

Bogdan, R., & Biklen, S. K. (1982). *Qualitative research for education*. Boston: Allyn & Bacon.

Brooks, V. R. (1982). Sex differences in student dominance behavior in female and male professors' classrooms. *Sex Roles, 8*, 683–690.

Butler, J. (1990). *Gender trouble: Feminism and the subversion of identity*. New York: Routledge.

Caldwell, M. A., & Peplau, L. A. (1982). Sex differences in same-sex friendship. *Sex Roles, 8*, 721–732.

Clinchy, B. M., & Zimmerman, C. (1982). Epistemology and agency in the development of undergraduate women. In O. Perun (Ed.), *The undergraduate women: Issues in educational equity*. Lexington, MA: D. C. Health.

Code, L. (1991). *What can she know? Feminist theory and the construction of knowledge*. Ithaca, NY: Cornell University Press.

Crawford, M., & MacLeod, M. (1990). Gender in the college classroom: An assessment of the "Chilly Climate" for women. *Sex Roles, 23*, 101–22.

Cronin, C. L. (1980). Dominance relations and females. In D. R. Omark, F. F. Strayer, & D. G. Freedman (Eds.), *Dominance relations: An ethological view of human conflict and social interaction*. New York: Garland.

Davidson, L. R., & Duberman, L. (1982). Friendship: Communication and interaction pattern in same-sex dyads. *Sex Roles, 8*, 809–822.

Dewey, J. (1916) *Democracy and education*. New York: Macmillan.

Dewey, J. (1930) *Individualism, old and new*. New York: Minton, Balch and Co.

Dewey, J. (1939). *Freedom and culture*. New York: G. P. Putnam's Sons.

Ely, M., Anzul, M., Friedman, T., Garner, D., & Steinmetz, A. McC. (1991). *Doing qualitative research: Circles within circles*. New York: The Falmer Press.

Fassinger, P. A. (1995). Understanding classroom interaction: Students' and professors' contributions to students' silence. *Journal of Higher Education, 66*(1), 82–96.

Friedman, M. (1993). *What are friends for?: Feminist perspectives on personal relationships and moral theory.* Ithaca, NY: Cornell University Press.

Gould, C. (1988). *Rethinking democracy: Freedom and social cooperation in politics, economy, and society.* New York: Cambridge University Press.

Grimshaw, J. (1986). *Philosophy and feminist thinking.* Minneapolis: University of Minnesota Press.

Guinier, L., Fine, M., & Balin, J. (1994). Becoming gentlemen: Women's experiences at one Ivy League law school. *University of Pennsylvania Law Review, 143*(1), 1–110.

Hall, E. T. (1976). *Beyond culture.* New York: Doubleday.

Hall, R. M., & Sandler, B. (1983). The classroom climate: A chilly one for women. Project on the status of education of women. Association of American Colleges, Washington, D.C.

Hall, R. M. (1985). Classroom climate for women: The tip of the iceberg. *Association for Communication Administration, 51,* 54–67.

Hays, R. B. (1989). The day-to-day functioning of close versus casual relationships. *Journal of Social and Personal Relationships, 6,* 21–37.

Heller, J. F., Puff, R. C., & Mills, C. J. (1985). Assessment of the chilly college climate for women. *Journal of Higher Education, 56*(4) 446–461.

Hill Collins, P. (1990). Black feminist thought: Knowledge, consciousness, and the politics of empowerment. New York: Routledge.

Holland, D. C., & Eisenhart, M. A. (1990). *Educated in romance: Women, achievement, and college culture.* Chicago: University of Chicago Press.

Howe, F. (1984). *Myths of coeducation: Selected essays, 1964–1983.* Bloomington: Indiana University Press.

Kramarae, C., & Treichler. P. A. ((1990). Power relationships in the classroom. In S. L. Gabriel and I. Smithson (Eds.), *Gender in the classroom: Power and pedagogy.* Urbana: University of Illinois Press.

Lather, P. (1991). *Feminist research in education: Within/against.* Geelong, Australia: Deakin University.

Latting, J. K., & Raffoul, P. R. (1991). Designing student work groups for increased learning: An empirical investigation. *Journal of Social Work Education, 27*(1), 48–59.

Levinger, G. (1980). Toward the analysis of close relationships. *Journal of Experimental Social Psychology. 16,* 510–544.

Lewis, M. G. (1993). *Without a word. Teaching beyond women's silence.* New York: Routledge.

Lincoln, Y. S., & Guba, E. G. (1985). *Naturalistic inquiry.* Newbury Park, CA: Sage.

Lockheed, M. E., & Hall, K. P. (1976). Conceptualizing sex as a status characteristic: Application to leadership training strategies. *Journal of Social Issues, 32*(3), 111–124.

Lugones, M. C. (1995). Sisterhood and friendship as feminist models. In M. Friedman, & P. A. Weiss (Eds.) *Feminism and community.* Philadelphia, PA: Temple University Press.

Maher, F. A., & Tetreault, M. K. T. (1994). *The feminist classroom.* New York: Basic Books.

Martin, B. (1988). Lesbian identity and autobiographical difference(s). In B. Brodski & C. Schenck (Eds.). *Lifelines: Theorizing women's autobiography.* Ithaca, NY: Cornell University Press.

Martínez Alemán, A. M. (1992). John Dewey: A feminist consideration of his concepts of the individual and sociality. Unpublished doctoral dissertation, University of Massachusetts, Amherst, MA.

Marton, F., Dall'alba, G., & Beaty, E. (1993). Conceptions of learning. *International Journal of Educational Research, 19*(3), 277–300.

McKeachie, W. J. (1990). Research on college teaching: The historical background. *Journal of Educational Psychology, 82,* 189–200.

Megargee, E. I. (1969). Influence of sex roles on the manifestation of leadership. *Journal of Applied Psychology, 53,* 377–382.

Noddings, N. (1984). *Caring: A feminine approach to ethics and moral education.* Berkeley: University of California Press.

Noddings, N., & Witherell, C. (1991). *Stories lives tell: Narrative and dialogue in education.* New York: Teachers College Press.

Patton, M. Q. (1990). *Qualitative evaluation and research methods.* Newbury Park, CA: Sage.

Pearson, C. S., Shavlik, D. L., & Touchton, J. G. (1991). *Educating the majority: Women challenge tradition in higher education.* New York: Macmillan.

Perry, W. G., Jr. (1978). Sharing the costs of growth. In C. A. Parker (Ed.), *Encouraging development in college students.* Minneapolis: University of Minnesota Press.

Perry, W. G., Jr. (1981). Cognitive and ethical growth: The making of meaning. In A. W. Chickering & associates, *The modern American college: Responding to the new realities of diverse students and a changing society.* San Francisco: Jossey-Bass.

Rankin, W. M. (1913). Friendship. In James Hasting (Ed.), *Encyclopaedia of religion and ethics.* New York: Charles Scribner Sons.

Raymond, J. G. (1986). *A passion for friends: Toward a philosophy of female affection.* Boston: Beacon Press.

Reinharz, S. (1992). *Feminist methods in social research.* New York: Oxford University Press.

Reisman, J. M. (1990). Intimacy in same-sex friendships. *Sex Roles, 23*(1–2), 65–82.

Rothman, S. M. (1978). *Woman's proper place: A history of changing ideals and practices, 1870 to the present.* New York: Basic Books.

Saljo, R. (1979). Learning about learning. *Higher Education, 8,* 443–451.

Shavlik, D. L., & Touchton, J. G. (1992). The new agenda of women revisited. *Educational Record, 73*(2), 47–55.

Sherrod, D, (1989) The Influence of gender on same-sex friendships. In C. Hendrick, *Close relationships.* Newbury Park, CA: Sage.

Snitow, A. (1990). A gender diary. In M. Hirsch & E. Fox-Keller (Eds.). *Conflicts in feminism.* New York: Routledge.

Solano, C. H. (1986). People without friends. In V. J. Derlega and B. A. Winstead (Eds.), *Friendship and social interaction.* New York: Springer.

Stein, A. H., & Smithells, J. (1969). Age and sex differences in children's sex-role standards about achievement, *Developmental Psychology, 1,* 252–259.

Walkerdine, V. (1994). Femininity as performance. In Lynda Stone (Ed.), *The Feminist Education Reader.* New York: Routledge.

Williams, D. (1990). Is the post-secondary classroom a chilly one for women? *The Canadian Journal of Education, 20*(3), 29–42.

Wohlgemuth, E., & Betz, N. E. (1991). Gender as a moderator of the relationships of stress and social support to physical health in college students. *Journal of Counseling Psychology, 5,* 295–309.

Wright, P. H. (1982). Men's friendships, women's friendships, and the alleged inferiority of the latter. *Sex Roles, 8*(1), 1–20.

CHAPTER 22

THE EVOLUTION OF EPISTEMOLOGY: REFINING CONTEXTUAL KNOWING AT TWENTYSOMETHING

MARCIA B. BAXTER MAGOLDA

Contemporary society requires complex thinking to manage ambiguity, continuous change, and multiple perspectives. This chapter describes how complex thinking evolved during the 20s on the basis of a longitudinal study with 39 men and women age 18 to 30. Themes that characterize this epistemological and intrapersonal growth are translated to implications for student affairs.

Life in 21st-century America promises to be increasingly complex. A college education is intended, in part, to help young people prepare for success and leadership in social roles. Educators hope that college graduates will experience a transformation from reliance on authority to complex ways of making meaning in which they are able to integrate multiple perspectives and make informed judgments. Parks Daloz, Keen, Keen and Daloz Parks (1996) write:

> The deep purpose of higher education is to steward this transformation so that students and faculty together continually move from naiveté through skepticism to commitment rather than becoming trapped in mere relativism and cynicism. This movement toward a mature capacity to hold firm convictions in a world which is both legitimately tentative and irreducibly interdependent is vitally important to the formation of citizens in a complex and changing world. (p. 223)

Parks Daloz et al. argue not simply for critical or logical analysis skills but rather for complex thinking from which adults can manage ambiguity, continuous change, and multiple interests in a collaborative way.

From annual interviews with young adults from college entrance to age 30, I have heard stories about the transformation from naiveté to commitment. These stories reveal that the mature capacity to hold firm convictions requires self-authorship, or "the ability to collect, interpret and analyze information and reflect on one's own beliefs in order to form judgments" (Baxter Magolda, 1998). The complex phases of self-authorship and how it evolves remain unclear, in part due to the scarcity of longitudinal studies following young people into adulthood. In this article I describe the complex phases of self-authorship in a group of 39 adults in their 20s using two participants' stories in depth to illustrate self-authorship. The annual interviews during college revealed their shift from accepting authority's knowledge to self-authoring knowledge. The postcollege interviews, conducted from their early 20s to age 30, unearthed how contextual knowing, or making informed judgments in context, became refined during these years and how it related to intrapersonal and interpersonal development. Following participants through their 20s offered the opportunity to trace the evolution of their ways of knowing in the context of commitments they made about their identities, relationships, and careers.

"The Evolution of Epistemology: Refining Contextual Knowledge at Twentysomething." Reprinted from *Journal of College Student Development* 40, no. 4 (1996), by permission of the American College Personnel Association.

Understanding how these dimensions integrate in young adult life is essential to help young adults move beyond skepticism and relativism to managing ongoing commitments.

On the Verge of Relativism

More is known about the move toward relativism than is known about the transformation to the mature capacity to hold firm convictions. As was the case in most studies of college students' intellectual development, participants in this study had not yet reached the mature capacity to hold firm convictions by the end of college. They had moved away from the naiveté of accepting the word of authority figures as the absolute truth and realized that in many arenas knowledge was uncertain (Baxter Magolda, 1992). They were on the verge of what William Perry (1970) called relativism, or the assumption that most knowledge is uncertain and choices must be made in the context of available information. Perry, the first to offer an extensive theory of college students' epistemic assumptions about the nature, limits, and certainty of knowledge, noted that the shift from assuming that knowledge is certain, to assuming that it is uncertain, constituted a revolutionary restructuring in one's view of knowledge and oneself. Because knowing and valuing becomes contingent upon context, and because contexts constantly change, what one knows and values can potentially change as well. Perry believed that these realizations prompted restructuring one's identity as the one who chooses what to devote one's energy, care, and identity to. Moving through the relativity of knowledge and choice to make commitments about what to believe and stand for represents the move to the mature capacity to hold a firm conviction in a tentative world.

Belenky, Clinchy, Goldberger, and Tarule (1986) also emphasized the link between identity and ways of knowing in women's development. Describing a similar shift away from receiving knowledge from authorities to listening to one's own inner authority, they identified "constructed knowing" in which one integrates one's own experience and external information to construct a perspective. This perspective became the basis of commitments to oneself, others, and one's community. Belenky and her colleagues noted that there was a paucity of this way of knowing in their college data.

King and Kitchener (1994) provided further specificity to the more complex phases of how knowledge is constructed and beliefs are justified. The last three stages of their seven-stage Reflective Judgment Model are characterized by the assumption that knowledge is relative. In Stage 5 individuals rely on evidence and rules of inquiry (e.g., faith or scientific evidence) in a particular context to form a perspective. Not until Stage 6 are they able to compare and contrast evidence across contexts, leading to the realization that "knowing as a process requires action on the part of the knower; the spectator view of the knower that characterizes earlier thinking will no longer suffice" (King & Kitchener, 1994, p. 66). This ability to compare and contrast evidence across contexts leads to Stage 7 thinking in which individuals "take on the role of inquirers; they are agents involved in constructing knowledge" (p. 70). They realize that inquiry is ongoing and that conclusions are open to reevaluation based on further inquiry.

Robert Kegan's (1994) self-evolution theory clarified the identity dimension of the transformation to the mature capacity to hold firm convictions. Kegan advocated an integrated view of development in which complex epistemological assumptions are accompanied by complex understanding of oneself (intrapersonal development) and one's relations to others (interpersonal development). His research describes many college-age persons as being in what he calls the third order of consciousness. The third order equips students with some of the cognitive processes to engage in knowledge construction (e.g., ability to think abstractly, hypothetically, deductively). Yet the intrapersonal dimensions of the third order embeds the student in making meaning through shared realities with others who are external to the self. Because the system by which meaning is made rests outside the self, self-authorship is not possible. The mature capacity to hold a firm conviction or to make a commitment in the context of continuous change requires what Kegan calls the fourth order of consciousness. In fourth order, values, beliefs, convictions, generalizations, ideals, abstractions, interpersonal loyalty and intrapersonal states of mind emerge from being coconstructed with others external to the self. Instead, the fourth order:

takes all of these as objects or elements of its system, rather than the system itself; it does not identify with them but views them as parts of a new whole. This new whole is an ideology, an internal identity, a *self-authorship* that can coordinate, integrate, act upon, or invent values, beliefs, convictions, generalizations, ideals, abstractions, interpersonal loyalties, and intrapersonal states. It is no longer *authored by* them, it *authors them* and thereby achieves a personal authority. (1994, 185, italics in original)

This system brings the creation of belief "inside" the self, separate from the shared realities and coconstructions of the third order. The existence of this system that generates beliefs makes self-authorship of knowledge possible. It also makes possible identity formation that is more enduring than the earlier coconstructed versions because the internal self—rather than the social context—is the source of belief. The ability to relate to one's own intrapersonal states, rather than being made up by them, makes it possible to see oneself as the maker (rather than experiencer) of one's inner psychological life.

The longitudinal participants stood at the threshold of relativism at the end of college. They recognized uncertainty in some areas and would recognize it as more prevalent soon after college. They left college with an initial awareness that they would have to make their own decisions, but without mechanisms to do so. Thus the college phase of my study, along with the research cited here, raised a number of questions for further inquiry, including: (a) are there finer distinctions within contextual knowing, and (b) how does epistemological evolution relate to intrapersonal evolution? In other words, what goes into the mature capacity to hold firm convictions? Hofer and Pintrich (1997), in a comprehensive synthesis of research on epistemology, point out that more needs to be known in this line of research about the nature of these constructs, their dimensions, and their relationship to other constructs. This article offers possibilities for the nature of contextual knowing and its relationship to the intrapersonal dimension of development. Although the longitudinal study is informed by the research noted here, I used an inductive approach, described next, to allow the participants' experience to take center stage.

Mode of Inquiry

The 39 adults upon whom this paper is based are participants in a 12-year longitudinal study that began in 1986 when they entered college; as a result portions of this description of method were previously published (Baxter Magolda, 1998). The primary goal of the college phase (Phase 1) was to explore the role of gender in epistemological development. The goal of the postcollege phase (Phase 2) was to explore epistemological development, including the role of gender, in young adulthood. Both phases involved annual interviews to explore participants' assumptions about the nature, limits and certainty of knowledge. I employed an inductive approach to allow students' constructions of their experience to surface. The inductive approach avoided restricting interpretation of the students experiences with preexisting theories. This was particularly important to the objective of describing a gender-inclusive model of epistemological development in Phase 1 of the study. It was equally important in allowing possibilities for pathways through young adult development.

The qualitative nature of the interviews allowed participants' stories to be the primary focus. Phase 2 interviews are best characterized as informal conversational interviews (Patton, 1990). Because few researchers have explored epistemological development after college via a longitudinal approach, the method especially needed to allow insights to emerge from the learners' experiences. The annual interview began with a summary of the focus of Phase 2 of the project; to continue to explore how participants learn and come to know. The participant was then asked to think about important learning experiences that took place since the previous interview. The participant volunteered those experiences, described them, and described their impact on her or his thinking. I asked questions to pursue why these experiences were important, factors that influenced the experiences, and how the learner was affected. Each year, I noted participants' reactions to the conversation to routinely enhance the interview process. By Year 9, the interview became more informal in response to participants' views regarding effective techniques for accessing their thinking. After the introduction, I then asked what life had been like for them since we talked last. These conversations included discussion of the dimensions of life they felt were most relevant, the demands of adult life they were experiencing, how they made meaning of these dimensions and demands, their sense of themselves, and how they decided what to believe. Interviews were conducted by telephone and ranged from 60 to 90 minutes. Seventy participants continued into the second phase during the 5th year; by Year 10 that number dropped to 39. During those 5 years, 7 participants withdrew and 24 participants were lost due to address changes or inability to schedule interviews after repeated attempts. These 39 remained through Year 12.

Of the 39 participants who continued through Year 12, 27 were married, 2 were divorced, and 11 had children. Sixteen were involved in advanced education: 11 had received master's degrees in education, psychology, social work, business administration, and economics. One had completed seminary, 2 had received their J.D., and 1 had completed a Ph.D. program. One was in medical school. The most prevalent occupations of these 39 participants were business (19) and education (8). Areas within business included sales in varied industries, financial work, public services, real estate, and marketing. The remaining participants were in social work, law, homemaking, and the Christian ministry.

Interview responses were analyzed using grounded theory methodology (Glaser & Strauss, 1967: Strauss & Corbin, 1994). Transcriptions of the taped interviews were reviewed and divided into units. The units were then sorted into categories to allow themes and patterns to emerge from the data. Credibility of the themes and patterns is addressed through prolonged engagement to build trust and understanding and member checking to assure accuracy of interpretations.

Due to the longitudinal nature of the study, a description of the participants as college students frames the context of the Phase 2 findings. The study began with 101 traditional-age college students (51 women and 50 men) who attended a state institution with a liberal focus. Admission is competitive and the entering class of which the study participants were a part had a mean ACT score of 25.8, and 70% ranked in the top 20% of their high school class. Their majors included all six divisions within the institution and involvement in college was high. Of the 70 participants continuing in Phase 2 of the study, 59 graduated within 4 years and the remaining 11 in 5 years. Twenty-one of the Phase 2 participants pursued additional academic preparation after college graduation including law school, seminary medical school, and various graduate degrees. Their occupations included business, education, social service, ministry, and government work.

One dynamic of this context is the small number of students from underrepresented groups on the campus. Only 3 of the original 101 participants were members of underrepresented groups; 2 of whom continued into the postcollege phase. Although none of these 3 withdrew from the study, all were unreachable by Year 10 due to changing addresses. This article offers a vision of contextual knowing based on the 39 participants described above. This vision is offered as a possibility; it is not assumed to fit for any young adults outside of this context. Transferability of other students and contexts is left to the judgment of the reader, as is customary in qualitative inquiry (Patton, 1990).

Knowing in a Contextual World

> I could read a text at [college], and say, "this is a feminist critique of this text," then whip on the other pair of glasses and say, "this is a Marxist critique of this text." I found conservative lenses in law school. I could figure out what various kinds of people would think. With Chinese philosophy, I've gotten closer to understanding what my own pair of eyes internally and externally are seeing. It is more fundamentally true to my human nature than political critiques. Getting toward more important questions than what is a critique of this movie—getting to what it means to be a human being with a soul. (Mark, age 30)

Participants' experiences in their 20s reveal that the mature capacity to hold firm convictions hinges on integration of epistemic assumptions and intrapersonal identity. Most adopted the epistemic assumptions of contextual knowing in the years immediately following college. They came to view knowledge as uncertain and created in context, understanding that some knowledge claims were better than others depending on the evidence relevant to the claim. Participants' initial approach to knowing in a contextual world was to use a formula—Mark's "pairs of glasses"—for deciding what to believe or do. This formula rose from the way they had been taught to think and the plans for success they had been exposed to during college. Following the formula, however, proved insufficient. Many participants were frustrated that their plans for success did not result in success; others who reached the goals of their plan found them unsatisfying. The latter was Mark's circumstance; the lack of meaning he experienced using these glasses led him to Chinese philosophy, and his own eyes, in his search for meaning. Both circumstances prompted participants to question their values, their priorities, and the tension between hearing their own voices and listening to the external voices guiding them toward success in their 20s. The increasing importance of one's own voice and self-understanding that grew out of this questioning formed a new basis for contextual knowing. Participants realized that they had the power to construct meaning of their experiences, yet simultaneously realized that the world was beyond their control. Their own voices and identity—their own eyes—became the foundation for accepting the inevitable and interpreting the world in a way that was workable for them. The foundation from which they authored their lives yielded an internal sense of peace labeled "spiritual" by many participants. This evolution from formula to foundation hinged on defining the self and making it a central part of knowing. Prior to the self becoming central to knowing, contextual knowing was a process detached from the self pairs of glasses that could be used without regard to the set of eyes behind them.

The evolution from formula to foundation can be heard most clearly by listening to each participant's experience over a number of years. Recounting 39 such stories is beyond the scope of this article. Thus rather than offer the experience of numerous participants here, I have chosen two participants' stories to illustrate the continuum of formula to foundation. Both Mark and Gwen had adopted contextual assumptions at the end of college, thus their stories offer an 8-year span of postcollege experience with contextual knowing. Their stories illustrate different contexts for this evolution and serve as examples of the larger collection of stories.

The Formula

Gwen articulated the formula concept most clearly. She explained, "We're taught to make [our] plan. 'Plan your work and work your plan and you're going to get where you want to go.' " She described the outcome of this way of thinking in her early 20s, saying,

> Things always came very easily to me. I could set my sights on something and it would happen. And I would generally know some of the things I needed to do to get there. "If you want this, then do this, this, and this," and it happened.

Mark was following a similar path, having learned the formula for getting to law school in college. He successfully used the formula to gain admission to the law school of his choice and proceeded there on the next plan for success. He described it like this:

> I tried to figure out what the legal culture figures is success. I knew a Supreme Court clerkship was, so one of my goals was to aim towards that. And if I didn't get it, I'd be so much the better off because I had aimed for it. I figured out, "Okay, to be a success here you have to get to know some professors who are influential with judges to get a good clerkship, to get in the pipeline, get in the star system here. Also get on *Law Review*. Write a paper here that you can publish." The ultimate plan for success in the legal culture, go to [this] law school and do these things, then you've got it made.

Mark initially persisted with his plan, despite recognizing that he had other interests. He reported attending a career fair during his first year at which tables for various involvement opportunities were set up. He shared:

> I went right to the law journal, that big prestige thing. I was thinking to myself "You've got to do this in order to get to being a law teacher." But on my way over to the law journal table, there was a table for street law, which involves teaching in the high schools around here. Real strong internal cues said, "Do this." So I picked up the information and was just like, "Damn! I just can't do it, because it's not going to get me there."

Following their plans for success initially brought both Gwen and Mark the success they sought.

Gwen was routinely promoted in her insurance job because she sought out the challenges that would help her move up. Mark acquired a seat on the law journal according to plan.

Mark, Gwen, and their peers were using eyeglass lenses borrowed from external sources. Although they viewed career and personal decisions as contextual, they hesitated to use their own eyes, or internal voices, to guide those decisions because they had not learned how to use them. Parker Palmer argued that "The academy has been dominated by an objectivist image of knowing that holds the knower at arm's length from the known so that 'subjective' biases will not distort our knowledge" (1990, p. 12). This objectivist way of knowing reality, prevalent in Mark's, Gwen's, and their peers' undergraduate experience, helped them develop what Palmer described as "the mind's eye," which sees fact and reason (1993, p. xxiii). Thus even when they realized that knowledge was subjective, they continued to use the mind's eye—to rely on logic and rationality, even in emotion-laden relationship decisions. Palmer identified a second eye, the eye of the heart, which sees love, community, and spirit. Although contextual knowing ushered in an invitation to use this eye, Mark and Gwen had not had opportunities to develop this line of vision. Their awareness of it, however, called their formulas into question.

In Search of Internal Authority

As Gwen, Mark, and their peers achieved success via their formulas, they often felt unfulfilled, or plagued by internal cues that called their success into question. Gwen and Mark described finally giving consideration to internal cues they had previously ignored, ushering in a shift toward internal reflection. Mark began to see his plan for success as a "careerist perspective," which he said "can get you in a place in 10 years where you really don't want to be because you didn't listen to your . . . feelings." He found his initial law school work boring. This dissatisfaction resulted in questioning and a change of direction, as he described:

> I started reading the books and I was like, "Whoa, this is pretty boring stuff." And it was painful. And I thought, "I don't want to go through"—and this took a long time, especially first semester and part of second semester and into the summer. I said, "Is this

map of success given to me by the legal culture really a map at all to success?" And it depends upon your definition of success. A great résumé or accolades, yeah, that's the map to . . . prestige. But I realized that I couldn't be a person who sacrificed happiness to that goal of prestige.

Law school was the first time that doing what was needed for success conflicted with Mark's values. It was also the pinnacle of what he had tried to achieve, and it left him dissatisfied. His struggle with these issues started during his first year of law school. During his third year of law school, he shared:

> I put major priority on "happiness success" now. That is my definite primary goal. And it took a lot of pain and thinking to change that, but for me you can be at the top of the prestige heap and life isn't worth living if you're not happy.

Mark chose to use happiness as the criterion for his career decisions after law school:

> I definitely didn't feel happy being in a firm. I put that on my list and looked at it objectively. Some of the things I put down, about working in a big law firm, on the pro side "Gives you more downward mobility (to go to a smaller firm)," than the prosecutor's office, for instance. On the con side I may write down "Yeah, but I'm not happy here." And, you know, happy is a feeling. Or, "I feel tense here," because of the evaluative process that's constantly going on. . . . one of the most important experiences for me at the DA's office was I went to the veteran prosecutor on staff and I asked him for names of prosecutors who had left the office who he respected a lot. And then I talked to all of them. I'd press them on issues about family and how you juggle that and time constraints and whether they liked being a lawyer or not, all kinds of stuff. It was really a profitable experience.

Mark continued to work on ways to listen to his internal cues as he sought happiness. Over the next 2 years he purposely pursued various resources, including Chinese philosophy, to learn more about how to grow in this direction.

Gwen was also giving up on her formula. Reflecting on her change of thinking, Gwen said:

> I think in the past it was definitely, "what is protocol?" How does someone get from Point A to Point B? Because I could pretty

much follow the rules to get there. If these are the things you need to do to be that, then I can do that and I can be that. I was pretty confident that that's how it worked. And now, thinking a little bit more outside the box. I have to look for a different way. It has definitely been an evolution for me.

Her evolution stemmed from feeling overwhelmed by the magnitude of career and personal decisions. She had terminated a long engagement after ascertaining that the relationship did not make her happy. Although she was satisfied for the time being with her job, she had other dreams for the future. Having concluded that "plan your work and work your plan" was a lie, she explained:

> If there's one thing I've learned it's when I don't feel comfortable and try to force something, I always regret it. I'm learning to trust my instincts more and more. Sometimes I think, 'Oh, that's okay,' even though inside I'm going, 'Nah.' And it always comes back to haunt me.

She described learning to trust her instincts:

> Make your little plan. Then check it out. Go on to the next step. Not that you are supposed to have this sequence of steps and then expect that you're happy with the end result. . . . It was learning to take smaller steps, look at things in pieces that are manageable instead of mountains that are overwhelming. I found myself writing a lot. That's a good way for me to kind of look inside a little bit more.

These excerpts hardly convey the magnitude of the struggle Gwen and Mark experienced during these years. Gwen's struggle with finding her intuition and her internal voice was the crux of our conversations over 4 years, from age 24 to 28. Mark devoted considerable time during his 3 years at law school and the 2 years following to work through his quest for happiness and what he calls the "good life." Both worked on hearing their internal voices, developing vision in their heart's eye, and determining how to make their way in a contextual world using both eyes. The major impetus for this intrapersonal work was the search for meaning, happiness, and peace that seemed unobtainable from the single vision of the mind's eye.

Of course, these young adults were searching during college as well. However, their search during college seemed to be for success. They assumed that by following the pathways to truth offered by authorities, they would achieve success and that meaning, happiness and peace would be inherent in their success. Questioning during college was also focused on, "Am I capable?" and "Is this right for me?" rather than "Does this satisfy me and have integrity with my values?" The shift in the nature of searching and questioning after college again reflects a move from external to internal. Like the participants in Belenky et al.'s study Gwen and Mark were seeking to "get beyond method" to reclaim themselves. The women in Belenky et al.'s study spoke of this as letting "the inside out and the outside in" (1986, p. 135). Rather than molding the self to match external methods for success, as had been done during college, Gwen, Mark, and their peers were trying to integrate their internal instincts, feelings and selves with the contextual realities of the external world. Their initial integration of their internal selves into knowing is similar to Stage 6 of Reflective Judgment (King & Kitchener, 1994) in which the belief that knowing requires action on the part of the knower occurs.

The Foundation

By the 10th interview, at which both Gwen and Mark were in their late 20s, both had arrived at a sense of self as the core of their way of knowing and being in the world. Gwen credited a book called *The Artists' Way* for introducing her to journaling, a process that helped her access and learn to trust her inner voice. She explained:

> The biggest thing in the last 6 months has been really coming to understand intuition. A couple of things came up recently—I probably knew the outcome long ago. I got little clues, ignored them, and pretended I didn't see them. They keep coming back until they are taken seriously. I listened to those instincts because they are strong—I'm learning to listen and trust them. That's been significant both professionally and personally. I am journaling every morning. . . . it is amazing what is dumping out of my head first thing in the morning—things seem insightful and logical—"ah-has." It is empowering; you caught me on a high. I used to ignore [instincts]; the message was inconvenient or disruptive to my lifestyle. Someone said the 20s are for defining who you are—still in

growing-up, but not in college. I feel a lot more centered, know about myself, my needs, the way that I am trying to pay attention to the way people interact. The way I'm thinking about it is less overwhelming. I used to think in terms of big huge overnight changes; now I'm thinking about little things on the way to a goal. I don't feel as afraid. It makes me hold on less tightly to what I know and what's familiar to make changes, take opportunities.

Knowing herself and listening to her instincts gave Gwen a solid foundation from which to approach the ambiguity of life. An earlier struggle between analyzing every decision to death and enjoying living seems to have dissipated. Gwen was still on this "high" a year later. At that point she shared:

I probably feel more content with my life now than any other time I have talked to you. I struggle less. There is so much peace in just *being* rather than searching—frees you to enjoy so many other things. There are things that come up, but I have tools, I know how to handle them, so they are not as offsetting as they were. I roll with the punches better than ever.

The existence of a solid foundation enabled Gwen to handle life's complexities with fewer struggles.

Mark's foundation came from his belief that he could construct his reaction to the realities of life. He explained:

Whatever I am in my life right now is primarily the product of decisions I made. This may have been something I believed before, but it wasn't a core belief, not internalized [until recent years]. It has made a tremendous difference—impacted every area of my life; spiritual, politically, socially in relationships, career; I believe I am the author of my life. I can make decisions right now that can change it in any direction. [That's a] tremendous amount of power; external influence pales in comparison.

As the author of his own life, Mark believes that he can make decisions and take actions that influence his life in a particular direction. Although he recognizes that external events are beyond his control, he believes that his response to those events is his responsibility. His response to life events is mediated by what he calls his spiritual core. He reported being engaged in "developing a personal philosophy that goes beyond a surface level of understanding." He clarified that this did "not mean the voice of deity, it means a kind of understanding beyond who I am, beyond a mere physical body, beyond levels of consciousness." Although he said it was a concept "beyond adequate linguistic description," he did his best to explain it to me in our 12th interview. He said:

One of the ways I have grown is to [accept or] come to peace with anything that happens to me. It will happen—people passing away, injuries, things that are inevitable. So with a broader understanding of context in mind, it would probably take a lot to shake me down to my boots. . . . As an undergraduate, intellect was my god. There is a syllabus for every class; you know when exams are and papers are due. In life, there is no syllabus! No finish line, no set time for exams. I really had to expand beyond the intellect when I got more into the real world. Intellect is no longer my god; used to think I could solve anything by thinking. It didn't lead to an understanding of who I really am. I decided to study emotions and spirituality more deeply. Have to go beyond intellect to understand those things, have to turn the intellect off.

When Mark says intellect was his god, he means that he thought rationality would solve anything. It was his foundation in college. As his quote at the outset of this section expresses, it was his various pairs of glasses to use in solving any problem. Now it is no longer the foundation, but instead a tool used in the service of the foundation. He explained:

I can see it [rationality, intellect] as a tool, a really sharp knife I can use to slice some things that are of importance to me. If you are using it constantly, 100%, you are cutting yourself off from yourself; you don't really understand who you are, and then you can't relate to others except the intellectual. That is not the way to relate to other people. One of the ways in which I brought the spiritual and emotional into daily life, and removed intellectual, is with arguments I have with [my wife]. Being intellectually right means nothing! First of all, the relationship is the most important thing and how can you extricate yourself from this without damaging that relationship? Hopefully it is through sympathy, understanding, a kind of detachment—I use this in just about any situation—when I am having a difficult time. Often times it manifests itself in detaching from intellect—it is chirping in my ear about career, money—those things don't matter emotionally or spiritually. It's like a waterfall of thoughts cascading down; you need to step behind that waterfall, no longer in the water, you can see it go by, but at a point of stillness. Not thinking. Letting thoughts just pass right through. It took me a long time. . . . Spirituality is the core—most important. Thoughts give rise to emotion. Intellect is not my master, I can turn it off. I was not like this when younger, before I learned meditative skills, and before I understood who I am. I [can] let the knife of intellect slip from my hand.

Mark's "intellect as god" portrays the objectivist image of knowing so prevalent in education—the mind's eye. As he searched for what he first called happiness, and later peace, he opened the other eye. Studying emotions and spirituality, the focus of the heart's eye, enhanced his vision to understand that knowing goes beyond the mind's eye. In his previous objectivist view of reality, who he was did not matter. Adopting a subjectivist view of reality necessitated finding out who he was and integrating that into knowing. Intellect shifted from being all encompassing to being one part of knowing. Who one is at the core, the kind of understanding reached by looking through the heart's eye, became a central part of his view of reality and thus of knowing.

Summary

Reflecting on her 20s, Gwen shared these thoughts:

> The five or six years that follow college are critical years for learning. Get out of the structured atmosphere; try your own wings, fly on your own! What is supposed to be good, what is important to me, what are my real values? For the first time I have a chance to listen to my own voice. I finally got to a point [in my mid-20s] where I was paying a lot of attention to that. During that time I was processing all that I had been gathering for the prior years. I was finally able to see a clear path, chart a course, and now am on the course.

Mark described the twenties as a time to articulate the questions, "What is going on that I am not happy? What would make me happy? Trying to understand that." His search around these questions yielded "peace, stillness, silence." While the 20s were a time to let go of the formula for success and recognize the ambiguity of the future, they were also a time of coming to terms with the core role of the internal self in facing ambiguity. Mark's *core* and Gwen's *intuition* became what Kegan (1994) called fourth order *systems*. This system brought the creation of knowledge, feelings, and self-identity inside, separate from what other people thought of it. Because these young adults create meaning from the foundation of this system, they are capable of authoring their thoughts, feelings, and relationships to others. Thus in a sense, they regain control in an uncontrollable world. Mark's ability to author his life or Gwen's ability to roll with the punches stems from their belief that despite the tentativeness of the world around them, they can control how they make meaning of it. The system, or foundation, constitutes a merger of the epistemological and intrapersonal dimensions of development and the mature capacity to hold firm convictions.

Stewarding the Transformation

Gwen, Mark, and their peers encountered a wide variety of life experiences after college. Analyzing the core similarities of their postcollege experiences, however, offers a framework for stewarding the transformation from formula to foundation. Their collective experience is marked by four dynamics: initial postcollege success, dissonance, learning to listen to internal cues, and the need to act on internal cues. Following their externally acquired plans for success, most reaped the initial rewards upon leaving college—jobs, admission to graduate or professional schools, or marriages that those around them valued. Within 1 or 2 years dissonance emerged in these settings because the choices were made without consideration of the participant's own voice. Mark found himself unhappy at law school; Gwen found herself struggling with instincts that went against protocol. As they consulted with supervisors, mentors, and friends, they were advised to learn how to listen to their internal voices. They began paying attention to their internal cues, writing them down, and exploring their career and life decisions in the context of their emerging internal voices. The need to "be happy" led participants to act congruently with their internal instincts and reorganize their thinking. Gwen's trusting her instincts and Mark's authoring his own life are their solutions to reducing the dissonance they felt. Disappointment from doing what others valued raised their awareness that one's own internal self was a necessary ingredient for finding success. The one-eyed vision they used upon leaving college proved insufficient.

Surfacing these four dynamics raises the question of whether institutions of higher learning can create conditions for transformation *during* college, to bring students' own voices, identities and eyes to the forefront earlier. Stories from contemporary forms of pedagogy suggest that it is. Contemporary pedagogy is shifting from a teaching-centered approach (in which educators deliver instruction and transfer knowledge to students), to a learning-centered approach (in which educators create conditions to produce learning and elicit student discovery and construction of knowledge) (Barr & Tagg, 1995). The learning-centered approach assumes that knowledge is uncertain and socially constructed—the core epistemic assumptions of contextual knowing. Inherent in this approach is the belief that who we are is central to how we know, thus incorporating the intrapersonal dimension necessary for contextual knowing. Teachers explore with students how existing knowledge was created and can be recreated, teaching students the process of knowledge creation in a way that develops the eyes of both the mind and heart. Students learn the discipline, learn to decide what they believe about it, and how to construct new knowledge. Learning is holistic, integrating intellectual, social, and emotional components (Love & Goodsell-Love, 1995). The value of the learning-centered approach in developing both the mind's and the heart's eye is demonstrated in liberatory (e.g., Shor 1996), critical (e.g., Ladson-Billings, 1994), feminist (e.g., Maher & Tetreault, 1994), constructivist (e.g., Twomey-Fosnot, 1996), and constructive-developmental (e.g., Baxter Magolda, in press; Kegan, 1993) stories about college teaching.

Student affairs professionals have the potential to improve even further on this learning-centered approach via their expertise in student development. Understanding how students think about knowledge and about themselves from various developmental vantage points helps student affairs educators understand the dissonance students routinely encounter in college life. Providing opportunities to work through this dissonance, and in doing so to learn to listen to internal cues, could create conditions similar to those Mark and Gwen encountered after college. For example, taking a cue from constructivist pedagogy, student affairs would move from telling students how to live in community (via rules and consequences for violation) to working together with students to construct community norms and mechanisms through which they could be maintained. Adding the developmental dimension, student affairs educators would organize this working together differently depending on the epistemological and intrapersonal development of the students involved. Absolute knowers who keep their feelings out of knowing would need guidance and a structure through which to entertain multiple perspectives and the role of their feelings in decision-making. Like constructivist teachers, student affairs educators would present living in community as socially constructed, as dependent on the persons who belong to the community, and model the process for learning how to do it—including facing the common dilemmas of diverse people in interdependent communities. Models of this approach already exist, the best example of which is the University of Nevada Community Standards Model (Piper, 1997). Staff maintain their voices in boundary-setting, yet invite students into the process of mutual boundary setting. The boundaries are narrow enough to avoid costly mistakes yet broad enough to shape rather than prescribe student growth. Students have opportunities to explore who they are and who they want to become in the context of learning to live with others. Mutually constructing meaning with staff and peers also promotes integration of epistemological and intrapersonal development. Using this approach to help students work through relationship issues, career decisions, and lifestyle choices would capitalize on the dissonance inherent in these arenas and give students a framework for developing and acting on their own internal voices.

Often, college students are in search of answers and readily accept advice regarding how to succeed in and after college. The struggles experienced by Mark, Gwen and their peers suggest that the best advice educators can give is to work on developing the internal authority so essential to defining and achieving success. Identifying internal authority as a goal, inviting and engaging with students in the struggle, and helping students find ways to develop both their mind's and their heart's eyes would steward the transformation to the mature capacity needed in life after college.

References

Barr, R. B., & Tagg, J. (1995 November/December). From teaching to learning—A new paradigm for undergraduate education. *Change, 27,* 13–25.

Baxter Magolda, M. B. (1992), *Knowing and reasoning in college: Gender-related patterns in students' intellectual development.* San Francisco: Jossey-Bass.

Baxter Magolda, M. B. (1998), Developing self-authorship in young adult life. *Journal of College Student Development, 39,* 143–156.

Baxter Magolda, M. B. (in press). *Creating contexts for learning and self-authorship: Constructive-developmental pedagogy.* Nashville, TN: Vanderbilt University Press.

Belenky, M., Clinchy, B., Goldberger, N., & Tarule, J. (1986). *Women's ways of knowing: The development of self, voice, and mind.* New York: Basic Books.

Glaser, B., & Strauss, A. (1967). *The discovery of grounded theory: Strategies for qualitative research.* Chicago. Aldine.

Hofer, B. K., & Pintrich, P. R. (1997). The development of epistemological theories: Beliefs about knowledge and knowing and their relation to learning. *Review of Educational Research, 67*(1), 88–140.

Kegan, R (1993). Minding the curriculum: Of student epistemology and faculty conspiracy. In A. Garrod (Ed.), *Approaches to moral development New research and emerging themes* (pp. 72–88). New York: Teachers College Press.

Kegan, R. (1994). *In over our heads: The mental demands of modern life.* Cambridge, Massachusetts: Harvard University Press.

King, P. M., & Kitchener, K. S. (1994). *Developing Reflective Judgment: Understanding and promoting intellectual growth and critical thinking in adolescents and adults.* San Francisco: Jossey-Bass.

Ladson-Billings, G. (1994). *The dreamkeepers: Successful teachers of African American children.* San Francisco: Jossey-Bass.

Love, P., & Goodsell-Love, A. (1995). *Enhancing student learning: Reintegrating intellectual, social, and emotional development* Washington. DC: George Washington University.

Maher, F. A., & Tetreault, M. K. T. (1994). *The feminist classroom: An inside look at how professors and students are transforming higher education for a diverse society* New York: Basic Books.

Palmer, P. J. (1990 January/February). Good teaching A matter of living the mystery. *Change, 22,* 11–16.

Palmer, P. J. (1993). *To know as we are known: A spirituality of education.* San Francisco, CA: Harper Collins.

Parks Daloz, L., Keen, C. H., Keen, J. P., & Daloz Parks, S. (1996). *Common fire: Lives of commitment in a complex world.* Boston: Beacon Press

Patton, M. Q. (1990). *Qualitative evaluation and research methods.* Newbury Park, CA: Sage.

Perry, W. G. (1970). *Forms of intellectual and ethical development in the college years: A scheme.* Troy, MO: Holt, Rinehart, & Winston.

Piper, T. D. (1997). Empowering students to create community standards *About Campus, 2*(3), 22–24.

Shor, I. (1996). *When students have power: Negotiating authority in a critical pedagogy.* Chicago: University of Chicago Press.

Strauss, A., & Corbin, J. (1994). Grounded theory methodology: An overview in N. Denzin & Y. Lincoln (Eds.), *Handbook of qualitative research* (pp. 273–285). Thousand Oaks, CA: Sage.

Twomey-Fosnot, C. (Ed.). (1996). *Constructivism: Theory, perspectives, and practice.* New York Teachers College Press.

CHAPTER 23

A MULTICULTURAL VIEW IS A
MORE COGNITIVELY COMPLEX VIEW
COGNITIVE DEVELOPMENT AND MULTICULTURAL EDUCATION

PATRICIA M. KING AND BETTINA C. SHUFORD

This chapter introduces the Reflective Judgment model of intellectual development (King & Kitch-ener, 1994), which illustrates how reasoning skills develop in adulthood, and shows how the devel-opment of these skills is relevant to multicultural education on college campuses. Many students do not understand the basis for differing points of view on controversial issues and develop their own judgments based on whim or others' opinions rather than on an analysis of the evidence. Instructors may better understand students' justifications for their beliefs in light of the students' different assump-tions about knowledge and how it is gained. Suggestions to faculty members for promoting intellec-tual development are offered in the context of multicultural education.

Is there a need for affirmative action policies for college admissions? Should courses on cultural diver-sity be required? Should campuses support and encourage organizations that have a monocultural perspective (e.g., Latino Student Union, Black Student Union, Women for Women, fraternities and sororities)? These are common questions on college campuses, and they show the degree to which multicultural issues permeate college campuses. How do students understand controversial ques-tions such as these, questions about which reasonable people disagree? Consider the following hypo-thetical responses to a question about whether affirmative action policies have achieved their purpose.

Student A: "My father says these programs just disadvantage Whites and that this is against the Constitution. . . . All people are created equal, so affirmative action policies aren't needed. . . . Once affirmative action policies are disbanded, then we'll know whether they were needed."

Student B: "Minorities were discriminated against before the Civil Rights movement, but now everyone has an equal opportunity to go to college and apply for whatever jobs they want. Minori-ties and women hold lots of different jobs now. How can you tell whether the effects of past dis-crimination still influence current hiring practices? It really depends on who you talk to, the political Left or the political Right. The two groups have valid arguments, but they can't seem to agree on this issue. I guess most people base their argument to continue or disband affirmative action on their po-litical beliefs. If you believe in conservative principles, then you believe affirmative action should be disbanded; if you believe in liberal principles, then you believe affirmative action should continue."

Student C: "It is true that women and minorities hold more faculty and staff positions than ever before. However, the flow of people of color and women into mid- and upper-management positions

"A Multicultural View Is a More Cognitively Complex View: Cognitive Development and Multicultural." Reprinted from *American Behavioral Scientist* 40, no. 2 (1996), by permission of Sage Publications, Inc.

is still not proportional to their numbers in the general population, despite the numbers of people from these groups who are earning advanced degrees. A number of institutions have recently conducted equity studies to investigate this question; these studies have looked not only at positions held (both faculty and administrative) but at rate of advancement, salaries, and how well the general climate or culture of the institution supports the success of these groups. At some and maybe most institutions, it appears that equity has not been achieved by women and persons of color in higher education."

These examples show increasingly complex ways of approaching or thinking about multicultural issues such as affirmative action policies. If Student A were to make this comment in class, a faculty member might interpret this comment as naïveté or lack of tolerance. In this article, we argue that such comments may also reflect the student's intellectual development, indicated by how complexly he or she processes information and understands the multifaceted nature of the problem itself. In student A's mind, there is only one simple answer; this approach reflects what is called prereflective thinking. Student B, on the other hand, has begun to recognize that knowledge is not always certain. The reasoning used to make a judgment was based on the student's political beliefs. Student C's reasoning was more complex than that of the first two students. Student C looked at the issue from more than one perspective and made a judgment on the basis of an evaluation of the evidence.

The purpose of this chapter is to introduce the Reflective Judgment model of intellectual development (King & Kitchener, 1994), which illustrates how reasoning skills develop in adulthood, and to show how the development of these skills is relevant to multicultural education on college campuses. To do this, we will briefly summarize the research on intellectual development during college and offer suggestions to faculty members for promoting intellectual development in the context of multicultural education.

The Reflective Judgment Model

How can instructors understand the divergent ways students explain and defend their beliefs? Why do some students seem to ignore the factual evidence in arriving at a point of view,

whereas others have a seemingly insatiable appetite for more and more information, thereby delaying or deferring judgment for long periods of time? Why do some students dismiss contradictory explanations as "merely different opinions," whereas others go to elaborate means to explain the basis for the differing perspectives? Why do some students quickly make judgments about complex problems, confidently asserting the correctness of their views? Why do others resist making judgments, worrying that to do so would be an irrevocable denial of the basis of different perspectives?

The Reflective Judgment model (Kitchener & King, 1981; King & Kitchener, 1994) offers an explanation for these observed differences in students, showing how students' assumptions about knowledge and the certainty of knowledge claims can affect such reasoning. It also shows how these assumptions develop over time as students become increasingly able to evaluate others' knowledge claims and to defend their own points of view about controversial issues. The model consists of seven distinct sets of assumptions about knowledge and how it is acquired; each set of assumptions constitutes a "stage" of development and is associated with a different strategy for approaching and resolving controversial problems. (The term *stage* has several meanings; it is used here to refer to a cluster of interrelated assumptions about knowledge. It is not intended to imply a lockstep view of development, nor that individuals only function in one stage at a time. For further explanation, see King & Kitchener, 1994.)

At the early stages of the model, students' reasoning is characterized by the assumption that knowledge is gained through direct, personal observation or through the word of an authority figure and is thought to be absolutely correct or certain. The first quote given above is consistent with these assumptions and may be described as "prereflective" (Stages 1, 2, and 3). A second example comes from a recent study (Guthrie, 1996) of the relationship between reflective thinking and tolerance for diversity. Guthrie defined tolerance as low levels of prejudice toward African Americans (using the New Racism Scale; Jacobson, 1985) and toward homosexuals (using the Attitudes Toward Lesbians and Gays Scale; Herek, 1988). She asked participants to describe the thinking processes, assumptions, and rationales they used when responding to these instruments. Participants reasoning at the *prereflective level* made comments such as the following: "It doesn't affect me really . . . I'm just going to worry about myself and what I'm doing." and "It's whoever you're exposed to—how they think. Those ideas tend to rub off on you" (p. 110). These students "illustrated a reliance on personal experience or authority as the basis for opinions, or alternately, an inability to accept the issue as problematic" (p. 110).

Absolute assumptions like these give way to more substantiated and qualified claims at the middle set of stages, where reasoning is characterized as "quasi-reflective" (Stages 4 and 5). Here, students are explicit in identifying evidence as a key ingredient in arriving at a point of view, and they are also clear in noting that evidence itself cannot be known with absolute certainty. With its emphasis on evidence and with the acknowledgment of the uncertainties associated with gathering and interpreting evidence, this type of reasoning is typically closer to what college instructors expect. However, the acknowledgment of this ambiguity also renders some students unable to make judgments about the issue. They note that since controversial questions have many possible answers and since evidence exists in support of contradictory answers, there is no clear way to adjudicate between answers. They see reasons people come to different conclusions, but not how to weigh the adequacy of competing interpretations. They conclude that knowledge claims are strictly idiosyncratic to the individual making the claim. Using a more developmentally advanced approach (Stage 5), other students argue that knowledge is contextual, with each perspective reflecting its rules of inquiry and valued concepts or principles. They emphasize that evidence must be interpreted, and that interpretations are informed by personal or disciplinary contextual factors. While this broader perspective offers a fuller view of the reasons for differences, it still is difficult for students working from these assumptions to evaluate or endorse competing interpretations. Student B's response was more contextual in nature: how one approaches the dilemma depends on one's political frame of reference.

In the Guthrie (1996) study, students reasoning at the *quasi-reflective level* "seemed to be caught up in the dilemma with no apparent means to reason their way to a solution." Several participants realized the impact of some authority on their thinking (e.g., society), but they could not seem to divorce themselves from this influence to bring their own reasoning abilities to bear and construct their own conclusion. Examples of their comments were: "I might have made some bad comments and I feel guilty every time that I do it, but I say it before I think. Because I think . . . society in general is homophobic and they don't like 'em. They like drill it into your brain that being gay is wrong so it just pops out and you can't help it." and "I try not to be prejudiced in any way because it's just not right—because who's to say that that's right or that's wrong? There's no right answer right now and there may never be, so you just have to accept it" (p. 111). Although this type of thinking does not reflect the espoused critical thinking goals listed in college catalogs, it is important to note that it reflects an important advance over prereflective thinking. Kroll (1992b) described this transition by noting that students are abandoning "ignorant certainty" in favor of "intelligent confusion."

By contrast, students whose thinking is fully reflective do not necessarily abandon "intelligent confusion" but find the weighing and judging function to be less problematic. At the *reflective level*, students work from the assumption that knowledge is not given but that they are responsible for constructing their own knowledge and take into consideration the context from which knowledge claims were generated. Further, they more readily evaluate knowledge claims, using criteria such as conceptual soundness, coherence, degree of fit with the data, meaningfulness, usefulness, and parsimony. These students demonstrate the kind of informed reasoning that most colleges aspire to teach their graduates. The knowledge claims of Student C were based on evidence gleaned from demographic data and gender equity studies. There was a clear recognition that knowledge is uncertain but that a reasonable judgment can be made on the basis of information one has at hand.

In the Guthrie (1996) study, students reasoning at the reflective level "illustrated complex cognitive ability, arguments justified on the basis of evidence, avoidance of simplistic or dualistic stances, and [a] willingness to critique their own thinking" (p. 112). They said,

> I don't understand what a person's orientation has to do with their ability to work in a job setting or teach or do anything outside of

their dating life and their sexual life. My orientation has no impact on anything else I do and I just assume nobody else's does either. I should qualify this . . . I know that a person's race and sexuality are at the core of their personality to some extent, but their other personality traits are more important.

I know that the stereotypes that I mentioned before are probably less true than people would think that they would be. But I know that I must have adopted them somehow still because as soon as I hear the word "lesbian" or try to picture a homosexual male, those are the images that I still bring to mind. And I don't think that they are accurate, but I think that I still somehow picked them up and adopted them.(p. 112)

These descriptions and examples offer a brief summary of the three major levels of reflective judgment (prereflective, quasi-reflective, and reflective thinking) and their associated patterns of reasoning. A more detailed description of the Reflective Judgment model may be found in King and Kitchener (1994). A summary of all seven stages is given in Appendix A.

Development of Reflective Judgment During College

Over the past 15 years, extensive longitudinal as well as cross-sectional research on the Reflective Judgment model has convincingly shown that the ways students respond to questions of what and how they know are related to their underlying assumptions about knowledge, assumptions that continue to change over the college years. In other words, the ability to think reflectively is not a static trait but rather the result of a developmental progression.

This body of research has also shown that even by graduation, most college students are not fully-reflective in their thinking styles. In a review of 20 studies (King & Kitchener, 1994) in which the intellectual development of 946 traditional-age college students was assessed, two thirds of the freshmen reasoned between Stages 3 and 4. In other words, the assumptions of prereflective thinking (Stage 3) were prevalent in their responses, for example, that knowing is limited to one's personal impressions or that absolute truth is temporarily inaccessible. Quasi-reflective thinking (Stage 4) was also prevalent among first-year students, indicating that they

also used reasoning that was more evidence based and were more accepting of uncertainty as part of the process of knowing.

By contrast, there was little evidence of prereflective thinking among the seniors in these studies: Their reasoning was typically consistent with the assumptions of quasi-reflective thinking. Only among advanced graduate students was fully reflective thinking consistently observed. Although educational level is frequently confounded with age in studies of college student development, education has been found to be a more powerful predictor than age alone. Adult learners, for example, have tended to enter college holding assumptions consistent with those of the class cohorts (e.g., other first-year students) but to progress more rapidly through the reflective judgment levels.

Implications for Teaching

How can educators promote reflective thinking to allow and encourage students to understand problems—especially multicultural problems—from a more complex perspective and in a way that enables them to speak with their own voices and from their own convictions? This section explores ways several educators have attempted to do so.

Faculty can play a key role in developing learning environments that enhance the process of learning to think more reflectively by providing adequate challenges matched by adequate supports. However, what students perceive as challenges will vary by developmental level. For example, students using prereflective assumptions will be challenged to provide factual evidence in support of their conclusions. Students using quasi-reflective assumptions will find this to be a fairly standard expectation that they understand and have come to expect; their challenge will come as they are asked to endorse a point of view as more defensible.

Faculty may begin by familiarizing students with controversial problems within the discipline they are teaching (King, 1992; King & Kitchener, 1994) and how these problems have been approached from different perspectives. Media such as movies, readings, simulations, case studies, debates, and interviews are effective ways to introduce conflicting views about an issue. Faculty can use these as opportunities for students to examine multiple points of view about complex problems in a reflective manner. Students should be encouraged to read different opinions about a topic and examine an issue from multiple perspectives and to examine the data that support each perspective. Classroom discussions or journal reflections are excellent mechanisms for engaging students in this kind of thinking. (For a detailed summary of this process, see Lynch, Kitchener & King, 1994.) Multicultural perspectives are often taught by examining problems from a race, class, and gender perspective (Rothenberg, 1996). Students' responses to such an exercise will vary according to their developmental level. Students holding prereflective assumptions may acknowledge that there are multiple views on a topic but assume that only one point of view is correct; students demonstrating quasi-reflective thinking may assume that all points of view are equally correct. It is important that students receive feedback about, and encouragement for, their efforts in thinking more reflectively. It is, after all, no small matter to change your fundamental assumptions about knowledge and how it is gained.

Once students have practiced examining issues from multiple points of view, the next step is to create opportunities for students to make judgments about controversial problems and to practice articulating what they believe. Before students are asked to make and defend judgments about such problems, faculty should model reflective thinking in the classroom.

> Students need to see examples of what it means to probe, question, compare, and evaluate sources of information, what it means to decide an issue on the basis of the soundest claims, the best evidence, and the most reliable experts. (Lynch et al., 1994, p. 57).

Making and defending judgments from a truly reflective perspective will be challenging for most undergraduate students; the critical role for faculty is to design challenges that are appropriate to students' developmental levels (see King & Baxter Magolda, 1996; King & Kitchener, 1994, chap. 9 for specific suggestions).

To do this, faculty should be cognizant of what skills are needed for selected activities or assignments. Kroll (1992a, 1992b) argued convincingly that teaching the skills of inquiry is a central responsibility of college teachers and offered an extended examination of how he has taught several types of inquiry (personal response,

literary judgment, critical analysis, and ethical reflection) in a course on the literature of the Vietnam War. His general approach was to present students with a complicated problem (such as investigating what happened during the events surrounding the battle of Hue) and ask them to make an informed judgment about these events. In the process, he assisted them in approaching the problem from several perspectives using the available evidence and a variety of tools of inquiry. Students read and discussed the events using a wide variety of sources: news reports from journalists from around the world; film footage of Defense Department briefings; independent journalists' interviews with survivors; literary accounts by Vietnam veterans, journalists, and others; and the biography of Ho Chi Minh. Asking students to view the question from the perspective of the Vietnamese was a new and uncomfortable experience for some students, but many began to understand the necessity of doing so if they were to fully glean the relevant information from these sources. Kroll described his course from the perspective of teaching students the skills and attributes of different aspects of inquiry, but his course can also be described as a multicultural experience, albeit a simulated one.

As he taught inquiry skills using this rich field of study, he also encouraged and cajoled students to think broadly but also to take a stance—however tentatively.

> The reflective judgment model . . . has guided my reactions to students' efforts: When their responses are dogmatic, I foster all their doubts; when they seem mired in skepticism or paralyzed by complexity, I push them to make judgments; when their tactics are not fully reflective, I encourage their best efforts to use critical, interrogative, or evaluative thinking. Thus, the model has enabled me to individualize my responses and craft them to the conceptual orientations that students bring to complex problems. (Kroll, 1992a, p. 13)

Teaching students to see problems and issues from multiple perspectives on the basis of available evidence is not the sole domain of the humanities or social sciences, as Finster (1992) has shown. He used current events to illustrate the uncertain nature of scientific problems and taught students the assumptions and skills involved in evaluating the validity of competing scientific claims, noting too that "it is humans who ask those questions" (p. 17). He deliberately used historical anecdotes about why some facts are gathered in the first place and noted where the chemists whose work was being discussed were female or from ethnic minority groups. "As Heisenberg (famous for his Uncertainty Principle) noted, 'What we observe is not nature itself, but nature exposed to our method of questioning' " (p. 17). Because methods of questioning are influenced by values and cultures, "the questions we ask as individual scientists and as a scientific culture dictate what answers we might—or might not—reveal" (p. 17).

Encouraging multiple voices to be heard in the classroom enriches classroom discussion. It also creates a challenge for faculty in trying to manage emotional responses that may ensue as a result of the discussion. Fried (1993) offered several valuable suggestions for assisting faculty to effectively manage emotionally laden discussions in the classroom. Her approach to bridging emotions and intellect is based on a constructivist approach in which there is an acknowledgment that personal experience plays an important role in how students interpret and value knowledge. Emotional responses are recognized as a legitimate—and desirable—part of the process of learning. The professor must help students understand the many factors that shape their responses. According to Fried (1993), "[t]his approach capitalizes on the professor's intellectual ability to examine issues from a number of different perspectives. Simultaneously, it helps students learn a vital developmental skill, the ability to manage their emotions" (p. 125). (For more information on this as a developmental task for young adults, see Chickering & Reisser, 1993.)

Students need to learn how to think critically about the content that is presented to them, as well as recognize the role that emotions, values, and personal experiences play in the ways they interpret information. Fried (1993) identified three sets of skills that faculty can use to address these issues. The first skill consists of *separating facts from cultural assumptions and beliefs about those facts*. Fried described the following scenario as an example of this skill. When the Europeans came to America, they set up property rights by dividing and cultivating the land; this act was viewed by Europeans as the progress of civilization. Native Americans, however, viewed this behavior as a desecration to mother earth.

Engaging in the analysis described above helps students "to realize that all facts are organized and presented within some frame of reference, which affects understanding and interpretation" (p. 127). The recognition of the role of factual evidence and the need to interpret evidence through frames of reference are hallmarks of quasi-reflective and reflective thinking.

The second skill is *teaching students how to shift perspectives*, a skill many students learn through compare-and-contrast assignments and classroom debates. "Students are much more likely to understand the value of such assignments when they have already begun to realize that culturally different classmates are likely to interpret information differently" (Fried, 1993, p. 127). Kegan (1994) argued that understanding cultural differences requires

> a mind that can stand enough apart from its own opinions, values, rules, and definitions to avoid being completely identified with them. It is able to keep from feeling that the whole self has been violated when its opinions, values, rules, or definitions are challenged. (p. 231)

Thus defined, understanding cultural differences requires at least quasi-reflective thinking; students who hold prereflective assumptions have great difficulty understanding cultural differences because they reason from an egocentric perspective that keeps them from acknowledging the basis for differing points of view.

The third skill involves *differentiating between personal discomfort and intellectual disagreement*. When students

> learn to think and speak in both realms, that of logic and fact, and that of beliefs, values, and personal experiences, they will begin to learn when it is appropriate to challenge and disagree and when it is appropriate to understand, accept, and self-disclose. (Fried, 1993, p. 127)

According to Fried, intellectual arguments alone cannot adequately address personal discomfort because they operate in two different domains. The ability to balance personal beliefs and experiences with other evidence is indicative of quasi-reflective and reflective thinking. Personal experience has some validity but should not be used as the only source of information when making a judgment.

Conclusion

Teaching students how to think about complex issues from different perspectives is a common goal of many multicultural education programs and curricula. As Junn (1994) noted, "Deepening students' multicultural knowledge and awareness affords them the potential of critically viewing the world and themselves from multiple, complex, and interrelated perspectives" (p. 130). Indeed, the understanding and appreciating of human differences as well as the ability to apply critical thinking skills to everyday problems are commonly cited as the kinds of attributes institutions of higher education aspire to teach (American College Personnel Association, 1994; Bok, 1986; Boyer, 1987).

The achievement of this goal may require the concerted effort of faculty and students alike. There is great variability in college students' abilities to construct reasoned judgments about controversial issues; simply put, students understand and interpret information differently, and those further along in the educational process are more likely to be able to make reasoned, interpretive judgments. Educators who recognize this developmental progression in their students can intentionally create learning environments that will enhance students' abilities to make reflective judgments by providing appropriate challenges (e.g., showing the evidence in support of more than one point of view) and supports (e.g., explicitly building on prior skills; acknowledging the difficulty in weighing competing explanations). The Reflective Judgment stages represent molar rather than micro developmental steps that tend to unfold slowly over time, so it is unlikely that students will abandon prereflective assumptions and become fully reflective thinkers in the course of one term. However, single one-term courses can reinforce existing skills, teach new skills, and lay the groundwork for further development. Students can produce more developmentally advanced reasoning when examples of good practice are provided (Kitchener, Lynch, Fischer & Wood, 1993) and when they are challenged to produce reflective responses in their course assignments and class discussions. Doing so will help prepare them to address many controversial topics, including multicultural issues.

Appendix A

Basic Elements of the Reflective Judgment Model

Prereflective Thinking (Stages 1, 2, and 3)

Stage 1. Beliefs need no justification because there is assumed to be an absolute correspondence between what is believed to be true (usually, what is directly observed) and what is true. Alternate beliefs are not perceived.

Stage 2. Beliefs are unexamined and unjustified, or justified by their correspondence with the beliefs of an authority figure (such as a teacher or parent). Most issues are assumed to have a right answer, so there is little or no conflict in making decisions about disputed issues.

Stage 3. In areas in which certain answers exist, beliefs are justified by reference to authorities' views. In areas in which answers do not exist, beliefs are defended as personal opinion because the link between evidence and beliefs is unclear.

Quasi-Reflective Thinking (Stages 4 and 5)

Stage 4. Beliefs are often justified by giving reasons and using evidence, but the use of evidence is often idiosyncratic (e.g., choosing evidence that fits an established belief), and situational variables (errors, data lost overtime, disparities in access to information) are emphasized as sources of ambiguity that preclude certain judgment.

Stage 5. Beliefs are justified within a particular context by means of the rules of inquiry for that context and by context-specific interpretations of evidence. Specific beliefs are assumed to be context specific or are balanced against other interpretations, which complicates (and sometimes delays) conclusions.

Reflective Thinking (Stages 6 and 7)

Stage 6. Beliefs are justified by comparing evidence and opinion from different perspectives on an issue or across different contexts and by constructing solutions that are evaluated by criteria such as the weight of the evidence, the utility of the solution, or the pragmatic need for action.

Stage 7. Beliefs are justified probabilistically on the basis of a variety of interpretive considerations, such as the weight of the evidence, the explanatory value of the interpretations, the risks of erroneous conclusions, consequences of alternative judgments, and the interrelationships of these factors. Conclusions are defended as representing the most complete, plausible, or compelling understanding of an issue on the basis of the available evidence.

NOTE: This appendix lists only a few of the characteristics associated with each Reflective Judgment stage; for a full description of the model, see King and Kitchener (1994), from which this text was adapted.

Appendix B

For Further Information

King, P. M. (Ed.). (1992). *Journal of Liberal Education.* This special issue on Reflective Judgment provides an introduction to Reflective Judgment and includes companion articles on the application of the model in four collegiate contexts: an English course, a chemistry course, an honors program, and students' cocurricular experiences.

King, P. M., & Kitchener, K. S. (1994). *Developing reflective judgment.* This book offers a detailed description of the Reflective Judgment Model and how it is measured, an extensive summary of the 10-year longitudinal study in which the model is grounded, a meta-analysis of numerous cross-sectional studies using this model, a discussion of the relationship between intellectual development and the development of character, and specific suggestions for fostering reflective thinking.

Kroll, B. M. (1992b). *Teaching hearts and minds.* This thoughtful, well-written book approaches college teaching in a manner that reflects the emotional as well as the cognitive dimensions of learning. Kroll discusses four threads of inquiry (connected, literary, critical, and ethical), showing how students learned each through a course on the Vietnam War Through Literature.

References

American College Personnel Association. (1994). *The student learning imperative: Implications for student affairs.* Washington, DC: Author.

Bok, D. C. (1986). *Higher learning.* Cambridge, MA: Harvard University Press.

Boyer, E. (1987). *College: The undergraduate experience in America.* New York: Carnegie Foundation for the Advancement of Teaching/Harper & Row.

Chickering, A. W., & Reisser, L. (1993). *Education and identity* (2nd ed.). San Francisco: Jossey-Bass.

Finster, D. C. (1992). New pathways for teaching chemistry. *Liberal Education, 78*(1), 14–19.

Fried, J. (1993). Bridging emotion and intellect: Classroom diversity in progress. *College Teaching, 41*(4), 123–128.

Guthrie, V. (1996). *The relationship of levels of intellectual development and levels of tolerance for diversity among college students.* Unpublished doctoral dissertation, Bowling Green State University, Bowling Green, OH.

Herek, G. M. (1988). Heterosexuals' attitudes toward lesbians and gay men: Correlates and gender differences. *Journal of Sex Research, 25*(4), 451–477.

Jacobson, C. K. (1985). Resistance to affirmative action: Self-interest or racism. *Journal of Conflict Resolution, 29,* 306–329.

Junn, E. N. (1994). Experiential approaches to enhancing cultural awareness. In D. F. Halpern & Associates (Eds.), *Changing college classrooms* (pp. 128–164). San Francisco: Jossey-Bass.

Kegan, R. (1994). *In over our heads: The mental demands of modern life.* Cambridge, MA: Harvard University Press.

King, P. M. (Ed.). (1992). Reflective Judgment [Special issue]. *Liberal Education, 78*(1, January/February).

King, P. M., & Baxter Magolda, S. (1996). A developmental perspective on learning. *Journal of College Student Development, 37*(2), 163–173.

King, P. M., & Kitchener, K. S. (1994). *Developing reflective judgment: Understanding and promoting intellectual growth and critical thinking in adolescents and adults.* San Francisco: Jossey-Bass.

Kitchener, K. S., & King, P. M. (1981). Reflective Judgment: Concepts of justification and their relationship to age and education. *Journal of Applied Developmental Psychology, 2,* 89–116.

Kitchener, K. S., Lynch, C. L., Fischer, K. W., & Wood, P. K. (1993). Developmental range of reflective judgment: The effect of contextual support and practice on developmental stage. *Developmental Psychology, 29*(5), 893–906.

Kroll, B. M. (1992a). Reflective inquiry in a college English class. *Liberal Education, 78* (1, January/February), 10–13.

Kroll, B. M. (1992b). *Teaching hearts and minds: College students reflect on the Vietnam War in literature.* Carbondale, IL: Southern Illinois University Press.

Lynch, C. L., Kitchener, K. S., & King, P. M. (1994). *Developing Reflective Judgment in the classroom: A manual for faculty.* U.S. Department of Education, Fund for the Improvement of Postsecondary Education Project No. P116B00926.

Rothenberg, P. (1996). The politics of discourse and the end of argument. In E. G. Friedman, W. K. Kolmar, C. B. Flint, & P. Rothenberg (Eds.), *Creating an inclusive college curriculum: A teaching sourcebook from the New Jersey project* (pp. 59–69). New York: Teachers College Press.

CHAPTER 24

A FRAMEWORK TO ENHANCE STUDENT LEARNING

LEMUEL W. WATSON AND FRANCES K. STAGE

Learning is often viewed as the unifying goal of teaching, research, and service for higher education. The term is widely used and difficult to define precisely. Learning has been described as knowing and interpreting the known, discovering the new, and bringing about desired change in cognitive and affective skills and characteristics of individuals (Bowen, 1977). Domjan (1993) describes learning as a change in behavior that meets three criteria. First, students think, perceive, or react to the environment in a new way; second, change is the result of students' experiences in repetition, study, practices, or observations; third, the change is relatively permanent.

This chapter introduces a framework that can be used for planning and discussing the complexities and factors in designing a campus to enhance learning, involvement, and educational outcomes. Here we describe the framework briefly, then present a case study involving learning on a college campus.

Student Affairs and Learning

The literature in student affairs is derived from a variety of fields that includes psychology, anthropology, sociology, organizational development, and counseling. Over the last decade, involvement has increasingly become the focus of research on college students. Involvement is characterized by the time and energy students expend in interacting with the resources and agents of an institution, as well as the amount of physical and psychological energy that students commit to their educational experience. Research has demonstrated that involvement on campus in a variety of ways is intrinsically linked to learning (Astin 1984; Pace 1984; Pascarella and Terenzini, 1991).

How do those of us in higher education ensure that we are acting responsibly in our attempts to foster student learning? We suggest engaging in wholistic planning. That is, we can examine a multitude of factors and avenues in order to maximize students learning and educational gains. Wholistic planning requires professionals to address issues within systems, examining how one factor affects another, rather than addressing them in hierarchical order. It is important for us to evaluate the links between the curriculum, co-curriculum, programs, services, community, learning and other social systems simultaneously while identifying our professional responsibilities and boundaries.

Student affairs professionals support the notion of wholistic learning for students. For example, one professional association declares that while students are maturing intellectually, they are also developing physically, psychologically, socially, aesthetically, ethically, sexually, and spiritually (National Association of Student Personnel Administrators, 1987, p. 11). It is equally important that we consider how students develop across the above dimensions prior to their enrollment within

"A Framework to Enhance Student Learning." Reprinted from *Enhancing Student Learning: Setting the Campus Context*, (1999), by permission of American College Personnel Association.

institutions of higher education. Are we doing enough for our students in planning programs and services without considering data that would assist us in maximizing their involvement in college and their educational gains? More recently, the American College Personnel Association sponsored *The Student Learning Imperative: Implications for Student Affairs* (SLI) (ACPA, 1994) which attempted to refocus the student affairs professional's role in student learning.

Such challenges have resulted in debates on some campuses as to what roles student affairs professionals might take regarding their responsibilities toward students' learning. For example, one Midwestern institution integrated the (SLI) into the strategic plan of their student affairs units. However, during the process, debates evolved among student affairs professionals regarding whether they should call themselves "services providers" or "educators." Some student affairs professionals wondered what faculty would think about student affairs professionals calling themselves educators. The problem is not really what we call ourselves as much as what our purpose and mission are as they relate to students' learning and development. Yet, the way we perceive ourselves does have an impact on the responsibilities and commitment we demonstrate in programs and services for student learning. We must ask "do we know enough about students in order to create opportunities to motivate them to become involved and committed to their educational experience?" Because it is important to design environments with learning opportunities to cause growth and development for our students, we need to incorporate techniques to encourage us to think simultaneously about several factors that affect educational outcomes.

A Conceptual Framework for Student Learning, Involvement, and Gains

Watson (1994, 1996) drew from Pace's (1984) and Astin's (1984) work to develop a conceptual framework for student learning, involvement, and gains. His model was designed to encourage a critical perspective for professionals when planning and addressing students' learning (see Figure 24-1). While the model employs familiar theoretical concepts, it is unique in proposing a simple and practical framework to spark a wholistic, creative, systematic, and critical thinking process that may be applied by student affairs professionals for enhancing student learning in the co-curriculum. The conceptual framework can be used as a planning tool. The framework is composed of three basic, dynamic, and interactive components.

- Input—Includes characteristics and experiences that students bring with them to college. We seem to do a great job of examining GPAs and standardized test scores; however we know little about students as we move away from these factors. For example, students' experiences in secondary institutions, home and community environments, as well as their age, gender, marital status, college class, housing, major, parents' schooling, and race all influence their college experience. The importance of self-efficacy, students' beliefs about their capabilities, and those effects on their lives before, during, and after college all are powerful factors in the educational experience.

- Process—Includes behavioral involvement of students on campus; quality of effort and time spent (in scholarly and intellectual activities, informal personal activities, use of group facilities, organizational activities); and influences from the college environment (agents, peers, resources, and places on-campus where students expend time and energies). Other environments represent agents, peers, resources, and places off-campus where students might spend their time and energies. These spaces may include off-campus housing, churches, community centers, bars, and sports centers.

- Output—Represents educational gains in personal, social, intellectual, vocational, and cultural preparation while attending an institution of higher education (Pace, 1988) as well as societal benefits and intergenerational effects. The literature on educational outcomes is plentiful. We know that as students proceed through college they develop along many dimensions (Pascarella and Terenzini, 1991). Central

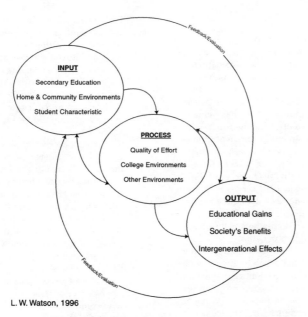

L. W. Watson, 1996

Figure 24-1 *Conceptual Framework for Student Learning, Involvement and Gains*

to most development theories is the notion of identity, those values and principles by which students live their lives. Raising consciousness to a higher level of understanding regarding the value of and respect for human existence, both collective and individual, is a major contribution to society.

In simple terms, this framework demonstrates the relationships and the influences that multiple factors may have on learning. When planning programs and services, we can consider how the program may interact with each component of the framework, input, process, and output; in addition, the opportunity should exist for program and service improvement through an evaluation or feedback process. Assessment and evaluation are the only means by which we, as professionals, can demonstrate the effectiveness of our efforts for students' growth and development. In Figure 24-1 the student's characteristics as input can play an important role in how an individual perceives him or herself within the college environment (input). In addition, the student's characteristics also may determine the quality of effort (process) with

institutional agents and resources. Students are also involved in and with various off campus activities and other environments (process) that affect the quality of effort while in college. Finally, students' characteristics, college environment, and quality of effort all have direct effects on educational gains (output).

Our conceptual framework provides student affairs professionals with a creative and critical way of thinking about the learning styles and theories of college students. The framework is designed to facilitate the use of theories in practical settings and to enhance the relationship between student affairs professionals and other units on and off the college campus. The conceptual framework highlights the importance of partnerships between high schools, two-year, and four-year institutions; the diversity of students, their learning styles and those effects on educational outcomes; and the training of future student affairs professionals to integrate the skills needed to enhance and create an environment where learning is maximized for each student. Below we describe the three major components of the model while incorporating a practical example to demonstrate the application of the conceptual framework in the campus context.

First, the case:

Central State University (CSU) was established in 1901 as a state normal school and is now a comprehensive public university controlled by a statewide board. The university includes six colleges, business, nursing, education, applied science and technology, arts and sciences, and music. CSU has publicly stated that its mission is undergraduate education. The enrollment of the institution is 10,000 undergraduate students. Graduate student enrollment is 1200 across master's degree programs in business, education, nursing, and music. CSU serves a diverse student population from across the region. Staying true to its mission, CSU has begun to evaluate ways of strengthening the undergraduate academic experience.

Dr. Durham, Dean for Undergraduate Education, has been asked by the provost, Dr. Pepper, to chair a committee that would develop a general education program for CSU. The idea was endorsed by President Harvey and his administrative council where the vice president of student affairs, Dr. Indyana, announced that she would like to also serve on the committee. She believed her division could offer assistance in improving the undergraduate educational experience at CSU. Although not all of the members of the administrative council understood how student "services" could enhance the academic experiences of students, Dr. Harvey agreed to appoint Dr. Indyana to the committee.

Dr. Pepper assembled the general education committee with faculty from across the colleges: four from the College of Arts and Science (CAS), one from the College of Music, one from the College of Applied Science and Technology, one from the College of Nursing, one from the College of Education, and one from the College of Business. Communication about the direction of the general education program was difficult; initially faculty could only discuss the general education curriculum from their own professional perspective. The committee's charge was to develop a program that would provide a common foundation for the baccalaureate degree. The foundation of the program needed to be liberal in its view of knowledge, have a focus on the development of the person, interdisciplinary in its educational approach, and global in its educational perspective. The general education program should develop skills and content knowledge from basic through higher levels of intellectual development. The common foundation was to be integrated and interactive with all majors, emphasizing the coherence of knowledge and learning across all areas and levels of study while retaining a commitment to the distinctive character of the general education program (within 39 credit hours).

The committee began by discussing courses that should be included in the 39 credit hours:

Professor Murphy (philosophy) "Students need to read things that will broaden their minds intellectually. I recommend that first year students use a book on advanced philosophy that gives them an idea of the expectations of graduate programs."

Associate Professor Rosales (women's studies) "Students need to understand the issues surrounding women's oppression in the world that none of us learned in our own undergraduate education."

Professor James (Education) "I can offer a perspective on issues we face with students who come with secondary educations that are often lacking."

Associate Professor Holmen (Business) "The general education program must include technical skill development for students."

Professor Hamrick (Computer Systems) "The entire general education program should include the latest in high technology for the well being of future generations of students."

Professor Needles (Nursing) "Why can't they just leave us to provide the courses that the students need for their professions."

Distinguished Professor Mbilizi (Music) "A general education must expose students to the importance of music and art across the centuries."

Assistant Professors Terry and Brady (English and Mathematics) both wonder why they have to cooperate with non arts and sciences faculty to create a general education program.

As the meeting goes on, Dr. Indyana becomes more frustrated with the direction the committee is taking. She realizes that she will need to be creative in order to help this faculty group improve undergraduate education.

This committee discussion is not unlike many such discussions on many campuses throughout the country. The chief student affairs officer must find a way to insinuate herself productively into this academic discussion even though the faculty members involved seem barely able to hear one another. In the sections that follow, we periodically revisit this case while examining the major components of our framework.

Input—Secondary Education, Home and Community Environments, and Student Characteristics—Makes a Difference in Students' Learning.

Does background affect who goes to college, where one goes to college, and how well one performs in college? Sociologists Pierre Bourdieu and Jean Claude Passeron are known for their work in social class, and cultural reproduction within educational systems. Bourdieu and Passeron (1990) view education as an important social and political force in the process of class reproduction. By appearing to be impartial and neutral "transmitters" of the benefits of a valued culture, educational institutions often inadvertently promote inequality in the name of fairness and objectivity. The Bourdieu and Passeron (1990) concept of cultural capital refers to the different sets of linguistic and cultural competencies that individuals "inherit" by way of the socioeconomic class of their families. In more specific terms, a child learns from his or her family sets of meanings, qualities of style, modes of thinking, and types of dispositions that are accorded a certain social value and status as a result of what the dominant class or classes label as most valued. These meanings, styles, modes, and dispositions can be called cultural capital. Secondary schools play a particularly important role in both legitimizing and reproducing the dominant culture.

At the level of higher education, colleges typically embody class interests and ideologies that capitalize on a kind of familiarity and set of skills that specific students have received by means of their family backgrounds and class relations (Bourdieu, 1977; Downey and Powell, 1993; Stage and Manning, 1992). A four year college degree has often been referred to as a ticket into the American middle class (Bowles and Gintis, 1976). Upward mobility in American society is defined by changes in occupational status and income and is inextricably linked to postsecondary education in modern American society (Pascarella and Terenzini, 1991).

Because we are sincere in our efforts to create maximum learning environments, we cannot afford to ignore the effects of family background and status experiences; more time in understanding students' communities, concerns, and problems is warranted. How are we to motivate and inspire if we do not know our students and their rationale for seeking enrollment? This question may seem rather trivial; however, we assume that the purpose of attending a post secondary institution is educational or vocational. If students were asked why they come to college, we can expect such responses as, "I had nothing better to do," "My parents wanted me to come," "For a better way of life," "To find a job," and "for the love of knowledge" (Stage, 1989, p. 390). These motivations are explicitly tied to the cultural capital students bring with them to college. And, whatever the reasons, student affairs professionals and faculty must work with students who are described in the literature as lonely, isolated, poorly guided, unequipped intellectually, unmotivated, and passive in their quest for learning. Students' differing motivations add complexity to an already diverse student population. Let us return to Central State University:

> The University's general education committee addresses one of their first tasks, to design a program with a common foundation for students who seek degrees. Dr. Indyana suggests to Dr. Durham that the committee might begin by examining the students themselves and looking at how they might have changed. She reminds the committee that twenty years ago the school accepted only students in the top 30% of their graduating classes. In recent years they have dipped slightly below the top 50% in order to maintain enrollments. As a result many students are first generation college attendees. Additionally, the committee sees more returning and part time students and, in the past decade, have seen increasing numbers of ethnic minority students matriculate. The committee launches into a discussion of various "deficits" in the preparation of their students. Many have never read an original Shakespeare play. Most lack basic algebra skills. Many declared science majors have no understanding of the phrase "scientific method."
>
> After lengthy discussion, Dr. Durham gets the group to grudgingly admit that, given the competitive climate for students, the

Admissions Office is probably recruiting the best students it can. Dr. Indyana volunteers to bring more detailed information about students to the next meeting, information in addition to the general admissions numbers, as well as some case studies that demonstrate the variety of students and their preparation for college. Next time, she thinks to herself, I will broach the matter of learning styles and students' motivations and decides to bring the data she has on that as well.

The committee's next task will be to create a curriculum with a foundation for all students' that is liberal while integrating knowledge and providing interaction between and among all majors, emphasizing the coherence of knowledge and learning across all areas and levels of study while retaining a commitment to developing the students toward life long learning. One might idealistically envision the faculty making fewer assumptions about knowledge levels of students in their classes and begin to reexamine some of their assumptions in the first days of class. An English professor might broaden the expectation that a student had read Shakespeare to the expectation that the student had read and/or had written or participated in writing a play. Developmental classes and special skills development activities might be used to take care of other perceived "deficits." At the very least, as a result of this experience, as committee members report back to their departments, faculty develop a better understanding of their students.

As the faculty committee begins to discuss what courses students should have in common, one can imagine disagreements that align themselves along the disciplines represented by the various professors. Because there are so many different departments in various locations, faculty rarely interact with each other. As student affairs professionals or educators, we enter the conversation to guide faculty attention toward discussion focusing on who their students are and the assets they bring to college.

The Process—Quality of Effort, College Environment, and Other Environments—Influences Student Learning

We have shown that student affairs professionals have access to information that faculty can benefit from in designing more inviting and meaningful learning experiences inside classrooms. Faculty and student affairs professionals can work together to inform each other in ways that can facilitate student learning. All too often, the objectives of programs, services, and classes are based on assumptions and traditions rather than facts. A campus that is committed to learning considers expanding boundaries and plans in a wholistic manner.

Today's students require more of faculty and student affairs professionals because of diversity in students' socioeconomic status, intellectual abilities, cultures, and ages. New and creative ways making the campus a welcoming environment for students we have actively recruited is indeed a challenge (Stage and Manning, 1992). Students from various backgrounds come together for a common goal, to learn. While learning, students also seek familiarity in other students, in college officials and faculty, and in the places and things they encounter (Stage and Manning, 1992). Faculty and student affairs professionals can work together to create "zones of familiarity" for students.

In a study using the College Student Experience Questionnaire (CSEQ), White students at small private liberal arts institutions described high level of educational gains but a low level of involvement in contrast to Black students who revealed the opposite (Watson, 1994; Watson and Kuh, 1996). One reason for this finding might be that White students had more options to become involved in activities in the local community (factors the CSEQ does not measure); hence, they spent less time on the college campus. The Black students were more involved on the college campus but reported significantly lower educational gains, implying that the college activities that were measured were unrelated to the educational gains of Black students at this particular institution. Additionally, the results suggest that assumptions we make based on experiences with populations of largely white students may need to be adjusted for more diverse groups of students.

As educators we are prompted to ask questions: "what kinds of activities are students engaged in off campus that would increase their educational gains?"; "what are Black students engaged in on campus that is not increasing their educational gains?" What is it about differences that exist between and among our students that affect their motivation, learning, involvement, and educational gains? As the student population continues to evolve, we must be equally concerned with the same basic questions for international students, returning students, and older students. In short, how do we provide adequate services and programs to challenge and support these groups of students to become involved in meaningful activities to maximize their learning and development? Additionally, we must remember that an institution of higher education should be a place where people grow through meaningful relationships that are developed among faculty, administrators, staff, and students for their mutual benefit. How can we assist students in these important ventures?

The person-environment theories are a major conceptual tool used by educators and practitioners to describe students' behavior and to understand how students adapt in the college environment (Chapman *and* Pascarella, 1983; Thompson and Fretz, 1991). Person-environment theories provide avenues for thinking about how the college environment affects student involvement, change, and development. Pervin (1968) hypothesized that an ideal environment for any given individual is one in which the congruence of individual and environment is not exact. The ideal environment would hold a predominance of individuals with many congruent characteristics but also present opportunities for change and personal growth. However, challenge without support to learn and develop can result in dissatisfaction and, in the campus setting, withdrawal.

Withdrawal from the institution is a major concern for educators, and Tinto's (1975) theory of retention hypothesizes that attrition results from sociopsychological interaction between a student and the educational environment. Each student brings to the college campus various factors, background, personal attributes, and experiences, and these factors influence college performance, initial goals and institutional commitment. Such factors and institutional environments lead to differences in integration into the academic and social systems of the institution. Bean's (1980) model of student attrition describes prematriculation characteristics of students that are expected to influence how the student interacts with the environment and intent to dropout or not.

Bean (1980) also looks at external factors or "non-intellectual" factors that play a major role in student persistence. Pascarella's general model for assessing change also emphasizes the student's background characteristics, interactions with major socializing agents, and the quality of student's effort (Pascarella and Terenzini, 1991). For most of the persistence models, the focus is primarily on the environments within the boundaries of the institution. However, the effects of external environments on student learning are also powerful. Student experiences working or volunteering in the community can motivate them when they see the applicability of theories. "Service learning" and its effect on the total educational experience is the topic of a later chapter.

The SLI supports the notion of collaborative efforts of all campus and community agents working together to integrate the curriculum and co-curriculum. The SLI suggests that enhancement of student learning is not only defined by faculty, but by those environments and conditions that encourage, inspire, and motivate students to actively participate in their educational pursuits. Collaboration between student affairs units and families, communities, and secondary schools has recently begun to draw more attention for creating ideal learning environments for college students (Lempert, 1996; Stage, 1996). By expanding our traditional boundaries to include secondary schools, business, and community, we can begin to better understand our students and their needs before they arrive on the college campus (Harper and Harston, 1996; Terrell and Watson, 1996; Weidman, 1989). Returning once again to our curriculum committee, we see some new ways of approaching old problems:

> Dr. Indyana comes to the next meeting armed with data. Throughout her presentation she prompts committee members to speculate about the differences between students of 20 years ago (for whom the current curriculum was designed) and today's students. From there she moves to a brief presentation on learning styles, discussing typical faculty styles as well as differences in styles for students of various ethnic groups. In the discussion that ensues Professors James and Terry describe activities in their own classes that are designed to vary learning tasks and student demonstrations of their learning. A heated discussion results in Professors Murphy and Hamrick wondering whether we will next be advocating an individual lesson plan for each student in the

classroom. Some around the table allow as how such innovation might be easy to implement in some practical courses like education or nursing but those ideas won't really help in courses where the students' job is to learn. Indyana makes a mental note to catch the student reporter for the Central State Issues to give her some more detail on the topic. The committee decides they would like to hear more from faculty who are actually trying some of these innovations especially those related to incorporating students' cultural backgrounds and community experiences in their classes. After two hours Durham calls the end of the meeting. Later Indyana catches Durham and suggests that Professor Rhoads' service learning project in criminal justice be one of the featured classes.

Learning and Development Benefit the Individual, Society and Future Generations

Pascarella and Terenzini (1991), in their review of 2,600 research studies, concluded that students make gains in cognitive skills, general verbal skills, general quantitative skills, and substantial advances in knowledge of a specific subject matter related to their field of study. The intellectual changes that occur from freshmen-to-senior year include: an improved ability to reason abstractly; the ability to solve problems or puzzles within a scientific paradigm; an enhanced skill in using reason and evidence to address issues and problems; and development as effective speakers and writers (Bowen, 1977; Pascarella and Terenzini, 1991).

In addition, students seem to move toward greater self-understanding, self-definition, personal commitment, and refinement of ego functioning as they move from their first year to senior status. The psychosocial changes experienced during college permeate throughout the students' lives in the manner in which they interact with other people and other aspects of their external world. Students show modest gains in personal adjustment, sense of psychological well-being, personal development, maturity, and tolerance of other people and ideas. "As the students become better learners, they also appear to become increasingly independent of parents, gain in their sense that they are in control of their world and what happens to them, and become somewhat more mature in their interpersonal relations, both in general and in their intimate relations with others whether of the same or

opposite sex" (Pascarella and Terenzini, 1991, p. 562).

Evidence connecting college experiences with the long-term gains and "quality of life indexes" is not very strong. When holding economic resources constant, many quality of life differences still exist (Pascarella and Terenzini, 1991). For example, the college experience has a moderate affect on one's health status, family size, consumer behavior, savings and investment, marital satisfaction, and life satisfaction index; it has a weak affect on marital stability, nurturance of children, cultured leisure, and job satisfaction (Pascarella and Terenzini, 1991). Much evidence suggests that having college-educated parents positively affects the socioeconomic achievement of sons and daughters and the educational attainment of children.

Yet, Pascarella and Terenzini acknowledge that having college-educated parents may enhance the cognitive development of young children through the indirect route of the home environment. As Bourdieu and Passeron (1990) discussed earlier, college-educated parents and particularly mothers pass on benefits to their children through time spent on developmental activities such as reading and teaching.

> The long-term trend of these intergenerational legacies appears to be not only toward greater socioeconomic security and well being but also toward greater cognitive growth and openness, tolerance, and concern for human rights and liberties. To a greater degree, the long-term effects of college on attitudes and values may also involve an intergenerational effect; the attitudes and values that students develop at least partially as a consequence of their college experience are passed on to their children. (Pascarella and Terenzini, 1991. p. 586).

Again we revisit the curriculum committee:

> By the third meeting Indyana feels that much of her work has been completed. She has used her leadership and influence to set the committee in a direction that broadens and informs their view of students as they consider the outcomes that they desire, and then begin to design the curriculum. She was successful in involving innovative faculty leaders to demonstrate their own ideas and to provide examples for other faculty rather than telling the faculty what she thought they ought to be doing. A final charge to the

committee was to develop a plan to ensure that the goals and objectives of the curriculum are met. She knows that as they move toward the end of the year and the committee turns its attention toward evaluation and assessment, her leadership skills will be critical to the committee work. For now, she welcomes participation as one of the ten committee members developing a plan to renew Central State University.

Conclusions and Recommendations

The framework presented in this chapter on student learning, involvement, and educational gains is designed to encourage us to think more broadly about our students when planning programs, enhancing services, and designing the cocurriculum. With the shortage of funds and demands on our time, it is often easy to rekindle last year's programs for this year's students. In fact, in times of reduced resources, keeping up with day to day operations can become overwhelming. Often little time exists to plan a program to stimulate growth for the diverse student population we encounter on our campuses. The diversity of our student body necessitates a wholistic understanding of students in order to assist them in their learning. How often do we really think about strategically planning our efforts to consider where a student is from and how that background might influence his or her participation in college experiences? Are we proactive in our efforts to identify students who may need support to become successful graduates? And, do we inform and identify those people who could and should get involved to support us in our efforts?

By using Watson's (1994, 1996) conceptual framework on learning, involvement, and gains, one may begin to focus more closely on the relationships among input, process, and output for the purpose of educational decision making regarding services and programming for students (Figure 24-1). A number of factors including student characteristics, college environment, and quality of effort influence students' educational gains. When employing the conceptual framework, here are some suggestions:

- Look at the programs that are currently in place. Ask such questions as: What are

the true purposes of the program and for whom were they designed? Consider the three areas of Watson's framework to evaluate and update programs to services. Assessment and feedback (Figure 24-1) of the "input, process, and output" factors should be conducted as regularly as possible due to the changing nature of students and society.

- In creating new programs, eliminate duplication of resources. Conduct research to see if outside organizations have similar programs that may be of help before instituting a new program. Ask such questions as: Will this program meet the needs of students? Have I considered those background characteristics that should be considered to enhance learning? What are the expected outcomes of the program and how will they be measured? How will feedback or assessment be reported for improvements or informational purposes?

- Encourage the creation of advisory or project teams, task forces, and committees that include students, faculty and administrators from across disciplines and the external community. Ensure strong support for collaboration with various groups.

- Plan to provide additional management training and recruitment support as needed to ensure the availability of qualified professionals who can discuss the nature of student learning and development with various groups in both the external and internal environments.

Because we are educators, it is imperative that we involve ourselves in the total education of students including teaching students how to be better learners; how to think critically in order to solve complex problems; and how to transfer skills from one situation to another. Now is the time for educators to make a commitment that focuses on building a community to maximize student learning. If we believe it is our responsibility as student affairs professionals to challenge and support students to their fullest potential, we should incorporate in our practices a wholistic approach to our work. Such an approach will require us to move out of our comfort zones and also challenge and support other professionals and colleagues across the university community to think of their work in different ways in order to enhance students' educational outcomes.

References

American College Personnel Association (ACPA). (1994). *The student learning imperative: Implications for student affairs*. Washington, DC: Author.

Astin, A. W. (1984). Student involvement: A developmental theory for higher education. *Journal of College Student Development, 26*, 297–308.

Bean, J. (1980). Dropout and turnover: The synthesis and test of a causal model of student attrition. *Research in Higher Education, 12*, 155–187.

Bourdieu, P. (1977). The cultural transmission of social inequality. *Harvard Educational Review, 47*, 545–555.

Bourdieu, P., and Passeron, J. (1990). *Reproduction in education, society and culture*. Beverly Hills: Sage.

Bowen, H. (1977). *Investment in learning: The individual and social values of American higher education*. San Francisco: Jossey-Bass.

Bowles, S., and Gintis, H. (1976). *Schooling in capitalist America*. New York: Basic Books.

Chapman, D., and Pascarella, E. (1983). Predictors of academic and social integration of college students. *Research in Higher Education, 19* 295–322.

Domjan, M. (1993). *The principles of learning and behavior*. Pacific Grove, CA: Brooks/Cole.

Downey, D. B. (1994). Understanding academic achievement among children in stephouseholds: The role of parental resources, sex of step-parent, and sex of child. *Social Forces, 73*(3), 875–894.

Downey, D. B. and Powell, B. (1993). Do children in singleparent households fare better living with samesex parents? *Journal of Marriage and the Family, 55*, 55–71.

Feldman, K., and Newcomb, T. (1969). *The impact of college on students*. San Francisco: Jossey-Bass.

Harper, J., and Harston, A. (1996). K16 Collaboration: University professionals of Illinois and the Chicago teacher union: *Universities 21*, 2, 47.

Lempert, D. H. (1996). *Escape from the ivory tower: Student adventures in democratic experiential education*. San Francisco: Jossey-Bass.

National Association of Student Personnel Administrators (NASPA), (1987). A perspective on student affairs. A statement issued on the 50th anniversary of The Student Personnel Point of View Washington, DC: Author.

Pace, C. R. (1984). *Measuring the quality of college students experiences*. University of California, Los Angeles: Higher Education Research Institute.

Pace, C. R. (1988). *CSEQ: Test manual & norms*. University of California, Los Angeles: Center for the study of evaluation.

Pascarella, E., and Terenzini, P. (1991). *How college affects students*. San Francisco: JosseyBass.

Pervin, L. A. (1968). Performance and satisfaction as a function of individualenvironment fit. *Psychological Bulletin, 69*, 565–8.

Stage, F. K. (1989). Motivation, academic and social integration, and the early dropout. *American Educational Research Journal, 26*.

Stage, F. K. (1996). Setting the context: Psychological theories of learning: *Journal of College Student Development, 37*(2), 227–235.

Stage, F., and Manning, K. (1992). *Enhancing the multicultural campus environment: A cultural brokering approach*: New Directions for Student Affairs, No. 60, 110. San Francisco: Jossey-Bass.

Terrell, M. and Watson, L. (1996). Collaborative Partnerships for a Diverse Campus Community: *Journal of College Student Development, 37*, 249253.

Tinto, V. (1975). Dropouts from higher education: A theoretical synthesis of recent research. *Review of Education Research, 45*, 89–125.

Thompson, C., and Fretz, B. (1991). Predicting the adjustment of black students at predominantly white institutions. *Journal of higher education, 62*, 437–450.

Watson, L. W. (1994). *An analysis of Black and White students' perceptions, involvement, and educational gains in private historically Black and White liberal arts institutions*. Unpublished doctoral dissertation, Indiana University, Bloomington, IN.

Watson, L. W. (1996). A collaborative approach to student learning: A model for administrators in higher education. *Planning and Changing: An Educational Leadership and Policy Journal*.

Watson, L. W. and Kuh, G. (1996). The influence of dominant race environments on student involvement, perceptions, and educational gains: A look at historically black and predominantly white liberal arts institutions. *Journal of College Student Development, 37*, 415–424.

Weidman, J. (1989). Undergraduate socialization: A conceptual approach. In J. Smart (ed.), *Higher education: Handbook of theory and research*. New York: Agathon.

CHAPTER 25

STUDENTS' OUT-OF-CLASS EXPERIENCES AND THEIR INFLUENCE ON LEARNING AND COGNITIVE DEVELOPMENT: A LITERATURE REVIEW

PATRICK T. TERENZINI, ERNEST T. PASCARELLA, AND GREGORY S. BLIMLING

The research literature examining the effects of students' out-of-class experiences on academic, intellectual, or cognitive learning outcomes is examined. Those aspects of students' out-of-class experiences over which student affairs professionals have some control through policy or programmatic interventions are identified.

In the 1920s and 1930s, an organismic psychology came to play an important role in the evolution of the mission and goals of higher education, forming the basis of the concept of developing the "whole student" as an educational goal. The student personnel movement subscribed to that concept and continued to grow throughout this century (see Caple, elsewhere in this issue). Nonetheless, the division of educational labor in America's colleges and universities continues to run essentially on two separate tracks: faculty and academic affairs administrators are charged with promoting students' academic and cognitive growth, whereas student affairs administrators are expected to enhance students' affective growth.

This functional and organizational dualism continues to conflict with holistic theories of how students learn and develop, and with the growing body of research on this topic. Over the last 30 years, numerous people have lamented the separation of cognitive and affective dimensions of student growth, defined student "learning" broadly, and asserted a role for student affairs professionals in promoting student growth. The most recent such effort is *The Student Learning Imperative (SLI)* (American College Personnel Association, 1994), designed "to stimulate discussion and debate on how student affairs professionals can intentionally create the conditions that enhance student learning and development" (p. 1). Indeed, according to the document, student affairs professionals have "responsibilities for fostering learning and personal development" (p. 2) and contributing to the achievement of their institution's *academic* mission.

A substantial body of literature exists on how students change and develop during the college years, as well as on what college experiences appear to shape those changes (Pascarella & Terenzini, 1991). Much of that literature, particularly studies examining the outcomes associated with students' nonacademic experiences, has been focused on psychosocial development. Substantially less is known about how students' out-of-class experiences influence their academic, intellectual, or

"Student's Out-of-Class Experiences and Their Influence on Learning and Cognitive Development: A Literature Review." Reprinted from *Journal of College Student Development* 37, (1996), by permission of the American College Personnel Association.

cognitive development. A growing body of research, however, suggests not only that students develop holistically (i.e., change in one area of a student's growth is accompanied by changes in other aspects of that student's being) but also that the sources of influence on student development are themselves holistic. Change along any given dimension appears to be shaped by multiple and often diverse experiences or conditions (Astin, 1993; Kuh, 1993, 1995; Pace, 1990: Pascarella & Terenzini, 1991).

This chapter provides a review of the empirical literature examining the influences of students' out-of-class experiences on learning. *Learning*, as used here, refers to any of a variety of academic or cognitive gains. It refers to grade performance; various forms of academic, intellectual, or cognitive development, and changes in learning-related attitudes or values. The term *out-of-class experiences* refers to structured and unstructured activities or conditions that are not directly part of an institution's formal, course-related, instructional processes. Particular attention is paid to those out-of-class experiences over which student affairs professionals have some control through policy or programmatic intervention and, thereby, the potential to contribute to the academic mission of their institutions.

Readers should keep in mind throughout this review that this body of research literature is dominated by studies of White, traditional-age, full-time students attending four-year, residential institutions. Studies of differential effects relating to race/ethnicity or gender are noted where relevant, but they are rare.

Other writers have reviewed the research on students' out-of-class experiences and their influence on student change and development (e.g., Kuh, Douglas, Lund, & Ramin-Gyurnek, 1994a, 1994b; Pascarella & Terenzini, 1991), and readers are encouraged to consult them for additional, related information. Because these reviews deal with a wide variety of educational outcomes, however, they are less focused on out-of-class influences on cognitive and academic growth, particularly those over which student affairs professionals, policies, and programs have some control. These reviews, moreover, cover all sources of influence that have been identified, many of which are beyond the control of student affairs units and professionals. The current review is intended to support campus-based *SLI* initiatives through a summary of the evidence

dealing specifically with academic, intellectual, or cognitive development among students, and through a presentation paralleling the organizational arrangements of most student affairs offices or divisions.

Residence

The largest body of research on the relation between students' out-of-class experiences and academic and cognitive development examines the influences of living in a residence hall as opposed to somewhere else (e.g.; at home, in a fraternity or sorority house, or in private, off-campus quarters). Because of the volume of the research, this section summarizes the findings of earlier, more detailed syntheses (Blimling, 1989, 1993; Pascarella, Terenzini, & Blimling, 1994).

After completing a meta-analysis of 21 studies published between 1966 and 1987, Blimling (1989) concluded that the findings that students who live in residence halls have an advantage in grade performance over commuting students tended to come from studies that lacked controls for precollege differences in academic performance. In the 10 studies in which previous achievement was controlled, thus providing a more rigorous and trustworthy test of the residential influence, Blimling found no statistically significant differences. This finding indicates that living in a residence hall provides students neither an advantage nor a disadvantage compared to living at home. He suggests that the absence of differences in grade performance is probably due to the fact that students' in-class experiences are so similar, regardless of where the students live.

Residence hall students appear to have a slight advantage in academic achievement over those living in fraternity or sorority houses, but the advantage is small and only two of the nine studies Blimling (1989) examined had controlled for previous academic achievement. Similarly, students living in conventional residence halls outperform those living in private, off-campus quarters by a statistically significant, but small, margin. Blimling identified only four studies of this relation, however, and warns that the findings might be unstable because of the small number of studies.

A number of institutions have experimented with their room assignment policies in efforts to enhance student learning. Where students are assigned on the basis of their academic performance, high-ability students assigned to live with other high-ability students perform better than high-ability students assigned at random, even after controlling for initial academic achievement. Such halls may create a peer culture that supports and promotes academic achievement through competition, status rewards for high performance, and perhaps informal peer tutoring arrangements in areas of common academic interest (Blimling, 1993). Consistent with this environmental hypothesis, students living on floors with an enforced study hours policy have been shown to perform better academically than students living on conventional residence hall floors without such policies (Blimling & Hample, 1979).

The evidence is mixed on assignment policies designed to enhance achievement by housing students according to their academic major field or interest. Blimling (1993) found two studies suggesting that students who live in a hall with other students in the same major field perform better academically than students in a conventional hall. Because of self-selection in both of these studies, however, living arrangement may be confounded with motivation. In two other studies in Blimling's review, the researchers found no differences between students assigned to a homogeneous hall and those assigned at random. Morishima (1966), however, found students assigned to hall floors by major field showed greater gains on a measure of scholarly orientation, but he found no differences in grade performance.

Studies of the effects on academic achievement of housing policies that assign entering students to all-freshman halls have also produced mixed results. Blimling (1993) found three studies reporting that students in an all-freshman hall performed better academically than those assigned to a hall with a mix of new and upper-division students. Three other studies in his review, however, were not so supportive. In one, researchers found that students in an all-freshman hall performed less well than those in mixed halls, and in the other two, the researchers reported finding no significant differences. Nor did any evidence suggest that a new student assigned to room with an upper division student has any advantage over a new student having another new student for a roommate. Some research (Beal & Williams, 1968; Schoeck, 1973)

indicates that the intellectual atmosphere was perceived to be somewhat lower in all-freshman halls than in mixed ones.

The academic performance of students in coed halls is neither better nor worse than that of their peers in single-sex halls. The only conclusive effect appears to be that students living in a coed residence hall (vs. a single-sex hall) are more likely to become socially involved with members of the opposite sex (Blimling, 1993).

Other alternative housing policies include pairing a high-ability student with an average-ability student and assigning a low- to average-ability student to room with a higher-ability student who has a similar personality profile. The number of studies of these alternatives, however, is too small or their results too are equivocal for researchers to recommend such alternatives for serious policy consideration.

One study included in Blimling's (1993) review led him to conclude that students who attend institutions housing a relatively small number of students (fewer than 4,000) and who share a room designed for two with one other student perform academically better than students assigned to a similar room that has been over-assigned to create a three-person room. In similar studies done at institutions housing more than 4,000 students, however, researchers have found no statistically significant differences in academic achievement. Blimling identified one study at a large university in which students in overassigned rooms outperformed their peers in rooms that were not overassigned. He suggests, among various possible explanations for these results, that students at larger institutions may have learned to cope with their institutions' size and the social density of the living centers; that students attending smaller institutions may have had a greater need for privacy than students at larger schools, and that the social density of the hall may have been more important than the total number of students living on campus.

Academic achievement, however, is only one of the academic and cognitive outcomes over which place of residence may have some influence. A growing body of research indicates that students' interpersonal interactions with peers and faculty members shape a number of dimensions of cognitive growth (Baxter Magolda, 1987, 1992; Pascarella & Terenzini, 1991; Perry, 1970), and that residence halls clearly afford more opportunities than other living arrangements for students to interact with peers and faculty members. The effects of place of residence on cognitive outcomes other than academic achievement, however, have received far less research attention (Pascarella et al., 1994).

The findings from studies on other learning outcomes are mixed. Although the evidence is limited, living in a residence hall may also facilitate the development of principled moral reasoning (Rest & Deemer, 1986). Hood (1984) found no significant relation between place of residence and gains in cognitive complexity. Winter, McClelland, and Stewart (1981), on the other hand, reported that level of involvement in residence hall activities had a statistically significant *negative* association with gains on a projective measure of critical thinking. They speculated that residence halls may prolong a protective, quasi-familial atmosphere rather than providing an intellectually-challenging living environment. However, because initial scores on their measure of critical thinking were left uncontrolled, several other factors are confounded with level of participation in hall activities.

In a more rigorously controlled study, Pascarella, Bohr, Nora, Zusman, Inman, and Desler (1993) examined students' first-year gains on measures of critical thinking, reading comprehension, and mathematical skills, while controlling for initial level of development on each of these measures, as well as precollege motivation, age, work responsibilities, and freshman-year credit hours taken. Students living on campus, compared with commuters, showed significantly larger gains in critical thinking and larger, but only marginally significant, gains in reading. No differences were found in math skill gains. These findings await replication, but they nevertheless suggest that residence halls may have an important role to play in promoting dimensions of students' cognitive development that are not closely tied to coursework activities and experiences.

Environments within residence halls vary (Moos, 1976, 1979), of course, and it is reasonable to suggest that some environments affect students' academic and intellectual development more than others. A moderately large and consistent body of research indicates that students who live in residence halls programmatically designed to promote academic and intellectual development experience greater cognitive gains than students in conventional residence halls. Such "living-learning centers" (LLCs) vary a

good deal in structure and activities, but they typically involve high levels of student-faculty interaction; targeted, intellectually oriented programming; academic advising and classes in the residence hall; and an academically and intellectually supportive peer environment. Students in LLCs not only perceive a stronger intellectual dimension to their living environment, but also perform better academically (even after controlling for precollege achievement). Only one study (Pemberton, 1969) found no academic achievement advantage to living in an LLC. In general, LLC students also show greater gains on measures of cognitive development and intellectual orientation (Lacy, 1978; Newcomb, Brown, Kulik, Reimer, & Revelle, 1970, 1971; Pascarella & Terenzini, 1980, 1981). The evidence is somewhat mixed on LLC's effects on other learning-related outcomes (e.g., aesthetic and cultural interests).

However, most of the influence of LLCs on students' intellectual and cognitive growth appears to occur indirectly, rather than directly, through the kinds of interpersonal interactions with peers and faculty members the LLCs promote and the greater opportunities they afford for such interactions (Lacy, 1978; Pascarella & Terenzini, 1980). These interpersonal contacts, in turn, exert a direct influence on various dimensions of student intellectual and cognitive development. This conclusion is supported by the growing evidence that many of colleges' effects are mediated through the interpersonal environments they create (Astin, 1993; Kuh, 1995; Pascarella & Terenzini, 1991).

Whatever mechanisms are involved, the evidence clearly supports Blimling's (1993) suggestion that residence hall interventions can be designed in ways that shape students' academic, intellectual, and cognitive growth. Discussion of what some of those interventions are is beyond the scope of this review, but numerous suggestions are provided elsewhere (e.g., in this issue; Schroeder & Mable, 1994).

Fraternities and Sororities

The evidence on the relation between membership in a fraternity or sorority house and students' intellectual and cognitive development is modestly consistent in suggesting that the general influences are negative, although not strong. As noted earlier, students living in a fraternity or sorority are at a slight disadvantage in terms of academic achievement when compared to students living in a residence hall (Astin, 1993; Blimling, 1989, 1993).

The evidence dealing with the effects of Greek society membership on first-year students' cognitive development is consistent with the research on academic achievement. Results from the 23-institution National Study of Student Learning (Pascarella, Nora, Edison, Hagedorn, & Terenzini, in press; see also Pascarella et al. elsewhere in this issue) indicates that, after taking into account precollege cognitive development and other potentially confounding variables, fraternity membership (vs. being an independent) during the first year of college was significantly and negatively related to reading, mathematics, and critical thinking skills, as well as to a measure of composite achievement. The negative effects were particularly pronounced for White males. For men of color, however, fraternity membership had a modest, positive influence on all four outcomes. Similar analyses for women indicated that first-year sorority membership also had a negative effect, but only those for reading and composite achievement were statistically significant, and the negative effects tended to be smaller for women than men. Results consistent with the general findings of this study are reported in Terenzini, Springer, Pascarella, and Nora (1994b).

In one study, fraternity and sorority members were found to have initially lower scores on a measure of cultural sophistication than independents, but freshman-to-senior gains were about-the same for both groups (Wilder, Hoyt, Doren, Hauck, & Zettle, 1978). In a replication of this study (Wilder, Hoyt, Surbeck, Wilder, & Carney, 1986), however, Greek society members showed smaller gains in cultural sophistication, but students who had pledged a fraternity or sorority but had subsequently withdrawn showed the greatest gains, suggesting that something in addition to Greek society membership was probably involved. Marlowe and Auvenshine (1982) found no differences in gains in principled moral reasoning over a 9-month period between fraternity-affiliated freshmen and independents Sanders (1990) report similar results.

Intercollegiate Athletics

The cognitive outcomes associated with participation in intercollegiate athletics have drawn only modest attention, and most of the existing evidence that exists focuses largely on academic achievement. Overall, the evidence indicates that after taking into account students' precollege aptitudes, achievements, and other relevant characteristics, intercollegiate athletes' academic achievement is approximately the same as that of their nonathlete peers (American College Testing Program & the Educational Testing Service, 1984; Hood et al., 1992; Pascarella & Smart, 1991; Smith & Dizney, 1966; Stuart, 1985). This parity holds even when the groups compared are in revenue producing sports (Hood, Craig, & Ferguson, 1992; Smith & Dizney, 1966; Stuart, 1985).

Only four studies were identified that dealt with the effects of intercollegiate sports participation on dimensions of academic and cognitive development other than achievement (Astin, 1977, 1993; Pascarella, Bohr, Nora, & Terenzini, 1995; Winter et al., 1981). According to the investigators in three of those four studies, the effects were negative, Only Winter et al. report a positive association (among both women and men) between participation in intercollegiate athletics and gains in a measure of critical thinking and broad analytical skills during college. Astin (1977) reports a series of findings that led him to conclude that intercollegiate sports participation tends to isolate athletes from their nonathlete peers and, consequently, from the effects of college mediated by other students. More recent evidence supports that conclusion. After controlling for relevant precollege characteristics, participation in intercollegiate athletics has been shown to be negatively related to scores on standardized graduate admissions tests such as the verbal portion of the Graduate Record Examination, the Law School Admission Test, and the National Teachers Examination (Astin, 1993).

Some evidence suggests that the negative effects for men may be sport-specific. After controlling for precollege ability, other student characteristics, and NCAA level of competition, Pascarella, Bohr, Nora, and Terenzini (1995) found that male football and basketball players (compared with male athletes in other intercollegiate sports and nonathletes) declined on measures of reading comprehension and math skills during their first year. No statistically significant differences were found between nonathletes and students participating in intercollegiate sports other than football or basketball. Interestingly, this relationship was apparent among football and basketball players, independent of the NCAA divisional level at which they played. This finding suggests that the disadvantages of first-year participation in intercollegiate football and basketball may be a function of the culture surrounding those sports in general rather than the intensity or competitive level at which they are played. That culture may promote a set of academic values and behaviors different from those of other intercollegiate sports and, as Astin (1977) suggests, afford greater insulation from interactions with non-athlete peers.

Women intercollegiate athletes (all sports combined) showed significantly smaller gains in reading comprehension compared to nonathletes, but there were no statistically significant differences between the two groups in the gains made in math and critical thinking skills (Pascarella, Bohr, Nora, & Terenzini, 1995). The evidence also suggests that the first-year reading disadvantage among women athletes may be greatest for those who enter college with the lowest reading skills.

The findings for both men and women intercollegiate athletes suggest that if steps are to be taken to reverse or reduce these learning disadvantages, any intervention will have to occur early in these students' college careers. Disadvantages identifiable after only year of college are likely to grow larger over time. The evidence clearly does not support current policies permitting freshmen to participate in intercollegiate athletics. If institutions continue to permit male freshmen to participate in intercollegiate football and basketball, the evidence suggests a clear need for early intervention and support to avoid the potential negative cognitive consequences of such participation.

Employment

The research relating to the learning effects of employment is limited, and the results are mixed. In two studies, no relationship was found between work experiences and gains in cognitive complexity (Hood, 1984) or in reading, math, or critical thinking skills (Pascarella, Bohr, Nora, Desler, & Zusman, 1994). Astin (1993), however, found that working full-time had a negative effect on grade-point average. Part-time off-campus work had a pattern of effects highly similar to that associated with full-time employment, but part-time *on-campus* work had a positive effect on virtually all areas of self-reported cognitive and affective growth. To the extent that part-time employment opportunities can be linked to students' academic experiences, however, they constitute additional opportunities to shape students' academic and cognitive development, as well as their interpersonal and practical skills (Kuh, 1995).

Other Extracurricular Activities

The literature relating students' participation in extra- or cocurricular activities to various forms of academic or cognitive development is small and diffuse. Formal extracurricular activities other than those discussed earlier have attracted little or no attention. Moreover, probably because of the large number and wide variety of sponsored activities that might fall under the rubric of "extracurricular activity," most researchers have either operationalized the concept as a global variable, or they have made no clear distinction between extracurricular and peer involvement (Pascarella & Terenzini, 1991).

Hood (1984) found no relation between participation in extracurricular activities and cognitive complexity, and Pascarella (1989) found no links between involvement in extracurricular activities and first-year gains in critical thinking when precollege critical thinking ability was taken into account. Terenzini, Springer, Pascarella, and Nora (1994a), on the other hand, report that involvement in clubs and organizations was positively related to first-year gains in critical thinking, even with a variety of precollege characteristics (including initial critical thinking ability) controlled.

After controlling for ability and other precollege characteristics, Astin (1993) found that students who participated in internships or study-abroad experiences had higher grades and self-reported gains in knowledge of a particular field, although this latter effect was weak. (Although internship and study-abroad programs on many campuses may be considered academic programs, they are included in this review because of the opportunities available to student affairs professionals to contribute through the identification and development of such opportunities, as well as to promote such programs among students.) Astin also found that students who had received vocational or career counseling reported greater gains in their critical thinking and analytical and problem-solving skills, although the latter effect was also a weak one.

Overall, the literature contains little consistent evidence suggesting that extracurricular involvement per se has a direct impact on students' academic or intellectual development (Pascarella & Terenzini, 1991). It seems reasonable to suggest, however, that formal extracurricular activities may have an indirect effect on learning gains through the kinds of interpersonal contacts and interactions they create between students and faculty members and between students and their peers.

Faculty Interactions

In addition to having strong instructional skills, most successful classroom teachers are also accessible to students outside of class (Wilson, Wood, & Gaff, 1974; Wilson, Gaff, Dienst, Wood, & Bavry, 1975). Wilson and his colleagues found that seniors who reported the greatest gains in such skills as the ability to comprehend, interpret, or extrapolate; to evaluate materials and methods; and to apply abstractions or principles also reported the most informal, out-of-class contact with faculty members. With some exceptions (e.g., Pascarella, 1989; Terenzini, Pascarella, & Lorang, 1982; Volkwein, King, & Terenzini, 1986), most researchers have reported positive associations between the nature and frequency of students' out-of-class contacts with faculty members and gains on one or another measure of academic or cognitive development (e.g., Astin, 1993; Baxter Magolda, 1987; Endo & Harpel, 1982, 1983; Kuh, 1995; Pascarella & Terenzini, 1980; Terenzini, Springer, Pascarella, & Nora, 1995; Terenzini, Theophilides, & Lorang, 1984; Terenzini & Wright, 1987). Although all of these studies are based on students' self-reported gains in knowledge and/or academic or intellectual skills, the evidence based on objective measures of cognitive skills leads to the same conclusion (e.g., Terenzini et al., 1994a, 1994b).

The causal direction of all these influences remains problematic, however. Are students who gain more in their cognitive capacities more likely to seek contact with faculty members, or does the contact promote the development? In terms of policy or practice, whether the learning gains are the catalyst or a consequence of student-faculty interaction is a less interesting or urgent question than how to promote it. Student—faculty contact

and student learning are positively related, and it would seem that finding ways to promote such contact is in the best educational interests of both students and institutions.

Peer Interactions

Students learn not only through their out-of-class contacts with faculty members but also through their interactions with peers. Such interactions can, of course, take many different forms, occur in many different settings, and have many different purposes. The evidence is generally clear, however, that when peer interactions involve educational or intellectual activities or topics, the effects are almost always beneficial to students.

Most of the recent research indicates, for example, that peer teaching or tutoring has a positive influence on learning (Annis, 1983; Astin, 1993; Bargh & Schul, 1980; Benware & Deci, 1984: Goldschmidt & Goldschmidt, 1976). The findings in this area are generally consistent in suggesting that peer tutoring increases student involvement in the learning process and enhances content mastery, particularly with conceptual content. Astin found that tutoring other students was positively related to grade-point average, analytical and problem-solving skills, a composite measure of overall academic development, and GRE-Quantitative scores. The causal direction of the last finding, however, remains unclear. Do capable students self-select themselves to be tutors, does the process of tutoring enhance learning, or is it both? As with the evidence on the positive benefits of student interactions with faculty, the question is an academic one, from the perspective of policy or practice. When tutoring takes place, students (both tutors and tutored) and institution benefit.

The character of the peer environment may also be important. Terenzini et al. (1995) found that students who characterized their relationships with other students as being competitive or uninvolved or as producing a sense of alienation were more likely to experience first-year gains in their intellectual orientation than were students who portrayed their peer relations as being friendly and supportive or as producing a sense of belonging. This finding would appear to pose a challenge to student affairs professionals: Can the peer environment be shaped in ways that promote students' learning and intellectual orientations without also creating a competitive atmosphere in which students feel separated or isolated?

Certain other specific forms of student-peer interactions appear to have statistically significant and positive effects. Discussing racial/ethnic issues appears to contribute to students' overall academic development and to gains in general knowledge, critical thinking, and analytical and problem-solving skills (Astin, 1993; Kuh, 1995). Students' socializing with people of different racial/ethnic groups has been related to enhanced overall academic development and to knowledge gains in a particular field or discipline (Astin, 1993), and participation in a racial/cultural awareness workshop appears to be positively related to first-year gains in critical thinking, even when precollege thinking skills are controlled (Terenzini et al., 1994b).

Not all student-peer interactions, however, produce benefits in the academic or cognitive domains. Astin (1993) identified several activities that appear to be negatively related to academic or cognitive development, including the number of hours per week spent in volunteer activities (on GRE-Verbal and GRE-Composite scores; no explanation for this finding was offered or apparent), the hours per week spent partying (on GPA), and the number of hours spent socializing with friends (on LSAT and GRE-Analytical scores). Terenzini et al. (1995) also found a negative relation between time spent socializing and development of students' intellectual orientations. These latter findings suggest that the peer influences on student learning are shaped not simply by the occurrence of peer interaction but also by the content of those interactions.

The whole, however, is probably greater than the sum of its parts. In their review, Pascarella and Terenzini's (1991) review indicate that the impact of any given collegiate experience is smaller than the cumulative effect of multiple experiences, particularly when they are mutually supportive and reinforcing. Other researchers have reached similar conclusions with respect to both overall student involvement in general and students' peers in particular (Astin, 1993; Kuh, 1995; MacKay & Kuh, 1994; Pace, 1984, 1990). Indeed, Astin has argued that students' peers are the single most important source of influence on most campuses. Kuh found that students attributed gains in knowledge and academic skills primarily to their academic experiences and

to faculty contact, but that reported gains in cognitive complexity (e.g., reflective thought and knowledge application) were attributed approximately equally to peers and academic activities (peers had a somewhat stronger influence among women than among men). Other researchers have found similar academic and out-of-class parity in the degree of influence on critical thinking gains (Terenzini, et al., 1994a, 1994b).

Conclusions

In the *SLI*, the American College Personnel Association (1994) calls for student affairs professionals to consider how they "can intentionally create the conditions that enhance student learning and development" (p. 1). The *SLI* further notes that "If learning is the primary measure of institutional productivity by which the quality of undergraduate education is determined, what and how much students learn also must be the criteria by which the value of student affairs is judged" (p. 2). The *SLI* defines "learning" in ways that extend beyond personal or psychosocial development to include students' academic, intellectual, and cognitive development as well. The current paper reviewed the research literature on the effects of students' out-of-class experiences on academic, intellectual, or cognitive learning outcomes. One purpose was to provide some sense of the extent to which those experiences, in fact, shape intellectual and cognitive growth. A second purpose was to identify those aspects of students' out-of-class lives that have some potential to enhance student learning and over which student affairs professionals have some control through their policy and programmatic interventions. This review suggests a number of conclusions.

First, students' out-of-class experiences appear to be far more influential in students' academic and intellectual development than many faculty members and academic and student affairs administrators think. Even when students' precollege academic learning and cognitive ability levels and other relevant characteristics are taken into account, academic and cognitive learning are positively shaped by a wide variety of out-of-class experiences. These influences include such specific experiences as living in a residence hall, particularly one in which the various dimensions of students' academic and nonacademic lives are purposefully-integrated; working part-time on campus; discussing racial or ethnic issues; socializing with others of different racial or ethnic groups; having an internship; spending a term studying abroad; and interacting with other students and faculty members, particularly when the topics of discussion are academically or intellectually related. Clear implications of this overall body of evidence are that revisions in current and widespread beliefs about how students develop cognitively and intellectually are needed, that such development occurs primarily in the classroom, and that students' out-of-class experiences have little if any influence on such growth (Terenzini & Pascarella, 1994). Consciousness-raising would appear to be in order. Although the politics of the process will be delicate, student affairs professionals might well consider ways in which they can constructively and collaboratively bring this body of evidence to the attention of faculty members, academic administrators, and their student affairs colleagues.

Second, not all out-of-class activities exert a positive influence on student learning. Compared to their peers, the students who show smaller gains on various measures of academic, intellectual, or cognitive growth are those who live at home while in college, belong to a fraternity or sorority, participate in men's intercollegiate football or basketball, work full-time, spend more hours socializing with friends, or have fewer academically or intellectually related out-of-class encounters with faculty members and other students.

Given that the negative effects of these experiences are observable at the end of students' first year, interventions will be needed early in students' college careers if the learning disadvantages associated with these experiences are to be avoided. Research in other areas (e.g., Pascarella, Brier, Smart, & Herzog, 1987; Walberg & Tsai, 1983) suggests that these differences may be only the first ones in a process of cumulative disadvantage that is likely to grow worse over time.

Third, student affairs programs may not be capitalizing on the potential of students' out-of-class experiences to enhance student learning. A growing body of evidence suggests that the learning advantages of living in a residence hall, for example, derive less from the *place* of residence than from the nature of the activities and interpersonal interactions with faculty and peers that they promote. The research quite consis-

tently points to the educational value and potency of the "living-learning" concept in residence halls. It seems reasonable to suggest that other student affairs programs can become more educationally potent to the degree that they, too, blur the boundaries between students' academic and out-of-class lives. Such opportunities might include speaker programs, cognitively substantive (rather than make-work) on-campus employment, internships, study-abroad opportunities, "study-abroad at-home" opportunities (i.e., studying for a term or two at another U.S. institution), and any of a variety of formal extracurricular activities specifically designed to promote academic or cognitive development.

Fourth, in virtually all cases where students' out-of-class experiences were found to enhance academic or cognitive learning, those experiences required, or at least afforded opportunities for, active student involvement. Other researchers have reached the same conclusion (Astin, 1993; Kuh, Schuh, Whitt, Andreas, et al., 1991; Pace, 1990; Pascarella & Terenzini, 1991). The learning potential of active student involvement suggests at least two courses of action. First, as student affairs professionals review current policies and programs, or develop new ones, they should consider the extent to which each policy or program permits or encourages active student responsibility for planning, organizing, and staging various student activities. Not taking advantage of the opportunities to involve students in the planning and staging of activities can deny students important opportunities to learn. Second, when student affairs professionals planning and implement policy or programmatic interventions, they should do so with the goal of promoting student learning clearly in mind. Indeed, the *SLI* involves a conscious attempt to "redefin[e] the role of student affairs to intentionally promote student learning and development" (American College Personnel Association, 1994, (p. 4); the operative word is *intentionally*. As Kuh (1995) points out, "many different out-of-class experiences have the potential to contribute to valued outcomes" (p. 145). To what extent do current student affairs policies and programs on our campuses have a clear, academically or cognitively relevant goal that can be articulated?

Fifth, the most powerful source of influence on student learning appears to be students' interpersonal interactions, whether with peers or faculty (and, one suspects, staff members). The evidence suggests that the influence of specific out-of-class experiences or activities (e.g., living in a residence hall, participating in extracurricular activities) is indirect rather than direct, being mediated by the amount and nature of the interpersonal interactions each activity involves. If one reviews the positive out-of-class influences on student learning listed earlier (e.g., living on campus, working on campus, discussing racial or ethnic issues, having an internship), it is clear that these activities bring students together with their peers or faculty members in situations with the potential for students to encounter new ideas and people different from themselves. Similarly, common to the out-of-class influences that appear to depress or impede student learning (e.g., living at home, working off campus, being a member of a Greek society) is their potential to isolate students from encounters with new ideas and different people. One implication of this conclusion is the importance of analyzing the nature of students' interpersonal interactions with peers, faculty, or staff and the extent to which learning-related encounters are promoted by current policies, programs, and services. Are all opportunities to facilitate or enhance academic or cognitive development being fully exploited? How can the learning potential of students' interactions with faculty and peers be increased? Are "weekend college" opportunities for commuting students feasible? Can financial aid packages be designed in ways that reduce the need for off-campus employment? Can fraternity and sorority policies, programs, practices, and customs be redesigned to reduce the potentially isolating influences of Greek society membership?

Sixth, the learning impacts of students' out-of-class experiences are probably cumulative rather than catalytic. Few of the specific or formal out-of-class experiences studied thus far have a clearly powerful influence on student learning. Virtually all of the effect sizes are small, even if statistically significant. In the aggregate, however, the magnitude of the impact may be substantially larger. Pascarella and Terenzini (1991) have suggested that a "majority of important changes that occur during college are probably the cumulative result of a set of interrelated experiences sustained over an extended period of time" (p. 610).

This conclusion suggests at least four implications, the first of which is that no single policy or programmatic intervention is likely to have as much influence on student learning as will multiple experiences, in multiple areas, that are educationally relevant. The cumulative impact is likely to be even stronger when those experiences are part of coordinated and mutually supportive and reinforcing sets of programmatic and policy interventions.

A second implication is the need to promote and sustain, purposefully and intentionally, a learning-centered environment or culture on a campus. How that can be done is beyond the scope of this paper, but a number of researchers have offered sound, practical advice (e.g., Kuh, 1993; Kuh, et al., 1994b; Kuh et al., 1991; Kuh, Schuh, Whitt, Andreas, et al., 1991; Schroeder & Mable, 1994).

A third implication of the cumulative nature of college's impact is the need to blur the functional (if not the structural) boundaries between academic and student affairs divisions. Some of the obstacles to accomplishing this end have been discussed elsewhere (e.g., Kuh, Shedd, & Whitt, 1987;Terenzini & Pascarella, 1994). The student affairs staff of the "involving colleges" Kuh (1993) studied

> understood that the academic mission of the institution was preeminent and approached their work with students accordingly. . . . More important (than organizational structure) were faculty and administrator expectations for students and a shared view of the institutional conditions that foster student learning and development. Said another way, the cultures of these colleges fostered student involvement. (p. 22)

Developing such a shared view will require more cooperative and collaborative program and policy planning than now occurs. Ways need to be identified in which greater collaboration between academic and student affairs units can be promoted in designing class and out-of-class experiences that are mutually reinforcing and supportive of learning goals. Such experiences as internships, work-study opportunities, speaker programs, orientation programs, and a variety of possible residence-based activities hold considerable potential for linking students' class and out-of-class experiences in ways that promote learning and cognitive development. Similarly, greater collaboration in planning and implementing programs *within* student affairs division units might also capitalize on potential interconnections between programs and services.

If student learning and cognitive development are, indeed, primary purposes of our colleges and universities, then the cumulative nature of how students learn has yet a fourth implication: learning-centered decision making should become a dominant philosophy in student and academic affairs divisions and units. This administrative orientation "consistently and systematically takes into account the potential consequences of alternative courses of administrative action for student learning" (Pascarella & Terenzini, 1991, p. 656). Whenever a decision is to be made, the learning-centered administrator will ask: "What will be the likely effect of my choosing this alternative (vs. any other) on our students' learning?" Student learning will be the better for such an approach.

Finally, it is well to remember, as noted earlier, that most of what is known about the influences of students' out-of-class experiences on their academic, intellectual, and cognitive development is based on studies of White, traditional-aged students attending four-year, residential institutions on a full-time basis. The clearest implication of this fact is the need for members of the higher education research community to devote a greater portion of their time and creative energies to studies of nontraditional students. The population to which the available evidence applies most directly is diminishing as a proportion of the total undergraduate student body on many campuses, and the evolution in the demographic profile of students entering higher education is projected to continue over the next decade (Hodgkinson, 1985; Levine & Associates, 1989; Upcraft, 1995). The extent to which the evidence reviewed here constitutes a faithful portrait of college's impacts on the academic, intellectual, and cognitive development of women, students of color, low-income students, older students, part-time students, and other segments of our undergraduate populations remains an open question. It cannot be allowed to remain so.

The *SLI* calls on student affairs professionals to consider how they can intentionally create conditions that enhance student learning. The research reviewed here clearly indicates that students' out-of-class experiences—and student affairs professionals and their programs, policies, and practices—have much to contribute to students' academic, intellectual, and cognitive development. Maximizing the opportunities to contribute, however, will require substantial rethinking of current programs and policies. It will also require student affairs professionals—as individuals—to rethink their conceptions of the appropriate roles for student affairs professionals in general and for themselves in particular.

References

American College Personnel Association. (1994). *The student learning imperative: Implications for student affairs.* Washington, DC: Author.

American College Testing Program & the Educational Testing Service. (1984). *Athletics and academics in the freshman year: A study of academic effects of freshman year participation in varsity sports.* Washington, DC: American Association of Collegiate Registrars and Admissions Officers.

Annis, L. (1983). The processes and effects of peer tutoring. *Human Learning, 2,* 39–47.

Astin, A. W. (1977). *Four critical years: Effects of college on beliefs, attitudes, and knowledge.* San Francisco: Jossey-Bass.

Astin, A. W. (1993). *What works in college? Four Critical Year revisited.* San Francisco: Jossey-Bass.

Bargh, J., & Schul, Y. (1980). On the cognitive benefits of teaching. *Journal of Educational Psychology, 72,* 593–604.

Baxter Magolda, M. (1987). The affective dimension of learning: Faculty-student relationships that enhance intellectual development. *College Student Journal, 21,* 46–58.

Baxter Magolda, M. (1992). *Knowing and reasoning in college: Gender-related patterns in students' intellectual development.* San Francisco: Jossey-Bass.

Beal, P., & Williams, D. (1968). *An experiment with mixed-class housing assignments at the University of Oregon.* Eugene, OR: Student Housing Research, Association of College and University Housing Officers Research and Information Committee.

Benware, C., & Deci. E. (1984). Quality of learning with an active versus passive motivational set. *American Educational Research Journal, 21,* 755–765.

Blimling, G. S. (1989). A meta-analysis of the influence of college residence halls on academic performance. *Journal of College Student Development, 30,* 298–308.

Blimling, G. S. (1993). The influence of college residence halls on students. In J. S. Smart (Ed.), *Higher education: Handbook of theory and research* (Vol. 9, pp. 248–307). New York: Agathon.

Blimling, G. S., & Hample, D. (1979). Structuring the peer environment in residence halls to increase academic performance in average-ability students. *Journal of College Student Development, 20,* 310–316.

Endo, J., & Harpel, R. (1982). The effect of student-faculty interaction on students' educational outcomes. *Research in Higher Education, 16,* 115–138.

Endo, J., & Harpel, R. (1983, May). *Student-faculty interaction and its effects on freshman year outcomes at a major state university.* Paper presented at the meeting of the Association for Institutional Research, Toronto.

Goldschmidt, B., & Goldschmidt, M. (1976). Peer teaching in higher education: A review. *Higher Education, 5,* 9–33.

Hodgkinson, H. L. (1985). *All one system: Demographics of education, kindergarten through graduate school.* Washington, DC: Institute for Educational Leadership.

Hood, A. (1984). Student development: Does participation affect growth? *Bulletin of the Association of College Unions-International, 54,* 16–19.

Hood, A., Craig, A., & Ferguson, B. (1992). The impact of athletics, part-time employment, and other activities on academic achievement. *Journal of College Student Development, 33,* 447–453.

Kuh, G. D. (1993, January). *The other curriculum: Out-of-class experiences associated with student learning and personal development.* Paper presented at the meeting of the Association for the Study of Higher Education, Minneapolis, MN.

Kuh, G. D. (1995). The other curriculum: Out-of-class experiences associated with student learning and personal development. *Journal of Higher Education, 66.,* 123–155.

Kuh, G. D., Douglas, K. B., Lund, J. P., & Ramin-Gyurnek, J. (1994a, November). *Student learning outside the classroom: A review of the literature.* Paper presented at the meeting of the Association for the Study of Higher Education, Tucson, AZ.

Kuh, G. D., Douglas, K. B., Lund, J. P., & Ramin-Gyurnek, J. (1994b). *That's all for today: Student learning outside the classroom* (ASHE-ERIC Higher Education Report No. 8). Washington, DC: George Washington University, School of Education and Human Development.

Kuh, G. D., Shedd, J. D., & Whitt, E. J. (1987). Student affairs and liberal education: Unrecognized (and unappreciated) common law partners. *Journal of College Student Personnel, 28,* 252–260.

Kuh, G. D., Schuh, J. H., & Whitt, E. J. (1991, September/October). Some good news about campus life: How 'involving colleges' promote learning outside the classroom. *Change,* 49–55.

Kuh, G. D., Schuh, J. H., Whitt, E. J., Andreas, R. E., Lyons, J. W., Strange, C. C., Krehbiel, L. E., & MacKay, K. A. (1991). *Involving colleges: Encouraging student learning and personal development through out-of-class experiences.* San Francisco: Jossey-Bass.

Lacy, W. (1978). Interpersonal relationships as mediators of structural effects: College student socialization in a traditional and experimental university environment. *Sociology of Education, 51,* 201–211.

Levine, A., and Associates. (1989). *Shaping higher education's future: Demographic realities and opportunities, 1990–2000.* San Francisco: Jossey-Bass.

MacKay, K. A., & Kuh, G. D. (1994). A comparison of student effort and educational gains of Caucasian and African-American students at predominantly White colleges. *Journal of College Student Development, 35,* 217–223.

Marlowe, A., & Auvenshine, C. (1982). Greek membership: Its impact on the moral development of college freshmen. *Journal of College Student Personnel, 23,* 53–57.

Moos, R., (1976). *The human context: Environmental determinants of behavior.* New York: Wiley.

Moos, R. (1979). *Evaluating educational environments: Procedures, measures, findings, and policy implications.* San Francisco: Jossey-Bass.

Morishima, J. K. (1966). Effects on student achievement of residence hall groupings based on academic major. In C. H. Bagley (Ed.), *Research on academic input: Proceedings of the sixth annual forum of the Association for Institutional Research* (pp. 163–170). Cortland, NY: State University of New York at Cortland, Office of Institutional Planning.

Newcomb, T. M., Brown, D., Kulik, J., Reimer, D., & Revelle, W. (1970). Self-selection and change. In J. G. Gaff (Ed.), *The cluster college* (pp. 137–160). San Francisco: Jossey-Bass.

Newcomb, T. M., Brown, D., Kulik, J., Reimer, D., & Revelle, W. (1971). The University of Michigan's residential college. In P. Dressel (Ed.), *The new colleges: Toward an appraisal.* Iowa City, IA: American College Testing Program & American Association for Higher Education.

Pace, C. R. (1984). *Measuring the quality of college student experiences.* Los Angeles: University of California-Los Angeles, Higher Education Research Institute.

Pace, C. R. (1990). *The undergraduates: A report of their activities and progress in college in the 1980s.* Los Angeles: University of California—Los Angeles, Center for the Study of Evaluation.

Pascarella, E. T. (1989). The development of critical thinking: Does college make a difference? *Journal of College Student Development, 30,* 19–26.

Pascarella, E. T., Bohr, L., Nora, A., Desler, M., & Zusman, B. (1994). Impacts of on-campus and off-campus work on first year cognitive outcomes. *Journal of College Student Development, 35,* 364–370.

Pascarella, E. T., Bohr, L., Nora, A., & Terenzini, P. T. (1995). Intercollegiate athletic participation and freshman year cognitive outcomes. *Journal of Higher Education.*

Pascarella, E. T., Bohr, L., Nora, A., Zusman, B., Inman, P., & Desler, M. (1993). Cognitive impacts of living on campus versus commuting to college. *Journal of College Student Development, 34,* 216–220.

Pascarella, E. T., Brier, E., Smart, J. S., & Herzog, L. (1987). Becoming a physician: The influence of the undergraduate experience. *Research in Higher Education, 26,* 180–201.

Pascarella, E. T., Nora, A., Edison, M., Hagedorn, L., & Terenzini, P. T. (in press). Cognitive effects of Greek affiliation during the first year of college. *NASPA Journal.*

Pascarella, E. T., & Smart, J. C. (1991). Impact of intercollegiate athletic participation for African-American and Caucasian men: Some further evidence. *Journal of College Student Development, 32,* 123–130.

Pascarella, E. T., & Terenzini, P. T. (1980). Student-faculty and student-peer relationships as mediators of the structural effects of undergraduate residence arrangement. *Journal of Educational Research, 73,* 344–353.

Pascarella, E. T., & Terenzini, P. T. (1981). Residence arrangement, student/faculty relationships, and freshman-year educational outcomes. *Journal of College Student Personnel, 22,* 147–156.

Pascarella, E. T., & Terenzini, P. T. (1991). *How college affects students: Findings and insights from twenty years of research.* San Francisco: Jossey-Bass.

Pascarella, E. T., Terenzini, P. T., & Blimling, G. S. (1994). The impact of residential life on students. In C. C. Schroeder & P. Mable (Eds.), *Realizing the educational potential of residence halls* (pp. 22–52). San Francisco: Jossey-Bass.

Pemberton, C. (1969). An evaluation of a living-learning residence hall program. Unpublished manuscript. Newark, DL: University of Delaware, Division of Academic Planning and Evaluation. (ERIC Document Reproduction Service No. ED 077 399)

Perry, W. (1970). *Forms of intellectual and ethical development in the college years: A scheme.* New York: Holt, Rinehart, & Winston.

Rest, J., & Deemer, D. (1986). Life experiences and developmental pathways. In J. Rest (Ed.), *Moral development: Advances in research and theory.* New York: Praeger.

Sanders, C. (1990). Moral reasoning of male freshmen. *Journal of College Student Development, 31,* 5–8.

Schoeck, T. J. (1973). Effects of class-year integrated housing on peership formation and environmental perceptions of freshmen. *Dissertation Abstracts International. 34*(11), 6986. (University Microfilms No. 74-9295)

Schroeder, C. C., & Mable, P. (1994). *Realizing the educational potential of residence halls.* San Francisco: Jossey-Bass.

Smith, E., & Dizney, H. (1966). Academic achievement and progress of participants in intercollegiate football. *Journal of College Student Personnel, 7,* 349–350.

Stuart, D. (1985). Academic preparation and subsequent performance in intercollegiate football players. *Journal of College Student Personnel, 26,* 124–129.

Terenzini, P. T., & Pascarella, E. T. (1994, January/February). Living with myths: Undergraduate education in America. *Change, 26,* 28–32.

Terenzini, P. T., Pascarella, E. T., & Lorang, W. G. (1982). An assessment of the academic and social influences on freshman year educational outcomes. *Review of Higher Education, 5,* 86–110.

Terenzini, P. T., Springer, L., Pascarella, E. T., & Nora, A. (1994a, May). *Influences affecting the development of students' critical thinking skills.* Paper presented at the annual meeting of the Association for Institutional Research, New Orleans.

Terenzini, P. T., Springer, L., Pascarella, E. T., & Nora, A. (1994b, November). *The multiple influences on college students' critical thinking skills.* Paper presented at the meeting of the Association for Study of Higher Education, Tucson, AZ.

Terenzini, P. T., Springer, L., Pascarella, E. T., & Nora, A. (1995). Academic and out-of-class influences on students' intellectual orientations. *Review of Higher Education, 19,* 23–44.

Terenzini, P. T., Theophilides, C., & Lorang, W. G. (1984). Influences on students' perceptions of their academic skill development during college. *Journal of Higher Education, 55,* 621–636.

Terenzini, P. T., & Wright, T. A. (1987). Influences on students' academic growth during four years of college. *Research in Higher Education, 26,* 161–179.

Upcraft, M. L. (1995) Teaching and today's college students. In R. Menges & M, Weimer (Eds.), *Teaching on solid ground: Using scholarship to improve practice.* San Francisco: Jossey-Bass.

Volkwein, J. F., King, M., & Terenzini, P. T. (1986). Student faculty relationships and intellectual growth among transfer students. *Journal of Higher Education, 57,* 413–430.

Walberg, H., & Tsai, S. (1983). Matthew effects in education. *American Educational Research Journal, 20,* 359–373.

Wilder, D., Hoyt, A., Doren, D., Hauck, W., & Zettle, R. (1978). The impact of fraternity or sorority membership on values and attitudes. *Journal of College Student Personnel, 19,* 445–449.

Wilder, D., Hoyt, A., Surbeck, B., Wilder, J., & Carney, P. (1986). Greek affiliation and attitude change in college students. *Journal of College Student Personnel, 27,* 510–519.

Wilson, R., Gaff, J., Dienst, Wood, L., & Bavry, J. (1975). *College professors and their impact on students.* New York: Wiley-Interscience.

Wilson, R., Wood, L., & Gaff, J. (1974). Social-psychological accessibility and faculty-student interaction beyond the classroom. *Sociology of Education, 47,* 74–92.

Winter, D., McClelland, D., & Stewart, A. (1981). *A new case for the liberal arts: Assessing institutional goals and student development.* San Francisco: Jossey-Bass.

CHAPTER 26

WHAT DO WE KNOW ABOUT STUDENTS' LEARNING, AND HOW DO WE KNOW IT?

K. PATRICIA CROSS

Within the past few years, there has been a flood of articles, books, and conference themes entreating colleges and universities to make student learning their top priority. Fortunately, there is more information about learning available to us than ever before in the history of the world; and the amount of research on learning continues to escalate. About 30 years ago, a large book entitled *The Impact of College on Students* by Feldman and Newcomb (1969) appeared, promising to tell us everything we ever wanted to know about student learning in college. The cover blurb assured us that "Everything written of any importance—during the last 40 years—has been thoroughly reviewed, analyzed, and distilled in this definitive compendium of research on higher education and college students . . .". (I doubt that any publisher today would be quite so confident that they had published the definitive book.) Nevertheless, the book lived up to its promise and ran to almost 500 pages, reviewing nearly 1500 research studies.

Almost a quarter of a century later, in 1991, an even larger volume appeared, entitled *How College Affects Students* by Pascarella and Terenzini, running to almost 1000 pages and reviewing nearly 2600 studies. At that rate, I figure that in ten years we should look forward to—if that is the correct terminology—a 2000 page treatise reviewing approximately 5000 studies, telling us perhaps more than we ever wanted to know about what and how students learn in college.

Despite the undeniable value of these books pulling together what we know about student learning in college, I doubt that we will ever see that next volume—either because such a huge compendium of information will no longer be presented via the printed page or because the research will change radically, not just in methodology and customization to more sharply defined issues, but in credibility and usefulness.

Right now we are struggling, as never before, to make research useful—to apply it to the improvement of undergraduate education. The current model for usefulness is to cope with the information explosion by ever-tighter syntheses and distillations. In our times, Pascarella and Terenzini have done the major work of synthesizing thousands of research studies into 1000 pages. Since most administrators and faculty don't have time to read the huge compendiums of information now available, the next step has been to condense 1000 pages into one or two pages of bulleted principles or conclusions.

I have on my desk right now a collection of such distillations of what we know about the learning of college students. The best known, certainly the most widely distributed list, is the "Seven Principles for Good Practice in Undergraduate Education." The Seven Principles were developed by

"What Do We Know About Students' Learning and How Do We Know It?" Reprinted from *Innovative Higher Education* 23, no. 4 (1999), by permission of Human Sciences Press, Inc.

convening a group of scholars of higher education and asking them to derive from their knowledge of the past 50 years of research a set of principles that could be applied to improve learning. Chickering and Gamson (1987) then formulated the conclusions into "seven principles," making them widely available to educators.

In addition to the seven principles, there are the "three critical conditions for excellence" formulated by the Study Group on the Conditions of Excellence in American Higher Education (1984), the nine strategies for improving student learning set forth by the Oxford Centre for Staff Development (1992) in England, and the twelve attributes of good practice published by the Education Commission of the States (1996). The Task Force on Psychology in Education established by the American Psychological Association has come forth with a dozen learner-centered principles representing psychology's accumulated knowledge about learning and instruction (McCombs, 1992).

We have been using what I call the mining approach to discovering and disseminating information. We are mining tons of ore to come up with a nugget of gold. True, our technology for bringing the ore to the surface is making the mining more feasible than ever before, but are we now faced with the prospect of mining old mines from which most of the gold has already been extracted? Pascarella and Terenzini admitted unabashedly that, "Our conclusions about the changes that occur during college differ in only minor ways from those of Feldman and Newcomb . . ." (p. 563).

I don't want to make light of the contributions of research to knowledge about how college affects students. I think those who have been mining the ore and those who have been extracting the gold have performed valuable services in making the results of research available to a wide audience. But I am going to suggest that we, as an educational community, are becoming too dependent on what the authorities in research tell us about learning.

John Naisbitt said, "We are living in the *time of the parenthesis*, the time between eras . . . a time of change and questioning." (1982, p. 249). Some believe that we are coming to the end of an era that the late Donald Schön, of MIT, called "technical rationality," and that there is little to be gained by trying to apply rigorous scientific methods to problems that may not lend them-

selves to easy answers. The professions are in the midst of a crisis of confidence and legitimacy, said Schön, because professional knowledge is mismatched to the conditions of practice. Schön (1983) put the dilemma this way:

"There is a high, hard ground where practitioners can make effective use of research-based theory and technique, and there is a swampy, lowland where situations are confusing 'messes' incapable of technical solution. The difficulty is that the problems of the high ground, however great their technical interest, are often relatively unimportant to clients or to the larger society, while in the swamp are the problems of greatest human concern. Shall the practitioner stay on the high, hard ground where he can practice rigorously, as he understands rigor, but where he is constrained to deal with problems of relatively little social importance? Or shall he descend into the swamp where he can engage the most important and challenging problems if he is willing to forsake technical rigor?" (1983, p. 42).

The assumption of most researchers is that further refinement of research methods, new statistical controls, more rigorous standards will lead to greater knowledge. Many are now questioning that assumption. It doesn't take much reading of the scholarly literature in education these days to see the huge question marks raised by the philosophical "isms"—constructionism, feminism, modernism, post-modernism. The "isms" are questioning the very nature of knowledge. Until we know what knowledge is, they say, we can't really say how to attain it. In a nutshell—which is perhaps not the way philosophers prefer to present their food for thought—the epistemological question is, do learners discover knowledge that exists "out there" in reality or do they construct it for themselves through a process of language, thought, and social interaction?

Kenneth Bruffee is a professor of English at Brooklyn college and an advocate of "nonfoundational social constructionism," which to my mind, is a rather awkward term for the belief that knowledge is socially constructed rather than discovered. "We construct and maintain knowledge," Bruffee says, "not by examining the world but by negotiating with one another in communities of knowledgeable peers" (1995, p. 9). Knowledge, he says, is "therefore not universal and absolute. It is local and historically changing. We construct it and reconstruct it, time and again, and build it up in layers." (p. 222).

In contrast, the foundational or conventional view of knowledge contends that there is a reality "out there," a foundation upon which all knowledge is built. The task of learners is to discover the world that exists. That means, of course, that there is a right answer and that the experts know what it is or have ways of eventually discovering it though objective scientific research.

The role of teachers and students is quite different in these two epistemologies. The difference is perhaps best illustrated in a series of articles in *Change* that contrasted cooperative and collaborative learning—frankly a topic which, at first blush, seemed to me not something I needed to get excited about. (Bruffee, 1995; Matthews, 1995; Whipple, 1987). But reading more deeply, I discovered that while both pedagogies seemed modern and enlightened in their agreement about the virtues of active learning, students teaching students, learning the skills of teamwork, benefiting from diversity, and most of the other advantages embedded in small group learning, cooperative and collaborative pedagogies had very different ideas about the nature of knowledge and how students should go about achieving knowledge.

Briefly, cooperative learning involves the more conventional notion of cooperation in that students work in small groups on an assigned project or problem under the guidance of the teacher who monitors the groups, making sure that students are staying on task and are coming up with the correct answers. This assumes, of course, that there is a right—or at least a best—answer and that the teacher knows what it is. Cooperative learning is what I think most faculty joining the learning revolution are thinking about.

Collaborative learning is a more radical departure. It involves students working together in small groups to develop their own answer—not necessarily a known answer—through interaction and reaching consensus. Monitoring the groups or correcting "wrong" impressions is not the role of the teacher, since the teacher is not considered the authority on what the answer should be. The teacher would be interacting along with students to arrive at a consensus.

Although the logic of social constructionism seems extreme to conventional education, the challenge it presents is worth serious consideration. Among other things, it lies behind some aspects of multiculturalism, in which the question is: Who says that the truth about the world lies in majority cultures?

Conventional instruction is based on a hierarchical model in which those who know teach those who do not know. Ultimately, there are answers to every question, and scholarship consists of knowing the answer or knowing how to find out. Once that epistemology is accepted, students—and, yes, faculty and administrators, too—can compete for who has the most or best answers. Gene Rice noted that today's colleges and universities are widely viewed as "the place where talented men and women—students, faculty, and administrators—contend for competitive advantage." (Rice, 1996, p. 4). And I can't argue with that. Students are rewarded for their right answers by high grades and selection to the best colleges; faculty are rewarded for their search for right answers by research grants and tenure; and administrators compete for fame for their campus by establishing the greatest storehouses of knowledge with large libraries, computer systems with huge memories, and a prominent research faculty. In sum, the epistemology on which our current educational system is built is that knowledge is accumulated by discovering the "truth" about the reality that exists. It can be discovered through scientific research, stored in libraries and computers, and disseminated via publications and teaching. And, yes, it can be transferred from researchers to practitioners.

The contrasting epistemology that is proposed by many of the "isms" holds that knowledge is constructed by humans through social interaction. Education, therefore, should be based in learning communities where teachers and students act interdependently to construct meaning and understanding. The model is collaborative and egalitarian. According to Bruffee, social constructionism contends that "knowledge is a consensus among the members of a community of knowledgeable peers—something people construct by talking together and reaching agreement" (1995, p. 3).

That is pretty close to what Schön recommended when he suggested that practitioners should engage in a search for knowledge by asking themselves what "kinds of knowing are already embedded in competent practice"

(Schön, 1983, p. 29). That would seem to call for communities of practitioners to generate relevant knowledge about the practice of their profession. Teachers would talk with one another about what they have observed in their own learning and the learning of their students.

Another strong sign of a radical shift in our view of how knowledge is generated is found in the work of feminist thinkers about women as learners. Belenky and her colleagues (1986) sparked a strong strain of sympathetic recognition among women teachers and students when they demonstrated that many women display different "ways of knowing" from the male model that has dominated academe for so many years. The male model is characterized by "separate knowing"—a way of learning that is impersonal and objective involving detachment, critical argument, analysis, and other descriptors that we associate with the "scientific method." Many women, however, are "connected learners." "Connected learners" said the authors, "develop procedures for gaining access to other people's knowledge. At the heart of these procedures is the capacity for empathy" (Belenky, 1986, p. 113).

Blythe Clinchy described a connected learner's search for knowledge this way: "She does not ask whether it is right; she asks what it means. When she says, 'Why do you think that?' She doesn't mean, 'What evidence do you have to back that up?' She means, 'What in your experience led you to that position'?" (Clinchy, 1990, p. 122). This student's search for knowledge, argued Clinchy, is best accomplished through connected conversations, "in which each person serves as midwife to each other person's thoughts, and each builds on the other's ideas" (p. 123). At heart, a connected conversation is a learning community at its best, and it is also a reflection of changing ideas about the source of knowledge and learning.

The cutting-edge books about the revolution taking place in business are yet another indication of the pervasiveness of a changing perspective about the origins of knowledge. Peter Senge, in his book on the *Fifth Discipline* (1990), goes on at some length about the emergence of new knowledge through dialogue with peers. He calls for "a shift of mind—from seeing ourselves as separate from the world to connected to the world, from seeing problems as caused by some-

one or something 'out there' to seeing how our own actions create the problems we experience. A learning organization is a place where people are continually discovering how they create their reality. And how they can change it" (pp. 12–13). Once again that sounds like a shift from discovering knowledge that lies in reality "out there," to creating knowledge that lies within human interchange.

If we are entering the 21st century in the parenthesis of philosophical questioning between scientific rigor and other ways of knowing, I cannot help noting the similarities between the developmental stages of personal growth and the developmental stages of society's pursuit of knowledge. Let me explain.

William Perry is perhaps the best known developmentalist to those of us in higher education. He posits nine positions of intellectual development for college students, but the three major positions can be presented briefly. The scheme starts at the low end of intellectual development, with students assuming that there is a right answer to every question and that the answer is known by an authority—namely the professors who are hired to teach them. Students entering college in the early stages of intellectual development have a low tolerance for ambiguity, but they can grant that in some cases we haven't found the answer yet. Their assumption, like ours as a society, is that authorities in research will tell us the answer; and, if they don't know it yet, they will eventually discover it. Like students who want quick and unqualified answers, we prefer that the experts make the answers available to us in brief, clear, unambiguous form, such as the three or seven or twelve principles of learning.

At the mid-level stages of Perry's student development theory, gray areas appear as students begin to discover that authorities often disagree and that the views of their fellow students often differ from their own. In an effort to resolve these inevitable discrepancies, students adopt an "everyone has a right to their own opinion" stance.

This middle stage seems to me to correspond in an eerie way to the developmental stage of society today, as we discover that there are many different views and that authorities often disagree. Certainly we have ample evidence that research authorities disagree on almost everything from the future of the economy to what causes cancer to how children should be raised. Thus we, as a society, have entered the mid-levels of intellectual development by contending that knowledge is a product of one's own experience and each person's experience is democratically and equally valuable. "Everyone has a right to their own opinion" we say. There is a seemingly inexhaustible demand for participatory discussion groups and internet exchanges on what other people think. It is not just television and radio talk shows that display an insatiable curiosity about other people's notions and experiences. Any educational conference that claims to be enlightened must present ample opportunity for discussion groups, workshops, and interactive conversations, and must keep lectures to a minimum—and I am in favor of that. There is a growing impatience and distrust with authoritative knowledge and "experts" in any field, but especially in the messy social sciences such as psychology, sociology, and education. *Time* magazine, in pondering the tendency of the American public to ignore the pronouncements of authorities, observed recently that, "Americans don't listen to pollsters and economists. They listen to neighbors, to friends, to family . . ." (January 5, 1997, p. 91). The questioning philosophical "isms" are controversial right now, but perhaps they are leading society into the mid-level stages of intellectual development by questioning authoritative answers and engaging in discourse, and listening more attentively to experience.

At the highest levels of intellectual development—a stage rarely reached by those who have been studied—there is an affirmation of identity through commitment and self-actualization. Developmental theorists are not very clear about the highest levels of personal development because they haven't seen much of it, and we are not very clear about what a fully-developed intellectual society would look like for the same reason. We haven't yet seen it. But most developmental psychologists are constructivists. They contend that the highest levels of personal development are reached as the person discovers that truth is relative and depends on context. There is not a single right answer, nor is one answer as good as any other. Rather, at the highest levels of development, the individual is able to evaluate truth in terms of the context in which it

occurs. In developmental theory, the periods of greatest personal growth are thought to lie in the unnamed and poorly-defined periods *between* stages. It is reasonable to assume that our societal position in the parenthesis offers an especially good opportunity for growth. Is there a societal developmental sequence that progresses from "right answers" to "everyone has a right to their own opinion" to commitment through careful and thoughtful evaluation of truth in context?

Today's theory about human development, it turns out, is not very different from what Socrates was promoting when he defended himself against the charge of corrupting the young by saying that democracy needs citizens who can think for themselves rather than simply defer to authority, who can reason together about choices rather than simply trade claims and counter claims. There are, as we know, charges today that universities are corrupting the young by exposing them to ideas that question the authority of traditional values. But the danger of corrupting the young by requiring them to think for themselves is no greater today than it was in the time of Socrates.

I entitled this chapter. "What do we know about student learning, and how do we know it?" The first question, "what do we know about student learning?" is intended to provide me with the opportunity to give a few "right answers;" the second question, How do we know it?" is intended to raise questions about authoritative knowledge.

The most efficient way to answer the first question about what we know about student learning is to collect the gold nuggets already mined from extensive research and melt them down into a gold bullion. In short, I could synthesize the condensed lists or "principles" and develop one or more meta-principles. If I were to do that, I would come up with a grand meta-principle that would say something like this: What we know about student learning is that students who are actively engaged in learning for deeper understanding are likely to learn more than students not so engaged. The disillusioning thing about that conclusion is that we already knew it from our own experience as learners—which is beginning to make the challenging epistemologies of knowledge based in personal and social experience more appealing.

Let us look specifically at the Seven Principles of Good Practice to see what they really tell us: The Seven Principles are stated as follows:

1. Good practice encourages student-faculty contact.

2. Good practice encourages cooperation among students.

3. Good practice encourages active learning.

4. Good practice gives prompt feedback

5. Good practice emphasizes time on task

6. Good practice communicates high expectations

7. Good practice respects diverse talents and ways of knowing. (Chickering & Gamson, 1987)

What the principles really tell us is how to get and keep students actively engaged in learning. Active learning is the grand meta-principle here. What troubles me is that the provision of the list violates its own advice. What we know about learning is that people have to find their own answers by working through the pathways to knowledge. Telling people what the "experts" know is not likely to result in the kind of deeper learning which we want to encourage. Peter Ewell (1997) makes the interesting observation in the *AAHE Bulletin* that our limited success so far in improving learning is due largely to our lack of a deep understanding of what "collegiate learning" really means, and to our implementation of piecemeal reform efforts that don't fit together very well. I wonder if our enthusiasm for bulleted distillations of research findings may not be responsible in part for our failure to understand at some deeper level what constitutes a program of learning.

Let us examine the first principle—good practice encourages student-faculty contact. How do we know that? Mostly through large-scale correlational studies that conclude that students who have frequent contact with faculty members in and out of class are better satisfied with their educational experience, less likely to drop out, and perceive themselves to have learned more than students with less faculty contact (Pascarella & Terenzini, 1991). Now, the experts who pass on that conclusion know the following things at a deeper level than we who receive the conclusion: First, that correlation tells what goes together, but not why. For instance,

it is quite possible that the correlation results from successful students being more likely than less successful students to seek contact with faculty. In other words, it is possible that success leads to faculty contact rather than that faculty contact leads to success. It is also possible that faculty who invite frequent student contacts are more likely to be the kind of people who stimulate educational satisfaction than faculty who are not so easily approachable. Thus, it is possible that the more successful we are in bringing about student-faculty contacts—that is spreading this piecemeal practice to include disinterested faculty and less scholarly students—the lower the correlations would become.

The second thing that any researcher working with data on human subjects knows is that there are always exceptions to the finding. In this case, there are students who are very successful and have virtually no contact with faculty; and there are students who have a lot of contact with faculty who drop out of college, dissatisfied and disillusioned.

Does that mean we have mined fool's gold in arriving at the first principle of good practice? Not at all. What it means, I think, is that rather than telling people the right answer, as expert researchers have discovered it, we should mix in a generous dollop of insight derived from our experience as learners and as teachers. What we know from our own experience—sometimes known as common sense—is that, it is not the *amount* of student-faculty contact that is important. Rather it is the quality of the contact. Truth, in this sense, is contextual. Student-faculty contact in one context is growth-enhancing; in another it is not.

What we actually know through combining research with experience is that when faculty show an interest in students, get to know them through informal as well as formal channels, engage in conversations with them, show interest in their intellectual development, then students respond with enthusiasm and engagement. We also know that when faculty take learning seriously, the attitudes of warmth and intellectual engagement are contagious; they are caught by students and colleagues, and the result is a caring campus that is seriously engaged in learning. Measuring the number of student contacts with faculty is at best a surrogate for the quality of interaction. But the kind of research that Schön calls "technical rationality" has a hard time dealing with the infinite variety of contexts that are involved in student/faculty contacts.

Our problem in this awkward time of the parenthesis is that we alternate between searching for "right answers" through research and discounting authoritative answers in favor of our own opinions. We hope that the research provides "right answers" that can be transferred from researcher to practitioner and from teacher to student. Or at the other extreme, we discount research, and insist on personal experience and political expediency—as witness the recent rush to reduce class size, despite conflicting research evidence regarding the efficacy of reduced class size. The question that begs to be answered is not whether small classes result in better learning than large classes, but rather in what teachers could and would do in the context of their own classrooms if class size were reduced. That answer is probably better sought through thoughtful conversations among experienced teachers than it is in the collection of data across large numbers of classrooms categorized only by size.

The challenge for society in the 21st century is to advance beyond the stages of development that result in the authoritarian search for right answers or the egalitarian notion that all ideas are equally valid. Those two stages have dominated our intellectual communities throughout this century.

Researchers—the acknowledged authorities of our times—talk about learning with no reference to the experience of teachers who have spent lifetimes accumulating knowledge about learning. And workshops on faculty development encourage faculty exchange with no reference to what scholars know through study of the matter. My colleague, Mimi Steadman, and I spent several years trying to bring research on learning and experience with teaching together in a book that attempts to integrate teachers' experience and insight with scholarly research on learning (Cross & Steadman, 1996). I am not certain that we have done it, but I am convinced that it can be done.

From our societal position inside the parenthesis as we approach the 21st century, we are questioning how we know what we know, and the developmentalists would say that is good— that offers the potential for growth. Frankly, I find what we know today about students and their learning, and how we know it, troubling

because it is so heavily dependent on categorizing students into groups—ironically, just as we are developing the technology for customizing education to individual requirements.

Knowledge about individual differences is lost in much of today's educational research. We purport to know about commuters, part-timers, adult learners, ethnic minorities, women, gays, or any other category that can be represented by checking a box on the measuring instrument. Most of us probably doubt that we could be fairly described by the characteristics of the single or multiple groups to which we belong. Toni Morrison has said "Race is the least reliable information you can have about someone. It's real information, but it tells you next to nothing" (*Time*, Jan. 19, 1998, p. 67).

Bloom (1980) has called the popular demographic descriptors of today "unalterable variables" because, as educators, we can do nothing to change them. Unfortunately, demographic descriptors predominate in the educational research of our times because barriers to equality lie in discrimination based on unalterable variables. Certainly we must continue to investigate the powerful impact of sociological variables on learning—most especially on the *opportunity* for learning—but we must also be constantly aware that there are almost always greater differences within demographic groups than between them. The difference between the height of the shortest and the tallest 14 year olds is far greater than the difference between the average height of 14 year olds and 16 year olds— even though that difference is consistently and statistically significant. Stereotyping 14 year olds as "short" does nothing to advance our knowledge about them.

A heavy dependence on group variables is defensible, I guess, when applied to the old school structures that were designed in times of assembly-line production. The greatest good for the greatest number is a reasonable approach if the task is to march the group through a standard set of learning procedures in a set period of time. But the efficiency of the assembly line approach depends on a normal curve that has a high hump in the middle—that is to say most people cluster in the middle around a fairly small range of difference. With the growing diversity of our student populations, that nice normal curve flattens out, so that there are not very many "average" students anymore—and especially not in open-admission colleges which span the full spectrum of human abilities and human conditions. The problem for us in this time of the parenthesis is that our educational structures are solidly anchored in assembly line procedures while in our future lies the potential for customization and individualization.

A second problem with our heavy dependence on demographic descriptors lies in the growing difficulty of finding that nice neat box on the survey form that places the student firmly and correctly in the appropriate group. The so-called Tiger Woods syndrome[1] applies to racial descriptors, but with participation in lifelong learning related more to life style than to age and with career options being more dependent on personal interest than on gender, group descriptors tell us less and less.

But the third and perhaps most serious barrier to taking learning seriously lies in our failure to take individual differences seriously. Studies of individual differences have almost disappeared from the research scene. It is almost as though there is something a bit unsavory—or at least undemocratic—about individual differences. But learning is about individuals, and improving learning is about understanding what goes on in the mind of the learner. Let me illustrate with a story.

Once upon a time, a young boy was given a beautiful old clock by his grandfather. He was thrilled with the clock, but it quit running after 8 days. Eager to know what was wrong with his clock, he took it to the researchers at the university. The boy thought maybe they would open up the clock to examine the running mechanism, but the researchers said that findings based on study of a single clock would not be generalizable. So they embarked upon a research project.

First they collected a sample of 100 clocks, including clocks of different sizes, colors, and country of manufacture. They then measured very precisely to the minute how long the clocks in each group ran. Upon analyzing their results, they found that while there did not seem to be a statistically significant differences in the running time of clocks of different colors, they did find that small clocks tended to run longer than large clocks; and they found one very exciting relationship. Controlling for color and size, they found that clocks made in Japan tended to run,

on average, significantly longer than those made in Switzerland.

Unbeknownst to them—because they didn't open up the clocks to investigate variables, such as quartz mechanisms and pendulums, that were relevant to how clocks ran—Switzerland continued to make some 8-day pendulum clocks whereas clocks from Japan were almost all quartz clocks, supplied with energizer batteries that just kept going on.

The researchers could assure the boy that if he bought a sufficiently large number of clocks from Japan, there was a better chance that he would get a long-running clock than if he bought the same number from Switzerland. Unfortunately, they could neither tell him why clocks from Japan tended to run longer, nor which clocks to buy, nor could they tell him what to do to get his own clock running.

The moral of my story is that if you want to know how students learn, find out what makes them tick. Looking carefully at how even one student learns is often quite revealing, and most of us have an opportunity to observe a wide variety of learners in the act of learning. Moreover, the students that we observe are *our* students in the process of learning *our* discipline; they are the most relevant sample of learners that we could imagine. The problem is that we have not trained ourselves to take learning seriously. Every student who writes a paper, takes a test, asks a question, participates in student activity as leader or follower or who comes to our office hours for conversation or help has a lesson to teach us about how students learn.

Although I may appear to be critical of educational research, I want to assure you that I think research is important to taking learning seriously. In criticizing what I see as our overdependence on correlational and experimental research that leans heavily on group variables, I do not mean to suggest that research on learning is at standstill. Indeed, the new research on neural networks of the brain, meta-cognition, motivation, and the like provides, even at these early stages of development, glimpses of a future rich with promise. That research, however, is going to require of all of us a deeper level of understanding than the research of the past. Research should become the working partner of both our own experience with learning and focused conversations about learning with our colleagues. If we are to take learning seriously, we will need to know what to look for (through research), to observe ourselves in the act of life-long learning (self-reflection), and to be much more sensitively aware of the learning of the students that we see before us everyday.

At present, I think we are prone to consider research findings as the *conclusion* of our investigations into learning. We might do better to think of them as the *start* of our investigations. For example, rather than assuming that the message of the first principle of the Seven Principles is that we should develop programs to increase student-faculty contact, we might use that research finding as a starting point for discussion about what it is about student-faculty contact that promotes learning. What role has it played in our own experience and why? What, exactly, is it about student-faculty contact that seems to enhance learning? Is it the nature of the individual conversations, or is it the affective feeling of belonging to a learning community? Is it the particular help on a sticking point that shows a student how to learn, or is it the fact that the teacher shows interest—or both? I don't think that researchers know the answers to these questions, and the answers are important if we are to take learning seriously.

But perhaps the most powerful advantage of using research findings to *start* the conversations about learning is that, it is a way to involve faculty and administrators actively in learning about learning. It is one way to push beyond the surface learning that is involved in knowing the slogan, "Good practice encourages student-faculty contact," to the deeper understanding that lies behind the research. People can comply with a new student-faculty contact initiative without fully comprehending that it is their own understanding of why they are engaging in the activity that will determine how well it works. Attending student-faculty get-togethers is one thing; understanding why they work to create a learning community is another; and working actively to assure success is still another.

In conclusion, we know a lot about student learning. We know it through research and scholarship; we know it through our own experience as learners; and we know it through the lessons our students teach us everyday. If we are serious about improving learning, we should use all the resources we can muster.

Notes

1. He resents being categorized by race and insists upon recognition of his multiracial heritage.

References

Belenky, M. F., Clinchy, B. M., Goldberger, N. R., & Tarule, J. M. (1986). *Women's ways of knowing: The development of self, voice, and mind.* New York: Basic Books.

Bloom, B. (1980). The new direction in educational research: Alterable variables. *Phi Delta Kappan* (Feb.), 382–385.

Bruffee, K. A. (1995). *Collaborative learning: Higher education, interdependence, and the authority of knowledge.* Baltimore: The Johns Hopkins University Press.

Chickering, A. W., & Gamson, Z. F. (1987). Seven principles for good practice in undergraduate education. *The Wingspread Journal, 9*(2). See also AAHE Bulletin, March, 1987.

Clinchy, B. (1990). Issues of gender in teaching and learning. *Journal on Excellence in College Teaching., 1.* Reprinted in Feldman, K. A., and Paulsen, M. B. (eds.) (1994) *Teaching and learning in the college classroom.* ASHE Reader Series. Needham Heights, MA: Ginn.

Cross, K. P., & Steadman, M. H. (1996). *Classroom research: Implementing the scholarship of teaching.* San Francisco: Jossey-Bass.

Education Commission of the States (1996). What research says about improving undergraduate education. *AAHE Bulletin, 48*(April), 5–8.

Ewell, P. T. (1997). Organizing for learning. *AAHE Bulletin, 50*(4), 3–6.

Feldman, K. A., & Newcomb, T. M. (1969). *The impact of college on students.* San Francisco: Jossey-Bass.

Matthews, R. S., Cooper, J. L., Davidson, N., & Hawkes, P. (1995). Building bridges between cooperative and collaborative learning. *Change, 27*(July/August), 34–40.

McCombs, B. L. (August, 1992). *Learner-centered psychological principles: Guidelines for school redesign and reform (revised edition).* Washington, DC: American Psychological Association, APA Task Force on Psychology in Education.

Morrison, T. (Jan. 19 1998). *Time Magazine,* p. 8.

Naisbitt, J. (1982). *Megatrends.* New York: Warner Books.

Oxford Centre for Staff Development (1992). *Improving student learning*. Oxford, England: Oxford Brookes University. Reprinted in "Deep Learning, Surface Learning," *AAHE Bulletin*, April 1993, pp. 10–11.

Pascarella, E. T., & Terenzini, P. T. (1991). *How college affects students*. San Francisco: Jossey-Bass.

Schön, D. A. (1983). *The reflective practitioner*. New York: Basic Books.

Study Group on the Conditions of Excellenc in American Higher Education (1984). *Involvement in learning: Realizing the potential of American higher education*. Washington, DC: National Institute of Education.

Time Magazine (Jan. 5 1997), p. 91.

Whipple, W. R. (1987). Collaborative learning. *AAHE Bulletin, 40*(2), 3–7.

PART V

SUMMARY & CONSIDERATIONS FOR FUTURE RESEARCH

SUMMARY AND CONSIDERATIONS
FOR FUTURE RESEARCH

Given the wealth and volume of research on college students, we are fortunate to have many who are willing to step back, take a deep breath, and tell us what it all means. The section begins with a classic piece, a snapshot from over a decade ago, of the state of knowledge on college students as well as two more recent commentaries on the status quo for students in higher education. Patrick Terenzini and Ernest Pascarella (1991), in "Twenty years of research on college students: Lessons for future research, " provide us with the definitive state of knowledge from a decade ago. Their exhaustive work is still basic reading for anyone who wants to study college students. Walter Allen, Robert Teranishi, Gniesha Dinwiddie, and Gloria González (2000), in "Knocking at Freedom's Door: Race, Equity and Affirmative Action in U.S. Higher Education," provide an analysis of the effects on racial equity of ten years of affirmative action. The authors describe the evolution of the concept and speculate on a future beyond its demise. In "Involvement in Learning Revisited: Lessons We Have Learned," Astin (1996) summarizes a decade's worth of research beyond his initial recommendations in involvement in learning.

The next set of readings provide recommendations for ways to make our research better informed and more relevant. Frances Stage(1989), provides a criticism of a bifurcation in the literature. "College Outcomes and Student Development: Filling the Gaps" provides suggestions for two groups of researchers who might better take advantage of and inform one another about college students. In "Theoretical Considerations in The Study of Minority Student Retention in Higher Education," Laura Rendon, Romero Jalomo, and Amaury Nora (2000) review research on minority students and examine it critically against conventional frameworks, they make theoretical and methodological recommendations for future study. Ed St. John, Alberto Cabrera, Amaury Nora and Eric Asker (2000) in "Economic Influences on Persistence Reconsidered: How Can Finance Research Inform the Reconceptualization of Persistence Models" review both theory and research. They argue that finance plays a greater role in college choice than previous theory describes and make suggestions for studying the influences of financial aid in future research.

The section closes with very specific advice regarding methodological approaches for research and assessment including Peter Magolda's (19990, "Using Ethnographic Fieldwork and Case Studies to Guide Student Affairs Practice" and Kathleen Manning's (1999) "Conducting Constructivist Inquiry."

CHAPTER 27

TWENTY YEARS OF RESEARCH ON COLLEGE STUDENTS: LESSONS FOR FUTURE RESEARCH

PATRICK T. TERENZINI AND ERNEST T. PASCARELLA

Based on a comprehensive review of the last twenty years of research on the influences of college on students, this chapter discusses conceptual and methodological recommendations for enhancing future assessment and college impact studies. The recommendations deal with isolating net college effects, studying the timing of change, estimating college effect sizes, examining indirect and conditional effects, and the potential benefits of qualitative approaches. Areas for future inquiry are also identified.

Twenty years have passed since Feldman and Newcomb (1969) published their landmark book, *The Impact of College on Students*, in which they reviewed forty years of theoretical propositions and empirical research on college students. Much has happened since then as the effects of college on students as a field of inquiry has grown qualitatively and quantitatively in both theory and method. Whole areas of inquiry, such as the effects of college on learning, cognitive development, moral reasoning, and various indices of status attainment, have developed into maturity. Theories of student development and change have emerged in sometimes daunting number and variety. Multivariate statistical procedures, adequate to the task of testing and extending these emergent and complex theories, have become increasingly accessible to scholars (a development with mixed blessings). History-altering advances in both mainframe and microcomputing hardware and software have been the handmaidens of these advances, facilitating both complex statistical analyses of equally complex theories and permitting the analysis of large, nationally representative databases.

In the last decade, the increasing costs of college attendance and operation, as well as mounting criticism of the quality of undergraduate education in the United States, have also spurred research on college outcomes. Earlier questions of cost, now answered, have been followed by questions of worth and value, of education's return on investment in both economic and noneconomic terms. Assessment of undergraduate student learning gained in popularity as a vehicle for a public accounting of an institution's stewardship of its resources and as a mechanism for improving the quality of the education offered.

The phenomenally productive conjuction of all these developments—in theory, methodological sophistication, computing, cost, criticism, and oversight—created a burgeoning literature on the effects of college on students that is more than double the size of that produced in the preceding four decades reviewed by Feldman and Newcomb (1969). What have we learned about studying college impacts from this enormous volume of research? What kinds of design, measurement, and analytical lessons can be drawn from it that might help researchers do better research in the future? This

"Twenty Years of Research on College Students: Lessons for Twenty Years of Research on College Students: Lessons." Reprinted from *Research in Higher Education* 32, (1991), by permission of Human Sciences Press, Inc.

chapter discusses eight such lessons. It offers a hopefully constructive critique of current research designs, methods, and substantive foci, suggesting ways in which research might be made more rigorous, informative, and supportive of educational programs and policy decision making.

Methods

Virtually all research relevant to student change during college and produced since 1967 was reviewed. To identify relevant studies, searches were made of various abstracting documents or databases, such as *Sociological Abstracts, Psychological Abstracts, Sociology of Education Abstracts, Dissertation Abstracts, College Student Personnel Abstracts, Higher Education Abstracts*, and the ERIC system. Recent conference proceedings from such scholarly and professional associations as the American Educational Research Association, the Association for the Study of Higher Education, and the Association for Institutional Research were also reviewed. Finally, an extensive network of colleagues was used to obtain unpublished papers or technical reports that dealt with college impact.

Despite the potential advantages of meta-analysis for synthesizing a large body of literature (see Cooper, 1982; Glass, 1977; Jackson, 1980; Pillemer and Light, 1980; Light and Pillemer, 1982), a number of factors led us to decide against using meta-analysis. First, meta-analytic techniques have come under close and often critical scrutiny in terms of their producing a truly objective and meaningful synthesis of evidence. These and related criticisms of meta-analysis are cogently reviewed by Slavin (1984), who concludes that meta-analysis can be a useful supplement to traditional narrative, explanatory reviews, but should not be seen as a replacement for them.

The second, and perhaps more important, reason for our deciding against meta-analysis as the primary method of synthesizing the evidence was simply the remarkable diversity of ways in which research on the impact of college on students is reported. The simple fact is that in many areas of inquiry the broad range of statistical evidence employed to report results makes the use of quantitative synthesis impractical if not impossible. Related to this issue was our concern that the requirements of quantifying study results

in a comparable metric would exclude studies based on naturalistic inquiry or other relevant investigations where the results were simply not amenable to the computation of effect sizes.

Thus, we turned to a narrative explanatory synthesis as our primary approach to the analysis of evidence. In this approach we were guided by the criterion of weight of evidence. That is, given a logical analysis of the studies conducted, what does the weight of evidence suggest about the influence of college or the influence of different aspects of the collegiate experience?

Findings and Conclusions

Eight lessons can be drawn from this review of more than 3,000 books, monographs, journal articles, papers, and other research reports:

1. *Simple change must be differentiated from the net effects of college.* The vast majority of studies we reviewed focus on change during the college years. Some of these studies were cross-sectional in design, based on a random sample of enrolled students (sometimes all class years, sometimes only seniors and freshmen). While the class year variable in cross-sectional studies can be argued to be a proxy for varying amounts of exposure to college, this design has numerous flaws that threaten its internal validity (see, for example, Pascarella, 1987; Pascarella and Terenzini, in press, Appendix A). Other studies were longitudinal panel studies, the same individuals in a cohort of entering freshmen being followed up one or more years later. Longitudinal designs using only college students, while generally much stronger designs for measuring change, shed no light on the extent to which any observed changes are due to the college experience, since the degree of exposure to college is the same for all study participants. In over twenty years of research, fewer than a dozen studies employed a control group of college-age individuals who did not attend college.

In short, virtually all of the studies done to date shed useful light on the extent to which students change *during the college years*, but change *during* college is not the same as change *due to* college. The drop-off in the volume of relevant research when one moves from studies of change during college to studies of change due to college attendance is striking and should be a source of some concern.

Change due to the college experience is sometimes referred to as the net effects of college. This phrase refers to the changes in students over time that can be attributed to the college experience and not to other sources of influence, such as normal maturation or conditions and events external to the campus. For example, if one is interested in assessing the extent to which increases in cognitive development can be attributed to college attendance (versus nonattendance), one must take into account those other variables *besides college attendance* that are likely to influence changes in critical thinking (e.g., intelligence, academic aptitude and high school achievement, cognitive development, socioeconomic status). If one were to compute the association between college attendance and a measure of cognitive development while statistically controlling for intelligence, the results would be an estimate of the effect of college on cognitive development *net* of (or independent of) the confounding influence of initial intelligence.

It is essential to the design of effective programs, professional integrity, and public credibility that claims about the benefits of college attendance be supportable with evidence that separates college effects from noncollege influences (e.g., precollege differences and normal maturation). Current claims about the benefits of college attendance frequently extend well beyond the empirical evidence to support them. Controlling the numerous alternative, noncollege sources of influence can be a daunting undertaking. It will require greater use of noncollege control groups and more extensive use of relevant theories in the design of studies. Such careful theoretical preparation and grounding is not one of the distinctive characteristics of most of the research done over the past two decades, but higher education as a field of inquiry has clearly started down that road, and we wish to encourage its continuation. Theory-based research will not only be more sharply focused and parsimonious but it is also likely to reflect more fully the complexity of college impacts.

2. *Effect sizes should be estimated.* Most studies identify statistically significant changes in students over time, but few examine the *magnitudes* of those changes. While it may be meaningful to report simply whether an independent variable is related to a dependent outcome variable at some level of statistical significance, it is much more meaningful, as well as theoretically and

practically informative, also to estimate the *strength* of the relation. Many of the studies we reviewed failed to report even the most rudimentary information (e.g., means and standard deviations) that might be used to estimate effect sizes.[1]

Reporting estimated effect size can reasonably be expected to lead to theories that are more parsimonious and better reflect the reality of college impact. It is necessary, but not sufficient, to know that group differences or changes are not due to chance. It is equally important to know whether the difference or change is *educationally* or *administratively* significant. Administrators can be expected to make programmatic, policy, and budgetary decisions at least in part on outcomes assessment information. They have a reasonable right to know—and institutional researchers have a corresponding obligation to provide information on—whether the impact of college or some aspect of the college experience is large enough to warrant attention, resources, and action.

3. *Little is known about when changes occur.* Much of the assessment literature examines change during the freshman year, or from freshman to senior years but not during the intervening years. Only a handful of the studies we reviewed monitored change on an annual, sequential basis. Thus, we know little about whether change is mostly linear and monotonic, or whether it is primarily episodic and discontinuous over the college years. Moreover, it seems reasonable to suggest (and there is some basis for believing) that the pacing of change varies across outcome areas. Much more attention needs to be given to the analysis of the *timing* of change during college. For policy and program planning purposes, it is, of course, important to know *whether* change occurs, but it is at least as important to know *when* an intervention will make a difference and when it won't so that institutional efforts and resources can be brought to bear when they are most likely to be effective.

4. *Important indirect college effects may be going unnoticed.* Much of the research on colleges' net effects indicates they tend to be small in size. That college effects are, in fact, small is only one of the possible explanations for this fairly consistent finding. Others include weak or unreliable measures; use of distal predictor measures (e.g., living on- vs. off-campus) instead of more

proximal ones (e.g., measures of the frequency and nature of students' interactions with peers and faculty members within the living environment); measures constructed to place a premium on test-retest reliability (and therefore perhaps biased against showing change) (Winter, 1979; Winter, McClelland, and Stewart, 1981), and the essentially conservative nature of the analytical procedures typically employed (e.g., hierarchical regression or path analytic models, which attribute variance jointly explained by precollege and college experience variables entirely to the precollege variable set).

Another possible explanation—often overlooked—is that a college effect may be *indirect*, as well as direct. A direct effect can be thought of as the unmediated influence of one variable on another (i.e., the impact is direct and does not pass through an intervening variable). Although the descriptor "direct" is seldom used in the research literature, direct effects are by far the most frequently estimated effects in educational or social science research. Using our previous example, if going to college has a significant association with cognitive development when intelligence is controlled, then it can be said to have a direct effect on cognitive development net of intelligence. Conversely, if the association between college attendance is nonsignificant when intelligence is taken into account, then college can be said to have no direct effect on cognitive development net of intelligence.

Although it is seldom estimated in the existing research, a variable may also have an indirect or mediated effect on an outcome. It occurs when that variable's effect is transmitted through an intervening variable(s). For example, it is possible that college attendance may have an important indirect effect on adult cognitive development by influencing a person's reading habits. Thus, the path of indirect influence would be college attendance directly affecting reading habits, and reading habits, in turn, directly affecting cognitive development. In this and similar ways college could have a significant impact on a range of outcomes without having a direct effect on them. In our synthesis of the research evidence, we have been impressed by how many of the effects of college are, or could be, indirect. For example, while major levers of institutional influence (e.g., residence halls) may not have substantial effects on student change in various areas, they *do* have important *indirect* effects,

influencing other variables which, in turn, have a substantial impact on students.

Thus, as much of the evidence we reviewed suggests, it is entirely possible that we may be underestimating or even misrepresenting the impact of many college influences by failing to consider their indirect effects. Because some source of influence in the causal chain is a step removed from having a direct effect on a given outcome makes it no less theoretically or practically important. Indeed, its consideration may add substantially to our knowledge of educational effects. Of course, any consideration of indirect effects means that one must typically conceptualize research questions in terms of theoretical models, but such a process is likely to reflect more fully and accurately the complexity of college impacts.

5. *Research on conditional effects will be increasingly important.* A general effect suggests that a particular collegiate experience is the same for all students who experience it. A conditional effect suggests that the magnitude of the effect is conditional upon, or varies according to, the specific characteristics of the individuals being considered (e.g., minority vs. nonminority, male vs. female, traditional-aged vs. older students). Conditional effects are sometimes referred to as interaction effects in that individual student differences are said to interact with the particular experience or condition thought to influence a particular outcome.

Despite many undoubtedly sincere statements about the importance of respecting individual student differences, relatively little attention has been given in the research and assessment literature to examining how college effects vary according to students' characteristics. Are the effects of college the same regardless of the student's sex? Race or ethnicity? Academic ability? Socioeconomic status? Answers to such questions are becoming increasingly important, particularly those related to race/ethnicity, sex, and age. If most demographic profiles of the college population for the next decade are anywhere near accurate, minority and older students will constitute a much larger proportion than they do at present. Current programs, designed primarily with traditional-aged white student populations in mind, may or may not have the same effects on different kinds of students. *If* more is known about how different kinds of students respond to similar experiences, programs and policies can be tailored and their effectiveness increased.

6. *Greater use should be made of qualitative research methods.* The current literature on college effects is almost exclusively quantitative. While the logical positivist, quantitative paradigm has served us well, judicious and creative qualitative approaches are capable of providing greater sensitivity to many of the subtle and fine-grained complexities of college impact than the more traditional quantitative approaches. Naturalistic and ethnographic inquiries may be particularly sensitive to the kinds of indirect and conditional effects just discussed. We expect that in the next decade, important contributions to our understanding of college impact will be produced by qualitative research approaches. Forewarned is forearmed, however: Qualitative methods are often thought to be less rigorous and less demanding than quantitative approaches. They are not.

7. *A single paradigm dominates current research on college effects.* Most of the prominent contributors to theory development and research on the impact of college on students have been or are psychologists. As a consequence, past and current research on college impacts is distinguished by its almost exclusive reliance on psychological models. Similarly, for the past quarter-century, graduate programs that have trained (and continue to train) many of higher education's researchers and administrators have had their conceptual origins largely in one theoretical genre. Theories from other fields have only recently begun to receive notice. Indeed, many researchers in higher education appear to be unaware of a substantial theoretical and empirical literature relating to collegiate effects based in other disciplines, especially sociology and anthropology.

The need for new perspectives on college impacts is particularly acute in studies of students' noncognitive, psychosocial changes. An alarming number of studies in these areas reflect little familiarity with the knowledge base outside the author's primary discipline. Whether many of the observed changes reported in the literature are due to developmental, psychosocial restructuring within students, or to learning through the socialization process of competencies, attitudes, values, and behaviors valued by important others remains very much an open and vital question. Single-paradigm research or assessment programs are likely to restrict the range of analytical vision, the depth of understanding, and, consequently, the effectiveness of academic and nonacademic programs.

8. *Certain areas of study are particularly in need of attention.* While the sheer volume of studies of the effects of college on students done over the past twenty years is truly impressive, several important holes in the research fabric are identifiable and become more glaringly so as time passes. One in particular that stands out is the impact of the academic program and the teaching-learning process. How do different teaching and instructional approaches influence not only how much content is learned but also what higher-order thinking skills are developed? How and in what ways does the academic program influence values and personal development? Are there particular teaching or instructional approaches that are differentially effective for different kinds of students? Answers to these and similar questions will constitute major contributions to our understanding of the impact of college.

A second important, but virtually unexplored, area of inquiry is the nature and dynamics of the collegiate experience for significant groups of nontraditional students. The absence of rigorous research on the effects of college on minority students and older students is particularly embarrassing to the higher education research community. As noted earlier, demographic forecasts for the next decade consistently indicate that the proportion of minority students in America's colleges and universities will increase, dramatically among some groups. Higher educational administrators cannot long delay responding to this and related trends. If researchers are to help prepare our higher educational system for these changes, much, much more must be learned about how the collegiate experience, academic and nonacademic, differs for minority versus majority groups, and for older versus traditional-aged students.

Other areas of inquiry that have been largely ignored in any detail include the dynamics of student and faculty interaction, the comparative influences of faculty and peer groups, and institutional subenvironments and subcultures that shape college's effects through their mediating influences on students' interactions with peers and faculty members. It will be particularly important to examine students' interpersonal experiences in both formal and informal learning settings. Continued research focusing on such distal environmental measures as living on- vs. off-campus, academic major, or similarly distal institutional characteristics, such as size, type of control, or even selectivity, is unlikely to advance our knowledge about college effects. More proximal and precise specification of the worlds in which students live are needed.

Summary

This chapter has attempted to help improve the quality of future student outcomes research on individual campuses by suggesting some of the future directions these studies might pursue. The maturation of this area of study over the years is apparent in studies of college impact published or reported in the last twenty years. Much remains to be done, however. In particular, we have argued, future research and assessment studies and programs should devote greater efforts to eight tasks: (1) to differentiating changes that occur *during* college from those that are *due* to college (so that current claims about the benefits of college attendance might be supported); (2) to estimating the magnitudes of college effects (so that the educational and administrative, as well as statistical, significance of results might be evaluated); (3) to examining not simply *whether* change occurs but also *when* it occurs (so that more tailored and effective programs and policies might be designed); (4) to exploring and measuring *indirect*, as well as direct, collegiate effects (so that the magnitude of college's effects will not be underestimated); (5) to the study of college effects that may be conditional on student characteristics such as race/ethnicity, age, and sex (so that important variations in college's effects might be better understood and more effective programs and policies might be designed); (6) to making greater use of qualitative research methods (so that important information inaccessible with quantitative methods will not be lost); (7) to expanding the theoretical perspectives that guide research and assessment study designs (so that theoretically myopic studies might be avoided); and (8) to focusing greater attention on the effects of the academic program and the teaching-learning process, the experiences of minority and older students, and the dynamics of students' interpersonal contacts with peers and faculty members (so that the educational experience might be maximized for *all* students).

Note

1. Effect sizes can be estimated as the average change in freshman-to-senior-year scores (whether for cross-sectional samples of, say freshmen and seniors, or for longitudinal panels) calculated in terms of standard deviation units. More specifically, an effect size can be estimated by subtracting a freshman-year mean score from the senior-year mean and then dividing that difference by the freshman-year standard deviation. When expressed in standard deviation units, an effect size can be converted (using the area under the normal curve) to a percentile point change estimate. For example, given an estimated effect size equal to one standard deviation, the area under the normal curve extends from the fiftieth to the eighty-fourth percentile, indicating a percentile point change of 34 percentile points from the freshman to senior year.

References

Cooper, H. (1982). Scientific guidelines for conducting integrative research reviews. *Review of Educational Research* 52: 291–302.

Feldman, K. A., and Newcomb, T. M. (1969). *The Impact of College on Students*. San Francisco: Jossey-Bass.

Glass, G. (1977). Integrating findings: The meta-analysis of research. In L. Shulman (ed.), *Review of Research in Education*. Itasca, IL: Peacock.

Jackson, G. (1980). Methods for integrative reviews. *Review of Educational Research* 50: 438–460.

Light, R., and Pillemer, D. (1982). Numbers and narrative: Combining their strengths in research reviews. *Harvard Educational Review* 52: 1–26.

Pascarella, E. T. (1987). Are value-added analyses valuable? In *Assessing the Outcomes of Higher Education* (pp. 71–91). Proceedings of the 1986 ETS Invitational Conference. Princeton, NJ: Educational Testing Service.

Pascarella, E. T., and Terenzini, P. T. (in press). *How College Affects Students: Findings and Insights from Twenty Years of Research*. San Francisco: Jossey-Bass.

Pillemer, D., and Light, R. (1980). Synthesizing outcomes: How to use research evidence from many studies. *Harvard Educational Review* 50: 176–195.

Slavin, R. (1984). Meta-analysis in education: How has it been used? *Educational Researcher* 13: 6–15.

Winter, D. G. (1979). Defining and measuring the competencies of a liberal arts education. In *Current Issues in Higher Education, Vol. 5* (pp. 1–9). Washington, DC: American Association for Higher Education.

Winter, D. G., McClelland, D., and Stewart, A. (1981). *A New Case for the Liberal Arts: Assessing Institutional Goals and Student Development.* San Francisco: Jossey-Bass.

CHAPTER 28

KNOCKING AT FREEDOM'S DOOR:
RACE, EQUITY AND AFFIRMATIVE ACTION IN
U.S. HIGHER EDUCATION

WALTER R. ALLEN, ROBERT TERANISHI,
ÒNIESHA DINWIDDIE AND GLORIA GONZÁLEZ

The American Dream lies at the very heart of the U.S. cultural ethos. At the center of this ideal is the emphatic conviction that, in this society, education opens the door to success. The belief that even the poorest citizen can achieve greatness with talent and hard work is one of this nation's most cherished cultural tenets (Hochschild, 1995). In most instances for those who adhere to these beliefs, talent is equated with educational attainment. African Americans have embraced this viewpoint to the extreme. Dating back to when slaves were forbidden to learn to read and write under threat of death or physical harm, African Americans have invested education with mythic qualities, holding it up as both hope and salvation for the future. Yet no matter how much education African Americans have achieved, they have still suffered discrimination based on skin color. Nevertheless, Black people in the United States have continued to crave and embrace education as the ultimate solution (Allen & Jewell, 1995). Despite the paradox of societal stereotypes depicting Blacks as lazy, ignorant, and mentally inferior—even as the nation developed history's most elaborate system of institutional barriers intent on denying them opportunities for schooling—African Americans continued to value and pursue education. The "holy grails" of education in general and higher education in particular have long embodied Black people's hopes and frustrations as they seek the "promised land" of freedom and opportunity.

Education has long been seen as an essential foundation of democracy. The extent to which citizens of any society are afforded equal educational opportunity speaks volumes about openness and power relations within that society. For African Americans, the centuries-old struggle for access to and success in higher education has been emblematic of a larger fight for personhood and equality. In this struggle, progress has come in fits and starts, interspersed with rollbacks and lost ground (Allen & Jewell, 1995). From 1965 to 1995, equal opportunity programs, and later affirmative action programs, represented rays of hope and promise for the nation's disenfranchised. For a relatively brief moment, U.S. society cracked open the doors of opportunity. Groups previously excluded from key positions and institutions slipped into those settings, although not necessarily in massive numbers. Nevertheless, they found some purchase where folks like themselves—Blacks, Latinos, Asians, and women—had not previously been allowed to set foot in any sizeable numbers, except

---

"Knocking at Freedom's Door: Race, Equity and Affirmative Action in U.S. Higher." Reprinted from *Journal of Negro Education* 69, no. 1 (2000), by permission of Howard University.

491

to clean or to serve food. In the case of African Americans, a country torn asunder by racial conflict and on the verge of precipitating a second Civil War cracked open the doors to higher education briefly. Under the imperatives of equity, inclusiveness, and diversity, U.S. universities enrolled African Americans from the tobacco fields of North Carolina, the ghettoes of New York City, the fruit and vegetable orchards of California, and the foundries of Saginaw. Equal opportunity and affirmative action programs gave minorities, women, and others who were routinely pushed to this society's fringes the chance to prove their worth. These programs did not guarantee success; they only provided the chance to compete and the opportunity to succeed—or fail—on one's own merit.

Having proven their value and effectiveness, affirmative action programs are today under severe, extensive attack. Yet, make no mistake about it: affirmative action is currently being challenged precisely because of its effectiveness. Affirmative action programs have made, or promise to continue to make, significant inroads against the established status quos of racial and patriarchal hierarchy. Powerful, vested interests see this progress and are determined to first stem and then reverse the gains.

Affirmative Action in Higher Education

In the midst of the national debate over affirmative action, the state of California is leading the rush to roll back the program in all its manifestations. In what truly must be seen as a moment of post-structuralist madness, the chief architect of this anti-affirmative action movement in California and nationally—Wardell Connerly, a Regent for the University of California (UC) system—is a Black man who readily admits that he was a beneficiary of affirmative action programs (Wallace, 1995). More recently, however, Connerly has posited numerous reasons to deny similar benefits to today's Black and Latino students who greatly need such assistance. Various rationales have been advanced by those opposed to affirmative action. Some say that affirmative action has served its purpose and is no longer necessary in our newly "colorblind" society. Others assert that affirmative action is unfair, that it represents "reverse discrimination" against guiltless Whites. Still others repeat the well-worn homily that the

poor and disenfranchised need simply to pull themselves up by their own bootstraps in order to advance in U.S. society. In the final analysis, however, none of these counterarguments is satisfactory or sufficient.

Affirmative action—and its predecessor equal opportunity programs—changed the "face" of this nation by tearing down the barriers that systematically blocked the access and prevented the full participation of Blacks, people of color, and women to the U.S. opportunity structure. Although the primary agenda of affirmative action was to remove unfair barriers to the equal participation of underrepresented racial groups and women would come to be equally represented in all sectors of society, the outcomes have been skewed. White women have been by far the greatest beneficiaries of affirmative action, realizing significant gains in all areas of education, employment, contracting, and careers (Wilson, 1998; Wise, 1998). As regards access to higher education in particular, White women increased their enrollment by 26% between 1978 and 1994 (Wilson, 1998), compared to lesser increases over the same period for both genders of African Americans (1%), Asian Americans (3.6%), and Chicanos/Latinos (2.9%).

As the predecessors of affirmative action programs, equal opportunity programs were rooted in the Constitutional guarantee of equal rights to all U.S. citizens. Despite the nation's political forefathers' emphasis on this ideal, Blacks were denied equal protection under the law for centuries. From 1619 to 1865, the enslavement of Americans of African descent was legal and protected by the U.S. Constitution. For 250 years, Blacks were categorized as chattel property, bartered, branded, brutalized, and dehumanized. For the next 100 years, from 1865 to 1965, Blacks were legally segregated, humiliated, and defined as inferior beings. By 1965, the legal barriers to Black progress were torn down, leaving in their place a heritage of opposition, denial, and restraint no less potent in denying Blacks equality of opportunity. What remained were the not-so-blind hands of structured inequality, market forces, stereotyping, and racial discrimination that continued to ensure the subordinate status of Blacks in U.S. society (Oliver & Shapiro, 1995; Wilson, 1996).

President Lyndon B. Johnson's 1965 Executive Order 11246, which mandated affirmative action, attempted to address the twin heritages of slavery and "Jim Crowism," or historic and contemporary racial oppression, that kept African Americans mired in poverty and despair (*Federal Register, 1967*). Moreover, the report to the United States Kerner Commission (1968), issued on the heels of riotous uprisings across the nation, made official what everyone already knew: the United States was a society divided by race, separate and unequal. In the language of his 1965 order, President Johnson invoked the powerful metaphor of a people in chains for 350 years, or 10 generations, being required to engage in a foot race against another people who were (and had long been) free of restraints. Over the years, he pointed out, the unchained had built up quite an advantage or head start over the chained. Therefore, Johnson argued, it was not sufficient in 1965 to declare the competition legal or even from that point on. According to the President:

> You do not take a person who, for years, has been hobbled by chains and liberate him, bring him up to the starting line of a race and then say, "You are free to compete with all the others," and still justly believe that you have been completely fair. (Johnson, 1965, p. 2)

Instead, he noted, special, systematic corrective actions were required to compensate for the accumulated disadvantage. After years of vigorously enforcing the exclusion of African Americans as well as other people of color, it was not sufficient for U.S. agencies and institutions to adopt the passive stance of "come if you like (read 'must')." Rather, Executive Order 11246 called for vigorous, proactive steps—affirmative action—to broaden and increase access to previously excluded, underrepresented groups.

In one sense, affirmative action as a policy recognized the root and branch nature of racism, in both its personal and institutional varieties, in the United States. Absent extraordinary efforts, proponents of the policy recognized that U.S. institutions would continue to conduct their business as usual, which translated into continued discrimination against Blacks and other people of color in opportunities for entry and progress, access and success. Ironically, equal opportunity legislation and policies, which evolved into what later became identified as affirmative action, stood the subordinate, degraded status of African Americans on its head. Given that the

U.S. racial caste system kept Whites at the top and Blacks at the very bottom of the social ladder, with other groups arranged in-between those poles based on various factors (e.g., skin color, physical features, U.S. geo-political interests, culture, etc.), a paradoxical national consensus arose. This unstated, but clearly understood, consensus declared that "What you would do for the *least* of us (i.e., Blacks), you most certainly should do for the *rest* of us" (i.e., non-Blacks). Thus, the affirmative action tent, its scope and parameters, was broadened beyond Blacks to include White women, Asians, Chicanos/Latinos, the physically impaired, those for whom English is a second language, and many, many others.

What this shift signaled was the eventual redefinition of affirmative action away from being a legal remedy or legal compensation for a distinct history of legally sanctioned racial discrimination to its being viewed as a tool for increasing diversity or improving the representation of underrepresented groups. Ironically, at day's end, affirmative action benefited the very White males who were at the pinnacle of the nation's systems of race, gender, class, and heterosexual oppression and who most fiercely resisted its advent. It did so by improving the economic status of White, two-earner families through improved opportunities for White women, who were their wives, mothers, sisters, and daughters. Although the purpose of affirmative action was to make the playing fields equal, on the flip side the economic progress of Blacks and other minorities continued to be hindered by substantial disparities in income, wealth, status, and employment as well as higher rates of poverty (Darity & Myers, 1998; Oliver & Shapiro, 1995).

Race, Equity, and Higher Education

The counterpoint to the concentration of wealth is the concentration of poverty. As the good times rolled for White couples and White families during the 1980s, Black couples and Black families withered under the grinding stones of poverty and deprivation (Wilson, 1996). Indeed, the number of African American children born into poverty actually increased from 43% in 1968 to 45% in 1998 (Public Broadcasting Services, 1999). In 1996, 22% of African Americans were not covered by any form of health insurance compared to only 12% of Whites (Public Broadcasting Services, 1999). The chronically poor economic status of Blacks has had direct consequences on their educational attainment, affecting early schooling opportunities, test performance, grades, and funding for college (Darity & Myers, 1998; Farley & Allen, 1987).

This is the history that brings us to the present, a moment when U.S. higher education is engaged in a process of resegregation. In particular, African Americans' current low rates of college enrollment and degree attainment are cause for concern. Black and Chicano/Latino enrollments at the University of California's most prestigious campuses, Berkeley and Los Angeles, have dropped by roughly 50% since the rollback of affirmative action policies in 1995 (Allen, Bonous-Hammarth, & Teranishi, 2001). The season of gains that African Americans realized in college enrollment and earned degrees has been reversed.

From the early 1960s until recently, African Americans made significant gains in enrollment and degree attainment at the university level. From 1962 to 1999, for example, the percentage of African Americans who completed four years of college or more rose from 4% to 15.5% (U.S. Bureau of the Census, 2000). Although this is positive news, the representation of African Americans among the college-educated was relatively poor compared to other racial groups. Although undergraduate enrollment for African Americans increased 8.3% since 1993, this is less than half the rates of increase for Chicanos/Latinos, Asian Americans, and Native Americans during the same period (Wilds, 2000). Compared to their White counterparts, Black disparities in enrollment are even more pervasive. Most recent data show that African Americans comprise less than 12% of the total undergraduate enrollment nationally, whereas Whites make up 71% of the student population (Wilds, 2000). Moreover, considering bachelor's degrees awarded in 1997, African Americans received only 8.1%, though they represented more than 11.2% of all undergraduate students (Wilds, 2000), while Whites were awarded 77% of bachelor's degrees, with 71% undergraduate enrollment. If the positive and disproportionate contributions of the nation's historically Black colleges and universities (HBCUs) were removed from the total Black student enrollment and earned degrees

rates, then these figures would be even more troubling.

College enrollment rates and participation in higher education for Chicanos/Latinos are often comparable to those of African Americans. Since 1974, for example, the percentage of Chicanos/Latinos of both genders who completed four years of college or more rose from 5.5% to 11% in 1999 (U.S. Bureau of the Census, 2000). Moreover, Chicano/Latino total enrollment in higher education increased 79.2% from 1988 to 1997 (Wilds, 2000), the highest gain among the four major racial groups. Although Chicanos/Latinos have a 45% completion rate at Division I U.S. colleges and their enrollment rates have increased 8 percentage points since 1990, they continue to trail both European Americans and African Americans in the completion of four-year degrees. Although Chicanos/Latinos represent 9% of undergraduate students, they were awarded only 5.3% of all bachelor's degrees in 1997 (Wilds, 2000). Asian Americans, on the other hand, made significant gains in enrollment, degree attainment, and participation in higher education over the period. For example, their enrollment in higher education increased 73% from 1988 to 1997, and they were awarded 6% of all bachelor's degrees in 1997 (Wilds, 2000).

In California particularly, the effects of antiaffirmative action legislation have directly impeded degree attainment and the participation of Blacks and Chicanos/Latinos in the UC system. For example, in 1997 nearly 50 Blacks and 50 Chicanos/Latinos enrolled in the University of California-Los Angeles (UCLA) Law School, this year's entering class counted only 2 Black students and 17 Chicanos/Latinos. *This* is the nature of the crisis currently confronting those who wish to address issues of race, equity, and affirmative action in U.S. higher education. It's déjà vu all over again, and a return to apartheid higher educational systems that either completely exclude or allow only a few token Blacks and similarly low numbers of Chicanos/Latinos.

Interestingly, much of this move to segregate U.S. higher education occurs under the banner of efforts to improve academic standards and academic quality. Under this banner, Blacks are implicitly and explicitly identified as threats to academic quality. Wherever their numbers grow, this reasoning implies, lowered academic standards cannot be far behind. Thus, the best way to improve an institution or community's academic reputation is to exclude African Americans or greatly limit their presence. This perspective has accompanied the multiplication of so-called high-stakes standardized tests: assessments whose results determine not only who will enter the next level but also who will qualify for graduation from the previous level. These instruments serve ably as mechanisms that can disqualify the educational goals or aspirations of a whole generation of Black students.

The state of California has provided much of the impetus for the anti-affirmative action movement, largely as a result of the state's own poor educational policy and planning. As Table 28-1 shows, California's population nearly doubled over the past three decades. From 1970 to 1998, the state's Black population grew by 71%—an impressive rate of population growth under most circumstances. However, this rapid growth was virtually insignificant alongside the astounding rates of increase for California's Chicano/Latino and Asian American populations. From 1970 to 1998, the former grew by over 450% (2,423,610 to 9,938,776) while the latter grew by over 500% (671,210 to 3,724,845) (California Department of Finance, 1999).

A series of state administrations did not anticipate or address the consequences of these population booms for the California higher education system, thus contributing to severe demand/supply discrepancies in higher education. Instead of adding beds in college dorms, these administrations invested exponentially in prisons and prison beds, an investment decision that made neither sound fiscal nor moral sense. Since 1984, there have been 21 prisons built in California, compared to 3 state university campuses and no UC campuses, even though prisoners cost the state 11 times as much to maintain compared to the standard in-state tuition for college students ($25,000 versus $2,250) (Families to Amend California's Three-Strikes, 2000). Moreover, largely due to implementation of the highly controversial "three-strikes law," the California prison population experienced a sevenfold increase from 23,511 in 1980 to 162,000 inmates by 2000 (California Department of Corrections, 2000). Thirty-nine percent of African American male Californians in their twenties are in prison, on probation, or paroled (Families to Amend, 2000). At the same time, Blacks, Chicanos/Latinos, Native Americans—and yes, even Asian Americans—are woefully underrepresented in college attendance and among those who wield positions of esteem and power in the state. Between 1989 and 1998, while California's African American population has remained consistent, the UC system has experienced an 18.1% decrease in the number of African American students (see Table 28.2).

The sum result of California's radically disproportionate investment in its criminal justice program has been to drastically increase the annual budget for the California Department of Corrections from $728 million in 1985 to $4.5 billion in 1998 (California Department of Corrections, 2000). Alongside these prodigious expenditures on corrections, the state is facing extreme shortages in K-12 and college educational facilities and personnel (Allen et al., 2001). In short, misplaced values and mis-investment caused a needless crisis whose unhappy, shortsighted solution has been to erect more and still more barriers to college opportunities. These barriers have taken the form of high-stakes standardized tests,

TABLE 28-1
California's Population, 1960 to 1990

Race/Ethnicity					
	Asian American	Black	Chicano/ Latino	Native American	White	Total
1960	—	—	—	—	—	15,717,204
1970	671,210	1,379,537	2,423,610	83,787	15,480,85 6	20,039,000
1980	1,257,408	1,794,051	4,615,711	164,710	15,950,120	23,782,000
1990	2,746,186	2,105,283	7,775,263	185,126	17,132,143	29,944,000
1998	3,724,845	2,357,377	9,938,776	197,521	17,275,835	33,494,354

Source: California Department of Finance, 1999

TABLE 28-2

Undergraduate Enrollment by Ethnicity in the University of California System, 1989 to 1998

Fall Term	Total Students	Asian/ Pacific Islander	Black	Filipino	Latino	Native American	Other	White	Total Declared Ethnicity	Non- Resident Alien	No Response
1989	123,441	22,993	5,796	4,102	13,071	1,121	1,609	68,187	116,879	2,554	4,008
1990	124,271	25,093	5,622	4,270	14,191	1,206	1,565	65,549	117,496	2,306	4,469
1991	124,627	27,224	5,327	4,334	14,778	1,301	1,504	62,602	117,070	2,443	5,114
1992	124,226	29,265	5,053	4,414	15,204	1,248	1,628	59,337	116,149	2,373	5,704
1993	122,271	31,642	4,911	4,469	15,395	1,194	1,710	54,840	114,161	2,317	5,793
1994	121,615	34,194	4,848	4,626	16,096	1,173	1,824	51,324	114,085	2,420	5,110
1995	123,737	36,327	5,009	4,982	16,956	1,234	2,024	49,804	116,336	2,569	4,832
1996	126,048	37,949	4,965	5,290	17,228	1,229	2,201	49,531	118,393	2,632	5,023
1997	128,689	39,257	4,988	5,644	17,131	1,195	2,482	50,240	120,937	2,800	4,952
1998	132,189	39,813	4,749	5,962	16,905	1,149	2,588	49,879	121,045	2,726	8,418
Percent Change	7.1%	73.2%	18.1%	45.3%	29.3%	2.5%	60.8%	26.8%	3.6%	6.7%	110.0%

Source: California Postsecondary Education Commission, 1999

higher thresholds of college eligibility, the dismantling of affirmative action, and the proposed mplementation of high school exit examinations.

What Future for Race, Economics, and Educational Opportunity?

In the dawning years of the 21st century, race and ethnicity continue to challenge U.S. society. The nation still wrestles with questions that ask whether race and ethnicity will be bases for unity or cause for division. What is valuable about the California case is the stark relief in which the complex intricacies of the nation's race problems in the new century are placed. In that microcosmic scenario, conflict is shown to result from both racial disputes *and* conflict based on national origin. This complexity propels the search for alternative models that can adequately address the roots of related struggles for power and personhood, such as those around gender, social class, and sexual orientation (Collins, 1998). Ultimately, the conflict in California, in Mississippi, in Michigan, across the United States, and across the world in places like Colombia, Kashmir, and the Congo traces back to sociopolitical and economic systems that require and thrive on exploitative relationships.

The emphasis in this nation on domination—and its companion, degradation—has wrought and continues to wreak profound human and societal havoc. The paradigm of White supremacy, domination, and exclusion has cut across the areas of education, health, politics, criminal justice, and the economy (Morris, Allen, Maurrasse, & Gilbert, 1995). Affirmative action's emphases on inclusiveness and diversity, however, have the power to enrich the higher education experience for all involved (Hurtado, Milem, Clayton-Pedersen, & Allen, 1999). Ultimately, exploitative relationships weaken not only those outside the mainstream—or in the shadows—but also those in the society at large. The choices are really quite simple: Will this nation opt to live up to the inspirational creed of the American Dream by offering freedom, opportunity, and equality to all, or will it continue to deny these ideals and by so doing lay the foundation for the destruction of yet another great civilization?

References

Allen, W. R., Bonous-Hammarth, M., & Teranishi, R. (2001). *Stony the road we trod. . . . The Black struggle for higher education in California.* Unpublished research report.

Allen, W. R., & Jewell, J. O. (1995). African American education since *An American dilemma*: An American dilemma revisited. *Daedalus, 124*(1), 77–100.

California Department of Corrections. (retrieved: 2000, September 6). *CDC facts: Second quarter 2000* [Online]. Available: http://www.cdc.state.ca.us/factsht.htm

California Department of Finance. (1999 [retrieved October 12, 2000]). *Race/ethnic population with age and sex detail, 1970–2040* [On-line]. Available: http://www.dof.ca.gov/html/demograp/race.htm

California Postsecondary Education Commision. (1999). *Student profiles, 1999* (Commission Report 99–5). Sacramento, CA: Author.

Collins, P. H. (1998). *Fighting words: Black women and the search for justice.* Minneapolis: University of Minnesota Press.

Darity, W., & Myers, S., Jr. (1998). *Persistent disparity: Race and economic inequality in the United States since 1945.* Cheltenham, UK: Edward Elgar.

Families to Amend California's Three-Strikes. (retrieved: 2000, July 13). *Latest statistics* [On-line]. Available: http://www.facts1.com/general/stats.htm

Farley, R., & Allen, W. R. (1987). *The color line and the quality of life in America.* Oxford: Oxford University Press.

Federal Register. (1967). Executive order 11246: Equal employment opportunity, by Lyndon B. Johnson (September 24, 1965; Code of Federal Regulations). Washington, DC: U.S. Government Printing Office.

Hochschild, J. L. (1995). *Facing up to the American dream: Race, class and the soul of the nation.* Princeton, NJ: Princeton University Press.

Hurtado, S., Milem, J., Clayton-Pedersen, A., & Allen, W. R. (1999). *Enacting diverse learning environments: Improving the climate for racial/ethnic diversity in higher education* (ASHE-ERIC Higher Education Report, 26[8]). Washington, DC: The George Washington University, Graduate School of Education and Human Development.

Johnson, L. B. (1965, June 4). *To fulfill these rights.* Commencement address presented at Howard University, Washington, DC.

Morris, A., Allen, W. R., Maurrasse, D., & Gilbert, D. (1995). White supremacy and higher education: The Alabama higher education desegregation case. *National Black Law Journal, 14*(1), 59–91.

Oliver, M. L., & Shapiro, T. M. (1995). *Black wealth/White wealth: A new perspective on racial inequality*. New York: Routledge.

Public Broadcasting Services. (1999; retrieved October 8, 2000). *Vital signs: Statistics that measure the state of racial inequality* [On-line]. Available: http://www.pbs.org/wgbh/pages/front/shows/race/economics/vital.html

United States Kerner Commission. (1968). *Report of the National Advisory Commission on Civil Disorders*. New York: Bantam Books.

U.S. Bureau of the Census. (2000). *Population profile of the United States: 1997*. Washington, DC: U.S. Government Printing Office.

Wallace, A. (1995, January 20). End race-based admissions, UC regent suggests. *Los Angeles Times*, p. 1.

Wilds, D. J. (2000). *Minorities in higher education, 1999–2000: Seventeenth annual status report*. Washington, DC: American Council on Education.

Wilson, H. (1998). Does affirmative action for Blacks harm Whites?: Some evidence from the higher education arena. *Western Journal of Black Studies, 22*(4), 218.

Wilson, W. J. (1996). *When work disappears: The world of the new urban poor*. New York: Knopf.

Wise, T. (1998). Is sisterhood conditional? White women and the rollback of affirmative action. *NWSA Journal, 10*(3), 1–26

Chapter 29

Involvement in Learning Revisited: Lessons We Have Learned

Alexander W. Astin

Given the rapidly changing political and economic circumstances of the past decade, we might expect a report that is now more than 11 years old to be somewhat out of date. However, with a few minor exceptions, the recommendations that were set forth in *Involvement in Learning* are just as relevant today as they were when they were first proposed by our Study Group in 1984. Indeed, much of the research that has been done since the report was issued not only has reinforced many of its recommendations but also has allowed us to elaborate on the recommendations in much more specific ways. In this essay I would like to review some of this research and comment on its special relevance for professionals in the field of student affairs. In the process I would also like to say a few things about another more recent report in which I was involved, the, *Student Learning Imperative* which was released in 1994 by the American College Personnel Association (ACPA).

To understand the interconnections among *Involvement in Learning*, the *Student Learning Imperative,* and our most recent research on student development, it is useful to keep in mind that each of these efforts is rooted in deeply held *values*. By focusing on these value issues, I will try to show how student affairs professionals can utilize our most recent research to help realize the full potential of the recommendations set forth in the two national reports.

Involvement in Learning

There are three sections of *Involvement in Learning* that seem to be most germane to the topic of this special issue of *JCSD*: "Shared Values" (pp. 2–4), the "Conditions of Excellence in Undergraduate Education" (pp. 15–22), and the "Recommendations" which make of the bulk of the report (pp. 23–81).

Shared Values

To understand the Study Group's shared values, it is useful to know the *process* that we followed in producing this report. Unlike many national commissions, our group did not meet for a few times to discuss drafts produced by staff; on the contrary, we met for many hours on several different occasions and actually wrote the report ourselves. After perhaps 40 to 50 hours of intense meetings often characterized by animated arguments and discussions, we came to realize that it would be very difficult to write a report that we could all endorse unless we could first define a common *value perspective*. The basic values on which we finally agreed might be characterized as "bullish."

"Involvement in Learning Revisited: Lessons We Have Learned." Reprinted from *Journal of College Student Development* 37, no. 2 (1996), by permission of the American College Personnel Association.

Borrowing a concept long promoted by one member of our group, Howard Bowen, we argued that "the United States must become a nation of educated people" (Study Group, 1984, p. 2). We asserted that to achieve this goal, the breadth and depth of American higher education needed to be expanded so that (a) larger proportions of the population would avail themselves of higher education and (b) larger proportions would complete their degree programs. In short, we argued that despite the many strengths of its higher education system, the United States was still a nation of "undereducated" people. Finally, we maintained that the quality of institutional performance should be judged ultimately in terms of *how effectively students were educated*, and that all institutions should employ publicly accountable assessment methods for demonstrating their effectiveness.

Although we argued that institutions needed to focus more on student outcomes, we avoided specifying what any of these outcomes should be, arguing instead that this task should be left largely to the individual institution. In retrospect, I think this was a mistake. If we had been more forthcoming about our own values with respect to some of the most important student outcomes, we certainly would have generated more controversy, but I think the controversy would have been healthy. More specifically, I wish we had spoken more directly about the importance of so-called affective outcomes such as self-understanding, tolerance, honesty, citizenship, and social responsibility.

If we stop for a moment to consider what the most critical problems of our society really are, they are at least as "affective" as they are "cognitive": racial tension, crime, drug abuse, teen pregnancy, school dropouts, disengagement from politics, and a growing unwillingness among the public to support governmental efforts to alleviate some of these problems. Certainly our colleges and universities bear some of the responsibility for preparing young people to deal constructively with such problems.

The issue of outcomes, of course, is ultimately a value question. What are the needs of our society and our students? What are the most desirable student qualities that we seek to develop? The problem with leaving such matters undiscussed is that academics, left to their own devices, will usually take refuge in "cognitive" outcomes like knowledge, cognitive skill,

critical thinking, and so on. Thus, even though colleges and universities are social institutions committed to serving the needs of the society, and even though the charters and mission statements of most institutions mention outcomes such as citizenship, character, and social responsibility, academics—especially faculty—tend to limit their conception of "outcomes" to the traditional cognitive side.

This issue of cognitive versus affective student outcomes has enormous implications for the work of people in the student affairs field. If higher education is really about cognitive *and* affective outcomes such as leadership, self-understanding, and citizenship, then student affairs has a central part to play in "educating" the student. If, on the other hand, we limit our concept of "education" to the content of academic textbooks and classroom lectures, the work of student affairs is more easily marginalized.

These distinctions are reflected in the terminology we use. Whereas most faculty talk about "student learning" (which implies the cognitive but not necessarily the affective side), most student affairs professionals talk about "student development" (which clearly encompasses both kinds of outcomes). Consider ACPA's *SLI*: the first four times the word *learning* appears, it is followed by *and student development*. The *SLI* then makes the following point: "the concepts of 'learning,' 'personal development,' and 'student development' are inextricably intertwined and inseparable" (p. 1). The word *learning* is subsequently used on 32 additional occasions throughout the *SLI*, and in fully 23 of these it is also accompanied by *student development*. Although it is easy to understand why student affairs professionals may wish to blur the distinction between "learning" and "development," there is another way to look at this problem: perhaps we need to expand the concept of "learning" to *include* affective as well as cognitive outcomes. Certainly it can be argued that students can and should "learn about" or "acquire skill in" such things as leadership, self-understanding, interpersonal relations, and citizenship.

The Pursuit of Excellence

The second relevant part of *Involvement in Learning* was our "Conditions of Excellence" section, which constituted a sort of minitheory of how students learn most effectively at the under-

graduate level. The cornerstone of this theory was the concept of *involvement* (Astin, 1975, 1977, 1984), which basically refers to the amount of time and physical and psychological energy that the student invests in the learning process. Literally hundreds of studies of college undergraduates (Pascarella & Terenzini, 1991) have shown clearly that the greater the student's degree of involvement, the greater the learning and personal development. The other two conditions of excellence were *high expectations* and *assessment and feedback*. Expectations give purpose and direction to involvement: toward what end is the student involved? Assessment and feedback not only help to make expectations explicit but also provide a basis for knowing the extent to which these expectations are actually being met by the combined efforts of the student and the institution.

Recommendation

The Study Group's recommendations were directed at faculty, staff, policymakers, and students. Of the 27 specific recommendations, those having to do with increasing student involvement (Recommendations 1–7) are most directly relevant to the work of student affairs professionals. These included such ideas as "frontloading" of more resources in the first year of undergraduate work, greater use of active teaching modes and learning communities, improved academic advisement and counseling, more support for the cocurriculum as a means of enhancing student involvement (especially among part-time or commuter students), and the use of learning technologies to increase, rather than decrease, student-faculty contact.

It is gratifying to realize that several of these recommendations have already been implemented on literally hundreds of campuses across the country. For example, since the report appeared, there has been a tremendous growth of interest in "Freshman 101" courses and similar devices for front-loading more resources into the first year or two of undergraduate work. There has also been a growing interest in active teaching modes and learning communities, especially in the area of cooperative learning. Although there has been a virtual explosion in the use of new learning technologies (especially personal computers) since our report was issued, it is not entirely clear whether these technologies

are really being used to enhance student-faculty contact. From certain perspectives it could be argued that computer technology has actually *reduced* the amount of such contact. And although we still have a long way to go in making better use of the cocurriculum to enhance involvement, there are some highly promising and exciting developments, such as the University of Houston's "Scholars Community" for part-time and commuter students.

Although the *Involvement in Learning* Study Group obviously cannot take all the credit for the "assessment movement" that seems to be sweeping our campuses, it is clear that much of what we recommended in the way of more and better assessment is now happening on many campuses. All of the regional accrediting associations—not to mention many state governments and even the federal government—are now actively promoting assessment on the campuses. And one of our major national organizations, the American Associates for Higher Education, has been operating a highly popular Annual Assessment Forum for the past 7 years.

Perhaps the biggest question mark concerns our eight recommendations regarding "high expectations." Certainly our recommendation for defining "scholarship" more broadly (Recommendation—14) is highly consistent with Boyer's *Scholarship Reconsidered* (1990). But whether colleges are more likely to make public statements of their learning goals for students or to make sure that curriculum content is consistent with these learning goals is more difficult to say. Also, our advocacy for more "liberal arts" courses, which was surely one of our most controversial recommendations, has probably *not* been implemented. This recommendation, interestingly enough, is one of the few that was not really grounded in prior research.

What does Recent Research Tell Us?

To what extent has the Higher Education Research Institute's more recent research on student development reinforced or confirmed the original recommendations in *Involvement in Learning*? Much of this newer research is summarized in *What Matters in College? Four Critical Years Revisited* (Astin, 1993b). This study provided us with an unprecedented opportunity to examine many educational questions that simply had not been researchable in earlier studies for lack of sufficient data. By a happy coincidence of multiple funding from public and private sources (primarily the Exxon Education Foundation and the National Science Foundation), we were able to put together what is probably the most comprehensive longitudinal, multi-institutional database on college student development ever assembled.

The Power of Involvement

Like most of the other studies of student development that we have been conducting at the Higher Education Research Institute for the past 20 years, this one relied on a large national sample of students who entered college as freshmen and were followed longitudinally during their undergraduate years. We used 82 different student outcome measures, including a variety of cognitive and affective measures that were pretested at entry and posttested 4 years later. In studying these diverse outcomes, we controlled for more than 140 characteristics of the entering students in order to examine the possible effects of some 190 environmental characteristics, including 57 different forms of student involvement.

The results strongly support the importance of involvement as a powerful means of enhancing almost all aspects of the undergraduate student's cognitive and affective development. The three most potent forms of involvement turn out to be academic involvement, involvement with faculty, and involvement with student peer groups. We also found that many important outcomes are *negatively* affected by various forms of "non-involvement" that either isolate the student from peers or remove the student physically from the campus. Specifically, I speak here of such things as living at home, commuting, attending part-time, being employed off campus, being employed full-time, and watching television.

But perhaps the most important generalization to be derived from this massive study is that the strongest single source of influence on cognitive and affective development is the student's *peer group*. In particular, the characteristics of the peer group and the extent of the student's interaction with that peer group have enormous potential for influencing virtually all aspects of the student's educational and personal development. Generally speaking, the greater the interaction with peers, the more favorable the outcome. Indeed, the study strongly suggests that the peer group is powerful because it has the capacity to *involve* the student more intensely in the educational experience.

If nothing else, our findings on the power of the peer group suggest that student affairs professionals and student affairs work in general should play a much more central role in academic planning and policy making. Most peer groups operate primarily outside of the formal classroom, and much of that out-of-class life falls under the purview of student affairs. In fact, discussions of formal classroom teaching techniques are beginning to focus more on the peer group. This focus can be seen, for example, in the growing literature on cooperative learning in higher education, and particularly in the work of Jim Cooper (1990) at the Dominguez Hills campus of California State University, Karl Smith of the University of Minnesota (Johnson, Johnson, & Smith, 1992), and Uri Triesman (1983, 1991), formerly of University of California at Berkeley and now at the University of Texas at Austin. What these teacher-scholars are showing is that cooperative learning—where students basically work together on classroom material in small groups where they serve as teachers of each other—is generally much more effective than traditional classroom instructional techniques. My own view of cooperative learning is that it works primarily because it get students much more actively involved in the learning process—both as students and as teachers and mentors of each other.

Teaching versus Research

What Matters in College? also provides strong support for what we have come to call the "student affairs point of view." Among the many environmental variables used in this study we identified two measures of the institutional climate that have powerful but contrasting effects on student development: the *research orientation* of the faculty and the *student orientation* of the faculty. Research orientation is defined in both behavioral and attitudinal terms: the publication rate of the faculty, the amount of time they spend conducting research, and their stated personal commitment to research. A faculty with a strong research orientation would thus publish many articles and books, spend a substantial amount of their working time on research, and attach a high personal priority to engaging in research. It is informative to see what other characteristics correlate with research orientation. For example, its correlation with the average faculty salary at the institution is an astounding .86. What this tells us, among other things, is that the primary factor that accounts for differences in what institutions pay their faculties is the faculty's degree of engagement in research. Research orientation also correlates highly ($r = .67$) with the institution's "Resources and Reputational Emphasis," which is another institutional "climate" measure reflecting the extent to which the institution is perceived as placing a high emphasis on the acquisition of resources and the enhancement of the institution's national image and reputation. For several years now I have been arguing that too many institutions define their "excellence" in terms of either (a) their level of resources or (b) their national reputation as reflected in various polls and surveys (Astin, 1985). Given that faculty research "stars" are considered to be one of the prime institutional "resources" for enhancing an institution's reputation, it is no surprise that research orientation is highly correlated with a resources and reputation emphasis.

What is perhaps most interesting is the fact that the research orientation of the faculty has its strongest *negative* correlations with factors having to do with teaching and being oriented toward students: hours per week spent teaching and advising ($r = -.83$), commitment to student development ($r = -.72$), use of active learning techniques in the classroom ($r = -.52$), and the percentage of faculty engaged in teaching general education courses ($r = -.52$).

Student orientation of the faculty is primarily a *perceptual* measure reflecting the extent to which faculty believe that their colleagues are interested in and focused on student development. Typical questionnaire items that make up this factor are "Faculty here are interested in students' academic problems," "Faculty here are interested in students' personal problems," "Faculty are easy to see outside of office hours," "Faculty here are committed to the welfare of the institution," and "There are many opportunities for student-faculty interaction." There is one questionnaire item that gets a *negative* weight in the student orientation score: "Students are treated like numbers in a book."

Interestingly enough, the student orientation of the faculty has its strongest correlation ($r = .78$)

with the institution's social activism and community orientation. This latter measure reflects the extent to which the institution is seen as being committed to goals such as teaching students how to change society, developing leadership ability among students, helping to solve major social and environmental problems, developing a sense of community among faculty and students, helping students to understand their own values, and facilitating student involvement in community service activities. Talk about "affective" values!

As would be expected, one is most likely to find a strongly student-oriented faculty in a private four-year college and a strongly research-oriented faculty in a public university.

What kinds of effects do these two different faculty measures have on student development? Let's start with research orientation. We will consider the negative effects first, because these are stronger than the positive effects. The strongest negative effect is on student satisfaction with faculty. Research orientation also has negative effects on the student's leadership, public-speaking skills, and interpersonal skills and reduces the student's likelihood of being elected to a student office or tutoring other students. Still other negative effects occur with college GPA, completion of the bachelor's degree, graduation with honors, participation in cultural activities, and satisfaction with the quality of instruction and the overall college experience. The only positive effects of research orientation are on the student's GRE and LSAT scores and on satisfaction with the institution's physical facilities. In short, with the exception of these last effects, there is a significant institutional price to be paid, in terms of student development, when the faculty puts a great emphasis on research.

Student orientation of the faculty produces a very different pattern of effects. Its strongest positive effects are on satisfaction with faculty, the quality of instruction, individual support services, opportunities to take interdisciplinary courses, and the overall college experience. The Student orientation of the faculty also has a number of positive effects on academic outcomes: bachelor's degree attainment, graduation with honors, intellectual self esteem, and growth in writing skills, critical-thinking abilities, analytical and problem-solving skills, preparation for graduate school, and overall academic development. Additional positive effects of student orientation are on leadership, election to a student office, and participation in cultural activities. In short, this pattern of results suggests that having a strongly student-oriented faculty pays rich dividends in terms of the affective and cognitive development of the undergraduate.

Even though research orientation and student orientation are substantially correlated in a negative direction ($r = -.69$), and have opposite patterns of effects on student development, it is important to realize that they are to a certain extent independent and that each contributes independently to predicting student outcomes. What this means, in effect, is that it is possible for some institutions to score high on both factors and for others to score low on both factors. A weak emphasis on research is thus not an *inevitable* consequence of having a student-oriented faculty, nor is a weak commitment to student development an *inevitable* consequence of having a strongly research-oriented faculty.

Given the obvious conflict between research and teaching documented in this research, we were naturally curious as to whether it is possible to emphasize both research and teaching in the interest of creating the "ideal" educational environment. To pursue this question, my colleague Mitchell J. Chang and I searched through our 217 institutions to identify those that were somehow able to emphasize both research and teaching simultaneously (Astin & Chang, 1995). An analysis of financial, student, faculty, and curricular practices at these institutions yielded the following findings:

- Faculties that manage to emphasize both teaching and research (the "high-high" institutions) must necessarily compromise somewhat between these two emphases, especially research. That is, none of the "high-highs" had extreme (top 10%) scores on *both* orientations.

- Compared to other types of institutions, the high-highs charge more tuition and spend more on instruction, student services, and financial aid.

- Students entering high-high institutions, compared to students in general, have much higher admission test scores, come from higher socioeconomic backgrounds, and are more liberal, feminist, and artistic. While in college they are more likely

to interact with faculty and with each other and to participate in campus protests. Despite their excellent academic preparation, they are less likely to compete with each other for grades.

- Students at the high-high institutions show a strong predilection for the liberal arts (especially social sciences and humanities) and little interest in professional fields (especially business, education, and allied health professions). They also end up taking more courses in history, foreign language, ethnic studies, and women's studies and fewer remedial and study skills courses.

- The curricula of the high-high colleges emphasize general education, interdisciplinary studies, independent study, freshman seminars, and a personalized/individualized approach to satisfying general education requirements.

- Faculty at the high-high institutions frequently engage undergraduates in their research, emphasize the humanities, incorporate issues relating to gender or race in their research, and develop new courses and engage in team teaching.

Investment in Student Affairs

One of the most interesting environmental variables identified in our study is the percentage of the institution's total expenditures invested in student services. That this measure is indeed an estimate of the priority that an institution gives to student services is reflected in the other variables that are strongly correlated with it. For example, this measure has its strongest positive correlations with such things as the priority that the faculty give to student development, the percentage of faculty involved in teaching general education courses, and the use of active learning techniques by the faculty. It has its strongest *negative* correlations with the use of teaching assistants in courses, the institutional priority given to research and graduate education, the size of the institution, and the institutional emphasis placed on resource acquisition and reputational enhancement.

But what is most interesting about student services expenditures is that it has direct positive effects on a number of student outcomes. Its strongest effects are on the degree of student satisfaction with faculty and on the students' perception of how student-oriented the faculty are. It also has direct positive effects on the students' perceptions of how oriented the institution is toward social change and of their level of trust in the administration, as well as on satisfaction with individual support services, the overall quality of instruction, general education requirements, and the overall college experience. The direct positive effect on satisfaction with individual support services shows that investing in student services actually pays off.

In the cognitive realm, the percentage of expenditures invested in student services has indirect positive effects on degree completion and on self-rated growth in leadership abilities, public-speaking skills, critical-thinking skills, and preparation for graduate school. It has positive effects on growth in writing skills, intellectual self-esteem, tutoring of other students, and participation in protests.

In short, here is one of those rare occasions when we are able to demonstrate empirically how institutions can strengthen their educational effectiveness by reallocating resources. Given that student services account for a relatively small proportion of educational and general expenditures (usually between 3% and 8%), it would appear that modest increases, in absolute terms, in such resources could yield significant educational benefits for students.

More Recent Findings

Since *What Matters in College?* appeared, we have completed a number of other studies with the data that also have important implications for student affairs work, and this more recent research has emphasized *values* and *affective* outcomes. This research is summarized in the three sections that follow.

Volunteerism and Service Learning

One of the most promising trends in American higher education is the rapidly growing campus interest in volunteerism and service learning. This interest is reflected not only in the establishment of President Clinton's Learn and Serve America: Higher Education program, but also in the burgeoning membership of the Campus Compact, a grassroots consortium of colleges and universities that is attempting to promote student involvement in community service activities.

One of the more troubling findings is that there is a substantial *decline* in student participation in community service activities between high school and college. Indeed, the number of students who are frequent participants in community services declines by more than half between high school and college, whereas the number of *non*participants more than doubles (from 22% to 52%). As a matter of fact, two in every five students who are frequent participants in high school never participate in college. What this suggests to me is that faculty and student affairs professionals are missing out on a great opportunity to maintain and promote student involvement in community service activities and volunteer work during the undergraduate years. In other words, there is a tremendous untapped potential in our undergraduate students for greater participation in volunteer work.

What factors in the college environment encourage or discourage volunteerism among undergraduates? As it turns out, we found a variety of influences related to such things as the curriculum, the faculty, the peer group, the type of institution, and individual student activities. Taking interdisciplinary courses or majoring in social science or education appears to enhance student involvement in volunteer service while in college. Given the emphasis in the field of education and in many of the social sciences on social and public policy issues, this result should not be surprising. Why interdisciplinary courses should be related to volunteer participation, however, is not entirely clear, although it is interesting to realize that, with few exceptions, most volunteer assignments are probably "multidisciplinary." It may well be that some of these interdisciplinary courses involve service-learning components.

As far as faculty influences are concerned, it appears that faculty who are themselves strongly committed to social change are successful in promoting greater student participation in volunteer activities among their students.

But perhaps the most significant finding of all concerns the effect of student peer groups. Of all the variables in our analysis—entering student characteristics as well as characteristics of the college environment—none had a positive effect on volunteer participation that rivalled the effect of frequency of interaction among students. One likely interpretation of this finding is that student engagement in volunteer and community service work operates through peer *networking*. Further, this finding suggests that one promising way to encourage greater student participation in volunteer activities and service learning would be simply to maximize the amount of interaction that occurs among students. Some of the specific forms of student—student interactions that have positive effects on volunteer participation include participation in religious activities, involvement in campus activism, and socializing with members of different ethnic groups. Each of these activities constitutes another form of student interaction.

The significance of these findings becomes even clearer when we look at some of the factors that negatively influence student volunteer participation. The peer group characteristic that has the largest negative effect on volunteer participation is the degree of involvement of the student body in outside work. That is, a student's chances of participating in volunteer work are lowest in those institutions where many students work at outside jobs. Other student activities that are negatively associated with volunteer participation include living at home and watching television. All of these activities—working at outside jobs, living at home, and watching television—would tend to reduce the student's opportunities for interacting with other students.

It is also of interest to note that the amount of interaction between faculty and students also has positive effects on volunteer participation. While *Involvement in Learning* and *SLI* both emphasize the importance of student-faculty interaction as a way of enhancing the learning process, our latest research shows that there are additional "affective" benefits associated with student-faculty interaction beyond any effects it might have on the student's "cognitive" development.

We have also been looking at factors that enhance the institution's degree of commitment to facilitate student involvement in community service. Two of the strongest factors are the priorities given to student development and to developing a sense of community among students and faculty. We also tend to find a strong emphasis on promoting student involvement in community service at institutions where the faculty themselves are committed to such things as influencing social values, helping others in difficulty, developing a meaningful philosophy of life, and promoting racial understanding.

The weakest commitment to promoting student involvement in community service tends to be found at institutions where there is a strong faculty research orientation and a high priority given to resource acquisition and reputational enhancement. A weak commitment to promoting involvement in community service is also associated with a lack of interest in students among administrators, a curriculum that is seen as suffering from overspecialization, and a lack of trust between minority students and administrators.

Given these patterns of positive and negative correlates, it is not surprising that there are differences by type of institution in the priorities assigned to facilitating student involvement in volunteer service. A particularly distressing finding is that *both* public 4-year colleges and especially public universities show a weak commitment to student involvement in community service, whereas the private 4-year colleges assign a much higher priority to involving students in community service. The private universities have an average level of commitment. These findings are ironic, if not troubling: Why do institutions that are presumably created to serve the public give such a low priority to public service?

Could the low level of commitment found in public institutions be attributable to their larger size? We conducted a series of analyses that showed, first, that size is indeed a negative factor in institutional commitment. But even after controlling for size, we still find a lower level of commitment in the public institutions.

More recently my colleague Linda Sax and I have been using a new 9-year follow-up of the *What Matters in College?* sample to examine the effects of volunteer service on postcollege development. While the analyses are still in progress, we have already determined that participating in volunteer service during the undergraduate years has positive effects on such postcollege outcomes as enrolling in graduate school, being committed to promoting racial understanding, and socializing across racial ethnic lines. It even increases the likelihood that the student will donate money to the college.

Diversity and Multiculturalism

We have been able to focus on three types of environmental measures relating to issues of diversity or multiculturalism: (a) institutional diversity emphasis, (b) faculty diversity emphasis, and (c) five specific student diversity experiences:

- took ethnic studies courses
- took women's studies courses
- attended racial/cultural awareness workshops
- discussed racial or ethnic issues
- socialized with someone of another racial/ethnic group

Recently, we (Astin, 1993a) have determined that all seven of these measures are associated with a similar pattern of student outcomes. Institutional and faculty diversity emphases and individual student diversity experiences have positive effects on two *value* outcomes: *cultural awareness* and *commitment to promoting racial understanding*. Cultural awareness reflects students' understanding and appreciation of other races and cultures. The positive effect on the student's commitment to promoting racial understanding is of special interest, given that some critics have alleged that emphasizing issues of race and multiculturalism tends to exacerbate racial tensions on the campus. Quite the opposite seems to be the case. That is, emphasizing matters of diversity seems to strengthen students' personal commitment to promoting understanding between the races.

Diversity emphases and experiences also have positive effects on the student's overall satisfaction with college and satisfaction with student life. Interestingly, these positive effects seem to be similar for Whites, African Americans, and Latinos (Villalpando, 1994). These results have obvious implications for student affairs that go well beyond the finding regarding expenditures for student services. If our institutions opt for a talent development philosophy, and if they want to take seriously their catalogue claims about developing talents like character, leadership, and citizenship, then the arena of student affairs assumes a role of central importance. Student affairs is not only the place where we can provide opportunities for students to become involved in community service activities, to learn about diversity, and to develop leadership skills, but it is also the place where we can maximize opportunities for positive peer group experiences.

The Role and Status of Student Affairs

The importance for student affairs professionals of *institutional values* is highlighted by the recent research of Ayala (1995), who used our longitudinal database of 217 institutions to study three outcomes of direct importance to student affairs: the *respect* evidenced for student affairs work by the institution, and two measures of *support*; namely, the *perceived* support (as reported by faculty at the institution) and the *actual* support (as evidenced by the proportion of educational and general expenditures allocated to student affairs). (As noted before, this latter resource allocation measure is associated with several positive student developmental outcomes.) Ayala's most important finding is that the principal environmental factors associated with respect and support are the extent to which the values of the faculty and the administration are consonant with the values traditionally espoused by student affairs practitioners. That is, the greater priority that the faculty or administration assign to student learning and development as an institutional goal, the greater the respect and support accorded to student affairs. In other words, student affairs is most likely to be respected and strongly supported when the faculty and the administration give a high priority to students and their development (as contrasted to other institutional priorities such as research, fund raising, or reputation building). Not surprisingly, Ayala also found that respect and support for student affairs is greater in smaller and privately controlled institutions than in larger public institutions. Most of these differences by institutional size and type, however, are directly attributable to differences in faculty and administrative values.

Some Final Thoughts on Assessment

Both *Involvement in Learning*, and the *SLI* make a strong case for more and better assessment of student learning and development. Given their special access to students, student affairs professionals are ideally situated to undertake major efforts at assessing student development. Although some institutions are already actively engaged in devising better ways to assess student learning using before-and-after longitudinal measures, we often forget that it is equally important to understand something about the institutional *environment* and *climate* to which students have been exposed. Here again is an area where student affairs can play a major role.

Given the demonstrated importance of student involvement, one of the things we should regularly assess is how much time students devote to various activities. Such information can reflect differing patterns of student involvement. For example, in *What Matters in College?* we found that the hours per week that students devote to studying and homework has substantial positive effects on a number of outcomes—cognitive as well as effective. By contrast, hours per week spent watching television has a widespread pattern of negative effects.

But perhaps the most important assessment issue has to do with the subject of *outcomes*. The fact is that any attempt at educational reform is ultimately driven by a consideration of what the desired outcomes should be. In higher education, the current "assessment movement" is driving us to operationalize certain student outcomes, and as I have already tried to say, our choices both of student outcomes and of instruments for measuring these outcomes are ultimately based on value judgments. We are long past the point where we can defend the argument that undergraduate education ought to be—or even *can* be—"value free." The findings reported in *What Matters in College?* show clearly that a particular educational program or environment might be judged as either desirable or undesirable, depending upon which outcomes are most valued. In fact, we found that the environmental factors that enhance performance on *standardized tests*, for example, are almost completely different from the environmental factors that favorably affect most other cognitive and affective outcomes. Mission statements and college catalogues are replete with statements of value, whether we are talking about cognitive outcomes such as critical thinking and scientific knowledge or affective outcomes such as citizenship and social responsibility. Even the idea that the only meaningful outcomes are cognitive is a value judgment.

In my judgment it is a serious mistake to limit our outcomes to the cognitive value. Considering the state of our society today, one could certainly make a strong argument in favor of developing talents such as cultural understanding, empathy, citizenship, volunteerism, and social responsibility. Given that our mission statements and catalogues are frequently focused on such affective outcomes, we have, in effect, given ourselves "permission" to include them in our outcomes assessments.

Assessment is a potentially powerful tool for assisting us in building a more efficient and effective educational program. Assessment, in other words, can enhance our educational mission directly—by strengthening the teaching-learning process—and indirectly—by informing or enlightening us about which of our programs, policies, and practices are most and least effective. If an institution succeeds in developing an assessment program that serves these two functions, the external critics of higher education who seek to make us more "accountable" will have little left to complain about.

Some readers may view the approach to assessment that I have described here as a sort of utopian ideal that has little chance of implementation in the real world. Paradoxically, such a *belief* may well be the principal obstacle to implementing a truly comprehensive and effective assessment program. In fact, the formal charters of most higher education institutions already provide the conceptual justification for such a program. The principal business of higher education is, after all, *education*. Assessment turns out to be an excellent device for helping us understand how effectively we are carrying out this mission.

In closing, I would like to return to the issue of institutional *values*. Values are at the center of virtually everything we do: Whether we get caught up in the mere pursuit of resources and reputation, or whether we follow instead the talent development conception of excellence; *which* student outcomes we choose to assess and *how* we choose to assess them; whether we continue to concentrate on the cognitive side, or whether we take the plunge and go into the affective realm in a significant way; whether we continue to ignore the environmental area of assessment or, instead, embark on a concerted effort to incorporate environmental data in our assessment programs; and whether we see ourselves narrowly as specialists doing "outcomes assessment," or whether we view ourselves instead as key players in a major effort directed at the institutional improvement and reform.

Most of the great philosophical and religious traditions have promoted, in one form or another, the maxim "Know thyself." Indeed, self-knowledge is regarded by most of these traditions as a prerequisite for all of the other virtues: honesty, love, compassion, empathy, maturity, and social responsibility. It seems to me that the individual benefits of self-understanding can be generalized with equal validity to the case of a higher education institution: an institution that really understands itself—its strength and weaknesses, its limitations and its potentials—is likely to be much more successful in carrying out its talent development mission than an institution that lacks such self-understanding. By becoming more aware of who we are and what impact our programs are having on our students, we greatly increase the odds that our institutions will be able to realize their full educational potential.

References

American College Personnel Association. (1994). *The Student Learning Imperative: Implications for student affairs*. Washington, DC: Author.

Astin, A. W. (1975). *Preventing students from dropping out*. San Francisco: Jossey-Bass.

Astin, A. W. (1977). *Four critical years*. San Francisco: Jossey-Bass.

Astin, A. W. (1984). Student involvement: A developmental theory for higher education. *Journal of College Student Personnel*. (A revised version appears as Chapter 6 in Achieving Educational Excellence).

Astin, A. W. (1985). *Achieving educational excellence*. San Francisco: Jossey-Bass.

Astin, A. W. (1993a). Diversity and multiculturalism on the campus: How are students affected? *Change, 25*(2), 44–49.

Astin, A. W. (1993b). *What matters in college? Four critical years revisited*. San Francisco: Jossey-Bass, 1993b.

Astin, A. W., & Chang, M. J. (1995). Colleges that emphasize research and teaching: Can you have your cake and eat it too? *Change, 27*(5), 44–49.

Ayala, F., Jr. (1995). *The status of student affairs work: Some factors critical to respect and support*. Unpublished doctoral dissertation, University of California, Los Angeles.

Boyer, E. L. (1990) *Scholarship reconsidered: Priorities of the professoriate*. Princeton, NJ: Carnegie Foundation for the Advancement of Teaching.

Cooper, J., et al. (1990). *Cooperative learning and college instruction: Effective use of student learning teams*. California State University Foundation on behalf of California State University Institute for Teaching and Learning. Office of the chancellor.

D'Souza, D. (1991). *Illiberal education: The politics of race and sex on campus*. New York: Free Press.

Johnson, D. W., Johnson, R. T., & Smith, K. A. (1991). *Cooperative learning: Increasing college faculty instructional productivity*. Washington, D.C.: George Washington University, School of Education and Human Development.

Johnson, D. W., Johnson, R. T., & Smith, K. A. (1991). *Active learning: Cooperating in the college classroom*. Edina, MN: Interaction Book Co.

Pascarella, E. T., & Terenzini, P. T. (1991). *How college affects student*. San Francisco. Jossey-Bass.

Study Group on the Conditions of Excellence in Higher Education (1984). *Involvement in learning: Realizing the potential of American higher education*. Washington, DC: National Institute of Education.

Treisman, P. U. (1985). *A study of the mathematics performance of Black students at the University of California, Berkeley*: Unpublished manuscript, University of California at Berkeley.

Treisman, P. U. (1991). *Developing the next generation of mathematics*. Washington, DC: Mathematical Association of America.

University of Houston. (1995, January). *The Scholar, 1*(1).

Villalpando, O. (1994, November). *Comparing the effects of multiculturalism and diversity on Minority and White students' overall satisfaction with college*. Paper presented at the Association for the Study of Higher Education annual meeting, Tucson, Arizona.

CHAPTER 30

ON-GOING DIALOGUE COLLEGE OUTCOMES AND STUDENT DEVELOPMENT: FILLING THE GAPS

FRANCES K. STAGE

Dr. Russell, a newly hired assistant professor, is asked to develop a course on student development theory and research. The course should contain a segment on special student populations. In addition, because the class will be mostly masters' students, it should touch on practical application. Her most recent administrative position was associate dean for academic affairs at a university of 18,000 students where her primary responsibility was to research student admissions and retention, track students within college, and follow the graduates. It has been six years since Russell earned her doctorate, and she does not want to rely on the syllabus from the class she took eight years ago.

Her colleague passes along a syllabus from a course on "The College Student" being taught in a similar program. Flipping to the bibliography, Russell is surprised to recognize few authors. From the list of Gilligan, Perry, King, Kitchener, Kegan, Astin, and Chickering only a few seem familiar. The names she expects—Tinto, Pascarella, Cross, Bean, Pace—are not there.

Realizing that the literature in which she has immersed herself for the past several years might have been "incomplete," she begins to reeducate herself. Again she is dismayed to discover that only a few of the readings mention the special populations whose problems she is to address in her class. She searches for more but finds only scattered articles, for the most part descriptive.

Finally, although Russell finds a few examples of a particular theory being implemented in very specific settings, she finds few "process models" to help her use a particular theory in more general circumstances.

In the past two decades, a great deal of research has focused on the college student. A shift from atheoretical to theoretical studies of college outcomes (satisfaction, progress, persistence, etc.) and the subsequent testing of those theories have spurred research on the topics. Additionally, a change of focus in the student affairs profession has sparked research on the nature of students and how they develop in college. However, I find gaps between these two bodies of research; if filled, they could provide broader insights into the college student experience.

Since the early seventies, colleges have gradually relinquished the *in loco parentis* role. Professionals have become less concerned with controlling and limiting student behavior and more concerned with enabling and fostering student development. This shift has led to further exploration of college student development. Additionally, institutional concerns with enrollment and retention have inspired research on student progress and satisfaction.

These relatively recent shifts in focus have yielded seemingly endless knowledge about the college student and the college process. With so much information on the topic, constructing a curriculum to inform practitioners might seem easy. However, closer examination of this literature brings some troublesome observations:

1. There are actually two separate literatures on the college student (sociological and psychological) and few clear links to meaningfully synthesize both the outcomes and the development literature.

2. Much college student literature is monocultural, focusing on white upper- and middle-class students at large residential research universities. Such research does little to inform us about students at nontraditional institutions or about the multicultural populations on most campuses.

3. Too few process models tie directly to specific theory and can be used to guide practice on college campuses.

I will discuss each of these observations in turn and offer some recommendations for researchers and those attempting to incorporate theory in practice.

Two Separate Literatures

Most research on college students is based either on sociology or on psychology. In general, those of us who study student outcomes view the college-going process at the macro level and tend to take a sociological approach in our research. We study students in large aggregates and place them in broad demographic classifications. We assess how these broadly defined groups of students react to their environment and attempt to determine how these variables relate to such outcomes as academic achievement, satisfaction, and persistence.

On the other hand, those of us who study the development of college students view the college-going process at more of a micro level and tend to take more of a psychological approach in our research. We may use one of many student development theories to identify developmental levels or tasks of the students being studied. Usually, as researchers we seek to link the theoretical development of students to specific kinds of campus experiences or activities.

Unfortunately, there is little current overlap in these two literatures. The research on student outcomes seeks to determine which aspects of college life can have positive influences on satisfaction, career choice, persistence, and grade point average. On the other hand, the student development research focuses on the students' development as college students and on what can be done to foster further development.

A few early, ambitious, and well-known studies conceptually and methodologically linked student psychological characteristics with sociological experiences and outcomes (Astin 1968; Feldman and Newcomb 1973). However, since the development of causal models in the study of college students, possible connections between these two bodies of literature have been weak and for the most part, remain unexplored (Stage 1988).

Student Development Research

Theories and research that focus on student development are, for the most part, psychologically based and provide a rich body of information for faculty as well as student affairs practitioners. The most widely used student development theories can be classified into three major families: cognitive theory, psychosocial theory, and typology theory.

Cognitive development theorists like Kohlberg, Gilligan, Perry, King, Kitchener, and Kegan focus on how students reason when faced with decisions (e.g., what thoughts guide a decision about career choice?). Generally, these theories delineate stages in a hierarchy of reasoning with higher levels representing broader, more sophisticated ways of making meaning of the world. Researchers exploring these theories tend to focus on classifying individuals into stages and determining what causes movement from one stage to another.

The psychosocial theorists include Chickening, Heath, Levinson, and Sheehy. They are more interested in the content or the developmental tasks with which students are dealing (e.g., is the student working on establishing autonomy or on establishing identity?). Researchers operating within these frameworks attempt to identify issues and to explain how such issues are resolved.

Both cognitive development theorists and psychosocial theorists believe that development results from an "optimal mismatch." That is, if a student feels challenged by a situation but also receives sufficient support to meet that challenge, he or she will likely develop. If the challenge is too great, if there is insufficient support, or if there is no challenge, development is unlikely.

Finally, typology theorists include Clark-Trow, Astin, Pace, Holland, and Myers-Briggs. These theorists focus on characteristics of the individual and of the environment, and the fit or lack of fit (interaction) between these two constructs (e.g., is the student an academic type or more of a social type?). Researchers using these theoretical frameworks may use physical, sociological, or perceptual measures of the campus environment. They contrast these measures with measures of a student's needs, personality, or sociological type, or perception of the ideal campus environment to identify discrepancies. These discrepancies then may explain lack of performance, dissatisfaction, or attrition.

As these theories became widely tested, replicated, and understood, researchers as well as college administrators began to recognize and appreciate their value in studying and dealing with college students. Currently these theories form the basis for most research on the development of the college student.

The Student Outcomes Research

During the past fifty years, much of the research in higher education focused on the study of such student outcomes as grade point average (GPA), persistence, intellectual achievement, change of major, and satisfaction with many aspects of the college environment (Ewell 1985; Pace 1984). The field of outcomes research, though not new, has changed radically in the last decade. Before the 1970s, researchers had explored the relationship of many individual variables (gender, socioeconomic status, religion, etc.) to any given outcome (grades, satisfaction, persistence, etc.). Only a few researchers attempted to tie characteristics, attitudes, experiences, and achievements together conceptually (Astin 1968; Feldman and Newcomb 1973). More recently, theorists developed models which provided structure and direction to subsequent research (Bean 1980; Ethington and Wolfle 1986; Pascarella and Staver 1985; Tinto 1975).

Theorists no longer view achievement and satisfaction as simple phenomena that can be predicted from a few easily gathered variables (Pace 1984). Rather they now view these outcomes as constellations of characteristics, attitudes, experiences, and subsequent changes in attitudes which can be depicted graphically. Studies conducted within the scope of the new theoretical frameworks have been replicated and modified so that we can now speak with greater confidence about a few consistent positive influences on persistence, grades, and satisfaction. Important environmental and experiential influences include the residence of the student, the perceived intellectual atmosphere of the campus, contacts with faculty members, perceived value of their education, and academic satisfaction (Tinto 1987). Student aspirations and attitudes about the importance of the college experience also help shape positive college outcomes (Astin 1985).

Despite the general coalescence of knowledge on the topic, a satisfactory explanation of outcomes eludes researchers. They cannot predict with assurance the success or failure, satisfaction or dissatisfaction, persistence or attrition of a student with certain background characteristics and attitudes, studying in a certain environment, and participating at a particular level of campus experiences. Researchers can advise administrators on strategies to promote positive outcomes, but large segments of the population go unaided by such recommendations. Outcomes phenomena seem to be complex webs of interaction that differ from student to student.

Any practitioner attempting to use these two bodies of research to incorporate theory in practice would find little guidance. Marcia Mentkowski and Arthur Chickering (1988) describe several possibilities for such study, but to date only a few recent researchers have begun to explore such links empirically (Pascarella 1987; Stage in press). In contrast, most of us seem to assume that students at widely differing levels of intellectual development will respond similarly to influences of the campus environment. Or we assume that students of widely differing psychosocial types are influenced positively or negatively by similar experiences. So rather than attempting to use developmental or psychosocial types to categorize students for analysis, we use only easily obtained demographic indicators. This method directly contradicts research based on student development theory, which tells us that students of differing psychological makeup respond in various ways to the same environmental stimulations.

A Monocultural Literature

Typically research conducted on college students focuses on the majority, middle- to upper-middle-class students attending a residential university. However, large segments of the population are not majority, and increasing numbers of students commute to and from home. Some work has been done to let us know who these students are, and strategies have been developed to help them negotiate a college campus that may seem alien to them.

Unfortunately most of the psychologically based student development theory is founded in studies of the mainstream college student. Little research has focused on the development of students outside the mainstream culture, although these are frequently the students who need the most help in negotiating a culturally different environment (Manning and Stage 1988).

Fortunately, the sociologically based outcomes research has begun to focus on some of these special populations (Fox 1986; Healy, Mitchell, and Mourton 1987; Pascarella, Smart, and Nettles 1987; Richardson and Bender 1987; Wolfle 1985). As positive as these nascent efforts are, some populations of students (e.g., the learning disabled, homosexuals, native Americans) are not easily identified nor numerous enough to be included in research currently being conducted. For these particular populations, qualitative approaches are probably needed.

Process Models for Practice

Identifying process models to help apply theory to research can prove frustrating. Only a few good process models link research and practice. Donald Blocher (1987) describes three basic types of conceptual frameworks in the counseling profession. First are the basic philosophical assumptions derived from global and abstract representations of human experience. They are empirically untestable but help professionals clarify their values. Second are the scientific theories focusing on and guiding empirical inquiry. And third are the process models, which serve as a guide for those attempting to implement theory.

Blocher described process models as cognitive maps that provide a direct and immediate guide for implementation and specify appropriate action in a given situation. Such models should be evaluated in terms of outcomes. Also important, they should be constantly polished and modified as experience provides more knowledge about their practical usefulness.

Several multi-dimensional process models are useful to guide the development of the college student. The COSPA II cube focuses on differing clientele, roles, and competencies. Similarly, the Colorado State University cube focuses on target, purpose, and method of intervention (see Rodgers 1980). An administrator attempting to solve a campus problem may refer to the Kuh (1984) cube, which requires the identification of disciplinary perspective, intervention theory, and student affairs function. The behavior engineering model (Gilbert 1978) focuses on the interplay between environmental supports and an individual's behavior in three categories: information, instrumentation, and motivation.

These models have provided rich fodder for those who study student development and student affairs organizations. They have also guided many administrators who are informed and sophisticated enough to choose a theory to fit their particular issue. Unfortunately, many of those who work with college students have just begun to explore student development and outcomes. Models with a wide range of possible options might not provide enough guidance for those with limited experience and insight.

At the other extreme, the literature is replete with idiosyncratic articles that discuss implementation of a particular theory at a particular institution with a particular set of problems. Such articles are too specific and do not help identify and match implementation strategies to wider environmental and institutional conditions.

Less experienced practitioners may need process models as defined by Donald Blocher (1987) that outline in a general way how to implement a specific theory and include guides for appraisal, action, and evaluation. Carole Widick and Deborah Simpson (1978) provide an excellent example of the Perry model applied to the college classroom. Similar models focusing on other aspects of the college experience would be useful.

Recommendations

In the midst of these discoveries and complex conditions, Professor Russell, who had thought she would be spending most of her first semester exploring and developing new research ideas, found herself spending more time than she wanted developing her course. Fortunately her efforts provided several options toward which to direct energy and research.

For each of the three problem areas, Professor Russell identified a solution to the short-term problem (information for the class), as well as the long-term problem (focus of research).

Two Separate Literatures

She drew from both bodies of literature in her course on development of the college student. College students generally do not develop where there are no positive outcomes. Those who work with students need to learn which aspects of the campus environment have positive effects on achievement, persistence, and satisfaction. Russell made sure her class read both bodies of research, drew parallels between them, and identified gaps in information.

As a researcher, Russell began to fill in the gap between the two literatures. For example, using student development theory to inform outcomes research, she studied predictors of changes in majors according to John Holland's (1985) framework. She hypothesized that satisfactory campus experiences might be rooted in different activities for an artistic type than for a social type.

Similarly, outcomes research guided a study of student development; possibly studies of developmental growth of students underestimated the importance of peer influences. Russell designed a study to explore the effects of peer pressure on cognitive development of college students.

The Monocultural Literature

To find readings for the class on students outside the mainstream culture, Russell supplemented higher education readings with those from other disciplines. Since the middle seventies, much counseling literature has focused on the problems counseling professionals have in dealing with those who are culturally different from themselves. Those cross-cultural perspectives provided rich resources to better understand students. Psychology, anthropology, and political science also provided insight into the difficulties

inherent in negotiating a culturally foreign system and the effects those adjustments might have on student satisfaction and motivation.

Another possibility for Russell was research on the development of particular student populations. Because there were too few nonmajority students to conduct the quantitative multivariable research traditionally used to predict outcomes, Russell had to shift her research style and "tool up" for a naturalistic study.

Process Models

Russell required students to read the "how we do it" articles as well as the broader, less directive process models. With a firm knowledge of a specific development theory, the class developed its own process models. Linking "scientific theory" to actual practice provided students with a sense of satisfaction and professionalism as well as a more thorough knowledge of the theory being studied.

This third problem presented Russell with a third possibility for research. She began to develop and polish a process model for her "favorite" student development theory. She designed the model to provide more direction for new professionals as well as for older professionals who had trouble applying theory in their daily practice.

Conclusion

We can learn from Russell's experiences. First, we can pay more attention to one another as researchers. It is tempting to focus our attention on those who are testing similar frameworks, operating within the same paradigm, and speaking our language. Unfortunately, this limited focus stifles creativity and reinforces narrow notions of research rather than encouraging us to explore new directions.

Second, research and researchers must be flexible. It is easier to use the same populations, types of variables, and modes of analysis than it is to expand our repertoires. Unfortunately, these self-limiting practices do little to enlarge our knowledge of the development and outcomes we study. To accommodate the nonmainstream students' experiences, which presumably differ from the majority students', we must use more open-ended ways of collecting information. Researchers may need to adopt more of a cultural perspective and focus at first on small numbers of students. Considering a broader range of situations and experiences may lead to new models of development and satisfaction.

Finally, we must work to develop process models with tangible links to practice. These models will enable professionals to use the knowledge that researchers are generating.

References

Astin, Alexander. *Achieving Educational Excellence*. San Francisco: Jossey-Bass, 1985.

———. *The College Environment*. Washington, D.C.: American Council on Education, 1968.

Bean, John. "Dropouts and Turnover: The Synthesis and Test of a Causal Model of Student Attrition." *Research in Higher Education* 12, no. 2 (1980): 155–87.

Blocher, Donald. "On the Uses and Misuses of the Term 'Theory.' " *Journal of Counseling and Development* 66 (October 1987): 67–68.

Ethington, Corinna, and Lee Wolfle. "A Structural Model of Mathematics Achievement for Men and Women." *American Educational Research Journal* 23 (Spring 1986): 65–75.

Ewell, Peter, ed. *Assessing Educational Outcomes*. New Directions for Institutional Research, No. 47. San Francisco: Jossey-Bass, 1985.

Feldman, Kenneth, and Theodore Newcomb. *The Impact of College on Students*. San Francisco: Jossey-Bass, 1973.

Fox, Richard. "Application of a Conceptual Model of College Withdrawal to Disadvantaged Students." *American Educational Research Journal* 23 (Fall 1986): 415–24.

Gilbert, Thomas. *Human Competence: Engineering Worthy Performance*. New York: McGraw-Hill, 1978.

Healy, Charles, Judith Mitchell, and Don Mourton. "Age and Grade Differences in Career Development among Community College Students." *Review of Higher Education* 10 (Spring 1987): 247–58.

Holland, John. *Making Vocational Choices: A Theory of Vocational Personalities and Work Environments*. Englewood Cliffs, N.J.: Prentice-Hall, 1986.

Kuh, George. "A Framework for Understanding Student Affairs Work." *Journal of College Student Personnel* 25 (January 1984): 25–38.

Manning, Kathleen, and Frances K. Stage. "Personalizing the College Context from a Cultural Perspective." Paper presented at the Annual Meeting of the National Association of Student Personnel Administrators, St. Louis, Missouri, March 1988. Copy in my possession.

Mentkowski, Marcia, and Arthur Chickering. "Linking Educators and Researchers in Setting a Research Agenda for Undergraduate Education." *Review of Higher Education* 11 (Winter 1987): 137–60.

Pace, Robert. "Historical Perspectives on Student Outcomes: Assessment with Implications for the Future." *NASPA Journal* 22 (Fall 1984): 10–18.

Pascarella, Ernest. "The Development of Critical Thinking: Does College Make a Difference?" *Journal of College Student Development* 30, no. 1 (January 1989): 19–26.

Pascarella, Ernest, John Smart, and Michael Nettles. "The Influence of College on Self-concept: A Consideration of Race and Gender Differences." *American Educational Research Journal* 24 (Spring 1987): 49–77.

Pascarella, Ernest, and J. R. Staver. "The Influence of On-campus Work in Science on Science Career Choice in College: A Causal Modeling Approach." *Review of Higher Education* 8 (Spring 1985): 229–45.

Richardson, Richard, and Louis Bender. *Fostering Minority Access and Achievement in Higher Education*. San Francisco: Jossey-Bass, 1987.

Rodgers, Robert. "Theories Underlying Student Development. In *Student Development in Higher Education*, edited by Don Creamer. Cincinnati: ACPA Media, 1980.

Stage, Frances K. "Motivation, Academic and Social Integration, and the Early Dropout." *American Educational Research Journal*, in press.

———. "Student Typologies and the Study of College Outcomes." *Review of Higher Education* 11 (Spring 1988): 247–57.

Tinto, Vincent. "Dropout from Higher Education: A Theoretical Synthesis of Recent Research." *Review of Educational Research* 45 (Winter 1975): 89–125.

———. *Leaving College: Rethinking the Causes and Cures of Student Attrition*. Chicago: University of Chicago Press, 1987.

Widick, Carole and Deborah Simpson. "Developmental Concepts in College Instruction." In *Encouraging Development in College Students*, edited by Clyde Parker. Minneapolis: University of Minnesota Press, 1978.

Wolfle, Lee. "Postsecondary Educational Attainment among Whites and Blacks." *American Educational Research Journal* 22 (Winter 1985): 501–25.

CHAPTER 31

THEORETICAL CONSIDERATIONS IN THE STUDY OF MINORITY STUDENT RETENTION IN HIGHER EDUCATION

LAURA I. RENDÓN, ROMERO E. JALOMO, AND AMAURY NORA

Research on college student persistence is by now voluminous. Much of this research is based on testing and validating Vincent Tinto's (1975, 1987, 1993) highly acclaimed model of student departure. The basic premise of Tinto's model is that social and academic integration are essential to student retention. Tinto's model (especially the 1975 and 1987 versions) has certainly provided a workable and testable foundation for analyzing the multiple factors involved with student departure, particularly employing quantitative methods. Quantitative researchers such as Nora and Cabrera (1996) note that there is sufficient empirical evidence establishing the validity of Tinto's (1975, 1987) model of student persistence. Others have modified and improved the model utilizing diverse study populations at different higher education institutions (Nora 1987; Nora, Attinasi, and Matonak 1990; Rendón 1982; Nora and Rendón 1990; Cabrera, Nora, and Castañeda, 1992; Nora and Cabrera 1993, 1996; Cabrera et al. 1992; Pavel 1992; Cabrera and Nora 1994; Pascarella and Terenzini 1991; Pascarella 1980; Terenzini, Lorang, and Pascarella 1981). Yet, more remains to be done.

Braxton, Sullivan, and Johnson's (1997) assessment of Tinto's theory (based on the 1975 version) found that, in the aggregate, assessment of empirical evidence regarding thirteen of Tinto's primary propositions indicated only partial support for the theory. The researchers cited problems with empirical internal consistency in multi-institutional or single-institutional assessments, in both residential and commuter universities, and across female and male college students. Further, Tierney (1992), Attinasi (1989, 1994), and Kraemer (1997) have questioned the validity of the model to fully and appropriately capture the experiences of nonwhite students, given that the model is based on an assimilation/acculturation framework.

It is worthy at this point to note the linkage between Tinto's interactionist theory and the assimilation/acculturation perspective. Interactionist theory is concerned with the impact of person- and institution-related characteristics on a particular phenomenon (Caplan and Nelson 1973; Braxton, Sullivan, and Johnson 1997). Tinto (1993) notes that his persistence model is an "interactional system" (p. 136) in which both students and institutions (through social and educational communities) are, over time, continually interacting with one another in a variety of formal and informal situations. Key to the interactionist view is that persistence is contingent on the extent to which students have become incorporated (integrated) into the social and academic communities of the college.

"Theoretical Considerations in the Study of Minority Student Retention in Higher Education." Reprinted from *Rethinking the Departure Puzzle: New Theory and Research on College Student Retention*, edited by John M. Braxton, (2000), by permission of Vanderbilt University Press.

Interactionalist theory may be linked to the acculturation/assimilation perspective that was prevalent during the 1960s when social scientists from various fields studied how members of minority groups became integrated into the dominant white society. It was believed that minority individuals were engaged in a self-perpetuating cycle of poverty and deprivation and that they could avoid societal alienation by becoming fully absorbed (assimilated) or adapted (acculturated) into the dominant culture (Hurtado 1997). Assimilation required a process of separation, a cultural adaptation that required minority individuals to break away from their traditions, customs, values, language, etc., in order to find full membership in the predominantly white American society. However, during the 1970s and 1980s critics contested this perspective, citing problems such as the use of mainstream cultural norms as evaluative criteria, as well as the problematic assumption that minority group norms and cultural patterns were inferior, deviant, and self-destructive when compared to those of the majority culture (de Anda 1984).

Along these lines, Caplan and Nelson (1973) provided important distinctions between person-centered and situation-centered problems, noting that the way a problem was identified gave way to specific solutions. For example, researchers focusing on person-centered problems would focus on individual characteristics as the root of the issue and the target of the solution, while ignoring situationally relevant factors. In the case of studying why minority cultures experience alienation, a person-centered definition would identify the pathology as residing with minority group characteristics. Conversely, Caplan and Nelson noted that situation-centered problems have a system change orientation. Here, the context in which individuals operate is examined and remedies are proposed to change the system.

Once in effect and legitimated, irrespective of their validity, these definitions resist replacement by other definitions or perspectives. For example, the idea that minority students are not motivated to learn or have low expectations has been around for decades and ignores how systemic inequities, racism, and discrimination have worked against minority populations. Within the past twenty years there has been greater emphasis on examining the interactions among individuals and systems. Yet Caplan and Nelson's

(1973) view that to the extent that problem definitions conform to and reinforce dominant cultural myths and clichés, as indeed most definitions must in order to become widely accepted, their change or replacement will be stubbornly resisted. People tend to conform to public definitions and expectations, even when there are doubts regarding their accuracy.

Because interactionalist retention theory adheres to some of the basic premises of the acculturation/assimilation framework, such as separation and incorporation, several researchers have challenged the way these processes have been conceptualized in relation to explaining minority student retention in college. In particular, the assumption that minority students must separate from their cultural realities and take the responsibility to become incorporated into colleges' academic and social fabric in order to succeed (with little or no concern to address systemic problems within institutions or to the notion that minority students are often able to operate in multiple contexts) becomes central to the critique of Tinto's student departure model.

At the same time, emerging scholarship that is beginning to take root not only in education but in fields such as psychology, anthropology, and sociology is revolutionizing the way we conceptualize different phenomena and the selection of empirical tools to guide this understanding (Hurtado 1997; Rosaldo 1989). For example, Hurtado (1997) explains that much feminist research advocates a multidisciplinary and multimethod approach that is nonhierarchical (i.e., one dominant group is not favored over another) and reflexive (i.e., invites critique and further analysis). Given these developments, we believe that revisionist models and theory refinements are needed. Also needed are new models that consider the key theoretical issues associated with the experiences of minority students in higher education.

It is important to note that researchers (primarily white) began studying student retention prior to the time that minorities had become a critical mass on college campuses. Few minority students resulted in small sample sizes or total exclusion from the samples. Consequently, much of the most widely acclaimed research guiding theories of students' transitions to college, departure, involvement, and learning was often based on white male students (Tierney 1992; Belenky et al. 1986). This research produced a monolithic view of students devoid of issues of race/ethnicity, culture, gender, politics, and identity (Hurtado 1997).

The research on minority college students is relatively young, and the majority focuses on African American and Hispanic (primarily Mexican American) students. Especially fertile territory is research on American Indians, Asians, Pacific Islanders, Filipinos, Puerto Ricans, Cubans, and immigrant students from Asia and Central and South America. As our society becomes more multicultural and complex, the experiences of multiracial students will merit careful investigation. In the 1970s only a few studies, such as Gurin and Epps (1975) and Olivas (1979), focused on minority students. Only within the past fifteen years have researchers, many of them nonwhite, begun to study minority students (Nora and Cabrera 1994; Nora and Rendón 1988, 1990; Rendón 1982, 1994; Jalomo 1995; Tierney 1992, 1993; Wright 1988; Allen 1984; Ogbu 1978, 1987; Thomas 1984; Harvey and Williams 1989; Attinasi 1989; Fleming 1984; Nettles et al. 1985; London 1978, 1989; Weis 1985; Hurtado and Garcia 1994; Kraemer 1997; Nora, Attinasi, and Matonak 1990; Cabrera, Nora, and Castañeda 1993; Lowe 1989; Melchior-Walsh 1994; Galindo and Escamilla 1995; Gandara 1993; Wycoff 1996; Valadez 1996; Mow and Nettles 1990). This relatively new research not only lifts the knowledge base of student retention and development theories, it advances policy and practice and calls to question the predominant ways of structuring student development services employing research that included few, if any, minority students.

Much of the research that provides important modifications to the problem definition, introduces new variables to the retention equation, and attempts to refine traditional paradigms of student retention is scattered and unconnected. Consequently, a new, coherent vision of minority student persistence has failed to evolve. Researchers and practitioners alike tend to view issues related to the retention of minority students as similar, if not identical, to those of majority students. What transpires is an almost universally entrenched view that Tinto's (1975, 1987) departure model, with all of its assumptions, is complete, appropriate, and valid for all students regardless of their varied ethnic, racial, economic, and social backgrounds. To his credit, Tinto (1993) elaborates on the importance of sup-portive student communities for students of color and adult students who may experience difficulties making the transition to college and becoming incorporated. Tinto (1993) also notes the need to build inclusive campuses, explaining that "to be fully effective, college communities, academic and social, must be inclusive of all students who enter" (p. 187). Yet researchers such as Hurtado (1997) would argue that linear models based on an assimilation/acculturation framework leave many questions unanswered, especially with regard to multiple group identifications and how both minority and majority groups change when they come into contact with each other.

Purpose

The purpose of this *chapter* is to (1) provide a critical analysis of Tinto's student departure theory (1975, 1987, 1993) with a specific focus on the separation and transition stage, (2) critique Tinto's concepts of academic and social integration, and (3) present future directions designed to take retention theory to a higher level. The main concern is not whether the Tinto theory works for minority students. Rather, the emphasis is on the kind of theoretical foundation and methodological approaches that are needed to more fully understand and facilitate the retention process for minority students in an increasingly complex and multiracial institutional environment. Our critique is not meant to assault or discredit the work of researchers who have devoted their careers to studying how students become engaged in college. Rather, we offer alternative perspectives that seek a similar aim: to more fully understand student retention in college. We believe scholars ought to periodically reassess their work and how they apply their empirically based perspectives to new contexts in order to advance knowledge. Indeed, even the ideas advanced here should be taken further, and we encourage researchers to do so.

Theoretical Considerations in Tinto's Student Departure Model

Tinto's (1975, 1987, 1993) model of student departure has been extensively employed to study how majority and minority students become academically and socially integrated into institutional life. To help develop his theory on student departure, Tinto employed the rites-of-passage framework of Dutch anthropologist Arnold Van Gennep (1960). Van Gennep was concerned with the movement of individuals and societies over time and the rituals designed to move individuals from youth to adulthood in order to ensure social stability. To facilitate a discussion of theoretical issues on the concepts of separation, as well as academic and social integration, a brief summary of Van Gennep's theory is presented.

Conceptual Issues in Van Gennep's Rites of Passage

The rites of passage as described by Van Gennep (1960) included a three-phase process of separation, transition, and incorporation. In stage one, separation, the individual became separated from past associations and a decline occurred in interactions with members of the group from which the individual originated. Specific ceremonies marked outmoded views and norms of the old group. In stage two, transition, the individual began to interact in new ways with members of the new group in which membership was being sought. Rituals such as isolation, training, and ordeals were used to facilitate separation, which ensured that the individual acquired the knowledge and skills of the new group. In the third stage, incorporation, the individual took on new patterns of interaction with members of the new group and established competent membership. Though able to interact with members of the old group, individuals now did so only as members of the new group. In this stage individuals became fully integrated into the culture of the new group (Tinto 1987). Tinto stressed that it was "possible to envision the process of student persistence as functionally similar to that of becoming incorporated in the life of human communities" (p. 94).

How generalizable are Van Gennep's perspectives and assumptions when studying minority college students? First, let us consider the concept of separation and the ways some scholars have interpreted the theory. One of the assumptions scholars have made is that individuals should disassociate themselves from their native cultural realities in order to assimilate into college life. The assumption made is that an individual's values and beliefs rooted in his or her cultural background must be abandoned to successfully incorporate the values and beliefs

not only of the institution but of the majority population upon which they are based. Only in this way can an individual student become integrated into the new environment. According to this assumption, minority students must reconcile the fact that they must leave the old world behind in order to find full membership in the new college world, since the two are distinctly different. A second assumption is that there is one "dominant" culture and that in order to succeed, members of minority cultures should become more similar to this dominant culture. A third assumption is that it will be relatively easy to find membership and acceptance in the new college world and that individuals who become integrated will have little or no contact with members of their old groups. Indeed, the hallmark of Tinto's (1993) revised model is that students should find social and intellectual communities to attain membership and receive support. Even students who initially resist separation will later determine that leaving their groups to succeed in college is appropriate and necessary. These assumptions are not entirely correct. Alternative views that challenge the three aforementioned assumptions are presented next.

A Critical Analysis of the Assumption of Separation

Scholars investigating how minority students make the transition to college should be familiar with the concepts of biculturalism and dual socialization, which challenge the assumption of separation. In addition, scholars should note the problematic issues in relation to the assumption of a dominant culture and the membership assumption.

The Concept of Biculturalism

While conducting an ethnographic study of poverty and Afro-Americans in a large northern city, Charles A. Valentine (1971) found that accepted cultural deficit and difference models of the time neglected and obscured important elements of the Afro-American culture. Referring to cultural deficit models as an alternative to analyze nonmainstream cultures, the researcher argued that "any theory of class or racial deficits of biological origin is quite undemonstrable, indeed scientifically untestable, in an ethically plural and structurally discriminatory society"

(p. 138). While not negating cultural distinctions between black and mainstream cultures, Valentine (1971) observed: "The central theoretical weakness of the 'difference model' is an implicit assumption that different cultures are necessarily competitive alternatives, that distinct cultural systems can enter human experience only as mutually exclusive alternatives, never as intertwined or simultaneously available repertoires" (p. 141). Valentine cited cultural difference models as incorrect and harmful when employed for establishing new educational policies and programs.

As an alternative to predominant cultural difference models, Valentine (1971) proposed the employment of a bicultural educational model. The researcher argued that since many blacks were simultaneously committed to both black and mainstream cultures, the two were not mutually exclusive of each other. Rather, blacks could be simultaneously socialized in two different cultures. He relied on the findings of Steven Polgar (1960), who had earlier found that individuals living on an Indian reservation regularly went through a process he termed "biculturation." Biculturation occurred when individuals were simultaneously enculturated and socialized in two different ways of life. In Polgar's example teenage Mesquakie boys experienced a contemporary form of their traditional Amerindian lifeways and mainstream Euro-American culture.

Valentine (1971) used Polgar's (1960) research to expand the concept of biculturation, the ability of a minority individual to step in and out of the repertoires of two cultures that were seen as distinct and separate (de Anda 1984; see figure 31-1). For Valentine, biculturation helps explain how people learn and practice both the mainstream culture and ethnic cultures at the same time. He indicates: "the Black community is bicultural in the sense that each Afro-American ethnic segment draws upon a distinctive repertoire of standardized Afro-American group behavior and, simultaneously, patterns derived from the mainstream cultural system of Euro-American deviation. Socialization into both systems begins at an early age, continues throughout life, and is generally of equal importance in most individual lives" (Valentine 1971, p. 143). The concept of bilculturalism seriously challenges the first two assumptions (noted earlier) of the separation stage.

The Concept of Dual Socialization

Diane de Anda (1984) elaborates on Valentine's (1971) concept of biculturation, citing six factors that affect biculturalism: (1) the degree of overlap of commonalty between the two cultures with regard to norms, values, beliefs, perceptions, and the like; (2) the availability of cultural translators, mediators, and models; (3) the amount and type (positive or negative) of corrective feedback provided by each culture regarding attempts to produce normative behavior; (4) the conceptual style and problem-solving approach of the minority

Two Separate Cultures

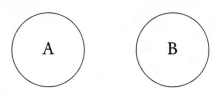

A = Majority Culture

B = Minority Culture

Source: de Anda, 1984

Figure 31-1 Two Separate Cultures

individual and their mesh with the prevalent or valued styles of the majority culture; (5) the individual's degree of bilingualism; and (6) the degree of dissimilarity in physical appearance from the majority culture, such as skin color and facial features (p. 102). Unlike Valentine, she indicates that the bicultural experience was possible not because the two cultures were totally disparate, but because there was some overlap between the two cultures (see figure 31-2). For de Anda, "dual socialization is made possible and facilitated by the amount of overlap between two cultures. That is, the extent to which an individual finds it possible to understand and predict successfully two cultural environments and adjust his or her behavior according to the norms of each culture depends on the extent to which these two cultures share common values, beliefs, perceptions, and norms for prescribed behaviors" (p. 102). In short, de Anda's model is not about individual separation from an old world in search of membership in a new one. Instead, de Anda argues that converging the two worlds could allow individuals to function more effectively and less stressfully in both worlds. This requires changing, indeed transforming, the academic and social culture of institutions of higher education to accommodate culturally diverse students.

Kuh and Whitt (1988) suggest that culture, in the context of higher education, could be described as a "social or normative glue" that is defined by the shared values and beliefs that exist within a college or university while serving four general purposes: (1) conveying a sense of identity; (2) facilitating commitment to an entity, such as the college or peer group, other than self; (3) enhancing the stability of a group's social system; and (4) providing a sense-making device that guides and shapes behavior (p. 10). In addition, the researchers propose that the culture of a college or university defines, identifies, and legitimates authority in educational settings. However, they caution that institutions may, perhaps even unwittingly, have "properties deeply embedded in their cultures that make it difficult for members of historically underrepresented groups to prosper socially and environmentally" (p. 15). In cases such as this, students already potentially at risk often find themselves decidedly at odds with prevailing social and cultural norms on campus.

Dual socialization does not occur naturally in a college environment that contains values, conventions, and traditions that are alien to first-generation students, many of whom are minority. Jalomo (1995) substantiates de Anda's dual socialization model in a study of Latino community college students who had completed their first semester. For these students the transition was not linear. Rather, Latino students were

Biculturation

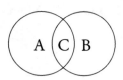

A = Majority Culture

B = Minority Culture

C = Shared Values and Norms

Source: de Anda, 1984

Figure 31-2 Biculturation

found to operate in multiple contexts: the Latino culture, comprised of four subcultures (family, work, barrio, and gang); and the prevailing culture of the community colleges they attended. In the study, students who conveyed difficulty in their transition to college spoke of the growing incongruence between their native environment and the newly encountered college arena. These students indicated that they had maneuvered a number of social domains in their native environment while attempting to meet the growing demands associated with college life. Upon transiting to college, Latinos experienced the downside and upside of college attendance. They expressed some tension and loss associated with separation, although at the same time they experienced excitement at learning new things and making new college friends. They also experienced culture clash as a result of the differences between their home lives and the world of college. To diminish this disjuncture, Jalomo proposes that individuals not totally separate but instead be supported to transit between two cultures.

Levy-Warren (1988) provides additional perspectives to the concept of separation. In analyzing disruptions that people experience in separating from their cultures of origin (culture loss, culture shock), Levy-Warren indicates that the passage involves cultural dislocation and relocation, a disjunctive process that is both internal and external. The internal level involves identity formation—an individual is shedding a part of the self and assuming a new, redefined identity. The external level is the actual move from one geographical location to another and involves the loss of familiar objects and people. Cultural relocation may be highly traumatic if the move is made before the individual has established mental representations of culture. That is, individuals must be able to distinguish differences between their own world and the new world. Consequently, Rendón (1996) argues that rather than asking students to disassociate themselves from their culture, they should be assisted to make modifications in their relationships. The passage to college needs to be gradual, giving students time to slowly break away and move toward healthy individualization.

Theoretically, the concept of dual socialization seriously challenges the assumptions of separation. In addition, there are retention policy considerations. Navigating two landscapes, one of which is almost entirely different from home

realities, requires both individual and institutional responsibility. To this end, the critical role of the institution cannot be overstated, yet is often diminished in retention and involvement studies. Tinto highlights the importance of the classroom as a learning community in his 1993 model. However, as noted earlier, Tinto's revised model has yet to gain widespread attention of the higher education research community. Connecting the world of the student to the world of college means that students must be able to find animate and inanimate objects in the new college culture that might evoke a sense of comfort that originates in their early cultural upbringing. That is why events and programs such as Black History Month, Women's Studies, and Cinco de Mayo celebrations are so important. Converging two worlds requires the use of cultural translators, mediators, and role models to (1) provide information and guidance that can help students decipher unfamiliar college customs and rituals, (2) mediate problems that arise from disjunctions between students' cultural traits and the prevailing campus culture, and (3) model behaviors that are amenable with the norms, values, and beliefs of the majority and minority cultures (Jalomo 1995; Rendón 1996; de Anda 1984).

The Assumption of a Dominant Culture

Tierney's (1992) critique of the Tinto model substantiates de Anda's convergence perspective. Tierney argues that Tinto did not consider an important point in Van Gennep's theory. The point was that Van Gennep uses the term *ritual* to speak of rites of passage within the same specific culture, i.e., some Indian cultures have puberty rituals designed specifically for girls and others specifically for boys. Here, the ritual is nondisruptive. However, Tinto employs the use of *ritual* in a way that "individuals from one culture, such as Apache, are to undergo a ritual in another culture, such as Anglo" (p. 609). In this case the transition constitutes a disjuncture—in effect, students from a minority culture enter a majority world that is vastly different from their sociocultural realities.

However, in his 1993 revised model Tinto argues that the majority of colleges are made up of several, if not many, communities or "subcultures." Rather than conforming to one dominant culture in order to persist, students would have to locate at least one community in which to find membership and support. Further, Tinto notes that membership does not require a full sharing of values. Instead, only some degree of consensus is necessary. Consequently, Tinto explains that the use of the term *membership* is more applicable than *integration*. Of course, safe havens and enclaves have their benefits and drawbacks. One of their key benefits is that they help students break down the institution into manageable parts. However, special communities and programs do not address the real challenge of today's institutions: the total transformation of colleges and universities from monocultural to multicultural institutions. This requires more convergence between the minority student's world and the college world. Further, Hurtado (1997) notes that research based on assimilation/acculturation views group contact as unidirectional in nature (i.e., the ethnic group changes to reflect the mainstream/dominant/ white group). Hurtado argues that "this type of approach effectively blocks the possibility that cultural contact can indeed bring change in both the minority and majority groups" (p. 305). In some areas of the nation and in some colleges and universities, minorities are the majority or are rapidly on their way to acquiring majority status. While white students have normally been viewed as the dominant or majority group, future research will have to take into account how group identities and power relationships are changing and the overall impact on student persistence.

The Membership Assumption

It is also important for scholars to consider that de Anda's concept of "dual socialization"— where individuals both develop and sustain membership in new and old cultures—has been the reality of behavior for most Americans who maintain an ethnic identity while coexisting within the dominant culture. In short, many minority students are not likely to give up their affiliations and lose contact with their cultural groups in order to find membership in a new college world. Just as many Latino immigrants maintain extensive and frequent contact with Mexico (Hurtado 1997), many minority students experience multiple associations with their own cultures and their new college realities. Tierney (1992) indicates that American Indian students value group membership over the individualized process of separation. In many Latino cultures separation is often not a viable option, as family is a source of rootedness and strength. This view that both minority and majority groups coexist and actually hold similar attitudes, values, and perceptions has been obliquely (indirectly) established by Nora and Cabrera (1996). Within this context, similarities between white and nonwhite students were noted in attitudes regarding the influence of family, perceptions of discrimination on campus, and educational goals and commitments. Nora and Cabrera's (1996) research validates de Anda's (1984) notion that groups (or minorities) do not need to break all ties with past communities in order to attain membership status in a new or an alien culture, as in the case of minority students who retain their sense of identity and cultural values while integrating in a predominately majority educational environment.

Moreover, the membership option often represents a false choice given the lack of acceptance of racial/ethnic minorities in many dimensions of college life. In fact, many minorities leave college due to "cultural assaults" (Zambrana 1988) to their sense of identity and self-esteem that lead to stress and tension. Though some students may leave, others may exhibit differential patterns of behavior. Some will become subservient to the codes of others, and others may deny their cultural heritage. Still others will manage to turn a negative into a positive—developing a strong sense of ethnic consciousness, i.e., pride in their cultural heritage and awareness of racism, discrimination, sexism, and elitism prevalent in higher education systems (Zambrana 1988).

While more research is needed to substantiate the multiple varieties of external and internal group memberships and their impact on retention, research has substantiated the view that different forms of encouragement and support from family and friends from the students' past communities not only continue to influence students during college enrollment but are instrumental in affecting persistence. These associations negate discriminatory experiences, enhance the social and academic integration of students, and positively affect students' commitments to earning a college degree (Nora and Cabrera 1993, 1996; Nora et al. 1996; Nora, Kraemer, and Itzen 1997; Cabrera, Nora, and Castañeda 1993; Cabrera et al. 1992).

Theoretical Considerations Regarding Academic/Social Integration

Separation and transition are the initial processes associated with Tinto's student retention model. The next stage involves incorporation in institutional life. Tinto (1987) notes that "eventual persistence requires that individuals make the transition to college and become incorporated into the ongoing social and intellectual life of the college" (p. 126). Incorporation is analogous to integration. The term "integration can be understood to refer to the extent which the individual shares the normative attitudes and values of peers and faculty in the institution and abides by the formal and informal structural requirements for membership in that community or in the sub-groups of which the individual is a part" (Pascarella and Terenzini 1991, p. 51). To learn more about how incorporation came about, Tinto turned to French sociologist Emile Durkheim (1951) and the study of suicide. Durkheim was interested in the character of the social environment, including social and intellectual characteristics, and its relationship to individual behavior, such as suicide. To draw an analogy between suicidal and dropout behavior, Tinto employed Durkheim's view of "egotistical suicide." Individuals who committed egotistical suicide were unable to become socially or intellectually integrated within communities of society. As noted earlier, interactionalist theory, when used to study minority student retention, has been called into question given that some of the theory's premises are based on an assimilation/acculturation framework.

Problems with the Use of an Acculturation/Assimilation Framework

Hurtado (1997) notes that during the 1960s an assimilation framework was the impetus of research on ethnicity, especially for Mexican Americans. Since assimilation was contingent on the minority group becoming incorporated into the life of the majority group, assimilation scales were developed to measure the quickest and most efficient ways to assimilate immigrants. In 1964 Gordon advanced the notion that individuals could be highly acculturated in one group but remain unassimilated in other dimensions of society. In short, biculturality became a viable option. But the assimilation/acculturation framework had multiple problems, which are listed below.

Focus on Academic Failure as Opposed to Success

Hurtado (1997) indicates that assimilation/acculturation research has focused on the left tail of the normal distribution curve, "that is, it has focused on cultural adaptations that are not particularly healthy, ones for which the only solutions are to assimilate to the dominant mainstream or spend a lifetime of psychological and social alienation" (p. 312). Some of the recent research (primarily within the past five to ten years) has called for a focus and examination of a variety of adaptations leading to academic success in addition to the repository of traditional research approaches examining academic failure (Hurtado and Garcia 1994).

Exclusion of Contextual and Historical Forces

Zambrana (1988) notes that during the 1960s and 1970s studies on racial/ethnic communities were in large part descriptive and ahistorical. These descriptions were in line with the cultural deficit model that emphasized the problems or "deficiencies" within these communities, for the most part pathological and disruptive. It was believed that these deficits led to a self-perpetuating cycle of poverty and deprivation. When applied to education, the cultural deficit model suggests that cultural patterns of marginalized groups are essentially inferior and predispose students within those groups to poor academic performance; de Anda (1984) notes that the discrediting of the cultural deficit model led to the ascendance of the cultural difference model that emphasized the uniqueness of each minority culture. An inherent assumption with both of these models was that upward mobility and acculturation were possible to the extent that minority groups approximated the values and norms of the dominant society. However, a model known as "internal colonialism" (Almaguer 1974; Blauner 1972) argued that cultural adaptations of ethnic/racial groups were due more to the organization of economics, labor, and power in the capitalist way the nation was structured than to differences in traits between minority and majority groups. As such, groups that had the experience of conquest were subject to race discrimination in every dimension of organized society, including education (Hurtado 1997).

In her review of cultural studies, Zambrana (1988) notes that "the most limiting aspect of the majority of studies has been their neglect of the relationship of racial/ethnic groups to the social structure" (p. 63). The lives of racial/ethnic minorities are shaped by social forces such as racism, sexism, and discrimination. Yet many researchers tend to view people of color as if they have all the options and privileges of white, middle-class Americans, when this is not often the case.

Lack of Focus on Systemic Barriers

Rather than focusing on systemic issues in the lives of oppressed people, most past researchers employing an assimilation/acculturation framework have tended to focus on perceived cultural traits or differences (i.e., poor motivation, academic deficiencies) as the source of a group's ability or inability to succeed and be upwardly mobile. This view suggests that students who possess or adopt mainstream cultural norms are capable of moving farther along the educational pipeline than those who lack these cultural traits (Nieto 1996). In opposition to this view, more recent educational research has documented that systemic barriers such as tracking, low expectations, and funding inequities, among others, play a critical role in hindering the educational achievements of ethnic/racial minorities (Oakes 1985; Brint and Karabel 1989; Nieto 1996). Nonetheless, perceptions of minority student inferiority persist to this day and have even been used as a rationale to place restrictions on college access for minorities.

Failure to Challenge Theoretical Assumptions and Paradigms

Even when minorities are studied, researchers often fail to challenge the philosophical assumptions made in traditional paradigms that are often grounded or developed from studies based on full-time, traditional-age, residential, middle-class, white, male students and/or fail to consider current research that presents a more comprehensive and contextual view of minority

student lives and educational experiences. The lack of a grounded historical perspective has led to the frequent omission of minority groups, or else they are identified as a source of their group's problems (a deficit perspective). Myths and stereotypes continue to prevail for racial and ethnic groups simply because there is a void in the incorporation of roles, characteristics, and perceptions of these subgroups. Many times variables are operationally defined in the same manner for all groups involved, thus excluding any cultural or racial differences in perceptions and attitudes. Rather than conducting culturally and racially based studies that can uncover new variables and that can offer insightful and meaningful findings to transform institutional structures that preclude academic success for minority students, invisible hierarchies are left intact. In these cases, minority students are measured simply by scales that reveal their level of acculturation and integration, or lack thereof (Zambrana 1988; Hurtado 1997).

Failure to Connect Theory to Practice

In his 1993 theory review Tinto acknowledges the importance of policy-relevant research and the importance of the institution in enhancing retention. When theoretical propositions are not compared across different subgroups or when diverse and culturally driven theoretical views are not incorporated in retention studies, institutional policies and practices cannot truly detect or address differences among student groups. Theories developed without using minority student perspectives and/or without "member checks" from the field may miss important details and nuances about the connection between student cultural realities and collegiate experiences. Tierney (1992) elaborates: "The search for an understanding about why students leave college is not merely of theoretical interest; if a model may be built that explains student departure then it may be possible for colleges to retain students" (p. 604).

Conceptual Issues in Interactionalist Theory

There are at least three conceptual problems with social/academic interactionalist theory as used in Tinto's (1975, 1987, 1993) student departure model.

Individual Responsibility as Opposed to Institutional Responsibility

The first conceptual problem is overemphasis on individual responsibility for change and adaptation. In 1987 Tinto emphasized the following points:

> The problems associated with separation and transition to college are conditions that, though stressful, need not in themselves lead to departure. It is the individual's response to those conditions that finally determines staying or leaving. Though external assistance may make a difference, it cannot do so without the individual's willingness to see the adjustments through. (p. 98)

> To adapt Durkheim's work to the question of individual departure from institutions of higher education we must move to a theory of individual behavior. (p. 105)

> To move to a theory of individual suicide, and therefore to a theory of individual departure, one has to take account of the personal attributes of individuals which predispose them to respond to given situations or conditions with particular forms of behavior. (p. 109)

While Tinto (1987) does indicate that "differences in institutional rates of departure may arise out of discernible differences in the structure of institutional academic and social systems" (p. 107), the overall tone of social/academic integration theory is that individuals, not the system, are responsible for departure. Elaborating on this point, Tierney (1992) argues that social integrationists tend to use anthropological terms in an individualist, rather than a collective, manner. Individuals attend college, become integrated or not, leave or stay, fail or succeed. Absent from the traditional social integrationist view are the distinctions among cultures; differences among students with regard to class, race, gender, and sexual orientation; and the role of group members and the institution in assisting students to succeed.

Nora, Kraemer, and Itzen (1997) and Nora and Cabrera (1993) argue that current quantitative models must include factors that are able to differentiate among racial and ethnic groups or must include measurement approaches (and techniques) that provide indicators of constructs that reflect racial, ethnic, and cultural differences. In a study of student persistence at an exclusively Hispanic two-year institution Nora,

Kraemer, and Itzen (1997) employed a different and more culturally sensitive set of items that more closely reflected the manner in which the study's Hispanic students became integrated on their campus. In doing so, the researchers reduced misspecification in the model. The researchers elaborate: "The measures of academic integration used to form the scale not only [represented] possible academic interest and involvement with faculty and staff, but . . . also [reflected] those circumstances (both financial and academic) that [were] prevalent among [the] Hispanic group" (p. 15).

Problems Associated with the Concept of Student Involvement

While interactionalist theory is concerned with the interaction among individuals and institutions, involvement is the mechanism through which student effort is engaged in the academic and social lives of the college. Tinto explains that the 1993 model is "at its core, a model of educational communities that highlights the critical importance of student engagement or involvement in the learning communities of the college" (1993, p. 132). Consequently, it becomes important to address problematic issues related to the involvement dimension implicit in the Tinto model.

Alexander Astin's (1985) theory of student involvement is perhaps the most widely adopted college impact model of student development. According to involvement theory, "the individual plays a central role in determining the extent and nature of growth according to the quality of effort or involvement with the resources provided by the institution" (Pascarella and Terenzini 1991, p. 51). Astin's involvement theory is based on the Freudian notion of cathexis, in which individuals invest psychological energy in objects outside themselves such as friends, families, schooling, jobs, and the like. Astin (1984) defines involvement as "the amount of energy that the student devotes to the academic experience" (p. 27). Indeed, research indicates that the more time and energy students devote to learning and the more intensely they engage in their own education, the greater the achievement, satisfaction with educational experiences, and persistence in college (Pascarella and Terenzini 1991; Tinto 1987).

While both Tinto and Astin would agree that the institution plays an important role in facilitating involvement, and in fact Tinto's 1993 revised model emphasizes this point, practitioners have concentrated on the aspect of individual responsibility. The result is that practitioners have resorted to offering programs to help students get involved but have not focused on active outreach to students. Consequently, few dropout-prone students actually get involved. If practitioners accept the cultural separation assumption without understanding its inherent trauma for nontraditional students, then practitioners will tend to see involvement as a relatively easy task since they will also assume that all students, regardless of background, are ready, willing, and able to get involved.

Researchers who have studied nontraditional students (Terenzini et al. 1994; Rendón 1994; Jalomo 1995) have contributed important findings and modifications to involvement theory. While the importance of involvement cannot be negated, these researchers note that many students, especially nontraditional students, find it difficult to get involved. Important differences between traditional and nontraditional students were not explained in the original conception of student involvement theory. Traditional students often come from upper- to middle-class backgrounds, are predominantly white, and come from families in which at least one parent has attended college and the expectation of college attendance is well established. For traditional students college attendance is a normal rite of passage and a part of family tradition. Consequently, they are more likely to understand and manipulate the values, traditions, and practices of college to their academic advantage. Involvement theory does not emphasize the fact that most two- and four-year colleges are set up to facilitate involvement for traditional students.

On the other hand, nontraditional students often come from working-class backgrounds, are older, work at least part-time, and are predominantly minority and first-generation—the first in their families to attend college (Rendón 1994; Terenzini et al. 1993; Jalomo 1995). Jalomo's (1995) study of Latino first-year community college students found that involvement was difficult for students who found the transition to college troublesome or whose background char-

acteristics did not "fit" the traditional student profile found on most college campuses today. Table 31-1 portrays the characteristics of students who found college involvement difficult. Moreover, Jalomo (1995) found that students required the assistance of cultural translators, mediators, and role models in order to survive or succeed in their first semester in college.

Rendón (1994) found that validation, as opposed to involvement, had transformed nontraditional students into powerful learners. While it is likely that most white and traditional students can become involved on their own in an institutional context that merely affords involvement opportunities (i.e., tutoring centers, clubs and organizations, extracurricular activities), nontraditional students expect active outreach and intervention in order to become involved. Rendón explains: "It appears that nontraditional students do not perceive involvement as *them* taking the initiative. They perceive it when someone takes an active role in assisting them" (p. 44).

Presenting a model of validation, Rendón (1994) notes that what had transformed nontraditional students into powerful learners and persisters were incidents in which some individual, either inside or outside class, had validated them. Validating agents made use of interpersonal and academic validation. Validating agents took an active interest in students. They provided encouragement for students and affirmed them as being capable of doing academic work and supported them in their academic endeavors and social adjustment. The critical role of the institution and its agents is underscored in Rendón's validation model. The role of the institution is not simply to offer involvement opportunities, but to take an active role in fostering validation. Faculty, counselors, coaches, and administrators take the initiative to reach out to students and design activities that promote active learning and interpersonal growth among students, faculty, and staff (Rendón 1994).

Focus on the Negative Impact of the External Community

A third conceptual problem with interactionalist theory is that external forces and cultures are seen as distinct and having mainly a negative

TABLE 31-1
Characteristics of Latino Students Who Found It Difficult to Get
Involved in Their Community College

Married students with family obligations

Single parents

Students who have been out of school for some time

Students who are the first in their families to attend college

Students who never liked high school or who were rebellious in high school

Students who have had negative experiences with former teachers or administrative staff in elementary and secondary schools

Students who were not involved in academic activities or student groups during high school

Students who did not participate in school-based social activities or student programs during high school

Students who are afraid or feel out of place in the mainstream college culture

Students who have had negative interactions with college faculty or administrative staff

Students who have a hard time adjusting to the fast pace of college

Students who take evening courses when little or no services are available.

Students who lack the financial resources to take additional courses or participate in campus-based academic and social activities in college

Source: Jalomo 1995

impact on student involvement. Tinto (1987) acknowledges that family and culture may play an important part in student decisions to depart from college. However, what Tinto (1987) stresses (and what scholars and practitioners are likely to emphasize) is that "in some situations, external social systems may work counter to the demands of institutional life. When the academic and social systems of the institution are weak, the countervailing external demands may seriously undermine the individual's ability to persist on completion" (p. 108). Even in his 1993 revised model, Tinto argues that external elements are secondary to those in college, conditioning but not determining the character of the experience on campus. Researchers have validated some of the negative effects of the external environment. For example, Terenzini et al. (1993) found that "friends who did not attend college could complicate the transition by anchoring students to old networks of friends and patterns of behavior rather than allowing them to explore and learn about their new college environment" (p. 5). Similarly, parents who feel anxious about students leaving home may

function as liabilities. Nora et al. (1996) found that minority students who needed to work off-campus for financial reasons were 36 percent more likely to drop out of college than those who did not. Moreover, researchers found that female students, as opposed to male students, who were required to leave campus immediately after class to help care for family members were 83 percent more likely to withdraw.

However, not everything external is a liability. For example, Terenzini et al. (1993) found that precollege friends performed a "bridge function," providing support and encouragement. And with few exceptions, students named family members when asked "Who are the most important people in your life right now?" Jalomo (1995) found that there were more out-of-class agents helping students to make connections on campus than in-class agents. Clearly, much more research is needed to assess the positive and negative influences of the external environment and how students negotiate external influences, not only during the first year of college but throughout the student's collegiate experience.

Taking Retention Theory to a Higher Level

The conceptual issues presented in this chapter, based both on empirical evidence and conceptual critiques, substantiate that Tinto's college student retention theory needs to be taken to an even higher level of theoretical development. Tinto has done this through extensions and refinements of his theory (Braxton, Sullivan, and Johnson 1997). However, Attinasi (1989, 1994) and Tierney (1992) would likely go as far as rejecting the theory and building another that is capable of reflecting subtle processes (particularly cultural and political and emerging from qualitative analysis) involved in persistence. We believe that with all that is now known about student retention, it is quite possible that a totally new theory is needed to take Tinto's theory to a different level. Moreover, knowledge from disciplines other than education can also be used to develop new theoretical perspectives regarding student retention. For example, Hurtado (1997) has developed a "social engagement model [that] takes into account gender as well as other significant social identities like ethnicity/race, class, and sexuality to study how groups change as they come into contact with each other" (p. 299).

Employing a social psychology perspective, Hurtado (1997) advocates that understanding cultural transformations in an increasingly complex and multicultural society, as in the case when students from one group enter the sphere of social engagement of another group, requires not an assimilation/acculturation framework, but a social engagement model. Hurtado (1994) has employed a social engagement framework to study the participation of Latino parents in school. Hurtado's analysis of Latino parents' participation in school is quite similar to how one might analyze college student retention.

For example, research findings illustrate that working-class Latino students are not as likely to get involved in the academic and social domains of the college as often as whites do. Engagement is usually defined as participating in clubs and organizations, meeting with faculty in and out of class, etc. Hurtado would argue that this narrow definition of student engagement is predominately based in the dominant group's perspective and not from the Latino stu-

dents' view of what is possible and desirable for them. Indeed, Rendón (1994), Jalomo (1995), and Terenzini et al. (1994) have found that involvement is not easy for nontraditional students from working-class backgrounds and that both in- and out-of-class validation were essential to their engagement and persistence. Validation is a powerful, interactive process involving a student and a validating agent. Much of the validation occurred out of class (with friends, parents, spouses, etc.), substantiating that there are other forms of engagement that can have a positive impact on persistence. These researchers employed qualitative methods that allowed students to express who and what was making a difference in their academic lives and why this was so.

If these researchers had relied only on an assimilation/acculturation framework (i.e., narrowly measuring student traits that restricted minority group involvement), then they most likely would have reached the following conclusions:

1. Latino students from working-class backgrounds are not as academically and socially integrated in college as are white students, leading to their higher dropout rate.

2. Traditional, primarily white students from upper- and middle-class backgrounds are more engaged in college than Latino students, which accounts for their higher levels of educational adjustment and attainment.

3. Consequently, we need to encourage working-class Latino students to avail themselves of services and opportunities that can increase their college retention rates. Further, because white students score the highest on scales of college involvement, they are the models all students should emulate.

An assimilation/acculturation framework would not allow Latino students to contribute their own perceptions and definitions of all that constitutes integration. Nor would their definitions influence the views of white students. We would also not be able to discuss the internal variations of each group, i.e., there are Hispanic students who exhibit very high achievement and engagement levels, and there are white students who do not. Many studies may not capture much of the variability in withdrawal decisions because of the misspecification of important constructs. Findings may turn out to be statistically significant, even though very little of the variance is explained. In these cases what may be most interesting is not what was statistically significant. Rather, the most important finding could be that there are other multiple, unaccounted factors that may be influencing retention.

Hurtado (1997) explains that a social engagement model, which has at its core a definitional approach to differences in social adaptations, would yield different results. Besides standard measures of college integration, there would be measures that allowed different groups of students to provide their own definitions of what they consider to be engagement and why. It could very well be that Latino students would report that they considered cultural activities, external relationships with family and friends, and race-based programs as essential and vital to their personal and academic development. Students could also identify the systemic barriers to integration. Similarities among the different ethnic/racial groups in terms of engagement and barriers related to involvement could also be identified. These variables could then be incorporated into quantitative models for statistical testing. Strategies for facilitating in- and out-of-class involvement for *both* minority and majority students could be generated from these findings. The key issue is that the sole use of an acculturation/assimilation framework to study retention does not go far enough.

Taking existing retention/involvement theory to a more sophisticated level will require a thorough, thoughtful, and critical analysis of all the quantitative and qualitative data that have been generated to date. Rather than operate in isolation, quantitative and qualitative researchers should be open to each other's methods, share findings, and probe further into the meaning of their results. We should also be open to theory developments in fields other than education. Multimethod approaches to the study of retention are likely to lift the current corpus of college persistence research. In short, we believe that the future of college student retention research offers exciting and viable possibilities both to uncover the dynamics involved in retention and to use data to shape practice and policy.

Conclusion

Researchers employing quantitative models based on Tinto's (1975, 1987) depiction of student persistence have conceptually advanced some of the factors and interrelationships postulated in Tinto's model (i.e., Nora and Cabrera 1993, 1996; Nora et al. 1996; Cabrera and Nora 1995; Cabrera, Nora, and Castañeda 1992, 1993). Qualitative studies also provide some support to Tinto's propositions (Terenzini et al. 1993; Jalomo 1995). But while traditional theories of student retention and involvement have been useful in providing a foundation for the study of persistence, they need to be taken further, as much more work needs to be done to uncover race, class, and gender issues (among others) that impact retention for diverse students in diverse institutions. Certainly, the theoretical issues regarding separation, transition, and incorporation presented in this chapter provide avenues for conducting future research. Yet we stress that the ideas presented here are intended to go beyond stirring intellectual discussion that will lift theory and research.

Minority students are altering the nature of higher education in many ways. Over the past twenty years we have witnessed dramatic changes in the classroom and the curriculum (with the inclusion of ethnic/racial perspectives and the use of learning communities), in student services (with race-based programs), and in faculty and staff composition, among other areas. While we believe that theory building is important, out of scholarly discussions and research should come advances in the development and dramatic transformation of academic and student services. Assuming that good social scientists are also caring humanitarians, the goal of student retention research transcends making conceptual modifications in theoretical models. In the end, students will elect to stay or leave college not so much because of a theory, but because college and university faculty and administrators have made transformative shifts in governance, curriculum development, in- and out-of-class teaching and learning, student programming, and other institutional dimensions that affect students on a daily basis. Consequently, connecting retention research to field practitioners and policy makers in new and creative ways that involve collaborative relationships and mutual learning experiences can take student retention research to a whole new level of theoretical accuracy and applicability.

References

Allen, W. R. 1984. Race consciousness and collective commitments among black students on white campuses. *Western Journal of Black Studies* 8 (3): 156–166.

Almaguer, T. 1974. Historical notes on Chicano oppression: The dialectics of racial and class domination in North America. *Aztlán* 5 (1–2): 27–56.

Astin, A. 1984. Student involvement: A developmental theory for higher education. *Journal of College Student Personnel* 12 (July): 297–308.

Astin, A. 1985. *Achieving educational excellence: A critical assessment of priorities and practices in higher education.* San Francisco: Jossey-Bass.

Attinasi, Jr., L. 1989. Getting in: Mexican Americans' perceptions of university attendance and the implications for freshman year persistence. *Journal of Higher Education* 60 (3): 247–277.

Attinasi, Jr., L. 1994. Is going to college a rite of passage? Paper presented at the annual meeting of the American Research Association, New Orleans, La.

Belenky, M., B. Clinchy, N. Goldberger, and J. Tarule. 1986. *Women's ways of knowing.* New York: Basic Books, Inc.

Blauner, R. 1972. *Racial oppression in America.* New York: Harper & Row.

Braxton, J. M., A. V. S. Sullivan, and R. M. Johnson. 1997. Appraising Tinto's theory of college student departure. In J. C. Smart (ed.), *Higher education: A handbook of theory and research,* vol. 12, pp. 107–164. New York: Agathon Press.

Brint, S., and J. Karabel. 1989. *The directed dream: Community colleges and the promise of educational opportunity in America, 1900–1985.* New York: Oxford University Press.

Cabrera, A. F., and A. Nora. 1994. College students' perceptions of prejudice and discrimination and their feelings of alienation. *Review of Education, Pedagogy, and Cultural Studies* 16: 387–409.

Cabrera, A. F., A. Nora, and M. B. Castañeda. 1992. The role of finances in the student persistence process: A structural model. *Research in Higher Education* 33 (5): 571–594.

Cabrera, A. F., A. Nora, and M. B. Castañeda. 1993. College persistence: Structural equations modeling test of an integrated model of student retention. *Journal of Higher Education* 64 (2): 123–139.

Cabrera, A. F., M. B. Castañeda, A. Nora, and D. Hengstler. 1992. The convergent and discriminant validity between two theories of college persistence. *Journal of Higher Education* 63 (2): 143–164.

Caplan, N., and S. Nelson. 1973. The nature and consequences of psychological research on social problems. *American Psychologist* 28 (3): 199–211.

de Anda, D. 1984. Bicultural socialization: Factors affecting the minority experience. *Social Work* 29 (2): 101–107.

Durkheim, E. 1951. *Suicide: A study in sociology.* Edited by G. Simpson. Translated by J. A. Spaulding and E. Simpson. Originally published in 1897. Glencoe, Ill.: The Free Press. Fleming, J. 1984. *Blacks in college.* San Francisco: Jossey-Bass.

Galindo, R., and K. Escamilla. 1995. A biographical perspective on Chicano educational success. *The Urban Review* 27 (1).

Gandara, P. 1993. *Choosing higher education: The educational mobility of Chicano students.* Report to the Latina/Latino Policy Research Program, California Policy Seminar. (ERIC Document Reproduction Service No. ED 374 942).

Gordon, M. M. 1964. *Assimilation in American life: The role of race, religion, and national origins.* New York: Oxford University Press.

Gurin, P., and E. Epps. 1975. *Black consciousness, identity and achievement.* New York: John Wiley & Sons.

Harvey, W. B., and L. Williams. 1989. Historically black colleges: Models for increasing minority representation. *Journal of Black Studies* 21 (3): 238.

Hurtado, A. 1997. Understanding multiple group identities: Inserting women into cultural transformations. *Journal of Social Issues* 53 (2): 299–328.

Hurtado, A., and E. Garcia. 1994. *The educational achievement of Latinos: Barriers and successes.* Santa Cruz: Regents of the University of California.

Jalomo, R. 1995. *Latino students in transition: An analysis of the first-year experience in community college.* Ph.D. diss., Arizona State University, Tempe.

Kraemer, B. A. 1997. The academic and social integration of Hispanic students into college. *Review of Higher Education* 20: 163–179.

Kuh, G., and E. Whitt. 1988. *The invisible tapestry: Culture in American colleges and universities.* ASHE-ERICD Higher Education Report.

Levy-Warren, M. H. 1988. Moving to a new culture: Cultural identity, loss, and mourning. In Bloom-Fesback & Associates (eds.), *The psychology of separation and loss.* San Francisco: Jossey-Bass.

London, H. 1978. *The culture of a community college.* New York: Praeger.

London, H. 1989. Breaking away: A study of first generation college students and their families. *American Journal of Education* 97 (February): 144–170.

Lowe, M. (1989). *Chicano students' perceptions of their community college experience with implications for persistence: A naturalistic inquiry*. Ph.D. diss., Arizona State University, Tempe.

Melchior-Walsh, S. 1994. *Sociocultural alienation: Experiences of North American Indian students in higher education*. Ph.D. diss., Arizona State University, Tempe.

Mow, S., and M. Nettles. 1990. Minority student access to, and persistence and performance in, college: A review of the trends and research literature. In J. C. Smart (ed.), *Higher education: A handbook of theory and research*, vol. 6, pp. 35–105. New York: Agathon Press.

Nettles, M., C. Gosman, A. Thoeny, and B. Dandrige. 1985. *The causes and consequences of college students' attrition rates, progression rates and grade point averages*. Nashville, Tenn.: Higher Education Commission.

Nieto, S. 1996. *Affirming diversity: The sociopolitical context of multicultural education*. 2d ed. New York: Longman.

Noel, L., R. Levitz, and D. Saluri. 1985. *Increasing student retention: Effective programs and practices for reducing the dropout rate*. San Francisco: Jossey-Bass.

Nora, A. 1987. Determinants of retention among Chicano college students: A structural model. *Research in Higher Education* 26 (1): 31–59.

Nora, A., and A. F. Cabrera. 1993. The construct validity of institutional commitment: A confirmatory factor analysis. *Research in Higher Education* 34 (2): 243–262.

Nora, A., and A. F. Cabrera. 1996. The role of perceptions of prejudice and discrimination on the adjustment of minority students to college. *Journal of Higher Education* 67 (2): 119–148.

Nora, A., and L. I. Rendón. 1988. Hispanic students in community colleges: Reconciling access with outcomes. In L. Weis (ed.), *Class, race, and gender in U.S. education*, pp. 126–143. New York: State University Press.

Nora, A., and L. I. Rendón. 1990. Determinants of predisposition to transfer among community college students: A structural model. *Research in Higher Education* 31: 235–255.

Nora, A., L. Attinasi, and A. Matonak. 1990. Testing qualitative indicators of precollege factors in Tinto's attrition model: A community college student population. *Review of Higher Education* 13 (3): 337–356.

Nora, A., B. Kraemer, and R. Itzen. 1997. Factors affecting the persistence of Hispanic college students. Paper presented at the annual meeting of the Association for the Study of Higher Education, November.

Nora, A., A. F. Cabrera, L. Hagedorn, and E. T. Pascarella. 1996. Differential impacts of academic and social experiences on college-related behavioral outcomes across different ethnic and gender groups at four-year institutions. *Research in Higher Education* 37 (4): 427–452.

Oakes, J. 1985. *Keeping track. How schools structure inequality*. New Haven, Conn.: Yale University Press.

Ogbu, J. U. 1978. *Minority education and caste: The American system in cross-cultural perspective*. New York: Academic Press.

Ogbu, J. U. 1987. Variability in minority school performance: A problem in search of an explanation. *Anthropology and Education Quarterly* 18 (4): 312–334.

Olivas, M. 1979. *The dilemma of access: Minorities in two year colleges*. Washington, D.C.: Howard University Press.

Pascarella, E. T. 1980. Student-faculty informal contact and college outcomes. *Review of Educational Research* 50:545–595.

Pascarella, E., and P. Terenzini. 1991. *How college affects students: Findings and insights from twenty years of research*. San Francisco: Jossey-Bass.

Pavel, M. 1992. The application of Tinto's model to a Native American student population. Paper presented at the annual meeting of the Association for the Study of Higher Education in November.

Polgar, S. 1960. Biculturation of Mesquakie teenage boys. *American Anthropologist* 62: 217–235.

Rendón, L. I. 1982. *Chicano students in south Texas community colleges: A study of student- and institution-related determinants of educational outcomes*. Ph.D. diss., University of Michigan, Ann Arbor.

Rendón, L. I. 1994. Validating culturally diverse students: Toward a new model of learning and student development. *Innovative Higher Education* 19 (1): 23–32.

Rendón, L. I., and R. O. Hope. 1996. *Educating a new majority*. San Francisco: Jossey-Bass.

Rosaldo, R. 1989. *Culture and truth: The remaking of social analysis*. Boston: Beacon Press.

Terenzini, P., K. Allison, P. Gregg, R. Jalomo, S. Millar, L. I. Rendón, and L. Upcraft. 1993. *The transition to college: Easing the passage. A summary of the research findings of the Out-of-Class Experiences Program*. University Park, Pa.: National Center on Post-secondary Teaching, Learning, & Assessment.

Terenzini, P., L. I. Rendón, L. Upcraft, S. Millar, K. Allison, P. Gregg, and R. Jalomo. 1994. The transition to college: Diverse students, diverse stories. *Research in Higher Education* 35 (1): 57–73.

Thomas, G. E. 1984. *Black college students and factors influencing their major field choice*. Atlanta: Southern Education Foundation.

Tierney, W. 1992. An anthropological analysis of student participation in college. *Journal of Higher Education* 63 (6): 603–618.

Tierney, W. 1993. *Building communities of difference: Higher education in the 21st Century.* Westport, Conn.: Bergin & Garvey.

Tinto, V. 1987. *Leaving college: Rethinking the causes and cures of student departure.* Chicago: University of Chicago Press.

Tinto, V. 1993. *Leaving college: Rethinking the causes and cures of student attrition.* Chicago: University of Chicago Press.

Valadez, J. 1996. Educational access and social mobility. *Review of Higher Education* 19 (4): 391–409.

Valentine, C. A. 1971. Deficit, difference, and bicultural models of Afro-American behavior. *Harvard Educational Review* 41 (2): 137–157.

Van Gennep, A. 1960. *The rites of passage.* Translated by M. B. Vizedom and G. I. Caffee. Chicago: University of Chicago Press.

Weis, L. 1985. *Between two worlds: Black students in an urban community college.* Boston: Routledge and Kegan Paul.

Wright, B. 1988. For the children of the infidels?: American Indian education in the colonial colleges. *American Indian Culture and Research Journal* 12: 1–14.

Wycoff, S. 1996. Academic performance of Mexican-American women: Sources of support that serve as motivating variables. *Journal of Multicultural Counseling and Development* 24 (July): 146–155.

Zambrana, R. E. 1988. Toward understanding the educational trajectory and socialization of Latina women. In T. McKenna and F. I. Ortiz (eds.), *The broken web: The educational experience of Hispanic American women,* pp. 61–77. Claremont, Calif.: The Tomás Rivera Center.

CHAPTER 32

ECONOMIC INFLUENCES ON PERSISTENCE RECONSIDERED

EDWARD P. ST. JOHN, ALBERTO E. CABRERA,
AMAURY NORA, AND ERIC H. ASKER

Financial assistance to college students increased from a meager $557 million in 1963–1964 (Lewis 1989) to a phenomenal $55.7 billion in 1996–1997 ("Average Cost of Tuition" 1997). Because of the enormity of this investment it is not surprising that a single policy question—How do prices and student subsidies influence the ability of students to persist?—has motivated much of the research on the economic aspects of persistence over three decades (St. John 1994). The economic studies examine how financial assistance equalized opportunities to persist in college for those students in need of financial support (St. John et al. 1994; Andrieu and St. John 1993; Astin 1975; Terkla 1985). However, because financial aid is not the only reason students persist in college (e.g., Stampen and Cabrera 1986, 1988), recently researchers have developed more complete models that seek to explain how finances interact with other factors that influence college persistence (e.g., Cabrera, Nora, and Castañeda 1993; St. John, Paulsen, and Starkey 1996). This recent line of inquiry can inform efforts to build a more complete understanding of the departure puzzle. In this chapter we first examine the evolution of economic models and then explore ways of integrating the logic of the new economic models into mainstream persistence research. We summarize by articulating a set of challenges facing persistence researchers.

The Evolution of Economic Models of Persistence

Research on factors believed to have an influence on college student persistence has been dominated by two distinct, yet overlapping, lines of inquiry: those studies that have focused on an economic perspective and those that have based their investigative efforts along a student-institution fit perspective. While both of these lines of inquiry address factors that influence a student to stay in college, they do so through competing explanations. Academic and social collegiate experiences emerge as primary determinants of persistence in studies that focus on student-institution fit (Pascarella and Terenzini 1991), while financial need, student aid packaging, and adequacy of aid are of central concern in those studies that focus on the economic perspective (Cabrera, Nora, and Castañeda 1992; Nora and Horvath 1989; St. John, Paulsen, and Starkey 1996). Moreover, the multiplicity of theoretical assumptions and conceptual frameworks has led to the suggestions of a

---

"Economic Influences on Persistence Reconsidered." Reprinted from *Rethinking the Departure Puzzle: New Theory and Research on College Student Retention*, edited by John M. Braxton, (2000), Vanderbilt University Press.

confusing array of intervention strategies. While financial aid from government and institutional sources supports access and persistence in college (Wilcox 1991), enhancing the cognitive and affective development as they relate to student-departure decisions would be stressed by those adhering to a student-institution fit model. Clearly, a better understanding of factors impacting student persistence in college emerges when both of these lines of conceptualization inquiry are considered.

The Economic Approach

Reliance on price-response theories and their allied theory of targeted subsidies is evident in research bringing about an economic approach to the investigation of student persistence (e.g., Manski and Wise 1983; St. John 1990; St. John, Kirshstein, and Noell 1991; Stampen and Cabrera 1986, 1988). Essentially, price-response theories focus in part on economic factors whereby the social and economic benefits of attending college are believed to outweigh any costs and benefits associated with alternative activities (e.g., working full-time). A critical component in these cost/benefit analyses is the student's perception of his or her ability (or inability) to pay for college (Becker 1964). While price-response theories provide a conceptual foundation for examining persistence, the theory of targeted subsidies suggests that the means to influence such behavior is through subsidies targeted at specific groups based on their ability to pay. Reduced tuition, direct grants, low-interest loans, and subsidized work-study programs all seek to equalize students on their ability to pay for college education and to increase the benefits derived from attending college (Bowen 1977; Cabrera, Stampen, and Hansen 1990). This line of research has focused on the overall effect of financial aid on persistence (e.g., Astin 1975; Murdock 1987; Stampen and Cabrera 1986, 1988); the sensitivity of persistence decisions to charges along with tuition reduction, grants, loans, and work-study awards (e.g., Astin 1975; Nora 1990; St. John 1990, 1994; St. John, Kirshstein, and Noell 1991; Voorhees 1985); and the effectiveness of particular student aid packages in the retention of minorities (e.g., Astin 1975; Olivas 1985; Nora 1990; Nora and Horvath 1989; St. John 1990). These studies focus on actual effects of student aid rather than on perceptions of aid adequacy

or the adequacy of aid relative to college costs.

However, economic studies provide an incomplete view of the true nature of financial influences on persistence in college, compared to recent integrative models. They focus on the influence of aid, along with the factors that need to be controlled to assess this effect, rather than attempting to construct a logical model that assesses interactions among all of the important factors that influence persistence. Two circumstances have handicapped this line of inquiry: methodological problems and shortcomings in the conceptualization of the persistence phenomenon.

First, some of the early economic studies on persistence were primarily impact-oriented (Cabrera, Stampen, and Hansen 1990; Nora 1990; Vorhees 1985).[1] While they took into account such important predictors of persistence as precollege motivational factors, precollege academic ability and achievement, demographic factors, students' socioeconomic status, and college performance, they did so with the purpose of controlling for sources of variance that substantially interact with the direct effects of prices and subsidies. The emphasis was on ascertaining the direct effects of financial aid on persistence, not the effects of noneconomic factors. This approach was limited in that it did not address the ways financial circumstances interacted with other factors in a manner more complex than would be evident from a measure of direct effect.

Second, the economic-impact approach underestimated the role that the institution plays in shaping persistence decisions. Factors such as student-support systems, interaction with faculty, and affective outcomes associated with college, while known to play a role (Pascarella and Terenzini 1991), were seldom sufficiently considered in economic-impact studies. Indeed the extant data sets typically used in this research usually do not include variables related to some of these forces. Further, to address the question of fit, which is important from an institutional perspective, most persistence researchers conducted supplemental surveys.

Student-Institution Fit Approach

Research utilizing this approach views persistence decisions as the end product of a successful match between a student and his or her academic and social environment in a higher-education setting (Bean 1980; Spady 1970, 1971; Tinto 1987, 1993). Experiences with the academic and social realms of an institution are seen as playing a key role in the cognitive and affective development of the student. In turn, these developmental changes are presumed to affect a student's commitments to an institution and to college completion. The stronger these commitments are, the greater the probability that a student will remain enrolled in college (Tinto 1987, 1993).

With the exception of Bean (1982), the early proponents of this approach did not incorporate finances as an independent variable. The underlying assumption was that personal or family finances were important only in helping to shape students' educational aspirations and their subsequent selection of institutions. In other words, once students enrolled in college, finances were disregarded as instrumental in playing a role in persistence decisions (Tinto 1987). The implicit assumption being made was that financial need was met.

In 1993 Tinto revisited his student integration model and included student finances as a key component in the adjustment of the student to college. Such a revision, while consistent with the mounting evidence highlighting the role of financial aid on persistence (e.g., Cabrera, Nora, and Castañeda 1992; Olivas 1985; Stampen and Cabrera 1986, 1988; Murdock 1987; Nora 1990; St. John 1989; St. John, Kirshstein, and Noell 1991; Voorhees 1985), did not substantially influence subsequent research. Most of the persistence research using the institutional-fit model continued to disregard finances (Braxton, Sullivan, and Johnson 1997). Below we review integrative studies that are an exception to this pattern of ignoring the crucial role of finances.

Integrative Approaches

Efforts at integrating both lines of research have followed two paths. Early studies by Voorhees (1985), Moline (1987), and Nora (1990) sought to explore the interconnections between financial aid and other variables (e.g., student grades) found to have an effect on student persistence. Later approaches, such as the ability-to-pay model (Cabrera, Stampen, and Hansen 1990; Cabrera, Nora, and Castañeda 1992) and the college choice—persistence nexus model (St. John, Paulsen, and Starkey 1996), have attempted to clarify the process by which ability to pay and financial aid are interrelated with collegiate experiences and the reenrollment decisions of students. Relying on path analysis, structural equation modeling, and sequential logistic regressions, the major thrust of this approach has been to uncover the interconnections that link financial factors and nonfinancial factors as much as documenting the direct and indirect effects of finances on persistence decisions.

The Early Integrative Models

In 1985 Voorhees examined the association between federal campus-based aid programs and the persistence of high-need first-year college students. His model of persistence reflected withdrawal decisions as the by-product of a two-stage process whereby financial resources that students bring to college, students' demographic characteristics, and academic ability would determine the type of campus-based financial aid programs granted, their academic performance in college, and, ultimately, persistence. Moline (1987), while examining persistence decisions among students also enrolled in a commuter institution, found that merit aid exerted an indirect effect on students' departure through the academic performance of students. Nora (1990) examined the effect of campus-based resources on the retention of Chicano community college students. Nora's model approached persistence decisions as a three-stage process involving the academic ability of students as they entered college, the financial need of those students, different forms of campus-based financial aid, and the academic performance of students during their first year in college. His model also explained three-quarters of the variance in the persistence process and highlighted the complex interplay among financial aid (both campus- and non-campus-based) and the academic performance of students.

While the notion of examining the process involved in the withdrawal of students from college furthered research on finances (the economic perspective) by stressing the need for a simultaneous analysis of numerous constructs, a common problem of this early research was not addressed; the adjustment of students to college in the persistence process was totally disregarded. For example, current institutional commitments were omitted. Nora and Horvath

(1989), as well as Stampen and Cabrera (1986), noted that the role of finances in the adjustment process needed to be explicitly examined from both conceptual and empirical bases.

The Ability-to-Pay Model

Cabrera, Stampen, and Hansen (1990) also argued that a more comprehensive view of college persistence could be secured by merging economic theory with persistence theory. They reasoned that researchers should disentangle the indirect and direct effects of finances from intellectual and nonintellectual factors related to collegiate experiences. Building upon educational attainment theory, organizational theory, cost/benefit theory, and institution-student fit theory, the model they advanced portrayed persistence as the product of a complex longitudinal process involving the interaction between the student and the institution. While acknowledging that prior academic skills, positive interactions with faculty and peers, as well as goals and institutional commitments are key for explaining persistence, they also recognized that such factors as encouragement and support from significant others and ability to pay could moderate the adjustment of the student with the institution. In this context they postulated that ability to pay was a precondition for the attainment of the cognitive and noncognitive outcomes, due to its role in removing or reducing a student's barriers to participate in the college academic and social dimensions of the institution while freeing such a student of the need to work long hours and from financial concern. Testing the model on a sample of college students drawn from the National Center for Educational Statistics (NCES) High School and Beyond 1980 Senior Cohort, Cabrera, Stampen, and Hansen (1990) found that adding college-related variables increased the proportion of variance explained over and above a model that presumed that persistence was primarily affected by economic factors (22.9 percent vs. 14.1 percent). They also found that finances, while having a direct effect on persistence decisions, moderated the effects of goal commitments. In short, students satisfied with their ability to pay for college had higher aspirations and higher chances to persist in college than their less-satisfied and lower-motivated counterparts.

Then Cabrera et al. (1992) postulated that finances could have a dual role in the persistence of college students, as a refinement to the ability-to-pay model. Finances were believed to increase the chances of persistence to graduation because of their role in increasing cost-related benefits while at the same time facilitating the social and academic integration of the student on campus. The researchers also argued that finances were comprised of two dimensions: an objective component, reflecting a student's availability of resources; and a subjective or intangible component that underscored a student's self-perceptions of ability to finance college-related expenses. They considered that the reception of financial aid could be a more reliable indicator of a student's ability to pay than his/her socioeconomic status. Cabrera et al. (1992) approached persistence as a complex process linking experiences with the institution, cognitive and affective changes resulting from collegiate experiences, a student's commitments to the institution and to the goal of college completion, his/her intent to persist at the institution, perceptions of finances, and the extent to which the student felt encouraged and supported by friends and family.

As a whole, results supported the proposition that persistence decisions underscore a process among cognitive and affective variables as well as financial-related factors. While financial aid was found to exert only indirect effects on persistence decisions, the total effect of this variable ranked third among all the constructs in the model. The results, however, emphasized the indirect nature of the role of finances on the adjustment of students to college. Receiving some form of financial aid facilitated a student's interactions with peers. Financial aid was also found to enhance the student's academic performance in college while increasing intent to persist. Being satisfied with one's ability to pay for college, on the other hand, facilitated the student's academic and intellectual development in college. While highlighting the indirect nature of finances, the study also emphasized that decisions to persist are the result of a complex process in which finances, however important, were but one of the many factors that played a role.

The College Choice-Persistence Nexus Model

Similar to other recent models (e.g., Cabrera et al. 1992; St. John et al. 1994), the nexus model (St. John, Paulsen, and Starkey 1996) reflected the need to merge the economic perspective with the student-institution fit perspective[2] However, St. John, Paulsen, and Starkey (1996) noted that efforts at integrating both perspectives had failed to incorporate a major component in the enrollment-persistence process: namely, the decision-making process in selecting a college (i.e., a student's college-choice phase) (Hossler, Braxton, and Coopersmith 1989). The omission of this component led to creating an "artificial" and isolated endeavor rather than being part of a continuous and interconnected student decision process. To compensate for this deficiency in earlier models, St. John and colleagues formulated a model that articulated a nexus between college choice and persistence, while at the same time clarifying the role that financial aid-related factors exert in student matriculation to and persistence in college.

The nexus model hypothesized that persistence was shaped through a three-stage process. In the first stage socioeconomic factors as well as academic ability were believed to affect a student's predisposition to pursue a college education and perceptions of financial circumstances. During the second stage the student estimated the benefits and costs associated with a particular institution that would induce the student to develop an initial commitment to enroll in college and further affect the decision to remain in college. Within this context, financial aid would not only positively influence thoughts of matriculation but would also predispose the student to select a particular institution. Once the student entered college (the third stage), college characteristics (e.g., the type of college attended), collegiate experiences, and academic performance in college helped modify or reinforce educational aspirations. Positive social and academic experiences in college and an adequate academic performance reinforced or even enhanced the student's perceptions of economic and noneconomic benefits associated with enrollment in and graduation from the institution. Financial aid was believed to positively affect persistence decisions by maintaining an equilibrium between the cost of attending college and the benefits to be derived from the attainment of an educational degree. Negative college experiences, such as increases in tuition, affected the benefits/cost equilibrium and pushed the student toward withdrawal.

St. John, Paulsen, and Starkey (1996) established support for the proposition that there existed a nexus between a student's college-choice stage and that student's subsequent persistence in college. They also reported that by incorporating college choice, along with college-experience variables included in the base model (St. John et al. 1994), the new choice-related variables modestly increased the proportion of variance explained. The nexus model revealed that financial factors were found to exert effects on both college choice and persistence in college. However, about half the total variance in this persistence process was explained by tuition, student financial aid, food and travel, housing, and other living costs. In addition, a follow-up study using the nexus model found that the direct effect of financial variables explained about half of the variance in persistence by students in both public and private colleges (Paulsen and St. John 1997).

New Understandings

Though differing in conceptualizations, unit of analysis (national cohorts vs. institutional cohorts), methodologies (logistic regression vs. linear structural equation modeling), and databases used, the integrative efforts by the nexus and the ability-to-pay models converge in reaching two major conclusions regarding finances. We state these as new understandings that can inform future research efforts.

First, both models substantiate the fact that a student's finances are comprised of tangible and intangible factors. The tangible element includes indicators of a student's ability to afford college-related costs—e.g., personal savings, reception of financial aid, financial-aid packaging (Cabrera, Stampen, and Hansen 1990; Cabrera, Nora, and Castañeda 1992, 1993; St. John 1994; St. John, Paulsen, and Starkey 1996). The second component of a student's finances is more psychological in nature; it embodies the student's perceptions regarding her/his financial circumstances. Integrative efforts also concur in depicting these perceptions as being cognitive and affective in nature. The cognitive strand represents calculations by which the student ponders the value of attending college against its costs. Satisfaction with cost of attendance, the affective component, is the outcome of this cognitive process. To be satisfied with the cost of attending means the student believes that the benefits of attending a particular institution outweigh its costs (Cabrera, Stampen, and Hansen 1990; Cabrera, Nora, and Castañeda 1992, 1993; St. John 1994; St. John, Paulsen, and Starkey 1996). Integrative efforts also concur in viewing satisfaction with finances as a dynamic process. Since satisfaction is closely associated with a delicate balance between perceived costs and benefits, it then follows that any factor affecting any component of the cost/benefit equation can trigger major changes in the correlated attitude. In the nexus model (St. John, Paulsen, and Starkey 1996), for instance, changes in the composition of the original student-aid package or unexpected increases in tuition and fees are seen to lead to dissatisfaction by the effect these changes have on the original cost/benefit computations. In the ability to pay model, another major source of change is played by those individuals who exert a significant role in the life of the student (Nora 1990; Cabrera, Stampen, and Hansen 1990; Cabrera, Nora, and Castañeda 1992, 1993). Both approaches support the proposition that the student can modify her/his original cost/benefit estimates as new significant people enter her/his life or when the original significant others revalue the benefits attached to a particular institution.

Second, these efforts concluded that finances exert both direct and indirect effects on persistence. While both the nexus and the ability-to-pay models have substantiated this connection empirically, they have provided little grounded discussion for this interconnection. Such a frame of reference, however, can be found in Maslow's (1954) motivation theory. Maslow argues that individuals evolve when they are driven to satisfy such higher-order needs as self-esteem and self-actualization. The pursuit of a college degree and a concurrent intellectual development clearly fit within Maslow's higher-order taxonomy. For Maslow the desire to satisfy higher-order needs can only take place once basic needs are satisfied. With regard to the student-institution fit model, the meeting of tangible and intangible financial needs provides the freedom to engage in and establish relationships with fac-

ulty and peers, to actively participate in classroom activities, and to commit enough time to all those endeavors that promote intellectual development. According to Maslow, dissatisfaction of basic needs can lead to stagnation and even regression to earlier developmental stages. For Maslow, these basic needs become prepotent; that is, they dominate an individual's life, diverting all efforts and thoughts to the satisfaction of those primary needs. Extending the Maslow concept of prepotency to integrative efforts portrays a situation where a student's pursuit of cognitive and affective development can be redirected when financial needs are no longer met. Financial need then becomes a psychological stressor compelling the student to divert his/her attention from academic endeavors to monetary concerns. If financial circumstances remain as such, the student is pulled away from the academic and social domains of the institution to pursue alternative activities (e.g., working, obsessing over financial problems).

Integrating Financial Variables into Student-Institution Fit Models

In their review of the research that has tested Tinto's student integration model, Braxton, Sullivan, and Johnson (1997) not only document the validity of the relationship among college-related variables but also stress that incorporation of financial variables in the student integration model is wanting. Our review of those efforts that integrate finances into models of student departure (Cabrera, Stampen, and Hansen 1990; Cabrera, Nora, and Castañeda 1992, 1993; St. John, Paulsen, and Starkey 1996) provides empirical evidence that this emerging approach offers the means to conceptualize the role of finances both in the adjustment to college and in persistence decisions. Below we explore ways the new understandings reached from these integrative studies can inform future efforts to refine and reconceptualize persistence models.

The Influence of Perceptions of Finances to Institutional Commitment

Research that focuses on the interactions between financial variables and the social and academic integration processes essentially treats perceptions of aid as integral to the formation of commitments. Cabrera et al. (1992) conducted a survey that asked students about the adequacy of their aid, receiving perceptual responses. Further, these perceptions of the ability to pay represented an aspect of the initial commitment students made to their college. In their nexus model St. John, Paulsen, and Starkey (1996) distinguished between the financial reasons for choosing a college and the actual prices and price subsidies students received. They treated these initial calculations about college affordability (e.g., choosing a college because of low tuition, high aid, proximity to home, or opportunity to work) as an integral part of the initial commitment process. Both these lines of inquiry clearly indicate that the early judgments students make about their financial circumstances influence the initial commitments they make to their institutions.

This research illustrates two ways of constructing variables related to perceptions about aid by considering: (1) whether students' decisions to enroll in the fall were influenced by high aid, low tuition, or other cost-related factors (the nexus approach); or (2) whether students thought their financial support was adequate, given the costs of attending (the integrated approach). Both of these approaches to constructing variables relate to perceptions of finance and provide insights that relate to, or take place at the same time as, the initial institutional commitments that are made to attend. There is a slightly different logic related to entering both types of variables into an integrated model.

The nexus model also offers a way of reconceptualizing the conceptual underpinning of initial commitment variables typically included in persistence research. Rather than treating initial commitment as a single variable with a scale, the model suggests identifying three sets of variables related to initial commitments that are integral to the college choice process and that, by extension, can have an influence on subsequent experiences in the persistence process. In other words, the college choice-persistence nexus provides an alternative way of conceptualizing how students make their initial commitments. The research clearly demonstrates that financial commitments are based on an understanding of the financial circumstances—including the ability to pay for college, as well as the ability to earn money for this purpose—and are not only part of this initial cost/benefit decision but also integral to the formation of initial institutional commitments.

The Influence of Perceptions on Social and Academic Integration

The initial financial commitments students make—in the form of finance-related reasons for choosing to attend a college as well as their perceptions of their ability to pay—have an influence on subsequent integration processes. The logic of the integrated model (Cabrera, Nora, and Castañeda 1993) argues that financial attitudes can directly influence the social and academic integration processes. In their research Cabrera, Nora, and Castañeda (1992, 1993) have documented that their question about finances had a direct influence on academic integration and college grades. Their study suggests that if students do not have sufficient resources, their academic work suffers. The underlying question addressed when this approach is used differs fundamentally from the questions that most economic analysts have been concerned with when they investigate the adequacy of student aid. Economic analyses assess whether subsidies are adequate to support students through the academic year (St. John et al. 1994; St. John 1999). However, students' perceptions of adequacy are also important because their perceptions influence commitments and integration processes. If students feel their aid is inadequate, then they may take fewer courses or find work off campus, behaviors that could limit opportunities for social and academic integration.

Thus, the integrated model (Cabrera, Nora, and Castañeda 1993) provides a complete approach for systematically examining the relationship between perceptions of financial circumstance on social and academic integration processes. By focusing on this set of interactions, researchers can discern how perceptions of the adequacy of student aid influence ways students interact in their academic environments, e.g., whether the time they have for informal interactions with faculty is influenced. However, this line of research does not incorporate information on the types and amounts of aid students actually were awarded or on actual family resources, data elements necessary to assess the direct effects of student aid.

The logic of the nexus approach argues that the initial commitments students make are of a specific nature: students reconsider the specific academic, social, and financial reasons they selected their colleges when they make their eventual persistence decisions. Paulsen and St. John (1997) and St. John, Paulsen, and Starkey (1996) identify three possible linkage structures: (1) from the financial reasons for choosing a college to the eventual experience of college affordability; (2) from the academic reasons for choosing a college to the eventual academic integration process; and (3) from the social reasons for choosing a college to the social integration process. Research to date verifies the financial nexus. These studies have found that the financial reasons for choosing to attend did interact with variables related to the college experience, including achievement in college (Paulsen and St. John 1997; St. John, Paulsen,and Starkey 1996). However, the logic of the other two approaches to examining the college choice-persistence nexus has not been explicitly examined and merits examination.

Thus, the nexus approach provides a second proven approach to integrating perceptions of finances into a complete persistence model. Further, the nexus model provides a way of examining how students' perceptions of affordability—including perceptions of tuition, work, and living costs, as well as perceptions of student aid—influence their integration processes and their subsequent cost/benefit calculations about persistence (i.e., commitments at the time the departure decision is made). The model also reveals that changes over time in financial-aid packages can influence students' academic and social integration processes, as well as their subsequent persistence decisions.

The Crucial Direct Effects of Aid and Tuition

There has long been a debate within the community of persistence researchers about whether finances actually influence persistence. Initially Tinto (1987) argued that if students said they were leaving college for financial reasons, it could be an excuse for other reasons, possibly a change in commitments. Such a claim could be true if a student truly had adequate resources to complete college. If students received adequate student aid, a condition that existed in many colleges in the 1970s because of generous federal financial aid, then such a statement could have valid logic. However, research that tested this proposition on students enrolled in the 1980s consistently found that aid was not adequate

(Paulsen and St. John 1997; St. John, Oescher, and Andrieu 1992; St. John et al. 1994; St. John, Paulsen, and Starkey 1996; St. John and Starkey 1995a, 1995b). Indeed, in national studies finance-related factors (student aid, tuition, and other costs, including living) explained about half of the total variance in the persistence process (Paulsen and St. John 1997; St. John, Paulsen, and Starkey 1996). Therefore it seems naive to overlook the direct effects of financial variables based on a self-sealing assumption such as: *if* students say they withdraw because of finances, *then* they are making polite excuses for changes in commitment.

If researchers who have access to information on family income and aid awards actually build appropriate controls for these factors into their persistence models, then they can assess the direct effects of aid. If they control for family income in a multi-institution study or in a study of a campus with differentiated tuition charges, then it is also possible to assess the effects of the tuition charges as well as aid subsidies. However, it is not logical to assume that influences on academic or social integration processes will influence the amount or type of aid awarded. Rather, aid awards are made based on certain criteria, which is why high school achievement and family income should be included in models that assess the effects of amounts of aid. Therefore, it is appropriate to treat student costs and subsidies as variables that directly influence withdrawal.

It is especially important to include income from aid applications because students do not accurately report parental income in response to surveys (Byce and Schmitt 1993). Recent research that includes this type of control has proven empirically that significant and negative coefficients for an aid variable indicate aid is inadequate and that a neutral and/or positive coefficient indicates aid is adequate (St. John forthcoming; St. John, Paulsen, and Starkey 1996). Thus, there are logical and empirical reasons to examine the direct effects of student aid, especially when researchers can attain accurate information on family finances and student aid awards.

Future Research

The review of the evolution of efforts to integrate economic variables into the student-institutional fit models frequently used to investigate student departure has illuminated three ways of integrating financial variables into persistence models. More important, it has been revealed that students' perceptions of their ability to pay are integral to the commitments students make to their institutions and, thus, need to be included for multiple logical reasons.

First, persistence researchers who work within the boundaries of the student-institutional fit model should consider the influence of the ability to pay (Bean 1982; Cabrera, Nora, and Castañeda 1992, 1993). Clearly students' perceptions of their ability to pay can influence their academic performance and the extent and nature of their academic integration (Cabrera, Nora, and Castañeda 1992, 1993). Further, it is relatively easy to modify the data-collection instruments used in these integration models to include questions about perceptions of affordability. Thus, such refinements to the student-institutional fit models are both desirable conceptually and feasible.

Second, the nexus approach merits consideration by researchers who are interested in reconceptualizing the initial commitment process and the ways this process influences the college experience (inclusive of variables typically treated as social- and academic-integration processes). The initial commitments students make to colleges and universities are really comprised of a set of judgments about affordability, academic opportunities, and potential social interactions. Research that has explored the financial aspect of this early commitment has found that student perceptions about affordability interact with their college experiences (St. John, Paulsen, and Starkey 1996) and their integration processes (Cabrera, Nora, and Castañeda 1993). More researchers should begin to explore the role of the financial nexus in the persistence process because it is linked to the basic financial commitments colleges and students make to each other in the recruitment process (Paulsen and St. John 1997).

However, more research is needed to assess the influence of choosing colleges for academic and social reasons on the college experiences and (social and academic) integration processes. The need for research on the nexus between college choice and persistence can be illustrated by several examples. First, consider the student who chose a private college for a middle-class-earning major (e.g., education) but is confronted by larger-than-expected debt. She may feel it is necessary to change to a higher-earning major or transfer to a less expensive college in order to complete the major she intended. Second, consider the student in the same college who had hopes of getting into a preferred major as an upper-division student but was unable to do so. She would be confronted by a decision to persist with another major or to change colleges to follow her interest. Financial perceptions are part of the choice process in the first instance; but they are not in the second case. Clearly, in order to untangle these types of interactions in persistence research it is necessary to include, along with finance-related reasons for choosing certain institutions, a variable related to choosing colleges based on specific majors.

Third, including variables related to actual family resources, tuition, and student aid awards is necessary in comprehensive persistence models. Research on the college choice-persistence nexus indicates no interaction between current postsecondary aspirations and finance-related variables (St. John et al. 1994; St. John, Paulsen, and Starkey 1996). In other words, students who leave college often still aspire to complete their college degrees, but their institutional commitments have changed by virtue of their decision to drop out. Thus, while affordability does influence institutional commitments through student perceptions, prices and financial aid also exert a large direct effect.

Research on the direct effects of student aid on persistence is especially important in colleges and universities with large percentages of low-income and adult students, since they are more price sensitive than traditional undergraduates (St. John and Starkey 1995a, 1995b). However, it is necessary to control for income to measure the direct effects of student aid. Therefore, if appropriate controls are included, it is possible to assess the adequacy of student aid. This means that researchers will need to integrate information from student and applications. A workable approach for this type of analysis has been proposed (St. John 1992) and tested (St. John forthcoming; Somers 1992). Given the decline in federal grants, it is increasingly important for financial planners to know when aid is not adequate. Therefore, the economic impact approach should not be abandoned in efforts to build more complete models.

Notes

1. Other researchers attempted to integrate variables related to commitments and college experiences (e.g., Andrieu and St. John 1993; St. John et al. 1994). This line of research provided the foundation for the nexus model (St. John, Paulsen, and Starkey 1996) discussed below.

2. St. John et al. (1994) merged the two perspectives by treating aspirations as an indicator of initial commitment and incorporating detailed information on college characteristics and experiences as being logically related to integration processes. The nexus model further adapted this approach.

References

Alexander, K., and B. Eckland. 1978. Basic attainment processes: A recapitalization and expansion. *Sociology of Education* 48: 457–495.

Andrieu, S. C., and E. P. St. John. 1993. The influence of prices on graduate student persistence. *Research in Higher Education* 34 (4): 399–419.

Astin, A. W. 1975. *Preventing students from dropping out.* San Francisco: Jossey-Bass.

Average cost of tuition is up 5 percent for 1997–98: Study by the College Board finds increases at 4-year colleges than at 2-year institutions. 1997. *The Chronicle of Higher Education*, October 3, pp. A49–A54.

Bean, J. 1982. Student attrition, intentions and confidence: Interaction effects in a path model. *Research in Higher Education* 14: 425–429.

Bean J. 1980. Dropouts and turnover. The synthesis and test of a causal model of student attrition. *Research in Higher Education* 55: 485–540.

Becker, G. S. 1964. *Human capital: A theoretical and empirical analysis with special reference to education.* New York: National Bureau of Economic Research.

Bowen, H. R. 1977. Investing in learning: *The individual and social value of American higher education.* San Francisco: Jossey-Bass.

Braxton, J. M., A.V.S., Sullivan, and R. M. Johnson. 1997. Appraising Tinto's theory of college student departure. In J. C. Smart (ed.), *Higher Education: A handbook of theory and research*, vol. 12, pp. 107–164. New York Agathon Press.

Byce, C., and C. Schmitt. 1993. *Quality of responses in the 1987 National Postsecondary Student Aid Study.* NCES-93-446. Washington, D.C.: Office of Educational Research and Improvement, U.S. Department of Education.

Cabrera, A. F., A. Nora, and M. B. Castañeda. 1992. The role of finances in the persistence process: A structural model. *Research in Higher Education* 33 (5): 571–593.

Cabrera, A. F., A. Nora, and M. B. Castañeda. 1993. College persistence: Structural equations modeling test of an integrated model of student retention. *Journal of Higher Education* 64 (2): 123–139.

Cabrera, A. F., J. O. Stampen, and W. L. Hansen. 1990. Exploring the effects of ability to pay on persistence in college. *Review of Higher Education* 13 (3): 303–336.

Cabrera, A. F., M. B. Castañeda, A. Nora, and D. Hengstler. 1992. The convergence between two theories of college persistence. *Journal of Higher Education* 63 (2): 143–164.

Clagett, C. 1992. Enrollment management. In M. A. Whiteley, J. D. Porter, and R. A. Fenske (eds.). *The primer for institutional research*, pp. 12–24. Washington, D.C.: Association for Institutional Research.

Hossler, D., J. Braxton, and G. Coopersmith. 1989. Understanding student choice. In J. C. Smart (ed.), *Higher education: A handbook of theory and research*, vol. 5, pp. 231–288. New York Agathon Press.

Lewis, G. L. 1989. Trends in student aid. 1963–64 to 1988–89. *Research in Higher Education* 30: 547–562.

Manski, C. F., and D. A. Wise. 1983. *College choice in America.* Cambridge, Mass.: Harvard University Press.

Maslow, A. H. 1954. *Motivation and personality.* New York: Harper & Row.

Moline, A. E. 1987. Financial aid and student persistence: An application of causal modeling. *Research in Higher Education* 26 (2): 130–147.

Murdock, T. A. 1987. It isn't just money. The effects of financial aid on student persistence. *Review of Higher Education* 11 (1): 75–101.

Nora, A. 1990. Campus-based programs as determinants of retention among Chicano college students. *Journal of Higher Education* 61 (3): 312–331.

Nora, A., and F. Horvath. 1989. Financial assistance: Minority enrollments and persistence. *Education and Urban Society* 21 (3): 299–309.

Olivas, M. A. 1985. Financial aid packaging policies: Access and ideology. *Journal of Higher Education* 56: 462–475.

Pascarella, E. T., and P. T. Terenzini. 1991. *How college affects students: Findings and insights from twenty years of research.* San Francisco: Jossey-Bass.

Paulsen, M. B., and E. P. St. John. 1997. The financial nexus between college choice and persistence. In R. A. Vorhees (ed.), *Researching student aid: Creating an action agenda*, pp. 65–82. New Directions in Institutional Research, no. 95. San Francisco: Jossey-Bass.

St. John, E. P. 1989. The influence of student aid on persistence. *Journal of Student Financial Aid* 19 (3): 52–68.

St. John, E. P. 1990. Price response in enrollment divisions: An analysis of the high school and beyond sophomore cohort. *Research in Higher Education* 31: 161–176.

St. John, E. P. 1992. Workable models for institutional research on the impact of student financial aid. *Journal of Student Financial Aid* 22 (3): 13–26.

St. John, E. P. 1994. *Prices, productivity, and investment: Assessing financial strategies in higher education.* ASHE-ERIC Higher Education Reports (1994 Report Three). Washington, D.C.: George Washington University.

St. John, E. P. 1999. Evaluating state grant programs: A case study. *Research in Higher Education* 40: 149–170.

St. John, E. P., and S. Andrieu. 1995. The influence of price subsidies on within-year persistence by graduate students. *Higher Education* 29: 143–168.

St. John, E. P., and J. B. Starkey. 1995a. An alternative to net price: Assessing the influence of prices and subsidies on within-year persistence. *Journal of Higher Education* 66 (2): 156–186.

St. John, E. P., and J. B. Starkey. 1995b. The influence of prices on the persistence of adult undergraduates. *Journal of Student Financial Aid* 25 (2): 7–17.

St. John, E.P.R. Kirshstein, and J. Noell. 1991. The effects of student aid on persistence: A sequential analysis of the High School and Beyond Senior Cohort. *Review of Higher Education* 14 (3): 383–406.

St. John, E. P., J. Oescher, and S. C. Andrieu. 1992. The influence of prices on within-year persistence by traditional college-age students in four-year colleges. *Journal of Student Financial Aid* 22 (1): 27–38.

St. John, E. P., M. B. Paulsen, and J. B. Starkey. 1996. The nexus between college choice and persistence. *Research in Higher Education.* 37 (2): 175–220.

St. John, E. P., S. C. Andrieu, J. Oescher, and J. B. Starkey. 1994. The influence of student aid on persistence by traditional college-age students in four-year colleges. *Research in Higher Education* 35 (4): 455–480.

Somers, P. 1992. A dynamic analysis of student matriculation decisions in urban public universities. Ph.D. diss., University of New Orleans.

Spady, W. 1970. Dropouts from higher education: An interdisciplinary review and synthesis. *Interchange* 1: 64–85.

Spady, W. 1971. Dropouts from higher education: Toward an empirical model. *Interchange* 2: 38–62.

Stage, F. K., and D. Hossler. 1989. Differences in family influences on college attendance plans for male and female ninth graders. *Research in Higher Education* 30 (3): 301–315.

Stampen, J. O., and A. F. Cabrera. 1986. Exploring the effects of student aid on attrition. *Journal of Student Financial Aid* 16:28–37.

Stampen, J. O., and A. F. Cabrera. 1988. Is the student aid system achieving its objectives? Evidence on targeting and attrition. *Economics of Education Review* 7: 29–46.

Terkla, D. G. 1985. Does financial aid enhance undergraduate persistence? *Journal of Student Financial Aid* 15 (3): 11–18.

Tinto, V. 1975. Dropout from higher education: A theoretical synthesis of recent research. *Review of Educational Research* 45: 89–125.

Tinto, V. 1987. *Leaving College: Rethinking the Causes and Cures of Student Attrition.* Chicago, Ill. University of Chicago Press.

Tinto, V. 1993. *Leaving college: Rethinking the causes and cures of student attrition.* 2d ed. Chicago: University of Chicago Press. (1st ed., 1987).

Voorhees, R. A. 1985. Financial aid and persistence: Do the federal campus-based aid programs make a difference? *Journal of Student Aid* 15: 21–30.

Wilcox, I. 1991. Evaluating the impact of financial aid on student recruitment and retention. In D. Hossler (ed.), *Evaluating student recruitment and retention programs,* pp. 47–60. New Directions for Institutional Research, no. 70. San Francisco: Jossey-Bass.

CHAPTER 33

USING ETHNOGRAPHIC FIELDWORK AND CASE STUDIES TO GUIDE STUDENT AFFAIRS PRACTICE

PETER M. MAGOLDA

The author advocates conducting and reading about ethnographic fieldwork as two ways for student affairs educators to enhance practice. He uses his most recent fieldwork experience along with published ethnographic texts about college students to illustrate three benefits of these ways of coming to know students.

Good practice in student affairs uses high-quality information about students, their learning, their needs, and campus environments to design programs, activities, policies, and systematic change strategies to achieve stated learning goals. (American College Personnel Association/National Association of Student Personnel Administrators, 1997, p. 38).

In this chapter advocate conducting and reading about ethnographic fieldwork as two ways for student affairs educators to enhance practice.

Witherell and Noddings (1991) argued that:

narrative and dialogue can serve as a model for teaching and learning across boundaries of disciplines, professions, and cultures. . . . The power of narrative and dialogue as contributors to reflective awareness in teachers and students is that they provide opportunities for deepened relations with others and serve as springboards for ethical action. (p. 8)

Hopefully, the narratives included in this article will encourage readers to use ethnographic fieldwork and case studies to guide student affairs practice. Through them, I invite readers to reflect and engage in dialogue leading to what Witherell and Noddings refer to as "ethical action."

A Personal Story

In 1987, I chaired my university's alcohol and other drug education committee (AODC). An eclectic mix of university and community representatives—a staff psychologist, a senior residence life administrator, three students, three faculty members, a police officer, the university's alcohol educator, a tavern owner, and an emergency medical technician (EMT)—attended the monthly meetings. Unlike other more conventional agenda-driven committee meetings, discussions about what we encountered in day-to-day practice dominated our time together.

Occasionally, the AODC invited students previously involved in drug-related incidents to attend meetings. Informal interviews conducted by the committee resulted in students telling

---

"Using Ethnographic Fieldwork and Case Studies to Guide Student Affairs Practice." Reprinted from *Journal of College Student Development* 40, no.1 (1999), by permission of the American College Personnel Association.

stories ranging from inspiring to tragic. These interviews were mutually beneficial. Committee members learned about student culture and students learned about the university's committee culture. The AODC periodically examined and discussed campus alcohol-related artifacts, ranging from the university alcohol policy to student-designed flyers advertising off-campus parties. Two primary aims of these physical artifact reviews were to reveal the implicit and explicit symbolic messages communicated by the administrators and students and to juxtapose espoused values with operational practices.

The AODC's discussions illuminated the inherent complexities of being a college student and administrator. But more importantly, the discussions altered the way members engaged in their day-to-day practice. Most notably, the committee recognized the importance of subscribing to a cultural perspective in higher education. Hays (1994) defined culture as:

> a social, durable, layered pattern of cognitive and normative systems that are at once material and ideal, objective and subjective, embodied in artifacts and embedded in behaviors, passed about in interaction, internalized in personalities and externalized in institutions. . . . Culture is a social structure with a logic of its own. (p. 65)

Culture, manifested in multiple forms (e.g., language, behaviors, architecture) was a theoretical lens through which AODC members interpreted students' cognitive and normative systems. This lens revealed the interplay of social, political, historical, and economic influences on the university as well as on student subcultures.

Toward the middle of the second semester, the AODC veered from its fieldwork-based discussions to administer a survey aimed at ascertaining students' use of alcohol and other drugs. At the end of the year, the vice president for student affairs requested an annual report from the committee; survey findings dominated the report. Stories based on participant observations, interviews, and document analysis were omitted because they just did not fit the committee's notions of "appropriate" content for an annual report. In retrospect, this decision was disappointing, because our case studies were abundant, enlightening, and useful.

Unknown to me in at the time the AODC's discussions and actions were a microcosm of a larger debate in higher education—specifically, the role of qualitative fieldwork in guiding practice (see Smith & Hesshusius, 1986). That is, should observations occurring in a natural setting (e.g., emergency room) where a person (e.g., an EMT) is the subjective instrument for data collection, leading to a particular interpretation, and presented in a case study format, "count" as credible ways to influence change? Although the AODC and individual members used case studies to alter their own thinking, they did not trust that the university would see them as acceptable ways to think about practice.

The AODC, with the exception of their survey activities, instinctively engaged in an ethnographic case study process, gathering data by using tools (e.g., observations, unstructured interviews, and document analysis) traditionally associated with qualitative inquiry. Schwandt (1997) defines ethnography as:

> The process and product of describing and interpreting cultural behavior . . . both anthropological and sociological definitions of ethnography stress the centrality of culture as the analytic concept that informs the doing of ethnography. Ethnography unites both process and product, fieldwork and written text. Fieldwork, undertaken as participant observation, is the process by which the ethnographer comes to know a culture; the ethnographic text is how culture is portrayed. (p. 44)

The AODC's ethnographic process involved qualitative methods to become intimately familiar with the various student cultures, interpreting the cultural behavior of students with the ultimate aim of enriching understanding of students' involvement with alcohol and other drugs. The committee's ethnographic processes and products were nowhere as purposeful, prolonged, or substantive as Schwandt's (1997) vision of ethnography; however these ethnographic case studies relied on a set of values commonly associated with qualitative ethnographic fieldwork. The committee focused on the particular, rather than theorizing grand schemes that explain substance abuse. Collectively, the committee advocated a personal rather than an impersonal or detached role when interacting with students, recognizing that the committee influenced students and vice versa. The committee also recognized and sought out multiple constructed realities, that is, avoiding the quest for "the" answer, opting for the identification of multiple perspectives from multiple stakeholders.

The AODC gathered cultural data using ethnographic methods, subscribed to values that underpin qualitative inquiry, and interpreted students' actions through a cultural lens. Yet, when asked to summarize the essence of their work, in the form of an annual report, the committee ignored their ethnographic case studies, favoring more conventional evidence, such as survey data. Although the latter were useful and educational and resulted in accolades for the committee, too many of the complexities, contradictions, and paradoxes intricately intertwined with students' use of alcohol and other drugs were discarded.

As student affairs educators, an informal version of the ethnographic process is part of our everyday professional practice. Like the AODC members these professionals experience a sense of competence and comfort in participating and observing students, formally and informally interviewing them, and studying and drawing conclusions about relevant physical artifacts. Yet, too often, like the AODC, student affairs staff members remain ill at ease with using ethnographic fieldwork case studies to guide practice. Ethnographic fieldwork as a method for collecting data appears too subjective and fieldwork-generated reports appear unsophisticated and lax. Fieldwork stories are typically ignored; if used they are bracketed, appended, or accompanied by a laundry list of disclaimers.

The reluctance to embrace ethnographic fieldwork case studies as a means of enhancing practice still exists in 1997. For example, I require graduate students enrolled in my program evaluation seminar to conduct a semester-long program evaluation. Students are attracted to qualitative approaches to program evaluation that are based on fieldwork (see Worthen, Sanders, & Fitzpatrick, 1997). Yet, they express lingering doubts about whether clients will value or take seriously their propensity toward qualitatively driven program evaluations.

What I advocate is more attention to the informal everyday ethnographic dynamics of student affairs work and the use of case studies to strengthen that work. Obviously, not every student affairs staff member can come to know and gather information about students through fieldwork. Learning to: design an ethnographic research study, gain informed consent, listen, watch, record, maintain confidentiality, analyze, theorize, and tell stories are skills that many ethnographers spend their lifetime refining. Although the complex task of conducting ethnographic research is best left to the trained and seasoned ethnographer, this does not preclude student affairs professionals from becoming ethnographic inquirers. That is, they can apply elements of qualitative research (e.g., open-ended interviews) and methodologies (e.g., ethnography) as one of many ways to come to know and gather information about students (for a full discussion of the nature of ethnographic research and corresponding assumptions see Denzin & Lincoln, 1994; Hammersley, 1992; Hammersley & Adkinson, 1983; Lareau & Schultz, 1996.)

My 1987 AODC experience spawned my interest in ethnography as a viable process and product of learning about students. Since then, I have engaged in several ethnographic field studies and I have become an avid reader of ethnographic texts that endorse the adaptation of a cultural perspective in student affairs practice (see Kuh, 1993; Kuh & Whitt, 1988), offer accounts of student culture (see Loeb, 1994; Moffatt, 1989; Sanday, 1990), and ethnographic journeys of faculty members (Brinkley, 1993; Kluge, 1993).

My uneasiness with ethnography, which was rooted in my inability to communicate to others its benefits, has subsided. From these field experiences and reading of ethnographic texts, I have identified three ways that doing and reading ethnographic case studies has enhanced my practice. A brief overview of my most recent fieldwork experience, along with published ethnographic texts about college students, illustrates these three benefits.

My most recent ethnographic undertaking was an intensive 6-week study of formal campus rituals that occurred just before and just after the first day of classes in late August, 1996. A sampling of the rituals included: convocation, first-year student move-in day, campus tours, international student orientation, and the first football game of the season. Of particular interest were the ways faculty, student affairs staff, and returning students used rituals to transmit to their newest members "their ways" with respect to becoming a contributing member of the university community.

The setting for this participant-observation study was a four-year medium sized public institution with an enrollment of 16,000 students. Data for this study were gathered via participant-observations (see Jogensen, 1989) of the public rituals, coupled with in-depth unstructured interviews (see Fontana & Frey, 1994) with ritual organizers and participants and analysis of written and audiovisual publications (see Hodder, 1994).

Benefits of Fieldwork and Ethnograpic Case Studies

Provide Access to Students' Experience and Culture

An underused strategy for accessing students' experience and culture is solicitation of their stories. When I formally interview students during my fieldwork, I usually begin by asking them to "tell me a story that would sensitize me to what it is like to be a student." This intentionally open-ended request provides interviewees maximum degrees of freedom to set the agenda for our discussion. During one interview after asking a student to tell me a story about his residential college experience, he paused for a few seconds (it felt like minutes) then apologetically replied that he was seldom asked to tell his story. As a student affairs educator, I should have been the one to apologize, not the student.

The student's apologetic confession provoked me to reflect on my interactions with students. I drew four tentative conclusions. First, we student affairs practitioners converse with students, but seldom ask them to tell their stories. Second, we structure informal conversations or formal interviews around what we want to know, not what students want to tell us. Third, students cherish the chance to tell their stories. And fourth, stories students deem as irrelevant and diversionary are anything but that. I recount two stories, one from my ritual study and the second from a published ethnographic case study about women to elaborate on these four points.

During my ritual study, I observed first-year students' moving into a men's residence hall their first day on campus. The hall housed one hundred eighty-six students, eight paraprofessional staff, and one full-time advisor. Through-out the day, I observed first hand and up close, numerous rituals associated with students' first day of college—checking into the residence hall, meeting roommates, saying good-bye to parents and loved ones, setting up the room, attending the first corridor meeting, and going off-campus for some late night (early morning) action.

Although students were my primary focus, I serendipitously met Helen, an elderly African American woman, in the residence hall lounge. Both of us were trying to locate a cool room to rest on that hot, humid August morning. We chatted as we sipped punch and snacked on cookies. Although I never intended to interview her, I explained my purpose for being in the hall and casually asked her to tell me a story about her day. After conveying her surprise that I was a professor she began her story. Without asking a single question, I learned that: (a) her grandson was moving into the hall as we spoke, (b) he was a first-year student, (c) the family was from Columbus, Ohio, (d) the college-bound entourage had arisen at 5:00 a.m. to pack the car and get a jump on the bumper-to-bumper traffic predicted for the sleepy college town, and (e) her grandson and his mother were in his room organizing his belongings. I followed Helen's lead by telling a short story about myself. I informed her that I taught graduate students in the school of education and described my research interests. Helen countered with a story about her daughter and granddaughter who are elementary school teachers.

With the perfunctory exchanging of introductory stories complete, we could have cordially parted ways. I was in no hurry to brave the sweltering heat outside. As I paused, not sure what to say next, Helen continued. She conveyed how proud she was that her grandson was attending a college "with a good reputation." She boasted about his scholarship, then lamented that he was attending a school so far away from home. The 2-hour trip to Columbus did not seem "far" to me, but as Helen talked about her grandson's close relationship with family and some of his unique contributions to the family, I better understood her concern. Our conversation reminded me that students were not the only ones who made adjustments when going off to college. As we refilled our punch cups, she began to divulge dreams, fears, aspirations, and career goals as they related to her grandson.

Soon after we parted, I relocated to the steps in the back of the building and began to record comments about our exchange. Later that week when I transcribed the tape, I was reminded of something that I already knew, that I probably learned more by listening to Helen's stories than by asking a predetermined set of questions aimed at eliciting responses to particular domains that interested me. I refrained from asking follow-up questions that would satisfy my curiosity. Listening patiently to Helen's story resulted in most of my questions being answered. I allowed Helen maximum degrees of freedom to tell her story, and a marvelous and moving story it was. Although at times I felt like I was imposing too much on her time, I took Helen's complimentary comments at face value; she told me that she enjoyed our conversation. As we parted ways, she speculated that her "ramblings" would not be useful for my study, but I knew otherwise. Helen's stories reminded me that students' experience is not limited to the campus; they are part of a larger family network that mediates their college experience.

Asking students to tell stories and listening carefully to them were two aims of Dorothy Holland and Margaret Eisenhart in *Educated in Romance* (1990), their ethnographic study about women's identity development, achievements, and campus culture. The following passage from this ethnography further illustrates the power of allowing students to tell their stories. This passage is about a college woman's reflections on high school:

> I did not date as much or as frequently or as seriously as my [high school] friends did. I was more into male friends. The guys I liked, I saw them, but they weren't by any stretch of the imagination, beaus. . . . My theory was you had to have a friendship first and then you could have a relationship, whereas some of my friends were just hot to trot, and they wanted the relationships and forget the friendships, and a lot of times, [the relationship] didn't work out. (p. 144–145)

Throughout their book, Holland and Eisenhart encouraged students to tell their stories and allowed students to focus on what was important to them, not what was important to the researchers. The students they interviewed were receptive to the storytelling requests and the sto-

ries enriched the researchers' understanding of student life.

A Robert Coles story (1989) that chronicled his medical school residency in a psychiatric unit of a hospital is focused on his relationship with two of his supervising psychiatrists. Cole's story crystallizes the benefits of encouraging storytelling and active listening.

During a supervisory meeting about a phobic patient, one supervisor, Dr. Binger, insisted that Coles read more extensively in the psychiatric literature to understand better the nature of the patient's phobias. Binger's primary concern was correctly diagnosing and treating the patient. Dr. Ludwig, Coles' other supervisor, offered different advice. During supervisory meetings, Ludwig seldom talked. Instead, he listened carefully to Coles' stories and encouraged Coles to do the same with his patients. Ludwig urged Coles to view patients as human storytellers, not as patients whom he had to "get a fix on." Ludwig argued that patients' stories contained reservoirs of wisdom that were essential for physicians' understanding and subsequent care. In Ludwig's model, patients were participants in the diagnosis and prognosis phases of recovery, not passive recipients. Coles struggled with the conflicting approaches to care. He eventually embraced Ludwig's model that advocated creating partnerships, encouraging the telling of stories, listening, recording impressions faithfully, and comprehending patients' stories as fully as possible.

Coles believed that in order to speak, one must listen—an axiom that should guide student affairs staffs' interactions with students. By genuinely listening, staff can access students' experiences from students' vantage points rather than their own. Often, when interacting with students, information is gathered with the intention of diagnosing and treating. My conversations with Helen, and Holland and Eisenhart's discussion with their respondent, were not intended to diagnose and treat their "afflictions." That is, I did not try to remedy Helen's concerns about her grandson's moving away from home, nor did Holland and Eisenhart try to respond to the woman's concern by designing an intervention. In both instances the advice of Coles—create partnerships, encourage storytelling, and listen carefully—was heeded.

Williams (1997) recognized the power of storytelling, and reminded readers that students tell stories in different ways. He noted:

> Our students bring us their stories, written in the language of their families and cultures. There are many chapters complete even before we make that first contact.... Our students usually tell their stories in less conventional forms through their opinions, their actions, their decisions. We must be receptive to each of these, and constantly on the lookout for other tales they tell. (p. 3)

Sage advice for student affairs professionals.

Provide Access to Student and Campus Culture

Patton's (1990) advice to qualitative researchers who are interpreting data—make the obvious obvious, make the obvious dubious, and make the hidden obvious—is sage advice for student affairs educators. Understanding student and campus culture can be deepened by affirming what we already know (i.e., making the obvious obvious), questioning what we think we already know (i.e., making the obvious dubious), and surfacing new insights (i.e., making the hidden obvious). As part of my 1996 ritual study, I took a campus tour conducted by the admissions office. My agenda was purposeful; I wanted to experience firsthand how cultural norms, values, beliefs, and so on were communicated to prospective members.

As we wound our way across campus, I paid careful attention to the physical surroundings and listened to the scripted and impromptu comments of the guide and questions asked by tour participants. The tour guide identified campus landmarks, rattled off university milestones, conveyed important demographic information about current students and faculty, casually mentioned admission expectations, conducted a crash course on the campus lexicon, offered helpful application hints, detailed curricular and cocurricular opportunities, and delivered a carefully crafted campus history lesson.

Not only did the guide provide concrete, uncontested campus information such as application deadlines, names of buildings, and graduation rates, he subtly conveyed numerous cherished values of the institution and institutional expectations for its members. For exam-

ple, at one point during the tour, the guide recounted a familiar campus folktale of how, when the new library opened, students and faculty stood side by side in a single-file line and passed books, one by one, from the old to the new building. Students and their parents smiled and nodded with approval as the story concluded. The tale subtly conveyed to prospective members of the campus community seminal campus values and ideals such as community service, teamwork, and close faculty-student interactions.

Certain segments of the tour made the obvious obvious; they affirmed what I already knew about the campus culture—the rhythms of the semester, the human scale of the campus, the homogeneous architectural style of campus buildings, the numerous curricular and cocurricular opportunities available to students, and the state-of-the art features of the new $22 million recreation facility. Some tour aspects made the obvious dubious by challenging my "conventional wisdom" on the topic. Prior to the tour, I predicted that the guide would concentrate on academic-related issues and prospective students and their parents would ask "big picture" questions about the university. Instead, issues of life outside the classroom dominated the guide's commentary, and participants asked specific questions such as, "Do the dorms have single or double beds?" "What kinds of computers does the university support, Mac or IBM?" "Why is sorority rush second semester?" These comments and questions challenged my tacit assumptions about campus and student cultures.

As the tour concluded, I realized that certain assumptions about the campus culture were hidden from me. That is, despite being a member of the community, I did not know about these aspects of the campus culture. For example, that (a) thousands of students visit the new recreation building daily, (b) the percentage of tenured faculty members who teach and collaborate on research with undergraduates is well above the national average, and (3) the institution has one of the largest study abroad programs in the United States.

Brief ethnographic field experiences, like the campus tour, can make the obvious obvious, the obvious dubious and the hidden obvious. Yet, similar benefits can be realized by reading and discussing ethnographic texts about college students or university environments. After reading Rhoads's (1995) ethnographic case study of a fraternity, his descriptions of the positive (e.g., brotherhood and social status associated with fraternity membership) and negative (e.g., drinking games and outlandish macho pranks and ordeals) aspects of fraternal life affirmed many of my preconceived views. These obvious aspects of fraternal life were recognizable in the opening passage of the manuscript:

> Around the table in a corner of the basement party room sits 10 fraternity brothers. In the middle of the table is a large pitcher of beer, and in front of the brothers are glasses filled with varying amounts of beer. Nine pairs of eyes fixate on one of the brothers, who appears to be telling some sort of story. The brothers lean forward to hear more clearly, as do the 12 or so onlookers, who encircle the 10 brothers seated around the table. The onlookers are mostly women, whose wrinkled brows, squinting eyes, and half-hearted smiles reveal both their confusion and amusement. (p. 306)

As Rhoads explained the inner workings of the fraternity, some of what was obvious to me became doubtful. For example, prior to reading the manuscript, I believed that the pledging process negatively influenced the fraternal socialization process. Yet, within this particular fraternity, this socialization occurred in different ways since the fraternity eliminated its formal pledge process. Rhoads' descriptions and interpretations revealed ways that other more subtle rituals, besides pledging, socialized new members. Rhoads' narratives and analyses challenged my conventional wisdom and invited me to revisit my preconceptions.

Most importantly, Rhoads' ethnographic case study made the hidden obvious. Numerous stories explicated the exploitation and victimization of women and how this particular fraternity continued to reproduce a culture of oppression. Rhoads included comments made by one woman who participated in one of the fraternity's lavaliering rituals to demonstrate the passive role of women within the fraternity structure:

> Several brothers came to my dorm room and blindfolded me. They told me that they couldn't tell me where or what was going on—although I had my suspicions. I was taken to a room in the basement of Alpha Beta, where rituals and ceremonies are normally performed. My blindfold was eventually removed, and I could see the room was filled with brothers wearing their robes used for fraternity rituals. . . . At first I was a bit nervous, but then I saw my boyfriend and I knew everything was all right. (p. 316)

Rhoads deconstructed this ritual focusing on the woman's powerlessness and requisite blind faith in a process over which she had no input or control. Although the woman spoke favorably of the ritual of which she was a part, Rhoads argued that while women were involved in fraternity life, their roles were subservient. Culture, although it may be hidden from the brothers, women, or the readers, becomes visible.

Not every ethnographic tale will be transformative, that is, provoke the reader to think dramatically differently about an experience. Yet a major benefit of using ethnographic fieldwork and case studies is that they allow readers to pause for a moment and reflect on the familiar or the new. Student affairs staff could benefit from affirming, disconfirming, or learning something new about student culture.

Enhance Practice Through Informed Theorizing

LeCompte and Preissle's (1993) discussion of how one engages in the process of ethnographic theorizing provides a necessary backdrop for understanding how ethnographic case studies can lead to sound theorizing on the part of student affairs faculty and staff. LeCompte and Preissle purport that ethnographic theorizing:

> consists of all modes of thinking upon which analysis is built: perceiving, comparing, contrasting, aggregating and ordering, establishing linkages and relationships, and speculating is a cognitive process of discovering or manipulating abstract categories and relationships among those categories. It consists of playing with data and ideas. (p. 238–239)

Although not as linear and rational a process as it appears, early steps in LeCompte and Preissle's theorizing process include uncovering conceptual categories embedded in the social phenomena, developing classification themes, then looking at how these classifications are similar and different from each other. Inductively, theory emerges from the field experience (LeCompte & Preissle).

LeCompte and Preissle (1993) define and operationalize the process of theorizing; however it is not something that most student affairs professionals recognize themselves doing as part of their daily routines. Strange and King's (1990) discussion about the nature of applied fields, like student affairs, clarifies the profession's estrangement from theory. They note:

> Success in an applied field tends to be gauged in terms of what an individual has done. Accomplishments accumulated over time lead to a successful "track record" which, in turn, becomes the mark of an experienced and "seasoned practitioner." Individuals must "pay their dues" as an apprentice, learning from those who have "been there." Advancement is contingent upon a succession of responsibilities and assignments. Basic knowledge, such as theory, that is acquired through traditional schooling is both a source of mistrust and perhaps even a threat to those already practicing in the field. It may be a source of mistrust for several reasons. Claims of expertise, grounded in "what you know" rather than "what you have done," will predictably be met with suspicion in an applied field. This is especially true of a field like student affairs where interaction with people is paramount. Nothing substitutes for experience and maturity in terms of learning about and responding to the complexities of human behaviors. Consequently, a status claim based on "what you know" (e.g., knowledge of current theory) rather than "what you have done" is understandably threatening because it tends to undercut the experiential foundation of the field. (pp. 18–19)

Although the profession persists in resisting theory, doing ethnographic fieldwork and reading case studies alter the ways one might understand, generate, and use theory. Two examples—the first based on my ritual study and the second on an ethnographic study of a college men's basketball program—illustrate this point.

In 1996, one formal campus ritual I attended was new student orientation. During one orientation session current and new students informally met to discuss campus life. A returning student made a seemingly innocuous comment about students heading uptown (the epicenter of off-campus social life) with a date to party after a long week of classes. Implicitly, he conveyed values, beliefs, and practices that were deemed "normal" by the dominant student culture. Carefully exploring the intent of his comment, I concluded that "normal" students were: heterosexual, unmarried, interested in dating, attending college full-time, prone to consuming alcohol, and living on campus. Although these assumptions apply to about 70% of the undergraduate population, I could not help but wonder how the other "abnormal" 30% of students interpreted this comment.

I would not draw any definitive conclusions about the student culture based on this one student's single comment. Nonetheless "conveying normalized expectations" was, in the words of LeCompte and Preissle (1993), a "conceptual category" that emerged while reflecting on many of the rituals I encountered. For example, the director of international education subtly conveyed to new international graduate students what "normal" international graduate students do when attending graduate school in the United States. Similarly, a science professor talking to her students during their first class, conveyed how "normal" aspiring scientists act. Although the word "normal" was never spoken by anyone I observed, this conceptual category led me to theorize about the connection between rituals and ritual organizers' desire to create and sustain normalized communities. Exploring how selective traditions sustain "normalizing" communities that legitimized the dominant culture moved to the forefront of my consciousness. I began to understand better the ways that normalizing communities define a cultural center or norm situating the "other[s]" on the margins and privilege some individuals who are represented as normal (see Carlson, 1994).

Adler and Adler (1991), in their ethnography about a men's college basketball team, engaged in a different form of theorizing. Their fieldwork revealed that the socialization of basketball players necessitated that they devalue nearly everything, especially academics, except activities that resulted in enhanced on-court performance. Role engulfment was the theoretical lens through which Adler and Adler came to understand the players' collegiate experience. A brief passage illustrates how, in the words of a player, basketball engulfed him:

In college the coaches are a lot more concerned on winning and the money comin' in. If they don't win, they may get the boot, and so they pass that pressure onto us athaletes [sic]. . . . I go to bed every night and I be thinkin' 'bout basketball. That's what college athaletics [sic] do to you. It take over your mind. (p. 85)

Ethnographic theorizing offers numerous benefits for practice. Theorizing helps develop a unified, systematic explanation of phenomena. For example, Adler and Adler's concept of role engulfment represents a unified systematic explanation of athletes' behaviors. Theorizing requires that one engage in a cognitive process of discovery based on playing with data and ideas. This form of theorizing necessitates a blending of what Strange and King (1990) refer to as what one has done and what one knows. The quality of ethnographic theorizing is influenced by experiential learning (e.g., fieldwork) and the establishment of interpersonal relationships with those in the field. Both are strengths of the student affairs profession according to Strange and King.

The doing and reading of ethnography closes the gap between student affairs practitioners and theory that Strange and King (1990) note, but more importantly, ethnographic theorizing is a prerequisite to altering oppressive cultural conditions (e.g. normalized communities, engulfed athletes). Rhoads and Black's (1995) discussion of a critical cultural perspective—a contemporary wave of student affairs theorizing—further clarifies how ethnographic theorizing can shape student affairs practice. Rhoads and Black's critical cultural perspective integrates four distinct yet interconnected theories: feminism, critical theory, postmodernism, and multiculturalism. This perspective places cultural understanding at the epicenter of theorizing and integrates theory and practice so that individuals and groups can illuminate contradictions and distortions in their beliefs and practices. The aim for those theorizing using a critical cultural perspective is to "help student affairs practitioners understand the power of culture, and, in so doing, enable them to engage in campus transformation intended to dismantle oppressive cultural conditions" (p. 413). If the student affairs profession is going to implement the transformative agenda that Rhoads and Black (1995) advocate, ethnographic theorizing must go hand-in-hand with practice.

Implications for Student Affairs Practice

Student affairs professionals must develop multiple, effective strategies that respond to the question: "How do we come to know about and gather useful information about students, their learning, their needs, and their environments?" This manuscript offers two effective strategies for student affairs staff to come to know and gather high-quality information—by conducting informal fieldwork and reading ethnographic texts based on others' fieldwork. Doing and reading about fieldwork can be effective prerequisites to designing programs, policies, activities, and change strategies. Incorporating these two strategies in student affairs would involve at least three components.

Making Better Use of Ethnographic Literature

Reading and collectively discussing ethnographic texts can enhance student affairs practice. Having a staff read and discuss an ethnographic text or having a student affairs staff member facilitate a discussion with a fraternity after, for example, reading Rhoads' (1995) ethnographic account and interpretation of a fraternity, can act as a springboard to substantively discuss complex problems (e.g., oppression of women) that too often are ignored or discussed in antiseptic or superficial ways. The reading and discussing of ethnographic texts can also model for students and staff ways to enhance the intellectual climate of the university and blur the archaic dualism between student affairs and academic affairs. Reading about and discussing higher education cultures is one way to reaffirm student affairs' role as centrally involved in intellectual, not simply affective, aspects of students' development.

Acting on "Ethnographic Instincts"

Schwandt (1997) argues that ethnography is a process (fieldwork) and product (written text). As the AODC narrative suggests, student affairs staff regularly employ informal ethnographic processes to enrich understanding about students. Specifically, they possess basic fieldwork skills, have access to cultural scenes, engage in fieldwork, gather cultural data, and describe culture (see Spradley & McCurdy, 1972). Student affairs staff: (a) recognize the value of engaging in fieldwork and listening to stories about other people's fieldwork experiences; (b) effectively employ "alternative" data collection techniques (i.e., participant-observations, interviews, document analysis) to gather information about students; (c) keenly understand the advantages of viewing student life through a cultural lens; and (d) recognize that listening to stories can simultaneously be affirming, disorienting, and enlightening.

Yet, student affairs staffs, like AODC members, are less comfortable with ethnographic products (e.g., incorporating ethnographic narratives into an annual report). What "counts" as evidence continues to be defined narrowly using traditional measures, despite the profession's intrigue, competencies, and propensities toward alternate ways of knowing and reporting. In the AODC example, surveys "counted" whereas the participant-observations, for example, were perceived as too particular, anecdotal, and subjective. Student affairs staff could benefit from incorporating their ethnographic instincts into their professional decision-making.

Enhancing Skills in Ethnographic Inquiry

Schwandt (1997), when discussing inquiry, makes a distinction between method and methodology. The former is a procedure, technique, or tool used to generate and analyze data. Schwandt defines the latter as a theory of how inquiry should proceed. He elaborates:

> The study of methodology includes examination of general theories about human behavior, society, and, more broadly, human nature itself; specific hypotheses about what phenomena are important to study; assumptions about the relationships between warrants, evidence, and the nature of inferences, and what constitutes legitimate knowledge; assumptions about the integrity, completeness, and thoroughness of various data sources; assumptions about casualty; and so on. (p. 94)

Conducting and reading about ethnographic fieldwork provides opportunities for student affairs staff to become better technicians or methods experts. They will likely become more proficient at observing, interviewing, analyzing documents, facilitating discussions, and writing.

All are important contributions to the profession, institutions, and students. More importantly, conducting and reading about ethnographic fieldwork invites student affairs staffs to grapple with methodological issues that are at the heart of many of the profession's struggles such as where should we devote our time, what should we study, what counts as evidence and legitimate knowledge. Embracing a qualitative methodology, among other benefits, reminds professionals that multiple constructed realities exist, that knowledge can be created by describing individual cases, and that history and context matter. Simply stated, enhancing skills in ethnographic inquiry leads to sound and theoretically grounded practice.

Conclusion

Witherell and Noddings (1991) note that:

> We live and grow in interpretive, or meaning-making, communities; that stories help us find our place in the world; and that caring, respectful dialogue among all engaged in educational settings—students, teachers, administrators—serves as the crucible for our coming to understand ourselves, others, and the possibilities life holds for us. (p. 10)

Doing ethnographic fieldwork and reading existing ethnographic case studies provide student affairs staff members with new ways to access and interpret these meaning-making communities and engage in respectful dialogue. More importantly both encourage staff to reexamine who they are and what they believe. My motivation for undertaking my ritual study was to learn about "the other." That is, I started out wanting to learn more about college students, in particular how they are socialized through participation in formal rituals sanctioned by the university. Eventually I realized that although I learned much about "the other" (e.g., students), I learned most about myself. Understanding oneself is essential to genuine engagement in the respectful dialogue Witherell and Noddings (1991) advocate. By understanding oneself, staff members can expand their professional roles to include interpreter, biographer, advocate, and transformative leader. These roles are particularly important as student affairs professionals continue the quest to better understand students and their needs in order to design programs and policies that meet these challenges as the next millennium approaches.

References

American College Personnel Association/The National Association of Student Personnel Administrators. (1997). *Defining principles of good practice for student affairs.* Washington, DC: Author.

Adler, P. A., & Adler, P. (1991). *Backboards and blackboards. College athletes and role engulfment.* New York: Columbia University Press.

Brinkley, D. (1993). *The majic bus: An American odyssey.* New York: Harcourt, Brace, & Company.

Carlson, D. (1994, Fall). Gayness, multicultural education, and community, *Educational Foundations,* 5–25.

Coles, R. (1989). *The call of stories: Teaching and the moral imagination.* Boston: Houghton Mifflin.

Denzin, N. K., & Lincoln, Y. S. (Eds.). (1994). *Handbook for qualitative research.* Newbury Park, CA: Sage.

Fontana, A., & Frey, J. H. (1994). Interviewing: The art of science. In N. K. Denzin & Y. S. Lincoln (Eds.), *Handbook of qualitative research* (pp. 361–376). Thousand Oaks, CA: Sage.

Hammersley, M. (1992). *What's wrong with ethnography?* London: Routledge.

Hammersley, M., & Atkinson, P. (1983). *Ethnography: Principles in practice.* London: Routledge.

Hays, S. (1994). Structure and agency and the sticky problem with culture. *Sociological Theory, 12*(1), 57–72.

Hodder, I. (1994). The interpretation of documents and material culture. In N. K. Denzin & Y. S. Lincoln (Eds.), *Handbook of qualitative research* (pp. 393–412). Thousand Oaks, CA: Sage.

Holland, D. C., & Eisenhart, M. A. (1990). *Educated in romance: Women, achievement, and college culture.* Chicago: University of Chicago Press.

Jorgensen, D. L. (1989). *Participant Observation: A methodology for human studies.* (Vol. 15). Newbury Park, CA: Sage.

Kluge, P. F. (1993). *Alma mater: A college homecoming.* Reading, MA: Addison-Wesley.

Kuh, G. D. (Ed.). (1993). *Using cultural perspectives in student affairs.* Washington, DC: American College Personnel Association.

Kuh, G. D., & Whitt, E. J. (1988). *The invisible tapestry: Culture in American colleges and universities.* Washington, DC: Association for the Study of Higher Education.

Lareau, A., & Shultz, J. (Eds.). (1996). *Journeys through ethnography: Realistic accounts of fieldwork.* Boulder, CO: Westview Press.

LeCompte, M. D., & Preissle, J. (1993). *Ethnography and qualitative design in educational research* (2nd ed.). San Diego, CA: Academic Press.

Loeb, P. R. (1994). *Generation at the crossroads: Apathy and action on the American campus.* New Brunswick, NJ: Rutgers University Press.

Moffatt, M. (1989). *Coming of age in New Jersey: College and American culture.* Rutgers, NJ: Rutgers University Press.

Patton, M. Q. (1990). *Qualitative evaluation and research methods.* Newbury Park, CA: Sage.

Rhoads, R. (1995). Whale tales, dog piles, and beer goggles: An ethnographic case study of fraternity life. *Anthropology and Education Quarterly, 26,* 306–323.

Rhoads, R., & Black, M. (1995). Student affairs practitioners as transformative educators: Advancing a critical cultural perspective. *Journal of College Student Development, 36,* 413–421.

Sanday, P. R. (1990). *Fraternity gang rape: Sex, brotherhood, and privilege on campus.* New York: New York University Press.

Schwandt, T. A. (1997). *Qualitative Inquiry: A dictionary of terms.* Thousand Oaks, CA: Sage.

Smith, J. K., & Heshusius, L. (1986, January). Closing down the conversation: The end of the quantitative-qualitative debate among educational inquirers. *Educational Researcher, 15,* 4–12.

Spradley, J., & McCurdy, D. W. (1972). *The cultural experience: Ethnography in complex society.* Chicago: Science Research Associates.

Strange, C. C., & King, P. A. (1990). The professional practice of student development. In D. G. Creamer (Ed.). *College student development: Theory and practice for the 1990s* (9–24). Alexandria. VA: American College Personnel Association.

Williams, L. B. (1997, May/June). Telling tales in school. *About Campus, 2,* 2–3.

Witherell, C., & Noddings, N. (Eds.). (1991). *Stories lives tell: Narrative and dialogue in education.* New York: Teachers College Press.

Worthen, B. R., Sanders, J. R., & Fitzpatrick, J. L. (1997). *Program evaluation: Alternative approaches and practical guidelines.* New York: Longman.

CHAPTER 34

CONDUCTING CONSTRUCTIVIST INQUIRY

KATHLEEN MANNING

Student affairs professionals have struggled since the field's inception to understand the complexities of student development and growth. In this search for knowledge, qualitative research, a method emphasizing depth of understanding over breadth, has been central to the formation of student affairs theory. Arthur Chickering (1969) used data from interviews with Goddard College students to construct his developmental vectors. Carol Gilligan (1982) used qualitative analysis to generate insights about women's psychological development. Marcia Baxter Magolda (1992) in her longitudinal study on epistemological stages used inductive reasoning, a qualitative research method.

Constructivist inquiry emphasizes the multiple perspectives of respondents, ethical obligations of the researcher to her or his respondents, and techniques required to meet standards of quality. Similar to many qualitative research methodologies, constructivist inquiry relies on interviewing, observation, and document analysis as a means of data collection. Data analysis is conducted through an inductive process of culling patterns and themes from the data rather than fitting the data, through deductive reasoning, into categories determined in advance.

Purposes of Constructivist Research

The purpose of constructivist inquiry is to produce depth of understanding about a particular topic or experience. This research differs from conventional quantitative research which defines average or normative behavior, makes generalizations about how all or most people act, and offers common characteristics shared across groups. Qualitative researchers seek *verstehen* or the "profound insight and comprehension of something's/one's essence" (Lincoln, 1988, p. 61). Holistic understanding, meaning-making, and interpretation are essential concerns in qualitative research (Patton, 1990). These methods can generate powerful insights about the complex issues students face in college.

Constructivist inquiry is well-suited to knowledge discovery about campus life. Through an open and trusting relationship between researcher and respondent, a "slice of life" or perspective is shared. These perspectives, expressed in a descriptive and interpretive written account (e.g., case study), are conveyed in all their emotional and personal distinction. The case, if it evokes emotions from the reader, can render a vicarious experience impossible through statistical and quantitative analysis.

Through the meaning communicated in the case studies, campus life can be better understood, college policy decisions more capably fashioned, and administrative decision-making skillfully achieved. The knowledge gained through qualitative research is as rich and complex as the lives upon whom the findings are based. The researcher is successful when she or he untangles the web of complexity that characterizes the respondents' lives and guides the reader to *verstehen*.

"Conducting Constructive Inquiry." Reprinted from *Giving Voice to Critical Campus Issues: Qualitative Research in Student Affairs*, (1999), by permission of American College Personnel Association.

Paradigm Considerations

Constructivist inquiry differs from quantitative research at the level of beliefs or assumptions; the emergent paradigm underscores this method. Assumptions include the idea that truth is not objective but rather socially constructed from the experiences, background, perceptions, and thought processes of humans. The researcher's task is to work diligently to understand the multiple realities of the respondents, research context, and others who influence the information being shared. Since research is generally conducted in communities, the task of sorting through, understanding, and conveying the multiple realities among respondents is one of the most difficult and interesting tasks of constructivist inquiry. The emergent paradigm is represented in physics by theory after Einstein (e.g., relativity, quantum physics), popular films such as "Jurassic Park," and popular business literature such as Peters and Waterman's (1982) *In Search of Excellence.*

Emergent Paradigm Assumptions

The assumptions of the emergent paradigm (Guba, 1985; Guba & Lincoln, 1989; Lincoln & Guba, 1985; Reason & Rowan, 1981) include the following:

1. The researcher and respondent have a close, subjective, collaborative relationship;

2. The research products are not generalizable to all or most circumstances but, rather, interpretable only within local contexts. Insight, meaning, and understanding, rather than broad application, are the goals of the research;

3. Rather than a singular Truth which holds reliably in all cases, multiple truths are socially constructed, time- and history-bound. Most important, there are many truths depending on the points of view of those involved in the research;

4. The methodology cannot escape, nor does it try to escape, the values of those involved: researcher, research setting, methodology, underlying theory, and respondents.

These emergent paradigm assumptions are expressed in several ways:

Trust

Trust was carefully built and scrupulously maintained between the researchers and respondents. The respondents were not simply means to acquire data. Data were obtained from respondents in a process emphasizing respect, collaboration, and reciprocity.

Co-constructed Interpretations

In keeping with the trust built through the data collection phase, the researchers did not single-handedly analyze the data, compile the findings, and write the case study. The researchers worked with their respondents to co-construct the interpretations, determine the information to be presented in the case studies, and choose a case study format in concert with the respondents' style. As such, the task of writing each case study, while the responsibility of the researcher, was guided by the respondent.

Value Driven

Values are understood always to affect research and can be used as lenses through which to interpret the data. To ignore the values of the researcher, respondents, or research setting means to overlook major sources of influence and insight: the perspectives through which people construct and view their realities and truths.

Researcher Assumptions

Since it is taken as a given that values will affect the study, an essential aspect of constructivist inquiry is an examination of the researcher's assumptions. The researcher scrutinizes her or his expectations, feelings about the topic under study, and fears and joys concerning the study. The goal of this effort is for the researcher to understand the lenses through which she or he constructs the study's focus, asks interview questions, and chooses the data depicted in the case study. This process of clarifying the researcher's taken for granted assumptions is significantly facilitated by peer debriefing (see High Quality and Rigor section) wherein peers discuss methodology issues, including assumptions "hidden" from the researcher.

Entry and Access to Respondents

Student affairs staff have unique advantages when it comes to gaining access and entry to respondents. Their significant interactions with students, accessibility to various campus offices, and exposure to a broad array of campus life expands their range of choices for research topics and respondents.

Entering a research site and identifying respondents are among the most difficult tasks of qualitative research. While people generally enjoy talking about themselves once contact is made, identifying respondents who are knowledgeable about the topic under study, have sufficient time, and are available through all stages of the research process can be frustrating and fraught with false starts and dead ends.

Entry and access negotiations are not completed when contact is made with the respondent, but take place throughout the research. The focus of the study, consent, and boundary negotiations are explained each time a new respondent is recruited for the study. Attention to the political nature of research and the discomfort that people have about "being studied" are to be heeded. After permission or consent to conduct the study is received from campus authorities, the characteristics necessary to build an adequate sample are determined.

Purposive Sampling

Purposive sampling was originated by Patton (1990) as a strategy by which one could learn or come to understand a particular subject. Unlike random sampling where representativeness for the purpose of generalizing is the goal, the researcher uses purposive sampling to identify people with particular characteristics. The researcher uses criteria to locate respondents who are likely to be knowledgeable about the topic being studied. Patton suggested four categories to guide respondent selection:

> (1) sampling extreme or deviant cases, (2) sampling typical cases, (3) sampling for maximum variation (picking three or four cases that represent a range on some dimension), (4) sampling critical cases, and (5) sampling politically important or sensitive cases (Lincoln, 1985, p. 146).

The emphasis for the enclosed studies centered on choosing respondents who were exemplar representatives of the topic under study. In other words, the respondents chosen included people who had done a significant amount of thinking about the focus of the study. They were people who could articulately express their distinctive experiences. While reticent respondents are not actively avoided in constructivist inquiry, data collected from respondents who enjoy talking about their experiences and point of view is richer and more extensive than data generated from shy, restrained interviewees.

The unethical practice of dual roles (e.g., friend and respondent; employee and respondent) was avoided by the researchers. They contacted respondents who were knowledgeable about the study's focus yet unknown to themselves. Gatekeepers were employed as "go betweens"—persons who serve as points of entry for the researchers (Bogdan & Biklen, 1992). The gatekeeper often made the first contact with the respondent so that the potential interviewee did not feel obligated or unduly pressured to participate in the study. The use of gatekeepers is especially important in research topics which are sensitive and could result in a breach of confidentiality (e.g., rape survival).

Responsibilities to the Respondents

Respondents were apprised of the time commitment being asked of them, degree to which confidentiality could be assured, and requirements of the methodology. Respondents were assured that the data, at all stages of the studies, belonged to them. If at any point the respondent changed her or his mind about participation in the study, she or he was free to cut off contact with the researcher. At this time the researcher was obligated to return all field notes and data. This commitment was reinforced through a consent form, signed by the researcher and respondent, outlining the parameters of the mutually agreed upon arrangement. In many cases, the researcher and respondent negotiated the consent form in a manner which set the tone for the collaborative and co-constructed nature of the research.

Data collection is not a primary concern during access, entry, and respondent identification. Realistically, however, data are collected from the first point of contact with potential respondents until the final parting.

Data Collection

The research summarized in this volume is based on data collection with one or two respondents. Not typical of constructivist or qualitative research, the purpose of this narrow range of respondents was to closely focus the data collection and meaning derived from data analysis. As the instructor of the qualitative research class in which these studies were undertaken, I felt that it would be unethical to ask students to undertake research with a wide, expansive scope. A completed, well-done study with a clearly defined focus is a more productive and preferable contribution to the student affairs field than an incomplete, broadly defined research project. Readers should note that sampling, particularly the appropriate number of respondents, is a highly contested issue in qualitative research. A sufficient number of respondents depends on the focus of the study, depth of data to be collected, and individual characteristics of the research context.

Data collection methods in constructivist research include interviewing (i.e., one-on-one conversations between the researcher and respondent), observation (e.g., meetings, student activities, class presentations), and document analysis (e.g., memos, college yearbooks, student journals, e-mail messages). Interviewing and observation were the predominant methods used in the studies in this book.

Interviews

Multiple interviews were held with the respondents until patterns and themes repeated. When this point of redundancy was reached, the researcher knew that the data collection was nearing an end. Trust was established during the interviewing by asking the respondents to choose the interview site. The emphasis was on the respondents' comfort, not the researchers' convenience.

The research foci were maintained by following Lincoln and Guba's (1985) advice of treating each interview as a "guided conversation" (Guba, 1985). While initially open ended, the guided conversations were not invitations for respondents to discuss anything that came to mind. Questions based on the foci were generated by the researchers in advance of the inter-

views. Many times, these questions were not explicitly asked because the respondents judged the information about the topic which was most important to share. Gentle prompting and competent listening skills often serve the researcher better than a formal interview protocol. But questions generated in advance of the interview assist the researcher when respondents are unsure of the research focus or need prodding to stay on topic.

Observation

In several cases, data were collected by observing the respondent in a particular situation (e.g., classroom, student activity). Skeffington observed her respondent in a class where his alcohol-related death experience became the inspiration for an art project. Wong observed and interviewed his respondent as she conducted her late night custodial responsibilities.

Document Analysis

While document analysis was not used in the studies contained here, the literate culture of higher education generates a rich array of written materials. Letters to home by students, memoranda documenting the evolution of a policy, and electronic mail archives are all sources of written documents. These can be collected and analyzed in the same manner as interview and observation data. The data generated from document analysis are a source of categories, themes, and interpretations.

Data Recording

Data, including direct quotations and respondent observer comments, were noted in a field journal (e.g., steno or legal pad) used during the interview or observation. The data from the field journal were then transcribed and expanded as field notes, usually via a computer. Some researchers, for example Regan with her research concerning acquaintance rape, recorded the respondents and transcribed the interviews verbatim from the audio tape recordings. Regardless of the method used (e.g., transcription or re-constructed notes from memory and the field journal), the field notes became the raw data of the analysis process.

Human as Instrument

The instrument or means of data collection in qualitative research is the human being or researcher. Different from quantitative paper and pencil surveys or instruments, the human as instrument is able to sense feelings, probe promising areas, and closely observe the nuances of human communication. As discussed earlier, the researcher uses his or her lens and personal perspective as a means through which to view the data. As such, she or he needs to be fully aware of how these lenses might distort as well as illuminate what is seen and heard. At all times, the researcher remains cognizant of the fact that the respondent, not the researcher, is the central focus of the research. A researcher with an ax to grind or point to make will over-represent her or himself in the findings and under-represent the respondents. Safeguards against these tendencies (e.g., peer debriefing, prolonged engagement, persistent observation) are discussed below (see High Quality and Rigor).

Data Analysis

Inductive Reasoning

Inductive reasoning begins with the data as a source of interpretation or explanation. This analysis contrasts with the investigative style of deductive reasoning where data verify and/or support hypotheses posited in advance. In other words, in quantitative research, the theory is proposed, data are collected, and the analysis of the data verifies or disproves the theory. In constructivist inquiry, data are collected prior to any theorizing. These data are then inductively analyzed into categories, expanded into themes, and folded into interpretations and findings. The resultant inductively generated interpretations are called grounded theory (Strauss & Corbin, 1990). A method used to generate grounded theory, constant comparative analysis (Glaser & Strauss, 1967), is described below.

Constant Comparative Analysis

In constant comparative analysis, the researcher separates the field notes into discrete, stand-alone ideas or units which are then printed onto index cards. These cards are sorted into categories based on their similarities and differences.

The researcher postpones naming the categories, but instead lets the inductive process of similarity and difference determine what data fit what groupings. These categories are then added to, adapted, and expanded as subsequent data collection activities are conducted. When the categories are saturated (i.e., additional information does not add meaning to the emerging themes), the data collection is complete. These categories become the backbone upon which to build the research interpretations and findings.

Although the inductive process of constant comparative analysis was used by the researchers in these studies, each went about the process in a different way. Wong used Hyperqual, a software package, to build the analysis and interpretation of his data. Hart and other researchers used the tried and true "cut and paste" method of physically dividing the data, printing it on index cards, and categorizing it manually (Lincoln & Guba, 1985). In all cases, the researchers combed the data for themes and categories from which they could build their interpretations.

Skillful analysis occurs when the researcher digs deeply into the data, examines underlying assumptions to ferret out meaning, and places the respondents' experiences into a fuller context of human living. This analysis becomes the source inspiration for interpretations which are then expressed through the case studies.

Data analysis is one of the most difficult steps in constructivist inquiry. A significant amount of insight, soul searching, and creativity is needed to generate findings which are conceptually rich, descriptively vivid, and analytically fruitful. Most of us can, with some effort, write a good story. But the purpose of constructivist inquiry is to collaborate with the respondents to write a case study which provides insight for practitioners, meaning for readers, and vision for educators.

Writing the Research Report

Qualitative research findings are often presented in case studies although documentary films, research reports, and other means are also used. During the writing of the case study, significant data analysis occurs. The researcher chooses the data to be presented in the case, makes interpretations of the data in conjunction with the respondents, and writes the case study as an interpretive text (Geertz, 1973). The case study is more than description; it is a conceptually and analytically rich piece of writing.

The case study form accommodates the grounded theory in the form of themes, interpretations, and working hypotheses providing a narrative account of the findings. Case studies can be organized in a variety of ways: thematically, question and answer, realist tale, first-person account, and researcher as narrator, among other forms.

Expressing the Voices of the Respondents

Respondents' and researchers' voices are expressed in case studies through a collaborative effort based on care, trust, and genuineness. These qualities are achieved through careful methodological procedures (e.g., authenticity) closely adhering to ethical practice (e.g., "do no harm").

A pressing issue regarding this collaborative effort is the presentation of the respondents' and researcher's voices. Substantial literature has been written about the privileges inherent in the researcher's position. When one has university titles and degrees, money with which to conduct the research, and confidentiality requirements directing that the respondents' names be withheld, the issue of who *really* owns the data becomes an issue.

Regardless of the choices made, the issues of authorship and voice remain contested:

> Ethical problems emerge in framing a case study. . . . how much of the researcher's "self" should be introduced into the case report? To what extent does the researcher speak with an "authorial voice," taking the role of the "professional stranger"? To what extent may the researcher be "informed and transformed" in the process? (Lincoln & Guba, 1989, p. 234).

In the end, while these issues can never be completely resolved, conversations with respondents and significant soul searching resulted in a satisfactory though still conflicted resolution about the location of the researcher's voice in the case study.

First-Person Voice

The first-person voice and case study format work well with topics that are personal, emo-

tional, and stirring. The reader should be warned that the first-person account is not the only or the predominant means of reporting qualitative data.

In addition to the first-person format, other case study styles are represented in this volume. Wong, for example, places himself squarely in the case study as the researcher. As the narrator and visitor to the respondent's place of work, Wong makes no effort to hide his presence. The conversations he had with the respondent during data collection are clearly evident in the case study. The voices of the respondents in Regan's study ring true as their words are placed, verbatim, into the case study. As she juxtaposes the respondents' words about acquaintance rape, one can hear the voices in her modified question and answer format case study.

High Quality and Rigor

High quality findings are a goal of constructivist inquiry. To that end, several techniques are recommended to constructivist researchers.

Consent Forms

Upon entry to the sites and respondents, each researcher negotiated informed consent. This process is a requirement of all human subjects research as well as an ethical consideration in constructivist inquiry. The form used to solidify consent assured the respondent that confidentiality would be maintained through the use of a pseudonym; he or she would be involved in decisions about data use; the data belonged to him or her and could be withdrawn at any point; and any aspect negotiated by researchers and respondents would be treated seriously. Furthermore, permission was obtained from the respondents for use of the research in both the course and this book.

The consent form was handled with extreme care in these research projects. Negotiated during the first contact with potential respondents, the manner in which the consent form was presented and negotiated set the tone for subsequent meetings. If the respondent felt that he or she was being "studied" without reciprocity or respect, that negative tone would have persisted throughout the research.

Member Checking

Member checking is the

> process of continuous, informal testing of information by soliciting reactions of respondents to the investigator's reconstruction . . . and to the constructions offered by other respondents or sources. (Lincoln & Guba, 1986, p. 77)

All field notes, patterns and themes gleaned from the data, summaries of interpretations, and drafts of case studies are checked by respondents for accuracy, clarification, and assurance that the findings generated are congruent with their perspectives (Manning, 1997).

Member checking is conducted to assure that the research findings emerge from, and remain true to, the respondent's experience. In keeping with the trusting, collaborative nature of constructivist inquiry, the respondents must be involved in each step of the process. While this means of assuring quality is often omitted in qualitative research, it is essential to the authenticity of any study (Lincoln & Guba, 1986; Manning, 1997). If the researcher does not stay close to and attuned with the respondents' meaning through member checking, data become distant from and irrelevant to their experiences.

Peer Debriefing

Each researcher was involved in a peer debriefing group for the duration of his or her project. This group was composed of fellow researchers who offered support, methodological checks, and insights about the projects. While the peer debriefing groups were initially given questions to consider (e.g., what's the focus of your study? how will you locate respondents? what are the themes emerging from your study?), these groups evolved in ways unique to the researchers' needs. The psychological and emotional support afforded within peer debriefing groups is invaluable.

An essential task of peer debriefing groups is to check the researcher's unacknowledged assumptions. As colleagues who have been with the researchers since the inception of the project, peer debriefers often recognize when themes are inductively generated from the data or when they reflect the researcher's perspectives with no accompanying corroboration in the data.

Prolonged Engagement

The researcher achieves prolonged engagement, and adds breadth to the study, by staying in the field sufficiently long enough to fully understand the context, issues at hand, and perspectives (Lincoln & Guba, 1986). In the case studies in this book, the short time frame of the studies is a concern. While the data collection and analysis were conducted over a limited period of time (e.g., four months), the researchers and I do not view this circumstance as a threat to the usefulness of the studies. Other measures of quality and rigor (e.g., member checking, co-construction and collaboration with respondents, member checking, and persistent observation) were met and add to the quality of the research.

Persistent Observation

The researcher is involved in the "lengthy and intensive contact with the phenomena (or respondents) in the field to . . . identify saliences in the situation" (Lincoln & Guba, 1986, p. 77). A researcher must stay engaged in the research site in such a way that he or she understands the important aspects of the respondents' lives and context. Adding depth, persistent observation permits the researcher to focus the research effort in a way that eliminates scattered and obscure data.

These techniques are only several of those available to assure rigor and quality in constructivist inquiry. A fuller discussion of authenticity and attendant techniques is available in Manning (1997).

Conclusion

This *chapter* provides a brief overview of constructivist inquiry for the purpose of apprising the reader of the methods used in these studies. Because a complete explanation of the methodology cannot be achieved in such a short space, the reader is encouraged to explore further the kind of research represented in this book.

student affairs professionals and other educators are encouraged to consider the following questions:

1. What insights, gleaned from the cases, can be folded into your knowledge base?

2. What practices, policies, and programs can be recommended as a result of the

vicarious experience acquired through your reading of the case studies?

3. How can these cases be used during professional and student staff training as examples of the crises they may experience in their work with students?

4. What institutional structures can be implemented for students, staff, and faculty in an effort to be proactive about the issues discussed in this book?

While qualitative methodology does not allow broad generalizations across all students or staff, the cases in this book can provide significant insights for policy making, program planning, program evaluation, and administrative practice. We hope you will find the results and recommendations as compelling as we did throughout the research process.

References

Baxter Magolda, M. (1992). *Knowing and reasoning in college: Gender-related patterns in students' intellectual development.* San Francisco, CA: Jossey-Bass.

Chickering, A. (1969). *Education and identity.* San Francisco, CA: Jossey-Bass.

Ely, M. with Anzul, M., Friedman, T., Garner, D., & Steinmetz, A. M. (1991). *Doing qualitative research: Circles within circles.* New York, NY: Falmer Press.

Geertz, C. (1973). *The interpretation of cultures.* New York, NY: Basic Books.

Gilligan, C. (1982). *In a different voice: Psychological theory and women's development.* Cambridge, MA: Harvard University Press.

Glaser, B., & Strauss, A. (1967). *The discovery of grounded theory: Strategies for qualitative research.* Chicago, IL: Aldine.

Guba, E. (1985). *The context of emergent paradigm research.* In Y. Lincoln (Ed.). Organizational theory and inquiry: The paradigm revolution. (79–104). Beverly Hills, CA: Sage.

Guba, E., & Lincoln, Y. (1989). *Fourth generation evaluation.* Beverly Hills, CA: Sage.

Lincoln, Y. (1985). The substance of the emergent paradigm: Implications for researchers. In Y. Lincoln (Ed.), *Organizational theory and inquiry: The paradigm revolution* (pp. 137–160). Beverly Hills, CA: Sage.

Lincoln, Y. (1988). "Naturalistic inquiry: Politics and implications for special education." Speech delivered for Project Directors' Meeting, Research in Education of the Handicapped.

Lincoln, Y., & Guba, E. (1985). *Naturalistic inquiry.* Beverly Hills, CA: Sage.

Lincoln, Y., & Guba, E. (1986). But is it rigorous? Trustworthiness and authenticity in naturalistic inquiry. In D. Williams (Ed.), *Naturalistic evaluation* (pp. 73–84). San Francisco, CA: Jossey-Bass.

Lincoln, Y., & Guba, E. (1989). Ethics: The failure of positivist science. *Review of Higher Education, 12,* 221–240.

Manning, K. (1997). Authenticity in constructivist inquiry: Methodological considerations without prescription. *Qualitative Inquiry, 3*(1), 93–115.

Patton, M. (2nd ed.) (1990). *Qualitative evaluation and research methods* (2nd ed.) Beverly Hills, CA: Sage.

Peters, T. J., & Waterman, R. H. (1982). *In search of excellence: Lessons from America's best-run companies.* New York, NY: Harper & Row Publishers.

Reason, P., & Rowan, J. (Ed.) (1981). *Human inquiry: A source-book of new paradigm research.* New York, NY: Wiley & Sons.

Strauss, A., & Corbin, J. (1990). *Basics of qualitative research:Grounded theory procedures and techniques.* Newbury Park, CA: Sage Publications.

ADDITIONAL READINGS

Arnett, J. J. (2000). "Emerging Adulthood: A Theory of Development From the Late Teens Through the Twenties." *American Psychologist* 55: 469–480.

Arnold, K. D. (1993). "The Fulfillment of Promise: Minority Valedictorians and Salutatorians." *The Review of Higher Education* 16(3): 257–283.

Astin, A. (1993). Chapter 12: Implications for Educational Theory and Practice. *What matters in College*: 396–437.

Astin, A. W. (1977). Summary of Effects. *Four Critical Years*. A. W. Astin. San Francisco, Jossey-Bass, Inc.: 211–241.

Astin, A. W. (1984). "Student Involvement: A Developmental Theory for Higher Education." *Journal of College Student Personnel* 25(4): 297–308.

Astin, A. W. (1985). The Changing College Student: Challenges Facing American Higher Education. *Achieving Educational Excellence*. A. W. Alexander. San Francisco, Jossey-Bass: 211–227.

Astin, A. W. (1993). Studying College Impact. *What Matters in College: Four Critical Years Revisited*. A. W. Astin, San Francisco, Jossey-Bass, Inc.:1–21, 25–31.

Astin, H. S. and K. Laura (1983). "Gender Roles in Transition: Research and Policy Implications for Higher Education." *Journal of Higher Education* 54(3).

Astone, B. and E. Nunez-Wormack (1990). Demographics and Diversity: What Colleges Should Know; Population Trends, Socioeconomic Status, and Geographic Distribution. Washington, D.C., ASHE-ERIC Higher Education Report.

Baxter Magolda, M. B. (1998). "Developing Self-Authorship in Young Adult Life." *Journal of College Student Development* 39(2): 143–156.

Baxter Magolda, M. B. (1998). "Learning and Gender: Complexity and Possibility." *Higher Education* 35(3): 351–355.

Baxter Magolda, M. B. (1999). "Constructing Adult Identities." *Journal of College Student Development* 40(6): 629–644.

Baxter Magolda, M. B. (2000). "Interpersonal Maturity: Integrating Agency and Communion." *Journal of College Student Development* 41: 141–155.

Bean, J. P. and B. S. Metzner (1986). "A Conceptual Model of Nontraditional Undergraduate Student Attrition." *Review of Educational Research* 55(4): 485–508, 520–528, 530.

Braxton, J. (2000). Reinvigorating Theory and Research on the Departure Puzzle. *Rethinking the Departure Puzzle: New Theory and Research on College Student Retention*. J. Braxton, Vanderbilt University Press.

Cheatham, H. E. (1991). Identity Development in a Pluralistic Society. *Cultural Pluralism on Campus*, American College of Personnel Association: 23–38.

Chickering, A. W. (1972). The young adult: An overview. *Education and Identity*. San Francisco, Jossey Bass: 8–19.

Cross, K. P. (1982). Participants in Adult Learning for Academic Credit. *Adults as Learners*. San Francisco, Jossey-Bass: 67–80.

Cross, W. E., Jr. (1971). "The Negro-to-Black Conversion Experience." *Black World* 20(9): 13–27.

Feldman, K. A. (1972). Difficulties in Measuring and Interpreting Change and Stability During College. *College and Student: Selected Readings in the Social Psychology of Higher Education*. K. A. Feldman, Pergamon Press: 127–142.

Feldman, K. A. and T. M. Newcomb (1969). Persistence and Change After College. *The Impact of College on Students*. K. A. Feldman and T. M. Newcomb. San Francisco, Jossey-Bass, Inc.: 308–324.

Feldman, K. A. and T. M. Newcomb (1969). The Sequence of Experiences. *The Impact of College on Students*. San Francisco, Jossey-Bass. 1.

Hossler, D. (1984). College Choice. *Enrollment Management: An Integrated Approach*. New York, College Entrance Examination Board.

Hurtado, S. (1992). "The Campus Racial Climate: Contexts of Conflict." *Journal of Higher Education* 63: 539–569.

Hurtado, S. and D. F. Carter (1994). *Latino Students' Sense of Belonging in the College Community: Rethinking the Concept of Integration on Campus*. Annual Meeting of the American Educational Research Association, New Orleans.

Hurtado, S. and D. F. Carter (1997). "Effects of College Transition and Perceptions of the Campus Racial Climate on Latino Students' Sense of Belonging." *Sociology of Education* 70(4): 324–345.

King, P. M. (1997). "Character and Civic Education: What Does it Take?" *Educational Record* 78(3–4): 87–93.

King, P. M. and M. B. Baxter Magolda (1999). "A Developmental Perspective on Learning." *Journal of College Student Development* 40(5): 599–609.

Kramer, G. L. and R. Washburn (1983). "The Perceived Orientation Needs of New Students." *Journal of College Student Personnel* 24(4): 311–319.

Kuh, G. D. (1981). From Indices of Quality in the Undergraduate Experience, ASHE-Higher Education Research Report.

Kuh, G. D. (1990). "Assessing Student Culture." *New Directions for Institutional Research* 17(4): 47–60.

Kuh, G. D. (1993). "In Their Own Words: What Students Learn Outside the Classroom." *American Educational Research Journal* 30(2): 277–304.

Kuh, G. D., J. P. Bean, et al. (1986). "Changes in Research on College Students Published in Selected Journals Between 1969 and 1983." *Review of Higher Education* 9(2): 177–192.

Love, P. (1998). "Cultural Barriers Facing Lesbian, Gay, and Bisexual Students at a Catholic College." *Journal of Higher Education* 69(3): 298–323.

Love, P. and V. Guthrie (1999). "Chapter 7: Synthesis, Assessment, and Application." *New Directions for Student Services* 88: 77–93.

Manning, K. (1992). "A Rationale for Using Qualitative Research in Student Affairs." *Journal of College Student Development* 33(2): 132–136.

McEwen, M. K., L. D. Roper, et al. (1990). "Incorporating the Development of African-American Students into Psychosocial Theories of Student Development." *Journal of College Student Development* 31: 429–436.

Moos, R. H. (1979). Architectural, Organizational, and Contextual Influences on Living Groups. *Evaluating Educational Environments*. R. H. Moos. San Francisco, Jossey-Bass: 67–90.

Newcomb, T. M. (1962). Student Peer-Group Influence. *The American College*. T. M. Newcomb, John Wiley and Sons, Inc.: 469–488.

Nora, A., L. C. Attinasi, et al. (1990). "Testing Qualitative Indicators of PreCollege Factors in Tinto's Attrition Model: A Community College Student Population." *The Review of Higher Education* 13(3): 337–355.

Olenchak, F. R. and T. P. Herbet (2002). "Endangered Academic Talent: Lessons Learned from Gifted First-Generation College Males." *Journal of College Student Development* 43(2): 195–212.

Olivas, M. A. (1992). Trout Fishing in Catfish Ponds. *Minorities in Higher Education: Pipelines, Policy, and Practice*, Educational Testing Service: 46–54.

Ortiz, A. M. (1999). "The Student Affairs Establishment and the Institutionalization of the Collegiate Ideal." *New Directions for Higher Education* 27(1): 47–57.

Pascarella, E. T. (1985). College Environmental Influences on Learning and Cognitive Development: A Critical Review and Synthesis. *Higher Education: Handbook of Theory and Research*. J. C. Smart, Agathon: 1–44, 54–61.

Pascarella, E. T. and P. T. Terenzini (1996). How Colleges Make a Difference: A Summary. *College Students: The Evolving Nature of Research*. F. K. Stage, G. L. Anaya, J. P. Bean, D. Hossler and G. D. Kuh. San Francisco, Jossey-Bass.

Peterson, M. and M. Spencer Understanding Academic Culture and Climate *New Directions for Institutional Research* no. 68 pp. 3–18 (1990)

Ponterotto, J. G. (2001). Chapter on Biracial Identity. *Handbook of multicultural counseling*. Thousand Oaks, CA, Sage Publications.

Reisser, L. (1995). "Revisiting the Seven Vectors." *Journal of College Student Development* 36: 505–511.

Rodgers, R. F. (1980). Theories Underlying Student Development. *Student Development in Higher Education*. D. G. Cramer, American College Personnel Association: 13–57.

Sedlacek, W. E. (1987). "Black Students on White Campuses: 20 Years of Research." *Journal of College Student Personnel* 28(6): 484–495.

Stage, F. K. and G. L. Anaya (1996). A Transformational View of College Student Research. *College Students: The Evolving Nature of Research*. F. K. Stage, G. L. Anaya, J. P. Bean, D. Hossler and G. D. Kuh. San Francisco, Jossey-Bass.

Stage, F. K. and K. M. Manning (2003). *Research in the College Context: Approaches and Methods*. New York, Bruner Routledge.

Stage, F. K. and S. Maple (1996). "Incompatible goals: Narratives of graduate women in the mathematics pipeline." *American Educational Research Journal* 22(1): 23–51.

Stage, F. K. and P. Muller (1999). Chapter 2: Theories of Learning for College Students. *Enhancing Student Learning: Setting the Campus Context*, F. K. Stage, L. Watson and M. Terrell: 25–41.

Stage, F. K., P. Muller, et al. (1998). *Creating Learning Centered Classrooms: What Does Learning Theory Have to Say?* Washington, D.C, ASHE/ERIC.

Statistics, N. C. f. E. (1997). Enrollment in Higher Education: Fall 1995. Washington, D.C., National Center for Education Statistics: 5–18.

Sternberg, R. J. (1996). "Myths, Countermyths, and Truths About Intelligence." *Educational Researcher* 25(2): 11–16.

Terenzini, P. T., L. I. Rendon, et al. (1994). "The Transition to College: Diverse Students, Diverse Stories." *Research in Higher Education* **35**(1): 57–73.

Tierney, W. G. (1992). "An Anthropological Analysis of Student Participation in College." *Journal of Higher Education* **63**(6): 603–618.

Tierney, W. G. (1995). "Addressing Failure: Factors Affecting Native American College Student Retention." *Journal of Navajo Education* **13**(1): 3–7.

Tierney, W. G. (1997). "The Parameters of Affirmative Action: Equity and Excellence in the Academy." *Review of Educational Research* **67**: 165–196.

Walsh, B. W. (1978). "Person/Environment Interaction." *National Association of Student Personnel Adminstrators*.

Warren, J. (1985). The Changing Characteristics of Community College Students. *Renewing the American Community College*. W. L. Deegan, T. Dale and a. Associates. San Francisco, Jossey-Bass: 53–79.

Watson, L. W. (1998). The college experience: A conceptual framework to consider for enhancing students' educational gains. *The African American Culture and Heritage in Higher Education Research and Practice*. K. Freeman, Greenwood Publishing: 73–92.

Whitt, E. Assessing student cultures-*Assessment in Student Affairs: A guide for Practioners*. (1996) pp. 189–216